FOR REFERENCE

Do Not Take From This Room

Encyclopedia of
GLOBAL
BRANDS

2nd Edition

Encyclopedia of

GLOBAL

BRANDS

VOLUME 2

2nd Edition

ST. JAMES PRESS
A part of Gale, Cengage Learning

Detroit • New York • San Francisco • New Haven, Conn • Waterville, Maine • London

**Encyclopedia of Global Brands,
2nd Edition**

**Written and edited by Kepos Media,
in collaboration with Thomas Riggs & Company**

Project Editor: Peggy Geeseman

Editorial: Miranda Ferrara

Composition and Electronic Prepress: Evi Seoud

Manufacturing: Rita Wimberley

Product Manager: Michele LaMeau

For product information and technology assistance, contact us at
Gale Customer Support, 1-800-877-4253.
For permission to use material from this text or product,
submit all requests online at **www.cengage.com/permissions.**
Further permissions questions can be emailed to
permissionrequest@cengage.com.

LIBRARY OF CONGRESS CATALOGING-IN-PUBLICATION DATA

Encyclopedia of global brands. — 2nd edition.
      volumes cm
   Includes bibliographical references and index.
   ISBN 978-1-55862-227-2 (set) — ISBN 978-1-55862-228-9 (vol. 1) —
ISBN 978-1-55862-229-6 (vol. 2)
      1. Brand name products–Encyclopedias. 2. Corporations–Encyclopedias.
I. St. James Press.
   HD69.B7E534 2013
   338.703—dc23   2013012023

Gale
27500 Drake Rd.
Farmington Hills, MI 48331-3535

ISBN-13: 978-1-55862-227-2 (set)   ISBN-10: 1-55862-277-6
ISBN-13: 978-1-55862-228-9 (vol. 1)   ISBN-10: 1-55862-228-4 (vol. 1)
ISBN-13: 978-1-55862-229-6 (vol. 2)   ISBN-10: 1-55862-229-2 (vol. 2)

This title is also available as an e-book.
ISBN 13: 978-1-55862-854-0 ISBN 10: 1-55862-854-1
Contact your Gale, a part of Cengage Learning, sales representative for ordering
information.

Printed in Mexico
1 2 3 4 5 6 7 17 16 15 14 13

Contents

Contents

KELLOGG'S

———— ◆ ————

AT A GLANCE

◆

Brand Synopsis: As a leading global food brand, Kellogg's helps consumers "Make Today Great."

Parent Company: Kellogg Company
One Kellogg Square
Battle Creek, Michigan 49016
United States
http://www.kelloggcompany.com

Sector: Consumer Staples

Industry Group: Food & Staples Retailing

Performance: *Sales*—US$14.1 billion (2012).

Principal Competitors: Nestle S.A.; Unilever N.V.; Kraft Foods Inc.; Danone S.A.; General Mills Inc.

BRAND ORIGINS

- The Kellogg Company was established by Will Keith (W.K.) Kellogg in 1906.
- W.K. Kellogg and his brother, Dr. John Harvey Kellogg, were responsible for the development of flake cereals.
- In 1922 the company reincorporated as the Kellogg Company.
- In the early 1950s Kellogg's success was tied to the postwar baby boom and television advertising.

The Kellogg Company was established by Will Keith (W.K.) Kellogg. By the time Kellogg launched his cereal company in 1906, he already had been in the cereal business for more than 10 years as an employee of the Adventist Battle Creek Sanitarium run by his brother, Dr. John Harvey Kellogg. One of the foods sold by Dr. Kellogg's Sanitas Food Company was called Granose, a wheat flake the Kellogg brothers had stumbled upon in 1894, following a long series of unsuccessful attempts to develop a more digestible form of bread.

In 1898 Sanitas introduced the corn flake, improving upon its flavor and shelf life over the subsequent years. By 1903 the company was advertising in newspapers and on billboards, sending salesmen into the wholesale market and introducing an ambitious door-to-door sampling program. By late 1905 Sanitas was producing 150 cases of corn flakes per day with sales of US$100,000 per year.

In 1906 W.K. Kellogg launched the Battle Creek Toasted Corn Flake Company, with the help of an enthusiastic former sanitarium patient. Kellogg recognized that advertising and promotion were the keys to success in a market flooded with look-alike products. The company spent one-third of its initial working capital on an ad in *Ladies' Home Journal.* Orders, fueled by early advertising efforts, continually outstripped production.

In May 1907 the company became the Toasted Corn Flake Company. By that time W.K. Kellogg had acquired his brother's share of the company, giving him more than 50 percent of its stock. W.K. Kellogg's company had become the Kellogg Toasted Corn Flake Company in 1909, but Dr. Kellogg's Sanitas Food Company had been renamed the Kellogg Food Company and used similar slogans and packaging. W.K. Kellogg sued his brother for rights to the family name and was finally successful in 1921.

In 1922 the company reincorporated as the Kellogg Company because it had lost its trademark claim to the name "Toasted Corn Flakes" and had expanded its product line so much that the name no longer accurately described the company. Kellogg had introduced Krumbles in 1912, followed by Bran Flakes in 1915, and All-Bran in 1916.

The company's upward sales curve continued through the Depression. In 1939 Kellogg named Watson H. Vanderploeg president. Vanderploeg expanded Kellogg's successful advertise-and-grow policy, adding new products and taking them into new markets. In the early 1950s Kellogg's continued success was tied to two outside developments: the postwar baby boom and television advertising.

To appeal to the new younger market, Kellogg and other cereal makers brought out new lines of presweetened cereals and unabashedly made the key ingredient part of the name. Kellogg's entries included Sugar Frosted Flakes, Sugar Smacks, Sugar Corn Pops, Sugar All-Stars, and Cocoa Crispies. The company created cartoon pitchmen to sell the products on Saturday morning television. Tony the Tiger was introduced in 1953 following a contest to name the ambassador for the new cereal, Kellogg's Sugar Frosted Flakes of Corn. The company continued adding new cereals, aiming some at adolescent baby boomers and others, like Special K and Product 19, at their parents.

BRAND ELEMENTS
- The Kellogg's brand is represented by a logo that displays the name "Kellogg's" in stylized red type.
- Midway through 2012 the Kellogg's brand received its most significant modification in over a century.
- In 2012 the phrase "Let's Make Today Great" was developed, reflecting Kellogg's identity as the best choice for consumers to start their day.
- Kellogg's branded products have been successfully adapted to the unique tastes and needs of international consumers.

The Kellogg's brand is represented by a logo that displays the name "Kellogg's" in stylized red type. Midway through 2012 the brand received the most significant modification in 106 years. In addition to the updated logo, there were brighter graphics, which impacted Kellogg's packaging, marketing materials, and advertising. These updates extended beyond packaging and print advertising to include the brand's various websites.

As part of its revitalization, Kellogg's also introduced a new tagline. The phrase "Let's Make Today Great" was developed. The statement reflected the brand's identity as the best choice for consumers to start their day. The tagline was somewhat reminiscent of the well-known phrase "They're Grrrrreat!" This was used by Kellogg's iconic

character, Tony the Tiger, who was introduced in 1953 as the ambassador for Kellogg's Frosted Flakes. Over the years Kellogg's branded products have been associated with other cartoon figures, including Snap, Crackle, and Pop, which were developed to represent Kellogg's Rice Krispies.

Kellogg's branded products have been successfully adapted to the unique tastes and needs of international consumers. For example Kellogg's Extra is marketed as an excellent choice with hot milk throughout Europe, while in France it is promoted alongside yogurt. Kellogg's began marketing All-Bran as something that could be poured into one's coffee after it discovered that Spanish consumers enjoyed the product that way.

BRAND IDENTITY
- The key aspects of Kellogg's identity were very much in sync with consumers' image of the brand. The 2012 American Customer Satisfaction Index measured the performance of approximately 225 companies in categories such as consumer expectations, loyalty, quality, and value. Among hundreds of companies within the food industry, Kellogg's was part of a select group of market share leaders measured by ACSI. Among those leaders, Kellogg's improved its score the most from 2011 to 2012, increasing 3.8 percent. In 2012 Kellogg's vision statement was "to enrich and delight the world through foods and brands that matter."
- Kellogg's has gained and maintained the trust of consumers by associating its name with good nutrition.
- The element of value is a key component of Kellogg's brand identity and is exemplified by efforts to introduce products specifically for low-income consumers.
- Among 14 leading food manufacturers, Kellogg's ranked 11th in the 2011 American Customer Satisfaction Index.

Several key elements are at the heart of the Kellogg's brand. In the company's 2012 annual report, President and CEO John A. Bryant and Chairman Jim Jenness shared the Kellogg's vision statement: "to enrich and delight the world through foods and brands that matter." The executives emphasized the importance of both gaining and maintaining trust with consumers. In part, Kellogg's has accomplished this by associating its name with good nutrition.

By late 2012 Kellogg's research had revealed a desire among consumers for food choices with fewer ingredients. Emphasizing the brand's association with high quality, simple foods, Kellogg's initiated its "Goodness of a Simple Grain" marketing campaign. The initiative emphasized heritage products such as Kellogg's Corn Flakes.

The element of value also is a key component of Kellogg's brand identity. The company's strategy includes efforts to market products specifically for low-income consumers. In South Africa Kellogg's Corn Flakes Porridge was introduced for this very reason. In the August 20, 2012, issue of *Advertising Age*, Kellogg International President Paul Norman revealed some of the strategy behind the value focus, explaining that the company intended to help consumers "bridge into a brand that they aspire to buy but can't always buy today, but in the future we expect them to buy."

BRAND STRATEGY

- Innovation and brand building were very much at the forefront of the Kellogg Company's strategic plan by 2012.
- Kellogg's has demonstrated its ability to meet the continuously changing needs of consumers.
- The Kellogg Company's strategy has involved adapting existing brands for new international markets.
- Kellogg's pursues philanthropic initiatives and partnerships that support the company's vision "to enrich and delight the world through foods and brands that matter."

A number of different products fall under the umbrella of the Kellogg Company's flagship brand. These include familiar registered trademarks such as Corn Flakes, Frosted Flakes, Special K, Rice Krispies, Mini-Wheats, Nutri-Grain, and Eggo. Although many of these tried-and-true products enjoy household name status, Kellogg's has struggled with innovation and new product development in recent years. For this reason, innovation and brand building were very much at the forefront of the company's strategic plan by 2012.

In the Kellogg Company's 2011 annual report, President and CEO John A. Bryant and Chairman Jim Jenness remarked, "In recent years we focused too little on innovating and the related increase in brand building, two things that drive not only our business, but also the categories in which we compete." This situation led to a renewed focus in these areas. Subsequently Kellogg's strengthened its ability to meet the continuously changing needs of consumers.

In the United Kingdom Kellogg's introduced Mini Max, its first new children's cereal in 20 years. The product was developed in order to provide a healthier cereal that was appealing to children, and also accepted by their mothers. Mini Max offered higher doses of fiber, while reducing levels of salt and fat. At the same time the company moved to lower the amount of sugar in Kellogg's Coco Pops.

The Kellogg Company's approach to innovation doesn't always involve the development of new products.

Sometimes it involves taking a successful product from one international market and introducing it to another. One example is the company's Crunchy Nut cereal. This formulation of honey-coated cornflakes with chopped nuts, marketed successfully in the United Kingdom since 1980 and eventually worth US$154 million per year, was slated for a U.S. rollout in 2011. This approach enabled the company to avoid research and development costs, while introducing a product that already had a proven track record in a similar market.

Kellogg's strategy also has involved philanthropic initiatives and partnerships that were in sync with its vision "to enrich and delight the world through foods and brands that matter," as described in the company's 2011 annual report. For example in 2011 Kellogg's agreed to sponsor the U.S. Olympic and Paralympic Teams through 2016. That same year the Kellogg's Corporate Citizenship Fund made a US$400,000 donation to the hunger-relief charity, Feeding America, following tornadoes that impacted the southern United States. Efforts such as these helped the brand gain and maintain consumer trust, while associating the Kellogg's name with good nutrition.

BRAND EQUITY

- In 2012 Interbrand ranked Kellogg's 29th on its list of the 100 Best Global Brands.
- In 2011 *Forbes* ranked the Kellogg's brand seventh in its Top Brands online survey.
- Citing data from the *Financial Times'* FT 500, *Market Share Reporter* indicated that Kellogg Co. ranked fifth among the most valuable U.S. food production companies in 2011, with a market value of nearly US$19.8 billion.
- Over more than a century, the Kellogg's brand has benefited from significant research and development investments, which totaled US$192 million in 2011 alone.

Kellogg's marketing and financial value are rooted in the brand's leadership position in cereal, snacks, and frozen food. The brand's value is confirmed in a number of rankings. In 2012 Interbrand ranked Kellogg's 29th on its list of the 100 Best Global Brands. In 2011 *Forbes* ranked the brand seventh in its Top Brands online survey.

Several other rankings also provide insight into Kellogg's brand equity. Citing data from the *Financial Times'* FT 500, *Market Share Reporter* indicated that Kellogg Co. ranked fifth among the most valuable U.S. food production companies in 2011, with a market value of nearly US$19.8 billion. In addition the company topped the *Manufacturing Confectioner'*s list of the leading breakfast/cereal/snack bar makers. With a commanding market share of 61.9 percent, Kellogg's was well ahead of competitors General Mills Inc. (8.8 percent) and Kraft Foods Inc. (5.7 percent).

Over more than a century, the Kellogg's brand has benefited from significant research and development investments. In 2011 Kellogg Co. devoted US$192 million to research and development. This compares to US$187 million in 2010 and US$181 million in 2009. Kellogg's brand equity is also supported by significant brand-building investments. According to Kellogg Co., it devotes more resources to advertising and consumer promotion, as a percentage of sales, than do its competitors.

BRAND AWARENESS

- The strong awareness surrounding the Kellogg's brand has a history dating back more than a century.
- Kellogg's pioneering role in the development of flaked cereals has, in many ways, allowed its brand name to become synonymous with such everyday products as corn flakes.
- Top-of-mind awareness of Kellogg's branded products is achieved through strong and growing levels of advertising support.
- Although specific expenditures were not available, the Kellogg Company has significantly elevated the status of its master brand in advertising efforts.

The strong awareness surrounding the Kellogg's brand has a history dating back more than a century. The company's pioneering role in the development of flaked cereals had, in many ways, allowed its brand name to become synonymous with such everyday products as corn flakes. By 2012 the Kellogg Company's portfolio of brands was marketed in 180 countries. Top-of-mind awareness was achieved through strong and growing levels of advertising support. Kellogg's advertising costs totaled US$1.13 billion in 2010 and increased to US$1.14 billion in 2011.

Although it did not report specific expenditures, the company had significantly elevated the status of its master Kellogg's brand through advertising. By late 2012 Kellogg's was promoting its "Goodness of a Simple Grain" campaign through numerous outlets. Beyond digital and print advertising, these included spots on the Food Network, Hispanic television, and the Country Music Awards. Advertising during the Olympics also provided broad exposure.

Generating global awareness of the Kellogg's brand has been accomplished in different ways. In India, Bollywood actresses have been retained to serve as brand ambassadors. Examples include Karisma Kapoor, who was chosen to represent Kellogg's Chocos and promote the product to mothers as a healthy snack, and Lara Dutta, who was selected to serve as the ambassador for Special K. In the United Kingdom Kellogg's Special K began

featuring plus-sized women in advertisements, as opposed to slimmer women in red swimsuits.

BRAND OUTLOOK

- To ensure long-term health and success, in 2011 Kellogg's invested US$70 million to expand an existing supply chain program to all of its North American production facilities.
- In 2012 the future growth of the Kellogg's brand rested largely on the potential of emerging markets.
- Kellogg's research and development activities are internationally focused.
- The development of products with lower levels of sodium and sugar was critical for Kellogg's, at a time when food manufacturers faced unprecedented pressure over rising levels of diabetes and obesity.

As the leading global cereals manufacturer, the Kellogg Company was in a strong position as the company headed into 2013. However, skyrocketing commodity costs and difficult economic conditions threatened its profits. To ensure health and success in the long term, in 2011 Kellogg's invested US$70 million to expand an existing supply chain program to all of its production facilities in North America. Support for this more robust supply chain initiative continued in 2012.

Kellogg's also recognizes that its future success hinges on the ability to innovate. In this regard, research and development are of great importance to the company. In 2011 Kellogg's devoted US$192 million to research and development expenses. This compares to US$187 million in 2010 and US$181 million in 2009. Efforts at the company's research facilities, including the W.K. Kellogg Institute in Battle Creek, Michigan, focused on developing new product variations, discovering different flavors, and enhancing product nutrition in response to consumer preferences.

Kellogg's research and development activities are internationally focused. For example, in 2010 a global research and development alliance was established with Japan-based Ajinomoto Company Inc. Together the two companies planned to concentrate on the creation of products with lower levels of sodium and sugar, as well as items focused on weight management. This was especially important at a time when food manufacturers faced unprecedented pressure from government and watchdog groups over rising levels of diabetes and obesity.

The future growth of the Kellogg's brand rested largely on the potential of emerging markets. In late 2012 the company established a joint venture in China with Wilmar International Limited and its Chinese subsidiary, Yihai Kerry Investments Co., Ltd., that focused on selling and distributing cereal, as well as savory and wholesome snacks.

In a September 24, 2012, *PR Newswire* release, Kellogg Company President and CEO John Bryant said the joint venture "fundamentally changes our game in China."

FURTHER READING

Baker, Rosie. "FOOD: Kellogg to Launch First New Kids' Cereal Brand in 20 Years." *Marketing Week*, August 25, 2011.

Beltrone, Gabriel. "Kellogg's Goes Back to the Land." *Adweek*, September 10, 2012.

"Best Global Brands 2012." Interbrand. Accessed October 31, 2012. http://www.interbrand.com/en/best-global-brands/2012/Best-Global-Brands-2012.aspx.

De La Merced, Michael J. "Kellogg to Buy Pringles for $2.7 Billion in Cash Deal." *New York Times*, February 16, 2012.

Kellogg Company. *Brands You Love. Foods That Delight. Kellogg Company 2011 Annual Report*. Accessed November 5, 2012. http://www.annualreport2011.kelloggcompany.com.

"Kellogg Company." *International Directory of Company Histories*. Ed. Tina Grant. Vol. 110. Detroit, MI: St. James Press, 2010.

"Kellogg Company and Wilmar International Limited Announce China Joint Venture." PR Newswire, September 24, 2012.

"Refreshing an Icon: Kellogg's Updates Brand to Keep Pace with Today's Consumers." Benzinga, May 14, 2012. Accessed December 7, 2012. http://www.benzinga.com/pressreleases/12/05/n2584562/refreshing-an-icon-kelloggs-updates-brand-to-keep-pace-with-todays-cons

Schultz, E. J. "Cereal Marketers Race for Global Bowl Domination." *Advertising Age*, August 20, 2012.

———. "Kellogg Plans British Invasion, Introduces Crunchy Nut to U.S. No. 1 Cereal Player Imports $154 Million Brand as It Looks for Innovation in Stale Category—and to Put Distance between It and a Gaining General Mills." *Advertising Age*, November 1, 2010.

KFC

BRAND ORIGINS

- Colonel Harland Sanders began developing a unique, quick method of spicing and pressure-frying chicken during the 1930s.
- The first franchise was awarded to Pete Harman, who owned a hamburger restaurant in Salt Lake City, Utah.
- In 1964 Colonel Sanders sold Kentucky Fried Chicken for US$2 million but continued involvement as a spokesperson.

- In 1991 Kentucky Fried Chicken changed its name to KFC.

Kentucky Fried Chicken was founded by Harland Sanders in Corbin, Kentucky. Sanders was born on a small farm in Henryville, Indiana, in 1890. In 1929 he opened a gas station in Corbin and cooked for his family and an occasional customer in the back room. Demand for Sanders' cooking rose, and he eventually moved across the street to a facility with a 142-seat restaurant, a motel, and a gas station.

During the 1930s an image that would become known throughout the world began to develop. First, Sanders was named an honorary Kentucky Colonel by the state's governor. Second, he developed a unique, quick method of spicing and pressure-frying chicken. A 1939 endorsement from Duncan Hines's *Adventures in Good Eating* put Sanders and his restaurant on the map. In 1952 the Colonel awarded his first franchise to Pete Harman, who owned a hamburger restaurant in Salt Lake City, Utah. Over the next four years he persuaded several other restaurant owners to add his Kentucky Fried Chicken to their menus.

In 1955 Sanders incorporated and the following year took his chicken recipe on the road, doing demonstrations onsite to sell his method. Clad in a white suit, white shirt, and black string tie, sporting a white mustache and goatee, and carrying a cane, Sanders' appearance was memorable and expressed his energy and enthusiasm. In 1956 Sanders moved the business to Shelbyville, Kentucky, 30 miles east of Louisville, to more easily ship his spices, pressure cookers, carryout cartons, and advertising material. By 1963 Sanders's recipe was franchised to more than 600 outlets in the United States and Canada.

In 1964 Sanders sold Kentucky Fried Chicken for US$2 million and an annual salary of US$40,000 for public appearances, which later increased to US$200,000. The offer came from an investor group headed by John Y. Brown, Jr., a 29-year-old University of Kentucky law school graduate, and Nashville financier John (Jack) Massey. A notable member of the investor group was Pete Harman, who had been the first to purchase Sanders' recipe 12 years earlier.

Massey and Brown changed the Colonel's concept of a sit-down Kentucky Fried Chicken dinner to a stand-up, take-out store emphasizing fast service and low labor costs. By 1970 this idea created 130 millionaires, all from selling the Colonel's famous pressure-cooked chicken. By August 1970 Colonel Harland Sanders and his grandson, Harland Adams, had resigned from the board of directors. After fighting leukemia for seven months, Harland Sanders died on December 16, 1980.

By 1983 Kentucky Fried Chicken had 4,500 stores in the United States and 1,400 units in 54 foreign countries. The company was the first American fast-food chain to establish operations in China in 1987. In February 1991 Kentucky Fried Chicken changed its name to KFC. The brand became part of Tricon Global Restaurants, Inc., which later became YUM! Brands, in October 1997 when owner Pepsi spun off its restaurant division.

BRAND ELEMENTS

- Although he died in 1980, Founder Colonel Harland Sanders continued to be a key element of the KFC brand during the early 21st century.
- Colonel Sanders' likeness, prominently featured in the KFC logo in 2012, has appeared on KFC signage since the 1950s.
- Colonel Sanders created KFC's now legendary Secret Original Recipe® of 11 herbs and spices.
- The KFC brand has been adapted to the unique tastes of different international markets.

Although he died in 1980, founder Colonel Harland Sanders continued to be a key element of the KFC brand during the early 21st century. The Colonel's likeness, prominently featured in the KFC logo in 2012, has appeared on KFC signage since the 1950s. A company museum situated inside the entrance to YUM! Brands' headquarters features a mechanical Colonel Sanders who tells guests about the organization.

In February 1991 Kentucky Fried Chicken changed its name to KFC. New packaging continued to include the classic red-and-white stripes that had long been part of the brand's color scheme. However, the stripes were made wider and on an angle, implying movement and rapid service. While the Colonel's image was retained, packaging was in modern graphics and bolder colors.

It was Colonel Sanders who developed a unique, quick method of spicing and pressure-frying chicken. In addition, he created KFC's now legendary Secret Original Recipe® of 11 herbs and spices. By 2011 KFC protected the special recipe in a custom-built safe, which weighed more than 770 pounds and was equipped with advanced security features.

In 2012 KFC's tagline was: "Today Tastes So Good." Recognizing that tastes vary throughout the world, the brand has been adapted to various international markets. For example, in the February 27, 2012, issue of *USA Today*, YUM! Brands CEO David Novak explained that consumers in Asia enjoy spicy food. Therefore, the company developed a spicy chicken filet sandwich named the Zinger for that market. Some consider KFC's practice of combining regional offerings with American flavors to be the gold standard for success in emerging markets.

BRAND IDENTITY

- By late 2012 KFC's advertising and public relations efforts had been emphasizing its use of fresh, on-the-bone chicken for more than 60 years.
- The KFC brand differentiated itself from the competition with its unique Original Recipe of 11 herbs and spices, created by founder Colonel Harland Sanders in 1952.
- Although he died in 1980, the legacy of founder Colonel Harland Sanders remained intertwined with KFC's brand identity more than three decades later.
- Like many other fast food brands, KFC has expanded its image beyond the fried chicken for which it is well-known to include healthier options.

Quality is the masthead of KFC's brand identity. By late 2012 the company's advertising and public relations efforts had been emphasizing its use of fresh, on-the-bone chicken for more than 60 years. Equally important is the element of taste. The KFC brand differentiated itself from the competition with its unique Original Recipe of 11 herbs and spices, created by founder Colonel Harland Sanders in 1952.

After he died in 1980, the legacy of Colonel Sanders remained intertwined with KFC's brand identity more than three decades later. As KFC PR Manager Rick Maynard explained in the August 2012 issue of *PR Week:* "We leverage the Colonel's story and remind people that he was a real person, a real cook, and a real entrepreneur with an amazing story, and this is the man who took a recipe for fried chicken and a Social Security check and built a business that now has 17,000 restaurants around the globe."

In November 2011 KFC accidentally discovered an autobiography written by Colonel Sanders in 1966. Distribution of the publication, titled *Colonel Harland Sanders: The Autobiography of the Original Celebrity Chef*, was done freely via Facebook, where the brand had amassed a base of approximately 5 million fans. The book also featured 33 previously unpublished recipes, along with rare photos of the colonel.

Like many other fast food brands, KFC has expanded its image beyond the fried chicken for which it is well-known to include healthier options. For example, consumers are able to choose from Kentucky Grilled Chicken, along with a broader range of salads.

BRAND STRATEGY

- International expansion is the driving force of KFC's growth strategy.
- Through franchising, YUM! Brands is reducing company ownership in KFC restaurants, especially in underperforming or highly penetrated markets.
- KFC is continuously expanding its menu, providing it with a sharper edge against McDonald's and other competitors.

International markets, especially China, are the driving force of KFC's growth strategy. KFC parent YUM! Brands generated more than half of its operating profit in China and 72 other emerging countries in 2011. In 2012 YUM! Brands planned to add 700 new restaurants in China, including KFC locations. In the July 21, 2012, issue of the *South China Morning Post*, CEO David Novak indicated that while the company had 60 restaurants for every 1 million people in the United States, in China that ratio was 4:1 million. On the Chinese mainland Novak indicated that the consumer population was projected to swell from roughly 300 million in 2012 to more than 600 million by 2020.

In addition to establishing traditional restaurant locations, KFC was employing other innovative brand building strategies in China. For example, in mid-2012 YUM! Brands formed a partnership with one of the country's largest electrical appliance retailers, Suning Appliance Co. Ltd., paving the way for the establishment of 150 in-store restaurants, including KFC units, over the course of five years.

Franchising is another key element of the KFC brand strategy. By 2011 YUM! Brands was focusing its resources more on emerging and underpenetrated markets while reducing company ownership in underperforming or highly penetrated markets. In keeping with this strategy, a refranchising program was established to reduce ownership in KFC restaurants to 5 percent by the end of 2012. In Russia, the company assumed full control of Rostiks-KFC in 2010. After rebranding the locations under the KFC banner, KFC's Russian restaurants led YUM! Brands in same-store sales growth.

The KFC brand is continuously expanding its menu to gain a sharper edge against McDonald's and other competitors. By 2011 KFC had introduced breakfast offerings at more than 600 locations, for example. In addition, it also had introduced espresso coffee, as well as its Krushers line of frozen drink concoction, available in flavors such as Mango Mania, Strawberry Lush, and Kookies N' Kream. Chicken-related menu items included Dip'ems, all-white Extra Crispy chicken tenders that customers could dip in six different sauces. In addition, after a 20-year absence, KFC reintroduced its slider-sized Chicken Littles sandwiches in 2012.

BRAND EQUITY

- According to *Nation's Restaurant News*, KFC held a commanding 33.19 percent share of the restaurant industry's chicken segment in 2012.
- Among U.S. quick service restaurants whose main offering is chicken-on-the-bone, The NPD Group Inc. reported that KFC's market share was a leading 39 percent in 2011.
- KFC placed 64th in Interbrand's ranking of the top 100 global brands in 2012.
- Citing data from Euromonitor, *Market Share Reporter* indicated that, in 2010, KFC was the leading fast-food restaurant chain in South Africa, with 44 percent market share.

According to *Nation's Restaurant News'* 2012 Top 100 Market Share Overview, chicken represented 6.74 percent of restaurant industry sales overall. With 33.19 percent of the market, KFC held a commanding lead within the segment. This compared to competitors Chick-fil-A (28.81 percent), Popeyes Louisiana Kitchen (12.30 percent), Church's Chicken (6.24 percent), and Zaxby's (6.06 percent). Among U.S. quick service restaurants whose main offering is chicken-on-the-bone, The NPD Group Inc. reported that KFC's market share was a leading 39 percent in 2011.

KFC's brand equity also is reflected in its inclusion in Interbrand's ranking of the top 100 global brands. KFC achieved a ranking of 64 in 2012, behind seventh-place McDonald's but ahead of sister company Pizza Hut (86) and Starbucks (88). KFC also was included in Millward Brown Optimor's 2012 BrandZ Top 100 ranking. KFC's ranking of 91 trailed behind other fast food industry brands, including Subway (52), Starbucks (42), and McDonald's (4).

KFC's brand equity is global in nature. For example, citing data from Euromonitor, *Market Share Reporter* indicated that in 2010 KFC was the leading fast-food restaurant chain in South Africa, with 44 percent market share. This compared to competitors Nando's (6 percent), Chicken Licken (5 percent), and McDonald's (5 percent).

BRAND AWARENESS

- With a commanding 33.19 percent of the restaurant industry's chicken segment in 2012, according to *Nation's Restaurant News*, KFC enjoyed the significant awareness that corresponds with a strong leadership position.
- In addition to strong brand awareness in its native country, KFC had achieved strong recognition worldwide by 2012, with operations in about 115 countries and territories worldwide.
- By August of 2012 the KFC brand had amassed more than 5 million fans on the social network, Facebook.

KFC enjoyed the significant awareness that corresponds with a strong leadership position. According to *Nation's Restaurant News*, KFC held a commanding 33.19 percent of the restaurant industry's chicken segment in 2012. By this time KFC's operations included more than 4,780 locations throughout the United States.

In addition to strong brand awareness in its native country, KFC had achieved strong global recognition by 2012, with operations in about 115 countries and territories worldwide. Each day, the company served approximately 12 million customers. By the end of 2011 YUM Restaurants International, the international division of KFC parent YUM! Brands, operated 8,920 KFC units. In China, where the brand was achieving significant growth, 3,701 KFC restaurants were in operation.

Social media is a prime example of the strong recognition surrounding KFC. By August of 2012 the brand had amassed more than 5 million fans on the social network, Facebook. That year, the brand held a "Bring Back a Classic" photo contest on Facebook, in which one lucky winner received a 1970 Dodge Charger, in connection with a promotion surrounding its classic menu item, Chunky Chicken Pot Pie. In addition, KFC also awarded a US$20,000 college scholarship for one tweeted photo on the micro-blogging site, Twitter.

BRAND OUTLOOK

- International expansion is the driving force of KFC's growth strategy.
- KFC parent YUM! Brands considers China the most promising growth opportunity for the 21st century, but India and Africa also were key markets for KFC.
- An increased focus on obesity and healthy eating has led KFC to offer healthier menu choices, including salads and grilled chicken.

- KFC's ability to develop new offerings is supported by YUM! Brands' strong investment in research and development, which totaled US$34 million in 2011.

Faced with a relatively mature domestic market, KFC looked to other countries for future growth. Beyond the United States, significant opportunities existed in China, according to the company, although sales in China declined steadily in 2012. In addition, India and Africa also were part of the brand's expansion strategy.

In its 2011 *Annual Customer Mania Report*, parent YUM! Brands indicated that it considered China to be "the best restaurant growth opportunity of the 21st century." During the late 1990s the company had determined that the casual dining operating model was the most successful in China. Since that time YUM! Brands devoted tremendous resources to expand in China. In 2012 the company announced plans to open about 500 new locations annually, especially in smaller Chinese cities, building on a base that already included more than 3,700 restaurants. KFC's future success in China was enhanced by a company-owned and operated Chinese distribution system for its restaurants. Still, industry analysts expressed skepticism as sales in China continued to decline following some unfavorable press on the KFC chicken suppliers in China. Yum! Brands CEO David Novak responded by suggesting KFC needed time for sales to recover, expressing confidence in "the resilience of the brand."

By 2015 YUM! Brands India had plans to establish 1,000 new locations in the country. A US$150 million investment would support the future growth of KFC and other YUM! restaurant brands. Specifically, the company planned to have 550 KFC locations in India by 2015, with projected sales of approximately US$1 billion. YUM! Brands planned to grow the KFC brand in India by mirroring the successful strategy it had employed in China. However, some indicated that the lack of a company-owned distribution system as well as more challenging government regulation were challenges that would need to be addressed in India.

Africa also was of great importance to KFC's future growth. By 2011 KFC operated approximately 660 restaurants in South Africa, eclipsing McDonald's and Nando's by a factor of four. In the March 19, 2012, issue of *Africa News*, KFC African Division General Manager Keith Warren estimated that KFC's locations across the African continent could potentially reach the 2,000 mark by 2020. In addition to South Africa, KFC already had made inroads in the markets of Kenya, Zambia, Ghana, and Nigeria by 2012. Moving forward, KFC was preparing to establish operations in Malawi, Angola, Tanzania, Uganda, Zimbabwe, and the Democratic Republic of Congo.

An increased focus on diabetes, obesity, and healthy eating has caused restaurants to offer healthier choices to consumers. In its June 4, 2012, issue, the *Financial Times* indicated that YUM! Brands has faced pressure from health advocates for contributing to health concerns such as these. However, KFC has added healthier choices to its menu, including salads and grilled chicken. In the same article, CEO David Novak remarked, "You can't be something that you're not," and argued that fried chicken can be part of a balanced diet.

KFC's future success also rests on its ability to continuously develop new offerings for consumers. Each year, YUM! Brands devotes considerable resources to research and development. In addition to a dedicated facility in Louisville, Kentucky, YUM! Brands' China Division also maintained a research and development center in Shanghai. Compared to US$31 million in 2009, the company's research and development investments totaled US$33 million in 2010 and US$34 million in 2011.

FURTHER READING

Chu, Kathy. "Yum Brands CEO Takes Global View on Fast Food; Novak Thinks Big in Terms of Expansion." *USA Today*, February 12, 2012.

"KFC Corporation." *International Directory of Company Histories.* Ed. Jay P. Pederson. Vol. 89. Detroit, MI: St. James Press, 2007.

"KFC Solves Double Dipping Dilemma with Introduction of Delicious and Satisfying New Dip'ems." Benzinga, October 15, 2012. Accessed February 28, 2013. http://www.benzinga.com/pressreleases/12/10/b2993941/kfc-solves-double-dipping-dilemma-with-introduction-of-delicious-and-sa.

"Newly Discovered Colonel Sanders Autobiography & Recipe Book Launched Exclusively on Facebook." *Business Wire*, May 29, 2012.

Perez, Bien. "Yum Ready to Gobble up More of Mainland Market." *South China Morning Post*, July 21, 2012.

Rappeport, Alan. "Finger Lickin' All over the World; Monday Interview." *Financial Times*, June 4, 2012.

———. "Yum Uses Chinese Model to Woo India; Food Retailers." *Financial Times*, June 4, 2012.

Robinson-Jacobs, Karen. "Doritos Taco Sales in U.S. Soar as KFC Sales in China Sink." *Dallas Morning News*, February 5, 2013.

"South Africa; KFC Colonel Leads the Charge into Africa." *Africa News*, March 19, 2012.

Stein, Lindsay. "Fast-Food Chains Use Heritage, Integrated Marketing Recipes." *PR Week*, August 2012.

"Top 100 Market Share Overview." *Nation's Restaurant News*, June 25, 2012.

2011 YUM! Brands Annual Customer Mania Report. Louisville, KY: YUM! Brands, Inc., 2012.

Van Landingham, Vanessa. "KFC Eyes Snack Market with Chicken Littles." *Nation's Restaurant News*, September 17, 2012.

"YUM! Eyes $1 Billion in Revenues in India by 2015 (Plans to Open 1,000 Outlets in India Investing $150 Million)." *India Business Insight*, September 24, 2011.

"Yum to Open Restaurants in Appliance Retail Stores." *Franchise Plus*, May 10, 2012.

KIA

———————————— ■ ————————————

BRAND ORIGINS

- Kia began life in 1944 as a manufacturer of steel tubing and bicycle parts.
- Much of Kia's early history is tied to the dictatorship of President Park Chung-hee, who used government policy to spur South Korea's economic growth.
- Under Park's tutelage, Kia sold its first truck in 1962 and began manufacturing automobiles in 1974.

- Park's successor, Chun Doo-hwan, designated Kia as just one of three Korean companies authorized to produce automobiles.

Kia began life as Kyungsung (or Kyeongseong) Precision Industry, a manufacturer of steel tubing and bicycle parts. Established in Seoul, South Korea, on June 9, 1944, the company began producing complete bicycles in 1951 and in 1952 changed its name to Kia. Only with the end of the Korean War in June 1953 did the company become fully operational, thereafter expanding its product line to include motorcycles in 1957. Yet it did not truly hit its stride until after General Park Chung-hee seized the South Korean presidency in a May 1961 coup.

Eager to spur economic growth, Park enlisted the help of the *chaebols*, business groups consisting of large companies owned or managed by relatives of one or two prominent families. He selected the Kia chaebol to concentrate on trucks and various industrial goods such as machine tools. Under Park's direction, Kia sold its first truck in 1962 and began manufacturing automobiles in 1974, producing a variant of the Mazda Familia that it marketed under the name Kia Brisa.

Park was assassinated in October 1979, and Chun Doo-hwan, who took power in a coup that December, became concerned about runaway growth in the Korean auto industry. Therefore in 1981 he designated Kia as one of just three companies allowed to produce automobiles, and the only one permitted to manufacture light trucks. Kia began looking toward the global marketplace, where it sought to fill the low-end, economy car segment vacated by up-and-coming Japanese automakers. In 1992 it incorporated Kia Motors America.

591

BRAND ELEMENTS

- The name "Kia" comes from the Chinese characters *Ki*, meaning "to arise or come up out of," and *a*, referring to Asia.
- The most distinctive feature in Kia's simple logotype is the absence of a crossbar on the *A*.
- In 2004 Kia reversed the color scheme of its logo, which had featured the company name in white against a red oval.
- Another Kia logo, used primarily in the Korean domestic market, features a stylized *K* on a baby-blue circle.

The name "Kia" comes from the Chinese characters *Ki*, meaning "to arise or come up out of," and *a*, referring to Asia. The most notable feature of its simple logo, which spells out the company name in all capital letters using a customized version of the Friz Quadrata bold OT font, is the absence of a crossbar on the *A*. Set into a horizontal oval shape, the logo sometimes appears in black and white, but more typically it is a combination of red and white.

For a decade following its adoption in 1994, the logotype appeared in white against the red background of the oval, itself surrounded by a band of white. In 2004, however, the company reversed this arrangement, rendering the brand name and the outline of the oval in red. Kia also switched to what it described in an August 2004 press release as "a richer, deeper red." The 1994 and the 2004 logos both appeared in a two-dimensional or typography version, as well as a three-dimensional version for mounting on the hood of a vehicle. In the three-dimensional version, the negative space is chrome rather than white.

Another Kia logo, used primarily in the Korean domestic market, features a stylized *K* that includes only the two angled legs, not the vertical one, thus giving it the appearance of taking off in flight. The *K* is in white or chrome, depending on whether the logo is two- or three-dimensional, and appears against a baby-blue circle inscribed within a larger circle of black containing the words "KIA MOTORS" in uppercase.

BRAND IDENTITY

- Unlike Ford or Toyota, which were simply named after their founders, Kia has a descriptive name that serves as its own form of advertising.
- Kia's slogan, "The power to surprise," emphasizes what the company calls "the exciting and enabling attributes of the Kia brand."
- In August 2004 Kia formally revealed its new corporate identity with a press release and a flurry of rebranding efforts worldwide.

A great number of automobile brands—for example, Ford or Toyota—were simply named after their founders and

their families. Kia, on the other hand, has a descriptive name that serves as its own form of advertising. Company literature stresses its meaning, "To arise or come out of Asia," which in turn conveys an image of a bold, fresh future.

Kia's logo likewise presents the brand as a powerful player in the global marketplace. According to a statement from the company, "The rich, deep red color" of the logo "suggests the passion of the sun and represents Kia's strong determination to move forward in a lively and entertaining fashion." The oval surrounding the brand name is a "refined ellipse [which] symbolizes the globe and alludes to Kia's stature as a major player on the world automotive stage." As for the company's brand slogan, "The power to surprise," this "represents Kia's global commitment to surpassing customer expectations through continuous automotive innovation, while embodying the 'exciting and enabling' attributes of the Kia brand."

In August 2004 Kia formally revealed its new corporate identity (CI) with a press release and a flurry of rebranding efforts worldwide, clear evidence of the importance its leadership placed on brand symbolism. The most obvious manifestation of the new CI involved changes to the logo, but as the press release explained, "Kia views the revamping of the CI as an opportunity to accelerate its overall brand-building strategy, with particular focus on international markets, where success in competition with the world's leading automakers increasingly hinges on differentiation and a continuous strengthening of brand value."

BRAND STRATEGY

- Kia and Hyundai originated as *chaebols*, business groups consisting of large companies owned or managed by relatives of one or two prominent families.
- By the end of the 1970s Kia had matured from an import processor, which received parts from overseas and assembled trucks locally, to a full-scale exporter.
- In the 1980s Kia systematically applied a strategy of filling the low-end automobile market segment from which Japanese carmakers had largely graduated.
- The Hyundai Group, which acquired a controlling share in the late 1990s, led Kia toward an increased focus on design.

Like the much larger Korean automaker Hyundai, Kia began its existence as one of its homeland's many *chaebols*, business groups consisting of large companies owned or managed by relatives of one or two prominent families. President Park Chung-hee, who seized power in May 1961, used the chaebols to advance Korean economic interests overseas, in the process developing a brand strategy for Kia that relied on a heavily managed system of government control.

Under Park's tutelage, Kia matured from an import processor, which received parts from overseas and assembled trucks locally, to a full-scale exporter of vehicles made with Kia parts. By the end of the 1970s, the company began preparing to take on the role of exporter, a move that would be hastened by outside events. First, Park was assassinated in October 1979, then Chun Doo-hwan seized power and in 1981 imposed restrictions aimed at curbing runaway growth in the Korean auto industry. His regime gave way to democracy in 1987, a change that, by ultimately bringing about the end of the chaebols, would further solidify Kia's break with its past.

During the 1980s, Kia systematically applied a strategy of filling the low-end automobile market slot which Japanese carmakers had largely vacated. This policy became manifest in a 1987 agreement to supply the Ford Festiva "microcar," sold at home as the Kia Pride. The midsize Concord, introduced soon afterward, was Kia's largest vehicle to date (aside from its pickup trucks), and thereafter Kia moved into larger models while continuing to produce compacts. The company introduced a full-size sedan (Potentia, 1991), a compact sport utility vehicle (SUV; Sportage, 1993), a minivan (Carnival, 1998), a multipurpose vehicle (MPV; Carens/Rondo, 1999), and a midsize SUV (Sorento, 2003).

The Hyundai Group, which acquired a controlling share in the late 1990s, led Kia toward an increased focus on design, an emphasis that kicked into high gear when Kia hired Peter Schreyer, formerly of Volkswagen and Audi, as its Chief Design Officer in 2006. The brand introduced a new face, literally, at the 2007 Frankfurt Motor Show when it unveiled its Tiger Nose grille. According to Shreyer, "A car needs a face and I think the new Kia face is strong and distinctive. Visibility is vital and that face should immediately allow you to identify a Kia even from a distance."

BRAND EQUITY

- The 2012 Interbrand "Best Global Brands" list included three newcomers, among them Kia, which entered the top 100 at number 87.
- Kia was one of only three automobile brands, out of thirteen on the 2012 Interbrand list, to increase U.S. sales for the three preceding years.
- After purchasing a 51 percent share in 1998, Hyundai placed Kia and itself on a program of streamlining and cost-cutting.
- When Kia sales figures are reported with those of its parent company, it ranks among the top five carmakers in the world.

The 2012 Interbrand "Best Global Brands" list included three newcomers, among them Kia, which entered the top 100 at number 87 with an estimated value of just

over US\$4 billion. Kia was one of only three automobile brands (out of thirteen on the list) to increase sales in the United States for each of the three preceding years. From 2011 to 2012 its overall U.S. sales figures had grown by about 15 percent to well over half a million units per year.

Kia had come a long way since 1997, when the Asian financial crisis dealt a brutal blow to a company already US\$5.7 billion in debt. At that point Kia had experienced three years' worth of negative income flow, and it went up for sale. The Hyundai Group purchased a 51 percent share and put both Kia and itself on an austerity program that involved selling off subsidiaries, consolidating manufacturing, and reducing the number of models produced. By the time Kia's 10-millionth vehicle rolled off the assembly line in 2002, its sales had grown to US\$11.7 billion and profits had climbed to US\$535 million.

Thenceforth Kia's sales figures would often be reported along with those of its parent, a change that helped catapult it into the realm of the world's top carmakers. Thus for 2011, Hyundai–Kia, with combined sales of 6.53 million vehicles globally, ranked fifth in the world, after General Motors, Volkswagen, Nissan/Renault, and Toyota. Yet though they enjoyed record U.S. sales in 2012, the two Korean carmakers had seen their market share drop for the first time in 20 years. Supply shortages and renewed competition from Japanese automakers (themselves finally coming out of a slump brought on by the earthquake and tsunami that hit their country the previous year) were blamed for the sales slump.

BRAND AWARENESS

- Kia earned a top-10 spot on J. D. Powers and Associates' Customer Service Index Ranking, Mass Market Brands in 2011 and 2012.
- Beginning in about 2008, the brand's advertising and marketing efforts began to shift toward an emphasis on design over mere affordability.
- With sponsorship of sporting events and the Vans Warped Tour, Kia targeted young buyers for its Soul compact MPV.
- "Space Babies," a 60-second Kia Sorento commercial aimed at young parents, ran during the 2013 Super Bowl.

Kia earned a 13th-place ranking on J. D. Powers and Associates' Customer Service Index Ranking Mass Market Brands in 2010, and climbed to fifth place in the following year. Also in 2011, the brand came in twentieth on Powers's Automotive Performance, Execution, and Layout Study, and rose to number 18 in 2012. Its position on the Customer Service Index Ranking, meanwhile, slipped slightly to eighth place.

The brand's advertising and marketing efforts have shifted apace with its growing emphasis on design over mere affordability. Michael Sprague, the company's vice president for marketing, told Karl Greenberg of *Media-Post* in February 2009, "In the past, a lot of our ads were more focused on humor rather than the product, and those were the right ads for the times, but now the products and features will be the heroes."

As it rolled out the youth-oriented Forte compact and the Soul compact MPV in 2008, Kia began shifting its marketing approach toward younger buyers. To this end, in 2009 it "moved into sports in a big way," as Greenberg noted, signing agreements with the National Basketball Association, the World Cup, the Asian Games, and the Australian Open tennis championship. Additionally, it continued as sponsor of the Vans Warped Tour, a summer rock concert series that had an obvious youth focus.

Kia advertised in the 2009 Super Bowl pregame show, and by 2013 it had greatly increased its stake in this highly important advertising venue with a 32nd spot in the third quarter of the game and a 60-second one in the fourth. "Kia has been red hot for the past few years," wrote Ryan Beene in *Automotive News*, "but at 3.8 percent market share [in the United States], it still has to work to get on consumer shopping lists. That's why the big game, and its 100 million-plus viewers, is a key part of Kia's ad strategy." The 60-second commercial, "Space Babies," was targeted to young parents, and offered what Sprague described as "an entertaining look at life's challenges and the many ways the [Kia] Sorento's long list of technologies and amenities can make getting through the day just a little better."

BRAND OUTLOOK

- During the U.S. financial crisis that began in the fall of 2008, Kia's stock continued to rise while that of its stateside competitors faltered.
- In 2012 Kia and Hyundai ran into trouble when the Environmental Protection Agency found that both had overstated fuel economy figures for 13 different models.
- In spite of an overall U.S. market-share drop for the Hyundai–Kia partnership in 2012, Kia itself had a better share than ever, at 3.85 percent.
- Byung Mo Ahn, group president and CEO of Kia Motors America, announced that KMA would launch seven new or revamped vehicles in 2013.

Kia entered the 21st century by expanding globally in a big way, opening large production facilities in China and Slovakia in 2005, a joint Hyundai–Kia European design center in 2007, and a US$1.2 billion factory in West Point, Georgia, in 2010. During the U.S. financial crisis that began in the fall of 2008, Kia's stock continued to rise, while that of its stateside competitors faltered.

In 2012, however, Kia and Hyundai ran into trouble when the Environmental Protection Agency found that both had overstated fuel economy figures for 13 different models. As a result, the two carmakers agreed to compensate some one million vehicle-owners, which would cost them about US$79 million annually for the next few years.

In spite of an overall market-share drop in the United States for the Hyundai–Kia partnership in 2012, Kia itself prospered, selling its 4-millionth vehicle in the United States that year. Viewed by itself, without its parent, Kia had a better U.S. market share than ever, at 3.85 percent.

The brand and its products showed up on dozens of consumer superlative lists during 2012. For example, the midsize Optima alone had been named "Best Car for the Budget-Minded Retiree" by Fox Business and "2012 Best New Car Value" from *Kiplinger's Personal Finance*, while earning recognition on *Consumer Guide's* "Best Buy" and *Parents* magazine's "Best Family Cars of 2012" rankings.

According to Byung Mo Ahn, president and CEO of Kia Motors America (KMA), "Kia is a completely different company from what it was just three years ago, and 2012 will go down as a milestone year that demonstrated the power of our brand transformation." Byung also announced that KMA would be launching seven new or revamped vehicles in 2013.

FURTHER READING

Beene, Ryan. "Hyundai–Kia Share Slips Despite Growth." *Automotive News*, January 3, 2013.

———. "Hyundai, Lincoln Bet Big on Super Bowl; GM, Honda Sit Game Out." *Automotive News*, January 28, 2013.

Greenberg, Karl. "Kia Leverages 'Power to Surprise' in Ads." *MediaPost*, February 16, 2009. Accessed January 26, 2013. http://www.mediapost.com/publications/article/100281/kia-leverages-power-to-surprise-in-ads.html#ixzz2J79dHUYd.

Kia Motors Corporation. *2011 Annual Report*. Seoul, South Korea: Kia, 2012.

"Kia Motors Corporation." *International Directory of Company Histories*. Ed. Derek Jacques and Paula Kepos. Vol. 136. Detroit, MI: St. James Press, 2012.

KIT KAT

AT A GLANCE

Brand Synopsis: Since its creation, the Kit Kat chocolate bar has been positioned as a snack that encourages people to take a break and enjoy a Kit Kat, anywhere and at any time.

Parent Company: Nestlé S.A.
Avenue Nestlé 55
CH-800 Vevey
Switzerland
http://www.nestle.com

Sector: Consumer Staples

Industry Group: Food, Beverage & Tobacco

Performance: *Market share*—1.70 percent worldwide (2006). *Sales*—US$1.6 billion (2004).

Principal Competitors: Kraft Foods Inc.; Cadbury; Mars Inc.; Hershey Company

BRAND ORIGINS

- The Kit Kat candy bar, originally known as Rowntree's Chocolate Crisp, was first developed by the Rowntree confectionary company of York, England, in 1935.
- Kit Kat is manufactured and sold in the United States through an agreement with the Hershey Foods Corporation.
- The international food conglomerate Nestlé acquired Rowntree in 1988.

The Kit Kat bar was first developed by the Rowntree confectionery company of York, England. The Rowntree company originated with a Quaker woman named Mary Tuke, a grocer in York who dealt in a variety of products but became well known for her coffee and tea. By 1785 she was also selling chocolate and cocoa, and in time the manufacturing of cocoa, chocolate, and chicory became a distinct, although relatively small, part of the Tuke business. When Tuke died, the business was carried on by her nephew, William, and later by his sons and grandsons. By 1862 the Tuke family was ready to disengage itself from various aspects of the business. The chocolate business was sold to Henry I. Rowntree, who, like Mary Tuke, was a devout Quaker.

In 1869 Joseph Rowntree joined his brother Henry in the business, eventually becoming the more active and influential of the two. H. I. Rowntree and Company began to experiment with the manufacture of gum sweets, a confectionery more popular at the time in France than in England, and in 1881 the company started to produce crystallized gums. The experiment was a success and soon led to Rowntree's first expansion.

Henry Rowntree died in 1883, leaving the business to Joseph, who was later joined by his two sons. At this time the firm manufactured two main cocoa products, but a Dutch cocoa —a pure cocoa powder from which the cocoa butter had been removed—began to gain in popularity. Rowntree devoted himself to manufacturing a pure cocoa essence using the Dutch method, which he began to sell in 1887 under the name Rowntree's Elect Cocoa. The cocoa was a success and led to even further expansion, and land was purchased on the outskirts of York in

1890 for the expansion of the company's manufacturing capacity. This estate became known as the Haxby Road factory, and by 1922 it had grown into a 220-acre complex of factories and other company buildings. In 1897, with more than 1,000 employees, the company reorganized as Rowntree and Company, Ltd.

In 1911 Rowntree trademarked the names "Kit Kat" and "Kit Cat." The names may have referred to an English political club of the 17th and 18th centuries that called itself the "Kit Kat club." It wasn't until the 1920s that Rowntree developed a box of chocolates that carried the name Kit Kat. During the early 1930s, the company decided that it was making too many different brands of chocolate and eventually phased out the Kit Kat box.

On August 29, 1935, the company debuted Rowntree's Chocolate Crisp after an employee suggested "a chocolate bar that a man could take to work in his pack." Rowntree's Chocolate Crisp consisted of four fingers, with each finger composed of three layered wafers covered in an outer layer of chocolate. The chocolate bar was initially sold in London and southern England; it was an immediate success and soon was sold throughout England. In 1937 the name was changed to Kit Kat Chocolate Crisp.

In the 1950s, Rowntree began to sell its products internationally in South Africa, Canada, Ireland, New Zealand, and Australia. Rowntree soon expanded into Germany, Belgium, Holland, and Italy. In 1969 Rowntree merged with John Mackintosh and Sons Ltd. to form Rowntree Mackintosh Limited. The new company had 28,000 employees at 22 factories making candy that was exported to 120 countries. Rowntree Mackintosh negotiated an agreement with Hershey Foods Corporation allowing Hershey to manufacture and market some Rowntree Mackintosh products, including Kit Kat, in the United States. Hershey holds this license in perpetuity unless the Hershey company is ever sold.

In 1988 two Swiss companies, Nestlé and Jacobs Suchard, began a bidding war for Rowntree. After a two-month battle, Rowntree was acquired by Nestlé, whose winning bid of £2.5 billion made the deal the largest takeover of a British company by a foreign firm to date. Nestlé agreed to keep Rowntree's headquarters in York and created a chocolate, confectionery, and biscuit group based in York that became responsible for Nestlé's worldwide chocolate and confectionery strategy.

BRAND ELEMENTS
- The first advertisements for Kit Kat in 1937 featured the concept of taking a break with a Kit Kat.
- The tagline "Have a break, have a Kit Kat" was first used in 1958.
- A shortage of fresh milk in England during World War II forced Rowntree to change its formula for Kit Kat bars.

- The Kit Kat logo used by Hershey in the United States features white lettering on a red background.
- Nestlé uses red lettering within a white circle for the Kit Kat logo in the rest of the international market.

As a Quaker with strong ideals, Joseph Rowntree disagreed with the concept of advertising and avoided the practice. He eventually dropped his objections, however, and full-page print advertisements helped make Rowntree's Elect Cocoa a success. In 1937 Rowntree began to advertise the Kit Kat bar. The first marketing campaigns for the brand featured the concept of taking a "break" with a Kit Kat; the theme has remained constant throughout the history of the brand. The Kit Kat was also labeled "The Biggest Little Meal in Britain."

Kit Kat's initial packaging featured an outer red label with the red letters of "Kit Kat" encircled in white above the white lettering of "Chocolate Crisp." During World War II, Rowntree was forced to adapt the recipe of the Kit Kat when fresh milk became scarce. Not wanting to confuse its loyal customers, Rowntree changed the packaging to a distinctive blue, deleted the words "Chocolate Crisp," and removed the oval logo, using block lettering instead for "Kit Kat."

By 1949 Rowntree was able to revert to its original chocolate formula, and the wrapping changed as well. The striking red color was back on the label, and the oval "Kit Kat" logo was placed in the center of the package and featured more prominently; the words "Chocolate Crisp" did not make a return to the packaging. The label for a Kit Kat bar has stayed remarkably constant over the years with one notable exception—the packaging by Hershey for the contemporary U.S. market features "Kit Kat" in bold white lettering on a red background.

In 1958 a series of television commercials was launched in Britain using the tagline "Have a break, have a Kit Kat." The marketing campaign was a runaway success and has stayed with the brand in various iterations. Over the years the tagline has become such an iconic part of the Kit Kat brand that it is now a trademark. In the United States a variation of the Kit Kat "break" theme has been used for ads with a jingle that was composed in 1986 for the "Gimme a Break" marketing campaign. Over the years the advertisements have featured celebrities singing the jingle.

BRAND IDENTITY
- The original elements of a Kit Kat—layers of wafers covered in chocolate—have remained constant since its creation.
- Nestlé tries to show how a Kit Kat allows people to enjoy chocolate while still making healthy choices.
- Kit Kat advertising focuses on the feelings of people enjoying themselves with a Kit Kat rather than the ingredients of the chocolate bar.

For more than 75 years, the original elements of a Kit Kat bar have remained constant: layered wafers covered in chocolate. Kit Kat's brand identity, too, has been constant—consumers around the world are reminded in myriad advertisements that eating a Kit Kat bar is an enjoyable way to have a break. In tough economic times, the Kit Kat is still a high-quality, moderately priced chocolate bar and a pleasant diversion at any time during the work day. The Kit Kat is at once traditional and modern.

Nestlé highlights that a Kit Kat can be the perfect snack as part of a balanced diet. A variety of sizes and types of Kit Kat bars allow consumers to choose the perfect Kit Kat to fit their budgets and calorie counts. Smaller and bite-sized Kit Kats are lower in calories and a good fit for people looking for a lighter snack.

Kit Kat advertising has featured people from all walks of life enjoying themselves while eating a Kit Kat. People in everyday scenarios take a break with a Kit Kat and then get back to the task at hand. The Kit Kat bar is not the focus of attention; rather, the feelings and emotions that people achieve while taking a break with a Kit Kat are on display.

BRAND STRATEGY

- The first extension of the Kit Kat brand was a two-finger multipack introduced in 1963.
- Kit Kats are popular throughout the world—to take advantage of cultural tastes, Kit Kat has made several line extensions that connect with each country's palate.
- Kit Kats are found in many flavors throughout the world, including more than 200 unique flavors in Japan.

In 1963 Rowntree introduced the two-finger, multipack Kit Kat as a way to sell its product in the biscuit aisle of grocery stores. This extension of the brand was such a success that it helped double the sales of Kit Kat within 10 years and encouraged more variations. By 2012 a range of sizes was available throughout the world: snack, king, and mini in the United States; balls in France and Japan; and bites in Singapore, Japan, and Canada. A 12-finger family block is popular in Australia. A three-finger Kit Kat is produced for the Middle East to match a denomination of the local currency, making the product a convenient, one-coin purchase.

This multicultural phenomenon continued as Kit Kat expanded its globalization. Its successes has made global line extensions a large part of the Kit Kat strategy. For example, the Kit Kat Chunky was launched in the United Kingdom in 1999 and became an instant success. In 2005 the Kit Kat Chunky sold at a rate of about 200,000 per day. Kit Kat Chunky is available in mini and snack sizes and in a king-sized bar called "Big Break." In the United States, the Kit Kat Chunky is known as the "Big Kat."

In the United Kingdom, where it has historically been the best-selling candy, Kit Kat is available in a range of flavors, including milk chocolate, dark chocolate, orange, mint, and caramel. Flavors in the United States include milk chocolate and white chocolate. Since 2000 Kit Kat has been available at various times in more than 200 flavors in Japan, including green tea, maple syrup, aloe vera yogurt, cola, sweet potato, miso, azuki red bean, roasted corn, and the most popular flavor of all, soy sauce. Cookie dough- and honeycomb-flavored Kit Kats are available in Australia, and a banana-flavored bar is sold in Canada.

BRAND EQUITY

- In 2012 Kit Kat had a brand value of US$3.3 billion, according to *Fortune*'s Global 500 list of top brands.
- Kit Kat is ranked in Brand Finance's "UK Top 50" and MPP Consulting's "Top 100 Most Expensive British Brands."
- In 2011 Nestlé, Kit Kat's parent company, was ranked as the most profitable company in the world.

In 2012, *Fortune*'s Global 500 list of the top brands ranked Kit Kat 346th, with a brand value of US$3.3 billion, a fall from 293rd place in 2011, when its brand value was estimated at US$3.6 billion. Brand Finance ranked Kit Kat 32nd, with a brand value of US$3.3 billion, in its 2012 ranking of the most valuable British brands, just behind international confectioner Cadbury, whose estimated brand value of US$3.6 billion was ranked 31st. MPP Consulting placed Kit Kat 11th, with a brand value of US$2.2 billion, in its "Top 100 Most Expensive British Brands," a ranking that includes only British goods or services or brands created in Great Britain. In 2011 Kit Kat's parent company, Nestlé, was listed as the most profitable company in the world in *Fortune*'s Global 500.

BRAND AWARENESS

- When most people hear the phrase "have a break," they immediately complete it with "have a Kit Kat."
- The *Guinness Book of World Records* calculated in 2010 that 540 Kit Kat fingers were eaten every second around the world.
- Fourteen different plants manufacture Kit Kat bars for sale in more than 100 countries.

According to the *Guinness Book of World Records*, in March 2010, 540 Kit Kat fingers were eaten every second somewhere in the world, translating to 17.6 billion fingers consumed every year. The distinctive red and white colors of the Kit Kat logo have made it one of the most recognizable brands around the globe. When Nestlé went through the trademark process for the Kit Kat tagline, it was able to prove in court that, when most people hear the phrase "have a break," they immediately complete it with "have a Kit Kat."

Kit Kat is the number one selling candy bar in England and Japan and the fifth-best seller in United States. The annual "Checkout Top 100" list of the biggest-selling brands in the Irish grocery industry ranked Kit Kat as the 41st-best-selling brand in 2012.

Kit Kat's global demand requires manufacturing plants around the world. In addition to York, England, Kit Kat is also manufactured in the United States, Canada, India, Germany, Malaysia, Japan, China, South Africa, Australia, Bulgaria, Turkey, Venezuela, and Russia. Consumers in more than 100 countries can purchase a Kit Kat bar.

BRAND OUTLOOK

- Kit Kat targets consumers of all ages, genders, and economic backgrounds.
- Growth of the Kit Kat brand slowed with the rise of low-carb diets and more healthful dietary choices by consumers.
- Nestlé has begun using fair-trade cocoa in the production of Kit Kat bars, a move popular with investors and consumers.

Nestlé has positioned the Kit Kat brand to be the candy of choice when consumers crave a high-quality chocolate snack. Kit Kat targets consumers of both genders, all ages, and every economic group with moderate pricing and a multitude of variations on the basic bar. Advertising for Kit Kat has been consistent and appealing.

As consumers around the world have become more conscious of their eating habits, growth of the Kit Kat brand in many parts of the world has stagnated. Formidable competition from Cadbury in the United Kingdom, Kit Kat's home market, has at times unseated the Kit Kat bar from its perch as England's best-selling chocolate. Kit Kat has countered by introducing new and unique flavors and sizes, marketing them as limited or special editions to drive demand.

In 2010 Nestlé began using fair-trade cocoa in its production of four-finger Kit Kat bars in the United Kingdom and Ireland. In 2012 the company announced that the two-finger bars will also use fair-trade cocoa. Nestlé buys about a 10th of the world's cocoa, and more than a third of that comes from Ivory Coast, the world's biggest cocoa producer. Companies that carry the fair-trade certification must cover the cost of sustainable farming and invest in community projects, including farmer training, new schools, and reduction of child labor and abuse in the region.

FURTHER READING

Doherty, Dermot. "Nestle U.K. to Produce More KitKat Bars under Fairtrade Label." *Bloomberg*, October 25, 2012.

Irvine, Dean. "How Did Kit Kat Become King of Candy in Japan?" *CNN*, February 2, 2012. Accessed October 31, 2012. http://eatocracy.cnn.com/2012/02/02/how-did-kit-kat-became-king-of-candy-in-japan/?hpt=hp_bn8.

"KitKat's 75th Anniversary Heralded." *Press* (York, England), October 12, 2010.

Madden, Normandy. "Soy-Sauce-Flavored Kit Kats? In Japan, They're No. 1: With 18 Other Exotic Flavors, Nestle Takes Product Localization in Country to Culinary Extremes." *AdvertisingAge*, March 4, 2010.

Nestlé Kit Kat. "Kit Kat." Accessed October 31, 2012. http://www.kitkat.com/about.aspx.

"Rowntree Mackintosh." *International Directory of Company Histories*. Ed. Lisa Mirabile. Vol. 2. Chicago, IL: St. James Press, 1990.

Silverstein, Barry. "Kit Kat: Extending Sweetness." *brandchannel*, August 13, 2010. Accessed October 31, 2012. http://www.brandchannel.com/features_profile.asp?pr_id=505.

"Top Chocolate Brands Worldwide, 2006." *Market Share Reporter*. Ed. Robert S. Lazich and Virgil L. Burton III. Detroit, MI: Gale, 2009.

KLEENEX

—■—

AT A GLANCE

Brand Synopsis: The Kleenex brand has continued its dominance in the facial tissue and personal care industries for nearly nine decades.

Parent Company: Kimberly-Clark Corporation
P.O. Box 619100, DFW Airport Station
Dallas, TX 75261-9100, USA
http://www.kimberly-clark.com, http://www.kleenex.com

Sector: Consumer Staples

Industry Group: Household & Personal Products

Performance: *Market share*—45.4%, U.S. (2012).
Sales—US$2.1 billion, global (2010).

Principal Competitors: Procter & Gamble; Georgia-Pacific Group; Johnson & Johnson

BRAND ORIGINS

- In 1872 Kimberly-Clark was founded in Neenah, Wisconsin, as a collective of paper mills.
- In 1924 Kimberly-Clark introduced Kleenex, which was developed from Cellucotton, a cotton substitute introduced during World War II.
- By the 1930s Kimberly-Clark was marketing Kleenex as a disposable handkerchief.
- In 1965 Kimberly-Clark's pop-up box design was recognized in a federal trademark registration.

- In 1941 Kleenex introduced the Kleenex Mansize Tissue, and in 1955 the Kleenex Dinner Napkin hit the consumer market.

Kleenex's parent company, Kimberly-Clark, was founded in Neenah, Wisconsin, in 1872 as a collective of paper mills. In little more than a decade, the company became the leading paper producer in the Midwest. In the 1890s, one of its divisions, Scott Paper, became the first company to put toilet paper on a roll, and in 1907, Scott introduced the first disposable paper towel.

In the early 20th century Kimberly-Clark developed Cellucotton, which was designed as a substitute for cotton in wartime hospitals and, later, filters for gas masks. Kimberly-Clark was left with a surplus of Cellucotton after World War I, and the company innovated ways to use the material, introducing Cellucotton-based Kotex sanitary napkins and then, in 1924, Kleenex. This was the first disposable facial tissue created in the Western hemisphere. A year later a Kleenex tissue ad in *Ladies Home Journal* touted the product as "the new secret of keeping a pretty skin as used by famous movie stars." Ads followed in other major women's magazines, and two years later Kleenex ads featured endorsements from Hollywood stars.

The product was initially marketed as a cold cream remover, but, according to Kimberly-Clark, the firm's head researcher suffered from hay fever and found Kleenex to be a suitable replacement for a handkerchief. By 1930 Kimberly-Clark had launched Kleenex as a disposable handkerchief. Sales doubled during the first year of this approach. The strategy to market Kleenex as disposable handkerchiefs was strengthened by the company's pop-box design. The company's engineers developed a technique of interfolding two rolls of tissues called the "quadrant design," adopted in 1938, that caused a new tissue to pop up after the consumer pulled a tissue through the slot on the top of the box. By 1949 Kimberly-Clark had devised a portable pop-up package, the Pocket-Pack, based on consumer requests. And in 1965 the pop-up box design was trademarked. Other Kleenex products included the Mansize Tissue (1941) and the Kleenex Dinner Napkin (1955).

BRAND ELEMENTS

- The Kleenex logo consists of the name "Kleenex" printed in a rounded script, followed by the much-smaller words "brand tissue."
- In 1980 Kimberly-Clark redesigned its blue and white box to incorporate other colors to complement consumers' homes.
- Kleenex introduced an oval-shaped package in 2005 and, in 2008, an oval box with Christmas lights that flashed as each tissue was removed.
- In 2010 Kleenex targeted summer sales by introducing triangular-shaped boxes featuring fruit-themed art in its "Slices of Summer" campaign.

The Kleenex logo consists of the name "Kleenex" printed in a rounded, light blue script. The word is slightly arched, and it is followed by the much-smaller words "brand tissue," which are stacked on top of each other. The logo is often printed in white on packaging.

Christine Mau, brand design director at Kimberly-Clark, told the *New York Times* that "with Kleenex we really consider the package as part of the product we're providing." The Kleenex slogan "pop up one at a time" and its packaging, which showcases the company's trademarked interfolding tissues, are an essential element of the Kleenex brand. The pop-up design was adopted by Kleenex in 1938. When a consumer pulled a tissue through the slot on the top of the box, another tissue popped up.

The Kleenex Boutique box, the consumer market's first upright tissue box, appeared in 1967. Mansize tissues, introduced in 1941, were made larger (11 x 11 1/2 inches) than the standard-size tissue, while Little Travelers tissues were made smaller (6 x 8 1/2 inches) than the standard. Until 1980 Kleenex tissues were available only in a blue and white box, which some consumers hid under their own box covers. Kleenex then introduced a variety of colors and patterns for its boxes, after which only about 12 percent of consumers continued to obscure the tissue box. The color and design combinations included oval-shaped boxes, introduced in 2005, and a Christmas-themed box (2008) with lights that flashed as a tissue was pulled out. In 2010 Kleenex introduced a triangular

package with "Slices of Summer" designs, such as a watermelon slice, to boost summer purchases of facial tissues. In 1990 the Kleenex brand introduced a premium bathroom tissue, and in 2010 the brand expanded to include Kleenex Hand Towels. The Kleenex logo—the brand name written in a rounded script set above the words "Brand Tissue"—is always well positioned on packaging.

BRAND IDENTITY

- Kleenex is so well known that the word is often used interchangeably with the term "facial tissue."
- Kleenex commissioned "Letting It Out in America: The Social Landscape for Expressing Emotions," a 2007 study that explored how Americans express their emotions.
- After an NFL coach cried in a team meeting following a difficult loss, Kleenex sent the team a supply of tissues for its locker room.
- Kleenex promotes its brand as contributing to health because disposable tissues offer a more sanitary way to deal with cold and flu symptoms than handkerchiefs.

Kleenex, which created the facial tissue market in the early 20th century, has such a strong presence in the market that the word "Kleenex" is often used interchangeably with the term "facial tissue."

Through its marketing initiatives Kleenex has tied its brand to emotional moments. In 2007 the brand commissioned "Letting It Out in America: The Social Landscape for Expressing Emotions," a study that explored how Americans express their emotions. To that end, Kleenex has sponsored events where tears are shed, such as movies and sporting events. After Rex Ryan, coach of the National Football League's New York Jets, cried during a team meeting following a difficult loss in 2009, Kimberly-Clark provided the team a supply of Kleenex tissues for its locker room.

Kleenex marketing campaigns often push the emotional aspects of the brand's identity, using slogans such as "It Feels Good to Feel." In a news release the company said "Kleenex brand wants to encourage Americans to express the emotions they might otherwise bottle up." In 2010 the company launched the "Softness Worth Sharing" campaign, which encouraged consumers to send a free pack of tissues to a friend or family member and relate their own stories of sharing on the brand's website.

Because disposable tissues are a cleaner way to deal with the symptoms of cold and flu than handkerchiefs are, Kleenex also promotes its brand as contributing to health. The Kleenex website offers facts about cold and flu, as well as tips for cold and flu season. Another health-related product is Kleenex hand towels, single-use towels for consumers to use after washing their hands. Customers are urged to become members of the "Clean Hands Campaign" by using the hand towels to avoid the build-up of germs on soiled linens.

BRAND STRATEGY

- Kleenex leads the United States in market share and has made efforts to expand its international market share in China, Russia, and Latin America.
- Using creative packaging and product design as part of its brand strategy, Kimberly-Clark has released a variety of Kleenex products.
- In 2011 Kleenex introduced tissues certified by the Forest Stewardship Council.
- Kleenex uses promotions and social media to share its brand and to strengthen its associations with health and emotional expression.
- Kleenex used a "sneeze catcher" campaign aimed at children to increase its market share among Hispanic consumers.

Kleenex, the first facial tissue product, is a billion-dollar international seller and leads the United States in market share (45.4 percent in 2012). The brand has also been expanding its international market share in China, Russia, and Latin America.

Kimberly-Clark continues to develop strategies to keep the product relevant, fresh, and popular by using creative packaging and product design. Among the available options are Pocket Packs; Space Saver packs in reduced-size packaging; Purse Packs; and the Boutique variety, which comes in an upright box. Other approaches include the addition of cold-aid components—such as lotion, menthol, and anti-viral features—to the tissues. In 2012 Kleenex introduced the "sneeze shield," a coating that is intended to prevent mucus from soaking through the tissues and getting on hands.

Kleenex makes efforts to expand its brand awareness throughout the year, particularly during the annual flu season. In 2010 the company launched the "Softness Worth Sharing" promotion, which encouraged consumers to send a free pack of tissues to a friend or family member. The recipients of the gifted tissues were encouraged to do the same for others. Kleenex sent approximately one million free packets during the first year of the promotion. The effort attached an "emotion to the promotion that could never be achieved if people were simply ordering samples for themselves," wrote Ian Bell on the *Euromonitor* global market research blog.

Kleenex relies on its website and Facebook page for promotions. For example, during cold and flu season, it asks consumers to nominate people in certain cities to receive a Special Care Delivery of a care pack containing Kleenex products and a cozy blanket. The Facebook page also reminds people that Kleenex brand tissues will be on hand at special events, such as the Super Bowl and the Academy Awards, to catch the tears of joy shed by the winners.

According to an August 20, 2011, article in *PRWeek*, Kleenex launched a campaign during the previous flu season specifically designed to increase its brand awareness among Hispanic consumers. In the *Atrapa estornudos* campaign, children were recruited to be "official sneeze catchers" and to persuade their parents to buy Kleenex. Participants received free gifts. As a result of the campaign, Kleenex saw a 1 percent market share increase among Hispanic consumers.

Kimberly-Clark has worked to tie the Kleenex brand to the recycling and "green" movements. In the 1990s Kleenex introduced recycled paperboard for its packaging, and the tissue boxes now include the 100 percent recycled symbol. In 2011, Kleenex adopted the sustainable requirements needed to add the Forest Stewardship Council certification stamp to its boxes, becoming the first U.S. tissue maker to do so. Kimberly-Clark announced its five-year Sustainability 2015 plan as "a holistic way of weaving sustainable business practices." The company planned to focus on "forest conservation, access to water and sanitation in communities, responsible solutions for postconsumer waste, and providing access to essentials for a better life."

BRAND EQUITY

- Kleenex, the dominant brand in the marketplace, held a 45.4 percent share of the U.S. market in 2012.
- Interbrand ranked Kleenex 80th among top global brands for 2012, with a brand value of US$4.36 billion.
- In 2012 *Brandirectory* ranked Kimberly-Clark number 201 among global brands, with a brand value of US$5.03 billion.

Kleenex, the dominant brand in the marketplace, held a 45.4 percent share in the United States in 2012 but was losing some ground to store brands, which rose almost 3 percentage points to 24.9 percent. Kleenex's main competitor, Puffs, held 24.4 percent of the market. Those numbers did not include sales of the brands at Walmart, which accounted for approximately 12 percent of Kleenex parent company Kimberly-Clark's net sales.

In 2012 *Brandirectory* ranked Kimberly-Clark at number 201 in its Global 500, with a brand value of US$5.03 billion. Interbrand's Best Global Brands 2012 ranked Kleenex at number 80 but dropped its brand value from more than US$5 billion in 2011 to US$4.36 billion. Interbrand reported that Kleenex had a strong social media presence and "outspent competitors in advertising" but that store brands had chipped away at its dominance.

BRAND AWARENESS

- Kleenex is one of Kimberly-Clark's top-selling international brands and is available in 150 countries.
- Kleenex is regarded as one of the classic examples of a brand with top-of-mind awareness.
- Kleenex has such high brand awareness that many consumers use the name "Kleenex" to mean facial tissue.
- Kimberly-Clark has had to run advertising campaigns to remind the public that Kleenex is a brand name, not a generic term.

Several of Kimberly-Clark's brands hold the number one or number two position in more than 80 countries, and its products are available in 175 countries. Kleenex is one of Kimberly-Clark's top-selling international brands and is available in 150 countries.

In fact, Kleenex is the classic example of a top-of-mind brand and is often cited in marketing studies of that concept. To most consumers, the name "Kleenex" is synonymous with "facial tissue." This nearly universal level of name recognition has been a problem as well as a benefit for Kimberly-Clark, which has had to spend millions in advertising to remind people that Kleenex is the brand name of a particular product, not a generic term.

BRAND OUTLOOK

- Kimberly-Clark made plans to increase its brand's presence in China, Russia, and Latin America, areas that already provided 50 percent of the company's sales.
- Kimberly-Clark instituted a cost-cutting program to save more than US$1.6 billion over eight years.
- Walmart, which provided 12 percent of Kimberly-Clark's net sales in 2011, could use its bargaining power to affect Kimberly-Clark's profits from Kleenex sales.

Although Kleenex has held a dominant brand position for nearly nine decades, Kimberly-Clark made plans to increase its brand's presence in China, Russia, and Latin America. Sales in those countries already provide 50 percent of Kimberly-Clark sales, according to Datamonitor, and are growing at a rate of 5 to 7 percent. At the same time the company instituted cost reductions intended to save more than US$1.6 billion over eight years, including a savings of up to US$500 million from 2011 to 2013.

The global recession weakened the Kleenex brand somewhat as price-conscious consumers chose to purchase store brands, which gained nearly 3 percent of the facial tissue market in 2012. According to Datamonitor, Kimberly-Clark faced serious competition from its competitors and needed to diversify its key retailers. Walmart, which Kimberly-Clark reported provided 12 percent of its net sales in 2011, could flex its bargaining strength and impact the manufacturer's profits.

FURTHER READING

Brand Finance. "Global 500 2012." *Brandirectory.* Accessed December 9, 2012. http://brandirectory.com/profile/kimberly-clark.

Interbrand. "Kleenex: Best Global Brands 2012." Accessed December 9, 2012. http://www.interbrand.com/en/best-global-brands/2012/Kleenex.

Kimberly-Clark. Accessed December 9, 2012. http://www.kimberly-clark.com.

Kimberly-Clark. "2011 Annual Report." Accessed January 19, 2013. http://www.cms.kimberly-clark.com/umbracoimages/UmbracoFileMedia/2011_AnnualReport_umbracoFile.PDF.

Kimberly-Clark. "Kimberly-Clark Fact Sheet 2012." Accessed December 9, 2012. http://www.cms.kimberly-clark.com/umbracoimages/UmbracoFileMedia/2012%20K-C%20Fact%20Sheet_umbracoFile.pdf.

Kleenex. Accessed December 9, 2012. http://www.kleenex.com.

Kroll, Dorothy. "Kleenex." *Encyclopedia of Consumer Brands.* Vol. 2. Ed. Janice Jorgensen. Detroit: St. James Press, 1994, 313-15.

Neff, Jack. "Creativity marks this spot: K-C thrives in tiny Neenah; Kimberly-Clark's marketing and design teams have taken the least glamorous of categories and given consumers something to talk about." *Advertising Age,* June 6, 2011. *Gale Power Search.* Accessed December 13, 2012. http://go.galegroup.com/ps/i.do?id=GALE%7CA258457096&v=2.1&u=itsbtrial&it=r&p=GPS&sw=w.

Newman, Andrew Adam. "With Kleenex, the Package Is Part of the Product." *New York Times,* July 8, 2010. Accessed December 13, 2012. https://www.nytimes.com/2010/07/09/business/media/09adco.html?_r=...1.

———. "For Kleenex, a Song and Dance to Sneeze To." *New York Times,* June 27, 2012. Accessed December 13, 2012. https://www.nytimes.com/2012/06/28/business/media/for-kleenex-a-song-and-dance-to-sneeze-to.html.

———. "Researching the Sneeze and How to Handle It." *New York Times,* September 27, 2012. Accessed December 13, 2012. https://www.nytimes.com/2011/09/28/business/media/researching-the-sneeze-and-how-to-handle-it.html.

KPMG

BRAND ORIGINS

- In 1897 James Marwick and Roger Mitchell founded the accounting firm Marwick, Mitchell & Co.
- In 1911 the company merged with a British accountancy firm to form Peat, Marwick, Mitchell & Co.
- After 75 years of continual growth, Peat Marwick formed Peat Marwick International in 1978 to expand global business.
- Peat Marwick merged with the Dutch firm KMG in 1987, creating the world's largest accounting firm, KPMG.

In 1897 James Marwick and Roger Mitchell, two Scottish immigrants, began Marwick, Mitchell & Co. in New York City. In the early years the company was focused mainly on accountancy services for the banking industry, but as the company grew, Marwick, Mitchell & Co. sought overseas markets. In 1911 the company merged with a British accountancy firm to form Peat, Marwick, Mitchell & Co. Both companies benefited by gaining access to overseas markets. The business grew steadily for the next 75 years, securing Peat, Marwick, Mitchell & Co. a ranking in the top eight U.S. accounting firms. Despite some reputational issues, by 1972 the company was the largest accountancy firm in the United States.

To accommodate its growing business and to ensure global expansion, Peat Marwick opened Peat Marwick International in 1978 to oversee operations outside the United States. The company then set up umbrella partnerships with different firms from around the world. This allowed the company to expand by combining a single corporate image with well-respected and established local accounting organizations. While the firm continued to grow, earning record-breaking revenues from its overseas operations, by the late 1980s the company faced increasing competition from the "big eight" firms as well as maturing markets for its services. In order to compete, the company implemented computerized auditing, made several acquisitions, and also took part in one of the biggest mergers in the accounting industry. In 1987

Peat Marwick completed a merger with Klynveld Main Goerdeler (KMG), a Dutch accounting firm with a strong U.S. arm that was the ninth-leading firm in the country. The merger of KMG and Peat Marwick, called KPMG, created the largest accounting firm in the world in terms of both size and revenue at the time.

While the global offices of KPMG earned financial success, the U.S. arm, KPMG Peat Marwick, had trouble growing in light of the collapse of the savings and loan industry in the late 1980s and the subsequent fallout in the market. To strengthen the U.S. portion of the company, KPMG Peat Marwick launched its first advertising campaign, aligned its brand with the international one by renaming itself KPMG LLC, and expanded its services, specifically in consulting services, to match new growth markets. These efforts paid off and demonstrated the direction of the entire company. Throughout the 1990s KPMG worked to align its core business and centralize its operations. The company divided its business into three geographic sections—the Americas (which now brought Mexico, Latin America, Australia, and several other member firms under the KPMG LLC name); Europe, Middle East, and Africa; and Asia-Pacific—and into three business sectors—tax, audit, and advisory services. By the turn of the millennium, the company was growing rapidly. While business was strong, the company experienced its share of scandals and reputational issues as the United States dealt with the Enron and Fannie Mae scandals, both of which affected the accountancy industry as a whole and KPMG individually. Other scandals plagued the company throughout the first decade of the new millennium. However, the company's revenues continued to increase rapidly despite these challenges.

BRAND ELEMENTS
- The company logo is KPMG's most recognizable image and helps to identify its member firms as part of the international organization.
- KPMG's tagline, "cutting through complexity," is a simple yet powerful expression of the company's brand.
- KPMG's tagline promises its clients clear and practical solutions that will add value to their business.

According to KPMG's "Brand Identity Guidelines," its logo, which consists of the company's name in white letters set in front of four rectangles outlined in white against a blue background, is its mark of authenticity—an instantly recognizable visual identification. This logo helps to identify the international cooperative as a whole, as well as its member firms. Because the cooperative is made up of so many different firms, it is important to present clients with a clear image of the company even when member firms are spread across the globe. The logo is a

clear way to communicate this image. Beyond company recognition, the logo, along with its trademarked tagline, "cutting through complexity," is a powerful expression of the KPMG brand. According to the company's logo guidelines, the bold and assertive tone of the tagline is meant to differentiate the company in the professional services market. Moreover, it delivers a promise to clients, shareholders, and communities alike that KMPG will cut through complex issues and deliver clear and practical solutions to bring value to people's lives.

BRAND IDENTITY
- At the heart of KPMG's brand is a culture of integrity supported by its seven core values.
- Skilled employees in more than 150 countries help deliver the KPMG promise of clear, concise business solutions.
- KPMG's global member firms provide with a cross-platform, integrated approach, a unique means of helping clients and communities address complex issues.
- In evidence of its commitment to service, KPMG has achieved 11 percent growth in its U.S. tax service sector and double-digit gains in high-growth markets like India and China.

KPMG's rebranding effort in 2010, "The KPMG Difference," was intended to show potential clients how KPMG stood apart from other financial service institutions. Its task was difficult because KMPG has member firms in more than 152 countries and offers a vast range of services, including tax advisory services, auditing services, and risk management. After extensive study of clients' expectations of financial services in the years to come, the company felt that the best way to identify its brand was to focus on its promise of integrity and service to clients. The company seeks to fulfill this promise by hiring high-performing employees and providing clear solutions that add value to client businesses.

Like most companies, KPMG seeks to hire the best of the best. Its ability to do so comes from its commitment to employees. By providing a challenging yet nurturing environment for staff, KPMG, according to Universum, is the world's second-most attractive place to work. With a vast network of employees, it is crucial that KMPG employees from all over the world provide a consistent delivery of its brand. In order to achieve this the company asks each of its member firms to adhere to a set of seven values. From working together and leading by example to seeking facts and providing clear insight, these values help to ensure that no matter where clients are being served, their business solutions will be delivered with integrity.

Most important to KPMG's promise of integrity is delivering clear, concise business solutions. With a commitment to adding value to all client businesses, KPMG accesses its global network of member services to provide "cross-functional, cross-KPMG solutions," a method that very few organizations can offer. For example, KPMG tax services can help domestic clients on an international level as consultants from the U.S. can collaborate with member firms in Europe to clarify difficult regulatory changes that may affect a client's interests. This support gives KPMG the best information on which to base advice that is clear, well researched, and effective. According to the KPMG website its "tax practice—which serves more than half of the Fortune 500—achieved revenue growth of more than 11 percent, outpacing all of our major competitors in the market last year. At the same time, practices in the high growth markets of India, Africa, China, Korea and Russia all posted double digits gains in tax revenues." The company credits this growth directly to the delivery of its brand's promise—the integrity, quality, and proven approaches that KMPG brings to the financial service industry.

BRAND STRATEGY

- KPMG's business strategy involves investing in new high-growth markets, narrowing its focus to five key industries, and pursuing acquisitions that boost service capabilities.
- KMPG has made many investments in high-growth markets, such as the 2012 plan to invest US$100 million in Africa.
- KPMG's involvement with the City of Johannesburg demonstrates its focus on government and infrastructure and its cross-platform approach to doing business.

Like many other corporations, KPMG is focused strategically on growing its business after several years of global recession. According to KPMG's 2011 annual report, the company's approach involves three decisive strategies: investing in new high-growth markets such as China, Russia, India, and Brazil; focusing on key industry segments such as financial services, healthcare, government and infrastructure, and energy; and pursuing acquisitions that expand high-demand service offerings like management consulting and tax services. Expanding these services, especially in key global markets, will allow KPMG to continue offering clients the kind of integrated services necessary to mitigate risks and manage opportunity wisely.

A good example of these strategies is KPMG's involvement in the restructuring of Africa's leading city, Johannesburg. KMPG's member firm in South Africa was chosen to help the city reorganize its revenue collection system. KPMG's ability to do this derives in part from a five-year plan, implemented in 2012, to invest US$100 million in the enhancement of service offerings in Africa.

Additionally, the South African member firm brought in a member of KPMG's Global Center of Excellence for Justice and Security, a leader in transformation projects, to assist with the project. Demonstrating KMPG's cross-platform approach and its continued focus on key industry segments—in this case government and infrastructure, KPMG in South Africa was able to adapt global best practices to meet the unique needs of the City of Johannesburg. Furthermore, this example demonstrates how the brand's strategies have contributed to the continued success of the firm.

BRAND EQUITY

- KPMG ranked fourth in size and sales among the "big four" commercial service firms, earning revenues of US$22.7 billion in 2011.
- KPMG sought to improve its brand value by strengthening its image with a new tagline and advertising campaign in 2010.
- In 2012 KPMG's brand value was assessed at US$10.5 billion, placing the company at number two among the "big four" and in *Brandirectory's* commercial services sector.

KPMG, as one of the "big four" commercial service firms, earned US$22.7 billion in revenue in 2011. While the company took the fourth spot in the "big four" in terms of size and sales, its brand value, reported at US$10.5 million by *Brandirectory*, earns it the second spot within the group, just behind PricewaterhouseCoopers. As part of a major rebranding effort in 2010 following the global economic crisis, KPMG launched new advertising featuring golfer Phil Mickelson and a new tagline, "cutting through complexity," to strengthen its brand image. Additionally, according to KPMG's annual report, the company operates a global quality and risk management department that monitors the quality effectiveness of the businesses within each KPMG member firm, ensuring that its services comply with international professional standards and meet regulatory expectations. These efforts in brand building appear to have worked, as *Brandirectory* placed KPMG at number 80 on its 2012 list of the top 500 global brands, with a brand value of $10.5 billion.

BRAND AWARENESS

- In 2011 the Information Technology Services Marketing Association's brand tracking study suggested that KPMG's brand awareness is on the rise.
- In 2010 marketing efforts like a social media campaign and the hiring of a chief marketing officer helped raise KPMG's brand awareness.
- KPMG's positive efforts in corporate citizenship brought additional awareness to its brand in the past several years.

As KPMG is one of the "big four" commercial service firms, its brand awareness is reasonably high. While all of the "big four" companies had their share of reputational issues stemming from the mortgage and lending crisis of 2009, many brands saw great improvements in the years afterward. According to the Information Technology Services Marketing Association's *Professional Services and Solutions 2011 Brand Tracking Study,* while IBM and HP are the most recognized brands in the service industry, with the highest top-of-mind awareness, companies like Deloitte, KPMG, and Capgemini are gaining ground. Due to marketing efforts by KPMG, the company's brand awareness was on the rise as the company entered the second decade of the 21st century. *Marketing Week Online* reports that in 2010, for example, KPMG hired its first chief marketing officer to raise awareness of KPMG's brand, ideas, and capabilities. During this effort, KPMG also featured golf champion Phil Mickelson on its promotional website about leadership. This social media campaign sought to demonstrate the company's ability to use leadership skills to "cut through complexity" and provide clear solutions to businesses.

Moreover, KPMG uses its leadership skills to support its efforts in global corporate citizenship. According to the company's annual report, KPMG focuses on three global issues: improving the environment, fighting poverty, and seeing problems through the lens of opportunity and solutions. By striving to resolve the world's most complex problems, KPMG hopes to help global communities as well as bring greater awareness to its brand.

BRAND OUTLOOK

- Being an expert in the evolving regulatory development of client industries and businesses is one of the keys to the success of KPMG.
- Global collaboration and shared solutions between member firms further enable KPMG to stay competitive within the services industry.
- Avoiding reputational adversity is a key concern of the professional services industry, and KPMG's efforts at risk mitigation bode well for the company's future.

Because KPMG operates in many segments where industries and regulations are constantly changing and becoming more complex, the company has endless growth opportunities. By leveraging its network of member firms that have expertise in different professional disciplines and in different global markets, KPMG can offer its clients a broad range of integrated services. KMPG can use knowledge from local firms to help clients at home, and it can also access global firms to help them abroad. According to KPMG's website, this collaborative approach is designed to help clients stay informed about the latest industry, market, and regulatory developments that may affect various aspects of their business.

Additionally, by staying committed to its strategic plan, KPMG not only endeavors to continue to deliver high-performance services, but also to ensure the future of the KPMG brand. By building business in high-growth global markets, acquiring more member firms to expand services, and hiring from a deep talent pool, KPMG will be well-positioned to keep up with the competition that exists within the other "big four" service firms and with emerging firms in the market. Furthermore, as all "big four" firms have had recurring reputational blemishes over the years, it is important to the future of KPMG that the company continues to stay abreast of risk mitigation as they have done with their Quality Performance Review program.

FURTHER READING

Brand Finance. "Global 500 2012." *Brandirectory.* Accessed November 28, 2012. http://brandirectory.com/profile/kpmg.

Information Technology Services Marketing Association. "IBM and HP Are Still the Top Brands for Consulting and Technology Services, According to ITSMA Study." January 26, 2012. Accessed December 2, 2012. http://www.itsma.com/news/ibm-and-hp-top-brands-consulting-and-technology-services/.

KPMG. "International Annual Report." 2011. Accessed November 27, 2012. http://www.kpmg.com/global/en/about/performance/annualreviews/documents/kpmg-international-annual-review-2011.pdf.

KPMG. "KPMG Launches New Website on Leadership Featuring Phil Mickelson." *PR Newswire,* September 10, 2010. *United Business Media.* Accessed December 2, 2012. http://www.prnewswire.com/news-releases/kpmg-launches-new-website-on-leadership-featuring-phil-mickelson-102616639.html.

KPMG. "Logo." *Brand Identity Guidelines.* Accessed November 27, 2012. http://www.kpmg.no/arch/_img/9629876.pdf.

"Largest Management Consulting Firms Worldwide, 2005." *Consultants News,* June 2006: 4. *Market Share Reporter.* Detroit: Gale, 2008. *Business and Company Resource Center.* Accessed November 27, 2012. http://galenet.galegroup.com/servlet/BCRC?vrsn=unknown&locID=itsbtrial&srchtp=adv&c=1&ste=31&tbst=tsVS&tab=2&RNN=A264103315&docNum=A264103315&bConts=2.

Parsons, Russell. "KPMG looks to integrate marketing with first CMO." *Marketing Week Online,* December 2, 2010. *General OneFile.* Accessed November 27, 2012. http://go.galegroup.com/ps/i.do?id=GALE%7CA243395188&v=2.1&u=itsbtrial&it=r&p=GPS&sw=w.

Rourke, Elizabeth, Mariko Fujinaka, and Kathleen Peippo. "KPMG International." *International Directory of Company Histories.* Ed. Jay P. Pederson. Vol. 108. Detroit: St. James Press, 2010. *Gale Virtual Reference Library.* Accessed November 26, 2012. http://go.galegroup.com/ps/i.do?id=GALE%7CCX1302600063&v=2.1&u=itsbtrial&it=r&p=GVRL&sw=w.

Universum. "The World's Top 50 Most Attractive Employers." 2012. *Rankingthebrands.com.* SyncForce, 2012. Accessed December 1, 2012. http://www.rankingthebrands.com/The-Brand-Rankings.aspx?rankingID=87&year=519.

LANCÔME

—◆—

AT A GLANCE

Brand Synopsis: Lancôme is an internationally recognized luxury beauty brand that embodies a sense of French elegance as well as innovation.

Parent Company: L'Oréal SA
41, Rue Martre
Clichy
France
http://www.loreal.com

Sector: Consumer Discretionary

Industry Group: Consumer Durables and Apparel

Performance: *Sales*—US$500 million (2012).

Principal Competitors: The Estee Lauder Companies Inc.; Shiseido Company Limited; Revlon, Inc.

BRAND ORIGINS

- Lancôme was established in France in 1935 by Armand Petitjean.
- Skincare product was added in 1936.
- Lancôme entered cosmetics market in 1938 with Rose de France lipstick.
- The Oceane line of skincare products was introduced in 1955.
- In 1964 L'Oréal acquired Lancôme.

The Lancôme brand originated in France in 1935 when 49-year-old Armand Petitjean started his own cosmetics company. He possessed an unusual business background, having imported European products to Latin America as well as serving as an advisor on Latin America to the French Foreign Ministry during World War I. He was also an executive at the company started by the renowned perfumer Francois Coty, who pioneered the concept of multiple price points for perfume. Previously, perfume had been a prohibitively expensive product marketed exclusively to the wealthy. When Petitjean decided to start his own beauty products firm, he lured key personnel away from Coty, including bottle designer Georges Delhomme, who would play a key role in the establishment of the Lancôme brand. Petitjean created five fragrances for his initial product line, introduced at the Universal Exhibition in Brussels, where he won a prize for innovation. The fragrances were christened Tendre Nutt, Bocages, Conquete, Kypre, and Tropiques. As for the name of his company, Petitjean drew inspiration from the ruins of a castle he visited, Le Chateau de Lancosme. The wild roses of the castle also inspired Petitjean to use the golden rose as a major element in his company's logo.

Petitjean launched a manufacturing operation in a former factory that made artificial pearls and opened a retail boutique on a prestigious Paris street, rue du Faubourg Saint-Honoré. Petitjean expanded beyond fragrances in 1936 with the introduction of a skincare product, branded Nutrix, that he developed with a horse veterinarian. (The product contained a 4 percent solution of an antitoxin horse serum.) Petitjean entered the cosmetics sector in 1938 with a rose-scented lipstick, a product that would be a bestseller for the next three decades. He christened it Rose de France, which he claimed made "lips shine like those of a child." In 1955 Petitjean introduced a new skincare line that relied on seaweed ingredients. It was marketed under the Oceane name, and helped Petitjean export his products to nearly 100 countries around the world. It was also around this time that Petitjean introduced Magie perfume and began exporting Lancôme products to the United States.

Petitjean was 80 years of age when he sold Lancôme to L'Oréal SA in 1964. By this time, he had ceased to have his thumb on the pulse of his customers and sales had fallen off for a number of years. He sold the business to L'Oréal on the condition that Lancôme remain a luxury brand. The new owner had no intention of changing the brand's image. Rather, L'Oréal used Lancôme to upgrade its own image as a luxury beauty products company. Other luxury brands were acquired to complement Lancôme. Under L'Oréal's ownership, Lancôme regained its place in the beauty industry, and it was marketed around the world as a premier, full-line, luxury cosmetics brand.

BRAND ELEMENTS

- The accent mark used in the Lancôme name was added as an allusion to France.
- The rose was a longtime component of the Lancôme logo.
- Some of the brand's original perfume flasks are now collector's items.
- Product innovation and performance are important aspects of the Lancôme brand.
- Celebrities play an important role in promoting the Lancôme image.

A variety of elements help to define Lancôme as a luxury brand, starting with the company name. The accent above the letter "o" is not warranted grammatically; its sole purpose is to create a connection to France, which in turn evokes sophistication. (This accent is often omitted in print.) To reinforce the point, the Lancôme logo incorporates the word "Paris." In most incarnations over the years, the Lancôme logo also made use of a rose, a symbol of femininity. According to Marc Gobe, author of *Emotional Branding: The New Paradigm for Connecting Brands to People*, "The combination of both symbols brings a powerful cocktail of exoticism and promise, which have been at the core of a universal language that has struck an emotional chord with women worldwide for decades."

Another important component of the Lancôme brand is innovation. And with innovation comes improved performance. Winning a prize at the Universal Exhibition in Brussels laid the foundation for the brand, and over the years Lancôme remained in the forefront of the beauty industry, introducing a number of groundbreaking products. In addition to Nutrix, Rose De France, and the Oceane products, Lancôme was the first to offer vibrating mascara. The company also collaborates with leading makeup artists, such as Fred Farrugia, who developed 13 color collections for Lancôme during his tenure as Lancôme's artistic makeup director. In 2000 he developed the industry's first lip gloss in a tube, Juicy Tubes. Invariably versions of Lancôme products are soon introduced by down-market brands, including L'Oréal sister brands.

Also important to the Lancôme brand is the packaging. It was no accident that Petitjean hired Coty's bottle designer Georges Delhomme. Petitjean knew full well the importance of packaging in the presentation of a luxury brand. The perfume flasks created by Delhomme were so distinctive that they have since become collector's items. Even when it comes to small items, Lancôme products are packaged in a box within a box, and handed to a customer in a Lancôme shopping bag. The shopping experience also reflects the brand. Salespeople provide free gifts with purchase, pampering customers in the spirit of a luxury brand.

Although Petitjean eschewed advertising, under L'Oréal's ownership Lancôme was advertised around the world. There have been slogans associated with the brand, such as "Release the beauty inside you," but they are not core to defining the brand's identity. Individual products have also made use of taglines. Of even greater importance to the marketing of Lancôme products, however, are the models and actresses hired to be the face of the brand or to represent specific products.

BRAND IDENTITY

- Lancôme established itself as a luxury brand from the beginning.
- Lancôme emphasizes its French attributes to portray the brand as chic.
- The retail experience supports Lancôme's brand identity.
- The Lancôme brand is about 'la femmme,' the universal woman, according to author Marc Gobe.
- Lancôme's identity is perceived positively in the United States, Europe, and Asia.

At the heart of Lancôme's brand identity is the sense of luxury. All aspects of a Lancôme product reflect this basic claim to luxury, from the high price tag to the quality of the product, the packaging, the person chosen to represent it, and the retailers allowed to sell the product. More than just luxury, the Lancôme brand expresses sophistication, specifically French sophistication. The logo includes the word "Paris," and many product names are French in nature, including Résolution, Absolue, Rénergie, Primordiale, Photôgenic, and Hypnôse.

While Lancôme portrays itself as chic and elegant, it also maintains a sense that it is warm and accessible.

Helping to emphasize that image are the types of celebrities who have represented the brand over the years. The retail experience also plays a role. The company liberally offers free gifts to its customers, emphasizing the warmth of the brand while strengthening the bonds with its customers.

Marc Gobe maintains that the Lancôme brand is "about 'la femmme,' the universal woman, and it crystallizes this universal woman's aspiration." Lancôme's "multi-dimensional brand character" is supported by its "powerful visual symbols." Gobe argues that "the Lancôme identity is an identity that is 'personal' and designed for 'contact' through its flexibility. Myths need symbols, and Lancôme's layered graphic expression creates a bridge between the brand and women worldwide. It puts the final accent on a wonderful story … the eternal beauty of the rose." The effectiveness of Lancôme in establishing a consistent identity with universal appeal is that the brand enjoys equal success in the United States, Europe, and Asia.

BRAND STRATEGY

- Petitjean wanted to associate his brand with the sophistication and elegance of France.
- Petitjean relied on word of mouth to promote Lancôme.
- Models and actresses served as the face of Lancôme under the ownership of L'Oréal.
- Actress Isabella Rossellini was the international face of Lancôme for 14 years.
- Lancôme signed first Muslim spokesmodel in 2012.

While Armand Petitjean may not have consciously set out to create a specific brand identity for Lancôme, he was a savvy marketer who carefully crafted an image for his company. As an exporter of European products to Latin America, he was very familiar with the way French products were associated with sophistication and elegance. Eager to take advantage of that appeal, Petitjean crafted the name of his company to include an unnecessary accent mark to connote French origins, and should the point be lost, he added "Paris" to the logo. Petitjean was also visually adept, using the evocative image of the rose to represent his new beauty company.

Elegant packaging was at the core of Petitjean's branding strategy, as demonstrated by his hiring of Coty's talented bottle designer, Georges Delhomme. In addition to its perfume flasks, Lancôme was recognized for its distinctive lipstick tubes, artistically rendered with gold or silver plating. Petitjean's image of elegance precluded the use of advertising, however. He relied on word of mouth, creating an air of exclusivity for the brand. Only a woman in the know, the right kind of person, was familiar with the brand. Distribution was also limited to upscale purveyors of beauty products.

Although during Petitjean's time Lancôme did not advertise, it did create taglines associated with its products that promoted a brand image. For example, Rose de France lipstick supposedly "made lips shine like those of a child." By the 1960s, Petitjean lost touch with consumer trends. Women, for example, no longer wished to carry bulky lipsticks in their purses, preferring instead the new disposable, plastic lipstick cases.

After L'Oréal acquired the brand, Lancôme maintained its image of a luxury brand. But L'Oréal was not reluctant to advertise, and it promoted Lancôme around the globe. The use of an internationally recognized model or actress to serve as the spokesperson for Lancôme products was a key component of the new brand strategy. In 1978 model Carol Alt served as the face of the brand. A year later, Nancy Dutiel became the spokesmodel in the United States. She was replaced in 1982 by actress Isabella Rossellini, who served as the international face of Lancôme for the next 14 years. She was closely associated with the fragrance Tresor. Other actresses who succeeded her included Juliette Binoche, Drew Barrymore, Uma Thurman, Mena Suvari, and Laura Morante.

In the new century, Kate Winslet and Emma Watson promote Lancôme products. To widen the appeal of the brand, Lancôme signed a wider array of actresses and models as spokespeople. In 2012 a Tunisian model named Hanaa Ben Abdessiem became the first Muslim face for the brand. In addition to new women representatives, Lancôme signed its first male spokesperson in 2007, when Clive Owen agreed to front an advertising campaign for a Lancôme fragrance and an anti-aging cream.

Under L'Oréal, Lancôme became one of the beauty industry's most advertised upscale brands. The medium of choice was print. With the support of leading photographers, the print ads appeared in such publications as *Elle, Essence, Harper's Bazaar, Vogue, W,* and *Women's Wear Daily.* Campaigns were often supported by outdoor advertising at such locations as New York's Grand Central Station as well as mallscapes and taxi tops. In the late 1990s Lancôme made an effort to appeal to a younger market, launching an ad campaign that featured the tagline "Believe in Beauty." The rose remained an important element of the brand's image, but in the early 2000s Lancôme began to deemphasize it. "Believe in Beauty" was also scrapped, as Lancôme now made more of an effort to convey a sense of newness to the brand, as well as to build a more emotional bond between its products and its customers. To help keep better tabs on changing consumer tastes, especially in important and growing markets, the company opened a new concept store in Hong Kong in 2001.

In 2011 Lancôme launched a new marketing strategy. It targeted women of all ethnic origins, especially younger women. Serving as the spine of the brand rejuvenation effort was the new Visionnaire line of skincare products, the first global skin corrector designed for women of all ethnic origins. Actress Emma Watson of Harry Potter fame served as the new face of the brand, a conscious appeal to the younger market. The strategy paid immediate dividends, as Lancôme enjoyed its best sales in 15 years. The United States and China performed especially well.

BRAND EQUITY

- Lancôme brand value was estimated at more than US$5 billion by Brand Finance in 2012.
- Forbes listed Lancôme No. 75 on its World's Most Powerful Brands in 2012.
- The *Financial Times* ranked Lancôme as the world's seventh most valuable personal care brand in 2012.

One measure of Lancôme's brand equity is the higher price its products can carry, compared to the price of comparable products of lesser brands, including those of L'Oréal sister brands. In absolute terms, the value of the Lancôme brand is estimated at more than US$5 billion by Brand Finance Plc, a brand evaluation consultancy. As such, Lancôme ranked No. 194 on Brand Finance's list of the top 500 Global brands in 2012. Lancôme was ranked No. 75 on the Forbes list of The World's Most Powerful Brands in 2012, with a US$5.5 billion brand value. In France, Lancôme trailed only L'Oréal as the country's most valuable cosmetics/personal care brands in 2011, according to *Business Rankings Annual*. Lancôme was valued at US$5 billion while L'Oréal was valued at US$7.75 billion. In 2012 the *Financial Times* listed Lancôme as the world's seventh most valuable personal care brand, assigning a US$4.15 billion value. Perhaps the most important number for Lancôme was the amount of business it did each year. In 2011 the brand generated more than US$550 million in sales.

BRAND AWARENESS

- Lancôme is well known around the world.
- Lancôme was the 11th most-searched luxury brand in China in 2012.
- Lancôme was the 18th most-searched luxury brand in Russia.

Lancôme is an internationally recognized brand, supported by an ample advertising budget. Over the years, the brand has associated itself with many internationally known models and actresses. In addition Lancôme has signed endorsement contracts to spread its name geographically. The signing of 22-year-old actress Emma Watson in 2011 helped the brand to reach out to a younger demographic than its traditional target customer. Tunisian model Hanaa Ben Abdessiem gave a Muslim face to the brand a year later.

Lancôme enjoys general brand awareness but is even better known among its target customers. That awareness is escalating in emerging new markets. One indicator of the brand's popularity is demonstrated by how often people search its name on the Internet. It was ranked as the 11th most-searched luxury brand in China in 2012, based on more than 150 consumer queries on the Google and Baidu search engines in China. Lancôme also ranked No. 18 for the most-searched luxury brands in Russia.

BRAND OUTLOOK

- Lancôme began to appeal to a younger market in the late 1990s.
- Lancôme controlled 21.3 percent of the prestige cosmetics market in 2000.
- Visionnaire line of skincare products introduced in 2011 laid the foundation for future growth.

Since the beginning, Lancôme established a well-defined identity, one centered on French elegance. The promise offered by the brand has been well delivered over the years, and Lancôme has always kept up with changing consumer tastes and market conditions, albeit somewhat belatedly at times. Armand Petitjean eventually lost touch with customers, but the brand was revitalized after L'Oréal acquired it. The brand ascended to a new level of awareness and sales, but by the end of the century had to contend with the problems associated with an aging customer base. In the late 1990s Lancôme took steps to appeal to a younger market, but it faced continued obstacles in the new century as the brand identity was tweaked.

In 2000 *Market Share Reporter* estimated that Lancôme controlled 21.3 percent of the prestige cosmetics market, trailing only Clinique, which boasted a 29.3 percent share. Lagging behind in third place with a 17.9 percent share of the market was Estee Lauder. A few years later, Estee Lauder surpassed Lancôme for second place. Changes to the Lancôme brand helped to rebuild sales by 2011. The changes included the introduction of the Visionnaire line of skincare products, which catered to women of all ethnic backgrounds, and an appeal to younger customers. A year later Lancôme signed its first Muslim model spokesperson to reach an even wider market. Looking forward, Lancôme is likely to make greater efforts with customers in the Middle East as well as China and other emerging markets for luxury brands.

FURTHER READING

Aktar, Alev. "Lancome Gets a Rosy New Look." *Women's Wear Daily*, October 29, 1999.

Born, Pete, and Janet Ozzard. "Lancome Stages a Youthquake." *Women's Wear Daily*, May 15, 1998.

Brand Finance. "Global 500 2012." *Brandirectory*. Accessed July 3, 2012. http://brandirectory.com/league_tables/table/global-500-2012.

Chesters, Anna. "A Brief History of Lancôme." *Guardian* (London), March 19, 2012.

Elliott, Stuart. "Lancome to Rely Less on the Rose and More on a Bold Signature to Reach Younger Cosmetics Users." *New York Times*, July 6, 2004.

Gobe, Marc. *Emotional Branding*. New York: Skyhorse Publishing, 2010.

Tungate, Mark. *Branded Beauty*. London: Kogan Page Publishers, 2011.

Weil, Jennifer, and Brid Costello. "Lancome Looks into Its Future." *Women's Wear Daily*, November 14, 2003.

Weisman, Katie. "Luxury in a Cold Climate." *New York Times*, December 4, 2003.

LEXUS

—■—

AT A GLANCE

■

Brand Synopsis: Conceived at a 1983 secret meeting, Lexus took six years and US$1 billion to develop, but it proved an enormous success with its 1989 debut, going on to lead the U.S. luxury market for many years.

Parent Company: Toyota Motor Corporation

1, Toyota-cho

Toyota 471-8571

Japan

http://www.lexus-global.com

Sector: Consumer Discretionary

Industry Group: Automobiles & Components

Performance: *Market share*—15.2 percent (parent company) (2010). *Sales*—JPY18.58 trillion (parent company) (US$226.7 billion) (2012).

Principal Competitors: Audi AS; Bayerische Motoren Werke AG; Mercedes-Benz

Lexus began as a secret project initiated by Toyota chairman Eiji Toyoda at a 1983 meeting. Codenamed F1 (for "Flagship One"), the vehicle would extend Toyota's product line and solidify its foothold in the luxury segment. The Japanese carmaker had already begun its expansion into the upper reaches of the automobile market with the Supra sports car and the upscale Cressida and Century sedans. However, the Century, only available in Japan, had been designed for affluent buyers in that country. By contrast, the car Toyoda proposed would be marketed globally, though primarily to U.S. buyers, and it would have a more powerful engine than any of its predecessors.

The process of creating the Lexus took six years and cost more than US$1 billion. It involved the efforts of some 60 designers, about 2,300 technicians, and 1,400 engineers on 24 engineering teams working with some 200 support personnel. Together they built about 450 prototypes. With rear-wheel drive and a 4.0 liter V8 engine, the LS 400 had design features unlike any existing Toyota. After its debut at the North American International Auto Show in Detroit in January 1989, the car officially went on sale at more than 80 new Lexus dealerships across the United States.

BRAND ORIGINS

- Lexus began as a secret project, codenamed F1 (for "Flagship One"), in 1983.
- The process of creating the Lexus took six years and cost more than US$1 billion.
- Some 60 designers, about 2,300 technicians, and 1,400 engineers, aided by more than 200 support personnel, created the Lexus.

BRAND ELEMENTS

- The principal feature of the Lexus logo is a stylized capital "L" whose vertical arm is canted 45 degrees to the right, conveying a sense of movement.
- The ellipse and the "L" in the logo form a single shape, designed to appear as though it had been drawn in a single flourish.

- Lexus guidelines permit only four colors in any of its corporate communications: Lexus Black, Gray, Gold, and White.

Legend has it that the Lexus logo, by Molly Designs and Hunter Communications, was created according to a precise mathematical formula. Its principal feature is a stylized capital "L" whose vertical arm is canted 45 degrees to the right, conveying a sense of movement, speed, and flight further enhanced by the fact that the outer corner of the "L" is aerodynamically curved.

The letter is set within an oval shape, described in corporate literature as an "openended ellipse that signifies the company's ever-expanding technological advancement and the limitless opportunities which lie ahead." The ellipse and the "L," which form a single shape, are designed to appear as though they had been drawn in a single flourish.

Accompanying this symbol in the Lexus brandmark is the Lexus logotype, which renders the brand name in all capital letters. The font is the same as that of the "L" in the logo proper, but the letters of the logotype are aligned along 90-degree angles rather than being tilted to the right. Lexus, which provides strict guidelines for the use of its brand symbols, permits use of only four colors in any of its corporate communications: Lexus Black, Gray, and Gold (designated as PANTONE® Black 3, 409, and 873 respectively), and white.

BRAND IDENTITY

- Image consultants created a list of 219 prospective brand names for the F1 car, of which the favorite was "Alexis."
- The name became "Lexus" in order to avoid confusion with a popular television character and an electronic database service.
- Lexus provides strict guidelines for the use of its brand symbolism, even in such specific situations as PowerPoint® presentations.

Many other car brands, including that of Lexus's parent, Toyota, came into being early in the 20th century, long before the emergence of modern marketing concepts. Lexus, on the other hand, began as a conscious plan, and its brand development was nearly as involved a process as its product development.

In 1986 the advertising firm Saatchi & Saatchi, with which Toyota had worked for years, formed a special marketing task force known as Team One. Among its first jobs was to give the secret F1 car a brand name, for which it turned to the image consulting-firm Lippincott & Margulies. The latter created a list of 219 prospective names, from which emerged 5 top candidates: Alexis, Calibre, Chaparel, Vectre, and Verone. "Alexis" quickly became the top choice, but it required some adjustments.

At the time, people were likely to associate the name with that of Alexis Carrington, Joan Collins's character on the enormously popular television drama Dynasty. Therefore, with the removal of the first letter and the replacement of the second from last, the name of the new car became "Lexus." Even so, just before the launch of the car brand, attorneys representing the LexisNexis database service obtained a temporary legal junction forbidding Toyota from using the name "Lexus" because this might cause confusion. However, a U.S. court of appeals ruled that there was little chance anyone would confuse the two products, and it lifted the injunction.

In 2004 Toyota issued *Lexus Brand Guidelines*, a detailed 50-page pamphlet designed to ensure that "all Lexus Associates and partners will capture the spirit of who we are … and be fully equipped to communicate the distinctive tone and personality that set us apart from less passionate luxury brands." The guide outlines exact stipulations regarding the use of the logo and other brand symbolism, even in such specific situations as PowerPoint® presentations.

BRAND STRATEGY

- Toyota conducted extensive research and consulted U.S. luxury buyers, even renting a luxury home in California to observe their target market firsthand.
- From the beginning, the creators of Lexus regarded it as an elite automobile separate from other Toyota products.
- The Lexus product line began with a midsize and full-size sedan, and expanded to include compacts, coupes, SUVs, and crossovers, including a hybrid.

The U.S. market for Japanese luxury cars opened up as a result of negotiations between the two nations' governments in the 1980s. Toyota competitor Honda led the way in 1986 with its Acura, and in 1989 Nissan introduced its Infiniti. In the meantime, Toyota researchers had been hard at work creating a product targeted to Americans of the upper-middle- and upper-class economic strata. In May 1985 they conducted market research and consulted focus groups composed of upscale consumers, and several designers even rented a luxury home in Laguna Beach, California, in order to observe their target market firsthand.

By creating a reputation for high quality and low price (relative to the standards of the luxury market), Lexus appealed to buyers upgrading from standard vehicles to the high end. From the beginning, its creators regarded it as an elite automobile separate from other Toyota products, an idea reflected in the "Lexus Covenant." The latter, an extended mission statement, says in part, "Over 50 years of Toyota automotive experience has culminated in the creation of Lexus cars. They will be the finest cars ever built. Lexus will win the race because: Lexus will do it right from the start. Lexus will have the finest dealer network in the industry. Lexus will treat each customer as we would a guest in our home."

As for product line, Lexus began with the midsize V20 sedan in the ES series and the full-size XF10 in the LS series. These have continued through the 2010s, with the addition of another line of midsize sedans (the GS series), as well as the compact IS and HS sedan series. Early in the 1990s the brand added the SC series of coupes, and in the middle of the decade the first Lexus sport utility vehicles (SUVs), the LX series. They augmented these with the RX crossover in the late 1990s (a hybrid version debuted in 2005) and the GX series of SUVs in the early 2000s. In 2007 Lexus created a sort of luxury brand within the luxury brand: the F marque performance division, which included the IS F sport sedan, and, in 2009, the LFA supercar.

BRAND EQUITY

- Industry analysts suggest that Lexus accounts for a significant portion of Toyota's profits.
- Lexus was on the Interbrand list of 100 Best Global Brands from 2006 to 2009, and in 2012 it earned eighth place on Interbrand's list of Japanese brands.
- Two coveted first-place rankings from J. D. Powers and Associates in 2012 are just some of the many awards Lexus has won over the years.

Though Lexus separated itself organizationally from Toyota in 2005, it remains a part of Toyota, and to some extent its fortunes rise and fall with those of its parent. Toyota does not provide information on Lexus's revenues or profitability, but an industry analyst told Alan Ohnsman of Bloomberg.com in April 2009 that "the contribution of Lexus to Toyota's profit probably is double or triple the proportion of the brand's volume to Toyota's sales." Another stated that "Lexus has been one of the drivers for Toyota's rapid earnings growth in North America in recent years."

This can be a two-edged sword: with America in a recession, Ohnsman wrote, slow sales on high-priced Lexus models were "magnifying the carmaker's financial pain in the biggest auto market." Ohnsman reported that Toyota's U.S. sales had dropped by 37 percent in the first quarter of 2009, "led by a drop in demand for the most expensive models." Toyota's first annual losses in six decades were forcing the carmaker "to more than quadruple discounts on Lexus models in the last two years."

In better times, Lexus entered the Interbrand list of the 100 Best Global Brands at number 92 in 2006, with an estimated brand value of just over US$3 billion. By 2010, as a 16 percent drop in brand value earned

Toyota recognition as one of the "top fallers" on the list, Lexus had dropped off completely. In 2012, however, it did earn eighth place on Interbrand's list of Japanese brands.

In 2012 Lexus earned ninth place in *Consumer Reports'* Best Car Brand Perception Survey; seventh place in J. D. Powers and Associates' Automotive Performance, Execution, and Layout Study, as well as the Buyology, Inc. "Most Desired Brands in the U.S.: Women" list; fourth place in the ADAC–AutomarxX Brand Ranking; and first place in J. D. Powers's Customer Service Index Ranking Luxury Brands and its Sales Satisfaction Index Ranking.

BRAND AWARENESS

- Lexus's original slogan, "The relentless pursuit of perfection," underwent a slight modification before being replaced by "Engineering the impossible" in 2010.
- The 1989 "Balance" commercial won awards, and influenced the creation of a number of other commercials, both by Lexus and its competitors.
- The brand has enhanced its profile with sponsorship of golf events, including an annual "Champions for Charity" series.

Team One, the Saatchi & Saatchi brand development task force established in 1986, created what would remain the Lexus slogan for many years: "The relentless pursuit of perfection." Lexus changed this slightly to "The passionate pursuit of perfection" in 2000, and in 2010 dropped the original theme altogether in favor of "Engineering the impossible."

Accompanying the introduction of Lexus in 1989 was a multimillion-dollar marketing campaign that began at the major auto shows the year before and ultimately involved both print and television coverage. Toyota introduced American audiences to Lexus in 1989 with a Team One–created commercial titled "Balance," which featured an LS 400 with fifteen champagne glasses stacked on the hood in a pyramid. As the engine reaches a speed of 145 miles per hour (233 kilometers per hour), the glasses remain in place, and a narrator explains that "the Lexus LS 400 is designed to stir the soul … and not much else."

The "Balance" commercial won several advertising awards, along with something perhaps even more valuable: imitation from competitors. Most notable was a 1993 spot for the Nissan Altima, which was considerably less expensive than a Lexus, operating with champagne glasses stacked on its hood. Lexus itself reprised the theme several times: its 2006 "Balance" commercial shows a driver using the vehicle's guidance system to park between two stacks of champagne glasses, while a 2010 spot for the new two-seat LFA involves a champagne flute breaking as the supercar's engine revs to just the right frequency.

Actor James Sloyan, nicknamed "Mr. Lexus," performed the voiceovers for Lexus commercials through 2009, when he was replaced by fellow actor James Remar. Lexus commercials in the 1990s, for which "Balance" set the tone, typically featured vehicles demonstrating their superior handling and performance. During the brand's first decade on the market, its commercials attempted to demonstrate the superiority of the Lexus driving experience, and the wording consisted primarily of single adjectives, including ones drawn from the Lexus slogan, "The relentless pursuit of perfection." Lexus commercials in the first decade of the 21st century, by contrast, tended to be wordier, and included more specific references to the brand's competitors.

At the end of each year, Lexus has typically run a "December to Remember" advertising campaign, featuring scenes of people surprising their loved ones with the gift of a new Lexus. The brand has enhanced its profile with sponsorship of golf events, including the U.S. Open, the Women's and Senior's opens, and the U.S. Amateur tournament. From 2005 to 2009, it sponsored the U.S. Open Grand Slam event in tennis, and since 1989 it has put on an annual "Champions for Charity" golf series in the United States.

BRAND OUTLOOK

- Lexus, along with Japan as a whole, was severely affected by the March 11, 2011 earthquake, the costliest natural disaster of all time.
- Ironically, March 2011 had been a strong month for Japanese carmakers in the U.S. market, but the quake cut deeply into their market share.
- Despite its challenges, the future of the Lexus brand looks bright, thanks to the loyalty of Lexus car owners.

Toyota's 2012 annual report includes a statement that "Reduced output due to Japanese Earthquake and Thailand floods as well as a stronger yen resulted in lower revenues and profits in the year ended March 31, 2012." The strong yen, which has been a problem for Japanese export businesses over the decades, made their products less affordable to overseas buyers. "Thailand floods" is a reference to a series of disasters that hit that country, site of major Toyota production facilities, in the second half of 2011.

As for the Great East Japan Earthquake, this was the worst in that nation's history, and one of the five most powerful quakes ever recorded. On March 11, 2011, a shockwave with a magnitude of 9.03 hit the country, triggering tsunami waves and setting off a series of nuclear accidents. It ultimately claimed nearly 16,000 lives, left another 3,000 missing, and injured some 6,000. More than a million buildings were affected, with about 130,000 destroyed completely. The World Bank estimated the total cost of the quake at US$235 billion, making it the costliest natural disaster in history.

A year later, Micheline Maynard in *Forbes* wrote that Japan's three largest automakers—Toyota, Honda, and Nissan—"have yet to fully recover the American market share that they lost when production was disrupted by the crisis." This was ironic because March 2011 had been a particularly strong month for Japanese carmakers in the U.S. market; but the earthquake, with its attendant "disruptions in supplies of parts and vehicles had a swift and devastating effect. By June 2011 the Japanese companies had lost a quarter of their American market share, a deeper blow than the recession had caused."

But as Hugo Moreno wrote in the same magazine in the same month, "2011 may prove to be no more than a very large speed bump for Lexus. Those reasons reside in the psyches of Lexus customers." For proof he cited a year-long marketing research study, conducted at *Forbes's* behest, that "gives us a sense of what Lexus has been doing right." The report noted in part that while Lexus won against Volvo, BMW, and Acura with regard to brand satisfaction, "it utterly dominates in Personal Promotion. Lexus owners clearly love their cars and will play them up to anyone who will listen, regardless of how difficult it may be to actually obtain one at the moment."

FURTHER READING

Dawson, Chester. *Lexus: The Relentless Pursuit: The Secret History of Toyota Motor's Quest to Conquer the Global Luxury Car Market.* Singapore: John Wiley & Sons (Asia), 2011.

Greimel, Hans. "Lexus Needs Excitement in Post-LFA Era." *Automotive News*, December 24, 2012.

Lexus Brand Guidelines. Toyota, Japan: Toyota Motor Corporation, 2004.

Mahler, Jonathan. *The Lexus Story.* 2nd ed. Foreword by Denny Clements, additional contributions by Maximillian Potter. Torrance, CA: Lexus, 2004.

Maynard, Micheline. "Earthquake's Aftermath Still Lingers for Japanese Automakers." *Forbes*, March 12, 2012.

Moreno, Hugo. "Will Lexus Surge Back This Year?" *Forbes*, March 20, 2012.

Ohnsman, Alan. "Toyota's U.S. Pain Amplified by Falling Lexus Sales." Bloomberg.com. Accessed February 2, 2013. http://www.bloomberg.com/apps/news?pid=newsarchive&sid=aJNPURUsO0Kg&refer=japan

Rechtin, Mark. "Lexus' Key Potential Growth Market? U.S." *Automotive News*, December 10, 2012.

Toyota Motor Corporation. *Annual Report 2012.* Accessed February 2, 2013. http://www.toyota-global.com/investors/ir_library/annual/pdf/2011/ar11_e.pdf.

Vlasic, Bill. "Toyota Moves to Revamp Its Lexus Luxury Line." *New York Times*, September 27, 2012.

LG ELECTRONICS

AT A GLANCE

Brand Synopsis: A mobile phone and consumer electronics brand, LG Electronics emphasizes the joy of using well-designed products.

Parent Company: LG Corporation

LG Twin Towers

20 Yeouido-dong

Yeongdeungpo-gu

Seoul 150-721

Republic of Korea

http://www.lg.com

Sector: Consumer Discretionary

Industry Group: Consumer Durables & Apparel

Performance: *Market share*—10.2 percent of televisions in the United States (2011); 18 percent of LED LCD monitors for mobile devices worldwide (2011); 6.6 percent of mobile phones worldwide (2010). *Sales*—KPW54.26 trillion (US$48.98 billion) (2011).

Principal Competitors: Apple Incorporated; Whirlpool Corporation; Samsung; Sony Corporation

BRAND ORIGINS

- The earliest incarnation of LG was the plastics firm Lak Hui (Lucky) Chemical Company, founded in Korea in 1947.
- In 1958 Lucky began its diversification into electronics, creating the electrical appliance manufacturer Goldstar Company, Ltd.

- Lucky and Goldstar were divisions of a chaebol that proposed South Korea's export earnings be improved through investment in better engineers.
- In 1983 Lucky-Goldstar became the first Korean brand to open a manufacturing plant in the United States.
- After Lee Hun Jo assumed control of Goldstar in 1994, sales in the United States and Korea began to climb.

The earliest incarnation of LG was the Lak Hui (Lucky) Chemical Company, founded in Korea in 1947. The brand produced cosmetic creams, petroleum products, and plastic molds. With the assistance of foreign aid from the United States, Lucky grew to be a strategic industrial resource, being Korea's only plastics manufacturer. Lucky created an export agency in 1953, developed the first domestic toothpaste in Korea in 1954, and in 1955 began production of the first PVC pipe in the country.

In 1958 Lucky began its diversification into electronics, creating the electrical appliance manufacturer Goldstar Company, Ltd. The first product to be released was an electric fan. In the following year, Goldstar produced the country's first line of domestically produced radios in its new factory in Pusan. The products manufactured at this time were unsophisticated, and Goldstar lacked the marketing skills to sell its wares abroad, and so for the next five years Lucky Chemical and Goldstar addressed domestic demand, marketing a refrigerator in 1965 and a television in 1966 (both the first domestically manufactured products of their kind).

Lucky and Goldstar were divisions of a *chaebol* (business group) that was approached in 1962 by Park Chung

Hee, a general who had come to power in South Korea and who desired to improve living standards in the country. Lucky Chemical and Goldstar responded by proposing South Korea's export earnings be improved through investment in better engineers. They applied for government funds to send students to top Western universities. From 1966 to 1979 Lucky Chemical entered joint ventures with foreign firms such as Continental Carbon (establishing Lucky Continental Carbon) and Caltex Petroleum (establishing the Honam Oil Refinery). During the 1970s, the parent company opened 20 subsidiaries and introduced the first Goldstar products in the United States, a 19-inch black-and-white television. At this time, Goldstar also invested in a semiconductor manufacturing division, with the long-term goal of competing in the advanced electronics and telecommunications industries.

The assassination of Park in 1979 meant political changes that required the chaebol to become more self-reliant. Lucky Chemical and Goldstar were made subsidiaries of a larger parent company, Lucky-Goldstar, which announced sales of US$4 billion in 1980. During the early 1980s, Lucky-Goldstar, which became known as LG, invested in Goldstar Co., intending to move away from chemical production and increase the output of its electronics and appliance division. In 1983 LG became the first Korean company to open a manufacturing plant in the United States, where it produced televisions, microwave ovens, and other household appliances. Another factory in Seoul was part of the brand's domestic growth strategy to make Goldstar a global supplier of VCRs, personal computers, and fax machines. During the 1980s, the brand's business strategy was represented by its slogan "Expensive electronics without the expense." Goldstar developed a strong presence in both domestic and international markets for household appliances. Despite this solidified position, competition from Samsung (also a chaebol-style business) and governmental restrictions on overseas financing caused Goldstar's global market share to fall again by the end of the 1980s.

Goldstar's exports to the United States broke down at last in 1990, due to management problems and the centralized, hierarchical structure of the chaebol, which was hindering the brand's ability to compete in Western markets. The latter problem was addressed when Lee Hun Jo assumed control of Goldstar in 1994. Through Lee's work in management, Goldstar's sales climbed from US$4 billion to US$6 billion in 1994, and Goldstar regained its number-one position in the South Korean home appliance market.

BRAND ELEMENTS

- LG Electronics' identifying taglines include "Delightfully Smart" and "Life's Good."

- The logo, with "LG" appearing within red circle, represents the globe, youth, humanity, and technology.
- LG has established research and development laboratories in more than 25 locations around the world.

LG Electronics' identifying taglines include "Delightfully Smart" and "Life's Good." The logo consists of the letters "LG" in gray and a stylized image of the human face in red. The red color is an essential aspect of the brand's marketing, symbolizing friendliness and a commitment to delivering the best. The "LG" within the circular logo represents the globe, youth, humanity, and technology. The simplicity and modernity of the corporate logo are repeated in its updated three-dimensional version.

LG Electronics' design philosophy consists of perfecting the concept, style, interface, and finish of each LG product. In addition to mobile phone and TV/audio/video products and services, LG Electronics also participates in the lucrative market for high-end household appliances and multimedia products. The brand particularly wishes to establish itself as an innovative technology firm with sophisticated design capabilities. LG has established research and development laboratories in more than 25 locations around the world as part of the brand's global strategy for growth.

BRAND IDENTITY

- LG Electronics tries to emphasize its brand as innovative yet functional.
- One of LG's slogans is the tagline "Delightfully Smart."
- LG Electronics wishes to be associated with its customers' self-expression.

In the heavily competitive category of electronics, LG tries to stand out by emphasizing its brand as innovative yet functional. It uses the slogan "Life's Good" and the tagline "Delightfully Smart" to send the message that the company wishes to enhance its customers' lives and lifestyles with intelligent, well-designed products, intuitive functionality, and top-rate performance. Choosing the LG brand is intended to be an act of self-expression; customers are promised objects of excellence built in an environment founded on the four basic principles of value, promise, benefits, and personality.

BRAND STRATEGY

- In 2003 LG Electronics led the U.S. CDMA mobile phone market for the first time.
- In 2004 LG Electronics received approval for E-VSB as the next-generation transmission standard in digital television.
- LG Electronics celebrated its 50th anniversary in 2008, when it also became a technology partner of Formula One auto racing.

- In 2011 LG Electronics launched the world's first smart appliances and introduced the LG Revolution, its first 4G smartphone.

LG Electronics has competed successfully in the electronics industry by consistently introducing new products and product applications. In 2003 the brand introduced several world's firsts: a 76-inch plasma TV, a DVD rewriter, and the synchronous–asynchronous IMT-2000 mobile phone, which earned the brand the lead in the U.S. CDMA mobile phone market for the first time. In 2004 the brand received approval for E-VSB as the next-generation transmission standard in digital television and led the global CDMA mobile phone market.

In 2005 LG Electronics introduced the first phones in the brand's Black Label Series, including the LG Chocolate, LG Shine, and LG Secret. The brand had shipped 15 million LG Chocolate phones by 2006. In 2008 the 50th anniversary of LG Electronics, the brand unveiled the world's first Bluetooth headset combined with a mobile phone. By 2009 the brand was the second-largest LCD TV provider worldwide and the third-largest supplier of mobile handsets. In the same year, LG Electronics agreed to become a technology partner with Formula One auto racing.

Yong Nam, vice chairman and CEO of LG Electronics, announced in 2012 that innovation was the key to brand growth and identified B2B solutions, smartphones, and intelligent TVs as products the company would focus on in future. In 2011 the brand launched the world's first smart appliances and introduced the LG Revolution, LG's first 4G smartphone, and the Optimus LTE, which would become the company's best-selling 4G smartphone.

BRAND EQUITY

- In 2011 the brand reported global sales of KPW54.26 trillion, operating profit of KPW280 billion, and net profit of KPW433 billion.
- The brand held 10.2 percent of the U.S. television market share and 18 percent of the global mobile market share in LED LCD monitors in 2011.
- In 2010 the brand's market share in mobile phones was 6.6 percent.
- In 2012 Brand Finance ranked LG 87th among the world's top-500 brands, with an estimated brand value of US$9.81 billion.

In 2011 LG Electronics operated in 117 locations around the world. The brand reported global sales of KPW54.26 trillion (US$49 billion). The brand's operating profit grew by 58.9 percent from 2010 to 2011. The brand held 10.2 percent of the U.S. television market and 18 percent of the global mobile market share in LED LCD monitors in 2011. In 2010 the brand's market share in mobile phones was 6.6 percent. In 2012 Brand Finance estimated LG's

brand value to be US$9.81 billion and ranked LG 87th among the world's top-500 brands, up from the 168th spot in 2011.

BRAND AWARENESS

- From 2002 to 2004 LG Electronics experienced a 45 percent jump in brand awareness in Nigeria.
- In 2010 LG was ranked second in TV technology and fifth in cell phones worldwide.
- In 2010 LG Electronics had a brand awareness in the United States of 94 percent, an increase of 20 percent higher from 2007.
- LG Electronics had achieved "global top three" status in almost every business area by 2010.

In 2010 LG Electronics had a brand awareness in the United States of 94 percent, 20 percent higher than in 2007. Some 48 percent of consumers recalled the brand without prompting. By this time, the brand had sold 15 million LG Chocolate mobile phones and gained further visibility when television host Oprah Winfrey showcased the LG HDTV refrigerator as one of her "favorite things." Marking its 50th anniversary in 2008, LG endeavored to achieve global significance by hiring its first marketing officer, Dermott Boden. In 2010 LG was ranked second in TV technology and fifth in cell phones worldwide, according to market research firm iSuppli.

Since 2004 LG had been using the tagline "Life's Good," and under Boden's direction, the brand began developing a new brand identity uniting "stylish design and smart technology." From 2002 to 2004 the brand experienced a 45 percent jump in brand awareness in Nigeria and enjoyed an unaided brand awareness of 69 percent in Saudi Arabia. In 2010 it was the number-one consumer electronics company in Canada. By 2010 LG Electronics had achieved "global top three" status in almost every business area and was the top sponsor of Formula 1 auto racing, claiming 16.6 percent of total on-screen coverage.

BRAND OUTLOOK

- By September 2012 LG had sold 7 million smartphones, an increase of 23 percent from the previous quarter.
- LG's stock climbed 29 percent during the first quarter of 2012.
- There was a consensus among investment analysts polled in November 2012 that LG Electronics would continue to outperform the market.

By September 2012 LG had sold seven million smartphones, an increase of 23 percent from the previous quarter. Although unable to compete with the smartphone sales of rivals Samsung and Apple, LG has come to stand above other competitors, such as Huawei, ZTE, and Motorola. LG's stock also climbed 29 percent during the first quarter of 2012. A poll of 48 investment analysts in November 2012 revealed a consensus that LG Electronics would continue to outperform the market. The LG brand strategy remains focused on innovation and creativity in consistently delivering new products characterized by careful design.

FURTHER READING

Berger, James T. "LG's Brilliant Marketing Strategy." *Wiglaf Journal: Sales, Marketing, & Entrepreneurship*, April 2012. Accessed November 14, 2012. http://www.wiglafjournal.com/marketing/2012/04/lgs-brilliant-marketing-strategy/.

Bulik, Beth Snyder, "LG's $100 Mil Charge Apes Samsung Tack." *Advertising Age*, June 21, 2004.

Byung, Hoo Suh. "S. Korea Conglomerates Move in on Record Biz." *Billboard*, April 30, 1994.

Carson, Phil, "LG's 'Mass Premium' Phones Bring Success." *RCR Wireless News*, April 17, 2006.

Institute for Supply Management. "Richter Awards: LG Electronics." Accessed November 13, 2012. http://www.ism.ws/files/RichterAwards/2010WinnerLGEExecSummary.pdf.

Just Marketing International. "Case Study: LG Motorsports." Accessed November 13, 2012. http://www.justmarketing.com/CMSPages/GetFile.aspx?guid=a9e0c815-f46a-4e70-b05c-2fe8064c6dba.

"LG Claims Top Global Market Share in LED LCD Monitors." ubergizmo.com. Accessed November 12, 2012. http://www.ubergizmo.com/2011/03/lg-top-global-market-share-led-lcd-monitors/.

LG Corporation. "LG Electronics CEO Sets Aggressive Innovation Targets." Accessed November 12, 2012. http://www.lg.com/global/press-release/article/lg-electronics-ceo-sets-aggressive-innovation-targets.jsp.

Mote, Dave, and Ellen Wernick. "LG Corporation." *International Directory of Company Histories*. Ed. Tina Grant. Vol. 94. Detroit, MI: St. James Press, 2008.

Woyke, Elizabeth. "Branding a New LG." *Forbes*, March 10, 2008.

LI-NING

■

AT A GLANCE

Brand Synopsis: One of the largest sports apparel companies in the world and dubbed the "Nike of China," Li-Ning hopes to take the global sporting goods market by storm.

Parent Company: Li Ning Company Limited
No. 8 Xing Guang 5th Street
Opto-Mechatronics Industrial Park, Zhongguancun Science & Technology Area
Tongzhou District, Beijing, 101111
People's Republic of China
http://www.li-ning.com/

Sector: Consumer Discretionary

Industry Group: Consumer Durables & Apparel

Performance: *Market share*—7.2 percent (2011). *Sales*—RMB8.93 billion (US$1.4 billion) (2011).

Principal Competitors: Nike, Inc.; Adidas AG; Puma SE; Lacoste S.A.; Anta Sports Products Ltd.; Xtep International Holdings Ltd.; Peak Sport Products Co., Ltd.; 361 Degrees International Ltd.

BRAND ORIGINS

- Li Ning, a Chinese gymnast who won numerous Olympic medals in 1984, founded the Li-Ning brand in 1992.
- The influx of high-profile international brands of sports apparel created a new demand for athletic shoes and other sportswear in China.

- The Li-Ning brand aimed to duplicate the success of foreign competitors, first within China and then worldwide.

The Li-Ning brand was founded by a Chinese gymnast of the same name, who won multiple medals at the Olympic Games in 1984. After retiring from his career as a gymnast, he opened a company in 1992 to design his own athletic shoes and establish a nationwide franchise system to market them. Li-Ning was the first national brand of sporting goods in China.

In 1993 the brand's principal domestic rival, Anta, was launched. Both firms were attempting to duplicate the extraordinary success of the American brand Nike and other international competitors during a time when the sports shoe market was changing dramatically. Before, most shoemakers had manufactured their own products. In contrast, Nike concentrated on brand promotion, handling the design and marketing while outsourcing production to low-cost factories in China and other developing countries. Nike's tremendous success forced other sports shoe manufacturers to follow suit.

This influx of high-profile foreign shoes and other athletic apparel created brand awareness among Chinese consumers and sparked a broader interest in sportswear. Unlike Western markets where athletic shoes and clothing had become everyday attire, the Chinese market was geared mostly toward people involved in sports. Rather than shopping for a specific brand, Chinese consumers previously had usually based their purchasing decisions on price and whether or not a store was conveniently located. However, economic reforms had given rise to a growing middle class of consumers who were eager to buy the much-admired international brands, part of a larger trend toward a more Westernized lifestyle. The people of China became even more interested in sports and related products when Beijing hosted the Olympic Games in 2008. During the opening ceremony, the legendary gymnast Li Ning lit the Olympic flame.

In the new but rapidly growing domestic sports shoe sector, Li-Ning became the leading Chinese brand while many other Chinese companies continued to manufacture shoes for export. Nevertheless, Nike generally maintained its dominance in China overall.

Over the years, Li-Ning expanded its inventory to include athletic clothing and equipment, and it established stores in neighboring Hong Kong. With hopes of challenging the leading brands globally, the company began to take steps toward expanding into Southeast Asia, Central Asia, and Europe. In 2010 Li-Ning opened a retail store in Portland, Oregon, only a few miles away from the headquarters of its greatest rival, Nike.

BRAND ELEMENTS

- The regiesterd trademark of the brand and company is Li-Ning, with a hyphen, though founder Li Ning's name is spelled without a hyphen.
- Although Li-Ning's original logo resembled the Nike "Swoosh," it changed to abstractly represent the letters L and N.
- The Li-Ning brand has a distinctive Chinese personality, sometimes incorporating such traditional elements as dragons and golden silk.

In 1989 founder Li Ning (no hyphen) registered Li-Ning (hyphenated) as a trademark, which became the name of the brand and the company when the business was launched in 1992. However, the company does not always include the hyphen in its name.

The brand's logo consists of "Li-Ning" in red capital letters, either below or beside two wide red lines that resemble brushstrokes. The company says these are meant to be a stylized representation of the letters L and N. This version of the logo was adopted in 2010 during a celebration of the brand's 20th anniversary. Previously, the graphic lines had been merged into one element resembling a checkmark with a wavy tail. Critics pointed out that it also looked much like an upside-down imitation of Nike's famous "Swoosh" logo.

The graphic part of the Li-Ning logo is featured on the side of all of the company's shoes, varying in color to match the product. The entire logo appears in red above the modern-looking front doors of Li-Ning stores, which feature large glass windows where mannequins model the latest sportswear. The firm maintains several websites with the logo positioned near photographs of attractive, perfectly conditioned athletes and the slogans "Be

unexpected," "Do different," "We the people of change," and "Join the movement."

Part of the brand's visual element is also a connection to its Chinese identity. For example, late in 2011 the company launched an online retail outlet called Digital Li-Ning. Based in Chicago, the website offered sportswear specifically made for U.S. consumers where people could get a feel for the distinctive Chinese character of the brand through photography and narrative descriptions that revealed the philosophy behind each design. One shoe was named the Liede after a bridge in China and was accompanied by the explanation "We like to think of our Liede as a bridge between China and America." In 2012 the Year of the Dragon, the site featured a collection of four shoes inspired by traditional Chinese art (complete with blue water dragons and the exact shade of golden silk that was used in an ancient emperor's robe) under the tagline, "Discover your inner dragon." These traditional Chinese images are an important part of Li-Ning's brand.

BRAND IDENTITY

- The brand's long-running slogans have included "China's New Generation of Hope" and "Anything Is Possible."
- Li-Ning was rebranded in 2010 with a revised logo and the slogan "Make the Change."
- The 2010 rebranding was intended to attract younger consumers and improve the brand's global appeal.

Named after a famous Olympic athlete, the Li-Ning brand has been presented as an inspiring example of how a person or organization can use the motivation and discipline of sports to achieve success. Li-Ning's slogan throughout the 1990s was "China's New Generation of Hope" as the firm worked to establish a brand that could compete with big names such as Nike. In 2002 the slogan became "Anything Is Possible." In 2010 Li-Ning was rebranded with a revised logo and the slogan "Make the Change" as the company launched an effort to move beyond China and market its products internationally.

After analyzing its sales, the firm realized that most of its customers were about the same age as the gymnast Li Ning, who was 49 at that time. To attract much younger consumers, the brand began to identify itself in a more lighthearted way with an emphasis on inventiveness, curiosity, and self-expression. The brand's U.S. website urged "new world thinkers" to embrace the unknown, set the pace, exceed the limits, and "create the next what's next."

This re-identification of the brand with young consumers also helped address another problem that was impeding the brand's global ambitions, namely China's image as a country with a history of marketing low-quality products and counterfeits of famous brands. The older generation of Americans and Europeans tended to hesitate before buying sportswear with a "made in China" label, but younger consumers (especially the affluent) were more inclined to try a new brand and judge it on performance alone.

The company's American website was launched in 2011 with the slogan "Straight Out of New China" to promote a more modern, appealing image of the homeland and to position Li-Ning as a quintessentially Chinese brand that embodies Eastern culture, values, philosophy, and principles of movement. This was the most significant factor that differentiated Li-Ning from its global competitors. The new brand image was intended to appeal directly to customers in the United States but also, and more importantly, to the company's vast customer base in China, where it inspired a sense of national pride.

BRAND STRATEGY

- Li-Ning initially borrowed ideas from competitors but later attempted to build its own distinctive Chinese brand identity.
- The company maintains a handful of other brands, but most of its merchandise is sold under the core Li-Ning brand.
- Li-Ning markets shoes, apparel, equipment, and accessories made specifically for various sports, from basketball to table tennis.

Over the years, Li-Ning has borrowed many ideas from Nike and other competitors, but it has also emphasized innovation, particularly in the design of its products. The company has been known to introduce 600 new styles of athletic shoes in one year, often incorporating elements that were uniquely Chinese. Li-Ning called this practice "connecting with China and sports in China," a concept it planned to continue promoting as the brand built a distinctive identity.

The business is focused primarily on developing, manufacturing, and marketing its core Li-Ning brand of apparel, shoes, sports equipment, and accessories, which accounted for 91 percent of sales in 2011. Over the years, the firm has also handled its own Z-DO brand, the Italian sports fashion brands Kappa and Lotto, the French brand Aigle, the Kason brand of badminton equipment, and the table tennis brand Double Happiness. In a country where counterfeiting has been an issue historically, Li-Ning in 2011 was operating more than 8,000 retail stores, where customers could be sure they were buying authentic brand-name merchandise.

As a brand that has served individual athletes, sports teams, and sporting events, Li-Ning has marketed products designed for each type of activity, including specialized sportswear for badminton and table tennis. In 2012 the company launched a campaign to greatly increase its sales of children's sportswear and leisure clothing in China, a potentially huge but competitive market.

BRAND EQUITY

- In 2011 Li-Ning controlled 7.2 percent of the domestic sportswear market, while Nike claimed 10.5 percent and Adidas, 7.9 percent.
- Li-Ning's revenues were RMB8.9 billion (US$1.4 billion) in 2011, down 5.8 percent from RMB9.5 billion in 2010.
- The market value of Li-Ning was estimated to be US$658 million in October 2012.

In 2011 Nike held its lead with 10.5 percent of the market for sportswear in China, while the German brand Adidas followed with 7.9 percent. In third place, Li-Ning claimed 7.2 percent of the market, and the Chinese brand Anta captured 7.1 percent. All of these companies have lost market share since 2009, when Nike captured 16.7 percent; Li-Ning, 14.2 percent; Adidas, 13.9 percent; and Anta, 9.9 percent.

Li-Ning was the largest Chinese sporting brand in terms of sales in 2011, while Anta was the largest Chinese sportswear company by market value, according to *Business Daily Update*. In October 2012 Reuters reported that Li-Ning had a market value of US$658 million. However, Li-Ning posted revenues of RMB8.9 billion (US$1.4 billion) in 2011, down 5.8 percent from 2010. During the first six months of 2012, revenues fell to RMB3.9 billion, down 9.5 percent from the same period in the previous year, while gross profits slipped 15.5 percent. According to BrandChannel, Li-Ning's brand value stands at 2.734 billion RMB (US$2 billion). This number certainly reflects its decrease in sales over the last few years.

BRAND AWARENESS

- People throughout the world have become aware of the Li-Ning brand because of its sponsorship of sports organizations.
- Shaquille O'Neal and other famous athletes have called attention to the brand through celebrity endorsements.
- Li-Ning has won numerous awards, including "My Favourite China Brand in 2005" and "The Most Respectable Enterprise in China."

Because Li-Ning's brand awareness is not yet top-of-mind, particularly in the United States, the company makes a constant effort to keep the brand in the public eye. Li-Ning has sponsored sports organizations throughout the world, and it has repeatedly sponsored the Chinese delegation to the Olympics. It has also forged strategic alliances and sponsorship agreements with such sports organizations as the U.S. National Basketball Association

(NBA), the U.S. National Basketball League (NBL), the Association of Tennis Professionals (ATP), the Argentine Basketball Federation, and the CCTV National Sports TV Channel.

Various athletes have served as celebrity spokespersons for Li-Ning: Jamaican track star Asafa Powell, Norwegian javelin thrower Andreas Thorkildsen, and most recently, Dwayne Wade of the NBA's Miami Heat. These collaborations are aimed solely at improving the brand awareness of Li-Ning. While domestic brand awareness might be lower than its competitors, it is growing—by October 2012 Li-Ning had more than 24,000 followers on Twitter and 372,000 "friends" on Facebook.

Within China, the company has also sought to keep itself in the public view. It has promoted physical fitness, provided funding for schools, and supported philanthropic endeavors such as disaster aid and the care of orphans. The company's brand awareness in China is considerably higher than it is elsewhere as can be seen by the following accolades: Li-Ning was named "My Favourite China Brand in 2005" in a survey by CCTV in China. It was honored as "The Most Respectable Enterprise in China" in 2005, 2006, and 2009. It won the 2006 "Best Enterprises' Public Image Award" and was recognized as the most creative organization at the First Grand Ceremony of Creative China in 2006. It was included in the 2010 list of the 100 most valuable footwear brands in China and ranked in the top 10 among sports shoe enterprises.

BRAND OUTLOOK

- Poor sales in 2011 and 2012 caused Li-Ning largely to abandon its global ambitions.
- In 2012 the company announced plans to focus on marketing its core brand in China.
- Analysts predict that large Chinese sportswear companies will soon begin buying out their smaller rivals.
- Li-Ning and Anta are considered to be the firms most likely to survive the expected consolidation.

After a dismal sales performance in 2011, Li-Ning was forced to rethink its global ambitions. The company's net profits fell 50 percent in the first six months of 2011, and revenues continued to drop during the following year. In February 2012 the Li-Ning retail store in Portland, Oregon, closed after only two years in business. The firm continued to publicize its Chicago-based online store,

developed plans for expansion into India, and expressed a determination to compete worldwide with Nike. By autumn of the same year, Li-Ning was closing operations in Hong Kong and announcing plans to concentrate almost exclusively on promoting its core brand within mainland China, the market that already accounted for 98 percent of the brand's revenues.

Also in 2012 the company restructured, with founder Li Ning returning temporarily as CEO, and measures were taken to cut costs, improve efficiency, and sell off an overstock of inventory. Demand for sportswear has declined in China, partly because the country's economic growth has slowed to its lowest rate since 1990. In addition, Li-Ning attributed its poor sales figures to escalating costs and increasing competition from other brands of sportswear and casual wear.

Many shoe companies were launched in China during the late 20th century and the beginning of the 21st, but analysts predict that there will soon be a consolidation as larger sportswear firms begin to acquire smaller competitors. Of the roughly 20 companies that now exist, only five or six are expected to survive. The two predicted to be the most likely to survive are the largest, Li-Ning and Anta.

FURTHER READING

Balfour, Frederik. "China's Li Ning Toe-to-Toe against Nike and Adidas." *BloombergBusinessweek*, April 30, 2008.

Chaney, Joseph. "Watch out Nike: China's Sports Brands Coming on Fast." Reuters, February 21, 2008.

Cheng, Allen T. "The Mainland's Sneaker King." *Time*, July 29, 2002.

"China's Sportswear Brands Nurse Olympics Hangover." *Business Daily Update*, July 2, 2012.

He, Sophie. "Li Ning Lets CEO Go As Prospects Appear Dim. *Business Daily Update*, July 6, 2012.

"Li-Ning Delivers Brand to the U.S. Market." *Manufacturing Close-Up*, March 30, 2012.

"Li Ning Goes Head to Head with Sportswear Giants." *Business Daily Update*, August 30, 2010.

"'Made in China' Gains Acceptance." *Business Daily Update*, June 18, 2012.

"Mark Ritson on Branding: China's Brands Imitate to Dominate." *Marketing*, August 20, 2008.

Voight, Joan. "The Great Brand of China: Hawking Its Own Computers, Sneakers and More, the Eastern Power Aims to Become a Formidable Player in the U.S. Marketplace." *ADWEEK*, October 29, 2012.

LIPTON

BRAND ORIGINS

- Thomas J. Lipton opened his first grocery store in Scotland in 1871; within 20 years he was operating more than 200 stores.
- Lipton began selling tea in 1890; he bought his tea directly from growers to ensure quality and to keep prices low.
- Global consumer goods company Unilever acquired Lipton through a series of transactions, with all Lipton businesses purchased by 1972.

Lipton bears the name of its founder, Thomas J. Lipton, an immigrant of Irish descent who sailed to the United States in 1865 at age 15. Lipton had fled his economically depressed homeland and arrived in New York with US$8 in his pocket. Had Lipton arrived at almost any other time he might have found work in New York. However, the Civil War was just ending, war factories were closing down, and veterans were returning home to take any jobs that were available. Lipton walked the streets of New York for several days before he finally got an offer from an agent to work in the tobacco fields of war-ravaged Virginia.

For the next three or four years, Lipton traveled up and down the eastern seaboard and the Mississippi River, chasing any job that became available. He worked in South Carolina rice fields; as a carman outside New Orleans; as a plantation bookkeeper; as a firefighter in Charleston, South Carolina; and as a department store clerk in New York before traveling to Scotland to work in his father's shop in Glasgow. He quickly became frustrated with his father's business practices, which he considered archaic, compared to what he had witnessed in New York. So, in 1871, at the age of 21, Lipton invested his small savings in his own store. A few years later, he opened a second shop. For the next several years, Lipton worked tirelessly to build his business, and within 10 years he was operating a chain of 20 profitable grocery stores.

In the 1880s, Lipton's thriving food business grew to more than 200 stores. Tea had become hugely popular in England during the 1880s, and tea brokers in London had been pressing Lipton to stock their chests of tea in his food stores, but Lipton had resisted. When he finally decided to start selling tea, Lipton traveled abroad to find his own tea supply rather than relying on middlemen.

Tea was selling for 50 cents per pound in 1890, which Lipton believed was too high a price for the working-class family. He believed that he could grow and sell tea himself for about 30 cents and still make a hefty profit. At the time tea was sold from large chests and weighed out for customers. Buyers often had no way of knowing if the tea was fresh or if the seller was giving them the proper amount. Lipton decided to sell tea in packets by the pound, half pound, and quarter pound. Besides being fresher, the tea would be easier to handle, and it would be more marketable in its neat, colorful packaging. Accompanied by aggressive marketing, Lipton tea was a runaway success.

After conquering the tea trade in Britain, Lipton moved to revolutionize tea drinking in the United States. As demand boomed, Lipton's tea operations quickly dwarfed the sales and profits from the Lipton grocery stores. Lipton was operating five tea plantations by the mid-1890s, and by the early 1900s, Lipton's tea empire had become vast, with stockyards in Europe and North America.

Lipton went public with its first stock offering in 1897 as Thomas J. Lipton, Ltd. The company was incorporated in 1915. Lipton left the company in the late 1920s. Consumer goods company Unilever acquired the U.S. and Canadian Lipton tea businesses in 1938 and bought the remainder of the global Lipton business in 1972.

BRAND ELEMENTS

- Thomas Lipton was the first to market tea in bags; the company patented the Flo-Thru Tea Bag in 1952.
- Lipton does not advertise specific tea lines, preferring instead to advertise the Lipton brand name.
- The Lipton logo consists of bold white lettering centered on a red shield.

Thomas Lipton was the first to market tea to consumers in a convenient and portable tea bag. The company spent years trying to improve upon the initial design, and in 1952 the company patented a four-sided tea bag called the Flo-Thru Tea Bag. This innovative tea bag was designed to improve flavor by exposing more of the tea to the hot water. In 2011 Lipton was awarded a U.S. patent for its method for processing whole-leaf tea.

Thomas Lipton used the slogan "Direct from the tea gardens to the tea pot" in his initial advertisements,

accompanied by a picture of an exotic Tamil woman sipping tea. The tagline focused on his company's control over the quality and price of the tea. Lipton spent prodigiously on advertising upon entering markets in the United Kingdom and the United States to ensure immediate dominance. Advertising for Lipton tea has focused on the overall brand instead of on particular varieties or flavors. The Lipton company believed that, by marketing the Lipton name, it could effectively market all types of tea at once.

A notable exception in the marketing scheme occurred in the United States in 1983, when Lipton launched a campaign for its iced tea mix with NutraSweet. The advertising featured the hugely popular tennis star Chris Evert-Lloyd relaxing with a Lipton iced tea. Another exception was a campaign for new decaffeinated tea bags that used the tagline "the newest way to be a Lipton Tea lover." Other taglines used over the years have included "This is Lipton Tea time" and "Lipton: A better tea bag. A perfect cup of tea."

The Lipton logo features bold white block lettering with the brand name "Lipton" centered in a red shield. Thomas Lipton included the logo on his initial packaging for Yellow Label tea in 1890; Lipton tea packaging has incorporated yellow and red ever since. The original logo was in use from 1890 until an update in 2002 included shades of yellow in the upper left corner of the shield.

BRAND IDENTITY

- By selling tea in prepackaged bags, Lipton was able to ensure freshness and flavor, a feature still important today for its brand identity.
- Lipton uses only the top leaves of a tea plant, which are the youngest, most tender, and most flavorful.
- Lipton highlights studies that suggest drinking tea may lower the risks of certain diseases, and the Lipton Institute of Tea participates in scientific conferences and invests in clinical trials investigating the health benefits of tea.

Lipton tea was an immediate success in the British Isles in 1889 for reasons that still guide its brand identity today: quality, freshness, and consumer satisfaction. Initially, Thomas Lipton set high standards for his blend, particularly with regard to taste and consistency. He used tea packets to preserve the freshness and flavor of the unique blend, and because weight, price, and quality were clearly marked on his products, they inspired consumer confidence. Today they still do.

Lipton continues to identify its brand in a similar way. In order to retain customer loyalty as the company expanded into a global empire, Lipton maintained high standards for its products. To ensure the best cup of tea, the company uses only the top leaves of the tea plant, which are the youngest, most tender, and most flavorful. Lipton also tries to appeal to diverse tastes throughout the world, employing master tea blenders and tasters to create new flavors and varieties best suited to regional preferences.

At the same time, Lipton is aware of consumer efforts to be more health conscious. Lipton tries to engage this movement by identifying the brightness, excitement, and uplifting effects that its products bring to the consumer's life. The company highlights how its teas are low in calories and can be part of a nutritionally balanced diet. It also emphasizes antioxidants in tea and the fact that some studies have shown that drinking tea may lower the risks of certain diseases.

Lipton takes the health aspect of their brand identity seriously. An example of their commitment to health can be seen in The Lipton Institute of Tea, home to scientists, biologists, nutritionists, aroma experts, and taste testers. Headquartered just north of London, the institute also has research centers in tea-growing regions and various key markets, including India, Kenya, France, the United States, Japan, and China. According to Lipton, the institute is designed "to promote awareness and understanding of tea, from bush to cup." In addition to growing samples of tea from around the world, the institute organizes and participates in scientific conferences and invests in clinical trials to support claims of the health benefits of tea.

BRAND STRATEGY

- In 1960 Lipton launched its first instant tea aimed at iced tea drinkers; by 1965 iced tea consumption had surpassed that of hot tea.
- Lipton sells a range of teas in pyramid-shaped tea bags, which allow tea leaves to expand more fully than traditional tea bags do.
- Lipton's joint venture with PepsiCo to market ready-to-drink teas has been extremely successful in the United States and Europe.

Approximately 75 percent of the tea produced and consumed globally is black tea; 20 percent is green tea. Black tea is popular in Europe, North America, and North Africa, while green tea is widely consumed in China, Japan, Korea, and Morocco. Tea bags are preferred in Australia, North America, and Western Europe, while loose-leaf tea is preferred in the Middle East and throughout Asia. To meet diverse consumer demands, Lipton sells a wide variety of bagged, loose-leaf, instant-mix, and ready-to-drink tea products.

Created by Thomas Lipton in 1890, the most popular Lipton tea worldwide is Yellow Label, a black tea blend sold in 150 countries. Lipton Linea, marketed as a "slimming" tea, is sold in Europe, while Lipton Milk

Tea, a black tea ready to be mixed with powdered milk and sugar, is available in East Asian markets. Lipton iced tea, fruit and herbal infusion teas, and fruity green teas are available throughout Great Britain. Sun tea, fruit and herbal infusion teas, Yellow Label, and the Sir Thomas Lipton line are marketed in France. South African consumers can purchase Wellbeing teas, and Australian consumers are able to buy Lipton herbal infusion teas, black tea, green tea, iced tea, and chai.

In 1992 Lipton's parent company, Unilever, entered into a joint venture with PepsiCo to grow the ready-to-drink tea line in North America. This agreement was expanded in 2003 to cover non-American markets and again in 2007 to cover European markets.

BRAND EQUITY

- In 2012 *Fortune* magazine placed Lipton's brand value at US$2.5 billion.
- Lipton beat Coke and Snapple in 2011 in rankings of popular vendors of canned or bottled tea.
- Lipton was the top bagged or loose-leaf tea brand in the United States in 2010 and 2011.

In *Fortune*'s Global 500 list of top brands, Lipton was ranked 477th in 2012, down from 413th in 2011, with a brand value of US$2.5 billion. Brand Finance ranked Lipton 10th in a 2012 ranking of the top brands in the Netherlands and 40th in a ranking of the top British brands, with a brand value of US$2.5 billion.

Lipton was the top bottled tea maker in the United States in 2010, with US$419.9 million in sales and a 12.86 percent market share, and it was the second most popular vendor of canned or bottled tea in 2011, with US$391 million in sales, beating Coke and Snapple. Lipton was the top bagged or loose-leaf tea brand in the United States in 2010, with a 22.3 percent market share, and in 2011, with US$167.5 million in sales. Lipton owned four of the top 10 ready-to-drink tea brands in 2011: Lipton Brisk was second (US$286.2 million in sales), Lipton was third (US$257 million in sales), Lipton Pure Leaf was fifth (US$149 million in sales), and Lipton Diet was 10th (US$75 million in sales).

BRAND AWARENESS

- Lipton is the second most popular brand of beverage in the world behind Coca Cola.
- Lipton teas are available in more than 150 countries, making the brand identifiable worldwide.
- Lipton uses social networking to raise brand awareness.

Tea is the second most popular beverage in the world behind water. Lipton is the second most popular brand of beverage behind Coca Cola. Lipton teas are available in more than 150 countries, and 9 percent of consumers preferred Lipton as their beverage of choice in 2009, which placed the brand third behind Coke and Pepsi. These kind of statistics demonstrate the kind of brand loyalty Lipton carries.

Its brand awareness is also high. In 2007 Lipton was the top tea brand worldwide, with a 15 percent market share, beating Twinings, which held a 6 percent market share. Lipton was the top tea marketer in the United States in 2011, with a 23.6 percent market share, including all canned and bottled tea, bagged and loose tea, refrigerated tea, and instant tea mixes. Lipton was the number one producer of herbal teas in France in 2006, with a 65 percent market share; one of every two tea bags sold in France is a Lipton brand. In 2005 Lipton was ranked third in the green tea market in Thailand, with an 8 percent market share. In Australia in 2004 Lipton held a 1.5 percent market share of top tea brands. It was among the top ready-to-drink tea brands in the Philippines in 2011.

Lipton has begun to use social networking to increase its brand awareness and boost sales in global markets. In 2010, for example, Lipton invited users of a major Chinese instant messaging service to send a video message to a friend. There was no direct push for a Lipton product, but a Lipton logo was attached to the message. For each message, the customer got a credit toward Lipton products. According to the China Daily website, "in a follow-up questionnaire, 46 percent of the 50,000 participants polled said that they bought at least one box of milk tea because of the online activity. In addition, Lipton's brand awareness increased by one to two percentage points in Beijing, Shanghai and Guangzhou, according to Gong"?

BRAND OUTLOOK

- As more consumers develop healthy eating habits they are drinking more tea, and Lipton has been able to capitalize on this trend.
- By 2015 all Lipton tea bags will be certified by the Rainforest Alliance conservation group.
- Lipton's "Trees 2000" initiative in Kenya plants thousands of trees each year in an effort to curb deforestation.

Lipton has sought to capitalize on the health-and-wellness trend in many of its larger markets by highlighting the healthy ingredients present across its tea lines. The beneficial properties of tea, along with its low calorie content, have helped to drive a global demand in general for tea. Lipton's convenient canned and bottled teas have been growing in market share worldwide. Lipton's agreement with PepsiCo to market its ready-to-drink teas also strengthens its global presence.

Lipton continues to operate tea plantations in Kenya and Tanzania. In 2007 Unilever announced that all tea bags sold by Lipton would be certified by the nonprofit conservation group Rainforest Alliance by 2015. Certified products show the company's commitment to practicing sustainable farming and investing in farmers and their families and communities. With Lipton's "Trees 2000" initiative in Kenya, the company plants 40,000 native trees each year in an effort to stem deforestation. The tea plantation in Kenya produces roughly 10 percent of all Lipton teas, resulting in a consistency of quality across the brand. These types of activities position Lipton as a brand that cares about quality and, at the same time, producing socially conscious products.

FURTHER READING

Boyle, Matthew. "Weak Tea at Unilever Persists amid Innovation at Rivals." *Bloomberg*, October 24, 2012.

"How Did Lipton Conquer Half the World (and Is Probably Planning to Invade the Other Half)?" Teaconomics, June 14, 2011. Accessed November 5, 2012. http://teaconomics.teatra.de/2011/06/14.

"Lipton Pyramid Fruit Teas to Enhance Women's 'Me-Time' Moments." *Al Bawaba Business*, May 9, 2011.

Lowenstein, Kate. "The Truth about the Health Benefits of Tea." *Health*, October 6, 2011. Accessed November 5, 2012. http://www.health.com/health/article/0,,20534999_2,00.html.

"Thomas J. Lipton Company." *International Directory of Company Histories*. Ed. Tina Grant. Vol. 14. Detroit, MI: St. James Press, 1996.

"Top Ready-to-Drink Tea Brands by Sales, 2011." *Business Rankings Annual*. Ed. Deborah J. Draper. Detroit, MI: Gale, 2013.

"Top Tea Marketers, 2011." *Market Share Reporter*. Detroit, MI: Gale, 2012.

Zmuda, Natalie. "Tea Titans Arizona, Lipton Tangle for First Place: Arizona's Price Play Has Given It the Lead, but Lipton Is Launching a Major Advertising Push to Reclaim the Title." *Advertising Age*, September 26, 2011.

L'ORÉAL

AT A GLANCE

Brand Synopsis: L'Oréal's emphasis on the self-worth and confidence people derive from their appearance has made it the world's leading beauty company.

Parent Company: L'Oréal SA
41, Rue Martre
92217 Clichy Cedex
France
http://www.loreal.com/

Sector: Consumer Staples

Industry Group: Household & Personal Products

Performance: *Sales*—EUR20.34 billion (US$26.4 billion) (2011).

Principal Competitors: Estée Lauder Companies Inc.; Bioré (owned by the Kao Corporation); Shiseido Company, Limited; Procter & Gamble Company; Unilever

BRAND ORIGINS

- In 1909 Eugène Schueller began a company named Société Française des Teintures Inoffensives pour Cheveux, which concentrated on hair and soap products.
- In 1939 the company's name was established as L'Oréal.
- Throughout the brand's existence, research has been a major focus. L'Oréal's facility in Aulnay-sous-Bois, France, works toward environmental friendliness, and there are also research divisions in Japan, Israel, and India.

In 1909 a chemist named Eugène Schueller began a company called Société Française des Teintures Inoffensives pour Cheveux (literal translation: "Safe Hair Dye Company of France"). His creations, which included a stable synthetic hair dye, new shampoos, and suntan lotion, were the beginning of a career in research and innovation.

During the Jazz Age in the 1920s, women began to wear shorter, bobbed hairstyles and show new interest in changing their hair color. Schueller invented a hair lightener, and when Hollywood embraced the platinum look, he created a bleaching powder called L'Oréal Blanc. He also created Dop, the first mass-market shampoo, which is still sold today. Interest in Schueller's products began to spread beyond France into Italy, Austria, the Netherlands, the United States, the United Kingdom, and Brazil. Schueller was keen on hygiene and invented soaps for all ages. In 1928 he made his first acquisition, purchasing the soap company Monsavon.

Rue Martre in Clichy, a suburb of Paris, became his company's new production site, and in 1939 the company's name was established as L'Oréal. Its brand presence continued to grow during the 1940s and 1950s. Schueller set up a school for hairstylists, invented a cold permanent wave product called Oréal, and created a temporary hair color that washed out in six to eight washings. During World War II, Schueller was involved with a political movement known as the Mouvement Social Révolutionnaire (MSR). Although the right-wing group's support of Nazi activities caused a scandal, L'Oréal's sales continued to grow.

L'Oréal's acquisition of Cosmair in 1954 was a major move. Cosmair became L'Oréal's main distributor in the United States, giving L'Oréal an international presence. Soon, pharmacies and perfumers began to sell L'Oréal products. The brand continued its expansion, with subsidiaries in Italy, Belgium, and Denmark.

Upon Schueller's death in 1957, François Dalle was appointed chairman and managing director of the company. Dalle offered sales classes and business meetings, where he encouraged input from participants. From 1957 to 1983 beauty products became more accessible to the public, and L'Oréal adopted the motto "Seize new opportunities." L'Oréal acquired Cadoricin and made its debut in the cosmetics market. Subsidiaries were formed in Brazil. In 1963 L'Oréal was added to the Paris stock exchange and continued to extend its boundaries with its acquisition of Lancôme, Garnier, Biotherm, and Gemey. In 1973 L'Oréal connected with women in a new way with its famous tagline "Because I'm worth it."

In 1983 L'Oréal opened a Japanese research center to focus on Japanese consumers and their needs. The company created the product Plénitude to address the skin care mass market. It also sought to attract male consumers with Drakkar Noir, Ralph Lauren, and Biotherm skin care products for men. Lindsay Owen-Jones, who became CEO in 1988, expanded L'Oréal's world presence by diversifying its product line and image. L'Oréal represented more than hair care, and Owen-Jones brought balance to the brand. Under his leadership, L'Oréal acquired new major brands, including Helena Rubinstein, Giorgio Armani, Maybelline New York, and Redken.

In the 1990s L'Oréal expanded its research efforts. Plants were opened in Israel and India. The company's ultramodern factory in Aulnay-sous-Bois, France, focused on environmental friendliness. L'Oréal acquired Soft-Sheen, a maker of hair-care products for black consumers, in the United States. Additionally, L'Oréal joined the World Business Council for Sustainable Development and established a bioengineering center in Lyon, France, to focus on skin reconstruction. BioMedic, a company specializing in skin care products for dermatology and plastic surgery patients, was acquired. The brand branched into oral cosmetics as well.

BRAND ELEMENTS

- The name L'Oréal was established in 1939.
- In 1971 the tagline "Because I'm worth it" became famous at a time when women were celebrating their individuality and self-worth.
- As of 2011, L'Oréal had expanded to 27 global brands in 130 countries and had applied for 613 patents.

L'Oréal SA is the parent company of 27 global brands, each with its own name and logo. In 1939 founder Eugène Schueller adopted the company name L'Oréal. This decision came shortly after he implemented the novel practice of profit sharing. L'Oréal was making a name for itself as a brand associated not only with innovative products for hair but with products that improved lives. L'Oréal's trademark uses a simple, classy, and clean design consisting of all-capital, sans-serif fonts. The French trademark has tailored accents and a slightly larger "O," which gives it a distinctive look.

L'Oréal manages to fulfill the needs of many customers through its own brand and through its subsidiaries. On L'Oréal's website, the phrase "Can I help you?" offers visitors the feeling that they are being cared for. Customers are so treated because they are "worth it." L'Oréal implemented the famous tagline "Because I'm worth it" in 1971, when women were embracing a stronger voice and experiencing an increased sense of self-worth. Throughout the years, the company has tweaked the slogan: in 1997 it became "Because you're worth it," and in 2010 it became "Because we're worth it." The company has also taken advantage of its position as the top cosmetics seller to bill itself as "the world's leading beauty company."

International research and innovation have always been important to L'Oréal. The company has taken advantage of current events and their effects on coinciding styles and fashions. It now comprises 27 global brands in 130 countries. By 2011 L'Oréal had filed for 613 patents for formulas and discoveries in the realm of hair care, makeup, and other personal products. L'Oréal's website declares, "There is no single type of beauty; it is a multi-faceted quality framed by different ethnic origins, aspirations, and expectations that reflect the world's intrinsic diversity."

BRAND IDENTITY

- L'Oréal's mission is to offer "all women and men worldwide the best of cosmetics innovation in terms of quality, efficacy and safety."
- Research centers worldwide continue to seek ways to improve the health of skin and hair.
- L'Oréal's sense of corporate responsibility is apparent in campaigns to support cancer patients, improve the lives of women and communities, and reduce animal testing.
- L'Oréal's stated ethical values are integrity, respect, excellence, courage, and transparency.

L'Oréal's mission is to offer "all women and men worldwide the best of cosmetics innovation in terms of quality, efficacy and safety." To meet the needs of the many, L'Oréal has acquired multiple brands, which are divided into five categories: Professional Products, such as L'Oréal Professionnel, Redken, and Shu Uemura; Consumer Products, which include the brands Maybelline New York, Garnier, and ShoftSheen-Carson; Active Cosmetics, which include Vichy and other brands that combine health awareness with beauty; the Body Shop, which focuses on ecological awareness; and L'Oréal Luxe, which includes luxury brands like Lancôme, Giorgio Armani, and Yves Saint Laurent.

L'Oréal is dedicated to global research. Among its many patents are those related to the discovery of molecules that help reduce the signs of aging of the skin, protect skin from UVB radiation, and repair damaged hair. In addition to conducting research and making wise investments, the brand is committed to corporate responsibility. In 1989 L'Oréal invested in "Look Good … Feel Better," a campaign to help cancer patients deal with the physical side effects of cancer. By 2011 L'Oréal had donated US$18 million toward research on ovarian cancer. The company celebrates women who make a difference by partnering with Women In Need (WIN), which helps women attain independence through classes that teach job skills and help bolster self-esteem.

L'Oréal also displays corporate responsibility toward animals. In the spring of 2012, the British news source *Mail Online* reported L'Oréal's donation of US$1.2 million to help abolish animal testing. Despite protests by animal rights groups that the company could act more quickly to end animal testing, in March 2012 the Ethisphere Institute recognized L'Oréal as "one of the world's most ethical cosmetic companies."

The Body Shop is a subsidiary division that emphasizes L'Oréal's eco-friendly agenda. The Body Shop's goals are to seek out natural ingredients for its products to enhance natural beauty. The division campaigns to end human trafficking and domestic violence and to find a cure for HIV.

According to Emmanuel Lulin, L'Oréal's group director of ethics, "L'Oréal has always had strong values which have shaped our culture and built our reputation. Our five ethical values are integrity, respect, excellence, courage, and transparency."

BRAND STRATEGY

- L'Oréal increased its customer base by taking on new companies and their brands.
- The company's alliance with Nestlé has opened doors for research in dermatology.
- By working on new products tailored to the needs of diverse communities, CEO Jean-Paul Agon's hope is to attract consumers in all tiers of the market.

L'Oréal's growth began with founder Eugène Schueller's keen attention to what women want in hair care and his ability to anticipate and accommodate new trends in the market. In the early 1930s Schueller's inspired use of the radio for advertising and his creation of the beauty magazine *Votre Beauté* heightened awareness of his products.

Schueller's acquisition of other companies, such as soap maker Monsavon, were only the earliest of L'Oréal's many successful investments. L'Oréal was able to increase its customer base by taking on new companies and their brands; its list of international brands includes Lancôme, Giorgio Armani, SoftSheen-Carson, Maybelline New York, Shu Uemura, and more.

When Cosmair, the U.S. distributor of L'Oréal products, changed its name to L'Oréal USA, Inc., Cosmair president and CEO Guy Peyrelongue said, "We will enjoy immediate brand recognition for outstanding achievement in beauty and technology." Lindsay Owen-Jones, L'Oréal's chairman and CEO at the time, said the name change was a strategy "to build corporate identity in every company behind one, recognizable name."

When L'Oréal discovered a large market in the United States for ethnic hair care products, it spent approximately US$370 million to buy SoftSheen Products and Carson, Inc., and picked up 20 percent of the market as a result.

According to the *International Directory of Company Histories*, L'Oréal's expansion into overseas markets, particularly Japan, was aided greatly by the company's new alliance with the Swiss food giant Nestlé, to whom Eugène Schueller's daughter, Liliane Bettencourt, sold nearly half of her L'Oréal stock in 1974. The two allies established a French holding company, Gesparal, of which Bettencourt owned 51 percent and Nestlé owned 49 percent. In 1981 L'Oréal engaged with Nestlé in a joint venture to build labs for Galderma, a company whose slogan is "Committed to the future of dermatology."

L'Oréal continues to research the hair care needs of diverse people around the world. According to Liz Alderman of the *New York Times*, L'Oréal is working on new "products for Garnier, Studio Line and other brands to be targeted to local hair." New colors are being developed to sell in markets around the world. Of CEO Jean-Paul Agon, Alderman writes, "Mr. Agon's dream is that people even in a third-tier Chinese city will wake up, shower with L'Oréal shampoos and soaps, and wear his creams and makeup before heading out the door."

BRAND EQUITY

- According to *Brandirectory*, L'Oréal ranked 122nd among top global brands in 2012.
- The brand value for L'Oréal in 2012 was US$7.7 billion, higher than its top competitor, Estée Lauder, with a 2012 brand value of US$3.7 billion.
- In 2012 L'Oréal's top subsidiary, Lancôme, was ranked 194th among the top global brands, with a brand value of US$5.1 billion.

According to *Brandirectory*, L'Oréal ranked 122nd among top global brands in 2012, one spot down from 2011. Among top cosmetic brands, its rank improved to third place. L'Oréal's brand value was estimated at US$7.7 billion in 2012 and US$7.6 billion in 2011.

L'Oréal's top subsidiary, Lancôme, was also ahead of the competition. In 2012 it ranked 194th among the top global brands, with a brand value of US$5.1 billion. In comparison, some of L'Oréal's top competitors lagged behind. In September 2012, Estée Lauder's brand value was US$3.7 billion, Bioré's was US$3.3 billion, and Shiseido's was US$2.9 billion. Revlon struggled with US$922 million.

BRAND AWARENESS

- As of 2012, L'Oréal comprised 27 global brands in 130 countries.
- China became the brand's top market in 2010.
- In 2011 Harris Poll EquiTrend ranked L'Oréal seventh place in the cosmetics category for Brand of the Year.

Over the last 100 years, L'Oréal has grown to include 27 global brands in 130 countries. According to its online magazine, China became the brand's number one market in 2010 when sales "exceeded the one billion euros of sales mark and became the group's number three subsidiary." The brand contributes this success to the "dynamism of the men's skincare, make-up and women's skincare segments."

In 2011 Harris Poll EquiTrend ranked L'Oréal seventh place in the cosmetics category for Brand of the Year. In comparison, Bobbi Brown Cosmetics took the top spot as Cosmetics Brand of the Year, followed by Sephora Cosmetics, Rimmel Cosmetics, and Shiseido Cosmetics in fourth place. Brand Keys Customer Loyalty Engagement Index ranked L'Oréal 48th on 2012's top 100 brands. In 2011, the brand came in 37th place. Its subsidiary Maybelline came in 22nd place, while competitors Mary Kay and Lancôme came in second and 40th place respectively.

BRAND OUTLOOK

- L'Oréal proposed an increase in payments on dividends in 2011 to EUR2 per share.
- The brand is committed to increasing its diverse pool of future managers by improving education around the world.
- L'Oréal aims to acquire one billion new customers during the next decade.

CEO Jean-Paul Agon reported that L'Oréal was in a position to "achieve another year of sales and profit growth in 2012." The company proposed an increase in payments on 2011 dividends to EUR2 per share. Agon said, "After a year of solid development, L'Oréal has emerged stronger, and has confirmed its position as the world leader in beauty.... We are beginning a new phase in our history."

L'Oréal's 2011 Annual Report states, "In a worldwide market undergoing a complete transformation, L'Oréal is making new advances to offer the best in cosmetics to as many people as possible." The report goes on to describe L'Oréal as making a "stronger commitment to responsible growth, … implementing the digital revolution, accelerating the globalisation of industrial organisation, [and] developing a relationship of trust." The brand plans to commit to the education of people around the world and to groom a diverse pool of managers for the future.

As the urban middle-class population grows, the number of prospective consumers of L'Oréal products will grow. According to *Forbes*, "L'Oréal targets to acquire 1 billion new customers over the next decade." One aspect of this effort is the company's investment of EUR100 million in a new hair research center, which opened in Paris in 2012.

FURTHER READING

Alderman, Liz. "Le Petit Prince of L'Oréal." *New York Times*, May 5, 2012.

Brand Finance. "L'Oréal." *Brandirectory*. Accessed September 5, 2012. http://brandirectory.com/profile/loral.

"Brand Keys Customer Loyalty Leaders 2012." *Brand Keys*. 2012. Accessed February 13, 2013. http://brandkeys.com/syndicated-studies/loyalty-leaders-list/.

"Harris Poll EquiTrend: Cosmetics Brand of the Year Rankings, 2011." *Harris Interactive*. 2012. Accessed February 13, 2013. http://www.harrisinteractive.com/SearchResults.aspx?Search=L'Oreal.

L'Oréal. "History of L'Oréal." Accessed September 8, 2012. http://www.lorealusa.com/_en/_us/html/our-company/history-of-l-oreal.aspx.

———. "2011 Annual Report." Accessed September 7, 2012. http://www.loreal.com/_en/_ww/html/company/pdf/LOREAL_RA2011_HD_27032012_EN.pdf.

"L'Oréal SA." *International Directory of Company Histories*, Vol. 109. St. James Press, 2010. Reproduced in Business and Company Resource Center. Farmington Hills, MI: Gale Group. 2012. http://galenet.galegroup.com/servlet/BCRC.

Morais, Richard C. "Cosmopolitan Genius." *Forbes*, November 27, 2000.

Osborne, Grant. "Cosmair to Become L'Oréal USA." Basenotes.net, June 26, 2000. Accessed September 5, 2012. http://www.basenotes.net/industry_news/20000626cosmair.html.

Ovarian Cancer Research Fund. "L'Oréal Paris." Accessed September 8, 2012. http://www.ocrf.org/index.php?option=com_content&view=article&id=137:loreal-paris-&catid=66:corporate-sponsors&Itemid=303.

Rand, Hannah. "L'Oréal Donates $1.2 Million to Help Abolish Animal Testing but Welfare Groups Say the Company Should Stop the Practice Now." *Daily Mail* (London), March 15, 2012.

Regan, James, and Pascale Denis. "L'Oréal Sees 2012 Growth, Heiress Steps Down." Reuters, February 13, 2012.

Roberts, Andrew. "L'Oréal Losing Mass-Market Share in Western Europe, CEO Says." *Bloomberg*, November 7, 2011.

Trefis Team. "L'Oréal Goes Global with Hair Research Center." *Forbes*, April 9, 2012.

LOUIS VUITTON

AT A GLANCE

Brand Synopsis: As the world's top luxury brand, Louis Vuitton is known for tradition, innovation, and quality.

Parent Company: LVMH Moët Hennessy Louis Vuitton S.A.

22 Avenue Montaigne

75008 Paris

France

http://www.lvmh.com/

Sector: Consumer Discretionary

Industry Group: Consumer Durables and Apparel

Performance: *Sales*—US$105 million (2012).

Principal Competitors: PPR SA; Rémy Cointreau Group; Compagnie Financière Richemont SA

BRAND ORIGINS

- The Parisian trunk maker Louis Vuitton started his own business in 1854.
- Louis Vuitton developed a distinctive pattern to ward off counterfeiters in 1876.
- The signature Louis Vuitton monogram canvas pattern was patented in 1896.
- Louis Vuitton introduced a new standard in luggage in 1959.
- LVMH Moët Hennessy Louis Vuitton S.A. was created in a 1987 merger.

As one of the most valuable luxury brands in the world, Louis Vuitton dates its history to 1835, when 15-year-old Louis Vuitton began an apprenticeship with a Paris trunk maker. He opened his own business in 1854 and made his mark by inventing stackable flat-topped trunks, which replaced traditional domed trunks. As a master trunk maker, Vuitton provided luggage to European royalty and aristocratic families. His work was also widely counterfeited, prompting him in 1876 to incorporate colored stripes in the canvas covers of his trunks. When these were imitated as well, Vuitton patented a checkered material. It may not have dissuaded counterfeiters, but it was an important step in the creation of the Louis Vuitton brand.

In 1885 Louis Vuitton's son, Georges, was dispatched to London to extend the Louis Vuitton brand to England. He then took over the business following his father's death in 1892. Like his father, Georges Vuitton had to contend with counterfeiters. In 1896 he invented a new canvas design, using a monogram of his father's initials. The patented monogram canvas was not only an immediate success but also it marked another important step in the development of the Louis Vuitton brand. Furthermore, it created such a distinctive look that rather than discouraging counterfeiters it made Louis Vuitton one of the most counterfeited fashion brands in history.

During the late 1800s and the early 1900s Louis Vuitton–branded products were introduced to Bangkok, Brussels, Buenos Aires, Montreal, Nice, and several cities in the United States, including Boston, Chicago, New York, Philadelphia, and San Francisco. Like his father, Georges Vuitton kept up with trends in transportation, the foundation on which the brand rested. In 1897 he introduced the first automobile trunk. It was an actual travel trunk that was lashed to the back of an automobile. Because it was so useful, automakers eventually provided for built-in storage, which in North America continued to be called the "trunk." Georges Vuitton would also design luggage that was suitable for hot air balloons and airplanes.

After devoting itself to the production of military trunks during World War I, Louis Vuitton returned its focus to supplying the luggage needs of aristocrats and a new breed of royalty: Hollywood movie stars. During the Great Depression of the 1930s the special orders declined and the company became increasingly dependent on catalog offerings, which included cases for books, rifles, radios, typewriters, and wine bottles. A third generation of the Vuitton family, Gaston Vuitton, took charge of the business during this period. After the company was shuttered because of World War II, he reestablished the Louis Vuitton brand.

Like previous generations in his family, Gaston Vuitton established his own reputation. In 1959 he created a new standard in luggage by introducing a new method of coating that made the bags waterproof, more durable, and better suited for shorter trips. He also began commissioning well-known artists to help in the design of accessories, which added to the luster of the luxury brand. His son-in-law, Henry Racamier, assumed control of the company in 1977, and he grew the brand further by opening Louis Vuitton shops around the world during the next decade. Brand awareness was also increased through a sponsorship with the America's Cup sailing competition. A preliminary competition among challengers became known as the Louis Vuitton Cup.

In 1987 Racamier merged Louis Vuitton with Moët-Hennessy to create LVMH Moët Hennessy Louis Vuitton S.A., the world's largest luxury goods conglomerate. Following the merger, the Louis Vuitton brand continued to grow in value. By the start of the 1990s there were 130 stores around the world that operated under the Louis Vuitton name. The first Chinese location opened in Beijing in 1992. The first store in Africa opened in 1999. The brand was also extended to new lines of leather goods and a line of women's and men's apparel. During the 21st century new and more luxurious stores opened around the world. The Louis Vuitton brand was applied to new product categories such as sunglasses, jewelry, and watches.

BRAND ELEMENTS

- The company's LV monogram is at the heart of the Louis Vuitton logo.
- The Louis Vuitton signature monogram pattern is used in numerous products.
- Advertising tag lines for Louis Vuitton often refer to the brand's travel heritage.

A key element of the Louis Vuitton brand is its monogram logo. The overlapping L and V letters are rendered in a custom, handmade typeface. The monogram is so important to the company's branding strategy that strict rules are maintained on the alignment of the monogram on products. The LV design should always be located on the front, center. In cases in which the shape of the product prevents the monogram from being centered, it is to be bilaterally symmetrical. The corporate logo also employs the monogram, with "Louis Vuitton" written below.

The monogram was created by Georges Vuitton to honor his father as well as to serve as part of the company's famous canvas monogram. The pattern was very much a Japanese-inspired flower motif, relying on a background of flowers and quatrefoils. Even though Japanese and Oriental imagery was in vogue at that time, it was a design that stood the test of time and was used by the company to create hundreds of products in a variety of colors. It became the ultimate status symbol, and as such was one of the most widely counterfeited images.

Louis Vuitton is not known for a single slogan. The brand's advertising has used a variety of taglines over the years, primarily drawing on the brand's close association with travel. For example, in 1921 Louis Vuitton coined "Show me your luggage and I'll tell you who you are." In 2008 the tagline used in ads with Sean Connery was "There are journeys that turn into legends." A campaign featuring the film director Francis Coppola used the line, "Inside every story, there is a beautiful journey." The company's advertising also plays on the concepts of tradition and innovation.

BRAND IDENTITY

- Louis Vuitton is positioned as a status symbol luxury brand.
- Louis Vuitton's high prices reinforce a luxury brand image.
- Quality workmanship plays an important role in maintaining Louis Vuitton's brand identity.
- Celebrity associations support Louis Vuitton's image.
- Louis Vuitton stores play a part in brand positioning.

Louis Vuitton presents itself as a luxury brand, one that is capable of imparting status on its customer. Moreover, it is an exclusive brand and not available to the ordinary person—a seeming contradiction, given that Louis Vuitton hopes to sell its products to as wide a market as possible without diluting the brand. The high price tag reinforces the luxury positioning. Quality workmanship and attention to the smallest detail are key to maintaining the image of Louis Vuitton products. For example, the company's iconic handbags feature handmade handles and naturally oak-tanned leather. Care is taken that all LV monograms appear whole and uninterrupted by seams. Bags are produced from a single, unbroken piece of leather or canvas. Not only does the quality of the products fulfill the brand promise inherent in a luxury brand but also it helps distinguish Louis Vuitton goods from the numerous knockoffs that are available for sale.

Louis Vuitton is also known by the company it keeps. The celebrities seen with Louis Vuitton goods—actors, models, musicians, and others—are an important aspect of the brand. To nurture that connection, Louis Vuitton has conducted marketing campaigns with the likes of Keith Richards, Jennifer Lopez, Sean Connery, and Kanye West. Even Mikhail Gorbachev, the former head of the Soviet Union, was featured in a Louis Vuitton advertising campaign for luggage in 2007.

Another important way Louis Vuitton positions its brand is through company-owned stores. They are found in prime locations and feature a decor that is in keeping with the upscale nature of the brand. Large flagship stores in major retail centers provide even greater exposure and prestige to the brand. To burnish its image further, Louis Vuitton sponsors activities that are associated with a wealthy lifestyle, including yachting and classic automobile racing.

BRAND STRATEGY
- From its inception, Louis Vuitton catered to an upscale clientele.
- Innovation elevated Louis Vuitton above other trunk makers of his day.
- The famous Louis Vuitton monogram pattern was adjusted in 1959.
- Sponsorships of sailing and automobile events were used to grow the brand.
- At the turn of the 21st century Asia became an important market for Louis Vuitton and other luxury brands.

When Louis Vuitton opened his own trunk shop in 1854, he was not consciously building a brand. Nevertheless, he laid a foundation for a luxury brand through his spirit of innovation and the wealthy customers he cultivated. Because only people of certain means traveled and required trunks, Vuitton's business was upscale by its very nature. After he invented his flat-topped trunks, Vuitton gained a reputation as a master luggage maker, attracting the attention of royalty and the wealthiest of customers. It was an association that would have a lasting impact on the Louis Vuitton brand well after its creator passed away.

Counterfeiting was an early problem for Louis Vuitton, and one that would forever plague the company. Imitators led Georges Vuitton to develop the monogram canvas pattern that would provide the graphic foundation for the Louis Vuitton brand. It did little to ward off imitators and actually led to even more counterfeit Louis Vuitton products. Regardless, it provided exponentially more benefits than problems for the company in the long term.

Another important aspect to building the Louis Vuitton brand was introducing it to new markets. Besides creating the LV monogram, Georges Vuitton began building a sales network to grow the brand. After opening a shop in London, he secured distribution partners in Argentina, Bangkok, Canada, and the United States. He also extended the brand to new modes of travel, in particular the automobile.

Innovative products combined with traditional styling that were sold to an upscale clientele was at the heart of the Louis Vuitton brand strategy in the 20th century. Following World War II the company began incorporating leather into its products, which allowed it to produce goods such as purses and wallets. Because of this shift in focus, the company's monogram pattern was changed slightly in 1959 to make it more workable. That same year Louis Vuitton introduced a new line of lightweight, waterproof luggage.

The Louis Vuitton brand was expanded during the late 1970s by the opening of stores around the world. To tie the brand closer to the wealthy lifestyle with which it was identified, the company began sponsoring the America's Cup sailing competition in 1983. It organized the challengers qualifying races under the Louis Vuitton Cup banner. In 1989 the brand associated itself with expensive automobiles by sponsoring the Louis Vuitton Classics Annual Automobile Race in Paris. Even though the race did not provide a great deal of exposure for the brand, it helped promote the brand's tradition, in light of Louis Vuitton's connection to the original automobile trunk.

In 1978 Louis Vuitton merged with Moët-Hennessy to form LVMH Moët Hennessy Louis Vuitton S.A. This merger enabled Louis Vuitton to achieve greater luster by being closely connected to luxury brands in other categories. Under new ownership, the Louis Vuitton brand was extended to new products, including the new Epi line of vibrantly colored handbags for women and the Taiga line of fine leather accessories for men. The brand was introduced in China during the early 1990s, where it thrived primarily because of its reputation. As the global economy deteriorated in 2008, Louis Vuitton aired its first television commercials. It also launched a "cores-values campaign," returning to the brand's travel roots by connecting it to the personal journey of celebrity endorsers.

BRAND EQUITY
- Brand Finance estimated a brand value of US$4.9 billion for Louis Vuitton in 2012.
- Louis Vuitton was awarded the 202nd position on Brand Finance's "Global 500 2012."
- Interbrand listed Louis Vuitton as the number-one brand in the fashion sector in 2012.

For a luxury brand like Louis Vuitton that makes a promise of bestowing status and prestige on its clientele, brand equity is everything, allowing its goods to command a higher price tag than comparable merchandise. Even during poor economic conditions in 2008 that led department stores to mark down many luxury brands, Louis Vuitton was able to hold the line. By continuing to charge full price, Louis Vuitton provided a vivid demonstration of its brand equity.

Several firms attempt to place a monetary value on Louis Vuitton's brand equity. Brand Finance, a brand evaluation consultancy, assigned a brand value of US$4.9 billion to Louis Vuitton in 2012. It was a performance that earned Louis Vuitton the 202nd position on Brand Finance's "Global 500 2012" list of the world's most valuable brands. Louis Vuitton also did well among the most valuable diversified holding company brands, ranked number two in 2011, behind Jardines but ahead of Dior.

Using its own methodology, Interbrand estimated the worth of the Louis Vuitton brand at US$23.6 billion in 2012. Not only did Interbrand list Louis Vuitton as number 17 on its Best Global Brands list in 2012 but also it named Louis Vuitton as the number-one brand in the fashion sector, worth significantly more than its closest rivals: H&M, Zara, and Gucci.

BRAND AWARENESS

- Longevity supports Louis Vuitton's brand awareness.
- Counterfeiting deprives revenues but grows awareness.
- Celebrities have always played an important role in increasing Louis Vuitton's brand awareness.

With a history that spans more than 150 years, Louis Vuitton enjoys excellent brand awareness, especially with the upscale clientele it has served since the beginning. The BrandZ Top 100 consistently ranks Louis Vuitton among the top brands in "brand contribution," a metric designed to measure the emotional bond that the brand inspires in consumers. The brand remains true to its message of luxury and status, one that continues to resonate not only with its core customers in the Western world but also with an emerging luxury market in Asia. Even counterfeiting, the long-time bane of Louis Vuitton, created greater visibility for the brand's iconic logo and monogram pattern, in the process fostering greater recognition of the brand.

Throughout its history the LV monogram has been on Louis Vuitton goods carried by the rich and famous, keeping the brand in the public eye. Even as Louis Vuitton holds fast to the traditions that underpin the brand, it remains current by associating the brand with actors, models, musicians, and other celebrities that foster brand awareness. In 2012, the brand aired its first-ever television commercial, starring supermodel Arizona Muse. Louis Vuitton has also embraced social media. It developed a

presence on Facebook and created an app that allowed customers to share their travel experiences. In that way, the name of a French trunk maker for royalty in the 19th century was kept alive for a new generation in the 21st century.

BRAND OUTLOOK

- Louis Vuitton is focusing some of its international growth on China.
- In 2012 Louis Vuitton opened a flagship store in Shanghai.
- In spite of being a top luxury brand, Louis Vuitton managed to maintain its price points during and after the recession that lasted from late 2007 to mid-2009.

As one of the world's top luxury brands, and the number-one fashion brand by some measures, Louis Vuitton faces a challenge in maintaining its illustrious position in the marketplace. As a venerable brand, it will have to retain its authenticity while adjusting to the times, a straddle that might be difficult to achieve. The brand showed its strength during poor financial conditions late in the first decade of the new century by being able to maintain its price points. It was an especially impressive performance because the luxury and travel markets, which are the core of the Louis Vuitton brand, were hard hit by the global recession.

Much of Louis Vuitton's growth in recent years has been in China. Already a powerful brand in China, it was further bolstered by the opening of a new flagship store in Shanghai in 2012. However, some industry analysts question whether the brand can continue growing in that market. Many Chinese consumers have traveled more widely and grown more sophisticated about the luxury goods they buy. To help ward off brand weariness, the new Shanghai store attempts to reengage the top-end customers who may have become jaded by offering invitation-only floors, where extremely expensive goods are available.

Louis Vuitton's trademark brown and gold LV bags, along with other merchandise, remain an attraction for first-generation status seekers in the emerging middle class in China and in other emerging nations, such as Brazil. Thus, millions of potential new Louis Vuitton customers are being created outside of the brand's traditional European and North American market.

FURTHER READING

Brand Finance. "Global 500 2012." *Brandirectory*. Accessed January 9, 2013. http://brandirectory.com/league_tables/table/global-500-2012.

Daneshkhhu, Scheherazade. "LVMH Faces Dilemma of Success." *Financial Times*, October 19, 2012.

Kiley, David. "Vuitton at the Rock." *Brandweek*, September 1, 1997.

Lamb, Rachel. "Louis Vuitton Is Most Valuable Luxury Brand: Top 100 List." *Luxury Daily*, May 23, 2012.

"LVMH Moët Hennessy Louis Vuitton S.A." *International Directory of Company Histories*. Ed. Tina Grant. Vol. 113. Detroit, MI: St. James Press, 2010.

Roberts, Andrew. "Louis Vuitton Risks Logo Fatigue as Chinese Taste Matures." Bloomberg.com, September 25, 2012.

Thompson, Derek. "Branding Louis Vuitton: Behind the World's Most Famous Luxury Label." *Atlantic*, May 2005.

"2011 Ranking of the Top 100 Brands." Interbrand. Accessed October 30, 2012. http://www.interbrand.com/en/best-global-brands/best-global-brands-2008/best-global-brands-2011.aspx.

Wheaton, Ken. "Vuitton Gets Its Rocks off with Rolling Stones' Keith Richards." *Advertising Age*, March 10, 2008.

LOWE'S

BRAND ORIGINS

- L. S. Lowe opened Mr. L. S. Lowe's North Wilkesboro Hardware store in 1921.
- Carl Buchan, L. S. Lowe's son-in-law, acquired full ownership of the business in 1952 and began expanding the company.
- Following the death of Carl Buchan in 1961, the company began trading publicly and was renamed Lowe's Companies, Inc.

- In 2012 Lowe's operated stores in the United States, Canada, and Mexico.

In 1921 L. S. Lowe opened a hardware store in the small town of North Wilkesboro, North Carolina, under the name Mr. L. S. Lowe's North Wilkesboro Hardware. Following his death, his son, James Lowe, took over the business. James Lowe and his brother-in-law, Carl Buchan, served in the U.S. Army during World War II, and during this period Lowe's sister and mother ran the business.

When Buchan was wounded and discharged from the army in 1943, he returned to North Wilkesboro to help operate the business, and in 1946 he became a partner. Buchan quickly sold off much of the store's inventory. He then reorganized the store, which became a wholesale-style seller of hardware and building supplies.

When Lowe was discharged from the army, he returned to aid Buchan in operating the business. The two opened a second store and used profits to buy an automobile dealership and a cattle farm. In 1952 Buchan bought out his brother-in-law. Three months later, Buchan opened a third store, in Asheville, North Carolina. The company was also incorporated as Lowe's North Wilkesboro Hardware, Inc. According to company lore, Buchan retained the Lowe's name so he could use the slogan "Lowe's low prices."

The post–World War II construction boom made the hardware business very profitable. By purchasing stock directly from the manufacturer, Lowe's was able to avoid paying the higher prices set by wholesalers, which meant lower prices for customers. By 1960 Buchan was operating 15 stores.

The big push to increase the presence of Lowe's in the home-building market came in 1960, when Buchan died and the office of company president was created. The company went public in 1961 and was renamed Lowe's Companies, Inc. By the late 1960s, Lowe's had more than 50 stores, and annual sales figures hovered around the US$100 million mark. At about this time, the burgeoning do-it-yourself market was beginning to change the face of the construction industry. Home centers were becoming the modern version of the neighborhood hardware store. By 1979 Lowe's had more than 200 stores and annual revenues of more than US$900 million.

When new home construction came nearly to a standstill in the later part of the 1970s, Lowe's made the decision to target consumers. While studying the track records of do-it-yourself stores that sold solely to consumers, Lowe's found that these stores were recording strong sales even during the home-building slumps. Lowe's embarked on a new marketing strategy. A consultant was hired to remodel the showrooms, and the resulting layout was similar to that of a supermarket.

By the late 1980s, the retail scene in the United States had once again been transformed, and the era of the "big-box" stores had begun. The Home Depot, Inc., led the way in the home improvement sector, and the proliferation of its 105,000-square-foot home improvement superstores quickly moved the upstart past Lowe's into the number-one position. Lowe's, meanwhile, had surpassed the 300-store mark in 1989, but those stores averaged barely more than 20,000 square feet in size. Lowe's then began to transform itself from a chain of small hardware stores into a chain of large, warehouse-style stores. By 1996 there were more than 400 Lowe's stores, averaging more than 75,000 square feet per store. By the end of 1999, the Lowe's store count had reached 550, and revenues of US$15.45 billion made Lowe's the 15th largest retailer in the country. The store count passed 1,000 in 2005, and by 2012 there were more than 1,700 locations.

Lowe's moved into the Canadian market in 2007, opening three stores in the Toronto area. By 2012 Lowe's operated 32 stores across Canada. The majority of these were located in Ontario, with several in Alberta, and one each in British Columbia and Saskatchewan. In 2007 Lowe's announced plans for expansion into Mexico. It opened two stores in the northern city of Monterrey in 2010. Approximately 430 employees were hired to staff the two stores and the company's office.

BRAND ELEMENTS

- Lowe's logo, a blue house with the brand name in the center, shows Lowe's goal of being at the center of every home-improvement project.
- The colors of the Lowe's logo are meant to impart the American flag and the quality of American products.

- Lowe's taglines are often aimed at female consumers because research shows that women make the majority of homeimprovement decisions.

The Lowe's logo features the brand name in white, block capitals against a blue background in the shape of a rectangle with a gable on top. The blue space is surrounded by a thin red outline. The shape of the house embodies the types of products that the store carries, while the central location of the brand name puts Lowe's at the center of any home-improvement project. The colors of the logo capture the colors of the American flag and suggests the durability and quality of the goods offered by Lowe's.

In 2001 Lowe's released its first national television advertising campaign, using the tag line "Improving Home Improvement" and touting its stores as cleaner, better organized, and better lit than those of its warehouse-style competitors. The campaign's themes were consistent with the company's push to attract female consumers, a strategy that a number of analysts considered a key to the company's success. Lowe's decided to cater to women because company research found that females made the vast majority of home-improvement decisions. This strategy is one that continues into the slogans today.

BRAND IDENTITY

- The Lowe's brand has always been about helping the customer improve their most valued asset—their home.
- Lowe's identifies its brand as consumer oriented.
- Lowe's used its first advertising slogan, "Improving Home Improvement," to bolster its long tradition in the hardware industry and in customer service.

The Lowe's brand is based on a tradition of building. What began as a small grocery and hardware store grew into a multinational, superstore chain. In order to keep the brand rooted in its small town heritage, Lowe's identifies itself as a place where customers can find the best products at the lowest possible price. Moreover, it is a place where the customer's needs always come first. Although the size of the stores has changed, the goal of the stores has not. They are still there to "help customers improve and maintain their biggest asset—their home."

The Lowe's brand is all about helping the customer help themselves. In fact, in the brand's first national television advertising campaign in 2001, the tagline, "Improving Home Improvement," showed that their stores were cleaner, better organized, and better lit than those of its warehouse-style competitors. Customers could go into any store and find the items, and the customer service, that they needed.

BRAND STRATEGY

- Lowe's carries roughly 40,000 items at each store, and each one is carefully selected to ensure customer satisfaction.
- In order to continue extending the brand globally, Lowe's expanded into Australia in 2011 through a joint venture with Woolworths Limited.
- Lowe's new domestic strategy includes a new ad campaign, "Never Stop Improving."

A typical Lowe's store carries about 40,000 items with thousands more items available through special order and online. Name brands include Whirlpool, Owens Corning, and KitchenAid. Lowe's also carries brands exclusive to the company, including Allen & Roth home decor, Portfolio lighting products, and Top Choice lumber. However, in order to expand these products, Lowe's has decided to go global.

While built upon American tradition, Lowe's has sought to globalize its brand in recent times. With successful stores in Mexico and Canada, Lowe's has continued to find new markets to expand their lines. The company entered the Australian home improvement market in 2011 through a joint venture with the Australian retail giant Woolworths Limited. Named Masters Home Improvement, the company boasted 22 stores in 2012 and continued the Lowe's format of brightly lit stores with easy-to-navigate layouts and colorful signing and displays. Under terms of the venture, Lowe's owns one-third of the home improvement chain.

In an effort to continue bolstering its brand domestically, Lowe's strategic advertising aims to fulfill its brand commitment to the customer. According to RetailingToday.com, in 2011 Lowe's introduced its newest strategy in the form of the ad campaign, "Never Stop Improving." With it comes a promise to customers that the brand "will constantly be innovating and improving ... to satisfy their ever changing needs." The new campaign brought new innovations to the market like MyLowes, an online tool to help customers manage their projects through every stage. Additionally, Lowe's uses social media to advance the brand. With about one million Facebook friends (twice as many as Home Depot), Lowe's generates interest in the brand through photos, product information, contests, and idea exchanges. Lowe's fields questions from Facebook fans and answers most questions within minutes.

BRAND EQUITY

- Lowe's placed 54th in the Fortune 500 rankings for 2012.
- Lowe's consistently ranks in the top tier of U.S. brands, with a brand value of approximately US$9 billion.
- Lowe's ranked 99th on Interbrand's "Global 500" with a brand value of US$8.8 billion, much below competitor Home Depot who ranked 23rd.

Lowe's is a Fortune 500 company, ranked 54th in 2012 with revenues of US$50 billion. With revenues that have increased over the last three years and a constant commitment to its customers, Lowe's also enjoys considerable brand value both domestically and globally. In Interbrand's "Best Retail Brands 2012," Lowe's placed 12th among U.S. brands, with a brand value of US$8.6 billion. According to Brand Finance's "Global 500," Lowe's came in at number 99 with a brand value of US$8.8 billion. Competitor Home Depot ranks higher at number 23 with a brand value of almost US$21 billion.

BRAND AWARENESS

- Lowe's enjoys both high brand awareness among consumers and rankings as one of the world's most valuable brands.
- In order to keep brand awareness high, Lowe's participates in social media events and sponsorships like that of NASCAR driver Jimmie Johnson.
- Awareness of Lowe's in Canada has been low because of the presence of Home Depot and Rona, an established regional competitor.

A major U.S. brand with a growing international presence, Lowe's enjoys a high level of awareness among U.S. consumers and consistently ranks among the world's most valuable brands. The *Financial Times* ranked Lowe's ninth, with a market value of US$34.8 billion, in its ranking of the world's most valuable general retailers in 2011.

Lowe's strives to keep its brand awareness high through social networking and promotional events. One example of this is the company's sponsorship of NASCAR Sprint Cup champion Jimmie Johnson and his No. 48 car. The sponsorship includes placement of the Lowe's logo on the car and on Johnson's racing suit. Johnson is one of the best drivers in NASCAR and had the best exposure value of any driver in 2010, ensuring generous display of the Lowe's logo and brand.

Globally, Lowe's brand awareness is not as high. Competition from Home Depot and regional home improvement retailer Rona kept Lowe's brand from achieving the high saturation of the market.

BRAND OUTLOOK

- Lowe's was able to navigate the U.S. economic downturn by attracting customers with its low price guarantee and strong customer service.
- The thriving home improvement industry in Australia provides opportunities for Lowe's continued strong growth there.

- Lowe's offers solar panels, wind turbines, and electric car-charging kits, in addition to its lines of energy-saving appliances.

In the early 21st century Lowe's weathered the collapse of the U.S. housing market and subsequent faltering of the economy by adhering to its core strategies of offering its everyday low price guarantee and establishing long-term relationships with shoppers. Employees moved beyond selling products to becoming partners with shoppers in the completion of their home improvement projects. A variety of national brands and strong private labels helped to match consumers' quality and price needs. Lowe's also closed underperforming stores to concentrate on its successful stores.

While expansion across Canada has been slower than anticipated, by 2012 Lowe's had opened 32 outlets in Canada. In Australia, where the housing market remained strong, home improvement was a booming business. In 2012 Masters Home Improvement operated 22 stores, with another 17 under construction and a further 50 stores planned.

Consumers and investors have been impressed by Lowe's commitment to being a good steward of the environment. The company has instituted an expansive recycling program, stocked Energy Star- and WaterSense-rated products, implemented programs to reduce emissions and fuel used in the transportation of goods, designed energy-efficient stores, and focused on timber sustainability in its lumber purchases.

FURTHER READING

Hoffer, Gail. "Lowe's Builds a New Brand Strategy," RetailingToday.com, September 19, 2011. Accessed October 5, 2012. http://www.retailingtoday.com/article/lowes-builds-new-brand-strategy.

"Home Improvement Professionals Have Strong Loyalty in Retail Arena, According to Latest TraQline PRO Report." *PR Web*, October 3, 2012. Accessed October 5, 2012. http://www.prweb.com/releases/2012/6/prweb9618957.htm.

"Lowe's Companies, Inc." *International Directory of Company Histories*. Ed. Jay P. Pederson. Vol. 81. Detroit, MI: St. James Press, 2007.

Perratore, Ed. "With MyLowe's Retailer Hopes to Be Your Go-to Store." *Consumer Reports*, October 17, 2011.

Sage, Alexandria, and Sonali Paul. "Lowe's Taps Australia Growth with Woolworths." Reuters, August 24, 2009.

Saler, Matt. "Touchdown! How the Building Industry Is Spending Money in Sports." *IMRE Build IQ*, July 12, 2011. Accessed October 5, 2012. http://imrebuildiq.com/2011/07/12/how-the-building-industry-is-spending-money-in-sports.

Walsh, Mark. "Lowe's Hopes Pinterest + Facebook = Higher Engagement." *Online Media Daily*, March 12, 2012.

"World's Largest Home Improvement Retailers Overall, 2011." *Business Rankings Annual*. Ed. Deborah J. Draper. Detroit, MI: Gale, 2013.

"World's Most Admired Diversified Specialty Retailers, 2012." *Business Rankings Annual*. Ed. Deborah J. Draper. Detroit, MI: Gale, 2013.

LUFTHANSA

―■―

AT A GLANCE

―■―

Brand Synopsis: German company Lufthansa is Europe's largest commercial air carrier and has placed in the top five of *Fortune*'s most admired airlines for several years.

Parent Company: Deutsch Lufthansa AG
Von-Goblenz-Strasse 2-6
D-50679 Cologne 21
Germany
http://konzern.lufthansa.com/en/

Sector: Industrials

Industry Group: Transportation

Performance: *Sales*—EUR 28.7 billion (US$37.1 billion) (2011).

Principal Competitors: British Airways; Air France-KLM; Air Berlin

BRAND ORIGINS

- Begun as a state-owned airline in 1926, Lufthansa ceased operations during World War II but resumed flying in the 1950s.
- Lufthansa had built a European-wide network before WWII.
- Lufthansa became a founding member of the Star Alliance in 1997.

Deutsche Luft Hansa (DLH) was formed by the Weimar government in 1926 through the merger of two private airlines, Deutcher Aero Lloyd and Junkers Luftverkehr. By 1931 DLH had built an extensive route network, Europe's largest and most comprehensive. It began serving what was then the Soviet Union in 1921 and China in 1930. It began the world's first trans-Atlantic air mail service from Berlin to Buenos Aires in 1934 and developed routes for air transport throughout South America.

The start of World War II brought an end to the airline's European operations, and soon after 1945 all operations ceased. However, in 1954 the Allies allowed Deutsche Lufthansa to recapitalize, and the airline started up again with domestic routes. At first, it went by a different name, but it soon adopted the name Deutsche Lufthansa and became familiarly known as Lufthansa rather than DLH. It then began flights to London and Paris, followed by flights to South America in 1956. Lufthansa then initiated routes between Germany and New York, Tokyo, and Cairo in the 1950s.

After the Allies relinquished control of Germany's airspace in 1990, Lufthansa finally was able to fly under its own colors for the first time since the war. Also in 1990, East Germany and West Germany became reunified, and Lufthansa was able to once again fly in and out of Berlin.

A code-sharing agreement with Air Canada occurred in 1996, and Lufthansa became a founding member of the Star Alliance, a global airline alliance, in 1997, along with Air Canada, Scandinavian Airlines, Thai Airways International, and United Airlines. The German government sold its stake in Lufthansa, which had been at 38 percent, in 1997, thus leaving the airline fully privatized.

In response to Air France's purchase of KLM, in 2007 Lufthansa took full ownership of SWISS, Switzerland's primary international airline. It also purchased a 45 percent equity stake in SN Airholding, parent of Brussels Airlines.

Today, Lufthansa employs more than 55,000 people. It owns almost 700 airplanes, flies to more than 200 destinations around the world, and carries more than 100 million passengers per year. It also owns almost 20 cargo planes that carry billions of tons of freight each year.

BRAND ELEMENTS

- The Lufthansa tagline is "There's no better way to fly."
- Lufthansa's logo is an encircled, stylized crane in flight, usually depicted in dark blue on a bright gold background.
- Lufthansa has two aural brand elements, an F-major musical motif and a corporate anthem called "Symphony of Angels."

Lufthansa's tagline is "There's no better way to fly." A new advertising campaign begun in 2012 also used the line of "Nonstop you," which was said to sum up the airline's pledge to customers.

Lufthansa's logo is a stylized bird, a crane in flight. It is enclosed within the outline of a circle. This logo was developed in 1918 and was used by the first German airline, Deutsche Luftreederei, although it was adopted by Lufthansa in 1926. Designed by Otto Firle, the crane logo signifies technical precision, aeronautical competence, and safe air travel. The logo formerly depicted a light bird on a dark background, but was changed to show a dark bird on a light background. Usually the bird is dark blue and the background is a bright golden yellow, similar to the gold in the German flag.

Lufthansa has two aural brand elements. One is an F-major musical motif of four ascending notes that precedes flight announcements and can be heard in Lufthansa broadcast advertising. In 2006 the airline introduced a corporate anthem called "Symphony of Angels," a pop song that is used as background music while passengers are boarding or when customers are on hold during telephone calls with the airline's representatives.

BRAND IDENTITY

- Lufthansa seeks to appeal to both business and leisure travelers.
- Lufthansa's branding focuses on its pledge to help customers meet their travel goals.
- Lufthansa aims for its brand to signify quality, reliability, and innovation.

With its 2012 advertising campaign, Lufthansa was trying to reach all its target market segments, both people

traveling on business and those traveling for leisure. Lufthansa has had a leading role in the business travel segment, and to meet business travelers' needs, it built up a dense route network, provided comfortable airport lounges, and promised personalized service. The 2012 campaign also aimed to attract leisure travelers and promised to focus on the wishes, dreams, and experiences that are the reasons they are flying. The "Nonstop you" tagline attempted to highlight Lufthansa's pledge to serve its customers. Lufthansa promised to see traveling from the passenger's point of view and to provide the experiences that make flying special.

Lufthansa aims for its brand to signify quality, reliability, and innovation. It provides quality services such as punctual flights on clean airplanes with crews that are efficient yet personable. However, while the company touts personalized service, Lufthansa customer reviews frequently note that the cabin crew does an efficient job quickly but without any personal touch at all.

BRAND STRATEGY

- Lufthansa acts as a house of brands in its travel segment.
- Lufthansa plans to transfer its non-hub short-haul flights in Europe to its Germanwings subsidiary in 2013.
- Lufthansa tried to establish a Lufthansa Italia brand, but after two years, it consolidated those flights under the Lufthansa brand and that of Air Dolomiti.

Lufthansa acts as a house of brands. In addition to Lufthansa, it also owns the passenger airlines Swiss International Airlines, Germanwings, and Austrian Airlines, as well as Lufthansa Cargo, Lufthansa Technik, Lufthansa Systems, and LS Sky Chefs. It was one of the founding members of the Star Alliance, which now includes 27 global airlines. This alliance has enabled Lufthansa to code-share seamlessly with the other member airlines, increasing its capacity to carry passengers around the globe.

In a move that went against its usual ubiquitous usage of its corporate name, Lufthansa transferred its flights within Europe to its low-cost subsidiary, Germanwings. This new airline, combining the old Germanwings operations with the non-hub European flights, operates almost 90 aircraft and covers all point-to-point markets outside the Lufthansa hubs of Frankfurt and Munich. The Lufthansa brand disappeared completely in this market segment, as the carrier is now positioning the brand exclusively as a long-haul and hub-and-spoke carrier.

This shift occurred because of the falling fares in the European segment. Traditionally, Lufthansa's profitable long-haul flights had subsidized these short-haul flights. It is obvious, through this move, that Lufthansa did not

Lufthansa

want its name connected to a low-price, no-frills service, thus maintaining its brand emphasis on caring about customers and providing comfort to them.

The new airline, as noted, continues to use the Germanwings branding and is based at the Cologne/Bonn Airport. This airline does not have business-class seating, although it will be positioned as a high-end yet low-cost carrier with features that appeal to the business traveler.

There are deep connections between Germanwings and Lufthansa, however, with both airlines cooperating in marketing and distribution as well as in frequent-flier programs. The Lufthansa Group brand is painted on the Germanwings aircraft, even though the company does not share the full corporate name.

Even though Lufthansa has a strong brand identity in Italy, it has recently decided to rethink its strategy in that market. In 2009, it had launched the Lufthansa Italia brand, primarily to serve the northern Italian market, which had been abandoned by Air Italia. However, the global recession that began in 2008 made it difficult to establish a separate brand at that time, and so in 2011, the airline announced it would end the Lufthansa Italia brand and streamline operations by running that carrier's flights as part of Lufthansa and its subsidiary Air Dolomiti.

In the United States Lufthansa offers non-stop service to Germany from 22 airports. It also has code-sharing agreements with US Airways, United Continental, and JetBlue, which provide service from an additional 100 cities.

BRAND EQUITY

- Lufthansa ranked number one on Brand Finance's list of the top 20 airline brands in 2011.
- Lufthansa's brand value in 2013 was estimated to be US$3.64 billion.
- Sixty percent of Lufthansa's revenue comes from those passengers who fly more than 10,000 miles per year.

Lufthansa is one of the world's leading airlines. It ranked first on Brand Finance's list of the top 20 airline brands in 2011. Although forced to cut costs during the recent economic downturn, Lufthansa managed to keep its AA+ brand rating, which indicates the strength of the brand. Brand Finance assessed Lufthansa's brand value at US$3.64 billion in 2013. This was up from its 2012 brand value of US$3.30 billion.

Lufthansa is neither a discount airline nor a luxury airline. It is well matched against British Airways, with large international routes. Demonstrating why Lufthansa leads other carriers when it comes to business travelers, 60 percent of the airline's revenue comes from passengers who fly more than 10,000 miles per year, even though

they make up only 20 percent of the airline's passenger volume.

BRAND AWARENESS

- Lufthansa has worldwide brand recognition, particularly among business travelers.
- Lufthansa has been in the top 275 of Brand Finance's Global 500 brands from at least 2007 through 2011.
- The MySkyStatus tool increased Lufthansa's brand awareness in the U.S. and global markets.
- In 2012, *Fortune* listed Lufthansa as the fifth-most admired airline in the world.

Lufthansa is a global airline, and as such, it has worldwide brand recognition, particularly among European business travelers. In addition to its number-one spot on a 2011 list of the top airline brands, it has been in the top 275 of Global 500 Brands from at least 2007 through 2011, although it did drop to number 341 in that index in 2012.

Lufthansa flies from many gateway cities throughout the world, enabling it to keep its name in front of many, if not all, airline travelers simply by having planes at the gate. Although it has enjoyed almost universal brand awareness in Europe, in 2010 Lufthansa took measures to raise its brand awareness in the United States. Consumers there had only about 50 percent unaided recognition of the Lufthansa brand. The 2010 launch of the MySkyStatus tool, which helps travelers monitor their flight information, proved highly popular and increased Lufthansa's brand awareness both in the United States and around the world.

In 2012, *Fortune* listed Lufthansa as the fifth-most admired airline in the world. Lufthansa has placed in the top five on this list every year since 2009.

BRAND OUTLOOK

- It has been estimated that travel and tourism could increase as much as 55 percent during the next decade.
- Lufthansa's passenger fleet carries over 161 million passengers each year on almost 700 airplanes.
- Lufthansa brings in about 50 percent more overall revenue than its nearest European rival, Air France-KLM, and more than twice the revenue of British Airways.

It has been estimated that travel and tourism could increase as much as 55 percent during the next decade. Consumer spending on business and international travel is highly important for airlines, since this is the travel most often requiring flight, rather than any other mode of transportation. Lufthansa excels in these two segments

ENCYCLOPEDIA OF GLOBAL BRANDS, 2ND EDITION

643

of the travel market. Leisure spending makes up about 75 percent of total travel spending, with business travel accounting for the remainder. Cross-border travel, at which Lufthansa also shines, accounts for approximately 30 percent of total travel. All segments share the 55 percent expected growth rate through 2021.

The unrest in the Middle East throughout 2011 and 2012 caused declines in both air travel and freight volumes, at the same time that increasing oil and jet fuel prices were causing airfares to rise. Business confidence, however, largely increased during the period, which helped boost the business travel numbers. Despite concerns regarding the Middle East and increasing fuel prices, Lufthansa continued to show revenue growth quarter over quarter.

Premium traffic, which is very important to airlines because the margins are higher than those for economy traffic, showed increases but at a relatively slow pace. There was even slower growth in the economy sections. Because of continuing economic problems in Europe, travel in that sector was sluggish. However, Lufthansa was poised to take advantage of both the leisure and business traveler segments, as it showed strong revenue throughout 2012. This is expected to continue. It had about 50 percent more overall revenue than its nearest European rival, Air France-KLM, and more than twice the revenue of British Airways. It had a positive net income, which allowed it to continue to invest in its future.

In its cargo business, Lufthansa has benefited from the boom in German exports. The Asia/Pacific region is its most important sales market; it generates about 50 percent of this division's revenue. With the level of continued outsourcing of manufacturing to Asia, particularly China, this continues to bode well for Lufthansa.

Overall, Lufthansa remains in good standing with its customers, even though passenger comfort remains an issue. Given its depth and breadth, as well as its founding membership status in the Star Alliance, Lufthansa's outlook appears favorable, even good.

FURTHER READING

Brand Finance. "Lufthansa." *Brandirectory*. Accessed December 20, 2012. http://brandirectory.com/profile/lufthansa.

Flottau, Jens. "Lufthansa Transfers Most Short-Haul Flights to Germanwings." *Aviation Week*, October 11, 2012. Accessed March 1, 2013. http://www.aviationweek.com/Article. aspx?id=/article-xml/awx_10_11_2012_p0-505710.xml.

Flottau, Jens, and Robert Wall. "Try, try again." *Aviation Week & Space Technology*, November 14, 2011. *Business Insights: Global*. Accessed March 1, 2013. http://bi.galegroup.com/ global/article/GALE%7CA276839751/7346a705337bef8859 dd2d66790a1c89?u=itsbtrial.

Lufthansa. "'Nonstop You'—Lufthansa launches new ad campaign." *Lufthansa Social Media Newsroom*, March 8, 2012. Accessed March 1, 2013. http://newsroom.lufthansa. com/news/%E2%80%9Cnonstop-you%E2%80%9D- %E2%80%93-lufthansa-launches-new-ad-campaign.

Lufthansa Group. "Lufthansa changes its Italy strategy." May 23, 2011. Accessed March 1, 2013. http://www. lufthansagroup.com/index.php?id=322&tx_ttnews%5Btt_ news%5D=1936&L=1&print=1&no_cache=1.

McAteer, Ian. "Branding: Design Choice—Lufthansa." *Brand Republic*, January 29, 2008. Accessed March 1, 2013. http://www.brandrepublic.com/news/780260/ Branding-Design-choice---Lufthansa/?DCMP=ILC-SEARCH.

Ziekursch, Kai, et al. "Lufthansa Airlines." *CEM Case Studies Series*. Accessed December 20, 2012. http://www.g-cem. org/papers/Design_a_Branded_Experience_for_Lufthansa_ Airlines.pdf.

LUX

AT A GLANCE

Brand Synopsis: As the best-selling bar soap in the world, Lux targets a largely female market with values such as glamour and beauty that is accessible.

Parent Company: Unilever
Unilever House
Springfield Drive
Leatherhead
KT22 7GR
United Kingdom
http://www.unilever.com/

Sector: Consumer Staples

Industry Group: Household & Personal Products

Performance: *Market share*—17 percent for bath and shower products (parent company Unilever) (2009). *Sales*—US$1.3 billion (2010).

Principal Competitors: Goodrich; Dial; Ivory; Liushen; Olay; Pantene; Parrot

BRAND ORIGINS

- Lux was introduced as a laundry soap in 1924 and as a beauty bar for women in 1925.
- During World War II, Lux expanded its advertising to target men.
- By the early 21st century, Lux was the number-one global brand of bar soap, sold primarily in Asia, the Middle East, and Latin America.

Created in 1899, Lux began as a laundry soap-flake product called Sunlight Flakes. In 1900 the brand's name was changed to Lux. It was widely advertised and sold well. Lux was a product of the British company Lever Brothers, which had been formed in 1855 by William Hesketh Lever and his brother James. Lever Brothers eventually became the world's largest soap seller and, after a merger with a Dutch company in 1930, was known as Unilever.

After Lever Brothers ran a contest in the mid-1920s, the company learned that women were using Lux not only as a laundry soap but also as a personal-care product. Lever Brothers then decided to relaunch Lux as a French-style beauty soap. The first mass-market toilet soap, Lux was promoted as an affordable beauty soap in the United States in 1925 for only 10 cents per bar, which was much cheaper than imported French soaps.

Beginning in 1929, Lux began using Hollywood stars to endorse the brand, making it a pioneer in the use of celebrity endorsements. By the 1930s the brand was using the tagline "the secret of their beauty" and promoting itself as the number-one beauty soap among movie stars. In 1931 the brand used female stars in its "I'm Over 30" campaign, in which it was stated that nine of ten movie stars used Lux. In 1934 the brand also became the sponsor of the long-running radio anthology series *Lux Radio Theatre*. In 1958 the show moved to television and became the *Lux Video Theatre*.

As Lux was building its celebrity endorsements, it was also expanding into international markets. Lux was introduced in the United Kingdom in 1928. Throughout the late 1920s and 1930s, Lux added more and more markets, including India, Argentina, and Thailand. During the 1950s Lux entered the Malaysian market. Additional markets were added over the years.

Lux advertising diverged in the 1940s. Until World War II, Lux's branding was still primarily female-focused, but during the war, Lux expanded its customer base by appealing to men. From 1939 to 1945, Lux targeted them by putting its advertisements in publications for the armed forces. Lux was promoted as a way to attract women. Because of such advertising campaigns, Lux became the best-selling brand among men during the war. To expand its market after the war, the brand introduced a larger, family-sized soap bar for the bath in 1947.

During the 1940s and 1950s, Lux's advertising was still primarily female-focused, however. The brand focused on everyday women, appealing to them through star endorsements by actresses like the wholesome Deanna Durbin. The brand also introduced the concept of the "Lux Girls," primarily stars who represented the brand's idealized image of its female consumers. To expand its base of customers, Lux updated its packaging and soaps in the late 1950s. Lux soap became available in pink, white, blue, green, and yellow. During the 1960s, Lux, already popular in the Middle East, launched soaps with rich scents in that region.

Lux remained extremely popular in the 1960s, and its branding evolved to emphasize bathing as a sensual act that was somewhat romantic in nature. Its advertising became more emotional, though the emphasis on star endorsements remained key. Actresses like Sandra Dee and Diana Rigg were Lux Girls, and ads from this period stated that "To him, you're just as lovely as a movie star." During the 1970s, Lux positioned itself as still affordable enough that the average woman could afford luxury, and its ads featured Brigitte Bardot as a Lux Girl. Actress Natalie Wood also appeared in ads, which emphasized down-to-earth women and natural beauty.

Lux used celebrity endorsers like Sophia Loren, Raquel Welch, and Cheryl Ladd during the 1980s, and was still touted as a beauty soap, not only for stars but for all beautiful women. To that end, Lux began using more and more local and regional celebrities to target its marketing. Lux also created a campaign that emphasized how its products were essential to good skin care, an important part of achieving beauty. To capitalize on its brand power, Lux offered extensions including body washes, lotions, and, in a few markets, hair care products in the 1990s and early 2000s.

By the early 21st century, Lux had long been the first globally popular beauty bar, which was still its primary product. Lux was no longer sold in the United States (though some of its products were sold under the Caress brand name), but it remained the number-one-selling beauty soap brand in the world, sold in more than 100 countries. Because its strongest markets were in Asia, Latin America, and the Middle East, Lux generally signed market-specific endorsers like Bollywood star Aishwayra Rai for India in 2005. India was a big market for Lux, where sales reached US$160 million in 2001. By 2012, Lux's tagline was "That Million Dollar Feeling," and the brand included Unilever's strongest performers in skin care.

BRAND ELEMENTS

- The Lux name comes from the Latin word for light as well as the first three letters of "luxury."
- By the early 21st century, Lux highlighted itself as a luxurious product by putting the brand's letters in gold.
- The Lux Girl was a successful marketing effort that began in the 1940s and transcended the brand.

Lux's name has been a definitive element of the brand from the first. Though the product was originally called Sunlight Flakes, the brand soon changed its name to Lux. The name was selected because it was the Latin word for light and also the first three letters of "luxury." Lever Brothers wanted to associate the brand of toilet soap, which was to be an affordable, mass-market version of expensive, imported French soaps, with these concepts to enhance its appeal to women. Lux's logo was simply Lux, in all capital letters, for many decades. Later versions featured the Lux name with a crown on top. By the early 21st century, Lux underscored its link to luxury by keeping the brand name in all capitals, but put them in gold and linked the L with the X in a way that emphasized the sensual luxury of the brand's products.

One of Lux's most successful advertising tactics was the concept of the Lux Girl. Introduced in the 1940s, the Lux Girl was the brand's attempt to create an ideal for its female customers as part of its use of Hollywood stars, primarily actresses, as product endorsers. A wide range of stars served as Lux Girls, from Deanna Durbin and Sandra Lee to Marilyn Monroe and Brigitte Bardot. In some advertisements, Lux Girls were ordinary users. By the 1980s Lux had phased out the use of the name Lux Girl, though celebrity endorsements remained the norm, to emphasize Lux as the soap of the stars. However, the Lux Girl name has remained in popular culture even in the 21st century.

BRAND IDENTITY

- Lux linked the brand with Hollywood stars as endorsers, beginning in 1929.
- By the 1980s Lux emphasized celebrity endorsements that were market-focused, such as using Bollywood stars in India.
- In 2004 Lux sponsored a reality show in Argentina.

Shortly after its introduction, Lux began associating itself with the leading Hollywood actresses of the day. As one of the first brands to use celebrity endorsements from these stars, Lux ensured that its target audience would know that using Lux beauty soap could make them as beautiful as the women who endorsed the product. On a print advertisement from the 1930s, Seena Owens proclaimed, "Years Haven't A Thing To Do With Charm" and "Stars know the secret of keeping youthful allure...." This ad was part of the "I'm Over 30" campaign, launched in 1931, which was also linked to the concept that nine of ten movies stars used Lux.

Many high-profile Hollywood stars appeared in Lux advertisements from the 1930s to the 1980s, including Elizabeth Taylor, Marlene Dietrich, Judy Garland, Grace Kelly, Natalie Wood, Sophia Loren, Raquel Welch, and Cheryl Ladd. Kelly's print ad from the 1950s proclaimed, "You don't have to be Grace Kelly to have a movie star complexion." The Lux Girl concept was introduced during the 1940s, linking the product to a certain type of star, representative of the era. In the late 1950s and early 1960s, Audrey Hepburn was a Lux Girl; during the 1970s, Brigitte Bardot took on the role.

Beginning in the 1980s, Lux began focusing more and more on targeted celebrity-endorsements specific to markets. In India, for example, the brand regularly used Bollywood stars, including Aishwarya Rai, beginning in 2005. In 2008 the brand had a major relaunch in 50 countries with the "Diva" campaign, using British actress Rachel Weisz globally and Bollywood actress Priyanka Chopra in India. By 2012 Lux had at least 400 different celebrity endorsers, including Rai, Argentine actress Mia Maestro, Bollywood star Katrina Kaif, actress Shu Qi (the face of Lux in Asia since 2008), Lebanese star singer Yara, and Pakistani actress Reema Khan.

Lux also regularly used radio and television to promote its brand. In 1934 *Lux Radio Theatre*, a dramatic anthology series, was one of the most popular shows of its era, airing for 20 years. In 1958 a television version of the anthology series, *Lux Video Theatre*, went on the air. Lux continued to use the television and film mediums in the 21st century. In 2004 Lux sponsored a three-month-long talent reality show in Argentina, *Lux Star, Nace una Estrella* ("Lux Star, a Star Is Born"). In 2008, to launch Lux shampoo in China and Japan, the brand created a seven-minute film featuring Academy Award nominee Catherine Zeta-Jones, which aired on television. Though television ads remained important to the brand in the early 2010s, Lux also had a presence on Facebook and YouTube. Linking Facebook to Lux's long-term connection with Hollywood glamour, the brand's website featured a "Glam Shot" promotion whereby users took pictures of themselves via webcam and had them processed by a Glam Shot app. The app modified the images to simulate the benefits of Lux beauty treatments, and the final images were loaded on Facebook.

BRAND STRATEGY

- Lux's only product until the 1990s was its toilet bar-soap/beauty bar-soap.
- The brand began experimenting with new scents as early as the 1960s and with special ingredients in the 1990s.
- Lux introduced brand extensions, some of them market-specific, beginning in the 1990s.

While Lux was originally a brand of laundry flakes, it became attached to a related toilet bar-soap in the mid-1920s and was essentially the brand's only product until the 1990s. The brand did try to capitalize on the popularity it created among men during World War II. It introduced a family-size bar for the bath in 1947 and new colors of soap to reflect the fashion trends of the day in 1958.

During the 1960s, Lux added more scents to its soaps to appeal to markets in the Middle East. By the 1990s, Lux focused on targeting its products. For example, the brand added new ingredients to its beauty soap, like milk cream, for specific skin types. Special ingredients were also added for regional appeal, beginning in the 1990s and through the early 2000s. For example, sandalwood was added for the Indian market and Chantilly cream and red wine for the Brazilian.

Also in the 1990s and early 2000s, various brand extensions were introduced, including body washes, body lotions, body scrubs, hand washes, shower gels, and bath additives. Some extensions were available only in certain markets. In 2005 liquid soaps debuted in the United Kingdom, while hair-care products were only available in Japan, China, and Taiwan after their 2008 debut. In 2012 Lux announced it would introduce a deodorant in India. By 2012 Lux's product line was divided into four categories: Classic Collection, Skin Perfectors, Mood Enhancers, and Fine Fragrance Elixirs. Specific products varied by market.

BRAND EQUITY

- Lux is the number-one bar soap brand in the world with sales of US$1.3 billion.
- Brand Finance ranked Lux 13th in its list of *Top Cosmetic Brands* for 2012.
- On MPP Consulting's list of the *Top 100 British Brands*, Lux was ranked 58th.

Lux is the number-one bar-soap brand in the world. Approximately 1.5 billion times per day, a Lux product is used, and 12 million are purchased daily. It is one of the top three beauty brands for Unilever, along with Pond's and Dove. By 2010 Lux's sales reached US$1.3 billion, and it was one of many one-billion-Euro brands for Unilever. In 2011 the personal care division of Unilever, which included Lux, had sales growth of 8.2 percent and volume growth of 4.2 percent, with total sales of EUR15.5 billion.

Because of its wide market, Lux is considered a truly global brand with high brand equity.

Brand Finance ranked Lux 13th in its 2012 list of *Top Cosmetic Brands*, a global list of the most valuable cosmetics (personal care) brands in the world. It had a brand value of US$2.541 billion. This was down from 12th in 2011. That year, it had a brand value of US$3.177 billion. Lux was also ranked 463rd in Brand Finance's *Global 500* for 2012 and 393rd in the *Global 500* in 2011. In 2012 Lux had an enterprise value of US$5.181 billion, while in 2011 its enterprise value was US$4.404 billion. MPP Consulting listed its *Top 100 British Brands*, which measured brand value, market position, and opportunities. Lux was ranked 58th, with a brand value of US$459 million.

BRAND AWARENESS

- Lux has high global brand-awareness, after decades of successful marketing of glamour to women.
- Lux's top markets were in Asia, the Middle East, and South America.
- Lux was especially popular in India, where consumers named it one of the most popular brands in 2011.

Sold in at least 100 countries, Lux was one of the most popular bar-soap brands in the world for women. About 600 million women per year use Lux. Because of its long-term use of celebrity endorsements from leading actresses, initially Hollywood and later more regionally specific, Lux has built high brand-awareness among its target audience. The brand focused on and was successful in emerging economies in Asia, the Middle East, and South America. For skin cleansing, the top markets for Lux were India, Brazil, the United States (as Caress), China, Saudi Arabia, Indonesia, Bangladesh, Thailand, South Africa, and Pakistan. Lux's hair-care items were a market leader in Japan. As a brand, Lux was also big in South Africa. The market in India was especially important to Lux. It had high top-of-mind awareness there and, by 2009, a 15.5 percent market share. In 2011 Lux was named one of the most popular brands for Indian consumers, along with Colgate and Airtel.

BRAND OUTLOOK

- Lux's sales were not particularly affected by the global economic downturn that began in 2008, primarily because it was heavily sold in the emerging and developing markets, markets which the brand expected to continue to emphasize.
- Lux was considering focusing on the African market.
- In 2010 Lux parent-company Unilever outlined its 10-year Unilever Sustainable Living Plan.

As a core global brand for Unilever, Lux was primarily sold and successful in the developing and emerging markets, with room for long-term growth. Despite the lingering effects from the global economic downturn that began in 2008, consumers still purchased personal care items like Lux, though the brand was challenged by local and regional offerings. Unilever's sales in emerging markets, including Lux, grew in double digits in 2011 and 2012, at 11.5 percent and 11.4 percent respectively. Because of Lux's mass market nature, the global recession did not have a huge impact on the brand. Lux was particularly effective in markets in Asia, the Middle East, and Latin America. South Africa was also a significant market for Lux, and the brand was considering exploring the sales potential of the whole African market in the future.

In 2010 Lux's producer, Unilever, outlined its Unilever Sustainable Living Plan, a 10-year plan for sustainable growth. The plan focused on improving health and well-being and enhancing the livelihoods of both Lux's employees and its consumers. The plan also emphasized the company's commitment to reducing its environmental impact through better controlling greenhouse-gas emissions, water use, and waste production.

FURTHER READING

Brand Finance. "Lux." *Brandirectory*. Accessed January 28, 2013. http://brandirectory.com/profile/lux.

"Lux." RankingTheBrands.com. Accessed January 28, 2013. http://www.rankingthebrands.com/Brand-detail.aspx?brandID=3255.

Madden, Normandy. "Unilever's Lux Grows Sales in Asia and Latin America." *Advertising Age*, July 22, 2010.

———. "Unilever Takes on P&G's Pantene with Lux Relaunch." *Advertising Age*, August 6, 2008.

Tanzer, Andrew, and Chandrani Ghosh. "Soap Opera in Bombay." *Forbes*, June 11, 2001.

Team, Trefis. "Unilever Doubles down On Booming Indian Personal Care Market." *Forbes*, December 29, 2012.

Unilever. *Annual Report and Accounts 2011*. Accessed January 29, 2013. http://www.unilever.co.uk/Images/Unilever_AR11_tcm28-283849.pdf.

MAGNIT

AT A GLANCE

Brand Synopsis: Like its American counterpart, Wal-Mart, Magnit is defined by aggressively low prices and its association with low- to middle-income rural consumers.

Parent Company: Magnit OAO (Magnit OJSC)
15/5 Solnechnaya st
Krasnodar 350072
Russia
http://www.magnit-info.ru

Sector: Consumer Staples

Industry Group: Food & Staples Retailing

Performance: *Market share*—4 percent of the Russian food and beverage market (2010). *Sales*—US$7.7 billion (2010).

Principal Competitors: X5 Retail Group N.V.; DIXY Group OJSC

BRAND ORIGINS

- In 1994 Sergei Galitsky started Tander, which quickly became a major distributor of household products and cosmetics in Russia.
- In 1998 Galitsky opened the first Magnit store, using Wal-Mart as his model, and absorbed Tander into the new company.
- In 2006 Magnit opened its first hypermarket and became a publicly traded company.

- In 2011 Magnit opened more than 1,000 convenience stores, 42 hypermarkets, and 208 cosmetic stores.

In 1994, only one year after graduating with a degree in economics from Kuban State University in southern Russia, Sergei Galitsky started his first company, Tander, which focused primarily on the sale of perfume and beauty products. Within four years Tander had become one of the major distributors of household products and cosmetics in Russia. Since founding Tander, Galitsky had become an admirer of the structure and operation of U.S.-based Wal-Mart Stores, Inc., the corporation well known for its multitude of store locations across the United States and its commitment to low prices. This admiration would form the basis for Galitsky's founding of the Magnit brand.

In 1998 Galitsky opened the first Magnit store in his home province of Krasnodar, immediately merging the successful and well-known Tander into the new company. Because Magnit was an undeveloped company, Galitsky decided to experiment by operating both convenience stores and superstore chain stores, but the overall Magnit concept was modeled after Wal-Mart. Even the Magnit slogan, "Always Low Prices," was similar to Wal-Mart's famous slogan of "Everyday Low Prices."

Galitsky set a goal of rolling out at least 250 Magnit stores throughout Russia each year, and the company expanded quickly, with 1,500 stores opening between 2001 and 2005. In 2001 the company instituted a policy of performance-linked compensation, meaning stores with higher sales would receive more stock options and bonuses. Magnit also adopted International Financial Reporting Standards (IFRS) during this period, which would allow the company to become an international operation if it decided to expand outside of Russia.

By 2006 Magnit had become the leading food retailer in Russia based on number of stores, surpassing competitors X5 and Dixy. It was also in 2006 that Magnit moved beyond convenience stores and began building "hypermarkets," or superstores that offer a full range of groceries and general merchandise under the same roof. The company started with 24 hypermarkets, which were rolled out over three years. During this time Magnit became a publicly traded company and continued to grow steadily. In 2009 alone, the company opened 636 Magnit convenience stores across Russia.

In 2012 Magnit's growth continued to accelerate. Although Galitsky's original goal had been to open 250 stores a year, in 2011 Magnit opened more than 1,000 convenience stores, 42 hypermarkets, and 208 cosmetics stores. That same year, the company had more than 150,000 employees.

BRAND ELEMENTS
- "Magnit" is the Russian word for "magnet."
- Magnit's slogan has been "Always Low Prices" since the company was formed in 1998.
- Magnit's target demographic is mid- to low-income consumers living in Russia's rural communities.
- Magnit's logo is a red-bordered, white rectangular lozenge with rounded corners that contains the company name in bold red, Cyrillic, italic, capital letters.
- Magnit is known for its wide range of merchandise, its consistently low prices, and its large number of locations throughout Russia.

The company name "Magnit" is the Russian word for "magnet." Since Sergei Galitsky founded the company in 1998, Magnit's slogan has been "Always Low Prices," which is modeled after the "Everyday Low Prices" slogan of Galitsky's inspiration, the U.S. company Wal-Mart. This slogan is intended to appeal to Magnit's target demographic, the mid- to low-income consumers who dominate Russia's population. To effectively target this market, Magnit builds stores only in rural locations and advertises only in areas that are home to Magnit stores.

The most recognizable brand element, the Magnit logo, consists of a white rectangular lozenge with rounded corners surrounded by a thin red border. Inside the logo is the company name, "Magnit", written in the Cyrillic alphabet, which is used for the Russian language. The name is printed in bold red, capital, italic letters. The company's fleet of trucks use the same color scheme: a red cab and a white trailer with the logo painted on the side.

Other recognizable elements of Magnit's brand include the company's extensive geographical reach in Russia, its wide array of merchandise, and its consistently low prices. Magnit hypermarkets, which are similar to Wal-Mart Supercenters in the United States, offer a large selection of consumer goods, including groceries, pharmaceuticals, clothing, and sporting goods, typically at prices lower than those offered by nearby competitors. These low prices and the wide selection of merchandise, paired with the company's success at reaching (or surpassing) its goal of opening at least 250 new locations each year, have helped Magnit eliminate competition and establish itself among Russian consumers as a widely available one-stop shop. Another element of the brand is that Magnit stores carry some 700 products under the Magnit private label.

BRAND IDENTITY
- Magnit's mission is to offer as many products to consumers at discounted prices as possible.
- Although a majority of Magnit locations are considered convenience stores, in 2006 the company began opening more hypermarkets.
- Magnit strives for efficiency in corporate structure, passing on the resulting benefits and savings to the consumer.
- Magnit is able to offer the lowest possible retail prices thanks in part to its use of modern technology in distribution, sales, finance, and strategy.
- Magnit promotes its identity with a fleet of company trucks and hundreds of private label items.

Magnit's mission is to offer as many products to consumers at discounted prices as possible. Although by 2012 the majority of Magnit stores were considered "convenience" stores, or stores with extended hours and convenient locations that stock a limited number of household goods and groceries, in 2006 Magnit began to broaden its identity by opening more hypermarkets throughout Russia. Magnit hypermarkets, similar to Wal-Mart Supercenters in the United States, combine the offerings of a grocery store and a department store, selling a wide variety of groceries, household goods, and clothing under one roof.

Another goal for Magnit's brand identity is to be perceived as a stronger performer than its competitors. This involves improving efficiency in corporate structure, which the company believes trickles down to the consumer. Magnit's corporate structure removes middle management, making communication from headquarters to sales associates efficient and effective. Magnit stores strive to streamline employee training, which helps maintain an efficient sales staff and project a customer-friendly store atmosphere. Through its use of modern technology in distribution, sales, finance, and strategy, Magnit is also able to offer the lowest possible retail prices in its stores.

Magnit also puts its brand identity before the public eye by using a large fleet of its own vehicles to ship cargo all over European Russia. In addition, the Magnit stores sell some 700 different products under the brand's private label. The company promotes this as a cost-savings to consumers because it does not have to spend money on advertising.

BRAND STRATEGY

- In 2012 Magnit had 5,523 convenience stores, 109 hypermarkets, and 480 cosmetics stores throughout Russia.
- Magnit's ultimate goal is to have a presence in all of Russia's rural communities.
- Magnit eliminates competition by buying out competitors or by slashing prices so deeply that competitors are driven out of business.
- Magnit's streamlined corporate structure and huge number of stores allow it to offer consistently discounted prices on a wide range of products.

To achieve its goal of "maximum density," Magnit set a corporate objective of opening a minimum of 250 stores each year. Since 1994 when Magnit's predecessor, Tander, opened, the company has rolled out an average of 340 stores each year, far surpassing its goal. Tander, already a successful cosmetics retail chain upon Magnit's founding, was absorbed into the Magnit corporation in 1998, and Magnit continues to operate cosmetics retail locations in addition to its convenience stores and hypermarkets. Magnit operated 5,523 convenience stores, 109 hypermarkets, and 480 cosmetic stores throughout Russia in 2012.

Magnit's ultimate goal is to operate a store in every rural community in Russia, which the company defines as any area with fewer than 500,000 residents. Its slogan of "Always Low Prices" is meant to appeal to the populations of those areas, made up largely of mid- and low-income consumers.

Magnit has maintained its success and rapid growth by buying out the competition in areas where it sought to establish a store. When researching a potential new store location, the company first assesses the area's competition to see if it's possible to simply purchase the competition and convert its store into a Magnit store. If this proves unsuccessful, Magnit will often go ahead and build a new store, where it will slash prices to the point that nearby competitors will eventually be forced out of business.

Magnit's ability to offer a variety of consumer products at consistently discounted prices is another important aspect of its brand strategy. The company is able to offer warehouse prices by streamlining its distribution, financing, and sales. Additionally, because it operates such a large number of retail locations, Magnit is able to make bulk deals with distributors in Europe and Asia, passing on those savings to the end consumer by marking down the retail prices.

BRAND EQUITY

- As of 2012, Magnit was the second largest grocer by sales volume in Russia, behind only competitor X5.
- The much-discussed possibility of Wal-Mart's entry into the Russian market, if realized, would provide stiff competition to Magnit's hypermarket stores.
- In 2012 Brand Finance's Global 500 ranked Magnit as the 451st most successful global brand, down from 423rd in 2011.

In 2012 Magnit was the second-largest grocer by sales volume in Russia, behind only competitor X5. Because the majority of Magnit's stores are convenience stores, which offer only a limited number of groceries and household goods, the company has not yet been able to compete directly with X5 in the retail food market. X5 was formed in the 2010 merger of Russia's two largest grocers, Pyaterochka and Kopeika, in an effort to compete with U.S. retail giant Wal-Mart, which was then poised to enter the Russian market.

Although Wal-Mart set up an office in Russia in 2008 and was seriously considering expanding into the country to take advantage of its booming economy, the company closed the office in 2010, and, as of 2012, Wal-Mart had not officially announced any further intentions of entering into business in the country. This withdrawal was good news for Magnit, which models its hypermarket stores after Wal-Mart Supercenters, operating under the same strategy of offering a wide array of discounted products in locations that are often sparsely populated and home to people with lower incomes. But Wal-Mart's withdrawal from Russia may have been only a temporary reprieve from the threat of a high-powered competitor with a similar business model. In 2012 a St. Petersburg-based Russian magazine reported that Wal-Mart was in talks to purchase Magnit competitor X5, which suggests the possibility of stiff competition for Magnit in the future.

In 2012 Brand Finance's Global 500, a ranking of the world's top 500 brands, placed Magnit 451st overall, with an estimated brand value of US$2.6 billion. Magnit's position on this list fell slightly from 2011, when it was ranked 423rd. Russian competitors X5 and Dixy were not ranked on this same list, although possible future competitor Wal-Mart was ranked fifth, with an estimated brand value of US$38.3 billion.

BRAND AWARENESS

- Due to the large number of its stores and its low prices, most Russian consumers associate Magnit with economy, savings, and convenience.
- The majority of Magnit's stores are convenience stores, offering extended hours for consumers who need grocery or household items beyond regular business hours.

- Magnit has continued to expand rapidly, adding more than 1,000 new convenience stores, 42 new hypermarkets, and 208 new cosmetics stores in 2011.

Thanks to Magnit's ability to offer a wide array of goods at discounted prices, most Russian consumers associate the brand with economy, savings, and convenience. Since 1998 the company's slogan has been "Always Low Prices," a promise the brand has continued to keep.

Magnit's sheer volume of stores across Russia encourages top-of-mind recall for most consumers in the country. In 2012 Magnit operated 5,523 convenience stores, which are different than its hypermarket and cosmetics retail locations. These convenience stores, similar to the stores of the 7-Eleven international chain, offer long hours and a limited selection of groceries and household goods, making them easily accessible for consumers needing items after regular business hours.

In 2011 the company opened more than 1,000 new convenience stores, 42 new hypermarkets, and 208 new cosmetic stores throughout Russia. Besides its convenience stores, in 2012 Magnit operated 109 hypermarkets and 480 cosmetics stores, and all indications were that these numbers would only continue to grow.

BRAND OUTLOOK

- The Russian economy saw consistent growth throughout the first decade of the 21st century, providing room for Magnit's corporate growth.
- As of 2012, Magnit had not announced plans to expand to other countries besides Russia.
- Magnit has surpassed its corporate goal of opening 250 new store locations every year, averaging 340 new stores annually as of 2012.
- Magnit has been able to destroy any competition in the rural areas it targets through purchase, through takeover, or by running competitors out of business.
- With Wal-Mart reportedly in talks to acquire X5, Magnit could soon face competition from the U.S. company that inspired its founder.

Russia's retail sector has been growing by 20 percent to 30 percent annually since 2000, and in 2008 the Global Retail Development Index ranked the country the third-most attractive retail market in the world, one that provides a strong platform for Magnit's continued corporate growth. As of 2012, Magnit had not announced any plans to expand its operations to other countries.

By 2012 Magnit was averaging 340 new store locations each year, far beyond its corporate goal of 250

new locations annually. Some analysts projected that Magnit would open at least 800 new locations in 2012. The company typically targets rural communities in Russia, and appeals to the mid- to low-income consumers often ignored by larger chains that operate in Russia's major cities.

Magnit has been able to eradicate competition through purchase, through takeover, or by running competitors out of business. The company reported revenues of US$7.7 billion in 2010, an increase from 2009. In November 2012 Magnit's sales were reported to have increased by 36 percent from the same period in 2011. In 2012 Magnit and its largest grocery rival, X5, accounted for 10 percent of all food sales in Russia, a country of approximately 141 million people.

In 2010 Wal-Mart halted its plans of entering the Russian market, but in 2012 news outlets reported that the corporation was in talks to purchase Magnit's competitor X5. If these reports are true, and if Wal-Mart chooses to move forward with such a plan, Magnit could potentially face as a new competitor the powerful international corporation whose structure provided the inspiration for Magnit's establishment.

FURTHER READING

Brand Finance. "Global 500 2012." *Brandirectory*. Accessed November 6, 2012. http://brandfinance.com/images/upload/bf_g500_2012_web_dp.pdf.

Kiselyova, Maria. "Russia's Magnit October Sales up 36 Pct Yr/Yr." *CNBC*, November 9, 2012. Accessed November 10, 2012. http://www.cnbc.com/id/49755374/Russia_s_Magnit_October_sales_up_36_pct_yr_yr.

———. "Timeline: Wal-Mart Eyeing Russian Market." Reuters, April 5, 2012.

Kramer, Andrew E. "Two Russian Grocers Move to Thwart Wal-Mart." *New York Times*, December 6, 2010.

Magnit OAO. "History." Accessed November 11, 2012. http://www.magnit-info.ru/en/about/history.

Oakman, Hannah. "The World's Top 100 Food & Beverage Companies." *Food Engineering*, October 4, 2012. Accessed November 7, 2012. http://www.foodengineeringmag.com/articles/89672-the-worlds-top-100-food-beverage-companies.

"Russia's Magnit Has Eyes on Smaller Competitors." Reuters, March 23, 2012.

"Sergei Galitsky." *Forbes*, March 2012.

"USDA Foreign Agricultural Service." U.S. Department of Agriculture, August 31, 2010. Accessed November 11, 2012. http://gain.fas.usda.gov/Recent%20GAIN%20Publications/Retail%20Foods_Moscow%20ATO_Russian%20Federation_8-30-2010.pdf.

MARKS & SPENCER

AT A GLANCE

Brand Synopsis: A leading British retailer, Marks & Spencer is known for selling quality, affordable apparel, personal items, housewares, and food items.

Parent Company: Marks and Spenser Group plc
Waterside House
35 North Wharf Road
London W2 1NW
United Kingdom
http://corporate.marksandspencer.com/

Sector: Consumer Discretionary

Industry Group: Retailing

Performance: *Market share*—3.8 percent of the UK food market (2012); 10.4 percent of the UK women's wear market (2012); 27.4 percent of the UK lingerie market (2012). *Sales*—£9.9 billion (US$15.54 billion) (2012).

Principal Competitors: Argos; ASDA; Boots; Debenhams; Harrods; John Lewis; Morrisons; Next; Sainsbury's; Selfridges; Tesco; Waitrose

BRAND ORIGINS

- Marks & Spencer was founded in 1894 in Manchester, England.
- Though it began as a clothing and household item store, in 1931 it added food, which eventually became its leading product category.

- M&S struggled in the early 21st century but saw potential in e-commerce and international markets like India.

Marks & Spencer (M&S) began in 1894 when Michael Marks and Tom Spencer entered into a partnership to open a shop in Manchester. The brand's slogan was "Don't ask the price, it's a penny." By 1900 M&S had 48 sales outlets. M&S continued to expand into new British markets, and by 1907 sales reached £355,000. Because goods had become more expensive and harder to obtain at the dawn of World War I, M&S had to give up its penny price-point.

By 1915 sales had reached more than £400,000 in M&S's 145 stores. After a power struggle behind the scenes, Marks's son Simon and his business partner Israel Sieff emerged as the leaders of the company in 1917, and they and their heirs would run the company through much of the 20th century. After M&S became a publicly traded company in 1926, a new price limit of five shillings per item was set, though there was a continued emphasis on value for the money. By 1930 there were 200 M&S stores. There was also an increasingly wide range of goods on sale. In 1931 M&S began selling food, and by 1932 the company had more than 20 distinct departments. Despite the ongoing effects of the Great Depression, there were 234 M&S stores and sales of £23.45 million annually by 1939.

During World War II and the post-war era, M&S tried to make the best use of its resources, but it struggled because of rationing. Because restaurants were not subject to rationing, M&S created Café Bars. By 1942 there were 82 of these restaurants inside stores. By the early 1950s, M&S again began upgrading stores and building new ones, with better quality fashions. By 1960 foods sales began increasing as M&S benefited from being in the forefront of using chilled food distribution and air-freighting fruits and vegetables to the United Kingdom. Sales increased greatly, from £95 million in 1954 to £148 million in 1960.

In addition to introducing a home-furnishings department in 1970, M&S put a greater emphasis on convenience foods. By 1973 sales reached £496 million. In the 1970s, M&S also expanded outside of the United Kingdom, beginning in Canada in 1972. By 1974 there were 17 overseas stores. For decades, M&S had primarily sold British-made clothing and other items, and it had supported British producers by exporting whenever possible. By 1973 M&S was the largest exporter of women's clothing in the UK.

Sales continued to grow, reaching £2.9 billion in 1984. In 1985 the Marks & Spencer Chargecard was launched nationwide. From the late 1980s through the first years of the 21st century, M&S had a particular focus on international expansion, through both company-owned and franchised stores in Europe, Asia, and Australia. M&S entered the U.S. market for the first time in 1988, when it acquired the Kings Super Markets grocery store chain.

As M&S expanded internationally, an M&S mail-order clothing catalog was introduced in the mid to late 1990s, the first time the company offered home shopping. By 1997 its revenue was £7.84 billion (US$12.84 billion), with a pre-tax profit of more than a billion pounds, the first time a British company reached the billion-pound mark in profits. M&S struggled greatly in the late 1990s, with profits plunging in 1998 and 1999 for many reasons, including significant drops in clothing sales and an inability to support its international expansion. M&S began closing or selling most of its international stores by 2002. Other changes included increasing the volume of clothes sourced outside of Britain and introducing new lines of branded clothing. Also in 2001, the brand debuted the successful Simply Foods stores, which were food-only, stand-alone outlets.

M&S remained the largest food and apparel retailer in the UK as of 2002, when it had about 300 stores. Though M&S had a brief turnaround in 2002 and 2003, it soon began flagging again. In 2004 M&S was pushed out as the number-one clothing retailer in the UK by Asda, after decades at the top. In 2006 M&S sold off its last non-M&S-branded business, King Super Markets, which was also its last remaining North American asset. M&S stores in the United Kingdom began being refurbished, with new product categories added, such as electronics, restaurants, and deli counters. There was also a greater emphasis on Internet retailing operations.

Just as M&S regained its footing, a global economic recession hit. This led to more store closings, but M&S continued to expand internationally. In 2008 it began

a joint venture with Reliance Retail, Marks & Spencer Reliance India, which led to successful store openings there. In addition to international expansion in emerging, developing, and developed markets, M&S increased its use of social media and e-commerce to build the brand. Though non-food sales continued to struggle, overall sales for M&S increased in 2011 and 2012, by which time it had 731 UK stores and 387 international stores in 44 territories in Europe, the Middle East, North Africa, and Asia.

BRAND ELEMENTS

- M&S sold its products under the name St Michael from 1928 to 2000.
- The first television advertising campaign featured the tagline "Exclusively for Everyone," but it failed to catch on.
- In about 2005, M&S adopted the tagline "Your M&S," which became the company's new tagline and logo.

While Marks & Spencer is the primary name of the brand, beginning in 1928 the company employed another brand name, St Michael (no period), for products sold in M&S stores. The use of St Michael was extended gradually until company chair Simon Marks referred to it for the first time in a speech in 1949. Even the in-house journal, *St Michael's News*, reflected the trademark name. St Michael stood for quality and reliability, and it was used on goods produced to the company's specifications. By 1950 all goods sold at M&S bore the St. Michael name. However, by the late 1990s M&S began de-emphasizing the St Michael brand name in favor of the Marks & Spencer name and soon dropped St Michael entirely. However, some clothing lines that were introduced had their own names, such as the women's line per una, which debuted in 2001. At the same time, M&S moved away from its brand name in another area in 2001 when it introduced Simply Food stores, a chain of food-only, stand-alone outlets.

After Marks & Spencer became once again the primary brand name of the products sold in M&S stores, it launched the first M&S television advertisements with the slogan "Exclusively for Everyone." Though this campaign did not catch on, in about 2005 M&S adopted a new tagline, "Your M&S," which came to define the brand in the early 21st century. "Your M&S," also modified to "Only at Your M&S" in later campaigns, was used to remind consumers that M&S stocked products that made it special and distinct from other retailers. The tagline was associated with advertising and marketing efforts which highlighted what was new and different at M&S. "Your M&S" became the logo for M&S, featured on its website and other media.

BRAND IDENTITY

- M&S emphasizes principles of quality, value, service, innovation, and trust.
- M&S is a British institution that focused on selling British-made goods until the late 20th century.
- M&S relies on celebrity endorsers and ambassadors to build the brand's identity.

Since its earliest days, Marks & Spencer (M&S), commonly called "Marks and Sparks" in the United Kingdom, has been guided by five key principles: quality, value, service, innovation, and trust. Value was a particular focus from the first. From its founding until the beginning of World War I, everything M&S sold cost one UK penny, giving birth to the slogan, "Don't ask the price, it's a penny." By the mid-1920s, a new price limit of five shillings per item was set.

Over the course of the 20th and into the 21st century, M&S became a national institution in the UK and its largest retailer. By 2013, 21 million customers visited M&S weekly. Since its founding and for much of the 20th century, M&S stocked goods, especially clothing, made in the UK. The company also exported hundreds of thousands of pounds of British-made items, beginning in the 1940s, and by 1973 M&S was the largest exporter of women's clothing in the UK. However, as M&S struggled in the late 20th and early 21st centuries, it moved away from British-made goods. By the first decades of the 2000s, most of its non-food items were sourced internationally.

To attract shoppers and build its brand, M&S often relied on celebrity endorsers and ambassadors. In 2002 soccer star David Beckham lent his name to a line of fashion clothing and accessories for boys, the Zip Project. After M&S launched the "Your M&S" marketing campaign in 2005, its advertisements featured celebrities like Dame Shirley Bassey, Twiggy, Gary Barlow, and Lisa Snowdon. When M&S launched its ambitious Plan A in 2007 to address issues like sustainability, actress Joanna Lumley served as Plan A ambassador. Model/actress Rosie Huntington-Whiteley and actor Ryan Reynolds were faces of M&S's trendy Autograph line in the 2010s.

Media also proved important to M&S and brand building. In addition to a successful partnership with the popular reality competition show *The X Factor*, M&S began focusing more on social media in 2009, building interest through Facebook, Twitter, and, later, Pinterest. By December 2012 the brand had more than a million fans on Facebook. M&S supported various charities through Facebook efforts like "Thanks a Million" from 2009. In 2012 the brand launched M&S Stories, an online community that offered brand-related news and expert insights.

BRAND STRATEGY

- M&S focused on apparel, footwear, products for the home, furniture, and food by the 2010s.
- M&S regularly added new products and items to its line to pique consumer interest.

- M&S has worked to increase its global reach by expanding the number of international stores and launching country-specific e-commerce websites.

Since its founding, Marks & Spencer (M&S) grew from selling various small goods at a penny to being a wide-ranging seller of apparel, personal care items, products for the home, furniture, and food in its stores, both in the UK and abroad. Beginning in 2001, M&S also had more than 140 Simply Food stores, which were small, stand-alone food outlets. Most M&S products are now sold under the M&S brand name, though it also has several private-label brand names, primarily for apparel. Food accounted for 51 percent of M&S sales by 2011.

Over the years, M&S regularly added new products to its lines to gain consumer interest. In 2012 alone, the brand added at least 700 new products. Since the turn of the 21st century, M&S's apparel sales struggled. In 2006 M&S introduced the Limited Collection, which allowed the brand to respond quickly to trends and put items on the shelf within weeks of their design. In 2012 the brand divided its apparel lines for adults into M&S Woman and M&S Man series to highlight the wardrobe staples M&S specialized in. The brand also introduced the "Savile Row Inspired" collection created by British tailor Richard James and a lingerie line created by Rosie Huntington-Whiteley, which became the best-selling lingerie line sold by M&S.

Since moving into international markets in the early 1970s, M&S has gone through periods of international expansion and contraction. Though more than 90 percent of M&S's sales came in the UK market by 2013, the brand wanted to expand its international reach through a new global growth plan. In 2012 M&S had 157 stores in Europe, 122 stores in the Middle East/North Africa, and 108 in Asia, and was targeting markets like China, India, Russia, Egypt, and the United Arab Emirates. According to the company's 2012 annual report, international sales were £1.1 billion, up 5.8 percent from 2011. To further penetrate international markets and as part of a larger strategy to increase online sales, M&S launched local M&S websites in European markets like France, Ireland, Germany, and Spain beginning in 2011.

BRAND EQUITY

- M&S had significant shares of the UK food and clothing/footwear markets in 2012.
- M&S was a valuable UK brand, ranking number two among UK brands according to Interbrand.
- In 2011 M&S was number five on a ranking of *Europe's Most Valuable General Retailers* by the *Financial Times*.

One of the leading retailers in the United Kingdom of food, clothing, and housewares, Marks & Spencer had 3.8 percent of the food market and 11.7 percent of the clothing and footwear market in the United Kingdom in 2012. That year its womens wear's UK market-share was 10.4 percent, its menswear's share was 12.1 percent, and its lingerie's share was 27.4 percent. Despite sluggish or declining non-food sales in 2011 and 2012, M&S was considered a highly valuable brand in the UK, in Europe, and globally.

In 2011 M&S was number five on a ranking of *Europe's Most Valuable General Retailers* by the *Financial Times*, with a brand value of US$8.553 billion. In 2012 Brand Finance ranked M&S number 25 on its list of the *Best Retail Brands*, with a brand value of US$4.575 billion and an enterprise value of US$11.266 billion. Brand Finance also ranked M&S at number 220 on its *Global 500* and number 24 in its *UK Top 50* for 2012. In 2012 Interbrand's *Best Retail Brands* included a ranking of the UK brands. M&S was number two after archrival Tesco, with a brand value of US$6.256 billion to Tesco's US$11.011 billion. Also in 2012 "BrandZ Top 100 Most Valuable Global Brands 2012" report featured a list of the *Top 10 UK Brands*. M&S was ranked number 10 with a brand value of US$4.327 billion. It was number nine in 2011.

BRAND AWARENESS

- M&S has higher brand awareness in the United Kingdom than globally.
- M&S is seen as a quality British brand in certain international markets.
- M&S was ranked the most meaningful brand in the United Kingdom in 2011.

In business in the United Kingdom since 1894, Marks and Spencer (M&S) is primarily a British brand and is identified within its mother country as one of the largest, best known retailers. Fondly nicknamed M&S or Marks and Sparks, the brand has become deeply ingrained as a major presence for British consumers, among whom it has high brand awareness. M&S primarily sold British-made goods until the late 20th century and was a major exporter of these goods for decades at mid-century. This contributed to its international brand awareness. While not a global entity, by 2012 M&S had entered some 44 international markets, where it was seen a a quality British brand. Various rankings underscore the brand's popularity, both in the United Kingdom and globally. In 2011 Havas Media ranked M&S number one in its list of UK's *Top 10 Most Meaningful Brands*, a measurement of how UK consumers feel about brands. The Reputation Institute's *Global RepTrak 100* measured consumer perception of brands. M&S ranked number 78 in 2012. The Reputation Institute also did a *UK RepTrak 100* on which M&S ranked number four in 2012.

BRAND OUTLOOK

- M&S is transforming into a multichannel, international retailer.
- M&S implemented Plan A in 2007 to become a more sustainable company.
- M&S became carbon neutral by 2012.

Many retail outlets have struggled in the wake of the global economic recession which began in 2008, and M&S is no exception as consumers seek out the best value for their money. While its overall sales increased in 2011 and 2012, M&S's apparel sales, a brand mainstay, have struggled, despite repeated efforts to increase them. As a result, M&S has seen its position as the top clothing retailer in the United Kingdom slip. To insure the brand's long-term viability, the company plans to grow what is still primarily a store-based, United Kingdom entity into a multichannel, international retailer in which consumers can buy its products in stores, online, and through mobile apps.

In 2007, just before the worldwide economic downturn, M&S announced Plan A, an effort to become the most sustainable major retailer in the world by 2015. Plan A was not just implemented to help the environment but also to ensure cost savings, motivate staff, and differentiate M&S as a brand. The plan covered such issues as climate change, waste, and health. In 2007 M&S made 100 social and environmental commitments to be delivered by March 2012 under Plan A. When the plan was renewed in 2010, 80 more commitments were added. As a result, M&S became carbon neutral at the beginning of 2012. As a result of Plan A, there was £185 million in net benefits as of 2012, to be reinvested over the next five years. M&S sales increased in 2011 and 2012, though the brand struggles in specific areas such as apparel.

FURTHER READING

"Best Retail Brands 2012." Interbrand. Accessed February 3, 2013. http://www.interbrand.com/en/BestRetailBrands/2012-Best-Retail-Brands.aspx.

Brand Finance. "Marks & Spencer." *Brandirectory*. Accessed February 3, 2013. http://brandirectory.com/profile/m-and-s.

"BrandZ Top 100 Most Valuable Global Brands 2012." Millward Brown. Accessed February 3, 2013. http://www.millwardbrown.com/brandz/2012/Documents/2012_BrandZ_Top100_Report.pdf.

Hennessey, Rachel. "British Retailer Marks & Spencer Struggles to Do It All." *Forbes*, January 11, 2013.

Marks and Spencer. *Only at Your M&S: Annual Report and Financial Statements 2012.* Accessed February 4, 2013. http://corporate.marksandspencer.com/documents/publications/2012/annual_report_2012.

"Marks & Spencer." RankingTheBrands.com. Accessed February 2, 2013. http://www.rankingthebrands.com/Brand-detail.aspx?brandID=83.

"Marks and Spencer Group p.l.c." *International Directory of Company Histories.* Ed. Jay P. Pederson. Vol. 85. Detroit, MI: St. James Press, 2007.

Ruddick, Graham. "M&S Missing Chinese Sales Targets." *Daily Telegraph* (London), January 29, 2013.

Wood, Zoe. "M&S Loses Further Ground in Battle for Vital Womens Wear Market." *Guardian* (London), June 8, 2012.

MARLBORO

———■———

AT A GLANCE

■

Brand Synopsis: The number-one cigarette brand in the world for decades, Marlboro is associated with an individualistic, adventure-seeking lifestyle.

Parent Company (within the United States): Altria Group Inc.
6601 West Broad Street
Richmond, Virginia 23230
United States
http://www.altria.com/

Parent Company (outside the United States): Philip Morris International
120 Park Avenue
New York, New York 10017
United States
http://www.pmi.com/

Sector: Consumer Staples

Industry Group: Food, Beverage & Tobacco

Performance: *Market share*—15 percent of the cigarette market worldwide (excluding the United States) (2011); 42 percent of the U.S. market (2011).

Principal Competitors: British American Tobacco PLC; Imperial Tobacco Group PLC; JT International SA; Lorillard Tobacco Company; R.J. Reynolds Tobacco Company

BRAND ORIGINS

- Marlboro cigarettes were originally introduced in the mid-1920s as a women's cigarette.
- Marlboro underwent a successful rebranding in the mid-1950s.
- In 1972 Marlboro became the best-selling cigarette in the world.

The Marlboro cigarette brand was introduced by the Philip Morris Tobacco Company in 1924 and specifically targeted to women smokers. Marlboro cigarettes came in two versions featuring a red or ivory hollow "beauty tip." Priced as a premium brand, Marlboro was marketed with the slogan "Mild as May." However, the brand never sold well and had limited market share. It was withdrawn from the market during World War II.

By the 1940s awareness grew of health problems linked to smoking, and filtered brands were thought to be less harmful. Philip Morris research indicated that filtered brands were likely to gain market share and that more women were beginning to smoke. Because of these factors, Philip Morris decided to reintroduce Marlboro as a filtered brand in 1954.

When it was rebranded, the new Marlboro cigarette featured cork filters and enriched tobacco. The brand was packaged in a flip-top, crush-resistant box with a distinctive crested red and white design. Along with new packaging came new advertising. A new advertising agency, Leo Burnett & Company, gave the brand a broader appeal. The goal was to position Marlboro as a masculine cigarette that also had appeal to women. After testing ads in a number of markets, the cowboy emerged as the most popular symbol in multiple markets. The cowboy featured in the ads became known as the Marlboro Man. Within eight months of his introduction, sales increased by 5,000 percent, rising from US$18 million in 1954 to more than US$5 billion in 1955. Marlboro became one of the most popular brands in the United States by the late 1950s, and Philip Morris began marketing Marlboro outside the United States for the first time.

In 1962 Leo Burnett purchased the rights to the film score from *The Magnificent Seven*, and its theme became indelibly identified with Marlboro through television and radio ads featuring the Marlboro Man as part of the successful "Marlboro Country" campaign. With the support of such advertising and other marketing efforts, Marlboro became the number-one selling cigarette in the world in 1972 and in the United States in 1975. About 150 billion Marlboro cigarettes were produced annually worldwide, and the brand had 26 percent of the American market in the mid-1970s.

Sales grew 10 percent annually well into the 1970s, even though cigarette advertising was banned from broadcast media in 1971. The brand moved to billboard and print ads to great effect, although some billboards and publications would no longer take advertising from tobacco companies. In 1998, as part a settlement of a class action law suit brought by 46 states against tobacco companies, there was a ban on nearly all outdoor advertising of tobacco products, including billboards, and tobacco logos on clothing or merchandise.

Despite increasing restrictions on advertising and marketing in the United States and other countries, Marlboro continued to have strong sales and growth from the 1970s to the early 2000s. It became the most recognized American brand in the world. By 1993, for example, Marlboro had a 25 percent market share in Argentina and 30 percent in Mexico; by 1994 it had a 26 percent of market share in the United States with sales of US$9 billion.

Yet Marlboro faced more challenges as cigarette consumption began declining in the United States beginning in the 1980s. To ensure continued growth, the brand engaged in ambitious efforts to develop foreign demand, to tap potentially lucrative international markets. In addition to discounting cigarette prices at times, Marlboro also introduced new products into various markets, including Marlboro Snus, a smokeless tobacco product in 2007. Such decisions ensured that Marlboro and Philip Morris remained number one worldwide and in the United States even as the market decreased for tobacco products overall.

BRAND ELEMENTS

- The Marlboro Man was created in 1954.
- Broadcast advertisements featuring the Marlboro Man used the theme from *The Magnificent Seven*, a song that became deeply associated with the brand decades after the ads went off the air.

- Marlboro was the first brand in the United States to use a flip-top box.

When Marlboro cigarettes underwent a rebranding in the mid-1950s, two iconic elements created by its advertising agency became indelibly associated with the brand: the Marlboro Man and the red and white flip-top box. In 1954 the agency tested advertisements featuring sailors, aviators, hunters, and cowboys, and the cowboy emerged as the most popular symbol in a variety of markets. The cowboy became known as the Marlboro Man, and his masculinity was further reinforced when in 1955 a macho anchor tattoo was added to his arm. A cowboy who lived in a rugged West known as "Marlboro Country," the Marlboro Man symbolized freedom and individuality, representing core qualities about Americans not only in the United States but abroad as well.

The Marlboro Man was featured in numerous television and radio advertisements, as well as print ads, beginning in the 1950s. All the Marlboro Men featured in Marlboro Country ads were real cowboys, never actors or models. Beginning in 1962, Marlboro's television and radio ads with the Marlboro Man featured the theme to *The Magnificent Seven*. Although tobacco ads were banned from broadcast media in the United States in 1971, the campaign was so successful that consumers still identified the theme with Marlboro decades after it ended. Marlboro Man continued to be featured in print ads and billboards, sometimes with little or no copy, until tobacco ads were banned from billboards in the United States in 1999. The Marlboro Man is still associated positively with the brand in the United States and abroad, even in nations with strong anti-American sentiment.

The Marlboro Man's cigarettes were packaged uniquely as well. Before rebranding, Marlboro cigarette packs were white with unremarkable graphics and a significant text. After rebranding, the cigarettes were packaged in a flip-top box whose design was licensed exclusively from the Molins Manufacturing Company in England. The cardboard box was sturdier and more crush-resistant than soft packs. There were also several incarnations of the graphics from red and white striped to a solid red design before the familiar crested layout with an inverted red v top and white bottom was adopted. Other items in the Marlboro product line used the same layout with different colors replacing the red.

BRAND IDENTITY

- Marlboro was consciously identified with masculinity, individualism, and the American West.
- In the 1990s Marlboro slightly shifted its identity from "Marlboro Country" to "Marlboro Unlimited."
- Outside the United States, Marlboro has sponsored the Ferrari Formula 1 racing team since the early 2000s.

Beginning in the 1950s, Marlboro—primarily through the Marlboro Man and the "Marlboro Country" campaigns—was consciously identified with masculinity, individualism, and the American West. Advertisements underscored the idea that consumers could share the Marlboro Man's qualities if they smoked Marlboro cigarettes. This concept was reinforced by the use of the theme from *The Magnificent Seven* in broadcast ads from 1962 until such broadcast tobacco ads were banned in 1971 in the United States. After 1971, Marlboro continued to reinforce this image through billboards and print ads, until they too became off limits to tobacco companies in the late 1990s in the United States.

From the first, Marlboro carefully chose its sponsorships to reinforce these ideas. In 1956 Marlboro became the first brand of any product to sponsor professional football at a time when the game was growing in popularity. After 1971 there were fewer sponsorship opportunities in the United States, although in 1988, Marlboro was the corporate sponsor for the American yacht competing in that year's defense of the America's Cup race. Beginning in 1988, Marlboro Music had a talent competition, the National Roundup, and sponsored concerts tours and festivals at military bases through the mid-1990s.

During the 1990s Marlboro slightly shifted its identity from "Marlboro Country" to "Marlboro Unlimited," a land that knows no limits, an unlimited mythic West. This move was made to appeal to younger smokers and widen the appeal of the brand. To that end, Philip Morris launched the "Marlboro Adventure Team" campaign in 1993. Smokers could acquire outdoor gear with the Marlboro logo and enter drawings for adventure trips based on the number of packs purchased. After the 1998 settlement of a class action lawsuit, no tobacco logos were allowed on clothing or merchandise, effectively ending this campaign in the United States though it continued in certain international markets until at least 2007. In 2010 Marlboro tried to further contemporize the brand by focusing on youthful images that sometimes did not include cowboys.

Outside the United States, Marlboro has sponsored the Ferrari Formula 1 racing ream since the early 2000s, renewing its sponsorship of the Italian team in 2005 and 2011. This sponsorship was controversial because the United Kingdom had restricted tobacco advertising in 2003, the European Union banned tobacco advertising in motorsports in 2007, and most stops on the F1 circuit had a total ban on tobacco advertising. Marlboro branding was only seen on cars in markets with no ban.

BRAND STRATEGY

- Marlboro has introduced a number of variations beginning with menthol in 1966.

- Marlboro Snus debuted in 2007 to take advantage of the growing smokeless tobacco market in the United States.
- Marlboro sought international markets as early as 1958.

While Marlboro has been the best-selling brand in the United States since the mid-1970s, it faced challenges in the marketplace as early as the 1950s because of market saturation. Beginning in the late 1950s, Marlboro began introducing differing packaging and variations. In 1958 Marlboro debuted soft-packs. A menthol version was added in 1966, and Marlboro Lights became available in 1972. In 2005 the brand introduced a new high-tech filter as part of its Marlboro Ultra Smooth in the United States, while in 2009, Blend No. 54, a menthol-flavored cigarette with a strong tobacco blend, became available.

As smokeless tobacco became more popular, especially among Marlboro's key 18 to 25 age demographic, Marlboro test-marketed Marlboro Snus in 2007 to broaden the brand's appeal. This spit-free tobacco pouch became available nationwide in 2010, then was revamped in 2011. It was sold in four varieties: rich, amber, spearmint, and peppermint. Marlboro also sometimes temporarily slashed prices and used special promotional pricing to appeal to consumers though it cut into profits.

In the United States, tobacco products became linked to health concerns even before the Marlboro was rebranded in the mid-1950s. To ensure long-term growth, the brand began seeking international markets as early as 1958, beginning with Switzerland. By the early 1960s there was a concentrated effort to grow new markets, sometimes in partnership with local investors instead of exporting Marlboro cigarettes from the United States. Blends were attuned to local tastes. By 1972 Marlboro was the best-selling cigarette in the world.

As more restrictions were placed on tobacco in the United States in the 1970s through 1990s, domestic consumption fell, and international markets were sought in Europe, Asia, and South America. Marlboro also introduced new products specifically for international markets such as a clove-flavored cigarette, Marlboro Mix 9, in 2007 in Indonesia, one of the largest tobacco markets in the world. By the 21st century, new growth markets were found in Brazil, China, India, and Russia.

BRAND EQUITY

- Marlboro has a 42 percent market share in the United States and is number one in every state.
- Marlboro has a high brand value despite restrictions on tobacco and declining tobacco sales overall.
- In the "BrandZ Top 100 Most Valuable Global Brands 2012," Marlboro ranked seventh with a value of US$73.6 billion, a 9 percent increase over 2011.

In 2011 Marlboro was the number-one selling cigarette brand in the world, with its production volume twice its next two competitors. That same year it was number one in the United States with a 42 percent market share and was number one in every state and among men and women in adult age groups. Despite restrictions on marketing tobacco in many countries and declining cigarette consumption overall, Marlboro had a high brand value.

According to the "BrandZ Top 100 Most Valuable Global Brands 2012," Marlboro ranked seventh with a value of US$73.6 billion, a 9 percent increase over 2011. It was also the top-rated tobacco brand and number seven among North American brands. Marlboro's brand value has increased annually according to BrandZ, moving from US$39.2 billion in 2007 to US$49.5 billion in 2009. Similarly, in the Brand Finance "Global 500" for 2012, Marlboro ranked 53rd with a brand value of US$15.2 billion, a brand rating of AAA-, and an enterprise value of US$180.7 billion. While its ranking on this list varied over the years, its brand and enterprise value have increased annually.

BRAND AWARENESS

- Marlboro has top-of-mind awareness among cigarette brands.
- It is the most recognized brand of American-produced cigarettes in the world.
- In 1996 Marlboro was the first tobacco product to be inducted into the Marketing Hall of Fame.

Because of the global penetration of its Marlboro Man symbol and longtime "Marlboro Country" campaign, Marlboro has had decades to build its top-of-mind awareness among cigarette brands. By the 1970s it was the most recognized American brand of cigarettes in the world and is currently sold in at least 180 countries. As a brand name, Marlboro is associated not only with cigarettes but with qualities like rugged individualism and the American West as well as American culture and commerce. Marlboro and the Marlboro Man are popular even in non-Western countries like the Philippines. The brand was coveted in the Soviet Union before *glasnost* and the breakup of the Eastern Bloc. Because of its consistent and effective image, created by marketing, Marlboro became the first tobacco product to be inducted into the Marketing Hall of Fame in 1996. In 2011 Marlboro was ranked 50th on the Sociagility list of the "Top 50 Most Social Brands." It was the only tobacco brand in the top 50 in the survey, which considered the social brand value of the brand including qualities such as popularity, receptiveness, network reach, and trust.

BRAND OUTLOOK

- Despite declining tobacco sales globally overall, Marlboro has generally had increased revenues and retained market share.

- In 2011 Marlboro had a slight loss of market share.
- Marlboro sought to expand its 0.3 percent of the Chinese market through initiatives like flu vaccines and less harmful cigarettes.

In 2011 the production volume of the cigarette industry was down by 3.5 percent because of a decrease in smoking overall worldwide. In the United States, cigarette volume declined by 10 percent in 2009 and 5 percent in 2010. Challenges included the packaging required in certain markets, such as the United States and Canada, which highlighted the dangers of smoking.

Despite the long-term decline of the tobacco industry, Marlboro had increased market share between 2002 and 2010, while revenues continued to rise in 2010. Because of its strength as a brand and long-term momentum, Marlboro was expected to rebound from a slight loss of market share in 2011. The brand was experienced in maximizing income. Marlboro also has cut costs, increased prices, and successfully entered the smokeless tobacco market. In addition, it added positively to its reputation by reducing the environmental impact of its production process, ensuring that its labor and tobacco farming were always above board, and investing in child education and domestic violence prevention initiatives.

In the 21st century Marlboro was successful in markets such as Indonesia and Korea, and in Eastern Europe, the Middle East, and Africa, while seeing a decline in parts of Europe and Latin America. Marlboro's international parent company, Philip Morris International, invested heavily in new growth markets such as Brazil, China, India, and Russia. China proved challenging to the brand, where Marlboro garnered only a 0.3 percent market share. To increase market share in China, Philip Morris was considering developing flu vaccines made from a certain type of tobacco plant and developing cigarettes that were less harmful.

FURTHER READING

"Best Global Brands 2010." Interbrand. Accessed January 18, 2013. http://www.interbrand.com/Libraries/Branding_Studies/Best_Global_Brands_2010.sflb.ashx.

Brand Finance. "Marlboro." *Brandirectory*. Accessed January 18, 2013. http://brandirectory.com/profile/marlboro.

"BrandZ Top 100 Most Valuable Global Brands 2012." Millward Brown. Accessed January 18, 2013. http://www.millwardbrown.com/brandz/2012/Documents/2012_BrandZ_Top100_Report.pdf.

De Guzman, and Noelle Francesca. "The Power of Advertising: Where There's Smoke, There's Marlboro." *BusinessWorld*, July 31, 2007.

Doward, Jamie. "Ferrari-Marlboro F1 Sponsorship Deal Provokes Anger of the Health Lobby." *Guardian Unlimited* (London), July 3, 2011.

Felberbaum, Michael. "Altria Cites Smokeless Items as Key for Business." Associated Press, May 19, 2009.

"Marlboro Man; Bob, I've Got Emphysema." *Medicine, Health, and Bioethics: Essential Primary Sources*. Ed. K. Lee Lerner and Brenda Wilmoth Lerner. Detroit, MI: Gale, 2006.

Ress, David. "Philip Morris Adds Another Cigarette to Marlboro Lineup." *Richmond (VA) Times-Dispatch*, July 22, 2009.

Simley, John. "Marlboro." *Encyclopedia of Consumer Brands, Vol. 1: Consumable Products*. Ed. Janice Jorgensen. Detroit, MI: St. James Press, 1994.

"Top 50 Most Social Brands." Sociagility, December 6, 2011. Accessed February 20, 2013. http://www.sociagility.com/top50/.

MARUBENI

AT A GLANCE

Brand Synopsis: Marubeni's longevity and commitment to improving the lives of others through goods and services has made it a trusted partner in global transactions in the energy, commodities, and utilities sectors.

Parent Company: Marubeni Corporation
4-2, Ohtemachi 1-chome
Chiyoda-ku, Tokyo
Japan
http://www.marubeni.com

Sector: Industrials

Industry Group: Capital Goods

Performance: *Revenues*—US$51.5 billion (2012).
Assets—US$56 billion (2012).

Principal Competitors: Itochu Corp.; Mitsubishi Corp.; Mitsui & Co. Ltd.; Sumitomo Corp.; Toyota Tsusho Corp.

BRAND ORIGINS

- Marubeni originated in 1858 when Chubei Itoh went into business for himself as a traveling peddler selling linens.
- During World War I Marubeni established international trading partnerships, filling the void of companies that were enlisted to manufacturing military supplies.
- Marubeni thrived in the 21st century through its ability to adapt to changing market conditions.

The founding of Marubeni can be traced to the traveling salesman Chubei Itoh, who established C. Itoh & Company in 1858 to sell linens made in his home region of Omi (now Shiga), Japan. In 1872 Chubei formalized his company by opening a drapery shop named Benichu in Osaka. In 1883 he created a simple logo for the shop in which the word "beni" (Japanese for "red") was placed inside a circle or "maru." Thus the origin of the company name. Over the next 20 years, Chubei expanded his business with foreign trading agents and eventually established his own international trading network. When World War I threw most of the planet into turmoil, C. Itoh took advantage of the situation by filling the void created when many companies switched production to manufacturing military supplies.

In response to financial difficulties brought on by a global recession, C. Itoh reorganized in 1921 under the name Marubeni Shoten, Ltd., with several of its subsidiaries regrouping as Daido Boeki Kaisha Ltd. Although Marubeni was primarily involved in textile trading, over the next decade it expanded into a variety of industrial and consumer goods. In September 1941 Marubeni reorganized again under the name Sanko Kabusiki Kaisya, Ltd. Three months later Japan attacked Pearl Harbor, Hawaii, and the United States entered World War II. In 1944 Sanko Kabusiki Kaisya merged with Daido Boeki Kaisha and Kureha Cotton Spinning Co., Ltd., to establish Daiken Co., Ltd. Chubei Itoh II, the son of Marubeni's founder, was named the president of the new company. By the end of the war in 1945, Japan's industrial capacity had been all but wiped out. An Allied military occupation was put in place to guide the rebuilding of the country's infrastructure and reorganization of its industry.

When the Korean War broke out in 1950, Marubeni was one of the many Japanese companies contracted by UN forces to manufacture military supplies. As a result of the postwar Allied occupation and industrial redevelopment, Japan was considered a valuable regional resource. However, when the war ended in 1953 most of the UN supply contracts ended with it. Japan fell into recession, and many companies struggled to survive. As it had done before in difficult times, Marubeni restructured, and on September 1, 1955, it merged with Iida & Co., Ltd., and became Marubeni-Iida & Co., Ltd. Iida was an established Japanese company that owned a chain of large department stores under the name Takashimaya. Iida also had diverse holdings, including 44 percent of its business in textiles and the other 56 percent in wool, leather, machinery, fuel, and much else. Iida also held a strong position in the domestic steel trade with connections to Yahata Steel and Fuji Steel. This single merger did more to advance Marubeni's position as a general trading company than anything prior. From the late-1950s into the mid-1960s Marubeni-Iida experienced explosive growth. When the two companies merged in 1955 their combined capital totaled ¥1.5 billion. By 1963 the new company's capital had increased to ¥15 billion. In 1966 Marubeni-Iida merged with Totsu Co., Ltd. and expanded its metals division to the point where metals sales rivaled those of its textiles division.

On August 15, 1971, U.S. President Richard Nixon disrupted worldwide currency values by removing the U.S. dollar from the gold standard. The value of the dollar dropped dramatically, making it difficult for Japan to export products to the United States. As a result, in an attempt to adapt to the sudden and adverse economic changes, Marubeni-Iida reorganized and by January 1972 changed its name to Marubeni Corporation. In August 1973 Marubeni acquired Nanyo Bussan, a trading firm that handled nonferrous metals such as copper, chrome, and nickel. This acquisition increased Marubeni's share of Japan's copper imports from 0.8 percent to 7 percent and refractory materials (materials that are resistant to heat at very high temperatures; most commonly used in industrial furnaces) from zero to 30 percent. The addition of Nanyo Bussan had further diversified Marubeni and strengthened its position in the metals market. By 1977 Marubeni had doubled its trading volume in just four years and expanded its businesses to Australia, Brazil, Sweden, the United Kingdom, the United States, and West Germany. During the 1980s it further diversified in the mining of coal, copper, and nonferrous metals.

A global recession during the 1980s was devastating for Marubeni, and it took the company until the mid-1990s to recover. It crippled the company so badly because as a general trading company, the majority of Marubeni's investments and revenues were involved in arbitrage (the simultaneous buying and selling of securities, currency, or commodities in different markets or in derivative forms). When the economic markets went into freefall, the value of many of Marubeni's assets collapsed. In 1995 Marubeni wrote off more than US$540 million in portfolio losses, lost real estate values, and the liquidation and restructuring of subsidiaries. In 1997 the company wrote off an additional US$144 million in losses.

During the first few years of the new millennium Marubeni worked to rebuild itself by focusing on commodities trading, natural resources, and power plants. In 2006 Marubeni formed a joint venture with the government of the United Arab Emirates to create investment opportunities in Abu Dhabi. In 2008 the company purchased Senoko Power, Ltd., in Singapore for US$2.8 billion and posted record profits for the fifth consecutive year. When a worldwide economic downturn struck in 2008, Marubeni returned to its long-standing formula for survival. The company reorganized in an effort to adapt to the stresses and uncertainties of the new global economy.

BRAND ELEMENTS
- Marubeni takes its name from the combination of two Japanese words, *maru* meaning circle, and *beni* meaning red.
- The name and logo of Marubeni were first used in 1883 by the company founder Chubei Itoh.
- In its modern rendering, the Marubeni icon logo is rendered as a stylized red character that combines *M* and *I* placed within a red diamond.

The Marubeni logo dates to 1883 and is based on an original concept of the company's founder, Chubei Itoh. In advertising his drapery shop, Benichu, in Osaka, Chubei simply formed a circle or "maru" enclosing the word "beni." *Beni* is the Japanese word for red, and *maru* is the Japanese word for circle. A modern rendering of the icon logo came into use following the merger of Marubeni and Iida & Co. in 1955. It positions the *I* from Iida through the center of the *M* from Marubeni to form a stylized character that is placed within a red diamond. The logo is often used together with the company name spelled out in red.

BRAND IDENTITY
- The Marubeni brand is based on a philosophy of fairness, innovation, and harmony.
- The international aspect of many of Marubeni's transactions has given the company an awareness of its "responsibility as a corporate citizen in the global community."
- Marubeni sponsors projects that uphold social welfare, international exchange, community development, environmental preservation, and Japanese culture.

Marubeni remains committed to the values handed down by the company's founder more than 150 years ago, seeking to improve the lives of others through goods and services. Because Marubeni operates largely in the business-to-business market, it strives to overcome the impersonal nature of its corporate dealings by emphasizing its social responsibility and adherence to a philosophy of fairness, innovation, and harmony. According to the company in 2012, "Being aware of our responsibility as a corporate citizen in the global community, we will actively pursue social contribution activities." These activities are concentrated in five primary areas: social welfare, international exchange, community development, environmental preservation, and cultural support. In the first area, since 1974 the Marubeni charitable foundation has provided over US$1 million in assistance to social welfare programs each year, totaling US$40 million and more than 2,100 projects. To the area of international exchange the Marubeni Scholarship Foundation has contributed over US$3 million to scholarship funds in six countries. Most of the grants go toward books, research courses, and student exchange programs. In the third area, community development, the company focuses on cleanup and improvement projects in local Japanese communities. In 2011 and 2012 Marubeni donated more than US$55 million to organizations helping in the recovery from the devastating Japanese earthquake of March 2011. With its close association to the energy and utilities sector, Marubeni is particularly active in environmental preservation and is involved in a number of renewable energy projects. The company has contributed to 10 wind farm projects in eight countries around the world. Finally, Marubeni supports cultural programs and the arts, including the Marubeni art collection, which comprises an estimated 600 paintings, 400 classical Japanese garments, and 600 garment design drawings that are often loaned out for cultural exhibitions.

BRAND STRATEGY

- Marubeni is a general trading company, or *sogo shosha*, a type of business unique to Japan.
- Marubeni and other general trading companies act as brokers in international commerce situations.
- In Japan, half of all exports and two-thirds of all imports are handled by general trading companies such as Marubeni.

Marubeni is a *sogo shosha*, or "general trading company," a uniquely Japanese business organization. General trading companies act as brokers in international commerce situations. On one side, they find large manufacturers or wholesalers to provide commodities or finished goods. On the other side, they act as an international sales force for companies of all sizes that do not necessarily have the

ability to create or maintain distribution channels in other countries. They are also often a key element in large projects such as building power plants, shopping malls, and mining operations. Sogo shosha companies like Marubeni are involved in handling nearly half of Japan's exports and two-thirds of its imports. Marubeni, as a business entity, does not primarily promote its own brand or any others for that matter. Instead, it brings together buyers, sellers, and project developers. Marubeni is also involved in the financial and logistical aspects of creating projects and is continually acquiring subsidiaries in order to participate in joint ventures. An example of this is the 2006 joint venture between Marubeni and the government of the United Arab Emirates to create a series of investment opportunities in the capital city of Abu Dhabi.

BRAND EQUITY

- Marubeni's longevity and ability to restructure in response to market pressures has made it a trusted partner in large-scale enterprises worldwide.
- Marubeni has total assets valued at US$62.6 billion and a market capitalization of US$13 billion.
- Marubeni ranked as number 286 on the *Forbes* list of the top 2000 companies in the world in 2012.

Marubeni is one of the largest and oldest companies in Japan. Started by a humble street peddler in 1858, it has grown into a multinational conglomerate with 12 divisions, 120 offices and 272 subsidiaries in 67 countries. Its longevity and ability to restructure in response to market pressures has made it a trusted partner in large-scale enterprises worldwide. In the four quarters ending in March 2012, the organization had total revenues of US$51.5 billion, assets totaling US$62.6 billion, gross trading profits of US$4.1 billion, and a market capitalization of US$13 billion. On the *Forbes* "Global 2000" list of the world's biggest public companies in 2012 Marubeni was ranked number 286. It was ranked number 191 in sales, number 377 in profit, number 392 in assets, and number 720 in market value.

BRAND AWARENESS

- Marubeni is well known globally among developers of large building projects.
- Because its transactions are largely business-to-business, Marubeni is not well known among general consumers.
- Marubeni fosters relationships and partnerships that promote the brand elements of its corporate clients, partners, and subsidiaries.

Marubeni's brand is based on performance, profits, and successful mergers and joint ventures. Nearly all of the company's business is conducted in the course of creating sales, purchases, and joint ventures for and with large corporations. Because of this business-to-business focus, Marubeni is well known globally in the import and export markets and among developers of large building and infrastructure projects. However, the company is little known among general consumers even though it trades in materials and services that are fundamental to everyday life, including food products, paper, metals, energy, real estate, and information technology. With 120 offices in 67 countries, Marubeni fosters relationships and partnerships that promote the brand elements of its corporate clients, partners, and subsidiaries rather than the corporate parent itself.

BRAND OUTLOOK

- Marubeni has secured many profitable commodities deals, joint ventures, and strategic alliances with particular success in energy production and distribution.
- Marubeni is collaborating with Mitsubishi on a joint venture to build the world's first floating wind farm off the coast of Fukushima, Japan.
- In 2012 Marubeni purchased the U.S. grain trader Gavilon Group LLC for US$5.6 billion, making Marubeni one of the five largest grain suppliers in the world.

Marubeni has succeeded on the global economic stage over the past 10 years and continues to actively pursue profitable commodities deals, joint ventures, and strategic alliances. In the energy field the company announced its participation in an offshore oil platform in the Gulf of Mexico and is currently in negotiations with the government of Myanmar to build an electric power plant there starting in 2015. Marubeni is also collaborating with Mitsubishi in a joint venture to build the world's first floating offshore wind farm. The power station is to be built off the coast of Fukushima, Japan, to replace a portion of the energy lost when three nuclear power plants in the region were destroyed by an earthquake and tsunami in March 2011. In January 2013 Marubeni announced the signing of a three-year deal with Canada Lithium Corp. to be its exclusive distributor of battery-grade lithium carbonate in Japan. The company also recently purchased the U.S. grain trader Gavilon Group LLC for US$3.6 billion. The acquisition elevates Marubeni to one of the top five grain suppliers in the world. Through such partnerships and acquisitions as these Marubeni continues to diversify its interests and increase its presence in the global commodities and energy markets.

FURTHER READING

"Global 2000 Leading Companies—Marubeni Corporation." *Forbes*, April 18, 2012. Accessed January 28, 2013. http://www.forbes.com/companies/marubeni/.

Inoue, Yuko, and Emi Emoto. "Marubeni Buys Gavilon for US$3.6 billion as It Eyes China." Reuters, May 29, 2012.

Marubeni Corporation. "Marubeni Signs Canadian Lithium Carbonate Distributorship Agreement." January 10, 2013. Accessed January 28, 2013. http://www.marubeni.com/news/2013/130110e.html.

"Marubeni Corporation." *International Directory of Company Histories.* Ed. Tina Grant. Vol. 104. Detroit, MI: St. James Press, 2009.

"Trading in Information—Throughout Marubeni and across the Globe." *Shosha* 95 (Spring 2008).

Young, Alexander K. *The Soga Shosha: Japan's Multinational Trading Companies.* Boulder, CO: Westview Press, 1979.

MATTEL

—◾—

BRAND ORIGINS

- Mattel was founded in California in 1945.
- Its most popular product, Barbie, debuted in 1959.
- Mattel faced a public relations struggle in the aftermath of a 2007 scandal involving toys with lead paint.
- Mattel was the world's leading toy company in 2012.

Mattel began in 1945 in a converted garage in California at a time when the toy industry was greatly expanding in the United States. The company was founded by Harold "Matt" Matson, Elliot Handler, and his wife, Ruth Handler. Their first product was furniture for dollhouses made from wood scraps left over from frame-making. Within a few years, Matson sold out to the Handlers, and Mattel was incorporated in 1948.

By 1952 Mattel added other products to its line, including musical toys like the Uke-A-Doodle and burp guns. Sales were in excess of US$5 million by 1955. That year Mattel ensured its name would be known to children by becoming the network television sponsor of the popular children's series *The Mickey Mouse Club*. It was the first time a toy company had sponsored a show, and it proved an effective means of reaching its core audience. Mattel became one of the first toy companies to run television advertisements all year round, not just at during the holiday shopping season, further stimulating demand.

One of the toys advertised by Mattel was the Barbie doll, the best-selling toy ever. Introduced in 1959, it was named for the Handlers' daughter, Barbara. Barbie was a hit as the first doll on the market that was not a baby doll but a teenaged, fashion-oriented toy. Mattel capitalized on the Barbie phenomenon by adding to her wardrobe and accessories, and over the years introduced hundreds of new Barbie models. Companion dolls were also created for the Barbie line, including a boyfriend named Ken, who debuted in 1961 and was named after the Handlers' son.

In 1960 Mattel introduced Chatty Cathy, a talking baby doll who was the second best-selling doll of the 1960s after Barbie. That year, Mattel had sales of US$25 million and went public. By 1962 sales had reached US$75 million. Mattel entered the educational preschool market with the innovative See 'N Say, an interactive talking toy in 1965. In 1968 Mattel launched Hot Wheels, a line of miniature die-cast cars with wheels that could move on a track. By the end of the 1960s, Mattel was the number-one toy company in the world.

However, Mattel faced challenges as the Barbie declined in popularity, and the company was near bankruptcy in the early 1970s. Accusations of financial improprieties forced the Handlers out of management in 1974. Despite the corporate turmoil, Mattel took part in the video game craze with handheld electronic games, including Auto Race (1976), Football (1977), and Hockey (1978). In 1979 Mattel released Intellivision, an early video game system.

By the mid-1980s the brand still had high sales volume, but there were steep overhead expenses and development costs. Mattel temporarily lost its position as the world's largest toymaker in 1985. Sales reached US$1 billion in 1987, but the company lost US$93 million on the year, prompting another consideration of bankruptcy. Mattel saved itself by cutting overhead and focusing on international sales growth. Having sold its products internationally beginning in the late 1950s, Mattel was selling in 100 countries worldwide by 1991.

During the early 1990s Mattel completed several acquisitions, including a merger in 1993 with Fisher-Price, a well-known maker of toys for preschool-aged children. In 1997 Mattel bought Tyco Toys, the number-three toymaker in the United States, responsible for such products as Tickle Me Elmo and Matchbox cars, and Pleasant Company in 1998. Pleasant Company was a mail-order business that made the popular American Girl dolls, books, and clothing.

During the first decade of the 21st century, Mattel expanded its licensing deals to include Barney, the purple dinosaur from the popular PBS television series, and focused more on educational learning toys. Mattel augmented its share in the electronic toy business in 2006 by buying Radica Games, a Hong Kong–based company that produced Pocket Poker, Pocket Slot, and other electronic card and casino games for older children and adults.

In 2007 Mattel faced a public relations nightmare when significant amounts of lead were found in Mattel toys made in China. The company had to recall millions of toys, pay millions of dollars to settle related claims, and ensure that its toys met standards for lower levels of lead. Soon after, the worldwide economic downturn that began in 2008 affected the brand with several years of declining sales as consumers limited toy purchases.

In 2010 Mattel introduced Monster High, its first original franchise since Hot Wheels. Debuting in 35 countries, Monster High dolls represent children of famous monsters with hip names like Draculaura. Like many Mattel lines, Monster High also had other branded items, in this case clothing, jewelry, a dedicated YouTube channel, and chapter books for teens. In 2013 Monster High had a straight-to-DVD animated feature called *Monster High: Ghouls Rule!*, with the Monster High characters. While Mattel lost a major lawsuit in 2011 over Bratz Dolls to MGA Entertainment, its sales recovered somewhat with the launch of Monster High, and Mattel remained the world's leading toy company as it successfully reorganized in 2012.

BRAND ELEMENTS

- Since 1969 the Mattel logo has been a red saw-toothed disc containing the company name in all capital letters.
- Mattel introduced the successful "You can tell it's Mattel, it's swell" campaign in the late 1950s.
- By 2012 the Mattel tagline "The Future of Play" emphasized the continued importance of play in the age of technology.

Mattel's first logo comprised a black saw-toothed disc in which the company's name, "Mattel, Inc. Toymakers," was printed in white surrounding an illustration of boy wearing a crown perched atop a capital M. In 1969 Mattel simplified the logo, changing to a red saw-toothed disc in which only the word Mattel appeared in white capital letters that were printed at a slight diagonal moving upward from left to right. The red disc logo, representing a stamp of quality on Matttel's many popular toys and games, became an iconic brand symbol for generations of toy buyers.

In tandem with its well-known logo, Mattel has used many memorable taglines and slogans to advertise its products throughout its history. During the late 1950s and 1960s, "You can tell it's Mattel, it's swell" was featured in ads that aired during *The Mickey Mouse Club*, establishing Mattel's importance as a toy manufacturer. With the successful introduction of Barbie in 1959, the doll was given its own advertising campaigns, including the "Barbie Look" in the 1960s.

By the 21st century, the demographic for toys had changed because of video games and other factors so that the maximum age for playing with toys was about eight years old in the United States. There was also a greater emphasis on toys that were educational. To respond to parents who wanted toys that brought together learning with play, Mattel introduced a new, memorable slogan, "Play. Laugh. Grow." in 2003 in print ads and television commercials. In 2004 the ads began airing in Spanish to attract Hispanic parents. This campaign increased Mattel sales by 7 percent. As video games and electronic toys became the norm, Mattel embraced the continued importance of play with its "The Future of Play" tagline, adopted in the second decade of the 21st century.

BRAND IDENTITY

- Mattel is known for innovative products, including the best-selling Barbie doll and Hot Wheels cars.
- The enormous popularity of Mattel toys during the mid-20th century baby boom led to a close identification of Mattel products with traditional notions of childhood play.
- Mattel was the first toy company to sponsor a network television program, *The Mickey Mouse Club*, in 1955.
- Mattel is dedicated to children's causes, including an emphasis on the importance of play.

Mattel is a brand known for being innovative in both its product lines and its marketing efforts. The enormous popularity of Mattel toys during the important baby boom years following World War II has led to a close identification of Mattel products with traditional notions of childhood play and with childhood in general. Toys such as Barbie and Hot Wheels are icons in the toy industry, launched in 1959 and 1968 respectively, and popular worldwide. Although sometimes criticized for being an unrealistic depiction of the female form, Barbie is the best-selling toy in the world, adored by generations of girls and collectors, who have dressed her and her friends up in various outfits and with the many available accessories. Hot Wheels were also unique when they hit the market as the miniature cars had wheels that worked on a track; the cars have been a perennial best seller.

Since Mattel's founding in the 1940s, it has been known for being pioneering and trend-setting in its marketing. It became the first toy company to sponsor a network television show, *The Mickey Mouse Club*, in the mid-1950s and aired advertisements for its products all year round, not just during the holiday shopping season. By the 21st century, Mattel had extended its advertising reach beyond traditional media ads in print, television, and radio. It developed a strong Internet presence, with many promotions on social media sites such as Facebook and Twitter as its target audience of children and their parents spent more and more time online.

Understanding its audience, Mattel generated goodwill by focusing on children's causes around the world through its Mattel Foundation, which was established in 1978. In the second decade of the 21st century, the brand instituted the 12 Days of Play program, through which company volunteers participated in events each December to underscore the importance of play in children's lives and development worldwide.

BRAND STRATEGY

- The successful Mattel toy Barbie essentially became a brand unto itself.
- Mattel manufactures many licensed products, often tied into children's films and television series.

- In 2012 Mattel reorganized into two distinct business segments, North America and International.

Since the 1950s many of the toys sold by Mattel have essentially become brands of their own, and Mattel marketed them successfully worldwide. For example, Mattel launched Barbie in 1959 and has since sold billions of Barbies to make it the number-one toy line among girls. Barbie has also been constantly reinvented and updated to reflect fashion and cultural trends of the time to keep young consumers interested. The Barbie product line encompassed many items, including accessories and clothing for Barbie and her friends, branded and/or licensed clothing for humans, cosmetics, bath and beauty items, computer games, MP3 players, eyewear, and a line of animated, straight-to-DVD movies. Similarly, Hot Wheels, which began as a line of miniature die-cast cars with movable wheels, has included related toy lines, plays sets, adult collectibles, and numerous other tie-ins. Mattel has had similar success with acquired lines such as the American Girl dolls.

Mattel also manufactures product tie-ins for movie releases and television shows through the many licenses it owns. It produces items featuring the children's television icon Barney the dinosaur, characters from the popular show *Thomas and Friends*, and those based on Disney and Warner Bros. films and characters like Looney Tunes, Batman, and Superman. In 2011 Mattel made toys that tied into the films *Cars 2* and *Green Lantern*. In 2010 Mattel launched a World Wrestling Entertainment (WWE) branded line of action figures and accessories. Even Mattel's leading games, UNO and Scrabble, had brand value of their own carefully cultivated by Mattel.

While Mattel has traditionally sold its toys through retail stores such as Wal-Mart, Toys "R" Us, and Target, in the 21st century the brand began placing more emphasis on its own catalog and online sales to limit its reliance on the declining retail model. In 2009 Mattel launched four specialty online stores for Barbie, Hot Wheels, Disney, and games. Mattel also had about 10 American Girl retail stores and operated some retail outlets in Europe, Latin America, and the United States.

In 2012 Mattel reorganized its operations into two distinct segments to further ensure optimal sales and marketing. The North American division included Mattel Girls & Boys Brands US, Fisher-Price US, American Girl, and Canada. The International division included the product lines offered in North America (with the exception of American Girl, which was only available in the United States and Canada) and a few additional products just for international markets.

BRAND EQUITY

- Mattel's leading product is Barbie, with one doll sold every two seconds globally.

- A majority of Mattel sales (52 percent) were generated inside the United States in 2011.
- Mattel has high brand value as one of the most valuable companies by category in the United States.

For decades Mattel has been the worldwide leader in toy designing, manufacturing, and marketing. A Barbie is sold every two seconds worldwide, and its global market share is about 16 percent, roughly 5 percent greater than its nearest rival, Hasbro. In 2011, 52 percent of Mattel sales were in the United States, with the rest coming internationally. Europe accounted for 26 percent of its sales, Latin America for 16 percent, and the Asia-Pacific region for 6 percent. Mattel had a high brand value as the global market leader. It is among the *Fortune* 500 "Top Miscellaneous Companies" for 2011 by revenue. Mattel is ranked number two on the "Most Valuable U.S. Leisure Goods Companies" for 2011 with a market value of US$8.7 billion and was the sixth largest U.S. household and personal products company in 2011. Mattel was also the fifth largest among U.S. miscellaneous manufacturers for 2010 by revenue. In 2009 *Brandirectory* ranked Mattel at number 358 on its "Global 500," with brand value of US$1.9 billion and an enterprise value of US$6.5 billion.

BRAND AWARENESS

- Mattel products are sold in 150 countries.
- In 2011 Mattel spent US$700 million on advertising.
- Mattel encompasses many toy lines with high awareness, including Barbie and Hot Wheels.

One of the most influential toy producers in the world since its founding in the mid-20th century, Mattel was the first real global toy brand and is currently sold in 150 countries. Since the 1950s Mattel has been cultivating strong brand recognition beginning with its sponsorship of *The Mickey Mouse Club* television program and continuing through memorable and effective ad campaigns in the 20th and 21st centuries like "Play. Laugh. Grow." and "The Future of Play." In 2011 alone, Mattel spent US$700 million on advertising.

Because of the company's long history, extensive product line, and effective advertising efforts, Mattel has high brand awareness among age groups from children to adults in the United States and many markets in the world. In addition to being the number-one toy brand in the United States and globally, it is the category and product leader in many market segments, adding to its name recognition, not only as Mattel but also as the owner of such successful toy lines as Barbie, Hot Wheels, and Monster High. In 2011 CoreBrand ranked Mattel number 42 on the "100-Top CoreBrand BrandPower Ranking," its annual list of best corporate brands.

BRAND OUTLOOK

- Mattel's sales rose in 2011 to a record-setting US$6.2 billion, a number expected to increase.
- Mattel focused on directly selling its products to consumers online and relying less on retailers.
- Mattel emphasized the importance of sustainability in its 2011 strategy, "Design It, Make It, Live It."

While Mattel is a strong brand structured for growth and with a proven ability to adapt to changing play patterns, fashion preferences, and cultural trends, it, like the toy industry as a whole, was not immune to changes in the world economy. During the worldwide economic downturn from about 2008 to 2010, Mattel's sales decreased. As recovery took hold in some parts of the world, sales cautiously increased in both 2010 and 2011. Mattel sales grew 7 percent between 2010 and 2011, to a record-setting US$6.2 billion. Mattel planned to continue this growth momentum by selling its products online and by relying less on its three biggest retailers, Wal-Mart (19 percent of Mattel's sales), Toys "R" Us (11 percent), and Target (8 percent). While there was growth in both its North American and International segments, Mattel was investing heavily in the development of international sales markets in Asia (particularly in China and India) and in Latin America.

Mattel also put an increasing emphasis on sustainability. In 2011 the brand announced its sustainability strategy, "Design It, Make It, Live It." This initiative was intended to reduce the environmental impact of its products through sustainable design, a reduced amount of packing materials, and greater use of recycled or sustainable fibers in its paper packaging.

FURTHER READING

Brand Finance. "Mattel." *Brandirectory*, 2013. Accessed January 21, 2013. http://brandirectory.com/search/?brand=mattel.

Bulik, Beth Snyder. "Mattel's Got a Monster Holiday Hit, but Will Franchise Have Staying Power?" *Advertising Age*, December 6, 2010.

Juliette, Peers. "Mattel." *Girl Culture: An Encyclopedia*. Ed. Claudia A Mitchell and Jacqueline Reid-Walsh. Vol. 2. Westport, CT: Greenwood Press, 2008.

"Mattel." RankingTheBrands.com. Accessed January 21, 2013. http://www.rankingthebrands.com/Brand-detail.aspx?brandID=412.

"Mattel, Inc." *International Directory of Company Histories*. Ed. Drew Johnson. Vol. 135. Detroit, MI: St. James Press, 2012.

McKinnon, Amy. "Ken." *Girl Culture: An Encyclopedia*. Ed. Claudia A. Mitchell and Jacqueline Reid-Walsh. Vol. 2. Westport, CT: Greenwood Press, 2008.

Oler, Tammy. "Hot Wheels." *Boy Culture: An Encyclopedia*. Ed. Shirley R. Steinberg, Michael Kehler, and Lindsay Cornish. Vol. 2. Santa Barbara, CA: Greenwood Press, 2010.

Teague, Kevin. "Mattel, Inc." *Encyclopedia of Major Marketing Campaigns*. Vol. 2. Detroit, MI: Gale, 2007.

MAZDA

—■—

AT A GLANCE

—◆—

Brand Synopsis: Japanese automotive brand Mazda's sporty styling and sense of fun is epitomized by the use of the promotional phrase "Zoom-Zoom."

Parent Company: Mazda Motor Corporation
3-1 Shinchi
Fuchu-cho, Aki-gun
Hiroshima 730-8670
Japan
http://www.mazda.com

Sector: Consumer Discretionary

Industry Group: Automobiles & Components

Performance: *Market share*—4.1 percent in Japan (2012); 2.4 percent in the United States (2012). *Revenues*—JPY2 trillion (US$21.8 billion) (2012).

Principal Competitors: Honda Motor Co., Ltd.; Nissan Motor Co., Ltd.; Toyota Motor Corporation; Daihatsu Motor Co.; Suzuki Motor Corporation; Fuji Heavy Industries Ltd (parent of Subaru); Mitsubishi Motors

BRAND ORIGINS

- Mazda Motor Corporation began in 1920 as a cork manufacturer, and later produced machine tools. Its first vehicle was a three-wheeled truck first sold in 1931.
- Toyo Kogyo introduced its first mass-produced automobile, the Mazda R360 coupe, in 1960. It took the

name Mazda from Ahura Mazda, an ancient Persian Zoroastrian sky god. Toyo Kogyo changed its name to Mazda Motor Corporation in 1984.

- One famous and best-selling Mazda car is the MX-5, known in Japan as the Eunos Roadster and in North America as the Miata.
- Mazda has had a long history with the American Ford Motor Company, building Ford Festiva models and Ford cars and trucks for the Japanese market and buying together an automotive plant in Flat Rock, Michigan, in 1987.
- After 2000 Mazda expanded its international efforts to China and Russia and introduced its promotional phrase "Zoom-Zoom," a phrase representing its commitment to fun.

Japanese automaker Mazda Motor Corporation began its history with the unlikely name of Toyo Cork Kogyo Company, Ltd., or East Sea Cork Manufacturing Company. Jujiro Matsuda founded this company in Hiroshima, Japan, in 1920 to make cork products. Also known as Toyo Kogyo, the company began making machine tools in the 1920s. In 1931 it introduced its first vehicle, a three-wheeled truck. It also began its relationship with Sumitomo industrial conglomerate around this time.

Like other Japanese companies, Toyo Kogyo manufactured military products during World War II. Near the end of the war, the Allied forces dropped an atomic bomb on Hiroshima, killing around 400 Toyo Kogyo employees among the estimated 100,000 to 140,000 Hiroshima residents who died in the attacks. Other Toyo Kogyo employees credited businesses like Toyo Kogyo with the rebuilding of the city after this bombing.

The company was rebuilding also. In 1960 it introduced its first mass-produced automobile, the Mazda R360 coupe. The company took the Mazda name from Ahura Mazda, a sky god who was the god of the Zoroastrians in ancient Persia. Toyo Kogyo also used the Mazda name because of its similarity to founder Jujiro Matsuda's name. After years of the success and high visibility of its automobiles, the company changed its name to Mazda Motor Corporation in 1984.

The Mazda R360 was a micro-mini car. Toyo Kogyo/Mazda has been known for manufacturing a number of small cars throughout its history. One famous small Mazda car is the MX-5, known at home in Japan as the Eunos Roadster and in North America as the Miata. Launched in the 1980s, the Miata "became the world's best-selling roadster as well as one of the most recognizable cars ever made, much like the Volkswagen Bug or Chevrolet Corvette," according to *Fortune* magazine contributor Doron Levin.

The company has also been involved in high-profile alliances with international companies. It has a long history with the American Ford Motor Company. Mazda's Japanese factories have built Ford Festiva models and Ford cars and trucks for the Japanese market, and Mazda and Ford bought an automotive plant in Flat Rock, Michigan in 1987. Ford became increasingly involved in Mazda in the 1980s and 1990s, buying more shares and supplying executives to serve as Mazda's chairpeople. Ford would reduce its Mazda holdings after 2000.

Mazda's international operations intensified after 2000. Already manufacturing and selling cars in several Asian and European countries and the United States, Mazda expanded these efforts to China and Russia. During this time, Mazda also introduced its promotional phrase "Zoom-Zoom," a phrase representing its commitment to fun.

BRAND ELEMENTS

- Wings superimposed over a ring shape form a stylized letter m in the Mazda brand logo. The wings also allude to winged sky god Ahura Mazda.
- Mazda's corporate identity symbol is lowercase block letters (usually blue) that read Mazda, with the letter z intersected by parallel white diagonal lines.
- Cars are other visual representations of the brand, appearing on its web pages and at the Mazda Museum in Hiroshima, Japan.

Wings superimposed over a ring shape form a stylized letter m. This winged m is the Mazda brand logo. In addition to signifying the Mazda name, Mazda has noted that the

wings symbolize "the company stretching its wings as it soars into the future." The wings also allude to the winged sky god Ahura Mazda, part of the inspiration for the company's name.

Another company symbol is Mazda's corporate image. This image is lowercase block letters (usually blue) that read "Mazda," with the letter z intersected by parallel white diagonal lines. These lines create movement and seem to signify the movement of the company and the vehicles it produces.

Cars are other visual representations of the brand. The company's cars appear everywhere on its websites. They appear on Mazda's home page, on pages devoted to specific Mazda models and technology, on pages discussing Mazda's involvement in motorsports, on pages targeted to Mazda owners, and on pages that help people purchase new and used Mazda vehicles. Cars are on display at the Mazda Museum on the grounds of the company's head office in Hiroshima, Japan, and cars race at Mazda Raceway Laguna Seca in Salinas, California. These pages and global attractions reinforce Mazda's identity as an automotive manufacturer with international interests.

BRAND IDENTITY

- Mazda's frequent use of the phrase Zoom-Zoom captures a spirit of playfulness and fun.
- A 1968 comic-book like brochure for Mazda demonstrated how the brand has long portrayed itself as fun and youthful.
- Mazda calls the components of its brand its brand DNA. The brand DNA uses the Zoom-Zoom phrase and defines the Mazda personality as "stylish" "inspired," and "spirited."

According to children, cars make the sound "zoom zoom." Mazda's use of the phrase Zoom-Zoom captures this spirit of playfulness and fun. Children have appeared in Mazda commercials using the phrase Zoom-Zoom. The company also frequently uses the phrase Zoom-Zoom in other commercials and promotional materials and posts *Zoom-Zoom*, an online magazine, on its website. Mazda's web pages also include a video showing children playing with cars and wheeled toys; this video stresses that adults do not have to lose this playfulness. These uses of the Zoom-Zoom phrase imply that Mazda's products are fun, like toys, and that adults can "play" with the fun cars of the Mazda brand.

Mazda has been linking its brand to fun for some time. Artist Tadanori Yokoo created a 1968 brochure for the Mazda 110S. The cover of the brochure featured photographs of a flying Mazda 110S surrounded by brightly colored cartoon graphics and the text "It's a bird! It's a plane! No, it's Supercar!!" Elsewhere in the brochure, another flying Mazda 110S was surrounded by more cartoon graphics and the word "Whammoo!" The brochure featured still more flying Mazdas and cartoons in a psychedelic style appropriate to its 1968 date. This document's bright colors, flying figures, and "It's a bird..." phrase linked the brochure to comic books, specifically a superhero comic book like Superman, linking Mazda to young people and fun.

Mazda calls the components of its brand its brand DNA, a name that recalls the genetic material that determines human characteristics. Human DNA is deeply ingrained and provides blueprints for the human body; similarly, Mazda considers the brand DNA's characteristics to be integral parts of its brand. It acknowledges that it wants "to create an excellent brand image through strong emotional ties with consumers." To do this, it again evokes fun. It uses the Zoom-Zoom phrase and defines the Mazda personality, using words like "stylish," "inspired," and "spirited." It also explains that product is another part of the Mazda brand DNA. It uses phrases like "distinctive design," "intuitive function," and "responsive drive" to describe Mazda products.

BRAND STRATEGY

- A 2011 promotional campaign targeted "people who are young at heart, people who buy cars because they are fun to drive," according to a Mazda executive. This campaign described the company's values and history and described the company and what it represents.
- To promote its SKYACTIV technology, Mazda offered driving demonstrations in 2011 and featured SKYACTIV engines and Mazda vehicles at the 2013 Rolex 24 at Daytona race.
- Mazda developed "Kodo: soul of motion," a design concept intended to capture "the most finely-honed balance of strength and streamlined beauty."

Youth and fun are two elements Mazda wanted to emphasize in a 2011 promotional campaign. This campaign targeted "people who are young at heart, people who buy cars because they are fun to drive," said Mazda chief marketing officer Don Romano upon the launch of the Anthem promotional campaign. This campaign described the company's values and history. Much like Mazda's brand DNA description, this campaign described the company and what it represents rather than providing detailed descriptions of Mazda's products.

The company has addressed specific products in other promotions. It promoted the release of its SKYACTIV technology with various events. SKYACTIV technology provides various improvements in fuel efficiency, driving performance, and structural safety. To illustrate these improvements, Mazda offered driving demonstrations in 2011. In 2013 the Rolex 24 at Daytona race featured Mazda6 cars that used Mazda's SKYACTIV-D, a clean, high-efficiency diesel engine with lower emissions. With drivers and fans from around the world, the Rolex 24 at Daytona race was a global showcase for Mazda's vehicles, parts, and technology.

In addition to promoting engineering work, Mazda has discussed its design work. Its 2010 Shinari concept car was Mazda's first car to utilize a design concept the company called "Kodo: soul of motion." The company explained that Kodo "Express[es] the living motion, strong and graceful" and that with its automotive designs, Mazda hoped to capture "the most finely-honed balance of strength and streamlined beauty." This discussion of its design concept is another instance of Mazda explaining what it represented, what it produced, and what it wanted to achieve.

BRAND EQUITY

- In 2010 Mazda captured a 5.1 percent share of the automotive market in Canada, 3.1 percent in Mexico, and 2 percent in the United States. In 2012 Mazda reportedly held 2.4 percent market share in the United States.
- In 2011 Mazda captured a 4.6 percent market share of the Japanese automotive market. It held the sixth-largest market share in Japan in both 2011 and 2012.
- In September 2012 Mazda captured a 10.7 percent share of the Australian automotive market, second only to Toyota's 18.3 percent.

As one of the world's largest automobile manufacturers, Mazda has captured significant market share in different countries. In 2010 in North America, it captured a 5.1 percent share of the automotive market in Canada, 3.1 percent in Mexico, and 2 percent in the United States. A few years later, in 2012, Doron Levin reported in *Fortune* magazine that Mazda held a 2.4 percent market share in the United States.

It held a similar portion of its domestic market. In 2011 Mazda captured a 4.6 percent market share of the Japanese automotive market. Similarly, Mazda averaged a 4.1 percent share of this market from January through and including April 2012. Automotive companies from Japan and a number of other countries produce vehicles for the Japanese market and Mazda held the sixth-largest share among all of these countries in both 2011 and 2012.

Mazda has enjoyed even more success on yet another continent. In September 2012 Mazda captured a 10.7 percent share of the Australian automotive market, second only to Toyota's 18.3 percent. Once again, Mazda and Toyota are among manufacturers from several countries that make cars for a specific market.

BRAND AWARENESS

- Almost 40 percent of U.S. consumers polled in 2010 by Complete Pulse correctly linked Mazda with its Zoom-Zoom phrase.
- Marketing consultant Jackie O'Dowd observed in 2011 that Mazda "is often seen as the sportiest of the Japanese brands."
- Even though the company experienced economic problems in 2011, Doron Levin noted that "Mazda still has strong brand awareness in the U.S. and a hardy band of enthusiasts," and observed that Mazda was known for its "sporty, fun-to-drive vehicles that don't cost much to own."
- A J.D. Power survey found that Mazda had the fourth-highest customer satisfaction ratings among German car owners in 2012; in 2011 Mazda received similarly high customer ratings in Italy and France.

Consumers are aware of Mazda's brand and its elements. A 2010 poll of U.S. Internet users posted on Compete Pulse found that almost 40 percent of these consumers correctly identified Mazda with the Zoom-Zoom phrase. In a 2010 *Advertising Age* article by Andrew Hampp, Mazda global marketing executive Masahiro Moro expressed similar sentiments. He noted that "every time I get to the United States and I'm passing through customs and they ask me what company I work for, they always point at me and say, 'Zoom-Zoom.'"

According to marketing consultant Jackie O'Dowd, Mazda also has a very specific image, especially in relation to design. In a 2011 article posted on Compete Pulse, O'Dowd noted that Mazda "recently adopted a new styling direction" in its adoption of the Kodo design concept and she observed that Mazda "is often seen as the sportiest of the Japanese brands." Others have discussed Mazda's automotive styling and the perception of its brand. *Fortune* magazine contributor Doron Levin wrote that Mazda has been known for producing "sporty, fun-to-drive vehicles that don't cost much to own." Even though the company experienced economic problems in 2011, Levin noted that "Mazda still has strong brand awareness in the U.S. and a hardy band of enthusiasts."

Mazda has enthusiasts and brand awareness in other countries as well. J.D. Power has conducted surveys of automobile owners around the world. In one J.D. Power consumer ranking, Mazda had the fourth-highest customer satisfaction ratings among German car owners in 2012. Mazda also tallied the fourth-highest owner satisfaction figures among Italian car owners and the sixth-highest rating among French car owners, both according to separate J.D. Power surveys in 2011.

BRAND OUTLOOK

- Like other automakers, Mazda has worked to comply with U.S. fuel efficiency mandates.
- Global economic problems, currency issues, natural disasters, and political disputes since 2000 have affected Mazda and other companies.
- Mazda reported a loss of more than JPY100 billion for the 2012 fiscal year and varying global sales totals in 2010, 2011, and 2012.
- By partnering to build cars with different companies in different countries, Mazda intends to strengthen its finances, global presence, and brand profile.

Mazda has utilized SKYACTIV technology in vehicles like the 2013 CX-5 for another reason: it reduces the weight of its vehicles. Mazda was just one of a number of automakers that looked to reduce the weight of their vehicles during this time, in part to improve their vehicles' fuel efficiency. This drive for improved fuel efficiency has followed U.S. government mandates that require new cars and trucks to average 54.5 miles per gallon by 2025. Mazda's reduction in car weight signals its compliance with these mandates and its environmental responsiveness.

In recent years, Mazda has grappled with international recessions, economic problems, and currency issues. It also faced disasters such as the earthquake, tsunami, and radiation leaks from damaged nuclear plants that damaged parts of eastern Japan and severe flooding in Thailand, all in 2011. In 2012 it briefly halted operations in China due to rioting in the country that erupted due to a territorial dispute between Japan and China. Mazda reported a loss of more than JPY100 billion for the 2012 fiscal year, and Mazda sales figures in different markets showed mixed results between 2010 and 2012.

In other international developments, Mazda has teamed with other automakers in joint ventures. Mazda sold US$1.9 billion (more than JPY150 billion) in public shares in 2012 to finance the building of a factory in Mexico to manufacture cars with Toyota. In another international venture, in 2012 Mazda and Italian automobile manufacturer Alfa Romeo announced their plans to jointly build a sports car. Mazda would manufacture this convertible, based on its MX-5 (Miata), at its plant in Hiroshima, Japan. By partnering with different companies in different countries, Mazda intends to strengthen its finances, global presence, and brand profile.

FURTHER READING

Hammerton, Ron. "VFACTS: Mazda Cracks 10,000 Sales Barrier." GoAuto.com.au, October 4, 2012. Accessed January 5, 2013. http://www.goauto.com.au/mellor/mellor.nsf/story2/20C9F0FF85A8E52DCA257A8D000C8FEF.

Hampp, Andrew. "Why 'Zoom-Zoom' Is Staying Put in a Year of Change for Mazda." *Advertising Age*, November 29, 2010.

Levin, Doron. "The Cloud Hanging over Mazda." *Fortune*, March 30, 2012.

Maloney, Val. "New Mazda Campaign to Focus on Brand Values." *strategy*, April 25, 2011. Accessed January 4, 2013. http://strategyonline.ca/2011/04/25/mazda-20110425/.

Mazda. "Kodo." Mazda Design. Accessed January 5, 2013. http://www.mazda.com/mazdaspirit/design/#/kodo.

———. *Mazda Annual Report 2012*. Accessed February 19, 2013. http://www.mazda.com/investors/library/annual/2012/pdf/ar12_02e.pdf.

———. *Mazda in Brief 2011*. Accessed January 4, 2013. http://www.mazda.com/profile/outline/library/2011/pdf/2011_all.pdf.

———. "Vision." Accessed January 4, 2013. http://www.mazda.com/profile/vision/brand.html

"Mazda." RankingTheBrands.com. Accessed February 18, 2013. http://www.rankingthebrands.com/Brand-detail.aspx?brandID=299.

"Mazda Motor Corporation." *International Directory of Company Histories*. Ed. Tina Grant. Vol. 138. Detroit, MI: St. James Press, 2013.

O'Dowd, Jackie. "The Mazda Evolution: Brand Awareness Driving Sales." Compete Pulse, January 24, 2011. Accessed January 5, 2013. http://blog.compete.com/2011/01/24/the-mazda-evolution-brand-awareness-driving-sales/.

Tuttle, Brad. "Losing Weight Is a Hot Trend—in the Auto Industry." *Time*, August 17, 2012.

MCDONALD'S

—◼—

AT A GLANCE

—◼—

Brand Synopsis: McDonald's is the world's largest and best-known chain of fast food restaurants and a symbol of American enterprise and culture.

Parent Company: McDonald's Corporation
2111 McDonald's Drive
Oak Brook, Illinois 60523
United States
http://www.mcdonalds.com

Sector: Consumer Discretionary

Industry Group: Consumer Services

Performance: *Market share*—19 percent (2012). *Sales*—US$27 billion (2011).

Principal Competitors: Burger King; Wendy's; Subway; Starbucks; Kentucky Fried Chicken

BRAND ORIGINS

- McDonald's signs and logos originated with the franchise's roadside restaurants.
- The Golden Arches logo and architecture has always been part of the McDonald's brand.
- Ronald McDonald has been the company mascot since the mid-1960s.

In 1940 Richard and Maurice McDonald opened a restaurant in San Bernardino, California. By 1948 the McDonald brothers had perfected their "Speedee Service System", establishing the basic elements of service—a limited menu, assembly-line preparation, and moving customers quickly through the store—that consumers recognize today as the hallmarks of fast food. In the restaurant's early years, Ray Kroc, a salesman for a food mixer company, sold the McDonald brothers several of his mixers and was greatly impressed by their operation. Kroc took over the franchising of the restaurants and personally opened his first restaurant in Des Plaines, Illinois, in 1955. Kroc bought the company for US$2.7 million in 1961 but kept the McDonald's name. Kroc oversaw the perfection of the McDonald's assembly line and expanded the business globally.

McDonald's first filed for a U.S. trademark for the name "McDonald's" on May 4, 1961, and in the same year the company filed to trademark its logo, an overlapping, double-arched "M." As a roadside restaurant, McDonald's needed a distinctive building and signage to attract travelers. The McDonald brothers were responsible for adding two golden arches to an architect's plan for a new building, and eventually the "Golden Arches" were incorporated into a sign that became the famous company logo. McDonald's restaurants and signs in the 1950s and 1960s incorporated many different versions of the single and double arches. The arch often featured Speedee, an early McDonald's mascot, on top and always included a rectangular space for advertising messages, including the widely recognized "Over [number in millions or billions] sold." The overlapping double-arched "M" logo was given trademark status in 1968. Speedee was eventually replaced with Ronald McDonald in 1967, when the company first filed a trademark on the clown-like mascot.

BRAND ELEMENTS

- McDonald's Golden Arches logo suggests modernity and efficiency.
- McDonald's stores and signage use bright, primary colors.
- The Ronald McDonald character suggests fun and happiness, especially for children.
- There is a sense of historic continuity in the McDonald's brand's signage and menus.

The first McDonald's brand mascot was Speedee, an image of a man with a chef's hat on top of a hamburger-shaped head. One of the franchise's earliest signs was a giant gold arch featuring Speedee on the top, holding a ladle. Red, white, and yellow or gold have long been the primary colors used in McDonald's buildings, signs, advertising, and product packaging. The company colors are bright and dynamic, and are intended to attract attention, especially the attention of children, who were to become one of the most profitable customer sectors for the company. The parabolic shape of the Golden Arches and the color schemes suggest modernity and point to the efficiency of fast food preparation, while the "Millions/Billions Sold" advertising signage points to the efficiency and the reach of McDonald's restaurants, which became ubiquitous in American cities and as roadside stopovers during the 1960s.

Speedee disappeared at the end of the 1950s and was replaced by Ronald McDonald, the clown character used as the primary mascot of the McDonald's fast food restaurant chain. Initially, Ronald McDonald was depicted in a fantasy world called McDonaldland, but over time this context was phased out and Ronald is now shown interacting with normal kids in their everyday lives. This was part of a very successful strategy aimed at making Ronald McDonald the leading figure in the company's outreach efforts, a strategy that was intended to improve the company's corporate image and its interface with individual communities. Ronald McDonald is designed to appeal to children, and his "smile known around the world" has earned him a place among mascots that enjoy global recognition, alongside Mickey Mouse.

The McDonald's logo, like many other fast food logos, was developed in the 1970s, and although the logo has undergone some minor upgrades through the years, the McDonald's "M" still possesses an old-fashioned feel.

BRAND IDENTITY

- The McDonald's brand is built on value for money, cleanliness, and fast service.
- McDonald's emphasizes the fun and happiness purportedly experienced by diners as part of its brand.
- The franchise's menu has retained old favorites but is also constantly updated to reflect changing attitudes and tastes.

Quality, service, cleanliness, and value are McDonald's stated operating principles. At the heart of the McDonald's brand is an emphasis on value for money: cheap food served quickly in reassuringly uniform surroundings. From the McDonald brothers' 15-cent hamburger to the "Dollar Meals" of today, the brand depends on low prices. The McDonald's experience is intended to be enjoyable, and happiness plays an important part in the company's brand identity. The company serves "Happy Meals," and Ronald McDonald is called the "Chief Happiness Officer" of the corporation. The slogan "i'm lovin' it" sums up what McDonald's would like its customers to feel. The emphasis on youthfulness and fun permeates the brand's advertising and image.

One of the advantages of the McDonald's franchise system is uniformity and the predictability that every McDonald's restaurant will feature the same menu, interior, and level of service. Although the company has continually amended its menu to accommodate food trends and changing attitudes towards fast food, it still offers the old standards that have been on the menu for decades. For example, the Big Mac dates back to the 1960s, and the Egg McMuffin and Filet-o-Fish first appeared in the 1970s.

BRAND STRATEGY

- The McDonald's brand is supported by highly effective marketing campaigns.
- McDonald's invests heavily in local communities to boost its brand awareness and its image as a socially responsible business.
- The company has repeatedly repositioned itself to keep pace with changing attitudes toward fast food.

McDonald's is an effective and relentless advertiser that uses many media outlets and social networks to promote its products and protect the reputation of the company and its franchisers. Effie Worldwide, a consortium of advertising firms and marketing research organizations, has often rated McDonald's advertising as exceptionally effective and recognized the company with its "Most Effective Brand" award. In addition to television, radio, and newspaper advertising, the company makes extensive use of billboards and signage, and it sponsors sporting events ranging from Little League to the Olympic Games. In most countries of the industrial West, McDonald's restaurants, signage, and products (including packaging) are ubiquitous. The company enjoys an almost 100 percent brand recognition rate in every global market, according to an August 2006 report in *Bloomberg Business Week* magazine.

Given the company's exclusive focus on selling food, the McDonald's menu has served as a major tool in developing brand strategy. The company built its reputation on a small number of products but has had to expand and redefine its menu to keep up with trends in the fast food industry and changing attitudes towards nutrition. Customers want more choices, and McDonald's has constantly added menu items to attract a more diverse clientele and to incorporate foods that have become popular since the 1950s, including Mexican and other regional food items.

In recent years, the widespread problem of obesity and an increased focus on nutrition and health have forced the company to defend its menu, especially the fat- and calorie-laden hamburger, and add more healthy food choices, such as salads, chicken, and fruit, to its offerings. The company has also changed its packaging, partly in response to documentaries such as *Super Size Me*, which criticized McDonald's large portions as a factor in obesity. McDonald's has extended its brand to represent a more diverse and healthy menu and promoted the McDonald's experience as part of a modern lifestyle that incorporates informed food choices. Thus, the company was able to use marketing vehicles like its sponsorship of the Olympic Games to promote a new identity for the brand that deflected many of the criticisms of its products.

McDonald's now operates on a global scale and, like many other companies that do business globally, it has had to adapt to completely different business and nutritional environments. It has tailored its products to meet local needs, and notable addition to its foreign menus have included the Japanese Ebi Filet-O; the Croque McDo, a version of classic French sandwich, the croque-monsieur; and the Big Spicy Paneer Wrap, an Indian menu specialty.

As a global representative of American business concepts, McDonald's has become a lightning rod for issues like child labor and cultural imperialism. The company has energetically defended its products and methods of operation in courtrooms, government investigations, and public forums, but equally important has been the repositioning of the McDonald's experience as involving something more than fast food. McDonald's has sought to defuse criticism and strengthen its brand by positioning itself as a friend of local communities and by publicizing its involvement with local charitable, sporting, and educational events. The company is heavily involved in American high schools through its "Growing Up Together" programs. Ronald McDonald is known for his good works, and many communities have Ronald McDonald Houses that provide accommodation for parents whose children are in hospital. McDonald's says it is "proud to be a part of the communities we serve ... giving back is an essential part of the way we operate every day." Although McDonald's has only been operating in Russia since 1990, it has become so well integrated into Russian social life, hosting birthday parties and other events,

that a survey found that Russians consider McDonald's restaurants to be local, indigenous restaurants rather than franchises of a foreign fast-food operation.

McDonald's brand strategy used to be cheap food quickly served, but recently the company has repositioned itself to appeal to a more upscale clientele by adding more sophisticated and higher-priced items to its menu and by redesigning its outlets to make them more comfortable and welcoming. It has copied Starbucks' success by introducing the McCafé experience and by introducing specialty coffee-based drinks, like the Frappé, that compete with Starbucks products. McDonald's has transformed its decor and its mode of operation by encouraging customers to stay longer in more attractive surroundings.

BRAND EQUITY

- McDonald's is considered one of the top 10 global brands.
- The value of the McDonald's brand is estimated to be in the range of US\$20 billion to US\$40 billion.
- The lackluster performance of its competitors in the early 21st century has helped boost McDonald's brand equity.

McDonald's has been consistently ranked in the top 10 global brands in various surveys, including those conducted by Interbrand and Brand Finance. Interbrand ranked McDonald's at number seven in 2012 and estimated the value of the brand at US\$40 billion. McDonald's was ranked 18th in *Brandirectory*'s Global 500 survey in 2012, with a valuation of US\$22 billion. While sales of its chief competitors, Burger King and Wendy's, have been falling since the global recession of the early 2000s, McDonald's has enjoyed strong sales during this time. Global sales in 2011 were up 5.6 percent over 2010, with revenues growing at a rate that was double that of the industry as a whole.

BRAND AWARENESS

- McDonald's invests heavily in advertising, spending approximately US\$2 billion annually on advertising.
- The sheer number of its stores gives the McDonald's brand a global presence.
- McDonald's high-profile presence on the global stage makes it a target for criticism as well.

With over 33,000 restaurants in 119 countries, McDonald's enjoys an extensive global presence. Heavy advertising via radio, television, print, social media, and packaging maintain the visibility of the McDonald's brand. With an annual advertising budget estimated at around US\$2 billion, the McDonald's name, logo, and slogans are everywhere. Not all brand awareness has been positive for the company, however. As a prominent example of the rapid globalization of the American fast food industry, McDonald's has become a symbol for American cultural imperialism for some and a target for anti-American sentiment. Activists in the environmental, anti-globalization, child protection, and healthy diet movements have chosen McDonald's as a major focus for their critiques. In response to such criticism, McDonald's has utilized its position as one of the world's best-known brands, with a multitude of advertising outlets at its disposal, to publicize changes intended to make the brand more socially and environmentally responsible.

BRAND OUTLOOK

- McDonald's effectively weathered the global economic downturn of the early 2000s.
- The brand has generally enjoyed increasing sales and brand awareness with each passing year.
- McDonald's future success will depend largely on its ability to adapt to changing customer tastes while not overlooking classically successful brand elements.
- McDonald's responded to a drop in sales in 2012 by making further changes to its menu, adding new items and bringing back old favorites.

McDonald's weathered the global economic downturn of the early 2000s and produced strong results as it entered the second decade of the 21st century, while its principal competitors continued to struggle. The company's sales grew by 5.6 percent in 2011, the eighth year that the company enjoyed a worldwide increase in sales. Additionally, the sales of its company-owned stores increased by 13 percent in 2011. The number of McDonald's stores and the customers these stores serve continue to increase with each year. McDonald's dominates the fast food industry in the United States and is still extending its brand in Europe and Asia.

Much of the future growth of the company will depend on the success of its efforts to reposition the McDonald's experience as more upscale and inviting while simultaneously not ignoring elements that have made the franchise so successful historically. The fast food industry has slowly been losing market share to slightly more upscale "fast-casual" chains, such as Panera and Chipotle, which offer more expensive but more varied and sophisticated menus in appealingly furnished restaurants. The global success of the Starbucks chain, with its inviting luxurious armchairs and more upscale décor, has made a strong impression on the fast food industry, which traditionally aimed at moving customers quickly in and out of stores.

In addition to adding higher-priced, more diverse items to its menu, McDonald's decided to change the look of the franchise's restaurants when it entered into the second decade of the 21st century. Brand staples such as the bright reds and yellows are being replaced with earth tones in many locations, and much of the utilitarian furniture is being replaced with more comfortable seats and tables that invite customer to linger and enjoy their meal rather than to "grab and go." The new look of the franchise's restaurants and the inclusion of healthier menu items are aimed at attracting new customer demographics. If the makeover does not succeed, however, McDonald's runs the risk of alienating its core clientele and diluting its brand value.

The immediate results of this shift in brand strategy have not been encouraging. In October 2012 McDonald's reported falling sales for the first time since 2003, during a month when it heavily promoted its value menu and rolled out its annual Monopoly promotion. This decline was probably due to the overall weaknesses of the global economy and strong performances by its main rivals. However, during the same period, Wendy's, Burger King, and Taco Bell all reported increases in sales and the successful introduction of new, more upscale coffee options and more innovative salads. These companies have quickly made up the ground lost to McDonald's since the economic downturn that began in 2007. In response to falling sales, McDonald's replaced its U.S. company president and promised to reinvigorate its menu with new items while at the same time bringing back such old favorites as the McRib sandwich for a limited time. The company has stressed its commitment to its low price "Dollar" menu, as the company's slightly higher-priced "Extra Value" menu has not been a success to date.

Much of the future growth of McDonald's depends on its ability to compete successfully with more upscale and aggressive competitors while remaining the choice for customers seeking value above all else.

FURTHER READING

"Best Global Brands, 2012." Interbrand. Accessed October 25, 2012. http://www.interbrand.com/en/best-global-brands/2012/McDonalds.

"Best Global Brands." *Bloomberg BusinessWeek*, August 6, 2006. Accessed February 22, 2013. http://www.businessweek.com/stories/2006-08-06/best-global-brands.

Brand Finance. "Global 500, 2012." *Brandirectory*. Accessed October 20, 2012. http://brandirectory.com/league_tables/table/global-500-2012.

Caldwell, Melissa. "Domesticating the French Fry: McDonald's and Consumerism in Moscow." *Journal of Consumer Culture* 4.1 (2004): 5-26.

Cowin, Erica. "The Ongoing Transformation of the McDonald's Logo." *Journal of Visual Literacy*, vol. 30, no. 2 (2011).

Horowitz, Bruce. "McDonald's 1st Monthly Sales Drop in a Decade." *USA Today*, November 8, 2012.

McDonald's Corp. "Annual Report, 2011." Accessed October 28, 2012.http://www.aboutmcdonalds.com/content/dam/AboutMcDonalds/Investors/Investors%202012/2011%20Annual%20Report%20Final.pdf.

Morrison, Maureen. "McDonald's Records 5.6% Global Sales Increase for 2011." *AdvertisingAge*, January 24, 2012.

O'Brian, Keith. "How McDonald's Came Back Bigger than Ever." *New York Times*, May 4, 2012.

Ritzer, George. *The McDonaldization of Society*. 5th ed. Thousand Oaks, CA: Pine Forge Press, 2007.

Schlosser, Eric. *Fast Food Nation: The Dark Side of the All-American Meal*. Boston, MA: Houghton Mifflin, 2001.

Watson, James L. "Golden Arches East." Stanford, CA: Stanford University Press, 2006.

MEDTRONIC

—■—

BRAND ORIGINS

- In 1949 Earl Bakken and Palmer Hermundslie founded Medtronic with the aim of creating medical equipment with minimal need for repairs.
- Medtronic created the world's first external, wearable, battery-powered pacemaker in 1957.
- Earl Bakken wrote in the company's mission statement in 1962 that Medtronic's goals are to alleviate pain, restore health, and extend life.

- On Medtronic's 50th anniversary in 1999, a new logo was created to represent the brand's focus on the restoration of patients' health.
- Through acquisition and innovation, Medtronic has become a leading brand in the treatment of such chronic illnesses as heart disease and diabetes.

Medtronic creates healthcare equipment that is used to treat more than 30 types of chronic disease. The company began in 1949 as a medical equipment repair business in founder Earl Bakken's garage. Bakken and his brother-in-law Palmer Hermundslie joined forces and named the company Medtronic.

The original vision of Bakken and Hermundslie was to create medical devices (to be implanted in or on the body) of such quality that the need for repair was minimal. In 1957 they created the world's first external, wearable, battery-powered pacemaker. The company was incorporated on April 23 the same year, and in 1964 it was listed on the New York Stock Exchange.

The 1960s were a time of innovation and expansion for the company. In 1960 Medtronic bought the rights to produce the first implantable pacemaker developed by Dr. William Chardack, Dr. Andrew Gage, and Wilson Greatbatch. Also during the 1960s, Bakken and Hermundslie began to experiment with electrical stimulation for parts of the body other than the heart. This led to the creation of a gastrointestinal pacemaker, providing relief from pain through stimulation of the spinal cord. The business expanded in the 1960s to Maryland; Washington, DC; and San Francisco and to locations in Africa, Australia, Canada, Cuba, Europe, and South America. At this time, Medtronic appointed Picker International Corporation in White Plains, New York, to be its sole distributor outside the United States (with the exception of Canada). Picker's 72 foreign sales offices made it possible for Medtronic to expand its brand even further. By 1968 the company reported sales of more than US$12 million.

As Medtronic continued to grow throughout the 1970s and 1980s, the company's vision remained true to its origins. Bakken and the company's board of directors had drafted the company's mission statement, which began with the pledge "to contribute to human welfare by application of biomedical engineering in the research, design, manufacture, and sale of instruments or appliances that alleviate pain, restore health, and extend life," at the company's inception. Medtronic's dedication to its mission and the continued success of Medtronic's products opened the door to funding opportunities.

During his term in the mid-1980s, Medtronic president and CEO Winston R. Wallin doubled diversification and research spending. Implantable cardioverter-defibrillators (ICDs) were developed, as was the SynchroMed drug delivery system. In 1989 William W. George stepped in as Medtronic's president and CEO. Annual revenues passed US$1 billion for the first time. Medtronic earned the status as a multinational, diversified medical technological corporation when it acquired Sofamor Danek, which specialized in spinal technology, and Arterial Vascular Engineering, which specialized in stents. The 1990s ushered in partnerships with leading hospitals and physicians, and long-term contractual agreements helped the company improve therapeutic outcomes and weather economic challenges.

Medtronic celebrated its 50th anniversary in 1999. At this time, the company's products were being used to treat heart disease, spinal conditions, diabetes, back pain, chronic pain, and Parkinson's disease. The company was voted one of the "100 Best Companies to Work For" in the United States by *Fortune* magazine. A new logo was created to represent the company's mission to restore health and extend life.

In 2001 a new facility in Fridley, Minnesota, became Medtronic's world headquarters, and Art Collins became the company CEO, taking the opportunity to focus on the long-term management of chronic diseases. The company also faced challenges, however, during the economic downturn of the early 21st century. A weak economy and negative publicity regarding defibrillator malfunctions led to a decreased demand in the market for Medtronic devices. Additionally, the company experienced a decline in sales of the brand's Infuse bone growth product due to a medical journal's accusations that researchers failed to disclose serious complications related to use of the product.

Changes in the healthcare industry and the economy have led Medtronic to increase its focus on hospital administrators, who are becoming the key decision makers in purchasing medical equipment. Omar Ishrak, who became chairman and CEO of Medtronic in 2011, stated that reviving "the company's growth by further expanding it internationally and improving its returns from research spending" will be a key strategy for the Medtronic brand. The company entered the second decade of the 21st century focused on raising brand awareness among patients. As of 2012, Medtronic's operations consisted of more than 250 manufacturing facilities, sales offices, research centers, education centers, and administration facilities serving 120 countries.

BRAND ELEMENTS

- Medtronic's first logo represented the bridge between medical therapy and electricity.
- The current Medtronic logo represents the brand's mission to restore people's health.
- Medtronic's main tagline is "Alleviating Pain. Restoring Health. Extending Life."
- Medtronic's brand also features Lenny the Lion, a Build-a-Bear character intended to encourage and comfort young patients who have diabetes.

The name Medtronic is a combination of the words "medical" and "electronic." Its first logo represented a bridge between the medical field and electricity. The company's tagline was "Bringing Electricity to Life" for many years. In 1999 a revamp of the logo concentrated more on the patient's experience. The bold, blue, semi-cursive letters of the company name appear beside a silver circle containing the profile of a man rising from a horizontal to vertical position.

Slogans for the brand have stressed the importance of its mission: "Alleviating Pain. Restoring Health. Extending Life"; "Transforming technology to change lives"; and "Innovating for a better world: innovating for life."

An additional element of the Medtronic brand is Lenny the Lion. Lenny is a Build-a-Bear character intended to encourage and comfort young patients who have diabetes. He wears an insulin pump and says, "I don't let diabetes hold me back."

BRAND IDENTITY

- Medtronic Academia educates medical professionals about new technologies and changes in the healthcare industry.
- It is important to the brand to respect employees and make them feel integral to Medtronic's success.
- Medtronic provides grants and product donations in communities where it operates, and it cultivates partnerships with global organizations.

- Interbrand helped refocus the brand in 2010 to communicate that "Medtronic is in the business of transforming lives through innovative technology."

Medtronic strives to be known for its innovative designs and methods of treating chronic disease. Medtronic Academia educates medical professionals about new technologies and changes in the healthcare industry. In 2010 Behrendt Graphic Design, a company based in the Netherlands, designed Medtronic Academia program materials with brightly colored illustrations. Brochures, foldout pamphlets, and various swag items, such as computer cases and book rests, reinforce the brand in creative ways.

It is important to the brand's mission that employees are respected and made to feel part of the company's success. Medtronic's hiring process involves a training program outlining the company's origin and values. Once the process is completed, each employee receives a bronze medallion with the brand logo and the statement: "Toward Full Life." On the back is the statement: "Your work here at Medtronic is not just to make money for yourself or the company, but to restore people to fuller lives."

Medtronic is involved in the communities in which the company operates. The company provides grants, practices product donation, and encourages employee volunteerism. Medtronic has also formed partnerships with global organizations such as the Center for Chronic Disease Control in India, Children's HeartLink, the International Center for AIDS Care and Treatment Programs, and the International Diabetes Federation.

While the 1999 logo and brand identity represented the general Medtronic brand vision, the company updated its focus in 2010 to support diversification. The brand consultancy Interbrand spoke with stakeholders about Medtronic's "unique ability to change the way chronic conditions are both managed and experienced." Interbrand also helped build an emotional appeal for the brand, emphasizing that "Medtronic is in the business of transforming lives through innovative technology."

BRAND STRATEGY

- Medtronic is divided into six areas of specialty and four cross-business groups to ensure consistent communication and the manageability of its specialties.
- Strategic acquisitions have helped the brand extend its therapeutic expertise to all areas of the body.
- Strategic allocation of investment dollars has allowed the company to improve therapies using new technologies.
- Medtronic's strategy of eliminating group-purchasing businesses is aimed at shifting bargaining power back to the brand.

Medtronic is an organization divided into six areas of specialty: Cardiac Rhythm Disease Management (CRDM), Spinal and Biologics, Cardiovascular Disease, Neuromodulation, Diabetes, and Surgical Technology. The Medtronic brand maintains cross-business groups to help ensure that communication is consistent and its specialties are more manageable. For example, Medtronic International manages global operations, sales, and distribution; Quality and Operations handles human resources and IT services; Strategy and Innovation finds ways to integrate research and technology into the company's six specialty areas; and Healthcare Policy and Regulatory helps keep government agencies and global peer groups up-to-date on changing aspects of the global healthcare industry's regulations, reimbursement processes, and cost–benefit analysis.

The Medtronic brand has become a global leader partly by keeping an eye on the market. Its strategic acquisitions have extended its treatment capabilities to many areas of chronic disease. Medtronic's purchase of the rights to the implantable pacemaker in 1960 was only the beginning. Sofamor Danek provided Medtronic with a specialization in spinal technology, Arterial Vascular Engineering added stents to the brand's capabilities, and the acquisition of MiniMed in 2007 helped the brand excel in treatments for diabetes. Also in 2007 Medtronic acquired Kyphon, a global leader in minimally invasive therapies that restore spinal function. Bill Hawkins, Medtronic's president and CEO at the time, said, "We expect this acquisition to help accelerate the growth of Medtronic's existing spinal business by extending our product offerings into some of the fastest growing product segments and enabling us to provide physicians with a broader range of therapies for use at all stages of the care continuum."

In 2008 Medtronic spent US$1.2 billion (about 10 percent of its total revenue) on research and development. A cross-business group, Strategy and Innovation, was formed at this time. The strategic allocation of investment dollars allowed the company to improve therapies using new technologies. In 2012 the company acquired Kanghui, a Chinese manufacturer of medical devices for use in the treatment of trauma and spinal injury. CEO Omar Ishrak stated that "Kanghui represents a significant investment in China, accelerating Medtronic's overall globalization strategy with an established value segment distribution network and strong R&D and operational capabilities."

In 2011 Medtronic made a controversial move and canceled five contracts with Novation, a large group-purchasing agent. Derrick Sung, a healthcare analyst with Bernstein Research, said the decision would save the company "$40 million to $60 million a year" by eliminating the "middleman" Novation and its administrative charges. Sung stated that Medtronic's "bold move could represent a positive shift in bargaining power away from the hospitals and back to the device manufacturers."

BRAND EQUITY

- Medtronic was listed 164th in the 2012 Fortune 500, down from 158th place in 2011.
- In 2012 Brand Finance ranked Medtronic 233rd among the top-500 global brands.
- In 2012 Medtronic was estimated at to have a brand value of approximately US$4.42 billion.

In 2012 Medtronic was ranked 164th in the Fortune 500 list of top companies, down from 158th place in 2011. It remained ahead of the competition, however, as Baxter International was ranked 195th; Stryker, 308th; Boston Scientific, 335th; and St. Jude Medical, 437th.

Per Brand Finance, the 2012 brand value of Medtronic was approximately US$4.42 billion. The brand was ranked 233rd on Brand Finance's 2012 Global 500, down from 212th in the 2011 ranking.

BRAND AWARENESS

- The Medtronic brand serves patients and medical professionals in more than 120 countries, and the company continues to expand its brand awareness through multiple channels.
- Medtronic launched a year-long advertising campaign in 2007 to educate people aged 50 or older about sudden cardiac arrest.
- The Medtronic Christmas party brings employees and patients together to celebrate the benefits of Medtronic's mission and to reinforce brand awareness and loyalty.
- Medtronic has focused on innovative new technologies, such as app technology, to continue to build awareness of its brand.

Medtronic is well known to physicians and hospitals. The brand serves patients and medical professionals in more than 120 countries. In 2007 the brand spent US$100 million on an advertising and education campaign to raise awareness of sudden cardiac arrest. Advertisements aimed at patients rather than physicians are traditionally rare in the medical equipment industry, but patients have become more proactive about their treatments. Martin Moylan of Minnesota Public Radio said, "During a year-long campaign, Medtronic will spend about $35 million on print, Web and TV advertising. To reach its target audience of people 50 years or older, Medtronic will run the ads on the History Channel, CNN, the Golf Channel, and morning news programs."

The company also promotes brand awareness and loyalty internally. A highlight of the year for employees and patients alike is the Medtronic Christmas party, held at the company's headquarters. At the party, patients and employees are brought together, and patients tell how Medtronic helped them. The inspirational stories remind employees why their work is important and reinforce the Medtronic viewpoint that patients are not statistics but individuals.

The company has been busy making use of app technology to further awareness to the Medtronic brand. Interviews with doctors and researchers were used to create a suite of 14 iPad apps. The apps are available to Medtronic employees to use as educational and marketing tools in meetings with vendors and other interested parties.

In the 21st century, Medtronic faces a growing need to increase brand awareness in developing global markets, and the company has made plans to address this need. For example, in India, the pilot program "Healthy Heart for All" identifies patients with heart disease through a diagnostics and referral network. The referral process is intended to ensure that patients receive care in a timely manner.

BRAND OUTLOOK

- Medtronic has begun to put more resources into well-performing divisions, and it is focusing on research and development as the sources of growth.
- In 2011 CEO Omar Ishrak announced plans to expand the company's international presence and improve returns on research spending.
- Medtronic is performance-driven in three areas: improving execution, accelerating globalization, and optimizing innovation.

Medtronic is performance-driven in three areas: improving execution, accelerating globalization, and optimizing innovation. In spite of the recent economic downturn, the company expects continued growth. Medtronic has begun to put more resources into well-performing divisions, and it is focusing on research and development to expand its role in the healthcare equipment industry.

According to an August 2011 report from Reuters, CEO Omar Ishrak planned to "revive the company's growth by further expanding it internationally and improving its returns from research spending." Ishrak expressed confidence that this direction is right for the company: "Our international revenue grew 11 percent, with emerging markets growing 21 percent—a rate I expect to continue to grow as our efforts to fully globalize the Company take effect."

FURTHER READING

Brand Finance. "Global 500 2012: Medtronic." *Brandirectory*. Accessed October 31, 2012. http://brandirectory.com/profile/medtronic.

"Fortune 500: Medtronic." *CNN Money*, May 21, 2012. Accessed October 31, 2012. http://money.cnn.com/magazines/fortune/fortune500/2012/snapshots/719.html.

"Medtronic." Interbrand. Accessed October 31, 2012. http://www.interbrand.com/en/our-work/Medtronic.aspx.

"Medtronic IPAD APPs." *Branding, Ads, Etc.*, January 3, 2012. Accessed November 4, 2012. http://robfranks.blogspot.com/2012/01/medtronic-ipad-apps.html.

"Medtronic's New Leader Outlines Growth Strategy." Reuters, August 23, 2011.

"Medtronic Signs Agreement to Acquire China Kanghui Holdings." *New York Times*, September 28, 2012.

Moylan, Martin. "Medtronic Begins TV Ad Campaign for Heart Devices." *MPR News*, February 22, 2007. Accessed November 5, 2012. http://minnesota.publicradio.org/display/web/2007/02/08/medtronicads/.

"Still on Target." *Medical Product Outsourcing*, July 1, 2009. Accessed November 3, 2012. http://www.thefreelibrary.com/Still+on+target.-a0205249828.

Wilson, Duff. "Medtronic Bypasses a Hospital Group Buyer." *New York Times*, February 25, 2011.

Yeh, Raymond T., with Stephanie H. Yeh. *The Art of Business: In the Footsteps of Giants*. Olathe, CO: Zero Time Publishing, 2004.

MERCEDES-BENZ

BRAND ORIGINS

- The founders of Mercedes-Benz are credited with inventing the world's first automobile in Germany during the 1880s.

- Gottlieb Daimler and Karl Benz operated separate companies until 1924, when the enterprises were merged to form Mercedes-Benz.
- The brand is now part of a parent company, Daimler AG, which makes cars, trucks, vans, buses, and accessories.

The *Guinness Book of World Records* credits the development of the first working car to Karl Benz in the 1880s. In 1885 Gottlieb Daimler, who would become Benz's partner at Mercedes-Benz, invented a wooden-spoked two-wheeler powered by a fraction of a horsepower, four-cycle internal combustion engine, and this vehicle is often considered the forerunner of all automobiles. There were predecessors to Daimler's motorcycle, but Daimler's was the first recognized internal-combustion vehicle and the first to incorporate a practical transmission system.

Shortly after Daimler applied for his combustion motor patent, Karl Benz of Mannheim, Germany, was granted a German patent for a three-wheel motor car he first constructed in 1844. This single-cylinder, 3/4 horsepower, benzene-fueled motor car had a combination of belts, chains, and gears to transmit power to the rubber-tired rear wheels, but no gear change was possible. Daimler's first four-wheeler, a Victoria-type motor-driven carriage, was built in 1886. By 1890 demands for Daimler's engine made expansion of his operation necessary, and a corporation was formed, the Daimler Motoren Gesellschaft, or Daimler Motor Company (DMG), as it became known in English. Benz, with several associates, formed another corporation, Benz & Company.

The first recorded auto race, sponsored by the *Petit-Journal* of Paris in 1894 and conducted over a course from

Paris to Rouen, attracted 46 entries and was anticipated as a test of the steam and electric engines against the gas-burning engines. The first three winning cars were powered by Daimler-built engines. From that time onward, the Daimler Mercedes and, later (after 1926), the Mercedes-Benz gained increasing prestige because of their high-speed performance.

At the beginning of World War I, both the Daimler and Benz factories were converted into production sites for war materials, although both resumed producing cars after the war. However, postwar Germany was beset by social unrest and a falling economy. There was little or no fuel for cars, and a 15 percent luxury tax made automobile production increasingly difficult. The disastrous market sent Benz seeking a strong partner, and the only one considered worthy of Benz was Daimler.

Merger negotiations began in 1910 and lasted for close to a decade, falling apart in 1919. Both automakers continued to struggle after negotiations collapsed, despite continued success on the racing circuit. Nearly 15 million cars were registered in the world in 1923. More than 80 percent of them were registered in the United States, and more than half of these were Fords. From sheer economic necessity, Benz and DMG signed an "Agreement of Mutual Interest" in 1924 and completed the merger by 1926. Although both companies retained their identities, the agreement was valid until the year 2000.

The new company did well. Production of Mercedes-Benz rose to 7,918 automobiles in 1927. The Mercedes-Benz diesel truck also went into production in 1927. The first two automobiles to bear the Mercedes-Benz name were the Stuttgart and the Mannheim. The merger not only helped the companies survive the Wall Street crash of 1929, but also helped to launch the brand as one for the wealthy.

In 2012 the brand, now under parent company Daimler AG, has several major divisions including Mercedes-Benz cars, Daimler trucks, Mercedes-Benz vans, Daimler buses, and Daimler financial services. The company also makes cars under the Smart and Maybach brands, and it collaborates in the manufacture of a wide range of products, from race cars to luxury furniture, via the divisions Mercedes-Benz Accessories and Mercedes-Benz Style.

BRAND ELEMENTS

- The parent company of the brand, Daimler AG, was named after one of its founders, Gottlieb Daimler.
- Mercedes-Benz was named after founder Karl Benz and a woman called Mercedes, the daughter of a businessman who marketed the brand.
- The brand's well-known trademark, a three-pointed star, is attached to the front of every Mercedes-Benz car.
- Instead of assigning a model name to its cars, Mercedes-Benz uses an unusual alphanumeric system.

The parent company of the brand, Daimler AG, was named after one of its founders, Gottlieb Daimler. Mercedes-Benz was named after another founder of the business (Karl Benz) and a woman named Mercedes (the daughter of Emil Jellinek, a businessman who was instrumental in marketing the brand during its early years). Mercedes is derived from a Spanish word that means "grace." It was legally registered as part of the brand name in 1902.

DMG began using a star as a trademark in 1909 as a tribute to founder Gottlieb Daimler, who had once predicted that a star would someday shine over his own factory as a symbol of prosperity. From 1910 onward, a three-pointed, three-dimensional star adorned the radiator at the front of each DMG car.

The DMG board immediately accepted the Daimler sons' proposal, and, in 1909, both a three-pointed and a four-pointed star were registered as trademarks. Although both designs were legally protected, only the three-pointed star was used. From 1910 onward, a three-dimensional star adorned the radiator at the front of each car.

The three-pointed star was supposed to symbolize Daimler's ambition of universal motorization "on land, on water and in the air." Over the years, various small additions were made. In 1916 the star's points were surrounded by a circle, in which four small stars and the word Mercedes were integrated. In November 1921, DMG applied for legal protection of utility patents for new variations on their trademark and lodged with the patent office a three-dimensional, three-pointed star enclosed in a circle, which included the design intended for use on the radiator grille. This design became a registered trademark in August 1923.

In addition, the Mercedes-Benz brand is known for its unique approach to car nomenclature. Unlike most other car manufacturers, who rely on model names, such as Toyota's "Camry," Mercedes-Benz uses an alphanumeric system for categorizing its cars that designates engine displacement as well as body style and engine type. To further emphasize the brand's nearly exclusive focus on luxury vehicles, Mercedes-Benz organizes its vehicles into "classes," again avoiding the more common nomenclature of "models."

The unique nomenclature, three-pointed star, and the easily recognizable grille of the Mercedes-Benz may make it the most identifiable car brand in the world.

BRAND IDENTITY

- Mercedes-Benz emphasizes meticulous engineering, powerful performance, constant innovation, extraordinary safety, and exquisite luxury.

- As "the brand of the future," Mercedes-Benz claims to set the standard for all other cars.
- Mercedes-Benz promises to stay true to timeless values and to operate in an environmentally responsible way.

Mercedes-Benz is presented as the brand that delivers meticulously engineered, powerful, innovative, luxurious automobiles that are exciting but safe to drive. As the creator of the world's first automobile, the company emphasizes a dedication to constantly improving its products: "Since inventing the car in 1886, we've simply never stopped reinventing it." Mercedes-Benz is portrayed as the brand of the future, making breakthroughs in safety, performance, and driving enjoyment that set the standard for all other cars. A slogan at the brand's website reads, "Iconic designs. Defining an era is one thing. Transcending it is another."

In describing the brand, the company uses words such as uncompromising, aggressive, advanced, groundbreaking, exquisite, extraordinary, and legendary. The brand promise includes remaining true to timeless values and manufacturing cars in an ecologically responsible way. Mercedes-Benz is promoted as the most sought-after brand on the planet: "Because to us, cars aren't just machines. And what they make us feel can't be measured."

BRAND STRATEGY

- Luxury cars are the core product line of the Mercedes-Benz brand.
- The company has tried extending the Mercedes-Benz line to include products such as helicopters and watches.
- In 2012 a line of furniture called Mercedes-Benz Style was launched as part of an attempt at global expansion.

Now a division of its parent company Daimler AG (owners domestically of the Chrysler group), Mercedes-Benz emphasizes its commitment to innovation, durability, and, most of all, luxury. Mercedes-Benz is considered to be one of the most reliable vehicles in production, and the *Guinness Book of World Records* calls the Mercedes S Class the "most durable car" ever made.

Though the brand maintains a financial services division and is associated with the manufacture of trucks, buses, and vans, the brand's strategy remains focused on the luxury car, with the emphasis on "luxury." Always trying to strengthen its image as the standard luxury car maker, the brand continues to extend itself in a variety of directions as a global symbol for high-end elegance. Past ventures have included everything from helicopters to watches, all bearing the familiar three-point-star logo and, perhaps more important, the subtle, sexy lines of Mercedes automobiles.

In 2012, for example, Mercedes-Benz extended its brand to the manufacture of high-end furniture. Produced under the label Mercedes-Benz Style, the furniture line is part of the effort to expand the brand's global footprint, sleek aesthetics, and engineering expertise to encompass a wider array of products and, in doing so, to influence the manufacture of everything from aircraft and boats to home accessories. In April 2012, the company unveiled its first chairs, tables, and other functional objects in the place perhaps best known for style, Milan. From cars to couches, the strategy for Mercedes-Benz is to imprint the brand as the label for luxury on a range of markets and on all aspects of daily living.

BRAND EQUITY

- Mercedes-Benz is frequently cited as one of the top five or ten brands in the world.
- In 2012 Harris Interactive named Mercedes-Benz the top luxury car manufacturer for a second consecutive year.
- Interbrand calculated the brand value of Mercedes-Benz at more than US$27 billion in 2011, up 9 percent from 2010.

Since 2007, Mercedes-Benz has ranked in or near the top 10 brands by SyncForce, a global brand recognition firm. J.D. Power & Associates consistently ranks Mercedes-Benz in the top five in everything from sales and owner satisfaction to vehicle performance, and consumers routinely rank the auto maker in the top five brands, according to Consumer Reports.

In 2012 Harris Interactive named Mercedes-Benz its top luxury car manufacturer for a second consecutive year. The 2012 Harris Poll EquiTrend Rankings, based on responses from more than 38,000 consumers, placed Mercedes-Benz just ahead of its closest competitor, BMW. A year earlier, Interbrand's "Best Global Brands 2011" ranked Mercedes-Benz twelfth, also naming it the "most valuable" European brand across all industry categories. According to Interbrand, Mercedes-Benz's brand value rose to more than US$27 billion in 2011, an increase of 9 percent from 2010. The Interbrand study's authors attribute the brand's success to customer satisfaction, which is the highest among automotive brands.

BRAND AWARENESS

- Mercedes-Benz is well known throughout the world for its high quality, durability, and precision engineering.
- Mercedes-Benz automobiles are manufactured and sold worldwide, a testimony to the brand's global reputation.

- The brand is widely known for its affiliation with auto racing, the Superdome in New Orleans, and soccer events.

Mercedes-Benz is well known throughout the world for its high quality, durability, and precision engineering. The global awareness of the Mercedes-Benz brand is evident in the number of countries that manufacture or assemble its luxury vehicles. As of 2012, Mercedes-Benz vehicles were constructed in at least 23 countries, from Argentina to Vietnam. Sales in these countries and elsewhere suggest that Mercedes-Benz is easily recognized as the preeminent luxury car brand. In 2011, for example, Mercedes-Benz sold more than 350,000 cars in Asia and the Pacific region, and it sold more than 250,000 cars in the United States.

Throughout its history, Mercedes-Benz has also maintained a strong presence in auto racing, with most of its recent attention focused on Formula One racing. Consumers in Europe, as well as those in India and in oil-producing nations like Saudi Arabia, most strongly associate Mercedes-Benz with racing. Finally, Mercedes-Benz holds the naming rights to the iconic Mercedes-Benz Superdome in New Orleans, and the brand also sponsors several prominent soccer players, clubs, and stadia in Germany, where soccer is by far the most popular sport.

BRAND OUTLOOK

- Because Mercedes-Benz increased in value during a global economic recession, the brand is expected to continue performing well.
- New car models and an emphasis on environmental responsibility are expected to broaden the brand's customer base.
- Mercedes-Benz has been winning awards for sustainable auto manufacturing, and the brand will be launching more "green" models soon.

Mercedes-Benz sold a total of 1.9 million vehicles in 2010, thereby exceeding the previous year's sales by 22 percent. Its brand value increased by more than US$7 billion in 2011, and, as a result, its overall brand rating jumped nineteen spots in 2011 to number 20, according to The Brand-Finance Global 500. Given the daunting global economic challenges of the early 21st century, these sales figures suggest that Mercedes-Benz will be able to maintain, if not enhance, its brand status in the years ahead.

The brand's identity is timeless, and its outlook as a car brand is strong. Given its commitment to innovation and responsibility as a car manufacturer, Mercedes-Benz should continue to be a top-20 or top-10 brand for the foreseeable future. New car models, particularly those designed to enhance the brand's "green" imprint, have

broadened the brand's reach. The S250 CDI, which features a turbocharged diesel engine, was declared the 2012 World Green Car at the New York International Auto Show in April 2012, and other hybrid, hydrogen-fuel, and concept cars aimed at maintaining luxury while reducing emissions demonstrate the brand's commitment to producing cleaner, more environmentally responsible vehicles. Mercedes-Benz has been ranked among the top 10 green brands in Germany and Italy, and, in 2012 the brand won a Plus X Award as the world's most sustainable automobile manufacturer. Moving forward, Mercedes-Benz is in position to become a global leader in green performance and innovation within the luxury automotive sector.

FURTHER READING

"Best Global Green Brands 2012: Top 50 Brands." Interbrand. Accessed September 6, 2012. http://www.interbrand.com/en/best-global-brands/Best-Global-Green-Brands/2012-Report/BestGlobalGreenBrandsTable-2012.aspx.

Brand Finance. "Mercedes-Benz." *Brandirectory*. Accessed September 6, 2012. http://brandirectory.com/profile/mercedes-benz.

Daimler AG. *Annual Report 2011*. Accessed August 29, 2012. http://www.daimler.com/dccom/0-5-1440977-1-1463300-1-0-0-0-0-0-36-7164-0-0-0-0-0-0-0.html.

————. "Facts on Sustainability 2011." Accessed September 6, 2012. http://sustainability.daimler.com/reports/daimler/annual/2011/nb/English/0/home.html.

Harris Interactive. "2012 Harris Poll EquiTrend Rankings: Luxury Automobile of the Year." Accessed August 28, 2012. http://www.harrisinteractive.com/insights/equitrendrankings.aspx.

"The History behind the Mercedes-Benz Brand and the Three-Pointed Star." *eMercedesBenz*, April 17, 2008. Accessed August 28, 2012. http://www.emercedesbenz.com/Apr08/17_001109_The_History_Behind_The_Mercedes_Benz_Brand_And_The_Three_Pointed_Star.html.

Jana, Reena. "Mercedes-Benz: Now a Luxury Furniture Brand, Too?" *SmartPlanet*, April 16 2012. Accessed August 29, 2012. http://www.smartplanet.com/blog/design-architecture/mercedes-benz-now-a-luxury-furniture-brand-too/5696.

"Mercedes-Benz." RankingTheBrands.com. Accessed September 7, 2012. http://www.rankingthebrands.com/Brand-detail.aspx?brandID=23.

Mercedes-Benz USA. "Leading through Innovation." Accessed September 4, 2012. http://www.mbusa.com/mercedes/benz/innovation.

Montagne, Lydia. "The History of Mercedes-Benz: How the Automobile Industry Came to Be." Yahoo.com, August 12, 2011. Accessed August 28, 2012. http://voices.yahoo.com/the-history-mercedes-benz-automobile-industry-8919341.html.

Silverstein, Barry. "Mercedes-Benz: Not Just a Car Brand." *Brandchannel*, May 7, 2010. Accessed August 29, 2012. http://www.brandchannel.com/home/post/2010/05/07/Mercedes-Benz-Expands-Design-Portfolio.aspx.

METRO CASH & CARRY

BRAND ORIGINS

- METRO Cash & Carry customers can buy a variety of goods at one site instead of through numerous vendors.
- Otto Beisheim founded METRO Cash & Carry in 1964 in what was then West Germany.
- METRO AG, METRO Cash & Carry's parent company, operates stores in more than 30 countries.
- Members of the Horeca (hotel, restaurant, and catering or café) industry form a core customer group for METRO Cash & Carry stores.

Looking for a better way to do business, Otto Beisheim created Metro SB-Grossmarkte, in Mülheim, West Germany (now Germany), in 1964. The store saved customers the hassle of "placing orders for the delivery of goods through multiple vendors" by allowing them to buy these items directly from a single store and then take them home, according to the METRO Cash & Carry website. These stores later became known as METRO Cash & Carry.

Beisheim's concept soon moved to other countries. METRO Cash & Carry opened Makro Cash & Carry in the Netherlands in 1968. Since then, it has opened a number of METRO and Makro stores in several countries in Europe and Asia, as well as in Egypt.

METRO Cash & Carry's international presence is matched by the global presence of its parent company, METRO AG, a retail behemoth. In addition to METRO Cash & Carry and Makro Cash & Carry, METRO AG owns the consumer electronics stores Media Markt and Saturn, the Real chain of hypermarkets (stores combining the offerings of department stores and grocery stores), and the department store chain Galeria Kaufhof, among other holdings. With these varied holdings, METRO AG is a huge company, employing more than 280,000 workers and operating in more than 30 countries.

The METRO Cash & Carry stores target business owners, in particular members of the Horeca, or HoReCa, industry. Horeca is an abbreviation for the hotel, restaurant, and catering industry (some sources say the abbreviation stands for "hotel, restaurant, and café industry"). METRO Cash & Carry stores carry food and beverages, glassware, utensils, appliances, office supplies, cleaning items, and other products for the industry.

BRAND ELEMENTS

- The wholesale stores of METRO Cash & Carry come in three sizes: Classic, Junior, and Eco.
- The stores of METRO Cash & Carry feature consistent signs, store layouts, and product placements to aid customers.
- The METRO Cash & Carry stores use the logo of the parent company, a blue rectangle with the word METRO in yellow.

METRO Cash & Carry locations are wholesale stores that sell a wide range of products to other businesses. To accommodate these products, the stores come in three different sizes. The Classic store format covers from 10,000 to 16,000 square meters, or around 108,000 to 172,000 square feet. The Junior format stores cover 7,000 to 9,000 square meters, or around 75,000 to 97,000 square feet. The Eco format stores, which are the smallest, are 2,500 to 4,000 square meters in size, or 27,000 to 43,000 square feet. In short, METRO Cash & Carry stores are large. Their size echoes the size of the parent company and its international reach. The stores are designed with their customers in mind. Their signage, layout, and placement of products all help customers find the products they want, and customers can use trolleys to help transport these products.

In addition to its stores, another visual element of METRO Cash & Carry is its logo, which is also the logo of its parent company, METRO AG. This logo consists of a blue rectangle with the word METRO in large yellow capital letters. METRO Cash & Carry stores display this logo in expected places, such as signs inside and outside of stores and on store products. The logo also appears in more unexpected places: on flags and employee uniforms, for example. In addition to bearing the logo, METRO uniforms sometimes relate to the local culture. For example, Chinese METRO hostesses wear Chinese dresses and badges with the METRO logo, thus reflecting METRO Cash & Carry's multinational and multicultural presence.

The brand's elements and retail interests can be seen in the METRO Cash & Carry's *Metro Retail Compendium 2012/2013,* a document which includes information about retailing around the world. The cover of this document features the familiar yellow METRO logo. It also features illustrations of different types of retailing. Representing the wholesale segment of the retail field is a drawing of a chef wearing the distinctive hat, clothes, and scarf of his profession. The chef pushes a trolley (cart) filled with bulk goods. The chef and his purchases illustrate the wholesale industry in general but METRO Cash Carry stores in particular, since they feature trolleys, bulk items for the food industry, and even clothing for chefs.

BRAND IDENTITY

- From its founder, METRO Cash & Carry gained an appreciation for courage, innovation, and ambition.
- METRO Cash & Carry views itself as a partner for professionals and seeks to provide them with a comprehensive array of products and innovative services.
- METRO Cash & Carry offers both high-end products and more cost-effective private-label brands. It also tries to help local economies by buying domestic products.
- The corporate culture emphasizes a performance-driven approach, openness, and internationalism.

The roots of METRO Cash & Carry's identity may lie in the personality of its founder, Otto Beisheim. After his death in February 2013, the company website featured an obituary that praised Beisheim as a pioneer and a legend. The obituary paid tribute to Beisheim for exhibiting three particular qualities: innovation, courage, and ambition. Those qualities may also apply to METRO Cash & Carry's view of itself as a brand.

On the "Company" page of its website, METRO Cash & Carry bills itself as "the leading international player in the self-service wholesale sector." The company presents itself as a partner for professionals, particularly those in the hotel, restaurant, and catering industries. METRO Cash & Carry offers a broad range of products and services customized to the specific demands of people working in its target professions. The specific focus of that partnership is providing a comprehensive array of products and efficient, innovative services.

The foundation for METRO Cash & Carry' identity was its initial business concept—that of providing businesses the opportunity to meet all their shopping needs under one roof. METRO Cash & Carry's core mission of "creating more value for the customer" is carried out in many ways. To ensure that its stores carry a comprehensive line of products, METRO Cash & Carry offers both well-known brands and more cost-effective private-label products. The company seeks to meet local needs by purchasing up to 90 percent of its stock from domestic producers and suppliers. METRO Cash & Carry stores also focus on helping their customers by offering tailored business solutions such as dedicated support for small traders in some locations.

METRO Cash & Carry sees its employees as an integral part of its customer-oriented mission, so it strives to create qualified, highly motivated employees. The corporate culture emphasizes a performance-driven approach, openness, and internationalism.

BRAND STRATEGY

- Private store brands at METRO Cash & Carry stores often target Horeca industry customers.

- Private store brands at METRO Cash & Carry stores include Aro, HORECA Select, Rioba, H-Line, Fine Food, and Sigma.
- METRO Cash & Carry stores began offering delivery services in 2009.
- Local products and suppliers are featured at METRO Cash & Carry stores.
- METRO Cash & Carry's environmentally conscious practices include packaging reduction, safety testing, and sustainable development measures.
- A 2010 television commercial for METRO Cash & Carry Ukraine demonstrates how the brand sells goods that can provide entertainment to people's lives.

METRO Cash & Carry stores feature their own private store brands, which are also referred to as own brands. These brands include Aro, a range of inexpensive products for budget-conscious consumers; HORECA Select, a line of kitchen-based items for the Horeca industry; Rioba, providing items for bars and cafes; H-Line, which includes two product lines for restaurants and the hotel/motel/boardinghouse industry; Fine Food, a line of high-quality food items; and Sigma, a line of office supplies. METRO Cash & Carry hopes to increase the sales of these brands to boost its overall financial health.

In addition to expanding its product lines, METRO Cash & Carry has also broadened its services. In another nod to customer convenience, it began offering delivery services in 2009. This move has proved profitable for the business, which reported EUR31.2 billion (about US$41 billion) in sales in 2011.

While it conducts a global business, METRO Cash & Carry thinks locally. It offers local goods from local suppliers in its stores. It has made commitments to sustainable development, reducing the amount of packaging for its brands and implementing tests of the safety and impact of its products.

As a strategy to help spread brand awareness, a 2010 television commercial for METRO Cash & Carry Ukraine incorporated brand elements and described how customers can use the brand. The spot featured long banquet tables with food, plates, glassware and other items. These tables appeared in a variety of settings that included homes, catering halls, and even METRO Cash & Carry stores (which featured METRO employees, uniforms, and logos). The spot showed people setting these tables, providing food for these banquets, and enjoying food and drink at parties. Since METRO Cash & Carry sells food, glassware, and food industry uniforms, the commercial portrays the brand as a convenient one-stop shop for people's various entertaining needs, a brand that therefore brings entertainment and enjoyment to people's lives.

BRAND EQUITY

- Brand Finance ranked METRO Cash & Carry 182nd among the 500 largest global brands and 21st on a list of top global retail brands.
- *STORES* magazine ranked METRO AG fourth on the list of the "2011 Top 250 Global Retailers."
- METRO Cash & Carry dominates the cash-and-carry wholesale market in Germany, with about a 58 percent share of that market.

In Brand Finance's list of the world's best retail brands of 2012, METRO Cash & Carry placed 21st, with a brand value of US$5.3 billion. In another Brand Finance ranking, the "Global 500 2012," which rates the world's largest brands in all industries, METRO Cash & Carry placed 182nd.

The parent company, METRO AG, also appears in international rankings. In *STORES* magazine's "2011 Top 250 Global Retailers" list, METRO AG placed fourth behind Wal-Mart Stores, Inc., Carrefour, and Tesco PLC, and ahead of fifth-place Kroger Co.

Given these rankings, it is not surprising that METRO Cash & Carry performs well in its home country. It is the leading cash-and-carry wholesaler in Germany, capturing around 58 percent of that market. Its closest competitor, FEGRO/SELGROS, holds only about a 16 percent market share.

BRAND AWARENESS

- To build awareness for its brand and the cash and carry concept, METRO Cash & Carry started outreach programs to communicate with small business owners.
- Some people have felt that METRO Cash & Carry should do a better job of communicating better about itself, especially regarding its store policies.
- METRO Cash & Carry continues it focus on the cash and carry concept internationally, providing consistency that can strengthen its brand awareness.

As it continues to open stores in new areas, METRO Cash & Carry has recognized that some people may not be familiar with its brand or the cash and carry concept. To address this, it has taken efforts to identify and reach potential customers. For example, it started outreach programs to communicate with small business owners about business, thus making them aware of METRO Cash & Carry in the process.

According to some writers, METRO Cash & Carry has not been successful in communicating about itself. In the 2009 article "Metro Cash and Carry—The INCONVENIENT Store," Marryam Chaudhry noted that her mother had difficulty shopping at a METRO Cash & Carry store in Lahore, Pakistan, in part because she did not know that only professionals could shop there. Chaudhry said that METRO Cash & Carry did not mention this fact anywhere at the store and thus was not effective in communicating vital information about the brand.

It appears that METRO Cash & Carry is attempting to reinforce the brand's activities to strengthen its awareness. When asked if METRO Cash & Carry would branch into regular customer retailing, a METRO executive noted that the company concentrates on cash and carry retailing internationally. This consistent focus can strengthen brand awareness since it informs customers what METRO Cash & Carry does and what its brand encompasses.

BRAND OUTLOOK

- METRO Cash & Carry began operating in India in 2003, had 10 stores there in 2010, and planned to open around 50 more by 2016.
- METRO Cash & Carry made 1 percent of its global revenue from Indian stores in 2012 but hoped the stores would eventually provide 5 percent.
- In the 2000s, METRO Cash & Carry faced the global economic problems and operated the La Doi Pasi (Two Steps Away) convenience stores in Romania.

Like other global companies, METRO Cash & Carry is turning to growing markets like India to build its business. The country has tremendous potential for a business and brand like METRO. A 2012 article stated that India's wholesale business had a value of US$150 billion. METRO Cash & Carry began operating in India in 2003, had 10 stores there in 2010, and planned to open around 50 more by 2016. This growth rivals its closest cash and carry competitor in India, Bharti-Walmart, which had 17 stores in the country in 2012 and planned to open more in the coming years. METRO Cash & Carry hoped that the new store growth would affect its global revenues. It made 1 percent of its global revenue from its Indian stores in 2012 but hoped to earn 5 percent of its total global revenue in the future.

Prolonged economic problems around the world hurt businesses in the early 2000s, and METRO Cash & Carry was not immune. The company, however, continued to expand, opening more stores in countries like India. It also began operating a new type of store for the company. By December 2012 it operated around 500 convenience stores in Romania under the name La Doi Pasi (Two Steps Away). These stores illustrate METRO Cash & Carry's ever-expanding involvement in global retail.

FURTHER READING

Best, Dean. "GERMANY: Metro Group Confirms 2011 Sales, Profit Fall." *just-food*, January 18, 2012. Accessed September 15, 2012. http://www.just-food.com/news/metro-group-confirms-2011-sales-profit-fall_id117972.aspx.

Braithwaite, Andy. "Metro Looks to Delivery and Private Label." *OPI*, March 21, 2012. Accessed September 15, 2012. http://www.opi.net/file/115144/metro-looks-to-delivery-and-private-label.html.

Brand Finance. "Global 500 2012." *Brandirectory*. Accessed September 17, 2012. http://brandirectory.com/league_tables/table/global-500-2012.

Chaudhry, Marryam. "Metro Cash and Carry—The INCONVENIENT Store." *HR Blog*, January 18, 2009. Accessed February 15, 2013. http://blog.ceesquare.com/2009/01/18/metro-cash-n-carry-the-inconvenient-store/.

"China Welcomes First Metro for Horeca Store." *China Retail News*, November 12, 2010.

"Germany's Metro Reorganizes Management Structures at Cash & Carry Unit." 4-traders, March 8, 2012. Accessed September 16, 2012. http://www.4-traders.com/METRO-AG-436626/news/Germany-s-Metro-Reorganizes-Management-Structures-At-Cash-Carry-Unit-14205626/.

METRO AG. "Metro Retail Compendium 2011/2012." Accessed September 15, 2012. http://www.metrogroup.de/internet/site/metrogroup/node/mgroup_retail_compendium/Len/index.html.

———. "2011 Annual Report." Accessed September 15, 2012. http://www.metrogroup.de/internet/site/annual2011/alias/mgroup_annual_report_2011/Len/index.html

METRO Cash & Carry Österreich GmbH. "METRO's Six Most Popular Own-Brands." Accessed September 16, 2012. http://www.metro.at/english/pages/metro-marken.cfm.

"Metro Cash & Carry to Launch Online Store in Q4 2012." *East-West Digital News*, June 12, 2012. Accessed September 15, 2012. http://www.ewdn.com/2012/06/12/metro-cash-carry-to-launch-online-store-in-q4-2012/.

"METRO Group." *International Directory of Company Histories*. Ed. Jay P. Pederson. Vol. 118. Detroit, MI: St. James Press, 2011.

Pandey, Onkar. "Why Wholesale Retail Is a Bigger Opportunity for Metro in India." *Business & Economy*, March 15, 2012. Accessed February 15, 2013. http://www.businessand-economy.org/15032012/storyd.asp?sid=6822&pageno=1/.

"Post-nod to FDI in Retail, Metro Cash and Carry Wholesale to Catch up on Bharti Walmart in Punjab." *Economic Times*, September 16, 2012.

"Rankings and Profiles of Food Retailers in Europe, America, Asia and Africa." Retail-index.com, 2012. Accessed September 15, 2012. http://www.retail-index.com/HomeSearch/RetailersinEuropedatabasebysectorEnglish/FoodRetailersinEuropeandworldwide.aspx.

"2011 Ranking of the Top 100 Brands." Interbrand. Accessed September 17, 2012. http://www.interbrand.com/en/best-global-brands/best-global-brands-2008/best-global-brands-2011.aspx.

"2011 Top 250 Global Retailers." *STORES*, January 2012. Accessed September 15, 2012. http://www.stores.org/2011/Top-250-List.

MICROSOFT

—■—

BRAND ORIGINS

- As teenagers, Microsoft founders Bill Gates and Paul Allen wrote computer programs for fun.
- Though it brought in just US$16,000 in its first year, Microsoft had US$1 million in annual revenues three years later.

- Some twelve thousand Microsoft employees have become millionaires, and four billionaires, from their shares in company stock.

Growing up in Seattle, Washington, during the 1960s, Bill Gates and Paul Allen were the best of friends. Technology enthusiasts from an early age, the two were writing computer programs for fun by the time they were 14 and 16 respectively. In 1972 they established a company called Traf-O-Data that sold a simple computer for recording and analyzing traffic information.

When the January 1975 issue of *Popular Electronics* featured MITS Computer's Altair 8800 microcomputer, the two decided to adapt the programming language BASIC for use on the new machine. Impressed by the result, MITS hired Allen, who had already dropped out of the University of Washington, and he moved to MITS headquarters in New Mexico. Gates, enrolled at Harvard, soon followed suit and joined his friend in Albuquerque, where on April 4, 1975, they established a partnership they named Microsoft. A year later, as Allen quit MITS to devote himself full-time to their new enterprise, the partners registered the company's trade name.

Microsoft brought in just US$16,000 in 1975, but it ended 1978 with US$1 million in revenues and a sales subsidiary in Japan. In 1979 Gates and Allen moved the company's headquarters to Bellevue, Washington, and incorporated in 1981. Microsoft moved yet again, to the town of Redmond in February 1986, and went public the following month. In the years that followed, the success of its stock would turn some twelve thousand employees into millionaires—and four into billionaires.

BRAND ELEMENTS

- The first Microsoft logo spelled out the company name on two lines, with the "O"s in "*MICRO*" and "*SOFT*" aligned vertically.
- Microsoft's third logo, introduced in 1982, included a curious-looking "*O*" that acquired the nickname "blibbet."
- A notch in the "o" of Microsoft's fourth logo made it look a little like a character in a popular video game, hence the nickname "Pac-Man logo."
- Though it went through a few versions with the addition of slogans, the "Pac-Man logo" remained in use for a quarter-century after its introduction in 1987.

The first Microsoft logo, introduced in 1975, consisted of the word "*MICRO*" above the word "*SOFT*," both in all capital letters and positioned in such a way that the "*O*"s aligned vertically. The letters themselves were each composed of seven pinstripes, which became increasingly more slender toward the inside of the letter. Near the end of the 1970s, Microsoft adopted the first of several logos that spelled out the brand name in a single line, adopting a logotype (a logo consisting only of lettering) in a bold, notched font with extended tails on several letters.

In contrast to these whimsical early logos, the third, adopted in 1982, had a much more businesslike appearance, its only flamboyant element being a curious-looking "*O*." The latter, which acquired the nickname "blibbet" (sometimes used for the logo as a whole), consisted of three concentric circles, the outermost made up of positive space, the innermost of negative, and the interior circle composed of alternating positive and negative horizontal lines. Though there was a black and white version, more often the blibbet logo appeared in a cream color against a horizontal bar of forest green.

The fourth logo, adopted in 1987, used a bold black Helvetica font, and here again the most distinctive feature involved "O," specifically the slash cut into its right side. Designer Scott Baker explained that he did this both to emphasize the word "soft" and to convey a sense of motion or speed. To some observers, however, the slash made the letter look like a figure in a popular video game, hence the nickname "Pac-Man logo." Periodically over the years, various slogans accompanied the principal logotype. Usually rendered in faint gray lettering, these included "Where do you want to go today?" (1994–2002) in centered capital letters below the company name; "Your potential. Our passion." (2006–2011) below and slightly to the right; and "Be what's next" (2011–2012) positioned all the way to the right.

On August 23, 2012, the company introduced its first completely new logo in a quarter-century, a multicolored square alongside the brand name in light gray. The square consisted of four quarters, separated from one another by white negative space and individually colored (clockwise, from upper left) red, green, blue, and yellow. According to Microsoft, the red stood for its Office productivity suite, green for the Xbox gaming system, and the blue for Windows. The yellow was not identified with any particular line. The symbol, which replicated the colors associated with the Windows logo (and, some critics noted, those of Microsoft competitor Google), had first appeared in a mid-1990s television commercial for Windows 95.

BRAND IDENTITY

- The success of the Microsoft brand and its leading products has depended in no small part on identifying them with technological innovation.
- Whereas its early logos were products of their time, later Microsoft symbols had a more timeless look.
- Taglines associated with Microsoft have tended to reinforce the idea that its products can help the consumer fulfill his or her needs and ambitions.

The success of the Microsoft brand and its leading products has depended in no small part on identifying them with technological innovation, and this in turn has meant establishing a link with both the present and the future. Looking back over the development of the brand's logos, one can see a shift in emphasis from the present to the future (and, correspondingly, from the timely to the timeless) as Microsoft's identity has developed and solidified.

The first logo, often described as "groovy" and discussed stylistically within the context of the disco era, was very much a part of its time. So too was the second version, with its wing-like, angular font that gave it a resemblance to the logotypes of heavy metal "hair bands" during that period. But with the 1982 "blibbet" logo, and to an even greater degree the enduring "Pac-Man logo" in 1987, Microsoft adopted a look that, while perhaps impersonal in comparison to earlier ones, had a timeless quality its predecessors had lacked. Rather than looking backward, Microsoft was clearly directed toward *The Road Ahead*, which was the title of its founder's 1995 bestseller.

At various times over the next quarter-century, the Pac-Man logo appeared with the taglines "Where do you want to go today?"; "Your potential. Our passion."; and "Be what's next." Each of these reinforced another key element in Microsoft's brand identity: the idea that Microsoft and its products could help the consumer fulfill his or her needs and ambitions. By contrast, the logo adopted in August 2012 eschewed slogans altogether. In their place was a four-colored square that established a clear visual link between Microsoft and its principal product, the Windows operating system.

BRAND STRATEGY

- Microsoft began as a brand marketed primarily to hardware manufacturers, but beginning in about 1990, it shifted its focus to consumers.
- A critical factor in Microsoft's early success was the deal it struck in 1980 regarding distribution of the DOS operating system on IBM PCs.
- Impressed by the graphical user interface on Apple computers, Bill Gates developed the Microsoft Windows operating system.
- Other key elements in the Microsoft product line are its Internet Explorer Web browser and the Office productivity suite.

Microsoft began as a brand marketed primarily to hardware manufacturers, but beginning in about 1990 it shifted its focus and began marketing directly to consumers. Its early successes came from its versions of existing computer languages, though it failed to capitalize on the first of these, Microsoft BASIC in 1977. Microsoft received a licensing fee of US$21,000 from Apple Computer, which went on to sell over a million machines, meaning that Microsoft only made about two cents per unit. More advantageous were its FORTRAN (1977) and COBOL (1978) versions. These had been written for an operating system used by Zenith, Sharp, and Sirius, major players in the market at the time, and this in turn made Microsoft the leading distributor for microcomputer languages in the late 1970s.

An even more important turning-point came in 1980, when IBM needed an operating system for its PC or Personal Computer and, after failing to reach an agreement with Digital Research, turned to the upstart Microsoft. After buying the rights to Seattle Computer Products' Q-DOS ("Quick and Dirty Operating System") for just US$75,000, Microsoft modified it and renamed it MS-DOS, known more commonly as just DOS. The PC quickly became a massive seller, driving sales of DOS. But even though IBM ultimately failed to maintain its dominance in the personal computer market, Microsoft prospered because it had retained the right to sell DOS to consumers and other manufacturers.

Microsoft worked closely with Apple on the development of Apple's Macintosh computer, introduced in 1984. In contrast to the typed DOS commands used on IBM PCs, the Mac had an icon-based graphical user interface that made its programs physically attractive and easier for novices to learn. Impressed, Gates set out to develop his own interface manager program, an endeavor in which he enlisted the support of hardware manufacturers and software publishers seeking to challenge the dominance of the IBM PC. The ultimate result was Windows, released in November 1985.

The year 1990 marked a watershed in several regards. Windows finally hit its stride with version 3.0, released in May, and November saw the introduction of the Microsoft Office suite. The latter included Word for word processing, Excel for spreadsheets, Powerpoint for presentations, and other programs, all packaged within an integrated system. (Later versions of Office would also include Outlook for email.) Windows and Office would, along with the Internet Explorer Web browser (introduced in 1995), become central to the Microsoft brand, though future decades saw it venture into such new realms as gaming, search engines, and cellular communications.

BRAND EQUITY

- According to Interbrand's "Best Global Brands" ranking for 2012, Microsoft is the fifth-most-valuable brand in the world, with a value estimated at nearly US$58 billion.
- While competitors Google and Apple saw their estimated value increase dramatically from 2011 to 2012, Microsoft's actually declined by 2 percent.
- On the *Forbes* list of "World's Most Powerful Brands" for 2012, Microsoft ranked highest in consumer perception.
- Though Microsoft earned a number of significant rankings in the period 2010–2012, it also saw its position decline on a number of lists.

Interbrand's 2012 "Best Global Brands" list ranked Microsoft fifth, with an estimated brand value of US$57.853 billion. This impressive ranking nevertheless placed it behind competitors Apple and Google, both of which had seen their values skyrocket: a 26 percent increase for Google, holding steady in fourth place, and an astounding 129 percent for Apple, which had jumped from eighth place to second. Microsoft, by contrast, had seen its brand value drop by 2 percent while its ranking slipped from third place.

Number one in consumer perception scores on *Forbes*'s 2012 list of "The World's Most Powerful Brands," Microsoft had nevertheless seen a 3 percent drop in its estimated brand value, rated at US$54.7 billion. This gave a second-place overall ranking behind Apple, which, though it ranked eleventh in consumer perception, had an estimated value of US$87.1 billion.

Microsoft earned a number of significant rankings in the period 2010–2012, but these also served to illustrate the challenges to its brand value. It climbed from fifth place in 2010 to second in the BrandFinance Global 500 rankings for 2011, but in the following year fell into third place. In several other indexes the changes were even less favorable. Microsoft's standing on the British Centre for Brand Analysis Business Superbrands list dropped from first to third to eleventh place, and the decline in its position on the Centre's Consumer Superbrands 500 list, from first to sixth to 45th, was even more abrupt.

BRAND AWARENESS

- From about 1990 onward, Microsoft enjoyed such prominence that brand awareness ceased to be an issue; what mattered more was public perception of the brand.
- The unwieldy and unpopular Windows Vista program, released in late 2006, had a negative impact on the Microsoft brand.
- Ironically, its very success has made Microsoft the target of scrutiny and challenges both in the marketplace and the courtroom.

From about 1990 onward, Microsoft enjoyed such prominence that brand awareness ceased to be an issue; what mattered instead was public perception of the brand. In the early 21st century consumer reaction to a couple of Windows releases illustrated the fact that Microsoft's powerful market presence could be a mixed blessing.

Windows Vista, released in late 2006, would earn negative attention for everything from its price to its security features to its performance. *PCWorld* ranked it as the worst technology disappointment of 2007, and *InfoWorld* put it in second place (behind only security cameras) in its January 2008 list of all-time technological failures. Even though Windows 7 fared much better in 2009, mixed reviews attended the August 2012 release of Windows 8. Its creators, who used the new "Metro" design language, emphasized touch screen operation and therefore removed the Start button and menus to which Windows users had long since become accustomed.

Ironically, the negative market reaction to changes in Windows also illustrated the pervasive nature of the operating system and its parent brand. During the 1990s, Microsoft had undergone a number of legal challenges precisely because it exerted what some regarded as undue influence over the market. The company weathered these cases, but its very success would almost inevitably make it a target of scrutiny.

BRAND OUTLOOK

- As it looked toward the future, Microsoft faced continued challenges from its two leading competitors, Apple and Google.
- Fields of conflict between Microsoft and its competitors included word processing, Web browsers, search engines, digital media, and smartphones.
- Throughout Microsoft's history, its products have tended to fare poorly upon release, only to improve with further adjustments and ultimately become dominant.
- Despite challenges, Microsoft, which underwent a thorough rebranding program in 2011 and 2012, still had a promising future ahead.

As it approached the future, Microsoft sought to head off challenges from its leading competitors in specific areas. Its Office productivity suite, which *Forbes* described as "Microsoft's biggest revenue driver," had seen a drop in its impressive market share, thanks to the rise of free applications such as Google Docs and Open Office. Microsoft's Internet Explorer, long the dominant browser, had begun to drop back even as the popularity of Google Chrome and Mozilla Firefox soared. Likewise the Windows digital media product line, Zune, failed to make a strong showing against Apple's iPod, while Google consistently outperformed Microsoft's Bing as the search engine of choice.

Microsoft had entered the smartphone market in 2010 and made a strong showing initially; but a rocky transition to touch screen operation resulted in a loss of position relative to Google's Android. The Windows Phone 7, however, enjoyed better results, and Microsoft teamed up with Nokia to do battle against Google and its partner Motorola. In an attempt to head off both major competitors in the realm of real-time video communications, Google Voice and Apple's FaceTime, Microsoft bought Skype for US$8.5 billion in 2011.

Yet throughout Microsoft's history, its products have tended to fare poorly upon release, only to improve with further adjustments and ultimately become dominant. Despite the challenges it had encountered in recent years, the future of Microsoft still looked strong. In a January 2013 overview explaining, as its title indicated, "Why Microsoft's Worth US$42" per share, *Forbes* estimated the brand's market share at 75 percent for operating systems and server software and 95 percent for productivity software.

A thorough rebranding in 2011 and 2012 resulted not only in a new logo but a new look consistent with the newly adopted Metro design language. In June 2012 the company introduced a product that represented a bold new step: the Microsoft Surface, a tablet computer and the first computer in its history with Microsoft's brand and hardware. Later that summer, Microsoft launched Outlook.com as a competitor to Google's Gmail service.

FURTHER READING

Badenhausen, Kurt. "Apple Tops List of the World's Most Powerful Brands." *Forbes*, October 22, 2012. Accessed January 11, 2013. http://www.forbes.com/pictures/mli45jglj/no-2-microsoft-2/.

Bott, Ed. "Microsoft Sizes up Its Competitors for 2013." ZDNet.com. Accessed January 13, 2013. http://www.zdnet.com/microsoft-sizes-up-its-competitors-for-2013-7000001816/.

Microsoft Corporation. *2012 Annual Report*. Accessed January 12, 2013. http://www.microsoft.com/investor/reports/ar12/index.html.

"Microsoft Corporation." *International Directory of Company Histories*. Ed. Derek Jacques and Paula Kepos. Vol. 125. Detroit, MI: St. James Press, 2011.

"An Overview Why Microsoft's Worth $42." *Forbes*, January 9, 2013.

Stampler, Laura. "Microsoft Unveils New Logo—Here's a History of the Design's Evolution." *Business Insider*. Accessed January 12, 2013. http://www.businessinsider.com/microsoft-unveils-new-logoheres-a-history-of-the-designs-evolution-2012-8?op=1.

Walton, Zach. "Premium Ads Drive Brand Awareness According to Microsoft." *WebProNews*, April 6, 2012. Accessed January 13, 2013. http://www.webpronews.com/premium-ads-drive-brand-awareness-according-to-microsoft-2012-04.

"Where Do You Want to Go Today? A Brief History of Microsoft's Marketing and Logos." *3B Tech*. Accessed January 12, 2013. http://blog.3btech.net/tech-news/where-do-you-want-to-go-today-a-brief-history-of-microsofts-marketing-and-logos/.

MITSUBISHI

BRAND ORIGINS

- Mitsubishi was started in 1870 by a trader named Yataro Iwasaki, who named the company in honor of his original three ships.
- The company expanded its divisions to include mining, shipbuilding, industrial manufacturing, electrical, and chemicals, the divisions later separating to form semiautonomous companies.
- After World War II, at first the company was split up under the supervision of the allied forces, but following the Treaty of San Francisco in 1951 the company came back together.
- Following an unprecedented production boom in the 1950s and 1960s, Mitsubishi further expanded its product line to include power companies and gas companies.

A well-established trader for the Tosa clan in Shikoku, Japan, Yataro Iwasaki established his own shipping company in 1870. The company, Tsukumo Shokai, started with only three chartered steamships. The company quickly expanded, and Yataro changed the company's name to Yubin Kisen Mitsubishi Kaisha. The name translates to the "Three-Diamond Mail Steamship Company." The three diamond name, Mitsubishi, hails back to Yataro's three original ships that brought him success. The company continued its expansion by offering service to China, becoming the first Japanese company to have an overseas route.

After Yataro succumbed to cancer in 1885, his brother Yanosuke succeeded him as president of the company. Under his guidance, and as competition increased in the shipping industry, Mitsubishi focused on mining. In order to save money, the company purchased the Yoshioka copper mine in Okayama and the Takashima coal mine in Nagasaki. The copper provided the materials for the company's ships and the coal helped fuel them. In 1884 the company also purchased the Nagasaki

Shipbuilding Yard from the Japanese government, helping to engineer Japan's first domestically produced steamship.

Following Yanosuke's retirement in 1893, Yataro's son, Hisaya, assumed Mitsubishi's presidency. Hisaya, a graduate from the University of Pennsylvania, restructured the company in order to support more diverse operations. Under his guidance, the company set up divisions for banking, real estate, marketing, administration, mining, and shipbuilding. Additionally, Hisaya purchased the Kobe Paper Mill, which still functioned in 2013 as Mitsubishi Paper Mills. Hisaya also backed the founding of Kirin Brewery. Mitsubishi continued its growth through World War I, as the company supplied many ships toward the war effort. The company had great success during the war under Hisaya's leadership. After the war ended, he retired at the age of 51, leaving the company to his cousin Koyata Iwasaki. Like his cousin, Koyata had received his education abroad, having graduated from Cambridge University.

Koyata continued Hisaya's work in diversifying the company, changing the previous corporate divisions into semiautonomous companies. Under his guidance, Mitsubishi began manufacturing machinery, electrical equipment, and chemicals. The two companies that were born out of this endeavor were Mitsubishi Heavy Industries, the manufacturer of automobiles, aircraft, and tanks, and Mitsubishi Electric, the manufacturer of electrical machinery and home appliances. During Koyata's time as president, the Iwasaki family relinquished some of its shares of Mitsubishi through a public offering. By the end of World War II, outside investors held almost half of the company's equity.

After the outbreak of World War II, Mitsubishi suffered losses in international business because a large part of the company's exports had gone to the United Kingdom and the United States, now Japan's opponents. Although the company was commissioned by Japan to build warships and aircraft during the war, under the allied occupation following the war, manufacturing in Japan was disbanded. Mitsubishi Headquarters was dissolved in 1946, breaking into smaller enterprises that abandoned the Mitsubishi brand. The holding company was also dissolved. However, the Treaty of San Francisco, acknowledging the end of World War II and signed in 1951, allowed international business to resume in Japan.

By 1954 the companies that had split off from Mitsubishi merged to reestablish the brand. The three-diamond logo and name were used again, although the companies functioned independently. Following the reconstruction of the brand, Japan's economy boomed and the country's industries, including Mitsubishi, saw unprecedented growth. As the company modernized, it added Mitsubishi Petrochemical, Mitsubishi Atomic Power Industries, Mitsubishi Liquefied Petroleum Gas, and Mitsubishi Petroleum Development to its already extensive list of allied companies.

BRAND ELEMENTS

- Yataro Iwasaki began calling his trading company Mitsubishi in the late 19th century, referring both to the three diamonds in the brand's logo as well as to his original three ships.
- The brand logo is derived from a combination of the Yataro family's and Tosa clan's crests, the result resembling a propeller.
- While Mitsubishi utilizes numerous slogans due to the diverse nature of the brand, the two most famous are "Driven to Thrill" and "Changes for the Better."

The brand name Mitsubishi applies to a large array of products. Mitsubishi deals in heavy industrial manufacturing, such as automobiles, ships, and aircraft, as well as electrical devices, mining, and pharmaceuticals. The name Mitsubishi was used by the founder of the company, Yataro Iwasaki, shortly after he formed his company in the late 19th century. The name translates to mean "three diamonds," paying tribute to Yataro's three original trading ships. Although the company name was briefly abandoned after the end of World War II, with the signing of the Treaty of San Francisco 1951, Mitsubishi quickly reemerged.

The brand's famous logo is three red diamonds, with their points connected to resemble a propeller. As Mitsubishi's first ships were coal-powered with propellers, the resemblance is not a coincidence. Additionally, the alignment of the diamonds is also similar to the three-leaf crest of the Tosa Clan, the first group Yataro traded for prior to starting Mitsubishi. Combined with the three-layer family crest of Yataro Iwasaki, the result is the three-diamond Mitsubishi logo. Although the exact thickness of the diamonds has changed slightly since they were first used in 1870, the logo remains basically intact.

Since Mitsubishi is comprised of many independent companies, the brand has several slogans. Mitsubishi Heavy Industries and Mitsubishi Electric both utilize the Mitsubishi logo, but differ in slogans, due to the difference in markets. Mitsubishi Motors, part of Mitsubishi Heavy Industries, uses the slogan "Driven to Thrill," encouraging consumers to purchase its automobiles based on speed and enjoyment while driving. Additionally, the company has used this longer slogan as more of a statement about the company's automobiles: "We are committed to providing the utmost driving pleasure and safety for our valued customers and our community. On these commitments we will never compromise. This is the Mitsubishi Motors way." Mitsubishi Electric has used the slogan "Changes for the Better" since 2001, as the company is continually working on advancements in appliances and other electric devices.

BRAND IDENTITY

- The Mitsubishi brand does not reflect one company but is utilized by approximately 500 independent companies that follow the same management philosophy.
- The brand is well-known for its philanthropy, as the independent companies are active with the charitable Mitsubishi Foundation.
- All the companies that fall under the Mitsubishi brand are required to follow three principles: Corporate Social Responsibility; Integrity and Fairness; and Global Understanding through Business.

The Mitsubishi brand is associated with a multitude of independent companies. There is no single "Mitsubishi" company, but there are approximately 500 independent companies that utilize the Mitsubishi brand and logo. The core of the Mitsubishi companies is run by a group of 28 members called the *Kinyokai*, which contains the largest companies of the Mitsubishi brand. Due to the independent nature and wide scope of the Mitsubishi companies, the brand is almost impossible to define. However, under the Mitsubishi brand umbrella, the companies maintain the same founding management philosophy. The companies also cooperate in areas of common interest, such as sporting events, cultural events, and public interest activities. All companies are also obligated to honor the three principles established by Koyata Iwasaki, the last president before the company was divested after World War II. The philosophies are summarized as: Corporate Social Responsibility; Integrity and Fairness; and Global Understanding through Business.

The brand is commonly associated with philanthropy, in part due to the Mitsubishi Foundation. However, because of the autonomous nature of the companies that make up the brand, philanthropic activities are left to the discretion of each company. Larger charities are approached by the brand as a whole, the companies acting jointly. The Mitsubishi Foundation is an organization that supports science and community activism under the Mitsubishi brand.

BRAND STRATEGY

- Under the Mitsubishi Corporation, the group that oversees the independent Mitsubishi businesses, the group is continually looking for new and diverse business prospects to further the brand diversification.
- Mitsubishi has significant global expansion, with offices in over 90 countries, and it utilizes its diverse businesses to provide an appropriate regional model.
- The Mitsubishi Corporation develops and operates businesses across virtually every industry, including industrial finances, energy, metals, machinery, chemicals, food, and environmental business.

As the Mitsubishi brand is not a single company, the brand does not have a single strategy, outside of continuing to diversify itself. In charge of the enterprise, the Mitsubishi Corporation develops and operates businesses across virtually every industry, including industrial finances, energy, metals, machinery, chemicals, food, and environmental business. The Mitsubishi Corporation, headed by CEO Ken Kobayashi, aims to expand the brand beyond its traditional trading operations and increase its business diversity. Mitsubishi Corporation has approximately 200 offices globally and employs nearly 60,000 people.

The Mitsubishi Corporation focuses its global strategy by region, allowing for differing economic needs. As the group is based in Japan, the companies that meet Japan's regional needs are on the forefront of the region's economy. In North America, the companies working in that region have struggled since the 2008 financial crisis, as the United States, Canada, and Mexico have close economic ties. Since the United States is still central in the global economy, Mitsubishi strives to build its brand on its existing businesses as well as creating new avenues when possible.

BRAND EQUITY

- Mitsubishi brand was dramatically affected by the Great East Japan Earthquake of 2011, but it remains one of the strongest brands in the world.
- Brand Finance ranked Mitsubishi as the 27th-most-valuable brand in the world, with competitor Sumitomo coming in 100th.
- In 2012 Brand Finance estimated Mitsubishi's brand value to be US$19.488 billion.

Mitsubishi's brand performance has increased dramatically since 2008, with a slight dip in 2012. The brand originally held a rating of AA-, but it was increased to an AA+ by 2010, with the brand value skyrocketing from US$3.002 billion to US$17.805 billion. The value of the brand dipped between 2011 and 2012, partly due to the Great East Japan Earthquake of 2011, which took a heavy toll on the Japanese economy. Mitsubishi UFJ Financial Group, Japan's largest bank holding group, had its profit fall by JPY56 billion. Mitsubishi Corporation suffered a 20 percent loss for the same period. Despite the financial struggle, Mitsubishi remains one of the strongest brands in the world, still seeing a high level of domestic brand equity.

Brand Finance's *Global 500 2012* ranked Mitsubishi 27th overall and estimates their brand value at US$19.488 billion. Competitor Sumitomo, also a Japanese-based miscellaneous manufacturer, is ranked 100th on the same list, with a brand value of US$8.881 billion. Suzuki, a Japanese competitor for Mitsubishi Motors, was ranked by Brand Finance as 232nd, with a value of US$4.433 billion.

BRAND AWARENESS

- The Mitsubishi brand is one of the strongest and most-recognized brands in the world.
- Due to the brand's diversity, the consumer awareness of the brand varies dramatically among the Mitsubishi companies.
- Because the many companies that fall under the Mitsubishi brand are very diverse in industry type, the markets and geographic locations of these companies are also very diverse, resulting in different consumer awareness for each company under the Mitsubishi brand.

The Mitsubishi brand is one of the strongest and most-recognized brands in the world. The notoriety is not due to advertisements and marketing, but is instead a result of both a long company history as well as a highly diversified brand. The company has been considered a reliable one since it was established as a trading company in the late 19th century. During its early years, Mitsubishi was expanded to include subsidiary companies in order to diversify the brand. After World War II ended and Mitsubishi was forced to dismantle, the company split into several independent companies, which, after the Treaty of San Francisco had been signed, would reunite in brand only and remain as independent companies. Because the companies are very diverse in industry type, the markets and geographic locations of the companies are also very diverse, resulting in different consumer awareness for each company under the Mitsubishi brand.

BRAND OUTLOOK

- Mitsubishi Motors has had poor performance in the United States, but has no plans to pull out of that market and is planning on releasing new vehicles after 2015.
- The Great East Japan Earthquake of 2011 dramatically affected Japan's economy, resulting in a decline of 20 percent in operating income for Mitsubishi.
- Mitsubishi Heavy Industries continues to do well, maintaining 29.5 percent of the domestic market for wind power, with plans to gain more of the global market by 2017.

As the Mitsubishi brand is involved in several different industries around the world, the outlook of the brand itself remains very strong, even if some of the companies are not performing as well as others. Mitsubishi Motors' sales decreased by 29 percent in the United States in 2012, despite the fact that the automobile market increased by 14 percent. Some of the company's problems stem from

a lack of new vehicles being released, although the company has reported it has several new vehicles planned for release beyond 2015. Japanese-based competitor Suzuki pulled out of the U.S. market at the end of 2012. However, despite the loss in sales, Mitsubishi Motors is aiming to bounce back.

Additionally, since Mitsubishi is Japan-based, the company was dramatically affected by the Great East Japan Earthquake of 2011. The disaster took a toll on the Japanese economy in terms of both infrastructure and economic activity. Mitsubishi Corporation reported a loss of 20 percent in operating income following the disaster. The Mitsubishi brand, however, remains one of the strongest in the world. The brand has not lost the domestic brand equity that had been established through the legacy of the brand.

Conversely, Mitsubishi Heavy Industries plans to capture a 10 percent share of the global offshore wind power market by 2017, using a new technology, not yet released, that will boost generator efficiency and lower costs. The company holds 29.5 percent of the domestic market share, with competitor Vestas Wind Systems slightly ahead with a 30.2 percent share of the Japanese market.

FURTHER READING

Brand Finance. "Global 500 2012." *Brandirectory*. Accessed September 3, 2012. http://brandirectory.com/league_tables/table/global-500-2012.

———. "Mitsubishi." *Brandirectory*. Accessed January 29, 2013. http://brandirectory.com/profile/mitsubishi.

"History of the Mitsubishi Logo." *Origin of the Mitsubishi Logo*. Mitsubishi Electric. Accessed January 26, 2013. http://www.mitsubishielectric.com/company/about/history/logo/index.html.

Johnson, Drew. "Mitsubishi, Suzuki Continue to Lose U.S. Market Share with No End in Sight." *Left Lane News*, August 27, 2012.

"Market Share Rankings in Japan." *Allon*. Accessed January 29, 2013. http://www.allon.info/japan-market-share.html.

"Origin." Mitsubishi.com. Accessed January 26, 2013. http://www.mitsubishi.com/e/history/index.html.

Vandezande, Luke. "Mitsubishi Outlines Plan to Regain Market Share in US." *AutoGuide*, November 12, 2012. Accessed January 28, 2013. http://www.autoguide.com/auto-news/2012/11/mitsubishi-outlines-plan-to-regain-market-share-in-us.html.

Watanabe, Chisaki. "Mitsubishi Heavy Seeks 10% of Offshore Wind Market." *Bloomberg*, January 24, 2013. Accessed January 28, 2013. http://www.bloomberg.com/news/2013-01-24/mitsubishi-heavy-seeks-10-share-in-global-offshore-wind-market.html.

MITSUI

■

AT A GLANCE

■

Brand Synopsis: Based in Japan, Mitsui is a highly diversified brand active in several industries, including chemicals, energy, and finance, with operations around the world.

Parent Company: Mitsui & Co., Ltd.
Mitsui & Co. Bldg. 2-1
Ohtemachi 1-chome
Chiyoda-ku
Tokyo 100-0004
Japan
http://www.mitsui.com/

Sector: Financials; Materials

Industry Group: Banks; Materials

Performance: *Revenues*—JPY5.25 trillion (US$63.92 billion) (2012). *Net income*—JPY434.5 billion (US$5.29 billion) (2012).

Principal Competitors: ITOCHU Corporation; Mitsubishi Corporation; Sumitomo Corporation

BRAND ORIGINS

- Mitsui & Co. is part of the *sogo shosha*, a Japanese term for general trading firms.
- Descendants of samurai warriors, the Mitsui family had founded retail stores and a bank in Japan by the 17th century.

- Beginning to trade internationally in 1874, the Mitsui family's business became known as the Mitsui Bussan Kaisha (the Mitsui Trading Company) in 1876.
- The two world wars benefited Mitsui & Co., but the company was broken up into 180 companies under postwar antimonopoly laws.
- In the 1950s Mitsui & Co. rebuilt at home and abroad, diversifying its international businesses and establishing operations in more than 60 countries.

Mitsui & Co. features diverse divisions and serves a variety of industries in countries around the world. The company is part of a *sogo shosha*, or general trading firm. This description is an accurate one for Mitsui & Co. The company has conducted business in several fields, as well as international trade, for years. Descended from samurai warriors, the Mitsui family claims an active history in business. By the 17th century the family had established a number of retail stores and a bank. Its business operated in a number of Japanese cities, and the bank even served as a fiscal representative for the Japanese government. The Mitsui company was known as one of the *zaibatsu* ("money cliques"), which were large, diversified Japanese companies that controlled large banks.

The company began international trading in 1874. It became known as the Mitsui Bussan Kaisha (the Mitsui Trading Company) in 1876, reflecting its participation in international commerce. The company opened its first foreign office in Shanghai, China, at this time as well, which enabled Mitsui to export coal and import cotton. Opened in 1892, Mitsui's Bombay (modern-day Mumbai) office imported Indian cotton. Mitsui's activities in the cotton trade helped the company provide more than 30 percent of Japan's cotton imports by 1897.

Around the beginning of the 20th century, Mitsui entered the shipping business. The company also participated in several other enterprises. Its bank profited during World War I, and, after the war, the company further prospered when it assisted other Asian countries in building industrial infrastructures. The company also benefited from Japan's increasing military activity and involvement in World War II in the 1930s and 1940s.

The aftermath of World War II, however, was a markedly different period for Mitsui. Wartime bombing had severely damaged much of Japan, including many of the company's factories and industrial facilities. The victorious Allied Powers felt that Mitsui Bussan Kaisha and similar businesses were monopolies and ordered the dissolution of these businesses. Mitsui Bussan Kaisha was broken up into 180 companies as a result of this decision, and it was denied the use of its prewar logo.

As the antimonopoly laws relaxed in the 1950s, Mitsui started to rebuild itself and began using its old logo once more. No longer part of the *zaibatsu* by 1959 Mitsui was part of the *sogo shosha* or *keiretsu* (group of banking conglomerates). The company established foreign offices, some of them in countries where Japan did not have diplomatic representation. In these instances, Mitsui sometimes served as an unofficial representative of the Japanese government.

As the company aged, it affiliated itself with a number of companies and industries in different countries. Some subsidiaries of Mitsui & Co. include Mitsui & Co. USA, Mitsui & Co. (Brazil), and Mitsui & Co. Europe PLC. One of the company's more renowned affiliates is Toyota, a company whose automobiles and parts Mitsui helps export to Canada and Chile. Mitsui & Co. has more than 150 offices in more than 60 countries. This number breaks down to approximately a dozen offices in Japan (including its Tokyo headquarters) and around 140 overseas offices, trading subsidiaries, and head offices.

BRAND ELEMENTS

- The Mitsui logo features three horizontal lines inside a diamond outline.
- According to centuries-old tradition, a man used coins found in one of three wells to start businesses, changing his name to Mitsui ("three wells").
- The logo for Mitsui Chemicals has features that correspond to and reinforce the logo of the parent brand.

The Mitsui logo features three horizontal lines inside a diamond outline. The logo incorporates three lines for the number three and the Japanese character for well (as in

an oil or water well). The word "Mitsui" is Japanese for "three wells." According to one story concerning the company's origins, around 1100 A.D., a member of the politically connected Fujiwara family found three wells on his newly purchased property. One of these wells contained gold coins, which Fujiwara used to start businesses. Fujiwara also changed his name to Mitsui to commemorate the discovery of the three wells.

The company's subsidiary logos incorporate visual and thematic elements of the Mitsui & Co. parent logo. The Mitsui Chemicals logo, for example, consists of three broad blue diagonal lines. These three lines correspond to the three lines of the Mitsui & Co. logo, while the lines' diagonal movement echoes the diagonal lines of the diamond outline of the Mitsui & Co. logo. By using recurring elements, these logos reinforce each other and solidify the Mitsui brand's visual image.

BRAND IDENTITY

- To promote its brand identity and raise its global brand awareness, Mitsui urges the use of its logo.
- Mitsui is pushing its brand in developing companies to solidify its global presence.
- Mitsui has used the phrase "challenge & innovation" in various places to reflect its use of innovation to meet challenges.

Mitsui & Co. uses its logo to promote its brand identity and raise global brand awareness. Mitsui Chemicals creates materials used in the manufacture of eyeglass lenses. In an interview in the September–October 2012 issue of *OpticPlus*, a periodical targeting the Indian eye care industry, Yasunori Nishiyama, a general manager at Mitsui Chemicals, noted that his company has been urging lens makers to use the Mitsui logo on their packaging. Using these logos would help make the Mitsui brand more visible in more markets, as this logo push is part of Mitsui's overall effort to promote itself in developing countries. Nishiyama's interview reflects the company's efforts to promote itself in a developing market, India, and once again demonstrates the global scope of Mitsui's businesses.

The phrase "challenge & innovation" appeared on Mitsui's 2012 annual report, in its advertising, and on its website. By using this phrase, Mitsui speaks volumes about its brand with just a few words and portrays Mitsui as a dynamic, progressive, capable brand.

BRAND STRATEGY

- In 2007 Mitsui & Co. sought to improve its brand awareness by changing the names of some of its financial subsidiaries.
- In 2012 Mitsui's Chuo Mitsui Trust and Banking and an affiliated bank merged with Sumitomo Trust and Banking to form Sumitomo Mitsui Trust Bank Ltd.

- Working with Interbrand, Mitsui Fudosan Group's Hotel Sun Garden changed its name to Mitsui Garden Hotel and emphasized relaxation, comfort, and luxury for business travelers.
- Mitsui & Co. owns a diverse range of brands, including the Mitsui Foods International brand.

Mitsui & Co. has taken measures to improve its corporate management and brand recognition. In 2007 the company strengthened its hold on some subsidiaries in its financial division by designating them direct subsidiaries entirely owned by Mitsui holding companies. It also renamed some of Mitsui's financial companies, creating Chuo Mitsui Asset Trust & Banking Co., Chuo Mitsui Trust Holdings, Inc., and Chuo Mitsui Trust Group. Mitsui made these name changes "to unify our corporate branding under the 'Chuo Mitsui' name and increase our brand awareness," according to a statement posted on the website *Private Banking.com*. In 2012 the company brand evolved once again, as Chuo Mitsui Trust and Banking, its affiliate Chuo Mitsui Asset Trust and Banking, and Sumitomo Trust and Banking merged to form Sumitomo Mitsui Trust Bank Ltd. (SMTB), a large trust bank.

At about the same time, Mitsui's hotel group also changed its brand strategy. Mitsui Fudosan Group worked with the brand management firm Interbrand to transform the brand image for its chain of Japanese hotels. In this rebranding, the Mitsui Fudosan Group's Hotel Sun Garden underwent a name change and became Mitsui Garden Hotel. Interbrand and Mitsui then determined that the hotel's target clientele would be businesspeople seeking relaxation and comfort after a hard day's work, who would pay more for accommodations that met these needs. The hotel has reinforced these concepts of relaxation, comfort, and luxury by providing special sleep pillows, bottled water with labels bearing the Mitsui Garden Hotel name, and other goods and services for its guests.

In addition to its many different divisions, affiliates, products, services, and locations, Mitsui owns a diverse range of brands. Mitsui Foods International provides food for the international market with its Empress and Pacific Premium brands and provides foods for the private brands of other companies, such as supermarkets and other store chains and food distributors. Mitsui Foods International is one example of the many companies in several fields that operate under the Mitsui corporate umbrella.

BRAND EQUITY

- The 2012 merger that formed Sumitomo Mitsui Trust Bank Ltd. (SMTB) created Japan's largest trust bank.
- Mitsui & Co. owns and operates two of the top five commercial banks in Japan.

- In Brand Finance's Global 500 brand rankings for 2012, Mitsui placed 49th, with a brand value of US$15.4 billion.

A large conglomerate, Mitsui & Co. consists of other large component companies. The 2012 merger between banks owned by Mitsui and the Sumitomo Corporation created the banking company Sumitomo Mitsui Trust Bank Ltd. (SMTB). SMTB is Japan's largest trust bank. It is also the fifth-largest commercial bank in the country. One of the four larger banks is the Sumitomo Mitsui Banking Corporation. Thus, the commercial banks of Mitsui & Co. compete against each other.

Its success in the financial sector and other areas, as well as its global presence, has made Mitsui a leading global brand. In 2012 Brand Finance's Global 500 brand ranking placed Mitsui 49th on the list of the 500 best global brands, with a brand value of US$15.4 billion. This was a significant jump from the previous year, when Mitsui placed 178th on the same list with a brand value of US$5.6 billion.

BRAND AWARENESS

- Awareness of the Mitsui brand is complicated by the fact that it is such a diversified brand.
- The Mitsui USA Foundation has received honors for its efforts in philanthropy, education, and cultural awareness
- Intel has given Mitsui Chemicals awards for its excellence as a supplier, illustrating the brand's interest and success in customer satisfaction.

Overall brand awareness of the Mitsui brand is complicated by the fact that it is such a diversified brand. Efforts have thus been made to promote international awareness through charitable works. Consumers may not be familiar with the brand's individual businesses but may at least recognize the brand name. For instance, in 2009, New York City's International House honored Mitsui for the work of the Mitsui USA Foundation, which encourages international awareness and cultural exchange, provides scholarships, assists the disabled, and performs other functions. Mitsui's participation in the Mitsui USA Foundation portrays it as a brand interested in philanthropy, education, cultural awareness, and other areas. Since Mitsui received honors for these endeavors, other people have recognized Mitsui's interest and success in these areas.

Other awards have recognized Mitsui's success in specific areas. Intel has given Mitsui Chemicals multiple Supplier Continuous Quality Improvement Awards. Intel uses this award to honor what it feels are its best suppliers; Intel suppliers like Mitsui Chemicals must earn high marks in several categories on Intel's achievement reports to receive this award. This award demonstrates the Mitsui brand's goal to satisfy its customers and the successful completion of this goal. It also demonstrates that other companies have acknowledged this success.

BRAND OUTLOOK

- Committing itself to developing markets, Mitsui has partnered with Dow Chemical Company in a joint venture to produce ethanol in Brazil.
- Since the 1990s, Mitsui has worked with the Chinese steel company Baosteel Group to provide products and services for the steel industry and other industries.
- In 2011 Mitsui became the first Japanese company to develop a housing sales business in southern China.

As a company with a long international history, Mitsui continues to diversify its global business. A website for its basic chemicals unit asserts that "[w]hile working to play a major role in Asia and in high growth emerging markets, we are investing in businesses in response to structural changes in the chemicals industry." One of these emerging markets is Brazil. In 2011 the company announced a partnership with the American Dow Chemical Company. In this partnership, Mitsui bought half of Dow's equity in a proposed venture in Brazil. This joint venture would use sugar cane to make ethanol for use in various applications, including packaging, medicine, and hygiene.

Mitsui is also heavily involved in emerging markets in China. In the 1990s, the company began working with the Chinese steel company Baosteel Group. This partnership provided products and services for the steel industry and industries requiring steel, such as the automotive industry. As China has become a major steel exporter, Mitsui's brand has also continued to grow alongside the emerging markets in which the company is involved.

The company has also entered the Chinese real estate market. In 2011 the Mitsui Fudosan Residential Co., Ltd., announced its intention to develop condominiums in Foshan, Guangdong province, China. This endeavor marks the first time a Japanese company has developed a housing sales business in southern China, and it is yet another example of the diverse global business operations of Mitsui & Co.

FURTHER READING

Bolar, Siraj. "In Conversation." *OpticPlus*, September–October 2012. Accessed October 29, 2012. http://opticplus. fourplusmedia.com/current-issue/in-conversation/.

Brand Finance. "Global 500 2012." *Brandirectory*. Accessed October 26, 2012. http://brandirectory.com/profile/mitsui.

"Chuo Mitsui Asset Trust & Banking Co Ltd." Privatebanking. com. Accessed October 26, 2012. http://www.privatebanking. com/user/extra_info.jsp?location_id=7023&category_id= 9&account_id=60342&published=1&page_id=0&.rnd= 0eed0ed64842479699e937dab3b3d6cb.

"Mitsui & Co., Ltd." *International Directory of Company Histories.* Ed. Tina Grant. Vol. 110. Detroit, MI: St. James Press, 2010.

Mitsui Fudosan Residential Co., Ltd. "Participation in Housing Sales in Southern China: a First for a Japanese Developer; Participation in Housing Sales Operations in Foshan Lingnan Tiandi in Foshan, Guangdong Province, China." December 1, 2011. Accessed October 29, 2012. http://www.mitsuifudosan. co.jp/english/corporate/news/2011/1201/index.html.

"Mitsui Garden Hotel." Interbrand. Accessed October 26, 2012. http://www.interbrand.com/en/our-work/MITSUI-GARDEN-HOTEL-MITSUI-GARDEN-HOTEL.aspx.

Mitsui Global Precious Metals. "The History of Mitsui & Co." Accessed October 26, 2012. http://www.mitprecious.com/about/history-mitsui-co/.

Mitsui-Soko (Europe). "Company Mitsui-Soko (Europe) S.R.O.—Warehousing, Logistics, Distribution, Forwarding, Customs Services." Accessed October 26, 2012. http://www. mitsui-soko.eu/introduction?lang=en.

Saito, Tokuhiko. "Japan's Largest Trust Bank Is Born." *Asahi Shimbun AJW*, April 2, 2012. Accessed October 26, 2012. http://ajw.asahi.com/article/economy/business/AJ201204020034.

MOËT & CHANDON

■

BRAND ORIGINS

- Moët & Chandon was established in 1743 and found early favor with royalty and aristocracy.
- Queen Victoria gave Moët & Chandon a royal warrant in the 19th century that was affirmed by Queen Elizabeth II in the 1950s.
- In 1987 Moët-Hennessy, Moët & Chandon's parent company, merged with Louis Vuitton to form the luxury conglomerate LVMH.

One of the oldest brands in the world, the House of Moët & Chandon was established in 1743 in the Champagne region of France. It was founded by Claude Moët as the House of Moët, the first champagne house in Epernay, the capital of the Champagne region. Though it was originally only popular regionally, Moët & Chandon was associated with the highest members of society from the beginning. The favorite mistress of Louis XV, Madame de Pompadour, was especially fond of Moët & Chandon champagne.

Claude Moët's heir, grandson Jean-Rémy Moët, further built the reputation of the champagne as a high-quality product and expanded its market, creating a pioneering sales network outside of France. Because of his efforts, Moët & Chandon was favored by the European aristocracy, which took up champagne as a luxury drink in the late 1700s. He sent cases to the Russian czar as well as courts in Russia and Spain, helping Moët & Chandon become a brand known throughout Europe. Napoleon Bonaparte celebrated his victories with Moët & Chandon.

Jean-Rémy Moët regarded the looting of his product as an opportunity to spread the word about Moët & Chandon. During the Napoleonic Wars, Cossack and Prussian troops looted the cellars located below the streets of Epernay where Moët & Chandon and other champagne houses fermented and stored their bottles. The soldiers praised Moët & Chandon champagne when they returned home.

The brand continued to expand internationally, sending its first bottles of champagne to China in 1843. Moët & Chandon became known worldwide in the 1800s and was regarded as innovative and an industry leader. For example, in 1842 it became the first champagne producer to make a vintage champagne (that is, produced from grapes from a single harvest, not a blend from different years). Queen Victoria favored Moët & Chandon champagne. In 1893 Victoria gave the brand a royal warrant (recognition for supplying a good or service for at least five years to the royal household). It was reaffirmed by Queen Elizabeth II in 1955.

By the early 20th century, Moët & Chandon was being exported to new markets such as Japan and Singapore. The champagne also found favor with the new aristocracy of the period: celebrities. Singer Josephine Baker and actress Sarah Bernhardt were two of many who favored Moët & Chandon and drank it in public early in the century. The brand became a favorite of Hollywood stars following actress Grace Kelly's marriage to a European aristocrat in the 1950s.

During the mid-20th century Moët & Chandon was revived as a company under the pioneering leadership of Count Robert-Jean de Vogüé. In addition to creating the Dom Pérignon champagne brand in 1936, he expanded Moët & Chandon into other luxury product areas, including perfume, after World War II. In 1971 Vogüé merged Moët-Chandon with Hennessy & Co., a producer of cognac, leading to the creation of the company Moët-Hennessy.

After Vogüé's death in the mid-1970s, Moët-Hennessy was helmed by Vogüé's protégé, Alain Chevalier. Under his leadership Moët-Hennessy merged with Louis Vuitton, a luxury luggage maker, forming the French luxury conglomerate LVMH in 1987. The US$4 billion deal linked Moët & Chandon with a number of luxury brands and items. In addition to champagne, wine, and spirits, LVMH produced perfumes, cosmetics, watches, jewelry, luxury leather goods, and handbags, and it owned department stores. By 2011 LVMH's wine and spirits division, which included Moët & Chandon, had revenues of US$5.1 billion.

BRAND ELEMENTS

- Moët & Chandon takes its names from Claude Moët, the brand's founder, and Pierre-Gabriel Chandon de Brialles, the husband of his great-granddaughter.
- The Moët & Chandon logo reflects its origins as a family business and champagne favored by royals.
- In 2005 Moët & Chandon launched the "Be Fabulous" advertising campaign.

As a brand, the Moët & Chandon name is a key element, a reminder of the champagne's French origins and long-term family commitment to excellence. Moët is the last name of the brand's founder, Claude Moët, a master vintner who, in the eighteenth century, established a vineyard near Epernay that became the basis for the champagne's

unique flavor. Claude Moët's son, grandson, and great-grandson also helmed Moët. The Chandon of the brand name was adopted in the 1830s when the husband of Claude Moët's great-granddaughter, Pierre-Gabriel Chandon de Brialles, joined the company and helped guide it to greater growth through expansion and a vast increase in bottle sales in the nineteenth century.

Though Moët & Chandon was transformed from a family-owned venture to a corporation in the mid-1950s, the brand's name reflects its commitment to heritage and tradition. This legacy is also echoed in Moët & Chandon's simple logo, which consists of the brand name at center in black, with the phrase "fonde en 1743" (established in 1743), a royal crown for its heritage as the champagne of French kings, and the word "Champagne," because its grapes come from the Champagne region in France, surrounding it.

In 2005 Moët & Chandon launched a new advertising campaign, "Be Fabulous," which included the tagline "Make a marvelous time more marvelous together with Moët & Chandon." This advertising underscored the link between the champagne and an upscale, luxurious lifestyle, a key element of the brand.

BRAND IDENTITY

- From its start, Moët & Chandon has been identified with high society, celebrity, and celebration.
- Moët & Chandon has sponsored London Fashion Week since 1998.
- In 2009 Moët & Chandon hired actress Scarlett Johansson as the first "face" of its champagne.

For nearly the entirety of Moët & Chandon's existence, an important aspect of the company's identity has been defined by those who drank the champagne. Brand founder Claude Moët and his heirs sought to associate Moët & Chandon with royalty, aristocracy, and other leading members of society. The champagne became famous for being consumed by such well-known leaders as King Louis XV, Napoleon Bonaparte, and Queen Victoria. As the culture of celebrity rose in status in the 20th and 21st centuries, Moët & Chandon ensured its brand would be identified itself with these modern-day elites including singers, actors, actresses, and athletes. Thus, Moët & Chandon is connected to the ideas of quality and a sense of privilege, like many luxury brands, and the concept of celebration, especially one that is high-end.

In the late 20th and early 21st centuries, Moët & Chandon selected sponsorships that reflected this brand identity. The company began sponsoring London Fashion Week in 1998 and continues to sponsor events at international fashion weeks in cities like Paris, Milan, Hong Kong, Madrid, and New York.

While the brand had been favored by mid-20th century film stars such as Cary Grant and Audrey Hepburn, Moët & Chandon associated its champagne with glamorous, often celebratory, events of the film industry as well. In 1953, it began a partnership with the Cannes International Film Festival. By 2008 Moët & Chandon was the official champagne of the opening ceremonies of the festival. Beginning in 1990, Moët & Chandon served as the official champagne of the Golden Globe Awards, and in 2008, the Academy Awards. In 2010 Moët & Chandon became the title sponsor of the British Independent Film Awards, which was renamed the Moët British Independent Film Awards.

The champagne industry struggled during the worldwide economic downturn that began in 2008, leading Moët & Chandon to take a new direction in its marketing and identity building worldwide. In 2009 Moët & Chandon became the first champagne house to have a Hollywood celebrity ambassador, actress Scarlett Johansson. She was featured in campaigns that emphasized celebration and cinema.

Since the early 20th century, Moët & Chandon sought out sporting events, such as international car and boat races, which further add to its identity as an elite drink consumed during celebrations. These have included Formula One racing, the 24 Hours of Le Mans, and the America's Cup. More recently, Moët & Chandon was the official champagne of the 2011 and 2012 U.S. Open tennis tournament, and in 2012, it became the first champagne to partner with the Kentucky Derby. As the brand moved toward high-end sports sponsorships, Moët & Chandon hired tennis star Roger Federer to serve as the "face" of the brand, replacing Johansson in late 2012.

BRAND STRATEGY

- Moët & Chandon introduced vintage champagnes in 1842.
- Moët & Chandon revitalized its brand with the introduction of Mini Moëts in the 1930s.
- Ice Imperial, which debuted in 2011, was the first champagne intended to be served with ice cubes.

While the quality of Moët & Chandon's champagne has remained high over its long history, the company has sought to be innovative, creating new products and ideas that have strengthened it as a brand. Moët & Chandon first devised the idea of a vintage champagne in 1842 and had produced only 70 vintage champagnes between 1842 and 2012. In the 1930s, Moët & Chandon introduced mini Moëts, miniature versions of the Moët & Chandon bottles. Mini Moëts became popular among the fashionable people who frequented cafés in Paris.

More recently, Moët & Chandon has introduced limited-edition offerings that have exceptional value because of their small quantities, thus underscoring the brand's luxury, high-end identity. In 2010, for example, the company sold a limited edition Gold Awards Moët & Chandon Imperial Bottle to celebrate its 20th anniversary as the official champagne of the Golden Globes.

Some campaigns were more long term. In the late 1990s, the company began working to increase the visibility of its new nonvintage rosé champagne, first with special advertising and packaging around Valentine's Day and later with a formal launch during London Fashion Week in 1998. As sales of Moët & Chandon Rosé Imperial increased in the early years of the 2000s, the marketing of rosé champagne was conducted throughout the year. Between 2000 and 2007 rosé champagne's share of the international market grew 7 percent, primarily because of Moët & Chandon's influential effort to promote the product. Moët & Chandon's rosé champagne sold particularly well among Japanese women.

As champagne sales dipped during the worldwide economic downturn that began in 2008, Moët & Chandon continued search for ways to gain new sales. In 2011 the company launched the first champagne to be served with ice cubes, Ice Imperial, which was targeted at beach resorts and warm-weather hot spots, such as Miami and Saint-Tropez.

BRAND EQUITY

- Moët & Chandon is the world market leader in champagne.
- Interbrand's Best Global Brands list included Moët & Chandon at number 98 in 2012, with a value of US$3.82 billion.
- Moët & Chandon is recognized as one of the most valuable luxury brands in the world.

Moët & Chandon is the market leader in champagne worldwide. According to the *Drinks Business* 2012 survey of the major champagne brands, Moët & Chandon remained number one by volume, with 2.21 million nine-liter cases sold. It was also one of the most valuable champagne brands and one of the top luxury brands. According to the Brand Finance's Global 500 list of top brands, Moët & Chandon had a brand value of US$2.82 billion in 2012 and an enterprise value of US$57.52 billion.

In 2012 Interbrand's Best Global Brands list included Moët & Chandon at number 98 with a brand value of US$3.82 billion—a 13 percent decline from 2011. On the Interbrand list of the top-100 brands of 2012, Moët & Chandon ranked ninth among luxury brands, with a brand value of US$4.22 billion. It had high brand momentum, despite an 8 percent decline in brand value from 2011 to 2012. The economic downturn, among other factors, affected the brand's value, though it was still considered strong.

BRAND AWARENESS

- Moët & Chandon is considered a pedigree brand.
- According to the BrandZ Top 100 Most Valuable Global Brands list, Moët & Chandon ranked number one in 2012 in terms of brand contribution.
- Moët & Chandon is the number one champagne brand worldwide in terms of volume sold.

Moët & Chandon has a long history and has been identified as a producer of high-quality champagne since the 1740s. It is a pedigree brand—that is, it is produced in the Champagne region of France. Pedigree brands are linked to certain contexts and qualities specific to the brands because of their backgrounds. Champagnes produced with grapes that do not come from the region of Champagne are known as sparkling wines and do not have the same level of prestige. This pedigree adds to Moët & Chandon's top-of-mind awareness worldwide.

According to the BrandZ Top 100 Most Valuable Global Brands list, Moët & Chandon was number one in 2012 in terms of brand contribution, a measurement of how a brand creates desire and encourages loyalty and how it distinguishes itself from its rival brands. A high brand contribution often includes an emotional connection for consumers. Moët & Chandon cultivates this deep awareness by linking its champagne with high-profile celebrations, high fashion, celebrity, film culture, and prestigious sporting events. Moët & Chandon has a particularly strong presence in France, the United States, Canada, Argentina, Australia, the United Kingdom, and Venezuela. The champagne division of Moët & Chandon's parent company dominates the U.S. market, controlling 67 percent, and translated its brand awareness to vastly increased sales in the Middle East and Africa, Asia Pacific, and Russia markets between 2001 and 2011.

BRAND OUTLOOK

- Moët & Chandon has invested heavily in advertising and has not discounted its product.
- Moët & Chandon has focused on growing markets in Asia, the Middle East, and Russia, a strategy that it will continue in the 21st century.
- Moët & Chandon and Dom Pérignon controlled about 80 percent of the champagne market in India in the early 21st century.

Moët & Chandon's brand value has made it a strong, long-term commodity and a market leader for many decades. The market for champagne struggled during the worldwide economic downturn that began in 2008, and Moët & Chandon's sales also slowed because of supply issues.

Nevertheless, the champagne industry was relatively steady compared to the markets for other alcoholic beverages. Strong marketing by brands such as Moët & Chandon led to champagne becoming an everyday drink, with more solo consumption becoming the norm. Such marketing also led to more champagne bars focusing on the beverage.

Moët & Chandon's ongoing success, expected to continue well into the 21st century, comes from heavily investing in advertising and maintaining its premium pricing instead of discounting to increase sales. Moët & Chandon also has worked to enhance the appeal of the brand and strengthen its distribution network. In addition to conducting a controlled increase in champagne volumes, the company saw demand recover in its traditional markets: Europe, North America, Australia, and the United Kingdom.

Moët & Chandon has, with much success, made a concentrated effort to grow in China, Japan, Singapore, and other Asian markets, as well as the Middle East and Russia. This was a strategy embraced by Moët & Chandon's parent company. In 2011 the LVMH wine and spirits division, which included several champagne brands, sold 55.5 million bottles of champagne and accounted for 14.9 percent of LVMH's revenues. These numbers marked an increase of about 8.7 percent over 2010 in a sagging economy. Moët & Chandon, along with fellow LVMH champagne brand Dom Pérignon, controlled about 80 percent of the champagne market in India, one of many emerging markets where the brand is expected to remain a leader.

FURTHER READING

"Best Global Brands of 2012." Interbrand. Accessed December 4, 2012. http://www.interbrand.com/en/best-global-brands/2012/MoëtChandon.

Brand Finance. "Global 500 2012." *Brandirectory*. Accessed December 4, 2012. http://brandirectory.com/league_tables/table/global-500-2012.

Carroll, Arati Menon. "'Champagne's Greatness Lies in Its Pleasure.'" *Economic Times*, February 27, 2010.

Millward Brown. "BrandZ Top 100 Most Valuable Global Brands 2012." Accessed December 4, 2012. http://www.millwardbrown.com/brandz/2012/Documents/2012_BrandZ_Top100_Report.pdf.

"Moët & Chandon." *Drinks Business*, September 6, 2012. Accessed December 3, 2012. http://www.thedrinksbusiness.com/2012/09/top-10-champagnes/2/.

"Moët & Chandon: The Vintage Brand." *Brand Royalty*. Ed. Matt Haig. London: Kogan Page, 2004.

Nassauer, Sarah. "How Moët & Chandon Made Rosé Champagne Fashionable." *Wall Street Journal*, February 15, 2007.

"A Study of Brands: Moët & Chandon: A Toast in Great Champagne." *Daily Yomiuri* (Tokyo, Japan), April 20, 2008.

"Worldwide 100." *Beverage Executive*, October 2012. Accessed December 4, 2012. http://www.beverageworld.com/userfiles/documents/BB_Top_100.pdf.

MORGAN STANLEY

—■—

BRAND ORIGINS

- The employees Henry S. Morgan and Harold Stanley left J.P. Morgan in 1935 to start their own company, Morgan Stanley.
- Morgan Stanley worked with many major companies over its history, including Apple Inc., the General Motors Company, and Google Inc.
- Morgan Stanley has also grown through acquisition, having acquired Dean Witter and Brooks, Harvey, & Co., which helped Morgan Stanley venture into the real estate market.

Morgan Stanley was founded in 1935 as a result of the Glass-Steagall Act of 1933. The act was an extensive reconstruction of the entire U.S. banking system. One part of the act obligated banks to separate commercial operations from investment operations, stating that one bank could no longer do both. Founded by John Pierpont Morgan in 1871, the bank J.P. Morgan opted to maintain the commercial portion of its company. Its employees Henry S. Morgan and Harold Stanley left to form a company that dealt with securities underwriting. The result was Morgan Stanley.

The new, independent company was immediately profitable, receiving over a quarter of the market share, over US$1 billion in its public offerings, during its founding year. The company gained notoriety during World War II because of its contributions to a campaign that raised US$1.5 million for the U.S. Committee for the Care of European Children. Following the war the company ventured into new projects. In 1952 Morgan Stanley co-managed the World Bank's US$50 million triple A-bond offering to help finance Europe's reconstruction. Also during the 1950s Morgan Stanley aided the General Motors Company with its US$300 million debt, the International Business Machines Corporation with its US$231 million stock offering, and the United States Steel Corp. with its US$300 million debt.

The 1960s and 1970s witnessed major corporate growth for Morgan Stanley. In 1962 the company introduced the first viable computer-based system for financial analysis, which brought about a new strategy for investments. The company also went multinational during the 1960s, opening its first office in Paris in 1967 under the name Morgan & Cie International S.A. The company also began growing through acquisition, starting with Brooks, Harvey, & Co., which led to the expansion of the company's real estate capabilities. In 1970 the company opened its first office in Tokyo, becoming the first international investment bank to have a presence there.

The 1980s were a time of international growth for the company, during which offices in Frankfurt, Hong Kong, Luxembourg, Melbourne, Milan, and Zurich were opened. In 1980 Morgan Stanley led Apple Inc.'s initial public offering (IPO). Four years later, in 1984, the company introduced the first automated trade processing system. Morgan Stanley went public in 1986.

By 1995 Morgan Stanley had ventured into Asia, merging with the China Construction Bank to form the China International Capital Corporation. The company furthered its expansion through acquisition in 1996, when it purchased Dean Witter, an American stock brokerage and securities firm that worked with retail clients. Thereafter, the company changed its name to Morgan Stanley Dean Witter Discover & Co. The name changed again in 1998 to Morgan Stanley Dean Witter & Co.; however, by 2001 the company was simply known as Morgan Stanley.

Morgan Stanley had offices in the World Trade Center during the terrorist attacks on September 11, 2001. The offices had originally been held by Dean Witter, but were acquired through the corporate merger. Morgan Stanley lost 13 employees during the attack, while the remaining 2,600 employees were safely evacuated. The company has since moved offices to lower Manhattan.

In 2004 the company aided in Google Inc.'s IPO, the largest Internet IPO in history as well as the largest auction-based IPO in U.S. history. Through 2012 the company had three core units: Institutional Services, Global Wealth Management, and Asset Management.

BRAND ELEMENTS

- Morgan Stanley's name comes from a combination of its two founders' names: Henry S. Morgan and Harold Stanley.
- Morgan Stanley's logo is simple, containing the company's name in white, black, or gray writing.
- Morgan Stanley has used two main slogans, "One client at a time" and "World Wise," the latter was released at the peak of the U.S. housing bubble of 2008.

The company's name is a simple combination of the founders' names: Henry S. Morgan and Harold Stanley. The Morgan Stanley logo is displayed as the company's name in thin sans-serif script and is often seen in black, white, or gray. The intent is to project the company as straightforward, elegant, and no frills. As an investment company, the majority of its clients want a direct approach, assistance in knowing where money should be invested, and assurance that the company is reliable. The logo emanates this concept with its simplistic and easy-to-spot design.

The company has used two noteworthy slogans. The first was "One client at a time," meaning that Morgan Stanley focuses on the individual client's needs as opposed to taking on several clients at a time. The intent of the slogan was to ensure that clients would have personalized attention and service. The most recent slogan, launched in 2008, was "World Wise." Being a play on the term *worldwide*, the slogan was poorly timed, as it came about very close to the housing bubble of 2008 in the United States. Because Morgan Stanley was involved with the real estate market, the company was affected by the economic downturn.

BRAND IDENTITY

- Morgan Stanley strives to be a community-oriented and environmentally friendly company by employing programs that help build affordable housing and create sustainability in new markets.
- Morgan Stanley's major priorities are responsible business practices and helping clients formulate a realistic strategy for investment success.
- In 2004 Morgan Stanley assisted with Google Inc.'s initial public offering, which was the largest Internet IPO in history as well as the largest auction-based IPO in U.S. history.

Morgan Stanley's brand identity is twofold; the company tries to meld being an attractive investment bank for large businesses with making positive contributions to society and the environment. On its website, Morgan Stanley states that it is "dedicated to making a positive contribution to society through our focus on the environment, our people, responsible business practices, community investment and strengthening the next generation of citizens." The firm strives to promote itself as a beneficial company for communities around the globe. To achieve this priority, Morgan Stanley has partnered with educational institutions, governments, agencies, and nonprofits to create affordable housing and aid in small business loans. Additionally, Morgan Stanley has worked on ensuring environmental sustainable development by focusing its global reach to developing new markets that can be directed to start out sustainable.

Morgan Stanley brings to its clients the notoriety of its long-used name, as well as the experience that comes along with it. The company utilizes some of the world's most-respected investment professionals who have an acute knowledge of financial opportunities and risks. Morgan Stanley also states that it creates strategies for its clients that address short- and long-term goals and can adjust those strategies as markets change. The company has worked with some very large corporate initial public offerings (IPOs), including Google Inc.'s IPO in 2004, which was the largest Internet IPO in history as well as the largest auction-based IPO in U.S. history.

BRAND STRATEGY

- The company split the Morgan Stanley brand into three core business units, offering a wide array of investments for customers.
- As of 2013, Morgan Stanley had a presence in 29 countries and was expanding the brand globally through social media.
- The brand is well known for working with high-profile initial public offerings, reinforcing the brand's abilities.

Morgan Stanley's name is a large part of the brand's identity and is used in all business activities for the company. Even though the company has broken down its businesses into three core units—Institutional Services, Global Wealth Management, and Asset Management—each unit still bears the Morgan Stanley brand. The three core units make up the services of the company and each represents part of the Morgan Stanley brand and its extensions. The two main reasons for the brand extensions are to expand the ventures of the brand and to customize the individual needs of customers.

As of 2013, Morgan Stanley had a presence in 29 countries and offered the same services at each location. The brand went global during the 1960s, but the bulk of the international offices did not open until the 1990s. Within the brand's global identity, Morgan Stanley aims to demonstrate that it is accessible to investors all around the world and that it offers a variety of investment options. In a different kind of marketing move to further the brand's reach, Morgan Stanley increased its social media marketing in 2012 to expand the awareness of the brand to younger potential investors.

A large part of the company's brand strategy has been dealing with high-profile initial public offerings (IPOs), which have generated a reputation for success of the brand. With the positive press that came from the Google IPO in 2004, the largest Internet IPO in U.S. history, Morgan Stanley demonstrated that it was a reliable investment brand that could handle any level of investors. Even though the Facebook IPO in 2012 proved to be an investment failure, the brand was still furthered due to the high-profile IPO with a well-known company.

BRAND EQUITY

- Morgan Stanley is ranked as the eighth best bank brand in the United States, of both commercial and investment banks.
- In 2012 Interbrand ranked Morgan Stanley 54th among the top-100 brands, with a brand value of US$7.2 billion.
- In 2012 Morgan Stanley was ranked 151st in Brand Finance's "Global 500" list, with a brand value of US$6.3 billion.
- In 2011 *Fortune* ranked Morgan Stanley 63rd among the top-500 corporations in the United States, with revenues of US$39.3 billion.

Of the banks in the United States, including both commercial and investment, Morgan Stanley is ranked eighth, according to Brand Finance. The agencies Standard & Poor, Fitch, and Moody indicate that Morgan Stanley's overall financial rating is AA-. This rating indicates that Morgan Stanley is a safe investment.

In 2012 Interbrand ranked Morgan Stanley 54th among the top-100 brands, with a brand value of US$7.2 billion. Brand Finance's "Global 500 2012" ranked Morgan Stanley 151st overall and estimated its brand value at US$6.3 billion. In *Fortune* magazine's listing of the 500 largest corporations in the United States in 2011, Morgan Stanley was ranked 63rd, with revenues of US$39.3 billion.

BRAND AWARENESS

- Morgan Stanley has had high brand awareness since the founding of the company, due to its history with the already established J.P. Morgan.
- According to *Fortune*, Morgan Stanley was the fifth most-successful commercial bank in 2012.
- In a study by the Centre for Brand Analysis, Morgan Stanley was listed as the 228th most-popular business brand in the world in 2012.

Since the company was founded in 1935, it has had high brand awareness due to its previous relationship with J.P. Morgan. As J.P. Morgan was already a well-established bank in the United States, Morgan Stanley's use of the name "Morgan" in its brand established an immediate connection for U.S. consumers. The brand's awareness is broad, with customers ranging from corporations and governments to financial institutions and individuals.

In the United States, Morgan Stanley is a top-of-mind brand in investment banking. *Fortune* magazine provides an annual ranking of the 500 most-successful companies. In the 2012 rankings, Morgan Stanley was the 68th most successful company and ranked fifth in the commercial banking industry. Morgan Stanley, while also being a commercially successful company, also makes the ranking due to high brand awareness and history. With over US$749.9 billion in assets under management and an average customer portfolio, Morgan Stanley attracts smart, wealthy investors.

The Centre for Brand Analysis conducts an annual study of the 500 most-popular business brands in the world. On the 2012 list, Morgan Stanley was ranked 228th, with a popularity index of 48.9 percent. By comparison, competitor Goldman Sachs was listed as the 143rd most-popular business brand with an index rating of 54.7 percent. The rankings are based on a wide array of criteria and research and the brands are voted on by the customers who use the brand.

BRAND OUTLOOK

- Morgan Stanley's brand image has been marred in recent years due to several high-profile and public investment scandals.
- The Morgan Stanley brand faced devastating scrutiny after it was forced to take a loan from the federal government following the 2008 financial crisis.
- Morgan Stanley has a relationship in the Asian market due to financial aid from the Mitsubishi UFJ Financial Group and the China Investment Corporation and aims to expand the brand further into the Asian market.

Given the strong brand awareness that Morgan Stanley has, the company has also experienced many publicized scandals in recent years. In 2005 Morgan Stanley received a US$19 million fine from the New York Stock Exchange, the largest fine in history, due to regulatory and supervisory lapses. That same year a Florida jury found Morgan Stanley guilty of providing inadequate information regarding an investment with the bankrupt company Sunbeam. The damages were listed at US$1.6 billion. Even though the verdict was overturned in 2007, the publicity surrounding it proved to be extremely negative for Morgan Stanley's brand image. The company has gone through several other lawsuits since then, further tarnishing its otherwise elite image.

More recently, Morgan Stanley handled the initial public offering for Facebook in 2012, which was a financial disaster for investors because shares sold at lower-than-expected prices and which resulted in heavy criticism and further marring Morgan Stanley's brand image. Despite the bad publicity, Morgan Stanley reported better-than-projected earnings for the third quarter of 2012, as it successfully boosted revenues in trading bonds. Even though bond trading had suffered a decrease during the summer of 2012, the company was able to rebound from this loss.

Despite the company's history of big business investments, by 2007 Morgan Stanley reported US$3.4 billion in earnings, which was a 62 percent drop from US$9.1 billion in 2006. During the fall of 2008 Morgan Stanley reported over US$15 billion in bad investments and appeared to be on the verge of financial collapse. Major competitor Goldman Sachs received more disapproval during this period, as the bank was criticized for making risky investments and, ultimately, was loaned US$589 billion by the federal government to avoid financial collapse. In comparison, Morgan Stanley borrowed US$107.3 billion from the federal government. By 2013 Morgan Stanley reported an increase in share price, but it was not fully recovered from the financial crisis. Morgan Stanley's fourth-quarter business for 2012 was worse than its rivals and was less than half of Goldman Sachs. In spite of the competition, Morgan Stanley still did better during the fourth quarter than was expected by financial analysts.

Besides the aid the company received from the federal government, Morgan Stanley received funding from the Mitsubishi UFJ Financial Group, a Japanese bank, and the China Investment Corporation, a wholly state owned company of the People's Republic of China. These two shareholders hold a combined 30 percent of Morgan Stanley. Because of this, Morgan Stanley has a massive Asian ownership interest at 31.3 percent of the company. As a result, Morgan Stanley suggested in 2013 of expanding its brand presence in the Asian market.

FURTHER READING

Blackden, Richard. "Morgan Stanley Takes Market Share from Rivals." *Telegraph* (London), July 21, 2011.

Brand Finance. "Global 500 2012." *Brandirectory*. Accessed February 4, 2013. http://brandfinance.com/images/upload/bf_g500_2012_web_dp.pdf.

Centre for Brand Analysis. "Official Top 500 2012." Business Superbrands. Accessed February 19, 2013. http://d3iixjhp5u37hr.cloudfront.net/files/2012/02/BSB12-Official-Top-500-yvd1Ux.pdf.

Dealbook. "Invesco to Buy Morgan Stanley Unit for $1.5 billion." *New York Times*, October 19, 2009.

"Directory of Financial Taglines." FinancialBrand.com. Accessed February 4, 2013. http://thefinancialbrand.com/taglines/.

Farrell, Greg. "Mortgage Meltdown Strikes at Morgan Stanley." *USA Today*, December 19, 2007.

"Fortune 500 U.S." *Fortune*. Accessed February 19, 2013. http://www.rankingthebrands.com/The-Brand-Rankings.aspx?rankingID=131&year=450.

"Global Investment-Banking Revenue." *Economist*, September 29, 2012.

Gomstyn, Alice, and Matthew Jaffe. "Bank CEOs Admit Mistakes at Financial Crisis Inquiry Commission Hearing." ABC News, January 13, 2009.

Griffin, Donal, and Michael J. Moore. "Morgan Stanley Will Buy More of Smith Barney from Citigroup." *Bloomberg Businessweek*, May 31, 2012.

LaCapra, Lauren Tara. "Morgan Stanley Beats Estimates on Big Bond Trade Gains." Reuters, October 18, 2012.

Lucchetti, Aaron. "Morgan Stanley Shares Soar on Earnings." *Wall Street Journal*, January 18, 2013.

"Morgan Stanley." History of Corporate. Accessed February 4, 2013. http://www.thehistoryofcorporate.com/companies-by-industry/finance/morgan-stanley/.

"Morgan Stanley Logo." Logo Inn, January 27, 2009. Accessed February 4, 2013. http://www.logoinn.org/famous-logos/morgan-stanley-logo.

Shayon, Sheila. "Morgan Stanley Expands Social Marketing on Twitter and LinkedIn." BrandChannel, June 25, 2012. Accessed February 18, 2013. http://www.brandchannel.com/home/post/2012/06/25/Morgan-Stanley-Social-Media-062512.aspx.

"2012 Ranking of the Top 100 Brands." Interbrand. Accessed February 4, 2013. http://www.interbrand.com/en/best-global-brands/best-global-brands-2008/best-global-brands-2011.aspx.

MORRISONS

—■—

AT A GLANCE

—■—

Brand Synopsis: Morrisons' realignment of brand identity allowed the company to refocus as "the food specialist for everyone" and highlight freshness, service, and value.

Parent Company: Wm Morrison Supermarkets plc
Hilmore House, Gain Lane
Bradford, BD3 7DL
United Kingdom
http://www.morrisons.co.uk

Sector: Consumer Staples

Industry Group: Food & Staples Retailing

Performance: *Market share*—12.3 percent (2012).
Sales—US$27.7 billion (2012).

Principal Competitors: Tesco plc; J. Sainsbury plc; Asda Group plc

BRAND ORIGINS

- William Morrison began his career in 1899 by selling eggs and butter wholesale, soon opening a shop stall at the market in Bradford, England.
- Ken Morrison transformed his father's business from a small family operation into a chain of supermarkets, beginning in 1956.
- Morrisons acquired rival supermarket chain Safeway in 2004, nearly tripling the number of Morrisons stores in England and Scotland.

William Morrison began his career selling eggs and butter wholesale, founding William Morrison (Provisions) Ltd. in 1899. Soon after, Morrison opened a stall in the Bradford, England, market, and then added stalls in other nearby markets. By the 1920s, Morrison's business had flourished enough to allow him to open his own retail stores, offering counter service by 1925. Morrison's operation remained a small business focused on the Bradford area; the company's warehouse was in the garage behind the family's home. Morrison had six children, the youngest of whom, Ken, the only boy, was born when Morrison was 57 years old.

The younger Morrison was working for his father by the age of five, running deliveries and later stocking goods in the warehouse. While his father encouraged Ken Morrison to study for a different future, Morrison joined the army at the age of 18. In 1950, with his health failing, William Morrison offered the family business to his son.

Ken Morrison approached the grocer's trade with a new perspective. Rather than the small, urban-center shops run by his father, Morrison saw the future in larger-scale supermarkets, particularly in exurban and suburban locations. At the same time, improvements in packaging and increasing branding of grocery products were occurring, coupled with a growing trend toward self-service shopping. Taking over as company chairman in 1956, Ken Morrison steered the family company into the newly developing supermarket industry, placing prices on all of its goods, and adding checkout lines, a first for the Bradford area.

Morrison next turned his attention to opening new stores. In 1962 he bought an abandoned theater in Bradford and converted it into a supermarket. Once transformed, the theater offered some 5,000 square feet of retail space and a parking lot for the company's increasingly mobile customers. The success of that store encouraged Morrison to begin opening new stores and making acquisitions of others. The company's expansion also took it into new territory. For the first time, the company began opening stores outside of its traditional northern stronghold, moving into the highly competitive southern regions of England.

The failing British economy of the late 1980s and early 1990s brought pressure on the company. Morrisons' competitors were leading a consolidation of the industry through a wave of takeovers and acquisitions that created four giant supermarket chains: Asda, Safeway, Tesco, and Sainsbury. In response to growing competition, the company focused on expansion into new markets and soon set its sights on acquiring competitor Safeway, whose stores were primarily in Scotland and southern England. The deal would nearly triple Morrisons' annual revenues as well as its store count. While the merger was met with opposition from England's Competition Commission, it eventually cleared and was finalized in 2004.

Ken Morrison's hands-on approach to his father's company remained an important factor in the firm's ability to compete in the crushing British supermarket climate. Ken Morrison was awarded knighthood in January 2000 for his contributions to England's food-retailing industry. With its history of strong sales and profit growth, Morrisons Supermarkets secured a position in 2001 on the venerable FTSE 100, a share index used to measure the financial health of London's most successful companies.

BRAND ELEMENTS

- A 1980 redesign of the Morrisons logo introduced the capital "M" on a yellow circle.
- In 2007 Morrisons redesigned its logo to make it more modern and more appealing to a wider audience, but kept the iconic yellow circle.
- To highlight a new brand image, Morrisons replaced its decades-old slogan with "The Food Specialist for Everyone."

Although formally registered as Wm Morrison Supermarkets plc, the company is usually referred to and branded as Morrisons. The original Morrisons logo was in use from 1961 to 1980. The rectangular logo featured a bold, brown-colored capital "M" placed next to "Morrison's Supermarkets Limited" on a red background. A complete redesign of the logo in 1980 featured a new block capital "M" in black on a yellow circle. "Morrisons" was positioned under the "M" and also appeared in black.

In 2007 the company redesigned its logo once again to make it more modern and more appealing to a wider

audience. The updated logo featured a thinner capital "M," now in green within the yellow circle. The Morrisons name was also now in green and featured much more prominently in the logo. The company chose to keep the yellow circle, which had become synonymous with the brand, but changed it from black to green to signify freshness and brightness.

Along with the logo update, Morrisons also changed its 30-year-old slogan from "More Reasons to Shop at Morrisons" to "The Food Specialist for Everyone." The slogan change was intended to reflect a new image as a purveyor of fresh and healthy food. Morrisons highlighted its new brand positioning with the tagline "Fresh for You Every Day." In 2010 Morrisons launched a marketing campaign revolving around the tagline "Eat Fresh. Pay Less."

BRAND IDENTITY

- Morrisons is the second-largest food producer in the United Kingdom, with its own butchers, bakeries, and fruit and vegetable warehouses.
- Morrisons stores feature a Market Street concept with separately staffed counters designed to resemble individual shops.
- Morrisons employs professional butchers, bakers, and fishmongers at each of its stores to provide personalized service to their customers.

As the second-largest food producer in the United Kingdom, Morrisons was a company with a commitment to fresh, high quality food. But faced with a stale brand image and poor customer perceptions, Morrisons relaunched the brand in 2007. Consumers were perceiving Morrisons as providing good value but decidedly inferior food. Morrisons thereupon embarked on a campaign to focus on the quality of food they could offer consumers.

Rather than buying all its food from suppliers, Morrisons has its own butchers, bakeries, and fruit and vegetable warehouses. This supply chain allows the company to ensure freshness, control quality, and reduce costs. Morrisons offers 100 percent British meats and sustainable fresh fish. Morrisons also promotes the professionalism of their skilled staff, with trained butchers, bakers, and fishmongers serving customers. These in-store professionals allow consumers the convenience of a supermarket but with a personal touch.

Morrisons seeks to appeal to customers with a Market Street concept that reproduces, around the periphery of the Morrison store, the feel of the stalls and small shops of a typical High Street. The Market Street concept utilizes a series of separately staffed counters designed to resemble individual shops. The various counters include a bakery, a butcher, a fishmonger, a pizzeria, a pie shop, an oven-fresh counter, a salad bar, and a counter of cooked meats and cheese. Market Street is a unique concept with a strong identity to Morrisons that allows the company to showcase their fresh food and on-site food preparation.

BRAND STRATEGY

- Morrisons operates over 455 stores in England and Scotland, stocking some 20,000 products and serving nearly 10 million customers each week.
- Morrisons initiated a complete redesign of its private-label brands in 2011, covering more than 10,000 products and introducing new brand lines such as M Savers, M Kitchen, and M Signature.
- In 2011 Morrisons entered the highly competitive convenience store market with a new small-store format branded M-local.

Morrisons operates over 455 stores in England and Scotland that serve nearly 10 million customers each week. Morrisons stores stock some 20,000 product lines. Morrison's private labels account for nearly 32 percent of its merchandise mix. The company initiated a complete redesign of its private-label brands in 2011, covering more than 10,000 products. The goal behind the redesign was to transform the private labels into a more coherent brand.

M Kitchen, a line of ready meals, was the first brand to be launched under this program. Created by Morrisons' chefs, it includes frozen dinners, vegetarian and Pan Asian selections, and Bistro, a line of restaurant-style dishes. M Savers, Morrisons' value-range of products, includes over 500 food and nonfood products in the brand. Morrisons touts this brand as "quality products even on the tightest budgets." It includes fruit, bread, lemonade, frozen dinners, dish-washing soap, and baby wipes.

The M Signature brand, Morrisons' premium food line, was launched in 2012. The product mix features over 700 food items, including spaghetti carbonara, chocolate and raspberry popcorn, and strawberry and champagne cream. Morrisons' NuMe brand, a line of healthy foods, replaced the previous Eat Smart line. NuMe includes 315 fresh, frozen, and refrigerated food items created by chefs and nutritionists who focus on healthier food choices for consumers.

In addition to its various food lines, Morrisons stores typically offer dry cleaning, photo printing, a pharmacy, a café, clothing, and a recycling facility. Many sites also feature a gas station, with car wash and vacuuming services available. Morrisons offers a loyalty-card program at its gas stations but not at the grocery stores.

In 2011 Morrisons launched a new smaller-store format called M-local. Reminiscent of a corner grocery store, the convenience-type store features over 100 lines of fresh fruits and vegetables, along with freshly baked bread, meats, and fish. The design of the store is intended to evoke a neighborhood shop with a marketplace feel that ties it to its parent store. Morrisons announced that it plans to open 70 M-local outlets by the end of 2013.

BRAND EQUITY

- Morrisons' 2012 brand value was placed at US$6.27 billion.
- Fortune magazine ranked Morrisons second in its *United Kingdom's Most Valuable Food Brands* and seventh in its *World's Most Valuable Food Brands* in 2011.
- The Reputation Institute ranked Morrisons 24th in its *UK Rep Trak 100*, a ranking of the most popular brands in the United Kingdom based on the strength of a positive reputation.

As part of its annual *Global 500*, *Fortune* magazine ranked Morrisons second in its rankings of the *United Kingdom's Most Valuable Food Brands, 2011*, and seventh in its *World's Most Valuable Food Brands, 2011*, with a brand value of US$6.27 billion.

Brand Finance rated Morrisons 18th in its rankings of *Best Retail Brands* in 2012, with a brand value of US$6.27 billion, ahead of 19th-ranked rival Sainsbury's. Interbrand ranked Morrisons eighth in its listing of *Most Valuable U.K. Retail Brands*, 2012, with a brand value of US$438 million. The Reputation Institute ranked Morrisons 24th in its *UK Rep Trak 100*, a ranking of the most popular brands in the United Kingdom based on the strength of their reputation.

BRAND AWARENESS

- Morrisons held a 12.3 percent market share among grocers in the United Kingdom in 2012, up from 11.5 percent in 2009.
- Morrisons has a higher market share in Scotland than it does in England.
- In 2009 Morrisons won several awards, including Retailer of the Year, Grocer of the Year, and Supermarket of the Year.

In 2006 Morrisons was the ninth-leading cake brand in the United Kingdom, with a 2.5 percent market share. In 2007 Morrisons ranked fourth among top private-label brands in the United Kingdom and it was the fifth-most-popular supermarket brand in the United Kingdom. In 2009 it was the fourth-leading grocery firm in the United Kingdom, with an 11.5 percent market share, and it was also fourth among retailers of home baking products in the United Kingdom, with a 9 percent market share. Morrisons ranked as the seventh-most-loved food-and-drink brand in the United Kingdom. Research firm Kantar Worldpanel reported that in 2012 Morrisons held a 12.3 percent market share among grocery stores in the United Kingdom.

Morrisons has tried to strengthen its brand awareness in southern England and Scotland through a series of initiatives. Morrisons enjoys a higher market share in

Scotland than elsewhere in Great Britain. In 2009 the company gained recognition for its efforts and won several industry awards, including "Retailer of the Year" from *Retail Week*, "Grocer of the Year" from the *Grocer*, and "Supermarket of the Year" at the Retail Industry Awards.

BRAND OUTLOOK

- Morrisons is the smallest of the "Big Four" grocery chains competing in the crushing British supermarket industry.
- In 2011 Morrisons bought a 10 percent stake in Fresh Direct, a New York-based online grocery retailer, as a way to gain knowledge and instruction in online grocery sales.
- Popular British television personalities Ant and Dec will be featured in new Morrisons' advertising in 2013.

As the smallest supermarket in the United Kingdom's "Big Four," which also includes rivals Tesco, Asda, and Sainsbury's, Morrisons has struggled to find its place. The integration of Safeway into the brand was a rocky transition that reverberated within the company for years. The redesign of its logo, tagline, and private-label brands are all part of an effort to strengthen the Morrison brand within England and Scotland.

In 2011 Morrisons bought British baby-goods retailer Kiddicare. The purchase of the established children's clothing, toy, and accessories brand may be a way for Morrisons to gain knowledge of online retailing and to expand its sales into nonfood arenas. The addition of Kiddicare to the Morrison portfolio should also help to attract more young families with children to the Morrisons brand.

Morrisons also announced in 2011 that they had purchased a 10 percent stake in New York–based online food retailer Fresh Direct. Fresh Direct, operating in the greater New York City area, stores, packages, and delivers groceries, including fresh meats, fruits, vegetables, and bakery items. As part of the deal, executives from Morrisons would be traveling to New York to learn the art of online food sales from an experienced retailer. The agreement comes ahead of Morrisons' expected announcement of its initiation of online grocery sales, an area where they lag considerably behind the competition.

In January 2013 Morrisons signed a brand endorsement partnership with well-known British television personalities Ant and Dec, who are to appear in an upcoming ad campaign. This marketing effort is intended to highlight Morrisons' fresh-food counters. Morrisons will also be the sponsor of ITV flagship television shows *Britain's Got Talent* and *Ant & Dec's Saturday Night Takeaway*.

FURTHER READING

Cameron, Greig. "Morrisons Hit by UK Sales Decline but Scottish Picture Remains Rosy." *Herald Scotland*, May 4, 2012.

Cohen, M. L., and Christina M. Stansell. "Wm. Morrison Supermarkets plc." *International Directory of Company Histories*. Ed. Tina Grant. Vol. 110. Detroit, MI: St. James Press, 2010.

Gordon, Kathy. "Top U.K. Supermarkets in Discount Challenge." *Wall Street Journal*, December 23, 2012.

"Morrisons Seals Safeway Takeover." *BBC News*, March 8, 2004.

Moulds, Josephine, and Rebecca Smithers. "Morrisons Considers Launching Online Store after Miserable Christmas: Sales Drop 2.5% over the Festive Period as Shoppers Favour Home Delivery from Supermarket's Rivals." *Guardian* (London), January 7, 2013.

Ruddick, Graham. "Morrisons Signs up Ant & Dec for New Advertising Campaign." *Telegraph* (London), January 4, 2013.

Spencer, Benjamin J. "FreshDirect Gets $50M to Expand outside NY." *Crain's New York Business*, March 10, 2011. Accessed January 25, 2013. http://www.crainsnewyork.com/article/20110310/SMALLBIZ/110319983.

Wood, Zoe, and Alex Hawkes. "Morrisons Buys Kiddicare for £70m." *Guardian* (London), February 15, 2011.

MOUNTAIN DEW

—■—

BRAND ORIGINS

- Mountain Dew began in the 1940s as a lemon-lime soda intended to be a mixer with whiskey.
- PepsiCo bought the Mountain Dew brand in 1964.
- Mountain Dew became the best-selling noncola product in the United States in 1996.

During the late 1940s the Hartman Beverage Company of Knoxville, Tennessee, launched Mountain Dew as a mixer for whiskey. It was invented by the Hartman brothers, Allie and Barney. The original version of Mountain Dew had a hillbilly brand image and a lemon-lime syrup base. The name Mountain Dew was first used on labels commercially in 1948 and became officially trademarked in 1953.

In 1958 Mountain Dew was sold to a regional bottler of Pepsi, the Tip Corporation of America. While Tip retained the hillbilly image, it changed the product in the early 1960s by adding orange flavoring and reducing the carbonation, creating a unique, citrus taste. Tip built Mountain Dew into a strong regional brand, featuring an animated spokesman, Willy the Hillbilly, and it sold as many as 10 million cases annually.

The Tip Corporation, including the Mountain Dew brand, was bought in 1964 by Pepsi-Cola Company (which became a subsidiary of PepsiCo in 1965). As part of PepsiCo, Willy was retained as brand spokesman, and the company expanded distribution nationally over the next few years. Mountain Dew soon became widely popular. Between 1964 and 1966, sales rose from 9.4 million cases to 39.3 million. It became the second-best-selling drink made by PepsiCo.

Though sales went flat in the late 1960s and early 1970s, beginning in 1973 Mountain Dew was reinvigorated when Pepsi began repositioning it to appeal more strongly to active youths. It mounted campaigns like "Hello Sunshine, Hello Mountain Dew." By 1978 Mountain Dew sold over 100 million cases annually and was the fastest growing soft drink in America.

During the 1980s, sales of Mountain Dew continued to soar, with volume doubling as brand awareness and growth potential seemed limitless. In addition to linking the brand with the outdoors through campaigns like "Give Me a Dew" and "Do It Country Cool," Mountain Dew introduced a diet version, Diet Mountain Dew, nationally in 1988. In that year Mountain Dew products had case sales of 52 million.

By the early 1990s, PepsiCo was facing declining market share overall, but Mountain Dew and Diet Mountain Dew were making gains among teens and young adults. Pepsi began greatly increasing the brand's advertising budget, with much success. By 1992 Diet Mountain Dew was experiencing an 18.4 percent increase in volume with help from such television advertising campaigns as "Get Vertical" and "Do Diet Dew."

By 1992 Mountain Dew had a 4.3 percent market share in the United States and was the number-six soft drink brand overall. A year later, it saw an increase in volume sales of 7.2 percent and market share of 5 percent. Mountain Dew's volume doubled between 1984 and 1993, resulting in US$2.2 billion in sales in 1993. By 1996 Mountain Dew had replaced Dr Pepper as the best-selling noncola product in the United States. That year it was introduced in the United Kingdom for the first time. However, it failed to catch on there and was withdrawn a few years later. In the United States, however, sales of Mountain Dew continued strong, with a volume growth of 9.9 percent in 1998 alone.

Yet carbonated soft drink sales continued to decline overall from the 1990s through the early 2000s in the United States and elsewhere as people began embracing healthy eating habits and drinking more healthy beverages. Mountain Dew was able to continue to grow, however, on the basis of campaigns like the popular "Do the Dew," which ran from 1997 through 2005. In 1999 sales grew by 7.1 percent, but after that the increases grew smaller and smaller.

To ensure continued strong growth, Mountain Dew introduced a number of extensions and variants in the first decades of the 21st century, beginning with Mountain Dew Code Red. New ad campaigns like "This Is How We Dew" and relationships with extreme sports, sports like NASCAR, and popular music helped maintain Mountain Dew's growth in the early 2000s. Diet Mountain Dew became one of the top ten soda brands in the United States in 2005, with a 1.4 percent market share. Over the next five years, market share continued to grow. By 2011 Mountain Dew was the fastest-growing, major carbonated-soft-drink trademark in North America.

BRAND ELEMENTS

- Willy the Hillbilly was the symbol of Mountain Dew from the late 1950s until 1969.
- Willy made a reappearance when throwback Mountain Dew hit the market in 2009.

- Mountain Dew became Mtn Dew in the United States in 2008 as part of a rebranding effort.

When Mountain Dew was still a product of the Tip Corporation, the brand rolled out what became its longtime animated spokesman, Willy the Hillbilly. The character represented Mountain Dew's origins, because the brand's name was slang for moonshine and the beverage was originally created to serve as a mixer with whiskey. Willy continued to symbolize the brand after Pepsi acquired it in 1964. He was part of a television and radio campaign that featured the slogan "Yahoo Mountain Dew … It'll Tickle Yore Innards." Willy was also featured in the "Yahoo Mountain Dew" ads of the mid-1960s. After 1972 Mountain Dew moved toward action-oriented advertisements, variations of which continue in the early 21st century. Willy reappeared in 2009 when Mountain Dew launched its throwback version of the soda, made with real sugar and using retro-looking cans.

From the earliest days of Mountain Dew, the brand's colors have been green, red, and white. Though the proportions and look have changed over the years, the brand's logo and packaging have been in distinctive shades of these colors. The Mountain Dew name was abbreviated to Mtn Dew for Mountain Dew products sold in the United States after a 2008 rebranding. The name has often been designed with a mountain shape. The green in the label reflects the unusual green color of Mountain Dew and Diet Mountain Dew, the brand's primary products. Mountain Dew also has a unique citrus taste. In addition, the soda has 50 percent more caffeine and 10 percent more sugar than most other carbonated soft drinks, adding to its appeal to its core audience.

BRAND IDENTITY

- Since the early 1970s, Mountain Dew has identified itself as the beverage of choice for active, young males.
- "Do the Dew" helped establish Mountain Dew's link to extreme sports.
- Mountain Dew has sponsored extreme sports competitions, skateboarders, NASCAR, and popular music.

Since the early 1970s, Mountain Dew has positioned itself as the beverage for active teenagers, primarily males, and for twentysomethings of either gender. The brand's 1973 slogan, "Put a Little Yahoo in Your Life," linked the brand to its hillbilly past and action-oriented present. Memorable campaigns from the 1970s to the 1990s reinforced this image, beginning with 1974's "Hello Sunshine, Hello Mountain Dew," "Reach for the Sun, Reach for Mountain Dew," "Give Me a Dew," and "Dew It to It."

The "Do the Dew" campaign, which began in the late 1990s and continued through the early 21st century, emphasized the brand's bold imagery and linked Mountain Dew to extreme sports. For many years Mountain Dew also sponsored the X Games, an extreme sports competition which aired on ESPN. Beginning in 2005, Mountain Dew became the title sponsor of the Mountain Dew Tour of Extreme Sports, an action sports tour which featured BMX, FMX, superbikes, quad bikes, and car drifting. A global event, it made stops in Saudi Arabia in 2008 and 2011, which helped increase awareness of the brand among Arab youths.

Mountain Dew linked its brand to other sports and games as well. The brand sponsored skateboarding and BMX events. In the early 2000s Mountain Dew became associated with video games in promotions related to the action-oriented games *Halo* and *Call of Duty*. In 2008 Mountain Dew began sponsoring the car of NASCAR driver Dale Earnhardt, Jr., and Diet Mountain Dew became his primary car sponsor in 2011.

Music was important to its target demographic, and Mountain Dew launched its Green Label Sound project in 2008. While originally dedicated to giving consumers free tracks from new artists, Green Label Sound later released albums by Cool Kids and Mac Miller. To help widen the brand's demographic, in 2012 it inked a deal with hip hop star Lil Wayne. He was featured in his own DEWeezy campaign as well as in the brand's wider "This Is How We Dew" campaign.

BRAND STRATEGY

- Diet Mountain Dew was the first brand extension, introduced across the United States in 1988.
- Beginning in 2003, Mountain Dew introduced a large number of extensions and variants.
- Mountain Dew found its greatest success in the U.S. market.

Mountain Dew was the brand's sole product until the mid-1980s, when the brand began introducing extensions and variants. Diet Mountain Dew was the first variant, introduced in test marketing in 1985 and available across the United States beginning in 1988. Diet Mountain Dew debuted when diet drinks were quite popular.

No successful new line extensions were introduced until 2001, when Mountain Dew Code Red hit the market. This cherry-flavored beverage had 55 milligrams of caffeine, like the original Mountain Dew, and it targeted younger teens from diverse socioeconomic backgrounds, primarily African American and Hispanic. This marked a broader attempt to reach more urban markets.

Beginning in 2003, Mountain Dew began introducing many brand extensions and variants, some with short-term availability and others becoming a permanent part of Mountain Dew's line. These included orange-flavored LiveWire (2003), grape-flavored Pitch Black (2004), ginseng- and raspberry citrus-flavored Voltage (2008), and the first diet extension, UltraViolet (2009), among many others. In 2012 Mountain Dew deviated from its basic soda formula by introducing Johnson City Gold, a more health-based, malt-flavored soda, in certain cities in the United States. Also in 2012 the brand debuted the limited-time flavor, Dark Berry, as part of its first global campaign, in conjunction with the film *The Dark Knight Rises*.

Mountain Dew is more popular in the United States than in any other country. Its top-selling U.S. markets are found from the Upper Midwest to the Carolinas and other parts of the Southeast. Internationally, Mountain Dew was introduced in the United Kingdom in 1996, but withdrawn after two years because of poor sales. However, it was successfully reintroduced in 2010. The brand also had success in the Russian market and in India, where Bollywood actor Salman Khan served as a spokesman for a few years. Mountain Dew used events like the Mountain Dew Extreme Sports Tour to build its brand worldwide.

BRAND EQUITY

- Mountain Dew and Diet Mountain Dew are billion-dollar products for PepsiCo.
- Mountain Dew was ranked eighth among soft drinks in "BrandZ Top 100 Most Valuable Global Brands 2012."
- In 2012 Mountain Dew had a brand value of US$3.487 billion, according to Brand Finance.

The number-four carbonated soft drink in the United States and a best-seller worldwide, Mountain Dew is a very valuable brand and has been for decades. It is one of PepsiCo's billion dollar products, based on sales. Diet Mountain Dew reached US$1 billion in sales in 2011. Mountain Dew doubled its volume over the previous decade. In "BrandZ Top 100 Most Valuable Global Brands 2012" report, Mountain Dew was number eight among soft drinks, with a brand value of US$2.577 billion, an increase of 4 percent over 2011. It ranked behind Coca-Cola, Diet Coke, Pepsi, Red Bull, Fanta, Sprite, and Gatorade. In 2011 Mountain Dew's brand value was US$2.478 billion.

According to Brand Finance's *Global 500*, Mountain Dew had a brand value of US$3.487 billion and an enterprise value of US$8.189 billion in 2012. It ranked 311th. This marked an increase from 2011, but was still lower than its 2010 results. In 2011 Mountain Dew's brand value was US$3.172 billion. Its enterprise value was US$8.518 billion, and it ranked 333rd. In 2010 its brand value was US$3.510 billion and its enterprise value was US$17.713 billion, with a ranking of 238. Though Mountain Dew has had strong sales, it has been impacted by the worldwide economic downturn, among other factors.

BRAND AWARENESS

- Mountain Dew knows its audience and picks its sponsorships, brand faces, and campaigns to create high brand awareness.
- Mountain Dew uses social media effectively to create brand awareness.
- Mountain Dew vastly increased its brand awareness in New Zealand by building a warehouse-sized skateboard park.

Mountain Dew is admired as a brand that knows its market and appeals to them with its sports, music, film, and gaming sponsorships, creating high brand awareness. Mountain Dew worked to broaden its primary market of young white males to a wider, urban audience. However, it carefully chose the flavors of its brand extensions, like Code Red, and the faces of its brand, like Lil Wayne, to appeal to young black and Hispanic males and increase their awareness of it as a brand made for them.

Mountain Dew uses social media effectively to increase brand awareness. In 2010 it was ranked 47th by Famecount in its ranking of Top Social Network Stars. This is a ranking of the most popular consumer and media brands globally, looking at Facebook, Twitter, and YouTube. In December 2012 Mountain Dew was ranked eighth by Famecount on its all-time, most-popular-in-social-media chart of soft drink brands. Famecount noted that Mountain Dew had 11.2 million fans on Facebook. It was number 157 on the website's all-time brand chart and number 39 on the all-time chart for food drink brands.

The brand aggressively builds up awareness in markets where this is lacking. For example, in New Zealand Mountain Dew had just 1 percent of the market and lacked significant brand awareness among core teenage males before 2011. Then Mountain Dew created a warehouse-sized skateboard park that was themed like a pinball table for use by skateboarders and BMXers. In addition to a related, 10-part documentary on the facility that aired on a youth-oriented television station, it was promoted along with the Mountain Dew name via social media and other publicity and via an invitational skateboard competition. Mountain Dew's share of the soft drink market in New Zealand grew by 123 percent as a result. In addition, this campaign brought global media attention to the brand.

BRAND OUTLOOK

- The market for carbonated soft drinks is in decline worldwide.
- Bucking industry trends, the Mountain Dew brand continues to grow.
- Mountain Dew accounts for about 20 percent of PepsiCo's sales in the United States.

The market for carbonated soft drinks (CSD) in the United States and worldwide has been on a decline for several years because of concerns about the increasing rate of obesity, the popularity of healthier foods and lifestyles, and economic issues related to the worldwide recession of 2008–09. Consumers have begun favoring healthier beverages that still taste good. Sodas have lost market share to noncarbonated beverages like juices, performance drinks, teas, and flavored water. PepsiCo suffered a 1 percent decline in North America and a 3 percent decline in CSD volume because of these factors.

Yet Mountain Dew has continued to thrive, outperforming many competitors, and it is expected to continue to do so because of its effective marketing, deep awareness of its target audience, and extended international outreach. In 2010, Diet Mountain Dew was the best performer among major soft drink brands, with 5.8 percent growth. Mountain Dew accounts for about 20 percent of PepsiCo's beverage sales in the United States, a figure that is expected to rise. The brand managers know where its strongest sales lie. The 20-ounce Mountain Dew was the number-one seller in convenience stores nationally by 2012, while industry leader Coca-Cola was only number five. It will be difficult for Mountain Dew to move up from being the fourth leading carbonated soft drink in the United States and in the world after Coke, Diet Coke, and Pepsi. However the brand is expected to build on sales of over US$5 billion for Mountain Dew and over US$1 billion for Diet Mountain Dew.

FURTHER READING

Brand Finance. "Mountain Dew." *Brandirectory*. Accessed December 29, 2012. http://brandirectory.com/profile/mountain-dew-mtn-dew.

"BrandZ Top 100 Most Valuable Global Brands 2012." Millward Brown. Accessed December 29, 2012. http://www.millward-brown.com/brandz/2012/Documents/2012_BrandZ_Top100_Report.pdf.

Brown, Abram. "Pepsi's Comeback Starts with Diet Dew's New Ads—and NASCAR." *Forbes*, March 5, 2012.

Leith, Scott. "Drinks Try to Sustain the Buzz." *Atlanta-Journal Constitution*, October 30, 2004.

McWilliams, Jeremiah. "Diet Coke Outpaces Rival Pepsi." *Atlanta-Journal Constitution*, March 18, 2012.

Pederson, Jay P. "Mountain Dew." *Encyclopedia of Global Brands. Volume 1: Consumable Products*. Ed. Janice Jorgensen. Detroit, MI: St. James Press, 1994.

"PepsiCo, Inc." *Encyclopedia of Major Marketing Campaigns*. Ed. Thomas Riggs. Vol. 2. Detroit, MI: Gale, 2007.

"Special Issue: U.S. Beverage Results for 2011." *Beverage-Digest*, March 20, 2012.

Stanford, Duane. "Mountain Dew Wants Some Street Cred." *Business Week*, April 26, 2012.

Zmuda, Natalie. "Mtn Dew Steps out from Shadow of Flagship Brand." *AdvertisingAge*, March 5, 2012.

MOVISTAR

—■—

BRAND ORIGINS

- Movistar's parent company, Telefónica S.A., was formerly a government company and a monopoly formed in 1924 and known as Compañía Telefónica Nacional de España S.A. (CTNE).

- Telefónica S.A., the parent company of Movistar, emerged after the deregulation of the Spanish telephone industry in 1998.

- Telefónica S.A. bought several mobile telecommunications companies in other countries and began offering Internet and mobile services under the Movistar and O2 brands it launched in the early 2000s.

- In Spain and Latin America Telefónica has rebranded its fixed and mobile services under the Movistar name. In Northern Europe Telefónica provides telecommunications services under the O2 brand.

A major telecommunications company in its home country of Spain and elsewhere, Movistar is part of Spanish telecommunications company Telefónica S.A. Telefónica started as an amalgamation of companies, formed after a Spanish company took control of International Telephone & Telegraph Corp. In 1924 the government of Spain allowed this new company, the Compañía Telefónica Nacional de España S.A. (CTNE), to operate as a telephone service monopoly in Spain.

During his rule of Spain from 1939 to 1975 Francisco Franco nationalized CTNE. The company extended its service within Spain and in other countries, and it expanded its product lines, offering car radio phones as well as working with communication satellites, data transmission, and television transmission. As had happened in other European countries in the later years of the 20th century, Spain deregulated its basic telephone industry in 1998, and CTNE was reorganized.

This 1998 reorganization led to the creation of a parent company, Telefónica S.A, and the telecommunications business moved to Telefónica de España. Telefónica worked in other countries and in new fields, such as Internet and mobile services, the latter initially under the name Telefónica Móviles. Telefónica became heavily involved in mobile telecommunications, buying several mobile firms in other countries. It began offering these services under the Movistar and O2 brands it launched in the early 2000s.

Telefónica uses the name O2 for its services in northern Europe. In Spain Telefónica rebranded its fixed and mobile services under the Movistar name in 2010, and it uses the Movistar name for these same services in Latin America. Similarly, in Colombia in 2012 Telefónica combined all of its telecommunications services under the Movistar name. The Colombian government owns 30 percent of this newly configured company.

BRAND ELEMENTS

- Movistar's logo is dominated by a large, cartoonish *M*, often in light green and yellow and sometimes in blue, usually accompanied by the word Movistar in all capital letters in blue or white.
- Web pages for Movistar frequently feature the green *M* logo and blue Movistar text. These pages often use blue and green, colors that refer to Movistar and Telefónica, Movistar's parent company.
- Interbrand and Movistar reshaped Movistar's brand identity and symbols in 2010, using sky blue to evoke images of inspiration and freedom.

For its logo Movistar uses a wide, cartoonish three-dimensional letter *M* that appears to be composed of a blob of liquid or gel rather than a product of traditional typography. The *M* is often light green and yellow and sometimes blue. The word Movistar in all capital letters often accompanies this logo, usually in blue or white letters.

The *M* logo and Movistar text appear in several places on Movistar web pages. These pages incorporate a number of blue and green images, which echo the *M* logo and text. The colors also echo the blue used by Movistar's parent company Telefónica and its various brands.

Interbrand helped Movistar reshape its brand identity and visual elements in 2010. According to Interbrand, Movistar's use of the color blue evokes "the brand's open, positive and expressive personality." Interbrand noted that the blue color symbolizes the sky, a connection that "evokes inspiration, aspiration and freedom," and that the sky metaphor also "expresses the brand proposition, which is capable of uniting communities … by suggesting a world without limits; a world of shared opportunities, ever growing in scope and dimension."

BRAND IDENTITY

- A hot air balloon featuring a giant version of Movistar's green *M* logo against a blue background provides a moving advertisement that travels to events in countries where Movistar does business.
- Movistar's web pages reflect its global business, featuring multiple maps with markings indicating the areas of Movistar's business and cartoons of geographic regions clutching mobile phones.
- With titles such as Movistar *en el mundo*, or Movistar in the world, and *servicios internacionales*, or international services, sections of Movistar's web pages also demonstrate its international scope.
- The Movistar slogan "Life is more when you share it" expresses the company's international work and its goal of bringing communications technology to people.

The blue in Movistar's logo is intended to evoke the kind of positive and inspirational images generally associated with a clear blue sky, and the brand has taken that imagery to a literal level. A giant version of Movistar's green *M* logo against a blue background appears on a hot air balloon that travels to events around the world, serving as a moving advertisement while illustrating Movistar's goals of "uniting communities" and creating "shared opportunities."

The company conducts business in several countries, and its web pages reflect its global presence, featuring multiple maps of the world with markings indicating where Movistar operates. The web pages also use drawings of various geographical regions to depict Movistar's services in unique ways. For example, they include cartoon depictions of South America and Mexico that appear as hands that clutch mobile phones, a visual depiction of how these regions have embraced Movistar's offerings.

Individual sections of Movistar's home page also explain the company's international business. These sections include Movistar *en el mundo*, or Movistar in the world, and *servicios internacionales*, or international services, and include detailed information on Movistar's work. Movistar's slogan, "Life is more when you share it," expresses the global approach of the brand and the company's goal of bringing communications technology to people.

BRAND STRATEGY

- Movistar sponsors a Spanish bicycle-racing team. Riders wear multiple Movistar logos during prominent races such as the Tour de France, and fans can buy merchandise affiliated with the team.
- Movistar sponsors other sporting events, such as motorcycle racing, sailing, and futsal, a scaled-down version of soccer.
- The Movistar name adorns the Movistar Arena in Santiago, Chile.

Movistar places a heavy emphasis on sporting events as a conduit for brand exposure. It sponsors a Spanish bicycle-racing team that competes at prominent cycling events, including the Tour de France and Vuelta de España (the tour of Spain). Members of Movistar cycling teams sport multiple green Movistar *M* logos on their clothing, and cycling fans can buy these and other Movistar items. The Movistar team consists of riders from various countries and competes in races in different areas, attracting fans from multiple regions.

Other racing sports have ties to Movistar. The *M* Movistar logo appears on the racing motorcycles that Movistar sponsors as well as the tractor-trailer truck that transports the motorcycles. Fans can buy and build kits featuring scale models of the motorcycles and trucks.

Movistar sponsors Formula One automobile racing and streamed broadcasts of some Formula One races to its mobile phones. Movistar has also been affiliated with sailing events and with futsal, a scaled-down version of soccer played primarily indoors.

In Santiago, Chile, the brand's name adorns the Movistar Arena.

BRAND EQUITY

- *Brandirectory* ranked Movistar 56th in the world among brands in all categories of business, with an estimated brand value of US$14,412 million, down from the previous year's ranking of 51.
- Movistar ranked sixth on *Brandirectory*'s list of the world's top telecom brands in 2011 and third on the list of Spain's top brands in 2010.
- *BrandZ* gave Movistar a ranking of 41st in the world among top brands in 2012, estimating the brand's value at US$17,113.

Movistar ranked 56th on *Brandirectory*'s listing of the top 500 global brands in 2012, with an estimated brand value of US$14,412 million. That was down from a ranking of 51 and an estimated brand value of US$14,935 million in 2011. In *Brandirectory*'s listing of the top global telecom brands in 2011 Movistar placed sixth, and in 2010 *Brandirectory* named Movistar the third-most-valuable brand in Spain.

Millward Brown's *BrandZ* rankings of the world's top brands placed Movistar at number 41 in 2012, with an estimated brand value of US$17,113, a drop from the brand's standing the previous year at number 21 with a brand value of US$27,249.

BRAND AWARENESS

- In September 2012 Movistar led Spain's mobile phone service market with a 36.96 percent market share.
- Movistar captured 32.2 percent of Venezuela's mobile service market in the fourth quarter of 2011.

- In Chile Movistar led the mobile phone service market in 2010 with a 41 percent share; by 2012 Movistar's share had dropped to 38 percent and ranked second behind Entel.

Offering multiple services in multiple countries, Movistar has captured significant portions of a number of markets, with especially strong performance in Spain and Chile. In Spain Movistar led the market for mobile phone service in September 2012, with a 36.96% market share. Its nearest competitor, Vodafone, held a 27.42 percent share of the market. Movistar claimed 32.2 percent of Venezuela's mobile service market in the fourth fiscal quarter of 2011.

In Chile Movistar led the mobile phone service market in 2010 with a 41 percent share. By 2012 Movistar's share in Chile had dropped to 38 percent and ranked second behind Entel, which led the market with a 38.4 percent share. In 2010 Movistar held a commanding lead in the landline market in Chile, pulling in a 56 percent share, well ahead of its nearest competitor, which held a 19 percent share. The brand also grabbed the largest slice of the Internet services market in 2010, with a 43 percent share of Chile's fixed Internet connections for homes and businesses.

BRAND OUTLOOK

- In addition to pursuing new markets, Movistar has begun selling new products and forging partnerships that create new ways for consumers to spend more time using Movistar's services.
- In 2011 Movistar partnered with Spanish company Mundo Reader's bq brand to introduce the Movistar ebook bq, a touchscreen reading device.
- Movistar partnered with MoreMagic Solutions to allow U.S. residents to buy airtime for Movistar mobile phone users in Mexico, Central America, and South America.

In addition to pursuing new markets, Movistar began selling new products to encourage existing consumers to use Movistar's services more often and in new ways. In 2011 it partnered with Spanish company Mundo Reader's bq brand to introduce the Movistar ebook bq, an electronic reader similar to the Amazon Kindle that can be used to download and read books, listen to music, browse the web, send e-mail messages, access social networks, or play games downloaded from the Movistar online store.

Movistar partnered with MoreMagic Solutions in a venture that allows United States residents to buy airtime for Movistar mobile phone users in Mexico, Central America, and South America. Movistar customers in Latin American countries can also conduct banking transactions with their mobile phones through a partnership between Movistar and MasterCard. In another joint operation, this time between Movistar and MoneyGram International, Movistar customers in Mexico, Spain, and other countries can transfer money.

FURTHER READING

Baigorri, Manuel, and Marie Mawad. "Orange Bets Spain Bargains Will Beat Telefónica." *Bloomberg*, November 22, 2012. Accessed January 17, 2013.

Brand Finance. "Movistar." *Brandirectory*. Accessed January 15, 2013. http://brandirectory.com/profile/movistar.

———. "Top 500 Telecom Brands 2012." *Brandirectory*. Accessed January 15, 2013. http://brandirectory.com/league_tables/table/top-500-telecom-brands-2012.

Business Monitor International. "Venezuela Telecommunications Report Q3 2012." MarketResearch.com, June 5, 2012. Accessed January 17, 2013. http://www.marketresearch.com/Business-Monitor-International-v304/Venezuela-Telecommunications-Q3-7026630/.

"Entel Beats Movistar Mobile Market Share in Chile." *Telecompaper*, July 16, 2012. Accessed January 17, 2013. http://www.telecompaper.com/news/entel-beats-movistar-mobile-market-share-in-chile--884835.

"Movistar." New York: Interbrand. Accessed January 16, 2013. http://www.interbrand.com/en/our-work/Telef%C3%B3nica-Movistar.aspx.

"Movistar Brand Identity." Advertolog. Accessed January 15, 2013. http://www.advertolog.com/movistar/design/movistar-brand-identity-15911305/.

PriMetrica, Inc. "Movistar Commits to Social Programme with Fixed Broadband Rollouts." *TeleGeography*, August 21, 2012. Accessed January 15, 2013. http://www.telegeography.com/products/commsupdate/articles/2012/08/21/movistar-commits-to-social-programme-with-fixed-broadband-rollouts/.

Ruano, Rafael, and Dennis Mahorney. "Market Profile: Chile." PwC. Accessed January 12, 2013. http://www.pwc.com/gx/en/communications/review/features/market-profile-chile.jhtml.

"Telefónica S.A." *International Directory of Company Histories*. Ed. Jay P. Pederson. Vol. 108. Detroit, MI: St. James Press, 2010.

MTV

■

AT A GLANCE

■

Brand Synopsis: Beginning as an American television network that broadcast music videos, MTV became a globally oriented multimedia promoter of youth culture.

Parent Company: MTV Networks, Inc.

1515 Broadway

New York, New York 10036-8901

United States

http://www.mtv.com

Sector: Consumer Discretionary

Industry Group: Media

Performance: *Sales*—US$1 billion (2011).

Principal Competitors: Cable networks, including Arts & Entertainment and The Learning Channel; digital cable channels; Internet sites

BRAND ORIGINS

- MTV was launched in 1981.
- The early MTV resembled a radio station, with video jockeys, countdowns, contests, and artist visits.
- In addition to broadcasting music videos, MTV has created its own programming, which has included awards presentations, animated series, and reality programs.

Although it eventually became synonymous with music videos, MTV was not the first to play them. A few television programs had experimented with showing music videos during the 1970s. Eventually, the Warner-Amex Satellite Entertainment Company (WASEC) became interested in developing a music channel. One of Warner-Amex's employees, Robert W. Pittman, had extensive experience in radio and helped create the programming for MTV. Known as "the father of MTV," Pittman later served as the president and chief executive officer of MTV Networks from 1983 to 1987.

After its August 1, 1981, launch, MTV in its early years resembled a radio station. The network featured a number of video jockeys, or VJs—similar to radio's disc jockeys (DJs)—who introduced and discussed music videos. MTV offered a countdown of the week's most popular videos, and musical artists visited the channel to promote their latest videos or help participate in the channel's contests. MTV also broadcast different shows highlighting music videos from different musical genres. These shows have included *Yo! MTV Raps* (rap), *120 Minutes* (alternative music), and *Headbangers Ball* (heavy metal).

Besides music videos, MTV showed other programs, including reruns of *The Monkees*, bringing music video programming full circle. MTV also produced its own shows, including the annual *Video Music Awards*, which began in 1984, and the *MTV Movie Awards*, which started in 1992. Other MTV programs included *Beavis and Butt-Head*, an animated program that began in the 1990s. Among their other activities, the teenaged characters in *Beavis and Butt-Head* watched and commented on live-action music videos.

Other MTV shows featuring music videos included *Total Request Live* (1998–2008), which played music videos requested by its viewers. By the time this show ended MTV had largely stopped broadcasting music videos. Instead, it continued to create other programs, including a number of reality shows. Critics have claimed that these reality shows did not belong on a channel founded to promote music programming. MTV's transition resembles that of other Viacom-owned channels such as VH1, Black Entertainment Television (BET), and Country Music Television (CMT), all of which initially broadcast music videos before offering other types of programming. MTV's programming also is part of a larger trend that saw broadcast and cable networks feature increasingly more reality programming in the 2000s.

BRAND ELEMENTS

- MTV has used its block M logo since its launch in 1981.
- MTV has used a "Moonman" symbol since 1981 in film footage and as its *Video Music Awards* statuette.
- The logo of MTV was designed to stand out from other networks; its fast-paced visual editing style also differentiated the network from others.

During MTV's first few minutes on the air on August 1, 1981, it broadcast footage of the 1969 Apollo 11 moon landing. The channel changed the appearance of the American flag in this footage to an animated flag with an MTV logo. This footage, accompanied by MTV's instrumental theme, aired frequently during MTV's early years. This identification continues to the present: the statue for MTV's *Video Music Awards* is the "Moonman," a silver statuette of an astronaut with an MTV flag. The Moonman actually spent time in space with Russian cosmonauts, who appeared on the 1996 *Video Music Awards*.

From the beginning MTV's logo has been a large block "M" with a smaller "TV" superimposed over it. The 1981 clip shows MTV logos in a variety of colors and patterns; other logo variations include the use of photographs from MTV shows to fill the logo's block M. This longstanding logo represents MTV in various ways, appearing on its television networks, Internet sites, and as part of its MTV Films logo. MTV's sister channel MTV2 also used variations of this block M logo before adopting the silhouette of a two-headed dog as its logo.

MTV's founders hoped that its original logo would distinguish it from other networks. They also created a distinctive visual style. MTV has often used a rapid succession of brief images and quick video cuts in its programming; its music videos often also featured these brief images. This style of rapid visual editing has been called the "MTV style" of editing.

BRAND IDENTITY

- MTV's graphics and logo have positioned the network to appeal to young people.
- In its focus on youth, MTV has featured young people in its shows and other programming as well as young people working at the network itself.
- Humor and an irreverent attitude have marked some of MTV's programming as an alternative to older, more serious networks.
- MTV has shifted its focus from youth music exclusively to young people and different aspects of their culture.

To MTV, its use of moon-landing footage and an animated logo symbolized the network's "giant leap" in music programming, a decisive shift to focus on younger viewers and their culture.

The network's focus on youth can be seen in its animated logos and other graphics, its youth-oriented music, and its attitudes, such as the irreverent humor of its awards shows. Its VJs and on-air personalities have been largely young people, as have many of the music artists featured on MTV and the people on its shows, in addition to the people working behind the scenes at MTV, such as programmers.

Early MTV commercials featured famous musical artists shouting "I want my MTV!" much like demanding children. The singer Sting also repeats "I want my MTV" in the 1985 Dire Straits song "Money for Nothing." In this song the narrator complains that musical groups featured on MTV do very little work but are paid well, getting money for nothing. The music video for this song is mostly animated; televisions in the music video feature live-action footage of the band Dire Straits (and the MTV astronaut footage and logo), creating a music video within the actual music video. MTV's frequent broadcast of this video is another example of its irreverence, its refusal to take many things—even itself—seriously. It instead hoped to provide a fun, funny alternative to more serious "adult" programming.

While the network has changed from a broadcaster of music videos to a broadcaster of reality programs, its focus on young people has not wavered. Popular MTV reality programs include the long-running *The Real World*, in which diverse groups of young people adjust to living with each other. Other programs featuring young people have included *16 and Pregnant* and its spin-off, *Teen Mom*, both of which chronicle the lives of teenagers during and after their pregnancies. Another popular MTV offering has been *Jersey Shore*, a show depicting the lives of a group of young New Jersey residents.

MTV, then, has shifted from focusing exclusively on the music of younger viewers to addressing younger viewers themselves, depicting different aspects of youth life and culture.

BRAND STRATEGY

- MTV's editing style and visuals assume that its young viewers were raised with television and are eager for a network different from their parents' networks.
- MTV offers television and Internet options for music videos, programs, and music in the United States and international markets.
- Political initiative Choose or Lose, public health campaigns, and programming about various social issues have demonstrated MTV's interest in social responsibility.
- Expanding to other areas, MTV has created films under MTV Films, published books under MTV Books, and has offered a wide range of merchandise.

MTV hoped that the animated MTV logo and other graphics would appeal to younger viewers looking for programming different from the programming on networks that their parents watched. MTV's frenetic visual style was also aimed at these young viewers, as MTV creators assumed that its viewers had grown up with television and had grown used to television's visual conventions.

Young people have a range of viewing options at MTV Networks. Music videos appear on MTV2, an MTV channel launched in 1996 as M2, and on MTV's digital channels, MTV Hits and the urban and hip hop-oriented MTV Jams. MTV2 also offers music programming and other programming, much like its counterpart Tr3s: MTV, Musica y Mas, a channel aimed at viewers of Spanish descent. Another MTV-related network is mtvU, a network catering to college students. MTV also appears around the world as MTV Canada, MTV Europe, and MTV channels in various countries. Music videos, MTV programming, and music also appear on the Internet as part of MTV's Internet sites.

The network has also involved itself in a number of social issues. In 2009 it began working with the Henry J. Kaiser Family Foundation in efforts to get young people tested for sexually transmitted diseases. MTV's programming has raised awareness of human trafficking, homelessness, poverty, and drug addiction. Since 1992 it also has tried to generate youth interest in politics with its Choose or Lose initiative, a campaign renamed the Power of 12 in 2012. These efforts have kept MTV's name in front of the public.

Besides its television and Internet offerings, MTV creates films under its MTV Films label and has published books through its MTV Books imprint. It has also offered a wide range of merchandise. With these offerings, MTV hopes to depict itself as a creative, hip voice for young consumers.

BRAND EQUITY

- In a 2011 Interbrand list of the top 500 international brands, MTV placed 58th.
- Another list, the "Global 500 2012" from Brand Finance, ranked MTV number 292 among 500 top international brands.
- According to MTV's parent company, Viacom, MTV and its affiliates are in about 99 million American homes and around 600 million households worldwide in 2011.
- Viacom also notes that MTV and its sister channels reach more than 150 countries and territories.
- Viacom, MTV's parent company, is among the world's largest international companies, according to *Forbes* magazine.

MTV's popularity and multimedia presence have helped make it a prominent brand in the United States and abroad. In Interbrand's list of the top 100 brands of 2011, MTV ranked 58th, with a brand value of about US$6.4 billion. Another media company, Disney, ranked ninth on this list with a brand value of around US$29 billion.

In another listing, Brand Finance's "Global 500 2012" listed MTV number 292 in a list of the top 500 global brands, with a brand value of around US$3.7 billion. On this list Disney ranked 50th, with a brand value of US$15.4 billion.

The parent company of MTV, Viacom, Inc., was listed number 376 in *Forbes* magazine's 2012 list of the 2,000 largest global companies. Discussing MTV's global presence, Viacom's 2011 annual report claims that "MTV reached approximately ninety-nine million domestic television households in September 2011 and more than 600 million households in more than 150 countries and territories worldwide via its fifty-eight MTV branded channels. It reaches many more households through branded programming blocks on third party broadcasters."

BRAND AWARENESS

- By the 2010s MTV was better known for reality-based programs than music videos on its television network.
- Music downloads, music videos, band information, and MTV programming can be found on MTV's various Internet sites, which often are separated by musical genres and geographical regions.
- In 2012, ratings for the original MTV channel dropped 30 percent from the previous year, leading to industry gossip that MTV was "broken."

For years MTV was synonymous with the music video. Now other representatives from music television brands say they do not consider MTV to be their competitor because MTV's programming has changed. By the 2010s, MTV was better known for its reality-based programs such as *Jersey Shore*.

MTV has also looked to move its brand awareness outside the United States. It has offered MTV channels in various locations. These international MTV affiliates sometimes feature MTV signature programming. For example, it draws on its tradition of awards presentations by broadcasting the *MTV Europe Music Awards*. This programming carries the MTV name and its products to new areas.

Similarly, MTV offers Internet sites targeted at different groups, such as MTV Desi for people of South Asian descent; MTV K, targeting Korean Americans, Asian Americans, and fans of Korean music; and a large number of MTV sites devoted to the MTV channels of different countries and regions as well as different types of music. These sites discuss bands and music, offer music and music videos, and feature MTV programming.

In spite of this diversification, MTV's brand awareness slipped considerably in the 2010s. In 2012, ratings for MTV's original cable channel dropped 30 percent lower than their levels of the year before. This led to gossip throughout the industry that MTV was "broken," reports that Viacom's leadership denied.

BRAND OUTLOOK

- Social media has helped MTV employees learn about fans.
- MTV hopes that its Internet site Artists.MTV will connect fans and musical artists and help guide MTV's strategy.
- MTV hires local talent when entering new markets; its recent global expansion includes more broadcasting channels and Internet sites.

Like other brands, MTV is turning to new communications technology and to other countries to expand its presence. MTV employees acknowledge that they learn about MTV viewers through social media services such as Facebook and Twitter.

Besides its interest in social media, MTV offers a number of Internet sites. In 2012 it started Artists.MTV, a website featuring famous and emerging artists and their music, merchandise, and other offerings. MTV hopes that this site will encourage the interaction between musical artists and fans and help direct the future strategy for the MTV brand.

The brand is increasingly global. When entering a new international market, MTV prefers to hire local people instead of importing its own employees. It now features television channels and Internet sites targeting different countries, ethnic groups, and types of music. While the MTV brand still offers young people music, it now offers more.

FURTHER READING

Bradshaw, Leslie. "Keeping the 'M' in MTV: MTV's Amy Doyle on Maintaining the Network's Musical Relevance," *Forbes*, September 6, 2012.

Brand Finance. "Global 500 2012." *Brandirectory*. Accessed September 6, 2012. http://brandirectory.com/league_tables/table/global-500-2012.

DeCarlo, Scott, ed. "The World's Biggest Public Companies." *Forbes*, April 18, 2012.

Hesse, Monica. "A Total End of an Era in Pop Videos." *Washington Post*, September 17, 2008.

Mianecki, Julie. "Air and Space Museum's 'Moon Man' Celebrates MTV's 30th Anniversary." Around the Mall. Smithsonian.com. August 1, 2011. Accessed September 5, 2012. http://blogs.smithsonianmag.com/aroundthemall/2011/08/nasms-moon-man-celebrates-mtvs-30th-anniversary/.

"MTV Networks, Inc." *Company Profiles for Students*. Ed. Donna Craft and Amanda Quick. Vol. 3. Detroit, MI: Gale, 2002.

"Napster and iTunes Most Recognized Brands in Fee-based Downloading in 2004," Ipsos MediaCT, December 7, 2004. Accessed September 6, 2012. http://www.ipsosmediact.com/knowledge/pressrelease.aspx?id=2484.

Rusch, Robin D. "MTV Networks Internationally." *Brandchannel*, July 26, 2004. Accessed September 6, 2012. http://www.brandchannel.com/features_effect.asp?pf_id=221.

Surette, Tim. "MTV Finally Gives up on Music." TV.com, February 10, 2010. Accessed September 5, 2012. http://www.tv.com/news/mtv-finally-gives-up-on-music-21327/.

"2011 Ranking of the Top 100 Brands." Interbrand. Accessed July 3, 2012. http://www.interbrand.com/en/best-global-brands/best-global-brands-2008/best-global-brands-2011.aspx.

"Viacom, Inc." *International Directory of Company Histories*. Ed. Jay P. Pederson and Miranda H. Ferrara. Vol. 67. Detroit, MI: St. James Press, 2005.

Viacom, Inc. "2011 Annual Report." New York: Viacom, Inc., 2011. Accessed September 6, 2012. http://www.annual-reports.com/Company/4471.

Warner, Charles. "Pittman, Robert W." Museum of Broadcast Communications. Accessed September 5, 2012. http://www.museum.tv/eotvsection.php?entrycode=pittmanrobe

NATIONAL BASKETBALL ASSOCIATION (NBA)

AT A GLANCE

Brand Synopsis: The National Basketball Association strives to bring the love of basketball to fans everywhere with a focus on talent, excitement, and the dynamic action of the game.

Parent Company: NBA, Inc.
645 Fifth Avenue
New York, NY, 10022
United States
http://www.nba.com

Sector: Consumer Discretionary

Industry Group: Media

Performance: *Sales*—US$3.96 billion (2011).

Principal Competitors: National Football League; Major League Baseball; National Hockey League

BRAND ORIGINS

- James Naismith, a YMCA instructor, invented basketball in 1891, and the sport eventually spread throughout the world.
- Professional basketball leagues were slow in gaining fan support and world attention; the NBA did not pick up momentum until the late 1960s.
- Not until individual stars like Larry Bird and Magic Johnson began to compete did the NBA become what it is today.

- The NBA earned its global reputation in the 1980s following the 1984 Olympic Games and Michael Jordan's entrance into the league.

In 1891 James Naismith, an instructor for a YMCA training school, attached two peach baskets on the railing of a gymnasium track and taught members to shoot balls into the baskets. This was the birth of modern-day basketball. The Y's missionaries spread the sport around the country and the world. They brought basketball to France, India, and China and to gyms in Brooklyn, Philadelphia, and other cities. In the early part of the 20th century, several professional leagues formed but soon failed. It was not until the National Basketball League (formed in 1937) and the Basketball Association of America (formed in 1946) joined together in 1949 that the National Basketball Association (NBA) emerged. And even then, the NBA had a difficult beginning. Teams were few and had difficulty staying in business. Additionally, the early rules of the game made it uneventful, with the result that attendance at games was often low.

In the 1960s the NBA made changes to the rules to quicken play and attract more types of players. The league started to capture fan attention as games became more challenging, and talented players and teams built exciting rivalries. With the start of the American Basketball Association (ABA), which recruited talented college players, competition increased, and in 1976 the ABA merged with the NBA, bringing additional teams to the NBA. By the late 1970s, however, the NBA had retired its best players, and teams' reputations' suffered as crime and drug use plagued the league. Fan interest dwindled.

Fortunately for the league, Larry Bird of the Boston Celtics and Earvin "Magic" Johnson of the L.A. Lakers continued their college basketball rivalry on the NBA courts in the early 1980s. Their presence saved the NBA, as their seven-game championship series in 1984 attracted the largest television audience in NBA history. It was also in 1984 that Michael Jordan entered the NBA. The game would never be the same. Jordan combined tremendous athletic skill, determination, and business savvy. He demonstrated the importance of the individually branded player within the league and helped turn NBA basketball into one of the most profitable entertainment properties in the world. Players like Jordan caught the attention of the world and contributed to the league's global expansion. During this time the entrance of professional basketball into the Olympics also thrust the NBA onto the global stage. While individual players continue to interest fans and increase licensing profits, the league is pushing to return to more team-oriented competition and a focus on the game itself.

BRAND ELEMENTS

- The NBA's logo, designed by Alan Siegel, is a white silhouette of a man dribbling a basketball on a rectangular, red-and-blue background.
- The colors and the image of Jerry West on the NBA logo represent the league's attempt to position basketball as an all-American sport.
- The logo is a classic symbol that readily identifies the league and earns the NBA about US$3 billion annually in licensing fees.

The NBA's classic logo was created in 1969 by Alan Siegel, a branding expert and lifelong basketball fan. The logo, a silhouette of a man dribbling a basketball in white on a rectangular, red-and-blue background, was designed as part of a strategy to rejuvenate the league's image. According to the *Los Angeles Times,* then-Commissioner J. Walter Kennedy accomplished this by choosing red, white, and blue colors for the logo—just as Siegel had done for Major League Baseball several years before—to position basketball as an all-American game. While the NBA will not confirm his claims, Siegel says the logo was designed based on a photograph of guard Jerry West during a Los Angeles Lakers' game because the picture of West captured the all-American image that the league was trying to portray. During a 2010 interview Siegel explained why the NBA wants to remain noncommittal about the logo: "They want to institutionalize it rather than individualize it. It's become such a ubiquitous, classic symbol and focal point of their identity and their licensing program that they don't necessarily want to identify it with one player."

Keeping the logo generalized also benefits the NBA's current brand strategy of returning its focus to the game itself. At a time when the league wants to downplay the showiness of individual star players, maintaining the classic logo is a good move, particularly in consideration of the fact that the image generates about US$3 billion a year in licensing and is synonymous with the pinnacle of excellence in professional basketball.

BRAND IDENTITY

- Since 2007 the NBA has tried to more clearly define its brand by reconnecting fans to the game rather than to individual players.
- The 2007 "Where Amazing Happens" advertising campaign aimed to ignite NBA fans' passion for the game of the basketball.
- The results of the NBA's rebranding effort have led to greater ticket sales, increased television viewership, and a jump in merchandise sales.

When most fans think about the National Basketball Association, oftentimes a particular player—such as Michael Jordan, Kobe Bryant, or LeBron James—comes to mind. In the not-too-distant past, the high-fashion, high-profile lifestyles of the league's players often overshadowed the purpose of the league itself: to entertain fans with the exciting, competitive game of basketball. However, in recent years, the NBA has tried hard to reconnect its brand image with the love of the game rather than the lives of its players. According to research conducted by the NBA in 2007, fans did not recognize a clear picture of the NBA brand. "The best of the game was being obscured: charisma was seen as ego, talent was being perceived as showboating, and captivating personalities were being misinterpreted as individualistic." The NBA's response to its fans' perceptions was to take control of its brand image and define it by refocusing on the dynamic and exciting action taking place on the court.

In 2007 the NBA launched an interactive, global advertising campaign titled "Where Amazing Happens." Rather than raising brand awareness, the campaign was aimed at reconnecting fans to everything they love about basketball: the competition, the coaches, the players, and, mostly, the passion shared by all involved. The strategy worked. Fans became more involved, game attendance increased, television viewership increased, and NBA-licensed merchandise sales jumped. Today, the NBA still uses this umbrella campaign, but it has created additional campaigns like "There Can Only Be One" that continue to push the love of the sport and the fans' involvement in the game.

BRAND STRATEGY

- Positioning basketball as the world's favorite sport is at the core of the NBA's brand strategy.
- The NBA strives to create multiple means of fan interaction with basketball and the NBA brand in order to expand globally.

- NBA initiatives, events, and access to large media networks aid in creating touch-points that maximize fan interaction on a global scale.

While the NBA has been a global presence since the emergence of Michael Jordan and the 1984 Olympic team, the league's current brand strategy focuses mainly on strengthening its position around the world. In 2008, alongside the rebranding effort aimed at rekindling the love of the game, the NBA worked to make basketball the world's most popular sport. To take this position from soccer, the NBA set out to be in every point where fans can interact with the game. According to an article by Charles Euchner in the *American* magazine, the strategy is an integrated one where "touch-points" are created to get fans to interact with the game: the NBA wants fans to play basketball, watch it on television, play NBA video games, buy NBA apparel, and interacting with the league via apps on smartphones and other devices. According to Heidi Ueberroth, top officer for global growth, "There must be constant promotion of the NBA's stamp, its corporate partners, and its larger-than-life players. The NBA brand must become as recognizable as Coca-Cola or McDonald's."

A good example of these "touch-points" came during the 2012 Olympic Games in London. The NBA opened the NBA House as a place for fans to gather, play ball, and share their love of the sport. According to *Marketing Event,* the house, where admission was free, was specifically targeted to open first in the United Kingdom because basketball is a developing sport there. The NBA wanted to create a tangible touch-point for British fans to experience the basketball lifestyle and the culture that goes with it.

In addition to creating global events, David Stern, NBA commissioner, put to work his great understanding of the importance of satellite networks and Internet capabilities to further advance the NBA brand. According to Charles Euchner in the *American* magazine, "More than 900 NBA games and 45,000 hours of NBA programming are seen in 215 countries in 41 languages with 188 TV partners." Likewise, the NBA's presence on the web is overwhelming. From its own interactive website to the Internet broadcasts of games around the world, the NBA has used media to strengthen its fan base and create touch-points in places where fans could not otherwise be reached.

BRAND EQUITY

- Despite difficult economic times, sports leagues continue to successfully earn revenue and turn a profit.
- In 2011 the NBA earned US$3.9 billion in revenues despite a shortened season caused by a lockout.

- In 2012 the NBA's average franchise value was an estimated US$393 million, a record high for the league.

Despite the world's slow climb out of the recent economic recession, professional sports have continued to do well. According to the *US Professional Sports Market & Franchise Value Report,* "All four major sports leagues have shown remarkable resilience and pricing power in the past, and appear poised to recover far faster than the economy overall." In the NBA, ticket sales, ticket prices, and regular season attendance all increased modestly in 2011 as compared to 2010. However, the 2011 lockout did disrupt the sales potential for the NBA. According to the *US Professional Sports Market & Franchise Value Report,* the lockout "led to a financial loss of an estimated US$800 million for owners and players alike." Although sales were less than they could have been, the NBA still took in revenues of US$3.9 billion during the 2011–2012 season. Overcoming the lockout also earned the NBA an all-time high in terms of its average franchise value, which was an estimated US$393 million, according to the 2012 *US Professional Sports Market & Franchise Value Report,* showing a strong rebound from a previous two-year lull.

BRAND AWARENESS

- The NBA has earned top-of-mind awareness both domestically and abroad.
- China provides an excellent example of the NBA's high recognition, with 89 percent of Chinese aged 15 to 54 aware of the NBA brand.
- In China the NBA brand is associated with the drive toward excellence.

The NBA's brand awareness domestically and throughout the world is top-of-mind. With international game coverage, player celebrities, global initiatives, slam-dunk contests, and philanthropic events, the NBA's brand works hard to promote its name. China provides an excellent example of the brand's level of recognition in other countries and its success as an all-American sport. According to the Charles Euchner, writing for the *American* magazine, "The NBA reckons that 300 million Chinese watch NBA games on TV or the Internet. That's roughly the entire U.S. population. Eighty-nine percent of Chinese aged 15 to 54 are aware of the NBA." At the Expo 2010 Shanghai, China's version of the World's Fair, the NBA was one of America's most recognizable brands, according to the *New York Times.* Because the NBA has been televised in China for more than 20 years, and because it continues to promote itself in China as a brand that exhibits American values, China has truly experienced a basketball craze. It identifies the brand as one that strives for excellence, a goal that is considered to be at the heart of the United

States. This type of global marketing is at the core of the NBA's brand strategy and the reason that its brand awareness is high all over the world.

BRAND OUTLOOK

- The success of the sports sector in general and its successful rebranding campaign gives the NBA brand a promising future.
- The "Where Amazing Happens" campaign continues to connect fans to the passion of basketball itself, which will lead to a longer-lasting brand image.
- The NBA's commitment to corporate responsibility also bodes well for the future success of the brand.

According to 2012 *US Professional Sports Market & Franchise Value Report,* the spectator sports' percentage share of total personal consumption has continued to rise because even in difficult economic times, professional sports appear to have a promising future. The NBA's outlook also appears bright due to its recent rebranding efforts. The NBA's research team reported that they "did not just set out to impact the NBA business short-term. Their hope was to create a long-term platform for the NBA that could continue to create emotional reengagement with the league and the game." Their 2008, and still-current, advertising campaign, "Where Amazing Happens," has achieved tremendous success in helping fans to re-embrace the game of basketball and remind them why they love the sport. This campaign has also significantly contributed to the NBA's success in marketing its brand around the globe. People everywhere connect with both the game and the culture that the NBA projects.

Moreover, the NBA has used its focus on the love of the game and its popularity to help the world around it. With many global initiatives like NBA Green and NBA Cares, the league and its players help to address social issues such as education, youth and family development, and health and wellness. Building a brand that uses its celebrity to help others is important to the league and to its continued success because it enables the world to see the NBA as more than just a sports league. It sees the league as a relevant part of culture that gives back to the world that it has the privilege to entertain.

FURTHER READING

Belson, Ken. "The NBA brand, on display in China." *Off the Dribble: The New York Times NBA Blog. New York Times,* June 30, 2010. Accessed December 8, 2012. http://offthedribble.blogs.nytimes.com/2010/06/30/the-n-b-a-brand-on-display-in-china/.

"Brand NBA: Court Judgment." *Marketing Event,* September 1, 2012. *General OneFile.* Accessed December 9, 2012. http://go.galegroup.com/ps/i.do?id=GALE%7CA301449342&v=2.1&u=itsbtrial&it=r&p=GPS&sw=w.

Crowe, Jerry. "That iconic NBA silhouette can be traced back to him." *Los Angeles Times,* April 27, 2010. Accessed December 5, 2012. http://articles.latimes.com/2010/apr/27/sports/la-sp-crowe-20100427.

Edelman, Rob. "National Basketball Association." *Bowling, Beatniks, and Bell-Bottoms: Pop Culture of 20th-Century America.* Ed. Sara Pendergast and Tom Pendergast. Vol. 3. Detroit: UXL, 2002. *Gale Virtual Reference Library.* Accessed December 5, 2012. http://go.galegroup.com/ps/i.do?id=GALE%7CCX3425100364&v=2.1&u=itsbtrial&it=r&p=GVRL&sw=w.

Euchner, Charles. "Hoop Dreams." *American,* January-February 2008. Accessed February 25, 2013. http://www.american.com/archive/2008/january-february-magazine-contents/hoop-dreams/?searchterm=nba.

Janof, Barry. "Playoff push 'splits' NBA players; Kia, IHOP join WNBA roster." *Brandweek,* April 7, 2008. *General OneFile.* Accessed December 9, 2012. http://go.galegroup.com/ps/i.do?id=GALE%7CA177872382&v=2.1&u=itsbtrial&it=r&p=GPS&sw=w.

Schnakenberg, Robert E. "National Basketball Association (NBA)." *St. James Encyclopedia of Popular Culture.* Ed. Sara Pendergast and Tom Pendergast. Vol. 3. Detroit: St. James Press, 2000. *Gale Virtual Reference Library.* Accessed December 6, 2012. http://go.galegroup.com/ps/i.do?id=GALE%7CCX3409001774&v=2.1&u=itsbtrial&it=r&p=GVRL&sw=w.

WR Hambrecht and Co. Sports Finance Group. *The US Professional Sports Market & Franchise Value Report 2012.* Accessed December 7, 2012. http://www.wrhambrecht.com/pdf/SportsMarketReport_2012.pdf.

NATIONAL FOOTBALL LEAGUE (NFL)

—■—

AT A GLANCE

—■—

Brand Synopsis: With its heavily armored players, aggressive style of play, and use of military language and music, the National Football League (NFL) defines itself as the sports league of warriors.

Parent Company: National Football League
280 Park Avenue, 15th Floor
New York, New York 10017
United States
http://www.nfl.com

Sector: Consumer Discretionary

Industry Group: Media

Performance: *Market share*—Number-one sports league in the United States. *Sales*—US$8.86 billion (2011).

Principal Competitors: National Basketball Association (NBA); Major League Baseball (MLB); National Hockey League (NHL); National Association of Stock Car Auto Racing (NASCAR)

BRAND ORIGINS

- Football was developed in the 1870s as a hybrid of rugby and soccer, and its first official rules were written in 1876.
- Professional leagues attempted to form in the early 1900s, and the NFL was established in 1920.
- The NFL grew in popularity quickly; by 1962 it had signed its first single-network television contract with CBS for US$4.6 million.

- With the help of business-savvy commissioners, a licensing firm, and multibillion-dollar television contracts, the NFL has become one of the best-run companies in the world.

Combining aspects of soccer and rugby, American football developed during the early 1870s, distinguishing itself as a separate sport in 1876 when the first rules for the game were written. The sport's popularity spread quickly, and by the 1890s the concept of paid players and professional teams was emerging. Intense competition, uncapped salary increases, and player movements from team to team became rampant, creating a need for standards. After various attempts were made to form professional leagues, the American Professional Football Association (APFA) was established in 1920. At the end of the first year, the APFA was composed of 14 professional teams. By 1922, when the name officially became the National Football League, it had grown to include 22 teams.

For the next 20 years, the NFL made many changes to improve the game and the league: rules were developed that distinguished the pro game from college-level play; the number of franchises was reduced, but the franchises' financial structure was strengthened; team schedules were organized into equal numbers of games, with the first playoff and championship series taking place in 1932; and the first televised game was broadcast in 1939. During the 1950s exposure on television and radio increased the popularity of professional football, and in 1962 the NFL signed the first single-network agreement with CBS for broadcasting all regular-season games. This contract, valued at US$4.6 million annually, marked the beginning of the bidding war waged by the networks to secure the rights for NFL games. Two years later, CBS paid US$14.1 million for broadcasting rights. These numbers demonstrate the popularity the NFL enjoyed in the United States in the 1960s as it surpassed baseball as the television's most lucrative sport. To help take advantage of the financial windfall, NFL Properties Inc. was formed in 1963 to serve as the licensing arm of the NFL.

Also contributing to the league's financial success were two major developments: a reorganization in the early 1960s of the way in which televised games were negotiated and shared among teams and the 1970 merger with the American Football League. NFL Commissioner Pete Rozelle spearheaded the idea of the separate franchises banding together to act as one big business. By the time Rozelle retired in 1989, the NFL had signed a four-year, US$3.6 billion contract with the three major television networks and two cable networks, the largest deal of its kind in television history. In the 1990s a new European league started, and with it came another historic multistation television contract for US$17.6 billion in 1998. While the new millennium brought legal issues for individual players, disputes with the NFL licensing company, and hazardous collective-bargaining negotiations, it also brought outstanding revenues, additional television contracts, an NFL-owned television network, and one of the strongest brands in history.

BRAND ELEMENTS

- The famous red, white, and blue shield logo has become synonymous with the NFL.
- The NFL logo was slightly modernized in 2008 to allow the league to better connect its fans to the game and the passion it creates.
- The eight stars on the logo represent the eight divisions of the NFL, and the image of the football closely resembles the league's championship trophy.

The NFL's identity is heavily associated with its famous red, white, and blue logo. The logo, which had a minor facelift before the 2008 season, is a blue-and-white shield, with "NFL" in red on the bottom and a white football flanked on each side by four white stars on the top. According to a report in *USA Today*, the number of stars was changed from 25 to 8 to represent the league's 8 divisions, and the football was redesigned to resemble the ball atop the Vince Lombardi championship trophy. Because the Lombardi trophy is now a part of the Super Bowl logo every year, connecting the league logo with the Super Bowl logo gives a streamlined visual identity to the brand. These changes link the logo more closely to the league and to the game, whereas the former logo's 25 stars had no symbolic purpose, and the football represented an old-fashioned pigskin and lacked a visual association with the championship. A large

part of the league's brand value comes from the passion of its fans. The use of a logo that conjures images of "their" teams, the competitive nature of the game, and the trophy that represents the best of the best further enhance what was already the premier sports brand.

BRAND IDENTITY

- The NFL has positioned itself as the premier sports and entertainment brand.
- The NFL brand is powered by the reciprocal passion of players, teams, and fans.
- Six core values guide the NFL brand: tradition, teamwork, excellence, community, integrity, and innovation.

The NFL has positioned itself as the premier sports and entertainment brand. It strives to remain relevant to its fans by bringing them together socially and emotionally. This unity is based upon the reciprocal passion between players, teams, and fans. The essence of the NFL brand comes from creating and capitalizing on that passion.

The league fosters passion among its fans by promoting its core values through everyone who represents the NFL. The values—tradition, teamwork, excellence, community, integrity, and innovation—are meant to guide all communication between the NFL and its consumers. Making sure that teams and coaches are diverse and connected to the communities in which they play is a crucial element of the professional excellence that the NFL brand represents. Fans are attracted to the league's ability to celebrate its own rich history while keeping the sport current and relevant.

BRAND STRATEGY

- Creating and protecting fan allegiance and passion is at the heart of the NFL's brand strategy.
- Capitalizing on changing demographics, such as the increasing number of female fans, has brought the NFL new audiences and new licensing opportunities.
- The NFL promotes its brand globally and in 2012 was reported to be considering the establishment of a permanent NFL franchise in London.

According to branding expert Rob Wolfe, "The NFL is not in the football business—its product is not football. The NFL is a media company that captures the mystique—the football aura—that pulses into the soul of the football fan." Creating and protecting that aura is at the heart of the NFL's brand strategy. It is clear from the amount of money spent on advertising during NFL broadcasts that its brand has earned its rank as the top sports league, perhaps even the number one prime-time television attraction, in the United States. However, the 2012 referee lockout offered an interesting example of how important fan passion is to the perseverance of the brand. During the lockout, fans became incensed at the plunging quality of the game, and they expressed their anger. It seemed a poor decision for a multibillion-dollar enterprise to let fans' spirit slip in an effort to save a few hundred thousand dollars. This blemish on an otherwise pristine brand offered an important lesson in brand strategy: invest in the game that pleases the fans because the end result will only bear more fruit.

A greater investment in fans is also at the core of another NFL brand strategy: appealing to broader demographics. Understanding how its fan base has changed over time has helped the league broaden its audience and increase its tickets sales and licensing revenues. A good example is the league's appeal to its fastest-growing demographic in recent years—women. According to a report in *Forbes*, by 2012 women had "become over 44 percent of its fan base, with 60 percent of females over the age of 12 identifying themselves as NFL fans. Last season, 80 million women watched NFL games and roughly 310,000 women attended NFL games each weekend." Cultivating this demographic is big business for the league. In recent years the NFL has begun an entire clothing and accessory line designed just for women. From Victoria's Secret loungewear and Marchesa clothing to boots and watches, the NFL has provided women with fashionable items in their favorite teams' colors. Additionally, the NFL launched "It's My Team," an advertising campaign aimed at women, to ensure that the business effort was worthwhile. According to the *Forbes* report, the ads, which featured high-profile female NFL fans such as former U.S. secretary of state Condoleezza Rice dressed in NFL apparel, helped push the NFL's total consumer product sales to US$3.2 million.

In addition to its U.S. fan base, the NFL also seeks to broaden its international reach. Since the 1980s, the NFL has made frequent forays into Europe, trying to establish a global connection to American football. Since 2006 the NFL has hosted the International Series at Wembley Stadium in London, a game that attracts an enormous crowd. In 2012 the NFL announced that the Jacksonville Jaguars would play one home game in London for each season from 2013 to 2016, a move that was seen as a test of the fan base in the United Kingdom, which the league is considering as the location for a permanent franchise in the future.

BRAND EQUITY

- Despite difficult economic times, the NFL has grown to be the richest sports league in the world, with annual revenues of about US$9 billion.
- The NFL's revenues derive largely from media contracts—in 2011 it reached an agreement with Fox, CBS, and NBC for US$28 billion over nine years.

- The NFL far surpasses its competition, with an average franchise value of more than US$1 billion.

Despite the world's slow recovery from economic recession, professional sports continued to fare well. The NFL grew steadily during the first decade of the 21st century. According to a report in the U.S. edition of the *International Business Times*, the league's growth is driven in large part by its highly profitable national TV contracts. In 2011 Fox, NBC, and CBS agreed to pay US$3.1 billion annually and a total of US$28 billion in fees over nine years for the rights to NFL broadcasting, a 63 percent increase over the US$1.9 billion paid annually under the previous contract.

Revenue gains and the brand's huge fan base have put the league far ahead of its competition. According to a report in the *International Business Times*, the NFL, rated by *Forbes* as the world's richest professional sports league, with more than US$9 billion in annual revenues, overshadows its rivals. With a far higher average franchise value (slightly more than US$1 billion), the NFL has demonstrated its superiority over its closest competitors in this regard, whose values are US$393 million (NBA) and US$523 million (MLB), respectively. The NFL's average team value rose by US$570 million over 10 years, according to the 2012 *US Professional Sports Market & Franchise Value Report*.

BRAND AWARENESS

- The NFL seeks top-of-mind awareness domestically and internationally.
- The NFL's cobranding efforts have led to brand awareness among non-NFL fans across the United States.
- The NFL seeks to push its global awareness beyond Europe and into China.

Present in all forms of public media, in video games, at the local shopping mall, and at many charitable events, the NFL brand has achieved top-of-mind awareness in the United States. According to branding expert Rob Wolfe, "For any individual, the NFL brand is with them from the earliest age they can remember through old age." Additionally, the NFL's cobranding efforts help it reach millions of other consumers who may not necessarily tune in to games each week, giving it an extremely recognizable brand domestically.

Part of the league's strategy is to achieve this brand awareness on a global scale. While football is becoming increasingly popular in Europe, the NFL is also seeking to extend its reach into Asia. Quoted in a Reuters report that was published in the *International Business Times* in 2012, Richard Young, the NFL's China managing director, said "Most people in China don't know what a quarterback does, but our research shows they recognize the NFL shield and the NFL brand quite well, actually a lot better than most people think and a lot higher than many leagues who are also in China." In 2011 more than 1 million people in China watched the Super Bowl online, while cumulative television viewership was at 80 million across the country for the season. The NFL will not hold any games in China until it can guarantee that the brand will hold, but it is investing in the market.

BRAND OUTLOOK

- The success of the sports sector in general and the NFL's ability to draw millions of fans each game day portend a promising future for the league.
- With rising ticket prices and steady fan attendance, the NFL continues to achieve record growth despite the recent slow economy.
- The NFL's successful contract negotiations in 2012 with players and referees fortified its brand for success for at least another decade.

According to the 2012 *US Professional Sports Market & Franchise Value Report*, because the percentage share of spectator sports in the total personal consumption category continues to rise, even in the current difficult economic times, professional sports appears to have a promising future. While spectators may have financial difficulties, their willingness to spend money on sports entertainment has not wavered much. The NFL's long history and harmonious balance of tradition and modernity helped keep fan attendance holding steady between 17.1 and 17.6 million during the five years leading up to the 2012 season. The league's average ticket price increased 4.4 percent during the same period. The average ticket price during the 2011 season was US$77.34.

In 2012 the NFL initiated a 10-year contract between the NFL Players Association and the franchise owners, as well as a contract with its referees. With those components in place for at least a decade, the league was able to turn its focus to expanding its brand to a global market. If the NFL can create the kind of successful brand identity internationally that it enjoys domestically, it will maintain its position as the world's richest and most popular sports entertainment league.

FURTHER READING

Breer, Albert. "NFL Team in London? League Entering New Phase of UK Project." National Football League, October 23, 2012. Accessed December 17, 2012. http://www.nfl.com/news/story/0ap1000000084365/article/nfl-team-in-london-league-entering-new-phase-of-uk-project.

Communicating the NFL Brand: Identity Guidelines. National Football League, 2007. Accessed December 11, 2012. http://sign2esymbol.files.wordpress.com/2010/05/nflbrandingguidelines.pdf.

Covell, Jeffrey L., and Stephen Meyer. "National Football League." *International Directory of Company Histories.* Ed. Derek Jacques and Paula Kepos. Vol. 115. Detroit, MI: St. James Press, 2010.

Jess, Alicia. "How New Marketing Approaches Helped the NFL Achieve Triple-Digit Growth in Women's Apparel Sales." *Forbes*, November 26, 2012.

McCarthy, Michael. "NFL to Revamp Shield with Redesigned Logo." *USA Today*, August 31, 2007.

"No NFL Game in China Anytime Soon." *International Business Times*, November 8, 2012.

W. R. Hambrecht and Co. Sports Finance Group. *The US Professional Sports Market & Franchise Value Report 2012.* Accessed December 7, 2012. http://www.wrhambrecht.com/pdf/SportsMarketReport_2012.pdf.

Wolfe, Rob. "Tis the Season for Hailing the NFL Brand." *Business to Community*, October 12, 2012. Accessed December 11, 2012. http://www.business2community.com/branding/tis-the-season-for-hailing-the-nfl-brand-0305565.

NESCAFÉ

—■—

AT A GLANCE

—■—

Brand Synopsis: Globally synonymous with instant coffee, Nescafé is the world's number-one brand.

Parent Company: Nestlé S.A.
Avenue Nestlé 55
Vevey CH-1800
Switzerland
http://www.nescafe.com/

Sector: Consumer Staples

Industry Group: Food, Beverage & Tobacco

Performance: *Market share*—51 percent in instant coffee (2010). *Revenues*—US$10.1 billion (2011).

Principal Competitors: Giraldo Farms; Green Mountain Coffee Roasters, Inc.; Hindustan Unilever Ltd.; The J.M. Smucker Co.; Massimo Zanetti Beverage Group; Mondelēz International; Rowland Coffee Roasters, Inc.; Starbucks Corp.; Wertform GmbH

BRAND ORIGINS

- Nescafé instant coffee was introduced in 1938.
- Nescafé instant coffee was well liked among U.S. military personnel during World War II, which helped spread its popularity.
- Nescafé introduced its Gold Blend, a freeze-dried water soluble version of Nescafé, in the mid-1960s.
- In the 21st century Nescafé was the second most valuable brand in the global drinks sector after Coca-Cola.

Nescafé was one of the first commercially available instant coffees, a creation of the Nestlé company, which previously had specialized in milk-based products such as chocolate and condensed milk. During the 1920s Nestlé invested in a condensed milk factory in Brazil. By 1930 the Brazilian Coffee Institute asked Nestlé if it could develop and manufacture what was termed "coffee cubes" that would be instantly soluble in hot water. Previously, instant coffee made from coffee crystals or liquid extracts had been attempted, but the experiments were unsuccessful as the coffee taste was not preserved.

Using its expertise in milk processing, Nescafé spent seven years on the project and developed a soluble powder. This instant coffee was created by spray-drying brewed coffee and adding carbohydrates to seal in the coffee flavor. Production capacity was limited, so the product was introduced in 1938 without much marketing. In 1939 Nescafé instant coffee was launched in the United States, France, and Great Britain.

Soon after the introduction of Nescafé, World War II broke out, disrupting coffee supplies and creating an inability to complete needed factories in Europe. Despite such setbacks, Nescafé proved popular in the United States. The U.S. military relied on Nescafé after entering the conflict in 1941. American soldiers took it all over the globe, introducing it to civilian populations in Europe and Asia, which added to its popularity. By 1944, one million cases were produced annually. Nescafé contributed to Nestlé's sales increasing from US$100 million before the war to US$225 million by 1945. In the United States most Nescafé production went to the military until after 1946, when a price war erupted among the instant coffees on the market.

Nestlé soon reintroduced Nescafé with a broad advertising campaign and built factories worldwide to keep up with consumer demand. By the early 1950s Nescafé had about 30 percent of the U.S. instant coffee market, but it lost market share over the next decade to other instant coffees, including the decaffeinated instant brand Sanka. By the mid-1960s, Nescafé only had about 12 percent market share in the United States.

Beginning in the mid-1960s, a new, more natural flavor Nescafé was introduced that could be made strong without any bitterness. About the same time, Nescafé Gold Blend, a freeze-dried water soluble version of Nescafé, hit the market. Nestlé then debuted another brand of freeze-dried coffee, Taster's Choice, which proved more successful than Nescafé in the United States, although Nescafé had become the best-selling brand of instant coffee in the world by this time.

From 1978 to the early 1980s, coffee consumption and total market volume were on a significant decline both in the United States and worldwide. Regular Nescafé saw its market share in the instant coffee category in the United States decline from 8.7 percent in 1978 to 7 percent in 1981, while Nescafé Decaffeinated slipped from 2.5 percent in 1978 to 2.1 percent in 1981. Nestlé tried to revitalize Nescafé in the United States by introducing Nescafé Custom Blended Instant, which had four flavors (Brava, Silka, Classic, and a decaffeinated Classic), in 1983. It was accompanied by an ad campaign, "Nescafé … taste your way."

During this period Nescafé added new blends such as Nescafé Mountain Blend, regular and decaf, which combined select mountain-grown coffee beans and a chicory flavor. The brand was trying to take advantage of rising coffee prices in the mid-1980s. By 1989 Nescafé Regular held 7.3 percent of U.S. market share, and Nescafé Decaffeinated comprised 2.7 percent. It was popular in international markets, including the United Kingdom, and held 70 percent of the Japanese market by 1989. Introduced in Korea in 1991, Nescafé quickly became a leading brand there as well.

Following on the success of iced coffee in Japan by 1990, Nescafé introduced Nescafé Mocha Cooler in select markets in the United States with ads calling it "The cooler for an uncool world." Iced coffee was expected to attract younger consumers who preferred cold, sweet beverages. In 1991 regular Nescafé was renamed Nescafé Classic, with ads that proclaimed, "Make a fresh start." In 1992 Nescafé was reformulated and called Nescafé Coffee Crystals. These changes led to a 9.7 market share in the U.S. instant coffee category by 1994 and contributed to its retaining its place as the best-selling instant coffee in the world.

To remain supreme, Nescafé continued to aggressively market itself and add new products to its product line in the early 21st century. In 2001 Nescafé began a US$30 million global advertising campaign targeting 16- to 24-year-olds. In 2003 it introduced Ice Java coffee syrup line in the United States, which allowed consumers to make iced coffee anytime. In 2008 Nescafé Café Menu coffee drinks and the Dolce Gusto system hit the market. As a result of such moves, Nescafé was the second most valuable brand in the global drinks sector after Coca-Cola, with almost 3,000 cups of Nescafé consumed every second by 2004. By 2009 Nescafé had four of the top 10 coffee brands in the United Kingdom, with Nescafé Original at one number, Nescafé Gold Blend at two, Nescafé Cappuccino at number eight, and Nescafé Decaf at number nine. By 2011 Nescafé was emphasizing quality products over convenience and supported brandwide environmental initiatives.

BRAND ELEMENTS

- The name Nescafé is a combination of Nestlé and café.
- The Nescafé name includes *café*, the Portuguese word for coffee.
- The Nescafé logo includes the brand name in all capital letters with a line stretching out from the top of the *N* over the rest of the letters.

Nescafé instant coffee is a signature product of the Switzerland-based Nestlé company, a global leader in the food and beverage business for decades. The first non-milk product produced by the company, Nescafé was created in Brazil during the 1930s when a large coffee surplus threatened to drive prices down worldwide. The name Nescafé links the coffee to the already globally popular Nestlé brand and emphasizes its Brazilian origins by combining the first three letters of *Nest*lé with *café*, the Portuguese word for coffee.

Since its introduction, Nescafé has had a distinctive logo that has remained essentially the same since the late 1930s. The Nescafé name appears in all capital letters with a line stretching out from the top of the upper stroke of the *N* over the rest of the letters. While originally the extension crossed the *E* and its accent and had a companion line from the bottom of the downward stroke of the *N*, more recent versions stretch only to the *F*, allowing the accent to remain in place. On Nescafé Classic labels, a red mug always appears, with red serving as a signature color of the brand.

BRAND IDENTITY

- Although a global brand, Nescafé strives to engage regional tastes with unique blends offered in different parts of the world.
- Nescafé's advertising emphasizes human relationships and the ability of coffee to bring people together.
- Nescafé television advertisements featuring the Gold Blend couple created a sensation in Britain in the 1980s and '90s and were later adapted for the U.S. market.
- In the 21st century Nescafé emphasized its natural purity and the restorative powers of coffee in the noisy modern world.

The global market leader in instant coffee and related coffee products, Nescafé created the market for instant coffee in the mid-20th century and embraces its identity as the best known instant coffee brand, especially in markets in Asia, Europe, Latin America, and Oceania. Although Nescafé has certain signature products generally available worldwide, the brand strives to engage regional tastes by offering blends that will appeal to local palettes. While Nescafé has had some global campaigns, most of its marketing and advertising is similarly tailored to specific markets making the brand's identity simultaneously global and local. To further build the brand identity, Nescafé has an active online presence, including Facebook, Twitter, and a dedicated YouTube channel.

Nescafé advertisements throughout the years have focused on home, relationships, and marriage. The brand's best known television campaign began in the United Kingdom in 1987 and ran for more than 10 years. To promote Nescafé Gold Blend, the brand introduced the Gold Blend couple, neighbors (played by Anthony Head and Sharon Maughan) who begin a flirtation when one borrows coffee from the other. The ads became a sensation in Britain, with 30 million British viewers tuned in for the episode in which the couple first kiss. Sales of Gold Blend increased by 70 percent during the time the ads ran. The commercials later were adapted for the U.S. market and used to promote another Nestlé instant coffee product, Taster's Choice.

Marketing in the 21st century emphasized the purity of Nescafé products and their ability to foster relationships and restore tranquility in the noisy modern world. In Argentina television ads for the Dolca line depicted people escaping from bothersome situations with a cup of Dolca. A British advertising campaign, "Coffee at Its Brightest" in 2009 and 2010, emphasized the quality and purity of Nescafe coffee in an attempt to overcome negative consumer perceptions about instant coffee. In India the "Know Your Neighbours" campaign featured Bollywood icons Deepika Padukone and Shahid Kapoor as brand ambassadors and included a related Facebook page that had attracted more than 2.2 million users as of February 2013.

BRAND STRATEGY

- Nescafé introduced its first variant in the mid-1960s, Nescafé Gold Blend.
- Nescafé had hundreds of products tailored to tastes in various markets worldwide.
- As single-cup brewed coffee became popular, Nescafé introduced its Dolce Gusto coffee machines and capsules in 2008.

Nescafé was introduced in 1938, but it was not until the mid-1960s that the brand began changing its core product and introducing new varieties. The first variant was Nescafé Gold Blend, a freeze-dried water soluble version of Nescafé. In 1975 Nestlé introduced Nescafé Decaffeinated, responding to industry trends and the popularity of Taster's Choice Decaf. (Taster's Choice was another Nestlé brand of instant coffee introduced in the United States as Nescafé lost market share there. Taster's Choice was rebranded Nescafé Taster's Choice for a time.)

Because Nescafé was responsive to local tastes and palettes, it developed hundreds of blends and types of Nescafé available in various markets worldwide. Many major Nescafé markets have a number of the brand's primary products available, including Alta Rica, Café Menu Cappuccino, Cap Colombie, Classic, Classic Decaf, Espresso, Gold Blend, Gold Blend Decaf, Green, and Original 3 in 1 (coffee with sugar and powdered creamer).

To capture more market share in the Middle East, Nescafé introduced Red Mug in 2002 and My Cup in 2005, which was a coffee and creamer blend available with or without sugar. By 2005 Nescafé had 88 percent of the Middle Eastern soluble coffee market. Nescafé Café Viet, introduced in 2008, targeted coffee drinkers in Vietnam who preferred strong coffee brewed in a traditional Vietnamese way by placing a coffee blend in a sachet. The successful introduction of Café Viet led to a leading market position in Vietnam. Much of Nescafé's focus was on emerging markets in Asia, including China and India, although its strongest markets still included Europe and Latin America.

Some products were developed and introduced specifically to attract younger coffee drinkers, including the Café Menu line, which included lattes, cappuccinos, and flavored coffees and which was released to the market in 2008. Nescafé's Frothe drinks, launched nationally in the United States in 2002, also targeted younger drinkers with such flavors as hazelnut mocha, white chocolate, and Butterfinger.

To take advantage of the single-cup brewed coffee trend revolutionizing the industry, Nescafé introduced its Dolce Gusto coffee machines and capsules in 2008. While the machine and the capsules were relatively expensive compared to other Nescafé products, Dolce Gusto was a success, selling two billion capsules through 2011.

BRAND EQUITY

- Nescafé is one of the most valuable coffee and beverage brands in the world.
- In 2011, 4,600 cups of Nescafé were consumed globally every second.
- *Forbes* ranked Nescafé number 20 on its list of most powerful global brands in 2012.

As the leading instant coffee brand in the world, Nescafé contributed to the combined instant coffee brands of Nestlé controlling 51 percent of the world market in 2010. By 2011, 4,600 cups of Nescafé were consumed globally every second. Though a best-selling coffee brand in the United States, Nescafé is more popular in Europe and other parts of the world. By 2011 it had about 51 percent of the market in India, and by 2012 it controlled two-thirds of the market in the Philippines.

Nescafé's brand equity peaked in 2009, and although Nescafé did not duplicate the same level of success in the following years, it remained one of the most valuable beverage brands in the world as of 2013. In 2012 *Forbes* listed Nescafé as number 20 on its ranking of the world's most powerful brands, with a brand value of US$17.4 billion. It was the second beverage on the list after Coca-Cola (US$50.2 billion), which was ranked number three.

In BrandFinance's "Global 500" in 2012, Nescafé was ranked number 248, with a brand performance of US$4.2 billion and an enterprise value of US$22.1 billion. According to Interbrand's 2012 list of "Best Global Brands," a ranking of the most valuable brands, Nescafé ranked number 35, with a brand value of US$11.1 billion. Interbrand also listed Nescafé as number one on its list of "Best Swiss Brands" in 2012, with a brand value of US$11.1 billion. This is higher than the brand of its parent company, Nestlé, which was ranked number five. Nescafé was number two on MPP Consulting's "SwissBrand Top 50" in 2012 after Nestlé. Nescafé had a brand value of US$5.3 billion.

BRAND AWARENESS

- Nescafé was the first internationally successful brand of instant coffee.
- In many markets, Nescafé has top-of-mind awareness as Nescafé means instant coffee.
- Nescafé regularly ranks as one of the best known brands in the world.

The first internationally successful brand of instant coffee, Nescafé has been the dominating brand of soluble coffee for decades in many major markets throughout the world. By 1994 it had name recognition of 90 percent among instant coffee consumers. By 2003 it was the second most recognized beverage brand in the world after Coca-Cola. Although it is a best-selling brand in the United States, Nescafé is more popular in Asia, Europe, and Latin America. In many markets, Nescafé has top-of-mind awareness as Nescafé means instant coffee. Studies underscore the popularity of the brand. In 2012 Nescafé was number 44 on the "Consumer Superbrands Official Top 500" of the Centre for Brand Analysis, a measure of brand popularity in Great Britain. In 2011 UNIC ranked Nescafé as number two on its list of the "Top Swiss Brands on Facebook" (after Toblerone), with more than one million fans at that time.

BRAND OUTLOOK

- Nescafé's growth primarily came in such developing markets as China, India, and Russia.

- Nescafé still saw growth in major developed markets including the United Kingdom and Ireland.
- In 2010 Nescafé outlined an environmental plan that included responsible consumption, responsible farming, and responsible production.

The demand and market for instant coffee has changed in the 21st century. Because of the worldwide economic downturn that began in 2008, many consumers sought value and instant coffee was generally inexpensive. There was also growing demand for instant coffee in developing markets such as China, India, and Russia, and Nescafé developed products and marketing strategies targeted to those regions. Even in developed markets, Nescafé was well positioned for future growth. By mid-2012 Nescafé showed value growth of 6.8 percent in the United Kingdom and Ireland. Such trends were expected to continue despite the entry of leading coffee chain Starbucks into the instant coffee market.

Nescafé also focused on becoming more environmentally responsible through its Nescafé Plan, introduced in 2010. The plan included three pillars—responsible consumption, responsible farming, and responsible production—which focused on becoming more energy efficient, ensuring it purchased coffee that met sustainability standards, and reducing its carbon footprint by using cleaner energy sources. The plan was to be implemented through 2015.

FURTHER READING

"Best Global Brands 2012." Interbrand. Accessed January 23, 2013. http://www.interbrand.com/en/best-global-brands/2012/Nescafé.

"Brandfame—Nescafé." *Marketing*, September 21, 2005, p. 34.

Brand Finance. "Nescafé." *Brandirectory*. Accessed January 23, 2013. http://brandirectory.com/profile/nescaf.

"Gold Blend Returns to Its Romantic Roots to Woo Women." *Marketing*, February 2003.

Haig, Matt. "Nescafé: The Instant Brand." *Brand Royalty*. London: Kogan Page, 2004.

Lewis, Scott. "Nescafé." *Encyclopedia of Consumer Brands, Volume 1: Consumable Brands*. Ed. Janice Jorgensen. Detroit, MI: St. James Press, 1994.

"Nescafé." RankingTheBrands.com. Accessed January 23, 2013. http://www.rankingthebrands.com/Brand-detail.aspx?brandID=144.

"Nestlé S.A." *International Directory of Company Histories*. Ed. Jay P. Pederson. Vol. 71. Detroit, MI: St. James Press, 2005.

Srivastava, Pallavi. "At Home." *Pitch*, May 11, 2012.

"Whoosh Whoosh, Bang Bang: Vietnam Production Company Sudest Dongnam Talks about Breaking the Barriers with Their Work on the Nescafé Cafe Viet TVC Blown Away." *Asia Image*, May–June 2011.

NESTLÉ

BRAND ORIGINS

- Nestlé was founded in the late 19th century, with early products including infant formula, condensed milk, and chocolate.
- One of the primary ways that Nestlé has grown in the 20th and 21st centuries is through acquisition.

- While Nestlé is primarily a food and beverage company, it has emphasized health and wellness in the first years of the 21st century.

The international conglomerate Nestlé began in 1843 when pharmacist Henri Nestlé bought a factory in Vevey, Switzerland. By the 1860s Nestlé noted the need for a substitute for breast milk for infants who could not be breastfed. He devised the first infant formula in 1867 and promoted it among doctors and mothers. Within a few years, demand exceeded his ability to produce supply in his factory, and Nestlé sold his company to Jules Monnerat in 1874.

By 1875 Nestlé was manufacturing its products in several countries and selling them in 16 nations worldwide. New items were added, including condensed milk in 1878 and milk chocolate in 1904. In 1905 Nestlé merged with its biggest rival, the Anglo-Swiss Condensed Milk Company, and the combined company retained the Nestlé name.

During World War I the growth of Nestlé was interrupted and its production stalled by limited milk supplies. The company sought new markets in countries less affected by the war, including the United States. By the 1920s Nestlé was again growing, this time by acquisition. Nestlé bought the chocolate companies Cailler and Swiss General in 1929, for example.

By the late 1920s one of Nestlé's best-selling products was chocolate, and the brand expanded into powdered chocolate and premium chocolate. Despite the economic effects of the Great Depression during the 1930s, Nestlé continued to develop new markets, opened new factories, and achieved steady sales with expanded offerings. It developed an instant coffee called Nescafé, released to the market in 1938. Other signature products introduced during this period included the Nestlé Crunch bar in 1938, Nestlé Toll House Morsels in 1939, and Nestea in 1939.

Nestlé struggled greatly during World War II because of food shortages, limited supplies of raw materials, and other effects of the war, especially in Europe. While profitability decreased in some markets, the United States again proved a strong source of sales for Nestlé. Nestlé quickly rebuilt after the conflict, and a period of rapid growth ensued primarily through acquisition for the next few decades. New products included Nestlé Quick chocolate milk powder, which debuted in 1948.

During the 1970s Nestlé bought more major food labels, including Stouffer's and Libby's, and opened factories in developing countries, firming up new markets. Also during this period, Nestlé expanded beyond the food and beverage business by buying the pharmaceutical firm Alcon Laboratories in 1971 and a major stake in the parent company of L'Oréal in 1974.

By the 1980s a new CEO, Helmut Maucher, focused on strengthening the Nestlé brand worldwide, making it less of a faceless conglomerate with a sometimes poor reputation. Nestlé had been highly criticized and the target of several boycotts because of the way it had promoted its infant formula over breast milk, especially in Third World countries. Despite this controversy, Nestlé remained global leader in market share for formula. By 1989 Nestlé had increased its market share as the largest food company in the world, selling 300 products in 160 countries.

Nestlé's acquisition spree continued during the 1980s and 1990s, including buying Carnation in 1985 and several candy companies in 1988. By the late 1990s Nestlé focused more on organic growth and launched Nestlé Pure Life bottled water in 1999. During the early years of the 21st century, Nestlé made many strategic acquisitions but put a greater emphasis on health and wellness. It bought Ralston Purina and Chef America, the maker of Hot Pockets and Lean Pockets. Nestlé also became the largest baby food company in the world after the acquisition of Gerber Products. In addition, Nestlé acquired the Jenny Craig diet company and, in 2007, the medical-nutrition business of Novartis, which made food for hospital patients in 40 countries.

Later acquisitions were also strategic, designed to consolidate Nestlé's market position in certain categories as well as to ensure access to emerging markets. In 2010 Nestlé bought Kraft's frozen food business in the United States and Canada which included such popular pizza brands as DiGiorno and Tombstone. To gain a foothold in China, Nestlé bought a 60 percent stake in Hsu Fu Chi, the second largest confectionary in China, in 2011 and a 60 percent stake in China's Yinlu Foods, a food product distributor, in 2012.

BRAND ELEMENTS

- Nestlé takes its name from the founder of the company, Henri Nestlé, an immigrant from Germany to Switzerland.
- The Nestlé bird's nest logo reflects the brand's origins and its concern for family, wellness, and health.
- The Nestlé tagline "Good Food, Good Life" emphasizes the brand's quality and benefits.

The brand name Nestlé serves as a link to the company's past. Nestlé takes its name from the founder of the company, Henri Nestlé. An immigrant from Germany to Switzerland, Nestlé was a pharmacist who founded his namesake company to manufacture and market the first infant formula. Originally called Farine lactée, it was a combination of wheat flour, sugar, and cow's milk. Nestlé invented the formula to save the life of a neighbor's infant, and he saw its potential to save the lives of infants who could not nurse due to illness or other circumstances. Nestlé's company did well, and after a few years he could not manage the demand for Farine lactée. Near retirement age, he sold Nestlé in 1874.

From the first, the Nestlé logo reflected the brand's origins and attitudes, including a concern for family, wellness, and health. The Nestlé logo, which was first used in the 1870s, featured a nest of baby birds being fed by a mother bird. This logo evoked the brand's first product, baby formula. The basic image of a nest with a mother and baby birds has remained a key element of the Nestlé logo through the 20th and early 21st centuries, although the details have changed and the nest has become less detailed overall. The only addition was the Nestlé brand name, which was superimposed over the nest image through versions introduced in the 1930s and 1960s but was placed below the image in 1988. The logo color is medium blue, and the Nestlé name is printed in a bold sans-serif font with a line stretching out from the top of the upper stroke of the *N* over the rest of the letters. In the 21st century the tagline "Good Food, Good Life" is printed in lighter type beneath or beside the logo, emphasizing the quality and benefits of Nestlé products.

BRAND IDENTITY

- Nestlé emphasizes convenience but also health consciousness, innovation, and a forward-thinking attitude.
- Nestlé is recognized for seeing a need in the marketplace and successfully developing a product to fit it.
- In 2012 Nestlé campaigns in various countries emphasized the value of its products in achieving a healthy lifestyle.

The name of a multinational company that focuses primarily on food and beverage products, Nestlé is not the brand name of every product it sells, but the brand is known for being innovative, forward thinking, health conscious, and, sometimes, paternalistic. From the introduction of the first commercially available infant formula on the market in the 1860s to the first milk chocolate and the first soluble coffee, Nestlé is recognized for seeing a need in the marketplace and successfully developing a product to fit it. For example, noodles are not consumed by Indians but masala is, so Maggi, a Nestlé brand, conducted consumer research to devise a masala product pleasing to the Indian palate. In 2011, showing its long-term commitment to health-related products and desire to be forward-thinking, Nestlé launched a subsidary called Nestlé Health Science to develop its interest in science-based nutrition and other health and wellness products.

Many of Nestlé's advertising and marketing campaigns reflect these ideals as well, often staying connected with consumers using online campaigns. In 2012, for example, a bilingual American campaign for Nestlé Pure Life bottled water targeted Latina parents and stressed the importance of adequate hydration and active lifestyles. Celebrity spokesperson Cristina Saralegui fronted the campaign, which included radio and print media as well as a Facebook page. A Nestlé campaign in Malaysia in 2012 called "How Am I?" promoted family nutrition and health and offered suggestions for healthy snack options through an online quiz. In 2012 in India, Nestlé conducted the "Nestlé Baby and Me" campaign for expectant and new mothers, offering educational information, including a related book about nutritional needs during pregnancy.

BRAND STRATEGY

- Nestlé products are marketed in 130 countries.
- Nestlé products include baking goods, beverages, canned milk, confections, chocolate, ice cream, and cereal.
- Nestlé's goal is to become the biggest health and wellness food company in the world.

Nestlé sells its products in 130 countries not only under the Nestlé brand name but also under numerous others, including Buitoni, Carnation, Gerber, DiGiorno, Dreyer's, Friskies, and Purina. Nestlé branded products include baking goods, beverages, canned milk, confections, chocolate, ice cream, and cereal. Through careful marketing, advertising, and positioning of its products, a number have become category leaders such as Nestlé Pure Life water in the United States and Nestlé Golden Morn, the best-selling cereal in Nigeria.

In addition to regularly adding new items to existing product lines, Nestlé frequently expands its product offerings through in-house development, acquisition, and partnership arrangements. In 1986 Nestlé introduced the Nespresso home brewing system for espresso and coffee. Although it lost money in its first decade on the market, sales of Nespresso reached US$3.4 billion by 2010, making it one of Nestlé's most profitable lines.

In the second decade of the 21st century, Nestlé set a goal of becoming the biggest health and wellness food company in the world, not only to diversify but to respond to increased consumer interest in healthier foods and lifestyles. The company launched the Nestlé Health Science unit in 2011. Because of changing consumer habits, Nestlé began reducing sodium content in its prepared food lines, including Stouffer's, Lean Cuisine, Buitoni, Hot Pockets, Lean Pockets.

While such decisions were made to help address slow growth in developed countries, Nestlé was employing strategies to increase sales in emerging markets. Nestlé especially focused on infant nutrition as well as health and nutrition for emerging markets. Its biggest growth was found in Brazil and China, and Nestlé began investing more in China beginning in 2011.

BRAND EQUITY

- Nestlé is the biggest food and beverage company in the world but experienced shrinking revenues between 2010 and 2011.
- Nestlé is consistently ranked one of the most valuable brands in the world.
- In 2012 Nestlé was number 33 on the *Forbes* list of the "World's Most Powerful Brands."

Nestlé is the largest food and beverage company in the world and the clear leader in the global food sector. Its biggest markets were Europe, which accounted for 33 percent of its sales, and North America (the United States and Canada), which accounted for 26 percent. The United States is the largest market for Nestlé, where it had sales of US$10 billion in 2011. Despite being a market leader in such categories as bottled water in North America with Nestlé Pure Life and efforts to grow market share in emerging markets in South America and Asia, Nestlé's revenues shrank considerably between 2010 and 2011, from US$116.6 billion to US$89 billion.

Despite short-term revenue issues, Nestlé consistently remained one of the most valuable brands. On the *Forbes* list of the "World's Most Powerful Brands" in 2012, it was ranked at number 33. On the *Fortune* "Global 500," a ranking of largest global companies by revenue, Nestlé was number 71 in 2012. That same year Nestlé was number 57 on Interbrand's list of "Best Global Brands," with a brand value of US$7 billion. Interbrand also ranked Nestlé number five on its "Best Swiss Brands" in 2012 with a brand value of US$6.1 billion. Also in 2012, Nestlé was number 41 on BrandFinance's "Global

500," with a brand value of US$16.7 billion and an enterprise value of US$63.2 billion.

BRAND AWARENESS

- Nestlé has had a long international history resulting in high brand awareness.
- Nestlé has built brand awareness through focused advertising campaigns, especially in emerging markets such as India.
- Nestlé is regularly ranked as a highly respected brand in global surveys.

Nestlé has been an international brand since the late 19th century, with a wide geographic reach and long-term investments in brand building. From the first, Nestlé created a reputation as a socially responsible brand, one that helped infants thrive through the use of Nestlé infant formula. While Nestlé later came under fire for promoting infant formula over breastfeeding in developing countries in the late 20th century, the brand has emerged with a generally positive reputation and effective campaigns to add to its already high brand awareness. To build brand awareness in developing markets such as India, for example, Nestlé employed popular Bollywood stars in its advertisements. Television ads stressed the health benefits of its milk, cereal, and formula products for infants and toddlers. Other advertising used humor, including daydreaming chocolate lovers who see dancing babies or singing squirrels while enjoying a Kit Kat break.

With its long history and wide presence in consumer products, Nestlé is a well-respected brand. On the Reputation Institute's "Global RepTrack 100," a survey that measures how consumers perceive brands worldwide, Nestlé was ranked at number 12 for 2012 after being number 16 in 2011. In 2012 Nestlé was number 31 on the *Fortune* list of the "World's Most Admired Companies" and was included on the "Top 25 Global Corporate Reputation Index," a ranking of reputation, performance, and citizenship compiled by Burson-Marsteller, Landor Associates, Penn Schoen Berland, and BrandAsset Consulting.

BRAND OUTLOOK

- Nestlé hopes to achieve 45 percent of its sales in emerging markets by 2020.
- Nestlé is investing heavily in developing markets, including Brazil, China, and India.
- Nestlé has positioned itself to capitalize on the growing interest in healthy foods in response to the obesity epidemic.
- In 2010 Nestlé announced plans to reduce the environmental impacts of its packaging.

While Nestlé has been the number-one food and beverage company worldwide for decades, it is facing challenges in the short term as there is slow to little growth and market loss in developed markets in Europe and North America. In the United States, Nestlé is losing market share to rival companies and cheaper private labels. Nestlé's sales and market share are being affected by political events, economic uncertainty in the wake of a worldwide economic downturn, and volatility in the price of raw materials.

Yet Nestlé has a global reach and is diversified in both its product line and markets. It has many products to appeal to consumers of all age groups in various regions of the world. Nestlé is especially investing in developing emerging markets, including Brazil, China, and India. In 2010 about 38 percent of sales came from emerging markets; Nestlé's goal is to reach 45 percent by 2020. Nestlé invested in new ways to reach them, including its first research and development center in India, which focused on Asian and Indian cooking, and adding two similar facilities in China.

Nestlé is also in a position to capitalize on the growing interest in healthy foods in response to the obesity epidemic. For example, Nestlé's bottled water business is a major player globally during a time when the world market is growing as consumers move away from carbonated soft drinks. Bottled water nearly outsells soda in the United States, where Nestlé Pure Life is the number-one brand of bottled water.

In addition, Nestlé emphasized sustainable practices in *Creating Shared Value*, a report published in 2010, and announced plans to reduce the environmental impacts of its packaging. In the United States in 2011, Nestlé began working to reduce water and energy use on a production volume basis.

FURTHER READING

"Best Global Brands 2012." Interbrand. Accessed January 22, 2013. http://www.interbrand.com/en/best-global-brands/2012/Best-Global-Brands-2012.aspx.

Brand Finance. "Nestlé." *Brandirectory*. Accessed January 22, 2013. http://brandirectory.com/profile/nestl.

Goel, Neha. "Nestlé: Keeping It Fresh.'" *Pitch*, December 31, 2011.

"Nestlé." *Fast Food and Junk Food: An Encyclopedia of What We Love to Eat.* Ed. Andrew F. Smith. Vol. 2. Santa Barbara, CA: Greenwood Press, 2012.

"Nestlé." RankingTheBrands.com. Accessed January 22, 2013. http://www.rankingthebrands.com/Brand-detail.aspx?brandID=156.

"Nestlé Reports New Accomplishments toward Creating Shared Value in the United States." *Business Wire*, May 29, 2012.

"Nestlé S.A." *International Directory of Company Histories.* Ed. Jay P. Pederson. Vol. 71. Detroit, MI: St. James Press, 2005.

Saltmarsh, Matthew. "Nestlé Places a Big Bet on Health-Oriented Food Products." *International Herald Tribune*, September 28, 2010.

NEXT

BRAND ORIGINS

- Next began as a men's tailor shop called Joseph Hepworth & Son in 1864 in Leeds, England.
- After a slowdown in sales, Joseph Hepworth & Son purchased a womenswear chain called Kendalls in the early 1980s to help diversify its product.

- The name Next was officially adopted in 1986.
- Following a massive expansion of stores and subsidiaries, Next suffered an equally substantial loss in profits in the late 1980s.
- In the late 1990s, Next closed all of its North American retail locations and focused on other international markets.

Joseph Hepworth, a tailor from Leeds, England, started his own tailor shop in 1864 under the name of Joseph Hepworth & Son. The company was considered a "gentleman's tailor," dealing exclusively with the sales of menswear. Over the next 50 years, Hepworth & Son expanded, forming a nationwide chain of menswear shops, which were primarily located in high-street shopping districts. The company continued its expansion into the 20th century and went public in 1948.

The company began to experience profit losses in the 1970s. The tailor shop was considered too conservative for the changing retail market. In order for the company to survive, it had to be rebranded. Led by chairman Terence Conran, Hepworth & Son made a bold move to completely remake its image by the 1980s. As part of this rebranding process, Hepworth & Son acquired the Kendalls retail chain. Kendalls, a womenswear retailer, operated more than 80 retail locations, complementing Hepworth & Son's already established menswear line. The acquisition not only allowed Hepworth & Son to revamp its conservative image but also allowed the company to become a full-service clothing retailer.

Following the acquisition of Kendalls, the company changed its name, along with its retail concept. The name "Next" was introduced at all the previous Kendalls locations, which continued to sell womenswear. In 1984 Next launched a men's line as the Next for Men retail chain began to take over the previous Hepworth & Son locations. In that same year, Next opened its first multidepartment retail store, offering both menswear and womenswear in the same location. Additionally, the store contained a shoe department and a café. The company continued its product expansion in 1985 by introducing its Next Interiors concept. Featuring home furnishings sold under the Next brand, Next Interiors were also included in Next's department stores. Also during 1985 the company acquired rival clothing retailer Lord John. By 1986 the company was operating more than 130 Next for Men retail locations.

Between 1986 and 1988 Next underwent a massive expansion. Apart from increasing the number of retail locations, the company also expanded as a mail-order business, acquiring jewelers Zales and Salsburys, as well as the newsstand operations of Dillons-Preedy. The company's revenue in 1986 was US$303 million; by 1988 the company had experienced a revenue increase of 578 percent, reaching US$1.6 billion. Additionally, Next began investing in the British Sky Broadcasting Company. Despite the increase in revenue, however, the company did not see an increase in profit, as its expanded operations led to increases in overhead costs. The company also experienced increased competition from trendier shops and suffered losses in 1989.

In response to the financial struggles of the late 1980s, Next streamlined its product base and went back to primarily selling clothing. It sold off its jewelry store holdings and mail-order subsidiary by 1991. Even with the corporate changes, Next still reported a net loss of US$710 million in 1991. The company began shutting down retail locations that were not bringing in enough revenue and focused solely on the department store format instead of a range of single-department stores. By the following year, the company reported a profit of US$17.4 million. As the company continued to recover, Next sought to expand beyond the British Isles. The first international location was opened in Boston in 1993, followed by locations in France and Belgium not long afterward.

By the late 1990s, Next had halted its North American expansion and shut down all Next locations within the United States, focusing instead on the Eastern European, Asian, and Middle Eastern markets.

BRAND ELEMENTS

- The company was renamed Next as part of a rebranding effort to direct sales toward younger consumers.
- Next is best known as a multidepartment store, selling clothing and shoes for all members of the family, as well as home furnishings.

- The Next logo is a well-known identifier of the company, despite the fact that it has undergone a number of transformations.

Next's name was adopted after Joseph Hepworth & Son acquired the womenswear chain Kendalls. Needing a new brand name and attempting to cater to a younger market, Hepworth introduced the brand name Next for the newly acquired Kendalls locations. The name was formally adopted in 1986 and all Hepworth locations were renamed Next for Men. Hepworth had decided to cater to a young audience in response to declining profits in the 1970s, as the menswear chain was considered too conservative and stuffy for younger shoppers. The name Next has been applied to all subsidiary ventures, and remained the primary brand name in 2012. Additionally, Next acquired Lipsy, a women's fashion brand directed at young women in 2008, furthering Next's youth-based branding.

The design of Next's multidepartment stores is an integral part of its branding, integrating every product Next has to offer under one roof. Having branched out from exclusively offering menswear, Next offers clothing for men, women, and children, as well as shoes and home furnishings. The company attempted to bring in other brand lines, such as jewelry and newsstands, but these ventures were short-lived. The company has maintained its success primarily by adhering to its origins in clothing retail, supplemented by sales of shoes and home furnishings.

The Next logo is also an integral part of the brand. Prior to 1991 the logo consisted of the word "Next" set in white, lowercase Courier on a black background. After 1991 the logo evolved to feature the name in white, uppercase letters, set in a Roman typeface on a black background. In 2007 Next launched a new logo featuring the brand name in lowercase with a half-crossed "t." Despite the introduction of the new logo in 2007, the company continued to use its previous logo as well.

BRAND IDENTITY

- Next strives to be a trendy and cutting-edge retailer that offers clothing for every member of the family.
- Next has been targeting younger consumers since undergoing a major rebranding in 1982.
- Next has sought to expand its product line strategically, incorporating a floral service and a wedding gift registry in the early 2000s.

Next strives to present itself as a trendy retailer that offers products for every member of the household. Its website describes the brand as "exciting, beautifully designed, excellent quality of clothing and home ware; presented in collections that reflect the aspirations and means of our customers." Next has striven to target the younger consumer market since the company rebranded itself in 1982 and acquired the womenswear retailer Kendalls. Prior to rebranding, Joseph Hepworth & Son was considered very conservative and did not relate to younger consumers. Continuing its effort to appeal to younger consumers, the company acquired Lipsy, a retailer of young women's clothing, in 2008.

Next has also leveraged its range in product offerings to establish itself as an all-encompassing multidepartment store. In addition to offering clothing for men, women, children, and infants, Next offers home furnishings and home products. In 2001 Next launched Next Flowers, further expanding its product lines to include fresh floral arrangements. Moreover, Next offers a wedding gift registry, enticing engaged couples to register with the company and encouraging wedding guests to shop exclusively at a Next retail location.

BRAND STRATEGY

- Although Next was unsuccessful in its North American retail pursuits, it has been successful in other international markets.
- Next has attempted many subsidiary concepts, including jewelry, flower delivery, online shopping, and newsstands.
- Next directly markets to young consumers, focusing on maintaining a trendy and cutting-edge brand image.

Part of Next's initial brand strategy was to expand the chain globally, pushing beyond the bounds of the United Kingdom. The first international location opened in Boston in 1993. The company hoped to expand throughout North America but ended by shutting down all North American operations by the late 1990s. Next could not compete with other well-established American department stores, such as Macy's. Next has continued to expand into other international locations, focusing primarily on Western and Eastern Europe, Asia, and the Middle East. In 2012 Next had locations in more than 50 countries.

Next has multiple subsidiaries, although the company's main branding focus is on the multidepartment store format. The company has experienced losses in several unsuccessful subsidiary brands in the past, including the Next jewelry line and the Next newsstand, which were cut to preserve forward motion and profitability. In 2001 Next launched the delivery florist Next Flowers. Next Online was launched in 2005 and has been a large part of Next's marketing plan, targeting consumers who do not live near a Next retail location. Additionally, the Next online shopping experience is available to consumers in North America. All Next subsidiaries function under the name Next, with the exception of the retailer Lipsy, which has retained its original name.

Next has continued to focus on maintaining a youth-based marketing strategy in the early 21st century. The acquisition of Lipsy in 2008 aided in Next's endeavors to keep the brand young and fresh in the eyes of consumers. Having added a strong online and social media presence to its marketing strategy, Next continues to market its youthful brand internationally.

BRAND EQUITY

- Next has locations in more than 50 countries, including more than 550 retail locations in the United Kingdom and Ireland.
- Brand Finance ranked Next as the 460th most valuable global brand in 2012.
- In 2011 Next reported revenues of US$5.5 billion.

Next's revenues for 2011 were US$5.5 billion. In 2007 Next claimed a 9.2 percent share of the British retail market for clothing and footwear. It held a 0.4 percent share of the global apparel market in 2007. Next is best known as a multidepartment store brand, offering apparel and shoes for all members within the household. Next has locations in more than 50 countries, with more than 550 stores located in the United Kingdom and Ireland.

According to Brand Finance, Next ranked 460th overall among the world's top-500 brands in 2012, with an estimated brand value of US$2.7 billion. Competitor Marks and Spencer was ranked 220th in the same list, with a brand value of US$4.58 billion.

BRAND AWARENESS

- Next operates a chain of multidepartment stores, offering clothing and shoes for all members of the family as well as home goods.
- The company's target market is in the 20–45 age range, focusing on attracting those looking for trendy, original styles.
- The simple Next logo, despite changes over the years, is easily recalled and recognized.

In the countries where Next operates, the ability of consumers to recall the Next brand is strongly related to the kinds of products that the retailer offers. Not only are the stores multidepartmental, but Next also offers exclusive designs and distinctive styling that have given the company a strong brand image. Additionally, Next targets its marketing toward consumers within the 20 to 45 age range, focusing on attracting those looking for trendy, original styles. Next's logo is easy to recall, despite the many design changes over the years. Since the early 1990s, the logo has simply featured the word "Next" in white lettering on a black background.

Consumer awareness received a boost in 2010 when Next was selected as the official supplier of clothing and home ware to the 2012 Olympic Games in London. Next also provided formalwear for members of Team Great Britain.

BRAND OUTLOOK

- Despite previous financial challenges, Next weathered the global recession and emerged intact.
- In 2011 Next reported revenues of US$5.2 billion and in 2012 US$5.5 billion, a 4.3 percent increase in revenue.
- Next operates 550 stores in the United Kingdom and 180 stores internationally.
- Next provided the formalwear for Team Great Britain at the 2012 London Olympics.

Next has had a challenging history as a brand, but it was ultimately in a strong place in the early 21st century. Weathering such obstacles as failed subsidiary brands and years of significant financial hardship, the brand nevertheless remains strong financially. In 2012 Next reported revenues of US$5.5 billion, an increase of 4.3 percent over the previous year.

In spite of the global recession of 2008, Next expanded its influence and market reach by purchasing the young women's clothing retailer Lipsy, launching Next Flowers, and developing a strong web and social media presence featuring a YouTube channel, an active Facebook page, and a Twitter account. The company has been most successful in the United Kingdom and Ireland, where it has more than 550 retail locations, although it also continued to operate more than 180 stores in more than 50 other countries in 2012. Additionally, in 2010 Next was selected as the official clothing and home-ware supplier to the London 2012 Olympic Games, and it also provided formalwear for Team Great Britain, giving the brand a significant boost in consumer awareness.

FURTHER READING

Brand Finance. "Global 500 2012, The Annual Report." *Brandirectory*. Accessed September 6, 2012. http://brandfinance.com/images/upload/bf_g500_2012_web_dp.pdf.

Dove, William. "Next plc Share Price Falls as Profits Boosted by Better Than Expected Christmas Sales." *IBTimes*, January 5, 2010. Accessed November 14, 2012. http://www.ibtimes.co.uk/articles/20100105/next-share-price-falls-profits-boosted-better-than-expected-christmas-sales_all.htm.

Finnegan, Kate. "London 2012 Olympics: The Fashion Olympics." *Telegraph* (London), July 22, 2012.

Hamilton, Scott. "U.K. Retail Sales Rise More than Forecast on Clothing Demand". *Bloomberg BusinessWeek*, October 18, 2012.

Next. "Annual Report." Accessed November 17, 2012. http://www.nextplc.co.uk/~/media/Files/N/Next-PLC/pdfs/latest-news/2012/ar2012.pdf.

"Next plc". *Bloomberg BusinessWeek*. Accessed November 15, 2012. http://investing.businessweek.com/research/stocks/snapshot/snapshot.asp?ticker=NXT:LN.

"Next plc." *International Directory of Company Histories*. Ed. Tina Grant. Vol. 29. Detroit, MI: St. James Press, 2000.

NIKE

—■—

AT A GLANCE

Brand Synopsis: Named for the winged goddess of victory, Nike is dedicated to bringing inspiration and innovation to athletic consumers around the world.

Parent Company: Nike, Inc.
One Bowerman Drive
Beaverton, Oregon 97005
United States
http://www.nike.com

Sector: Consumer Discretionary

Industry Group: Consumer Durables & Apparel

Performance: *Sales*—US$24.1 billion (2011).

Principal Competitors: adidas AG; PUMA SE; New Balance Athletic Shoe, Inc.

BRAND ORIGINS

- Founder Philip Knight originally imports running shoes to the United States from Japan.
- Nike, the name for the Greek goddess of victory, is chosen in 1978.
- California design student was paid US$35 for the Nike "swoosh" logo design.
- Initial public offering in 1980 raises funds for international expansion.
- The "Just Do It" tagline appears in 1988.

Founded in the United States, Nike embraced a global perspective from the beginning. Founder Philip H.

Knight, while a student at the Stanford Business School in San Francisco, wrote a business plan for a class assignment that sought to take advantage of Japan's low cost of production to offer inexpensive shoes in the U.S. market. A former member of the University of Oregon track team, Knight was particularly interested in athletic shoes, and after graduating from Stanford, he pursued his business plan while working as an accountant.

He traveled to Japan in 1962 and contacted the Tiger division of Onitsuka Company Ltd., a maker of running shoes eager to export to the United States. Knight became Tiger's U.S. distributor by claiming that he had a shoe company, Blue Ribbon Sports (BRS), which he would not actually establish with partner Bill Bowerman until 1964. Knight sold the Tiger-made shoes designed for U.S. runners under the Blue Ribbon label out of the trunk of his car.

To promote the Blue Ribbon name, the company soon began placing its logo on apparel and increased the brand's exposure further by providing free shoes to star athletes. Knight and Bowerman then decided to launch their own shoe line. Knight nearly christened the new brand Dimension Six, but his marketing head, Jeff Johnson, a former Stanford Track athlete, offered a name that he said came to him in a dream: Nike, the goddess of victory. For a logo, Knight turned to a college design student, Caroline Davie, who for US$35 created the brand's iconic "swoosh" logo. A soccer shoe became the first Nike-branded product.

Nike was positioned as a premium brand, one that offered high performance and catered to the serious athlete. To improve traction, BRS introduced a waffled sole. Dubbed Nike Moon Shoes, a new athletic shoe line was introduced at the U.S. Olympic time trials for track and field. The shoes sold well, leading Nike to expand to Canada in 1973 and to Australia the following year. The Nike brand name grew more valuable, and in 1978 BRS changed its name to Nike, Inc.

By the end of the 1970s about half of the running shoes sold in the United States bore the Nike swoosh, and soon Nike surpassed Adidas as the country's top-selling athletic shoe company. Nike went public in 1980, using the proceeds of the stock offering to expand into Latin America, Europe, Africa, and Asia. In the mid-1980s the Nike brand was extended to include golf shoes, tennis gear, and women's apparel.

In 1988 Nike launched a "Just Do It" marketing campaign that would lay the foundation for continued growth around the world. In the final years of the 1990s Nike evolved into something of a lifestyle brand, espousing the "Nike attitude." To further develop the Nike brand beyond the United States, the company embraced hockey and soccer, becoming major equipment suppliers in those sports. Of even greater import was Nike's association with athletes having international appeal, such as basketball star Michael Jordan and golfer Tiger Woods. By 2003 Nike's international sales exceeded domestic sales for the first time. Nike turned its attention to China as well, adapting its Just Do It message to a new culture, its advertising paying tribute to young Chinese who succeeded in sports despite personal obstacles. By this stage, all of the elements of the Nike brand were well established around the world.

BRAND ELEMENTS

- Ilie Nastase was Nike's first celebrity athlete endorser.
- Michael Jordan endorsement led to the "Be Like Mike" ad campaign
- "Just Do It" tagline was unveiled in 1988 ad campaign.
- Nike does not shy away from controversial athlete endorsers.
- Innovative technology is an important element of the Nike brand.

Its name, logo, tagline, product features, and celebrity athlete associations combine to create a distinct brand identity for Nike. The Nike name, drawn from Greek mythology, offers several associations that resonate with the athletic market. The winged goddess Nike presided over victory in both war and peaceful competitions, such as the Olympic Games of ancient Greece. The swoosh logo is another key element in the Nike brand, so well established in the marketplace that it immediately brings to mind the Nike name.

In the early 1980s the public face of the Nike brand was Michael Jordan. While the company did well with its "Be Like Mike" slogan, encouraging customers to identify

with the basketball star by buying his signature shoes, the vast majority of people knew they could never actually perform like Jordon. A more universal tagline, one that would enjoy greater staying power, followed in 1988: "Just Do It." It was consistently positioned with the swoosh logo, whether in television or print advertisements. Together, the logo and tagline reflected the brand's association with athleticism and victory.

From the beginning, well before its relationship with Michael Jordan, another key element of the Nike brand was its ties to internationally recognized athletes, but almost as important as success was the provocative personality of many of the stars. Nike's first professional endorser was tennis player Ilie ("Nasty") Nastase. John McEnroe, another tennis player with a bad boy image, would later sign as well. Controversial figure skater Tonya Harding became an endorser in the 1990s. Other stars such as Michael Jordon and Tiger Woods also possessed a combative side to their personalities that many disliked but that perfectly suited the Just Do It image Nike sought to foster.

As a premium brand, Nike incorporates groundbreaking technology to help athletes maximize their talents to secure victory, or to provide other less-talented consumers with a vicarious fulfillment of their own dreams of athletic success. The most significant new features that became an important element in the Nike brand were the waffle-like soles that improve traction and Nike's patented "Air" technology that provided better heel cushioning.

BRAND IDENTITY

- Nike mission is to bring inspiration and innovation to every athlete in the world.
- Nike's definition of an athlete: "If you have a body, you are an athlete."
- First significant innovation is waffle-like running shoe sole.
- Just Do It slogan embodies a lifestyle image.
- Nike will tolerate personal shortcomings in athlete endorsers, but not cheaters.

Over the years Nike has carefully crafted the image it wishes to portray to consumers around the world. Using a variety of elements at its disposal in a coordinated manner, Nike creates a brand identity that is embodied in its mission statement: "To bring inspiration and innovation to every athlete in the world." Nike also offers its own expansive definition of an athlete: "If you have a body, you are an athlete."

While most consumers are not aware that Nike is the name of the Greek goddess of victory, the company's effective brand messaging essentially renders that knowledge unnecessary. The company's iconic logo does much of the heavy lifting. Essentially a stylized check mark, Nike's swoosh logo implies a completed task and presumably a job well done, all in keeping the brand promise of success. Moreover, the swoosh looks similar to a wing, which not only provides a tie-in to the goddess Nike but also the winged feet of another Greek god, Hermes, who is associated with athletics. The wing imagery by itself implies speed, again reflecting an important aspect of Nike brand identity.

The Just Do It phrase also plays an important role in Nike's brand identity. In essence, the tagline is a call for action, but one that people in their own way can answer. Further, the meaning can be extended beyond athletics and exercise to encompass other aspects of life. In this way, Just Do It became an attitude embraced by a generation worldwide and elevates Nike beyond a sporting goods brand, making it akin to a lifestyle brand.

Nike is also a brand that portrays itself as an innovator, with an implicit promise that it provides the customers with a winning edge. The first significant innovation, the waffle-like running shoe sole, was a crude research and development effort, formed by molding rubber on a household waffle iron. Since then, Nike has invested heavily in the development of sporting goods technology, resulting in more than a thousand U.S. patents and foreign utility patents for components, manufacturing techniques, and product features.

Another aspect of Nike's identity is winning. Hence, Nike is keen to associate itself with winners, highly successful athletes recognized across the globe. Even when some of Nike's star endorsers experience scandal in their personal lives, such as Tiger Woods did with marital difficulties, Nike has remained loyal. Nike draws the line in protection of its brand identity when one of its endorsers is caught cheating to win in the athletic arena. In those cases, Nike acts quickly to sever ties.

BRAND STRATEGY

- Nike brands are considered premium, and Michael Jordan's Air Jordan brand is particularly valuable.
- Nike brands controlled through acquisition include Cole Haan, Converse, Hurley, and Umbro.
- Manufacturing moves overseas drew criticism and the brand, according to Philip Knight, for a time was "synonymous with slave wages, forced overtime and arbitrary abuse."

Nike's brand strategy is multifaceted. Nike is positioned as a premium brand, applied to products in a wide category of sports, including running, basketball, football, soccer, baseball, men's and women's training, baseball, golf, tennis, skateboarding, surfing, and snowboarding. The Nike name is also extended to the Nike+ brand of sports devices, used to measure performance for serious athletes

as well as everyday activities for other customers. Another brand, NIKEiD, focuses on customized footwear, apparel, and other products. Other brands employing the Nike name include Nike Aerobics shoes, Nike Grind Sporting goods, Nike Maxsight optical lenses, Nike Regrind shoes, Nikefit apparel and accessories, and Nike Shox running shoes. In addition, the Air Jordan brand promoted by Michael Jordan since the 1980s remains a valuable Nike property, and both Air and Jordan are used as sub-brands for Nike products. Nike's brand portfolio has also grown over the years through acquisitions. Brands controlled through subsidiaries include Cole Haan, Converse, Hurley, and Umbro.

From its headquarters in the Pacific Northwest of the United States, Nike has successfully expanded around the world. For the most part, the company has had little difficulty in transferring the Nike brand to new cultures. One notable exception was a 2004 marketing campaign in China that featured basketball player LeBron James defeating a computer-generated Kung Fu master. Chinese consumers found the ad offensive, leading it to being banned in the country. Nike changed ad agencies and soon unveiled a new marketing campaign that instead of famous athletes, Chinese or otherwise, featured everyday young Chinese who pursued their sports despite obstacles.

Nike's problems in China, however, were modest compared to the controversy surrounding the company's manufacturing practices that threatened to subvert its carefully crafted brand image. During a recession in the early 1990s Nike was vilified by many in the United States for moving its factories overseas. The criticism grew even louder as the working conditions and low wages in the company's Asian factories were documented. Nike was accused of profiting from sweatshops and child labor. In 1998, according to *Marketing Magazine*, Knight observed that the Nike brand had become "synonymous with slave wages, forced overtime and arbitrary abuse." To combat this assault on the Nike brand, Knight implemented a plan that included raising minimum working age requirements, introduced independent monitoring, and established formal targets to improve the condition of workers in Nike's contract factories. To ensure that factories remained in compliance, Nike employed about 100 inspectors to monitor factories and help improve problems. The company also allowed the Fair Labor Association monitoring organization to conduct random factory visits. To further repair the damage done to its brand, Nike has made efforts to decrease the use of natural resources and save energy, donates sporting equipment to impoverished youth populations, and through the Nike Foundation invests in projects designed to benefit adolescent girls in the developing world.

BRAND EQUITY

- Nike's revenues grew tenfold from 1990 to 2011, when sales reached US$20.8 billion.
- Nike ranked 136 in the Fortune 500 in 2011.
- Nike is the undisputed market share leader in athletic apparel and athletic footwear.
- Interbrand ranked Nike 26th on its list of top global brands in 2011.
- Nike brand value was estimated by Interbrand in 2011 at US$15.1 billion.

The value of its brand to the performance of Nike Inc. is undeniable, albeit difficult to quantify. What is not in question is that Nike is the world's top seller of athletic footwear and apparel. The company's rise to market dominance has been methodical. At the start of the 1990s annual revenues totaled US$2.2 billion. Ten years later, sales approached US$9 million. With annual sales of US$20.8 billion in 2011, Nike ranked No. 136 in the illustrious Fortune 500. In terms of global market share, Nike's 7 percent leads Adidas Group's 5.5 percent, and Under Armour's 2.6 percent among athletic apparel producers in 2011, according to *Market Share Reporter*. As an athletic footwear manufacturer, Nike controls about one-third of the market. Its closest competitor, Adidas, has a 16 percent share, followed by Puma at 7 percent, according 2009 statistics provided by *Market Share Reporter*.

Interbrand, one of the world's leading brand consultants, places Nike 26th on its ranking of the top 100 global brands. According to Interbrand's methodology that assigns a monetary value to a brand, Nike's brand equity has grown steadily over the years. In 2012 Nike held a brand value of US$15.126 billion, a 4 percent increase over the previous year. Brand Finance plc, a brand evaluation consultancy, assigns a brand value of US$18.6 billion, or about half of Nike's US$35.6 billion market capitalization.

BRAND AWARENESS

- Nike-branded products are sold in more than 160 countries.
- More than 800 Nike stores around the world serve to increase brand awareness.
- According to TheSportsOneSource survey of consumers, Nike enjoyed a 98.9 percent brand awareness.
- Women, according to TheSportsOneSource survey, were slightly more aware of the Nike brand than are men.

Nike is a well-known brand across the globe, as shown by its consistent top-100 rankings in the Brandz and Interbrand "most valuable brands" rankings. The company sells athletic footwear, apparel, and equipment in more than 160 countries. The brand is well supported by

advertising, social media, an e-commerce site, and more than 800 company-owned Nike-branded retail stores. Moreover, world famous athletes endorse the brand and display the Nike swoosh on their shoes, apparel, and equipment when competing. Even when Nike is not an official sponsor of a sporting event, such as at the 2012 London Olympic Games, its athlete endorsers promote the Nike brand.

Even before the Olympics, Nike enjoyed excellent brand awareness. In a survey conducted by TheSportsOneSource Group in 2012, the Nike brand was recognized by 98.9 percent of all respondents aged 13 and older who had purchased athletic footwear or apparel over the past year. Female respondents were even more familiar with the brand, displaying 99.1 percent awareness. The rest of the top five in brand awareness was Adidas at 95.2 percent; Reebok/RBK at 93.2 percent; Converse, another Nike brand, at 87.6 percent; and Puma at 86.1 percent.

BRAND OUTLOOK

- The NIKE and Swoosh Design trademarks are registered in about 150 jurisdictions.
- Nike uses social media and sponsors The Chance, an athletic talent search.
- Nike seeks to improve its track record for social and environmental responsibility.

Nike is a well-established brand around the world with few markets left to conquer. The NIKE and Swoosh Design trademarks are registered in about 150 jurisdictions. More important to the growth of the company is extending the Nike brand to new product categories. In October 2010, for example, Nike revealed plans to extend its Nike+ running monitor to other sports, part of an effort to position the brand as a performance aid.

Another part of Nike's long-term growth strategy was a plan to sell its Cole Haan and Umbro units. In this way, Nike hoped to focus more attention to growing its Nike, Jordan, Converse, and Hurley brands. Key to fostering such growth would be a growing reliance on social media to stimulate awareness and interest in Nike's brand portfolio. The Chance, an athletic talent search, was an example of the kind of company-sponsored event Nike also hoped to exploit in order to increase the value of its brands.

Just as important as brand growth for Nike was brand preservation. After suffering through the negative publicity surrounding the conditions of its manufacturing operations, Nike was expected to take pains to portray itself as a socially responsible brand. To improve its environmental record, Nike launched the "Zero Discharge of Hazardous Chemicals" initiative, slated to be met by 2020.

FURTHER READING

Baird, Roger. "Game, Set and Match." *Marketing Week*, August 28, 1997.

Brand Finance. "Global 500 2012." *Brandirectory.com*.

Grimm, Matthew. "Nike Vision." *Brandweek*, March 29, 1993.

———. "Swoosh Over Europe: Nike Goes Global." *Brandweek*, February 1, 1993.

O'Malley, Gavin. "Who's Leading the Way in Web Marketing? It's Nike, Of Course." *Advertising Age*, October 16, 2006.

Madden, Normandy. "Nike Drops Its American Idols." *Advertising Age*, March 20, 2006.

Mullen, Jeremy. "For Nike, the Tiger Woods Brand Was Too Big to Fail." *Advertising Age*, April 12, 2010.

"Nike, Inc." *International Directory of Company Histories*. Ed. Jay P. Pederson. Vol. 75. Detroit, MI: St. James Press, 2006.

"Social Responsibility: The Nike Story." *Marketing Magazine*, July 25, 2008.

"2011 Ranking of the Top 100 Brands." Interbrand. Accessed February 15, 2013. http://www.interbrand.com/en/best-global-brands/previous-years/best-global-brands-2011.aspx.

NINTENDO

———— ♦ ————

BRAND ORIGINS

- In 1889 Fusajiro Yamauchi founded a company that made hanafuda (flower) playing cards and, later, Western-style playing cards, in Kyoto, Japan.
- In the 1970s, Nintendo began manufacturing electronic projection games, arcade video games, and tabletop video games, as well as home video game consoles.
- Nintendo's game consoles have included the Famicom (family computer) home video game system, the Super Nintendo Entertainment System, Nintendo 64, GameCube, Wii, and the Wii U.
- Along with its console systems, Nintendo has sold handheld electronic video games and handheld video game systems with interchangeable game cartridges.
- International subsidiaries of Nintendo include Nintendo of America, Nintendo of Europe, and Nintendo UK.

"It's me, Mario!" shouted the Nintendo character Mario in the 1996 video game *Super Mario 64*. By this point, he did not need an introduction. Millions of viewers knew who he was and the company he represented: Nintendo.

Although Nintendo is now known for its video game technology, the company has existed for more than one hundred years. In 1889 Fusajiro Yamauchi created a company to make hanafuda (flower) playing cards in Kyoto, Japan, still the site of Nintendo's headquarters today. In the early 1900s, Yamauchi began creating Western-style playing cards for domestic use and export, a precursor to the company's tremendous global success decades later.

In 1933 Yamauchi's founded the Yamauchi Nintendo & Co., and the company became known as the Nintendo Playing Card Co. Ltd. in 1951. "Nintendo" is a Japanese term with various translations, including "you work hard but, in the end, it's in heaven's hands" and "to leave one's fortune in the hands of fate." Given the company's history of manufacturing hanafuda cards, some writers contend that the name means "the temple of free hanafuda" or "the company that is allowed to make (or sell) hanafuda." In addition to cards, the company also made board games during its early years of operation.

In an agreement with the Walt Disney Company, Nintendo produced in 1959 cards featuring Disney characters for the international market. The company began producing electronic games in the 1970s. One of these games was a laser clay pigeon shooting system that required players to shoot beams of light at targets projected on screens. Nintendo originally released these Beam Gun games and other projection games in Japan and began exporting them to Europe and the United States in 1974. It sold other arcade video games and tabletop video games to the Japanese and international markets in the 1970s and 1980s, including popular arcade games like *Donkey Kong*.

During this time, the company also developed home video game systems. These systems incorporated increasingly sophisticated technology, including electronic video recording (EVR) players and microprocessors. Working with Mitsubishi Electric, Nintendo produced the home video game systems Color TV Game 6 in 1977, Color TV Game 15 in 1978, Color TV Game Racing 112 (which used a steering wheel as a controller) in 1978, the Color TV Game Block Breaker (also known as Color TV Game Block Kuzushi) in 1979, and the Computer TV Game in 1980.

These Nintendo and Mitsubishi Color TV Games products were for the Japanese market. Products that followed would have wider distribution. Nintendo released its Famicom (family computer) home video game system in Japan in 1984. This system was so popular that, eventually, more than 35 percent of Japanese households owned it. In 1985 Nintendo released a successful American version of the system, the Nintendo Entertainment System (NES). The system also sold well in Europe.

Later Nintendo console systems released around the world included the Super Nintendo Entertainment System (also known as the Super NES, Super Nintendo, and Super Family Computer), the Nintendo 64 (N64), the GameCube, the Wii (which used motion-sensing technology), and the Wii U. These consoles have been joined by Nintendo's wildly successful handheld games. The company produced handheld games as early as the 1980s, and it later produced handheld gaming systems with interchangeable game cartridges, including Game Boy (1989), Super Game Boy (1994), and Game Boy Color (1998). In 2004 Nintendo released the Nintendo DS, a handheld system with two screens. It later released the Nintendo 3DS, a DS system with three-dimensional effects. Nintendo would also market and sell game cartridges for their console and handheld systems.

Nintendo markets and sells its systems, games, accessories, merchandise, and other products all over the world. In addition to its Kyoto headquarters, Nintendo owns the subsidiary Nintendo of America, a company based in Redmond, Washington. Other Nintendo affiliates include Nintendo of Europe and Nintendo UK.

BRAND ELEMENTS

- Famous characters from Nintendo video games include Mario, Luigi, Donkey Kong, Pokemon, and Link.
- Characters from Nintendo's games and images of its video game systems and controllers appear in a wide range of merchandise.
- The Nintendo logo consists of the word "Nintendo" within a capsule-shaped outline.
- Music and sound effects from Nintendo video games have been featured in commercials and phone ringtones; at concerts and sporting events; and on websites and albums.

Mario, Luigi, Donkey Kong, Pokemon, and Link: all started as Nintendo video game characters but are now popular, even iconic characters in international pop culture. All appear in video games and many other Nintendo products, ranging from toys and collectibles, costumes, clothing and accessories, housewares, and food items. These characters are the faces of the Nintendo brand.

The company also uses other images, such as the likenesses of Nintendo's game systems and their controllers. The company's logo is famous as a standalone image. The logo, a registered trademark, features the word "Nintendo" surrounded by a capsule-shaped outline. Both the name and outline are usually a silvery gray color, though other colors, such as red, have been used, depending on the context.

Some sounds associated with Nintendo are also famous. Music and sound effects from its games are featured on its websites and in its commercials, as well as in albums and phone ringtones and at concerts and sporting events. Koji Kondo composed music for a number of Nintendo games, and when Kondo met former Beatle Paul McCartney and his wife, Linda, the McCartneys sang Kondo's music from the Nintendo Mario games. The fact that a member of one of the most famous rock bands in history knew a Nintendo theme song confirms the wide reach of Nintendo's music, the Nintendo games featuring this music, and Nintendo itself as a brand.

BRAND IDENTITY

- The bright colors and familiar characters from Nintendo games have appeared on company communication like its annual reports, reinforcing the company's status as a gaming brand.
- Nintendo commercials clearly portray it as a gaming brand, using video game images and music and sometimes the slogan, "Now you're playing with power."

- Nintendo store displays allow potential customers to play sample systems and games and reinforce the idea that Nintendo is a gaming brand.

The company's consistent use of its visual images has created a strong brand identity and demonstrates clearly its desire to be viewed as the ultimate gaming brand. Familiar characters and bright colors not only appear in Nintendo's games but even appear in company communications like its annual report. While annual reports can be somewhat dull and generic, Nintendo's 2011 annual report featured an icon from one of its video games on the cover. This immediately identified the Nintendo brand and demonstrated the fame of its games and systems. Since the company used a video game icon to represent itself on the document cover, Nintendo clearly portrayed itself as a gaming brand.

Nintendo has furthered strengthened this brand identity in its commercials. These commercials have depicted Nintendo systems and games as well as people playing with these games and systems. The spots incorporated brand elements like Nintendo characters, video game symbols, and game music, all of which reminded people of the brand and its products. Some of these spots also incorporated the Nintendo slogan, "Now you're playing with power," a phrase that further emphasized how people can play with Nintendo brand products.

The brand does encourage people to play. Its store displays—which feature the Nintendo name logo prominently—offer more than shelves of games and systems. They also offer consoles and games that allow people to play with Nintendo products before (or instead of) buying. These sample games and systems provide interactive demonstrations of Nintendo products and further reinforce the company's image as being all about games.

BRAND STRATEGY

- Analysts have observed that Nintendo attained success by seeking new markets, hiring skilled designers, and shifting its focus from high-tech development.
- Nintendo targeted new markets with its Brain Age games for its handheld DS system. The first Brain Age game sold millions of units in the United States and was Europe's top-selling game in 2007.
- Nintendo products targeting new markets include the My Coach series, a line of self-improvement games for the DS, as well as the Wii system's fitness games.

In addition to creating memorable characters, Nintendo has been successful for other reasons. In the 2010 article "Nintendo: Japan's Brand Story of the Decade." marketing executive David Aaker and business professor Satoshi Akutsu noted that Nintendo has achieved success by deciding to "[m]ove away from competing on high-tech innovation," "[t]arget a different, broader market," and "[e]mploy a talented product design group."

Nintendo offers educational games in addition to its traditional adventure and sports-based games. The company began selling its Brain Age games for its handheld DS system in 2005. A company website claims that playing these Brain Age games can "stimulate your brain" and "keep your mind in shape." These games proved to be wildly popular worldwide, selling more than 4.4 million units in the United States from 2006 to 2008 and becoming Europe's top-selling game in 2007.

Other educational games for the Nintendo DS followed, including the My Coach series, which helps DS users learn to cook, use other languages, lose weight, become more physically fit, prepare for tests, and even stop smoking. These titles have attracted buyers interested in self-improvement. These buyers may not have used Nintendo's more traditional lineup of entertaining adventure games, and so these self-improvement games have been a way for Nintendo to gain entry to new markets.

Other Nintendo products attract different kinds of consumers. The Wii console system features fitness games and accessories like a balance board. Users can use the balance board to perform the physical activities featured in Wii games and even use it to weigh themselves. Like the My Coach series for the DS, the Nintendo Wii fitness game system has tapped into the self-improvement and fitness markets.

BRAND EQUITY

- A 2012 study found that the Nintendo Wii system captured a 22.2 percent share of the global video game console market.
- The handheld Nintendo DS system captured a 41.8 percent share of its market and the Nintendo 3DS, a 72.3 percent share of its market.
- By late 2011 game software for the Nintendo DS software claimed a 36 percent share of the portable software market.
- Interbrand named Nintendo the 56th most valuable brand in the world in 2012, with a brand value of US$7.08 billion.

Nintendo's products have captured significant shares of some markets. In July 2012 the Nintendo Wii system captured a 22.2 percent share of the global video game console market. Competitor Sony's PlayStation 3 claimed a 44.5 percent share of the market, and Microsoft's Xbox 360 held a 33.3 percent share. Nintendo's handheld video game systems have also performed well in global markets. In 2012 the Nintendo DS captured a 41.8 percent global market share, compared to the Sony PSP's 58.2 percent share. With regard to other handheld games, the Nintendo 3DS captured a 72.3 percent global market share, and Sony's PS Vita claimed a 27.7 percent share.

A 2011 study published on the *Flurry Analytics* blog compared the U.S. market share for Nintendo DS game software and games for Sony's PSP, Google's Android system, and Apple's iOS system. This study found that market share had declined considerably for both the DS and PSP, an indication that handheld gaming devices are being supplanted by devices that offer capabilities in addition to gaming, as well as cheaper, digitally distributed games. Nevertheless, in late 2011 users of handheld devices still gave Nintendo DS software a sizable 36 percent share of the portable software market; the Android and iOS systems, a combined share of 58 percent; and PSP, a share of 6 percent.

Nintendo's significant shares in the hardware and software markets have made it one of the most prominent brands in the world. In 2012 Interbrand named Nintendo the 56th most valuable brand in the world, with a brand value of US$7.08 billion.

BRAND AWARENESS

- A survey of schoolchildren conducted in the 1990s found that Nintendo's Mario character was more popular than Mickey Mouse.
- Respondents from 28 different countries named Nintendo the 15th-coolest brand in a 2010 survey by the Spanish company Allegro 234 Strategic Marketing & Branding.
- Investor Teodor Rasa compared Nintendo with the extraordinarily successful Coca-Cola brand, noting the international fame, pop culture presence, and successful products of both brands.

With the introduction of its first video games in the late 1970s and early 1980s, Nintendo achieved great popularity quickly. By the 1990s, a survey of schoolchildren found that the Mario character was more popular than Mickey Mouse. Decades later, adults continued to hold positive opinions about the company. In 2010 respondents from 28 different countries named Nintendo the 15th-coolest brand in a survey by the Spanish company Allegro 234 Strategic Marketing & Branding.

Investor Teodor Rasa compared Nintendo's success and visibility with that of another successful brand, Coca-Cola, Interbrand's most valuable global brand in 2012 (with a brand value of approximately US$77.8 billion). In 2012 Rasa observed that "[o]ne could compare Nintendo's 'Super Mario Bros' as the Coca-Cola of video games. This brand is known worldwide and has become a cornerstone of pop culture. Nintendo has successfully leveraged this brand to produce games in multiple categories without dilution." The comparison is apt. Both Nintendo and Coca-Cola have highly recognizable brand identities and produce popular products sold in large numbers around the world.

BRAND OUTLOOK

- Gaming on electronic devices like smartphones has cut into Nintendo's share of the software market for handheld games.
- Nintendo entered the application and small electronic devices markets with the 2012 introduction of the Wii U, a console system that also features a tablet computer.
- The Nintendo Wii U system's tablet provides Internet access, enabling users to play games, watch television and other content, and connect with others.

Nintendo DS claimed 36 percent of the U.S. software market for handheld devices in 2011, while Android and iOS systems together captured 58 percent of that market. The same study also determined that only a year previously, the figures had been almost reversed, with the Nintendo DS holding 57 percent of the market and the Android and iOS systems holding 34 percent.

The rise of gaming on electronic devices like smartphones has clearly cut into Nintendo's software market share. To address this development, Nintendo entered the app (application) and small electronic devices markets in 2012, when it introduced the Wii U system, a console system that also features a tablet computer. This tablet controls the game but also offers Internet access, enabling users to surf the Internet, watch television and other content, and connect with others through the Nintendo Miiverse social network.

FURTHER READING

Aaker, David, and Satoshi Akutsu. "Nintendo: Japan's Brand Story of the Decade." *Marketing News*, October 30, 2010. Accessed October 23, 2012. http://www.marketingpower.com/AboutAMA/pages/davidaakercontributor.aspx.

Allegro 234 Strategic Marketing & Branding. "Coolest & Gaps 2010 Branding Survey." *Rethinking Business*, 2010. Accessed October 24, 2012. http://www.rethinkingbusiness.es/en/news/2010-coolest-gaps-branding-survey.

"Best Global Brands 2012." Interbrand. Accessed October 23, 2012. http://www.interbrand.com/en/best-global-brands/2012/Best-Global-Brands-2012.aspx.

D'Angelo, William. "2012 Year on Year Sales and Market Share Update to July 28th." *VGChartz*, August 4, 2012. Accessed October 23, 2012. http://www.vgchartz.com/article/250310/2012-year-on-year-sales-and-market-share-update-to-july-28th/.

Farago, Peter. "Is It Game over for Nintendo DS and Sony PSP?" *Flurry Analytics*, November 9, 2011. Accessed October 24, 2012. http://blog.flurry .com/bid/77424/Is-it-Game-Over-for-Nintendo-DS-and-Sony-PSP.

Irwin, Mary Jane. "Nintendo's Brainy Strategy." *Forbes*, October 8, 2008. Accessed October 24, 2012. http://www.forbes. com/2008/10/08/games-smart-brain-tech-personal-cx_ mji_1008games.html.

"Nintendo Company, Ltd." *International Directory of Company Histories*. Ed. Jay P. Pederson and Miranda H. Ferrara. Vol. 67. Detroit, MI: St. James Press, 2005.

Nintendo Company, Ltd. "2012 Annual Report." Accessed October 23, 2012. http://www.nintendo.co.jp/ir/en/index.html.

Rasa, Teodor. "Nintendo's Hidden Competitive Advantage." *Seeking Alpha*, April 13, 2012. Accessed October 24, 2012. http://seekingalpha.com/ article/495791-nintendo-s-hidden-competitive-advantage.

NTT GROUP

BRAND ORIGINS

- Nippon Telegraph and Telephone Corp. (NTT) provides telephone, mobile phone, smartphone, personal handyphone, and Internet services and the hardware for these services.
- NTT has 220,000 employees working at many companies, including more than 750 subsidiaries, on five continents.
- The Japanese government originally controlled Nippon Telegraph and Telephone Public Corp. (NTTPC), a company founded in 1952.
- NTT took its current name when it was partially privatized in 1985. The Japanese government still owns 34 percent of the company.
- After its partial privatization, NTT increased its foreign operations, founding NTT International Corp. in 1985.

The Japanese telecommunications firm Nippon Telegraph and Telephone Corp. (NTT) is one of the largest companies in the world. It provides telephone, mobile phone, smartphone, personal handyphone, and Internet services. It develops, manufactures, and sells the phones and devices that use these services, develops technology to support its goods and services, and works with business data and information systems.

NTT originally developed handyphones for Asian markets. A handyphone functions as a mobile phone and as a more conventional cordless phone. The company operates in several markets on five continents. Its operations include the NTT Group and more than 750 consolidated subsidiaries. Some parts of the company include Nippon Telegraph and Telephone East Corp. (NTT East), Nippon Telegraph and Telephone West Corp. (NTT West), NTT Communications Corp., Dimension Data Holdings PLC, NTT Docomo, Inc., and NTT Data Corp.

The company's history somewhat parallels the history of the American company AT&T. The U.S. government permitted AT&T to operate as a monopoly until antitrust lawsuits in the 1980s forced the company to break up into seven smaller entities. AT&T maintains local, long-distance, cellular, and Internet services; continues its technological involvement; and has more than 240,000 employees around the world.

Nippon Telegraph and Telephone Public Corp. (NTTPC) began in 1952. The Japanese government controlled NTTPC until it became the partially privatized company Nippon Telegraph and Telephone Corp. in 1985. The Japanese government continues to own 34 percent of the company. Like AT&T, NTT has a large number of employees—220,000—who work at NTT or one of its several international subsidiaries. During the 1980s, NTT, AT&T, and the British telecommunications company British Telecommunications (known as British Telecom or BT) all shifted from government control to more privatized operations.

Before the 1980s, NTTPC had operated on an international level by training foreign workers, sending its own workers abroad, participating in exchanges and agreements, and establishing foreign offices. After its partial privatization, NTT increased its foreign operations, founding NTT International Corp. in 1985. Its international operations have continued since then, as NTT and its companies have worked to promote their goods, services, and names to users in countries all over the world.

BRAND ELEMENTS

- A blue circle with a loop at the top forms part of the logo for the NTT Group and various NTT companies such as NTT East, NTT West, and NTT Electronics.
- The logo for NTT Communications consists of the words "NTT Communications" with a golden yellow mark surrounding half of the words.
- NTT Docomo's logo features "NTT" in capital letters and "docomo" in lowercase letters, all in red.
- Dimension Data, an NTT Group affiliate, uses a logo featuring a green-and-white triangle and the words "dimension data" in gray lowercase letters.
- Adopted in 2012, the NTT Data logo uses blue-violet letters that spell "NTT DATA."

The NTT Group is a large company made up of smaller companies that use a number of different logos. The NTT Group logo is a blue circle with an inward loop at the top followed by the words "NTT Group" in black. NTT uses this circle logo for NTT East and NTT West as well as some of its other companies, such as NTT Electronics. NTT Data began using its blue logo in 2012, replacing the logo it had used since the 1980s. On a company website, NTT Data explained that this newer version "carries over aspects from the current logo, while also giving

the name 'NTT DATA' increased presence as a means of acquiring greater awareness within the global market." NTT Data first used this logo in January 2012 in the Americas as the company expanded and reorganized, and it started using the logo in Japan the following April, with plans to introduce the new logo in other regions as the reorganization progressed.

The logos of NTT Communications companies feature the words "NTT Communications" with a golden yellow mark surrounding half of the words, similar to the rings of the planet Saturn. In 2008 the NTT Group's NTT Docomo began using a new logo featuring "NTT" in capital letters and "docomo" in lowercase letters, all in red. Beginning in 2012 NTT Data Corp. used a logo featuring blue-violet lettering.

Some NTT affiliates do not use the NTT name as part of their part logos. Dimension Data's logo features the words "dimension data" in gray lowercase letters. These words precede a green-and-white triangle. These logos sometimes are displayed with the NTT Group's circle logo on websites and online documents.

BRAND IDENTITY

- NTT's mission is supplying "ongoing, safe, and secure communications services to become a company continually trusted by customers through adapting changes in the ICT market."
- The NTT group wants to be proactive in a rapidly changing market.
- NTT wants to provide ICT services for a variety of fields, so each of NTT's business groups is customized to meet a particular need.

According to the "Message from the President" on the corporate website, the NTT Group sees its mission as supplying "ongoing, safe, and secure communications services to become a company continually trusted by customers through adapting changes in the ICT market." The NTT group wants to be proactive in a rapidly changing market by pursuing the highest levels of research and development and offering safe, secure, convenient, and cutting edge services and opportunities.

NTT believes it should be possible for information and communications technology (ICT) to be used "anytime, anywhere, for anything and by anybody." NTT seeks to make that possible by reinforcing high-speed and comfortable networks as well as providing handsets and service content. The company wants to provide ICT services for a variety of fields, so each of NTT's business groups is customized to meet a particular need, whether the telephone or Internet needs of the individual consumer or the software needs of international businesses.

BRAND STRATEGY

- In 2010, NTT acquired Dimension Data to strengthen its business in South American, African, and Middle Eastern markets.
- In 2011, in accordance with its globalization strategy, NTT Data acquired the company Value Team to bolster its presence in South America.
- Value Team changed its name to NTT Data, but its home page was written in Italian and used the NTT Data logo in English.
- Other NTT acquisitions with international ties include Germany's Cirquent as well as Keane, Intelligroup, and Verio, which were based in the United States.
- The website for NTT Communications highlights its global commitment, with sections titled "Our Global Strengths" and "Our Global Coverage."

In response to rapid changes in the telecommunications market, the NTT Group announced its Medium-Term Management Strategy in November 2004. This strategy included the goals of creating a broadband access infrastructure that includes the Next-Generation Network (NGN) and offering ubiquitous broadband services to meet diverse customer needs. Further, NTT began commercial-use NGN services. In May 2008, NTT announced a new Medium-Term Management Strategy called the "Road to a Service Creation Business Group," whose goal was to develop and offer new services compatible with full IP networks that cover both fixed-line and mobile communications. NTT's more recent goals include emphases on fiber optics, high-speed wireless, multi-devices, and cloud services.

Expanding globally is another one of NTT's most important brand strategies. In 2010, NTT acquired the business technology firm Dimension Data, which is based in Johannesburg, South Africa,. Acquiring Dimension Data was an attempt to compete in the South American, African, and Middle Eastern markets. Dimension Data already had several offices in those regions, and business analysts said that Dimension Data had a stronger brand presence in those markets than NTT did. Dimension Data also had offices in Europe and North America, further emphasizing the international scope of its—and NTT's—business.

In 2011 NTT Data acquired the engineering and consulting firm Value Team SpA in hopes of expanding its business in South America, where Value Team had already established offices and businesses. Value Team changed its name to NTT Data but kept its headquarters in Italy. As a consequence, the company's home page uses Italian as its primary language, yet the NTT Data logo still appears in English for both the Japanese parent company and the

Italian subsidiary. The Italian website also uses English for some of its links, with links to other pages in Italian.

The 2012 restructuring of NTT Data also reflected NTT's global reach. This reorganization incorporated some of NTT's latest acquisitions, technology companies based in various countries: Value Team in Italy as well as Cirquent in Germany and Keane and Intelligroup in the United States.

NTT Communications has offices in approximately 30 countries. Looking to broaden its business in the United States and Asia, NTT Communications finished its buyout of the Colorado-based Internet company Verio in 2000. The home page of NTT Communications also demonstrates NTT's global commitment. It features two large tabs situated prominently at the top of the page reading "Our Global Strengths" and "Our Global Coverage." These tabs provide links to NTT websites in other countries as well as information about international projects, services, and other aspects of NTT Communications.

BRAND EQUITY

- A 2012 report by Japan's Ministry of Internal Affairs found that NTT East and NTT West captured a 79.2 percent share of the subscriber telephone market.
- A 2012 report found that NTT Docomo captured 45.3 percent of the mobile phone and personal handyphone market.
- With a value of US$26.3 billion, Brand Finance ranked NTT 14th on its list of the top global brands in 2012, down from 13th place in 2011.
- In 2012, *Fortune* magazine named the NTT Group the 29th-largest company in the world and the third-largest in Japan.

The various components of NTT hold significant shares of a number of markets. A 2012 report by Japan's Ministry of Internal Affairs and Communications found that, in Japan, NTT East and NTT West captured a 79.2 percent share of the subscriber telephone market, 74.2 percent of the fiber optic cable market, and 34.6 percent of the DSL (digital subscriber lines for Internet access) market. Meanwhile NTT Docomo captured 45.3 percent of the mobile phone and personal handyphone market.

These market shares helped NTT land a place on Brand Finance's 2012 list of the largest global brands. NTT placed 14th on the list with a brand value of about US$26.3 billion versus a 2011 value of about US$26.9 billion when it took the 13th spot. In 2012, *Fortune* magazine ranked NTT the 29th-largest company in the world and the third-largest in Japan.

BRAND AWARENESS

- NTT has had low brand awareness outside Japan.
- In its 2012 global restructuring, NTT Data worked to raise its international brand profile and create a unified brand identity and organization.
- NTT Docomo significantly raised its brand awareness with a targeted Internet campaign.
- A 2008 poll found that NTT West and KDDI Corp tied as the Internet protocol (IP) telephone providers with the highest customer satisfaction ratings.
- J. D. Power Asia Pacific reported that NTT Docomo had the most satisfied business users of mobile phone and personal handyphones from 2009 to 2012.

Outside Japan, NTT has traditionally had low brand awareness. In its 2012 global restructuring, NTT Data worked to raise its international brand profile. It incorporated companies from Italy, Germany, and other countries known for their work in different regions. These companies were linked with the NTT Data name to create a single brand identity and organization. NTT Data hired public relations firms to raise the company's visibility and reputation in Italy, Germany, Brazil, and the United Kingdom. One result was an agreement to sponsor the Open Championship golf tournament, commonly known as the British Open—a prestigious partnership that should bring NTT Data a sharp increase in its global brand awareness.

Similarly, NTT Docomo, the mobile communications group, tried to raise its brand awareness with an Internet campaign that targeted its ads to users based on their online behavior, according to the website AudienceScience. NTT Docomo saw its brand awareness increase significantly. Familiarity with the brand name rose by 45 percent and association of the brand with the key attribute of being a "pioneer" rose 89 percent.

NTT customers rate its companies highly. In a 2008 poll by J. D. Power Asia Pacific, NTT West and fellow Japanese telecommunications company KDDI Corp. tied as the Internet protocol (IP) telephone providers with the highest customer satisfaction ratings. NTT Communications also performed above the industry average. J. D. Power Asia Pacific also reported that NTT Docomo had the most satisfied business users of mobile phone and personal handyphones for four straight years, from 2009 to 2012.

BRAND OUTLOOK

- An earthquake and tsunami and radiation leaks in eastern Japan in 2011 caused NTT to lose about 30 billion yen in operating income.
- In 2012, NTT Docomo released multiple smartphones, feature phones, and a tablet computer.
- In 2012, NTT Docomo announced its alliance with fellow telecommunications companies Fujitsu and NEC to develop, manufacture, and sell chips for smartphones.
- In 2012, NTT Communications opened a branch in Myanmar (Burma), becoming the first foreign telecommunications company to do so.

In March 2011 an earthquake and tsunami that hit parts of eastern Japan caused extensive destruction and resulted in radiation leaks from damaged nuclear power plants. The disaster hit NTT, which estimated that it lost about 30 billion yen in operating income. The company bounced back, however, and worked to restore services in affected areas. Its brand value remained steady. According to Brand Finance, NTT had a 2012 brand value of about US$26.3 billion versus a 2011 value of about US$26.9 billion.

The company has continued to develop and release new products. In 2012, NTT Docomo unveiled multiple smartphones and feature phones (mobile phones with extra features), as well as a tablet computer. The company announced it was joining with fellow telecommunications companies Fujitsu and NEC to develop, manufacture, and sell chips for smartphones. NTT Docomo worked with these companies and others to develop various technologies.

In addition to its development of new technologies, NTT expanded into new territories. In 2012, NTT Communications opened a branch in Myanmar (Burma) to become the first foreign telecommunications firm to enter the country. Myanmar had been under military rule until 2011; its new government, resources, and workforce made it an attractive new market. These efforts contribute to a bright future for the brand.

FURTHER READING

Brand Finance. "Global 500 2012." *Brandirectory*. Accessed October 15, 2012. http://brandirectory.com/league_tables/table/global-500-2012.

J. D. Power Asia Pacific. "J. D. Power Asia Pacific Reports: KDDI and NTT West Rank Highest in Customer Satisfaction with IP Phone Service in Japan." Accessed October 17, 2012. http://businesscenter.jdpower.com/JDPAContent/CorpComm/News/content/Releases/pdf/2009004.pdf.

Keane. "NTT DATA Expands to Form Single Brand and Organisation." February 28, 2012. Accessed October 17, 2012. http://www.keane.com/keane-insights/press-releases-28-feb-2012.aspx.

Kubo, Nobuhiro, and Paul Sandle. "Japan's NTT to Buy Dimension Data for $3.2 Billion." *Reuters*, July 15, 2010. Accessed October 16, 2012. http://www.reuters.com/article/2010/07/15/us-dimension-data-ntt-idUSTRE66E0SH20100715.

Lewis PR. "NTT DATA Selects LEWIS PR to Drive Campaign across EMEA and Brazil." September 23, 2012. Accessed October 17, 2012. http://live.lewispr.com/LEWISPR/2012/09/23/ntt-data-selects-lewis-pr-to-drive-campaign-across-emea-and-brazil-301210.

Ministry of Internal Affairs and Communications. "Official Announcement of Quarterly Data on Telecommunications Service Contract Number and Market Share (FY2011 Q4 (End of March 2012)." Tokyo: June 22, 2012. Accessed October 16, 2012. http://www.soumu.go.jp/main_sosiki/joho_tsusin/eng/Releases/Telecommunications/120622_01.html.

"Nippon Telegraph and Telephone Corporation." *International Directory of Company Histories*. Ed. Tina Grant. Vol. 117. Detroit: St. James Press, 2011. *Gale Virtual Reference Library*. Accessed October 15, 2012. http://go.galegroup.com/ps/i.do?id=GALE%7CCX2845500079&v=2.1&u=itsbtrial&it=r&p=GPS&sw=w.

NTT. Accessed October 15, 2012. http://www.ntt.co.jp/index_e.html.

NTT Data Corp. "Changes to the Corporate Logo Design." Accessed October 15, 2012. http://www.nttdata.com/global/en/news-center/global/2011/120900.html.

NTT Docomo. "DOCOMO Ranked Top for Fourth Straight Year in Business-Customer Satisfaction for Mobile Phone and PHS Services." Accessed October 17, 2012. http://www.nttdocomo.com/pr/2012/001609.html.

NISSAN

◆

AT A GLANCE

Brand Synopsis: Though it ranks among the world's leading carmakers, Nissan, which until the mid-1980s primarily marketed its vehicles under the Datsun brand name, has suffered from a lack of name recognition that it sought to redress with a global marketing campaign.

Parent Company: Nissan Motor Co., Ltd.
1-1, Takashima 1-chome, Nishi-ku
Yokohama-shi, Kanagawa 220-8686
Japan
http://www.nissan-global.com

Sector: Consumer Discretionary

Industry Group: Automobiles & Components

Performance: *Market share*—5.8 percent (2010). *Sales*—US$114.32 billion (2011).

Principal Competitors: Ford Motor Company; General Motors Company; Honda Motor Company, Ltd.; Hyundai Motor Company; Toyota Motor Corporation

BRAND ORIGINS

- The foundations of Nissan go back to 1911, when U.S.-trained engineer Masujiro Hashimoto established Kwaishinsha Motor Car Works.
- Hashimoto's company, which became DAT Automobile Manufacturing in 1926, began producing a car called the "Datson" in 1931.
- DAT became Jidosha-Seizo Company, which in 1934 merged with the automobile parts division of Tobata Casting to form Nissan Motor Company.

In Tokyo in 1911, U.S.-trained engineer Masujiro Hashimoto established Kwaishinsha Motor Car Works, which became DAT Motorcar Company in 1925. A 1926 merger with Jitsuyo Motors made it the DAT Automobile Manufacturing Company, which in 1931 began producing a car called the "Datson."

Entrepreneur Yoshisuke Aikawa purchased a controlling interest in DAT, and placed it under his holding company, Nippon Sangyo, which would ultimately become the fourth-largest *zaibatsu* or conglomerate in prewar Japan. In 1934 Aikawa merged the automaker (now known as Jidosha-Seizo Company) with the automobile parts division of Tobata Casting, another of his companies. The newly formed Nissan Motor Company began producing cars at its Yokohama plant under the guidance of American industrial engineers, but the Datsun, with a new spelling, faced overwhelming competition from the products of U.S. automobile companies.

Then came World War II, during which Nissan directed its effort toward producing military trucks, airplane engines, and torpedo boats. Nissan struggled to regain its footing in the postwar years, and for a period in 1947 and 1948 it was called Nissan Heavy Industries. By the 1950s, however, it had returned to manufacturing vehicles, this time for Britain's Austin Motor Company.

As it began developing its export business, the company established Nissan Motor Corporation U.S.A. in 1959. A 1966 merger with Prince Motor Company broadened Nissan's market to include upscale sports cars. Foreign sales grew dramatically, reaching one million units in 1969, and the 1973 oil crisis further spurred interest in gas-saving models such as the Datsun 210 Honeybee, which offered 41 miles to the gallon. In the early 1980s, Nissan phased out the Datsun name, and in 1989 it introduced the upscale Infiniti line.

BRAND ELEMENTS

- The Tokyo stock exchange abbreviation for Nippon Sangyo, which acquired the carmaker in 1930, was Nissan.
- Datsun's name commemorates the surnames of three investors who underwrote the original company in 1911: Den, Auyama, and Takeuchi.
- In Japanese, the name Datsun connotes "fast, fleeing rabbit," an image of speed appropriate for an automobile.
- Both Datsun and Nissan used a logo that included a large sun-like circle, much like the one that appears on the flag of Japan.

The Nissan brand name comes from that of the holding company that acquired it in 1930: Nippon Sangyo or "Japan Industries," whose abbreviation on the Tokyo stock exchange was *Nissan.*

The Datsun brand name has a curious history, making it the subject of urban legend and at least one joke. (The latter involves a Japanese auto executive telling his German counterpart that he needs a name for a new car brand, but he has to have it by tomorrow. The German replies, "Dat soon?") In fact the first part of the name commemorates the surnames of three investors who underwrote the original company in 1911: Den, Auyama, and Takeuchi. Originally the brand name was Datson, which blended DAT with a widely recognized English word to mean "son of DAT." But because "son" means "loss" in Japanese, the second syllable became "sun," the English word for one of Japan's most important national symbols. The name took on further meaning because when "dat" is pronounced in Japanese, it becomes *datto,* meaning "fast, fleeing rabbit," an image of speed appropriate for an automobile.

Beginning in the early 1950s, Nissan and Datsun used a succession of logotypes with various cursive and block fonts. Then in the 1970s, the company introduced a logotype with the name in plain capital block letters surrounded by a horizontal rectangle. It later added a large sun-like circle, much like the one that appears on the flag of Japan, behind the rectangle. Versions of this logo appeared in chrome and black or in color, with the brand name in white surrounded by blue and the sun in red. This pattern would continue for a quarter century as the Nissan name ultimately replaced that of Datsun, Then in

2001, Nissan returned to a plain logotype, with the company name in plain red capital letters.

Infiniti has its own logo, which appears either in chrome or black. It consists of a horizontal oval with a notch cut into the bottom, like an inverted "V," which symbolizes the infinite open road.

BRAND IDENTITY

- The term "innovative" is at the center of Nissan's efforts to provide greater definition to its brand.
- In the 2010s Nissan launched a marketing campaign built around the tagline "Innovation that excites."
- Earlier Nissan campaigns were built around the words "Driven" (1998–2002) and "Shift" (2002–2010).
- Nissan spent more than US$200 million on an advertising campaign in the 1980s to support its transition from the Datsun brand name.

Nissan's vision statement is "Enriching people's lives," and its mission statement is almost as lean: "Nissan provides unique and innovative automotive products and services that deliver superior measurable values to all stakeholders in alliance with Renault." An asterisk beside "stakeholders" points to a footnote explaining that "Our stakeholders include customers, shareholders, employees, dealers and suppliers, as well as the communities where we work and operate."

But perhaps the most important word in the company's statements of identity is innovative, a term at the center of Nissan's efforts to provide greater definition to its brand. "It's something that Nissan historically hasn't done very well, which is show a common face around the world," executive vice president Andy Palmer admitted to Hans Greimel in *Automotive News.* But as Greimel went on to add, "that is changing," thanks in large part to a global campaign in the 2010s using the tagline "Innovation that excites."

Prior to the "Innovation" tagline, which was introduced in 2010 and became the basis for the brand's first global marketing campaign in 2012, Nissan had built earlier campaigns around the words "Driven" (1998–2002) and "Shift" (2002–2010), for example, "Shift your expectations."

A much earlier campaign involved a shift of a different kind, as Nissan phased out the Datsun brand name in favor of its own. Beginning in 1981, the company placed "Datsun by Nissan" badges on Datsun vehicles and spent about US$30 million on changing signage at some 1,100 dealerships. An estimated US$200 million went into an advertising campaign that introduced the new brand. Datsun had enjoyed strong name recognition with its "We are driven" campaign in the 1970s, and between 1982 and 1986 the automaker sought to reeducate customers with a theme built around the phrase "The name is Nissan." Yet by the beginning of the 1990s, half a decade after the name change, consumers were still more familiar with Datsun than with Nissan.

BRAND STRATEGY

- For many years, Nissan manufactured a wide array of vehicles under both the Nissan and Datsun brand names.
- The Nissan lineup came more clearly into focus in the 1980s, with the phasing out of the Datsun brand and the introduction of Infiniti in the luxury segment.
- By the 2010s Nissan's North American line included cars, sport utility vehicles, multipurpose vehicles, and trucks in a broad range of sizes.

For many years, Nissan manufactured a wide array of cars, trucks, and later vans under both the Nissan and Datsun brand names, with little clear differentiation as to market segment. However, the Nissan lineup came more clearly into focus in the 1980s, a decade that began with the phasing out of the Datsun brand and ended with the introduction of Infiniti in the luxury segment.

By the 2010s Nissan's North American road car lineup consisted of the subcompact Versa, the compact Sentra, the midsize Altima, and the full-size Maxima. Other significant models included the Leaf, a five-door, electric-powered hatchback introduced in 2010, and several sports cars, such as the 370Z. The brand's sport utility vehicles (SUVs) ranged from the compact Xterra to the midsize Pathfinder and the full-size Armada. Nissan also offered a mini MPV (multipurpose vehicle), the Cube, named for its distinctive body design. Its trucks ran the gamut from the Juke, a mini-crossover (a vehicle built on a car platform that combines elements of an SUV with other body styles), to the Titan, a full-size pickup available in two- and four-door versions.

Infiniti, rather than using model names, developed a system that uses one letter for coupes and sedans and two letters for SUVs, along with a number that usually indicates engine displacement. Some models also include letter extensions—x, s, h, d, or t—that designate all-wheel drive, sport, hybrid, diesel, and touring models respectively. Beginning in 2013, coupe and sedan names would use the letter "Q," and SUVs and crossovers, "QX," along with a number indicating the model's position within the Infiniti hierarchy.

BRAND EQUITY

- During the 1990s, the strength of the yen, along with the resurgence of the U.S. auto industry, hurt Nissan's export business.
- A March 1999 alliance with French automaker Renault saved the Nissan brand with cash, a restructuring plan, and common production platforms.

- With 30 percent growth in value, Nissan earned a designation of "top riser" among automotive brands on Interbrand's 2012 Best Global Brand list.

During the 1990s a series of calamities hit Nissan. The strength of the yen, along with the resurgence of the U.S. auto industry, hurt Japanese exports, and the coming of a global recession early in the decade caught the company at a time when it had already stretched its resources in an effort to unseat Toyota as the number-one Japanese carmaker. An aggressive austerity program helped bring it back from the brink, but its failure to move into such emerging markets as minivans and SUVs hurt Nissan's standing, both at home and abroad, and it lost market share to competitors Toyota and Honda.

The coming of the Asian financial crisis in 1997 very nearly spelled doom for Nissan, but fortunately it struck an alliance with French automaker Renault S.A. that saved the company and its brand. Not only did the March 1999 agreement bring a much-needed infusion of cash, but it included more long-term benefits in the form of a highly successful restructuring and streamlining plan, as well as a strategy of using common production platforms for Renault and Nissan products.

Despite further calamities, such as another financial crisis in 2008, as well as an earthquake and tsunami that hit Japan in 2011, Nissan prospered in the early 2010s. In 2011 it entered the Interbrand Best Global Brands list at number 90 with an estimated value of almost US$3.82 billion, and in 2012 it climbed to number 73 with a value estimated at US$4.97 billion. Its growth of 30 percent earned it a designation as "top riser" among the 13 automobile brands on the list. In 2012 the combined sales of Nissan and Renault made the alliance the third-biggest automaker in the world after General Motors and Volkswagen.

BRAND AWARENESS

- Despite its global presence, Nissan has suffered from a lack of brand differentiation, if not brand awareness.
- To improve brand awareness, Nissan has begun focusing its communications and using its marketing to tell stories.
- In May 2012 Nissan launched its first global marketing campaign with a series of billboards built around "What if?" questions.

Despite its global presence, Nissan has suffered from a lack of brand differentiation, if not brand awareness. Industry analysts have offered a number of reasons for this, not least being lingering confusion regarding the switch from the Datsun brand name in the 1980s.

In an August 2012 interview with Jon Brancheau, marketing vice president for Nissan North America, Lindsay Chappell of *Automotive News* posed this question: "Your senior management has said a number of times that Nissan has suffered from a lack of brand awareness. Nissan has been around 50 years successfully selling cars; why are people fuzzy about the brand?" Brancheau did not dispute the point, but observed that "we've changed our strategy. We're going to strategically align more of our resources against fewer models." Brancheau added that "Our resources will be disproportionately focused on those cars that are both high volume and can drive favorable perception of the brand."

Discussing Nissan's past challenges with brand awareness, Michael Barnett in *Marketing Week* quoted executive vice president Andy Palmer, who observed that Nissan had "always been a company of '*monozukuri*'—Japanese for the science of making things … but awful at '*kotozukuri*', the art of storytelling." With its new marketing efforts, Barnett observed, Nissan would use storytelling "to take its branding up a gear and grab more of the upmarket and green vehicle sectors."

As for those new marketing efforts, in May 2012 Hans Greimel reported in *Automotive News* that "an increasingly brand-conscious Nissan Motor Co. is embarking on its first global marketing campaign in an attempt to build a cohesive public image worldwide." Built around a series of "What if?" questions, the campaign would begin with billboards at major airports and would expand to include corporate sponsorship of sporting activities.

BRAND OUTLOOK

- In March 2012 Nissan announced its intention to bring back the Datsun name as a low-cost marque in emerging markets.
- Marketing forecasters predicted that by 2015 Nissan would have an 11 percent share of the electric-vehicle market, behind only Toyota and Ford.
- Nissan announced in January 2013 that it begin making its product names consistent around the globe.
- In June 2011 Renault/Nissan CEO Carlos Ghosn presented a roadmap for the next six years known as Nissan Power 88.

In March 2012 Nissan announced its intention to bring back an old name: Datsun, which would become a new, low-cost marque for the emerging markets of Russia, India, and Indonesia beginning in 2014. Of greater significance to the company's future plans, however, was the Leaf, a fully electric vehicle (as opposed to a gas–electric hybrid) introduced in 2010. Marketing forecasters Baum and Associates predicted that by 2015 Nissan would have an 11 percent share of the electric vehicle market, behind only Toyota and Ford.

Nissan announced in January 2013 that it would, as Lindsay Chappell reported in *Automotive News*, "press for more consistent global product names this year—an acknowledgement that customers now read about foreign-market cars online." Thus, for instance, the vehicle sold in the United States as the Versa Hatchback would become the Versa Note, as it was already known in Japan and Europe. In the past, Chappell noted, Americans had "famously resisted names handed to them from the home [i.e., Japanese] market." An example was the 370Z sports car, called the Fairlady (after the film *My Fair Lady*) in Japan. Perhaps not surprisingly, "U.S. sales executives scoffed at the name." But now, as a senior Nissan executive told Chappell, "We have received clear direction from upper management in the company that global names are preferred."

The brand's future planning would take place within the context of its alliance with Renault, which in April 2010 grew to include Daimler AG as a partner with a mutual 3.9 percent share. In June 2011 Carlos Ghosn (rhymes with "bone"), CEO of Renault and Nissan, presented a roadmap for the next six years called Nissan Power 88. The name refers to Ghosn's goal of expanding both global market share and operating profit to 8 percent by 2016. Power 88 involved ambitious plans such as introducing a new vehicle every six weeks for six years, which would enable the company to cover 92 percent of all market segments by the end of the 2016 fiscal year.

FURTHER READING

Barnett, Michael. "What's Driving Nissan?" *Marketing Week*, August 30, 2012.

Chappell, Lindsay. "Global Names for Nissan Models." *Automotive News*, January 28, 2013.

———. "Nissan's Brand Ads Push the Image of Innovation." *Automotive News*, August 27, 2012.

Eisenstein, Paul. "Nissan Reveals Power 88 Plan: 8% Profit Margin, 8% Market Share and New Model Every 6 Weeks." The Detroit Bureau. Accessed January 29, 2013. http://www.thedetroitbureau.com/2011/06/nissan-reveals-power-88-plan-8-profit-margin-8-market-share-and-new-model-every-6-weeks/.

Elliott, Stuart. "Nissan Shifts from 'Shift' to 'Innovation.'" *New York Times*, August 24, 2010.

Greimel, Hans. "Nissan Begins 1st Global Branding Bid." *Automotive News*, May 14, 2012.

"Nissan Motor Company Ltd." *International Directory of Company Histories*. Ed. Tina Grant. Vol. 92. Detroit, MI: St. James Press, 2008.

NIVEA

―◆―

BRAND ORIGINS

- In 1911 Dr. Oscar Troplowitz worked with Dr. Paul Gerson Unna to develop Nivea, a stable oil-and-water-based skin cream.
- Nivea's research has led to a global presence with the creation of skin whiteners, skin softeners, sun care, baby care, and creams including Q10.
- In 2011 Nivea's centennial year, Beiersdorf celebrated the brand's values of trust, honesty, reliability, quality, and family.

In 1911 Dr. Oscar Troplowitz, a pharmacist from Silesia and owner of Beiersdorf & Co., a Hamburg-based manufacturer of bandages and skin care products established in 1880, bought the patent for Eucerit, a stable water-soluble foundation for medicinal salves. He worked with Dr. Paul Gerson Unna to develop a stable oil-and-water-based skin cream. The result was a white cream with the scent of rose and lily of the valley. They named the product Nivea, which was derived from the Latin word for snow.

Beiersdorf was already present in foreign markets when Nivea Crème was invented. By the beginning of World War I, the company had production facilities in New York, Austria-Hungary, Vienna, London, Buenos Aires, Copenhagen, Mexico, Moscow, Paris, and Sydney, with sales representatives in 29 countries around the world.

World War I stalled foreign trade and the production of Nivea Crème, but production began again after the war. During the 1920s, new facilities were built in Hamburg to handle increased production. Responding to a culture that embraced youth and leisure time, Beiersdorf redesigned Nivea's folk-art-styled container, giving it a simple blue background and white lettering. This design is still in use and continues to be a symbol of freshness and new beginnings.

Beiersdorf's success enabled it to avoid layoffs during the Great Depression, and the company's research during the period focused on the needs of different skin types. A new shaving soap was developed for men, who often used Nivea Crème as an aftershave treatment. In Asia the desire for pale white complexions led to the creation of Nivea Whitening Paste. Shampoo and Nivea Ultra-oil (the world's first sunscreen) were also included in the

769

brand range, and sales increased on a global scale. Even during World War II, Beiersdorf's workforce and revenues continued to grow. Elly Heuss-Knapp was in charge of advertising at this time and managed to keep Nivea's reputation from harm during the Nazi era in Germany.

Following World War II, production slowed in response to shortages of materials and energy as well as the regulations put in place by the military government of the occupying Allies. Beiersdorf continued to advertise to maintain recognition of its brands, and in 1947 the company received permission to resume production of Nivea Crème and toothpaste. Though materials shortages during the 1950s limited the quantities produced, Nivea managed to extend its global presence to the Middle East.

The baby boom inspired the addition of baby care products to Nivea's sub-brands. Postwar prosperity and the car culture led families to spend more leisure time outdoors. Nivea used a blue beach ball featuring the brand's distinctive white lettering to advertise the brand and its sunscreen at beaches of international resorts. The Nivea ball proved popular: by 2012, 20 million of the balls had been produced and distributed.

By the 1970s, Nivea had emerged as a leader in the European market. To consumers, the brand represented gentle, caring products at a reasonable price. During the 1980s and 1990s, Nivea launched Nivea Visage, a line of face care products; Nivea for Men; Nivea Hair Care; Nivea Sun; and Nivea Bath Care. In 1994 the Nivea Vital line was created for mature skin. In 1998 Nivea researchers discovered Q10, an element in skin that becomes depleted with age. Nivea Visage Anti-Wrinkle Q10 Day Cream, formulated to reduce the loss of Q10, became a best seller.

Finding new ways to reach global consumers became a priority during the 2000s. Nivea Haus spas opened in Hamburg, Dubai, Berlin, and Vienna. New products introduced in the early 21st century included Nivea Visage Aqua Sensation, with Hydra Q10 to improve moisture in the deep layers of the skin, and Nivea Pure & Natural, a line featuring natural and organic ingredients.

In 2011 Beiersdorf celebrated Nivea's centennial and, seeking to expand the brand's audience and modernize its image, hired English R&B singer Rihanna to appear in Nivea promotions. Public events and social media were used to reinforce the values associated with Nivea: trust, honesty, reliability, quality, and family.

BRAND ELEMENTS

- The name Nivea comes from the Latin word for snow, and Nivea Crème's original white color and floral scent have not changed.
- A cobalt-blue tin with simple, white lettering replaced Nivea Crème's original folk-art inspired container in 1925.

- Nivea's message is "Touch and be touched," and its goal is to provide better skincare for all cultures and ages.

The name Nivea is derived from the Latin word for snow. The product's color, texture, and scent have endeared it to consumers for more than a century. The familiar tins are popular with consumers, who have been known to reuse them as storage containers that are enhanced by the lingering scent of roses and lily of the valley.

The original Nivea tin was round and yellow, with a folk-art border, but a new container, inspired by the Bauhaus movement, was devised in 1925. A white ring circled the name Nivea Crème on a background of cobalt blue. The lettering was straight and simple, giving a fresh, clean look to the product. The essential design of the container has not changed, but in the United States the tin has been replaced by plastic. The logo for Nivea sub-brands is the word "Nivea" in white against a cobalt blue rectangle. With the message "Touch and be touched," Nivea promotes skincare products for skin of all cultures and ages.

BRAND IDENTITY

- Nivea is a company that stands for trust, family, and reliability.
- Nivea balls provide a simple yet effective way to highlight the brand's message that family time is a key value of the Nivea brand.
- Nivea promotes itself as a leader in skincare by investing in continuing research.

Stephan Heidenreich, CEO of Beiersdorf, said, "Nivea is a company which stands for trust, family and reliability." Nivea presents itself with a consistent, ongoing mission: to help all people live life to the fullest with healthy skin. To promote this brand image, Nivea advertisements typically show diverse families, young people in love and at play, and older generations enjoying memories of lives well-spent. The Nivea website reaches out to its global audience: "No matter what you do, or where you live, we're here to help you enjoy better skincare for life. Whether you're male or female. Young or old. Fair or dark. Oily or dry. Sensitive or normal. Or anything in between. We care for all your skin. For life."

In the 1930s "Nivea caravans" began to show up at international resorts to deliver Nivea balls to consumers who had purchased Nivea sun protection products. The ball served as a simple way to emphasize Nivea's key values of family time and an active lifestyle.

Nivea demonstrates its goals to protect skin with continuing research. Whether the skin needs protection from the sun or age, new discoveries reinforce the brand's desire to help keep skin healthy. It also promotes Nivea as a brand with scientific credibility.

BRAND STRATEGY

- Nivea continues to research new ways to care for different types of skin.
- The extensive range of sub-brands allows for high-quality products at reasonable prices and meets a wide variety of consumer needs.
- Nivea's "Million Moments of Touch Movement" in 2012 encouraged consumers to make the world more affectionate by using the power of touch.

Nivea is an umbrella brand of Beiersdorf AG. Nivea Crème is the popular force behind the brand's success, but the company continues to research new ways to care for different types of skin and assures consumers that "no matter what your age, race, location or culture, Nivea has you covered."

The extensive range of sub-brands reinforces Nivea's association with high-quality products at reasonable prices and meets a wide variety of consumer needs. A majority of young girls did not want medicated products for their skin, for example, and so Nivea created Nivea Visage, a product line aimed at helping girls begin a regular beauty routine. These young girls then grow to become part of Nivea's loyal consumer base. In Asia consumers were interested in whiter skin; Nivea Visage Whitening Cream 20+ SPF 15 was developed for Asian skin. For consumers that wished to be tan, Nivea created a line of self-tanning moisturizers that hydrate skin. Nivea has expanded to more than 170 countries and offers some 500 personal products.

In 2011 Beiersdorf streamlined the range of Nivea-branded products, a move that Interbrand described as an effort to refocus the brand on skincare, because decorative cosmetics (make-up) were not a good fit. In 2012 the Nivea USA website promoted the "Million Moments of Touch Movement." Each day throughout the year, a couple was chosen from Facebook entries and awarded a date night. The campaign encouraged consumers to get away from social media and reconnect with the power of touch as a way to "make the world a more affectionate place."

BRAND EQUITY

- In 2012 *Brandirectory* ranked Nivea 172nd among the top-500 global brands.
- *Brandirectory* estimated Nivea's brand value at US$5.6 billion in 2012.
- Nivea did not make Interbrand's top-100 global brands in 2012, but it was ranked 87th in the fast-moving consumer goods category in 2011.

In 2012 *Brandirectory* ranked Nivea number 172 in the top-500 global brands with a brand value of US$5.6 billion. Nivea ranked 13th in *Brandirectory's* "Germany 30" and fifth among the top-50 cosmetics brands.

Interbrand did not place Nivea among the top-100 global brands in 2012, but in 2011 Nivea was ranked 87th among producers of fast-moving consumer goods. Its brand value in 2011, according to Interbrand, was US$3.9 billion, up 4 percent over the previous year.

BRAND AWARENESS

- Nivea is known for its heritage, affordability, and loyal customer base.
- Nivea was named the "most trusted brand" by European *Reader's Digest* readers in 2012.
- The connection with Rihanna during Nivea's centennial year enabled the brand to reach a large consumer base through social networks and other media.
- Nivea enjoys almost 100 percent brand awareness in Germany.

Interbrand notes that Nivea is known for its heritage, affordability, and loyal customer base. *Reader's Digest* readers in Europe named Nivea the "most trusted brand" in skincare in 2012.

During the 1920s Nivea promoted its fresh, healthy, family oriented image with an advertisement that featured a photo of three brothers in Hamburg, Germany. The "Nivea boys" were said to be so popular that people addressed them with "Hello, Nivea!" when they walked down the street.

According to the newsletter *CosmeticsDesign-Asia.com*, the activities surrounding Nivea's 100th anniversary were a key source of momentum, and around 1.6 million consulting sessions were held at over 75,000 promotional stands in retail stores in 52 countries as part of the company's skin advisory tour. The anniversary celebration was also an opportunity to increase brand awareness among a younger crowd, and social networks were used extensively, with 10 percent of the campaign budget dedicated to digital activities. The global campaign featured the song "California King Bed" by British pop star Rihanna. Nivea offered opportunities to win tickets to Rihanna concerts in the media, on the Nivea website, and at retail outlets in more than 40 countries. The skincare brand recorded around one billion internet hits, including more than 200 million on social networks.

Beiersdorf claims on its website that, in Germany, Nivea "enjoys brand awareness of almost 100 percent."

BRAND OUTLOOK

- Nivea intends to focus more strongly on its core values in the coming years.
- Nivea plans to adapt its advertising and marketing campaigns to reflect its renewed commitment to its core values.

- In response to economic struggles and limited supplies, the company plans to reduce its dependence on particular suppliers and specific raw materials.

In a 2012 interview with CBS News, Beiersdorf CEO Stefan Heidenreich said Nivea's future brand positioning would focus "more than ever on its core values. This leads to a change in advertising strategy as well as marketing campaigns."

According to Beiersdorf's 2012 annual report, continued growth was expected in Asia, in spite of struggles in China with fiscal and monetary policies being introduced by the government. The ongoing decline in crude oil prices was a good sign for the brand, but limited supplier capacity was expected to affect the availability of materials needed for production. Beiersdorf said it was looking to reduce its dependence on certain individual suppliers and specific raw materials.

FURTHER READING

Beiersdorf AG. "History: Nivea Haus: A Spa Experience." Accessed October 25, 2012. http://www.nivea.ie/about-us/beiersdorf/NIVEAHistory#!stories/story36.

————. "100 Years Skincare for Life: Nivea Makes Billion-Euro Investment in Its Biggest Global Campaign Ever." Accessed October 5, 2012. http://www.beiersdorf.com/Press/Press_Releases_News/NIVEA_100_Years_Skincare_for_Life.html.

"Beiersdorf AG." *International Directory of Company Histories.* Ed. Jay P. Pederson. Vol. 137. Detroit, MI: St. James Press, 2012.

"Best Global Brands: 2011–2012." Interbrand. Accessed October 2, 2012. http://www.interbrand.com/en/best-global-brands/2012/Best-Global-Brands-2012.aspx.

Brand Finance. "Global 500 2012." *Brandirectory*, 2012. Accessed October 2, 2012. http://brandirectory.com/league_tables/table/global-500-2012.

Bryan, Victoria. "Update 2-Beiersdorf Profit Surprises as Nivea Focus Pays Off." Reuters, January 25, 2012.

Derschowitz, Jessica. "Rihanna Deemed Too Sexy for Nivea?" CBS News, August 8, 2012. Accessed October 5, 2012. http://www.cbsnews.com/8301-31749_162-57489469-10391698/rihanna-deemed-too-sexy-for-Nivea/.

Mansour, T. Abi. "Celebrating 100 Years of NIVEA." *Beirut-Online*, September 9, 2011. Accessed October 2, 2012. http://www.beirut-online.net/portal/article.php?id=9855.

McDougall, Andrew. "Beiersdorf Announces Positive 2012 Outlook as Nivea Brand Takes Centre Stage." CosmeticsDesign-Asia.com, March 2, 2012. Accessed October 1, 2012. http://www.cosmeticsdesign-asia.com/Business-Financial/Beiersdorf-announces-positive-2012-outlook-as-Nivea-brand-takes-centre-stage.

Nudd, Tim. "Nivea Apologizes for Wanting to 'Re-civilize' Black Man: Draftfcb Ad Ran Once, Won't Run Again." *Ad Week*, August 18, 2011.

NOKIA

—◼—

AT A GLANCE

Brand Synopsis: Nokia is a telecommunications equipment manufacturer with a vision of "Connecting People."

Parent Company: Nokia Oyj
Keilalahdentie 2-4, Fl-02150
Espoo
Finland
http://www.nokia.com

Sector: Information Technology

Industry Group: Technology Hardware & Equipment

Performance: *Sales*—EUR38.7 billion (2011)

Principal Competitors: Apple; Samsung; HTC

BRAND ORIGINS

- Nokia began as a pulp and paper mill in 1865.
- The company began doing more work in telecommunications in the 1970s.
- Nokia divested itself of all non-telecommunications businesses in the 1990s.
- Nokia became a leading supplier of cellular phones in the 1990s and early 2000s.
- In 2011 Nokia formed an alliance with Microsoft to develop wireless phones using the Microsoft Mobile operating system.
- Nokia has 130,000 employees in 10 countries.

Nokia, now one of the world's leading makers of cell phones, actually started as a pulp and paper mill founded by Fredrik Idestam in 1865. Idestam, a mining engineer, grew the company to two mills, with the second being near the town of Nokia. After the retirement of Idestam, his friend, Leo Mechelin, was able to expand the company into the electricity business. It effectively added electricity generation to its pulp and paper business.

In 1898 a rubber works, making galoshes and other products, was established near Nokia and the company took on that name as its product brand. This company later became Nokia's rubber business. In 1912 Finnish Cable Works was established. This was the foundation of Nokia's cable and electronics business.

All of these companies did not come together, however, until after World War I. While jointly owned, they were not merged into one industrial conglomerate, Nokia Corporation (or, in Finnish, Nokia Oyj), until 1967. The conglomerate manufactured many different kinds of products, from its original paper to rubber galoshes to robotics, military communications equipment, plastics, aluminum, and chemicals.

In the 1970s Nokia started doing more work in the telecommunications sphere by developing digital switches for telephone exchanges. It worked on equipment that came before today's cellular and wireless technology and developed its first cellular telephone as early as 1981. It then went on to become one of the key developers of GSM (Global System for Mobile Communications) technology, a second-generation cellular technology widely adopted in Europe and many other parts of the world.

The company began focusing more on telecommunications and divested itself of all of its non-telecommunications businesses in the 1990s. Digital phones came on the market in 1993, and in 1998 the company sold 40 million mobile phones, leapfrogging Motorola as the world's number-one mobile phone company. Early in the 2000s, with handset sales slowing, Nokia teamed with phone makers and wireless providers to develop a common global standard for 3G phone software. It developed the Symbian operating system utilized on its phones. However, that proved to be a double-edged sword. Nokia phones remained popular for quite some time, but then began to rapidly lose ground to smartphones such as Apple's iPhone.

Then, in 2011 Nokia announced that it had formed an alliance with Microsoft and would now produce phones with the Windows Phone operating system. Only its lowest-end phones would continue to use Symbian.

Nokia has about 130,000 employees located in 10 countries, with the largest percentage located in Europe. This is down about 2 percent from previous years. Its revenue is driven largely from Europe, the Asia-Pacific region, the Middle East, and Africa. Other regions in which it sells include Greater China, Latin America, and North America.

BRAND ELEMENTS

- The Nokia slogan is "Connecting People."
- The logo features two people almost joining hands.
- The company name is printed in a custom font in a bold blue hue.

The Nokia slogan is "Connecting People." Its logo features a portrait of two people almost joining hands with each other. The company name is written in a bold blue color, which is intended to signify the firm's durability and credibility. The font utilized is fairly plain, intended to symbolize easygoingness. The font is a custom corporate typeface called Nokia Pure, designed by Dalton Maag in 2011.

BRAND IDENTITY

- Nokia sells its products in more than 160 countries around the world.
- China is its largest single-country market.
- Nokia was once the dominant wireless-device provider, but it has now slipped to third behind Samsung and Apple.
- Nokia's brand identity suffered when it ignored smartphone technology, instead focusing on basic mobile phones geared toward its emerging growth markets.
- Nokia provided luxury mobile phones through its Vertu unit, recently divested.

Nokia has products in more than 160 countries, with the largest single-country market being China, although by region, Europe is Nokia's largest. Nokia was once the dominant wireless-device provider, but it faced increasing competition in both devices and operating systems. It is still the third-largest producer of mobile devices, behind Samsung and Apple, but its original operating system, Symbian, could not compete with these companies. Thus, Nokia developed a partnership with Microsoft to use its operating system on all its smartphones.

Nokia's brand identity suffered as it tended to ignore smartphone technology for too long, clinging to the fact that its largest markets were in emerging growth countries, where consumers had no need for those kinds of capabilities. Thus, it was overtaken by Samsung, who understood that while connections were important, what people were focusing on now was computing power in their handsets.

Nokia did attempt to jump into the luxury phone market, however, with Vertu. Similar to NAVTEQ, Vertu was an independently run subsidiary of Nokia until it was divested in 2012. These phones are targeted to a very small audience of those willing to spend as much as US$300,000 for a telephone. While that was its highest price, all these phones were and are being sold for prices ranging from five to six figures. The Vertu phones had been utilizing the Symbian operating system, but the company has now made the switch to Android (notably, not to the Microsoft Windows Phone operating system that the Nokia brand is using). There is an assumption that the newest Vertu phone, launched in January 2013, is still being made by Nokia, because the model number is similar to model numbers of Nokia's Lumia line. However, the Nokia brand does not appear on the any of these phones, so they are not strengthening Nokia's brand identity.

BRAND STRATEGY

- Nokia's goal is to provide mobile products that enable billions of people to enjoy what life has to offer.
- Nokia offers a very broad range of mobile phones; while each series has its own brand, all phones carry the Nokia name prominently, just above the screen.
- Nokia's partnership with Microsoft is the focus of the Nokia Smart Devices team.
- NAVTEQ in the United States is a wholly owned subsidiary of Nokia and is the only division that does not carry the Nokia name.

Nokia's goal is to "build great mobile products that enable billions of people worldwide to enjoy more of what life has to offer." Their overall corporate strategy is fourfold: to build a mobile ecosystem in concert with Microsoft; to bring "the next billion" in emerging markets online; to invest in so-called disruptive technologies; and to increase its focus on speed to market, as well as results and accountability.

Nokia currently has a very broad range of mobile smartphones on the market, almost too many to count. While they each have a brand name, such as Lumia and Asha, they all still carry the Nokia name as well, prominently displayed at the top of each phone, just above the screen.

Nokia's Smart-Devices team focuses on developing Nokia smartphones and smart devices within the Microsoft partnership. The first phone to be developed under this partnership was launched with the Nokia Lumia name in late 2011.

The Nokia Mobile Phones team brings Internet-capable mobile phones to growth markets, often offering its customers their first Internet experience, not only on a mobile device, but ever. Again, all phones bear the Nokia brand name.

The Nokia Location-and-Commerce business works on a range of consumer location-based products and services. It also offers platform services for device manufacturers, application developers, Internet service providers, merchants, and advertisers. This business was formed by combining Nokia's Devices and Services operations with the acquisition of NAVTEQ in the United States. While this division works under the NAVTEQ name, its services do use the Nokia brand name, for example, Nokia Maps, Nokia Drive, Nokia Transport, and Nokia City Lens. At the NAVTEQ website, there is no mention at all of Nokia's ownership. It operates completely independently from the parent company.

BRAND EQUITY

- Nokia was the largest company in Finland in 2010.
- Nokia was the third-largest aerospace and electronics company in Europe in 2010.
- Nokia had been known for its speed to market and its meritocratic, quirky culture.

There is no financial information available for measuring Nokia's financial brand equity. However, Business Rankings Annual lists Nokia as the largest company in Finland in 2010 and the third-largest aerospace and electronics company in Europe in the same year.

For a long time, Nokia was noted for its speed to market and for a meritocratic culture that was considered quirky. People wanted to work for the company and people wanted to buy its products. Demand for the brand diminished greatly as it essentially ignored the smartphone market.

BRAND AWARENESS

- More than 1.3 billion people worldwide use a Nokia device every day.
- Nokia is a very well-known brand worldwide.
- While it might be known in North America, it has a very small market share in a region of the world with very high sales of mobile phones.
- The company is continuing to focus on emerging growth markets, where it is expected that awareness of the brand will continue to grow.

According to the Nokia website, each day more than 1.3 billion people use a Nokia product. Nokia claims that its technological and design innovations have made the brand one of the most recognized around the world. This may be true, but still it has a very small market share in the United States, which contains some of the most voracious buyers of smartphones in the world. It is probably best known in Europe, where it controls just over a 30 percent market share, based on sales. In comparison, North America accounts for only about 4 percent of its sales. By comparison, the Middle East/Africa region accounts for about a 14 percent market share.

These figures show that, while Nokia is certainly not an unknown brand worldwide, it has work to do in its North American market. It is unknown if a simple lack of awareness of the brand is the issue there, or whether Nokia's long stretch of ignoring smartphone technology before its alliance with Microsoft cost it too dearly in brand interest and support. Whatever may be the case, the Android operating system and phones from Apple have come to dominate the United States market.

From information posted on the Nokia website, it appears that the company will continue to focus on its emerging markets, seeking to provide "even more people their first Internet and application experience." While this will certainly increase Nokia's brand awareness in emerging markets, it will do little in the developed world.

BRAND OUTLOOK

- The success of Nokia's alliance with Microsoft remains to be seen, as phones using this operating system continue to be rolled out.
- Nokia has been aided by the slower-than-expected fall in sales of feature phones.
- Nokia is building an ecosystem around the Microsoft Windows Phone operating system it has adopted.
- The company feels that the ecosystem built around the Microsoft Windows Phone operating system will be a viable alternative to compete with those formed around Android and Apple products.

Nokia seems to have awakened from its smartphone slumber of the early 2000s, but it is still struggling to gain traction once again in the market for feature-rich smartphones. The success of its alliance with Microsoft, whereby it is building its phones with the Windows Phone operating system, remains to be seen. The company's recent financial reports have largely been on the negative side.

In addition, the growth of the smartphone market has slowed appreciably, although the growth percentage appears to be robust at about 36 percent at the end of 2012. However, that was below projections and far below the 55 percent growth rate seen in 2011. Research firm IDC, however, noted that sales of feature phones, those with less functionality than smartphones and for which Nokia has been more recently known, are declining more slowly than expected. This gap remained available to Nokia to exploit with its older phone technology until its Microsoft smartphones could gain momentum.

Nokia firmly believes that it can build an effective "ecosystem" around its Windows smartphones, and it is actively working toward that. The company has stated that this will be a third ecosystem, along with the ones that have developed around the Android operating system and around the products coming out of Apple. The company sees this as a key area of differentiation that will drive value, prices, and margins in the marketplace. Nokia's Chief Executive Officer has expressed the belief that, if Nokia had adopted the Android operating system, they would not have been able to differentiate on anything other than price. That would have resulted in lower margins for Nokia.

FURTHER READING

"Company Vitae: Nokia." *Management Today*, June 1, 2012.

Florin. "Luxurious Vertu Ti RM-282V with Android Shows up, It's a Nokia-Made Device." Unwiredview.com. Accessed January 31, 2013. http://www.unwiredview.com/2013/01/30/luxurious-vertu-ti-rm-828v-with-android-shows-up-its-a-nokia-made-device/?utm_source=feedburner&utm_medium=feed&utm_campaign=Feed%3A+UnwiredView+%28Unwired+View%29"

"Friday Review: Drowning in Espoo." *Total Telecom Online*, April 20, 2012.

Kuittinen, Tero. "Smartphone Growth Is Slowing Rapidly, but Feature Phone Surprise Aids Nokia." BGR. Accessed January 30, 2013. http://bgr.com/2013/01/28/smartphone-market-growth-analysis-q4-2012-309650/?utm_source=feedburner&utm_medium=feed&utm_campaign=Feed%3A+TheBoyGeniusReport+%28BGR+|+Boy+Genius+Report%29

"Nokia Completes Divestment of Vertu to EQT VI." *Telecom Tiger*, October 15, 2012.

"Opinion." *Marketing*, May 9, 2012.

"Q1 2011 Nokia Oyj Earnings Conference Call—Final." *Fair Disclosure Wire*. Accessed January 30, 2013. http://seeking alpha.com/article/510541-nokia-s-ceo-discusses-q1-2012-results-earnings-call-transcript

NORDSTROM

—◆—

AT A GLANCE

Brand Synopsis: Nordstrom is known for its superior customer service, upscale merchandise, and elegant settings.

Parent Company: Nordstrom, Inc.
1617 6th Avenue
Seattle, Washington 98101
United States
http://www.nordstrom

Sector: Consumer Discretionary

Industry Group: Consumer Durables and Apparel

Performance: Nordstrom operates more than 100 full-line Nordstrom department stores and about the same number of Nordstrom Racks discount stores in 31 states. With sales of $10.9 billion in 2011, Nordstrom, Inc., ranked 242 on the 2012 Fortune 500.

Principal Competitors: Bloomingdale's, Inc.; Neiman Marcus, Inc.; Saks Fifth Avenue, Inc.

BRAND ORIGINS

- Business established in Seattle in 1901 as a shoe store, Wallin & Nordstrom.
- By 1960, Nordstrom became the largest independent shoe store chain in the United States.
- Nordstrom entered the department store sector in the 1960s as Nordstrom Best.
- Nordstrom, Inc., name was adopted in 1973.

- Brand identity centering on customer service took shape in the 1980s.

The heart of the Nordstrom brand was established by the founder of the Nordstrom, Inc. retail empire: John W. Nordstrom. Born in Sweden, he immigrated to the United States in 1887 as a 16-year-old boy. He made his way to Seattle, where in 1897 he learned that gold had been discovered in the Klondike of Alaska. Like many young men, he rushed to the new gold fields, but unlike most, he left with $13,000 he earned from a gold mine stake. With those funds, he and a shoemaker he met in the Klondike, Carl Wallin, opened a shoe store in downtown Seattle in 1901 called Wallin & Nordstrom. Nordstrom's focus on quality merchandise, value, and attentive service not only proved a winning combination at the time, allowing the shop to build a loyal cadre of customers, it helped to create the character of what would become the Nordstrom brand.

Nordstrom and Wallin opened a second shoe store in 1923. Five years later, John Nordstrom retired, selling his share of the business to two sons. In 1929, Wallin retired as well and sold his interest to the Nordstrom brothers, who were soon joined by a third brother. Shoes remained the focus of the store, which took the Nordstrom's name in 1930. By 1960, there were eight Nordstrom's stores in Washington and Oregon, creating the largest independent shoe store chain in the United States. Nordstrom's flagship store in downtown Seattle was the nation's largest shoe store. In addition, Nordstrom leased 13 shoe departments in Washington, Oregon, and California.

At a crossroads, the Nordstrom brothers decided to extended its brand to apparel rather than expand its shoe business to other parts of the country. In 1963, they acquired Seattle-based Best Apparel, a women's clothing store. Three years later, a Portland, Oregon, retail outlet was combined with a Nordstrom shoe store to create a hybrid that assumed the Nordstrom Best name, setting the stage for the Nordstrom family to enter the department store business. Other Nordstrom Best stores selling shoes and women's apparel were opened, and by the end of the decade, men's and children's clothing were added to the product mix.

It was also in the late 1960s that the next generation of the Nordstrom family took the helm. The company was taken public in 1971 as Nordstrom Best, and two years later, when annuals sales cracked the $100 million mark for the first time, the company changed its name to Nordstrom, Inc., an important step in solidifying the Nordstrom brand. During this period, the company expanded into Alaska. In 1978, Nordstrom opened a store in southern California, the success of which set the stage for the opening of larger stores in the state.

By 1980 Nordstrom operated 31 stores, making it the third largest specialty retailer in the United States, trailing only Saks Fifth Avenue and Lord & Taylor. Over the course of the next decade, Nordstrom expanded aggressively, while at the same time building a reputation for operating upscale full-service department stores. More importantly, it established strong customer service as the essence of the Nordstrom brand, in keeping with the character of Swedish immigrant who co-founded the business decades earlier.

BRAND ELEMENTS
- Customer service is a key element of the Nordstrom brand.
- Luxurious atmosphere plays an important role.
- Graphic elements include a wordmark logo and the Nordstrom crest.
- Nordstrom seldom uses taglines or slogans.

The Nordstrom brand is most closely associated with its legendary approach to customer service, and a customer-friendly atmosphere in general is a key element. Pampering customers is another, and many Nordstrom stores offer free coat checks and live piano music. Luxury is another important aspect of the Nordstrom brand. In addition to the elegant décor of its stores, the chain allies itself with top designer names.

Visually, the Nordstrom brand is supported by two elements. Like competitors Saks Fifth Avenue, Macy's, Bloomingdale's Neiman Marcus, and Lord & Taylor, Nordstrom makes use of a wordmark for its corporate logo. The simple block letters of the Nordstrom name are used on signage, products, advertising, shopping bags, and promotional materials. In addition, the company employs

the Nordstrom Crest, a white "N" set against a black background surrounded by a white border. Although the crest is sometimes used as a corporate symbol, it is generally combined with the Nordstrom logo. In such cases, the crest is always positioned above the wordmark. Store names and departments are located below the wordmark when the logo is used in signage. For vendor-procured merchandise, the phrases "Exclusively at" and "Available at" are italicized and placed above the wordmark.

The Nordstrom wordmark is primarily reproduced in metallic bronze on a white background. Other corporate colors include metallic dark bronze, metallic silver, and black. Corporate foils are used sparingly. Acceptable colors include bright silver, matte silver, and matte gold.

Taglines and slogans are rarely used in Nordstrom advertising. In 2000 the retailer launched its first national branding campaign, one intended to attract younger shoppers. It was centered on the "Reinvent Yourself" tagline. The campaign was terminated less than a year later. Another tagline, "Customers are the only one," is rarely used but embodies the most important element of the Nordstrom brand.

BRAND IDENTITY
- Customer care is the heart of Nordstrom's brand identity.
- Customers are pampered like royalty.
- Suburban career women are key target customers.
- Nordstrom is still known for its shoes.

Nordstrom's brand identity is well established in the marketplace: customer care is the most important goal of the store and its employees. Nordstrom personnel are given wide latitude in servicing customers, epitomized by an extremely liberal returns policy. For many years, new employees were given a 75-word employee handbook, the heart of which was a simple direction: "Use best judgment in all situations. There will be no additional rules." In a famous and most likely apocryphal story, related by Douglas Albertson on Brandchannel.com, a Nordstrom employee in the Alaska store once provided a refund on a tire despite the chain not offering tires in any of its stores. The message of the tale, and the heart of the Nordstrom brand, is that customers are always right, even when they're wrong. Nordstrom's has not commented on the story, and Albertson suggests that "they figure if the stories are good enough, word-of-mouth will take them to the marketplace and the stories will carry even more credibility than if Nordstrom is caught tooting their own horn."

Part of Nordstrom's identity is the retailer's commitment to treating its customers like royalty. Nordstrom salespeople have been known to pay customers' parking tickets, carry packages to cars, and liberally hand out business cards, urging customers to contact them directly if needed. The royal treatment also extends to the upscale décor and atmosphere, accentuated in many cases by live piano playing. In keeping with this approach is the merchandise itself. As a retailer catering to upper-income customers, Nordstrom offers high quality merchandise and associates itself with leading designer names.

Additionally, Nordstrom is identified with friendliness. The target customers are suburban career women, who not only respond well to being pampered, but also appreciate the social atmosphere Nordstrom creates. In essence, Nordstrom's approach was well received by customers, creating an ideal mood for the merchandising of upscale fashion lines, including shoes. Nordstrom was founded as a shoe store and more than a century later, the quality shoes the department store chain offers remain an enduring part of Nordstrom's identity.

BRAND STRATEGY

- Nordstrom Best brand was shortened to Nordstrom in the 1970s.
- Nordstrom Rack brand introduced in 1970s.
- Effort to enter Eastern markets was launched in 1986.
- "Reinvent Yourself" branding campaign fell short.
- Nordstrom and Nordstrom Rack brands effectively coexist.

It wasn't until the 1960s that the Nordstrom family expanded beyond shoes to become involved in the department store sector. Gradually, the Nordstrom brand evolved to include upscale merchandise and superior costumer service. Through the merger with Seattle women's clothing store Best Apparel in 1963, the nascent department store chain operated under the Nordstrom Best brand for several years. It wasn't until the 1970s that the brand name was shortened to Nordstrom. At the same time, however, the company applied the Nordstrom name to an outlet store: Nordstrom Rack. This operated out of the basement of the downtown Seattle flagship store, and as a result did not diminish the value of the growing Nordstrom brand. The Nordstrom family also launched another division in 1976. Known as Place Two, it was a brand assigned to smaller department stores, offering select women's and men's apparel and shoes.

The Nordstrom brand came to full bloom in the 1980s. The chain's focus on custom service was joined with a growing image of Nordstrom as a well-run, upscale, full-service department store. With 53 stores in six western states in 1986, Nordstrom began an effort to expand its brand to the Eastern United States. By the end of the decade, there were two Nordstrom stores in the Washington, D.C., area. In addition, the chain

opened it largest store, 350,000 square feet in size, in downtown San Francisco. Offering a host of luxurious amenities, this new store enhanced the upscale nature of the Nordstrom brand.

Nordstrom's dedication to unmatched customer care, however, created a problem for the brand. Some union employees complained about not being paid for providing the kind of extra services to customers on which Nordstrom prided itself. Following an investigation, the Washington State Department of Labor & Industries ordered Nordstrom to pay back wages to many employees because the chain's practice of having employees perform such duties as delivering merchandise violated state laws. Nordstrom also had to contend with civil suits, which were finally settled out of court in 1993. Between the state charges and the civil settlement, Nordstrom paid between $35 million and $45 million. The bad publicity did little to diminish the growth of the department store chain.

Nordstrom opened its first Midwest store, located in a Chicago suburb, in 1991. In that same year, Nordstrom opened new stores in Riverside, California; Edison, New Jersey; and Bethesda, Maryland. As the decade progressed, the Nordstrom brand was taken to such major markets as Dallas, Denver, Detroit, and Philadelphia. Additionally, a new brand, Façonnable, a men's boutique, opened in New York. In the final years of the 1990s Nordstrom opened stores in Arizona, Connecticut, Georgia, Kansas, Ohio, and Rhode Island. By the turn of the century, the Nordstrom group numbered 77 full-line department stores, 38 Nordstrom Racks, and 23 Façonnable boutiques. The Nordstrom brand also received greater prominence when the stock of Nordstrom, Inc. began trading on the New York Stock Exchange in 1999.

Although Nordstrom grew in size, it did not effectively keep pace with the changing tastes of its customers, many of whom began to consider Nordstrom merchandise too formal. It was against this backdrop that Nordstrom launched its first national branding campaign in 2000, employing the "Reinvent Yourself" tagline. In order to appeal to a younger market, the chain emphasized more youthful fashions. For Nordstrom's core customers, members of the baby-boom generation, it was a betrayal of the brand, and sales suffered as a result. The campaign was scrapped and Nordstrom's management ranks were shaken.

Nordstrom continued to open new stores in Sunbelt states such as Texas and Florida, despite a downturn in the economy, and found a way to attract younger shoppers without alienating core customer by creating a department called "via C" that offered edgier fashion apparel. More new Nordstrom stores were added in the early 2000s, though like other luxury retailers, Nordstrom was adversely impacted by the recession at the end of the decade. After navigating the worst of the economic downturn, Nordstrom shifted its strategy on the use of the Nordstrom Rack brand. New Rack stores opened near full-line Nordstrom department stores, leading some in the retail industry to question whether the Nordstrom brand might be diluted. In fact, the two brands complemented one another, especially when located close by. Shoppers at the Rack could purchase merchandise at a steep discount, and in many cases they developed an affinity for the brand and would shop at the full-line store for the latest styles.

BRAND EQUITY

- Nordstrom's high markups depend on its brand equity.
- Brand Finance plc assigned a 2012 brand value of $4.45 billion to Nordstrom.
- Nordstrom ranks 231st on Brand Finance's list of the world's 500 most valuable brands.
- Interbrand ranked Nordstrom as the 11th most valuable retail brand in the United States in 2012.

For a luxury retailer like Nordstrom, the importance of brand equity is apparent. Some of the same merchandise can be found elsewhere at a lower price, yet Nordstrom's core customers are willing to pay a higher price for the Nordstrom shopping experience. The customer care they receive and easy product return, if necessary, help offset the price differential, as do the selection of finer merchandise and store atmosphere.

According to the methodology employed by Brand Finance plc, a brand evaluation consultancy, Nordstrom's brand value in 2012 was $4.45 billion. It was a performance that provided Nordstrom with the 231st position on *Brand Finance*'s list of the world's 500 most valuable brands. Interbrand, one of the world's leading brand consultancies, lists Nordstrom as the 11th most valuable retail brand in the United States, assigning a brand value of nearly $9.5 billion in 2012.

Another measure of Nordstrom's brand equity is the performance of Nordstrom, Inc. The growth of net sales has risen steadily over the years, increasing from $2.9 billion in 1990, to $5.53 billion in 2000, and nearly $10.9 billion in 2011. According to the FrogDog business strategy firm: "In shareholder-value terms, Nordstrom's historical adherence to its brand promise helped invested funds grow six times their original amount, while comparison companies that did not hold true to their brand promises and core ideologies yielded only two times the amount invested."

BRAND AWARENESS

- Nordstrom's brand awareness is mostly confined to the United States.
- Nordstrom brand is well known to ultra-affluent consumers.
- Nordstrom brand also resonates with more moderate income consumers.

Nordstrom's brand awareness is primarily limited to the United States. Within that market, Nordstrom's name recognition is mostly confined to large urban markets. Nevertheless, the department store chain's reach extends evenly across the country. There are 27 full-line Nordstrom department stores located on the East Coast, 35 stores in the Central States/South division, and another 35 stores in the Southwest. While there are only 20 stores in the Northwest, the Nordstrom brand has historical ties to this area and enjoys even strong brand recognition.

More important to general awareness of Nordstrom's brand is its recognition among targeted customers. According to a survey conducted by Unity Marketing in 2011, Nordstrom was the second most popular luxury department store, trailing only Barney's, New York, with ultra-affluent consumers (those with annual incomes of $250,000 and above, representing about the two 2 percent of American households). A study conducted by Unity Marketing earlier in the decade also revealed that Nordstrom enjoyed the same level of brand awareness as Neiman Marcus in the luxury consumer market, the top 5 percent of American households. Unlike Neiman Marcus, however, Nordstrom was able to attract shoppers at more moderate income levels, between $75,000 and $150,000, comprised of about 22.4 million households. As a result, Nordstrom enjoyed greater brand recognition among a wider section of the U.S. population than many other luxury retailers. The brand topped the Harris Poll EquiTrend rankings for Luxury Department Store Brand in 2012.

BRAND OUTLOOK

- Nordstrom ranked fifth in market share among the top department store chains in the North America in 2010.
- Consolidation among retailers poses greater competition for Nordstrom.
- HauteLook.com acquisition added to Nordstrom's online shopping strategy.
- Nordstrom began testing the New York City market with the 2011 opening of Treasure & Bond.

The Nordstrom brand is well positioned in the luxury retailing market, as well as the wider retail sector. According to *Market Share Reporter*, Nordstrom ranked fifth in market share among the top department store chains in the North America in 2010, trailing only Sears, Macy's, J.C. Penney, and Kohl's. Among apparel makers in 2010, Nordstrom was only surpassed by Nike, The Gap, and Limited Brands.

While the strategy of operating lower-price point Rack stores in close proximity to full-line Nordstrom department stores has proven effective, there is no guarantee that the Nordstrom brand might not be diluted over time. Moreover, the chain faces growing competition in a retailing industry that continues to see smaller players acquired by major operations. To help maintain its brand equity, Nordstrom has added in-store wedding boutiques, expanded its complimentary personal stylist program, and incorporated digital technology to its sales floor. In 2011 Nordstrom completed an acquisition to bolster its position: HauteLook.com, a members-only site with limited-time sales events, helped to improve Nordstrom's online shopping business.

In 2011 Nordstrom also opened Treasure & Bond in the trendy SoHo district of New York City. The profits of the small boutique were earmarked for charity, but more importantly it allowed Nordstrom to learn more about the New York market. To date, Nordstrom was only represented with a Rack store in this key retailing market. Perhaps in the years to come, a full-line Nordstrom store would finally come to New York City. There was also a possibility that the Nordstrom brand might one day take root in foreign soil. The most likely starting point would be Canada.

FURTHER READING

"Aiming Low at the High End." *Floor Covering Weekly,* June 2, 2005.

Albertson, Douglas E. "The Importance of Storytelling in Branding." *Brandchannel.com.*

Andruss, Paula. "Secrets of the 10 Most-Trusted Brands." *Entrepreneur,* March 20, 2012.

Brand Finance. "Global 500 2012." *Brandirectory.com.*

Clifford, Stephanie. "Nordstrom in New York to Use an Alias." *New York Times,* August 15, 2011.

Cuneo, Alice Z. "Fallon's Strategic Thinking was Behind Nordstrom Win." *Advertising Age,* April 6, 1998.

———. "Nordstrom Breaks With Traditional Media Plan." *Advertising Age,* February 14, 2000.

Gustafson, Krystina. "Will Nordstrom's Discount Stores Hurt the Brand?" *CNBC,* April 14, 2010.

Interbrand. "Best Retail Brands 2012." New York: Interbrand, 2012.

"Nordstrom, Inc." *International Directory of Company Histories.* Ed. Jay P. Pederson and Miranda H. Ferrara. Vol. 67. Detroit: St. James Press, 2005.

"Using Brands to Make Business Decisions." *FrogDog.com.*

NOVARTIS

BRAND ORIGINS

- The roots of J.R. Geigy S.A. date to the mid-1700s.
- Ciba Ltd. was established in the mid-1800s.
- Sandoz Ltd. was founded in 1886.
- Geigy and Ciba merged in 1970.
- Ciga-Geigy and Sandoz merged to create Novartis AG in 1996.

Novartis is a brand created out of the 1996 merger of Ciba-Geigy Ltd. and Sandoz Ltd. that resulted in the creation of Switzerland-based Novartis AG. The oldest of these corporate entities is J.R. Geigy S.A., the roots of which date back to the mid-1700s when Johan Rudolf Geigy began making drugs, as well as dyes and spices. Ciba Ltd. was established 100 years later by a French silk maker and dyer, Alexander Clavel, who moved to Switzerland to establish a dyeworks. It was called Gesellschaft fur Chemische Industrie im Basel, known by the abbreviation of Ciba. Sandoz Ltd. was also originally involved in the manufacture of dyes. It was established in Switzerland in 1886 as Kern & Sandoz by businessman Edouard Sandoz and Dr. Alfred Kern.

The Swiss chemical companies were able to survive at the turn of the 20th century, despite the power of IG Farben, a German cartel that for many years stifled the American chemical industry but tolerated the Swiss companies because they provided an outlet for excess raw materials. Following World War I, Ciba, Geigy, and Sandoz formed their own cartel, Basler IG. The Swiss chemical companies no longer competed against one another, agreeing to share knowledge as well as profits. Basler soon diversified into drug manufacturing. It also created the Dual Cartel by joining forces with Farben in 1929. The French cartel was soon added to create the Tripartite Cartel, and in 1932 the British chemical cartel was admitted into a pan-European enterprise known as the Quadrapartite Cartel. War was brewing in Europe, however, and such an alliance would be impossible to maintain for very long.

After World War II, the Swiss cartel was pried apart as well, due to antitrust laws in the United States that affected Ciga, Geigy, and Sandoz subsidiaries in that country. The United States market was too important to abandon, and in 1951 Basler IG was dissolved. The three Swiss chemical companies went their own ways, competing against one another as diversified manufacturers of pharmaceuticals, dyes, plastics, specialty chemicals, and other products. In 1970 Ciba and Geigy decided to merge, but in order to pass regulatory muster in the United States, Ciga sold its American dyeworks and Geigy sold its American pharmaceutical assets. Ciba-Geigy Ltd. prospered as a combined company, becoming one of the world's five largest chemical companies by the early 1990s.

As an independent company, Sandoz Ltd. enjoyed success with its pharmaceutical division, primarily in the development of synthetic compounds used in the treatment of mental illness and migraine. One of these compounds was Delysid, which would later be known popularly as LSD. Sandoz was not limited to this category of drugs or pharmaceuticals in general. The company diversified through a series of acquisitions, including U.S. companies that took Sandoz into the business of providing chemicals for the construction industry. In 1994 Sandoz acquired Gerber baby food in an attempt to create a nutrition business.

The 1990s brought significant change to the international drug market. Heightened competition and managed healthcare that squeezed margins led to the formation of large multinational conglomerates that possessed both the finances and technical resources necessary to operate on the global stage. The Swiss companies took note, and in a surprise move, Ciga-Geigy and Sandoz announced in March 1996 that they intended to merge, creating the world's second-largest pharmaceutical company with a global market share of 4.4 percent. They also planned within a year to sell off Ciba's specialty-chemicals division and Sandoz's chemical and building technology divisions. Because it was a merger of equals, the combined, pure-play pharmaceutical company would also adopt a new name and brand: Novartis.

BRAND ELEMENTS

- The Novartis name is derived from the Latin words *novae* and *artes*, or "new skills."
- The logo image depicts the flower of life or a mortar and pestle.
- The "caring and curing" tagline is only used in corporate logo applications.
- Novartis Blue is used exclusively with the logo signature.
- Novartis makes use of five warm colors in its advertisements.

Several elements are key to the Novartis brand. The name itself is the first to consider. It was derived by joining the Latin words *novae* and *artes*, or "new skills." As such, it was a name well suited for a brand that placed innovation at the core of its identity. Novartis was just one of

18 names provided to the company by the Siegel & Gale brand consultancy, which also created the Novartis logo, another important brand element.

There are three parts to the logo: the Novartis signature, a graphic image, and a tagline. The image is divided into three parts. Two inward-facing curved lines, one red and one yellow, create a bulb shape. A turquoise arrowhead intersects the bulb, which Siegel & Gale's managing director Malcolm Parkinson told the *Wall Street Journal* was meant to suggest "the flower of life, or a mortar and pestle." The red and yellow colors symbolized the warmth from the sun or the flame of a Bunsen burner used in research laboratories. Parkinson added, "The arrow is to indicate precision." The tagline that is placed below and to the right of the corporate signature is "caring and curing." It is not included in business unit logos, such as Novartis Vaccines or Novartis Oncology. In those uses, the name of the business unit replaces the tagline.

Certain colors are also associated with the Novartis brand. Red and gold are used to create the bulb in the logo, and so-called Novartis Blue is used exclusively in the arrow and the name. Novartis also makes use of five warm colors in orange, brown, and yellow shades. They are prominent in Novartis advertisements, as are close-up photographs.

BRAND IDENTITY

- Novartis portrays itself as a caring and innovative company.
- The "caring and curing" tagline is at the heart of Novartis' brand identity.
- Imagery and copy in print media are crafted to reinforce Novartis' brand identity.
- Demonstrable research and development results are perhaps the greatest proof that Novartis is true to its brand identity.

The brand identity of Novartis, the way the company wishes to be perceived, is of a caring and innovative company, dedicated to the needs of individual patients. This vision is supported in a variety of ways. The "caring and curing" slogan represents the heart of the brand in a literal yet alliterative manner. In internal and external print media created by Novartis, warm colors are used to elicit a sense of warmth and proximity for the audience, implying a close connection between medication and the patient. Novartis is also artful in its use of imagery. Photographs tend to be tighter shots, emphasizing intimacy, as does the soft lighting and focus. The content of the images is important as well. They show people in situations or engaged in actions that reinforce intimacy and caring. Moreover, Novartis takes care with its imagery to include people of differing ethnic backgrounds and all ages. Copy is also written with the brand's identity in mind.

Language is intended to be fact-based, avoiding puffery and unrealistic promises. By being straightforward and honest, Novartis will, therefore, display transparency with patients and customers, and lay a foundation of credibility and trust.

Aside from artful appeals to emotion, Novartis attempts to lend credence to its brand identity through its actions. Corporate social responsibility initiatives help to portray Novartis as a responsible global citizen—that is, a caring brand. The company works with the World Health Organization to make many of its medicines available in poor countries. It also seeks to lower its impact on the environment by pursuing energy efficiency and reduced carbon dioxide emissions. Novartis was one of the first companies to sign the UN Global Compact, which promoted responsible corporate citizenship.

Novartis also made a financial commitment to research and development to support its claim to innovation and dedication to finding cures for patients. The ultimate proof is the success of Novartis in developing new products. In the new century, the company boasted a strong record of receiving drug approvals in both Europe and the United States.

BRAND STRATEGY

- As a former practicing physician, Novartis' Chairman and Chief Executive Officer Daniel Vasella embodied the brand's identity.
- Novartis Institutes for Biomedical Research was created as an independent unit to help fulfill the brand promise.
- Some group companies maintain their own identities apart from the Novartis corporate brand.
- The Sandoz brand was brought out of retirement for use with Novartis' generic drug business.
- Individual Novartis products and services employ unique brand names.

After the merger of Ciba-Geigy Ltd. and Sandoz Ltd., the combined company made the conscious decision to adopt a new brand as a way to avoid infighting between employees of the two merger partners. There was no old way of doing things, there was the Novartis way. What precisely was the Novartis way, and the company's branding strategy, was a bit vague at first. A commitment to innovation, as reflected by the Latinized brand name, was a given, but it was hardly surprising for a drug development company. It was the caring component that put flesh on the bones, and it was that attribute that emanated from the top ranks of management. Novartis' Chairman and Chief Executive Officer Daniel Vasella was uniquely suited to promote the "curing and caring" identity. As a child growing up in Switzerland, he survived both tuberculosis and meningitis, while losing a sister to cancer. His tribulations led

him to become a medical doctor, and before becoming an executive, he practiced medicine. Caring for patients and fighting to cure them was not a marketing abstraction for Vasella. Thus, the promise made by the Novartis brand to listen to the concerns of patients and to do what was necessary to bring effective medications to market was a personal commitment that trickled down from the top of the organization.

Novartis' corporate brand strategy evolved further in 2002 when Vasella hired a new head of the company's global research effort, Mark Fishman, a cardiologist at Boston's General Hospital. Vasella and Fishman established the Novartis Institutes for Biomedical Research (NIBR), and rather than tuck it inside the pharmaceutical division, they had it report directly to Vasella. As a result, the influence of the commercial side of the business was greatly reduced. A new corporate culture, more in line with the brand, began to evolve. The focus shifted from the development of blockbuster drugs to meeting unmet medical needs, as researchers were given more latitude, and scientific achievements were rewarded, not just commercial success.

Novartis primarily pursued a corporate branding strategy, applying its name to most of the group companies, such as Novartis Pharmaceutical Company, Novartis Oncology, Novartis Vaccines, Novartis Diagnostics, and Novartis Animal Health. A provider of diagnostic testing and services, Genoptix, Inc., maintained its own identity within Novartis Pharmaceuticals. The eye care sector was served by two subsidiaries that enjoyed strong brand equity in their own right, Alcon and Ciba Vision. At the time of the Novartis merger, the Sandoz brand had been retired, but it was brought back in 2002 as the brand for Novartis' generic drug business. Because generics competed against the primary business of Novartis, the development of proprietary treatments, it made sense to create some distance by making use of a different name. With Sandoz a well-known pharmaceutical brand on the shelf, Novartis elected to revive it. Within its different business units, a host of product brands were crafted and promoted, filling out Novartis' overall brand strategy.

BRAND EQUITY

- Estimates of Novartis' brand value fluctuate greatly between methodologies.
- Brand Finance assigned a US$3.07 billion brand value at the end of 2011.
- Brand Finance listed Novartis number 369 on its 2012 Global 500 list of the world's most valuable brands.
- According to European Brand Institute, Novartis was the world's 39th most valuable brand in 2012.
- Interbrand ranked Novartis the third most valuable brand in Switzerland in 2012.

Because at the heart of the Novartis business are proprietary drugs, many of which are chosen on the basis of efficacy alone, it is difficult to claim that the equity of the Novartis brand can be measured by the higher price the company can charge in relation to the competition. In the case of generics, of course, there is always a significant difference in price between a branded product and one that only touts the active ingredient. There is no clear difference, however, between the equity of Novartis and other major pharmaceutical brands compared to generic equivalents.

According to brand consulting firm Brand Finance, Novartis had a brand value of US$3.07 billion at the end of 2011. It was a performance that placed Novartis number 369 in Brand Finance's Global 500 list of the world's most valuable brands in 2012. That ranking was somewhat misleading. In 2009 Novartis was awarded a brand value of US$7.707 billion and was listed as the world's 74th most valuable brand. Between 2007 and 2011 the company's annual revenues increased from US$43.7 billion to US$58.6 billion. The ranking of a brand might fluctuate a great deal because of the methodology rather than the underlying strength of the brand. According to the European Brand Institute, Novartis was the world's 39th most valuable brand in 2012, an improvement on the prior year when Novartis was listed at number 54.

Novartis' standing in its home country also displayed a wide divergence. According to branding firm Interbrand, Novartis was the third most valuable brand in Switzerland in 2012. MPP Consulting, on the other hand, listed Novartis at number 45 on its SwissBrand Top 50 in 2012.

BRAND AWARENESS

- Because Novartis is a relatively young brand, it is not as widely known by general consumers as other pharmaceutical brands.
- The Alcon, Ciba Vision, and Sandoz brands enjoy their own strong level of awareness.
- Novartis is well known and respected within the healthcare industry.
- According to a 2012 *Fortune* survey, Novartis was considered the world's most admired pharmaceutical company.

As a relatively young brand, Novartis does not enjoy the level of awareness with general consumers that comes with older established brands. Moreover, many pharmaceutical manufacturers do not enjoy the same level of awareness as the products they sell. According to a 2002 study conducted by the Monitor Group, Novartis was listed 12th in aided awareness of pharmaceutical manufacturers among American consumers with 29 percent. The leader was Johnson & Johnson with 96 percent.

The scope of Novartis' operations helps to improve brand awareness around the world. Novartis maintains a presence in about 140 countries and operates five divisions, offering a wide range of products. Some of those units—Alcon, Ciba Vision, and Sandoz—are well established brands in their own right. They also enjoy improved brand awareness that comes with longevity.

Within the pharmaceutical and healthcare industries, where recognition is more important to the fortunes of the company, Novartis is both well known and respected. According to a survey conducted in 2012 by *Fortune*, Novartis was ranked number 1 on the list of the World's Most Admired Pharmaceuticals Companies. Companies were judged on the basis of innovation, financial soundness, employee talent, use of corporate assets, long-term investment value, social responsibility, quality of management, and quality of products and services. Respondents included industry executives, directors, and securities analysts who covered the pharmaceutical industry. Thus, where it counted the most, the Novartis brand was both familiar and highly regarded.

BRAND OUTLOOK

- Novartis is a brand that is likely to increase in recognition and value in the years ahead.
- Because delivery of product is key to its identity, Novartis needs to produce innovative new drugs to maintain its brand promise.
- Consolidation and increased competition in the pharmaceutical industry could impact Novartis, but the needs of an aging population, the brand's global reach, and the breadth of its product offerings bode well for the future.

With a strong reputation in the healthcare field and a limited history, Novartis is a brand that is likely to increase in recognition and value in the years ahead. The company's research unit is still relatively new and only beginning to turn out treatments that fulfill the brand's mandate of filling unmet medical needs. The development of new patented drugs is key to the future health of the company and the brand. Like other global pharmaceutical companies, Novartis depends on proprietary drugs and has to contend with the challenge of patent expirations in the years ahead. Regardless of its brand identity, Novartis must produce innovative new drugs to maintain its brand promise. Delivery, not imagery, has always been the key to the future of Novartis.

There is no shortage of competition. Aside from other global pharmaceutical firms, Novartis has to contend with smaller drug discovery and development companies and biotechnology companies. There are also changing industry standards and evolving business models. A fresh wave of consolidation in the pharmaceutical industry could escalate competitive pressures and might well have a dramatic impact on the future of the Novartis business and brand.

On the other hand, there are ample opportunities to take advantage of the positive image of the Novartis brand. An aging population that requires an increasing level of medical solutions plays to the company's strength. The global reach of Novartis and breadth of its product offerings also bode well for the future. Ultimately, the key to the success of Novartis is its ability to fulfill the promises of its brand, to be a champion of innovation and a company that both cares and cures.

FURTHER READING

Brand Finance. "Global 500 2012." *Brandirectory*. Accessed February 12, 2013. http://brandirectory.com/league_tables/table/global-500-2012.

Collins, Glenn. "2 Swiss Drug Giants in a Surprise Merger to Be 2d in World." *New York Times*, March 7, 1996.

Gwynne, Peter. "A Different Approach to Drug Discovery." *Research-Technology Management*, July–August 2011.

"Naming of New Company No Novice Task." *Chicago Tribune*, March 24, 1996.

"Novartis AG." *International Directory of Company Histories*. Ed. Jay P. Pederson. Vol. 105. Detroit, MI: St. James Press, 2010.

Quain, John R. "From Pipeline to Lifeline." *NYSE Magazine*, May–June 2004.

Singer, Natasha. "Drug Firms Apply Brand to Generics." *New York Times*, February 16, 2010.

O_2

AT A GLANCE

Brand Synopsis: O_2 is a bold and innovative yet trust-worthy brand that strives to be as essential in people's lives as the air they breathe.

Parent Company: Telefónica O_2 UK Limited
260 Bath Road
Slough
United Kingdom
http://www.o2.co.uk

Sector: Telecommunication Services

Industry Group: Telecommunication Services

Performance: *Revenues*—US$84 billion (parent company Telefónica S.A.) (2011).

Principal Competitors: Orange S.A.; T-Mobile (UK) Limited; Vodafone Limited

BRAND ORIGINS

- O_2's roots date to the launch of the Cellnet service in 1985.
- The O_2 brand was introduced in 2002.
- O_2 was acquired in 2005 by Telefónica S.A.
- O_2 grew to become the United Kingdom's largest mobile communications provider.

O_2 is a brand used by Spain's Telefónica S.A., a major global telecommunications company, in its operations in the United Kingdom, Ireland, Germany, the Czech Republic, and Slovakia. The brand originated in the United Kingdom, its lineage dating to January 1984, when British Telecommunications (BT) and Securicor Group created a 60-40 joint venture, Telecom Securicor Cellular Radio Limited. At the start of 1985, this subsidiary launched the United Kingdom's first cellular telephone service, Cellnet, which replaced BT's radiophone service. That same year rival Vodaphone was launched and quickly became the more innovative of the two services. Despite an earlier start in the market, Cellnet was also upstaged by the later arrivals One2One and Orange.

BT acquired 100 percent of Cellnet in 1999 and rebranded the service BT Cellnet. Because BT was a landline brand and *cell* was an out-of-date term, BT Cellnet was a brand that presented a dowdy image and as a result was not embraced by the British public. The name changed again in 2000, becoming Genie, as part of an effort to emphasize mobile Internet services. The brand promised that users could easily "surf the net," but the promise failed to come to fruition, and Genie was retired the following year.

In September 2001 BT's wireless service was spun off as a new public company, mmO_2 plc, which included operations in Ireland, Germany, and the Netherlands. It would operate in all four countries under the O_2 brand, which was launched in May 2002. The corporate parent would also align itself with the brand, becoming O_2 plc. (The company is referred to as O_2 and the brand as O_2, but other than the logo, O_2 is not used consistently in corporate communications or the media.) At the heart of the rebranding strategy was the preparation for the third generation in wireless network technologies, which would allow for the introduction of new services and content. In keeping with this goal, O_2 adopted the tagline "See what you can do."

The new brand was now better able to compete, but was still at a disadvantage because it lacked the deep pockets of its rivals. This shortcoming was rectified in 2005, when O_2 plc was acquired by Telefónica S.A. Hence, O_2 plc became Telefónica UK Limited, but continued to maintain its London headquarters and British management team and do business as O_2. Telefónica's non-Spanish European telecommunications properties were folded into the O_2 brand, adding operations in Germany and the Czech Republic. The remainder of Telefónica's mobile telecommunications properties operated under the Movistar banner. With the backing of Telefónica, O_2 grew to become the largest mobile telephone services provider in the United Kingdom. The brand also expanded into other areas and began the process of transcending the mobile communications sector.

BRAND ELEMENTS

- The O_2 brand name refers to the chemical symbol for oxygen.
- Water is an important part of the O_2 brand's symbology.
- The O_2 brand's first tagline was "It's your O_2. See what you can do."
- The O_2 entertainment complex is an important brand element, especially in the United Kingdom but also in other markets that are served by the brand.

The O_2 brand is defined and supported by several means. At the heart of the brand is the name O_2, the chemical symbol for oxygen. For a pan-European brand, it is a recognizable name regardless of the language. More important, oxygen is essential to life, implying that O_2 and mobile communications are essential to modern life. The brand also closely associates itself with water. The O_2 logo is either presented in blue or in white against a blue background. Oxygen bubbles suspended in water are sometimes used in the logo.

Taglines are another important support for O_2. For the first several years the brand relied on "It's your O_2. See what you can do." As a promise of what mobile communications could provide in the new third-generation world, the slogan served a narrow purpose. By 2008, however, the market had changed, and O_2 sought to create more of an emotional bond with consumers, who were living in an increasingly fragmented society. The new tagline was "We're better, connected." It was supported by advertising that showed more warmth and humanity than had been seen in previous campaigns. Another new

tagline was unveiled in 2012: "Fresh thinking, new possibilities." The theme was used to move the brand beyond mobile communications into other product and service categories. The resulting marketing campaign was supported by the 1960s anti-establishment song *Little Boxes*, which questioned the conformity of modern life.

In 2007 O_2 secured the naming rights to The O_2, the southeast London entertainment district, which grew out of the Millennium Dome project. It included an indoor arena, an exhibition space, a music club, a cinema multiplex, restaurants, and taverns. When O_2 secured the naming rights for 15 years at a cost of £90 million, it was viewed as a questionable investment, especially because the old Millennium Dome had been sitting empty for some time and was considered by the British public to have been a boondoggle. The revamped facility changed that perception, as The O_2 became one of the world's most popular entertainment venues. According to the Marketing Society of the United Kingdom, awareness of The O_2 reached 72 percent within two years, redounding greatly to the benefit of the O_2 brand. In addition, O_2 used the complex to reward its customers, allowing them to buy concert and other event tickets two days before the general public, enjoy fast-track entry, and gain access to exclusive zones.

BRAND IDENTITY

- O_2 portrays itself as a bold and trustworthy innovator that is devoted to serving the needs of customers.
- O_2 claims to be an essential part of customers' lives.
- Oxygen and water imagery support the idea that the O_2 brand is essential to life.
- The "Fresh thinking, new possibilities" tagline supports O_2's brand identity while opening up new opportunities for brand growth.

All the elements of the O_2 brand serve to establish a unique personality, or identity. O_2 portrays itself as a bold and trustworthy innovator that is devoted to serving the needs of customers. More than that, O_2 claims to be an essential part of customers' lives, an idea that has been at the heart of the brand since it was introduced in 2002. The symbol for oxygen was chosen as the name, and water became another important graphic element. Without either compound, human life is not possible. In a similar way, people have come to consider their mobile telephones as a staple of life, and O_2 aligns itself with this connection through its symbolic name and imagery.

The taglines that O_2 has employed over the years have reinforced the brand's identity as well. The first one, "It's your O_2. See what you can do," was crafted at a time that third generation was opening up new service possibilities. The tagline not only promised an abundance of new possibilities but also claimed that the brand was devoted to meeting the needs of its customers. The further suggestion was that the brand and the customer were synonymous: *You* are the brand, the brand is you.

O_2 sought to deepen its bond with customers with the new tagline "We're better, connected." It was a reflection of a world in which convergence—the coming together of voice, data, and video—was becoming a reality in the mobile communications realm. The phrase also reinforced the idea that the brand and the customer were inextricably linked. More than that, the tagline claimed this was a mutually beneficial relationship.

Used to support a further evolution in brand strategy was the tagline "Fresh thinking, new possibilities." By this stage, the fundamental planks of the brand had been well established: the essential need for the brand and the close connection between the brand and the customer. O_2 had also branched into new areas, such as credit cards, but harbored much greater ambitions for the O_2 brand. The new tagline was preparing the ground for the next stage in the brand's development while staying in character and supporting the innovative side of the brand's identity.

BRAND STRATEGY

- O_2's brand strategy has evolved since the introduction of the O_2 brand.
- The O_2 brand has extended beyond mobile telephone service to include broadband, financial, travel insurance, and health care services.
- Launched in 2012, the "Fresh thinking, new possibilities" campaign opened the door to further O_2's brand extensions.

The brand strategy for O_2 has evolved significantly over time. Initially, it was simply a mobile telecommunications brand that was positioned to compete against Vodafone and Orange. As a result, the once disappointing Cellnet service emerged as O_2 and ultimately became the United Kingdom's market share leader. With this foundation, as well as with the financial backing of its Spanish corporate parent, O_2 began extending the O_2 brand to other products and services. In June 2006 the company paid £50 million for Be, a British broadband provider that was in the process of building a national broadband network. This acquisition allowed O_2 to extend the O_2 brand to the broadband and home phone markets. Later, O_2 Wifi was created to allow O_2 customers to connect their mobile devices to wireless local area network hotspots when they were away from home.

The O_2 brand was expanded beyond telecommunications when an agreement was reached in 2009 with the National Westminster Bank to offer prepaid Visa debit cards to O_2 customers under the O_2 Money label. The agreement lasted only a year, after which O_2 Money dropped physical currency in favor of a mobile wallet

application for iOS and Android devices, which were introduced in 2011. During this period O_2 also offered travel insurance through Mondial Assistance, but that venture was eventually discontinued. In 2010 O_2 Health was established to help health care organizations take better advantage of technology.

In support of its brand extension strategy, O_2 launched a £5 million "Think Big" campaign to build greater trust with younger consumers, who were the target for its new branded products and services. It also awarded cash to young people to fund innovative ideas that helped local communities. Another goal of the campaign was to persuade a large portion of the O_2 workforce to be involved in the "Think Big" initiative by making social responsibility a part of the brand's basic structure.

O_2 reached another stage in its development with the launch of the "Fresh thinking, new possibilities" campaign in 2012, which represented a new business strategy as much as it did a new branding strategy. In fact, the O_2 marketing and consumer director Sally Cowdry told Lara O'Reilly of *Marketing Week* in a March 7, 2012, interview, "Our brand strategy is our business strategy." She explained, "At O_2 the brand really is the entire company. It's all-pervasive; we see every touch point with our people as a brand experience." Thus, when O_2 considered a new product, the question "What is fresh about it?" naturally arose. While the company remained devoted to the products and services that a new generation of mobile devices could offer, the focus on new possibilities no longer limited the brand to the telecommunications industry alone.

BRAND EQUITY

- In 2011 Brand Finance estimated the worth of the O_2 brand at US$6.8 billion.
- O_2 ranked 141st on Brand Finance's 2012 "Global 500" list of the world's most valuable brands.
- In 2012 O_2 was listed number 16 on Brand Finance's "UK Top 50" list.
- The 2012 "BrandZ Top 100" of the world's most valuable brands listed O_2 number 94.
- According to MPP Consulting, O_2 is the United Kingdom's third-most valuable brand.

Success in extending O_2 beyond mobile telephone service demonstrates the underlying equity of the brand. Determining a brand's true equity is a difficult task, but to compare brands some brand consultancies and business publications have created brand value models that are based on quantifiable data, such as net sales. One prominent consultancy, Brand Finance, estimated the worth of the O_2 brand at US$6.8 billion in 2011. It was a valuation that in 2012 ranked O_2 number 141 on Brand Finance's "Global 500" list of the world's most valuable brands and number 16 on the "UK Top 50" list. In 2011 O_2 was number 16 on Brand Finance's "Top 500 Telecom Brands."

Another consultancy, Millward Brown, estimated the value of the O$_2$ brand at US$8.6 billion in 2012. As a result, O$_2$ was ranked 94th on Millward Brown's "BrandZ Top 100" brand ranking. The Centre for Brand Analysis placed O$_2$ 41st on its 2012 "Business Superbrands Official Top 500 (100)" list of the United Kingdom's most valuable business-to-business brands. According to the methodology used by MPP Consulting, O$_2$ is the United Kingdom's third-most valuable brand.

BRAND AWARENESS

- According to Harris Interactive, 52 percent of the British public was familiar with the O$_2$ brand in 2013.
- In 2013 the O$_2$ brand was "loved" by 10 percent of the British public, according to Harris Interactive.
- O$_2$ was the eighth most admired brand by British marketers in 2012.

O$_2$ enjoys strong brand awareness in the countries in which it operates, especially the United Kingdom. Even though brand awareness studies are generally proprietary information, some surveys conducted by the Harris Interactive polling agency shed light on how O$_2$ is perceived by the British public. In a survey published in 2013 regarding familiarity of electronic devices and other media properties, 52 percent of respondents said they were familiar with O$_2$. Only eight other properties ranked higher; the television providers BBC and ITV stood at the top, with 90 percent familiarity. The percentage of people who said they "loved" the O$_2$ brand was 10 percent. Even though O$_2$ was down the list at 26th, it was well ahead of the rival mobile telephone brands Orange and Vodafone. Respectively, only 6 percent and 5 percent of people had an emotional connection to these brands. O$_2$ was also a brand that was very popular with British marketers. In 2012 *Marketing Week* listed O$_2$ as the eighth most admired brand by marketers in the United Kingdom.

BRAND OUTLOOK

- The strength and weakness of Telefónica may determine the future health of the O$_2$ brand.
- Continued growth in the telecommunications industry bodes well for O$_2$.
- O$_2$ may become more of a lifestyle brand in the years ahead.

The prospects for the O$_2$ brand appear to be bright. It is well established in the mobile telephone markets in the countries in which it operates, and the brand has been successfully extended to the broadband, home phone, and financial sectors. As a part of Telefónica, O$_2$ has the backing of a global telecommunications company and shares many of the same strengths and weaknesses. Research and development efforts are strong, boding well for the future, as does continued growth in the telecommunications market. However, competition in the industry will likely grow even more intense in the years ahead.

What is especially intriguing about the O$_2$ brand is its potential to transcend the telecommunications sector entirely. O$_2$ has staked a claim on the idea that it offers the essentials of life, like oxygen and water, while also embracing "fresh thinking" and "new possibilities." O$_2$ is essentially developing a lifestyle brand identity that could be extended to any number of products and services. A ready example of such an all-encompassing brand is the direct competitor Virgin Mobile, part of the British conglomerate Virgin Group Ltd., which operates more than 400 travel, entertainment, and lifestyle companies around the world. Even though it is unlikely that the O$_2$ brand will become as ubiquitous as Virgin, there is a chance that O$_2$ might emulate Virgin on a small scale and extend the O$_2$ brand beyond mobile communications and the products and services that are directly connected to it. Whether O$_2$ will find currency in other sectors is a question that remains to be answered.

FURTHER READING

"Close-Up: The Advocates—O$_2$ Finds Marketing Success with Its 'Ruthless Execution.'" *Campaign*, January 29, 2010.

Curtis, James. "Battling for a 3G Future." *Marketing*, May 9, 2002.

Darling, Andrew. "Bursting with Optimism." *New Media Age*, May 1, 2003.

O'Reilly, Lara. "Q&A: O$_2$ Marketing and Consumer Director Sally Cowdry." *Marketing Week*, March 7, 2012.

"O$_2$ Brand Campaign to Trumpet New Strategy." *Marketing Week*, March 8, 2012.

"O$_2$ Brand Is in the Right Place to Extend Reach beyond Telecoms." *Marketing Week*, February 4, 2010.

"O$_2$: Does Your Brand Have the Stretch Factor?" *Marketing Week*, November 19, 2009.

Timmons, Heather. "Telefonica of Spain to Buy British Mobile Phone Concern." *New York Times*, November 1, 2005.

OLAY

———— ◆ ————

AT A GLANCE

Brand Synopsis: Olay, one of the most recognizable brands in the world, emphasizes timeless feminine beauty in its line of skincare products.

Parent Company: Procter & Gamble
One Procter & Gamble Plaza
Cincinnati, Ohio 45202
United States
http://www.olay.com

Sector: Consumer Staples

Industry Group: Household & Personal Products

Performance: *Market share*—10 percent (2011). *Sales*—US$42.6 billion (2011).

Principal Competitors: Avon; Dove; Neutrogena; Nivea

BRAND ORIGINS

- Graham Wulff invented Oil of Olay Beauty Fluid for his wife in the early 1950s.
- Wulff's business partner used newspaper and magazine articles to reach Oil of Olay's original consumer base.
- Procter & Gamble acquired Oil of Olay and its parent company in 1985.
- Oil of Olay was rebranded in 1999 as "Olay" and grew to include numerous sub-brands, attracting women and men of all ages worldwide.

South African chemist Graham Wulff created Olay as a gift to his wife, who was unhappy with the greasy beauty creams on the market in the 1950s. He worked with her input to create the pink, quick-absorbing Oil of Olay Beauty Fluid. The first batches were made by hand and sold to stores on request.

When Wulff met Jack Lowe, an account executive for an advertising agency, they partnered and founded Adams National Industries to make and sell the product. An accomplished marketer, Lowe offered beauty tips in newspapers and magazines and recommended Oil of Olay as part of a successful beauty routine. By 1959 the brand had expanded to the United Kingdom, the United States, the Netherlands, Canada, and Germany.

After Lowe died, Wulff sold the company in 1970 to Richardson-Merrell, Inc., which became Richardson-Vicks, Inc., in 1980. Five years later, Procter & Gamble bought Richardson-Vicks, Inc., and the Oil of Olay brand.

By the late 1990s, consumers had come to associate Oil of Olay with an older generation of women, and the brand was not maintaining its previous rate of growth. Procter & Gamble rebranded the product and simplified the name to "Olay" in 1999. This helped give the brand a uniform presence throughout its global affiliates. Even with some of the changes made to the product over the years, Olay maintained its reputation as a light, greaseless formula that absorbed quickly into the skin. Procter & Gamble introduced Olay Total Effects and began to highlight Olay's anti-aging properties.

The expanding product line reached a new generation of users. Younger women who wished to keep their skin fresh and young were attracted to the brand. The

Olay Pro-X, Definity, and Regenerist products achieved prestige among consumers. The emerging metrosexual market inspired the creation of Olay for Men.

A weak economy did not inhibit consumer demand for anti-aging and grooming products. The Olay brand led Brand Finance's 2011 rankings and retained the top position in 2012.

BRAND ELEMENTS

- Oil of Olay was called Oil of Ulay, Oil of Olaz, or Oil of Olan in various international markets until the name was simplified as "Olay" in 1999.
- Olay's design was simplified in the rebranding process, with the name in black letters on a light background giving the product a more elegant appearance.
- New Olay sub-brands each have their own look and feel.
- Taglines for the brand have included "Love the skin you're in" "Look good, feel good," and "Skin so beautiful, it sings."

Before 1999 the name of Olay-branded products varied according to region. It was Oil of Olay in South Africa and North America; Oil of Ulay in the United Kingdom; Oil of Olaz in some European countries; and Oil of Olan in Australia. Rebranding to the simpler "Olay" took place in 1999 to bring more consistency to the brand's global presence.

The product began as a pink, uniquely scented moisturizing fluid packaged in glass bottles. Intriguing print advertisements urged women to find the "beauty secret" within. The Oil of Olay name was written in pink letters on a black, house-shaped background, which contrasted again with the pink box (and the pink fluid in the bottle). Logo and packaging were easily recognized. The original logo was the black outline of a woman holding her hands to her face.

Today's "classic" beauty fluid has a more elegant label. The word "Olay" is presented in black letters against a light background. The woman's face has been redesigned and placed on a gold coin-like circle, giving it the appearance of a wax seal.

Each Olay sub-brand has its own look and feel. For example, Olay Regenerist is packaged in eye-catching red and black with white lettering. Though Olay's name is on the front of all sub-brand packaging, the logo of the woman's face is not. Packaging for most of the Regenerist, Total Effects, and Complete lines still shows the logo, while packaging for Pro-X, Fresh Effects, and the Age Defying Series does not.

Recent advertising has included the tagline "Love the skin you're in." Another is "Look good, feel good." A tagline that emphasized the fight against aging was "I'm not gonna grow old gracefully. I'm gonna fight it every step of the way." And a recent advertisement featuring country singer Carrie Underwood used the slogan "Skin so beautiful, it sings."

BRAND IDENTITY

- Olay is constantly evolving, with innovation and new technology providing the impetus for new products.
- The brand strives for a personal relationship with the consumer.
- Olay presents itself as a brand with a commitment to safety and environmental responsibility.
- Olay strives to represent itself as a "masstige" item.

As Olay celebrated 60 years in 2012, Michael Kuremsky, Procter & Gamble's global vice president and general manager of skin care, said the brand tries "to be at the forefront of innovation, with new ingredients and technologies that really transform the skin." Olay's philosophy is "to maintain a deep understanding of women's changing needs and to combine products that fit their needs with the latest advances in skin care technology." Olay brings "healthy, beautiful skin to more than 80 million women on five continents." To connect more closely with consumers, the website OlayForYou.com was launched as a source of personal skin-care and beauty advice.

To compliment the brand's presence in technology is the brand's goal to demonstrate its commitment to the safety and environmental responsibility of its products. Numerous quality tests are performed every year. From 2011 to 2012, 250 safety evaluations were made for new Olay product formulations. The Olay brand also presents itself as a "masstige" item by selling prestigious products at affordable prices to the masses.

BRAND STRATEGY

- Olay has branched out into sub-brands that meet the needs of different consumers.
- The sophisticated look and promise of a new improved anti-aging formula enabled Olay to charge more for Olay Total Effects products.
- Changes in Olay packaging not only improved the brand's reputation as sustainable, it reduced the cost of production.

By the 1990s, Oil of Olay's identity had become tied to an older generation of women. In an attempt to attract younger consumers, the brand was relaunched in 1999 as "Olay."

Over the years the brand has branched out, with many of its sub-brands concentrating on restoring, rejuvenating, and regenerating skin while reducing the effects of aging. Olay Total Effects was introduced to the market with a sophisticated look and the promise of a better anti-aging formula. The improved product attracted a wider, younger audience seeking ways to keep skin fresh and youthful. Its design and quality made it possible to charge up to three times more for Total Effects products. The brand was made available at mass retailers such as Walmart and Walgreens. Newer products in the Olay line, such as Regenerist, Definity, and Pro-X, have given added boosts to the customer base. The company spent more than US$50 million to promote Regenerist in 2003.

In 2009 Twiggy, a model known for her beautiful eyes, was featured in an advertisement for Olay Definity with the line "Because younger looking eyes never go out of fashion." In the ad, Twiggy, who first achieved fame as a model in the 1960s, seems ageless and is an alluring example of beauty. Unfortunately, the ad was banned in the United Kingdom because of its heavy use of photo-enhancement techniques.

Changes in Olay packaging from a clamshell to a blister-based design reduced the amount of plastic used and helped to position the brand as more environmentally conscious. Olay also improved the pump design for Total Effects, which, according to Procter & Gamble, is "expected to save 800,000 pounds of plastic a year—equivalent to the weight of a Boeing 747." These changes in packaging helped reduce the cost of production.

BRAND EQUITY

- Olay was named the top beauty brand by Brand Finance in 2011 and 2012.
- Olay's 2012 brand value was US$11.8 billion.
- In 2012 Olay ranked 71st among the top-500 global brands.

Brand Finance named Olay the top beauty brand in 2012 for the second year in a row, with a brand value of US$11.8 billion. Avon was ranked second. Olay ranked 71st in the top-500 global brands in 2012, up five spots from 2011.

BRAND AWARENESS

- Olay is a multibillion-dollar brand for Procter & Gamble.
- The Olay brand and its sub-brands have received numerous beauty awards in magazines, including *Allure*, *Elle*, and *Marie Claire*.
- Per Procter & Gamble "eight out of 10 dermatologists would recommend Olay for the care of skin."
- A go-to-market approach for Olay Regenerist Micro-Sculpting Cream propelled Olay to an 8 percent share in Mexico's highly competitive facial moisturizer market.
- In China Olay's White Radiance received a design excellence award at the International Package Design Awards.

One of Procter & Gamble's multibillion-dollar brands, Olay has been characterized by *Forbes* as a "legacy brand"—a brand that has been active for 60 to 100 years. Consumer loyalty has played a large part in the ongoing popularity of the Olay brand during that period. On the one hand, anti-aging products increased in popularity as the first of the baby boom generation moved beyond age 60. On the other hand, Olay actively cultivated a younger image in various ways, including an association with American gymnasts Alicia Sacramone and Jordyn Wieber during the 2012 Olympic games.

Olay and its sub-brands have received numerous awards and is recognized by consumers as a leader in skincare. *Elle* magazine gave its Beauty Genius Award to Olay's Smooth Finish Facial Hair Removal Duo for Medium to Coarse Hair before the product arrived on store shelves. Other beauty awards were received from the magazines *Life & Style*, *Allure*, *Good Housekeeping*, *Essence*, and *Marie Claire*.

Olay offers quality products at good value, and it validates its moisturizing and anti-aging properties with positive reviews from the dermatological community. Procter & Gamble reported that "eight out of 10 dermatologists surveyed at the World Congress of Dermatology said they would recommend Olay for the care of skin."

Olay's sub-brands play an important part in its international popularity. In 2009 Olay Regenerist Micro-Sculpting Cream was introduced in Mexico. The campaign introduced the product with samples, using a go-to-market approach to make the product visible to retailers and consumers. Procter & Gamble's 2010 annual report said the launch "propelled Olay to an 8 percent share in Mexico's highly competitive facial moisturizer market."

In Asia the cultural desire for lighter skin opened the door for products, such as Olay Natural White, developed specifically for the market. Olay's White Radiance is exclusive to the Chinese market. The design agency Libby Perszyk Kathman received a design excellence award in the mass skin care category for Olay White Radiance's packaging at the International Package Design Awards.

BRAND OUTLOOK

- Procter & Gamble's long-term goals for Olay include growth in organic sales, earnings per share, and cash flow.
- The effort to meet Procter & Gamble's goals will require increases in innovation, productivity, and use of renewable energy.
- Olay's innovations are intended to improve people's everyday lives in every part of the world.

Among Procter & Gamble's long-term goals for its many brands are growth in organic sales, increased earnings per share, and growth in "free cash flow productivity of 90 percent or greater." The company plans to meet these goals through innovation, increased productivity, and the use of renewable materials and energy.

The ongoing effort to simplify Olay's packaging while increasing consumer awareness through digital and mobile technologies will continue to enhance the equity of the brand. As a premium product, Olay Pro-X will help the brand as it is marketed in more countries.

Procter & Gamble's 2011 annual report says that Olay's innovations are intended to improve people's everyday lives in every part of the world and to expand the company's "portfolio of innovation up and down price tiers, into new markets, and into new and existing product categories."

FURTHER READING

Begoun, Paula. "Olay." *Beautypedia Reviews.* Accessed October 25, 2012. http://www.beautypedia.com/Brand/Olay/174.aspx.

Brand Finance. "Olay." *Brandirectory.* Accessed October 22, 2012. http://brandirectory.com/profile/olay.

———. "Olay the Most Valuable Beauty Brand in the World." April 17 2012. Accessed October 22, 2012. http://brandfinance.com/news/in_the_news/olay-is-the-most-valuable-beauty-brand-in-the-world.

Canada, Alonzo, and Joyce Chen. "Revitalizing Your Business." *Jump.* Accessed October 25, 2012. http://www.jumpassociates.com/revitalizing-your-business.html.

"DMI Members—Creating Brand Value." Design Management Institute. Accessed October 24, 2012. http://www.dmi.org/dmi/html/members/news/membernewswinter06.pdf.

Goudreau, Jenna. "The Top 10 Global Beauty Brands." *Forbes,* April 20, 2012.

Idler, Sabina. "Case Study: The Emotional Pull of Beauty Brands." *Usabilla,* March 8, 2012. Accessed October 24, 2012. http://blog.usabilla.com/case-study-the-emotional-pull-of-beauty-brands/.

Kats, Rimma. "Procter & Gamble's Olay Aims to Bolster New Product Sales via Mobile Ads." *Mobile Commerce Daily,* September 7, 2012.

"Olay: Brand Profile (US)." Adbrands.net. Accessed October 23, 2012. http://www.adbrands.net/us/olay_us.htm.

Patrick, Monica. "Oil of Olay." *Love to Know Skincare.* Accessed October 26, 2012. http://skincare.lovetoknow.com/Oil_of_Olay.

Procter & Gamble. "Olay." Accessed October 25, 2012. http://www.olay.com.

———. "Olay." Accessed October 24, 2012. http://www.pg.com/en_US/brands/beauty_grooming/olay.shtml.

ORACLE

——— ■ ———

AT A GLANCE

——— ■ ———

Brand Synopsis: Representing the world's largest enterprise software company, Oracle is a visionary brand boasting all-encompassing, integrated enterprise technology solutions.

Parent Company: Oracle Corporation
500 Oracle Parkway
Redwood City, California 94065
United States
http://www.oracle.com

Sector: Information Technology

Industry Group: Software & Services

Performance: *Market share*—70 percent in enterprise software (2011). *Sales*—US$37.1 billion (2012).

Principal Competitors: International Business Machines Corporation; Microsoft Corporation; SAP AG

BRAND ORIGINS

- Oracle Corporation was founded in 1977 as Software Development Laboratories.
- Oracle was initially a code name for a Central Intelligence Agency proprietary database project.
- The first commercial Oracle database product was released in 1979.
- The Oracle Corporation name was adopted in 1983.
- Oracle Corporation was taken public in 1986.

Oracle is the overarching brand of Oracle Corporation, the world's largest enterprise software company. In many respects the Oracle brand reflects the personality of its cofounder and longtime chief executive officer, Larry Ellison. Born in New York City in 1944 but raised by adoptive parents in Chicago, Ellison displayed an aptitude for math and science but little patience with his academic studies. His time at college, however, introduced him to computer programming, which in the mid-1960s he found to be a lucrative endeavor that suited his personality. He moved to California and became an itinerant programmer, moving from one company to the next to earn enough money to support his interests in hiking and rock climbing.

Ellison became vice president of research and development at a company called Omex in 1976, working on a mass storage concept. Rather than report to managers whose abilities he did not respect, Ellison decided to start his own company. Thus, in 1977 he founded a software consultancy business with a pair of programmer friends, Edward Oates and Robert Miner. Ellison was the chief executive and majority owner of the venture, called Software Development Laboratories (SDL). The partners had worked on various government projects over the years and now used their experience to persuade the Central Intelligence Agency to award a lapsed US$50,000 contract to build a proprietary database. Ellison used Oracle as the code name for the project.

Rather than work only as consultants, the partners wanted to become software developers to meet the growing demand for prepackaged software programs. What they needed was a flagship product, a program that could be sold to a wide range of businesses. Ellison found the inspiration for such a product in a paper written by an IBM researcher about a new way of organizing large amounts of data. His conceived relational database management system (RDBMS) would allow for ad hoc queries, rather than requiring a program be written for each query. Ellison understood the potential commercial uses of such a program and realized that IBM was not energetically pursuing the idea. Ellison and his partners decided to beat IBM to the market with a salable product.

Ellison again drew on the Oracle name for the RDBMS. Oracle 1 was written in assembly language in 1978, and the following year Oracle Version 2 was released and became commercially available. Another two years would pass before IBM was able to release its first relational database. In the meantime, SDL changed its name to Relational Software Inc. With the release of Oracle Version 3, the company aligned itself with the product brand, changing its name to Oracle Corporation in 1983. The company went public in 1986 but remained a bit player until the mid-1990s when Ellison, foreseeing the declining importance of the personal computer, turned his attention to the Internet. Proving more nimble than IBM, Oracle was able to establish its database as an essential business platform on the Internet, transforming Oracle into one of Silicon Valley's most powerful companies and Ellison into one of the world's richest entrepreneurs. In the new century, the company expanded its horizons, broadening its range of products and services and growing the value of the Oracle brand.

BRAND ELEMENTS

- The Oracle name, drawn from the ancient Greeks, retains powerful associations of foretelling the future with authority.
- The Oracle word mark serves as the corporate logo.
- The Oracle logo uses a custom-designed typeface and a particular shade of bright red.
- Oracle's primary tagline is "Hardware and Software. Engineered to Work Together."
- Founder Larry Ellison's personality is an important aspect of the Oracle brand.

Of the elements that comprise the Oracle brand, the name is perhaps the most important. The word "Oracle" appealed to Ellison, who used it as a project code name, then a product name, and finally as the name of his company. The word resonates with meaning, referring to the ancient Greek priestesses through whom a deity was believed to speak. An oracle also foretold the future with authority. Such associations are useful to a high-tech company, and the Oracle name connects these values to the Oracle brand.

The Oracle name has such power that there is little need for a corporate logo beyond a word mark. The Oracle logo is simply the name in upper-case letters using a custom-designed typeface. The mark is either rendered in Oracle Red or presented in white letters within an Oracle red rectangle. The word mark is also combined with product categories, such as Oracle Cloud or Oracle Database, or education certification, like Oracle Certified Master or Oracle Professional. In any case, the Oracle name always stands out, both in terms of color and font size.

Because they are not prominently displayed, taglines are as not as important to the Oracle brand as the name. When the company was trying to emphasize the reliability and security of Oracle Database, the slogan "Can't break it, can't break in" was used. Another slogan—"Software. Hardware. Complete."—was crafted after the acquisition of Sun Microsystems to emphasize the totality of what Oracle now had to offer. The tagline was then refined as "Hardware and Software. Engineered to Work Together." It supported the idea that Oracle simplified information technology.

Another element of the Oracle brand not to be discounted is Larry Ellison. In some respects Ellison is like Microsoft's Bill Gates, who is arguably a brand unto himself. Ellison is not as well known to the general public as Gates, but Oracle does not sell to the general public. Within the smaller world of information technology, no one individual dominates the running of a major company like Larry Ellison. Even Gates turned over day-to-day control of Microsoft, content to serve as chairman of the board. Ellison, on the other hand, allowed someone else to have the chairmanship while he continued to act as CEO. The close association of Ellison with Oracle means that many of his attributes, both beneficial and detrimental, adhered to the Oracle brand.

BRAND IDENTITY

- Oracle's identity is that of a visionary company with an all-encompassing, integrated enterprise technology solution.
- The connotations of an "oracle" as foretelling the future with authority support the Oracle brand image.
- The candid, confident personality of CEO Larry Ellison supports Oracle's identity.
- CEO Larry Ellison's outspokenness has an impact, both good and bad, on Oracle's image.

The image that the Oracle brand seeks to convey to the world, its identity, is that of a visionary company with all-encompassing, integrated enterprise technology solutions. The farsighted nature of the brand is suggested by the Oracle name. Not only do oracles divine the future; they speak with authority. Once the oracle has spoken, there is nothing more to be said. Similarly, the Oracle brand has fashioned an identity that claims certainty. In other words, Oracle has all of the answers to a customer's IT needs. Providing further reinforcement of this assertion is the tagline "Hardware and Software. Engineered to Work Together." Not only is what Oracle has to offer a complete package of hardware and software, the promise is that the components are designed to work together to meet customer needs.

Founder and CEO Larry Ellison's personality reinforces Oracle's brand identity. He is considered a Silicon Valley visionary, who recognized the importance of relational databases before anyone else, understood the impact the Internet would have on personal computing, and realized the true potential of network computing. He also enjoys the spotlight and offers his opinions at every opportunity in any forum, thus building recognition for himself and the Oracle brand and tying the two together. His message is unwavering: Oracle not only offers great technology, but it is an ideal provider because it offers everything a client might need, from databases to business applications.

Ellison also gives voice to another element of Oracle's brand identity: Oracle is so advanced that the competition can never hope to catch up. Moreover, he is seldom reluctant to name names as he dismisses Oracle's rivals. While such candor helps to promote Oracle's identity as an IT authority, it in some ways tarnishes Oracle's image—the way the brand is actually perceived by the outside world. Ellison is seen by many as brash and ruthless, a dictator who runs his company with an iron fist and is involved in virtually every significant decision. In much of Silicon Valley, Ellison is as despised as he is respected. It turn, Oracle is seen in a similar light, overly aggressive and ruthless, taking advantage of its domination of the database market. "Capitalizing on such an edge," according to a 2010 *New York Times* article, "Oracle's sales representatives have earned a fearsome reputation as hard-line negotiators determined to squeeze customers."

BRAND STRATEGY

- Oracle pursues a master brand strategy.
- There are six levels to Oracle's brand architecture.
- The name Jia Gu Wen is used in China as an equivalent to the Oracle brand.
- Oracle allowed Java to act as a standalone brand with limited ties to the Oracle master brand.
- Oracle discontinued the Sun Microsystems brand after acquiring the highly regarded tech company.

Oracle Corporation primarily pursues a corporate branding strategy, applying Oracle as a prefix to its divisions, products, and services. There are six levels to Oracle's branch architecture. At the top is the master brand, followed by the category level, which covers database and storage systems, including Oracle Database, Oracle

Storage, and Oracle Cloud. Next is the suite level, which includes Oracle Fusion Middleware. At the fourth level are product descriptions, such as Oracle Content Management and Oracle Identity Management. The next level is reserved for components, including Oracle Sales Prospector and Oracle FS Probability Analytics. The sixth and final level of Oracle's brand architecture is product editions, such as Oracle Database 11g, which are further distinguished by release numbers.

As much as possible the Oracle name is used throughout the world. In China, however, the company uses Jia Gu Wen. It is a brand name that resonates with the local market. With a lineage that dates back more than 3,000 years, Jia Gu Wen was once a cutting edge way to store information. In addition, it was used in prophecy. Both of these attributes are in keeping with the Oracle brand. As a result, Jia Gu Wen was as close to being a Chinese equivalent of Oracle as possible.

Oracle Corporation expanded greatly through acquisitions in the early 2000s. Major additions included JD Edwards & Company, PeopleSoft, Siebels Systems Inc., and Sun Microsystems Inc. Much of the technology acquired from these companies was incorporated into existing Oracle products. The PeopleSoft, Siebel, and JD Edwards names continued to be used as product brands, as are other acquired corporate brands, but they are relegated to a much lower level of importance than the Oracle master brand. This focus on the master brand was evident when the acquisition of Sun brought several products with overlapping functions. Hence, Sun Directory Server Enterprise Edition became Oracle Directory Server Enterprise Edition; Sun OpenDS was renamed Oracle Unified Directory; and Sun Role Manager was rebranded as Oracle Identity Analytics. Sun also brought the highly popular Java object-oriented computer programming language used on billions of personal computers, smartphones, and other devices. Java was a brand that possessed considerable value and was allowed to act as a standalone brand with limited ties to the Oracle master brand. The same could not be said for Sun Microsystems, Inc. It was merged with Oracle USA, Inc. to become Oracle America, Inc., and Sun's former Menlo Park, California, campus was subsequently sold to Facebook. Sun, once a prized Silicon Valley tech brand, became little more than a memory.

BRAND EQUITY

- Brand Finance estimated at the end of 2011 that the value of the Oracle brand was US$17 billion.
- Oracle was number 39 on Brand Finance's 2012 "Global 500."
- Interbrand recognized Oracle as the 18th most valuable brand in 2012.
- According to *Forbes* magazine, Oracle is the 11th most valuable brand in the world.

Oracle is a highly valuable tech brand and one of the world's most valuable brands no matter the industry. Measuring the true equity of a brand is always difficult, given that many benefits of a strong brand are not tangible. Some branding consultancies and business publications attempt to compare brands to one another by assigning a monetary value based on measurable criteria. One of the most reputable brand consultancies, Brand Finance, placed a US$17 billion brand value on Oracle at the end of 2011. It was a rating good enough to give Oracle the 39th ranking on Brand Finance's 2012 "Global 500" list of the world's most valuable brands. According to Brand Finance, Oracle's brand worth has increased steadily, growing more than 60 percent between 2008 and 2011.

Another important brand consultancy, Interbrand, ranks Oracle highly as well. According to its methodology, Oracle was the 18th most valuable brand in 2012, worth US$22.1 billion, a 28 percent increase over the previous year. The Millward Brown agency estimates a similar value, US$22.5 billion, and places Oracle as the 27th most valuable brand in its "Brandz Top 100" brand listing.

Business publications also highly rate the value of Oracle, but they differ on how Oracle compares to other brands. *Forbes* magazine estimates that the Oracle brand is worth US$25.9 billion, making it the 11th most valuable brand in the world, according to its "World's Most Valuable Brands" list. The last time *BusinessWeek* issued its "100 Best Global Brands" list, in 2009, Oracle was ranked 31st. Since that time, however, Oracle acquired Sun Microsystems, a transaction that would significantly enhance the value of Oracle in *BusinessWeek*'s brand evaluation modeling.

BRAND AWARENESS
- Oracle is especially well known among information technology decision-makers.
- An early 2000s marketing study revealed 16 percent top-of-mind brand awareness for Oracle among information technology decision-makers.
- Growth in middleware and hardware expands the number of Oracle customers, further increasing its brand awareness.
- Larry Ellison's sporting exploits and personal life increase awareness of the Oracle brand.

Doing business around the world, Oracle enjoys strong brand awareness. Although the company does not sell directly to consumers, the Oracle name is generally well known. It is with business customers, especially chief technology officers and other managers directly involved in the procurement of software, hardware, and database services, that Oracle enjoys excellent brand awareness. While marketing studies that measure brand awareness are generally not available for public consumption, a survey conducted in the early 2000s by the Yankee Group provides some insight. The research and advisory firm produced a report that tested the corporate image of enterprise resource planning vendors among business decision-makers. When asked unprompted, 32 percent of respondents said that SAP came to mind. Oracle was second with 16 percent. It was a performance that surprised the researchers. Moreover, 32 percent of respondents said they were willing to recommend Oracle, compared with only 26 percent who said they would recommend SAP. In the years since that study was conducted, Oracle has greatly expanded into middleware and hardware to broaden its customer base. As a result, it is very likely that Oracle has significantly increased its brand awareness among business decision-makers.

The personal exploits of Larry Ellison should not be discounted in the consideration of Oracle's brand awareness. The company's charismatic chief executive has made for interesting news coverage over the years. On one hand, he is a visionary who seeks the spotlight, but on the other he is brash and arrogant and came close to crashing the company in the early 1990s before building Oracle into a true powerhouse. He also gained notoriety for allegedly hiring a private investigation firm to search the trash dumpsters of business rivals. In 2012 he paid US$100 million to settle an insider stock trading suit.

Ellison's sporting exploits have also made news. An aerial enthusiast, he likes to engage in mock air battles. He once attempted to buy a vintage Russian MiG fighter, but the transaction was thwarted by the U.S. Department of Justice. He is also an accomplished sailor. In 2010 he headed the syndicate that won the prestigious America's Cup for the United States for the first time since 1992. Defending the cup would bring further attention to Ellison's Oracle Team USA and the Oracle brand.

BRAND OUTLOOK
- Oracle has a strong position in the expanding cloud computing market, and its long-term outlook for information technology services appears strong.
- As of 2013, Oracle's hardware business was experiencing diminishing profitability and margins.
- Oracle's future depended on the expected leadership transition from founder Larry Ellison to the next generation of Oracle managers.

Oracle has grown into a highly valuable brand, especially during the early 2000s. In a matter of five years, more than 60 companies were acquired to expand Oracle's product offerings. Annual revenues increased to US$37.1 billion in 2012. The company set a target of US$100 billion, but it faced a number of challenges in reaching that number. Oracle's hardware business was experiencing diminishing profitability and margins. The company was also highly dependent on resellers and independent software vendors. There were many opportunities, however. Oracle had a strong position in the expanding cloud computing market, and the long-term outlook for IT services appeared strong. With its market-leading position, Oracle was well placed to leverage its strength to take advantage of that growing demand.

Many of Oracle's prospects were dependent on the value of the Oracle brand. It was a well-known and respected brand but hardly a beloved brand, one that connected with the world on an emotional level. The bond between the Oracle brand and the marketplace was purely a transactional one. Because it was all business and no love, this relationship brought with it some degree of uncertainty. As long as Oracle delivered on its promises, the brand was on solid footing. Should the brand fail to meet expectations, however, there was no irrational attraction to the brand that would overcome any significant shortfall in performance. Adding to the uncertainty was Oracle's dependence on Larry Ellison, who is now past traditional retirement age. Whether he is willing to give

up some control of the company, and in turn lessen his impact on the Oracle brand, remains to be seen.

FURTHER READING

"Back from the Brink: How Larry Ellison Pulled off One of the Biggest Comebacks of the 1990s." *Success*, August 2009.

"Best Global Brands 2012." Interbrand. Accessed February 18, 2013. http://www.interbrand.com/en/best-global-brands/2012/Oracle.

Brand Finance. "Global 500 2012." *Brandirectory*. Accessed February 18, 2013. http://brandirectory.com/league_tables/table/global-500-2012.

"Larry Ellison." *International Directory of Business Biographies*. Ed. Neil Schlager. Vol. 4. Detroit, MI: St. James Press, 2005.

"Oracle Corporation." *International Directory of Company Histories*. Ed. Tina Grant. Vol. 138. Detroit, MI: St. James Press, 2012.

Stamler, Bernard. "Oracle Defies Wisdom by Using Itself to Pitch Its Software Products." *New York Times*, February 23, 2001.

Vance, Ashlee. "Oracle Growth Plans Worry Rivals and Customers." *New York Times*, September 21, 2010.

ORANGE

BRAND ORIGINS

- The Orange brand was launched in the United Kingdom in 1994.
- Despite being the fourth mobile carrier entrant in the United Kingdom, Orange quickly grew market share through savvy branding.
- Orange established itself as an innovative brand that was also aspirational.
- Orange became the face of France Telecom's Internet and television service.

Orange was launched as a mobile telephone brand in the United Kingdom by Hutchison Whampoa, a Hong Kong–based conglomerate. The mobile provider had been established in 1990, when Microtel Communications Ltd. was formed by British Aerospace, Millicom, Matra, and Pactel Corporation. After British Aerospace assumed full ownership, Hutchison acquired a 65 percent controlling interest through a stock exchange. By this time, Microtel had secured a license to develop a mobile telephone network in the United Kingdom.

Microtel was renamed Orange Personal Communications Services Ltd. and in April 1994 began offering mobile telephone service under the Orange brand. As the fourth entrant in the United Kingdom's mobile telephone market, which was dominated by Vodafone and BT Cellnet, Orange was at a distinct disadvantage. It was largely due to excellent branding, something that was neglected by the other mobile providers, that Orange prospered. Charged with creating the company's corporate and brand identity was Wolff Olins, an international brand consultancy, which was supported by the work of the SCRS advertising agency.

Orange was able to differentiate itself in a highly competitive marketplace by forging a reputation as a service innovator. It became the first mobile carrier to bill by the second, rather than by the minute, and it offered monthly subscriptions and free insurance. It was also the first to offer caller ID and dual band handsets, and the first brand to text message numbers to subscribers' phones. Moreover, through clever advertising and adroit brand positioning, Orange became an aspirational brand. It offered a vision of a wireless future, one in which mobile phones would liberate everyone, not just the young professionals who had been the industry's core customers. The product offerings and messaging were especially appealing to a wide range of consumers, especially young people.

To align itself with its brand, Orange Personal Communications Services became Orange plc in 1995. The following year the company was taken public on the London Stock Exchange and the NASDAQ. By July 1997 Orange topped the 1 million mark in subscribers. Because it was better able to retain subscribers, it became the most profitable of the mobile carriers in its market. Orange extended its brand to Hong Kong during the fall of 1998, and within a matter of months it became that market's top mobile provider. The Orange brand was then introduced in Austria, Belgium, and Switzerland and licensed to providers in Australia, India, and Israel.

Changes in ownership would play a significant role in changes to the Orange brand in the new century. The German conglomerate Mannesmann AG acquired Orange for US$33 billion in October 1999. A few months later Vodafone acquired Mannesmann in an even larger transaction. To satisfy regulatory concerns over a company holding two mobile licenses, Vodafone was forced to divest Orange. The company was acquired by France Telecom in August 2000. The following year France Telecom's mobile brand, Mobicarte, was replaced by the Orange brand. In 2005 the Orange brand was extended to include France Telecom's Internet and television services. Shortly thereafter, France Telecom affiliates from around the world began marketing their services under the Orange brand. As a result, Orange became known throughout Europe, the Caribbean, the Middle East, Africa, and Asia.

BRAND ELEMENTS

- The color orange is a fundamental element of the brand.
- The original Orange logo was minimalist in nature.
- Innovation was a key element in growing the Orange brand.
- "The Future's Bright, the Future's Orange" proved to be an effective tagline.

Orange was one of the most exciting brands to emerge during the 1990s. The name alone was provocative. It was simple, a common color, and the name of a common fruit. As such, the brand was provided with a readymade corporate color. The original minimalist logo was rendered in orange but assumed a square shape, defying expectations of a round orange. Within the box was written "orange" in white lowercase letters. A black border surrounded the orange box.

Another important element of the Orange brand was its memorable tagline, "The Future's Bright, the Future's Orange." It was a message with multiple meanings. It announced the brand's intention to dominate its market and tied the brand to the qualities of optimism and positive thinking. It also suggested a bright future made possible by wireless communication.

Service offerings played an important role in the growth of the brand. Orange made its mark in the United Kingdom market by adopting new billing methods and features before its competitors. Coupled with innovative advertising, it became a trendy brand with the youth market, which led the way to greater general acceptance. As time went on, however, other carriers caught up and Orange found it difficult to differentiate itself on the level of service and features.

The Orange brand was later extended by its parent, France Telecom, to market all of its voice, Internet, and television services around the world. Orange retained its distinctive look and introduced a new tagline, "Today changes with Orange." The brand now became a champion for a digital future.

BRAND IDENTITY

- Novelty was at the core of Orange's early identity.
- The young brand was especially appealing to a youth market.
- Orange's identity evolved under new ownership.

Orange's identity has shifted over time. Orange presented itself as something new and different when it was introduced in 1994. It was a sensory brand, one that on the surface had no connection to mobile telephone service. Nevertheless, the novelty of the branding approach fit perfectly with the core message: mobile communications was novel, and among the mobile carriers doing business in the United Kingdom, Orange presented itself as the freshest new face. It was a young brand geared toward young customers. Orange reinforced its trendy image through its unusual logo and hip advertisements. The introduction of new billing plans and service features also supported this concept.

Just as young customers grow older, Orange became an established brand. Its identity evolved slightly over time, partly because of changes in the marketplace and partly because of changes in ownership. The name was applied to Internet and television service, leading Orange to portray itself as a brand committed to bringing the digital universe to as many people as possible. The brand was still a champion, but instead of a wireless future, the emphasis was on a digital future. In this way, Orange continued to lay claim to the mantle of novelty and hope for the future.

BRAND STRATEGY

- Early brand efforts focused on emotion rather than on products.
- In 2005 France Telecom decided to make Orange the corporate and consumer face of the company.
- The tagline "Today changes with Orange" was adopted in 2010.
- Three words define Orange's new brand strategy: simplicity, service, and segmenting.

As a late entrant in the United Kingdom mobile telephone business, Orange used clever advertising backed by innovative service to carve out a share of the market during the mid- to late 1990s. Orange advertisements did not feature mobile phones. Rather, the focus was on human emotions engendered by Orange. The tagline "The Future's Bright, the Future's Orange" performed a similar sleight of hand. Mobile telephone service became a mere bonus to what Orange was really selling: hope. It was a strategy that paid off, as Orange built a devoted subscriber base.

After a change in ownership, Orange pursued more of a global branding strategy. In 2000 the brand took a more conventional approach by becoming a sponsor of the Arrows Formula One automobile racing team. Because Formula One enjoyed worldwide appeal, the relationship made sense from a traditional marketing point of view. After completing its three-year commitment to the Arrows team, however, Orange severed its ties with Formula One.

Orange's brand strategy lost focus during the first decade of the 21st century. Ben Carter, writing for *Marketing* in 2004, said the strategy now had an "air of desperation." He explained, "Orange seems content to leap on the next technology innovation, while showing no concern for consumer confusion." Rather than returning to a strategy of simplifying the brand, however, France Telecom expanded it in 2005. Orange now became the corporate and consumer face of the company, representing all of France Telecom's global mobile, Internet, and fixed-line interests, as well as television. In November 2010 Orange launched a new marketing approach that was embodied in the tagline "Today changes with Orange." The new tagline was meant to represent a commitment to making the world's digital transformation a simple and useful reality for all. Orange was no longer the plucky anticorporate mobile telephone brand that had proven so attractive in the United Kingdom during the 1990s. It was now a global brand crafted to appeal to a wider market and to diverse cultures and customers.

Orange emphasized three concepts that defined its new strategy: simplicity, service, and segmenting. The idea of simplicity meant that Orange provided convenience to customers by bundling services, offering them all-in-one solutions that included mobile, fixed-line, Internet, and television plans. Orange also viewed simplicity in terms of offering innovations that made technology more customer friendly.

Service was another key to Orange's new brand strategy. The goal was to provide customers with the industry's best customer service. This commitment even preceded the sales by offering simple and easily understood products and services, as well as demonstrations and helpful advice at Orange stores. Service also included installation and the resolution of problems after the sale in a streamlined manner.

Through segmenting, Orange hoped to establish a reputation for meeting the needs of its customers by only offering what delivered maximum benefit. For example, in 2011 Orange introduced a web-only mobile service in France. To help in the development of new service offerings, Orange labs and customer test centers were opened around the world to evaluate customer response before the product was officially launched.

BRAND EQUITY

- Orange was ranked as the 50th most valuable brand on BrandZ Top 100 Most Valuable Global Brands in 2012.
- With a value of US$18.6 billion in 2012, Orange was ranked 31st on the Brand Finance Global 500.
- Orange was ranked fifth on Brand Finance's "Top 500 Telecom Brands" in 2012.

Orange is considered to be one of the world's most valuable brands. It was ranked as the 50th most valuable brand on BrandZ Top 100 Most Valuable Global Brands in 2012. It was assigned a brand value of US$15.4 billion, a decrease of 13 percent over the previous year, when Orange was listed as 36th among the top-100 brands.

According to Brand Finance, Orange was valued at US$18.6 billion in 2012, a performance that garnered the 31st position on the Brand Finance Global 500. A year earlier, however, Orange was rated as the 29th most valuable brand. Among telecommunications brands, Orange was regarded as the fifth most valuable brand on Brand Finance's "Top 500 Telecom Brands" in 2012. Only Vodafone, AT&T, Verizon, and Apple (handsets) were ranked higher.

BRAND AWARENESS

- As of December 31, 2011, the Orange brand operated in 35 countries.
- In 2011 approximately 147 million customers subscribed to Orange-branded mobile, Internet, or television services.
- Orange is particularly well known in the United Kingdom, where it is considered to be one of the country's most valuable brands.

Orange is a highly recognized brand around the world, as demonstrated by its high rankings on Brand Finance's Global 500 list and the BrandZ Top 100 Most Valuable Global Brands. It is also among the top handful of the most valuable global telecommunications brands. Its parent company, France Telecom, had operations in 35 countries and 226 million customers at the end of 2011. Approximately 147 million of those customers subscribed to Orange-branded mobile, Internet, or television services.

Orange is especially well known in Europe, but it also enjoys strong brand awareness in parts of Africa, the Middle East, the Caribbean, and Asia. In the United Kingdom, where the brand originated, Orange enjoys top-of-mind awareness. It is also considered to be one of the country's most valuable brands. Brand Finance affords Orange the number 5 ranking on its UK Top 50 list of the most valuable brands in the United Kingdom. The Orange name also gains wider recognition through Orange Business Services, providing telecommunication services to multinational companies.

BRAND OUTLOOK

- In 2010 the Orange brand was merged with the T-Mobile brand to create the new company Everything Everywhere.
- In 2012 Orange began exploring opportunities to expand to new markets, with the first country being South Africa.

Even though the brand was launched in the United Kingdom, Orange faced a number of challenges in its home country because of the creation of a 50-50 joint venture between France Telecom and Deutsche Telekom that brought together Orange with the mobile telephone competitor T-Mobile. The transaction was completed in 2010 and resulted in a new company called Everything Everywhere, which elected to keep both the Orange and T-Mobile brands. The plan was to allow both brands to maintain and grow their distinct identities.

Orange and T-Mobile attempted to coexist, in some cases marketing their brands together. The situation grew more complicated, however, when Everything Everywhere unveiled yet another brand in September 2012. Called EE, it was created to operate on a new fourth-generation (4G) network and act as Everything Everywhere's high-speed service brand. Again, Orange and T-Mobile were expected to maintain their own identities and unique propositions. The role of Orange was to serve as a brand for third-generation monthly subscribers, while T-Mobile became more of a value-oriented brand.

Everything Everywhere was expected to urge its customers to upgrade to the more expensive EE service. By 2014 EE's 4G network was expected to be available to 98 percent of the United Kingdom. If most of Everything Everywhere's customer base eventually transferred to the 4G network, there was a question whether the Orange and T-Mobile brands would remain viable. Orange was clearly the more valuable of the two legacy brands, and as of 2012 it was more valuable than the nondescript EE brand. In the future, Orange might face elimination in the country of its birth. However, it might prove so valuable a brand that it might supplant EE as Everything Everywhere's premiere brand.

From an international perspective, Orange continued to serve as France Telecom's primary consumer brand. In August 2012 a new unit was formed by France Telecom to nurture the Orange brand in countries where there were no current operations. The first country to be targeted was South Africa, where Orange began sponsoring major sporting events to lay the groundwork for possible entry into the market. Because of such efforts, Orange is likely to grow even more valuable in the years ahead as France Telecom remains aggressive in introducing the brand in new markets around the world.

FURTHER READING

Alarcon, Camille. "T-Mobile and Orange Face New Challenge." *MarketingWeek*. September 8, 2009.

Brand Finance. "Global 500 2012." *Brandirectory*. Accessed January 24, 2013. http://brandirectory.com/league_tables/table/global-500-2012.

Carter, Ben. "Brand Health Check: Orange." *Marketing*, April 21, 2004.

"France Telecom S.A." *International Directory of Company Histories*. Ed. Jay P. Pederson. Vol. 99. Detroit, MI: St. James Press, 2009.

"France Telecom to Adopt Orange as Global Brand." *Marketing*, September 1, 2005.

McGill, Adrienne. "Orange Driven by Zest for Brighter Future." *News Letter* (Belfast, Northern Ireland), October 3, 2000.

"Orange: A Bright Future?" *Marketing*, October 24, 2001.

"Orange Man Beats the Drum." *Sunday Business* (London), June 4, 2000.

"Orange and T-Mobile to Rework Brand Alignment." *Marketing*, March 16, 2011.

O'Reilly, Lara. "EE Launch Casts Doubts over Orange and T-Mobile Brands." *MarketingWeek*, September 2012.

Shearman, Sarah. "EE's Top Marketers Discuss 'Magnificent' Brand Launch and 'Churlish' Rivals." *Marketing*, September 11, 2012.

PANASONIC

—■—

BRAND ORIGINS

- Company was founded as Matsushita Electric Industrial Co. in Japan in 1918 to manufacture electric plugs.
- National was Matsushita's first brand, introduced in 1925.
- The Panasonic brand was coined in 1955 for audio speakers.
- The Technics brand was introduced in 1965 for upper-end stereo equipment.
- Panasonic was adopted as a corporate brand in 2008.

For many years, Panasonic was just one of the brands controlled by Japan's Matsushita Electric Industrial Co., Ltd. The origins of the company date to 1918 when 23-year-old Konosuke Matsushita quit his job in a light bulb factory in Osaka, Japan, to start a company with his brother-in-law to manufacture electric plugs. After diversifying into the production of bicycle lights, he registered the National brand name for his new product line in 1925. As Matsushita applied the brand to a host of consumer appliances over the ensuing decades, National became one of Japan's best known brands.

While Matsushita prospered during Japan's military buildup in the 1930s and World War II, it faced the daunting challenge of rebuilding after Japan's defeat. Only support from unionized labor allowed Konosuke Matsushita to remain as chairman, after the American occupation authority had originally demanded his resignation because of his support for Japan's war effort. The company revived the National brand in Japan during the postwar years and applied it to such new product lines as washing machines, refrigerators, vacuum cleaners, and televisions. Matsushita also looked to new markets, in particular the United States, which Konosuke Matsushita visited for the first time in 1951.

During the 1950s, Matsushita began producing audio speakers, which led to the creation of a new brand. The prefix "pan," meaning "all" or "every," was joined with "sonic," for "sound," to create "Panasonic." The brand, introduced in 1955, was used in Japan, and in the 1960s it became well known in North America and Europe. In 1965 Matsushita introduced another brand, Technics, for high-end speakers. Initially used exclusively in Japan, the Technics name soon gained international currency.

Matsushita maintained its portfolio of three brands into the next century. Although they all enjoyed individual success, the combination of three brands and a parent company of a different name resulted in confusion among consumers. As a result, in 2008 Matsushita unified its business under its best-known international brand. Matsushita Electric was renamed Panasonic Corporation, while the National and Technics brands were retired in favor of the Panasonic corporate brand. In this way, the company hoped to be better equipped to compete against such rivals as Sony, Hitachi, and Samsung.

BRAND ELEMENTS
- Original meaning of the Panasonic name was lost over time.
- "Panasonic" is colored blue in the corporate logo.
- "Ideas for life" is the Panasonic slogan.
- "Ideas for life" also serves as an advertising tagline.

The Panasonic name no longer maintains its original connection to audio speakers. The company continues to produce audio products, but "Panasonic," unfettered to its original purpose, is also applied to a wide variety of consumer electronic products. An array of home appliances, beauty and healthcare products, and products and services catering to the business market also bear the Panasonic brand. In the company logo, the Panasonic name is rendered in upper- and lower-case letters in simple block letters, using a distinctive shade of blue. The same unobtrusive graphic is also found on the company's various products.

Another important brand element is the slogan "ideas for life." When used as part of the corporate logo, the phrase is depicted in gray, lower-case letters. It is centered beneath "Panasonic," and by way of color and placement maintains a secondary position to the corporate name. The "ideas for life" phrase also serves as a tagline for Panasonic advertisements. The Panasonic slogan suggests another important brand element: Panasonic products. They are, in effect, ideas for life and serve as the ultimate reflection of the brand.

BRAND IDENTITY
- Panasonic still adheres to the management objective laid out by its founder in 1929.
- The "ideas for life" slogan simplifies Konosuke Matsushita's vision.
- Panasonic's brand promise is to enrich the lives of its customers around the world.
- Panasonic products are the ultimate embodiment of Panasonic's brand identity.
- Panasonic seeks to be a leading green company as a way to reinforce its identity.

As a global company that appeals to customers in a variety of cultures, Panasonic embraces an expansive vision, as reflected by the company's stated management objective: "We will devote ourselves to the progress and development of society and the well-being of people through our business activities, thereby enhancing the quality of life throughout the world." Given that Konosuke Matsushita crafted this statement in 1929, it was a remarkable elucidation of Panasonic's enduring brand identity even before the Panasonic name was created.

The "ideas for life" slogan is essentially a refined version of Matsushita's vision, and it remains at the heart of Panasonic's brand identity, as well as its history. Starting with electric plugs, Konosuke Matsushita was devoted to the manufacture of practical, everyday products. While Panasonic ultimately manufactured industrial products, the core focus remained on consumer products, and the company kept up with consumer needs to meet its brand promise of enriching the lives of its customers around the world. The slogan implies that the source of product ideas comes from the close observation of daily life, and that the products themselves will better the lives of Panasonic customers. Moreover, there is a suggestion of longevity: that Panasonic products will last a lifetime. The further implication, and brand promise, is that Panasonic products are of the highest quality and able to withstand the rigors of everyday life. The greatest proof of this proposition is, of course, the products themselves.

To reinforce the idea that Panasonic is a trusted brand across cultures, the company advertises in many languages. More importantly, the advertisements depict everyday people from these cultures, interacting with Panasonic products in a way that enriches the lives they lead. From a global perspective, Panasonic seeks to demonstrate a commitment to the improvement of all lives by pursuing environmental initiatives. In light of global warming, the company seeks to become an industrial leader in creating a "green revolution." The company has made a public pledge to make the environment central to all of its business endeavors, and it set a goal of becoming the No. 1 green innovation company in the electronics industry by the time it celebrates its 100th anniversary in fiscal 2019. In keeping with that aspiration, Panasonic pledges to promote lifestyles "with virtually zero CO_2 emissions all throughout the world."

BRAND STRATEGY
- Three brand names unconnected to the parent company caused confusion with consumers.
- Because manufacturing divisions and regional operations were given marketing latitude, there was no consistency to Panasonic's branding.

- The "Panasonic — just slightly ahead of our time" tagline provided little if any brand lift.
- North American unit crafted the "ideas for life" tagline.
- Panasonic adopted as a unified corporate brand in 2008.

Throughout much of its history, Matsushita Electric Industrial Co. applied a loose hand to its brand strategy. The company's first brand, National, was far from distinctive and applied to whatever products Matsushita Electric had to offer. The National logo of the 1930s featured lightning bolts within a globe, along with the Japanese spelling of National, creating a general association with electrical products but little more. In the 1950s, the National logo was updated, with the globe of the 1930s placed within a large, block-lettered "N." More importantly, Matsushita Electric coined the Panasonic name for the export market during this period. The original capitalization of "PanaSonic" placed emphasis on the individual parts of the brand name to reinforce the connection to sound. In the 1960s Panasonic was rendered in all capital letters, and the following decade the contemporary upper- and lower-case spelling of Panasonic was adopted.

It was also in the 1960s that the Technics brand was introduced for high-end speakers sold in Japan. The brand would then be extended to international markets, but unlike National and Panasonic, its use was limited to stereo systems and components. None of the three brands reinforced the others or Matsushita Electric. Because of the upper-end market to which it appealed, the Technics brand created the impression that Panasonic products, in contrast, were down-market and of lower quality. Most consumers, however, were not aware of the corporate connection between the two brands and were simply confused or unaware of Matsushita Electric's brand strategy.

Much of this brand confusion was the result of Matsushita Electric's traditional policy of allowing manufacturing divisions and geographic operations to pursue their own marketing efforts with little regard for brand consistency. Branding at the Matsushita Electric units was little more than deciding where to place the logo in a marketing piece. At any one time, there might be 20 different taglines in use around the world. The most memorable slogan, "Panasonic — just slightly ahead of our time," was hardly a rallying cry. There was little wonder that in the eyes of most consumers Panasonic was viewed as a second-tier brand compared to Sony, despite the notable achievements of Matsushita Electric's engineers and the high quality of products carrying the Panasonic, Technics, and National labels. Because Matsushita Electric spent far less on marketing than its competitors, and what money it spent was uncoordinated, whatever brand equity Panasonic had to offer was negligible.

It was Matsushita Electric Corp. of America that in 1997 began the process of bringing clarity to the Panasonic brand, at least for its region, by engaging a brand consultancy for the first time in corporate history. Working with Landor Associates, the American marketing team took stock of the Panasonic brand and realized that it lacked a strong emotional connection to customers, especially younger ones. In 1999 the division's brand marketing group, armed with the results of its research, began the process of developing a formal brand repositioning. The group eventually drew on the words of Konosuke Matsushita, distilling them down to the tagline "ideas for life."

Matsushita Electric Corp. of America introduced the new tagline in the fall of 2002 and launched a US$100 million "Ideas for Life" branding campaign in 2003. The effort began to show results, leading to inquiries from sister divisions in other regions of the world. The tagline was adopted elsewhere, but there was no consistency to the look and little regard for the underlying brand identity contained in the tagline.

In 2004 a new chairman and chief executive officer took the helm at Matsushita Electric. The following year, the North American marketers were brought in to discuss a global branding effort. After a two-year process, Matsushita Electric announced in early 2008 that it was unifying its corporate brand under the Panasonic name and phasing out the Technics and National brands by the end of fiscal 2010. To reinforce its branding strategy, Matsushita Electric also changed its name to Panasonic Corporation. It was a highly unusual step: Japanese companies are usually fiercely loyal to tradition regardless of branding implications. The move by itself was a reflection of the commitment the company was making to the growth of the Panasonic brand.

BRAND EQUITY

- Brand Finance Plc estimates a brand value of US$9.233 billion for Panasonic.
- Interbrand estimates Panasonic's brand value at US$5.765 billion.
- Panasonic ranked No. 94 on Brand Finance's Global 500 in 2012.
- Panasonic is considered the world's 65th most valuable brand, according to Interbrand.

For many years, determining the value of the Panasonic brand to Matsushita Electric was especially difficult. There was overlap between Panasonic and sister brands National and Technics, and there was no consistent use of the brand between product categories or geographic markets. That confusion began to lift in 2008 when Matsushita Electric adopted the Panasonic Corporation name, and Panasonic began to take its place as a truly global brand.

In 2012 brand evaluation consultancy Brand Finance Plc, employing a proprietary methodology to assign a monetary value to a brand, estimated the worth of the Panasonic brand at US$9.233 billion, which garnered it 94th place on Brand Finance's Global 500, 2012, list of the world's most valuable brands. The brand had actually ranked higher in 2011, however, reaching the No. 64 position on the Global 500. The earthquake that devastated Japan in 2011 had severely harmed Panasonic's business because of disrupted supplies and other problems. As a result, the Panasonic brand lost value even as its long-term potential continued to grow.

Another leading brand consultancy, Interbrand, also ranks Panasonic high on its list of the world's most valuable brands. Using its own method of measuring the monetary value of a brand, Interbrand estimates Panasonic to be worth US$5.765 billion, placing it No. 65 on the Interbrand list of the world's most valuable brands in 2012.

BRAND AWARENESS

- The Panasonic brand is promoted by about 600 corporate entities around the world.
- Panasonic enjoys strong brand awareness with general consumers as well as the business community.
- While Panasonic is one of the world's most valuable brands, the company recognizes that it still needs to increase brand awareness.

With its parent company operating globally through about 600 subsidiaries, Panasonic is a well-respected brand around the world. In the Reputation Institute's 2012 RepTrak survey, Panasonic ranked as the fourteenth most reputable company in the world. It enjoys strong brand awareness in the consumer electronics field, where it is a major manufacturer of televisions, blue-ray disc and DVD players, digital cameras, and audio system. A 2012 Harris Equitrend poll of U.S. consumers ranked Panasonic as the fourth-best consumer electronics brand, behind Sony, Samsung, and LG. While the Panasonic brand is also well known in other consumer product categories, most consumers do not appreciate the breadth of the brand's products and services. Panasonic's scope is so far-reaching there is virtually no corner of the world the brand does not touch and few sectors of the global economy in which it does not participate. In the summer of 2012, Panasonic Corporation of North America launched a new brand awareness campaign to call more attention to Panasonic's scope, a tacit admission that recognition of the brand was still lacking.

BRAND OUTLOOK

- Panasonic has enjoyed strong growth in its brand value since the 2008 corporate branding initiative.

- Most consumers around the world are still unaware of the scope of Panasonic's products and services.
- Panasonic is already regarded as one of the leading green companies in the world and is likely to improve its standing.

For a well-established brand, Panasonic retains a great deal of unused potential, due in large measure to improper nurturing of the brand over the course of many years. The crafting of the "ideas for life" slogan, the adoption of Panasonic as a corporate brand in 2008, and the elimination of sister brands were strong first steps in tapping the full value of the Panasonic brand. The earthquake that devastated Japan lowered the value of the brand and hindered its growth somewhat. But Panasonic, while in the early stages of developing a consistent approach to communicating the brand, appears to be making progress. In some respects, the lack of a clear brand message throughout its history played to the benefit of the parent company. The Panasonic name was well known, but what the brand stood for was unclear in the minds of many consumers. They were also unaware of the wide range of products and services Panasonic had to offer. With something of a blank slate, Panasonic was given greater latitude in crafting a desired image around the "ideas for life" proposition. In addition, Panasonic would likely enjoy success in casting itself as the top green company in the consumer electronics field. Already Panasonic was listed No. 6 on Interbrand's 2012 Best Global Green Brands. After about a century in operation, Panasonic Corporation appeared to be finally hitting its stride in building what was already a valuable brand.

FURTHER READING

Brand Finance. "Global 500 2012." *Brandirectory*. Accessed December 26, 2012. http://brandirectory.com/league_tables/table/global-500-2012.

Ebenkamp, Becky, and Kenneth Hein. "Panasonic Has 'Ideas' for Lara Croft, MLS (Tie-ins)." *Brandweek*, March 31, 2003.

Gregory, James R., and Timothy Robinson. "Matsushita out, Panasonic Welcomes a New Brand." *Wiglaf Journal*, September 2008.

Hein, Kenneth. "Panasonic Puts $50m into 'Fascinating' Push." *Brandweek*, May 10, 2004.

"Matsushita Electric Industrial Co., Ltd." *International Directory of Company Histories*. Ed. Tina Grant. Vol. 64. Detroit, MI: St. James Press, 2008.

"Panasonic to Unveil New Brand Strategy." *Economic Times*, July 11, 2003.

Schmitt, Bernd H., and David L. Rogers. *Handbook on Brand and Experience Management*. Northhampton, MA: Edward Elgar Publishing, 2008.

"2012 Ranking of the Top 100 Brands." Interbrand. Accessed December 26, 2012. http://www.interbrand.com/en/best-global-brands/2012/Best-Global-Brands-2012.aspx

PÃO DE AÇÚCAR

BRAND ORIGINS

- Grupo Pão de Açúcar, which began as a bakery in 1948, takes its name from a famous mountain in Rio de Janeiro, Brazil.
- From the 1950s through the 1970s, Pão de Açúcar opened additional bakeries, supermarkets, and Jumbo hypermarkets in such locations as Brazil, Portugal, and Angola.
- Today's Grupo Pão de Açúcar stores include the store chains Extra Hiper, Extra Supermercado,

Mini Mercado Extras, Drogaria Extras, and Posto Extras.
- Other Grupo Pão de Açúcar enterprises include the Pontofrio and Casas Bahia general merchandise stores, online retailing sites, and the wholesaler Assai.
- In 2012 Grupo Pão de Açúcar had more than 1,800 stores and more than 140,000 employees.

The name Grupo Pão de Açúcar is an appropriate name for a Brazilian company. Pão de Açúcar is a famous mountain in Rio de Janeiro. By using the name Grupo Pão de Açúcar, the company reminds people of the mountain and thus the company's country of origin. The English translation for Pão de Açúcar is Sugarloaf Mountain. Since Pão de Açúcar began as a bakery, the Sugarloaf name suits the company well for yet another reason.

Portuguese immigrant Valentim Dos Santos Diniz founded the Pão de Açúcar bakery in São Paolo, Brazil, in 1948. He opened additional branches throughout Brazil in the 1950s and 1960s. The fledgling company also opened Brazilian supermarkets, the first Brazilian hypermarket, Jumbo (in 1971), and even automotive dealerships, auto parts stores, and travel agencies. It also introduced its private brand during this time. Internationally, it opened stores in Portugal as well as a Jumbo hypermarket in Angola. The company would eventually sell its interest in its Jumbo stores. It also once owned other enterprises, including the Sandiz department store chain.

Today, Grupo Pão de Açúcar encompasses different types of stores under its Extra brand. These include Extra Hiper, a chain of hypermarkets. A hypermarket combines a department store and a supermarket under one roof. The group's other food retailers include the supermarket chain

Extra Supermercado as well as Mini Mercado Extra, a chain of smaller markets with a more limited selection of foods. Drogaria Extra stores are drugstores, and the Posto Extra chain combines gas stations with convenience stores.

Grupo Pão de Açúcar acquired the Brazilian Pontofrio stores in 2009. Pontofrios sell a wide range of goods. The store name comes from the Portuguese translation of Coldpoint, a line of refrigerators the stores once imported from the American company Sears Roebuck & Co. Other recent Grupo Pão de Açúcar acquisitions include the supermarket chains CompreBem and Senda. The company enlarged its retailing group even more when it acquired the Casas Bahia chain of general merchandise stores in 2010. Other parts of Grupo Pão de Açúcar include the wholesaler Assai and online retailing sites related to its brick and mortar stores. These holdings add up to more than 1,800 stores with more than 140,000 employees.

BRAND ELEMENTS

- The hills in Pão de Açúcar's logo represent Sugarloaf Mountain, and their transparent green colors refer to the chain's fresh food.
- Logos for Grupo Pão de Açúcar's Extra stores include a red square with the word "extra" in white as well as a red and blue pennant shape.
- Another Grupo Pão de Açúcar company, Pontofrio ("cold spot"), uses an image of a penguin as part of its logo.
- The logo for CompreBem, another Grupo Pão de Açúcar supermarket chain, features the letters C and B with a heart drawn between them.

With all of its stores and brands, Grupo Pão de Açúcar has several brand elements. Visual elements of Pão de Açúcar include its logo, which features the name in green below a dark green transparent hill shape that overlaps a lighter green transparent hill shape. These shapes are known as *morrinhos*, or little hills. The morrinhos' green colors and transparency reflect the company's fresh food, as noted by Pão de Açúcar executive José Roberto Tambasco. He added that the logo's morrinhos represent the "reliability and quality" of the brand. These morrinhos represent a play on words, since Pão de Açúcar shares its name with the famous Sugarloaf Mountain in Rio de Janeiro.

Individual stores within Grupo Pão de Açúcar have their own identifying characteristics. The Extra stores use a red square with the lowercase word "extra" in white for their logos. A red and blue pennant shape appears above the word "extra" in this logo. The words "Supermercado", "Hiper", "Drogaria", or "Posto" also appear in the red square logo to identify the individual business in question.

The red and blue pennant shape also appears in the logo of Mini Mercado Extra markets, while the stores of Pontofrio, which means "cold spot" in English, use an image of a penguin drawing as part of their logo. Pão de Açúcar's CompreBem supermarket chain's evocative logo includes the letters *C* and *B* with a heart drawn between them. These logos are some of the many ways Grupo Pão de Açúcar visually represents itself.

BRAND IDENTITY

- A Grupo Pão de Açúcar website describes the company's commitment to humbleness, discipline, determination and grit, and emotional balance.
- "The recipe for happiness is yours. Some of the ingredients are Pão de Açúcar" is the message of a 2010 Grupo Pão de Açúcar advertising campaign.
- One Grupo Pão de Açúcar store chain, Casas Bahia, allows customers to pay for purchases in installments, which encourages customer loyalty.
- Grupo Pão de Açúcar awards points to customers that can be applied toward the purchase of goods and services, another example of the brand's customer focus.

Pão de Açúcar's mission to serve its customers is based on a number of values. According to a Pão de Açúcar website, these values include a commitment to humbleness, discipline, determination and grit, and emotional balance. These commitments are joined to other company interests, including technology, capital, and sustainability. It has demonstrated these interests through words (its promotional campaigns) and deeds (its services and other offerings).

Positive customer emotions are at the heart of a Pão de Açúcar 2010 advertising campaign. Stressing happiness and simple pleasures, this campaign used the slogan "A receita para ser feliz é sua. Alguns dos ingredientes estão no Pão de Açúcar," which translates as "The recipe for happiness is yours. Some of the ingredients are Pão de Açúcar." According to this campaign, then, Pão de Açúcar is a brand that can bring happiness to customers' lives.

Pão de Açúcar stores strive to make their customers happy through various programs. At Casas Bahia, customers may pay for their purchases in small installments over a period of time. This is convenient for customers and establishes a relationship between the stores and the customers, who revisit the stores to make their payments. This arrangement establishes Pão de Açúcar as a sensitive, compassionate brand that is aware of customers and their circumstances and willing to make accommodations.

Like other retailers around the world, Grupo Pão de Açúcar offers customers an incentive system. Known as Pão de Açúcar Mais, "mais" meaning "more" in English, this program awards customers points that correspond to the amounts of money they spend. These points can be used toward the purchase of various goods and services. This is another example of the Pão de Açúcar brand's interest in customers, and not coincidentally, another way it encourages customers to revisit the store in the future.

BRAND STRATEGY

- More than 1,200 health, personal care, and home products are sold under Grupo Pão de Açúcar's private Taeq brand.
- The Grupo Pão de Açúcar private Qualitá brand includes more than 1,300 food, beverage, hygiene, cleaning, and houseware products and the Qualitá Kids food line.
- Pão de Açúcar exports its private brands to other companies as well.
- After buying the CompreBem and Senda supermarket chains, Grupo Pão de Açúcar changed the names of many stores to Extra Supermercado.

Due to its numerous stores and their varied logos, Pão de Açúcar has connections to several brands. It also has private store brands. The Taeq private brand is a line of more than 1,200 products related to health, personal care, and the home. Qualitá is a private brand that began in 2008. It encompasses more than 1,300 food, beverage, hygiene, and cleaning products, as well as housewares, and it also includes the Qualitá Kids food line for children. Started in 2000, the private brand Club des Sommeliers is a line of wines from all over the world.

These products appear in numerous Pão de Açúcar stores. The company also exports products to other companies, including other companies belonging to its parent corporation, Groupe Casino. Such product distribution has broadened the company's reach and has further expanded Pão de Açúcar's brand identity.

The company has also expanded its brand through name changes. It gave the Extra Supermercado name to many of its newly acquired CompreBem and Senda stores. This adds to the already sizable number of Extra stores in different formats and repeats and reinforces the Extra brand name.

BRAND EQUITY

- A 2012 report stated that Pão de Açúcar enjoyed an 18 percent share of the Brazilian retail market.
- Interbrand's "Best Brazilian Brands 2011" ranked Pão de Açúcar the 22nd best brand in Brazil.
- *Forbes* magazine named Grupo Pão de Açúcar one the world's 2000 largest global public companies.

Pão de Açúcar enjoyed an 18 percent share of the Brazilian retail market, according to a 2012 report by Thomas White Global Investing. This report added that French competitor Carrefour had 14.5 percent of this market, while Walmart Brazil enjoyed a 12 percent share.

Not surprisingly, Pão de Açúcar has a large presence in its native country. In 2011 Interbrand Brazil's "Best Brazilian Brands 2011," a survey of thousands of consumers and buyers, ranked Pão de Açúcar the 22nd best Brazilian brand, citing the company's commitment to its customers, health, and other causes.

Its market share has made Pão de Açúcar a powerful international brand. In 2012 the company appeared in *Forbes* magazine's Global 2000, a list of the largest global public companies.

BRAND AWARENESS

- In 1997 Grupo Pão de Açúcar joined the New York Stock Exchange, the first Brazilian retailer to list American depositary receipts on the exchange.
- A poll published in 2012 reported that middle-class Brazilian consumers named Casas Bahia their favorite brand for retail electronics.
- Large numbers of diverse stores and their distribution across Brazil have made Extra and Pão de Açúcar well-known brands.
- The Reputation Institute named Pão de Açúcar the world's 40th most reputable company in 2007.

Brazilian consumers know about and enjoy Pão de Açúcar brands. For example, middle-class Brazilians named Casas Bahia their favorite brand for retail electronics, according to results of a poll published in 2012.

Size, variety, and geography have contributed to brand awareness for Pão de Açúcar and its stores. For example, the Extra brand represents multiple chains of different types of stores. These stores appear in states across Brazil, their numbers and geographical dispersal contributing to the widespread success of the company's multiple brands.

Pão de Açúcar has also enjoyed a good reputation along with this high brand awareness. The Reputation Institute's "RepTrak 200" ranks the reputation of the world's largest companies and incorporates customer ratings from the companies' home countries. Pão de Açúcar has appeared on this multiple times, placing 40th on this list in 2007.

BRAND OUTLOOK

- In 2012 the French company Groupe Casino took over the majority of Grupo Pão de Açúcar's shares, raising the international profile of both companies.
- Cuts in Brazil's interest rates and consumer taxes helped boost sales and stock prices for Pão de Açúcar in 2012.
- Pão de Açúcar and other Brazilian supermarkets held 80 percent of the food retailing market in 2012.

In 2012 the French company Groupe Casino took over the majority of Grupo Pão de Açúcar's shares. This move transferred power from the company's founders, the Diniz family, to Groupe Casino. Groupe Casino's retailers include hypermarkets, supermarkets, convenience stores, discount stores, organic stores, and online retailers. These stores are in France as well as various countries in South America, Southeast Asia, and the Indian Ocean region. Grupo Pão de Açúcar's involvement with Groupe Casino raises the international profile of both companies and illustrates the fact that big business is global business.

Conditions closer to home also affected Pão de Açúcar in 2012. Brazil's president cut interest rates and consumer taxes, which boosted sales for Pão de Açúcar and other Brazilian retailers, who enjoyed a 10 percent sales increase through August 2012. The price of Pão de Açúcar's stock also rose dramatically, experiencing a 39 percent increase that year. During that year, Pão de Açúcar and other companies awaited other factors that could bring further economic benefits to the country, such as Brazil's hosting of soccer's World Cup in 2014 and Rio de Janeiro's hosting of the 2016 Summer Olympics.

Other economic factors have influenced Pão de Açúcar. A 2012 report by Thomas White Global Investing valued Brazil's retail market at an estimated US$230 billion and noted that the country experienced a 40 percent increase in its gross domestic profit (GDP) per capita in the previous eight years. The report also named the rise of rise of Brazil's middle class and the expansion of consumer credit as other factors fueling the highly competitive field of Brazilian food retailing. It noted that supermarkets like Pão de Açúcar contributed to 80 percent of the country's food sales. Since Pão de Açúcar accounted for 18 percent of all retail sales in Brazil, it is clearly a prominent brand.

FURTHER READING

"Best Brazilian Brands 2011." Interbrand Brazil. Accessed November 20, 2012. http://www.interbrand.com/Libraries/Branding_Studies/Best_Brazilian_Brands_2011.sflb.ashx.

DuPont. "Packaging That Reduces Food Waste Captures Top DuPont Packaging Award." May 10, 2012. Accessed November 21, 2012. http://www2.dupont.com/Packaging_Resins/en_US/whats_new/article20120511_dupont_award_winners.html.

Ferraz Magalhães, Gladys. "De Nestlé a Fiat, conheça as marcas favoritas do consumidor da classe C." *InfoMoney*, September 5, 2012.

Grupo Pão de Açúcar. "Extra." Accessed November 21, 2012. http://www.grupopaodeacucar.com.br/nossas-lojas/extra/extra.htm.

———. "Missão, Visão, Valores e Pilares." Accessed November 21, 2012. http://www.gpari.com.br/conteudo_en.asp?idioma=1&conta=44&tipo=29949.

Halasz, Robert. "Companhia Brasiliera de Distribuiçao." *International Directory of Company Histories*. Ed. Tina Grant. Vol. 76. Detroit, MI: St. James Press, 2006.

Leite, Julia, and Denyse Godoy. "Pao de Acucar Driving Retail Rally on Stimulus: Corporate Brazil." Bloomberg, October 31, 2012. Accessed February 20, 2013. http://www.bloomberg.com/news/2012-10-31/pao-de-acucar-driving-retail-rally-on-stimulus-corporate-brazil.html.

Neuwirth, Benjamin. "Marketing Channel Strategies in Rural Emerging Markets: Unlocking Business Potential." Northwestern University, Kellogg School of Management, 2012.

"Nova marca: Grupo Pão de Açúcar." *Guia sobre Design*, April 24, 2010.

Pontofrio. "Conheça o Pontofrio." Accessed November 20, 2012. http://www.pontofrio.com.br/&prev=/search%3Fq%3Dpontofrio%26hl%3Den%26tbo%3Dd%26biw%3D1440%26bih%3D754&sa=X&ei=IgCsUNbiA7S80QHPy4DoDg&ved=0CDEQ7gEwAA.

Reputation Institute. "LEGO and IKEA Top 29 Country Study of the Reputations of the World's Largest Companies. AWB and Halliburton Least Respected Internationally." May 21, 2007. Accessed February 20, 2013. http://www.reputationinstitute.com/events/RepTrak_Pulse2007_PressRelease_May2007_USltr.pdf.

Thomas White Global Investing. "Retail Sector in Brazil: Riding the Wave of Middle Class Growth and Consumer Credit Boom." March 2012. Accessed November 20, 2012. http://www.thomaswhite.com/explore-the-world/bric-spotlight/brazil-retail.aspx.

PEARSON

—■—

BRAND ORIGINS

- Pearson, which traces its roots back to 1844, began as a highly diversified company with interests in sewerage, construction, oil, electricity, manufacturing, and finance.
- Pearson's foray into publishing began after World War I, when it acquired complete control of London newspaper the *Westminster Gazette*.
- Pearson acquired the *Financial Times* newspaper in 1957, and the Financial Times (FT) Group is now one of Pearson's three main divisions.

- Pearson Education, the second of the company's three divisions, was officially formed in 1998.
- Pearson entered into trade publishing in the 1970s; it combined its consumer publishing imprints to form Penguin Group, its third main division.

Formerly a highly diversified company, Pearson today is a leader in publishing, information, and education solutions. The company's history can be traced back to Samuel Pearson, who became a partner in a building and contracting firm in Huddersfield, England, in 1844. When Samuel's son George joined the firm in 1856, it became S. Pearson & Son. The company provided water supply, drainage, and sewerage facilities to expanding cities, also offering brickmaking, glazed tile, and sanitary pipe services. A third Pearson generation entered the business when Samuel's grandson Weetman Dickinson Pearson (later known as First Viscount Cowdray) joined the company in 1873. Eventually, the company would change its name to the much simpler Pearson.

In the 1870s the growing company began working on contracts outside of England, providing port works, railway construction and tunneling, and water supply and drainage services to several countries. Pearson at that time was particularly active in Mexico, where it completed a number of large and profitable projects. The company also remained active in its home country, working on several projects for the British government and moving its head office to London in 1884.

Entering yet another industry, Pearson established Whitehall Trust Ltd. in 1919 as a finance and issuing house, acquiring a substantial interest in the merchant bank Lazard Brothers & Company that same year. Pearson's operations in the electrical industry in Mexico, South America, and the United Kingdom helped sustain the company when it closed its construction division in the 1920s.

Meanwhile, Pearson was becoming increasingly active in publishing. In 1908 a large syndicate that included Weetman Pearson acquired the *Westminster Gazette*, a London evening newspaper. After World War I, Pearson acquired complete control of the newspaper, converting it into a morning daily. In the 1920s, Pearson also acquired a group of provincial British newspapers that were combined to form the foundation of Westminster Press.

In 1957 Pearson acquired the financial newspaper the *Financial Times*, which, along with several financial periodicals, magazines, and online publications, came to form Pearson's Financial Times (FT) Group, one of the company's three main divisions. Besides its principal publications, the FT Group is a joint owner of BDFM Publishers, which produces the weekly South African business magazine *Financial Mail* and similar publications in the region. The Economist Group, publisher of the *Economist* and other business-focused print media, is also partly owned by Pearson's FT Group.

By 1960 Pearson had abandoned its interests in the electricity industry, and by the 1980s, it had divested its interests in the oil industry as well. In 1968 Pearson acquired the British publisher Longman, adding the company to its publishing arm alongside Westminster Press and the *Financial Times*. In 1988 Pearson acquired math and science publisher Addison-Wesley, merging the company with Longman to create Addison-Wesley Longman. In 1998 Pearson Education, now one of the company's three main divisions, was officially formed by the merger of Addison-Wesley Longman with the newly purchased education division of Simon & Schuster.

Pearson's foray into trade publishing began in the 1970s. In 1969 Pearson went public on the London Stock Exchange, and the following year it acquired Penguin Books, which in 1975 merged with prestigious New York-based publisher Viking Press. Other acquisitions followed, including the 1983 purchases of prominent children's book publishers Grosset & Dunlap and Frederick Warne. Pearson would eventually group these imprints and many others under Penguin Group, its international consumer publishing division.

In the early 21st century Pearson expanded its existing publishing activities into new markets while continuing to acquire new businesses. Most notably, Pearson paid US$2.4 billion for National Computer Systems, a leading U.S. educational testing and data management company, in 2000, establishing in the process what has become the main aim of Pearson's education division. Renamed NCS Pearson, this subsidiary now forms the cornerstone of Pearson Education's goal of creating an integrated education company that connects the home and school by combining educational content, online learning, and enterprise applications. Meanwhile, in big news on the

trade publishing front, in 2012 Pearson announced it had entered into an agreement with Bertelsmann to combine Penguin Group with Random House. Should the deal move forward, the newly formed Penguin Random House would control a quarter of the global book market.

BRAND ELEMENTS

- The Pearson brand is represented by a logo bar, a long, colored bar with "Pearson" at one end and the tagline "Always Learning" at the other.
- Pearson employs strict guidelines for correct use of its logo bar, including exact dimensions and color values.
- The salmon-colored paper of the *Financial Times* print version is widely known, as is the Penguin Group's symbol, a black and white penguin.

The Pearson brand is represented by an element that the company calls a "logo bar." The logo bar is a long, colored bar with "Pearson" appearing at one end and the tagline "Always Learning" at the other. Both text elements appear in white, all-capital letters, although the font size for the word "Pearson" is slightly larger. The logo bar is used at the top or bottom of Pearson applications, and it can appear in one of four approved colors, which include specific shades of blue, green, orange, and purple. Through the Pearson website, users can download and view specific guidelines on the correct use of the logo bar, including exact dimensions and placement on the page.

Pearson's three main divisions have their own visual identities, although the branding for Pearson Education closely mirrors that of Pearson's overall corporate branding. The Financial Times (FT) Group uses the name of the company in black, all-capital letters, which fittingly appear somewhat like the title of a newspaper. Additionally, the print version of the *Financial Times* newspaper is widely recognized for the salmon-colored paper it's printed on. Pearson's Penguin Group also employs a fitting image, a black and white penguin in an orange oval. The same orange and black colors are used on Penguin Group's books and websites, establishing a consistent visual image for the trade book publisher.

BRAND IDENTITY

- "Always learning" is Pearson's slogan, tying the brand to education and information.
- The Pearson-published 2012 report "The Learning Curve." discussed global education and reflected Pearson's interest in the field.
- Pearson and Penguin's We Give Books initiative reinforces the company's commitment to transmitting information.

Pearson's slogan, "Always Learning," is an appropriate one for the publisher, since it succinctly describes several of its brands and products. The brand contains the numerous publications of the Financial Times Group, the publications and educational centers of Pearson education, and the myriad publishing imprints of Penguin Random House. These brands provide a lot of information in several areas. "Always Learning" conveys a double meaning: the brand can help customers continue to learn, and the company itself is always learning and striving for ways to improve itself.

A Pearson publication that symbolized the brand and its interests was the Pearson-published 2012 report "The Learning Curve." Written by the Economist Intelligence Unit (EIU), a group of international analysts affiliated with the news magazine the *Economist*, the report included extensive data and interviews with international educators, political figures, and others. Featured prominently on the Pearson home page, the report demonstrated Pearson's international scope, its many publications and affiliations, and the brand's interests in education and information.

The Pearson Foundation and Penguin have also transmitted information through another effort, the We Give Books initiative. As the name says, the initiative gives books in various ways. It allows Internet users to read some books for free online and has donated books to readers and libraries around the world. The initiative uses the penguin logo of the Penguin brand accompanied by a stack of orange, white, and black books—the colors of the Penguin brand. We Give Books, then, reminds people of the familiar visual elements of the Penguin brand and connects the Penguin and Pearson brands to the transmission of information and philanthropic endeavors.

BRAND STRATEGY

- According to Pearson, its strategy for growth involves "[l]ong-term organic investment in content … [d]igital products and services businesses … [i]nternational expansion … [and] efficiency."
- Pearson Campus Ambassadors learn job skills, help college students learn with Pearson products, and help Pearson improve by relaying product feedback.
- Pearson Education, Pearson VUE, the Financial Times Group, and Penguin Random House are all Pearson brands that convey the brand's interest in transmitting information.

On one of its web pages, Pearson describes its goals and strategies. It states that it is working toward becoming "the world's leading learning company, serving the citizens of a brain-based economy wherever and whenever they are learning." To accomplish these goals, Pearson says it will utilize "[l]ong-term organic investment in content … [d]igital products and services businesses … [i]nternational expansion … [and] efficiency." These statements position Pearson as a goal-oriented brand that is technologically aware, globally minded, and skilled in business.

Pearson has also made efforts to demonstrate the brand's interests in information and education. It employs college students as Pearson Campus Ambassadors to assist other students with Pearson technological products and transmit student feedback on these products to Pearson. The Pearson student ambassadors learn job skills while they help students learn by accessing Pearson products. The feedback the ambassadors transmit helps Pearson improve its products. The ambassador program exemplifies Pearson's "Always Learning" slogan, as it allows students and Pearson to learn and improve.

Pearson provides this ability to learn and improve by offering a wide variety of brands under its own name and others. The Pearson Education brand offers textbooks under several imprints, online education websites, university and college websites, and education centers. Pearson VUE, meanwhile, helps administer tests. Both Pearson Education and Pearson VUE are international brands. Other international Pearson-affiliated brands are the Financial Times Group and Penguin Random House. Even though these two brands do not use the Pearson name, they too deal with information. All of these companies help portray Pearson as a brand interested in information and education.

BRAND EQUITY

- Pearson was the world's largest publishing company in 2009, 2010, and 2011, according to *Publishers Weekly*.
- In 2011 Pearson made 67 percent of its profits in North America, 21 percent in Europe, 6 percent in Asia, and 6 percent in other regions.
- North American Education is Pearson's largest business.
- Brand Finance assigned Pearson an estimated brand value of US$2.7 billion in 2012, placing it at number 437 on the Global 500.

Publishers Weekly named Pearson the largest publishing company in the world in 2009, 2010, and 2011. As a reflection of the company's international scope, Pearson's profits in 2011 came from many parts of the world. In that year, the company made 67 percent of its profits in the North American market, 21 percent in Europe, 6 percent in Asia, and 6 percent in other regions. Sales figures from 2011 also showed that Pearson made 11 percent of its profits in developing markets.

North American Education is Pearson's largest business, accounting for £2.6 billion (US$3.2 billion) in sales in 2011. Pearson enjoyed a 37 percent "win rate" (defined by the company as new business based on market share by value) for American school publishing in 2011, up from a win rate of 28 percent for the same market in 2010.

Solid sales figures and an international presence have made Pearson a strong brand. In 2012 Brand Finance assigned Pearson an estimated brand value of US$2.7 billion, ranking it at number 437 on its Global 500 list of top brands for that year. This was a slight fall from 2011, when Brand Finance gave Pearson a brand value of US$2.8 billion and ranked it in the 400th spot on the Global 500. In 2010 Brand Finance ranked Pearson at number 34 on its UK Top 50 list.

BRAND AWARENESS

- As one of the world's largest trade book publishers, Pearson's Penguin Group and its imprints are recognizable to many outside of the publishing industry.
- In 2011 the Bookseller Industry Awards named Penguin Children's Books the children's publisher of the year.
- Pearson divisions Pearson Education and the Financial Times (FT) Group also enjoy strong brand recognition around the world.

In 2012 Kate Wilson of Nosy Crow, an independent British publisher and digital application (app) creator, discussed Pearson's Penguin Group, particularly its plans to merge with Bertelsmann's Random House to form the largest trade book publisher in the world. Wilson noted that Penguin, Puffin, and Ladybird, all imprints of Penguin Group, are "among the few publishing brands that the general public is aware of," adding that those imprints are essentially brands on their own merit. Indeed, in a time of mass consolidation in the publishing industry, Penguin Group is one of the world's "Big Six" publishing companies (or "Big Five," following its merger with Random House), with a name that is recognizable to many outside the industry.

Critical recognition for Penguin Group has accompanied its strong brand recognition. In 2011 the Bookseller Industry Awards, which honor publishers, libraries, and book retailers in the United Kingdom and Ireland, named Penguin Children's Books the children's publisher of the year. Pearson and its divisions also received multiple Bookseller Industry Award nominations in 2012.

Pearson Education, an international leader in nearly every sector of educational publishing, is also widely recognized around the world. This is due largely to the huge number of textbooks, digital technologies, and other learning materials the company produces, in addition to its administering of international tests like the Graduate Management Admission Test (GMAT). Meanwhile, the *Financial Times* newspaper, part of Pearson's Financial Times (FT) Group division, boasted an average daily print and online readership of 2.1 million people worldwide in 2012.

BRAND OUTLOOK

- In 2012 Pearson purchased Author Solutions, which offers self-publishing services to writers.
- In 2012 Pearson's Penguin Group and Bertelsmann's Random House announced plans to merge.
- Pearson Education India announced in 2011 that it hoped to capture 10 percent of the Indian education and school publishing market by 2013.

Pearson has continued to expand in the 21st century. In 2012 it purchased Author Solutions, which helps authors publish, market, and sell their written works. Like other Pearson subsidiaries, Author Solutions consists of a number of divisions, including those providing editing, design, marketing, and retailing.

Pearson's involvement in international mergers and buyouts has also continued. In October 2012 Pearson's Penguin Group announced its plans to merge with Bertelsmann's Random House to create Penguin Random House. Pearson would own 47 percent of this new company, and Bertelsmann would own 53 percent. Combining two of the "Big Six" publishing companies would create the world's largest trade book publisher, giving Penguin Random House control over a quarter of the global book market. Despite concerns that the merger will create an unfair competitive advantage, many expect the deal to go forward, and similar mergers are expected to take place in the years ahead as the declining publishing industry seeks out ways to stay afloat and compete with online giants like Amazon. Writing for the *New York Times Magazine*, Adam Davidson noted that the Big Six may eventually be whittled down to the "Big Three and perhaps one day even the Big One."

Like many companies in the 21st century, Pearson is also looking to expand in developing markets, particularly in India. In recent years Pearson Education India has invested in Indian education solution companies and online education sites. In 2011 Pearson Education India announced its goal of capturing a 10 percent share of the Indian education and school publishing market by 2013.

FURTHER READING

Davidson, Adam. "How Dead Is the Book Business?" *New York Times Magazine*, November 13, 2012.

"The Global 50: The World's Largest Book Publishers, 2012." *Publishers Weekly*, June 25, 2012.

Orbell, John, Christina M. Stansell, and Paul R. Greenland. "Pearson plc." *International Directory of Company Histories*. Ed. Jay P. Pederson. Vol. 103. Detroit, MI: St. James Press, 2009.

Pearson PLC. "Education." Accessed December 6, 2012. http://www.pearson.com/about-us/education.html.

———. "Financial Highlights." Accessed December 3, 2012. http://ar2011.pearson.com/browse/overview/financial-highlights.aspx.

———. "Pearsonapos;s Strategy." Accessed February 14, 2013. http://www.pearson.com/investors/strategy.html.

"Penguin and Random House to Merge in £2.4bn Deal." *Telegraph* (London), October 29, 2012.

Reid, Calvin. "Pearson Acquires Self-Publishing Vendor Author Solutions for $116 Million." *Publishers Weekly*, July 19, 2012.

Shah, Sneha, and Khushboo Narayan. "Pearson Education Eyes Acquisitions, Tie-Up." *Mint*, June 7, 2011. Accessed December 3, 2012. http://www.livemint.com/Companies/KWQ37Ha6PrHriij16IbXPI/Pearson-Education-eyes-acquisitions-tieups.html.

Wilson, Kate. "Penguin Random House." *Nosy Crow Blog*, October 29, 2012. Accessed December 5, 2012. http://nosycrow.com/blog/penguin-random-house.

"Y&R Malaysia's Books for Every Interest." *Campaign Brief Asia*, October 9, 2012. Accessed December 18, 2012. http://www.campaignbrief.com/asia/2012/10/yr-malaysias-books-for-every-i.html.

PEPSI

— ■ —

AT A GLANCE

— ■ —

Brand Synopsis: In opposition to Coca-Cola's time-less appeal, Pepsi is "timely," espousing the attributes of youth, innovation, excitement, and celebrity.

Parent Company: PepsiCo, Inc.

700 Anderson Hill Road

Purchase, New York 10577

United States

http://www.pepsico.com

Sector: Consumer Staples

Industry Group: Food, Beverage & Tobacco

Performance: *Market share*—10 percent.

Principal Competitors: The Coca-Cola Company; Dr. Pepper Snapple Group, Inc.; National Beverage Corp.

BRAND ORIGINS

- Pepsi-Cola was trademarked on June 16, 1903, five years after the name was adopted.
- Years of difficult decisions and poor management led to bankruptcies in 1923 and 1931, but Pepsi emerged with a new focus.
- Pepsi went international in 1934 and was represented in the United States, Canada, Cuba, and England by 1936.
- In 1965 Pepsi began its transformation into a food and beverage conglomerate when it merged with Frito-Lay, Inc.

In 1893 Caleb D. Bradham, a 31-year-old pharmacist, developed his own soft drink syrup made from kola-nut extract. Bradham's intent was to create a soft drink that was both refreshing and delicious. First sold simply as "Brad's Drink" in Bradham's New Bern, North Carolina, drugstore, the carbonated beverage proved quite popular. In 1898 it was renamed "Pepsi-Cola."

During the early 1900s, soda fountain drinks needed a healthy ingredient in order to overcome the negative stigma they carried at the time. The new name was an allusion to one of the cola's main ingredients, pepsin, a digestive enzyme. Its presence allowed Branham to market the product under its first tagline, "Exhilarating, Invigorating, Aids Digestion." The popularity of Pepsi-Cola grew exponentially, requiring Bradham to close his drugstore in 1902 to focus on his growing soft-drink business. Bradham trademarked the Pepsi-Cola name in 1903, and by 1910 the production of his syrup grew to over one million gallons per year.

During World War I, Bradham ran into a road-block when sugar-rationing started. Bradham had to either continue buying sugar and hope the prices would eventually drop or stock up on sugar in case the prices continued to rise. Bradham chose the latter option, but after the war his gamble went sour: rationing was loosened and sugar prices fell. By 1923 Bradham was forced into bankruptcy. Under new management, Pepsi-Cola became National Pepsi-Cola Company in 1928, but this venture also fell into bankruptcy just three years later. Then a partnership developed with future majority-owner Charles Guth that proved to be very beneficial for the company. Guth was the owner of Loft, Inc., a candy and fountain store that had fallen out with Coca-Cola the previous year. This partnership revitalized Pepsi-Cola, and in 1933 Guth obtained a 91 percent ownership of the company.

Under Guth, Pepsi-Cola became an international brand, branching out to Canada in 1934 with the establishment of the Pepsi-Cola Company of Canada. In 1935 Campania Pepsi-Cola de Cuba was established in that country, and in 1936 Pepsi-Cola Ltd. of London, England, opened its doors. The operation in Cuba became a key strategic placement. With sugar rationing reinstituted in the United States during World War II, sugar prices reached all-time highs, but the Pepsi-Cola sugar plantation in Cuba allowed Pepsi to keep the cost of sugar down and profit margins up.

In 1940 Loft, Inc. and National Pepsi-Cola Company merged to become Pepsi-Cola Company, which instituted a board of directors after years of rocky ownership. Pepsi shares were sold for the first time on the New York Stock Exchange in 1941.

Pepsi became more than just a beverage company in 1965 when CEO Donald M. Kendall met Herman Lay, owner of Frito-Lay, Inc. The two companies soon merged, becoming PepsiCo, Inc. Herman Lay retired a few years after the merger, retaining some ownership of his company, but giving control over to Kendall. This marked the first move toward a broadening of the Pepsi brand, which would later include fast-food restaurants such as Taco-Bell, Kentucky Fried Chicken, and Pizza Hut, as well as snack-food brand Quaker.

In 2012 PepsiCo, Inc., was divided into three divisions: PepsiCo American Foods, PepsiCo American Beverages, and PepsiCo International.

BRAND ELEMENTS

- The Pepsi-Cola brand name was simplified to Pepsi in 1962.
- The red, white, and blue Pepsi Globe represents the global audience Pepsi hopes to reach with its products.
- The "Live for Now" marketing campaign launched in May 2012 was Pepsi's first global marketing campaign.

In 1959, while future CEO Donald M. Kendall was visiting the Moscow Trade Fair in Russia to introduce the Pepsi product, he was able to position his good friend, the visiting U.S. Vice President Richard M. Nixon, and Russian Premier Nikita Khrushchev next to one another. While Khrushchev enjoyed a Pepsi, photographers snapped their front-page picture under the caption "Khrushchev Learns to be Sociable," echoing the Pepsi tagline "Be Sociable, Have a Pepsi." This was during a time when other brands refused to do business with the Soviet Union, and it opened up a market as yet untapped by most American companies.

Pepsi-Cola shortened its brand name to Pepsi in 1962 and rolled out its highly successful Pepsi Generation marketing campaign, which was designed to develop a connection with the younger generation of the time. After 30 years, the younger crowd of the 1960s became the older generation, and Pepsi was forced to revitalize its tagline. In 2012 it instituted a "Live for Now" campaign. In its first global marketing effort, Pepsi launched an interactive campaign that enabled fans from all over the world to communicate via "Pepsi Pulse," a digital platform that, according to Pepsi's press release, was to operate in real time, curating and serving up trending pop-culture content, entertainment news, and consumer incentives. "Mi Pepsi" was to target the Hispanic consumers by offering a similar platform to present content relevant to that market.

In 2012 PepsiCo held over 400 patents dating back to 1965 that created such innovations as new designs for bottles and beverage dispensers, new ways to keep beverages cold, and even a way to control the bubble size in a carbonated liquid. The most notable patent Pepsi holds is the design for the red, white, and blue Pepsi Globe, the name of Pepsi's logo.

BRAND IDENTITY

- In 2011 Pepsi's loss of the number-two cola spot and a 0.3 percent drop in market share led to a realignment of brand identity.
- In 2012 Pepsi and Twitter agreed to a year-long partnership in Pepsi's "Live for Now" promotion.
- In 2012 Pepsi planned to establish a more global identity with a television advertising campaign in 40 countries.

Pepsi has long been associated with its competitor Coca-Cola in the "Cola Wars," and much of its identity developed in relation to this competition. While both companies developed into juggernauts of the beverage industry, by 2011, according to a Beverage Digest market-share report, Pepsi had fallen to the number-three soda spot behind both Coca-Cola and Diet Coke. It experienced a 0.3 percent drop in market share in 2011 alone. In 2012 Pepsi CEO Indra Nooyi called for a ceasefire in the Cola Wars. The brand had already obtained much of the athletic beverage market with the purchase of Gatorade, and it owned a plurality of the noncarbonated juice market with Tropicana. Calling an end to the Cola Wars was the next step in revitalizing and broadening a stagnant brand.

In 2012 the soda industry plateaued, resulting in an unsettling reaction from investors in the company and a restructuring of the Pepsi brand. In that year Pepsi inked the largest agreement in the history of Twitter, the social networking website, to initiate a "Live for Now" campaign. This web-heavy marketing campaign furthered the youth-oriented focus Pepsi had become known for since its introduction of the Pepsi Generation campaign in 1963. Pepsi's 2012 marketing strategy includes a 40-country advertising campaign focused on international consumers rather than just U.S. consumers.

BRAND STRATEGY

- Pepsi divested its restaurant holdings in 1997 to Tricon Global Restaurants and focused on the snack food and beverage industries.
- Pepsi Next, released in 2012, was a mid-calorie, low-sugar alternative to Pepsi and Diet Pepsi designed to attract more health-conscious consumers.
- A US$600 million marketing campaign commenced in 2012, covering all PepsiCo brands.
- Pepsi created the Global Beverage Group in 2012 in order to focus its attention on its failing beverage brands.

Starting with the mergers of the 1960s, PepsiCo underwent several different brand strategy changes. The divestments of several of its bottling companies as well as sporting goods businesses and freight lines in the 1980s helped PepsiCo to narrow its focus to the food and beverage industry. In 1997 PepsiCo sold Taco Bell, Kentucky Fried Chicken, and Pizza Hut to Tricon Global Restaurants, Inc., later known as Yum! Brands, Inc. With the divestiture of these three restaurants PepsiCo was able to focus on the snack food and beverage industry. It rebranded itself into three divisions: PepsiCo American Foods, PepsiCo American Beverages, and PepsiCo International. In 2006 Pepsi signed a 25-year agreement to bottle single servings of Ocean Spray–brand juice. In an effort to increase sales in the global market, Pepsi acquired a controlling interest in Russia's largest food and beverage business, Wimm-Bill-Dann, and built a snack and beverage plant in Azov, Russia, in 2009.

In 2012 the soda market leveled out as consumers around the world became more health conscious. Many consumers switched to drinking tea instead of soda. In response, Pepsi released Pepsi Next, a mid-calorie soft drink designed to draw consumers back to the brand. Over the years, Pepsi's mid-calorie soft drinks have gone through several incarnations, including short-lived brands Pepsi XL (launched and discontinued in 1995) and Pepsi Edge (introduced in 2004 and discontinued in 2005).

In May 2012 Pepsi announced a US$600 million marketing campaign that will cover all of their existing brands, including Pepsi Next, in the hopes of regenerating lost business and developing new consumers. Pepsi also teamed up with Wal-Mart stores in the United States in 2012 for in-store taste tests of Pepsi Next.

Also in May 2012 Pepsi drew the attention of Relational Investors LLC, a San Diego, California, activist hedge fund, and its cofounder Ralph Whitworth. Relational Investors bought a small but influential stake in PepsiCo worth US$609 million, and it helped to slow speculation that Pepsi was going to split its food and beverage brands into two separate companies. PepsiCo soon indicated it had no plans to divide the two companies. Looking ahead in its new global marketing campaign, Pepsi sought to add the iconic Michael Jackson to the labels of a billion cans.

Pepsi has been identifying new possibilities by developing a Global Beverage Group focused on the North American, European, Asian, Middle Eastern, and African markets. Pepsi has established divisions dedicated to each of those areas. The Global Beverage Group was to add guidance to counteract the failing Pepsi market. Pepsi was also considering a Global Snacks Group.

BRAND EQUITY

- Pepsi lost a little market share in 2012 but still held the number-two rank in beverages behind Coca-Cola, according to Beverage Digest.
- In 2011 Pepsi was ranked 22nd as an overall global brand, but archrival Coca-Cola was ranked first, according to Interbrand.
- In 2012 PepsiCo-owned Lays was the number-one global food brand, according to the PepsiCo 2012 Annual Report.

According to Ad Age, in 2011 one out of every two soft drinks consumed was marketed by Coca-Cola, while only one out of every four soft drinks was marketed by Pepsi. Beverage Digest lists Pepsi as the world's second-largest carbonated-soft-drink brand, holding a 28.5 percent market share, down slightly from 29.3 percent in 2010. Pepsi's attempts to broaden its products globally had already benefited the brand by producing a 1 percent increase in stock value. According to PepsiCo's 2010 annual report, over 45 percent of Pepsi's business came from international sales.

According to Interbrand's *2011 Ranking of the Top 100 Brands*, PepsiCo ranked 22nd, with a brand value of US$14 billion, whereas Coca-Cola ranked first, with a US$71 billion brand value. Pepsi ranked second in the beverage sector according to the same survey, but only held a US$2 billion edge over the next closest beverage, Nescafé. Brand Finance's *Global 500 2012* ranked Pepsi 38th overall and estimated the brand value at US$17.1 billion; Coca-Cola ranked 8th. According to PepsiCo's 2012 Annual Report, PepsiCo's Lays was ranked as the number-one global food brand.

BRAND AWARENESS

- As of 2012 Pepsi was available in over 200 countries and territories with a multibillion-dollar focus on international marketing.
- In 2012 Pepsi was considered the brand associated with cricket.
- Pepsi ranked fourth in market share in Western Europe in 2012, well behind Coca-Cola.

The Pepsi brand dates back over 100 years, and with the exception of the removal of a digestive aid, the original formula changed very little. PepsiCo had a US$22 billion marketing business worldwide, and the soft drink was available in over 200 countries and territories. The Pepsi brand held a strong presence in the Middle East. In 2011, according to the *Times of India*, Pepsi and Hero Honda were the two brands with the highest consumer awareness. In 2012 Pepsi was also the brand most associated with cricket, one of the world's most popular bat-and-ball sports. Pepsi had good top-of-mind awareness, making Pepsi synonymous with cola drinks in the Middle East and India. As of 2012 Pepsi trailed Coca-Cola, Nestlé, and Danone Groupe in Western Europe, ranking fourth with approximately 4 percent of the overall beverage market in that region. In comparison, Coca-Cola held a commanding 15 percent of the soft drink market.

BRAND OUTLOOK

- According to the PepsiCo 2010 Annual Report, Pepsi planned to try to expand at twice the global GDP growth rate in international revenues by 2013.
- In 2011 Wall Street analysts advised PepsiCo to split into separate food and beverage companies, advice the company had not yet accepted.
- In 2011 and 2012 Pepsi increased its efforts to design products aimed at the eco-friendly and health conscious markets.

In the PepsiCo 2010 Annual Report, the company unveiled almost 50 goals it wanted to achieve from 2011 to 2013, focusing on Performance, Human Sustainability, Environmental Sustainability, and Talent Sustainability. The company planned to grow its international revenues to twice the global GDP growth rate. According to the 2010 Annual Report, Pepsi faced a stagnating global carbonated-soft-drink market and new competition in the global market in the form of carbonated energy drinks,

whose market shares were growing. In 2010, even though PepsiCo assured its investors that it would not divide its beverage and snack brands, Wall Street analysts were advising that very action. Combined with the loss in rank and market share to Diet Coke, this caused great concern among investors.

In 2011 Pepsi continued to try to stay in step with the ever-more environmentally minded consumer market by developing eco-friendly bottles and facilities. Pepsi also increased its global presence with a multibillion-dollar marketing campaign. In 2012 the company strengthened its cola brand by releasing mid-calorie Pepsi Next, which along with Diet Pepsi and sugar-free Pepsi Max served the needs of the more health-conscious consumers. Playing off its popularity in India, Pepsi was to be a sponsor of the 2015 World Cup of Cricket.

FURTHER READING

"Activist Firm Takes $600 Million Stake in PepsiCo." *SeattlePI*, May 15, 2012.

Brand Finance. "Global 500 2012." *Brandirectory*. Accessed July 3, 2012. http://brandirectory.com/league_tables/table/global-500-2012.

Parekh, Rupal, and Natalie Zmuda. "Pepsi Shops Not Feeling the Love as Marketer Trims Their Ranks 65%." *Advertising Age*, February 13, 2012.

"Pepsi Launches First Global Campaign, 'Live for Now.'" PR Newswire, April 3, 2012.

PepsiCo. *2010 Annual Report*. Accessed July 3, 2012. http://www.pepsico.com/Download/PepsiCo_Annual_Report_2010_Full_Annual_Report.pdf.

"PepsiCo, Inc." *International Directory of Company Histories*. Ed. Jay P. Pederson. Vol. 93. Detroit, MI: St. James Press, 2008.

Sharma, Samidha. "Pepsi, Hero Honda Win WC Brand War." *Times of India*, May 24, 2011.

Thomson Reuters. "Edited Transcript: PEP-PepsiCo at Consumer Analyst Group of New York Conference." *Thomson Reuters StreetEvents*, May 10, 2012. Accessed July 3, 2012. http://www.pepsico.com/Download/PEP-Transcript-2012-05-10T15_35.pdf.

"2011 Ranking of the Top 100 Brands." Interbrand, 2012. Accessed July 3, 2012. http://www.interbrand.com/en/best-global-brands/best-global-brands-2008/best-global-brands-2011.aspx.

Zmuda, Natalie. "Pepsi Beverage Guru Unveils His Plan to Win the World Over." *Advertising Age*, July 11, 2011.

———. "Pepsi Tackles Identity Crisis." *Advertising Age*, May 7, 2012.

PERFETTI VAN MELLE

———————— ■ ————————

BRAND ORIGINS

- Perfetti Van Melle is the product of a 2001 merger between Perfetti S.p.A. and Van Melle NV of the Netherlands.

- Van Melle was founded in 1841 as a bakery that eventually began producing sugar candy alongside its baked goods.
- Perfetti originated as a small Italian company and began expanding in the 1950s, a time when the brand became known for its chewing gum.
- The merger in 2001 made Perfetti Van Melle the third largest confectionery manufacturer in the world.

Perfetti Van Melle is the product of a 2001 merger between Italian company Perfetti S.p.A. and Van Melle NV of the Netherlands. Van Melle, the older of the two operations, was founded in 1841 as a bakery that gradually began producing sugar candy alongside its baked goods. In 1900, Van Melle opened its first large-scale factory for making candy, and by the 1920s, its products were being sold in international markets. Company owner Izaak van Melle traveled often to promote the company's goods, returning to his factory with ideas for new candy and confectionery items. By the 1930s the company was shipping so many products outside the local area that it purchased an airplane for the task. However, during World War II, production was cut, and bombing raids destroyed the Van Melle factory.

In 1946, Van Melle relaunched production in Rotterdam, the Netherlands, and by 1950 the factory had returned to its full production capacity. The company continued to launch initiatives in new markets throughout the 1950s, 1960s, and 1970s while also narrowing its confectionery line to focus on smaller ranges of candy brands. Van Melle also introduced roll-type packaging for some of its candy products, including Fruittella and Mentos. Most candies up until that time had been sold loose and bagged, and the new packaging helped turn Fruittella and Mentos into top-selling international brands. During this time, Van Melle also began expanding its production, opening foreign sales and marketing subsidiaries in Belgium (1950), Germany (1953), and France (1960). A production facility was opened in Brazil in 1956, and in 1972 Van Melle entered the United States, expanding into India, Singapore, and Vietnam in the same decade.

Van Melle made its first acquisition in 1982, buying small candy producer PPW. Acquisitions of Peco Suikerwerken and Look-O-Look were made in the following years. During this time, Van Melle also formed a connection with the Italian confectionery Perfetti, which prompted several joint marketing projects. In 1986, Van Melle launched the Air Heads candy brand in the United States, which would become one of the best-known candy brands in the country. In the 1990s the company made a considerable move into Eastern European markets, acquiring VDG, which operated in the Czech Republic, Slovakia, and Hungary. In the latter half of the decade, Van Melle opened a production plant in Poland, a packaging plant in Russia, and factories and sales and production subsidiaries in Indonesia, India, and China. Van Melle went on to acquire the Klene, CandyTech, Fundy, and Wybert brands, and eventually moved its stock listing to the Euronext Amsterdam stock exchange.

By 2000, Perfetti had become a major shareholder in Van Melle, owning a 36 percent stake in the company. Perfetti started as a small Italian company and began expanding in the 1950s. The expansion coincided with Perfetti's growing reputation as a maker of chewing gum, which many Italians had become familiar with when American soldiers arrived in Italy during World War II. By the end of the 1970s, Perfetti was carrying multiple confectionery brands and appeared a valuable ally to Van Melle. Van Melle was focused on northern Europe, while Perfetti wished to control the markets in southern Europe. Perfetti acquired the brands Caremoli, La Giulia, and Gelco in the 1980s, and had opened production operations in Turkey, India, China, and Brazil by 1999. In 2001, Perfetti and Van Melle merged to become Perfetti Van Melle, and by 2011 the new company was billing itself as the third largest confectionery manufacturer in the world. Perfetti Van Melle now operates 35 subsidiary companies, including one in the United States, and distributes its products in more than 150 countries around the world.

BRAND ELEMENTS

- The Perfetti Van Melle logo features the word "Perfetti" in simple, uppercase white letters, while "Van Melle" appears underneath in an elaborate red font.

- The Perfetti Van Melle brand is divided into three major product groups: snacks, confectionery, and health care.
- Perfetti Van Melle relies heavily on its global subsidiaries to manufacture and advertise versions of its products that appeal to regional preferences.

The Perfetti Van Melle name reflects the names of the two merged companies' founders, the Italian brothers Ambrogio and Egidio Perfetti and the Dutchman Izaak van Melle. The Perfetti Van Melle logo features two distinct elements, the first being the word "Perfetti" written in simple, uppercase white letters. The word appears on a dark blue rectangular shape that has two sharp edges and two rounded edges. Just beneath the last five letters in "Perfetti" is the second element, the words "Van Melle" written in an elaborate red font, with a swirl from the capitalized "M" encircling the word "Van." Another swirly shape, also in red, forms a partial oval around the two words, with its upper portion disappearing behind the blue rectangle.

The Perfetti Van Melle brand is divided into three major product groups: snacks, confectionery, and health care. The best-known products from these groups include the brands Mentos, Frisk, Fruittella, Alpenliebe, Golia, Happydent, Vivident, Big Babol, Air Heads, Chupa Chups, and Smint, all of which are popular in countries around the world.

When manufacturing in and advertising to specific regions, Perfetti Van Melle relies largely on the versatility and innovation of its global subsidiaries. For example, Perfetti Van Melle India owns 15 brands, all of which were developed after market research was conducted to study the tastes and preferences of the region's consumers. Similarly, in other Asian subsidiaries, Alpenliebe products are produced and packaged according to local preferences. In European markets, Perfetti Van Melle has begun offering more items to meet the rising demand for healthy products, while in the United States, the company distributes its top brand, Mentos, in a range of exclusive flavors and colors.

BRAND IDENTITY

- Perfetti Van Melle is a privately owned company with 35 subsidiaries around the world.
- Perfetti Van Melle is known largely for the many brands it produces, including candy items, sugar-free candy lines, and oral health lines.
- The Perfetti Van Melle brand relies on consistent innovation, quality, and strong marketing strategies.

Perfetti Van Melle is a privately owned company with headquarters located in Lainate, Italy, and Breda, the Netherlands. It distributes products in more than 150 countries around the world through its 35 subsidiary companies. The Perfetti Van Melle brand relies on consistent innovation, quality, and strong marketing strategies, while its corporate identity is based on its core values and code of conduct. The Perfetti Van Melle vision states that the brand's position in the international market is founded on the principles of integrity without compromise, desire to achieve excellence, dedication to the customer, and social and environmental responsibility.

While its brand identity shapes its behavior, Perfetti Van Melle is known less for its corporate brand than for the many brands it produces, such as the popular candies Mentos, Fruittella, and Air Heads. In addition to its popular international candy brands, Perfetti Van Melle manufactures a variety of products for individual local and regional markets. In some markets, such as the United Kingdom and United States, the company offers sugar-free candy lines, and it also markets products purported to offer health benefits, including the Vivident and Hyperdent lines, which promise fresher breath and whiter teeth in their marketing advertisements.

BRAND STRATEGY

- The Perfetti Van Melle brand strategy has been based on the company's ability to acquire smaller brands and to market its products globally.
- In 2006, Perfetti Van Melle acquired Spanish company Chupa Chups, maker of the popular Chupa Chups lollipops and Smint mints and gum.
- In 2011, Perfetti Van Melle hired Essential Communications PR & Media Consultants to help establish the brand in the travel retail confectionery sector.
- The Mentos Helpline, a spoof call center, was introduced in India in 2008 to help introduce the Mentos brand in the country.

The growth of the Perfetti Van Melle brand has benefited from the company's ability to acquire smaller brands and successfully introduce its products in locations around the globe. A key example of this business strategy is Perfetti's acquisition of Van Melle in 2001, which brought together the many acquisitions of both companies. In 2006, Perfetti Van Melle acquired Spanish company Chupa Chups, adding Chupa Chups lollipops and Smint mints and gum to Perfetti Van Melle's collection of globally known brands. In the same year, the brand announced that it was in the process of building a factory in Russia and doubling the size of its operation in Kentucky in the United States.

In 2011, Perfetti Van Melle announced its hiring of Essential Communications PR & Media Consultants, a consultancy that had previously worked with Imperial Tobacco and Nestlé International Travel Retail, to promote the Mentos and Chupa Chups brands via retail trade magazines, online news media venues, and other relevant press outlets. This venture was part of Perfetti Van Melle's strategy to become a force in the travel retail confectionery sector. Essential Communications was also tasked with creating a tactical advertising and sponsorship program and to eventually represent the brand's products in duty-free shops worldwide.

This marketing strategy carried over to India, where Perfetti Van Melle introduced the Mentos brand in 2008. With the help of public relations firm Ogilvy, Perfetti Van Melle created animated advertising campaigns and commercials based around the theme of "smart thinking." This included the launch of the Mentos Helpline, a spoof call center that used flash-based video to interact with users and offer answers to everyday problems. The quirky nature of the campaign was designed to appeal to India's younger consumers.

BRAND EQUITY

- Perfetti Van Melle's 2011 net sales were US$2.92 billion, having risen slowly but steadily since 2009.
- Perfetti Van Melle is a privately owned company and is not listed on any world stock exchanges.
- In 2011, *Candy Industry* magazine ranked Perfetti Van Melle sixth on its list of the top 100 candy manufacturers worldwide.
- In 2012, Perfetti Van Melle was the third largest sugar confectionery and chewing gum processing operation in the world and the second largest in Europe.

Perfetti Van Melle's revenues in 2011 were US$2.92 billion, with candies representing 59 percent of sales and chewing gum representing 41 percent. Net sales have been steadily increasing over the past several years, creeping up from EUR2.1 billion (US$2.74 billion) in 2009 to EUR2.2 billion (US$2.87 billion) in 2010. Perfetti Van Melle has approximately 19,000 employees, 31 manufacturing sites, and 35 operating companies worldwide. Its products are sold in more than 150 countries.

Because Perfetti Van Melle is a privately owned company, it is not listed on any world stock exchanges, and most of its financial and performance information is unavailable to the public. The January 2011 issue of *Candy Industry* magazine ranked Perfetti Van Melle sixth on its list of the top 100 global candy manufacturers, while in 2012 Perfetti Van Melle was ranked as the third largest sugar confectionery and chewing gum processing operation in the world and the second largest in Europe. The company also enjoys a high rate of brand recall in India, thanks largely to its successful 2008 Mentos advertising campaign in the country.

Other studies have ranked Perfetti Van Melle well in terms of advertising and human resources. In 2011 Nielsen ranked Perfetti Van Melle 75th on its Top 100 Dutch Advertisers list, while in 2009 Dutch company Effectory en Vkbanen named Perfetti Van Melle the 18th best employer in the Netherlands.

BRAND AWARENESS

- During a 2003 election in California, Perfetti Van Melle introduced a microsite advertising Mentos mints as the "official chewy mint" of the election.
- In 2011, Perfetti Van Melle used Facebook to introduce the first Mentos stick gum to be sold in the United States.
- In 2011, the global travel retail division of Perfetti Van Melle sought to introduce key brands Mentos and Chupa Chups to the travel retail market.

While Perfetti Van Melle's corporate brand may not be top-of-mind for consumers, it is certainly noteworthy within the industry and high for the specific sub-brands. The brand ranked sixth on the January 2011 issue of *Candy Industry* magazine's list of the top 100 global candy manufacturers, while in 2012 Perfetti Van Melle was ranked as the third largest sugar confectionery and chewing gum processing operation in the world. Additionally, the company also enjoys a high rate of brand recall in India, thanks largely to its successful 2008 Mentos advertising campaign in the country.

Perfetti Van Melle also uses social media to great effect in promoting its products to increase brand awareness. During a 2003 election in California, the Mentos brand introduced a microsite advertising Mentos boxed mints as the "official chewy mint" of the election. In 2011, Perfetti Van Melle used social media platform Facebook to introduce Mentos UP2U, the brand's first stick gum to be sold in the United States. The first 1,000 visitors to "like" the product's Facebook fan page received free gum, and the page ultimately received more than 95,000 "likes."

Also in 2011, Perfetti Van Melle's global travel retail division attended the Tax Free World Association (TFWA) world exhibition in Cannes, France, with the aim of introducing the company's key brands, Chupa Chups and Mentos, to the travel retail market. The company also took part in the Middle East Duty Free Association (MEDFA) conference in Dubai. Perfetti Van Melle considers the Middle East to be its second largest travel retail region after Europe.

BRAND OUTLOOK

- The brands Mentos, Fruittella, Meller, and Air Heads are sold in more than 125 countries, with new markets being added frequently.
- In 2011, Perfetti Van Melle announced the implementation of new environmental management systems, with the aim of obtaining the ISO 14001 environmental certification.

- Perfetti Van Melle plans to create more products that are sugar free, use natural coloring and flavoring, and are packaged in smaller portions.

Perfetti Van Melle has seen steady increases in annual sales in recent years, thanks in part to its acquisition of Chupa Chups in 2006 and to the targeted regional marketing of popular brands like Mentos, Fruittella, Meller, and Air Heads, which are sold in more than 125 countries around the world. The Mentos brand and several lines of chewing gum are available in Serbia and Montenegro, and in 2012 Perfetti Van Melle announced plans to enter the Burmese market through a partnership with market expansion firm DKSH.

Like many brands in the 21st century, Perfetti Van Melle has been strengthening its commitment to social and environmental responsibility. In 2011, Perfetti Van Melle announced it would be implementing new environmental management systems with the aim of obtaining the ISO 14001 certification, an international standard for the continuous improvement of environmental performance and organization.

Reflecting a growing concern in many markets about the negative health effects associated with consuming sugar and processed foods, the Perfetti Van Melle Benelux Annual Social Report for 2010 noted the company's emphasis on the "responsible eating of sweets." This new focus included the goal of producing more products that are free from sugar and artificial flavoring. The report stated that approximately 50 percent of the company's recent marketing budget was spent on products without sugar, products with natural coloring and flavoring, and products packaged in smaller portions. All of these efforts combined seem to point to a bright future for the brand.

FURTHER READING

Bhattacharya, Sindhu J. "Perfetti's Sweet Success." *Business Line,* October 7, 2004, 19.

Bickerton, Ian. "Van Melle Gives Consent for Takeover by Perfetti." *Financial Times,* January 16, 2001, 32.

"Chups Links to Fruittella." *Grocer,* March 19, 2005, 8.

Cohen, M. L. "Perfetti Van Melle S.p.A." *International Directory of Company Histories.* Ed. Tina Grant. Vol. 72. Detroit: St. James Press, 2006. *Gale Virtual Reference Library.* Web. Accessed November 28, 2012. http://go.galegroup.com/ps/i.do?id=GALE%7CCX3444900084&v=2.1&u=itsbtrial&it=r&p=GVRL&sw=w.

Delta DMD. "Portfolio: Perfetti Van Melle S.p.A." Accessed November 30, 2012. http://www.deltadmd.rs/code/navigate.php?Id=69&country=2&type=20&pr=55.

Elliot, Stuart. "Building a Buzz in Social Media Ahead of Traditional Marketing." *New York Times,* June 22, 2011. Accessed November 27, 2012. http://www.nytimes.com/2011/06/23/business/media/23adco.html?_r=0.

IBS Center for Management Research. "Perfetto Van Melle: Marketing Mentos in India." 2008. Accessed November 27, 2012. http://www.icmrindia.org/casestudies/catalogue/Marketing/Perfetti%20Van%20Melle-Marketing%20Mentos%20Case%20Study.htm.

Perfetti Van Melle Benelux. "Caring for Excellence: Perfetti Van Melle Benelux Annual Social Report on the year 2010." July 2011. Accessed December 7, 2012. http://www.perfettivanmelle.nl/media/PVM_mvo_jaarverslag_ENG_03.pdf.

"Perfetti Van Melle Group Market Analysis in Packaged Food." *Euromonitor International,* December 2011. Accessed November 26, 2012. http://www.reportlinker.com/p0715657/Perfetti-Van-Melle-Group-in-Packaged-Food-World.html.

Rogers, Paul. "The Big Get Bigger." *Candy Industry,* January 2011. Accessed December 7, 2012. http://digital.bnpmedia.com/publication/?i=57718&p=49.

PETROCHINA

———— ■ ————

AT A GLANCE

Brand Synopsis: PetroChina, a producer and seller of oil and gas, is one of the largest public companies in the world.

Parent Company: PetroChina Company Limited
9 Dongzihimen North Street, Dongcheng District
Beijing, 100011
P.R. China
http://www.petrochina.com.cn

Sector: Energy

Industry Group: Energy

Performance: *Market share*—39.2% of the domestic retail market (2011). *Sales*—RMB$2 billion (US$321.27 billion) (2011).

Principal Competitors: Royal Dutch Shell; BP; Exxon Mobile Corp.; Chevron

China's state-run oil company, China National Petroleum Corporation (CNPC), has been through a series of changes throughout the years as the Chinese government has restructured its integrated oil and gas services. As China's domestic oil fields matured and its population continued to grow, the need to import oil increased tremendously in the 1980s and 1990s. At the same time, crude oil prices increased, as did exploration costs to meet the need for more oil. The government's solution to these mounting financial burdens was to sell stock in the company through an initial public offering (IPO). CNPC thus formed a limited liability company called PetroChina in 1999 that would operate in upstream and downstream activities, particularly in the domestic sector. CNPC, which still owns 86 percent of PetroChina, hoped to raise US$7 billion on the IPO in 2000, but the sale fell short, raising only US$2.9 billion.

A decade later, PetroChina and CNPC had made significant strides since implementing the strategy to internationalize. According to *Forbes,* "PetroChina can now say it produces more daily barrels of oil than Exxon Mobil. The Chinese company produced 2.43 million barrels of oil per day in 2011, climbing above Exxon's 2.3 million barrels." While those numbers represent only crude oil and do not take into account natural gas production, the figures demonstrate PetroChina's progress toward joining the ranks of the global oil giants. It is one of the fastest growing companies in the oil industry.

BRAND ORIGINS

- China's state-run oil company, CNPC, created Petro-China in 1999 in order to conduct an IPO and to aid in domestic upstream and downstream activities.
- In 2000, PetroChina's IPO raised US$2.9 billion, far short of the goal of US$7 billion.
- By 2011, PetroChina was producing more barrels of oil per day than competitor Exxon Mobil, thanks in large part to an internationalization strategy.

BRAND ELEMENTS

- PetroChina shares its logo, tagline, and strategy with state-run CNPC.

- PetroChina's flower-shaped logo symbolizes both the company's desire to be in harmony with nature and its drive to expand its business.
- The tagline "Energize, Harmonize, Realize" expresses the message symbolized in PetroChina's logo: the brand's strategy of responsibly expanding its business.

Because PetroChina is owned predominantly by the Chinese government's China National Petroleum Corporation (CNPC), the two firms share the same logo, tagline, and strategy. According to the PetroChina website, the logo—a flower-shaped, red-and-orange circle with a sunburst in the center—symbolizes the company's commitment to ensuring harmony between the development of energy and the environment. The logo's colors are those of China's national flag, and the 10 petals of the flower represent the group's core businesses. The solid red base illustrates PetroChina's strength and cohesion, while the rising sun highlights the hope for a brilliant future. Similarly, the company's tagline, "Energize, Harmonize, Realize," encapsulates the brand's objective to provide energy in an environmentally responsible manner while at the same time expanding business on an international level.

BRAND IDENTITY

- PetroChina aims to be a competitive international energy company that promotes harmony within the scope of its business.
- PetroChina's stated mission, "Caring for Energy, Caring for You," is about ensuring a responsible energy supply while building economic and social growth.
- International cooperation is crucial to ensuring oil and gas supplies and exploring new possibilities for green energy.
- Corporate citizenship and mutual cooperation in the communities where it operates are key elements of PetroChina's aim to promote harmony among people.

PetroChina aims to be a highly competitive international energy firm. At the same time, the company strives to evoke a sense of global harmony—one that unites people and the environment. PetroChina's mission, articulated as "Caring for Energy, Caring for You," expresses its commitment to ensuring an environmentally responsible oil and gas supply while promoting social development and economic growth. One way the company seeks to provide energy to the world without exhausting natural resources or human relationships is by creating cooperative partnerships with other large oil companies. According to PetroChina's 2011 sustainability report, "Win-lose competition is being replaced by win-win cooperation, a realistic

option that emphasizes complementary advantages and mutual benefits." By working together to solve problems and share costs, PetroChina hopes to build its resources so that it can continue to grow its business.

PetroChina also hopes to identify its brand as one that aids in the social and economic development of the countries where it operates. Becoming a loyal and trustworthy corporate citizen is important to PetroChina domestically and abroad. This means bringing excellent returns to its shareholders, growth to communities, and benefits to its employees. According to its sustainability report, PetroChina has "shown great enthusiasm in public welfare work, such as supporting education, alleviating poverty, and building public facilities and infrastructure. More efforts have been made to boost local socio-economic growth, for example, purchasing local products and services, hiring local labor, etc." Just as it does with major corporations, PetroChina employs its philosophy of the mutual benefits of cooperative partnerships within the communities where it operates. Sharing advantages with communities proves to be beneficial to both parties. PetroChina believes that identifying the brand with this type of harmony is an essential part of its future success.

BRAND STRATEGY

- PetroChina's main brand strategy has been to internationalize its business through overseas acquisitions and corporate partnerships.
- Opening operational hubs throughout Europe, North America, and Asia has helped PetroChina expand its global trade, refining, and storage.
- Effective marketing of refined products has led to an increase in domestic gas sales and market share.
- Increasing yearly revenues have demonstrated the effectiveness of PetroChina's strategies emphasizing resources, marketing, and internationalization.

While initially launched in 2000 to serve as the publicly traded arm of China National Petroleum Corporation (CNPC), with a focus on domestic upstream and downstream activity, PetroChina has since refocused its business strategy and has taken great strides in internationalizing its brand. By investing in resources throughout the world, PetroChina is trying to become a competitive player in the global energy market. According to *Business Daily Update*, in 2010 PetroChina pledged to boost acquisitions and form partnerships with oil giants to increase its international reach. It planned to spend about US$60 billion throughout the 2010s on such overseas activities as a 2011 joint venture with petrochemical company Ineos in Europe, the 2010 formation of Arrow Energy with Royal Dutch Shell in Australia, and the Rumalia Project with BP in Iraq. In addition to positive financial returns, these ventures also aid the company in finding alternative resources, such as coal steam and shale gases, that will become more important to energy companies as traditional resources decline. Moreover, PetroChina has expanded its global trading and storage capacities throughout the world with operational hubs in Europe, North America, and Asia.

Focusing on efficient and effective marketing to help the company capitalize on the resources it has produced is also a large part of the overall brand strategy. According to the company's 2011 annual report, "the group steadily pushed forward the building of high-performance and strategic markets, including the construction of service stations in urban areas and on expressways. As a result, more than 1,300 new service stations were developed" domestically in 2011. These stations led to a 20.4 percent increase in gasoline, kerosene, and diesel sales and contributed to a total retail market share of 39.2 percent. This increase is a clear example of the success of the company's brand strategies focusing on "resources, marketing, and internationalization." By expanding international business, the company has been able to find resources, refine them, and turn them into profit—profits that have led to steady increases in total revenue for PetroChina since 2009.

BRAND EQUITY

- Due to high import prices and tax increases, Petro-China experienced a 5 percent decline in net profits in 2011.
- PetroChina's financial performance brought steady increases in revenue for the five years leading up to 2011, when revenues reached about US$321.27 billion.
- With a brand value of US$10.4 billion, PetroChina was the fifth most valuable brand in the oil and gas sector on *Brandirectory*'s Global 500 list.

According to PetroChina's annual report, increases in taxes and natural gas import prices led to a decline in profits in 2011. The group's performance, however, was excellent. It earned revenues of RMB2 billion (US$321.27 billion), a 36.7 percent increase over 2010. The increase is indicative of the strength of the brand. According to *Brandirectory*, PetroChina's financial success is due to the company's implementation of its key strategies and the strengthening of the overall balance among its activities related to production, transportation, marketing, and storage.

For these reasons the company's brand value has experienced a steady increase as well. From 2009 to 2012, the brand's value increased more than US$7 billion. According to *Brandirectory*'s Global 500 report of 2012, Petro-China was rated as the world's fifth most valuable brand

in the oil and gas sector, with a value of US$10.4 billion. Coming in at number 81 on the overall list, PetroChina moved up from 114th place in 2010. With continued emphasis on expanding exploration and development and marketing products internationally, PetroChina looked to ensure a successful future.

BRAND AWARENESS

- PetroChina derives much of its brand awareness from the Chinese government's connection with the company.
- Operating more than 17,000 gas stations in China has contributed to PetroChina's high domestic brand awareness.
- Building brand awareness overseas will be more difficult for PetroChina because it is a relatively new company on the global energy scene.

Because PetroChina's largest stakeholder is the Chinese government and because its parent company, state-run China National Petroleum Corporation (CNPC), held a monopoly in the oil industry in China until recently, PetroChina enjoys good brand awareness domestically. Additionally, as PetroChina continues to employ effective marketing of its refined products, its brand awareness is expected to rise. According to *BrandZ*'s Most Valuable Chinese Brands Top 50 report, "PetroChina serves 17,000 gas stations in China, which produces high brand awareness. The company increased communications activities in recent years to include sponsorship of major sporting events." With activities like this, and with key strategies to internationalize its company, PetroChina also seeks to build a brand with top-of-mind awareness abroad. The key challenge is to build brand equity around a strong proposition that will help make PetroChina, a large, mostly state-owned entity, more accessible. On the world stage, PetroChina will have to make a name for itself without the domestic comforts of government connections.

BRAND OUTLOOK

- The future of PetroChina is linked closely to the governmental policies that guide its parent company, China National Petroleum Corporation (CNPC).
- PetroChina believes that, for its brand to be successful, it must build an environmentally friendly, international, and sustainable company.
- Continuing to expand international oil and gas production, create clean energy, and employ effective marketing are key strategies necessary for PetroChina to meet its business goals.

Because PetroChina operates in the world's most populous country—a country with a need for energy that is growing at an extremely fast pace—its future seems promising.

PetroChina is the publicly traded arm of the government-owned China National Petroleum Corporation (CNPC), so its success is partly dependent on how the government operates. According to the company's 2011 annual report, PetroChina will have a favorable environment in which to grow in the coming years as the Chinese government continues to implement beneficial fiscal and currency policies, encourage the clean use of conventional energy resources, and speed up the streamlining of the pricing structure of energy resources. To further its progress, PetroChina will, according to its website, "explore new areas of growth while focusing on its core oil and gas activities so as to continuously propel its expansion and to build an environmentally-friendly, international, and sustainable company."

The company plans to provide cleaner and more efficient energy, particularly in the natural gas sector, which PetroChina considers the main source of its future growth. The company plans to continue building cooperative relationships and joint investments with international companies while at the same time expanding global trade. In the area of sustainability, the company plans to develop exploration and production, strengthen its market competitiveness through innovation and technology, and improve its oil and gas supply network to ensure efficient and safe distribution. With a plan for these three areas in place, PetroChina will attempt to deliver the bright future symbolized by its logo.

FURTHER READING

Brand Finance. "Global 500 2012." *Brandirectory.* Accessed October 30, 2012. http://brandirectory.com/profile/petrochina.

Fontevecchia, Agustino. "The End of Exxon's Reign? PetroChina Now the Biggest Oil Producer." *Forbes,* March 29, 2012. Accessed November 5, 2012. http://www.forbes.com/sites/afontevecchia/2012/03/29/the-end-of-exxons-rein-petrochina-now-the-biggest-oil-producer/.

Millward Brown. "Most Valuable Chinese Brands Top 50." *BrandZ.* Accessed November 4, 2012. http://www.millward-brown.com/Libraries/Optimor_BrandZ_Files/2012-BrandZ_Top50_ChineseBrands_EN.sflb.ashx.

PetroChina Company Limited. "2011 Annual Report." Accessed November 1, 2012. http://www.petrochina.com.cn/Resource/Petrochina/img/2012bg/2011ndbg_en.pdf.

PetroChina Company Limited. "2011 Sustainability Report." Accessed November 3, 2012. http://www.petrochina.com.cn/Resource/Petrochina/img/2012bg/2011kcxbg-en.pdf?COLLCC=2522875356&.

"PetroChina overtakes Exxon as biggest oil producer." *BBC,* March 29, 2012. Accessed October 30, 2012. http://www.bbc.co.uk/news/business-17556938.

"PetroChina to step up global expansion." *Business Daily Update,* August 27, 2010. *General OneFile.* Accessed October 30, 2012. http://go.galegroup.com/ps/i.do?id=GALE%7CA235849391&v=2.1&u=itsbtrial&it=r&p=GPS&sw=w.

"Refining and marketing." *Petroleum Economist,* February 2011. *General OneFile.* Accessed October 30, 2012. http://go.galegroup.com/ps/i.do?id=GALE%7CA250434475&v=2.1&u=itsbtrial&it=r&p=GPS&sw=w.

PEUGEOT

AT A GLANCE

Brand Synopsis: The Peugeot brand promises high-quality, stylish mobility solutions, from cars to scooters and bicycles.

Parent Company: Peugeot S.A.
75 Avenue de la Grand Armeé
Paris
France
http://www.psa-peugeot-citroen.com

Sector: Consumer Discretionary

Industry Group: Automobiles & Components

Performance: *Market share*—33.2 percent of the French automotive industry (2009); 15.4 percent of the European automotive industry (2009). *Sales*—US$77.6 billion (2011).

Principal Competitors: Renault; Fiat S.p.A.; Volkswagen AG

BRAND ORIGINS

- Peugeot was originally involved in the manufacture of coffee, salt, and pepper grinders.
- Peugeot began using the lion as its corporate symbol in 1847.
- Peugeot became involved in car manufacturing in the late 1800s.
- Peugeot and Citroën merged in 1976.

- Citroën was rebranded in 2009, followed by a Peugeot rebranding in 2010.

The brand history of Peugeot S.A. dates back to the first half of the 19th century. Although now known as one of the world's most recognizable automobile, bicycle, and scooter brands, Peugeot was founded in France in 1842 as a manufacturer of coffee, salt, and pepper grinders. In 1847 the company adopted the lion as its trademark, an image that would evolve over the years but remain a fixture even as Peugeot evolved as a business. Later in the 1800s, the company produced steel rods used as supports in crinoline dresses. These rods proved ideal as umbrella frames and, in turn, wheel spokes, which led Peugeot to become a bicycle manufacturer. It was Armand Peugeot who shifted the focus to automobiles, developing a three-wheel, steam-powered vehicle in 1889. It was after he met with Gottlieb Daimler, pioneer of the gasoline internal combustion engine, that Peugeot produced its first true modern car, a four-wheel vehicle powered by a Daimler engine. Soon Peugeot was producing its own engines and unveiling a number of automotive innovations, including the first rubber tire wheels.

Peugeot was far from innovative, however, in the branding of its automotive models, merely assigning them Type numbers. The company showed more marketing savvy when it entered several three-horsepower Type 12 cars in the world's first automobile race, the Paris–Rouen *Le Petit Journal* Competition for Horseless Carriages, with one of the 12s winning the event. Peugeot refrained from participating in motor sports for a while, but returned with a flourish in 1913 by winning the Indianapolis 500. By this time the company was manufacturing a full range of cars, including the world's first compact in 1905, dubbed Le Beb. Peugeot factories also began turning out motorcycles, starting with a motorized bicycle in 1901.

Following World War I, Peugeot prospered as the automobile became commonplace rather than a luxury item. In 1929 the company began numbering its cars, starting with the first 201 model, a system that Peugeot would now trademark. The automaker managed to survive the depression of the early 1930s, only to fall victim to a greater calamity: the conquest of France by Nazi Germany in 1940. With its production commandeered by the German war machine, Peugeot, its factories severely damaged by Allied bombing, would not return to automobile manufacturing until 1948, when the 203 model resumed production.

During the postwar era, Peugeot elected to position itself as an exclusive carmaker, one that focused on the sale of high-quality, high-margin vehicles rather than mass producing less profitable models. It proved to be a successful formula and led to Peugeot's entering the US market in 1958. It was also during this period that the company began the production of motor scooters.

To expand its automotive business without jeopardizing the positioning of the Peugeot brand, the company acquired a stake in another French automobile manufacturer, Citroën. In 1976 Peugeot and Citroën merged to create PSA Peugeot-Citroën. The two brands were designed and marketed individually but shared one another's technical achievements and the economies of scale that came with being part of a larger concern.

Peugeot expanded further in 1978 with the acquisition of former Chrysler plants in Europe. Cars produced at these facilities were sold under the Talbot name. When sales plummeted, the line was soon discontinued. In the 1980s Peugeot enjoyed success entering new markets, especially in the Pacific region. After negotiating a recession at the start of the following decade, Peugeot regained some lost luster with the introduction of the Peugeot 06 line and the Citroën Xantia and Xsara models. Successful participation in motor racing once again helped to promote the Peugeot brand. By 2007 Peugeot's dual-branded strategy led to its emergence as Europe's second-largest car company, trailing only Volkswagen. Like all automakers, Peugeot was adversely impacted by the financial crisis of 2008. To regain its footing, Peugeot revived the Talbot brand to compete in the entry-level car market while preserving the brand equity of both the Peugeot and Citroën brands. A new chief executive was also installed in 2009, setting the stage for a complete rebranding of Citroën, followed by a rebranding of Peugeot the following year, an effort that covered Peugeot automobiles, vans, bicycles, and scooters.

BRAND ELEMENTS
- Peugeot first used the lion as a logo in 1847.
- Various lion shapes were used as radiator caps and hood ornaments on Peugeot cars until 1958.
- A new Peugeot logo and slogan was introduced in 2010.
- The creation of Citroën's logo was inspired by a new design in milling gears.
- The Citroën logo was revamped in 2009 as part of a rebranding effort.

The most recognizable Peugeot brand element is the lion logo. It was introduced by the company in 1847, decades before Peugeot became associated with automobiles. The lion was first used to promote the company's saw blades, symbolizing the strength of the teeth, flexibility of the blade, and quick cutting ability. Although the lion did not enjoy the same connection to other Peugeot products, it was registered as the company's trademark in 1858. Two other logos were created, but the lion was reserved for Peugeot's highest quality products.

In 1905 a lion signature stamp crowned the grill of Peugeot cars, and in 1923 a lion sculpture was introduced as a radiator cap. A different lion hood ornament followed in 1933. Because of security reasons, the hood ornaments were withdrawn in 1958. In the meantime the corporate logo underwent a number of changes, evolving from a realistic to a heraldic lion in profile. This lion would be replaced in turn by a lion's head encased in a triangular shield in 1960, followed a few years later by an unframed lion's head. In 1975 the company returned to a stylized version of the heraldic lion. Greater depth was provided to the image in 1998, and as part of the Peugeot rebranding effort of 2010, the image was given a bimetal look through the use of contrasting matting and lustrous finishing details.

Citroën relies on its own distinctive logo, a pair of upward-pointing chevrons. The image was the creation of 22-year-old André Citroën, who in the early 1900s while on a trip to Poland was impressed by a new chevron-shaped gear used in milling. The logo represented the intermeshing of these gears. Later, when he became involved in the automotive industry, Citroën used the image as a logo for his cars. The logo evolved over the years, with the chevron coming to appear more like herringbones. In the 1980s the image became white chevron shapes presented against a red background. When Citroën underwent its rebranding in 2009, the logo was given a three-dimensional metallic treatment. It was also accompanied by a new slogan, "Créative Technologie."

In addition to a revamped logo, the Peugeot rebranding also resulted in a new slogan, "Motion & Emotion." It replaced the previous slogan, "Engineered to be Enjoyed," and represented a shift in the company's brand identity. The focus was now on the driving experience, rather than on touting engineering prowess.

BRAND IDENTITY

- Peugeot's brand identity is consistent, regardless of product line.
- "Motion & Emotion" embodies Peugeot's brand identity.
- The lion symbol helps to reinforce Peugeot's commitment to excellence.
- Citroën's identity is expressed by the "Créative Technologie" slogan.

Peugeot is a generalist brand for automobiles as well as the company's bicycles and motor scooters. Its identity is embodied in the slogan "Motion & Emotion," part of the 2010 rebranding program and used to promote all three product categories. Whether it has two wheels or four, a Peugeot-branded product is portrayed as well engineered and of the highest quality. Not only are Peugeot products reliable, they are touted as safe. While the lion was originally used by Peugeot to promote saw blades, it has long been one of the world's most potent symbols, representing royalty, strength, courage, wisdom, and many other virtues. As such, the lion remains an apt symbol for a company like Peugeot, which seeks to present an image of a manufacturer of high quality, safe, and reliable products.

Moreover, the Peugeot brand promises flair and sophisticated styling, whether the product is a sedan, bicycle, or scooter. The slogan "Motion & Emotion" also suggests that joy will accompany the driving or riding experience of a Peugeot customer. The slogan replaced "Engineered to be Enjoyed" as a way to help forge a closer bond between Peugeot and its customers.

In addition to offering several product lines under the Peugeot brand, Peugeot S.A. maintains the distinct Citroën brand. In Citroën's rebranding of 2009, the "Créative Technologie" slogan was adopted. Like the new Peugeot slogan, it exemplified Citroën's revamped brand image. At its heart is the idea of creativity, both in terms of innovative engineering and the driving experience. Citroën also portrays itself as a forward-looking brand, especially in terms of ecological performance.

BRAND STRATEGY

- Peugeot S.A. offers multiple products under one brand, while also selling the same product under multiple brands.
- Whether it's a bicycle, scooter, or car, the Peugeot brand image remains consistent.
- Despite sharing many of the same parts, Peugeot and Citroën maintain distinct brand images.
- An international orientation is a key element of Peugeot's brand strategy.
- The Talbot brand was revived as a way to participate in the low end of the automotive market without diluting the brand equity of Peugeot or Citroën.

Peugeot S.A. employs a multifaceted brand strategy. On the one hand, it offers multiple products under one brand, while on the other, it sells the same product under multiple brands. The Peugeot name is found on automobiles, vans, bicycles, and motor scooters, while automobiles are also produced under the Citroën and Talbot brands.

At the heart of marketing under the Peugeot name, regardless of product, is upscale positioning. Peugeot-branded cars, bicycles, and scooters are presented as premium products, worthy of the high price-points they command. Another important component of Peugeot marketing is an international approach. Although the brand is best known in Europe, especially its home country of France, Peugeot markets to the world. As a result, the company's "Motion & Emotion" slogan was crafted to appeal across cultures, to promote four-wheel or two-wheel vehicles. Also part of Peugeot's appeal to the international market was a strengthened commitment to environmental responsibility. This was demonstrated by the introduction of a new micro-hybrid diesel technology and three full-hybrid diesel models, which complemented Peugeot's electrical car efforts. A further reflection of Peugeot's international orientation was a commitment to begin production of new car models around the world within months of their introduction in Europe. Additionally, Peugeot developed cars for specific markets, including Latin America, Russia, and China.

The Citroën and Talbot brands carved out their own niches in the automotive market. Given that Citroën cars shared about 60 percent of their parts with Peugeots, it was no easy task for these two brands to differentiate themselves one from the other. By maintaining separate design and marketing teams, the two were not only able to coexist but to excel individually. The down-market Talbot, a long-dormant brand, was revived in 2009 mainly to compete against Renault's Dacia brand in emerging markets. By relying on this third brand, Peugeot S.A. was able to compete in the entry-level sector of the market without the risk of compromising the brand equity of either Peugeot or Citroën.

Preserving the value of these brands was especially important at this juncture because Citroën was introducing its new DS line as a way to become a more upmarket brand. The rebranding of Peugeot also coincided with the launch of the stylish RCZ coupe in the spring of 2010, along with the SR1 Roadster concept car. These developments plus the reintroduction of the Talbot brand helped the parent company to expand sales at both ends of the automotive market.

As a diversified company, Peugeot S.A. is involved in other business activities as well, maintaining several lesser brands. Faurecia is a major manufacturer of certain automotive components, including car seats and exhaust systems. Gefco is a provider of transportation and logistics services, and in 2012 a controlling stake in the business was sold to Russian Railways. Banque PSA Financial offers financing for Peugeot and Citroën vehicles in 24 countries. Peugeot Citroën Moteurs adapts the parent company's automotive engines for other automakers and industrial manufacturers. Finally, Process Conception Ingénierie designs and manufactures industrial equipment for sister units as well as other automakers.

BRAND EQUITY

- According to Brand Finance, the Citroën brand was valued at US$4.175 billion in 2012.
- Citroën was the 246th most valuable brand in the world in 2012.
- The Peugeot brand was worth US$7.976 in 2012, according to Brand Finance.
- Peugeot was listed No. 116 on the Global 500 in 2012.
- Peugeot is France's second most valuable automotive brand.

Peugeot S.A. enjoys strong brand equity for both of its primary brands. According to brand evaluation consultancy Brand Finance, which has developed a method to assign a monetary value to a brand, Citroën was worth US$4.175 billion in 2012. It was a performance that placed Citroën No. 246 on Brand Finance's Global 500 list of the world's most valuable brands in 2012. The brand's value actually decreased over the previous year when its worth was estimated at US$4.456 billion. Since its rebranding, however, Citroën has enjoyed significant growth. In 2009 it held a Brand Finance value of US$2.343 billion.

Peugeot was assigned a US$7.976 billion brand value in 2012 by Brand Finance. As a result, Peugeot was listed No. 116 on the Global 500, a significant improvement over the previous year's No. 141 ranking. Like Citroën, Peugeot enjoyed the fruits of a rebranding strategy. The company's 2009 brand value was estimated at US$3.78 billion, or less than half of the 2012 valuation. Peugeot's value also placed it No. 8 among France's most valuable brands, according to Brand Finance. It was also France's second most valuable automotive brand, trailing only Renault. Because of its varied product lines and multiple brands, Peugeot S.A. was far larger than Renault S. A. According to Business Rankings Annual, it posted 2010 revenues of about US$76 billion, compared to Renault's US$38.7 billion. Peugeot S.A. was second only to retailer Carrefour S. A. as France's largest company, while Renault was ranked No. 10.

BRAND AWARENESS

- Citroën and Peugeot are both well-known automotive brands in Europe.

- Citroën and Peugeot combined for a 33.2 percent market share in France and a 15.4 percent share in western Europe, according to 2009 statistics.
- Peugeot's brand awareness is supported by multiple product lines.

Both Citroën and Peugeot are well known automotive brands in Europe, especially in France. According to 2009 statistics, they combined for a 33.2 percent market share in France and a 15.4 percent share in the 25 countries of western Europe. They also controlled 5.8 percent of the worldwide market.

By itself, Peugeot enjoyed strong brand awareness. It maintained an automotive presence in 160 countries, and in 2011 about half of its car sales were made outside of Europe. Peugeot bicycles and motor scooters also enjoyed a worldwide following. A major contributor to the global recognition of Peugeot was the deep history of the brand, which dated to the start of the automotive industry. The Peugeot name was also long associated with bicycles, motorcycles, and scooters. Thus, Peugeot's brand awareness was aided by sheer duration and supported by cross-product reinforcement.

BRAND OUTLOOK

- Peugeot looked to emerging markets for future growth.
- Restructuring led to plant closing in 2012.
- Company denied merger rumors in late 2012.

Peugeot is a venerable brand, deep into its second century. Citroën is well known as well, albeit it has traveled a rougher road, having been rescued out of bankruptcy by Peugeot. The primary line bearing the Peugeot brand is cars. Peugeot will seek to grow its automotive brand outside of France and Europe in the years ahead. In addition to China and Russia, Peugeot has targeted Latin America, especially Argentina and Brazil.

The rebranding effort of Citroën in 2009 and Peugeot in 2010 helped to improve the fortunes of Peugeot S.A., but the company still faced significant challenges. It dealt with a painful restructuring in 2012 that included a plant closing and the loss of 8,000 jobs. Rumors also began circulating that a possible alliance with General Motors' Opel division was turning into a merger. In late 2012 Peugeot S.A. dismissed the possibility. Regardless, the company's future prospects, and the health of its main brands, remained far from certain.

FURTHER READING

Brand Finance. "Global 500 2012." *Brandirectory*. Accessed December 26, 2012. http://brandirectory.com/league_tables/table/global-500-2012.

"France's Largest Auto and Truck Manufacturers Overall, 2011." *Business Rankings Annual*. Ed. Deborah J. Draper. Detroit, MI: Gale, 2013.

"France's Most Valuable Brands, 2011." *Business Rankings Annual.* Ed. Deborah J. Draper. Detroit, MI: Gale, 2013.

Kreindler, Derek. "PSA Peugeot-Citroën to Revive Talbot Brand for Low-Priced Cars." Autoguide.com. July 9, 2010.

"Largest Companies in France, 2010." *Business Rankings Annual.* Ed. Deborah J. Draper. Detroit, MI: Gale, 2013.

"Market Chatter: Peugeot Manager Rules out Merger with GM's Opel: Report." *MidnightTrader Live Briefs*, December 24, 2012.

"New Effort in the U.S. by Peugeot." *New York Times*, July 28, 1988.

"PSA Peugeot-Citroën S.A." *International Directory of Company Histories.* Ed. Drew D. Johnson. Vol. 124. Detroit, MI: St. James Press, 2011.

Thuermer, Karen E. "Regions: Europe—Profile: Renault/PSA Peugeot-Citroën—Fighting Back." *Foreign Direct Investment 1. December 2008.*

PFIZER

BRAND ORIGINS

- In 1849 chemist Charles Pfizer and confectioner Charles Erhart began a partnership to manufacture bulk chemicals and named it Charles Pfizer & Company.
- In 1946 Pfizer purchased a World War II shipyard and renovated it for mass production of penicillin, marking its official entrance into pharmaceutical manufacturing.
- Pfizer was the first pharmaceutical company to circumvent traditional drug-distribution companies when it began selling directly to hospitals and retailers.

- In 1998 Pfizer introduced Viagra, a pill for treating erectile dysfunction, and it became a blockbuster.

In 1849 chemist Charles Pfizer and confectioner Charles Erhart began a partnership in Brooklyn, New York, to manufacture bulk chemicals, and they named it Charles Pfizer & Company. While producing iodine preparation and boric and tartaric acids, Pfizer pioneered the production of citric acid, using large-scale fermentation technology. By the end of the 19th century Pfizer was producing a wide range of industrial and pharmacological products and had offices in New York and Chicago. In 1900 the company was incorporated in New Jersey as Charles Pfizer & Company Inc.

While Pfizer technicians became experts in fermentation technology, across the Atlantic Ocean Sir Alexander Fleming made his historic discovery of penicillin in 1928. Recognizing penicillin's potential to revolutionize health care, scientists struggled for years on how to prepare a large quantity of the drug and at high quality. By 1942 Pfizer divided the first flask of penicillin into vials for the medical departments of the Army and Navy. That year Pfizer reincorporated in Delaware and went public with an offering of 240,000 shares of common stock. In 1946 Pfizer renovated a World War II shipyard for mass production of penicillin, marking the company's official entrance into pharmaceutical manufacturing.

In the postwar years, pharmaceutical companies searched for new, broad-spectrum antibiotics to treat a wide range of bacterial infections. Pfizer's breakthrough came with the discovery of oxytetracycline, a broad-scope antibiotic that it trademarked as Terramycin. The company circumvented traditional drug-distribution companies and began selling Terramycin directly to hospitals and retailers. Pfizer's minuscule retail force of pharmaceutical salespeople would target one small region at a time and promote their product to every accessible health care professional. The sales force left generous samples of the drug at every sales call, sponsored golf tournaments, and provided lively hospitality receptions at conventions.

Beyond its modern marketing strategies, Pfizer was very successful at developing a diversified line of pharmaceuticals. Whereas many companies concentrated their efforts on developing innovative drugs, Pfizer borrowed research from its competitors and generously released variants of these drugs. Ultimately this enabled the company to reduce its dependence on sales of antibiotics by releasing a variety of other pharmaceuticals.

As Pfizer's domestic sales increased, the company was quietly improving its presence on the foreign market. By 1965 Pfizer had expanded into 100 countries and reached US$175 million in annual sales. It would be years before any competitor came close to achieving similar success in the foreign market.

In 1970 the company changed its name to the more modern-sounding Pfizer Inc. In 1998 Pfizer introduced Viagra, a pill for treating erectile dysfunction. By far the most famous of the new "lifestyle drugs," Viagra was an instant blockbuster. More than 350,000 prescriptions were written in the first three weeks, and sales for 1998 totaled US$788 million. Less than a year after the launch of Viagra, Pfizer began comarketing Celebrex, a treatment for arthritic pain which had been developed by G.D. Searle & Co. It became the most successful pharmaceutical launched in U.S. history, with 19 million prescriptions written in the first 12 months.

BRAND ELEMENTS
- Pfizer's name originated in 1849 with chemist Charles Pfizer.
- The Pfizer brand is represented by a logo that uses a blue and white color scheme and contains the company's name within an oval.
- Pfizer promotes its brand through the tagline, "Working Together for a Healthier World."

Pfizer's name originated in 1849 with chemist Charles Pfizer. At that time Pfizer partnered with confectioner Charles Erhart to establish a bulk chemical manufacturing partnership named Charles Pfizer & Company. The company name was changed to Charles Pfizer & Company Inc. in 1900, and to the more modern-sounding Pfizer Inc. in 1970.

The Pfizer brand is represented by a logo that was created in 1987 by Gene Grossman. It contains the company's name within an oval. The letter "f" is different from the other characters in the logo in that the base of the character extends all the way to the bottom of the oval.

In addition, the letter "f" also is directly connected to the letter "i." The special treatment of the letter "f" takes the emphasis off the silent "P" in the Pfizer name.

In 2009 Pfizer revised its logo. The oval was given an upward-angled appearance, conveying motion. In addition, slight modifications were made to the typeface used to represent the Pfizer name. The Pfizer logo depicts the company name either in white on a blue background or in blue on a white background.

Pfizer promotes its brand through the tagline, "Working Together for a Healthier World." The slogan represents the brand's commitment to bettering health and well-being at all stages of life. The company accomplishes this through scientific advancements and the application of global resources.

BRAND IDENTITY
- In 2013 the Pfizer brand was supported by the tagline "Working Together for a Healthier World," which embodied its identity of developing promising treatments for a wide range of diseases.
- Consumers mainly connect with Pfizer through the brand-name drugs it has produced and through publicity campaigns related to specific conditions, as opposed to initiatives specifically branded under the Pfizer name.
- A key aspect of Pfizer's brand identity is improving people's well-being and health at various life stages.

In 2013 the Pfizer brand was supported by the tagline, "Working Together for a Healthier World." More than just a catchy phrase, the statement embodies the essence of Pfizer's brand identity of developing promising treatments for a wide range of diseases. As Pfizer explains on its website, "Good health is vital to all of us, and finding sustainable solutions to the most pressing health care challenges of our world cannot wait."

Consumers mainly connect with Pfizer through the brand-name drugs it has produced and through publicity campaigns related to specific health conditions, as opposed to initiatives specifically branded under the Pfizer name. Through Viagra, Pfizer is well known for providing a solution to erectile dysfunction. The company's position in this regard was reinforced by its ability to be first to market with this type of drug. Beyond prescription drugs, Pfizer developed Advil, which is synonymous with over-the-counter pain relief. This association has been reinforced through advertising campaigns featuring musician Jon Bon Jovi and talk show host Regis Philbin, who demonstrate how Advil helps them overcome pain and engage in the activities they love.

A key aspect of Pfizer's brand identity is improving people's well-being and health at various life stages. In 2012 Pfizer unveiled a campaign called Get Old in an attempt to reinforce this aspect. The company developed the microsite www.getold.com to help people address the challenges associated with longer life spans. In addition Pfizer began working with other organizations and leaders, such as the U.S. Conference of Mayors, to develop strategies for addressing an aging population.

In the August 20, 2012, issue of *ADWEEK*, Pfizer Corporate Affairs Chief Sally Susman commented on the campaign as follows: "There was a conversation out there that people were very interested in, and it really has to do with moving through the turnstiles of the different chapters of your life. The young woman who becomes a mother, that person who has the midlife moment, the elderly person leaving home for a retirement center—at these turnstiles of life, people were having a conversation about what information and what support they need to help them make that decision more productively, more smoothly. This was a conversation on the top of their mind where they felt we might have something to say of value."

BRAND STRATEGY

- Pfizer's brand strategy is highly targeted, concentrating on specific patient populations.
- Lifestyle advertising is utilized to connect Pfizer's branded pharmaceuticals with consumers.
- Pfizer's strategy sometimes involves the adaptation of its drugs for specific global markets.
- Globally, Pfizer has lived out its tagline "Working Together for a Healthier World" through innovative partnerships with other industry leaders to accelerate the development of cancer treatments in Asia.

Pfizer's brand strategy is highly targeted, concentrating on specific patient populations. Pfizer uses lifestyle advertising to connect its branded pharmaceuticals with consumers through print and television advertising, and it employs an interactive strategy that involves websites devoted to specific drugs. Regardless of the drug being promoted, the prospect of relief is a common thread.

In the case of Celebrex, Pfizer's treatment for conditions such as rheumatoid arthritis, osteoarthritis, and the management of acute pain in adults, Pfizer speaks to the target audience by depicting middle-aged and older adults engaging in activities such as throwing a Frisbee on the beach, riding a bicycle, or swimming. These images are supported by the tagline, "For a body in motion." A similar approach is taken with other popular Pfizer drugs. Lyrica, which is used for treating pain from conditions such as shingles, spinal cord injury, fibromyalgia, and diabetes, is promoted with the tagline "Relief is possible with Lyrica." In the case of Viagra, Pfizer targets advertisements toward middle-aged men, using the catchphrase, "This is the age of taking action."

Pfizer's strategy sometimes involves the adaptation of its drugs for specific global markets. For example, Pfizer has piloted Viagra as an over-the-counter drug in the United Kingdom, with only a pharmacist consultation required. In Mexico a chewable form of the drug, named Viagra Jet, was introduced in 2011 after the company discovered men were grinding up the traditional tablet form with hopes of making it faster-acting or easier to swallow. At that time, Mexico was the developing world's largest market for Viagra.

Globally, Pfizer has lived out its tagline "Working Together for a Healthier World" through innovative partnerships. For example, it formed the Asian Cancer Research Group Inc. in partnership with Eli Lilly & Co. and Merck & Co. By working together, the three industry leaders hoped to accelerate the development of treatments for the most common cancers in Asian nations, beginning with gastric and lung cancers.

BRAND EQUITY

- Pfizer ranked 40th on the 2012 Fortune 500 list, ahead of competitors such as Merck (57th) and Abbott Laboratories (71st).
- The *Financial Times* ranked Pfizer 19th in its FT Global 500 ranking in September 2012, at which time its market value was US$185.6 billion.
- According to data from *IMS Health World Review Analyst 2012*, Pfizer held the largest share of the global pharmaceutical market in 2011 at 6.6 percent.
- According to *Pharm Exec's* 2012 ranking of the top 50 pharmaceutical companies, Pfizer was first, ahead of second-place Novartis and third-place Merck.

Pfizer ranked 40th on the 2012 Fortune 500 list, ahead of competitors such as Merck (57th) and Abbott Laboratories (71st). The *Financial Times* ranked Pfizer 19th in its FT Global 500 ranking in September 2012, ahead of competitors Novartis (25th), Roche (26th), and Merck (32nd). At that time the *Financial Times* indicated that Pfizer's market value was US$185.6 billion. According to data from *IMS Health World Review Analyst 2012*, Pfizer held the largest share of the global pharmaceutical market in 2011 at 6.6 percent, ahead of Novartis (6.0 percent) and Merck (4.7 percent).

In *Pharm Exec's* 2012 ranking of the top 50 pharmaceutical companies, Pfizer was first, ahead of second-place Novartis and third-place Merck. According to the publication, Pfizer had five products with sales of at least US$2 billion. With more than US$500 million in revenues generated from 18 countries beyond the United States, Pfizer maintained strong value despite the patent expiration for its well-known, brand-name cholesterol drug, Lipitor.

Pfizer's high value is also reflected in other, more specific rankings. For example the company is a significant player in areas outside of prescription-drug manufacturing. According to information from SymphonyIRI Group Inc.'s *2011–2012 Nonfoods Handbook*, in 2011 Pfizer held 18.2 percent of the lip-care market, behind GlaxoSmithKline (21.3 percent), but ahead of Blistex (11.9 percent), Burt's Bees (9.2 percent), and Carma Labs (8.1 percent).

BRAND AWARENESS

- Pfizer has long had strong brand-awareness within the professional community, dating back to its pioneering role in the mass production of penicillin during World War II.
- Among consumers Pfizer is mainly known for the brand-name pharmaceuticals it has trademarked.
- In the fourth quarter of 2012, four of Pfizer's drugs were among the most-prescribed medicines in the United States.

Beginning with its pioneering role in the mass production of penicillin during World War II and its primary role in creating the contemporary pharmaceutical marketing approach during the 1950s, Pfizer has developed strong brand-awareness within the professional community. This is especially true among pharmacists and physicians. However, to consumers Pfizer is known more for the brand-name pharmaceuticals it has trademarked.

Consumer awareness of the Pfizer brand has been accomplished through the introduction of a number of popular drugs. The most famous of these was probably Viagra, a pill for treating erectile dysfunction introduced in 1998. This example of the new breed of "lifestyle drugs" was an instant blockbuster; more than 350,000 prescriptions were written in the first three weeks after its release. Another popular medication is Celebrex, which had the most successful pharmaceutical launch in U.S. history; 19 million prescriptions were written in the first 12 months after release.

In the fourth quarter of 2012, four of Pfizer's drugs were among the most-prescribed medicines in the United States, according to pharmaceutical sales figures monitored by Drugs.com. In addition to Pfizer's well-known drugs Celebrex and Viagra, these included the antibiotic Zyvox, used for treating skin and bacterial infections that were resistant to other forms of antibiotics, and Lyrica, for treating pain associated with conditions such as shingles, spinal cord injury, fibromyalgia, and diabetes.

BRAND OUTLOOK

- Like many other pharmaceutical companies, Pfizer has been challenged with the expiration of patents for popular, brand-name drugs, but the company has responded with innovative programs for maintaining market share.
- Pfizer has taken strides to position itself for global success with both prescription and over-the-counter drugs.
- In 2012 Pfizer's use of incentives to generate prescriptions from physicians in emerging countries resulted in a US$60 million fine from the Justice Department for violating the Foreign Corrupt Practices Act.

Like many other pharmaceutical companies, Pfizer has been challenged with the expiration of patents for popular brand-name drugs. A prime example of this is the expiration of patent protection for Celebrex which takes place in 2014. This comes on the heels of the expiration of Pfizer's patent for its popular cholesterol drug Lipitor in late 2011.

In order to protect erosion of market share related to expiring patents, Pfizer has pursued a number of innovative tactics, which bodes well for its future success. In the case of Lipitor, Pfizer has employed a program that offers home delivery of the drug to patients for only US$4 per month. The company also has co-marketed an "authorized generic" version of Lipitor in partnership with Watson Pharmaceuticals. Finally, Pfizer was exploring the possibility of making Lipitor an over-the-counter drug, although analysts were skeptical about the chances of this happening.

Pfizer has taken strides to position itself for global success with both prescription and over-the-counter drugs. For example, in order to promote Viagra in Africa and the Middle East, the company hired the Connecticut-based marketing agency Adams & Knight Inc. to develop a promotional campaign targeting pharmacists, physicians, and patients. Additionally the company acquired the consumer health business of Ferrosan, securing lifestyle products and dietary supplements needed to bolster its over-the-counter offerings in emerging markets, including the Ukraine, Russia, and certain Nordic countries.

As Pfizer looks to expand in emerging markets, the company has encountered some roadblocks. Unlike the case in the United States, many pharmaceutical companies in emerging countries are more aggressive in utilizing incentives or gifts to generate prescriptions from physicians. However, in 2012 Pfizer was required to pay a US$60 million fine when the U.S. Justice Department found the company in violation of the Foreign Corrupt Practices Act. Specifically, the act equates gifts with bribes in the case of government workers, a category that often includes state-employed doctors.

FURTHER READING

"Lipitor's Patent Loss Signals Future for Other Top Drugs." *Drug Store News*, January 30, 2012.

McMains, Andrew. "A New Spin on an Old Topic: Pharmaceutical Giant Pfizer Eschews Sentimental TV Spots in Favor of a Frank Online Conversation with Consumers about the Topic of Aging." *Adweek*, August 20, 2012, 13.

Pfizer Inc. "Who We Are. What We Stand For." Accessed February 9, 2013. http://www.pfizer.com/about.

"Pfizer Inc." *International Directory of Company Histories*. Ed. Jay P. Pederson. Vol. 79. Detroit, MI: St. James Press, 2006.

"Pfizer Won't Let Go of Lipitor, to Begin Home Delivery." *India Business Insight*, November 24, 2011.

"Taking Its Medicine; Pfizer." *Economist*, August 11, 2012.

Wilson, Duff. "As Generics Near, Makers Tweak Erectile Drugs." *New York Times*, April 14, 2011.

PHILIPS

BRAND ORIGINS

- Philips was founded in Eindhoven, the Netherlands, by members of the Philips family in 1891.
- Philips played an integral part in the development of lightbulbs, radio, television, CDs, DVDs, and many other inventions.

- The company is one of the world's largest makers of lighting products, home electronics, and medical devices.
- During the last third of the 20th century, Philips struggled in a market flooded with inexpensive Japanese electronics products.
- Although it has remained a consistent global leader among electronics companies in the 21st century, Philips posted losses in 2002, 2008, and 2011.

Philips was founded as Philips & Company in 1891 during the Industrial Revolution by a young engineer named Gerard Philips and his father, Frederik Philips, who financed the venture. Gerard's teenage brother Anton was enlisted as business manager in 1895 and became the company chairman after Gerard retired in 1922.

At its factory in Eindhoven, the Netherlands, the firm manufactured carbon-filament lightbulbs and other electrical products, soon establishing itself as a leading innovator in the burgeoning electrical industry. Over the years, Philips has used its research laboratory to help pioneer the development of incandescent lightbulbs, radios, televisions, electric shavers, compact audiocassettes, compact discs, DVDs, LaserVision optical discs, high-definition satellite hardware, medical X-ray technology, transistors, integrated circuits, nuclear control instruments, portable defibrillators, and numerous other inventions.

Philips flourished initially, employing 2,000 individuals in the Netherlands by 1910. By 1939 the company had expanded to include 45,000 employees in both the Netherlands and in other countries, and it grew to encompass more than 165,000 employees in 60 countries by 2012. By 2010 Philips was the ninth largest conglomerate in the world. However, the firm has also survived daunting setbacks.

During World War I Philips set up factories to produce some of the materials needed for the company's operations. During World War II, those factories in the Netherlands were bombed, first by the Allies and later by the Nazis as they withdrew from their occupation of the country. Philips rebuilt after World War II and began a steady global expansion that lasted into the 1970s, at which time Japanese companies flooding the market with inexpensive electronics products challenged the Philips brand. Despite efforts to increase its worldwide customer base, improve efficiency, and cultivate successful product lines, Philips continued to struggle throughout the 1980s and 1990s, laying off thousands of workers, closing factories, and closing or selling dozens of subsidiary companies. In 2002 Philips posted record losses of EUR3.21 billion; nevertheless, the company was still the global leader in lighting, electric shavers, and CD drives, and it was the second-largest producer of color televisions. For most of the next decade, the company posted profits, but it operated at a loss in 2008 and 2011, due in large part to the worldwide economic recession.

BRAND ELEMENTS
- The Philips brand derives its name from the family that started the company.
- Although the name of the company has been changed repeatedly, its core identity as "Philips" has remained constant.
- Numerous subsidiaries have also been identified and united under the Philips brand name.
- The parent company has been referred to as "Big Philips" while some subsidiaries have been called "Little Philips."
- The brand's primary logo is simply the name "Philips" in dark blue capital letters.

As founders of the enterprise, members of the Philips family used their own surname as the brand name that has remained a defining element for more than a century, despite numerous changes in the business itself. Philips & Company was incorporated in 1912 as N.V. Philips Gloeilampenfabrieken, although the company continued to be known informally as Philips. In 1920 a holding company, N.V. Gemeenschappelijk Benzit van Aandeelen Philips Gloeilampenfabrieken (known as N.V. Benzit) was formed and assumed ownership of Philips and other businesses. In 1991 the holding company was dissolved, Philips became the holding company for the entire group, and its name was changed to Philips Electronics N.V. In 1999 the name was changed again, to Koninklijke Philips Electronics N.V. The company is also called Royal Philips Electronics N.V. and Royal Philips Electronics of the Netherlands.

Throughout its long history the corporation has operated numerous subsidiary businesses, some bearing the Philips name, including Philips Research Laboratories, Philips Lamp Works, Philips Medical Systems, Philips Consumer Communications, Philips Industries, the North American Philips Corporation, and the North American Philips Lighting Corp. The corporation grew into a complex multinational conglomerate with headquarters in the Netherlands and with certain subsidiaries functioning as virtually independent businesses. These were called "Little Philips," while the parent corporation was called "Big Philips."

The brand's logo is simply the name "Philips" in blue, block capital letters. In its early years, the company used various forms of the name as a logo and as part of the graphic design in advertisements. For instance, a campaign launched in 1898 involved postcards with pictures of Dutch costumes. The name "Philips" was spelled out on a row of light bulbs across the top of each card.

Another familiar logo features "Philips" in white letters on a black rectangle with a tan shield behind it. Below is a red circle with stars and three wavy lines, representing radio waves making their way through the evening sky. This logo has been used since the 1920s on radios and other audio equipment and in advertisements.

BRAND IDENTITY
- Philips is promoted as a brand that delivers innovative products to help improve people's lives.
- During the 1990s the brand's promise was expressed in the slogan "Let's make things better."
- Since 2004 the Philips slogan has been "Sense and Simplicity," promising advanced products that are easy to use.

Philips is positioned as the brand that uses research and cutting-edge technology to improve people's lives. The company stresses the word "innovation," not only in technological inventiveness but also in the way the business itself operates, including the way it relates to its customers. The slogan "Let's make things better" was adopted in 1995 to announce the company's intention to sell products that would help people. Instead of being aimed at building a coherent brand image, however, the marketing emphasis was more on the technology itself.

In 2004, responding to focus groups that said new technology was often too complex, the company adopted the brand promise "Sense and Simplicity" in an effort to change its image and speak to consumers in more relatable language. The slogan expressed a commitment to deliver sensibly designed, highly advanced products that would be simple to use. Over the next few years, the company was restructured into three divisions: lighting, health care, and consumer lifestyle. The aim was to reinforce the idea that Philips is an organization that revolves around its customers and is structured to meet their needs. The Philips brand has since been portrayed as "people-centric" and "market-driven," created to meet the needs of customers around the world.

In keeping with the goal of making the world a better place, Philips promotes sustainability and conservation of resources. By marketing technology such as LED lighting, Philips also expects to accelerate its own growth as the world shifts toward more energy-efficient products.

BRAND STRATEGY

- Koninklijke Philips Electronics N.V. is a parent company operating in three market segments called the Philips Group.
- The Philips brand has sometimes become entangled with other brands because the corporation owns numerous subsidiaries.
- The vast conglomerate adopted the slogan "One Philips" to unite its diverse businesses under one banner.

Koninklijke Philips Electronics N.V. is a parent company operating in three segments called the Philips Group: lighting; consumer lifestyle (products such as televisions, home audio systems, electric shavers, and small appliances); and health care (products such as medical imaging equipment and patient monitoring systems).

Over the years the Philips brand became somewhat tangled with other brands as a great many subsidiaries were bought, sold, merged, and reorganized. The company markets electronics under various brand names, including Philips, Magnavox, and Sylvania. It has also owned countless businesses that have marketed a wide assortment of brands, including Norelco electric shavers, Lifeline medical emergency pendants, Genie garage door openers, Selmer musical instruments, and Polygram Records. Occasionally, brand names have been combined, as in Philips-Magnavox and Philips-Norelco, to inform consumers that the product was made by Philips or to introduce one brand into a country where the other brand was already known.

Since the 1990s Philips has worked to improve coordination among its subsidiaries. The slogan "One Philips" has been used worldwide in all markets and on all products since 1995 to unite the conglomerate's myriad businesses under one banner. The corporation still owns many subsidiaries but is tightening its focus on its core brand.

BRAND EQUITY

- After operating at a loss in 2011, Philips underwent restructuring, cut thousands of jobs, and rebounded in 2012.
- The Philips brand was valued at US$6.7 billion at the end of 2011, down from US$9 billion in 2010.
- Philips was ranked number 144 among the world's top 500 brands in 2012, down considerably from number 85 in 2008.

The Philips Group had sales of EUR20.1 billion in 2009, EUR22.3 billion in 2010, and EUR22.6 billion (about US$29.5 billion) in 2011. Net income was EUR4.88 billion in 2007, EUR0.42 billion in 2009, and EUR1.45 billion in 2010. The company posted losses of EUR0.9 billion in 2008 and EUR1.3 billion (about US$1.7 billion) in 2011. In 2009 and 2010 Philips claimed 30 percent of the U.S. market for lighting and bulbs, followed closely by Siemens AG and General Electric Co. Philips ranked eighth in the world for electronics and instruments patents in 2010 and second for industrial components and fixtures patents in 2009, close behind France-based Schneider Electric SA.

In response to the poor performance of 2011, the firm was drastically overhauled and thousands of jobs were cut. After a loss of EUR160 million (US$211 million) in the final quarter of 2011, Philips rebounded to post a net profit of EUR249 million (about US$324.8 million) for the first quarter of 2012. Sales increased 7 percent for the quarter.

Brand Finance, a brand valuation consultancy firm, calculated the value of the Philips brand at US$6.7 billion at the end of 2011, down from US$9 billion in 2010 and US$8.3 billion in 2009 but up from US$5.6 billion in 2008. The brand's rating was AA+ in three of those years and AAA in 2010.

Among the world's top 500 brands in 2012, Brand Finance ranked Philips at number 144, down from 103 in 2011 and 85 in 2008. Philips was ranked fourth among the top 50 companies in the Netherlands in 2012, down from second in 2011. Of the world's most valuable electronics brands, Toshiba was ranked first with a brand rating of US$14.2 billion, Philips was second at US$6.7 billion, NEC was third at US$3.6 billion, and Thermo Fisher Scientific was fourth at US$3.1 billion. The *Financial Times* cited Philips as the third most valuable leisure goods company in the world in 2011, up from fourth in 2010.

BRAND AWARENESS

- *Fortune* magazine ranked Philips seventh among the world's most admired electronics companies in 2010.
- An annual survey named Philips as the Dutch company with the highest rated reputation from 2009 through 2012.
- Philips has been rated twelfth among the world's most meaningful brands.

During the past century, the Philips brand became a household name as the firm introduced one invention after another, and customers purchased hundreds of millions of the company's products. In 2010 *Fortune* magazine ranked Philips seventh among the world's most admired electronics companies and fourth among the most admired companies in the Netherlands. Philips often places high on both of these annual lists.

In the Reputation Institute's Dutch Reputation Award, an annual survey of how Dutch companies are perceived, Philips ranked number one every year from 2009 through 2012. Philips was ranked 23rd in 2011 and 25th in 2012 on the "Global RepTrak 100," the Reputation Institute's worldwide survey, which calculates how consumers perceive companies and how their perceptions affect their purchasing decisions. The Dutch Empathy Monitor, a measure of how well a brand meets the needs of its customers, placed Philips seventh in 2010 and tenth in 2011.

Ethisphere magazine placed Philips second on its list of the world's most ethical medical devices companies for 2011. Also in 2011 Philips placed 12th on the "Top 20 Global Meaningful Brands Index," a measure of how much a brand contributes to individuals, communities, and the environment.

BRAND OUTLOOK

- As a multinational corporation, Philips is attempting to expand its brand globally while tailoring products to specific local markets.
- Philips expects to generate great interest in its brand in developing nations with large populations, such as China.
- The corporation reorganized and increased sales in 2012 but expected slow growth for 2013 due to the ongoing worldwide economic slump.

As a multinational corporation with a presence in more than 60 countries, Philips is attempting to expand its worldwide operations while still adapting its brand to customers at the local level. The company has four regional hubs for manufacturing products, two of which were acquired in 2011, Preethi, in India, and Povos, in China. This approach will allow Philips to speed up the invention and production of items designed for specific cultures. For example, demand for kitchen appliances has been growing rapidly in many countries, especially in Asia. In 2011 Philips moved its base of operations for kitchen appliances to Shanghai, China, to become more attuned to customers there and to be able to deliver merchandise as quickly as competitors can.

China presents opportunities in the healthcare sector as well, since it must provide health care to more than 1.3 billion people, including a growing middle class and regions that have not previously had access to sufficient services. The nation is investing heavily in the necessary infrastructure, and Philips plans to develop innovative technology to help meet China's healthcare needs. Philips has already become one of the leading firms that provide medical imaging technology to

China. From 2007 through 2010, the company's sales of CT and MR technology tripled in China, and growth continued into 2011.

In 2012 Philips formed a partnership with Jones Lang LaSalle, a real estate services firm, to change the way industrial and commercial buildings are illuminated. This switch to more energy-efficient lighting systems is expected to help businesses around the world conserve electricity. Philips wants to be perceived as a leader in sustainability and has established sustainable energy goals for each of its business segments to accomplish by the end of 2015.

Philips has reorganized repeatedly over the years, often in response to lagging sales figures, and was in the process of restructuring under new management throughout 2012. After operating at a loss in 2011, the firm showed marked improvement by the spring of 2012, particularly in its healthcare and consumer products segments. Nevertheless, widespread economic recession continued to dampen spending by both consumers and governments. Chief Executive Frans van Houten said the company would require additional restructuring and should take steps to launch new products more swiftly. Philips projected sales growth of 4 percent to 6 percent for 2013.

FURTHER READING

Brand Finance. "Most Valuable Brands in Electronics." *Brandirectory*. Accessed October 1, 2012. http://brandirectory.com/brands/industry_group/Electronics/.

———. "Philips Profile." *Brandirectory*. Accessed October 1, 2012. http://brandirectory.com/profile/philips.

Capell, Kerry. "Global Economics; How Philips Got Brand Buzz." *Bloomberg BusinessWeek*, July 30, 2006.

Cohen, Kerstan. "Koninklijke Philips Electronics N.V." *International Directory of Company Histories*. Ed. Karen Hill. Vol. 119. Detroit, MI: St. James Press, 2011.

"Koninklijke Philips Electronics NV." *Notable Corporate Chronologies*. Detroit, MI: Gale, 2010.

"Philips Announces Vision 2015 Strategic Plan Focused on Growth and Strengthening Leadership in Health and Well-Being." *Investment Weekly News*, October 2, 2010.

"Philips Axes 2,200 More Jobs after Losing 1.3bn." *Daily Mail* (London), September 12, 2012.

"Q2 2012 Koninklijke Philips Electronics NV Earnings Conference Call—Final." *Fair Disclosure Wire*, July 23, 2012.

"Ranking the Brands; Philips." RankingTheBrands.com. Accessed October 9, 2012. http://www.rankingthebrands.com/Brand-detail.aspx?brandID=361.

Wang, Andrew. "Global LED Lighting's Production Value to Hit US$66.67 b. in 2020." *Taiwan Economic News*, September 10, 2012.

Webb, Sara. "Philips Surprises with Q1 Turnaround." Reuters, April 23, 2012.

PIZZA HUT

—————■—————

BRAND ORIGINS

- Pizza Hut was founded in 1958 by brothers Dan and Frank Carney in their home town of Wichita, Kansas.
- In 1971 Pizza Hut became the world's largest pizza chain, according to sales and number of restaurants.
- In 1976 Pizza Hut established the 35-by-65-meter, red-roofed Pizza Hut restaurant building as the regulation size and design for all of its new establishments.
- Pizza Hut's Personal Pan Pizza was introduced in 1983.

Pizza Hut was founded in 1958 by brothers Dan and Frank Carney in their home town of Wichita, Kansas. When a friend suggested opening a pizza parlor, then a rarity, they agreed that the idea could prove successful, and they borrowed US$600 from their mother to start a business with partner John Bender. Renting a small building at 503 South Bluff in downtown Wichita and purchasing secondhand equipment to make pizzas, the Carneys and Bender opened the first Pizza Hut restaurant. On opening night they gave pizza away to encourage community interest. A year later, in 1959, Pizza Hut was incorporated in Kansas, and Dick Hassur opened the first franchise unit in Topeka, Kansas.

In the early 1960s Pizza Hut grew on the strength of aggressive marketing of the pizza restaurant idea. In 1970 Pizza Hut opened units in Munich, Germany, and Sydney, Australia. That same year the chain's 500th restaurant opened in Nashville, Tennessee. In 1971 Pizza Hut became the world's largest pizza chain, according to sales and number of restaurants, then amounting to just a little more than 1,000. At the end of 1972, Pizza Hut made its first, long-anticipated IPO offer of 410,000 shares of common stock to the public on the New York Stock Exchange.

In 1976 the 35-by-65-meter, red-roofed Pizza Hut restaurant building was introduced as the regulation size and design for all new establishments. In 1977 Pizza Hut merged with PepsiCo, becoming a division of the global soft drink and food conglomerate. Pizza Hut introduced the Pan Pizza in 1980, followed by the Personal Pan Pizza in 1983. In the late 1990s PepsiCo combined its restaurant businesses, including Pizza Hut, Taco Bell, and KFC, into a single division. In October 1997 the company spun off the restaurant division, creating an independent, publicly traded company called Tricon Global Restaurants, Inc., which eventually was named Yum! Brands. Pizza Hut celebrated its 50th birthday in 2008.

BRAND ELEMENTS

- The red-roofed Pizza Hut building, featured on the brand's logo, originated in 1976.
- An abbreviated version of Pizza Hut's name, "The Hut," complete with a special logo, is sometimes used in marketing campaigns.
- Pizza Hut has utilized various marketing taglines, including "Making It Great," "America's Favorite Pizza," and "Your Favorites. Your Pizza Hut."
- The Pizza Hut brand has been adapted to the unique tastes of different international markets.

In 2012 the Pizza Hut logo consisted of several components. The brand name was featured in stylized white type on a black background. The word "Pizza," which included a green dot over the "i," appeared directly beneath a graphic depiction of the distinctive red roof that sits atop the company's restaurants. On a second line, the word "Hut" was underscored by a yellow diagonal line. The red-roofed Pizza Hut building-style originated in 1976, when the company first introduced the now-iconic restaurant architecture. At that time, a 35-by-65-meter building became the regulation size and design for new Pizza Hut establishments.

The Pizza Hut brand has been subject to a certain amount of experimentation over the years. For example, in 2008 the company employed an "April Fool's" publicity stunt in the United States, explaining that it was changing its name to Pasta Hut. A new modified logo and temporary signage were developed. Six months later the company announced that it was rebranding its restaurants in the United Kingdom under the Pasta Hut name for real, as part of a more health-conscious focus. Although the exterior signage on some of its restaurants was changed, Pizza Hut ultimately reverted back to its original name in 2009.

Pizza Hut also has experimented with an abbreviated version of its name: "The Hut." A special logo, similar to the original one, has been used for this approach. The company indicated that this was not a name change, but only part of its marketing strategy. However, some restaurants have used both logos, prompting some industry observers to question whether the company was considering a rebranding effort. In addition to its name, Pizza Hut also has utilized various taglines, including "Making It Great," "Your Favorites. Your Pizza Hut," and "America's Favorite Pizza."

The Pizza Hut brand has been adapted to the unique tastes of different international markets. For example, in the February 27, 2012, issue of *USA Today*, YUM! Brands CEO David Novak explained that consumers in India have special preferences in flavors and sauces. For this reason, Pizza Hut offers Indian customers the Masala line of pizzas.

BRAND IDENTITY

- Pizza Hut has expanded the identity of its brand beyond pizza.
- "The Hut," an abbreviated, more all-encompassing version of the Pizza Hut brand name, is sometimes used in marketing communications and restaurant signage.
- Pizza Hut's approach to communicating its broader offerings to potential customers is a global one.

Pizza Hut has expanded beyond its pizza roots to offer customers items such as pasta and wings. In promoting its broader offerings, the brand's very name has been subject to experimentation. For example, in 2008 and 2009 some Pizza Hut restaurants were temporarily rebranded under the Pasta Hut name as part of a more health-conscious focus. In addition, an abbreviated, more all-encompassing version of the brand's name, "The Hut," is sometimes used in marketing communications and restaurant signage. These moves have prompted criticism from some industry analysts, who argue that Pizza Hut has created confusion around its brand image.

Pizza Hut's approach to communicating its broader offerings to potential customers is a global one. For example, in India the brand utilized the tagline, "Pizzas and Much More" in 2012. At that time Pizza Hut was introducing pasta in India. This was a challenge because the Italian dish was new to Indian tastes. The Pasta Masti campaign was developed to alleviate negative perceptions about pasta among Indian consumers and encourage them to explore the new food.

Pizza Hut has also promoted the brand as an appropriate choice during special times of the year. For example, in Pakistan an All-You-Can-Eat promotion was replaced with the Ramazan Fiesta during Ramadan, an annual observance in which Muslims practice fasting from dawn to sunset. In its August 7, 2012, issue, the *Daily Times* (Lahore, Pakistan), commented that the new offer would discourage food waste, explaining: "The former 'All You Can Eat' format served as an unrestrained invitation to gluttony and waste, colliding with the very spirit of Ramadan."

BRAND STRATEGY

- International economic expansion is the driving force of Pizza Hut's growth strategy.
- Through franchising, YUM! Brands is reducing company ownership in Pizza Hut restaurants, especially in underperforming or highly penetrated markets.
- Pizza Hut employs a brand strategy that relies heavily on public relations.

International growth is the driving force of Pizza Hut's expansion strategy. Pizza Hut parent YUM! Brands generated more than half of its operating profit in China and 72 other emerging countries in 2011. In China, Pizza Hut followed a strategy centered on value and variety, and a commitment to change 25 percent of its menu twice annually.

In early 2012 Pizza Hut revealed plans to establish 150 new locations in China by the end of the year, building on its existing base of 764 units. In addition to focusing on promising third- and fourth-tier cities, Pizza Hut was employing other innovative brand-building strategies in China. For example, in mid-2012 YUM! Brands formed a partnership with one of the country's largest electrical appliance retailers, Suning Appliance Co. Ltd., paving the way for the establishment of 150 in-store restaurants, including Pizza Hut units, over the course of five years.

Franchising is another key element of the Pizza Hut brand strategy. By 2011 YUM! Brands was focusing its resources more on emerging and underpenetrated markets, while reducing company ownership in underperforming or highly penetrated markets. In keeping with this strategy, a refranchising program was established to reduce ownership in Pizza Hut restaurants to 5 percent by the end of 2012. In addition, plans also were made to sell the company's 380 UK Pizza Hut operations to a master franchisee.

According to an interview with Pizza Hut Chief Marketing Officer Kurt Kane in the August 1, 2012, issue of *PR Week*, Pizza Hut's brand strategy relies heavily on public relations. Kane explained that Pizza Hut attempts to identify a "PR hook" first before developing an advertising campaign. One example was a 2012 campaign to promote the P'Zolo, which touted the new sandwich-pizza combination as a better alternative to the traditional sub sandwich. In Chicago, Pizza Hut wrapped a subway car in large format P'Zolo graphics and distributed samples to travelers.

BRAND EQUITY

- According to *Nation's Restaurant News*, Pizza Hut held a commanding 38.75 percent share of the restaurant industry's pizza segment in 2012.
- Citing figures from *Pizza Today*, *Market Share Reporter* indicated that Pizza Hut was the market leader by sales in 2011 at US$11 billion.
- In 2010 Pizza Hut was named the "Most Trusted Food Service Brand" in India for the sixth consecutive year by the *Economic Times*.

According to the *Nation's Restaurant News* 2012 Top 100 Market Share Overview, pizza represented 6.9 percent of restaurant industry sales overall. With 38.75 percent

of the pizza market, Pizza Hut held a commanding lead within the segment. This compared to competitors Domino's Pizza (24.26 percent), Papa John's Pizza (15.53 percent), Little Caesars Pizza (10.05 percent), and Papa Murphy's (4.90 percent).

Citing figures from *Pizza Today's* ranking of the leading pizza firms for 2011, *Market Share Reporter* indicated that Pizza Hut was the clear leader, with annual sales of US$11 billion. Ranking second was Domino's Pizza (US$6.7 billion), followed by Papa John's International (US$2.4 billion), and Little Caesars Pizza (US$1.35 billion). Noteworthy competition also came from California Pizza Kitchen (US$710.0 million), Papa Murphy's Take 'N Bake Pizza (US$653.3 million), and Sbarro (US$620 million).

Pizza Hut's brand equity is global in nature. For example, for the sixth consecutive year the *Economic Times'* Brand Equity Most Trusted Brands Survey found Pizza Hut to be the "Most Trusted Food Service Brand" in India. In addition, Pizza Hut was the only restaurant included in the survey's ranking of the Top 20 Service Brands.

BRAND AWARENESS

- With a commanding 38.75 percent of the restaurant industry's pizza segment in 2012, Pizza Hut enjoyed the significant awareness that corresponds with a strong leadership position.
- Pizza Hut had achieved strong recognition worldwide by 2012, with operations in about 97 countries and territories.
- By August 2012 the Pizza Hut brand had amassed more than 7 million fans on Facebook.

In October 2012, *PR Week* revealed that 93 percent of Americans eat pizza at least once per month. With a commanding 38.75 percent of the restaurant industry's pizza segment in 2012, according to *Nation's Restaurant News*, Pizza Hut enjoyed the significant awareness that corresponds with a strong leadership position. By this time Pizza Hut operated approximately 7,600 restaurants in the United States, and America's relationship with the brand spanned more than five decades.

In addition to strong brand awareness in its native country, Pizza Hut had achieved strong recognition worldwide, with operations in about 97 countries and territories worldwide. At that time, YUM! Restaurants International, the international division of Pizza Hut parent YUM! Brands, operated 5,383 units. In China, where the brand was achieving significant growth, 764 Pizza Hut locations were in operation by the end of 2011.

Social media is a prime example of the strong recognition surrounding Pizza Hut. By August 2012 the brand had amassed more than 7 million fans on the social network Facebook. In addition Pizza Hut had made significant inroads on other social channels, including Pinterest and Twitter, providing additional opportunities for consumer engagement. Following the 2012 launch of the P'Zolo, a new sandwich-pizza combination, Pizza Hut Chief Marketing Officer Kurt Kane indicated that corresponding photos and reviews appeared online within 12 hours of the first television advertising.

BRAND OUTLOOK

- International economic expansion is the driving force of Pizza Hut's growth strategy.
- YUM! Brands considers China to be Pizza Hut's most promising growth opportunity for the 21st century.
- Pizza Hut has responded to difficult economic conditions by offering value-based promotions.
- An increased focus on obesity and healthy eating has led Pizza Hut to use better ingredients and modify menu choices.

Faced with a relatively mature domestic market, Pizza Hut looked to international markets for future growth. Beyond the United States, significant opportunities existed in China. In addition, India and Thailand also were part of the brand's expansion strategy.

In its *Annual Customer Mania Report*, parent YUM! Brands indicated that it considered China to be "the best restaurant growth opportunity of the 21st century." During the late 1990s the company determined that the casual-dining operating model was achieving its greatest successes in China. Since that time YUM! Brands has devoted tremendous resources to expanding in China. In 2012 alone, plans were in place to establish 150 new Pizza Hut locations throughout the country, where it already operated more than 700 restaurants. Pizza Hut enhanced its chances for future success in China with a company-owned and company-operated Chinese distribution system for its restaurants.

India and Thailand were also of great importance to Pizza Hut's future growth. By 2015, YUM! Brands India had plans to establish 1,000 new locations in the country. A US$150 million investment would support the future growth of Pizza Hut, Pizza Hut Delivery, and other YUM! restaurant brands. In Thailand, where only 35 percent of the country was urbanized in 2012, YUM! Brands expected to double its restaurant locations to 1,000 by 2020. In 2012 the company owned and operated 70 Pizza Hut locations in Thailand.

In 2012 difficult economic conditions challenged Pizza Hut and other leading restaurant players. Pizza Hut has responded to this challenge by offering value-based promotions, including a US$10 Dinner Box that includes a one-topping medium pizza, along with 10 cinnamon sticks and 5 breadsticks. Although Domino's Pizza has followed a similar approach, some competitors, including Papa John's International, have resisted discounting.

In addition, an increased focus on obesity and healthy eating has pressured restaurants to offer healthier choices to consumers. After introducing a pizza called "The Natural" in 2008, Pizza Hut began using all-natural ingredients chain-wide in 2009. The company has also expanded its menu beyond pizza to include pasta and other options. In the United Kingdom, Pizza Hut upgraded its salad bar and took measures to reduce saturated fat and salt in its products in 2008.

FURTHER READING

Chu, Kathy. "Yum Brands CEO Takes Global View on Fast Food." *USA Today*, February 12, 2012.

Mehra, Priyanka. "Will Pastas Do It for Pizza Hut?" *Pitch*, August 13, 2012.

O'Leary, Noreen. "Hard Times for 'The Hut.'" *Brandweek*, June 7, 2010.

"Pizza Hut, Inc." *International Directory of Company Histories.* Ed. Derek Jacques and Paula Kepos. Vol. 121. Detroit, MI: St. James Press, 2011.

"Pizza Hut Named Most Trusted Food Service Brand in India by the Economic Times for the Sixth Year." Benzinga, September 3, 2010.

"Pizza Hut Rejects Criticism of New Offer." *Daily Times* (Lahore, Pakistan), August 7, 2012.

Stein, Lindsay. "CMO Q&A: Kurt Kane, Pizza Hut (Extended)." *PR Week*, August 1, 2012.

"Top 100 Market Share Overview." *Nation's Restaurant News*, June 25, 2012.

"Top Pizza Firms, 2011." *Market Share Reporter*. Detroit, MI: Gale, 2012.

Yum! Brands, Inc. *2011 YUM! Brands Annual Customer Mania Report*. Accessed October 5, 2012. http://www.yum.com/annualreport/pdf/2011_AR.pdf.

"YUM! Eyes $1 Billion in Revenues in India by 2015." *India Business Insight*, September 24, 2011.

"Yum to Open Restaurants in Appliance Retail Stores." *Franchise Plus*, May 10, 2012.

PLAYSTATION

BRAND ORIGINS

- After working with Nintendo to create a video game system in the 1980s, Sony developed what became PlayStation One.
- PlayStation 2 launched in 2000, and PlayStation 3 was introduced in North America in 2006.
- Sony introduced its PlayStation Portable in North America in 2005 and PlayStation Vita, another handheld device, in 2012.
- Games for PlayStation are available on CDs and memory cards, via the Internet, and on Sony tablet computers and smartphones.

"Long Live Play" is the slogan for a Sony PlayStation advertising campaign, and millions of video game players around the world would agree. Founded in Tokyo in 1946, Sony has long been a popular producer of electronic products such as televisions, audio and video recording devices, and music players. It entered the video game market in the 1990s with the introduction of the PlayStation system.

In the 1980s, Sony had worked with Nintendo to develop a video game system that incorporated Sony's CD-ROM drive with the graphic capabilities of a computer system. While Nintendo abandoned the project, Sony Computer Entertainment continued its work. It introduced the initial PlayStation console, also known as PlayStation One or PS One, in Japan in 1994 and in the United States in 1995. This system achieved instant and massive success.

This success continued with the launch of other PlayStation systems, such as PlayStation 2 (PS2, launched in 2000) and PlayStation 3 (PS3, introduced in North America in 2006). These were not just game consoles; they were entertainment units that could play CDs and DVDs, such as those containing the movies and music released by parent company Sony. Other Sony game hardware systems include the handheld systems PlayStation

Portable (PSP), introduced in North America in 2005, and the PlayStation Vita (PS Vita), introduced worldwide in 2012.

Sony also markets and sells other content, including hundreds of games for its PlayStation systems. These games are available on CDs or memory cards for consoles and handheld systems. The PlayStation 3 console and the handheld PSP and Vita also have Internet capabilities that allow users to access games through the PlayStation Network, which offers sites for downloading music, movies, television programs, and sporting events as well as PlayStation Home sites for social games and other offerings. The PlayStation Network also features PlayStation Plus, a subscription service that offers games and other content. Gamers can also purchase and play PlayStation Mobile games for Sony's tablet computers, smartphones, and other portable electronic devices.

Another PlayStation development, PlayStation Move, can be attached to a PlayStation 3 console to capture players' movements and then incorporate those actions into a video game. The system competes with the motion-capture systems of other video game systems, such as the Nintendo Wii MotionPlus and the Microsoft Xbox Kinect. The PlayStation Move demonstrates how Sony and its PlayStation brand have applied different technologies for home entertainment purposes.

BRAND ELEMENTS

- The PlayStation consists of a capital P and a capital S and appears in different colors depending on its placement.
- PlayStation 3 consoles feature the Homoarakhn font, which also appeared in posters for *Spider-Man, Spider-Man 2,* and *Spider-Man 3.*
- Some PlayStation commercials feature a clinking or crashing sound accompanying the brand identification and a robotic-sounding voice pronouncing the name as "Play Sta-tion."
- The PlayStation logo appears in *PlayStation* magazine, on PlayStation's websites covering different global regions, and in advertisements.
- The PlayStation logo appears on a multitude of products and other items: game consoles, handheld systems, controllers, games, accessories, and packaging.

The PlayStation logo is an upright, red capital P and a yellow, green, and blue capital S. The capital P appears to be three-dimensional and is at a slight angle. The capital S appears at an angle as well and appears on a plane perpendicular to the base of the capital P. This logo appears entirely in one color in certain instances.

PlayStation also has other distinctive brand elements. PlayStation 3 consoles feature the Homoarakhn font,

which also appeared in posters for the movies *Spider-Man, Spider-Man 2,* and *Spider-Man 3,* which were released by Columbia Pictures, a division of Sony Corporation. Users of PlayStation consoles and handheld devices can play a number of Spider-Man games, which link the PlayStation brand and the Spider-Man character in a number of ways.

PlayStation's game system has distinctive sounds. A number of PlayStation commercials feature a clinking or crashing sound accompanying the brand identification. Advertisements also include the PlayStation logo accompanied by a robotic-sounding voice that pronounces the brand as "Play Sta-tion." This voice and pronunciation have appeared in commercials since the 1990s, although not continuously. PlayStation thus uses a number of visual and auditory cues to identify its brand.

The PlayStation P and S logo appears in various places, such as *PlayStation* magazine, PlayStation websites for different global regions, and advertisements. The logo also appears on myriad PlayStation products: game consoles, handheld systems, controllers, games, accessories, and packaging.

Aspects of these games have become famous parts of the PlayStation brand. A 2011 advertisement in the "Long Live Play" campaign illustrates this. The commercial features live-action versions of PlayStation characters celebrating a video game player named Michael, thus highlighting the characters and emphasizing their connection to PlayStation video games. It also confirms the fame and popularity of PlayStation, its games, and the games' characters.

BRAND IDENTITY

- PlayStation's original goal was that of "creating a gaming platform that would become as pervasive as the VCR and change the industry forever."
- PlayStation launched an interactive relationship marketing program called Playstation Underground to reward its more loyal users and to create a subculture of gaming.
- PlayStation continued to reset the bar higher and revolutionize gaming by launching new systems that provided gamers with experiences they had never had before.

According to the PlayStation website, the PlayStation brand started with the lofty goal of "creating a gaming platform that would become as pervasive as the VCR and change the industry forever." However, the company wasn't satisfied with simply creating a gaming system that sold more than a million units in its first six months. It wanted to create a unique and long-lasting relationship with the gamers who were its primary consumers. To accomplish this, it instituted an interactive relationship marketing program called Playstation Underground, which recognizes and rewards loyal gamers by providing them with new challenges and giving them insider news on games, merchandise, and offers. PlayStation views itself not just as a brand, but as a subculture for intense gamers.

After its successful start, PlayStation continued to revolutionize gaming by launching new systems that provided gamers with experiences they had never had before. One of PlayStation's goals is to continually reset the bar higher and higher by developing the most advanced gaming systems. It aims to be the "must-have" console for all gamers and an all-in-one entertainment hub for the home. To that end, its innovations have included features like more lifelike animation, the ability to play DVDs and Blu-ray, portable gaming, Internet browsing, and social connectivity.

BRAND STRATEGY

- In 2006 PlayStation's "Play Beyond" promotional campaign used traditional print advertising, commercials, and billboards, as well as online advertisements linked to a PlayStation website.
- PlayStation has showcased products through the PlayStation Experience, a traveling exhibition of PlayStation systems and games.
- In 2008, PlayStation and media channel InStadium made televisions at U.S. football stadiums look like giant PSP devices to promote Sony's Madden Entertainment Bundle.

Sony has employed various strategies to highlight PlayStation systems and games. In 2006 it launched the "Play Beyond" campaign to advertise PlayStation 3 in North America. The campaign used traditional tools such as television commercials, print advertisements, and billboards. It also used online advertisements that were linked to a website with PlayStation information. PlayStation 3 consoles could connect to this site as well.

As part of the "Play Beyond" campaign, Sony placed kiosks with PlayStation hardware, software, and Internet connections at several stores. The PlayStation Experience, a traveling exhibition of PlayStation systems and games that accompanied concerts and other events, was used to demonstrate the brand's products. The PlayStation Experience also made appearances at events in London and India.

In 2008 Sony partnered with media channel InStadium to make televisions look like giant PlayStation Portable (PSP) devices. To promote PlayStation, the technology was used with televisions at stadiums hosting American professional football games. The promotion advertised Sony's Madden Entertainment Bundle, a package consisting of a PSP and a PlayStation Madden NFL

game, a popular game featuring John Madden, a former American football coach and television commentator. The pseudo-PSPs/stadium televisions displaying real football games in progress looked like PSP systems with PlayStation football games, thus reminding people of what they could get by purchasing the Madden Entertainment Bundle.

BRAND EQUITY

- By 1998, PlayStation One held about a 40 percent share of the global game market.
- The PlayStation unit helped Sony Computer Entertainment earn 10 percent of Sony's worldwide revenues and 22.5 percent of its operating income.
- In October 2012, PlayStation 3 held a 45.1 percent global market share, and the handheld PSP had a 54.9 percent global market share.
- Young people in India named PlayStation the top gaming brand in Nielsen's "Most Exciting Youth Brands," a poll published in 2012.
- In 2012 PlayStation's brand value was US$3.69 billion.

In 1998, just a few years after the launch of PlayStation One, the console held about a 40 percent share of the global video game market. By this time, Sony Computer Entertainment had already generated sizable profits for the parent company—10 percent of Sony's worldwide revenues and 22.5 percent of its operating income.

Millions of people worldwide have continued to buy PlayStation systems and games. In October 2012, PlayStation 3 held the largest market share for video game consoles, with a 45.1 percent global market share, compared to the Microsoft Xbox 360's 34.6 percent share and the Nintendo Wii's 20.3 percent share. In the handheld market, Sony's PSP system captured a 54.9 percent global market share, while Nintendo's DS claimed a 45.1 percent share. The other PlayStation handheld system, the PS Vita, held a 24.3 percent share in a market dominated by Nintendo's 3DS, with a 75.7 percent share.

PlayStation's strong market performance has translated into global consumer excitement. Published in 2012, Nielsen's "Most Exciting Youth Brands" survey named PlayStation the top gaming brand. The poll surveyed young people in India from the ages of 15 to 24. They ranked PlayStation 2, PlayStation 3, and the PSP higher than the Microsoft Xbox 360 console, Nintendo's DS handheld system, and Nintendo's Wii console.

In 2012 Brand Finance reported that PlayStation's brand value was US$3.69 billion, up from US$3.34 billion the year before. It received user ratings of four stars for reliability and performance but only three stars in the category value for money.

BRAND AWARENESS

- A 2006 poll found that 72 percent of North American consumers knew about the PlayStation 3 before its release, and 6 percent intended to buy one.
- In the same poll, 65 percent of the respondents were aware of the PSP, and about 3 percent intended to purchase one.
- In 2012 a Sony employee claimed that about 93 percent of PlayStation Plus subscribers planned to renew their subscriptions.
- North American college students represent Sony and PlayStation in the PlayStation Ambassador Program, which promotes the PlayStation brand on college campuses.
- College students can learn about the video game industry through the PlayStation Summer Internship Program.

Consumers around the world are very familiar with PlayStation products. A poll of North American consumers before the release of the PlayStation 3 in 2006 revealed that 72 percent were aware of the PlayStation 3, and 6 percent intended to purchase one. In the same poll, 65 percent of the respondents were aware of the PSP, with about 3 percent of these consumers intending to purchase one.

Consumer satisfaction with the PlayStation Plus (PS Plus) game and content subscription service has led to brand awareness and sales for the PlayStation Network. A Sony employee claimed in 2012 that about 93 percent of PS Plus subscribers planned to renew their subscriptions.

Sony and PlayStation have taken various steps to increase awareness of the PlayStation brand among students. In Sony Computer Entertainment America's PlayStation Ambassador Program, North American college students work with other students and faculty members to promote the brand on college campuses. College students can also learn about the video game industry in the PlayStation Summer Internship Program.

BRAND OUTLOOK

- In 2012, PlayStation launched its Vita handheld system, which provides access to software updates and content via a broadband network.
- Sony installed PlayStation 3 and Vita gaming systems, as well as its Bravia televisions, in London's O2 arena in 2012.
- Sony planned to launch the PlayStation 4 console in time for Christmas 2013 and to offer significantly increased power and new features.
- Continuing to adapt to new technological developments, Sony Computer Entertainment bought the California cloud-gaming company Gaikai in 2013.

In 2012, PlayStation launched its Vita handheld system, which offers delivery of software updates and content over a broadband network. That same year, it installed PlayStation 3 and Vita systems, as well as Sony Bravia televisions, in the O2 arena in London. In 2012 and 2013, Sony also worked on developing the PlayStation 4, which it announced would go on sale in time for Christmas 2013. This new generation of PlayStation was expected to be much more powerful than its predecessor with more lifelike graphics and more believable virtual worlds. Other features expected to be part of the new system were a motion-sensing system, connectivity with smartphones, and the ability to record gameplay. One open question was whether the system would have backwards compatibility, allowing gamers to use games from their previous systems on the new model. This is a feature much desired by the gaming community and could play a major factor in the new rollout's success. Microsoft is expected to launch a new version of Xbox about the same time, so PlayStation will need every advantage it can muster to keep a competitive edge over its rival.

In addition to its work on hardware and systems, Sony has also focused on developing games for the PlayStation systems. In 2012, Sony Computer Entertainment bought Gaikai, a California company specializing in cloud gaming, which allows users to stream games onto devices connected to the Internet. This acquisition will likely change the way many PlayStation users get their games as the technology is being incorporated into PlayStation 4. The deal also demonstrated Sony continues to pursue relationships with changing technologies.

FURTHER READING

Balakrishnan, Ravi. "Sony PlayStation Tops Most Exciting Youth Brands in Gaming." *Economic Times,* February 22, 2012. Accessed November 5, 2012. http://articles.economictimes.indiatimes.com/2012-02-22/news/31086946_1_ps2-ps3-atindriya-bose.

D'Angelo, William. "2012 Year on Year Sales and Market Share Update to October 20th." *VGChartz,* October 26, 2012. Accessed November 5, 2012. http://www.vgchartz.com/article/250505/2012-year-on-year-sales-and-market-share-update-to-october-20th/.

"In-Stadium Turns Stadium TV's into Sony PSP Branding Pieces." *Partnership Activation,* December 8, 2008. Accessed November 5, 2012. http://www.partnershipactivation.com/headlines/2008/12/8/in-stadium-turns-stadium-tvs-into-sony-psp-branding-pieces.html.

Ngak, Chenda. "PlayStation 3 'Michael' Commercial Is a Sweet Tribute to Gamers." *CBS News,* October 5, 2011. Accessed November 5, 2012. http://www.cbsnews.com/8301-501465_162-20116142-501465.html.

"PlayStation Plus 'Contributing in a Big Way' to Increase PSN Sales and Awareness.'" *Player Essence,* October 25, 2012. Accessed November 5, 2012. http://playeressence.com/ playstation-plus-contributing-in-a-big-way-to-increase-psn-sales-and-awareness/.

"PS3 'Play Beyond' Marketing Campaign Press Release from North America." *Three Speech,* November 24, 2006. Accessed November 5, 2012. http://threespeech.com/blog/2006/11/ps3-play-beyond-marketing-campaign-press-release-from-north-america/.

Quilty-Harper, Conrad. "Sony's PlayStation Brand Strongest in the Industry." *joystiq,* February 24, 2006. Accessed November 5, 2012. http://www.joystiq.com/2006/02/24/ sonys-playstation-brand-strongest-in-the-industry/.

Sony Corporation. "Business Highlights." Accessed November 5, 2012. http://www.sony.net/SonyInfo/IR/financial/ar/2012/ financial/.

"Sony Corporation." *International Directory of Company Histories.* Ed. Jay P. Pederson. Vol. 108. Detroit: St. James Press, 2010. http://bi.galegroup.com/essentials/article/GALE %7CI2501313435/8a03994a8b059132fbf4f2936e736e78? u=itsbtrial.

PORSCHE

AT A GLANCE

Brand Synopsis: An elite sports car with a romantic image, Porsche is a high-quality, prestigious German brand for people who value status and luxury.

Parent Company: Porsche Automobil Holding SE
Porscheplatz 1
Stuttgart D-70435
Germany
http://www.porsche.com

Sector: Consumer Discretionary

Industry Group: Automobiles and Components

Performance: *Market share*—less than 1 percent (2012). *Sales*—EUR10.93 billion (US$14.15 billion) (2011).

Principal Competitors: Aston Martin; BMW; Ferrari; Lamborghini; Maserati; Mercedes-Benz

BRAND ORIGINS

- Ferdinand Porsche began his career building coaches for Austrian emperor Franz Josef and in 1901 created the world's first gas-electric hybrid vehicle.
- At the direction of Adolf Hitler, Ferdinand Porsche developed several prototypes for the Nazi "people's car," or Volkswagen.
- The company fell on such hard times after World War II that it survived by performing auto repairs.

- The Type 356, released in 1948, was the first car to bear the Porsche brand name.

Born in 1875 in what was then Austria-Hungary, Ferdinand Porsche began his career building coaches for Emperor Franz Josef. Improving on a design for a battery-powered automobile, in 1901 he created the world's first gas-electric hybrid. During World War I, he designed vehicles for the Austrian military, and in 1923 he took a job in Germany with Daimler, for which he designed the Mercedes SKK. In April 1931, he opened his own firm.

Adolf Hitler's accession to power in 1933 proved fortuitous for Porsche. Fascinated by automotive power as an expression of political power, Hitler immediately announced plans both for a nationwide racing initiative as well as the development of a cheap, reliable car for German workers. Porsche's P-Wagen would become prominent in racing circles, but he would achieve much greater impact with the "people's car," or Volkswagen. Between 1935 and 1939, he designed several prototypes for what became known as the Beetle, but the project had to be abandoned when World War II began.

During the war, Porsche designed tanks for the German army, and after Germany's defeat, the Allies relocated him to France to develop the Volkswagen. Amid unrest in the French automotive industry, the country's government arrested Porsche for war crimes and put him to work creating designs for French automaker Renault. He was imprisoned in a medieval fortress at Dijon, and his health suffered. Following a bail payment by his son Ferry, he was released in April 1947, having never stood trial, and died of a stroke in December 1951.

Ferry Porsche had assumed leadership of the company during his father's imprisonment. The company had been forced by war, and later by the Allied seizure of its property in Stuttgart, to relocate to Gmünd, Austria. The firm struggled to survive during those years, even performing auto repairs for a time. Its fortunes changed dramatically, however, with the 1948 release of the Type 356, the first car to bear the Porsche brand name.

BRAND ELEMENTS

- Ferdinand Porsche used the title associated with his honorary engineering doctorate, "Dr. Ing. h. c." (*honorus causa*), in his company's original name.
- Both the Porsche and Ferrari logos feature rearing (rampant, in heraldic terminology) horses.
- Native English speakers often pronounce the Porsche brand name as a single syllable, but it should be pronounced "Porsh-uh."

For many years Porsche's parent company bore the curious-sounding name "Dr. Ing. h. c. Ferdinand Porsche KG." This is a reference to the fact that Ferdinand Porsche earned an honorary engineering doctorate ("Dr. Ing. h. c." [*honorus causa*]) from the Vienna University of Technology during World War I. The name was later simplified to become Porsche Automobil Holding SE.

Porsche's logo, like that of its competitor Ferrari, depicts a rampant, or rearing, horse. The design pays tribute to Porsche's hometown, Stuttgart (whose name comes from a medieval German term meaning "stud farm"), the state of Württemberg-Baden, and the region of Swabia. The name *Stuttgart* appears in black letters above the horse, also in black, which dominates the central and smallest of the concentric shields that make up the logo. Around the central shield is a larger one, divided into quadrants, with the upper left- and bottom right-hand sections each bearing a trio of antlers, and with the opposite sections each containing four alternating stripes of black and red. Running above this shield in a shallow arc, set apart by a narrow border, is the name *PORSCHE* in all capital letters. Each of these elements has its own thin black border, outside of which is a narrow strip of gold (also the background color of the entire logo) that surrounds all of the logo's elements, and then another thin black border.

In addition to memorable advertising campaigns and taglines such as "There is no substitute," Porsche is known for its sequential numbering of its cars (for example, 356, 550, 911, 914, and so on) and for an ongoing dispute over the pronunciation of its name. Native English speakers often pronounce it as a single syllable ("Porsh"), but in keeping with its German origins, it should be pronounced "Porsh-ə," with the second syllable voiced as an unaccented schwa, or "uh"-sound.

BRAND IDENTITY

- Porsches have long had a romantic image, thanks in part to association with flamboyant and sometimes tragic figures such as James Dean and Janis Joplin.
- Hollywood has often celebrated the Porsche, which featured memorably in Tom Cruise's breakthrough 1983 comedy *Risky Business*.
- The tagline "Porsche: there is no substitute" speaks both to the brand's exclusivity and to its reputation for streamlining and adherence to tradition.

Porsche cars have long had a romantic image. In part this is due to the many celebrities who have been known to drive them. The fact that a number of them were tragic figures only adds to the mystique. Janis Joplin owned a flamboyantly painted 356 and mentioned the brand (along with one of its competitors) in her song "Mercedes Benz." James Dean died in his 550 Spyder, and Hollywood hair stylist Jay Sebring was driving his 911 just a few hours before his murder at the hands of the Manson Family at actress Sharon Tate's house in 1969.

In a memorable sequence from his breakthrough 1983 comedy *Risky Business,* the young Tom Cruise eludes Guido the Killer Pimp by skillfully handling his father's 928 on a nighttime chase through the streets of a Chicago suburb. Afterward, he turns to Rebecca De Mornay and says: "Porsche: there is no substitute." This, the most famous of the brand's advertising taglines, succinctly expresses its identity. On the one hand, it speaks of the elitism that distinguishes it and other high-end marques from more workaday brands such as Ford or Toyota. However, it also calls to mind characteristics specific to Porsche: simplicity, streamlining, and adherence to tradition.

Whereas other car companies offer a wide array of models, Porsche in 2012 concentrated on just five. A highly acclaimed Internet commercial from 2012 celebrated this fidelity to basics: over stirring music and iconic images of Porsches past and present, a voice proclaims, "We keep reinventing ourselves … and still remain true to ourselves. We challenge the turn of every screw and bolt … but never our origins."

BRAND STRATEGY

- For decades Porsche targeted a narrow market of consumers who could afford a high-priced, high-performance sports car.
- Facing imminent bankruptcy in 1993, Porsche began to diversify its product line despite protests from loyal customers.
- Because Porsche has introduced several models outside its traditional image, customers worry that the brand is losing its identity.

For many years Porsche was a brand that targeted a narrow market of consumers who could afford a high-priced, high-performance sports car. The brand rolled out a few new models each year, all of them fitting comfortably into the brand's traditional image, and customers enjoyed the fact that they belonged to a small group of people who owned a Porsche. However, by 1993 this strategy was not financially viable. High production costs, economic recession, and other factors brought the company to the verge of bankruptcy.

In need of revenues, Porsche diversified to appeal to a wider consumer base with a less expensive model called the Boxster, introduced in 1996 despite protests from loyal customers. Brand loyalists were even more upset in 2002 when Porsche targeted the lucrative American market by launching a five-seat, mid-size luxury SUV (sports utility vehicle) called the Cayenne. By 2010 the Cayenne accounted for approximately half of Porsche's sales. Although this model generated impressive profits and helped the company recover financially, the heavy SUV represented a giant step away from Porsche's traditional image as a sleek, fast sports car.

Porsche has always had close ties to Volkswagen (VW), a less prestigious line of cars designed for everyday use. In fact, it was Ferdinand Porsche who designed the original Volkswagen Beetle. In 2009 Porsche unveiled its first four-door luxury sedan, the Panamera, during a time when the firm was being taken over by Volkswagen, joining a group of automobiles that included Audi, Lamborghini, and Bentley. Again, the brand's traditional customers complained, saying that Porsche was losing its identity.

In 2012, as Porsche was preparing to introduce another entry-level SUV called the Macan and hinting that other models might be on the way, the company's head of sales and marketing reassured customers with the promise, "No matter what we build, we build sports cars."

In 2012 Porsche made both consumer and racing automobiles, as well as aircraft engines and even tractors. Its consumer lineup consisted of five basic vehicles: the 911, Boxster, and Cayman sports cars; the Panamera four-seat sedan; and the Cayenne SUV, with the Macan SUV scheduled for launch in 2013.

BRAND EQUITY

- In 2012, for the third year in a row, Porsche placed 72nd in Interbrand's ranking of the best global brands.
- In 2012, Interbrand estimated Porsche's brand value at US$5.15 billion, an increase of 12 percent over the previous year.
- Also in 2012, Porsche placed first in the J. D. Power Automotive Performance, Execution, and Layout Study for the eighth year in a row.

In 2012, for the third year in a row, Porsche placed 72nd in Interbrand's ranking of the best global brands. Interbrand estimated Porsche's brand value at US$5.15 billion, an increase of 12 percent over the previous year. Of the 13 automotive brands on the list, Porsche ranked 9th, behind competitors Mercedes-Benz and BMW (ranked 2nd and 3rd, respectively, in the automotive sector) but well ahead of Ferrari (13th in the automotive sector and 99th overall.)

Also in 2012, Porsche placed first in the J. D. Power Automotive Performance, Execution, and Layout Study for the eighth year in a row. In addition to this award, which reflected the overall popularity of the Porsche marque, the 911 and Cayenne won in their respective sectors. Porsche also earned top-10 rankings in the J. D. Power Customer Service Index Ranking for luxury brands in 2011 and 2012, and in the Sales Satisfaction Index Ranking from 2009 through 2012.

Despite these successes, Porsche has endured financial challenges in the 21st century, particularly in the wake of the global financial crisis that began in 2008. The timing could hardly have been worse for the company, which was in the process of attempting to purchase Volkswagen. In the process, Porsche took on about EUR9 billion (US$11.80 billion) in debt, and this development ultimately brought about a role reversal, with VW purchasing a 49.9 percent stake in Porsche in 2009.

BRAND AWARENESS

- The success of the Porsche scene in the film *Risky Business* owes a great deal to the fact that the brand had a memorable slogan.
- In contrast to competitor Ferrari, Porsche advertises and in 2011 undertook the marketing campaign with the slogan "Engineered for Magic. Every Day."
- The Porsche Design Group, founded by Ferdinand Porsche's grandson, handles Porsche's extensive merchandising efforts.

Porsche enjoys top-of-mind awareness all over the world. The following example pays great tribute to the brand's popularity and its allure. In what must rank as one of the all-time greatest examples of product placement in a film, a chase scene in the 1983 coming-of-comedy *Risky Business* showcases the smooth handling of a Porsche 928 and ends with the protagonist facing the camera and repeating the brand's advertising tagline: "Porsche: there is no substitute." The scene owes a great deal, no doubt, to the skills of a promising young actor named Tom Cruise, not to mention the stunt driver, but it would have fallen flat if viewers had not readily recognized the slogan.

Inasmuch as it *has* a memorable advertising slogan, Porsche contrasts sharply with its rival Ferrari, which has reinforced its image of inaccessibility by not advertising at all. In March 2011, Porsche widened this marketing gap with Ferrari by undertaking an aggressive integrated marketing campaign that incorporated the use of television, the Internet, direct mail, and mobile marketing. Porsche and advertising firm Cramer-Kasselt developed the campaign, which featured the slogan "Engineered for Magic. Everyday," after consumer research showed that a large segment of potential buyers considered a Porsche out of reach financially.

Porsche has long promoted itself through the sale of merchandise, and in this it is not atypical of luxury carmakers. Ferrari may not advertise, but it has certainly increased awareness (and profits) through the sale of branded goods. What is unusual about Porsche's merchandising, however, is the fact that an entirely separate, though closely linked, company handles the production and sale of these items. This is Porsche Design, formed by F. A. Porsche, son of Ferry, after he left the company due to differences with his cousin Ferdinand Piëch.

Porsche Design's first product in 1973 was a luxury chronograph wristwatch, which proved so successful that the company received contracts from several NATO (North Atlantic Treaty Organization) countries to make watches for their armed forces. The company marketed other traditional types of branded merchandise, including sunglasses and luggage, as well as products like machines and furniture. Some of these did not even bear the Porsche logo, but sales undoubtedly benefited from the products' association with the luxury carmaker. In 2003, Porsche Design became Porsche Design Group, and it continues to handle all Porsche-licensed merchandising.

BRAND OUTLOOK

- In the early 21st century, Porsche set out to buy Volkswagen AG but ended up being acquired by VW.
- The overturning of a German law enabled Porsche to acquire a majority stake in Volkswagen, but Porsche consequently became burdened with debt.
- Heavily in debt, Porsche was already financially vulnerable when the global financial crisis struck in 2008.
- Looking toward the future, Porsche plans to produce more hybrids, SUVs, and even station wagons, with a goal of 200,000 sales annually by 2018.

Since the beginning, Porsche and Volkswagen have had strong links. As Jack Ewing of the *New York Times* observed, the fact that "fancy Porsches contain some plebeian Volkswagen genes has never been a secret." Yet, for two-thirds of a century, "Porsche and Volkswagen have been like a couple who never quite moved in together." That all changed in the early 21st century, though not quite in the way that Porsche's leadership had hoped.

In late 2005, Porsche purchased slightly less than a 20 percent stake in Volkswagen AG, and in March 2007 it upped this holding to more than 30 percent. Later that year, the European Court of Justice struck down Germany's so-called "Volkswagen Law," which had been implemented to prevent a takeover of VW by limiting the power of shareholders possessing more than a 20 percent stake in the company. Thereafter, Porsche made no secret of its plans for a takeover, and by the beginning of 2008 it held a majority stake in VW.

Unfortunately for Porsche, it had gone heavily into debt in its effort to buy up VW shares, which put it in a highly vulnerable position just as the global financial crisis struck in the fall of 2008. When a merger was finally announced, in August 2009, it was Volkswagen that held the upper hand in the new "integrated automotive group." The fact that the chairman of Volkswagen AG was Ferdinand Piëch, grandson of Porsche's founder, only intensified the irony. In July 2012, Volkswagen AG announced that it would assume full ownership of Porsche the following month.

Though it had taken an unexpected course, the Volkswagen deal brought Porsche back to its origins by joining it with Ferdinand Porsche's other car brand. Given that Ferdinand had created the world's first gas-electric hybrid in 1901, it was only fitting that, as hybrids became an emerging trend a century later, his company would catch on and launch its own Cayenne, Panamera, and 918 Spyder hybrids. At the same time, the SUV segment at Porsche continued to grow, and the company's leadership discussed plans for a Panamera station wagon. CEO Matthias Mueller told *Automotive News* that he planned to introduce at least one new Porsche every year and to increase sales to 200,000 automobiles a year by 2018. With this new partnership and an effort to increase models, the Porsche brand is prepared to go the long haul.

FURTHER READING

Bayley, Stephen. "Can the Porsche Mythology Survive Under VW?" *Times* (London), July 30, 2009, 22.

Ewing, Jack. "Will Porsche Still Shine in Volkswagen's Garage?" *New York Times*, August 29, 2010, BU-1.

Hamprecht, Harald. "Porsche Boss: A Launch Every Year; 200,000 Sales by 2018." *Automotive News*, February 21, 2011, 18.

"Porsche AG." *International Directory of Company Histories*. Ed. Tina Grant. Vol. 31. Detroit: St. James Press, 2000. *Business Insights: Essentials*. Accessed December 12, 2012. http://bi.galegroup.com/essentials/article/GALEpercent7CI2501304075/3d7b1e625296fcfa0a949cb276af6d19?u=itsbtrial.

"Porsche Looks Beyond Sports Cars; Station Wagon, SUV, Coupe Are Possibilities." *Automotive News*, September 10, 2012. *Business Insights: Essentials*. Accessed December 12, 2012.

http://bi.galegroup.com/essentials/article/GALEpercent7CA3022
72891/4f3ed026107d77d264969ea2ec086e45?u=itsbtrial.

Reiter, Chris, and Christian Wuestner. "Porsche Has
an Identity Crisis amid Its SUV Success." *Business-Week,* July 5, 2012. Accessed December 12, 2012.
http://www.businessweek.com/articles/2012-07-05/
porsche-has-an-identity-crisis-amid-its-suv-success.

Schafer, Daniel. "Porsche Vows to Fix Dented Brand Image."
Financial Times, March 3, 2010. Accessed December 12,
2012. http://www.ft.com/intl/cms/s/1950cb0a-26f0-11df-8c08-00144feabdc0,Authorised=false.html?_i_location=htt
ppercent3Apercent2Fpercent2Fwww.ft.compercent2Fcmsp
ercent2Fspercent2F0percent2F1950cb0a-26f0-11df-8c08-00144feabdc0.html&_i_referer#axzz2Es0JLd7W.

Welsh, Jonathan. "Porsche Touts Versatility in New Ad Cam-paign." *Wall Street Journal,* March 24, 2011. Accessed Decem-ber 12, 2012. http://blogs.wsj.com/drivers-seat/2011/03/24/
porsche-touts-versatility-in-new-ad-campaign/.

PRADA

■

Brand Synopsis: Prada is a luxury brand known for its sense of innovation, modern elegance, and style.

Parent Company: PRADA S.p.A.
Via Antonio Fogazzaro 28
Milan
Italy
http://www.pradagroup.com

Sector: Consumer Discretionary

Industry Group: Consumer Durables and Apparel

Performance: Prada luxury goods, including luggage, shoes, apparel, and accessories, are sold in 70 countries around the world in luxury department stores, specialty stores, and about 400 company-directed shops. The brand generates nearly $3 billion in annual sales for Prada.

Principal Competitors: LVMH—Moet Hennessy Louis Vuitton S.A.; Gucci Group

BRAND ORIGINS

- Mario Prada founded a leather shop in Milan, Italy, in 1913.
- Prada became the official supplier to the Italian Royal Household in 1919.
- Miuccia Prada inherited the family business in 1978 and began expanding the Prada brand.
- Miu Miu brand was added in 1993.

- Church's and Cart Shoe brands were added through acquisition.

The Prada brand traces its origins to 1913 when Mario Prada opened a leather goods store in Milan, Italy, offering handbags, traveling trunks, beauty cases, and other luxury leather accessories. Prada quickly became known for its well-designed, handcrafted products, which caught the attention of Italy's noble families. Prada solidified its place in the luxury market in 1919 when it became the official supplier to the Italian Royal Household. It was a commercial arrangement that provided the company with the right to incorporate the House of Savoy's coat of arms and knotted rope design into the Prada logo.

For the next several decades, Prada remained a relatively obscure luxury brand, albeit one favored by Europe's upper class, including Princess Grace of Monaco. The direction of the Prada business and brand began to change in the mid-1950s with the death of Mario Prada. The wife of his son ran the shop for the next 20 years, and in 1970 her daughter, Miuccia Prada, joined the business. Luxury merchandise and the fashion industry had been of little interest to the young woman, who had earned a Ph.D. in political science and for several years studied mime. Nevertheless, she would make good use of her unconventional preparation to help Prada become one of the world's most influential luxury brands.

A turning point in the history of Prada came in 1977 when Miuccia Prada met leather manufacturer Patrizio Bertelli, maker of fine leather shoes and bags. The following year, when Miuccia Prada inherited Prada, she and Bertelli became business associates and a decade later a married couple. While Bertelli revamped Prada's operations, dropping English suppliers and updating luggage styles, Miuccia turned her attention to design. Using the military-grade black nylon her grandfather used as protective covering for steamer trunks, she produced backpacks and totes that became her first commercial success, due in large part to the lack of logo that provided anti-status cache. Soon, however, the bags carried a silver triangle Prada logo.

The Prada brand was not yet supported by advertising at this stage. In 1983, Prada opened a second, modern boutique in Milan. Over the next few years, awareness of the Prada brand was nurtured through the addition of a new line of footwear in 1985 and a collection of women's ready-to-wear apparel in 1989. In the meantime, Prada stores opened in Florence, Paris, Madrid, and New York.

A concerted effort was made to develop the Prada name in the United States. In 1993 the company launched a second brand called Miu Miu (Miuccia Prada's nickname). This new line offered less expensive women's apparel targeting a younger market. The Prada label would also continue to expand into new categories. In the mid-1990s men's clothing was added. The Prada Sport collection of outdoor gear was introduced in 1997. A Miu Miu line for men was introduced in 1999 as well.

At the heart of Prada's strong growth was Miuccia's fashion sense and ability to continually surprise the market. Bertelli also supported Prada through a vertical corporate structure that brought continuity to the brand. New retail stores opened around the world, and to reinforce the brand message of exclusivity the retail space displayed minimal amounts of merchandise. Moreover, the company discontinued products that grew too popular.

In keeping with the consolidation of luxury brands in the late 1990s Prada added several brands during an acquisition spree. Unable to support the heavy debt load it acquired, most of those properties were ultimately divested. Two brands were retained, however, joining Prada and Miu Miu to create the Prada group of brands. They were Church's, an English men's shoe brand, and Car Shoe, an Italian brand of handmade moccasins especially suited for sports car driving.

BRAND ELEMENTS

- Brand features two logos.
- Prada goods are functional, yet classic and elegant in styling.
- Miu Miu brand features more sensual styling.
- Retail experience plays a key role in Prada's brand.
- An integrated value chain ensures highly quality merchandise.

Prada merchandise is well crafted, made from unconventional fabrics, and employs design innovations. Moreover, Prada goods are functional, yet classic and elegant in styling. Prada merchandise bears one of two logos. The older

one, a knotted-rope oval surrounding "Prada, Milano" rendered in a simple typeface, reinforces the brand's venerability. The newer triangular logo offers a more modern look, although the Savoy coat of arms helps tie the brand to its deeper roots. The Miu Miu logo is futuristic: the brand is spelled out in lower case letters, and white space interrupts the "m" and the "u" to create a wave sensation.

Prada styling is also a key brand element. In some respects, Miuccia Prada is the embodiment of the brand. Bringing unconventional training to the art of fashion design, she has continually surprised the fashion industry. In essence, Prada goods reflect her taste as well as her restlessness. Rather than following trends, she sets them, a trait that is also at the heart of the Prada brand. She also developed Miu Miu into a brand with its own distinct identity that relied on more sensual styling.

An important element to both the Prada and Miu Miu brands is the retail experience. Not only does the décor of the boutiques separate Prada from its competitors but also from its younger sibling. Colors are used to help differentiate the brands further. While Prada stores emphasize chartreuse shading, Miu Miu uses brilliant vermilion as its signature color.

In addition, Prada considers its integrated value chain to be an important element in the success of its brands. Not only does Prada design and create new collections in house, it produces most of its own prototypes and samples. As a result, Prada is able to create detailed specifications for its products to provide greater control over the quality of its outsourced production. Such attention to detail ensures that high-quality merchandise remains an important Prada brand element.

BRAND IDENTITY

- Prada boasts lengthy ties to the luxury market.
- The Prada brand reflects customers who consider themselves intellectual, creative, and innovative.
- Celebrities are an important part of maintaining Prada's brand identity.
- Associations with contemporary art reinforce brand identity.

The Prada name has long been associated with luxury merchandise, at least with a narrow slice of a regional market market. Since the early 1980s, however, the brand has gained recognition with a broader swath of upscale consumers around the world. Primarily women, the target customers consider themselves intellectual, creative, and innovative. These traits are at the heart of Prada's brand identity and are reflected in Prada's high quality apparel, which combines unconventional fabrics with original modern designs.

Prada's two logos reinforce the brand's identity. One old, one new, they reflect a classic appeal and an innovative spirit, and together help to extend a brand promise to core customers who value superior taste as well as self-expression. Prada styling is crucial to this image. The brand projects elegant minimalism and, most of all, modernity. The styling of the Miu Miu brand plays an equally key role. While still of high quality in materials and construction, the brand is less expensive than Prada and more sensual and futuristic in spirit, in keeping with the younger market it targets.

The retail stores have long been an important way to present Prada's image. The Prada "epicenter" that opened in the SoHo section of New York City in 2001, for example, took customers and retailers by surprise, reinforcing the idea of Prada as an innovative brand. It featured plasma-screen monitors, now commonplace but unusual for the time, as well as glass dressing-room doors that could frost over electronically, and the first round glass elevator in the United States. To further reinforce the Prada brand, retail stores display a minimum amount of merchandise on the selling floor, so that scarcity brings to mind exclusivity. The décor of Miu Miu boutiques are also carefully designed to reflect that brand's image, combining classic materials with a futuristic air.

Not only does Miuccia Prada reflect the identity of the Prada brand, so too do the celebrities that wear Prada apparel and accessories. The brand received unsolicited attention with the 2003 publication of the novel "The Devil Wears Prada," featuring a thinly-veiled depiction of renowned fashion editor Anna Wintour. The book and the Prada brand received even greater notice three years later with the release of a motion picture version of the property starring Meryl Streep. While demanding and abrasive, Streep's character also reflected key aspects of Prada's brand identity and target customers: well heeled intellectual, creative, fashionable women.

Several other celebrity women in the fashion industry and arts were also known to wear Prada, helping to reinforce Prada's image. To help carve out its own identity in the mid-1990s, Miu Miu made use of actress Drew Barrymore, then in her early 20s, in advertisements to increase the brand's appeal to a younger market. In addition to creative advertising campaigns, Prada's brand identity was burnished through its well-executed fashion shows and company-sponsored events. Prada sponsored contemporary art exhibits and incorporated contemporary art into the backdrop of some of its fashion shows. In one 2012 show, for example, the seating configuration resembled a sea of 600 blue flowers set against a green field. In keeping with its luxury image, Prada also tied its brand to the upscale sport of sailing, a personal passion of Bertelli. Not only did the company sponsor his America's Cup bid, Prada outfitted the 2012 Italian Olympic sailing team.

BRAND STRATEGY

- In 1983, a new Milan boutique highlighted Prada's evolving image.
- Prada footwear was introduced in 1985.
- Men's products were added in mid-1990s.
- Prada Epicenters opened in New York, Tokyo, and Beverly Hills
- Branded perfumes and a men's fragrance were launched.

Through much of its history, Prada relied on the association with the Italian Royal Household to maintain its place as a luxury trunk and luggage brand in Europe. After Miuccia Prada inherited the business and forged a creative partnership with her future husband, the brand expanded beyond its roots, both in terms of product lines and geography. Miuccia's nylon bag set the stage. In 1983 a new, more modern Prada boutique opened in Milan to highlight the brand's evolving image. Prada moved beyond bags and luggage in 1985 with the launch of a footwear line. Next, Prada expanded its retail presence, opening boutiques in Florence, Madrid, London Paris, and New York. In 1989, Prada launched a successful ready-to-wear collection of women's apparel.

Prada made a concerted effort to develop its brand in the United States in the early 1990s. A secondary line was created under the Miu Miu name in 1993 to appeal to a younger market without diluting the Prada brand that catered to older, financially well-off women. By the mid-1990s Prada had established itself as a prestigious luxury brand in the United States. During this period, the company sought to extend the brand to male customers, launching a men's line of fashion. A Miu Miu men's line would follow by the end of the decade. In 1997 the Prada sport collection of mountain gear and other outdoor wear was introduced.

Late in the 1990s Prada bolstered its brand through its retail outlets, seeking to add its twist to the shopping experience. The company enlisted innovative architects Rem Koolhaas and Herzog & de Meuron to create what were called Prada Epicenters, which incorporated cultural stimuli and cutting edge technology. The first opened in New York City's SoHo neighborhood in 2001. Two years later, an Epicenter opened in Tokyo, followed by one in Beverly Hills, California, in 2004. Not only did these stores support the Prada brand, they helped the company keep tabs on market trends to maintain the innovative spirit of the brand.

Also in the late 1990s Prada's brand strategy included acquisitions, as rivals Gucci and LVMH began assembling stables of luxury brands. In 1999 Church & Company was acquired. The Church's brand was already well established in the luxury market. Founded in Northampton, England, in 1873, the shoemaker began exporting in the early 1900s. The brand became famous for its fine leather and high-quality craftsmanship. In 2001 Prada gained majority control of Car Shoe. The focus of this luxury brand, founded in Italy in 1963, was on handmade moccasins with soles that incorporated small rubber studs especially suited for driving sports cars. Prada acquired other luxury brands as well at the turn of the millennium, but because of heavy debt and difficult economic conditions they were soon divested.

Prada continued to extend its brand to other product categories in the new century. Both Prada and Miu Miu introduced branded sunglasses in 2000. Through a licensing agreement in 2003, Prada added eyewear products. A Prada perfume, Amber, was introduced in 2004, followed by a men's fragrance in 2006. A second women's perfume, Infusion d'Iris, was unveiled in 2007, and a third, Prada Candy, was launched in 2011. In addition, Prada forged an alliance with LG Electronics to become involved in mobile telephones. "The Prada Phone by LG" was introduced in Europe in 2007. In 2011, a Prada-branded smartphone was launched.

BRAND EQUITY

- Prada was No. 84 on Interbrand's 2012 ranking of the top 100 global brands.
- Interbrand calculated Prada's brand equity at $4.271 billion in 2012.
- Initial public offering of stock in 2011 raised $2.15 billion.
- Prada became first Italian company to list its stock in Hong Kong.

As with any luxury brand, Prada's name and reputation play a significant role in the price a customer is willing to pay. Interbrand, a leading brand consultancy, lists Prada 84th on its 2012 ranking of the top 100 global brands. According to Interbrand's methodology, Prada's brand equity is value at $4.271 billion. Brand Finance plc, a brand evaluation consultancy, claims that Prada's brand is worth 27.3 percent of the company's market capitalization, giving Prada a brand value of $3.346 billion.

Prada S.p.A. posted annual revenues of $2.75 billion in 2004. That amount dipped below $2 billion the following year, as Prada and other luxury brands had to contend with poor economic conditions that hampered growth for the next several years. Growth in China and Russia helped the brand to rebound following the financial crisis of 2008 and 2009. Revenues improved to $2.8 billion and net income to $341.2 million in 2011. It was a performance that allowed the company to raise about $2.15 billion in a long-delayed initial public offering of stock in Hong Kong in 2011. (Although the company had hoped to raise about $2.5 billion.) The equity of the Prada brand played an important part in that valuation. It was also the first time that an Italian company was listed in Hong Kong,

reflected a growing importance of the Asian market for luxury brands. Prada's, brand equity, in fact, was growing increasingly dependent on the loyalty of Asian customer.

BRAND AWARENESS

- Prada was not listed on 2001 survey of 100 most recognizable international fashion brands.
- "Devil Wears Prada," both novel and film, brought attention to the brand.
- Retail outlets play an important role in expanding brand awareness.

Despite a century-long heritage, the general awareness of Prada's brand has been limited. Even in the mid-1990s, when Prada was a trend setter in the fashion world and its merchandise was an undisputed status symbol, the brand was not particularly well known. Despite having grown sales to about $1.4 billion by the turn of the century, Prada was unable to find a place on the 100 most recognizable international fashion brands in a survey released by *Women's Wear Daily* survey in 2001. The "Devil Wears Prada," however, played an important role in Prada's growing brand awareness in the early 2000s. Soon, Prada was listed among the top luxury brands in a number of countries, and ultimately joined the ranks of Interbrand's top 100 global brands.

Another important contributor to Prada's growing brand awareness was its retail presence. The Prada Epicentres located in major cities helped to promote the brand to a host of potential new customers. All told, Prada products were sold in more than 70 countries through nearly 400 company-operated stores, luxury department stores, and multi-brand stores. While the affiliated brands of Miu Miu, Church's, and Car Shoe possess far less general brand awareness, they too are well known in their individual markets.

BRAND OUTLOOK

- The Prada brand is well established in the luxury marketplace, especially in Asia.
- In recent years Prada has blended contemporary art into its fashion shows.
- Prada's future plans may include expanding beyond the luxury category.

The Prada brand has a well established identity in the luxury marketplace, one that the company looks to exploit in emerging markets. Prada has enjoyed especially strong success in Asia, where sales increased at a much faster clip than in Europe or the United States, growing to more than 40 percent of total revenues. Indonesia holds particular promise for Prada and other luxury brands. The Middle East is another area that appears ripe for future growth. The market is expected to double by 2015. Prada has displayed a more cautious approach to India, reluctant to open retail stores in the market.

In the years ahead, Prada might very well expand beyond the luxury category. Writing for CCP-Luxury.com, Oliver Petcu claimed that Prada has already become an institutional lifestyle brand. "Probably the best illustration of how PRADA ascends to an institutional lifestyle luxury brand," he argued," is Miuccia Prada's love for contemporary art." In 2012, as a case in point, an art installation was organized at Prada's SoHo store to honor an exhibit at The Metropolitan Museum of Art. Contemporary art was also blended into Prada's fashion shows.

FURTHER READING

Barone, Amy B. "Patrizio Bertelli: Prada." *Advertising Age,* December 8, 1997.

Cartner-Morley, Jess. "Prada, the Brand that Never Follows Trends." *Guardian,* November 25, 2010.

Forden, Sara Gay. "Prada on the Prowl." *WWD,* December 10, 1997.

———. "Prada Using Star Status to Expand Its Role on Global Stage." *WWD,* February 15, 1996.

Interbrand. "2011 Ranking of the Top 100 Brands." New York: Interbrand, 2012.

Petcu, Oliver. "Have Luxury Powerhouses Prada and Ralph Lauren Reached Institutional Lifestyle Brand Status?" *cpp-luxury.com,* May 4, 2012.

"Prada S.p.A." *International Directory of Company Histories.* Ed. Tina Grant. Vol. 138. Detroit: St. James Press, 2012.

Ritson, Mark. "Show Me the Founders, I'll Show You the Brand." *Marketing,* August 18, 2004.

Trebay, Guy and Ginia Bellafante. "Prada: Luxury Brand with World-Class Anxiety." *New York Times,* December 18, 2001.

Wilson, Eric. "Adventures in Design: Prada's Vision of Techno Chic Comes to SoHo." *WWD,* December 17, 2001.

PURINA

—■—

AT A GLANCE

Brand Synopsis: Purina is a leading manufacturer of pet food that touts itself as "a company of pet lovers."

Parent Company: Nestlé S.A.
Checkerboard Square
St. Louis, Missouri 63164, USA
http://www.nestlepurina.com

Sector: Consumer Staples

Industry Group: Food, Beverage & Tobacco

Performance: *Market share*—10.48% worldwide (2006); 43.5% of the U.S. dog food market (2010); 72.2% of the U.S. cat food market (2010). *Sales*—US$12.5 billion (2010).

Principal Competitors: The Iams Company; Hill's Pet Nutrition Inc.; Del Monte Foods; Procter & Gamble; Mars Inc., Agrolimen S.A.

BRAND ORIGINS

- William Danforth and two church friends formed an animal feed business in 1894 called the Robinson-Danforth Commission Company.
- Danforth bought control of the business and changed the name to Ralston Purina in 1902.
- In 1957, Ralston Purina debuted its highly successful dog food, Purina Dog Chow, selling the dry pet food in grocery stores.

- International conglomerate Nestlé acquired Ralston Purina in 2001 and merged it with another of its businesses to form Nestlé Purina PetCare Company.

The founding of Purina was largely the result of the vision of one man: William Henry Danforth. In 1893, Danforth joined two church acquaintances in St. Louis in mixing and selling feed for mules and horses. The blend of oats and corn, billed as "cheaper than oats and safer than corn," sold well among the farmers along the Mississippi River. In 1894 the company incorporated as the Robinson-Danforth Commission Company, and in 1896, Danforth bought control of the firm. One day after the purchase was completed, the company's new mill—on the site of what is now known as Checkerboard Square, Purina's headquarters—was destroyed by a tornado. With the help of a sympathetic banker, Danforth rebuilt the mill, and his business continued to thrive.

In 1898, Danforth learned of a Kansas miller who had found a way to prevent wheat from turning rancid. Danforth introduced the miller's hot breakfast cereal made from cracked wheat. A clever marketing strategist, Danforth persuaded a Dr. Ralston, the head of a string of faddish health clubs, to give the cereal his official sponsorship. The doctor agreed on the condition that it be renamed Ralston Cereal. To advertise the growing success of both the cereal and the feeds—now called Purina to signify purity—Danforth changed the name of his company in 1902 to Ralston Purina and adopted the familiar checkerboard logo, which began to appear on all of Ralston Purina's packages.

One of Danforth's marketing techniques emerged from his stint as YMCA secretary for the Third Army

Division during World War I. While serving in France, the savvy Danforth noticed that solders' rations were often endearingly called "chow." When he returned from the war, Danforth substituted the word "chow" for "feed" on all of Purina's animal products. He also created the company's Chow Division, which was later to become subsidiary Purina Mills.

With a successful line of breakfast cereals and animal feed in its portfolio, Ralston Purina launched a new line of pet food in 1957. Named Dog Chow, this commercial pet food was sold in grocery stores for the burgeoning number of pets in U.S. households. Packaged as puffed biscuits instead of canned, wet food, Dog Chow was less messy and cheaper than other leading brands. Within 15 months, Purina was the leader in the dog food market. Purina launched Cat Chow in 1962.

After William Danforth died in 1955, Purina began expanding outside the United States and soon became co-owner of feed companies in France, West Germany, and Italy and bought plants in Mexico, Guatemala, Colombia, Venezuela, and Argentina. Ralston Purina International expanded operations further in 1992, entering new markets in China, the Philippines, and Thailand, eventually selling Ralston Purina products in more than 50 countries.

In 1986, Ralston Purina sold Purina Mills—the animal feed business that had been the basis of the company's inception—to London-based conglomerate British Petroleum. The sale did not include the pet food lines, which were kept by Ralston Purina. British Petroleum sold Purina Mills in 1992, and after a 1999 bankruptcy, Land O'Lakes purchased the feed business and formed Land O'Lakes Purina Feed.

In 1994, Ralston Purina spun off its food lines for people to Ralcorp Holdings, which subsequently sold the cereal line to General Mills. Ralston Purina and its lines of pet food were acquired by the Swiss company Nestlé in 2001 and merged with Nestlé's Friskies PetCare Company to form Nestlé Purina PetCare Company.

BRAND ELEMENTS

- William Danforth incorporated a checkerboard motif as part of the Purina brand to make the products more visible and to set them apart from competitors.
- Purina's marketing has always emphasized the nutritional quality of its pet foods as well as the emotional side of pet ownership.
- Purina uses different taglines to market its different brands of pet food; Nestlé Purina's corporate slogan is "Your pet. Our passion."

Looking for a way to set Purina products apart and make them easy to spot, Danforth remembered a family he

had known from his childhood in Missouri who always wore clothing made from a red-and-white checkerboard-patterned cloth. Danforth decided to try using the distinctive checkerboard pattern on his product packaging. The ploy was highly successful, and Danforth took to wearing checkerboard ties, shirts, and coats. He established a "Checker Gallery," containing pictures of his employees wearing checkered clothing, and he designated an annual Checker Day. The company's headquarters became known as Checkerboard Square. The checkerboard has remained synonymous with the Purina brand.

From the very beginning Purina emphasized the nutritional value of its products and the emotional side of being a pet owner, eventually developing the slogan "All you add is love." Nestlé Purina's contemporary line of pet foods incorporates many different taglines. The Alpo brand employs "A great dog deserves Alpo," while Felix cat food brand uses "Cats like Felix like Felix." Purina Puppy Chow uses "Incredible puppy food, incredible puppies," and the Fancy Feast brand uses "Fancy Feast. Good taste is easy to recognize." The Happy Dog tagline is "Happy Dog. Naturally healthier!" Nestlé Purina's corporate slogan is "Your pet. Our passion."

The contemporary Purina logo, as used by Land O'Lakes and Nestlé, features the red-and-white square checkerboard with Purina in white, capital letters on a rectangle-shaped black background.

BRAND IDENTITY

- Each Purina brand of dog and cat food has its own web page and Facebook page.
- Nestlé Purina formed Project Pet Slim Down in an effort to impart information about better nutrition and exercise habits for pets and their owners.
- Lines of premium Purina pet foods are sold at veterinary clinics and pet shops instead of grocery stores.

Purina strives for its products to be an integral part of pet ownership and focuses much of its marketing on the bond pet owners have with their pets. Purina wants to develop a trusting relationship with pet owners by sharing its expertise in nutrition through dedicated professionals who, according to Purina, "seek to enrich the lives of pets and the people who love them." Purina understands that a healthy dog or cat can translate into the pet's ability to live a longer, happier life. Purina employees love their own pets, and in many offices they bring their pets to work with them.

Purina has a wide and varied presence online designed to promote its identity as a resource for pet owners and the pets they love. The "About Us" page states, "For more than 80 years, we've been guided by the belief that pets and people are better together." The company sees itself as more than just a purveyor of food: "Our passion for pets goes beyond pushing pet nutrition forward, and into forging partnerships in the pet welfare world and raising awareness of what pets truly need." To accomplish that, the Purina website targets consumers by country and may include advice on choosing a dog or cat as a pet, understanding pet behavior, dog training, and keeping your pet healthy through all stages of its life, in addition to information on brands of pet food. The Purina website also includes an "Experts on Hand" section with answers from pet professionals to common questions about pets. Purina also gives each brand its own web page and Facebook page with details about each brand, including variations within the brand, such as available flavors.

Ralston Purina developed new channels for distribution of pet food by targeting pet owners at pet shops and veterinary clinics, a method also employed by Nestlé Purina. Premium pet foods that are more expensive are marketed to pet owners who feel they are getting a better quality pet food by shopping at a veterinary clinic rather than at the grocery store. Purina Pro Plan and Purina Veterinary Diet brands are part of this marketing strategy.

To further promote pet health, Nestlé formed a collaboration between Purina and its weight-loss brand, Jenny Craig, to form Project Pet Slim Down. The collaboration strives to get pet owners to make a resolution for themselves and their furry friends to achieve a more healthful lifestyle.

BRAND STRATEGY

- Initially, Purina's biggest competitor was the farmer who fed his animals ordinary grain.
- Today, Purina's main competition comes from pet owners who feed their pets table scraps.
- Growth for Purina has come mainly through extensions of different brands, with variations of flavors and pet treats.
- In 2011, Purina became the sponsor of the elite Westminster Kennel Club Dog Show in New York City.

Growth for the company has come in the form of new brands, line extensions, and variations of flavors, particularly for cats, since it is perceived that cats need variety in their dinner. Dog treats and snacks have also become a burgeoning business as pet owners seek to show their affection for their dogs by giving them extra treats.

Purina has also sought to grow its brand by expanding into the pet health insurance business, beginning in 2008. By 2010, it was available in all 50 states and the District of Columbia. Health insurance is one of the fastest growing sectors of the pet industry.

Much of Purina's growth is happening on a global level. Initially, Purina's biggest competitor was the farmer who fed his animals ordinary grain. While consumers in

mature markets for pet food, including the United States and Great Britain, now overwhelmingly feed their pets store-bought pet food, pet owners in smaller and emerging markets often still feed their pets table scraps. To continue its global expansion and to meet increasing demand as owners turn to packaged food, Purina has been investing in plants in countries such as Hungary and Russia.

Although plants are not in every country, Nestlé Purina pet food can be purchased worldwide, and food lines vary by country. Dog and cat food brands available in the United Kingdom include Felix, Bakers, Purina One, GoCat, Purina Pro Plan, Purina Beta, Purina Veterinary Diets, and Purina Winalot. Consumers in Australia can purchase Purina Pro Plan, Purina One, Fancy Feast, SuperCoat, Beneful, Friskies, Lucky Dog, Bonnie, and Ruffs. In Italy, Purina Pro Plan, Purina Veterinary Diets, Purina One, Gourmet, Tidy Cats, Purina Professional Care, Friskies, Felix, Tonus, Fido, Beneful, and Purina ProCare are available. Purina Arabia brands include Alpo, Purina Dog Chow, Little Bites, Fit & Trim, Fancy Feast, Friskies, Purina Cat Chow, and Purina Pro Plan.

In addition to global expansion, part of Purina's brand strategy is to promote the Purina name domestically. In 2011, Purina signed a multi-year contract to be the primary sponsor of the Westminster Kennel Club Dog Show. The show, held each year at Madison Square Garden in New York City, is the pinnacle of dog-show events and gives Purina an unprecedented opportunity to showcase the company and its pet products. Purina also sponsors the Purina Incredible Dog Challenge at Purina Farms in Gray Summit, Missouri. The Incredible Dog Challenge is a series of competitive events for top canine athletes. Events include dog diving, agility competitions, freestyle flying disc, 60-weave pole racing, and Jack Russell hurdle racing.

BRAND EQUITY

- In 2006, Nestlé Purina PetCare held a worldwide 10.48 percent share of the pet food market and was assigned a brand value of US$4.12 billion.
- In 2012, Nestlé Purina was ranked 251st in *Fortune*'s Global 500, a ranking of the top international corporations by revenue.
- Purina was ranked second among dog treat makers, behind Del Monte Foods and its brand of Milk-Bone dog treats.

In 2006 global sales of dog and cat food reached US$45.1 billion, and Nestlé Purina PetCare held a 10.48 percent market share. In 2010, Purina had a 43.5 percent market share of dog food and a 72.2 percent market share of cat food in the United States. In 2012, Purina was ranked 251st in *Fortune*'s Global 500, with a brand value of US$4.12 billion, up one spot from its 2011 ranking.

In 2010, Purina owned four of the top 10 dry dog food brands in the United States, with Purina One holding a 5.6 percent market share; Beneful, a 5.5 percent market share; Purina Dog Chow, a 5.1 percent market share; and Beneful Health Weight, a 4.6 percent market share. In 2011, Purina brands in the top 10 of dry dog foods included Purina Dog Chow, with an 11.7 percent market share; Beneful, with a 7.8 percent market share; and Purina One, with a 4.7 percent market share. Nestlé Purina was ranked second among dog treat makers, with a 21.4 percent market share, behind Del Monte Foods, which held a 35.4 percent market share.

BRAND AWARENESS

- In 2009, 66 percent of dog and cat owners were able spontaneously to recall Nestlé Purina as a pet food company.
- Nestlé Purina PetCare Company products are available in more than 100 countries.
- Purina dog and cat food lines are consistent best sellers throughout the world.

Nestlé Purina PetCare employs 14,500 people worldwide in 24 manufacturing plants and 13 sales offices. Purina dog and cat food, treats, and litter are available in more than 100 countries. In 2009, Purina enjoyed double-digit unaided brand awareness, with 66 percent of dog and cat owners able spontaneously to mention Purina as a pet food company.

In Canada, Purina Dog Chow was the fifth most popular pet food, with a 4.7 percent market share in 2009. In Poland, Nestlé Purina was ranked second among pet food suppliers in 2009, with an 11 percent market share, behind Mars Inc., which held a 49.2 percent market share. In Japan in 2007, Purina held a 9.2 percent market share among pet food makers and a 21 percent market share of the cat food market. In 2000, in the dry dog food market, Ralston Purina held a 10 percent market share in Austria, a 5 percent market share in Germany, and a 15 percent market share in France. In 2004, Purina held a 22 percent share of Brazil's cat food market and a 25 percent market share in Australia.

BRAND OUTLOOK

- The trust pet owners have in Purina products has been tested through multiple food recalls and a controversy involving dog treats.
- Purina invests heavily in research to develop new formulas to meet growing demands for specialized pet food formulas, especially those for aging animals.
- Nestlé Purina has multiple programs in place to help animal shelters throughout the United States feed their animals and to promote adoptions.

Nestlé Purina PetCare and Land O'Lakes Purina Feed were involved in multiple recalls in 2012 because of questionable safety practices in the production of some of their food lines. The biggest controversy involved Nestlé Purina and its chicken jerky treats, which were manufactured in China. Hundreds of pet owners implicated Purina in the illnesses and deaths of dogs that had eaten tainted treats sold by Purina. In late 2012 and early 2013, some pet owners also began to report illnesses caused by Purina's Beneful lines, but Nestlé Purina issued a statement that there were no known problems with Beneful and that false information about its product was circulating on social media. Purina continues to stress that all sourcing and processing of its pet food ingredients meet or exceed all government standards. Additionally, Purina mandates that all suppliers of ingredients for Purina products must meet stringent standards for product safety and sanitation. As of the end of 2012, Purina sales were not significantly affected by the problems, but if the recalls continued, they could hurt the brand's reputation.

The trend to apply human characteristics to pets has led to specialized pet foods intended to support arthritis relief, heart health, digestive tract health, the immune system, and mental health. Pet foods focused on aging and senior pet populations that are less active and potentially overweight are becoming particularly popular. Consumer attraction to products that tout themselves as natural, organic, grain-free, and eco-friendly will continue to be a potent trend and to drive the marketing of new pet food products. Purina invests heavily in research and develops new formulas to meet this growing demand.

In 2010, Purina assisted in disaster relief across the United States with significant donations of money and food. Additionally, Purina programs such as Pets for People, Purina Pro Plan Rally to Rescue, and the One Hope Network by Purina One promoted adoptions and supported animal welfare at shelters by giving more than US$20 million in money, food, and litter. In Europe, Purina supports pet care education programs in such countries as France, Estonia, Austria, Germany, and Italy. The pet care programs target mainly children, the potential pet owners of the future, to build up its prospective customer base.

Also, by expanding into popular services such as the pet health insurance, Purina is tapping into a market that is expected to continue to grow. This bodes well for the brand's outlook.

FURTHER READING

Becker, Karen. "Nestlé Purina TV Ad Is Going to the Dogs." *Healthy Pets with Dr. Karen Becker,* November 1, 2011. Accessed November 16, 2012. http://healthypets.mercola.com/sites/healthypets/archive/2011/11/01/nestle-purina-tv-ad-is-for-dogs.aspx.

Brown, Lisa. "Nestlé Purina nabs Westminster Kennel Club sponsorship." *St. Louis Post-Dispatch,* June 7, 2011. Accessed November 16, 2012. http://www.stltoday.com/business/columns/lisa-brown/nestl-purina-nabs-westminster-kennel-club-sponsorship/article_68dd45ec-9119-11e0-8510-001a4bcf6878.html.

Donaldson, Debbie Phillips. "Nestlé Purina: building on a tradition of trust." *Pet Food Industry.com,* March 7, 2011. Accessed November 16, 2012. http://www.petfoodindustry.com/Nestl%C3%A9_Purina__building_on_a_tradition_of_trust.html.

Nestlé Purina. *Nestlé Purina 2011 Corporate Responsibility Report.* Accessed November 16, 2012. http://www.nestlepurina.com/_res/pdf/sharedvalue.pdf.

"Nestlé Purina celebrates a decade of passion for pets." *Nestle.com,* December 12, 2011. Accessed November 16, 2012. http://www.nestle.com/Media/NewsAndFeatures/Pages/Purina_celebrates_decade.aspx.

"Purina Mills, Inc." *International Directory of Company Histories.* Ed. Jay P. Pederson. Vol. 32. Detroit: St. James Press, 2000. *Gale Virtual Reference Library.* Accessed November 16, 2012. http://go.galegroup.com/ps/i.do?id=GALE%7CCX2843600097&v=2.1&u=itsbtrial&it=r&p=GVRL&sw=w.

"Steady Growth in $4B Market for Natural Pet Products." *Internet Wire,* November 5, 2012. *Business Insights: Global.* Accessed November 16, 2012. http://bi.galegroup.com/global/article/GALE%7CA307385362/c4c8be13b651e57f5a5f1b7b54edf490?u=itsbtria.

Taylor, Jessica. "Top Pet Food Companies." *Pet Food Industry.com,* December 5, 2011. Accessed November 16, 2012. http://www.petfoodindustry.com/2012topcompanies.html.

RANDSTAD

AT A GLANCE

Brand Synopsis: Randstad is a multinational consulting brand that specializes in both temporary and professional staffing for companies of every size and type of employment needs.

Parent Company: Randstad Holding n.v.
Diemermere 25
1112 TC Diemen
The Netherlands
http://www.randstad.com

Sector: Industrials

Industry Group: Commercial & Professional Services

Performance: *Market share*—3.6 percent worldwide (2011). *Revenues*—US$22 billion (2011).

Principal Competitors: Adecco S.A.; Allegis Group, Inc.; Kelly Services, Inc.; Manpower Inc.; USG People N.V.

BRAND ORIGINS

- Randstad Holding originated as the result of a master's thesis by graduate student Frits J. D. Goldschmeding in 1960.
- In 2007 Randstad became the world's second-largest staffing company following the acquisition of Vedior NV.
- Randstad celebrated its 50th anniversary in 2010.

Randstad originated as the master's thesis of a graduate student in 1960. While studying at Amsterdam's Vrije Universiteit, Frits J. D. Goldschmeding was working on the subject of temporary employment. His work inspired him to start his own temporary services company, Uitzendbureau Amstelveen, from his dorm room along with his close friend and classmate Ger Daleboudt. The company was eventually a success, and by 1964 it was renamed Randstad Uitzendbureau. From there, the company began to expand quickly. In 1965 its first international branch, Interlabor, opened in Belgium. It opened branch offices in Germany in 1968. By 1970 there were a total of 32 offices in three countries. The corporate name was changed to Randstad Holding n.v. in 1978, and the following year the company opened its 100th office.

Until the late 1970s most of the jobs focused on by Randstad were office positions, such as secretaries, accountants, and administrators, or cleaning service jobs. In 1980 the company formed the new division Randon to supply guards, surveillance services, and home security systems. Three years later, in 1983, it purchased the midsized rival Tempo-Team, which offered industrial, tech, and cleaning services. In 1985 Randstad celebrated its 25th year in business. It had amassed 257 offices in four countries, 1,600 full-time staff, over 35,000 temps, and revenues totaling US$617 million. The following year Randstad opened its first training center for cashiers, computer jobs, and telemarketing positions. The company went public in 1990 and was listed on the Amsterdam Stock Exchange. In 1992 Randstad claimed its largest acquisition to date with the purchase of the Flex Group and its 700 branches. By the end of the year Randstad made nearly US$1.8 billion in revenues. The following year the company expanded for the first time into Spain with the formation of Randstad Trabajo Temporal, and broke into the U.S. market with the purchase of Temp Force and Jane Jones Enterprises, taking over 37 American offices.

In 1996 Randstad signed a contract to supply employees for the 1996 Olympic Games in Atlanta, Georgia, then decided to become an official sponsor as well. The company provided a total of 16,000 employees for the event, including more than 4,000 bus drivers for the public transportation system. Even though the staffing contract lost Randstad money in the short run, both strategies proved to be incredibly lucrative in the long run. Just prior to the Olympics, the Randstad name had a 15 percent recognition rate in the Atlanta area, where there were a dozen branch offices. After the Olympics, its recognition rose to 99.5 percent. Randstad finished the year with nearly US$3.7 billion in total revenues.

Randstad expanded its North American operations in 1998, when it acquired Strategix Solutions, a major division of the competitor AccuStaff, Inc., for US$850 million. The purchase increased Randstad's locations in the United States from 89 to 478, providing the company with offices in 34 states. The following year Randstad expanded its European operations with the purchase of Time Power Personal-Dienstleistungen in Germany and Tempo Grup in Spain. By that point, Randstad was the staffing leader in Belgium, Germany, the Netherlands, and even the southeastern United States and the third-largest staffing company in the world.

Shortly after Randstad celebrated its 40th anniversary in 2000, it began experiencing some financial setbacks. Due to lower than expected revenues that year, the company sold its cleaning services subsidiary Lavold. Randstad finished the year with a respectable US$7.9 billion in revenues. However, income problems continued into 2001 as its total revenues decreased 11.3 percent to US$5.2 billion, while its net income plunged nearly 73 percent, from US$200 million to US$53 million.

The forward momentum of this huge company had apparently stalled out, and something had to be done to get it moving forward again. In 2002 Cleem Farla was appointed chief executive officer (CEO), and his strategy was to go back to the basics: find the best people, make the best matches between client and staff, and develop strong concepts and superior branding. Farla stepped down as CEO in 2003 due to health reasons, but his replacement, Ben Noteboom, continued what Farla had started and soon the company was seeing progress and profits again. By 2004 the back-to-basics strategy, along with carefully analyzed cost-cutting measures, earned Randstad US$7.8 billion in sales with US$272 million in net profits. In 2007 Randstad became the world's second-largest staffing

company following the acquisition of the Dutch competitor Vedior NV for US$5.1 billion.

Randstad expanded into the Japanese market in 2008, when it acquired a 10 percent stake in FujiStaff Holdings, Inc., a major staffing company in Japan. The end of 2008 also saw the start of the global economic recession. Despite the challenging business climate, Randstad managed to persevere through strategic cost-cutting measures: Randstad Portugal was sold to Kelly Services, Inc.; the Randstad subsidiary CIAN, a human resource and payroll outsourcing service, was sold to Northgate Arinso; and Randstad's French-based Selpro was sold to Activa Capital, a French private equity firm. In 2010 Randstad purchased the remaining 90 percent of FujiStaff Holdings, making it the top staffing firm in Japan. That same year the company celebrated its 50th year in business.

BRAND ELEMENTS
- The Randstad name is based on a large urban area in the southwestern Netherlands that contains the four largest Dutch cities.
- The Randstad company logo consists of the letter *r* and its reflection and is meant to give the appearance of welcoming with open arms.
- The mirrored *r*s in the Randstad logo are meant to symbolize the company's position as an intermediary between its flex workers and its business clients.

The Randstad name comes from a region in southwestern Netherlands that consists of the four largest Dutch cities: Amsterdam, Rotterdam, The Hague, and Utrecht. The area that is occupied by these cities is so densely populated that it has essentially grown into one continuous urban and industrial development. The reason the founders named their company after this area is because, at that time, their business covered the entire region.

The Randstad logo is based on a stylized version of a lowercased *r* because the look was considered to be "contemporary without being trendy." A reversed *r* was used to balance the logo visually, and it represented that Randstad was an intermediary between its flex workers and its business clients. The logo also gives the appearance of welcoming with open arms, which is obviously a very positive association. There have been minor variations in the logo over the years, with the double *r*s placed either to the left or above the company name. Other than that the rest of the logo elements have remained consistent—the two *r*s and the company name are all lowercased letters and the color scheme is either the lettering in blue on a white background or white lettering on a blue background. The blue color is known as Kone blue and over the years has been used by many companies, including General Motors, Qualcomm, the Orlando Magic basketball team, and the Kone Corporation, which is believed to be the inspiration for the color name.

BRAND IDENTITY

- Randstad regularly fills 80 percent of its own top management positions from within.
- In 2011 Randstad saw a 17 percent increase in traffic to its websites, which was a much higher increase in comparison to similar employment websites.
- In 2011 Randstad was named the "most valuable brand" in its industry by Brand Finance and was ranked 185th among the top-500 global brands.

Shortly after Randstad had reached its 40th anniversary in 2000, the business began a noticeable decline. In 2001 the company experienced an 11.3 percent decrease in total revenues, and its net income dropped a staggering 73 percent, from US$200 million down to US$53 million. When the downward trend continued into 2002, it was obvious that something significant had to be done to get the company back on tract. In October 2002 Cleem Farla was appointed chief executive officer of Randstad, and his strategy was to focus the company back to the basics that made it so successful in the first place.

Randstad's brand identity consists of four building blocks. The first of these is "Best People." Randstad believes that the true value of any business is the quality of its employees. This means an emphasis on finding quality people, giving them further training and development, and then providing them the opportunities that will help them realize their full potential. Randstad applies this principle each year by filling 80 percent of its own top management positions from within.

The next building block is "Excellent Execution." This refers to Randstad's variety of blueprints that are based on the best real-world, hands-on processes it has developed and standardized over the years. This standardization then enables individual work processes to be plugged into different market situations with only minor adjustments.

The third building block is "Superior Brands." The understanding here is that if the company has a highly recognizable brand that is also superior, it ensures that the company's services will always be in demand and that penetration into new territories will be much easier. In 2011 Randstad experienced a 17 percent increase in traffic to its websites, a percentage that was higher in comparison to other similar employment websites. In its 2011 analysis, Brand Finance rated Randstad the "most valuable brand in the industry" and gave it an overall ranking of 185th among the top-500 global brands.

Finally, the fourth building block, "Strong Concepts," addresses the strategy of offering five distinct global service concepts—Staffing, HR Solutions, Professional Services, Search and Selection, and Inhouse Services—that are based on the needs of both clients and candidates. The strength of each of these five concepts is in their consistency and quality of process and their flexibility in adapting to specific situations.

BRAND STRATEGY

- Randstad offers five separate service concepts, and each one is promoted by a combination of Randstad brand companies.
- Staffing is a US$300 billion per year business worldwide and accounts for 81 percent of Randstad's revenues.
- Professional Services is valued at US$120 billion globally and accounts for 19 percent of Randstad's revenues.

As its services have become more sophisticated over the years, Randstad has developed a series of five specific service concepts to better serve both the present and future needs of its clients and candidates. Each of these service concepts is supported by a combination of Randstad brand companies.

Staffing constitutes the largest business sector for Randstad, accounting for 81 percent of revenues and is worth approximately US$300 billion worldwide. Staffing focuses on recruiting candidates with a secondary education and places them in either temporary staffing positions or permanent placements. This service is conducted under three brands: Randstad, Tempo-Team, and Spherion.

HR Solutions provides clients with a range of services, including outplacement and outsourcing, payroll services, and consulting. These services are provided by four brands: Randstad, Randstad Managed Services, SourceRight Solutions, and Tempo-Team.

Professional Services focuses on middle and senior management positions, including supervisors, managers, interim specialists, and others with a wide range of backgrounds and disciplines. Specific sectors addressed include information technology, engineering, communications, finance, and health care. This service accounts for the other 19 percent of Randstad's revenues and is worth approximately US$120 billion globally. This set of services is covered by four brands: Randstad, Randstad Construction/Property/Engineering, Randstad Technologies, and Technisource.

Search and Selection recruits middle and senior managers for permanent positions that are usually fee based. The Randstad brands for this service include Expectra and Yacht.

Inhouse Services is aimed at clients that have a significant need for labor flexibility, such as companies that may operate in seasonal cycles and will need more employees during some parts of the year and less during others. Clients of this type are usually in the manufacturing sectors. These services are handled by the brands Randstad and Tempo-Team.

BRAND EQUITY

- In 2011 Randstad had a total of 4,711 offices in 43 countries and 28,700 full-time employees.
- In 2011 Randstad generated US$22 billion in revenues and a gross profit of US$4 billion.
- In 2011 Randstad had a worldwide market share of 3.6 percent.

Randstad is the world's second-largest human resource and employment brand, and in 2011 it had a market share of 3.6 percent. That same year Randstad had 3,566 branch offices and 1,145 in-house locations in 43 countries around the world and 28,700 full-time employees. As of December 31, 2011, its total revenues were US$22 billion, with a gross profit of US$4 billion. The company's market capitalization was US$5.3 billion. According to *Forbes* "Global 2000" for 2012, Randstad ranked 421st in sales, 1,723rd in assets, 1,317th in market value, and 1,243rd overall.

BRAND AWARENESS

- Through its global network of over 4,700 branch offices, Randstad places over 576,000 of its candidates each day.
- Having placed 16,000 of its candidates in jobs during the Atlanta Olympic Games, Randstad's brand recognition in Atlanta increased from 15 percent prior to the games to an 99.5 percent afterward.
- Randstad is a partner of Voluntary Service Overseas, which is the world's largest independent, international volunteering agency.

The Randstad brand goes back over 50 years to its humble beginnings as the materialization of a graduate student's thesis. By 2013 the company had grown to become the world's second-largest human resources organization with over 4,700 offices in 43 countries. It was also the top firm in many of those nations, including the Netherlands where it originated, most of the countries of the European Union, Japan, and even the southeastern United States. Currently, Randstad places over 576,000 of its candidates daily. Randstad is also a master at gathering attention in a variety of ways. In 1996 it received a contract to place 16,000 of its candidates in jobs during the Atlanta Olympic Games. Randstad's brand recognition in Atlanta increased from 15 percent prior to the Olympics to an astounding 99.5 percent afterward. Randstad is also an official partner of the Formula 1 Williams Racing Team.

Aside from assisting people to find employment opportunities, Randstad also takes part in helping to alleviate poverty on a global scale. Randstad is a partner of Voluntary Service Overseas, which is the world's largest independent, international volunteering agency. Through this partnership, Randstad is able to leverage a more positive change in battling the difficulties that face the world.

BRAND OUTLOOK

- With the 2011 purchase of the SFN Group, Inc., a rival U.S. staffing firm, Randstad became the third-largest staffing company in the United States.
- Through its Indian subsidiary Ma Foi Randstad, Randstad will be able to capitalize on strong business growth in India.
- Recognizing the significant business growth due to global outsourcing demands in India and China, Randstad is positioning itself to dominate those markets.

Randstad plans to expand by acquiring companies in specific key markets during the second decade of the 21st century. In 2011 it purchased rival SFN Group, Inc., the 13th-largest staffing firm in the world. The merging of the two companies was a major strategic win for both, as the combined company became the third-largest staffing company in the United States. Growth in the Asian and Pacific markets has been positive and offers Randstad huge potential for expansion. The brand gained a major foothold in the Asian market in 2010, when it purchased FujiStaff Holdings, Inc., Japan's largest staffing company. Randstad also wants to expand in India and China, as both nations continue to show significant business growth due to global outsourcing demands. India in particular has had significant growth in the banking, financial services, telecommunications, media, and retail sectors. Randstad maintains a presence in India through its subsidiary Ma Foi Randstad. Such strong continued growth in both India and China will present great demand for people to fill opened positions, and Randstad will be more than ready to offer its help in filling those shortages.

FURTHER READING

"Europe's Most Valuable Support Services Companies, 2011." *Business Rankings Annual.* Ed. Deborah J. Draper. Detroit, MI: Gale, 2012.

"Global 2000 Leading Companies: Randstad Holding." *Forbes.* Accessed January 31, 2013. http://www.forbes.com/companies/randstad-holding.

"Logo: Randstad." Goodlogo.com. Accessed January 31, 2013. http://goodlogo.com/extended.info/randstad-logo-3531.

Randstad. "Company History." Accessed January 31, 2013. http://www.randstad.com/about-us/company-information/history#1975.

Randstad Holding. *2011 Annual Report.* Accessed January 31, 2013. http://files.shareholder.com/downloads/RANJ F/2297309487x0x542828/73bc94c4-18b1-4818-b582-e461a6931e00/Annual_Report_2011.pdf.

"Randstad Holding." Yahoo.com. Accessed January 31, 2013. http://finance.yahoo.com/q?s=RAND.AS&ql=1.

"Randstad Holding: Financial and Strategic Analysis Review." *SWOT Report*. Accessed January 31, 2013. http://callisto. ggsrv.com.ezproxy.lib.indiana.edu/imgsrv/FastFetch/UBER1/ 503559_GDBCS34602FSA.

"Randstad Holding nv." *International Directory of Company Histories*. Ed. Tina Grant. Vol. 113. Detroit, MI: St. James Press, 2010.

"Top Human Resource and Employment Firms Worldwide, 2011." *Market Share Reporter*. Detroit, MI: Gale, 2012.

RAYTHEON COMPANY

—◆—

BRAND ORIGINS

- Raytheon began as a radio technology company in Cambridge, Massachusetts, in 1922.
- A Raytheon engineer discovered microwave cooking in 1945 when he observed that a radar device he was operating had melted a candy bar in his pocket.
- Raytheon gained recognition in 1969 for the guidance systems it built for the Apollo 11 mission to the moon.

- Raytheon is best known for its Patriot and Tomahawk missiles developed for the U.S. military.

Raytheon began on July 7, 1922, in Cambridge, Massachusetts, when a partnership between Vannevar Bush, Laurence Marshall, and Charles Smith resulted in one of history's earliest technology startups: the American Appliance Company. Smith, a young scientist who had done work on the electrical properties of gases, began experimenting with a new type of gas tube that would allow radios to be powered by home electrical outlets. At that time radios were powered by expensive and short-lived batteries and were therefore a luxury item affordable only by the wealthy. The tube Smith developed, known as a gaseous rectifier, would not only change the radio manufacturing industry but would make the devices affordable for nearly every home. It was introduced to the public in 1925 under the brand name Raytheon. In a little over a year this invention would earn the company more than US$1 million in sales. At about the same time, the firm was renamed Raytheon Manufacturing Co. to distinguish it from an Indiana firm already using the name American Appliance Co.

During the early years of World War II, scientists in Great Britain invented a special microwave-generating electron tube known as a "magnetron." It was a key component in significantly boosting the ability of radar to detect enemy aircraft. In 1941 Raytheon received a contract to mass produce the devices and the U.S. Navy appropriated US$2 million to build a manufacturing facility for Raytheon in Waltham, Massachusetts. By war's end, Raytheon had accounted for 80 percent of all the magnetrons manufactured. During the war years

Raytheon had also pioneered special components in the operation of ship-based radar systems, specifically for submarine detection, proximity fuses in antiaircraft shells, and in 1945, Raytheon engineer Percy Spencer accidentally invented microwave cooking, when he discovered a candy bar in his pocket melted as he stood in front of an active magnetron. He then decided to test his observation on a handful of popcorn kernels. Two years later, Raytheon developed the first microwave oven.

In 1962 the management of Raytheon decided that the company was becoming too dependent on government contracts and needed to diversify. Beginning in 1964 Raytheon expanded its offerings with the purchase of Packard-Bell's computer operations as well as several small electronics companies. In 1965 it acquired Amana Refrigeration, Inc. Although Raytheon had invented the microwave oven 20 years earlier, they needed Amana's experience and resources in order to begin mass producing a home appliance that could be marketed to the general public. This collaboration came to fruition in 1967 when Amana unveiled the first countertop microwave oven priced at US$500 (approximately US$3,500 in 2013 dollars). In 1969 Raytheon received significant publicity as the company that had built the guidance systems for the Apollo 11 spacecraft and lunar landing module, as well as the microwave tubes in the onboard radio and television equipment that allowed more than 500 million people around the world to witness the historic landing live.

In February 1980 Raytheon made its largest purchase to date with the acquisition of Beech Aircraft for US$800 million. Beech manufactured single- and twin-engine airplanes. By this time, Raytheon's diversification strategy had worked well. Government contracts now made up only 40 percent of the company's total sales, and commercial computing, consumer products, and construction made up the other 60 percent. With the collapse of the Soviet Union and the end of the Cold War in 1991, most other major defense contractors were looking to expand civilian contracts as Raytheon had. During the first Gulf War, Raytheon received tremendous notoriety for making claims that their Patriot missile in combination with a sophisticated radar system could intercept and destroy incoming enemy missiles. During live televised news feeds from the front line, the missiles were shown to do just that, and Raytheon's world reputation increased. Between 1990 and 1994 Raytheon missile sales to international governments amounted to US$2.5 billion.

During the late 1990s Raytheon focused on strengthening its defense business capabilities by expanding subsidiaries in those areas. In 1995 it merged its missile systems and equipment divisions to form Raytheon Electronics Systems. Later that year it acquired E-Systems Inc. for US$2.3 billion and in 1996 purchased two of Chrysler's defense firms for US$475 million. In 1997 Raytheon went on to purchase the defense divisions of Texas Instruments for US$2.9 billion and Hughes Electronics for US$9.5 billion. The addition of these two businesses enhanced Raytheon's expertise in the fields of laser-guided weapons, night-vision systems, airborne radar, and electronic warfare systems. All together the acquisitions Raytheon completed during the late 1990s put it among the top three defense contractors globally and made it the number-one defense electronics contractor.

In 1998 it consolidated all of its military businesses into Raytheon Systems Company. However, as the century was coming to a close, Raytheon experienced a number of setbacks—cost overruns, missed deadlines, contract delays, earnings losses, and corporate debt that reached US$9.5 billion. By 2001 Raytheon showed a loss of US$755 million, and the following year it suffered a loss of US$640 million. In 2002 Raytheon's shares dropped in value by 3.6 percent, while in comparison, shares in its competitor Lockheed Martin went up by more than 25 percent.

With the terrorist attacks in the United States on September 11, 2001, and the outbreak of wars in Afghanistan and Iraq, Raytheon and other defense contractors saw a surge in business. In December 2003 Raytheon was awarded a US$1 billion contract by the U.S. Navy followed by a second large Navy contract in 2004 for Tomahawk missiles. This was followed by a US$1 billion contract with the U.S. Army for a new missile defense system. In 2009 the United Arab Emirates awarded Raytheon a contract worth US$3 billion for its Patriot missile system. Raytheon was back on track financially, earning US$2.6 billion in net profits for 2007 alone. With both wars in full swing, Raytheon's future looked bright.

BRAND ELEMENTS
- Raytheon is named after the company's first product, a gas-filled tube that made it possible to plug radios into electrical outlets instead of being dependent on batteries.
- The name Raytheon comes from two words: *Ray*, meaning "a beam of light," and *theon*, meaning "from the gods."
- Raytheon's motto, "Customer Success Is Our Mission," reflects its commitment to manufacturing world-class defense and aerospace products.

Raytheon is named after the company's first product, a gas-filled tube that made it possible to plug radios into electrical outlets instead of being dependent on batteries. The Raytheon name originates from two words: *Ray*, meaning "a beam of light," and *theon*, a Greek word meaning "from the gods." Its logo is simply the company name in upper and lower case letters presented in a bold, red, sans-serif font.

The Raytheon name is synonymous with high-tech weapons, defense and communication systems, and cutting-edge technical services. A majority of the company's contracts are with the U.S. Department of Defense, and Raytheon uses the motto "Customer Success Is Our Mission" to reflect its commitment to manufacturing and delivering world-class products, systems, and support to customers, whether on the battlefield, in an office environment, or even out in space.

BRAND IDENTITY

- Raytheon prides itself on its successes in developing state-of-the-art solutions for the defense and aerospace industries.
- Raytheon boasts a large pool of talented, dedicated engineers whose work puts the company at the forefront of the defense and aerospace industries.
- Raytheon celebrates its legacy as a leader in high-tech solutions, from the invention of microwave cooking to its Patriot missile defense system.

Raytheon has been a technology and innovation leader for more than 90 years, and it prides itself on its successes in developing state-of-the-art solutions for the defense and aerospace industries. Key areas it promotes include Raytheon advancements in sensing technologies, effects technologies, communications, intelligence technologies, mission support services, cyber security, and homeland security. With 68,000 employees worldwide, Raytheon emphasizes the talent and dedication of its large pool of engineers whose work puts the company at the forefront of the defense and aerospace industries. It celebrates its legacy as a leader in high-tech solutions, from its invention of the microwave oven right after World War II, to the guidance and communications systems used during the Apollo 11 moon landing and the Patriot missile defense shield that protected coalition troops during the first Gulf War.

BRAND STRATEGY

- In 1962 Raytheon received more than 90 percent of its business from the U.S. Defense Department.
- Government contracts made up 40 percent of Raytheon's business in 1980, and private sector ventures accounted for the other 60 percent.
- In 2006 Raytheon recommitted to the government sector when it sold its private aircraft subsidiary to Hawker Beechcraft Corp.
- Raytheon is shifting emphasis from military contracts to other government operations, including homeland security and aerospace programs.

During the early 1960s Raytheon management became concerned that the company was potentially setting itself up for significant problems by focusing all of its business on Defense Department contracts. They believed the company should be more diversified, and over the next two decades worked hard to reshape and expand the products and services offered by Raytheon. By 1980 their diversification strategy had worked, and government contracts made up only 40 percent of Raytheon's business, while private sector ventures accounted for the other 60 percent. With the end of the Cold War at the beginning of the 1990s, defense spending began to decrease, and competition for contracts became more intense. Because of its diversification, Raytheon continued to have high levels of revenues, but in the competitive private sector, the profits were comparatively small.

Beginning with the terrorist attacks on the United States in September 2001 and escalating to the wars in Afghanistan and Iraq, Raytheon reversed its strategy and decided to focus again primarily on military projects. In 2003, soon after the start of the Iraq war, Raytheon received a US$1 billion contract to upgrade the Navy's Cobra Judy radar system. Another Navy contract in 2004 brought a large order for Tomahawk missiles. By 2007 Raytheon delivered its 1,000th Tomahawk Block IV missile to the U.S. Navy. In 2006 Raytheon made a big step in shifting business to the government sector by selling off its Raytheon Aircraft Co. subsidiary to Hawker Beechcraft Corp. for US$3.3 billion. Raytheon was now out of the private aircraft business. In 2009 the United Arab Emirates paid Raytheon US$3 billion to supply the country with a Patriot defensive system. In 2013, as the war in Iraq had ended, and the Afghan war was winding down, Raytheon again began a shift, but not so much away from the military sector as toward other government agencies, including the homeland security and aerospace markets.

BRAND EQUITY

- Raytheon is the fourth largest defense contractor behind Boeing, Lockheed Martin, and Northrop Grumman.
- In 2012 Raytheon had sales of US$24.4 billion with gross profits totaling US$5.2 billion, and a total market capitalization of US$17.5 billion.
- Raytheon is ranked number 342 on the *Forbes* "Global 2000" list of the world's largest companies.

Raytheon is the fourth largest U.S. defense company with 2012 contracts totaling US$24.4 billion. (Boeing is the leading contractor with earnings of US$81.7 billion.) Raytheon's 2012 gross profits were US$5.2 billion, and its total market capitalization is calculated at US$17.5 billion. Raytheon is headquartered in Waltham, Massachusetts, and has 68,000 full-time employees. According to the *Forbes* "Global 2000" list of the world's largest companies, Raytheon was ranked at number 357 in sales, number 335 in profits, number 798 in assets, number 493 in market value, and an overall placement of number 342 among the largest corporations on the planet.

BRAND AWARENESS

- Although Raytheon is primarily known as a defense contractor, it has earned recognition in the private sector for its innovative technologies.
- Raytheon increases its market profile through new media outlets including Facebook, Twitter, YouTube, LinkedIn, and the student website MathMovesU.com.
- Raytheon sponsors the Sum of All Thrills attraction at Disney's Epcot theme park, where users can design and simulate an imagined thrill ride.

Although Raytheon is primarily known as a defense contractor, it has earned recognition in the private sector as well. In 1967, through its Amana Refrigeration subsidiary, Raytheon produced the first consumer microwave oven. During the Apollo 11 mission to the moon in 1969, Raytheon earned respect as the designer and manufacturer of guidance and communications systems for both the command and lunar landing modules. In the 21st century Raytheon gains market awareness through its new media channels, including its website, Twitter, YouTube, Facebook, LinkedIn, and RSS feeds. In addition, Raytheon sponsors the Sum of All Thrills attraction at Disney's Epcot theme park, where users can design and simulate an imagined thrill ride, using science and engineering to determine the height and velocity of hill climbs, rolls, and corkscrews. Raytheon also operates MathMovesU.com, a website that connects students with scholarships, games, and educational initiatives in an effort to encourage children to get more involved in math and science as possible future careers.

BRAND OUTLOOK

- A cutting-edge technology firm engaged in high-level military contracts, Raytheon is poised for further growth.
- Raytheon is working on the Space Fence Initiative, a system designed to detect and monitor space debris near the earth.

- Raytheon is developing a kinetic weapon that can shoot down incoming missiles in a manner similar to "hitting a bullet with a bullet."
- Raytheon continues to invest in research and development efforts to strengthen key markets such as missile defense, reconnaissance, and cybersecurity.

As one of the cutting-edge technology firms engaged in high-level military contracts, Raytheon is poised for further growth. Its reputation is strong following the successes of such missile projects as the Patriot and Tomahawk systems in use during conflicts in the Middle East. In the second decade of the 21st century many of Raytheon's contracts are considered top secret, but some projects in development have been discussed publicly. One such program is the Space Fence Initiative, a system being designed for the U.S. Air Force that will have enhanced surveillance capabilities to detect and monitor thousands of pieces of space debris. Another project is the Standard Missile-3 (commonly called the SM-3), a defensive weapon designed to shoot down short to medium range ballistic missiles by actually colliding with them with tremendous force. Raytheon describes the system as "hitting a bullet with a bullet." The company is also investing heavily in research and development efforts to strengthen key markets such as missile defense, reconnaissance, surveillance, electronic warfare, and cyber security.

FURTHER READING

"Global 2000: Raytheon." *Forbes*, April 2012.

Lynem, Julie. "Q&A with Bill Swanson of Raytheon." Sanluisobispo.com, February 5, 2013. Accessed February 5, 2013. http://www.sanluisobispo.com/2013/02/05/2382596/bill-swanson-raytheon-interview.html#storylink=cpy.

"MDA Successfully Tests Standard Missile-3 Maneuvering System." *Defense Daily*, January 11, 2005.

"Raytheon Company." *International Directory of Company Histories.* Ed. Jay P. Pederson. Vol. 105. Detroit, MI: St. James Press, 2010.

Raytheon Company. "Raytheon Company History." Accessed February 4, 2013. http://www.raytheon.com/ourcompany/history/index.html.

"Raytheon Space Fence Set for Acquisition Phase after Passing Military PDR." *Satellite Today*, April 20, 2012.

RBC

———————————■———————————

AT A GLANCE

———————■———————

Brand Synopsis: Canada's top brand, RBC emphasizes reliability in banking and financial services.

Parent Company: RBC
1 Place Ville Marie
Post Office Box 6001
Montreal, Quebec H3C 3A9
Canada
http://www.royalbank.com

Sector: Financials

Industry Group: Banks

Performance: *Market share*—RBC was the sixth-largest bank in the world in terms of assets under management (US$435 billion) (2010). *Sales*—CAD27.4 billion (US$26.9 billion) (2011)

Principal Competitors: Toronto Dominion Bank; Bank of Montreal; Scotiabank

BRAND ORIGINS

- RBC was founded in 1864 as Merchants Bank, a private commercial bank, on Bedford Row in Halifax; obtaining a federal charter after confederation, the bank expanded into the rest of the Canadian maritimes.
- Starting in 1910 Royal Bank began purchasing other banks, helping to vault Royal Bank over its competitors, and by the mid-1920s it owned 668 branches.

- Expertise in commodity trade financing enabled Royal Bank to participate in trades of Caribbean goods, leading to the establishment of a Havana branch. By 1925 Royal Bank held 121 international branches.
- In the 1950s Royal Bank entered the oil industry, facilitating national growth by investing in the Alberta oil patch and earning itself the nickname "R-Oil."
- From 1970 to 1980 Royal Bank developed Chargex/Visa, personal checking, and the automated banking system.

The foundation of the Royal Bank of Canada was laid as early as 1864 on the wharves of Halifax, Nova Scotia, where the Merchants Bank was begun as a private commercial bank on Bedford Row. Following confederation, the bank, which had previously held closer links with England and the Caribbean, obtained a federal charter and expanded into the Canadian maritimes. By 1887 the bank, now known as the Merchants' Bank of Halifax, opened a branch in Montreal, placing it at the center of Canadian finance. After considerable expansion into British Columbia, Manitoba, Saskatchewan, and Alberta the board of directors in 1901 decided to leave behind the bank's moniker in favor of Royal Bank of Canada, and six years later the head office was moved to 147 St. James Street.

Expertise in commodity trade financing enabled Royal Bank to participate in trades of sugar, cocoa, tobacco, and other Caribbean goods, leading to the establishment of a Havana branch. By 1925 Royal Bank boasted 121 such international branches, and was established in key centers of North American and European Finance. Beginning in

1910 Royal Bank began purchasing other banks in order to gain access to new territory; Union Bank of Halifax, the Traders Bank of Canada, and the Quebec Bank were among several financial institutions acquired that helped to vault Royal Bank over its competitors, and by the mid-1920s it was Canada's largest bank, with 668 branches.

Although viewed with suspicion alongside other banks during the economic crash of the 1930s, Royal Bank under Morris Wilson rebuilt its credibility from 1934 to 1946, and the bank's headquarters were subsequently moved to 360 St. James Street, then the tallest building in the British Empire. In the 1950s Royal Bank made its first foray into the oil industry, facilitating national growth by investing in the Alberta oil patch and earning itself the nickname "R-Oil." Royal Bank also became the preferred provider of home mortgages. Under the leadership of Earle McLaughlin Royal Bank developed new products such as Chargex/Visa, personal checking accounts, and in 1972 the automated banking system.

To compete with major international banks in the wake of the recession of the 1980s Royal Bank integrated Dominion Securities, Voyageur Insurance Company, and Royal Trust into its services, all of which helped increase revenue generation enough to overcome debt problems of the early 1980s. Royal Bank also committed itself to corporate social responsibility and gradually developed one of the largest philanthropic budgets of any Canadian business.

BRAND ELEMENTS

- The focal point of Royal Bank's logo and brand representation is the word "Royal" and the accompanying emblem that recalls the British royal coat of arms.
- In 1962 a new emblem—the lion, crown, and globe—was introduced to suggest RBC's growing global presence as well as its traditional values.
- In 2001 Royal Bank updated its master brand and adopted the name RBC Financial Group to express the diverse services and businesses that were part of Royal Bank's operations.

The focal point of Royal Bank's logo is the "Royal" name and an emblem closely resembling the British royal coat of arms. This insignia symbolizes tradition and stability. In 1962 a newer, simpler emblem was adopted—a lion and crown, to hark back to the authoritative values suggested by the old heraldic symbol, and a globe, to announce Royal Bank's new global presence. The visually simple logo was identifiable at the top of a building or on the cover of a checkbook. In 2001 Royal Bank updated its master brand and adopted the name RBC Financial Group to express the diverse services and businesses that were part of its operations. A new logo to accompany the

new brand name maintained the lion and globe and was intended to define RBC Financial Group's growth strategy in North America and niche markets worldwide.

Royal Bank's transformation from a traditional commercial bank to a broad-based financial group involved strategic alliances with technology partners, such as a relationship with AOL Canada Inc. to make e-banking alternatives available to clients. To expand the bank's North American presence a new global brand strategy was launched under the RBC Financial Group title in which the RBC prefix was added to each business platform and operating subsidiary.

BRAND IDENTITY

- RBC's fundamental principles are centered around a desire to "earn the right to be [their] clients' first choice."
- The RBC brand cultivates a warm and approachable identity through the character "Arbie."
- RBC communicates with its customers annually through the RBC "Letter."

RBC' defining principles are centered around a desire to "earn the right to be [their] clients' first choice." RBC characterizes the brand as one open to diversity and inclusion, a strong culture of employee engagement, and a foundation on which everyone can succeed. Cultivating a banking community that comprises many different skill sets, ideas, and people prepares the brand to better anticipate a wide range of customer needs.

RBC's "Letter" (archived since 1943) reflects RBC's interest in corporate citizenship and reflects the brand's perspective on a range of relevant topics from healthcare to environmentalism. In an effort to cultivate an identity of warmth and approachability RBC adopted the brand character "Arbie" to give customers an accessible touch-point with which to connect to the bank.

BRAND STRATEGY

- In 2008 RBC acquired RBTT Financial Group with the aim of controlling its expansive banking network in the Caribbean, helping the brand establish a common operating program to support growth in the region.
- Royal Bank launched the campaign tagline "Advice you can bank on" in 2010.
- RBC expanded its branches and ATM networks from 2009 to 2010.

In 2008 RBC acquired the RBTT Financial Group, an expansive Caribbean banking network. RBC's headquarters in Port of Spain, Trinidad and Tobago, established a common operating program to support growth in the region. RBC's Caribbean headquarters represents the second largest banking network in the English speaking Caribbean, and it resulted in enhanced value for the brand's shareholders. RBC Dexia Investor Services is ranked as a top 10 global custodian by its assets under administration and provides unique offshore and onshore solutions to businesses worldwide in 16 countries.

In 2010 RBC withstood the financial conditions that caused its global competitors to fail, and it remained the leading Canadian financial institution. To continue this leadership RBC plans to leverage its distribution and brand strength to expand the business, increase global capability by placing two-thirds of its employees in the United States and the United Kingdom, increase market shares by servicing client needs more efficiently than the brand's peers, continue as the top performing Canadian asset manager, and attract the best advisors in North America and globally.

RBC's strategy from 2009 to 2010 involved extending the branches and ATM networks of its retail bank to make these services more accessible to clients. RBC invested in more efficient methods of serving clients by adding client-facing employees to branches; this resulted in more business from new and existing clients; higher market shares in consumer lending, business loans, and business deposits; and recognition by other organizations, including Synovate and Forrester Research Inc.

BRAND EQUITY

- RBC was ranked as Canada's top brand in 2011.
- RBC's market capitalization in 2009 was more than CAD30 billion, and its return on equity was 11.9 percent.
- Approximately 60 percent of RBC's revenue comes from outside of Canada.

In a brand value study released by London's Brand Finance in 2011 RBC was ranked as Canada's top brand, valued at US$7.55 billion. The corporate brand has put a strong focus on baby boomers in sponsorship and philanthropic projects, hoping to target educated, moneyed opinion leaders with complicated financial needs.

Royal Bank holds a top-tier market share in nearly all of its businesses. It has a diversified segment generating 25 percent to 30 percent of RBC's revenue and earnings that is made up of a broad range of businesses, geographies, and clientele. Approximately 60 percent of RBC's revenue comes from outside of Canada. RBC has assets of CAD609 billion and a net income of CAD3.6 billion. The brand's market capitalization in 2009 was more than CAD30 billion, and its return on equity was 11.9 percent. Its average return on equity was 20 percent in the

same year. RBC also holds the highest senior debt ratings among banks globally.

BRAND AWARENESS

- In 2007 RBC was ranked among the Top 100 Most Powerful Brands in the world in Millward Brown's second annual BrandZ survey.
- RBC reported that brand recall was the highest it had ever been in 2011.
- RBC was named the third best Canadian brand by Interbrand in 2013.

In 2007 RBC was ranked among the Top 100 Most Powerful Brands in the world in Millward Brown's second annual BrandZ survey. Ranking 39th, RBC was the first Canadian company to make the list at the time. RBC earned Outstanding Private Bank—North America honors from *Private Banker International* in 2009 for the brand's growth potential, stability, and national leadership. RBC was also named Dealmaker of the Year in Canada by the *Financial Post* and Best Investment Bank in Canada by *Euromoney*. Bloomberg and Thomson Reuters named RBC the leader in Canadian equity underwriting and corporate debt financing.

In 2012 RBC had only fallen one position on BrandZ's Top 100 Brand Ranking, to the 40th position. RBC was ranked 17th on Global Finance's World's 50 Safest Banks in the same year. In 2013 RBC was named the third best Canadian brand by Interbrand. RBC says that brand recall was the highest it had ever been in 2011, the fifth year that RBC had sponsored the Toronto International Film Festival. In the same year RBC renewed its commitment to making the bank known globally and launched a new advertising campaign that reminded customers of the strength, stability, and global reach that the brand embodies.

BRAND OUTLOOK

- In the summer report of 2012 RBC's total assets were tallied at more than CAD800 billion, with a tier 1 capital ratio of 13.2 percent.
- RBC's net income for 2011 was CAD6.97 billion.
- In 2012 RBC received numerous awards, including the Best Retail Bank in North America by *Retail Banker International*.

RBC is Canada's leading financial institution and one of the leading diversified financial services brands. In RBC's summer report of 2012 the brand's total assets were tallied at more than CAD800 billion with a tier 1 capital ratio of 13.2 percent. RBC's net income for 2011 was CAD6.97 billion, with revenue of CAD27.64 billion and a return on equity of 20.5 percent. In 2012 RBC was named Best Retail Bank in North America by *Retail Banker International*.

FURTHER READING

"Banking on RBC." *Strategy: Bold Vision Brand New Ideas.* Accessed September 20, 2012. http://strategyonline.ca/2011/10/05/banking-on-rbc/.

Baragar, Geoff. "Reflections of a Royal Banker," *Canadian Business Review*, Summer 1987.

Darroch, James L. *Canadian Banks and Global Competitiveness.* Montreal, Canada: McGill-Queen's University Press, 1994.

Ince, Clifford. *The Royal Bank of Canada: A Chronology, 1864–1969.* Montreal, Canada: Royal Bank of Canada, 1969.

McDowell, Duncan. *Quick to the Frontier: Canada's Royal Bank.* Toronto, Canada: McClelland & Stewart, 1993.

Simon, Bernard. "Each to His Own." *Banker*, August 1994.

RBC. "Corporate Responsibility and Sustainability Report and Public Accountability Report." Accessed September 20, 2012. http://www.rbc.com/community-sustainability/_assets-custom/pdf/RBC-CRR-Report-e.pdf

"The Royal Bank of Canada." *International Directory of Company Histories.* Ed. Lisa Mirabile. Vol. 2. Detroit, MI: St. James Press, 1990.

RENAULT

BRAND ORIGINS

- Renault was founded in 1898 by the Renault brothers, Louis, Marcel, and Fernand.
- In the post–World War II period, Renault became primarily owned by the French government.
- Though Renaults had been sold in the American market as early as the late 1950s, the brand withdrew in 1987 after sustaining large financial losses.

Renault has its origins in France in 1898 when Marcel and Fernand Renault helped found Renault Freres (Renault Brothers) with their brother Louis. That year the first Renault Voiturette automobile was produced. By 1901 Renault was the eighth-largest automobile company because of the popularity of its small, inexpensive, reliable car.

To promote the young brand, Louis and Marcel became expert racing drivers and won numerous international races. However, Marcel died in 1903 while competing in a Paris-to-Madrid race. Louis stopped racing, and though the Renault car was withdrawn from the racing circuit for several years, the brand would be linked to auto racing on into the 21st century.

Because of strong sales, including a best-selling taxicab sold both in France and abroad, Renault became the most important French auto company by 1905. Renault continued to grow, and by 1912 it was exporting cars, primarily cabs, to markets like Mexico City and Melbourne. By 1914 Renault had dealers in 31 foreign countries, and Louis Renault had taken out 700 patents related to his company.

During World War I, Renault manufactured military equipment, such as aviation engines, trucks, ambulances, and the first light machine-gun tank, the FT17. During the 1920s, Renault diversified production to include passenger cars, commercial vehicles, boat engines, aircraft engines, and motor units. Particular success was found with its 10CV and 40CV automobiles.

Despite the onset of the Great Depression in 1929, Renault remained relatively strong in the 1930s because of good management and diversified production. In 1936 Renault produced 61,146 cars, a yearly record, and launched another popular model, the Juvaquatre. During World War II, its main factory was occupied and used by Germans. Renault's fortunes were further impacted when Louis Renault was imprisoned on charges of Nazi collaboration in 1945 and died in prison. The French government soon nationalized Renault but allowed it to operate and develop as a commercial entity.

The new Renault's fortunes reached new heights with a miniature car called Quatre Chevaux (or 4CV), which was launched in 1946 and went into production in 1948. Secretly developed during the war by Renault technicians, it reflected the company philosophy that a car was a social instrument that every family had the right to possess. In 1956, the Dauphine, a midpriced model which replaced the 4CV, became popular, outselling all other models for five years. Renault still emphasized exports. By 1959 Renault was the sixth-largest automaker in the world, having spent the mid-1950s focusing on expansion outside of France and its colonial markets.

In the early 1960s, Renault developed the R-16 to meet the demands of the American motorist. Other popular models in the 1960s and early 1970s included the Estafette, a commercial vehicle designed for deliveries, the Renault 8 Gordini, and the R-5, a well-designed and highly reliable vehicle that helped ensure that Renault would remain a leading European vehicle manufacturer. When the R-5 debuted in 1974, it accounted for 60 percent of Renault sales in the wake of the oil crisis brought on by the Organization of Petroleum Exporting Countries.

To further build brand awareness in the United States, Renault struck an agreement with American Motors Corp. (AMC) in 1979 in which American Motors became the exclusive North American importer and distributor of Renault cars, while Renault marketed AMC products in France and other countries. The Renault Alliance and Encore were sold in the United States. Despite this agreement, and while still remaining the leading vehicle manufacturer in Europe, Renault began losing market share and money steadily through the mid-1980s. Despite campaigns to build brand awareness, like 1984's "One Small Step Ahead," and the introduction of an improved Renault 5, by the mid-1980s Renault had losses of US$1.5 billion and sank from number one to number six domestically. In 1986 AMC had huge losses as well, compelling Renault to withdraw from the U.S. market in 1987.

Renault thereupon returned to profitability in that same year and launched the Renault 19 in 1989. Its advertising helped build the perception of the brand as a quality

car. Renault continued to introduce popular models in the 1990s. In 1991 the Renault Clio debuted and became the best-selling car in France. Other successes included the Twingo, introduced in 1993, the Laguna, introduced in 1995, larger vehicles like the Megane, which became the number-two selling car in France, the minivan Espace, and 1997's hit, the Kangoo. Renault also focused on expanding its international presence in countries such as Turkey, Romania, China, and the Czech Republic, as well as strengthening the company's Latin American and Asian operations and entering the Russian market. By 1997, 20 percent of its sales came in foreign markets.

In the late 1990s, the French government began reducing its 80 percent ownership-share, reaching 16 percent by 2003. In 1999 Renault launched a successful, long-term partnership with Nissan Motor Company. By 2003 the Renault-Nissan alliance was the fourth-largest vehicle manufacturer in the world. And by 2004 Renault had again become the most successful auto manufacturer in Europe, with revenues reaching US$55 billion. To further boost sales outside of Western Europe, Renault introduced a budget vehicle, the Logan, to sell in China, Eastern Europe, and other emerging markets in 2004. The Logan later launched in developed markets like France in 2005 and sold extremely well.

Though Renault's overall sales in Western and Central Europe fell, beginning in 2005, Renault worked hard to sell more vehicles in markets such as France. In 2008 it was still the top automaker in France, with a 21.9 percent market share. To stay abreast of current industry trends, Renault announced its *Renault Commitment 2009* statement, which included initiatives to promote electric vehicles and related technology. Still struggling, however, Renault received the equivalent of US$3.9 billion in a loan from the French government to keep it afloat.

In 2012 Renault had sales of 2.55 million units globally, a drop of 6.3 percent from 2011. Its share of the European market, which still struggled economically because of a global recession that started in 2008, shrank to 8.5 percent. To compensate for the decline in Western Europe, Renault focused on building its markets in Australia, Asia, South America, and Africa. Renault was also guided by a new strategic plan introduced in 2011 called *Renault 2016—Drive the Change*, which promoted the goal of creating widespread access to sustainable mobility.

BRAND ELEMENTS
- The first Renault logo included the initials of the brand's three founding brothers.
- In 1925 the Renault diamond was introduced.
- In 2007 the Renault logo was updated to include the brand's signature warm yellow, the diamond, and the Renault name.

The Renault brand name is deeply linked to the brothers who founded the brand and their heritage of innovativeness. Louis Renault alone held at least 700 patents for his inventions and innovations. Early logos for the brand reflect this family legacy, with the original 1900 logo consisting of a medallion with the initials of Louis, Fernand, and Marcel at the center. While subsequent logos consisted of images of cars and tanks, in 1923 a circular logo in the shape of a grille was introduced which featured the Renault name at center.

Two years later the same elements were fashioned into a diamond shape, with the Renault brand name at center. This led to Renault being known as the "diamond brand." After Renault became nationalized in 1946, the company name was changed to Régie Nationale des Usines Renault. While "Régie Nationale" appeared on the logo for over a decade, the most important element introduced was a shade of yellow that would be a key part of the brand's logo and branding in the early 21st century.

In 1972 Renault's logo underwent an overhaul. The new version no longer featured lines representing a grill or the Renault name, but was reimagined as a 3D diamond with bold lines forming the diamond shape. These lines were dropped in favor of a boxy diamond shape and the Renault name underneath in 1992. A yellow background and spare diamond symbol came into use in 2004, with an update in 2007 in which the diamond and the Renault name were contained within a yellow square, bringing together the Renault history in one simple, yet modern symbol.

BRAND IDENTITY

- Renault is a definitive French brand of automobiles.
- By 2012 Renault was promising to "Drive the Change."
- Its founders associated Renault with auto racing in 1901, and the brand had a long-term relationship with Formula 1.

From its earliest days, Renault has been inextricably identified with France as one of the first and arguably best-known French car brands. Though Renault was founded by three French brothers, the French identity became more deeply entrenched when the French government took a major stake in the brand in 1946. While government's share was originally 80 percent, it had declined to only 15 percent by 2013. However, many Renaults were still manufactured in France, including the popular Clio model, and one of its most significant markets remained its country of origin.

Over the years, many Renault taglines defined the brand as being in step with customer needs, including 1984's "One Small Step Ahead" and 1993's "A Private View." The latter was used to launch a high-end executive model, the Safrane, and it emphasized this model's exclusivity and top-of-range status. Labeling itself a pioneering brand, Renault recognized its one-hundredth anniversary in 1998 in the tagline, "Renault, 100 Years of Driving Innovation." After the introduction of the Renault SA's new strategic plan, *Renault 2016—Drive the Change*, in 2012, the brand emphasized its commitment to widespread and sustainable mobility with its "Drive the Change" tagline.

A few years after the Renault brothers founded their car company, they began associating the Renault brand with autosports. Both Louis and Marcel won numerous international races, though Marcel died in 1903 while competing in a race. Renault later won what is generally considered the first Grand Prix in Le Mans in 1906. Renault later joined Formula 1 (F1) racing, powering its own successful F1 team from 1977 to 1986 and again from 2002 to 2009. By 2012 Renault was supplying engines for four F1 teams.

BRAND STRATEGY

- Renault's brand strategy after 1948 was to ensure that every family had the right to own a car, and it provided many inexpensive models to meet that need.
- In 2011 Renault introduced its first electric vehicles.
- As Renault's sales fell in Western Europe in the early 2010s, the brand saw its presence expand in Brazil, India, China, Morocco, and Algeria.

From Renault's founding in 1898 until present day, the brand has focused on producing numerous vehicles under the Renault name, from passenger cars to taxi cabs to commercial vehicles. During World War I, it also made military equipment like airplane engines and even tanks. In 1948, after Renault became 80 percent owned by the French government, it launched one of its most popular models, the the very small 4CV (Quatre Chevaux). The brand's new philosophy was that every family had the right to own a car, and Renault focused on producing many small, inexpensive models in this time period. It then expanded its offerings over time as incomes and markets grew, though many of its most popular models, such as the Clio, Logan, and Twingo, were affordable. In 2011 Renault launched its first electric vehicles, including the Kangoo Z.E. and Fluence Z.E., with plans to introduce more models to cover all market segments.

Renault also produced models under other brand names. The Logan, for example, was originally produced by Dacia, Renault's subsidiary in Romania. Renault had begun working with Dacia in the early 1960s and took over the company in 1999, using the Dacia brand name to grow its presence in Eastern Europe and other growth markets. In 2000 Renault acquired the automotive division of the Samsung group and founded Renault Samsung Motors, which became the fourth-ranked automotive company in South Korea by 2009.

Because of the weak market in Western Europe, where Renault S.A. sales fell by 18 percent in 2012, Renault has focused on developing a presence in various growth markets. These markets include Russia, where it had a 5.8 percent market share in 2011, and Brazil, Renault S.A.'s second best market in 2011. Asia had a number of growth markets for the carmaker, such as India, where Renault introduced the specially developed compact Pluse debuted in 2012, and China, where sales grew nearly 23 percent in 2012. African markets were also targets, especially Morocco and Algeria, two markets where Renault was the number-one car brand in 2011, and South Africa, a market it had reentered in 2002 and where it now strove to improve on its 4 percent market share.

BRAND EQUITY

- Renault sold 2.55 million units in 2012, though more than half were outside of Europe for the first time.
- Renault remained the number-one passenger car brand in France in 2012.
- According to Brand Finance, Renault's brand value was US$8.064 billion in 2012.

Though Renault is a quintessentially French and, by extension, European brand, in 2012 for the first time it sold more cars outside of Europe than inside. Overall, it sold 2.55 million units worldwide in 2012, and saw its European market share drop to 8.5 percent. Renault did dominate the European LCV (light commercial vehicle) market with a 15.5 percent market share, and it remained the number-one passenger car brand in Europe. Renault's investment in international growth paid off in markets like Brazil, Renault's second-biggest market, where it had a 6.6 percent market share, India, where it had a 1.1 percent market share, and Algeria, where it had a 26 percent market share.

Despite Renault's uneven performance and struggles in key European markets, it was still a highly valued brand. In Brand Finance's *Global 500* for 2012, Renault placed number 115, with a brand value of US$8.064 billion and an enterprise value of US$30.616 billion. MPP Consulting ranked the value of brands that were created in France in its *FranBrand Top 100 French Brand*. Renault ranked number 14 for 2011, with a brand value of US$2.135 billion.

BRAND AWARENESS

- By 2012 Renaults were available in 118 countries.
- Renault was associated with auto racing, particularly Formula 1.

- Renault's three biggest markets as of 2012 were, in order, France, Brazil, and Russia.

As a brand, Renault has existed since the late 19th century. It is best-known in its home country of France and in former French colonies, including Algeria and Morocco. However, it has established a global reputation as a builder of reliable vehicles, including cars, minivans, light commercial vehicles, and electric cars. Renault products were sold in 118 countries as of 2012. Many of its best-selling and most popular models in markets from Europe to Asia to South America are small and inexpensive, such as the 4CV, the Logan, and the Clio. Though Renault only sold cars in the U.S. market from the late 1950s until 1987, the brand is still known there and in other global markets because of Renault's long history with auto racing. It all started with the first Grand Prix at Lemans in 1906 and led to Renault's ownership of a Formula 1 racing team from 1977 to 1986 and from 2002 to 2009, and then to its role as an engine supplier for four F1 teams in 2012. Surveys also showed Renault had a strong overall image and awareness. ADAC's *AutomarxX Brand Ranking*, which considered concepts like brand image, market strength, customer satisfaction, and product strength, ranked Renault at number 24 for 2012.

BRAND OUTLOOK

- Car sales were slowing in Europe in the early 2010s, contributing to an 18 percent decline in Renault sales in 2012.
- Renault had more success in international markets like Brazil, Russia, India, and China where it had made significant investments.
- *Renault 2016—Drive the Change* outlined Renault's five-year plan for growth.

Globally, most car brands saw their value significantly decline between 2011 and 2012. This trend began with the onset of the global economic recession in 2008. Most European car brands lost value in that continent's troubled economy. Car sales slowed in most countries, except Germany, during the economic crisis. Renault saw its car sales in Europe decline by 18 percent in 2012 alone, leaving a market share of 9.1 percent, and contraction was expected to continue in the early to mid-2010s. However, Renault made significant investments in markets outside of Western Europe, including Eastern Europe, China, India, Russia, and Brazil, where it had years of positive growth. In 2012 Renault set a sales record outside of Europe with a 9.1 percent increase, to 1.28 million vehicles. This trend was expected to continue as the global automotive market had much positive momentum. Renault also had the support of the French government, which lent the automaker the equivalent of US$3.5 billion in 2009. In 2011 Renault released its report *Renault 2016—Drive the Change*, which outlined its ambitious plan for growth through 2016. In addition to setting a goal of selling over three million vehicles in 2013, the brand committed to innovating, strengthening its product line, pursuing international growth, and strengthening Renault's brand image.

FURTHER READING

Brand Finance. "Renault." *Brandirectory*. Accessed February 14, 2013. http://brandirectory.com/profile/renault.

"Driver of Change: New Renault COO Carlos Tavares Wants to Radically Change the Company's Corporate Culture." *Automotive News Europe*, November 1, 2011, 45.

Jolly, David. "Renault Reports Lower Sales and Profits for 2012." *New York Times*, February 14, 2013.

"Renault." *Forbes*. Accessed February 14, 2013. http://www.forbes.com/companies/renault/.

"Renault." RankingTheBrands.com. Accessed February 14, 2013. http://www.rankingthebrands.com/Brand-detail.aspx?brandID=394.

"Renault S.A." *International Directory of Company Histories*. Ed. Tina Grant. Vol. 74. Detroit, MI: St. James Press, 2006.

Wright, Clinton. "Renault in the Fast Lane." *Automotive Industries*, Fall 2007.

ROCHE

BRAND ORIGINS

- Roche traces its history to Switzerland, 1896.
- An orange-flavored cough syrup called Sirolin was one of Roche's early successful brand products.
- The "Roche" trademark was adopted circa 1920.
- Valium, introduced in 1963, became one of Roche's best known product brands.
- Roche restructured its operations in 2002 to focus on pharmaceuticals and diagnostics.

The Roche brand traces its origins in the pharmaceutical industry to 1896 when Fritz Hoffmann-La Roche bought out a partner to form F. Hoffmann-La Roche & Co. The Basel, Switzerland-based company manufactured a variety of medicinal and household remedies. In 1898 La Roche introduced an orange-flavored cough syrup called Sirolin, one of many successfully branded products the company would offer over the years. Early in the following decade, Hoffmann-La Roche introduced Digalen, a heart condition treatment, and Pantopon, a pain killer. These products proved so popular that by 1912 the company was operating on three continents through branches in nine countries, including the United States.

The difficulties of doing business on a large scale during World War I led to a bank bailout in 1919, reducing La Roche to minority ownership status until his death in 1920. Under new leadership, the restructured company rebounded, in part by standardizing its brand around the world. "Roche" was trademarked and applied to all of the company's products and services. The company also continued to market products under individual brand names, such as Somnifen and Allonal.

In 1933 Roche became involved in the lucrative vitamin business when it introduced Redoxin, the first mass-produced vitamin C. It was followed over the next dozen years by branded vitamins B1, E, B2, and B6. Following World War II, the company enjoyed strong growth in its pharmaceutical and cosmetics segments as well. Tranquilizers proved especially successful. In 1960 the company introduced Librium, followed three years later by what would become one of Roche's best known brands, a tranquilizer named Valium.

Roche expanded on multiple fronts in the final decades of the century. By the early 1970s, Roche was selling about half of the world's vitamins, but it was Valium and Librium that were the company's flagship product brands. Together, they accounted for about US$500 million of Roche's US$1.2 billion in sales in 1973. When the Valium patent in the United States expired in 1985, Roche was dealt a significant blow, but following a series of acquisitions, it was now a more diversified company. External growth continued in the 1990s, when Roche acquired majority control of Genentech, helping Roche to become a leading biotechnology company.

The Roche brand was tarnished in the late 1990s when Roche and other vitamin manufacturers in the United States were charged with price fixing by the U.S. Department of Justice. To settle the matter, Roche paid a US$500 million fine, the highest ever imposed at the time. In 2001 the European Commission also issued a record fine against Roche for the same transgression. The company decided to restructure in 2002, divesting its vitamins business and other units to focus on its pharmaceuticals and diagnostics segments. Subsequent acquisitions bolstered these areas, as the Roche name became solely associated around the world with drug treatments and diagnostics tools.

BRAND ELEMENTS

- The Roche name has served as a trademark for nearly a century.
- The hexagonal shape of the Roche logo is used in chemistry for skeleton formulas.
- The Roche slogan is "We Innovate Healthcare."
- A second slogan, "Make your Mark. Improve Lives," is used to recruit and retain employees.

Roche uses a variety of means to support both its corporate brand and individual product brands. The overarching Roche brand strikes a general tone. The Roche name, tied to its founder, has been in use for nearly a century. In truth, Fritz Hoffmann-La Roche was born Fritz Hoffmann in 1868. When he married Adele La Roche in 1895, he adopted his wife's last name. He aggressively expanded into countries around the world. To bring some continuity to the brand, a shortened version of the La Roche name was adopted as the company's trademark and corporate brand.

Like the name, the Roche logo is simple. Presented all in blue, "Roche" is enclosed within a hexagon. While simple in shape, the hexagon carries significance because in chemistry such shapes are known as skeleton formulas. They contain shorthand representations of molecules. For a pharmaceutical manufacturer like Roche, the connection to chemistry is highly relevant. By placing the Roche name within this evocative symbol, Roche not only says that it uses chemistry, it suggests that it is chemistry.

Roche supports its brand message through the slogan "We Innovate Healthcare." On its face, the slogan identifies the primary sector the company serves, healthcare. More than that, the slogan reveals the company's dedication to the production of cutting-edge therapies, especially in the biotechnology field. More than half of Roche's drug sales and five of its top ten products come from biopharmaceuticals.

Roche employs a second slogan, "Make your Mark. Improve Lives," used to recruit and retain employees. It appeals to the desire of potential employees to not only forge a career but to make a difference in the world. By implication, Roche claims to be pursuing the same ends. The slogan suggests that the company make its mark by improving healthcare through the development of innovative diagnostic products and therapies.

BRAND IDENTITY

- At the core of Roche's identity is a commitment to innovation.
- Much of Roche's identity is aimed at key decision makers in the healthcare field.
- Part of Roche's identity is a commitment to serve as a catalyst for personalized healthcare.
- To employees, Roche emphasizes an identity that reflects compassion for others.

The way that Roche wishes to be perceived, the identity it presents to the world, is revealed in its slogan, "We Innovate Healthcare." Innovation is at the heart of the Roche brand. The company does not manufacture generic drugs, or what it calls "me-too" treatments. Rather, the focus is on the development of new treatments using cutting-edge methods, in particular biotechnology. The company's Genentech subsidiary was a biotechnology pioneer, lending further credence to Roche's claim to the mantle of innovation. Most consumers are not aware of this background. Rather, they are prescribed Roche products by their physicians. Therefore Roche seeks to shape its identity to meet the expectations of these key decision-makers.

More than just asserting that Roche creates innovative treatments and diagnostic products, the corporate slogan expands the brand promise to include changing healthcare through innovation. The claim extends to the future as well. Roche is investing heavily in the field of personalized healthcare, a commitment that has become part of the brand's identity. Using biotechnology, Roche is moving toward the development of treatments that are modified at the molecular level to meet the requirements of specific patient populations.

In addition to innovation, Roche's brand identity includes commitment and compassion. Roche invests heavily in research and development, a reflection of its brand promise. The company's employee-oriented slogan, "Make your Mark. Improve Lives," supports the concept of compassion. Roche implies that it is also dedicated to improving the lives of everyday people, espousing a culture of "patients before profit." At a secondary level, Roche extends that compassion to employees, presenting itself as a company that wants to provide its people with ample opportunities to achieve professional and personal growth.

BRAND STRATEGY

- Roche is involved in corporate branding as well as product branding.
- Subsidiary Genentech pursues its own corporate branding within the parameters of the Roche brand identity.
- In projects in which Roche and Genentech are both involved, the Genentech brand is used in projects focused on the United States.
- Product branding is mostly aimed at physicians rather than consumers.
- Rocephin is a shining example of successful pharmaceutical product-branding by Roche.

Roche pursues both a corporate- and a product-branding strategy. The Roche name serves as the master brand, under which the company's diagnostics products and services operate. The company's main subsidiaries maintain their own brand identities, while still acknowledging a connection to Roche. Genentech, for example, identifies itself as "A member of the Roche Group," while at the same time promoting its own brand image centered on the slogan "To us, science is personal." Like its parent brand, Genentech emphasizes innovation and a commitment to improving the lives of patients as well as the healthcare system as a whole. When it comes to working on a specific project, the Genentech brand is generally used for activities focused in the United States, while the Roche name is mostly used in other parts of the world. In this way, Roche avoids the problem of appearing as if it were two separate companies and thereby diluting the brands. Roche would rather appear like a single, unified company than insist on promoting the Roche name as much as possible.

Because consumers do not directly buy Roche Group products or specifically request these products from their physicians, there is little value in building awareness of the Roche brand with the general public. Roche does, however, promote a stable of consumer brands to physicians. Some of the better known product brands include Berocca, Rennie, Tamiflu, and Rocephin.

Rocephin (ceftriaxone sodium) is one of Roche's most successful efforts at product branding. From the mid-1980s into the new century, Rocephin was the leading injectable broad-spectrum antibiotic. To promote the product, Roche used the apple as a brand icon that served as an image for the logo and inspired the tagline "once-a-day." The branding played on the traditional belief in the medicinal properties of the apple, as embodied in the old saying "An apple a day keeps the doctor away." In print ads, the apple took on a variety of personas, depending on the type of disease the product was intended to treat. When the indication was pneumonia, for example, the apple was pictured in a snowstorm. There was little need for blaring headlines or extensive copy in promoting Rocephin. The conceptual branding that linked the apple to good health and in turn to Rocephin created a standard of excellence in pharmaceutical branding for both Roche and the pharmaceutical industry.

BRAND EQUITY

- Avoiding "me-too" drugs helps Roche to maintain its brand equity.
- Brand Finance placed a US$2.388 billion brand value on Roche at the end of 2011.
- Roche was ranked No. 497 on the 2012 Global 500 list of the world's most valuable brands.
- Roche was listed as the world's 115th-most-valuable brand in 2007.

Maintaining the equity of its brand is of key importance to Roche and its operating companies. Roche eschews "me-too" drugs, instead focusing its attention on the development of innovative products. Moreover, innovation is at the core of its brand identity, making it imperative that Roche Group companies demonstrate they are in the vanguard of the pharmaceutical industry. Helping to distinguish Roche drugs from their generic equivalents are the company's efforts at building its corporate brand as well as the individual product brands. At a fundamental level, the equity of these brands working in concert can be measured by the difference in price between the generic version of a drug and Roche's branded equivalent.

The general value of the Roche brand is more difficult to pin down. A leading branding consultancy, Brand Finance Plc, employs its own methodology in determining the monetary worth of a brand. According to Brand Finance, at the end of 2011 Roche enjoyed a brand value of US$2.388 billion. It was a performance that garnered the No. 497 position on Brand Finance's 2012 Global 500 list of the world's most valuable brands. A year earlier, however, Roche possessed a brand value of US$5.599 billion and the No. 148 place on the Global 500. The steep decline in brand value was mainly caused by harsh market conditions created by the debt crisis in the United States and Europe that resulted in governments mandating deep cuts in the price of pharmaceuticals. Before the global economy entered a difficult strait, Roche was listed No. 115 in 2007 on what was then known as the Global 250.

BRAND AWARENESS

- Awareness of the Roche brand by healthcare decision makers is more important than general recognition.
- With operations around the world, Roche creates a certain level of brand awareness through basic proximity.
- Longevity of the Roche trademark has also raised awareness of the brand over time.

The Roche brand is less well known to the general public than one would expect for a company of its size. For example, in the 2011 Harris Poll EquiTrend rankings, Roche was below the index average for pharmaceutical company brands. However, it could be argued that for a healthcare company like Roche, brand awareness is more important in terms of who, rather than how many, know about the brand.

The company has tried to use the strong name recognition of some of its products to increase awareness of the Roche brand. In 2003 Roche used the opportunity of Valium's fortieth anniversary to celebrate the Roche scientist who created one of the most famous drugs in the history of pharmacology, as well as the company's own tradition of research and innovation. Other Roche products with strong brand recognition include the osteoporosis drug Boniva, which enjoys high recall in studies despite competing products outspending it in advertising.

The company also raises awareness of the brand through charitable work, such as the Children's Walk that roughly 20,000 Roche employees participate in yearly, which raises money for pediatric HIV and AIDS. The brand's profile is also raised by industry accolades, such as being ranked on *Fortune's* "25 Best Global Companies to Work For" and the company's strong showing on the DOW Jones Sustainability World Index.

BRAND OUTLOOK

- The aging of the population bodes well for healthcare brands like Roche.
- Biotechnology companies like Genentech are likely to enjoy continued strong growth.
- Roche might transition to a single corporate brand in the future.

Despite difficult economic conditions that have depressed the performance of the Roche Group, the company and its brand are set to enjoy strong growth in the years ahead. The members of the massive baby boom generation who were born in the years following World War II have begun their retirement years, creating a growing demand for the pharmaceutical and diagnostic products and services Roche Group has to offer. With life expectancies increasing, this period of heightened demand will likely extend well into the future.

Roche is also well positioned to enjoy its leading role as a biotechnology company, primarily through Genentech but also with Chugai. The potential of biotechnology is still largely untapped, and might very well redound to the benefit of Roche's brand equity. After it fully acquired Genentech in 2009, Roche elected to retain the Genentech brand to avoid confusion in the marketplace, choosing instead to portray Genentech as a Roche Group company. Such an accommodation for Genentech and other subsidiaries might be a transitional strategy, however. In the years ahead, Roche might very well bring all of its operations under the Roche name, creating a unified, potentially stronger brand.

FURTHER READING

"Avon to Launch Roche Tie-In." *Marketing Week*, May 3, 2001.

Brand Finance. "Global 500 2012." *Brandirectory*. Accessed January 7, 2013. http://brandirectory.com/league_tables/table/global-500-2012.

Domanico, Tom. "Private View." *Medical Marketing & Media*, July 2003.

"Roche: A Leader in Biotechnology." *Research*, March 2010.

"Roche Holding AG." *International Directory of Company Histories*. Ed. Derek Jacques and Paula Kepos. Vol. 109. Detroit, MI: St. James Press, 2010.

"Roche to Develop an Ethical Culture Solution for Staff." *Marketing*, October 11, 2001.

ROLLS-ROYCE

■

AT A GLANCE

■

Brand Synopsis: One of the best-known engineering brands in the world, Rolls-Royce is "Trusted to deliver excellence."

Parent Company: Rolls-Royce Holdings plc
65 Buckingham Gate
London, SW1E 6AT
United Kingdom
http://www.rolls-royce.com/

Sector: Industrials

Industry Group: Capital Goods

Performance: *Market share*—8 percent of the global aircraft engine market (2011). *Sales*—£12.161 billion (US$18.870 billion) (parent company Rolls-Royce Holdings plc) (2012).

Principal Competitors: CFM International; European Aeronautic Defense & Space Company; General Electric; Honeywell; Pratt and Whitney

BRAND ORIGINS

- Rolls-Royce began as an automotive manufacturer in 1904.
- Rolls-Royce began making aircraft engines in 1907.
- By 2004 Rolls-Royce was both the second-largest civil aeroengine company and the second-largest defense aeroengine company in the world.

Rolls-Royce began in 1904 as a joint venture between dealership owner Charles Rolls and engineer Henry Royce. Royce owned electrical engineering firms, including Royce Ltd., and had developed a sparkless electric dynamo. Both Rolls and Royce had an early interest in motor cars. They became business partners after Royce built a smooth-running car that was introduced at the 1904 Paris car show as a Rolls-Royce. In 1906 there was a formal merger between Rolls-Royce distributor C.S. Rolls & Company and the car-making division of Royce Ltd. to form Rolls-Royce Ltd.

While Rolls-Royce introduced such classic models as the Silver Ghost in 1907, Rolls had an interest in another burgeoning technology: powered aircraft. In 1907 Rolls-Royce began making aircraft engines, and Rolls-Royce models were used in the some of the world's first powered aircraft. In 1910 Rolls resigned from Rolls-Royce Ltd. to focus on airplanes, dying a few months later in a plane crash. Though Royce was not particularly interested in aircraft, he continued to build aircraft engines, including the Hawk and the Falcon.

In 1914 Rolls-Royce Ltd. began building airplane engines for the British government for use in World War I. The company produced 60 percent of all British-built airplane engines used in the conflict. Royce designed the Eagle, which was used extensively by the allies. The Eagle was later employed on the aircraft that completed the first direct transatlantic flight and the first flight from England to Australia. By 1919 Rolls-Royce accounted for more than half of Britain's total aeroengine production.

During this time period, Rolls-Royce became as well-known for making airplane engines as for luxury automobiles, including the Phantom engine in 1925. In the late 1920s, Rolls-Royce developed another aeroengine, the R, which was used in the British entry in the International Schneider Trophy and set a world air-speed record in 1931. Royce himself worked on the development of his brand's next major aeroengine, the Merlin, until his death in 1933.

Rolls-Royce engines were coveted for their handmade attention to detail. They were widely used and were considered high quality. Rolls-Royce engines would also prove key to the British war effort during World War II. In 1939, as Britain prepared for the war, the 1,260-horsepower Merlin began to be used in military planes in Great Britain and the United States. During the war Rolls-Royce suspended automobile operations to devote its productive capacity to the manufacture of aircraft engines.

The demand created for the Merlin engine made Rolls-Royce a leader in aero propulsion. In 1943 British aircraft power was greatly increased with Rolls-Royce's new 2,000-horsepower Griffon engine. Also in 1943 Rolls-Royce began to develop a jet engine called the Welland, which was used at the end of the war and continued to be developed in the postwar period. Later in the 1940s, Rolls-Royce introduced more new engines, including the Derwent and the Nene. The Avon jet engine was modified for commercial purposes and was eventually used for the Comet jetliner, the world's first passenger jet.

By the 1950s Rolls-Royce was an industry leader in aircraft-engine development in Europe and the United States. The Dart engine was a turboprop model that marked Rolls-Royce's entry into civil aviation in 1953. In 1960 the Conway engine was used in the Boeing 707 to become the first turbofan to be used in airline service. By 1960 more than 80 percent of Rolls-Royce's revenues were generated by the aeroengine division. The brand began to be aggressively marketed in the United States, concentrating on the promising jumbo-jet market, for which Rolls-Royce engineers began designing their most powerful engine to date, the RB211.

Development problems emerged as the RB211 was rushed to market in the late 1960s. As a result, Rolls-Royce started losing money. In 1970 the British government loaned Rolls-Royce Ltd. £60 million to keep the company from bankruptcy. A few days later, Rolls-Royce Ltd. was nationalized. In 1973 the motor-car division was spun off as a public company, Rolls-Royce Motor Cars, Ltd. As the government reorganized Rolls-Royce, the modified RB211 came on the market and was used in widely acclaimed planes, such as the Lockheed L-1011 and the Boeing 757. The RB211 firmly established Rolls-Royce as a world-class aeroengine maker.

During the 1980s Rolls-Royce suffered from low productivity, and thousands of employees lost their jobs ahead of privatization. In May 1986 Rolls-Royce again went private. Over at least the next three decades, Rolls-Royce merged with and acquired numerous companies so that it could create a variety of engines for planes, boats, and land vehicles, as well as enter new areas like power plants and steam turbine generators. In the late 1990s, for example, Rolls-Royce acquired Vickers plc, which made Rolls-Royce a worldwide leader in the manufacture of marine power systems.

Airplane engines remained the heart of Rolls-Royce, with such engines as the Trent 700 and Trent 800 being certified by aviation authorities for use in the mid-1990s. The Trent 500 made its first flight in 2000. After the September 11, 2001, terrorist attacks on the United States, there was a severe drop in engine sales worldwide, which lasted for several years. By 2004, however, Rolls-Royce was the second-largest civil aeroengine company and also second-largest defense aeroengine company. It was also a worldwide leader in marine propulsion and was still engaged in the energy solutions business. It also provided numerous related engine services. Between 2006 and 2012 Rolls-Royce landed major contracts to install its engines, such as the Trent 1000, on airplanes for Air China, China Southern Airlines, Gulf Air, and other airlines. By 2012 Rolls-Royce Holdings plc, as the Rolls Royce Group plc became known, had revenues of £12.161 billion.

BRAND ELEMENTS

- The Rolls-Royce name is a combination of the last names of the brand's founders, Charles Rolls and Henry Royce.
- The Rolls-Royce logo, in use since 1911, is a simple design of two overlapping Rs, representing the founders.
- When the logo is used on cars as a grille monogram, the lettering is black, as it has been since the death of Royce in 1933.

Whether referring to Rolls-Royce cars or airplane engines, the Rolls-Royce name is associated with reliability, innovation, and integrity. Rolls-Royce is a brand name well-known unto itself, as symbol of quality and, when referring to cars, luxury. The name has its origins in the brand's founders, Charles Rolls, a motoring enthusiast and the owner of one of the first car dealerships in the world, and Henry Royce, an engineer. Rolls and Royce began their partnership when Rolls began marketing a two-seater, quality car built by Royce. The Rolls-Royce name debuted at the 1904 Paris car show. Rolls's name came first because he was better-known in motoring circles of the time, though it was Royce who created and built the car. It was Rolls's enthusiasm for the relatively new technology of powered aircraft that would involve Rolls-Royce in one of its most lucrative businesses, airplane engines. Long after the passing of both Rolls and

Royce, their names live on, not only in the few thousand Rolls-Royce automobiles that are made each year, but also in the engines made by their still-existent company. Their partnership has been highlighted by the hyphen which has linked their name since the brand's inception.

Though the Rolls-Royce car design and manufacturing business split from its engine business in 1973, both aspects of the Rolls-Royce brand continued to use the same logo that they had when part of the same company. Since its introduction around 1911, the Rolls-Royce logo has consisted of two overlapping Rs at the center, with the "Rolls" name above and the "Royce" name below in a simple, rectangular box with simple, narrow lines bringing all the elements together. The logo itself is a distinctive blue, with white lettering and lines. The "RR grille monogram," as it is called when used on Rolls-Royce automobiles, featured red lettering when it was introduced. However, when Royce died in 1933, the color was changed to black, which has been used on most models ever since.

BRAND IDENTITY

- Rolls-Royce cars have defined the Rolls-Royce brand name more than Rolls-Royce's engine business.
- Rolls-Royce is defined as a quality, reliable, and innovative brand.
- In 2011 Rolls-Royce's tagline stated "Trusted to deliver excellence."

As a brand, Rolls-Royce automobiles are perhaps much better known to the general public than Rolls-Royce engines for aircraft, marine craft, land, and energy uses. From handcrafted leather and walnut interiors to their legendary "Spirit of Ecstasy" grille mascots, Rolls-Royce automobiles have represented the ultimate in motoring elegance since their introduction in 1904. Like Rolls-Royce cars, Rolls-Royce engines and related businesses have made the Rolls-Royce name synonymous with quality engineering, integrity, reliability, and innovation, though they are more mass-market and are widely available within their target industries. Rolls-Royce is one of the best-known engineering names globally, having provided aircraft engines for key moments in history, like World War I, World War II, and the introduction of passenger jet aircraft. The brand crafts its image through its website and limited advertising, primarily focusing on its products and high-profile contracts to define itself.

Rolls-Royce has used a limited amount of advertising and taglines to reinforce its brand identity over the years. In 1999, for example, it created posters to bring attention to gas turbines, which formed the core of its identity as they are used in most Rolls-Royce engines. The posters also highlighted the fact that Rolls-Royce was a leading global engineering brand which produced engines for the leading airlines in the world, various defense agencies,

and energy markets. These posters were placed in major airports in the United Kingdom, the United States, and France, and targeted international business travelers. One poster, which focused on the Rolls-Royce Trent engine, claimed it "Lifts 300 tons, travels at 500 mph. Now that's what you call an engine." Another poster focused on reliability, claiming the Rolls-Royce engine was "The best reason in the world for choosing a window seat." By 2011 the brand's definitive tagline stated that Rolls-Royce is "Trusted to deliver excellence," further underscoring its leading position globally among aircraft engine manufacturers as well as its reputation for quality.

BRAND STRATEGY

- Rolls-Royce has invested in producing ever more sophisticated models of aircraft engines since 1907.
- In 1989 Rolls-Royce moved into power generation.
- Rolls-Royce had particular success in China in the 1990s and the early 21st century.

The Rolls-Royce brand began to be engine-focused as early as 1907, when it created aircraft engines used in some of the first powered aircraft. Though automobiles remained a key, if not definitive, part of the brand throughout the 20th century and into the 21st century, airplane engines became a lucrative source of continued innovation and were generally produced under the Rolls-Royce brand name. With technological advances came new airplane engine models, from early entries to the Phantom (1925) and the Merlin (1939). In the 1940s Rolls-Royce moved into the jet age with its aero gas turbine jet called the Welland and the modified Avon jet engine, a turbojet engine used in the first passenger jet, the Comet. By 1960, 80 percent of Rolls-Royce's revenues came from aeroengines.

It was only with the problematic, rushed development process of the powerful RB211 engine in the late 1960s that the company ran into serious problems. It nearly went bankrupt, and then it was nationalized and spun off the automotive business. While Rolls-Royce had been focused on both civilian and military aircraft engines for decades, it entered new businesses in part because of the RB211, which was used in land-based and offshore installations for drilling by oil and natural gas companies. In 1989 Rolls-Royce moved into power generation after acquiring Northern Engineering Industries plc. In the late 1990s Rolls-Royce acquired Vickers plc, which transformed Rolls-Royce into a world leader in the production of marine gas turbines and other power systems. In the early 2000s airlines increasingly sought to outsource their service and repair operations, and Rolls-Royce responded by expanding its capacity in this area, sometimes by acquisition. Rolls-Royce Engine Services represented almost 50 percent of the company's profits by 2004.

Rolls-Royce continued to create innovative engines in the early 21st century, including the Trent 1000, which it sold in an ever-expanding airline marketplace. While Rolls-Royce is a distinctly British firm, it has sought new markets abroad for its engines from the first. Some its earliest successes came in wartime when it provided engines for planes used in the war effort by British allies, including the United States. Rolls-Royce targeted the civilian airliner and American markets in earnest during the 1950s. In the 1990s Rolls-Royce paid particular attention to a new class of super jumbo jets and to fast-growing markets in the Middle East and the Asia-Pacific region, especially China. By the mid-1990s, Rolls-Royce had one-third of China's aeroengine orders, a trend that continued into the early 2000s with large orders for Air China and China Southern Airlines.

BRAND EQUITY

- Rolls-Royce's revenues increased from £11.124 billion to £12.161 billion between 2011 and 2012.
- Rolls-Royce is regarded as one of the most valuable brands in the United Kingdom, ranked number 33 in 2012 by the *UK Most Valuable Brands*.
- On *Forbes's* ranking of the *Global 2000*, Rolls-Royce was number 372 in 2012.

A leading brand of aircraft engines controlling 8 percent of the global aircraft engine market by 2011, Rolls-Royce was also the number-five gas-turbine maker in the world, with 3 percent of the global market in 2009. Its revenues increased 9 percent between 2011 and 2012, going from £11.124 billion to £12.161 billion. Because of this success, Rolls-Royce was one of the most valuable brands in the United Kingdom and the world. According to Brand Finance's *UK Most Valuable Brands*, Rolls-Royce was number 33 for 2012, with a brand value of US$3.175 billion and an enterprise value of US$17.107 billion. Brand Finance also ranked Rolls-Royce 356th in its 2012 *Global 500*. MPP Consulting listed the most valuable British brands in its 2011 ranking of the *Top 100 British Brands*. Rolls-Royce's value was listed at US$1.521 billion and it ranked 15th. In 2012 Rolls-Royce Holdings was number 372 on *Forbes' Global 2000*.

BRAND AWARENESS

- The Rolls-Royce brand is better-known for its automobiles than for its engine-related businesses.
- Rolls-Royce is a leader in the aircraft engine industry.
- Rolls-Royce has customers in 150 countries and operations in 50 countries.

The Rolls-Royce brand has been in existence since 1904. The average consumer is mainly aware of it as a brand of automobiles, rather than as a producer of aircraft, marine, and land engines and related energy services. In the 20th

century and into the 21st century, Rolls-Royce has been arguably the most famous brand of automobile in the world, because of the limited availability of the cars—only a few thousand are made and sold each year—and their handcrafted elegance and luxury. In contrast, the engine-focused aspect of the brand does not have top-of-mind awareness for consumers, despite several small campaigns to promote the brand. However, Rolls-Royce is still a global leader in its industry, with customers in 150 countries and operations in 50 of them in one or more of its four main sectors: civil aerospace, defense aerospace, marine, and energy. Rolls-Royce is the number-four aircraft-engine maker in the world, with an 8 percent market share, and it is known for being technically capable and committed to excellence.

BRAND OUTLOOK

- Rolls-Royce was regarded as a globally innovative company, which positioned it well for future growth.
- Rolls-Royce had already taken advantage of growth in Asia, and was expected to continue to do so in the future.
- Rolls-Royce estimated that the demand for civilian aircraft engines and services will reach US$1.400 billion over the next two decades.

Rolls-Royce is regarded as a highly inventive company, regularly ranked on *Forbes's* list of the most *Innovative Companies*. Rolls-Royce was number 76 in 2011 and number 81 in 2012. This commitment to continued advancement, improvement, and technological investment has positioned Rolls-Royce well for future growth. Rolls-Royce already had a track record for impressive annual growth and financial performance, with revenues increasing 9 percent between 2011 and 2012 alone, and it was making inroads into growing markets in Asia. Looking ahead, the brand believed that there would be faster growth rates for long-haul markets, as well as markets within Asia, for civil aeroengines and related services, projecting revenues of US$1.400 billion over the next two decades. While military demand for engines and related services is expected to be smaller globally, Rolls-Royce still forecast a market of US$415 billion over the next 20 years. Rolls-Royce's marine and energy sectors were also expected to be lucrative, with marine power and propulsion systems and services generating an estimated US$340 billion, with energy engine and services reaching an estimated US$120 billion into the 2030s.

FURTHER READING

Brand Finance. "Rolls-Royce." *Brandirectory*. Accessed February 17, 2013. http://brandirectory.com/profile/rolls-royce.

Elliott, Hannah. "Despite Slump in China, Rolls-Royce Posts Record Year." *Forbes*, January 10, 2013.

"Rolls-Royce." *Encyclopedia of Consumer Brands, Volume 3: Durable Goods.* Ed. Janice Jorgensen. Detroit, MI: St. James Press, 1994.

"Rolls-Royce." RankingTheBrands.com. Accessed February 17, 2013. http://www.rankingthebrands.com/Brand-detail. aspx?brandID=1773.

"Rolls-Royce Group PLC." *International Directory of Company Histories.* Ed. Jay P. Pederson. Vol. 67. Detroit, MI: St. James Press, 2005.

"Rolls-Royce Holdings." *Forbes.* Accessed February 17, 2013. http://www.forbes.com/companies/rolls-royce/.

Rolls-Royce Holdings plc. *Annual Report 2011.* Accessed February 18, 2013. http://www.rolls-royce.com/reports/2011/.

Thomaselli, Rich. "Ultra-Targeted Marketer Rolls-Royce Taps KBS&P as First Agency of Record." *Advertising Age,* October 11, 2011.

SABMILLER

—————— ◆ ——————

AT A GLANCE

—— ◆ ——

Brand Synopsis: The world's second-largest brewer seeks to be the world's most admired brewer while at the same time nurturing local and international brands that are the first choice of consumers.

Parent Company: SABMiller plc
One Stanhope Gate
London, W1K 1AF
United Kingdom
http://www.sabmiller.com/

Sector: Consumer Staples

Industry Group: Food, Beverage & Tobacco

Performance: *Market share*—11.8 percent (2010). *Sales*—US$31.2 billion (2011).

Principal Competitors: Anheuser-Busch InBev SA/NV; Carlsberg A/S; Heineken N.V.

BRAND ORIGINS

- The South African United Breweries was formed in 1892; a reincorporation in 1895 changed the name to South African Breweries Limited (SAB).
- The South African government's policies of beer taxation, foreign investments, and apartheid all shaped SAB's development.
- After the acquisition of Miller Brewing Company in 2002, SAB changed its name to SABMiller and became the world's second-largest brewer.

The history of SABMiller is in many ways the history of the South African brewing industry, which was greatly influenced by the policies of the South African government. In 1875 the discovery of gold on the Witwatersrand, a region encompassing Johannesburg, brought large numbers of prospectors to South Africa. Small outposts for white settlers were transformed into busy cities with new industries. Several brewmasters, most with little experience, began producing a variety of beers that immediately gained popularity with the settlers.

In 1889 a British sailor named Frederick Mead left his ship in Durban and took a job working in the canteen of a local army garrison at Fort Napier. While there, Mead, who was only 20, became acquainted with George Raw, a businessman in Pietermaritzburg. Neither of them knew anything about brewing, but they persuaded the local residents to help establish the Natal Brewery Syndicate. The company brewed its first beer in July 1891.

In 1892 Mead purchased the Castle Brewery in Johannesburg. The expansion of this facility, however, was beyond the means of the Natal Brewery Syndicate, so Mead returned to England to attract new investors. In the final arrangement, Mead formed another larger company based in London called the South African United Breweries. This company took over the operations of both the Natal Brewery Syndicate and the Castle Brewery. South African United Breweries released Castle Lager to the market in 1898 and the beer gained such widespread popularity that competing breweries rushed to introduce their own lagers.

Growth of the company precipitated a restructuring and reincorporation in London in 1895, as the South African Breweries Limited (SAB). SAB was listed on the London Stock Exchange in 1895 and two years later became the first industrial company to be listed on the Johannesburg Stock Exchange.

In 1899 a war broke out between British colonial forces and Dutch and Huguenot settlers known as Boers. The war drove residents of Johannesburg out of the city and forced the Castle Brewery to close for almost a year. After the war's end in 1902, SAB was able to continue its expansion across southern Africa through acquisitions of existing breweries.

Exorbitant excises on beer by the government made it the most heavily taxed beverage in South Africa, causing a decline in beer consumption that showed no sign of slowing. In response, SAB bought out Ohlsson's Cape Breweries and United Breweries to form one large brewing concern, merging production capabilities and eliminating competition.

The South African government barred SAB from further investment in the liquor industry and limited its ability to invest overseas. Furthermore, the South African government's system of racial separation (apartheid) had become an international issue and many foreign-owned companies sold their South African subsidiaries and closed their offices in South Africa. SAB was able to take control of Amalgamated Beverage Industries Ltd., a Coca-Cola bottler, from the Coca-Cola Company in 1977.

The dismantling of apartheid began in 1990 and in 1994 the first nationwide free elections were held, with Nelson Mandela elected president. However, the threat of a government-forced breakup of SAB's beer monopoly hung over the company following the end of apartheid. Partly in response to this threat and partly because of loosening laws regarding foreign investment, SAB aggressively expanded outside its home country starting in 1993. The drive into emerging markets included expansion into new African markets, China, Colombia, Ecuador, El Salvador, Honduras, Hungary, India, Panama, Peru, Poland, Romania, Russia, and Slovakia.

SAB made a pivotal deal in 2002, when it acquired Miller Brewing Company, the number-two beer maker in the world's largest beer market: the United States. Upon completion of the acquisition, SAB changed its name to SABMiller plc and became the world's number-two brewer behind Anheuser-Busch InBev SA/NV.

SABMiller continued its strategy of expansion and acquisitions to include holdings in Angola, Argentina, Australia, China, India, Italy, Namibia, Poland, South America, and Vietnam, and as well as the formation of MillerCoors from a joint venture between SABMiller and Molson Coors Brewing Company.

BRAND ELEMENTS

- SABMiller owns over 200 brands that are sold in 75 countries across the globe.
- SABMiller adapts advertising for different brands to reflect regional preferences in customs, traditions, and attitudes.
- The popular Czech Republic beer Pilsner Urquell uses the tagline "The World's First Golden Beer."

SABMiller has over 200 brands in its portfolio that are spread over six continents and 75 countries across the globe. Each brand is tailored for the market it serves, with its own logo, slogan, and campaign. The company believes that the key to winning market share is to appeal to a home country by featuring regional customs, traditions, and outlooks in its advertising. SABMiller has employed regional historians, anthropologists, and sociologists to help with marketing campaigns that will spur organic growth.

In Peru bottles of Cusquena beer feature stones from an Incan wall that pay tribute to Incan craftsmanship, while Arequipena beer portrays the popular sport of bull fighting. In Romania television ads for Timisoreana beer show beer barrels being rolled through picturesque landscapes before being filled at the original 18th-century brewery.

At the MillerCoors subsidiary, Coors beer features the tagline "The Silver Bullet," while Miller beer uses "It's Miller Time." The Foster's subsidiary utilizes the tagline "The Amber Nectar" in Australia and the United Kingdom and "Foster's—Australian for Beer" elsewhere overseas. The Peroni Brewery features "Italian Style in a Bottle," while Pilsner Urquell employs "The World's First Golden Beer." Grolsch beer uses the slogan "As Unique as Grolsch," Castle beer uses "The taste that has stood the test of time," and Carling Beer features "Carling. Spot On."

BRAND IDENTITY

- SABMiller's brand identity as a global conglomerate is far different than its genesis as a brewery centered in South Africa.
- SABMiller strives to excel with strong local beer brands in regional markets that appeal to a majority of consumers.
- SABMiller's premium international brands are marketed as being trendy and cosmopolitan.

The SABMiller of the early 21st century, a globally active company with a sharp focus on beverages, is a far different company from the apartheid-era South African Breweries Limited (SAB), which was centered largely in South Africa, where it had diversified interests. SAB built itself through a bold yet focused program of international expansion. SABMiller seeks to capture market share and win consumers with a portfolio of brands in each region that are appealing at every price point.

In both developed and emerging markets, SABMiller aspires to excel locally with strong local brands. Local brands often appeal to the everyday consumer, with an identity close to home and an affordable price. SABMiller also features leading premium international beers that the company is turning into lifestyle "must have's"; beers that are trendy, cool, and cosmopolitan. SABMiller states that its premium international beers "offer a premium drinking experience wherever you are in the world."

BRAND STRATEGY

- SABMiller has achieved growth through licensing agreements, mergers, and acquisitions around the world.
- SABMiller's international premium brands are Pilsner Urquell, Peroni Nastro Azzurro, Miller Genuine Draft, and Grolsch.
- SABMiller is one of the world's largest Coca-Cola bottlers.

SABMiller's growth strategy has been one of mergers and acquisitions instead of establishing its own brands. SABMiller has had a history of acquiring companies and transforming them according to its own model. The company now operates approximately 140 breweries with over 76,000 employees.

SABMiller's international premium brands are Pilsner Urquell, Peroni Nastro Azzurro, Miller Genuine Draft, and Grolsch. The company also features 80 flagship brands, or leading local brands, including Lion Lager of South Africa, Cristal of Peru, Snow of China, Blue Moon of the United States, and Atlas of Panama. Additional beers include the Bluetongue, Dirty Granny, and Fat Yak brands of Australia, De Klok beer of the Netherlands, Sarita of South Africa, and Nile brand of Uganda.

Besides producing and marketing beer, the company is one of the world's largest Coca-Cola bottlers and has carbonated soft drink bottling operations in 14 markets. The South African Breweries subsidiary soft drink division is also the country's largest producer of products for the Coca-Cola Company.

BRAND EQUITY

- In 2012 *Forbes* "Global 2000" ranked SABMiller number 247.
- In 2008 *Fortune* "Global 500" ranked SABMiller number 493.
- SABMiller had a brand value of US$18.9 billion in 2012.

In 2012 SABMiller was ranked 247 in the *Forbes* "Global 2000," with sales of US$15.1 billion. SABMiller was ranked number 493 in the *Fortune* "Global 500" in 2008, with revenues of US$17 billion; SABMiller has not made the list since that ranking.

The European Brand Institute ranked SABMiller 10th in its 2011 ranking of Europe's Most Valuable Brand Corporations, with a brand value of US$17.9 billion, and 32nd in its 2012 Top 100 Brand Corporations Worldwide, with a brand value of US$18.9 billion. The company was also ranked 31st in the *South Africa 50 2012*, with a brand value of US$303 million.

BRAND AWARENESS

- SABMiller is the world's second-largest brewer, behind only Anheuser-Busch InBev SA/NV, with an 11.8 percent market share in 2010.
- The world's most popular beer, the Chinese brand Snow, belongs to SABMiller.
- SABMiller has a market value of approximately US$56 billion.

SABMiller operates in over 75 countries around the world and has worked diligently to expand its business. The company has solidified its position as one of the largest brewers in the world, with holdings in Africa, Asia, Australasia, Europe, North America, and South America. In 2010 SABMiller had an 11.8 percent market share globally, trailing only Anheuser-Busch InBev SA/NV, with an 18.8 percent market share. The company is among the top marketers in Colombia, the Czech Republic, Ecuador, Peru, South Africa, Tanzania, and Uganda.

Twelve of SABMiller's brands are number-one sellers in local markets. In 2011 three of the top-10 most popular beers in the world belonged to the company. Miller Light, the fourth most popular beer in the United States, was the eighth most popular globally. Coors Light was the second most popular in the United States and the seventh most popular in the world, while Snow beer, the most popular beer in China, was also the most popular beer in the world.

In 2011 SABMiller was ranked as the fourth-largest beverage company in the world. It also ranked fifth in the world's most valuable beverage companies and second in the most valuable European beverage companies, with market values of US$56.2 billion. In 2010 the company ranked sixth in the world's top beverage companies, with sales of US$18 billion.

BRAND OUTLOOK

- Uncertainty about economic recovery in Europe and North America has slowed sales in these traditional beer markets; as a result, SABMiller is looking to emerging markets for future growth.
- In Africa the company's biggest competition comes from homemade alcohol.

- Rumors continue in the beer industry that Anheuser-Busch InBev SA/NV is considering purchasing SABMiller; analysts consider the deal unlikely.

Sales in traditional beer markets have been slowly declining due to tough economic conditions and uncertainties about the pace of economic recovery in Europe and North America. In response, SABMiller has been looking to emerging markets for future growth from expansion of existing businesses. Regardless, fewer opportunities exist in the global market for further mergers and acquisitions. SABMiller's strong presence in developing markets, particularly in Latin America and China, has enabled the company to deliver solid growth numbers to investors.

In Africa the company's biggest competitor comes from homemade alcohol from bootleggers and moonshiners. SABMiller has concentrated its efforts there on lobbying government officials to lower taxes on beer. It is also emphasizing local beers with new products and packaging that are tailored to specific African regions.

Rumors persist that Anheuser-Busch InBev SA/NV is considering acquiring SABMiller. A combined company would likely have a global market share at over 35 percent, giving Anheuser-Busch InBev a highly valued global presence in greater developing markets that it currently does not possess. Even though analysts believe such a deal is unlikely, industry insiders continue speculation.

FURTHER READING

Davie, Kevin. "SABMiller: Brewing up a Global Brand." South-Africa.info, October 14, 2010. Accessed January 3, 2013. http://www.southafrica.info/business/success/sabmiller.htm#.UNTexm_LTkM.

Fontevecchia, Agustino. "Is Anheuser Busch-InBev about to Buy SABMiller for $80B? They Could, But Won't." *Forbes*, October 7, 2011.

Kowitt, Beth. "Big Beer's Response to Craft: If You Can't Beat 'Em, Join 'Em." *CNN Money*, December 12, 2012. Accessed January 3, 2013. http://management.fortune.cnn.com/2012/12/12/sabmiller-big-beer-craft-brewers.

Salamie, David E., and Christina M. Stansell. "SABMiller plc." *International Directory of Company Histories*. Ed. Tina Grant. Vol. 134. Detroit, MI: St. James Press, 2012.

Shultz, E. J. "How SABMiller Fights Bootleggers in Africa." *Advertising Age*, February 23, 2011.

———. "SABMiller Thinks Globally, But Gets 'Intimate' Locally." *Advertising Age*, October 4, 2010.

Tepper, Rachel. "World's Most Popular Beers: 'The Drinks Business' Names Top 10 Biggest Brands of 2011." *Huffington Post*, September 26, 2012.

SAINSBURY'S

AT A GLANCE

Brand Synopsis: Representing a United Kingdom supermarket chain, the Sainsbury's brand focuses on quality, service, and fair prices.

Parent Company: J Sainsbury plc
33 Holborn
London
United Kingdom
http://www.j-sainsbury.co.uk

Sector: Consumer Staples

Industry Group: Food & Staples Retailing

Performance: *Sales*—US$35.6 billion (2012).

Principal Competitors: ASDA Group Limited; Tesco PLC; Wm Morrison Supermarkets PLC

BRAND ORIGINS

- Sainsbury's was founded in 1869 in London as a dairy store.
- New store in 1882 transformed Sainsbury's into an upscale brand.
- First self-service Sainsbury's store opened in 1950.
- Sainsbury's brand tarnished by the mid-1990s.
- Poor economic conditions of the early 2000s led Sainsbury's to add a value proposition to its brand message.

Known as Sainsbury's, J Sainsbury plc has deep roots. The United Kingdom-based supermarket operator was founded in 1869 in London by 25-year-old John James Sainsbury and his 19-year-old wife, Mary Ann Staples. Shortly after their wedding, they opened a dairy store on the ground floor of their Drury Lane home. The couple were well familiar with the retail trade. He had previously worked for a grocer as well as a hardware merchant, while she had grown up in the dairy business of her father. They offered customers an alternative to unsanitary street carts and stalls and untidy family-run shops. Theirs was a clean, orderly shop offering high-quality merchandise. These were still hallmarks of the Sainsbury's brand a century-and-a-half later.

The Sainsbury's approach proved so successful that James and Mary Ann opened a second shop seven years after opening the first, and as their sons came to age, six in all, more stores were opened to accommodate their employment. The retailing brand burnished its image further in 1882 when a new ground-breaking branch opened in Croydon. Compared to the competition, it was both opulent and easy to keep clean. It featured tiled floors, walls, and counter fronts, and marble slabs for countertops. Bentwood chairs were provided to customers, who were waited on by attentive Sainsbury's clerks. The store attracted a better class of customer. Similar stores soon opened and Sainsbury's gained a reputation as an upscale brand. In 1882 the grocer began selling products under its own name, adding further luster to the Sainsbury's brand.

While Lipton's became the largest grocery chain in the United Kingdom, Sainsbury's grew at a steady pace over the years, all the while retaining a reputation for cleanliness and high quality foods. The business was incorporated in 1922, by which time the number of branches

897

totaled 136. It was a period of transition in the grocery business. In the United States, the self-serve concept was being pioneered by the Piggly Wiggly chain, leading to the growth of larger-format stores, which would eventually become known as supermarkets. Following the war, Sainsbury's took notice of these developments and in 1950 opened its first self-service store. Over the next decade, existing stores were converted into supermarkets and new supermarkets were built from the ground up, albeit the company refrained from using the word "supermarket," a term a bit too common for the brand's image of refinement. Behind the scenes, however, the chain was progressive, becoming the first British retailer to computerize its distribution system.

Sainsbury's launched a diversification program in the 1970s. It began adding gas stations to its stores and became involved in the hypermarket and home center segments through joint ventures. In the early 1980s the company began making investments in the United States, acquiring a stake in Shaw's Supermarkets, gaining full control by the end of the decade. In 1994 Sainsbury's acquired a stake in another U.S. supermarket chain, Giant Food Inc. To maintain its standing in the United Kingdom, Sainsbury's launched a private-label program. Some of the products, like the company's Novon laundry detergent and Classic Cola, challenged national brands.

Also during this period, the company launched its own magazine, *Sainsbury's: The Magazine*. Not only was it a new profit center, the magazine served to promote the Sainsbury's brand, which became associated with the lifestyle espoused in editorial content. Diversification came with a price, however. The company lost focus on its core supermarket business, and the brand's perception with shoppers began to deteriorate. Sainsbury's became associated with high prices, a lack of brand name products, insufficient staff in the aisles, and long checkout lines. Unlike competitors, Sainsbury's eschewed the use of loyalty cards.

To restore its image as an innovative brand, Sainsbury's launched its own Reward Card and in the late 1990s became the first supermarket chain in the country to open its own fully licensed bank. In 1999 Sainsbury's introduced a new corporate identity, embodied in the slogan "Making life taste better." Further refinements followed in the new century, as difficult economic conditions mandated a different approach. In 2011 Sainsbury's launched a new brand positioning effort centered around the "Live Well for Less" tagline. Nevertheless, the Sainsbury's brand continued to emphasize quality at the core of its message.

BRAND ELEMENTS
- Sainsbury's employs a wordmark for its logo.
- Corporate colors are living orange and blue.

- "Live Well for Less" slogan was introduced in 2011.
- High-quality private label products support the brand image.

The Sainsbury's logo is a wordmark, the name of the retailer in upper- and lower-case letters, rendered in a shade called "living orange." A previous incarnation, used from 1960 to 1999, employed capital letters. The lettering of the new logo was also more rounded. The word mark is sometimes used in conjunction with a slogan. Beginning in 2011, the slogan was "Live Well for Less." A price comparison program used the brand name as well: "Sainsbury's Brand Match." Although the lettering was black, living orange was used to color a circle enclosing the logo.

In addition to orange, blue became one of Sainsbury's corporate colors. Since 1999 Sainsbury's stores have used blue walls and orange wall panels. Moreover, the J. Sainsbury name that graced the exterior signage was replaced at the vast majority of stores by the Sainsbury's name, further reinforcing the brand. The stores themselves are bright, clean, and inviting, attributes that have been the heart of the brand since the 1800s. In-store signage uses the corporate colors to lend consistency to the brand. The products on the shelves play a significant role in portraying the Sainsbury's brand as well. This is particularly true of private label products. Not only do they bear the Sainsbury's wordmark, they are of high quality, a key aspect of the brand.

In the early 2000s celebrity chef Jamie Oliver was signed as brand ambassador. Over the next 11 years, he appeared in more than 100 television advertisements for the supermarket chain. He was also an outspoken advocate for food standards and animal welfare. His positive public perception added value to the Sainsbury's brand. His relationship with Sainsbury's came to an end in the summer of 2011.

BRAND IDENTITY
- Quality and low prices were at the heart of the Sainsbury's brand in the 1800s.
- Consumers grew to perceive Sainsbury's as a high-price retailer.
- Sainsbury's portrays its prices as "fair."
- The company's 20 by 20 Sustainability Plan reinforces the brand's commitment to the improvement of the lives of its customers.

Sainsbury's has presented a fairly consistent brand image for more than a century. The brand has always laid claim to offering quality goods. In the late 1800s, for example, storefronts boasted "Quality perfect, prices lower." The message of quality was reinforced by the stores themselves, from the marble countertops of the late 1800s to the supermarkets of the 1950s and new formats at the turn of the millennium. At the same time, Sainsbury's fostered an image of being the purveyor of fine foods to those of discerning tastes, people for whom price was not a key consideration.

A diminishing emphasis on price had an adverse impact on Sainsbury's brand image by the late 1900s. Although customers continued to believe that Sainsbury's offered high quality goods, there was a perception that the stores were much more expensive than the competition, such as the Tesco and Asda supermarket chains. Since 2010 Sainsbury's has attempted to establish the premise that, given the quality of its products, its pricing is fair.

A major part of Sainsbury's brand identity is an abiding concern for customers. The company maintains that its business strategy and objective comes down to a simple proposition: "We put the customer at the heart of everything we do, aiming to make their lives easier every day by offering great quality and service at fair prices." Consistent with concern for its customers is a concern for the communities in which its customers live. The company's 20 by 20 Sustainability Plan lays out goals Sainsbury's pledges to meet by the year 2020, including steps to reduce its impact on the environment, improve the health of customers, and promote charitable causes.

BRAND STRATEGY
- Cast-iron "J SAINSBURY" signs promoted the brand in the late 1800s.
- Sainsbury's gained a reputation as an upscale retailer by the 1900s.
- Logo and tagline from the 1960s were used for more than three decades.
- New logo was unveiled in 1999.
- "Making Sainsbury's great again" campaign was launched in 2005.

For much of its history, Sainsbury's was more concerned with its reputation than with its brand, per se. John and Mary Sainsbury opened their dairy store to offer an alternative to the shopping experience of their day. A reputation for quality goods sold in a sanitary, tidy retail environment was a key to the growth of the business and led to the opening of additional branches, which in turn nurtured Sainsbury's reputation. With the opening of the Croydon branch in 1882, with its mosaic floor, tiled walls, marble-slab counters, and white-aproned staff, Sainsbury's was well on its way to becoming a true brand. Stores with a consistent look followed, each with a cast-iron "J SAINSBURY" sign to catch the attention of customers. Helping to promote the brand was the opening of new branches, which drew large opening-day crowds.

Sainsbury's retained its brand identity as an upscale purveyor of quality foods in the 1900s, while adapting to changing times. Instead of old-fashioned cast-iron, a new

Sainsbury's sign was fashioned out of gilded glass. New slogans also kept the brand fresh while emphasizing the core message. They included "Sainsbury's for Quality. Sainsbury's for Value" and "Sainsbury's. Essentials for the Essentials." To help maintain consistency with the brand, the company launched the *JS Journal* in 1946 to keep employees up-to-date on the industry and on company policies. The Sainsbury family also kept abreast of changes in grocery retailing and opened new supermarkets, while retaining brand identity.

In 1960 the company introduced a modern-looking logo, an orange wordmark that simply proclaimed "Sainsbury's" in capital letters. It would remain unchanged for the next 39 years. It was also in the 1960s that the company coined a slogan that would be used nearly as long as the logo: "Good Food Costs Less At Sainsbury's." The company did not remain static, however. It extended the Sainsbury's brand to gas stations and private label products, as well as a magazine. But by the end of the century, the company realized its brand had grown stale. With a host of strong competitors, Sainsbury's had become associated with high prices, despite a slogan in the mid-1990s that declared "Sainsbury's. Where good food costs less."

Working with M&C Saatchi, Sainsbury's developed a new corporate image that was unveiled in 1999. It included a new rendering of the Sainsbury's wordmark in a different shade of orange. A new advertising tagline, "Sainsbury's makes life taste better," was unveiled to go along with the "Making life taste better" slogan. To reinforce the change, employees were outfitted in new staff uniforms. A new range of products developed under the Well Being banner was also introduced, including foods for special diets, sports drinks, beauty products made without artificial ingredients, fair-trade products, and environmentally responsible household products. The makeover did not prove especially effective, however.

In 2005 Sainsbury's launched a "Making Sainsbury's great again" campaign. A new advertising agency was brought in and a fresh brand statement was introduced: "Try something new today." The company continued to refine the brand image over the next few years, responding to deteriorating economic conditions as well as societal changes. In late 2010 the company adopted the "Value where it matters" tagline. A year later Sainsbury's launched its "Live Well For Less" initiative, one that presented the case to shoppers that they could make their money go further without sacrificing quality. As part of the effort, Sainsbury's offered a "coupons at till" program, which provided customers with discount coupons on regularly purchased products. Another program, "Brand Match," issued coupons to make up the difference on the price for branded products if either Tesco or Asda offered those products for less. Aside from a value message, Sainsbury's also placed greater emphasis on fresh food offerings and took steps to build an image as a socially and environmentally responsible retailer.

BRAND EQUITY

- Sainsbury's generates more than US$35 billion in annual sales.
- In 2012 Sainsbury's brand value was estimated at US$5.85 billion.
- Sainsbury's was ranked as the 162nd most valuable global brand in 2012.
- Sainsbury's was ranked as the 19th most valuable global retail brand in 2012.
- Sainsbury's was listed No. 19 on Brand Finance's list of the most valuable British brands in 2012.

One measure of Sainsbury's brand equity is the high prices the retailer is able to charge compared to rival supermarket chains that are more price oriented. On the other end of the scale are upscale supermarket chains like M&S and Waitrose. Traditionally Sainsbury's has competed on value rather than on low prices alone. As the economy soured in the early 2000s, however, Sainsbury's was forced to adjust. It began to match the prices of its competitors on certain branded products through a checkout register coupon program. Nevertheless, the Sainsbury's brand still carried a measure of equity in the minds of shoppers that justified higher prices in general. From a bottom-line point of view, Sainsbury's generated more than US$35 billion in annual sales, a performance that afforded the company a place on the FTSE 100 Index, representing the top 100 companies on the London Stock Exchange in terms of market capitalization.

According to brand-evaluation consultancy Brand Finance Plc, the value of the Sainsbury's brand in 2012 was US$5.85 billion. As a result, Brand Finances ranked Sainsbury's No. 162 on its list of the 500 most valuable brands in the world. Among the top global retail brands, Sainsbury's came in at No. 19 in 2012. Rival supermarket retailer Tesco was listed at No. 4, by way of comparison. Coincidentally, in Brand Finance's list of the most valuable British brands in 2012, Sainsbury's was slotted again as No. 19 and Tesco was No. 4. Brand consultancy Interbrand, using its own methodology, assigned a brand value of US$976 million to Sainsbury's, making it the sixth most valuable retail brand in the United Kingdom.

BRAND AWARENESS

- Sainsbury's brand has been well known in the United Kingdom since the 1880s.
- Brand awareness is supported by nearly 600 supermarkets bearing the Sainsbury's name.

- Brand awareness is supported by local convenience stores carrying Sainsbury's products.

Sainsbury's enjoys strong brand awareness in the United Kingdom, where it has been a leading grocery retailing brand since the late 1800s. Outside of that market, however, it is little known, but that does not limit the value of the brand where the company does business; it was able to rank among the top 20 retail brands worldwide in the 2011 BrandZ survey. Playing an important role in Sainsbury's brand awareness are about 575 supermarkets that operate under its banner throughout the United Kingdom. The Sainsbury's name is also promoted in a jointly owned Sainsbury's Bank. Further, the parent company owns 424 local convenience stores, which carry many products bearing the Sainsbury's name, again increasing brand awareness.

BRAND OUTLOOK

- Key personnel losses could adversely impact brand in the short term.
- Online shopping offers an opportunity to extend the brand.
- Expansion to emerging markets is a long-term opportunity for the brand.

In late 2011 brand ambassador Jamie Oliver ended his 11-year relationship with Sainsbury's. For many consumers, he was the public face of the brand. His influence was significant, as demonstrated in 2005 when as part of Sainsbury's "Try something different" promotion he suggested that cooks grate nutmeg over spaghetti Bolognese. Customers responded by purchasing nine tons of nutmeg, an amount that normally took the chain two years to sell. The loss of Oliver's created some uncertainty about the short-term prospects of the Sainsbury's brand, as did the sudden departure of the company's brand director in February 2012. In addition, a newly hired marketing director changed his mind and decided not to join the company, leaving Sainsbury's with a number of gaps to fill.

The loss of key players was clearly a temporary setback to the brand, but there remained long-term opportunities. Sainsbury's had already begun to sell online, but because of its brand recognition, it was very well positioned to exploit this channel to a greater extent in the years to come. There was also an opportunity to introduce the Sainsbury's brand to such emerging markets as India, Russia, China, and the United Arab Emirates.

FURTHER READING

Baker, Rosie. "Interview: Sainsbury's Marketing Chief Explains Route to Success." *MarketingWeek*, May 24, 2010.

———. "Sainsbury's Loses Marketing and Brand Chiefs." *MarketingWeek*, December 14, 2011.

———. "Sainsbury's Says Its Marketing 'Inspires' Shoppers." *MarketingWeek*, March 21, 2012.

Brand Finance. "Global 500 2012." *Brandirectory*. Accessed July 3, 2012. http://brandirectory.com/league_tables/table/global-500-2012.

"J Sainsbury plc." *International Directory of Company Histories*. Ed. Jay P. Pederson. Vol. 95. Detroit, MI: St. James Press, 2008.

Parsons, Russell. "Sainsbury's Cites 'Compelling' Marketing for Sales Lift." *MarketingWeek*, May 9, 2012.

Seth, Andrew. *The Grocers: The Rise and Rise of the Supermarket Chains*. London: Kogan Page, 2001.

Stogel, Chuck. "The Once and Future King." *Brandweek*, May 8, 1995.

Tylee, John. "M&C Saatchi Sainsbury's Films Use 'Makes Life Taste Better' Line." *Campaign*, April 16, 1999.

SAINT-GOBAIN

AT A GLANCE

Brand Synopsis: Saint-Gobain is a global leader in the habitat and construction markets and is the largest building materials company in the world.

Parent Company: Compagnie de Saint-Gobain
Tour Les Miroirs
18, avenue d'Alsace
92 096 La Défense cedex
France
http://www.saint-gobain.com

Sector: Materials

Industry Group: Materials

Performance: *Market share*—Saint-Gobain's flat glass, building products, manufacturing, and distribution divisions all rank first in Europe and third worldwide; its automotive glazing and solar energy solutions rank first in Europe and second worldwide. *Sales*—US$55.5 billion (2011).

Principal Competitors: NSG Group; Asahi Glass Co., Ltd.; Guardian Industries; PPG Industries; Şişecam Group; Schott AG; 3M Company; E. I. du Pont de Nemours and Company; Lafarge SA; Owens Corning; BASF Group

BRAND ORIGINS

- The company that would eventually become Saint-Gobain was formed in 1665 by French finance

minister Jean-Baptiste Colbert to challenge Venice's dominance of Europe's glassmaking industry.
- In 1688, Saint-Gobain began using glassware casting, an innovative process that allowed for the creation of larger sheets of glass.
- The company began using the name Saint-Gobain in 1858, when it officially became known as Manufacture des Glaces et Produits Chimiques de Saint-Gobain, Chauny et Cirey.
- In 1968, Saint-Gobain merged with cast-iron-pipe manufacturer Pont-à-Mousson to avoid a hostile takeover attempt by another French glass manufacturer.
- Through aggressive acquisitions in the 1990s and early 21st century, Saint-Gobain has become a top player in a variety of international construction material markets.

In the mid-1600s mirrors were quite fashionable among European high society, and the highest-quality glass and mirror products were being produced in Venice. Jean-Baptiste Colbert, France's minister of finance at the time, did not believe his country should be purchasing luxury items from foreign sources, and so in 1665, with the backing of King Louis XIV and financier Nicolas du Noyer, Colbert established the Manufacture des Glaces de Miroirs (Royal Mirror-Glass Factory). To more fully undermine Venice's supremacy in Europe's glassmaking industry, Colbert granted the new company numerous tax advantages and a temporary but renewable monopoly on the manufacture and sale of glass in France. He also hired several former Venetian glassmaking experts to oversee production, with the goal of improving overall product quality.

Colbert's efforts quickly paid off, and competition between the French and the Italians was intense for the next two decades. In 1684 the French company received a large and prestigious order in the form of 357 mirrors to be installed in the Hall of Mirrors at the Palace of Versailles. In 1688 the company began using a process called glassware casting, which involved rolling out the glass on a flat surface to create larger sheets. In 1692 the company opened a factory in the village of Saint-Gobain, near Paris, to accommodate increasing demand. Nevertheless, the business struggled, and after declaring bankruptcy in 1702, it was purchased by a Swiss bank and renamed Dagincourt.

Dagincourt's sales quadrupled between 1720 and 1786, making it the largest revenue-generating company in France. The French Revolution (1789-99) created major operations disruptions and financial losses, and after the war, the company lost its monopoly and had to face competition from manufacturers in France, England, and Belgium. In 1853 the glassmaker built a factory in Mannheim, Germany, its first outside France. This was followed by factories in Italy (1899), Belgium (1900), and Spain (1904). In 1858 the company merged with its main domestic rival, Saint-Quirin, and the new company was called Manufacture des Glaces et Produits Chimiques de Saint-Gobain, Chauny et Cirey (or Saint-Gobain, for short). During this period the company also began to diversify into other products and commodities, such as wood, paper, petroleum, nitrogen, and sodium carbonate. The new and diversified product lines included skylights, roofing materials, room dividers, laminated glass and mirrors, and embossed mirrors and windowpanes.

During the early part of the 20th century, Saint-Gobain dramatically expanded its product lines to include bottles, jars, glassware, tableware, and fiberglass products. Between 1950 and 1970, following the global devastations of World War II, Saint-Gobain made a dramatic recovery. Sales of glass and fiberglass products soared thanks to the booming construction industry. Glass production increased from 38 million square feet in 1950 to nearly 500 million square feet by 1969. Near the end of 1968, Saint-Gobain initiated a merger with Pont-à-Mousson, a French industrial group producing cast-iron pipes, to thwart a hostile takeover attempt by Boussois-Souchon-Neuvesel (BSN), a much smaller French glass manufacturer. Although the merger between Saint-Gobain and Pont-à-Mousson was initially completed for financial reasons, the leaders of the combined organization gradually created a new management structure, which in 1978 led to the replacement of the company's basic 6 market departments with 10 production-oriented branches.

In the early 1990s, Saint-Gobain made several major acquisitions that would further diversify and strengthen its position in the world market. In 1990, Saint-Gobain acquired the U.S. company Norton, the world leader in abrasives products, for US$1.9 billion. The following year, Saint-Gobain purchased two major German glassmakers, thus establishing itself as the world's leading glass manufacturer. In the early 1990s a recession across Europe dramatically reduced demand for Saint-Gobain's products, causing its profits to plunge by 45 percent in 1993 and forcing the company to sell off its paper, pulp, and packaging divisions. The loss of the paper division was estimated to have cost Saint-Gobain 10 percent in overall sales, but the US$1.1 billion earned from the sell-off was critical to the future of the company's operations. The economy rebounded within the year, and Saint-Gobain's profits recovered. The company again began to focus on acquisitions, becoming the world's largest glass-packaging manufacturer when it paid US$1 billion in 1995 for a controlling share of Ball Corporation and Foster Forbes, two major glass-packaging manufacturers. This was followed by the 1996 purchase of Poliet Group, a French building and construction distribution business, and all of its subsidiaries. By 2005, with the acquisition of British Plaster Board (BPB), the world's largest plasterboard manufacturer, Saint-Gobain could claim domination of a complete range of construction material product markets.

BRAND ELEMENTS

- Saint-Gobain is named after a small French village located outside Paris, where in 1692 the company opened one of its first factories.
- In 1665, when Saint-Gobain was first created, it used as its company trademark the royal coat of arms of Louis XIV.
- Following its 1968 merger with Pont-à-Mousson, Saint-Gobain adopted the logo of its new partner, a simple depiction of a seven-arch bridge.
- Saint-Gobain's slogan as of 2012 was "The future is made of Saint-Gobain," representing the company's reputation for producing innovative, high-quality, and environmentally sound building materials.

Saint-Gobain is named after a small French village of the same name, where the glass manufacturer opened a factory in 1692. Although the company has gone through several name changes during its nearly 350 years in business, its identification with the town of Saint-Gobain was used as a primary identifier of the organization in one manner or another until the name became formalized in 1858, following the company's merger with former rival Saint-Quirin.

Saint-Gobain has used many logos throughout its long and intricate history—so many, in fact, that a book titled *Saint-Gobain, Logos through Time: Signs, Symbols & Messages,* authored by Maurice Hamon, was published in 2003. In 1665, when the company first formed, it was represented by the royal coat of arms of Louis XIV, primarily to let the public know that the company was under the legal protection of the king. Of the numerous symbolic representations that would follow, none did a very good job of capturing the essence of the Saint-Gobain brand. The company's longest-lived logo, used from 1806 to 1970, was an image of three salamanders inside an octagon.

It would appear that Saint-Gobain never made it a priority to develop a meaningful iconic symbol of its brand, or that the company was simply unable to create or locate a symbol it deemed appropriate. This held true in 1968, when Saint-Gobain merged with fellow French conglomerate Pont-à-Mousson. Rather than create a new symbol that incorporated the blended ideals of the two companies, Saint-Gobain simply took on Pont-à-Mousson's corporate logo as its own. This logo, still in use in 2012, is a simple depiction of a seven-arch bridge found in the village of Pont-à-Mousson, located in northeastern France.

Saint-Gobain combines its standard logo with the brand logos of its subsidiaries, a branding strategy common among complex conglomerates. This practice demonstrates that each secondary business has the parent organization's seal of approval, while also promoting and enhancing the brands of both the parent company and the subsidiary.

Saint-Gobain's slogan as of 2012 was "The future is made of Saint-Gobain." This tagline was created to emphasize the organization's focus on creating products and building materials that are innovative, high in quality, energy-efficient, cost-effective, and environmentally friendly. Saint-Gobain has stated that its goal is not only to improve the quality of life at home and in the work environment but also to create structures that function in harmony with the environment.

BRAND IDENTITY

- Saint-Gobain has been in business since 1665, making it one of the oldest continuously operated companies on the planet.
- Despite its more than three centuries of existence, Saint-Gobain focuses on innovative and progressive business practices.
- Saint-Gobain has phased out from its manufacturing processes many heavy metals, including cadmium and lead, due to their adverse effects on the environment.

Despite its nearly 350 years in existence, Saint-Gobain brands itself not in terms of past strengths but in terms of the ways in which it is building the future. The company's slogan, "The future is made of Saint-Gobain," represents this strategy of looking forward, and it is rare to find in

Saint-Gobain's literature any mention of the fact that the company has been in operation for well over three centuries. Instead, Saint-Gobain's corporate literature and websites use words like "innovation," "potential," "efficiency," "research," and "solutions."

To further highlight its focus on the future, Saint-Gobain presents and demonstrates on its websites numerous examples of current and future products designed to improve the quality of people's lives and to interact harmoniously with the natural environment. For instance, the company notes that 100 percent of the polyvinyls used in its automotive glazing division are recycled. Similarly, the amount of water used in the company's manufacturing processes has been reduced by an average of 2 percent each year, while environmentally destructive heavy metals, such as cadmium and lead, have been phased out completely.

BRAND STRATEGY

- Saint-Gobain is made up of four major business sectors: Innovative Materials, Construction Products, Building Distribution, and Packaging.
- About one of every three residential buildings in Europe and more than half of the region's vehicles incorporate glazing products created by Saint-Gobain's Innovative Materials sector.
- Saint-Gobain has a presence in about 64 countries worldwide.
- In 2012, all of Saint-Gobain's divisions were ranked first in their sectors, either in the European markets or worldwide, based on total market share.

Saint-Gobain is made up of four major business sectors: Innovative Materials, Construction Products, Building Distribution, and Packaging. Each sector includes divisions and companies that promote their own brands under the Saint-Gobain umbrella. The Innovative Materials sector, which accounts for nearly two-thirds of Saint-Gobain's total research for development operations, consists of the flat glass and high-performance materials divisions and includes a wide variety of materials and processes for the home, construction, and industrial markets. Approximately one of every three residential buildings in Europe and more than 50 percent of all vehicles in the region incorporate glazing products created by this sector of Saint-Gobain. The Construction Products sector includes acoustic and thermal insulation products, roofing materials, wall facings, pipes, and a wide variety of other products and solutions designed with efficiency, economy, and low environmental impact in mind. The Building Distribution sector supplies the needs of the commercial construction market, while the Packaging sector, led by subsidiary brand Verallia, is the world's second-largest manufacturer of glass containers, including bottles for beverages and jars for food products.

Saint-Gobain maintains a presence in about 64 countries around the world, successfully promoting its diversified brands by cobranding them under the umbrella of the larger Saint-Gobain corporation. The company's ongoing strategies of expansion, diversification, innovation, and branding appear to have paid off, as each of Saint-Gobain's divisions ranked in the top spot in the European or global markets, based on total market share, in 2012.

BRAND EQUITY

- In 2011, Saint-Gobain generated more than US$55.5 billion in worldwide net sales.
- Saint-Gobain employs more than 194,000 people in 64 countries.
- In 2012, Brand Finance ranked Saint-Gobain 146th on its Global 500 list, estimating the company's brand value at US$6.6 billion.
- In 2011, Saint-Gobain was ranked 155th on *Fortune* magazine's Global 500 list.

In 2011, Saint-Gobain generated more than US$55.5 billion in net sales worldwide, with its total equity valued at US$24 billion and total assets estimated at US$39.4 billion. Headquartered in France, the company maintains a large international presence, with more than 194,000 full-time employees at 4,100 facilities in 64 countries.

Saint-Gobain's dominant market share is one of the most significant indicators of the strength of its brand. Every one of its business and product divisions ranks in the top spot of its sector, either in Europe or worldwide, based on market share. For example, Saint-Gobain's flat glass, building products, manufacturing, and distribution divisions all rank first in Europe and third worldwide. Similarly, its automotive glazing and solar energy solutions rank first in Europe and second worldwide.

In 2012, Brand Finance estimated Saint-Gobain's brand value to be US$6.6 billion and ranked it 146th among the top 500 global brands. This was a minor step up from 2011, when Saint-Gobain held the 149th spot on the same list, with a brand value of US$6.5 billion. In 2011, *Fortune* magazine also ranked the French conglomerate 155th on its list of the top 500 global brands, a decline from its ranking of 132nd on the same list in 2010.

BRAND AWARENESS

- Saint-Gobain emphasizes the brand awareness of its subsidiaries over that of the larger parent corporation.
- In 2011, 27 percent of Saint-Gobain's total sales came from France, 41 percent from the remainder of Western Europe, and 13 percent from North America.

- In North America, Saint-Gobain's products are better known by the names of the individual subsidiaries that operate and sell their products in the region.

Despite its presence in more than 60 countries around the world, the Saint-Gobain brand is not well recognized by the general public. This is because Saint-Gobain places far more emphasis on the brand awareness of its subsidiaries than on that of the parent company. Because Saint-Gobain has diversified into so many areas, it is much easier and more practical to lean on the strength of the brands operating within its individual sectors.

In 2011, France accounted for more than 27 percent of Saint-Gobain's business. The Saint-Gobain brand is well-known in its home country because the corporation operates in (and, in many cases, dominates) many of France's business sectors. The rest of Western Europe accounted for 41 percent of Saint-Gobain's business in 2011, while North America accounted for 13 percent. Saint-Gobain may be one of the largest construction and high-performance material manufacturers in the world, but in the United States and Canada, where its individual subsidiaries promote their own brands, the company's products are better known by such names as Norton, Carborundum, SageGlass, Meyer Decorative Surfaces, and Verallia North America, all major components of the Saint-Gobain brand portfolio.

BRAND OUTLOOK

- In 2011, *Reuters* placed Saint-Gobain on its Top 100 World Leaders in Innovation list.
- Saint-Gobain allocated EUR 431 million (US$583 million) for research and innovation projects and filed 396 patents in 2011.
- Saint-Gobain estimates growth of up to 80 percent in solar solutions between 2011 and 2015, particularly in China and Latin America.

In the 21st century, Saint-Gobain has continued to expand into international markets through aggressive acquisitions, the creation of quality products, and continuous innovation. However, the effects of the global recession that lasted from approximately 2008 to 2012, along with the resulting austerity measures enacted in many countries, have left the company facing an uncertain future that may be difficult to navigate. Despite this, Saint-Gobain remains fairly confident in the development of its top markets, saying it will continue to focus on several main areas, including strategic innovation.

In 2011, *Reuters* named Saint-Gobain one of the top 100 international leaders in innovation, making the French conglomerate the only company from the habitat and construction industry on the list. That same year, Saint-Gobain invested EUR 431 million (US$583 million) in research and innovation projects, resulting in the filing of 396 patents for the year. Between 2011 and 2015, Saint-Gobain expects to see growth of up to 80 percent in solar solutions, with China and Latin America predicted to account for 65 percent of that growth. Saint-Gobain is also aiming to raise its construction sector's contribution to total net sales from 52 percent in 2011 to 60 percent by 2015. As to future expansion and acquisitions, Saint-Gobain has announced plans for significant activities in China, India, and the United States.

FURTHER READING

Brand Finance. "Best Global Brands: Saint-Gobain." *Brandirectory.* December 31, 2011. Accessed December 16, 2012. http://brandirectory.com/profile/saint-gobain.

Compagnie de Saint-Gobain. "2011 Annual Report." Accessed December 16, 2012. http://www.saint-gobain.com/en/press/corporate-publications.

Compagnie de Saint-Gobain. "Saint-Gobain at a Glance." Accessed December 16, 2012. http://www.saint-gobain.com/en/press/saintgobain-glance.

Hamon, Maurice. *Saint-Gobain 1665-1990: The Making of a French Multinational.* Paris: Jean-Claude Lattès, 1998. Print.

———. *Saint-Gobain, Logos through Time: Signs, Symbols & Messages.* Paris: Somogy Editions d'Arts, 2003. Print.

Miller, Peter W., A. Woodward, and Christina M. Stansell. "Compagnie de Saint-Gobain." *International Directory of Company Histories.* Ed. Tina Grant and Miranda H. Ferrara. Vol. 64. Detroit: St. James Press, 2005. *Gale Virtual Reference Library.* Accessed December 16, 2012. http://go.galegroup.com/ps/i.do?id=GALE%7CCX3429100030&v=2.1&u=itsbtrial&it=r&p=GVRL&sw=w.

Miller, William H. "Compagnie de Saint-Gobain." *Industry Week,* June 7, 1999. Accessed December 16, 2012. http://www.industryweek.com/companies-amp-executives/compagnie-de-saint-gobain.

SAM'S CLUB

———————————————————

AT A GLANCE

Brand Synopsis: As a leading warehouse club brand, Sam's Club promises its members "Savings Made Simple."

Parent Company: Sam's West Inc.

702 S.W. Eighth Street

Bentonville, Arkansas 72716

United States

http://www.samsclub.com

Sector: Consumer Discretionary

Industry Group: Retailing

Performance: *Market share*—41 percent (2009).

Principal Competitors: Office Depot, Inc.; Costco Wholesale Corporation; BJ's Wholesale Club, Inc.

BRAND ORIGINS

- Sam's Club was created by Sam Walton, the retailer who brought the nation Wal-Mart stores.
- The first Sam's location opened in Oklahoma City in 1983.
- In 1990 Sam's Wholesale Club shortened its name to Sam's Club.

Sam's Club was created by Sam Walton, the remarkable retailer who brought the nation Walmart stores. Walton had built a chain of Arkansas five-and-dimes in the 1960s and increased this to almost 300 stores in the South in the 1970s. Walmart Stores, incorporated in 1971, was a billion-dollar operation by 1980. Walmart stores were initially located in small towns, usually in markets so small that other retailers avoided them. The stores offered deeply discounted goods, and people flocked to them. Wal-Mart continued to expand across the nation in the 1980s, mainly in small towns. Sam's Club debuted in 1983 as something of a corollary to the Walmart small-town strategy. The warehouse stores were designed for an urban market, giving Walmart Stores, Inc., access to customers it did not otherwise reach.

The warehouse club idea did not originate with Sam Walton. The designated father of the warehouse club industry was the aptly named Sol Price, who ran Price Club. Sol Price opened his first Price Club in San Diego in 1976. The chain spread across the West Coast in the 1980s. Price Club stores were huge, on average 108,000 square feet, and ran with no frills and a minimum of employees. Sol Price guided Sam Walton through one of his stores in the early 1980s, and Walton acknowledged that his Sam's Club stores were patterned after the Price chain.

The first Sam's Club opened in Oklahoma City in 1983. It was called Sam's Wholesale Club, a name that stuck with the chain until 1990. By the end of 1983 there were two more stores, one in Kansas City, Missouri, and one in Dallas. Sales the first year were US$40 million. In 1984 the chain added eight stores, and these 11 stores brought in US$225 million total that year.

Sam's stores were located in leased warehouses, usually in rather desolate areas. They were huge and bare of decoration. Goods were displayed on shipping pallets or on steel shelves that reached almost to the ceiling. Items were often stacked inside torn-open packing boxes, but the goods were brand-name, at prices much lower than elsewhere. Customers usually had to buy large sizes or multiple packs of things. Sam's took advantage of the distribution know-how of the Walmart chain.

Sam's then opened in urban markets in the South and Southwest. The chain entered the Midwest in 1986. By 1987 Sam's had 84 stores. This included stores it bought in 1987 when Sam's took over the warehouse chain Super Saver Wholesale. Super Saver had gone head-to-head with Sam's in ten southern cities, and had another 11 warehouse stores in the South. However, it was not profitable, and in 1987 Sam's took over the chain, closing some stores and reopening others under the Sam's banner. In 1989 Sam's began moving into the Northeast. This region had little exposure to the warehouse store concept and was not a Walmart stronghold either.

By 1989 the Sam's Wholesale Club division brought in US$4.8 billion in sales, rising more than 25 percent over the previous year. The chain continued to account for a larger portion of Wal-Mart's total sales each year. By 1989 it was providing more than 18 percent of Walmart's total sales.

In 1990 Sam's Wholesale Club changed its name to Sam's Club. A judge in North Carolina had ruled that the chain was not entitled to the word "wholesale" in its name. State law required that at least 50 percent of goods sold be intended for resale in order to merit the "wholesale" appellation, and at Sam's that percentage was between 11 and 15. Although the ruling only applied to North Carolina, the chain thought it would be confusing to have different names in different states, so it adopted the simpler Sam's Club name overall.

BRAND ELEMENTS
- The Sam's Club brand name appears in serif type within a large blue diamond, beneath two smaller blue and green interlocking diamonds.
- The Sam's Club logo often appears in conjunction with the tagline, "Savings Made Simple."
- The graphic elements and color scheme used in the Sam's Club logo also are featured in the stores on aisle markers, promotional banners, and kiosks.
- Sam's Club's Simple Steps to Saving Green campaign includes a specialized logo utilizing the same color scheme as the brand's main logo.

The Sam's Club brand is represented by a distinct logo treatment, separate from that of Walmart. The word "Sam's" appears in large serif type in the center of a blue diamond, atop the word "CLUB," which is displayed in all capital letters. Two smaller blue and green interlocking diamonds appear within the larger blue diamond, above

the word, "Sam's." In 2013 Sam's Club continued to use its logo in conjunction with the tagline, "Savings Made Simple."

The graphic elements and color scheme used in the Sam's Club logo also are used in other ways within club locations. For example, aisle markers display aisle numbers within the smaller blue and green interlocking diamonds. Promotional banners and in-store kiosks feature complementary blue and green color schemes.

In the interest of environmental sustainability, Sam's Club also created its Simple Steps to Saving Green campaign. These words appear within the store along with a specialized logo. The logo features a green leaf that touches a blue diamond containing what appears to be concentric water ripples. The logo appears on reusable shopping totes and also is used within the store to designate when a product "has taken a step toward being more environmentally responsible in the way it was created, processed and/or distributed," according to Sam's Club's website.

Interactive technology often is a key aspect of the way in which members experience the Sam's Club brand. One example is a mobile app that includes features such as featured items, club map, club locator, scanner, product search, and feedback tool. The app features the blue and green interlocking diamond element, as well as the blue and green color scheme utilized in the brand's logo.

BRAND IDENTITY
- A key aspect of Sam's Club's brand identity is that it represents clubs, as opposed to stores, and members, as opposed to customers.
- Sam's Club brand identity is expressed by the tagline, "Savings Made Simple."
- Sam's Club uses data mining to understand and respond to its members' needs.

As its name suggests, Sam's Club is a fee-based club, and not a typical retail operation. This is a key aspect of a brand identity that represents clubs, as opposed to stores, and members, as opposed to customers. Within this context, Sam's Club focuses on delivering as much value as possible to its members, while helping them to make smart choices and have an enjoyable shopping experience. These objectives support the brand's tagline: "Savings Made Simple."

Sam's Club employs several tactics to ensure that its brand identity is in sync with consumers' image of the brand. These include selling name brand products at the lowest prices and offering unique merchandise. In addition, the company also relies on product sampling and interactive technologies to enhance members' shopping experience. As Walmart explains in its 2012 annual report, elements such as these "make Sam's Club a fun and exciting place to shop."

Sam's Club also ensures that it is delivering on its brand promise by maintaining an understanding of its members' needs. In the September 2012 issue of *Black Enterprise*, Sam's Club CEO Rosalind Brewer explained: "One thing that we're doing different in this era is to really speak to the member. We're data mining, but we're activating against that data we have on our members. It allows us to speak back to them in a way they've never been spoken to before. What we'd like to do is to be able to understand how they're shopping and their purchasing habits—and let them know that we're sensitive to their issues."

BRAND STRATEGY

- In the company's 2012 annual report, Walmart summarized its strategy for Sam's Club in eight words: "Leveraging Member insights to deliver value and quality."
- Sam's Club uses interactive technology to help members to make informed choices and customize their shopping experience.
- Sam's Club's interactive strategy includes the development of specialized mobile apps for members.
- Although Sam's Club sells a wide range of merchandise, a core aspect of the club's strategy is the health and wellness category.
- Sam's Club's utilizes health screenings to benefit its members' health and support the sale of both prescription and over-the-counter products.

In the company's 2012 annual report, Walmart summarized its strategy for Sam's Club in eight words: "Leveraging Member insights to deliver value and quality." A key aspect of this strategy is member engagement. Sam's Club continuously gathers feedback from its members to ensure that their expectations are met or exceeded. It combines competitively priced national brands and distinctive "roadshow merchandise" with exceptional customer service to create an optimal experience. The company also focuses on maximizing the productivity of its operations, so that savings can be used to create additional value for members.

Sam's Club's strategy also involves helping members make informed choices and customize their shopping experience. This is largely accomplished through the use of interactive technologies. For example, a Sam's Club mobile app allows members to create custom shopping lists, peruse in-club and online inventories, and manage their membership. Within the club, members are able to scan QR codes on select merchandise that link to short video reviews from related experts.

Sam's Club utilizes social media outlets such as Twitter and Facebook to engage with members in different ways. For example, to promote its proprietary Simply Right baby care product line, Sam's Club held a "#SimpleSavings Twitter Party," allowing members to obtain product information, learn about baby care tips, and also enter a chance to win products. Sam's Club also partnered with Triad Retail Media to develop Pet Central, an online offering for pet owners with interactive information on pet health and nutrition. Through social media, members were able to pose questions to pet expert Dr. Louise Murray.

Sam's Club's interactive strategies also have included the development of specialized mobile apps for members. For example, the company partnered with Triad to create a mobile weight loss app that was co-branded with Slim-Fast. The app provided members with tools to meet their weight loss goals, locate products, and take advantage of special offers at Sam's Club locations.

Although Sam's Club sells a wide range of merchandise, a core aspect of the club's strategy is the health and wellness category. In addition to its own SIMPLY RIGHT line of health and wellness products, Sam's Club has made exclusive arrangements with other leading brands on behalf of its members. Examples include the availability of private label products from General Nutrition Centers Inc., as well as nutritional supplements from Naturade.

Sam's Club health and wellness strategy extends beyond products. In 2012 the company published its first issue of *Healthy Living Made Simple*, a family wellness magazine distributed via mail, in-store, and online to more than 7.4 million members. In addition, Sam's Club also has established exclusive retail partnerships with health experts, including author Heidi Murkoff and her What to Expect parenting and pregnancy brand.

Although many retailers offer basic health screenings, Sam's Club's offerings are much more extensive. In 2011 alone Sam's Club provided more than 1 million health screenings. Beyond blood pressure, cholesterol, and glucose screenings, Sam's Club has provided prostate-specific antigen screenings, thyroid screenings, and allergy screenings. In addition to increasing health awareness and disease prevention, screening such as these also support the sale of both prescription and over-the-counter products at Sam's Club.

BRAND EQUITY

- In 2012 Sam's Club generated US$53.8 billion in net sales, placing it among the ranks of many of the United States' leading companies, including Coca-Cola.
- Sam's Club ranked eighth on Interbrand's 50 Most Valuable U.S. Retail Brands list for 2012, ahead of 15th-place Costco.
- Interbrand valued the Sam's Club brand at US$12.85 billion in 2012, a 4 percent increase from the previous year.

In 2012 Sam's Club generated US$53.8 billion in net sales. Although that figure only represented 12 percent of Walmart's US$443.9 billion in net sales, the figure places Sam's Club among the ranks of many of the United States' leading companies, including Coca-Cola. In 2012 Sam's Club ranked eighth on Interbrand's 50 Most Valuable U.S. Retail Brands list, ahead of 15th-place Costco. That year, Interbrand valued the Sam's Club brand at US$12.85 billion, a 4 percent increase from the previous year.

An Insider's Guide to Retail Success 2011–2012, a report from Barclays Capital, Kantar Retail, and Citigroup, ranked Sam's Club as the second-leading North American warehouse club in 2010, with a market share of 33.63 percent. Sam's Club was second to Costco (55.06 percent), but ahead of BJ's (8.31 percent). That year, Sam's Club's sales totaled US$46.7 billion, behind Costco (US$70.2 billion), but ahead of BJ's (US$10.6 billion).

BRAND AWARENESS

- Because it is one of only a few warehouse club operators, Sam's Club enjoys a high level of top-of-mind awareness.
- In 2012 the majority of Sam's Clubs' 611 locations were in the United States, where it had the strongest brand awareness.
- Sam's Club operates customized websites for its operations in Mexico, Brazil, and Puerto Rico.
- Sam's Club was one of only eight companies to receive an "excellent" rating from consumers in the 2012 Temkin Experience Ratings, which involved 206 large companies across 18 different industries.

In 2012 the majority of Sam's Clubs' 611 locations were in the United States, where it had the strongest brand awareness. That year the company also had 99 locations in Mexico, 24 in Brazil, 11 in Puerto Rico, and 4 in China. With the exception of China, Sam's Club operated websites that were customized for each of the aforementioned countries. This enabled members to interact with the brand in their native language. Sam's Club's Brazilian site included robust video elements, including a virtual tour and a link to a dedicated Brazilian You-Tube channel.

Because it is one of only a few warehouse club operators, Sam's Club enjoys a high level of top-of-mind awareness. However, the brand also is on consumers' shortlist for excellent customer service. In 2012 the Temkin Group gathered customer experience data from 10,000 consumers in the United States. The information was used to compile the Temkin Experience Ratings, which spanned 18 different industries and pertained to 206 large companies. Sam's Club was one of only eight companies to receive an "excellent" rating from consumers. In addition, Sam's Club was the only retailer, and one of only seven organizations overall, to achieve a double-digit lead over the average ranking for its industry.

BRAND OUTLOOK

- In its 2012 annual report Walmart explained: "Members are shopping more frequently, shopping more categories and spending a greater share of their wallet with Sam's Club."
- The challenging and uncertain economic climate of 2012 and 2013 was advantageous for Sam's Club as individuals, families, and businesses sought ways to stretch their budgets.
- In 2013 Sam's Club appeared to be well positioned for both domestic and international growth.

Sam's Club ended 2012 on a strong note, with net sales increasing 8.8 percent from the previous year. In addition, the company's operating income achieved a 9 percent increase over 2011. In its 2012 annual report Walmart explained: "Members are shopping more frequently, shopping more categories and spending a greater share of their wallet with Sam's Club." Considering these factors, Walmart concluded: "Sam's Club has strong momentum that sets the stage for continued growth in the warehouse club segment."

A challenging and uncertain economic climate was, in one respect, advantageous for Sam's Club. As individuals, families, and businesses sought ways to stretch their budgets, warehouse clubs provided them with additional options. In addition to providing members with an opportunity to buy a wide range of merchandise in bulk, Sam's Club also was focusing on developing its prepared home meals segment as a cost-effective alternative to restaurant dining. Likewise, the company was experiencing excellent performance in its produce, frozen, and fresh foods segments, as well as the health and wellness category.

From 605 locations in 2010, Sam's Club had grown its network of clubs to 609 sites in 2011 and 611 in 2012. The company's growth plans for its 2013 fiscal year were the most ambitious in several years. In addition to establishing nine new clubs, Sam's Club planned to expand or relocate six other locations. Although it was unclear if any of the new clubs would be located outside of the United States, in 2013 Sam's Club appeared to be well positioned for both domestic and international growth.

FURTHER READING

Alleyne, Sonia. "Rosalind Brewer's Second Act: Changing Jobs at the Height of Her Career Led to the CEO Spot at Sam's Club." *Black Enterprise*, September 2012.

"Breaking through at Sam's Club: Focus on Members, Not Brands Reiser Tells Mack Elevation Forum." *Drug Store News*, August 1, 2011.

"Digital Media Radically Transforming Marcom Process; Sam's Club, Publix Top-Rated in Customer Experience." *PR News*, March 5, 2012.

DeArment, Alaric. "Connecting Dots of Awareness, Prevention and Solutions." *Drug Store News*, April 2, 2012.

"Interbrand Releases the 2012 Best Retail Brands Report." Interbrand, February 21 2012. Available from: http://www.interbranddesignforum.com.

"Sam's Club." *International Directory of Company Histories*. Ed. Derek Jacques and Paula Kepos. Vol. 115. Farmington Hills, MI: St. James Press, 2010.

"Sam's Club Announces New Simply Right Vitamin Line." *India Pharma News*, January 24, 2012.

"Sam's Club and WhatToExpect.com Unveil Retail Program." *Professional Services Close-Up*, March 16, 2012.

Walmart Stores, Inc. *2012 Annual Report*. Accessed February 28, 2013. http://www.walmartstores.com/sites/annual-report/2012/WalMart_AR.pdf.

SAMSUNG

BRAND ORIGINS

- Lee Byung-chull founded Samsung in Taegu, Korea (now known as Daegu, South Korea), in 1938. He refounded the company after the Communist invasions of the early 1950s.

- Samsung is a chaebol, a Korean term for a large, diversified parent company connected to smaller subsidiary companies. Samsung is the largest chaebol in South Korea.
- Samsung Electronics began in 1969. Its first product was a small black and white television.
- Other Samsung companies include Samsung Heavy Industries and Samsung Life Insurance. Samsung Life Insurance is one of the largest companies in South Korea.
- Other Samsung holdings include high-tech, chemical, finance, and engineering companies, as well as hotels, research and education centers, and the Samsung Medical Center. Samsung also participates in cultural, athletic, and charitable efforts.

In 1938 Lee Byung-chull, a Korean entrepreneur, founded Samsung Group (Samsung) as a trading company in Taegu, Korea, which is now known as Daegu, South Korea. Looting during the 1950 North Korean invasion of South Korea depleted the company's inventory, and Byung-chull refounded the company in the early 1950s. Today Samsung operates on a much larger scale. Samsung is a *chaebol*, a Korean term for a large, diversified conglomerate made up of a parent company that is connected to a number of smaller subsidiary companies. Samsung is the largest chaebol in South Korea, and a number of Samsung's subsidiaries are large companies in their own right.

For example, Samsung Electronics Co., Ltd. (Samsung Electronics), is one of the largest technology companies in the world in terms of sales. In 1969 Samsung Electronics released its first product, a small black and white television. The company would eventually sell more televisions than any other company in the world. Although it is the largest and most profitable subsidiary of Samsung Group, Samsung Electronics is just one part of the Samsung chaebol. The conglomerate also includes Samsung Heavy Industries Co., Ltd. (Samsung Heavy Industries), one of the largest shipbuilders in the world, and Samsung Techwin, which focuses on physical security, video surveillance, and imaging.

In addition to its high-tech and industrial presence, Samsung Group is a major figure in the South Korean financial industry. Samsung Life Insurance Co., Ltd. (Samsung Life Insurance), is one of the largest companies in South Korea and one of the world's largest insurance underwriters. Samsung also owns and operates a number of companies and organizations in different fields, including high-tech companies, chemical and petrochemical companies, finance and investment companies, engineering firms, research and education centers, hotels, and a hospital (the Samsung Medical Center).

Samsung's community activities have extended the Samsung name even further. The company's involvement in cultural activities includes its founding of the Leeum, Samsung Museum of Art in Seoul, South Korea. The company also sponsors a number of sports and leisure activities. Its charitable work includes the establishment of the Samsung Life Public Welfare Foundation, which operates child care centers for low-income South Koreans.

BRAND ELEMENTS

- The Samsung logo uses white letters on a blue elliptical shape that represents the universe. The white and blue color scheme represents stability, reliability, and warmth.
- Although Samsung is a South Korean company, its logo uses the Latin alphabet as a sign of its international presence.
- Samsung means "three stars" in Korean. Some products and product lines evoke astronomical theme.

Samsung brands its products and services with the word "Samsung" in all capital letters. The color of the letters changes according to the accompanying product or service, but the font remains the same. This font's appearance echoes the Samsung logo, which consists of the word "Samsung" in white capital letters over a blue ellipse. This elliptical shape represents the universe and signifies change and advancement. Samsung chose the blue and white color scheme to represent stability, reliability, and warmth.

The name Samsung means "three stars" in Korean. The names of some Samsung products evoke this astronomical theme. For example, the Samsung Star is one of the company's feature phones (cell phones that, while not considered smartphones, offer more functions than standard phones), and the Galaxy line contains Samsung's best-selling Android smartphones and Android tablets.

BRAND IDENTITY

- Samsung wishes to be perceived as an innovative and "cool" company.
- A Samsung commercial featuring the tagline, "The next big thing is already here," portrayed Samsung as a brand offering the latest technology.
- Samsung hopes to become one of the world's top brands by 2020.

Samsung is a diversified brand, and it has taken great strides in the 21st century to promote its brand as innovative and "cool," particularly in the mobile telephone market. To convince consumers of its prowess, the company spent more than US$349 million on marketing in the U.S. alone in 2012. In addition, to support its image as an innovation leader, Samsung poured US$8.7 billion into research and development in 2011.

Samsung has used commercials for its phones to describe its brand. One commercial depicted a line of people waiting outside a store to buy the latest technological device. People outside the line showed their Samsung phones and its features to the people in waiting in line, who seemed impressed by the Samsung devices. The advertisement's tagline, "The next big thing is already here," portrayed Samsung as a brand offering the latest technology. It also implied that Samsung was a worthy rival to competitors like Apple, a company so popular that consumers sometimes wait in long lines to purchase its products.

The Samsung philosophy is "to devote our talent and technology to creating superior products and services that contribute to a better global society." For the second decade of the 21st century Samsung added a new motto to its philosophy: "Inspire the World, Create the Future." The new motto tries to signal to the world that Samsung is even more devoted to technological breakthroughs, creative solutions, and innovative products. Samsung also declared on its website that it hopes to become one of the top five brands in the world by 2020.

BRAND STRATEGY

- Samsung Electronics is the largest, most visible, and most profitable part of the Samsung brand.
- In addition to electronics, Samsung has extended its brand with companies like Samsung Heavy Industries.
- Samsung subsidiary Samsung Life Insurance is South Korea's largest insurer and is another prominent extension of the Samsung brand.

Although they all use the Samsung name, Samsung's different subsidiaries operate in different fields, serving as diverse extensions of the overall Samsung brand. Samsung Electronics Co., Ltd. (Samsung Electronics) is the largest and most visible subsidiary of Samsung Group. It manufactures phones and phone accessories, computers and computer accessories, televisions, cameras, MP3 players, home appliances, medical equipment, and other electronic devices. Samsung Electronics is the most lucrative subsidiary of Samsung Group, accounting for more than half of the conglomerate's 2011 sales and net income.

Electronics are not Samsung's only concern, however. The Samsung brand is actually quite diverse and contains other large companies that earn substantial profits. These include Samsung Heavy Industries Co., Ltd. (Samsung Heavy Industries), with a 2011 net income of about US$777.9 million (KRW863.9 billion), and Samsung Life Insurance Co., Ltd. (Samsung Life Insurance), with a 2011 net income of about US$853.9 million (KRW948.4 billion). Samsung Life Insurance, which offers loan, investment, and pension services in addition to life insurance, is South Korea's largest insurer.

BRAND EQUITY

- Samsung sells more televisions, memory chips, and cell phones than any other company in the world.
- Between 2006 and 2009, Samsung sold more digital televisions in the United States than any other company. It sold 50 percent of Iran's televisions in 2009.
- In South Korea, Samsung Life Insurance holds a 26 percent share of the insurance market.
- Brand Finance and Interbrand both ranked Samsung as one of the top 10 global brands in 2012. *Fortune* magazine said that Samsung Electronics and Samsung Life Insurance were among the world's largest 500 companies in 2011.
- Samsung accounts for around 20 percent of South Korea's gross domestic product.

Samsung's high visibility echoes its large market share. The company sells more televisions, memory chips, and cell phones than any other company in the world. It also sells large numbers of other product types. There is some debate as to whether Samsung Electronics Co., Ltd. (Samsung Electronics), or Apple Inc. is the world's largest smartphone maker. Samsung Electronics sold more digital televisions in the United States than any other company between 2006 and 2009, and Samsung televisions accounted for half of all televisions sold in Iran in 2009. Other subsidiaries of Samsung also capture significant market share. In South Korea, Samsung Life Insurance Co., Ltd. (Samsung Life Insurance), holds a 26 percent share of the insurance market.

This success has made Samsung a valuable international brand. Brand Finance's Global 500 2012, a list of the top brands in the world, named Samsung the sixth best global brand in 2012, with a brand value of US$38.2 billion. Similarly, on leading brand consultancy Interbrand's 2012 list of the top 100 brands in the world,

Samsung placed ninth, with a brand value of about US$32.9 billion. In *Fortune* magazine's 2011 list of the 500 largest corporations in the world, the Global 500, Samsung Electronics Co., Ltd. (Samsung Electronics), placed 22nd, while Samsung Life Insurance placed 333rd.

Samsung's prominence in the electronics and insurance markets has made the company a powerful economic force in its home country. Samsung accounts for around 20 percent of South Korea's gross domestic product. This means the value of Samsung's products and services amounts to approximately one-fifth of the total amount of South Korea's goods and services in a given year.

BRAND AWARENESS

- In the LoveBrands 2011 poll, Russian consumers named Samsung as the top brand they associate with the word "love" and also named Samsung's electronics and household appliances as "love brands." This study was similar to a top-of-mind awareness poll.
- In the Asia's Top 1,000 Brands poll, conducted by *Campaign Asia-Pacific* magazine and published in 2012, consumers in the eastern Asia and Pacific regions named Samsung the top brand in Asia.
- After a U.S. jury ruled in August 2012 that Samsung had infringed on products and patents belonging to Apple, Samsung's reputation fell but quickly recovered by September 2012.

Samsung's market success has been accompanied by consumer respect. In the LoveBrands 2011 study, a poll that sought to determine top-of-mind brand awareness by asking Russian consumers to name the brands they associate with the word "love," Samsung was the top brand overall and the top brand for both electronics and household appliances. In a poll titled "Asia's Top 1,000 Brands," a similar top-of-mind awareness poll conducted by *Campaign Asia-Pacific* magazine and published in 2012, consumers in the eastern Asia and Pacific regions named Samsung the top brand in Asia. This poll asked consumers to name the best brand in a number of consumer categories.

Samsung's brand reputation wavered in 2012. In August of that year, a jury in the United States ruled that Samsung had infringed on a number of electronic products and patents belonging to Apple Inc. (Apple). The jury ruled that Apple should receive more than US$1 billion in compensation. Although Samsung countersued, it did not receive anything. This ruling may have initially hurt consumers' perceptions of Samsung, but the company's reputation quickly recovered. By September 2012, early technology adopters and technology users between the ages of 18 and 34 reported positive perceptions of Samsung, largely similar to their perceptions of Apple. Thus, the court ruling did not seem to hurt Samsung's overall long-term reputation.

BRAND OUTLOOK

- In 2009 Samsung restructured and announced its goal of becoming one of the five largest brands and 10 largest companies in the world by 2020 and to earn US$400 billion by that same year.
- In 2009 Samsung India released the Solar Guru, an affordable cell phone that was the first of its kind to be charged with solar power.
- Samsung India first offered the Solar Guru cell phone to the Indian market before later selling the phone under the name Crest Solar in other countries.
- In 2011 Samsung resumed investing overseas. It had stopped such investments during the global economic recession of the preceding years.

Samsung restructured in 2009. That same year it announced its plans for the future. Samsung said it wanted to become one of the top-five brands in the world, become one of the top-10 companies in the world, and earn US$400 billion in revenue by 2020.

In another 2009 development, Samsung India released the first cell phone that could be charged with solar power, the Solar Guru. Samsung India first released this affordable phone to the Indian market before later offering it to other countries around the world, where it was known as the Crest Solar. This release epitomized Samsung's interests in innovation, new products, and global markets.

In other global news for Samsung, in 2011 the company began investing overseas again after the global economic recession of the preceding years forced it to temporarily stop such investments. A major company in its native South Korea and around the world, Samsung looks to expand even further in the years ahead.

FURTHER READING

"Best Global Brands 2012." Interbrand. Accessed October 3, 2012. http://www.interbrand.com/en/best-global-brands/2012/Best-Global-Brands-2012-Brand-View.aspx.

Brand Finance. "Global 500 2012." *Brandirectory*. Accessed October 1, 2012. http://brandirectory.com/league_tables/table/global-500-2012.

Lev-Ram, Michal. "Samsung' Road to Global Domination." *Fortune*, January 22, 2013. Accessed February 22, 2013. http://tech.fortune.cnn.com/2013/01/22/Samsung-apple-smartphone/.

Marzilli, Ted. "Samsung Buzz Bounces Back from Lawsuit." YouGov BrandIndex, September 10, 2012. Accessed October 3, 2012. http://www.brandindex.com/article/samsung-buzz-bounces-back-lawsuit.

Naidu-Ghelani, Rajeshni. "South Korea's 10 Biggest Companies." CNBC.com, July 20, 2012. Accessed October 1, 2012. http://www.cnbc.com/id/48237596/South_Korea_s_10_Biggest_Companies.

Otremba, Jolene. "Asia's Top 1000 Brands: Samsung Takes No. 1 Spot in Exclusive Consumer Research." Campaign Asia-Pacific, July 5, 2012. Accessed October 3, 2012. http://www.campaignasia.com/Article/307374,asias-top-1000-brands-samsung-takes-no-1-spot-in-exclusive-consumer-research.aspx.

"Our Products, Your Technology: Russians Love Global Technological Brands." Online Market Intelligence, January 11, 2012. Accessed October 3, 2012. http://www.omirussia.ru/en/analytics/press_releases/2012/01/news134.html.

"Samsung: A Success Story in Branding Strategy." *VARIndia*, January 2009. Accessed October 1, 2012. http://www.varindia.com/Jan_BrandBuilding.htm.

"Samsung Electronics Co., Ltd." *International Directory of Company Histories*. Ed. Jay P. Pederson. Vol. 108. Detroit, MI: St. James Press, 2010.

Samsung Group. "2011 Annual Report." Accessed October 1, 2012. http://www.samsung.com/us/aboutsamsung/ir/financialinformation/annualreport/IR_Annual2011.html.

"Samsung US Homepage." Samsung Group. Accessed October 1, 2012. http://www.samsung.com/us/#latest-home.

SANTANDER

◼

BRAND ORIGINS

- Banco Santander originated in the merger of two of Spain's banking empires, Banco Central and Banco Santander.
- Banco Central, founded in 1919, achieved growth by investing in emerging industries and later moving into a continuing strategy of acquisition.

- By 1980 Banco Central was Spain's largest bank, while Banco Santander looked to its rival for a merger, which took place in 1999.
- In 2007 the bank was officially renamed Banco Santander, S.A. (Santander).

Banco Santander, S.A. (Santander) is the product of the 1999 merger between two of Spain's banking empires, Banco Central and Banco Santander. Banco Santander was formed in 1857 and, under the leadership of the Botín family (who would assume majority control of the newly merged bank in the 1990s), had achieved a top position among Spain's financial institutions by World War I. Banco Central was founded in 1919, achieving growth by investment in emerging industries, such as coal, steel, shipping, and papermaking. Banco Central later adopted an ongoing strategy of acquisition. The end of World War I led to economic nationalism and a desire for financial expansion among the Spanish banks. Banco Central's position in the industry saw it through the global depression of the 1930s and prepared it to eventually fill the void left when the Bank of Spain fell under new government measures that prevented it from serving the public.

Following World War I, the Spanish government under Francisco Franco joined the International Monetary Fund (IMF) and the International Bank for Reconstruction and Development (IBRD), eventually creating laws that institutionalized Spain's major banks. In this new environment, Banco Central continued to develop and offer more consumer services, such as credit and checking accounts, as the standard of living increased for the middle class. The large number of banks in Spain in the 1970s led to many failing financial entities, which Banco Central then bought, bringing its total number of offices to more than 1,000. By 1980 Banco Central was the largest Spanish bank but was as yet unable to compete effectively in the liberalized and internationalized Spanish economy. Banco Central merged briefly with Banco Español de Credito, lost the partnership at the end of the 1980s, and merged with Banco Hispano Americano in 1991. Meanwhile, Banco Santander had seen its profits slip gradually and was now looking to its rival, the newly formed Banco Central Hispanoamericano (BCH), for a merger, which took place in 1999.

The new bank, Banco Santander Central Hispano (BSCH), owned more than US$330 billion in assets and immediately moved to increase its holdings by buying Mexico's Grupo Financiero Serfin, Champalimaud of Portugal, and Argentinian online brokerage Patagon.com (in order to boost its online service options). By 2002 the remaining Banco Central executives had left the bank, leaving Emilio Botín in command. BSCH established a new consumer banking franchise the following year and made significant inroads in the United Kingdom. In 2007 the bank was officially renamed Banco Santander, S.A. (Santander). It became the world's largest bank in terms of market capitalization and the seventh-largest in terms of profits.

BRAND ELEMENTS

- The Santander brand is represented by the Santander flame and the color red, which promote the concepts of light, transparency, warmth, and proximity.
- Banco Santander was named after the port of Santander in northern Spain.
- The "Together. We Are Santander" advertising campaign used a bridge-building theme with the bank's red branding to showcase the brand's strength and stability.

The essence of the Santander brand is purportedly leadership, strength, and dynamism. The brand is represented by its corporate symbols, the Santander flame and the color red, which when combined are intended to promote the concepts of light, transparency, warmth, and proximity. These visual cues convey to the public Santander's values of global access and local visibility, as well as the bank's history of business. The Santander brand's tagline is "Santander, a bank for your ideas."

The original Banco Santander was involved in trade between the port of Santander in northern Spain and Latin America. By adopting and maintaining the name Santander, the firm conveys its commitment to its roots and long history.

The "Together. We Are Santander" advertising campaign utilized the bank's red branding in a bridge-building theme to broadcast Santander's strength and stability. The

company carried the motif into further advertising venues by creating the "Red Brick Game," a bridge-building iPhone application (app), mobile game, and Facebook widget. In Latin America Santander is known as a "football bank" for its sponsorship of the Copa Santander Libertadores, an international club soccer competition.

BRAND IDENTITY

- Santander launched a brand unification campaign in 2004.
- Santander faced brand image issues in the United Kingdom in the 2010s and changed its tagline and marketing approach as a result.
- In 2012 Santander focused on establishing itself as a global bank and international finance group.

In 2004 Santander initiated a brand unification campaign in order to present a single, cohesive brand in the numerous countries where it operates. According to the Santander corporate website, "Santander is a unique global brand that conveys a homogeneous, consistent image, with a single communication code."

Though Santander lists customer satisfaction and service among its corporate values, the company faced some challenges in conveying this message to consumers. In the United Kingdom in particular in the early 21st century, Santander banks faced some brand image issues after merging the banks Abbey, Alliance & Leicester, and Bradford & Bingley under the Santander umbrella. Complaints about poor customer service prompted Santander to change its tagline from "Together. We are Santander" to "Driven to do better" and to launch a major marketing campaign in 2011.

The bank's vision as of 2012 was focused on establishing itself as a global bank and international financial group, with the aim of providing high return to shareholders and meeting all of the financial needs of customers by retaining a strong presence in local markets as well as global ones.

BRAND STRATEGY

- In the late 1990s Emilio Botín assumed chairmanship of Banco Santander Central Hispano (BSCH) and initiated an accelerated period of expansion for the bank.
- Launched in Spain in 2006, a new campaign, "We Want to be Your Bank," drew thousands of customers in its first year.
- In 2007 BSCH formed a consortium with the Royal Bank of Scotland and Fortis to buy and divide Dutch bank ABN AMRO.

Santander's expansion outside Spain was initiated by Emilio Botín, who assumed chairmanship of the bank in the 1990s. In 2003 the bank, which until 2007 was named Banco Santander Central Hispano (BSCH), established a new consumer banking franchise through the merger of its subsidiary Hispamer with CC Bank in Germany and the Italian consumer credit company Finconsumo. The following year BSCH paid US$15.6 billion for Abbey National plc and made a significant move into the United Kingdom. Back in Spain, a new campaign called "We Want to be Your Bank" ("Quermos Ser Tu Banco") was launched in 2006. As part of the campaign's promotion, the bank canceled fees and commissions for customers using a minimum of one BSCH product, which drew thousands of customers in the promotion's first year. The numbers of consumers holding debit and credit cards, personal loans, and life insurance package from the bank rose, which produced record profits for the bank in 2006.

By 2005 BSCH had become the largest shareholder of Pennsylvania-based Sovereign Bancorp, a savings and loan association, which gave BSCH the right to acquire Sovereign within the following two years. In 2007 BSCH formed a consortium with the Royal Bank of Scotland and Fortis (a now-defunct insurance, banking, and investment management company) to buy and divide Dutch bank ABN AMRO just as world markets were sinking into the credit crisis created by the collapse of the U.S. subprime mortgage market. BSCH reacted by selling its Italian operation and retaining its more valuable Brazilian banking franchise. A year later BSCH renamed itself Banco Santander, SA (Santander). It was officially the world's largest bank in terms of market capitalization and seventh-largest in terms of profit.

During the difficult economic climate of the global recession that began in 2008, Santander devised a new strategy for success, which involved strict focus on retail and commercial banking, increased access to technology, and a renewed emphasis on risk management. In 2011 Santander opened 836,000 new bank accounts and 543,000 new credit cards. The bank has a distribution network of 1,400 branches and 28 corporate banking centers.

BRAND EQUITY
- In 2010 Santander ranked 68th on Interbrand's Most Valuable Global Brands list.
- In 2011 the Santander brand reported a profit of EUR 5.4 billion (US$7.1 billion).
- In 2011 Santander's net operating income was EUR 24.4 billion (US$32 billion), while the bank's core capital ratio was 9 percent.

In 2007 Millward Brown's BrandZ ranked Santander 47th in its Top 100 Most Powerful Brands list. In 2010 Santander entered Interbrand's Most Valuable Global Brands list, ranked at number 68. Santander suffered in

2011 due to the economic downturn affecting Europe, but the brand has gained awareness thanks to a celebrity-driven branding campaign. In 2011 Santander reported a profit of EUR 5.4 billion (US$7.1 billion). Net operating income was EUR 24.4 billion (US$32 billion), and the bank's core capital ratio stood at 9 percent.

BRAND AWARENESS
- In 2009 Santander strategically partnered with two of the most successful Formula One auto racing teams, Ferrari and McLaren.
- In 2010 Santander began an ad campaign with the tagline "Together. We are Santander" to raise awareness of the brand in the United Kingdom.
- Brand awareness in the United Kingdom rose to more than 92 percent around 2010.

In the early 2000s the Santander brand began gaining a reputation among the world's leading brand consultancy firms, including Interbrand, Millward Brown, and Brand Finance. The brand continued to gain visibility in key markets in Brazil, the United Kingdom, and Germany, and the need to form a single Santander brand in the United States and Poland was reflected in the bank's efforts to unify its global segments in advertising and rebranding projects.

Although the bank's primary goal was global expansion, in 2006 Banco Santander Central Hispano (BSCH), as Santander was then named, launched a Spain-based advertising campaign carrying the tagline "We Want to be Your Bank." In 2009 Santander strategically partnered with two of the most successful Formula One auto racing teams, Ferrari and McLaren, for the following five years. In 2010, following the 2004 acquisition of Abbey National plc, Santander launched an advertising campaign with the tagline "Together. We are Santander" to build its presence in the United Kingdom. The result of that multimillion-dollar multimedia campaign was a brand awareness of more than 92 percent and a brand that was closing in on the top position among U.K. financial services.

BRAND OUTLOOK
- In 2011 Santander recorded total assets of EUR 1.3 trillion (US$1.7 trillion).
- Santander's profit is divided between developed countries (46 percent) and emerging markets (54 percent).
- Santander's profits declined 59 percent in 2012, but the bank expected profits to rise considerably in 2013.

In 2011 Santander opened 836,000 new bank accounts and 543,000 new credit cards. The bank has a distribution network of 1,400 branches and 28 corporate banking centers. In 2011 Santander recorded total assets of EUR 1.3 trillion (US$1.7 trillion), shareholder funds of EUR 80.6 billion (US$105.5 billion), and a net operating income of EUR 24.4 billion (US$32 billion). Santander achieved a geographic positioning centered on its 10 markets, with a balance between developed countries (which accounted for 46 percent of the brand's profits) and emerging markets (which accounted for 54 percent of the brand's profits).

The outlook for Spanish banks declined considerably in the 2010s, and in 2012 Moody's, the ratings agency, cut Santander's rating along with the ratings of 15 other Spanish banks. By early 2013, however, Santander's outlook had improved, and many analysts voiced hope for a turnaround. The bank's 2012 profit declined 59 percent, but Santander said 2012 was a turning point, and that earnings would increase considerably in 2013.

FURTHER READING

"Banco Santander Central Hispano S.A." *International Directory of Company Histories*. Ed. Jay P. Pederson. Vol. 36. Detroit: St. James Press, 2001. *Gale Virtual Reference Library*. Accessed October 18, 2012. http://go.galegroup.com/ps/i.do?id=GALE%7CCCX2844000022&v=2.1&u=itsbtrial&it=r&p=GVRL&sw=w.

"Banco Santander's Emilio Botín takes on the world." *CNNMoney*, March 23, 2012. Accessed October 18, 2012. http://finance.fortune.cnn.com/2012/03/23/banco-santander-emilio-botin.

Brownsell, Alex. "Santander Marketing Overhaul Aims to Tackle Image Problems." *Marketing Magazine*, June 14, 2011. Accessed February 28, 2013.

Kaihla, Paul. "Riding the Iberian Tiger." *Canadian Business*, October 29, 1999, 21.

Nash, Elizabeth. "Spanish Banks in £20bn Merger." *Independent*, January 16, 1999, 20.

Santander. "Santander Annual Report 2011." Accessed October 18, 2012. http://www.santander.com/csgs/StaticBS?ssbinary=true&blobtable=MungoBlobs&blobkey=id&SSURIsscontext=Satellite+Server&blobcol=urldata&SSURIcontainer=Default&SSURIsession=false&blobwhere=1278681725312&blobheader=application%2Fpdf&SSURIapptype=BlobServer#satellitefragment.

"Santander: Building bridges with mixed metaphors." *Marketing Communications Weblog*, January 22, 2010. Accessed October 18, 2012. http://www.marketing-comms.com/blog/blog-5-santander-building-bridges-with-mixed-metaphors.

Sine Qua Non. "Banco Santander: brand awareness and brand recognition via Formula 1." Accessed October 16, 2012. http://www.sinequanon-intl.com/news-views/article/banco-santander-brand-awareness-and-brand-recognition-via-formula-1.

"A Titan Looks Way Past the Pyrenees." *Business Week International*, February 1, 1999, 27.

SANYO

—■—

AT A GLANCE

—■—

Brand Synopsis: The Sanyo brand represents the pursuit of a better quality of life and a pristine environment all made possible through the wonders of technology.

Parent Company: Panasonic Corporation

5-5, Keihan-Hondori 2-Chome

Moriguchi City, Osaka

Japan

http://panasonic.net/sanyo

Sector: Consumer Discretionary

Industry Group: Consumer Durables & Apparel

Performance: *Sales*—JPY1.59 trillion (US$17.18 billion) (2010).

Principal Competitors: LG Electronics; Samsung; Toshiba

BRAND ORIGINS

- Toshio Iue, founder of Sanyo, was the brother-in-law of Konosuke Matsushita, founder of Matsushita Electric, which is today known as Panasonic.
- In 1962 Sanyo invented the first rechargeable battery, made with cadmium and nickel, and named the product Cadnia.
- By 1998 Sanyo was manufacturing 30 percent of all digital cameras sold in the world.

- Sanyo was purchased by Panasonic in 2009, essentially the same company which 62 years earlier had given it birth as a subsidiary.

After the end of World War II the Allied Occupation Authority known as SCAP (Supreme Command Allied Powers) was set up in Japan to monitor, reorganize, and help rebuild the devastated Japanese economic infrastructure. Part of its process was to eliminate any perceived monopolies. One of these, the Matsushita Electric Industrial Co., was divided into two smaller companies. In 1947 a subsidiary of one of these two companies was started by Toshio Iue, which he named Sanyo Electric Works. Iue was the brother-in-law of Konosuke Matsushita and an original partner in Matsushita Electric. The purpose of the factory was to manufacture and export bicycle lamp generators. Sanyo's first major order was for 5,000 bicycle generator lamps to the GHQ (General Headquarters) of the Allied Forces. Business was good and by April 1, 1950, after paying off the remainder of its unsecured loans, the company incorporated as Sanyo Electric Co. Ltd. Later that year the company secured a contract with Channel Master, an American antenna manufacturer, to distribute Sanyo transistor radios in the United States. Over the next few years Sanyo quickly expanded its product lines to include radios, tape recorders, washers, air conditioners, vacuum cleaners, and even televisions, in response to the strengthening Japanese economy and the increasing number of domestic consumers who were purchasing home products. In 1961 Sanyo established its first overseas factory in Hong Kong. The following year the company put into production a revolutionary new cadmium and nickel battery, named Cadnia, which was not only durable but rechargeable. The battery was very popular and presented a profitable product line.

In 1974 the worldwide energy crisis inspired Sanyo to expand into the alternative energy field, studying solar-powered devices and home heating units. The following year Sanyo was credited with creating lithium ion batteries and also expanding into the home video market.

Beginning in 1991 Japan went through a lengthy recession which is today known as the "Lost Decade." Sanyo, like most other Japanese companies, was not immune. In 1994 Sanyo finally posted a profit of US$114.5 million on revenue of US$17.12 billion and in 1995 had major breakthroughs as it unveiled its first digital camera. Sanyo cameras turned out to be very popular and by 1998 the company was producing 30 percent of the world's digital cameras. But in 1997 Japan was struck a second economic blow as the Japanese recession was magnified by an economic downturn in Asia. As a result, for 1999 Sanyo posted a US$216 million loss. In response, a major reorganization was initiated merging all of its operations into five newly created companies—Multimedia, Home Appliances, Commercial Equipment Systems, Semiconductor, and Soft Energy—each with its own president and its own business strategies.

The year 2000 marked the 50th anniversary of Sanyo Electric's incorporation. In February the company formed a strategic alliance with Maytag Corp to develop and market a number of home appliances, specifically cooking, laundry, and floor care. In 2001 Sanyo became the world leader in sales of batteries for digital devices. Sanyo held a 30 percent market share of all lithium ion batteries produced, and even more impressively, over 50 percent of all nickel-metal hydride batteries. Sanyo further strengthened its dominance by purchasing Toshiba's nickel-metal hydride battery business. Later in the year Sanyo also secured contracts with Ford Motor Company and Honda Motor Co., Ltd., to supply rechargeable batteries for their hybrid gas-electric cars.

In October 2004 Sanyo's semiconductor plant in Niigata was severely damaged by a strong earthquake. By the end of fiscal 2005 the company had lost more than JPY73.3 billion (US$684 million) due to extensive damage to the plant and inventory, as well as financial losses from the plant not producing. By early 2006 Sanyo was on the brink of collapse and was forced to raise US$2.56 billion through the sale of preferred stock to outside investors represented by Goldman Sachs and Japanese brokerage house Daiwa Securities SMBC. But it was too little, too late. On December 21, 2009, Panasonic acquired a majority ownership in Sanyo Electric and soon after announced that it would stop selling Sanyo brand appliances after April 2011. In 2012 Panasonic proceeded to convert all 1,500 Sanyo-affiliated stores to Panasonic stores, and by December 2012 all buildings, including the Sanyo corporate office, were now displaying the Panasonic name. The Sanyo history had come full circle. The company had begun as an offshoot of Matsushita and 62 years later returned to that same company, which in 2008 changed its name from Matsushita Electric Industrial Co., Ltd, to the Panasonic Corporation.

BRAND ELEMENTS
- The word "Sanyo" is a generic Japanese term which means "three oceans," referring to the Pacific, Atlantic, and Indian Oceans.
- The Sanyo logo has remained fairly consistent, since the first single-word logo was used in 1949.
- "Think GAIA" was a slogan Sanyo developed to promote the company as a leader in both research and application of environmentally friendly technologies.

In 1947 Toshio Iue founded the Sanyo Electric Works. He dreamed of one day having hundreds of factories all over the world. This dream was the inspiration for the name as Sanyo is a generic Japanese term which means "three oceans," referring to the Pacific, Atlantic, and Indian Oceans. He would live to see his dream eventually come true, as Sanyo did grow and spread throughout the world.

The Sanyo logo has remained fairly consistent over the years. The very first logo, created at the company's inception in 1947, was the most unique. The main symbol was a circle containing a lightning bolt. The word "National" was in large bold letters in front of the circle, and underneath the circle was the name "Sanyo Electric Co. Ltd." in cursive. In 1949 this was altered to an upward-angled "Sanyo" in cursive, underscored with a lightning bolt. There were more logos after this but nearly all were variations of the one-word "Sanyo" name in either blue or red lettering.

There have been quite a few slogans over the years, but there were three in particular which were most memorable. The first, "Sanyo. Quality Above All," was used for several years to promote the company's audio line of products. The most notable slogan and jingle was "That's Life! Sanyo" which was sung throughout a great number of television commercials, often by well-known, glamorous female celebrities. Finally "Think GAIA. For Life and the Earth" was part of Sanyo's push to establish an image for the company as one which was at the forefront of both research and application of environmentally friendly technologies and natural, alternative energy solutions, in particular solar energy applications. Sanyo was the first manufacturer to employ CFC-free refrigerants in all the home and industrial refrigerators and freezers it manufactured. It was also one of the first companies to apply a variety of environmentally friendly standards throughout its manufacturing processes as part of its Sanyo Green initiative.

BRAND IDENTITY

- In 1998 Sanyo was manufacturing 30 percent of all digital cameras sold in the world.
- Sanyo is the world leader in sales of rechargeable batteries with a 30 percent market share of all lithium-ion batteries sold and over 50 percent of all nickel-metal hydride batteries.
- Sanyo's Solar Ark is a massive solar energy collector and includes inside the Solar Energy Museum and the Solar Field Lab and Gallery.

Sanyo has always worked hard to develop and maintain a brand name which represents quality and value based on cutting-edge technology. The company mission statement reads "Our ultimate goal is to restore a beautiful earth for the generations to come." Throughout its history this company has focused on three main areas of production, all of which have the end goal of improving quality of life for people or improving the environment. In 1952 Sanyo began mass producing the first plastic radio, an inexpensive and easily portable device which was affordable by almost anyone. This product opened the door for Sanyo to enter the home electric appliance market. In 1953 Sanyo developed the pulsating washing machine. In the coming years it would become an industry leader in manufacturing products such as televisions, stereo components, cell phones, cameras, and much more. By 1998 Sanyo was manufacturing 30 percent of all digital cameras sold in the world. That figure does not include Sanyo components used in other manufacturers' cameras. By 2001 Sanyo's marketing efforts and high-quality products had helped the company to become the world leader in the sale of batteries for digital devices. Sanyo held a 30 percent market share of all lithium ion batteries sold and over 50 percent of all nickel-metal hydride batteries.

Sanyo also gained worldwide attention when it unveiled the Solar Ark in December 2001. This huge structure is 315 meters (1,033.5 feet) wide and 37 meters (121.4 feet) tall. It is not only a massive collector of solar energy, but also contains the Solar Energy Museum and the Solar Field Lab and Gallery. Further signs of commitment to the environment have included the Sanyo Green initiative, which has focused both research and production on product designs which are less intrusive to the environment such as CFC-free refrigerants, energy-efficient devices and appliances, noise reduction, RoHS compliance (Restriction of Hazardous Substances), and storage volume efficiency.

BRAND STRATEGY

- Since the company was first founded in 1947 all of Sanyo's products have been sold under the single Sanyo brand label.

- In 1969 Karou Iue introduced the "one-third marketing strategy" that divided Sanyo's manufacturing resources into three equal divisions.
- The downfall of Sanyo began in 1991 at the start of the Japanese recession known as the "Lost Decade" and ended in 2009 when the company was taken over by Panasonic, which eliminated the Sanyo brand.

Sanyo has had a variety of brand strategies over the years, most of which turned out to be successful. In each case all products were represented in one of two ways. They were manufactured and sold under the Sanyo name brand or they were produced for use under the name brands of companies which had purchased them as components in their own products. In 1969 Kaoru Iue, brother of founder Toshio and newly chosen president of Sanyo, had his own ideas on how to run the company and introduced the "one-third marketing strategy." This would consist of dividing Sanyo's manufacturing resources into three equal divisions—domestic manufacture for domestic markets, domestic manufacture for foreign markets, and foreign manufacture for other foreign markets. Over the next few years the new system reduced overall risk and promoted a balanced growth globally. In 1986 Sanyo made a key business move when it merged with one of its largest subsidiaries, Tokyo Sanyo Electric, to form Sanyo Electric, Ltd. The merger made the new company the largest manufacturer of televisions in Japan as well as Japan's largest exporter.

In 1997 Japan had suffered through seven years of a domestic recession when it was struck further down by an economic downturn in Asia. Sanyo was losing hundreds of millions of dollars, and was forced to reorganize in an attempt to stem the financial hemorrhaging. The plan was to merge all of the company operations into five new and independent companies. Though the new strategy slowed losses somewhat, it was unsuccessful overall, and in 2009 Sanyo was purchased by Panasonic Corporation, which over the next couple of years absorbed it and all of its resources into its own name brand. Today, except for several lines of Sanyo labeled inventory, the company brand no longer exists.

BRAND EQUITY

- At the end of 2010 Sanyo had total revenues of JPY1.59 trillion (US$17.18 billion) with net losses of JPY48.79 billion (US$530 million).
- In 2010 Sanyo had approximately 250 subsidiaries worldwide, with 57 percent of all revenues generated coming from foreign markets.
- In 2010 Sanyo's largest revenue-producing markets were 43 percent from Japan, 29 percent from Asia, 17 percent from North America, and 8 percent from Europe.

At the end of 2010 when Sanyo was still compiling its own annual reports, the company had total revenues of JPY1.59 trillion (US$17.18 billion) with net losses of JPY48.79 billion (US$530 million). At this point Sanyo had approximately 250 subsidiaries and affiliates worldwide. Approximately 43 percent of all revenues were generated domestically, while 57 percent were generated in foreign markets. This included 29 percent of revenues coming from Asia, 17 percent from North America, and about 8 percent from Europe. Sanyo's total assets were valued at JPY1,391 billion (US$14.98 billion).

BRAND AWARENESS

- The Sanyo brand name became particularly well known between the late 1970s and the mid-1990s.
- The "That's Life. Sanyo" jingle is the most commonly remembered tune and ran on television for nearly ten years from the mid-1970s to the early 1980s.
- In a Harris Interactive Poll conducted in December 2012 with nearly 2,000 UK respondents, 89 percent reported recognizing the Sanyo brand and only 6 percent of those familiar with the brand reported a negative association.

Though Sanyo had been a global brand since the early 1950s, its name became particularly ubiquitous between the late 1970s and the mid-1990s. The Sanyo brand label was prominent in most electronics and appliance stores selling televisions, projectors and recording equipment, as well as cameras, batteries and other components. During the late 1970s and early 1980s actress and model Susan Anton was the face and voice of Sanyo products, singing the "That's Life. Sanyo" jingle on a number of television commercials and in magazine advertisements. According to a Harris Interactive Poll conducted in December 2012 from a pool of approximately 2,000 respondents from the UK, 47 percent of the respondents were familiar with the brand, 42 percent had heard of the brand but were not familiar with it, and the remaining 11 percent had not heard of Sanyo. To further break down the consumer awareness responses, of the 937 respondents familiar with the brand, 34 percent reported a positive association to the brand name, 60 percent of respondents were neutral, and only 6 percent reported any sort of negative association with the brand.

BRAND OUTLOOK

- On December 21, 2009, Panasonic purchased a 50.2 percent majority stake in Sanyo for JPY400 billion (US$4.6 billion).
- After 2012 the Sanyo brand name will have been fully taken over by Panasonic and will no longer exist except for several discontinued product lines which will still display the Sanyo name until that stock is sold out.
- Sanyo Taiwan received permission from Panasonic to continue using the Sanyo brand name until 2018, after which its name changes to Sanlux.

As of December 2012 Sanyo is officially no longer an existing company. After prolonged financial problems which had dragged on for several years, Sanyo was on the verge of financial collapse and needed investors for financial backing to keep the company solvent. On December 21, 2009, Panasonic purchased a 50.2 percent majority stake in Sanyo for JPY400 billion (US$4.6 billion), making the company its subsidiary. As of April 2011 Panasonic began the transition of removing the Sanyo brand name from nearly all of its products and locations and replacing it with the Panasonic brand. In one of the few exceptions, the subsidiary Sanyo Taiwan reached an agreement allowing it permission to continue using the Sanyo brand name until 2018, after which point it will change its name to Sanlux.

FURTHER READING

Ku, Helen. "Sanyo Taiwan to Buy Out Parent Firm." *Taipei Times*, January 16, 2013.

Panasonic. "Sanyo Company History." Accessed February 4, 2013. http://panasonic.net/sanyo/corporate/profile/history/history01.html

———. *Sanyo 2010 Annual Report*. Accessed February 4, 2013. http://panasonic.net/sanyo/corporate/ir_library/annualreports.html

"Sanyo Electric Company Ltd." *Notable Corporate Chronologies*. Detroit, MI: Gale, 2012. Accessed February 4, 2013.

"Sanyo Electric Co., Ltd." *International Directory of Company Histories*. Ed. Jay P. Pederson. Vol. 95. Detroit, MI: St. James Press, 2008.

"Sanyo Logos." Logopedia. Accessed February 4, 2013. http://logos.wikia.com/wiki/Sanyo

Tse, Andrea. "Panasonic Buys Sanyo for $4.6 Billion." *The Street*, December 10, 2009.

SAP

BRAND ORIGINS

- SAP was founded in 1972 in Germany by five former IBM employees.

- SAP originally stood for Systemanalyse und Programmentwicklung (Systems Analysis and Program Development); the acronym later stood for Systeme, Anwendungen, und Produkte in der Datenverarbeitung (Systems, Applications, and Products in Data Processing).
- SAP released its hugely successful business software suite, R/2, in 1979 and a subsequent leading-edge product, R/3, in 1992.
- SAP software can be converted into over 35 different languages, including Chinese, Czech, Dutch, Greek, Korean, and Thai.

SAP was founded in 1972 by five German IBM engineers. When a client asked IBM to provide enterprise-wide software to run on its mainframe, the five began writing the program only to be told the assignment was being transferred to another unit. Rather than abandon the project altogether, the five engineers left IBM and founded SAP in Walldorf, near Heidelberg. Even though the company originally took its name from the abbreviation for Systemanalyse und Programmenentwicklung (Systems Analysis and Program Development), SAP eventually came to stand for Systeme, Anwendungen, und Produkte in der Datenverarbeitung (Systems, Applications, and Products in Data Processing).

Without the benefit of loans from banks, venture capitalists, or the German government, SAP began fashioning its software business gradually through the cash flow that was generated by an ever-growing stable of customers. Working at night on borrowed computers to land their first contracts, the colleagues built SAP's client list with regional firms, beginning with a German subsidiary of the global chemical company ICI and later adding major German multinationals such as Siemens and BMW.

Because SAP operated in a corporate computing climate in which business programs were designed to provide only specific, isolated solutions with no relevance to a company's other applications, its concept of a fully integrated software product that could be tailored to any company's business was originally greeted with resistance. However, because SAP produced software, a nonlabor-intensive product, it was able to avoid the labor agreements and high costs that dogged many German manufacturing start-ups. In 1976 SAP declared itself a Gesellschaft mit beschränkter Haftung (GmbH) corporation, and by 1978 it was selling its financial accounting software to 40 corporate customers.

In 1979 SAP released R/2, a mainframe-based, standard business software suite in which integratable modules for accounting, sales and distribution, and production enabled customers to consolidate their financial and operational data into a single database and eliminate costly paperwork and data entry. R/2 soon established itself as the standard for integrated corporate business software in Europe.

Relying on word-of-mouth that filtered through the overseas branches of its German customers, SAP eventually began selling its software outside Europe. With the corporate giants Dow Chemical and Bayer already running R/2, SAP could rely on the fear of obsolescence by its customers' rivals to sell its software to the major competitors in each industry. Among the large corporations that adopted R/2 were du Pont, General Mills, Goodyear Tire and Rubber, Heinz, and Shell Oil, as well as 80 of the 100 largest companies in Germany, such as Hoechst, Daimler Benz, and BASF.

During the mid-1980s IBM announced a new system applications architecture technology in which all IBM operating systems and platforms would be fully harmonized, such that code written for one product would work with any other. Seeing the ramifications of such integratability for its own products, SAP began developing R/3 for use in the decentralized, nonmainframe computing environment known as client-server.

In 1988 SAP GmbH formally converted itself to a publicly traded Aktiengesellschaft (AG) to raise capital for research and development. SAP had established its first operations outside Germany in the mid-1980s, but it was not until the creation of the Swiss-based subsidiary SAP International in the late 1980s that it began the expansion that would make it a truly international player in the global client-server software market.

The company established SAP America in Philadelphia, Pennsylvania, in 1988. Fueled by the release of R/3 in 1992, SAP America soon became SAP AG's most profitable subsidiary. On the strength of R/3's rocketing international sales, SAP traveled from relative anonymity to the business applications vendor of choice for nine of the 10 largest U.S. corporations, one-third of the *Fortune* 500, seven of the 10 largest *Business Week* Global 1000, and 80 percent of the *Fortune* 100 companies in software, computers, peripherals, and semiconductors.

By 2013 SAP was one of the largest global brands in the world, with over 100,000 business clients. Its software can be converted into over 35 different languages, including Chinese, Croatian, Dutch, English, French, Italian, Polish, Portuguese, Russian, Spanish, and Swedish. Additionally, SAP has over 115 subsidiaries with research and development centers in Canada, China, Germany, Hungary, India, and the United States.

BRAND ELEMENTS

- SAP is pronounced by its individual letters rather than as a one-syllable word.
- In 2000 SAP established its current logo, which consists of the company name in white capital letters set in a blue trapezoid.
- SAP has used a myriad of taglines over the years and in 2013 its slogan was "The Best-Run Businesses Run SAP."

According to the company, the acronym SAP stands for Systeme, Anwendungen, und Produkte in der Datenverarbeitung (Systems, Applications, and Products in Data Processing). In spoken form, SAP is pronounced by its individual letters rather than as a one-syllable word.

SAP's logo has evolved over the company's history. Originally, the logo consisted of the company name in bold white capital letters that were fixed at the bottom of a blue square. A blue triangle was positioned adjacent to the square. In 1999 the logo was replaced entirely by new branding, mySAP.com. SAP was still in white on a blue background, but the two shapes were merged into one to form a trapezoid and the rest of the logo appeared in bright, multicolored letters.

The logo was altered for a third time in 2000. SAP dropped the logo branding of mySAP.com and reverted back to using only the company name. To reflect the growing stature of the brand, the company increased the SAP logotype inside the blue trapezoid. The background changed to gradients of blue, evoking both the digital marketplace and innovation. The company also inserted a "smile" in the logo by curving the crossbar in the letter *A*, reflecting the friendly and approachable nature of the brand.

SAP has used a variety of taglines over the years, including "We Can Change Your Business Perspective," "A Better Return on Information," "The City of 'e,'" "The Time of New Management," and "You Can. It Does." In 2013 the company slogan was "The Best-Run Businesses Run SAP."

BRAND IDENTITY

- As global sales increased, SAP's marketing became fragmented and its brand identity became increasingly confused.
- In 2000 SAP began a realignment of its brand within the business software industry by accentuating innovation and the strength of its products.
- SAP has created a consistency across the brand by implementing new branding on brochures, the company website, product packaging, and graphics.

SAP's brand identity has evolved over the course of the company's history. From the outset, SAP delivered a product that was effective and reliable. As sales outside of Germany rapidly increased, the brand expression became blurred, with inconsistent branding occurring in each sales market. Even as a global market leader in enterprise software, SAP found itself coming from behind the competition in Internet products and sales. The perception among consumers and critics was that SAP was unable to remain cutting-edge and that the company was stumbling. A lack of clear brand identity was damaging the reputation of the company.

A realignment of SAP's brand identity in 1999 sought to capitalize on a new suite of software products that were now designed for the Internet. The SAP logo was replaced by the mySAP.com logo on all branded products, including the company website, brochures, and product packaging. The identity of SAP became that of a single product.

In 2000 SAP began the arduous task of repositioning itself once again within the business software industry. The company sought to make itself relevant to consumers by highlighting the quality of products that made it a leader in every market. A new company logo, taglines, and branding throughout all of SAP's products were implemented to create consistency across the brand.

SAP has revolutionized the business marketplace by using technology to boost business productivity and ultimately increase profitability for its customers. SAP software products are an essential factor to the success of a myriad of businesses around the globe. Through a newly sharpened marketing focus, the company has transformed its brand identity from being reliable but stodgy to being a dominant leader once again, whose products are at the forefront of innovation and technology. SAP reminds consumers that it has not only built itself into an enterprise software leader but also that it has become a pioneer in the blistering-fast domain of Internet software and sales.

BRAND STRATEGY

- SAP offers over 1,200 software products that are designed to help other companies run more efficiently.

- Besides licensing its software products, SAP offers consulting and training for its business systems as well as maintenance programs.
- As part of its brand strategy, SAP invests billions of dollars into research and development of new software and technology.

SAP's brand strategy focuses on the creation of software that enables other businesses to run effectively. It offers more than 1,200 software products that help companies manage their sales, customers, costs, inventory, and staff. Its core software products fall under the category of enterprise resource planning, which aims to help businesses run their day-to-day operations. When daily operations run at peak performance, companies are able to maximize profits. Diverse activities for a single business are integrated using the SAP brand and are offered under the classifications of business applications, database and technology, analytics, cloud, and mobile. SAP provides businesses support in various operations, including finance, information technology, human resources, marketing, sales, sustainability, supply chain, procurement, and manufacturing.

The brand offers over 20 industry-specific software products, including packages for retail, utilities, public sector, telecommunications, aerospace, and health care. It also sells an extensive range of software for large companies, including asset management, risk and compliance, warehouse management, human resource management, and business intelligence.

Another aspect of SAP's brand strategy concentrates on developing strategic partnerships throughout the computer industry. The company has cooperated with computer manufacturers such as Compaq and IBM in tailoring SAP products to new hardware developments. By participating with other software vendors in industry-wide initiatives to determine standards for new technologies, SAP is demonstrating its willingness to cooperate with potential competitors to ensure the continued functionality and influence of its products.

A final aspect of the company's brand strategy centers on research and development. In this regard, the brand has spent billions of dollars, and the direct result is that it has achieved expansion of the brand primarily through its product offerings and related services. In recent years SAP has begun acquiring companies that can be integrated into the SAP portfolio and that can offer specific technologies and capabilities for its customers.

BRAND EQUITY

- In 2012 SAP was ranked 227th in *Forbes* "Global 2000," with a market value of US$88.1 billion.
- Interbrand placed SAP at number 25, with a brand value of US$15.6 billion, in its rankings of the "Best Global Brands 2012."

- In 2012 Brand Finance ranked SAP ninth in its rankings of the "German Top 30," with a brand value of EUR6.8 billion.

In its listing of "The World's Most Powerful Brands" for 2012, *Forbes* ranked SAP 31st, with a brand value of US$15.3 billion. *Forbes* also ranked SAP 227th in its "Global 2000" list, with a market value of US$88.1 billion. That same year the European Brand Institute ranked SAP 88th in the "Top 100 Brand Corporations Worldwide," with a brand value of EUR10.7 billion. The *Financial Times* ranked SAP sixth in its "World's Most Valuable Technology Brands" for 2012.

With a brand value of US$15.6 billion, SAP was ranked 25th in Interbrand's list of the best global brands for 2012. Brand Finance placed SAP at number 96 in its 2012 "Global 500" list, with a brand value of US$9 billion, and at number nine in the "German Top 30" list, with a brand value of EUR6.8 billion. Millward Brown's "Brandz Top 100 Brand Ranking" ranked SAP at 22nd, with a brand value of US$25.7 billion in 2012.

BRAND AWARENESS

- SAP operates in over 120 countries in Europe, North American, the Middle East, Africa, Asia, Japan, Australia, and India.
- The United States is SAP's largest market, accounting for nearly 26 percent of group sales.
- In 2012 SAP held a 22 percent market share worldwide in enterprise management software.

As a world leader in enterprise software, the SAP brand is widely recognized around the globe. SAP's operational markets include over 120 countries in Europe, the Middle East, Africa, Asia, Japan, Australia, and India. The United States is SAP's largest market, at nearly 26 percent of group sales. Germany remains a prominent market as well, at nearly 16.5 percent. Europe, the Middle East, and Africa combine to account for 32 percent of group sales.

In 2011 SAP held a 25.5 percent market share worldwide of the enterprise resource planning (ERP) market. In 2012 SAP slipped, but still held a 22 percent market share in the ERP market, with arch rival Oracle claiming a 15 percent market share.

BRAND OUTLOOK

- SAP is one of the largest cloud computing companies.

- To increase market share, SAP is targeting small and medium-sized business consumers who view the brand as reliable but expensive and unwieldy.
- SAP is expanding into cloud computing technology to capitalize on the expanding use of smartphones and tablet computers by consumers.

Traditionally, SAP has courted large businesses, but in recent years it has begun targeting the small and medium enterprise (SME) segment as a way to increase market share. Brand awareness is already high among midsized business consumers, who view SAP as the dominant leader in enterprise resource planning software, with the reliability and expertise that personifies the brand. However, SAP is also viewed as too expensive and too cumbersome to be utilized by smaller companies. SAP's challenge is to become more accessible to the SME segment.

With the recent acquisition of two cloud computing businesses, SAP has become one of the largest cloud computing companies. Cloud computing allows companies to run applications online, rather than installing the software on computers located in data centers. Cloud computing is seen as the future of enterprise software due to the proliferation of tablet computers and smartphones. SAP hopes to become profitable in this new segment by 2015 and that its extension into the mobile and cloud-computing markets will help it consolidate its leading position in the business management software industry.

FURTHER READING

Greenbaum, Joshua. "SAP Has Edge in Battle with Oracle." Datamation, December 30, 2005. Accessed January 14, 2013. http://www.datamation.com/columns/entad/article.php/3574396/SAP-has-Edge-in-Battle-with-Oracle.htm.

Krigsman, Michale. "ERP Implementation Benchmark: Comparing SAP, Oracle, and Microsoft." ZDNet, July 16, 2012. Accessed February 22, 2013. http://www.zdnet.com/erp-implementation-benchmark-comparing-sap-oracle-and-microsoft-7000000971.

"Market Awareness Is SAP's Biggest SME Challenge." Tigris Technology Solutions, December 13, 2010. Accessed January 14, 2013. http://www.tigristech.com/archives/market-awareness-is-saps-biggest-sme-challenge-partners.

SAP. "2011 Annual Report." Accessed January 14, 2013. http://www.sap.com/corporate-en/investors/reports/annualreport/2011/pdf/SAP-2011-Annual-Report.pdf.

"SAP AG." *International Directory of Company Histories*. Ed. Jay P. Pederson. Vol. 137. Detroit, MI: St. James Press, 2012.

Schultes, Renee. "SAP's Journey into the Clouds." *Wall Street Journal*, October 24, 2012.

Woods, Dan. "How SAP Is Betting Its Growth on Partnerships." *Forbes*, September 12, 2011.

SBERBANK

BRAND ORIGINS

- Sberbank originated in 1841, when the czar of Russia ordered the national treasuries to accept savings deposits from citizens.
- The national bank was the only option for savings accounts under the centralized control of the Soviet Union.
- Sberbank became a separate financial institution in the 1980s, providing savings and loan services to average citizens.
- Sberbank was privatized in the 1990s but remained largely under the control of the Russian government.
- The Sberbank brand expanded to several nearby European countries, beginning with Kazakhstan in 2006, but remains primarily Russian.

Sberbank of Russia is one of the oldest financial brands in that country. Its origin can be traced to 1841 when Emperor Nikolai I ordered the treasury houses in Moscow and St. Petersburg to open offices where the general public could deposit money in the safekeeping of a bank. After the State Bank of Russia (also known as Gosbank) was established in 1860 the savings institutions were placed under its jurisdiction. By 1895 there were 4,000 branch offices in urban and rural areas.

More than other European countries, Russia used the state bank to manage the economy. Gosbank funded railroads, manufacturing plants, war enterprises, and aristocratic land ownership in a way that foreshadowed the central command of the Soviet Union. After the Bolsheviks seized control of Russia in 1917, commercial banks were nationalized, the economy collapsed, the private savings system failed, and the country returned briefly to the barter system. In 1923, Gosbank was resurrected as the State Bank of the USSR. The savings banks were restored, growing to 42,000 branches in the 1950s and 79,000 in the 1980s. However, the Soviet Union had a floundering economy: government funds were drained by inefficiency and military expenditures. During the economic stagnation of 1970-85, citizens brought their money to Gosbank because they had no other option.

In the 1980s, under the leadership of Mikhail Gorbachev, the banking system was reorganized. Gosbank became a central regulatory institution, while five separate banks were created to serve specific purposes, such as foreign trade and loans to industry. One of those firms was Sberbank, responsible for operating a savings and loan system for average citizens. At this time the government also allowed the founding of commercial and cooperative banks that would compete with the Sberbank brand, although at first they attracted only a few depositors.

During the collapse of the Soviet Union in the early 1990s, Sberbank was privatized as a joint stock company of about 75 regional banks. The government-operated Russian Central Bank soon acquired a majority stake in Sberbank but was never allowed to assume full command of the business. By 2005 the company was aiming to become one of the top 20 banks in the world. Despite global economic turmoil, the brand expanded into nearby Kazakhstan in 2006 and Ukraine in 2007, followed by Belarus and Germany. In 2012, Sberbank had 257,000 employees and was operating more than 20,000 branches and offices across a wide geographic area.

BRAND ELEMENTS

- The Sberbank logo is a solid green circle with white wedges beside the words "Sberbank" and "By your side."
- Another version of the logo included the words "Established in 1841."
- Sberbank is a shortened version of the words "savings bank" in Russian.

The Sberbank logo is a solid green circle with the upper half covered by several white wedges that are canted to the left and thus resemble checkmarks. To the right is the name "Sberbank," and in smaller letters below is the slogan "By your side." Before 2009 the logo read "Sberbank Rossii," with no slogan. In another version the brand name was positioned below the words "Established in 1841." On the company's bright green automated teller machines the logo is prominently displayed in white—simply the brand name below the graphic circle.

Sberbank is a contraction of the words "savings bank" in Russian. The brand name was launched in 1988 when the State Bank of Russia (also known as Gosbank) was reorganized and its savings outlets became the Bank of Labor Savings and Lending for the Population (also known as Sberbank of the USSR). In 1991 the name was changed to the Joint-Stock Commercial Savings Bank of the Russian Federation. The firm is also known as Sberbank of Russia, Sberbank Rossii OAO, the Savings Bank of the Russian Federation, Sberbank Rossiyskoy Federatsii, and simply Sberbank.

BRAND IDENTITY

- Sberbank is an established brand that earns a small profit while helping the Russian government maintain social order.
- For decades the brand has remained competitive by offering stability during times of economic turbulence.
- Although dependable, the brand has been associated with the inefficient, slow bureaucracy of the USSR.
- Sberbank has attempted to improve its brand image by promising integrity, responsibility, professionalism, versatility, friendliness, and respect for tradition.

Sberbank is a pillar of the Russian national economy, an old, well-established brand that generates relatively small revenues while helping the government maintain social stability. During its long history, it became known for dependability, but it was also associated with the cumbersome, often unfriendly bureaucracy of the USSR. In recent years the company has worked to change the brand image, promising to conduct its business with friendliness, integrity, prudence, responsibility, professionalism, and respect for tradition. The organization also wants to be perceived as a modern and versatile financial institution, serving all types of customers and beginning to expand internationally. Above all Sberbank intends to be the brand that people can trust to safeguard their money.

The fact that Sberbank holds a monopoly in certain areas has added to its imposing reputation. Because the government guarantees deposits at Sberbank only, customers have remained confident in the brand despite economic turbulence over the years. When newer, smaller banks failed and citizens' savings became nearly worthless, many depositors returned to the well-established brand that survived each crisis.

Throughout the past two decades, Sberbank has modernized its brand image by offering new technology and services and by remodeling some of its buildings with marble and glass to dispel their reputation for dinginess. In partnership with the state, Sberbank contributes to socially and environmentally responsible pursuits such as education, science, culture, and sports to encourage the development of Russia and its people.

BRAND STRATEGY

- For many years, Sberbank faced little or no competition, because Russia's government did not allow it.
- Under Soviet rule, Sberbank was generally managed by regional bureaucrats who failed to coordinate with each other.
- Competition from other banks in the early 1990s initially reduced Sberbank's market share but eventually prompted a substantial, modern rebranding.

As a brand owned by the government of Russia, Sberbank faced little or no competition for many years. Therefore, its basic method of operation was to safeguard money and to encourage clients to use the bank's services. The enterprise grew slowly in its first two decades because most of country's population was made up of serfs, who had little wealth. After serfdom was abolished in 1861, savings accounts became more widespread. When citizens deposited their earnings in the bank, the czars of Russia used that money to fund industries, wars, and other ventures as they saw fit. This destabilized the national currency and caused a loss of trust in the brand.

Later, under communist rule, the bank functioned as an extension of the government: printing money, providing credit for industries and savings accounts for individuals, and managing federal money transfers and accounting. The bank was partitioned into 17 regional offices, each of which followed its own procedures and did not communicate much with the others. The brand had a monopoly: citizens had no choice but to use the state bank.

Sberbank began to encounter its first real competition in the late 1980s when the government permitted the founding of commercial and cooperative banks. Sberbank was privatized in the early 1990s and lost market share to new rivals offering better interest rates, but then it regained some clients after rival banks failed. Unlike its competitors, Sberbank was saddled with unprofitable operations, such as processing payments for public utilities and operating branches in provinces served by no other bank.

Within the past decade, the brand has been transformed considerably as the firm has become a universal commercial bank with regional offices following standard, modern procedures established by the central headquarters. The bank offers a full range of savings, investment, and lending services. In a country where cash is still used for 96 percent of transactions, Sberbank introduced credit cards in 2009. Online banking and other technology have also been part of the transformation, along with a friendlier, customer-oriented approach. In 2009, as part of its rebranding effort, the company embarked on a large-scale plan titled "Sberbank Development Strategy until 2014," which was intended to increase efficiency, improve customer service, incorporate the latest technology, and develop international operations, especially within the Commonwealth of Independent States.

The firm operates subsidiary banks in Kazakhstan, Ukraine, and Belarus; offices in Germany and China; and a branch in India. The company's international ventures benefit from partnerships and memberships in such organizations as the International Chamber of Commerce, the International Securities Market Association, the International Bank Security Association, and the U.S.-Russia Business Council. In recent years Sberbank has been moving toward becoming one of the most important brands throughout Europe.

BRAND EQUITY

- Sberbank was Russia's top bank in July 2012, with US$26.9 billion of tier 1 capital.
- As of April 2012, Sberbank had annual sales of US$31.8 billion and a company market value of US$74 billion.
- Brand Finance calculated Sberbank's brand value at US$10.78 billion in January 2012.
- Sberbank had a brand rating of AA+ in 2011 and 2012.

In July 2012, according to the *Banker* magazine, Sberbank was the leading bank in Russia, with US$26.9 billion of tier 1 capital, down from US$29.5 billion in 2011. VTB Bank was second, with US$13 billion in 2012, down from US$18 billion in 2011.

Forbes calculated that, as of April 2012, Sberbank had annual sales of US$31.8 billion, assets of US$282.4 billion, and a company market value of US$74 billion. *Forbes* ranked Sberbank at number 90 on its 2011 list of the world's leading companies.

In 2012, Millward Brown valued the brand at US$10.65 billion, up from US$8.53 billion in 2011, and placed Sberbank at number 74 on its BrandZ list of the most valuable brands in the world.

Brand Finance calculated the brand value at US$10.78 billion at the start of 2012, down from US$12.0 billion in 2011. On Brand Finance's Global 500 list of the world's top companies, Sberbank ranked 78th in 2012, down from 65th in 2011 but up from 260th in 2008. On Brand Finance's Banking 500 list, Sberbank ranked 17th in 2012, up from 19th in 2011 and 56th in 2008. Sberbank had a brand rating of AA+ in 2011 and 2012.

In January 2011, Sberbank was accepting more deposits than any other bank in Russia, with 47.9 percent of retail deposits. Sberbank is also the largest credit organization both in Russia and the Commonwealth of Independent States.

BRAND AWARENESS

- Most Russians are familiar with the Sberbank brand, while most people outside Russia are not.
- In 2011, among banks in Central and Eastern Europe, Sberbank was named the best overall and the ninth safest.
- Sberbank was ranked 20th among the strongest banks in the world in 2011.

The Sberbank brand has nearly universal awareness within Russia but is not well known internationally. During the economic turbulence of the early 1990s, nearly 90 percent of citizens with savings accounts chose Sberbank, even though it paid low interest rates, because it was a well-known brand guaranteed by the government. When other banks began offering higher interest rates, some customers were lured away, and Sberbank's share of the individual savings market shrank to 60 percent, but a financial crisis in 1995 sent people back to Sberbank, raising its market share to 70 percent as consumers chose familiarity and stability over profit.

In 2011, the *Banker* magazine cited Sberbank as the best bank in Central and Eastern Europe. *Global Finance* ranked Sberbank as the ninth-safest bank in Central and Eastern Europe, based on total assets and long-term credit ratings from Moody's, Standard & Poor's, and Fitch. *Bloomberg Markets* magazine placed Sberbank at number 20 on its list of the world's top 20 strongest banks. Kommersant-Renaissance named Herman Gref, CEO and chairman of Sberbank's management board, as businessman of the year.

BRAND OUTLOOK

- Foreign bankers see great opportunities in Russia but hesitate to invest there because the venture would present serious risks.
- The Sberbank brand became more daunting to competitors after the firm merged with Troika Dialog to create an enormous company.
- While primary rival VTB Capital has been expanding internationally, the Sberbank brand has focused more on clients within Russia.
- In 2012 the Russian government began the process of selling part of its share in Sberbank.

Although analysts predict that investment banks could reap huge profits in Russia, many international firms hesitate to pursue the opportunity because a serious default happened there in 1998. Foreign competitors have also been hindered by a widespread economic recession that began in Europe in 2008 and then spread to the United States and beyond. In January 2012, Sberbank merged with Troika Dialog, an independent corporate finance house, creating such an enormous investment bank that foreign competitors wondered if they should retreat from Russia.

On the domestic front, rival VTB Capital has expanded aggressively and in 2011 became the top-ranked investment bank in Russia in terms of revenues. VTB Capital hired hundreds of experienced executives away from companies in London and other locations, and it has been establishing operations in China and the Middle East.

Meanwhile, taking a more conservative path, Sberbank hired an executive from Bank of America Merrill Lynch to manage its investment bank segment, with a strong focus on domestic clients in Russia and the Commonwealth of Independent States. In 2011 the brand's share of the trade finance market increased significantly in Belarus, Ukraine, and Kazakhstan. The recent acquisitions of Volksbank International AG (based in Austria) and DenizBank (based in Turkey), along with their subsidiaries in neighboring countries, have expanded the brand's European presence. The company has also begun to establish its brand in Germany, India, and China. Sberbank has announced that by 2014 it expects to generate about 5 to 7 percent of its net income from sources outside Russia.

In September 2012 the government of Russia began the process of selling about 7.6 percent of its share in Sberbank, a move designed to increase private ownership of the business.

FURTHER READING

"Abacus to ATM; Russian banking." *Economist,* June 23, 2012. *General OneFile.* Accessed October 16, 2012. http://go.galegroup.com/ps/i.do?id=GALE%7CA293899658&v=2.1&u=itsbtrial&it=r&p=ITOF&sw=w.

"Banks walk Russian tightrope as Sberbank builds." *Euroweek,* February 3, 2012. *General OneFile.* Accessed October 16, 2012. http://go.galegroup.com/ps/i.do?id=GALE%7CA284423184&v=2.1&u=itsbtrial&it=r&p=ITOF&sw=w.

Brand Finance. "Global 500 2012." *Brandirectory.* Accessed October 15, 2012. http://brandirectory.com/league_tables/table/global-500-2012.

Brand Finance. "Profile: Sberbank." *Brandirectory.* Accessed October 15, 2012. http://brandirectory.com/profile/sberbank.

"Company Profile, Sberbank Joint Stock Co." *Gale Business Insights Online Collection,* 2012. *Business Insights: Essentials.* Accessed October 17, 2012. http://bi.galegroup.com/essentials/company/1244924?u=itsbtrial.

"Emerging Europe: Sberbank takes a breather after DenizBank deal." *Euromoney,* July 2012. *General OneFile.* Accessed October 16, 2012. http://go.galegroup.com/ps/i.do?id=GALE%7CA299392261&v=2.1&u=itsbtrial&it=r&p=ITOF&sw=w.

Lorenz, Sarah Ruth, and Christina M. Stansell. "Sberbank." *International Directory of Company Histories.* Ed. Tina Grant. Vol. 138. Detroit: St. James Press, 2013. *Business Insights: Essentials.* Accessed October 16, 2012. http://bi.galegroup.com/essentials/article/GALE%7CCX2577700086/56dc0a4cbff1dd0c1e105778174c5576?u=itsbtrial.

"Sberbank adds sparkle to somnolent banking sector." *Euromoney,* May 2012. *General OneFile.* Accessed October 16, 2012. http://go.galegroup.com/ps/i.do?id=GALE%7CA291625814&v=2.1&u=itsbtrial&it=r&p=ITOF&sw=w.

"Top 1000 world banks: Central & Eastern Europe—CEE sees capital fall." *Banker,* July 1, 2012. *General OneFile.* Accessed October 16, 2012. http://go.galegroup.com/ps/i.do?id=GALE%7CA295461458&v=2.1&u=itsbtrial&it=r&p=ITOF&sw=w.

"The World's Biggest Public Companies 2011." *Forbes.* Accessed October 12, 2012. http://www.forbes.com/lists/2012/18/global2000_2011.html.

SCHNEIDER ELECTRIC

———◆———

AT A GLANCE

Brand Synopsis: Among the world's top providers of energy management solutions, Schneider Electric has worked to strengthen brand recognition by consolidating its many arms under the Schneider Electric name.

Parent Company: Schneider Electric SA

35 rue Joseph Monier

92500 Rueil Malmaison

France

http://www.schneider-electric.com

Sector: Industrials

Industry Group: Capital Goods

Performance: *Market Share*—15.8% of electronic components, worldwide (2011). *Sales*—EUR $27.62 billion (US$37.17 billion) (2011).

Principal Competitors: ABB, Ltd.; Siemens; Furukawa Electric

BRAND ORIGINS

- Adolphe and Eugène Schneider formed Schneider Frères & Cie. in 1836 after they took over the foundries and mines in Creusot, France.
- The Schneiders' original operations were in machinery and steel production; they entered into the electricity industry in the early 1900s.

- A 20-year period of aggressive acquisitions and divestitures produced Schneider Electric SA, a company focused solely on electrical holdings, by 1999.

In 1836 two brothers, Adolphe and Eugène Schneider, took over the foundries, mines, and forges in Creusot, France. This event marked the beginning of Schneider Electric, then named Schneider Frères & Cie. Although its roots were in complex industrial mechanisms, like the building of France's first steam locomotive, followed by steel manufacturing, the company got involved producing electrical equipment by the early 1900s. Schneider did well until World War II, when the Germans overran most of its factories. By the time the war was over, these factories were bombed or obsolete. However, Charles Schneider, the last family member to run the company, led a recovery effort that saved it. He turned the firm into a holdings company that eventually operated subsidiaries in civil and electrical engineering, manufacturing, and construction.

Throughout the second half of the 19th century, Schneider went through a number of major reorganizations: a merging with another family-run industrial group, Empain, from the 1960s through 1980, a forced restructuring by the socialist government in 1981, and then additional reorganization between the years 1981-87 that transformed the company from a complex family financial trust with many diverse interests to a leading international industrial group named Schneider SA. As a result of this reorganization Schneider divested all of its machinery, steel, and telecommunications operations. What remained were electric-power plants and power-distribution systems, building and civil-engineering projects, industrial infrastructure, and a wide variety of industrial electronics systems. For the next 10 years, the company aggressively acquired many companies, and divested more, to achieve its goal: to eventually reduce itself to its electrical holdings alone.

By 1997 the group was successfully focused on electrical equipment and industrial control and automation products. By 1999 the group had changed its name to Schneider Electric S.A. and begun to sell all its acquired groups with their original brand names under Schneider Electric. Moving into the new century with a continued international acquisition-growth strategy, Schneider Electric doubled its revenues between 2002 and 2008, with 32 percent of sales coming from emerging global economies like South Korea and Russia. Additionally, Schneider began to focus on new technology and energy-efficiency products. The global recession in 2009, however, led to a temporary freeze on acquisitions, streamlining of operations, and condensing its array of brands from 120 into just 10 by 2011. These efforts were rewarded as the company produced record high sales of over EUR 22 billion (US$29 billion) in 2011.

BRAND ELEMENTS

- Schneider Electric's logo originated concurrently with the renaming of the company to Schneider Electric S.A. to place emphasis on its expertise in electricity.
- The green color of the logo signifies Schneider Electric's connection to nature and its font helps to portray the company's straightforward communication.
- The company's logo and tagline are currently being used to unify and strengthen the Schneider Electric corporate brand.

In May 1999, after years of acquisitions and divestitures, Schneider S.A. renamed its company Schneider Electric S.A. to emphasize its expertise in electricity. At this time the company introduced a new logo. The trademarked logo is typically displayed in one of three green colors to show the company's connection to nature, according to the company's 2008 graphic standards. There are also white/green and black variations. The logo and all company literature are printed in "SE Optimist" font to give the information an open and friendly feel. The Schneider name is set in bolded font above the word "electric," and between the two words is an "s" within an oval. While the company name emphasizes the company's expertise in electricity, the larger size and boldness of the name are designed to place importance on its long and rich business history.

Moreover, since 2008, the company has used the Schneider Electric logo as an important tool to help align its most popular brands under the corporate brand.

Following the mission of their trademarked taglines, "The Global Specialist in Energy Management" and "Make the Most of Your Energy," the group hopes to unify the identity of its brand as a one-stop shop for energy solutions. According to the U.S. version of the company's website, Schneider Electric has migrated the Telemecanique and Merlin Gerin products to the corporate brand and logo to help strengthen the Schneider Electric brand and present one face to its customers. Moreover, the brand names that remain separate have "by Schneider Electric" following their names to reinforce the unity of the line extensions.

BRAND IDENTITY

- Schneider Electric strives to be the global specialist in energy management that helps people make the most of their energy.
- Schneider Electric hopes to identify its brand as one that employs "energy optimists" who help solve the world's energy crisis.
- Four core values—passion, openness, straightforwardness, and efficiency—help guide Schneider Electric's brand identity.

Schneider Electric strives to be the global specialist in energy management. With operations in more than 100 countries, Schneider Electric markets itself as an integrated energy solutions firm that helps people make the most of their energy by offering products that are safe, reliable, efficient, productive, and green. According to its 2008 brand platform report, Schneider Electric hopes to indentify itself as a company of energy optimists who can find solutions that fulfill people's true potential while reducing the impact on the environment.

To do this successfully, Schneider Electric promotes four core values that guide its operations. The company promises to be passionate about its business and customers, open to new ideas and diverse people, straightforward about commitments and information, and efficient in its performance. These values are meant to inspire trust in Schneider Electric customers and ensure sustainable growth for the company.

BRAND STRATEGY

- Schneider Electric implements a company program every two to three years that outlines the short- and long-term business and brand strategies.
- The success of Schneider Electric's strategic programs led the company to double in size and revenue between 2003 and 2008.
- By 2011 Schneider Electric had merged 120 brands into just 10 and launched its first global marketing campaign.

Since the time that Schneider emerged as Schneider Electric in 1999, the firm introduced short-term company programs every two years that were designed to grow the company. According to the company website, the first such program, 2000+, supported a strategy of faster, more competitive growth that pushed back the limits of products and services and geographic and cultural limits. NEW 2004, implemented in 2002-04, focused on growth and efficiency, the establishment of a dedicated sustainable development department, and the publication of a Principles of Responsibility statement. For the years 2005-08, New2, which built upon the successes of NEW, was implemented to drive change by reorganizing Schneider's management. These programs pushed Schneider Electric to new levels of success, as the company doubled in size between 2003 and 2008 and sales jumped from EUR 9.06 billion (US$12.19 billion) in 2002 to EUR 18.3 billion (US$24.63 billion) in 2008.

Continuing on the success of these types of short-term programs, Schneider made further progress from 2009 to 2011 under the ONE program. This program focused on finding ways to boost customer satisfaction with the brand and on streamlining and unifying the brand as well as extending it to new markets. Through the streamlining effort, 120 brands were merged into just 10 by 2011, the same year in which the company launched its first-ever global marketing campaign. In aligning the company's core brands under the Schneider Electric brand, the company sought to strengthen its image as a market leader by showing confidence in the brands it had invested in over the years. According to *Air Conditioning, Heating & Refrigeration News,* this "migration to one company under Schneider Electric will offer customers increased access to a wider range of integrated solutions."

BRAND EQUITY

- Schneider Electric's financial success has grown significantly, earning them record sales of EUR 27.62 billion (US$37.17 billion) in 2011.
- Schneider Electric is a leading global provider of low-voltage power, medium-voltage power and automation in the infrastructure industry, and critical power and cooling in the IT industry.
- In 2012, Brand Finance ranked Schneider Electric 305th on its Global 500 list, with a brand value of US$3.5 million.

Schneider Electric produced record-high sales of EUR 27.62 billion (US$37.17 billion) in 2011 partly because of the company's strategic program, ONE. The program increased efficiency, led to improvements in acquisitions and the development of products and solutions, and unified operations and marketing efforts under the Schneider brand. These improvements helped Schneider Electric reach the number-one position in three of the five markets in which it operates: low voltage in the power industry, medium voltage and automation in the infrastructure industry, and critical power and cooling in the IT industry. These leading positions, along with a new focus on the corporate brand, enabled Schneider Electric to claim 305th place on Brand Finance's Global 500 list in 2012, with a brand value of US$3.5 billion.

BRAND AWARENESS

- Schneider Electric's brand awareness is difficult to measure, as it has acquired more than 120 brands during the last 25 years.
- The 2009 ONE initiative was designed to raise brand awareness by consolidating most brands under the Schneider Electric name.
- In 2011 Schneider Electric launched its first-ever global advertising campaign to further boost the corporate brand.

Because Schneider Electric acquired more than 120 brands during the past 25 years, brand awareness is difficult to measure. In 2009 the company began the ONE initiative, under which it sought to strengthen its corporate identity and unify most of its brands under the corporate name. According to a 2008 company newsletter, the recognition of the Schneider Electric name surpassed its historical brands in most countries; thus, unifying these brands under the corporate brand was essential to gaining additional brand awareness throughout the world as a trusted solutions provider.

In order to further boost brand awareness and push the identification of the corporate brand, Schneider Electric launched its first-ever integrated, global advertising campaign in 2011. According to the Schneider website, the message of the campaign was about "bringing together the broad scope of solutions and services in a single value proposition: 'You Deserve an Efficient Enterprise!'" The results were impressive gains in web impact, revenue opportunities, and new customer acquisition. In addition to record sales in 2011, awareness of the brand appeared to be taking off globally.

BRAND OUTLOOK

- Schneider Electric feels that it is perfectly positioned to capitalize on the world's growing need for energy.
- Schneider Electric has taken leading positions in three of its five markets.
- Using the Planet & Society Barometer, Schneider Electric ensures the success of its brand by measuring its level of corporate responsibility.
- Schneider Electric has positioned itself to grow in the coming years by implementing new technologies.

According to most analysts, the growing population, along with climate change, will cause energy consumption to grow at an alarming pace over the next 25 years. In its annual report Schneider Electric has said it is "perfectly positioned to take advantage of growth opportunities linked to the energy challenges facing the planet and to the development of emerging economies." The company's research and development of new energy products, like the Smart Grid, and its ability to seize new business opportunities by installing these technologies, gives Schneider Electric's brand a promising future. In fact, the company has already begun to capitalize on these activities. The markets in which Schneider Electric occupies a number-one or number-two position globally accounted for more than 90 percent of its revenue in 2011, compared with 50 percent in 2000, according to its annual report.

Additionally, the company's ability to aggressively acquire leading brands within the electricity industry has given Schneider Electric a vast portfolio of products and energy solutions to help achieve its business objectives. Continuing to place those brands under its corporate identity will help the company realize its mission of becoming the global specialist in energy management. Moreover, the company's efforts in environmental and social responsibility give the brand an impressive edge. Through their Planet & Society Barometer the company directly monitors the group's actions. They seek to improve their responsiveness to the environment through energy conservation and low emissions and to their people by improving safety, employee training, and social development in emerging markets.

FURTHER READING

Brand Finance. "Global 500 2012." *Brandirectory.* Accessed November 7, 2012. http://brandirectory.com/profile/gazprom.

Salamie, David E. "Schneider Electric SA." *International Directory of Company Histories.* Ed. Jay P. Pederson. Vol. 108. Detroit: St. James Press, 2010. *Gale Virtual Reference Library.* Accessed November 15, 2012. http://go.galegroup.com/ps/i.do?id=GALE percent7CCX1302600087&v=2.1&u=itsbtrial&it=r&p=GVRL&sw=w.

Schneider Electric. "Brand Migration Story." *Distributor,* August 2008: Corporate Section. Accessed November 18, 2012. http://www.magnonclients.com/schneider-e-newletter/distribution/brand-migration-story.html.

Schneider Electric. "Registration Document 2011: Financial and Sustainable Development Annual Report." Accessed November 17, 2012. http://www2.schneider-electriccom/documents/presentation/en/local/2012/03/schneider_electric_annual-report-2011.pdf.

Schneider Electric. "The Story to Tell: Schneider Electric Brand Platform 2008." Accessed November 17, 2012. http://www.hotlinet.schneider-electric.com/download/1-The_story_to_tell.pdf.

"Schneider Electric Named to 2011 InformationWeek 500 List of Top Technology Innovators Across America." *Entertainment Close-up,* September 24, 2011. *General OneFile.* Accessed November 17, 2012. http://go.galegroup.com/ps/i.do?id=GALE%7CA267926913&v=2.1&u=itsbtrial&it=r&p=ITOF&sw=w.

"TAC to become Schneider Electric." *Air Conditioning, Heating & Refrigeration News,* July 27, 2009. *General OneFile.* Accessed November 17, 2012. http://go.galegroup.com/ps/i.do?id=GALE percent7CA206535594&v=2.1&u=itsbtrial&it=r&p=GPS&sw=w.

"Top Electronic Component Firms Worldwide, 2011." *Market Share Reporter.* Detroit: Gale, 2012. *Business Insights: Essentials.* Accessed November 15, 2012. http://bi.galegroup.com/essentials/article/GALE|I2502042559/9d14c9b17366ae14a5dcf2289f488735?u=itsbtrial.

SCHWARZKOPF

—■—

AT A GLANCE

—■—

Brand Synopsis: Focused on fashionable and quality hair care at all levels, Schwarzkopf ranks third in the world in sales in the global hair salon business.

Parent Company: Henkel AG & Co. KGaA

Henkelstrasse 67, 40191 Düsseldorf,

Germany

http://www.henkel.com

Sector: Consumer Staples

Industry Group: Household & Personal Products

Performance: *Market share*—11% (2010). *Sales*—US$4.25 billion (2010).

Principal Competitors: L'Oréal; Procter & Gamble; Unilever; Redken; Goldwell

BRAND ORIGINS

- Hans Schwarzkopf began creating products for hair care in 1903.
- Schwarzkopf's early products included a powder that mixed with water to make shampoo, the first liquid shampoo, and the first non-alkaline shampoo.
- The Schwarzkopf method, drafted in 1972, addressed all aspects of hair care: consultation, technology, products, and training.

- After its acquisition by Henkel in 1995, Schwarzkopf became a leading European supplier of hair cosmetics.

In 1898 chemist Hans Schwarzkopf opened a drugstore in Berlin, and five years later he devised a powder that dissolved in water to create shampoo. The product was less oily and less expensive than shampoos on the market at the time. By 1904 all drugstores in Berlin carried the product, and expansion into Holland and Russia soon followed.

Schwarzkopf created a liquid shampoo in 1927, and the product was an instant success. He went on to open the first hairdresser training center, the Schwarzkopf Institute for Hair Hygiene. In 1933, Schwarzkopf created Onakali, the first non-alkaline shampoo on the market, and in 1947 he introduced the first cold permanent wave to the German market as well as Poly Color, the first home hair-coloring product.

Schwarzkopf's first hairspray, Taft, was introduced in 1951, inspiring popular usage of the verb "taften," meaning "to spray with hairspray." Igora Royal was added to Schwarzkopf's top professional coloring range in 1960, and it continues to perform well among salon products today. In 1969, Schwarzkopf introduced Igora Toning, the first color mousse used in European salons. It made a broader range of colors available to hair stylists and their clients.

In 1960, Schwarzkopf introduced Poly Color's first home permanent wave, and in 1962 the company expanded its Poly Hair Cosmetics line to include products in all market segments of the hair product industry, including colorants, perms, hair care, and hair treatment.

The Schwarzkopf method, drafted in 1972, was an outline of service for Schwarzkopf brand perms and included consultation, products, technology, and training. In the early 1970s Poly Kur delivered Schwarzkopf's first hair-care system, composed of shampoo, conditioner, and treatment. Poly Soft Toner, a temporary liquid hair color, was launched in Germany in 1988, and the line of Poly Brilliance products was launched in 1990.

Natural ingredients and products became important to consumers in the early 1990s, and Schwarzkopf responded in 1991, launching Igora Botanic, a plant-based colorant in the Igora line that offered semi-permanent color in a biodegradable, vegetable-based formula. It was free from pesticides, herbicides, and fungicides.

In 1995, Schwarzkopf was acquired by Henkel, which helped it become a leading European supplier of hair cosmetics. In 1998, Schwarzkopf marked its 100th anniversary and launched "Re-Nature," a home hair-care product that restores gray hair to its natural color.

Schwarzkopf Professional launched OSIS in 2000. This new styling brand for professional hairdressers was endorsed by the British salon chain Umberto Giannini. Its slightly edgy quality made it a hit in the fashion world. Schwarzkopf's ASK Academy, an educational program for hairdressers, was initiated in Tokyo in 2003, and a London ASK Academy opened in 2004.

Targeting a younger generation, Schwarzkopf launched the got2b line of styling products in 2000 in California and New York City and began selling got2b products in Europe in 2004. Since 2004 the line's presence has expanded to 24 countries, including Australia, China, and Scandinavia.

Schwarzkopf's range of Seah Hairspa products, a line intended to enable nonprofessionals to administer spa treatments to hair, was launched in 2004. Many other Schwarzkopf offerings made their debut in the first decade of the 21st century, including a product to replenish thinning hair for men and women that used an ingredient called Carnitintartrat to stimulate the hair root.

The brand marked its 111th anniversary in 2009 with celebrations that included an exhibition in Düsseldorf and the release of the book *We Love Hair,* which covered a range of topics related to hair.

BRAND ELEMENTS
- The tagline "professional haircare for you" accompanies the Schwarzkopf brand name on its website and products.
- Schwarzkopf connects with its consumers using the catchphrase "Together. A passion for hair."
- The brand's silhouette logo appears on product packaging and in advertising.

- Birdboy, the "got2b hero," endorses the got2b sub-brand, which is marketed to younger consumers.

Accompanied by the phrase "professional haircare for you," the Schwarzkopf logo consists of a silhouette of a head. The silhouette appears on all of the company's products and features prominently in its advertising. The brand's slogan is "Together. A passion for hair."

In contrast to the more glamorous elements of the brand, Schwarzkopf also uses images and messages in social media to appeal to a more street-savvy generation. The sub-brand got2b was promoted via YouTube videos featuring Birdboy, a practitioner of parkour, a type of noncompetitive urban gymnastics. Birdboy used Schwarzkopf's got2b Glued Blasting Freeze Spray to achieve his signature spiked hairstyle. He is referred to as the "got2b hero" in the videos. Schwarzkopf used the phrase "got2b-where u r" to connect with the target audience for the product line.

BRAND IDENTITY
- The Schwarzkopf brand presents itself as the consummate provider of hair-care products to professionals and nonprofessionals alike.
- The Schwarzkopf website, which makes use of videos and interactive technology, is designed to be a constantly evolving magazine about hair.
- Schwarzkopf demonstrated a commitment to environmental responsibility when it began introducing CDC-free products in 1980.

The Schwarzkopf brand presents itself as the consummate provider of hair-care products to professionals and nonprofessionals alike. It presents itself to the world mainly through salon professionals, websites, and YouTube videos.

The company seeks to connect its brand with high fashion and celebrity. Messages are directed at a global audience, with discussion of all hair types and colors: how to curl and straighten, how to color, and how to cut and style. Hairdressers can access Schwarzkopf's ASK Academy, an online tutorial that is frequently updated. Schwarzkopf brick-and-mortar academies also provide specialist seminars and training courses.

The Schwarzkopf website has elements of a top-flight fashion magazine. Videos show women and men with hairdos suitable for all hair types and shades. The images recall catwalks and photo shoots; many of the images are of celebrities who use the products. The site also features practical how-to videos for the average female or male consumer.

Schwarzkopf's parent company, Henkel, has invested heavily in research work for the cosmetics and toiletries segment of its operations. Its contributions to sustainability and performance show a desire to meet the public demands of environmental responsibility. Schwarzkopf created CDC-free products beginning in 1980 and claims to have been the first international cosmetics manufacturer to do so.

During the brand's 111th anniversary celebration, Schwarzkopf produced a book to celebrate hair. Titled *We Love Hair,* the book was filled with the work of such photographers as Karl Lagerfeld, Roxanne Lowit, Russell James, and Gabo; illustrations by Olaf Hajek; and stories by Nick Hornby, Patrice Leconte, and Roger Moore. Senior Executive Vice President Tina Müller said of the anniversary year, "The three ones in 111 represent innovation, market leadership and consumer trust."

BRAND STRATEGY

- Salons provide major word-of-mouth marketing for Schwarzkopf, and Schwarzkopf provides participating salons with posters, displays, and equipment for hairdressers.
- By sponsoring the Eurovision Song Contest in 2011, Schwarzkopf was able to reach a large number of potential consumers.
- Birdboy, "the got2b hero," was part of a YouTube video campaign that demonstrated the holding properties of got2b hair products.
- Schwarzkopf recently rolled out a product line intended to prevent hair loss and its first 10-minute hair color.
- Schwarzkopf has been growing internationally and is focusing on Latin America and Asia-Pacific.

Schwarzkopf is the umbrella brand of a portfolio that includes Schauma, Drei Wetter, Fa, Taft, and Brilliance. Salons provide the main thoroughfare for Schwarzkopf's market. They carry Schwarzkopf products for their clientele, and their stylists provide word-of-mouth advertising for the brand. For those salons associated with Schwarzkopf Professional, the company provides advertising materials to use in their facilities, including posters, displays, capes, aprons, trolleys, tool holders, and scissors.

Schwarzkopf was a presenting partner of the Eurovision Song Contest in 2011. The television program aired throughout Europe during prime time and online, reaching more than 100 million viewers and potential consumers.

One of Schwarzkopf' recent strategies has been targeting new market segments. The got2b line of styling products attracted a large following among younger consumers with the help of Brass, an ad agency specializing in social media. The campaign was designed to provide "haircare with attitude" for 14- to 24-year-olds, who consume a large proportion of their media online. Brass said the goal was to project "a young, funky, innovative,

extrovert image for [Schwarzkopf] to fuel online [conversations] and propel Schwarzkopf into the limelight as a leading hair care brand amongst a youth audience." The project featured Birdboy, a parkour practitioner who used got2b Glued Blasting Freeze Spray to create his signature "liberty spikes." He demonstrated the hold of the product while performing his athletic feats, as seen in YouTube videos. The campaign received significant media coverage.

Schwarzkopf recently rolled out other product lines with significant growth potential. One of these was the 2007 introduction of the ACTIV Dr. Hoting product line, designed to help prevent hair loss. Another was the 2008 launch of Coloriste, Schwarzkopf's first product designed to color hair within ten minutes and at the same time minimize damage.

In a 2009 press release, Executive Vice President Hans Van Bylen also discussed Schwarzkopf's international growth. "We have expanded our positions in Western Europe, and our hair coloring and styling products have long dominated their markets in Eastern Europe and Russia. Through focused investments in Latin America and Asia-Pacific, we are participating in the market growth on these continents. Schwarzkopf Professional has achieved remarkable growth rates in recent years, evolving into a business with a global presence."

BRAND EQUITY

- Schwarzkopf is considered the number one hair-care brand for German consumers.
- Schwarzkopf ranked 11th in *Brandirectory*'s listing of the top 50 cosmetics Brands 2012.
- Brand Finance assigned Schwarzkopf a brand value of US$2.68 billion in 2012.

Schwarzkopf is considered the number one hair-care brand for German consumers. Brand Finance's *Brandirectory* assigned a brand value of US$2.68 million to Schwarzkopf in 2012 and ranked it 432nd in its Global 500 list of the top brands worldwide. The brand ranked 11th in *Brandirectory*'s listing of the top 50 cosmetics brands in 2012.

BRAND AWARENESS

- Schwarzkopf received *Reader's Digest*'s "Most Trusted Brand" award from 2001 to 2012.
- Schwarzkopf products were used to style the hair of catwalk models during the 2010 German Hairdresser of the Year Award ceremony.
- The Schwarzkopf brand is represented in more than 100 countries.
- By using social media, Schwarzkopf turns brand users into "brand ambassadors."

Schwarzkopf received *Reader's Digest*'s "Most Trusted Brand" award from 2001 to 2012. The Schwarzkopf brand is represented in more than 100 countries. Schwarzkopf's website has pages in languages for 30 countries.

During the 2010 German Hairdresser of the Year Award ceremony, Schwarzkopf products were used to style the hair of the catwalk models. The event was attended by 1,300 guests, including celebrities and specialists in the German professional hairdressing field, thus keeping the brand in the forefront of their minds.

Schwarzkopf's brand awareness among younger demographics has increased via online and word-of-mouth promotions. The got2b line of hair-care products has also appealed successfully to younger consumers. By successfully using popular social media such as Facebook and Pinterest, Schwarzkopf turns brand users into "brand ambassadors" who promote their products for free.

BRAND OUTLOOK

- Schwarzkopf ranked third in sales in the global hair salon business.
- Negative factors in the global marketplace made it important for the company to keep the Schwarzkopf brand present through inexpensive, creative advertising.
- Successful innovations by the Schwarzkopf brand have helped expand Henkel's market shares.

The Schwarzkopf brand ranks third globally in sales in the hair salon business. Successful innovations by the Schwarzkopf brand helped boost Henkel's market shares in recent years.

A number of factors have contributed to declining sales overall in the global market. Among them are poor economic conditions since the onset of the global recession in 2008, the unresolved debt crises in Europe and the United States, and political unrest in Africa and the Middle East. Money-conscious consumers and competition in the cosmetic and hair-care sector are making it necessary to work harder for recognition in the marketplace. Promotional activities are still important; yet, it is necessary to keep costs down with creative advertising.

The increased cost of materials and packaging has had its impact on profits for global businesses. Henkel was able to balance increasing costs by raising prices. Investments in property, plants, and equipment rose from EUR 40 million (US$52.53 million) in 2010 to EUR 66 million (US$86.67 million) in 2011. These investments were intended to improve efficiency in production and supply and to reduce annual cost increases. Henkel was able to maintain profits in the mid-single-digit range by accelerating business expansion during the second half of 2012. The company looked to expand further in the European and North American markets as well as in emerging markets.

In order to keep their brands strong in the future, Henkel plans to remain focused on strict cost discipline in its administration. Another goal is to increase the quality of service to customers with efficiency improvements in shared service centers.

FURTHER READING

Bakker, Sietse. "Schwarzkopf Presenting Partner of Eurovision Song Contest 2011." *Eurovision,* October 21, 2010. Accessed November 27, 2012. http://www.eurovision.tv/page/news?id=20603&_t=schwarzkopf_presenting_partner_of_eurovision_song_contest_2011.

"Beauty Products Maker Henkel Lauds U.S. Recovery: An interview with Kasper Rorsted, CEO of Henkel." *WSJ Live,* n.d. Accessed November 28, 2012. http://on.aol.com/partner/wsjlive-517302109?redirected=true#_videoid=517630868.

Brass. "Turning Heads for Schwarzkopf with an Extreme Haircare Launch." Accessed December 1, 2012. http://www.brassagency.com/our-work/schwarzkopf.aspx.

Henkel. Accessed December 1, 2012. http://henkel.com.

Jameson, Alison. "Winners Announced at HJ's British Hairdressing Awards." *ResponseSource: Enquiry Service,* November 27, 2012. Accessed December 1, 2012. http://www.responsesource.com/news/75403/winners-announced-at-hj-s-british-hairdressing-awards.

Rao, Sree Rama. "Salon Brands—Reaching the Consumer." *citeMAN: Global Corporate Community Knowledgebase,* October 4, 2008. Accessed December 1, 2012. http://www.citeman.com/4133-salon-brands-reaching-the-consumer.html.

"Richard Povian aka Birdboy, got2b hero: How to style all over liberty spikes." *YouTube,* June 9, 2009. Accessed December 1, 2012. http://www.youtube.com/watch?v=yqT2zCyl7eI.

Schwarzkopf International. Accessed November 27, 2012. http://www.schwarzkopf.com.

Schwarzkopf Professional. Accessed November 27, 2012. http://www.schwarzkopf-professionalusa.com.

7-ELEVEN

BRAND ORIGINS

- Convenience store concept was established in Dallas in 1927.
- Totem poles provided 7-Eleven with the first brand name: Tote'm Stores.
- The 7-Eleven name was coined in 1946.
- International expansion began in 1969.
- Proprietary ready-to-eat foods were introduced in the 1990s.

The leading convenience store brand in the world, 7-Eleven, had its origins in Dallas, Texas, in 1927 when John Jefferson Green persuaded his employer at the Southland Ice Company to allow him to sell milk, eggs, and bread from a retail ice dock during the evening hours and on Sundays. The concept soon spread to Southland's 20 other retail ice docks. In 1928 a Southland manager returned from a trip to Alaska with a souvenir totem pole, which he planted in front of the store. Whether intentional or not, it was the first act of branding by the fledgling business. Totem poles were erected at other Southland stores. And because it was a cash-and-carry business, customers "toted" away their purchases. Hence the stores became known as Tote'm Stores. Thompson then brought continuity to the young brand by making sure each store offered the same level of quality and service.

By the time World War II came to an end in 1945, there were Tote'm Stores spread across north-central Texas, open seven days a week from seven in the morning until eleven at night. In 1946 the TracyLocke marketing firm was commissioned to craft a name to replace "Tote'em Stores." Because of the consistent and convenient hours of operation, the "7-Eleven" name was selected. At the same time, the chain remodeled all of its stores, doubling the floor space while bringing even more standardization to the brand.

In the late 1950s, the 7-Eleven concept was taken to new markets in Virginia, Maryland, and eastern Pennsylvania. After going public under the Southland Corporation name, the convenience-store chain expanded rapidly, often through the acquisition of smaller convenience-store operators emulating the 7-Eleven model. They included 100 SpeeDee Marts in California in 1963, an acquisition that was of particular importance because it introduced Southland to the idea of franchising, which accelerated the chain's growth. It was also during this period that Southland began experimenting with a 24-hour store in Las Vegas, and 7-Eleven introduced the Icee, a semifrozen carbonated drink that would later be relaunched as the Slurpee drink, a name that came to rival 7-Eleven as a brand.

In 1969 7-Eleven used franchising to begin an international push, starting with Canada. The following decade saw the brand introduced to Mexico in 1971, Japan in 1974, Australia in 1977, and Sweden in 1978. Southland entered the United Kingdom market through the acquisition of the retail operations of Cavenham Ltd. The 24-hour format was also embraced by the chain in the United States, so that by the mid-1970s there were nearly 4,000 continuous-operation stores.

International expansion continued in the final decades of the century. The 7-Eleven brand entered Taiwan in 1980s and Hong Kong a year later. Singapore followed in 1983, the Philippines and Malaysia in 1984, and Norway in 1986. In 1989 South Korea and Thailand were added. Guangdong was introduced to the brand in 1992 and Denmark the following year.

During this period, 7-Eleven revamped its operation, offering fresh perishables and new ready-to-eat fresh foods, leading ultimately to the introduction of dinner entrees. The chain also added financial services, such as ATMs and the sale of money orders, as 7-Eleven moved away from the brand image of a purveyor of beer, tobacco, soda, and overpriced staples. New proprietary products were introduced, including Café Select coffees, Deli Central sandwiches, World Ovens Pastry baked goods, and Café Cooler frozen cappuccinos. Southland also changed its name to 7-Eleven, Inc., in 1999, aligning the company with its flagship brand.

In the early 2000s, 7-Eleven expanded its brand to new locations through the introduction of a smaller footprint that permitted stores in such high-traffic locations as office buildings and airports. Asia became the chain's greatest area of growth. In 2004 7-Eleven was granted permission to enter the Chinese market, and the first stores opened in Beijing. A year later, ownership of the 7-Eleven chain passed into the hands of Japanese retail conglomerate Seven & I Holdings. The chain began marketing fuel under its own name, rather than that of long-time partner Citgo. Following the financial crisis of 2008 and 2009, the brand continued its expansion in the Far East, entering Indonesia in 2009. Chengdu and Shanghai followed in 2011.

BRAND ELEMENTS
- 7-Eleven logo was introduced in 1969.
- "Oh thank Heaven for 7-Eleven" tagline was developed in 1969.

- Brand colors include orange, green, white, and red.
- Consistent store layout is an important brand element.

Several elements combine to make up the unique brand of 7-Eleven. The name has become anachronistic because the stores are now open 24 hours a day instead of just from 7:00 in the morning to 11:00 at night, but it remains effective because of longtime use. The rhyming nature of the name is also effective in making the brand memorable to consumers. In a similar way, the company's longtime advertising tagline, "Oh thank Heaven for 7-Eleven," gains resonance. The catchy phrase, developed by the Stanford Agency, has been in use since 1969. Consumers are so familiar with it that a shorter version of the slogan, "Oh thank Heaven," was employed and trademarked.

Also enjoying longevity and lending consistency to the brand is the 7-Eleven logo. It includes a large, stylized orange numeral 7 with the word "eleven" written through the stem in orange in capital letters, with the exception of the "n," which is rendered as lowercase. The same shade of green is used to provide the logo's border, enclosing a white background. Orange, green, and white, as well as red, are the 7-Eleven brand colors, found in signage, packages, and elsewhere.

The 7-Eleven stores themselves are another important brand element. Not only do the stores make use of the corporate colors inside and out, but also layouts are the same throughout the chain. Thus 7-Eleven enjoys brand consistency and customers know where they can find desired products anywhere in the world. The merchandise itself supports the 7-Eleven brand. Outside, gas is marketed under the brand name. Inside, the focus on coffee and ready-to-eat foods, many of them carrying their own brand names, reinforces a friendly brand image. Not to be forgotten, the very idea of convenience is perhaps the most important element of the 7-Eleven brand.

BRAND IDENTITY
- At the core of 7-Eleven's brand identity is convenience.
- A wide range of products and services reinforces 7-Eleven's brand identity.
- 7-Eleven emphasizes its role as a good neighbor.
- Corporate charitable contributions focus on youth programs.

7-Eleven has created an identity recognized by customers around the world and embodied by the corporation's stated intent to be a convenient neighborhood store: "At 7-Eleven, our purpose and mission is to make life a little easier for our guests by being where they need us, whenever they need us." From the very beginning, the foundation of the 7-Eleven brand was convenience. The original Tote'm Stores were popular because people could buy staples, such as milk, bread, and eggs, without having to make a full shopping trip. It was one of those modern conveniences that consumers had already come to appreciate. Being open early in the morning and late at night was part of the 7-Eleven brand promise, which was expanded upon when the stores became 24-hour operations.

What 7-Eleven offered its customers also grew over the years, adding further to the chain's identification with the idea of convenience. Gas pumps were added so that customers could fill up their tanks while making other purchases. 7-Eleven was a pioneer in the sale of hot coffee, another convenience that commuters embraced. As consumer tastes in coffee grew more sophisticated, 7-Eleven kept pace and developed a branded line of Café Select coffees. 7-Eleven offered snack foods and, over the years, added fast foods, which evolved into higher quality ready-to-eat and meal-replacement options. This was another convenience that was appreciated by singles as well as families. The addition of ATMs and the sale of money orders reinforced the brand promise of convenience. In many countries, customers could also pick up videos, pay utility bills, top up their mobile phones, and purchase concert tickets at their local 7-Eleven. By becoming more of a one-stop shop, 7-Eleven presented itself as a paragon of convenience.

7-Eleven portrays itself as a good "neighborhood," the equivalent of the general store of a bygone time, a place where people gathered. In many parts of the world, the local 7-Eleven store became a hub of activity for young people. Homey and friendly, the brand extends an invitation to its neighbors. The stores are bright, colorful, and clean. The consistent store layout makes nonlocals feel welcome as well. The universal availability of the Slurpee, Big Gulp, and other branded products also creates an emotional connection to customers. Additionally the stores offer regular deals to reward regular customers and foster even greater brand loyalty.

In keeping with its promise to be a good neighbor, 7-Eleven is diligent about the sale of age-restricted products, such as alcohol and tobacco. 7-Eleven stores also support the communities in which they do business. The chain mostly contributes to youth programs, focusing on safety, education, health and wellness, and community revitalization. Monetary contributions are made to public schools, libraries, police departments, government agencies, and nonprofit organizations.

BRAND STRATEGY

- From the start, 7-Eleven made wise use of branding techniques.
- 7-Eleven brand grew stale by the 1990s.
- The rise of major oil company competition in the convenience store sector prompted changes to the 7-Eleven formula.

- 7-Eleven remodeled stores and introduced new products during a 1990s' reinvention.
- A lifestyle marketing strategy was adopted in the early 2000s.

When the 7-Eleven chain started out selling everyday staples from the retail dock of an ice house in 1927, developing a brand was not even a consideration. Nevertheless, the use of a totem pole as a symbol for the business, while unplanned, planted the seeds for a brand strategy. It created an identity, as did the nature of the business itself, embodying the idea of convenience. Following World War II, the retail chain took the next step in the evolution of its brand by adopting the 7-Eleven name. As such, the brand was taken to other parts of the country and expansion accelerated after a franchising model was embraced in the early 1960s.

The success of 7-Eleven prompted the emergence of the modern convenience store industry. 7-Eleven solidified its place as the best-known brand in the late 1960s with the creation of its iconic logo and crafting of the "Oh thank Heaven for 7-Eleven" tagline. In addition the Slurpee drink was created, helping to build the brand further. The company also began an international expansion program, introducing the 7-Eleven brand to countries around the world.

By the 1990s, however, 7-Eleven's brand had lost some of its luster. The format had grown stale and the stores had become the butt of comedians' jokes. 7-Eleven also faced growing competition in the convenience store category by the gasoline retailing operations run by the major oil companies. Lapsing into bankruptcy in 1990 hurt the image of the brand even further. The relationship with franchisees was strained as well, resulting in competing lawsuits that led to Southland cutting off formal communications with the leadership of a franchisee coalition. In the early 1990s Southland's management took steps to reinvigorate the brand, launching a national advertising campaign, a step franchisees had been clamoring for, while initiating a remodeling and remerchandising effort. New products replaced less popular fare. They included several proprietary beverages and ready-to-eat foods. Exterior and interior lighting were improved, while aisles were widened and merchandise reorganized. An "everyday fair pricing" policy was instituted, doing away with the high markups on many convenience items that had become a black mark on the brand.

During this time of transition, Southland divested a variety of assets it had acquired over the years. As part of focusing on its core operation, Southland aligned itself with the brand in 1999, becoming 7-Eleven, Inc. When ownership of the chain passed to a Japanese company, the focus of the 7-Eleven brand grew more international in scope, and it enjoyed growth in China and other Asian markets. The new owners also took steps to burnish the 7-Eleven brand. As part of a lifestyle marketing strategy, 7-Eleven sought to increase its relevance in the lives of its customers and become more of a neighborhood store. In addition the company extended the 7-Eleven name to a line of products, such as snack cakes and breakfast pastries, that would be priced below national brands. This best-value branding strategy, supported by new packaging and the 7-Eleven logo, served to enhance shopper loyalty.

BRAND EQUITY

- *Convenience Store News* listed 7-Eleven as the top convenience store chain in 2010.
- 7-Eleven operates the most convenience stores in the world.
- The 2012 value of the 7-Eleven brand was estimated at US$4.55 billion by Brand Finance Plc.
- Brand Finance ranked 7-Eleven 225th on its list of the top 500 Global brands in 2012.

As a globally recognized and respected brand, 7-Eleven holds significant value. The chain generates nearly US$4.5 billion in annual sales from company-owned and franchised stores around the world, making it the globe's number-one convenience store operator. In 2010 *Convenience Store News* listed 7-Eleven as the top convenience store chain, well ahead of the next four competitors, all of which were controlled by oil companies. Moreover, in 2010 7-Eleven operated the second-largest worldwide franchise system in terms of revenues, according to *Franchise Times*, trailing only McDonald's but significantly ahead of KFC. With more than 40,000 locations around the world, 7-Eleven topped McDonalds in that category. In the United States, 7-Eleven operated the third-largest overall franchise system, behind Hampton Hotels and Subway, according to the *Entrepreneur* list of top franchise systems in 2012.

The value of the 7-Eleven brand to the business is estimated at US$4.55 billion by Brand Finance Plc, a brand evaluation consultancy. As a result, Brand Finance ranks 7-Eleven number 225 on its list of the top 500 Global brands in 2012. It was a significant improvement over the previous year's number 268 ranking.

BRAND AWARENESS

- For many consumers, 7-Eleven is a generic term for convenience stores.
- Brand awareness is supported by more than 40,000 store locations around the world.
- Brand awareness for 7-Eleven is especially high in Asian markets.

With more than 40,000 stores in the United States and about a dozen other countries and with a logo that is instantly recognized and understood, 7-Eleven enjoys excellent brand awareness. It enjoys such top-of-mind brand awareness that 7-Eleven is almost a generic term for convenience stores for many people, especially in large parts of the United States. It is one of the great American brands, so much a part of the culture that it has been satirized in popular culture over the years.

Awareness of the 7-Eleven brand is strong beyond the United States. In Japan young people are especially connected to 7-Eleven, where it is known as a *combini*. Many Japanese customers do their banking at the local 7-Eleven. "The average 25-year-old here has grown up with all this being normal," according to *Advertising Age*. "To the young people, having a new drink on the shelf every time they visit their local combini is absolutely the norm."

A study conducted in Malaysia reveals the depth of 7-Eleven's brand awareness in that market. Every one of the 100 respondents had heard of 7-Eleven, 81 percent through their outlets. In addition, 87 percent recognized the Slurpee and Big Gulp as signature 7-Eleven products. By that same percentage, respondents reported they had easy access to a 7-Eleven store. Three-quarters recognized that the layout was consistent from store to store.

BRAND OUTLOOK

- Growth opportunities remain in the United States for 7-Eleven, especially in Southern California.
- Chinese market is not yet fully tapped.
- Best-value branding strategy is likely to continue.

With a history that dates to the 1920s, as well as a logo and tagline virtually unchanged since the late 1960s, 7-Eleven is a brand that remains vibrant well into the 21st century. Although the chain numbers more than 40,000 units, there remains ample room for continued expansion. In the United States, 7-Eleven stores only operate in 30 states. Southern California remains a promising new target market for the brand. The same holds true for the rest of the world. 7-Eleven stores are only found in 16 countries. Moreover, in the massive China market the brand has only scratched the surface. With the deep pockets of its Japanese parent, 7-Eleven is likely to pursue a global expansion program in the years to come, but it is just as likely to make certain there is a need for the brand before entering a new market.

While the brand is firmly connected to the convenience store concept, 7-Eleven could be expected to evolve further in the years ahead. The best-value branding approach is likely to grow, as the 7-Eleven name is

944

applied to a variety of new products. Making 7-Eleven feel more like a neighborhood store through a lifestyle marketing approach will also remain a key strategy. There is every reason to believe that these other efforts will continue to deepen consumer loyalty to the 7-Eleven brand.

FURTHER READING

Benezra, Karen. "Southland Maps C-Store Empire to Vie on Price." *Brandweek*, December 5, 1994.

Brand Finance. "Global 500 2012." *Brandirectory*. Accessed July 3, 2012. http://brandirectory.com/league_tables/table/global-500-2012.

McCarthy, Michael. "7-Eleven Stores Face Fresh Food Showdown." *Brandweek*, February 28, 1994.

———. "Shakeup at 7-Eleven." *Brandweek*, July 11, 1994.

McCaughan, Dave. "Does Your Brand Bore the Japanese? Blame 7-Eleven." *Advertising Age*, August 13, 2007.

"7-Eleven Builds a Best-Value Branding Strategy." *Packaging World*, December 7, 2009.

"7-Eleven, Inc." *International Directory of Company Histories*. Ed. Derek Jacques and Paula Kepos. Vol. 112. Detroit, MI: St. James Press, 2010.

Sharrah, Kim. "7-11's New Marketing Man." *Convenience Store Decisions*, May 1, 2007.

Weddington, Randy. "Reinventing Convenience." *Supermarket News*, July 2, 2001.

SHANGHAI TANG

AT A GLANCE

Brand Synopsis: "The first Chinese luxury brand in the world," Shanghai Tang is noted for its use of bright and flamboyant colors.

Parent Company: Shanghai Tang (subsidiary of Compagnie Financière Richemont SA)

25th Floor, Guangdong Investment Tower

148 Connaught Road Central

Hong Kong

http://www.shanghaitang.com

Sector: Consumer Discretionary

Industry Group: Retailing

Performance: *Market share*—5.3 percent of the luxury market worldwide (parent company Compagnie Financière Richemont SA) (2012).

Principal Competitors: Armani; Gucci; Hugo Boss; Prada

BRAND ORIGINS

- David Tang opened Shanghai Tang as a custom-tailor business in 1994.
- Compagnie Financière Richemont SA took control of Shanghai Tang in 1998 and attempted to continue its expansion internationally.
- After Shanghai Tang was unsuccessful in the global market, the company rebranded itself by hiring new staff in 2001 to bridge the gap between Chinese style and modern taste.

David Tang, a Hong Kong businessman and socialite, launched the luxury retailer Shanghai Tang in 1994 as a custom-tailoring business. Because Hong Kong was going to be released back to China by the British in 1997, Tang decided to sell Chinese ready-to-wear in preparation of the tourist inundation. The company specialized in distinctive Chinese-styled clothing by combining traditional design with contemporary fashion. The concept was to satisfy consumers' desire to maintain their cultural identity prior to Hong Kong being returned to mainland China. The store was an instant success, which Tang followed up with by opening locations in New York, London, and throughout Asia.

In 1998 Tang sold his controlling shares of the company to the Swiss-owned luxury goods company Compagnie Financière Richemont SA, which owned other types of luxury brands such as Cartier and Jaeger-LeCoultre. Richemont quickly discovered that Shanghai Tang was not winning popularity in the Western market. The company responded by hiring a new CEO, Raphael le Masne de Chermont, in 2001 to help rebrand and transform the company to make it more appealing to Western consumers. The company also hired a new creative director, Joanne Ooi, to help revitalize the brand. Some of the changes were dramatic, such as altering the brand's style to be more Westernized, while maintaining hints of Chinese design. The brand struggled to maintain the Chinese elements to satisfy the domestic market, which made up 20 percent of revenues for the company, while still achieving international expansion. The ultimate goal of the rebrand was to establish Shanghai Tang as an ambassador of Chinese taste and style.

As of 2013, the brand continued its focus on the Asian market, while gradually opening stores in cities worldwide. Under the control of Richemont, the company's principal executives have been recruited from across the globe, with hopes that the diversity will help the brand's international expansion.

BRAND ELEMENTS

- The name Shanghai Tang combines the founder's name with one of the largest cities in China, identifying itself in the global market as a Chinese brand.
- The company's two primary slogans, "Made in China" and "Re-Orient Yourself," both play on the company's cultural identity to appeal to the international market.
- The brand's style is unique in the luxury industry, combining traditional Chinese elements with Western styles and bright colors.

The company's name, Shanghai Tang, is the most recognizable element of the brand's identity. The name reflects the company's founder, David Tang, and one of the largest cities in China. Because Tang intended to create a Chinese luxury brand, he wanted the name to be recognized globally as a Chinese brand. Shanghai Tang was the first luxury brand from China, as previous brands sold in China were Western. The style was also intended to reflect Chinese culture, appealing to its domestic market.

Shanghai Tang's well-known slogan is "Made in China," making a play at the fact that many foreign retailers have their merchandise made in China. Given that Shanghai Tang is a Chinese-based company, its clothes are obviously made in China, but at a higher quality than the merchandise that is made for foreign retailers. The company also uses the slogan "Re-Orient Yourself" in its marketing, which also plays on the Asian-based company. Shanghai Tang urges consumers to expose themselves to Asian and Chinese culture while enjoying luxury fashion.

The brand's merchandise is noted for its distinctive elements. Even though the brand originally was entirely Chinese fashion, the company began incorporating more Western elements in the early 2000s as an effort to expand the brand further into the global market. The style is still distinctly Chinese, with touches of traditional design, while embracing popular Western fashion. The company is also well known for its use of bright and flamboyant colors, in contrast to luxury competitors such as Armani.

BRAND IDENTITY

- Shanghai Tang's original brand image was to offer custom-tailored Chinese luxury fashions for Chinese consumers and later to offer the same designs ready-to-wear.

- After the brand was failing internationally, Shanghai Tang rebranded itself to have more Western-designed apparel with Chinese elements to appeal to the global market.
- Shanghai Tang markets its exotic elements, utilizing slogans such as "Re-Orient Yourself," with the goal of the clothing transporting consumers mentally to "someplace exotic."

Shanghai Tang was originally opened as a custom-tailor shop in Hong Kong, hiring tailors who had left Shanghai after the Communist Party of China took control. The concept was to offer authentic Chinese custom-tailored designs for Chinese consumers. As luxury markets began to infiltrate China, the country did not have a brand of its own to enter into the steadily growing market. David Tang, Shanghai Tang's founder, wanted to give Chinese fashion to the consumers who would wear it. As the transfer of Hong Kong from Great Britain back to China approached, Tang began offering ready-to-wear high-end fashions in Chinese design, marketing toward tourists who would soon be infiltrating the country.

When Shanghai Tang's international sales began to falter, the company realized that it needed to rebrand itself to succeed globally. The brand's styles were considered too authentic Chinese to be worn regularly outside of China. Under the direction of Richemont's newly hired staff, Shanghai Tang went from traditional Chinese wear to Western styles with Chinese elements. The result was to incorporate Shanghai Tang's styles into clothing that would work on the international luxury scene. The brand's identity is still a delicate balance, however, of keeping styles that will be purchased by Chinese consumers while mixing in Western designs to appeal to the global luxury market.

In the brand's marketing, the company reminds consumers that it is an Asian brand while aiming to appeal to luxury consumers who opt for more exotic clothing. The most-recent slogan the company has used is "Re-Orient Yourself," calling on consumers to reevaluate Chinese style and embrace the elements featured in the brand's apparel. Even though the brand lost some of its original authentic design in its rebranding, the designs still contain elements that are distinctly Chinese, which is the company's marketing focus. The brand's chief designer, Joanne Ooi, has stated that the goal behind Shanghai Tang's collections is wearability: "Every item should transport the wearer mentally to someplace exotic."

BRAND STRATEGY

- Shanghai Tang's clothing designs were altered from the original authentic Chinese designs to make the brand more appealing to the global market.
- Even though Shanghai Tang has been expanding stores gradually throughout the global market, the company's target market is in Asia, where 70 percent of the stores reside.

- Shanghai Tang uses the social network website Pinterest to release previews of new fashion lines, spreading designs to potential customers who may not have been looking for the brand.

David Tang, Shanghai Tang's founder, wanted to create luxury apparel that was made in China for Chinese. While the company was originally a custom-tailor for Chinese fashion, Tang expanded his brand to include ready-to-wear fashions, a concept that worked best with tourists traveling to Hong Kong who wanted to purchase the clothing as a fine souvenir. Tang intended to hone in on the tourist market as Hong Kong was returned to China in 1997, after the 99-year agreement between China and the United Kingdom ended. The concept was successful with both high-spending tourists and Chinese and led to the acquisition of Shanghai Tang by Compagnie Financière Richemont SA in 1998.

Prior to the Richemont takeover, Tang had attempted to expand his stores into the Western market by opening locations in New York, London, and throughout Asia in 1997. However, the New York location closed in 1999, less than two years after opening, due to a lack of interest. The company opened a smaller location in New York in 2001. Even though Tang had hoped that his brand would be an international success, its reception in the Western market proved to be lackluster. Most Western consumers considered the Chinese style to be costume wear, rather than items to be worn daily. The result was a rebranding of the company's image.

Under the direction of CEO Raphael le Masne de Chermont, Shanghai Tang hired an American designer to help with the Westernization of the clothing to increase its appeal to a broader market. Even though the clothing adhered to Westernized style, it still contained authentic Chinese elements. Richemont does not divulge Shanghai Tang's revenues publicly, but it has stated that Shanghai Tang's profits have been growing 40 percent on average each year, with only limited attention on the U.S. market. Le Masne de Chermont has stated that he intends to roll out additional U.S. locations, but it is not the focus of the company. Approximately 70 percent of the brand's locations reside within Asia and the Asian market remains the target for the company. As of 2013, 50 percent of the company's revenues came from Asia, with 20 percent from China alone.

Shanghai Tang uses new media as a way of expanding awareness of the company's brand, releasing previews of upcoming designs on the social network website Pinterest. Through the use of Pinterest, the company is able to spread its fashion designs to consumers who would not have been searching for the brand, in that a design can be "repined" on Pinterest boards thousands of times and thus reaching potential consumers at random. This form of marketing also appeals to younger consumers, who are more technologically savvy and involved in social networking, furthering Shanghai Tang's exposure to a younger demographic.

BRAND EQUITY

- Half of Shanghai Tang's sales are from its domestic market and half are from the global market, with the company focus on continuing expansion in Asian.
- As the luxury market continues its growth throughout China, Shanghai Tang's parent company, Compagnie Financière Richemont SA, will profit from the fact that the company already has a Chinese market.
- Shanghai Tang does not appear in the major brand rankings, as the company has limited exposure in the global marketplace and little popularity in the United States.

Despite the fact that Western luxury brands have been expanding into the Chinese market, Shanghai Tang has been infiltrating both its domestic market as well as the global market. For the brand's parent company, Compagnie Financière Richemont SA, Shanghai Tang is a potentially high-profit investment as the luxury market continues to expand in China. Because Shanghai Tang is a Chinese-based company with Chinese elements, it has already been gaining popularity throughout the domestic market, with China making 20 percent of the company's sales. More broadly, half of Shanghai Tang's revenues came from Asia and half from the global market in 2013.

Because Shanghai Tang is still more of a fledgling luxury brand, it does not appear on the major global rankings provided by Interbrand and Brand Finance. High-end fashion competitor Gucci was ranked 420th on Brand Finance's "Global 500 2012" and 38th on Interbrand's "Ranking of the Top 100 Brands" in 2012. Competitor Armani did not make either of the rankings.

BRAND AWARENESS

- Historically, the Shanghai Tang brand was known by high-end tourists to Hong Kong, who sought authentic Chinese style with luxury quality.
- Approximately 50 percent of Shanghai Tang's revenues come from Asia, which indicates how important the Asian market is to the brand and where the company's focus should rest.
- Shanghai Tang has been more successful in Europe after the brand image was altered to appeal to Western consumers; it contains enough Chinese touches to appeal to consumers who want the exotic flair of the brand's designs.

Shanghai Tang's primary focus was originally international tourists to Hong Kong who were interested in luxury fashions as well as Hong Kong's authentic style. Because

Shanghai Tang combines authentic designs with high-end flair and quality, the chain is well known among affluent tourists to China. In the Western world, however, the brand is less known. Having been forced to shut down its original New York location less than two years after opening, Shanghai Tang has struggled in the American market, with difficulty marketing its authentic designs to high-end consumers. The company's CEO has stated that while it would be beneficial to expand the brand further into North America, he acknowledged that the company is more exposed and has a better future within China. Because China is expected to continue to expand as a more capitalistic country, its large population has the potential to provide massive profits for Chinese retailers.

While 50 percent of Shanghai Tang's revenues come from Asia and 20 percent of its total revenues come from China, the brand has already established itself as a premium Asian company. However, the brand is not as well known among the main population of China, because the average consumer is not a luxury consumer. As a result, Shanghai Tang is better known to tourists or emigrants who are trying to grasp the exotic elements of the designs.

To appeal to Western consumers, the brand has altered its style to be more Westernized; it includes elements of Chinese authenticity without making the clothing only appropriate for Chinese consumers. Combined with the new designs, rebranding the company's slogan to "Re-Orient Yourself" has been successful in the European market, in that consumers have been encouraged to indulge in the exotic nature of the brand.

BRAND OUTLOOK

- Material costs for Shanghai Tang have been steadily increasing, with the price of silk increasing 60 percent and cotton increasing 45 percent.
- While the brand continues to expand globally, Shanghai Tang's primary focus is on the domestic market.
- The Chinese economy has been creating more millionaires, with an estimated 960,000 in 2011.

Even though Shanghai Tang's sales have been reported as improving since Compagnie Financière Richemont SA rebranded it, the brand still faces strong challenges in its future. The company has said it anticipates large growth in revenue, which is not reported because Richemont is private and does not release financial information, but higher costs of material are becoming more of a challenge. Silk, for example, went up in cost by 60 percent in 2011, while cotton increased by 45 percent. Despite the rising costs in material, the company has reported increases in sales.

Shanghai Tang plans to continue expanding the brand internationally; however, the brand's main focus is on China. Marketing itself as "the first Chinese luxury brand in the world," Shanghai Tang hopes to pursue wealthy Chinese consumers by encouraging them to take pride in domestic brands. As of 2013, the company was aiming to double the amount of stores in Asia. In 2011 the number of millionaires in China was 960,000. As the Chinese economy continues to progress, it will create more high-end consumers who can purchase luxury brands.

FURTHER READING

Brand Finance. "Global 500 2012." *Brandirectory*. Accessed September 3, 2012. http://brandirectory.com/league_tables/table/global-500-2012.

Howells, Chris. "Shanghai Tang Plots Asian Expansion." Channel NewsAsia.com, April 1, 2011. Accessed February 5, 2013. http://www.channelnewsasia.com/stories/singaporebusiness-news/view/1120169/1/.html.

Jana, Reena. "China Goes Luxury." *Bloomberg BusinessWeek*, November 30, 2005.

Khan, Natasha and Frederik Balfour. "Richemont's Shanghai Tang to Double Chinese Stores as Luxury Demand Climbs." *Bloomberg*, October 6, 2011.

"Shanghai Tang: Branding the Chinese Consumer's Mind." *Modern Living*, February 26, 2012.

"Shanghai Tang Expands in Mainland China." *Red-Luxury*, April 7, 2011. Accessed February 5, 2013. http://red-luxury.com/2011/04/07/shanghai-tang-expands-in-mainland-china/.

"Shanghai Tang, Richemont's Secret Weapon." *Fashion United*, October 19, 2011.

"The Story Shanghai Tang." *eTeacherChinese*. Accessed February 3, 2013. http://blog.eteacherchinese.com/china-economy/the-story-of-shanghai-tang/.

Tischler, Linda. "The Gucci Killers." *Fast Company*, January 1, 2006. Accessed February 3, 2013. http://www.fastcompany.com/54589/gucci-killers.

SHARP

AT A GLANCE

Brand Synopsis: A well-established brand of consumer and business electronics, Sharp's focus on invention and innovation has made it a success in North America, Europe, and in its home country of Japan.

Parent Company: Sharp Corporation
22-22 Nagaike-cho
Abeno-ku, Osaka 545-8522
Japan
http://www.sharp-world.com/index.html

Sector: Consumer Discretionary

Industry Group: Consumer Durables & Apparel

Performance: *Market share*—The leading manufacturer of cell phones in Japan, with a 23.50% market share (2012). *Net sales*—JPY1.18 trillion (US$14.58 billion), domestic (2012); JPY1.27 trillion (US$15.74 billion), international (2012).

Principal Competitors: Samsung Electronics Co., Ltd.; Sony Corporation; Panasonic Corporation

- By 2012, the Sharp Group employed more than 60,000 people: 31,100 in Japan and 32,000 overseas.
- The American part of Sharp, Sharp Electronics Corporation, opened in 1962 and is based in New Jersey.
- Recent Sharp products include televisions, mobile phones, Blu-ray disc players, refrigerators, vacuum cleaners, air purifiers, and LED lighting.

A leading manufacturer of electronics in the 21st century, the Sharp Corporation's first product was definitely not electronic. It was a snapping, self-fastening belt buckle. Tokuji Hayakawa invented this belt buckle in 1912. His later inventions included mechanical pencils that proved to be very popular in Japan, Europe, and the United States. In the 1920s, Hayakawa's company, known then as Hayakawa Metal Works, made crystal radios, a forerunner of the electronic devices that his company would later manufacture with great success. These products included televisions in the 1950s, color televisions in the 1960s, and LCD (liquid crystal display) televisions in later decades.

Hayakawa's inventions helped create and build the Sharp Corporation. In 2012, the Sharp Group employed more than 60,000 people worldwide—31,000 in its home country of Japan and 32,000 overseas. These numbers reflect the brand's global presence.

In 1962, Sharp opened its first overseas office in the United States. The American part of Sharp is known as the Sharp Electronics Corporation and is based in Mahwah, New Jersey. Also in the 1960s, Sharp opened sales subsidiaries in the United Kingdom and West Germany (now part of the reunified Germany). A decade later, in

BRAND ORIGINS

- Tokuji Hayakawa's self-fastening belt buckle was the first invention for his company, which would eventually become known worldwide as the Sharp Corporation.

1979, the company founded Sharp Manufacturing Company of America (SMCA) in Memphis, Tennessee, adding manufacturing facilities to its overseas businesses.

These manufacturing plants do not make the belt buckles and mechanical pencils of the company's earliest days. Sharp's 2012 annual report lists two major product categories, with a number of subcategories. It describes several of its products as consumer/information products. The first subcategory in this division is audiovisual and communication equipment: televisions, mobile phones, DVD and Blu-ray disc players, calculators, and other equipment. The second subcategory is health and environmental equipment, which includes refrigerators, vacuum cleaners, humidifiers, air purifiers, and LED lighting. The final subcategory includes information products, such as electronic cash registers and multifunction printers.

Sharp's second major product category is electronic components, which includes the LCD product subcategory, which is devoted to solar cell technology, and a subcategory for other electronic components, which includes microprocessors, laser diodes, and optical sensors.

Sharp continues to operate internationally. It has offices and regional headquarters around the world. It makes and markets its products in different areas, targeting its products to specific global regions.

Although it has operated under different names (Hayakawa Metal Works, Hayakawa Electric Industry Co., Ltd., and Sharp Corporation) during its history and manufactured a wide variety of products (from belt buckles and radios to solar cell products), Sharp has always focused on invention, adaptation, and geographic expansion.

BRAND ELEMENTS

- Sharp takes its company name from a 1915 invention by Tokuji Hayakawa, a mechanical pencil that became known as the Ever-Sharp Pencil.
- The Sharp logo features the company name in large capital letters, usually in red.
- To celebrate its 100th anniversary, Sharp used a golden 100th Anniversary logo that featured two intersecting laurel wreaths as the two zeros in 100.

Sharp takes its company name from one of Tokuji Hayakawa's early inventions, the mechanical pencil. Hayakawa invented this pencil in 1915, and it became known as the Ever-Ready Sharp Pencil and later as the Ever-Sharp Pencil. The company was granted a patent for the pencil in Japan in 1920 and in the United States in 1926. The popularity of this pencil helped build the company, and Sharp's name continues to provide a historical link to one of its successful early products. A company website states that the name Sharp symbolizes its "broad vision and competencies."

The Sharp logo consists of the company's name in large capital letters, usually in red. Sharp Electronics uses the capitalized Sharp logo accompanied by the word Electronics in a smaller typeface. This logo appears on the company's products, promotions, advertisements, and other materials.

The company has also used other logos. To commemorate its 100th anniversary in 2012, the company used a golden 100th Anniversary logo that featured two intersecting laurel wreaths as the two zeros in 100. Ancient civilizations used laurel wreaths to celebrate victories, and the images of wreaths in the logo represent Sharp's achievement of a significant milestone. Sharp noted that the intersection of the wreaths symbolized the company's ties to its past and its future. The company used the anniversary logo in 2012 on its websites as well as in advertisements, publications, presentations, and other materials. The company's website included information about the anniversary as well as the company's history. Given Sharp's status as an international company, this historical information was made available in Japanese, Chinese, and English.

BRAND IDENTITY

- Sharp's goal is to "Make products that others want to imitate."
- Sharp emphasizes that expanding business is not its primary goal.
- The Sharp advertising slogan "From Sharp minds come Sharp products" plays on the fact that the English word sharp can mean "smart" or "clever."

Sharp's global website reveals the goal of the Sharp brand and the dream of its founder: "Make products that others want to imitate." Additionally, the company's two principal ideals are "sincerity and creativity," and Sharp emphasizes the increasing business volume is not its primary goal. The company website provides an extensive history of Sharp founder Tokuji Hayakawa and uses language designed to stress sincerity and creativity, such as "A Spirit of Service that Impressed the Social Entrepreneurs of the World" and "A Life of Always Moving Forward, Always Looking One Step Ahead."

Sharp's logo has appeared in some memorable advertising campaigns. One campaign used the slogan "From Sharp minds come Sharp products." This slogan takes advantage of the fact that in the English language, the word sharp can mean "clever" or "smart." The slogan thus hints that the Sharp company and its workers are clever and that they make clever products. It captures the Sharp brand's spirit of invention and innovation. This slogan also repeats the name of the company twice, reinforcing the audience's awareness of the brand.

BRAND STRATEGY

- In 1995 the company established Sharp Laboratories of America as a site for research collaborations between the United States, Japan, and the United Kingdom.
- In response to operating losses incurred in 2012, Sharp committed to strengthening regional operations and focusing more closely on its customers.
- Sharp gained prominent international exposure by serving as the shirt sponsor for the Manchester United Football Club from 1982 to 2000.

Because Sharp has always focused on offering quality products, while at the same time globalizing its brand, the company established Sharp Laboratories of America in Camas, Washington, in 1995. This laboratory develops technology for use in many Sharp products and is the site of various Sharp operations, including its solar energy group. Sharp's American laboratories represent a research coalition between the United States, Japan, and the United Kingdom.

Despite these efforts, however, in 2012, Sharp experienced operating losses. Its annual report attributed these losses to Sharp's international performance. To remedy these losses, the company vowed to become even more globally oriented: it opened regional headquarters, beginning with the Americas, China, and Europe; it created new products that Sharp hopes will generate new demand in new markets; and it also took steps to strengthen its regional operations and to focus more closely on marketing and its customers.

For many years, from 1982 to 2000, Sharp sponsored the Manchester United Football Club. For the 1982–83 season, the words Sharp Electronics appeared in capital letters on Manchester uniforms. The following season, the team's shirts carried only the name Sharp. In some years, the uniforms featured the words Sharp Viewcam, which advertised both the Sharp brand and its Viewcam camcorder. In other years, the uniforms featured the words Sharp Digital. Thus, for almost 20 years, the word Sharp appeared prominently on the uniforms of one of the most popular sports teams in the world. In light of the 2012 operating losses, promotions and marketing like this will again become part of the Sharp brand strategy.

BRAND EQUITY

- Two studies published in 2007 found that Sharp controlled different percentages of the global market for flat panel televisions.
- From December 2011 through February 2012, Sharp captured 23.5 percent of the market for mobile phones in Japan.
- In 2010, Sharp manufactured 27.1 percent of the photovoltaic modules sold on the global market.

- Brand Finance assigned Sharp a brand value of US$5.584 billion and named it the world's 171st most valuable brand in 2012.
- Interbrand named Sharp the 13th best brand in Japan in 2012 with a brand value of US$1.884 billion.

Different studies published in 2007 found Sharp controlling different percentages of the same market. May Wong noted in *USA Today* that market researcher iSuppli Corporation reported that Sharp held a 13.3 percent share of the global market for flat panel televisions. In the same article, Wong added that another market researcher, DisplaySearch, calculated that Sharp held an 11.4 percent share of the same market. A few years later, in 2012, Sharp's share of the market had dwindled to 5 percent.

Sharp's mobile phones have enjoyed greater market share. International technology analyst comScore, Inc. reported that, from December 2011 through February 2012, Sharp accounted for the largest share of the Japanese mobile phone market—23.5 percent. Sharp's nearest competitors during this period were Panasonic, with a 13.8 percent share, and Fujitsu, with an 11.8 percent share.

Sharp products also performed well in emerging markets. For example, Sharp manufactures solar cells and photovoltaic (PV) modules, which are used to capture solar energy, in Japan, Europe, and the United States. In 2010 the German solar website SolarServer reported that Sharp manufactured 27.1 percent of the PV modules sold throughout the world. These statistics demonstrate Sharp's prominent position in the markets for various products throughout the world.

These global market share figures have helped build Sharp's brand value. In its annual ranking of top global brands, the "Global 500," Brand Finance determined that Sharp was the 171st most valuable global brand in the world, with a brand value of US$5.584 billion in 2012. This same ranking determined that Sharp was the 16th most valuable brand in Japan that year. This brand value is also consistent. Brand Finance determined that Sharp was the 179th most valuable global brand in the world in 2011, with a brand value of US$5.517 billion. Similarly, Interbrand named Sharp to its "Japan's Best Global Brands" lists in 2009, 2010, 2011, and 2012. In 2012, it placed 13th on Interbrand's list with a brand value of US$1.884 billion, compared to its 12th place ranking and brand value of US$2.003 in 2011.

BRAND AWARENESS

- A study published in 2013 found that consumers recalled the Sharp brand name in "unaided free recall," or without memory prompts.

- In a Harris Interactive poll published in 2012, American consumers named Sharp their sixth-favorite mobile phone brand and ninth-favorite electronics brand.
- In 2012, the Superbrands Council named Sharp a "superbrand," citing its history of quality manufacturing and strong global presence.

In his technology and society blog, analyst Steve Webster has questioned Sharp's brand strength. He noted that the company lacks an iconic product and added that customers do not seem to feel the "attachment" to the brand that they appear to feel for the products of other technology manufacturers, such as Sony or Apple. Other Sharp products, however, seem to enjoy greater customer approval. In 2012, Sharp's solar panels were judged to be the top brand by EuPD Research, an international research firm that analyzes sustainable business. The rating was based on reports from consumers and installers of solar panels.

Other studies have shown that consumers recognize the Sharp brand. TFCinfo, a firm that studies the audio visual industry, polled a number of projector users and released the results of this poll in 2013. TFCinfo discovered that several audio visual consumers could recall the Sharp brand name without memory prompts, a phenomenon known as "unaided free recall." Sharp joined Epson and NEC as the electronic brands with the highest unaided free recall measurements. Other consumers have voiced their opinions about the Sharp brand and its products. In a Harris Interactive poll published in 2012, more than 38,000 American consumers named Sharp the sixth-best mobile phone brand and the ninth-best electronics brand.

Sharp also remains a strong brand in the eyes of business analysts. Brand analyst the Superbrands Council has studied the strength of brands in various countries. In 2012 this organization named Sharp a "superbrand," citing Sharp's history of quality and its international presence.

BRAND OUTLOOK

- Sharp's "new one-of-a-kind strategy" aims to create new demand by creating products that no other brand offers.
- Sharp is expanding its involvement in sustainable energy, selling solar power systems to Japanese homes and undertaking solar power ventures in other areas.
- In its 2012 annual report, Sharp announced its intention to "[b]reak away from a self-sufficient mindset."

Sharp has changed the way it operates in the 21st century. Its 2012 annual report describes the company's plan to "[b]reak away from a self-sufficient mindset." In light of this plan, Taiwan's Hon Hai Group and Sharp began providing joint management and capital in 2012 for Sharp Display Products Corporation, a manufacturer of large LCD (liquid crystal display) panels. Sharp hoped that this move would help it produce more, offset its 2012 losses, and thrive in a competitive marketplace. This joint venture stands as yet another example of the company's international focus.

The 2012 annual report also described what Sharp called its "new one-of-a-kind strategy." This strategy emphasizes the creation of new products that Sharp hopes will generate new demand. For example, it added air purification technology and robotic functions to vacuum cleaners in an effort to give its products an edge over more ordinary vacuum cleaners.

Sharp has also begun to expand its efforts in different business areas and geographic regions. It has sold increasing numbers of solar power systems to Japanese consumers and also operates solar power ventures in Europe, Asia, and the United States. These efforts demonstrate Sharp's growing involvement in the field of sustainable (renewable) energy and position Sharp to stay competitive in a market that demands constant innovation.

FURTHER READING

Brand Finance. "Sharp." *Brandirectory*. Accessed February 22, 2013. http://brandirectory.com/league_tables/table/global-500-2012.

comScore, Inc. "In Japan, Smartphones Surpass Feature Phones among Newly Acquired Devices for First Time Ever." By Sarah Radwanick. April 23, 2012. Accessed November 24, 2012. http://www.comscore.com/Insights/Press_Releases/2012/4/1_in_5_Mobile_Phone_Users_in_Japan_Now_Owns_a_Smartphone.

EuPD Research. "Sharp Also Receives 'Top Brand PV' Seal of Quality." *PV Magazine,* February 21, 2012. Accessed November 23, 2012. http://www.pv-magazine.com/services/press-releases/details/beitrag/sharp-also-receives-top-brand-pv-seal-of-quality_100005826/#axzz2D5oWIW2w.

Harris Interactive. "Apple Is Still King, but Android-based HTC Follows Closely Behind as Top Mobile Phone Brands," April 26, 2012. Accessed February 22, 2013. http://www.harrisinteractive.com/NewsRoom/PressReleases/tabid/446/mid/1506/articleId/1011/ctl/ReadCustom%20Default/Default.aspx.

rAVe Publications. "Epson, Sharp, NEC and Panasonic Dominate ProAV Brand Image according to TFCnet." January 28, 2013. Accessed February 22, 2013. http://ravepubs.com/index.php?option=com_content&view=article&id=9612&Itemid=180.

Sharp. "Annual Report 2012." Accessed November 23, 2012. http://www.sharp-world.com/corporate/ir/library/annual/pdf/annual_2012.pdf.

Sharp. "Company Profile." Accessed November 24, 2012. http://www.sharpusa.com/AboutSharp/CompanyProfile/SharpAndTechnologyHistory.aspx.

Sharp. "Sharp 100th Anniversary Logo and Web Site Created, Corporate Homepage Renewed." December 27, 2011. Accessed November 23, 2012. http://www.sharp-world.com/corporate/news/111227.html.

"Sharp Is 'UAE Superbrand.'" *Khaleej Times,* July 4, 2012. Accessed November 23, 2012. http://www.khaleejtimes.com/biz/inside.asp?xfile=/data/uaebusiness/2012/July/uaebusiness_July22.xml&section=uaebusiness.

SolarServer. "Sharp Electronics (Europe) GmbH." Accessed November 24, 2012. http://www.solarserver.com/yellow-pages/companies/company-search/sharp-electronics-europe-gmbh.html.

Statista. "Global Market Share of Leading Flat Panel TV Brands from 3rd Quarter 2010 to 2nd Quarter 2012." 2012. Accessed November 24, 2012. http://www.statista.com/statistics/180255/worldwide-market-shares-of-leading-flat-panel-tv-brands-by-quarter/.

SyncForce. "Sharp." *Ranking The Brands.com*, 2013. Accessed February 22, 2013. http://www.rankingthebrands.com/Brand-detail.aspx?brandID=286.

Webster, Steve. "From Sharp Minds Come Sharp Products." *Seeking 2020,* November 6, 2012. Accessed November 23, 2012. http://seeking2020.com/.

Wong, May. "Sharp Loses Lead in LCD-TV Market to Samsung." *USA Today,* February 14, 2007. Accessed November 24, 2012. http://usatoday30.usatoday.com/tech/products/2007-02-14-samsung-flat-panel-sales_x.htm.

SHELL

―――――――― ◼ ――――――――

AT A GLANCE

Brand Synopsis: A leading global energy brand, Shell provides global energy solutions in a responsible, forward-thinking manner.

Parent Company: Royal Dutch Shell plc/Shell Group
Carel van Bylandtlaan 16
2596 HR The Hague
The Netherlands
http://www.shell.com/

Sector: Energy

Industry Group: Oil, Gas & Consumable Fuels

Performance: *Market share*—4.19 percent of petroleum refineries worldwide (2011); 12.2 percent of U.S. top gas station firms (2011). *Sales*—US$470.2 billion (2011).

Principal Competitors: BP; Chevron; ConocoPhillips; ExxonMobil; Gazprom; Petrobas; PetroChina; Sinopec; Total

BRAND ORIGINS

- The Shell brand name came into use in 1897 when The Shell Transport and Trading Company Plc was founded.
- Shell moved into the manufacture of chemicals in 1929.
- By 1991 Shell had become the world's largest public oil company, with sales exceeding US$100 billion.

What became Shell began in Great Britain and the Netherlands in the late 19th century. Samuel Samuel formed The Shell Transport and Trading Company Plc in 1897 to search for a secure source of oil nearer to the Far Eastern markets. His family's trading company had been selling Russian oil as early as 1878. By 1898 Shell discovered a major oil field in Dutch Borneo and grew rapidly over the next few years. Within two years, it owned oil fields, a refinery in Borneo, and a fleet of oil tankers.

In 1903 Royal Dutch Petroleum and Shell became partners in the oil marketing company Asiatic Petroleum Company. Royal Dutch had been founded in 1890 in the Netherlands after receiving a concession to drill for oil in the Dutch East Indies. Royal Dutch and Shell officially merged in 1907 to form the Royal Dutch/Shell Group and further expand production options outside of Russia. The new business developed rapidly, with assets growing more than two-and-a-half times between 1907 and 1914. The Shell brand became widely known when it was used in high-profile flights and motor races in the early 20th century.

By 1913 Royal Dutch/Shell owned major production facilities in Russia and Venezuela, and it moved into the U.S. market when it acquired Roxana Petroleum. Within two years Shell was producing more than six billion barrels of crude oil annually in the United States. During World War I, Shell played an important role in the Allied war effort, supplying gasoline, aviation fuel, and TNT to the British.

The 1920s was a decade of growth, globally and in the United States, for the oil industry and for Shell because of the expanded use of automobiles and greater demand for gasoline. By the end of the 1920s, Shell was the leading oil company in the world, supplying 10 percent of all the crude oil and possessing 10 percent of all tanker tonnage. Its ads in the late 1920s claimed "You can be sure of Shell." In 1929 Shell moved into a new business, chemicals, initially manufacturing nitrogenous fertilizer and refining chemicals made from oil.

Shell struggled during the Great Depression, in part because of a chronic problem with overcapacity in the oil industry that began in 1929. But the brand's ads emphasized that the product was powerful, pure, and reliable, and could help users get away from it all. During World War II, Shell continued to face challenges as its Netherlands-based headquarters had to move to the Dutch West Indies after Germany invaded the Netherlands in 1940. As part of the war effort, Shell refineries in the United States produced large quantities of high octane aviation fuel, while Shell Chemical manufactured butadiene for synthetic rubber products.

The 1950s and 1960s were golden years of growth for oil companies like Shell. Demand for petroleum products grew as more cars were on the road and other uses for petroleum were developed. During this time period, Shell supplied one-seventh of the world's oil products. In 1959 Shell became able to further extend its product line when, as part of a joint venture, it discovered a natural-gas field in the Netherlands that turned out to be one of the largest in the world.

Shell's exploration activities proved fruitful, leading to oil in the North Sea and natural gas offshore in Australia in 1971. However, the Organization of Petroleum Exporting Countries started a global oil and energy crisis when it unilaterally raised crude oil prices in 1973. Oil companies like Shell faced difficult political decisions on how to allocate their scarce oil supplies. In response to these developments, Shell diversified into nuclear energy, coal, metal, solar, biomass, and biofuels, while also growing its chemical business.

In the early 1980s, Shell Chemicals remained the world leader in production of petrochemicals and a leading supplier of agrochemicals. Despite global economic difficulties, Royal Dutch/Shell had record sales of US$83.8 billion in 1982. By 1991 Shell had become the world's largest public oil company, with sales exceeding US$100 billion. During the 1990s, Shell continued to expand its exploration, refining, and gas station activities globally, including its first oil exploration in India. It also further developed its liquefied natural gas business, an area which remained important in the early 21st century.

Shell struggled in the late 1990s and early 2000s, with sales falling 9.3 percent to US$135 billion in 2001. While trying to turn the tide through acquisition and a refocusing of its business, Shell faced public criticism about its actions in South Africa and Nigeria and the ire

of environmentalists because of issues related to drilling. There was greater fallout, including investigations by the U.S. Justice Department and the European Commission, in 2004 when Shell revealed that its proved reserves were overestimated by 20 percent.

Despite this challenge, in 2005 Shell's parent companies merged into a single firm, Royal Dutch Shell Plc, which was incorporated in the United Kingdom but based in the Netherlands. While oil and related operations remained central to Shell, there was an ever-increasing investment in alternative energy sources, including wind. By 2010 Shell was the second-largest oil and gas company in the world after Exxon Mobil. By 2011 it was operating in 80 countries, producing 3.2 million barrels of oil per day, running 43,000 Shell service stations globally, and earning revenues of US$470.2 billion, up from US$368.06 billion in 2010. A Shell tagline that debuted in 2012 summarized its broad, new corporate attitude by declaring "Let's Go."

BRAND ELEMENTS
- Shell's name, logo, and colors are among the most recognizable in the world.
- The Shell name was adopted because the company's origins lay in the sale of shells.
- The familiar pecten Shell logo came into use in 1904.

The Shell name and logo are among the most recognizable corporate brand-names and trademarks in the world, and have been in use since the late 19th century. Samuel Samuel named his enterprise The Shell Transport and Trading Company Plc in 1897 in recognition of a commodity that was the basis of business success for his father, Marcus Samuel, Sr. The elder Samuel had a store in Great Britain in the 1830s which sold antiques and bric-a-brac. He expanded into importing and exporting from the Far East to take advantage of the popularity of shells from the Orient. Marcus Samuel, Sr., sold boxes made from shells, among other items. Buying and selling the shells made his business a success, transforming it into an international trading firm.

By 1900 an associated logo had been created for Shell Transport. The first version was a mussel shell, face down. In 1904 the logo was changed to the more familiar upright, scalloped pecten, or scallop shell, after the merger between the Royal Dutch Petroleum Company and The Shell Transport and Trading Company Plc. "Shell" was adopted as its brand name. From the first, the depiction of the pecten was fairly accurate, though it also reflected trends in graphic design. The current version, which came into use in 1971, is based on a design by the famous industrial designer Raymond Loewy. From 1948 to 1999 the Shell name appeared as part of the logo.

The Shell logo had been depicted in the brand's colors of red and yellow for decades, though the shades have changed over time. The first use of Shell red and yellow came in 1915 when the Shell Company of California began building service stations, but faced competition. Because of the state's strong cultural connection to Spain and Shell's desire to use bright colors, the red and yellow of that country's flag were adopted.

BRAND IDENTITY

- Shell fuels have been associated with groundbreaking events like the first transatlantic flight.
- Shell has been a sponsor of Ferrari's Formula One team since 1950.
- Shell's tagline "Let's Go" emphasized that Shell was working to address long-term global energy needs.

Though Shell engages in the production and distribution of many forms of energy, as well as other, often related businesses, it is primarily known as an innovative oil and gas company. From its earliest years, Shell fuels were used in ground breaking events, linking the brand to excitement and pioneering endeavors. In 1907 Prince Borghese won the Peking to Paris motor rally using Shell gasoline, while Louis Bleriot became the first man to fly across the English Channel using Shell Spirit fuel in 1909. Antarctic explorers Sir Ernest Shackleton (1908) and Robert Falcon Scott (1911–12) used Shell fuel on their expeditions. British aviators John Alcock and Arthur Whitten Brown made the first transatlantic flight using Shell fuels in 1919.

Shell remains a brand linked to motor racing to the present day. In 1950 it began a long-term association with Ferrari and Formula One racing. As part of its sponsorship of the Ferrari team, Shell developed lubricants and advanced fuels to power Ferrari's entries in Formula One races. In the 2010s Shell also had technical partnerships with Ducati motorcycles and NASCAR, the American stock car racing circuit.

Shell's advertising and marketing efforts also reflected a sense of adventure, reliability, and information. In the late 1920s its ads proclaimed "You can be sure of Shell," while in the 1930s Shell's advertising themes emphasized power, purity, and the ability to get away from it all. In Britain in the early 1950s, Shell sponsored a series of road guides which helped build the brand. From 1976 to 1982 its American "Come to Shell for Answers" campaign included television commercials, print ads, and informative booklets related to driving and car maintenance. By 2012 Shell was using the tagline "Let's Go," which not only emphasized that Shell was working to address long-term global energy needs but also that Shell fuel could help take consumers places. Active on YouTube, Facebook, Twitter, Flickr, and various blogs, Shell created apps like the Shell Motorist and Insider Energy to inform consumers about Shell products and disseminate information related to driving, energy, and related topics.

BRAND STRATEGY

- Shell generally branded its divisions, subsidiaries, and products with the Shell name.
- In 1980 Shell introduced Formula Shell, its branded unleaded fuel.
- In 2010 Shell food brand Deli2go, sold at Shell petrol stations in the United Kingdom, was an example of a non-Shell branded product line.

Since the early 20th century, Shell generally has branded its divisions and product lines with the Shell name. Shell's first emphasis was on petroleum and gas, and by 1915 it had Shell-branded gas stations. As Shell moved into new business areas, the Shell name came with it. In 1929, for example, what became part of Shell Chemicals was launched in the United States as Shell Chemical Company. In the early 1970s, as Shell diversified its energy portfolio, it acquired coal businesses that were renamed Shell Coal International. When the brand unveiled an early unleaded gasoline in 1980, it was dubbed Formula Shell and helped start a trend to the use of unleaded gas. There were some exceptions, however. In 2010 Shell launched Deli2go, a food brand sold at Shell petrol stations in the United Kingdom and later available in certain other global markets.

Shell's parent company, Royal Dutch Shell, gave most of its international subsidiaries, which managed Shell's activities within defined geographic areas, the Shell name as well. In 2009, for example, Shell Energy Europe was formed after the company combined its European power, gas, and carbon marketing and trading operations. Specific Shell products for consumers and businesses were often rolled out with the Shell name. There were branded credit card services, fuels, loyalty programs, oils and lubricants, and gas stations. By 2011 there were 43,000 Shell service stations around the world, making it the largest retail fuel-network worldwide. Shell's business operations included Shell Aviation, Shell Bitumen, Shell Commercial Fuels, Shell Marine Products, and Shell Sulphur Solutions. In the 2010s Shell placed an emphasis on growing both its consumer and business interests in developing markets like China, India, and Brazil.

BRAND EQUITY

- Shell was the number-two petroleum refiner worldwide.
- According to *Forbes*, Shell was the 91st-most-powerful brand in 2012, with a brand value of US$7.3 billion.
- Shell has the highest brand value of any company in the Netherlands, according to Brand Finance.

Shell was the largest non-U.S. company in the world by sales, with revenues of US$470.2 billion in 2011. It had operations in 80 countries. In 2011 it was the top gas station brand in the United States, with 12.2 percent of the market. In 2011 Shell was number two on a ranking of top petroleum refiners worldwide, after ExxonMobil. Shell had 4.19 percent of the market. The largest company in the Netherlands, according to *Forbes*, Shell was also widely considered to have high brand value. On *Forbes's* ranking of *The World's Most Powerful Brands* for 2012, Shell was 91st, with a brand value of US$7.3 billion.

Shell had high brand value according to other entities as well. In 2012 Brand Finance listed Shell as number one on its *Netherlands 50*, number three on its *UK Top 50*, and number 19 on its *Global 500*. According to Brand Finance, Shell's brand value was US$22.022 billion and its enterprise value was US$236.670 billion. Interbrand also listed Shell as number 75 on its "Best Global Brands 2012" ranking, with a brand value of US$4.788 billion. Recognizing Shell's environmental efforts, Interbrand also ranked it at number 34 on its "Best Global Green Brands 2012." In the "BrandZ Top 100 Most Valuable Global Brands 2012" ranking, Shell was 39th, with a brand value of US$17.781 billion. Shell was also number two on this report's ranking of *Oil & Gas Movers and Shakers*, after ExxonMobil.

BRAND AWARENESS

- By 2011 Shell was operating in 80 countries and had 43,000 service stations globally.
- Shell is regularly ranked the top gasoline brand in the United States.
- In 2012 Shell ranked 59th on The Centre for Brand Analysis's *Consumer Superbrands Official Top 500*.

The Shell brand name has been used since 1897, and since the early 20th century, Shell has been one of the top oil and gas companies in the world. With its indelible name, pecten logo, and distinctive red and yellow color scheme, the brand is one consumers worldwide have long associated with Shell as an energy company. Despite a major oil spill off the coast of Nigeria, controversial Arctic drilling, and several other high-profile incidents across the globe, Shell has retained a strong brand image and positive brand awareness because of its reputation for responsibility. By 2011 it was operating in 80 countries with 43,000 service stations, ensuring widespread awareness and recognition. In the United States, for example, Shell is the top gas-station brand, with 12.2 percent of the market. Various surveys and studies underscore the widespread awareness for Shell. In 2010, for the second consecutive year, *Popular Mechanics* named Shell the top gasoline brand, as part of its Readers' Choice Awards. The Reputation Institute's *Dutch Reputation Award*, a ranking

of Dutch perception of companies and services, placed Shell at number 25 for 2012.

BRAND OUTLOOK

- Shell has diverse business interests which should help its future profitability.
- Shell has made long-term investments in non-oil energy sources such as biofuels and natural gas to serve the energy needs of future generations.
- Shell has made significant investments in fast-growing markets in Asia, where much growth is expected.

As the global economic recession eased in the early 2010s, Shell posted impressive revenues of US$470.2 billion, in part because it had long diversified its business interests. Though Shell is still primarily known as an oil and gas brand, the company has been pursuing other types of business since 1929, when it began developing, producing, and selling chemicals, an area in which Shell continues to operate.

Shell considers itself primarily an energy company and understands there is a limit to the amount of oil available in the long term. While pursuing costly, challenging projects to explore oil reserves in Russia and the Arctic, among other locales, Shell has made long-term investments in other energy sources like biofuels, natural gas, and wind energy. Shell is a leading distributor of new biofuels and has long been a market leader in natural gas in various markets. Between 2006 and 2011, Shell spent US$2.3 billion on developing alternative energy sources, as well as carbon capture and storage and carbon dioxide research and development. Shell's pursuit of alternative energy is also related to its commitment to protect the environment. Shell had been concerned with environmental issues and sustainable development since at least the mid-1990s.

Shell understands that the demand for energy will only grow, as the world's population is expected to reach nine billion by 2050. To ensure its long-term growth, Shell has invested in fast-growing markets in Asia, such as China and India, to help build the brand for the future. About US$125 million was spent on voluntary social investments in 2011. Brazil and Russia are also seen as key to Shell's future profitability.

FURTHER READING

"Best Global Brands 2012." Interbrand. Accessed February 9, 2013. http://www.interbrand.com/en/best-global-brands/2012/Best-Global-Brands-2012.aspx.

Brand Finance. "Shell." *Brandirectory*. Accessed February 9, 2013. http://brandirectory.com/profile/shell.

"BrandZ Top 100 Most Valuable Global Brands 2012." Millward Brown. Accessed February 9, 2013. http://www.millwardbrown.com/brandz/2012/Documents/2012_BrandZ_Top100_Report.pdf.

"Royal Dutch Shell." *Forbes*. Accessed February 9, 2013. http://www.forbes.com/companies/royal-dutch-shell/.

Royal Dutch Shell plc. *Annual Report and Form 20-F for the Year Ended December 31, 2011*. Accessed February 9, 2013. http://reports.shell.com/annual-report/2011/servicepages/downloads/files/entire_shell_20f_11.pdf.

———. *2012 Investor Fact Sheet*. Accessed February 9, 2013. http://www.shell.com/content/dam/shell/static/investor/downloads/shell-at-a-glance/shell-2012-ir-factsheetenglish.pdf.

"Royal Dutch Shell plc." *International Directory of Company Histories*. Ed. Jay P. Pederson. Vol. 108. Detroit, MI: St. James Press, 2010.

"Shell." RankingTheBrands.com. Accessed February 9, 2013. http://www.rankingthebrands.com/Brand-detail.aspx?brandID=204.

SHISEIDO

—■—

BRAND ORIGINS

- On April 8, 1872, Arinobu Fukuhara opened Japan's first Western-style pharmacy in Tokyo's Ginza district and named it Shiseido.
- Shinzo Fukuhara, the first president of Shiseido, designed the camellia logo and developed the company's corporate philosophy.

- Miss Shiseido, a consultancy service, and the Camellia Club were early ways of interacting with the consumer.
- As the company spread to other countries, Shiseido diversified its line of products by adding non-Shiseido brands, such as IPSA, NARS, and Bare Escentuals.
- During Shiseido's 125th and 140th anniversary celebrations, it re-released its Eudermine moisturizer and increased marketing efforts via the Internet and life quality seminars.

On April 8, 1872, Arinobu Fukuhara opened Shiseido, Japan's first Western-style pharmacy in Tokyo's Ginza district. The first products sold were medicinal, using both traditional and Western methods of pharmacology. The innovative moisturizing lotion Eudermine was introduced in 1897. The cherry-colored liquid was sold in decorative glass bottles and tied with a bow. Its moisturizing properties were immediately popular with Japanese women, who prized clear, healthy skin.

Shiseido added the food market to its portfolio in the early 1900s. It opened Japan's first soda fountain in 1902. In 1941 the brand entered the markets for restaurant management and confectionery sales. There is still a Shiseido restaurant chain in Japan today.

When Japan implemented import restrictions, Shiseido's share of the country's cosmetics market grew. In 1915, Shinzo Fukuhara, the first president of Shiseido, began to concentrate on the brand's manufacture of cosmetics. Shinzo designed the Art Nouveau camellia logo in 1915, and in 1921 the company developed its corporate philosophy, which featured "Shiseido's Five Principles": Quality First, Coexistence and Co-Prosperity, Respect for Retailers, Corporate Stability, and Sincerity. Quality assurance and new products were researched in Shiseido's first laboratory.

In 1917 the brand created Hydrogen Peroxide Cucumber, the first brightening lotion. In 1923, Shiseido launched Univiolin, one of world's first sunscreen products. Ingredients such as Flower Leaf Zinc Oxide and PH-Responsive Titanium Dioxide provided protection, water-resistance, and easy removal. The company claimed that *Ginkgo biloba* extract in the product elevated the body's biological protection system to inhibit damage from the sun's ultraviolet rays.

Unfortunately, the Ginza district burned during the Kanto Earthquake of 1923. This incident and the worldwide economic depression of the 1930s caused a decrease in sales. Nevertheless, Shiseido partnered with stores to form the Shiseido Cosmetics Chain Store System. This marketing strategy allowed the brand to expand throughout Japan. During World War II, the company's research facility was destroyed. Shiseido's tenacity was demonstrated again with its reorganization four years later. In 1949, Shiseido was listed on the Tokyo Stock Exchange.

Miss Shiseido was the 1934 counterpart to today's beauty consultant. The Camellia Club, a mail-order service for Shiseido customers, was created in 1937. The personal contact with consumers established by the service laid the groundwork for the brand's commitment to service and loyalty.

The company's first expansion outside Japan occurred in Taiwan in 1957, and the Shiseido facility there was soon exporting to Singapore and Hong Kong. Shiseido expanded to Hawaii in 1962 and to the continental United States in 1965. In Europe, Shiseido products were first sold in Italy.

Interest in the company's broad product line began to wane in the 1970s. Shiseido then took a new approach and offered an exclusive product line to several top fashion retailers, such as Bloomingdale's in New York and Bullock's in Los Angeles. By the mid-1980s, these lines were earning US$75 million annually and sales were growing by 40 percent each year.

As the brand spread to other countries, Shiseido diversified its product lines with non-Shiseido brands. The IPSA cosmetics brand was launched in 1986. The company also added designer fragrance brands, including Issey Miyake and Jean-Paul Gaultier. During the 1990s, Shiseido continued to acquire new brands, adding Beauté Prestige International S.A., D'icilà, Ettusais, Ayura, and NARS. In 2010 the acquisition of Bare Escentuals increased the brand's presence in the United States.

Shiseido has also sought to increase its visibility by operating beauty salons. In the 1980s, Shiseido acquired Carita S.A., the French beauty salon and beautician school chain, and Zotos International Inc., a leading U.S. supplier of professional hair and salon products. In 1996, Shiseido acquired the North America Hair Salon Division of Helene Curtis Inc. from Unilever United States, Inc.

In 1994 the brand debuted its highly successful, high-end Aupres line of cosmetics, which was developed exclusively for the Chinese market. By mid-1997, Shiseido products were available in 130 stores in 32 Chinese cities.

The 1991 price deregulations in Japan meant competition at home for the first time in the brand's history. In response, Shiseido began to offer lower-priced products and divided its domestic cosmetic lines into consultation-oriented products and "cosmenity" (self-selected products). The company also opened a European production facility in Gien, France.

Shiseido's 125th anniversary was in 1997. To celebrate, Eudermine was introduced to markets outside of Japan. A second Shiseido plant was established in Taiwan, and the company acquired its fourth factory in New Jersey, with the goal of creating one of the largest cosmetics plants in the world. By this time, Shiseido products were being marketed in more than 50 countries worldwide. In 2010, Shiseido opened a factory in Vietnam.

Shiseido joined the United Nations Global Compact of 2004 to demonstrate its commitment to the international community and to developing sustainable business practices. The year 2012 marked the 140th anniversary of the brand, making it one of the longest existing global brands. It renewed its release of Eudermine and celebrated the anniversary throughout the world on the Internet and in life quality seminars.

BRAND ELEMENTS

- Shiseido's name is derived from the Chinese "Book of Changes" and represents its important message to honor virtue, life, and values.
- The camellia flower epitomizes Shiseido's philosophy, symbolizing loveliness and faithfulness.
- The mission of Shiseido is summed up in its tagline: "This moment. This life. Beautifully."

The name Shiseido originated from a passage in *Yi Jing*, a classic Chinese "Book of Changes." The Japanese translation, "Ban butsu shi sei," means, "Praise the virtues of the great Earth, which nurtures new life and brings forth new values."

Camellia flowers adorn the Shiseido brand's Art Nouveau logo with simple lines and curves. Red is the prominent color. Shiseido explains that its logo represents camellia blossoms "floating in a bowl of water."

Eudermine is the product with the oldest association to the Shiseido brand. The unique red liquid moisturizer has been a part of the brand since its introduction in 1897.

"This moment. This life. Beautifully": these words allude to the brand's mission. The full statement of that mission is "For Shiseido, making cosmetics isn't just about caring for people's skin. It's about caring for people."

BRAND IDENTITY

- Working on an emotional level, Shiseido aspires to relate to its consumers in a way that makes them feeling valued, healthy, and beautiful.
- Shiseido's life quality seminars emphasize one-on-one relationships with high school students, people with cancer, and others.
- Shiseido has sought to associate its brand with the larger culture through its support of poetry and the visual arts.

Shiseido made a promise to consumers 140 years ago: "Experience your best skin. Forever." The Shiseido brand works on an emotional level to attract customers. The company's 2011 annual report states, "We cultivate relationships with people. We appreciate genuine, meaningful values. We create beauty, we create wellness."

Shiseido's core values embrace three ideals: "Rich," an experience of purity and beauty; "Human Science," research "[b]eyond chemistry and biology"; and "Omotenashi." In an article for *WAttention,* a magazine focusing on Japanese culture, Muneyuki Joraku explains that Omotenashi is deeper than hospitality: "[I]t is based on a one-to-one relationship... The host anticipates the needs of the guest in advance and offers a pleasant service that guests don't expect."

Shiseido life quality seminars exemplify the brand's ideal of helping people improve their quality of life through cosmetics. Originally held to help high school graduates prepare for their appearance in the business world, the program has been extended to help senior citizens, persons with disabilities, and individuals with emotional issues. Shiseido has also partnered with the Cancer and Careers program in the United States and provided makeup, skincare products, and cosmetic training for cancer patients. The life quality seminars go beyond the application of makeup: their use of the sense of touch builds feelings of trust and self-esteem.

The brand also invests in cultural activities, including support for poetry, contemporary art galleries, the Shiseido Corporate Museum, and the corporate culture magazine, *Hanatsubaki,* which was first published by Shiseido in 1937.

BRAND STRATEGY

- Shiseido offers its varied global markets both Shiseido and non-Shiseido brands.
- The acquisition of Bare Escentuals in 2010 helped Shiseido expand its presence in the United States.
- Strategies to strengthen Shiseido's corporate structure in the United States involved sharing service platforms among premier consumer brands and centralizing distribution.

Shiseido reaches its diverse consumer base through a combination of its own brands and brands that it has acquired. Global Shiseido brands include Shiseido White Lucent and Shiseido Bio-Performance skincare lines, as well as other cosmetic, sun care, and fragrance brands. Acquired brands include Clé de Peau Beauté; Za, a cosmetics line for middle-income consumers; and the Issey Miyake and Jean-Paul Gaultier fragrance brands.

In Shanghai and other urban areas in China, women spend a great deal of money on skincare. In 1994, Shiseido captured this market with its "Chinese national brand," Aupres. The company's research and development center in Beijing has continued its work to take advantage of this evolving market. In 2008 a renewal of the Aupres skincare line included the launch of Aupres Time Lock and Aupres Whitening. The Chinese actress Sun Li portrayed Chinese women of the new era in a series of Aupres advertisements and television commercials. Media events were held in Beijing and Shanghai, as well as other important regional cities.

Shiseido acquired Bare Escentuals for US$1.7 billion in 2010. This gave the Japanese brand a larger presence in the U.S. market. The shrinking population of Japan heightened the need for expanding Shiseido's global consumer base. The yen's value against the dollar made it a wise time to purchase the company. Tatsuyoshi Endo, a Shiseido spokesman in Tokyo, said, "Asia is still the most important market to us, but we wanted more of a boost in the U.S." With the acquisition, Shiseido became the fourth-largest cosmetics company in the world in terms of sales.

In the early spring of 2012, Shiseido's subsidiary bareMinerals designed a lipstick called "Upper Class Red" for the first-class cabin flight attendants of Virgin Airlines. The color was developed to match the red suits worn by the flight attendants. Samples were given to first-class passengers.

During the fiscal year ended March 31, 2012, there was a decrease in domestic sales (which account for over 50 percent of total sales). In response, Shiseido cut new the number of new product launches in half and focused on existing lines. To strengthen the corporate structure in the United States, a shared services platform was created for the financial, legal, and human resources of the company's premier consumer brands; the distribution operations were moved to the distribution center in Columbus, Ohio; and the U.S. manufacturing business and Shiseido America Inc. (SAI) were merged into the umbrella organization Shiseido Americas Corporation (SAC). According to Carsten Fischer, chairman and CEO of Shiseido Americas Corporation, "Together these changes create a seamless, world-class corporate, manufacturing and distribution platform in the US that will benefit all of our brands in the region." The brand planned to continue to concentrate on the Asian market, place greater emphasis on Web-based marketing, and put the consumer first in the spirit of Omotenashi.

BRAND EQUITY

- Shiseido was ranked 387th on Brand Finance's list of the top 500 global brands and 10th among the top cosmetics brands in 2012.
- Interbrand ranked Shiseido 10th on its list of "Japan's top 30 global brands" in 2011.
- Shiseido was the first brand not linked with the auto or electronics industries to make the top 10 on Interbrand's list of top Japanese brands.

Brand Finance estimated Shiseido's 2012 brand value to be US$2.91 billion. Shiseido was ranked 387th in Brand Finance's list of the top 500 global brands in 2012 and 10th among the top 50 cosmetic brands.

In 2011 Interbrand ranked Shiseido tenth among Japan's top 30 global brands. To make this list, a company's overseas sales must make up 30 percent or more of its total sales. Shiseido's rise in the Chinese market is a substantial reason for its success. It was the first Japanese brand not associated with the auto or electronics industries to break into the top 10 on Interbrand's list.

BRAND AWARENESS

- Shiseido's strong brand recognition is the result of word-of-mouth testimonials, its presence in an area, and its community activities.
- China is the largest global market for Shiseido after Japan.
- Shiseido has won numerous awards and has been cited in leading publications for dermatology and beauty.

Shiseido is a strong global brand. Its high brand recognition is the result of word-of-mouth testimonials, its presence in an area, and its community activity. Shiseido's beauty consultants have established consumer trust, and the Camellia Club and the beauty magazine *Hanatsubaki* have helped personalize the brand.

Shiseido's greatest presence has been in the Asia Pacific region, with China as the brand's second-largest global market after Japan. In a 2010 study by the Pao Principle, a global business consulting firm in New York, Shiseido skincare had the highest percentage of Chinese participants, at 8.2 percent. Almost 45 percent of Shiseido's sales come from its international markets.

Shiseido has won top awards from the International Federation of Societies of Cosmetic Chemists (IFSCC) numerous times between the years 2006 and 2011 for its innovations in skincare. The brand has been cited in numerous papers in leading cosmetics, fragrance, and dermatological publications.

During its 140th anniversary, Shiseido used its website to share stories about the brand's history, its approach to management and development, and the role beauty consultants play in its mission. Social responsibility takes precedence at Shiseido. The Mirai-Tsubaki Project is an outward expression of the brand to thank customers and the global community. Shiseido employees engaged in such activities as beauty seminars, raising cancer awareness, and working for Habitat for Humanity both to create a more beautiful world and to bring the brand to a wider global audience. The brand's Facebook project, "140 Campaign's 'Wishes for the World,' " invites people to write a wish for making the world a better place. For every 140 wishes, Shiseido will plant a cherry tree in New York City in collaboration with the New York Restoration Project.

BRAND OUTLOOK

- In 2011 Shiseido's president and CEO, Hisayuki Suekawa, said the company needs to "accelerate globalization to get Shiseido into a growth trajectory."
- Shiseido will need to reduce debt and stabilize sales and profits in domestic and overseas cosmetics.
- The goal for 2018 is for the company to reach consolidated net sales in excess of 1 trillion yen (US$10.7 billion).

In April 2011 Hisayuki Suekawa became the president and CEO of Shiseido. He said, "We must quickly achieve a domestic business turnaround and accelerate globalization to get Shiseido into a growth trajectory."

China has been a major consumer of Shiseido products, but recently China's poor economic situation and a dispute with Japan over islands in the East China Sea caused an unexpected drop in sales. Related protests have caused many manufacturers of global Japanese brands to suspend operations in China. According to *Reuters,* "On Nov. 6, 2012, Standard & Poor's Rating Services revised the outlook on its long-term rating on Japan-based Shiseido Co. Ltd. to negative from stable…[however] Shiseido maintains high brand recognition worldwide and holds a leading position in Japan's cosmetics market, with strong capabilities in product development and market research.

Our assessment of Shiseido's business risk profile remains 'strong.'"

Shiseido's "First Half Results and Outlook," dated October 31, 2012, reported that the protests in China brought no harm to employees or damage to facilities. The Beijing and Shanghai plants stayed open. More than 100 department stores that had been closed were reopened, and one-quarter of the cosmetics specialty stores that had stopped selling Japanese products were selling them again.

Suekawa stated that the plan is to streamline Shiseido's business structure by integrating functions globally. The goals are consistent sales growth and an operating margin of 8 percent. Shiseido's goal for the year ending March 2018 "is to become a company with a consolidated net sales in excess of 1 trillion yen [US$10.7 billion] and an overseas sales ratio of more than 50 percent that can consistently achieve operating profitability of 12 percent or higher and return on equity (ROE) of 15 percent or higher."

FURTHER READING

Brand Finance. "Shiseido." *Brandirectory,* 2012. Accessed November 13, 2012. http://brandirectory.com/profile/shiseido.

Interbrand. "Japan's Best Global Brands: 2011." Accessed November 13, 2012. http://www.interbrand.com/en/newsroom/press-releases/2011-02-01-ea9205c.aspx.

"The International Top 30: 6. Shiseido." *Happi: Household and Personal Products Industry,* n.d. Accessed November 12, 2012. http://www.happi.com/articles/2012/08/6-shiseido.

Joraku, Muneyuki. "Omotenashi: The Heart of Japanese Hospitality." *WAttention,* February 2011. Accessed November 15, 2012. http://www.wattention.com/archives/omotenashi-the-heart-of-japanese-hospitality/.

Ogura, Junko, and Jethro Mullen. "Fresh Anti-Japanese Protests in China on Symbolic Anniversary." *CNN,* September 19, 2012. Accessed November 19, 2012. http://www.cnn.com/2012/09/18/world/asia/china-japan-islands-dispute/index.html.

Pao, Patricia. "Why Shiseido Beats Western Beauty Marketers." *Ad Age China,* September 1, 2010. Accessed November 19, 2012. http://adage.com/china/article/viewpoint/why-shiseido-beats-western-beauty-marketers-in-china/145645/.

Prasso, Sheridan. "Battle for the Face of China." *CNN Money,* December 12, 2005. Accessed November 13, 2012. http://money.cnn.com/magazines/fortune/fortune_archive/2005/12/12/8363110/index.htm.

"S&P: Outlook on Shiseido Negative; 'A' Rtgs Affirmed." *Reuters,* November 6, 2010. Accessed November 19, 2012. http://www.reuters.com/article/2012/11/06/idUSWLA578420121106.

Sanchanta, Mariko, and Ayai Tomisawa and Anjali Cordeiro. "Japan's Shiseido Agrees to Acquire Bare Escentuals." *Wall Street Journal,* January 13, 2010. Accessed November 13, 2012. http://online.wsj.com/article/SB10001424052748704363504575003844097292162.html.

Shiseido. Accessed November 12, 2012. http://www.shiseido.com.

"Shiseido Company Ltd." *Notable Corporate Chronologies.* Detroit: Gale, 2012. *Business and Company Resource Center.* Accessed February 26, 2013. http://galenet.galegroup.com/servlet/BCRC?rsic=PK&rcp=CO&vrsn=unknown&locID=itsbtrial&srchtp=cmp&cc=1&c=1&mode=c&ste=74&tbst=tsCM&tab=4&ccmp=Shiseido+Company+Ltd.&tcp=shiseido&n=25&docNum=I2501151534&bConts=13119.

Yamaguchi, Yuki. "Shiseido to Unveil Cost Cutting Plan to Boost Profit." *Bloomberg,* July 26, 2012. Accessed November 13, 2012. http://www.bloomberg.com/news/2012-07-25/shiseido-to-unveil-cost-cutting-plan-to-boost-profit.html.

SIEMENS

———◆———

AT A GLANCE

———◆———

Brand Synopsis: Siemens, one of the oldest and most diverse industrial brands in the world, strives to become a more recognizable and formidable global competitor in the 21st century.

Parent Company: Siemens Aktiengesellschaft
Wittelsbacherplatz 2
Munich D-80333
Germany
http://www.siemens.com

Sector: Industrials; Energy

Industry Group: Commercial & Professional Services; Energy

Performance: *Sales*—US$100 billion (2011).

Principal Competitors: ABB Group; Emerson Electric; General Electric; Philips Electronics; Honeywell International; Mitsubishi Heavy Industries; Rockwell Automation; United Technologies

BRAND ORIGINS

- Siemens founder Ernst Werner Siemens invented a machine that made it possible to send messages via telegraph in plain language instead of Morse code.
- The company flourished in the late nineteenth century as it became involved in power generation, electric trains, and the production of lightbulbs.

- Siemens AG was established in 1966, when Siemens & Halske merged with Siemens-Schuckertwerke and Siemens-Reiniger-Werke AG.

In the 1840s a young German engineer named Ernst Werner Siemens invented a machine that used a special needle to point to sequences of letters, thus making it possible to send messages via telegraph in plain language instead of Morse code. This became the basis for the first incarnation of the company that today bears the young engineer's name: Telegraphen-Bauanstalt von Siemens & Halske, established on October 12, 1847.

The company flourished in the following decades as it expanded its focus from communication to power generation, electric trains, and the production of lightbulbs. The acquisition of another firm in 1903 resulted in the establishment of Siemens-Schuckertwerke GmbH, the second of the three parent companies that later formed Siemens AG. The last of these came into existence in 1932 as the medical engineering company Siemens-Reiniger-Werke AG.

By this time, Siemens had also begun producing heaters and appliances, but with the rise of the Nazi regime in Germany, it began redirecting its energy and communication divisions toward military applications. The company's leadership actively supported the Nazis and made extensive use of slave labor in concentration camps during World War II. The end of the war left Siemens greatly diminished, reduced to producing such basic necessities as cooking pots. Like Germany itself, the company underwent a period of rehabilitation and reconstruction. By the mid-1950s, Siemens had begun producing semiconductors.

In 1966 the existing three parent companies merged to form Siemens AG. The company spread into a number of new areas, including nuclear power production in the 1970s, digital telephony in the 1980s, and personal computing in the 1990s. The reunification of Germany in 1990 breathed new life into Siemens, which expanded in central and eastern Europe, as well as eastern Asia, during the years that followed.

BRAND ELEMENTS

- The first Siemens & Halske logos, which appeared in 1897, featured the superimposed letters *S* and *H* in various configurations.
- The contemporary Siemens logo is a variation on a basic design introduced in 1973.
- Blending a cool blue with a warm, friendly green, the color of the Siemens logo suggests technical competence combined with a human touch.

The history of Siemens is written in its logos, the first of which appeared in 1897, when Siemens & Halske marked a half-century in business and was incorporated. These early logos included the superimposed letters *S* and *H* and generally took two forms. The first had a shape similar to a dollar sign with two vertical lines, usually in a font that bore a superficial resemblance to the flowery script in common use at the time. However, there is a muscular, Gothic quality to the Siemens logos that evokes the bold and aggressive atmosphere of the German Empire of the late nineteenth century.

The second basic type of logo that emerged in the company's early years seems, in retrospect at least, to foreshadow a German Empire even more dynamic and dangerous than the kaiser's. Most variations on this design use a strong, unadorned sans-serif font, invariably rendered in a striking black, with an elongated *S* and a much smaller capital *H,* set at a 45-degree angle to the left, which straddles the *S*'s middle. The result bears a strong resemblance to the Nazi swastika. Succeeding versions of this design dominated Siemens brand symbolism during the Nazi era, but its use did not come to an end with World War II. This memorable brand mark remained in widespread use until the 1970s, and according to a 2002 official history of Siemens logos (which makes no reference to the swastika), "was used until very recently for components that were too small for the present Siemens logo."

The contemporary Siemens logo is a variation on a basic design introduced in 1973, which consists simply of the logotype "Siemens" rendered in strong, sleek, black capitals. A new version, slightly rounded and light blue in color, appeared in 1991. Simple as it is, the Siemens logo is extremely specific in its design, and the rules governing its usage are very precise. The font of the logotype is proprietary, as is the shade of blue, Pantone 321 or "petrel." In 2006 the company reset color values for the old Pantone 320 by increasing the ratio of yellow, resulting in a shade that blends a cool, almost cold, blue with a warm, friendly green. The effect suggests a marriage of serious-minded technical competence with a restful, comforting human touch.

BRAND IDENTITY

- Siemens has used so many logos in its history that in 2002 it published a 42-page booklet chronicling their evolution.
- Only in the third quarter of the 20th century did Siemens develop a consistent global branding effort.
- The blue-green 1973 logotype—Siemens's first official logo—reflected its emerging global emphasis.
- As a company involved in diverse industrial sectors, Siemens has long grappled with the challenge of establishing a clear, consistent image.

Over the course of more than one-and-a-half centuries, the Siemens brand has encompassed a variety of companies—the three "parent corporations," various joint ventures, wholly owned subsidiaries, and finally Siemens AG itself—that have operated in a wide array of industrial sectors. Understandably, then, the company has represented itself in numerous ways through the symbolism of logos and advertising, an evolution chronicled in a 42-page booklet published by Siemens in 2002.

Through the mid-20th century, Siemens focused primarily on the German market, and its symbolism reflected this fact. Not only did it direct its advertising primarily toward regional consumers, but its logos had a bold, apparently militaristic quality reflective of pre-1945 German design. As it expanded into larger geographic markets during the postwar years, however, Siemens began to develop a consistent global branding effort with a distinctly different focus. This fact became manifest in 1973 as the company for the first time adopted an official logo.

Whereas the old symbol had appeared almost invariably in black, the new logotype (a logo consisting exclusively of text) used a soft bluish green that suggested peace and globalism. Its rounded letters, in sharp contrast with the angular shape of the old symbol, likewise reinforced a friendly, inclusive image. Siemens's global character became such a fundamental aspect of its brand image that in 2001 it added the slogan "Global network of innovation" to the logotype. According to the booklet on the history of Siemens's logos, this step reflected the influence of "global trends," and though Siemens eventually dropped the four-word slogan, its emphasis on globalism has remained its defining quality. As a company involved in diverse industrial sectors, many of which do not involve direct contact with the general public, Siemens has long grappled with the challenge of establishing a clear, consistent image among consumers. Summing up this challenge, a Siemens creative director told Diane Anderson of *Brandweek,* "Our company is ubiquitous but invisible; we're behind the scenes—that's the dilemma."

BRAND STRATEGY

- At various times, Siemens has been involved in personal computing, cellular phone communications, nuclear power, lightbulbs, and a range of other products and services.
- In an attempt to focus its activities, Siemens has gone through numerous restructuring and reorganization efforts.
- Two-fifths of Siemens's business comes from the Industry division, which includes industry automation, mobility, motion control, and building technology.
- The Energy division, which accounts for one-third of Siemens's business, includes fossil power generation, oil and gas extraction, and renewable energy.

It began life as a communications company, but ultimately Siemens would involve itself in a wide array of businesses ranging from energy production to medical engineering and the manufacture of home appliances. For a few years during the early part of the twentieth century, it even made cars, but in the aftermath of World War II, it was relegated to manufacturing humble but necessary products, such as coal shovels and wood-burning stoves. At various times the company has been involved in personal computing, cellular phone communications, nuclear power, lightbulbs, and a range of other products and services.

Given this diversity of activities, Siemens has long faced a challenge in defining a unified corporate brand strategy. "For decades," according to a 2010 profile in the *Economist,* "Siemens was the problem child of European heavy industry," with a problem that could be attributed in part to an "inability to decide on whether to concentrate on making the guts of modern industrial societies such as trains, turbines, and transformers, or … clever, zippy things such as mobile phones and computer chips."

In part to address this apparent lack of focus, the company has reorganized itself numerous times, and by 2012 it had settled into five major divisions: Industry, Energy, Health Care, Infrastructure and Cities, and Financial Services. Industry, which accounted for 44 percent of Siemens's business in 2010, includes automation, mobility systems, motion control, lightbulbs and light-emitting diodes, and building technology. Energy, which comprised 33 percent of sales for 2010, includes fossil power generation, oil and gas extraction, power distribution and transmission, renewable (wind) energy, and power plant services and operations. Under the Health Care division (16 percent) are diagnostics, imaging and networking, and health care systems and services. Much of the remaining 7 percent belongs to Infrastructure and Cities, which applies expertise from the Industry and Energy sectors to areas such as rail systems and smart grids.

BRAND EQUITY

- In 2010, *Forbes* ranked Siemens AG among the 10 largest conglomerates in the world.
- Siemens ranked second only to rival General Electric on the *Financial Times'* list of the world's most valuable industrial companies in 2011.
- In 2011, Siemens employed some 360,000 people, operated in more than 190 countries worldwide, and generated revenues of approximately US$100 million.
- Although eclipsed by GE on Interbrand's ranking of global brands for 2012, Siemens has emerged from financial troubles to become increasingly profitable.

The vast Siemens enterprise is among the world's largest corporations, a fact reflected in its placement along with competitors General Electric, Honeywell International, Philips Electronics, and United Technologies on *Forbes*'s unranked list of the "World's Largest Conglomerates Overall" for 2010. The *Financial Times* ranked it second on its 2011 list of "World's Most Valuable General Industrial Companies," with a market value of US$125.5 billion, compared to US$212.9 billion for GE. In 2011, Siemens employed some 360,000 people, operated in more than 190 countries worldwide, and generated revenues of approximately US$100 million. In Interbrand's 2012 ranking of the best global brands, Siemens was in 51st place, with a brand value of US$7.5 billion.

This valuation represented a five-percent drop from 2011, and in any case Siemens's brand value paled in comparison to that of sixth-ranked GE, with an estimated worth of US$43.7 billion. Nevertheless, Siemens had come a long way since the late twentieth century, when, in the words of the *Economist,* it came to be known as "the problem child of European heavy industry.… lurching from profit to loss almost quarter by quarter as big infrastructure projects went wrong or spending spiraled out of control."

By the fall of 2010, this had changed, and Siemens's stock performance had, in the words of Christopher C. Williams in *Barron's,* left competitors such as GE and ABB "in the dust." Thanks to astute planning, the 163-year-old corporation was "acting as nimble as a teenager." The *Economist* noted that, although GE remained twice as big as Siemens in terms of market capitalization, in 2007 it had been three times as big, and the gradual narrowing of the gap could be attributed to wise changes in Siemens's structure and operations.

BRAND AWARENESS

- Siemens has garnered negative publicity for its association with totalitarian regimes and bribery scandals.

- As part of its effort to overcome past negative associations, Siemens is heavily committed to a number of charitable corporate activities.
- Through the "Spin the globe" and "Siemens answers" campaigns, Siemens in the early twenty-first century has sought to increase awareness of its brand worldwide.

Despite the overall success of Siemens as a company, the Siemens brand has sometimes made headlines for negative reasons. Like other world-famous brands such as Bayer, Kodak, Porsche, and Hugo Boss, it bears the taint of association with the Nazi regime in the 1930s and 1940s. More recently, the brand's global dealings also attracted unwanted attention. In 2007, the European Union fined Siemens and other major corporations for price-fixing through a cartel, and a worldwide series of bribery scandals around the same time resulted in additional fines of more than US$1.3 billion. In 2009, telecommunications equipment supplied through a joint venture with Nokia put the Siemens name in the news when the Islamic fundamentalist regime in Iran used its monitoring capabilities in an effort to suppress protests.

Siemens invests heavily in various corporate citizenship efforts, including education and science initiatives, arts sponsorships, and environmental awareness projects. Such efforts may help the brand overcome past negative associations, but Siemens's marketing has had to confront what may be in some ways a greater challenge: lack of brand awareness. As Diane Anderson wrote in *Brandweek,* "While many people have heard of Siemens, few know what it actually does."

To change this situation, Siemens launched a series of advertising campaigns in the early twenty-first century, built around the tagline "Spin the globe," that emphasized a personal association with the brand's technological solutions. It even invested in developing soundscapes with the help of German branding firm Metadesign, whose 10 composers created a variety of aural signatures to reflect the brand's history and core values.

The US$145-million "Siemens answers" campaign, launched in conjunction with the company's 160th anniversary in 2007, conveyed the message that Siemens could provide solutions in a number of areas. Brand consultant Jim Gregory told Kate Maddox of *B to B,* "Anything they can do to simplify their business, which is hugely complex, and put more effort behind explaining what the company actually is and what their value proposition is, the better their corporate brand will be."

BRAND OUTLOOK

- In 2011, Siemens ended its involvement in the nuclear industry, which dated back to 1959.
- The future of the Siemens brand includes greater emphasis on renewable energy, global markets, and the Infrastructure and Cities division.

- Thanks to a restructuring effort that began in 1998, Siemens has become increasingly profitable and competitive in the global marketplace.

In September 2011, Siemens ended more than a half-century of involvement in the nuclear industry. Spurred by fears arising from the Fukushima disaster in Japan in March of that year, when an earthquake caused a series of equipment failures and the release of hazardous materials from a nuclear power plant, Germany began to put the brakes on its own nuclear industry. Siemens, which had built all 17 nuclear plants in Germany, had already begun moving toward an emphasis on alternative energy sources, notably wind power.

Another emerging area of focus was the Infrastructure and Cities division, created in 2011, which merged expertise from the Energy and Industry divisions to provide technological and logistical solutions for rapidly growing urban areas in China, India, Russia, and other countries. These developing regions promised to hold increasing interest for Siemens in coming years, although the mature markets of Europe and North America still accounted for the greater portion of its business: in 2010 the company earned 55 percent of its revenues from Europe, and another 19 percent from the United States.

As part of a streamlining effort that began in 1998, the company continued to sell off businesses in an effort to maximize the value of both its portfolio and its brand. In 2011, for instance, it divested itself of the Industry division's Information Technology and Services unit and announced plans to sell most of Osram, its lighting business. As Siemens marked its 165th birthday in the fall of 2012, profits and expectations were rising, suggesting that many new ventures lay ahead for one of the world's oldest brands.

FURTHER READING

Anderson, Diane. "Siemens Engineers Name Recognition." *Brandweek,* December 5, 2005, 6.

Klaffke, Thomas. *The History of the Siemens Logo 1878-2001.* Munich: Siemens, 2002. Accessed October 24, 2012. https://www.cee.siemens.com/web/ua/ru/about/Documents/Siemens-LogoHistory3.pdf.

Maddox, Kate. "Siemens Rolls out Global Ad Campaign." *B to B,* November 12, 2007, 3.

Siemens AG. Accessed October 24, 2012. http://www.siemens.com.

"Siemens: A Giant Awakens." *Economist,* September 9, 2010. Accessed October 24, 2012. http://www.economist.com/node/16990709?story_id=16990709&fsrc=rss.

Williams, Christopher C. "Slimmed-Down Siemens Girds for Growth." *Barron's,* November 27, 2010. Accessed October 24, 2012. http://online.barrons.com/article/SB50001424052970204474604575632480683950368.html.

Wylie, Ian. "Sounds to Brand By." *Fast Company,* January 2004, 38.

SINGAPORE AIRLINES

———————●———————

AT A GLANCE

●

Brand Synopsis: Singapore Airlines is a brand known for its exemplary cabin service and innovation, represented by its iconic "Singapore Girls" air hostesses.

Parent Company: Singapore Airlines Limited
Airline House
Singapore
http://www.singaporeair.com

Sector: Industrials

Industry Group: Transportation

Performance: *Sales*—US$12 billion (2012.)

Principal Competitors: Cathay Pacific Airways Limited; Japan Airlines Co., Ltd.; Malaysian Airline System Berhad

BRAND ORIGINS

- Singapore Airlines Limited was established in 1972.
- With no domestic routes, Singapore Airlines had to market itself as an international carrier.
- The Singapore Girls became the face of the Singapore Airlines brand.
- Singapore Airlines established itself as an innovative airline, the first to offer hot towels, hot meals, and free alcoholic and nonalcoholic beverages.
- Singapore Airline became known for operating one of the industry's newest fleets.

As one of the most respected brands in the airline industry, Singapore Airlines (SIA) traces its history to 1936, when the British government and Imperial Airways formed Malayan Airways Limited (MAL). It was formally incorporated the following year but because of competition with an Australian carrier and the Japanese occupation of the region during World War II, MAL did not become operational until 1947. Renamed Malaysia-Singapore Airlines (MSA), the carrier was a joint venture owned by the Malaysian and Singapore governments, but after Singapore separated from Malaysia, the Malaysian government announced in 1970 that it would establish its own national airline. MSA was dissolved and the assets were divided between the two governments. In June 1972 SIA was established.

SIA faced a unique challenge that would place a greater emphasis on marketing and branding. Because it had no domestic routes to provide a steady source of unopposed business, the fledgling airline had to establish itself as a viable alternative to established international airlines. Not only did it have to gain access to airports and negotiate landing rights but also it had to attract customers. SIA decided on a marketing strategy that would build a brand associated with excellent customer care, premium service, and the best available technologies.

At the heart of SIA's branding effort were its air hostesses, who were known as the Singapore Girls. Young, attractive, and fluent in English, they were trained to pamper SIA passengers by providing friendly and efficient service. Soon, they were outfitted in custom-designed sarongs to emphasize their Geisha-like qualities and distinguish them further from the flight attendants of other airlines. The Singapore Girls became the focal point of the Singapore Airlines brand and SIA's advertising.

In 1981 a new Singapore airport opened, allowing SIA to improve its service to visitors. With the Singapore Girls serving as the public face, SIA bolstered its brand by being the first airline to offer hot towels, hot meals, and free alcoholic and nonalcoholic beverages. The airline also invested heavily in new aircraft, maintaining one of the newest fleets in the industry. As a result of all these factors, by the early 1980s SIA was named the Asia-Pacific region's top airline according to customer preference.

The Singapore Girls remained the key to SIA's successful marketing. They gained almost celebrity status in the Far East. Thousands of girls in the region vied to become Singapore Girls. At the turn of the new century SIA continued to emphasize hospitality and innovation by becoming the first airline to offer personal entertainment systems and video-on-demand in all cabins. However, as the first decade of the new century came to a close, SIA faced increasing competition. Despite protests that the Singapore Girl was outdated and sexist, the airline continued to rely on the distinctive hostess as a way to distinguish its brand.

BRAND ELEMENTS

- The Singapore Girl was a creation of Batey Ads Ltd.
- The sarong kebaya flight hostess uniform was designed by the Parisian couturier Pierre Balmain.
- In-flight comforts are an important brand element.
- Singapore Airlines was the first carrier to fly the Airbus A380.

The most important element of the SIA brand is the Singapore Girl. It was created by Ian Batey, who ran Batey Ads Ltd., Singapore's largest advertising agency. According to Philip Shenon in the *New York Times*, Batey "decided that the best way to lure passengers, especially male business passengers, to the airline was by promoting attentive, luxurious in-flight service from pretty, young women." Initially, the air hostesses wore skirts and blouses, but in 1974 SIA introduced a new uniform that, in the words of *Brandweek*'s Bernadette Doran, "embodies every aspect of the Singapore Airlines brand promise: An authentic Asian experience dedicated to service, comfort, luxury and perfection." Designed by the Parisian couturier Pierre Balmain, the new frock was based on a traditional Malay garment, the sarong kebaya. It was customer-fitted for each hostess and cut tight to emphasize slender figures, so tight in fact that blouses sometimes split when hostesses closed overhead bins. The new uniform came in four colors, representing different ranks.

SIA took great pains in the recruitment and training of its Singapore Girls. While about 90 percent of the hostesses were born in Singapore or Malaysia, the airline also recruited in China, India, Indonesia, Japan, Korea, and Taiwan. Shenon noted that aside from an ability to speak fluent English, applicants were required to be younger than 26 years old, at least 5 feet 2 inches tall, "slim and attractive with a good complexion and a warm personality." Successful applicants then underwent four months of training. Not only did they learn life-saving and firefighting techniques, train in simulated crashes, and learn the proper way to handle disruptive passengers, but also they were taught hair and makeup and how to sit, walk, and climb stairs with poise and deportment. They were hired under five years contracts and were initially required to retire from flight duty at age 35. The rule was modified in 1986 so that mandatory retirement was changed to 15 years of service. At that point, many Singapore Girls stayed with the airline but with on-ground positions. More than just the employees who represented the brand directly to passengers, the Singapore Girls were also the focus of SIA's advertisements. Complementing these images was the tagline "A Great Way to Fly."

In-flight comforts became another important aspect of the Singapore Airlines brand. Hot towels were handed out to passengers, a traditional Singaporean gesture of hospitality. It was a service so distinctive that it soon become a standard practice for airlines around the world. SIA developed its own unique scent, Stafan Floridian Waters, which became another trademark of the brand. Blended into the hot towels, the distinctive scent soon permeated the SIA fleet. Other passenger comforts were introduced as well over the years. In many respects, SIA positioned itself as an entertainment company as much as an airline. However, it never forgot its brand promise: luxury, superior service, and comfort with an Asian flair.

The SIA fleet also played a key role in the growth of the Singapore Airlines brand. A month after it was formed, SIA bought its first Boeing 747s, which served as the backbone of the fleet for a number of years. SIA continued to upgrade its fleet with new aircraft. During the late 1970s SIA flew the Concorde in a joint operation with British Airways. In the early 1980s SIA replaced its entire fleet and continued to upgrade it in the 1990s. During the first decade of the 21st century SIA became the launch customer for the new Airbus A380, the world's largest airliner. For a few years, the A380 was almost as important a marketing hook as the Singapore Girls, until other airlines began flying the A380.

BRAND IDENTITY

- Since its founding in 1972, Singapore Airlines has pursued a service differentiation strategy.

- The Singapore Girls embody a brand promise of Asian warmth and hospitality.
- Singapore Airline promotes a reputation as an innovator and trendsetter.
- Maintaining a new fleet is an important part of Singapore Air's brand identity.

Singapore Airlines has presented a clear brand identity throughout its history, based on a service differentiation strategy. As a young airline forced to compete against established international carriers, SIA elected to create a reputation for offering the highest quality service. The Singapore Girls who serve as air hostesses epitomize the brand. Possessing archetypal Asian beauty, they are poised, attentive, and caring. Their uniforms give them a Geisha look, further emphasizing the promise of Asian warmth and hospitality.

In keeping with its best-in-brand approach, SIA seeks to maintain a reputation as an innovator and trendsetter. During the 1970s it was the first airline to offer free headsets and a choice of meals and free drinks to economy-class passengers. In 1991 SIA became the first airline to offer satellite-based in-flight telephones. Ahead of the curve, SIA installed a "cabin management interactive system" in every seat, providing passengers with six-inch video screens and a choice of movies and video games.

Another aspect of SIA's brand identity is its fleet. The aircraft are regularly upgraded. Not only are they new and presumed more reliable but also they are often the latest generation of aircraft, such as the Airbus A380. The young fleet reinforces SIA's reputation as an innovator, and also makes a promise of greater passenger safety. Given that SIA aircraft are required to make extended flights, primarily over the ocean, the assurance of a safe flight is important to passengers and SIA's brand image.

BRAND STRATEGY

- The first advertisement by Singapore Airlines combined the image of a Singapore Girl with the tagline "This girl's in love with you."
- The "Singapore Girl, you're a great way to fly" slogan was eventually shortened to "A Great Way to Fly."
- Passenger amenities are an important part of the strategy by Singapore Airlines.
- During the early 2000s the A380 served as a point of differentiation for Singapore Airlines.

To set itself apart from its better-established competition, Singapore Airlines took immediate steps after its founding in 1972 to differentiate itself in terms of service by forging a marketing strategy that emphasized passenger comfort. At the heart of that effort were the airline's hostesses, the Singapore Girls, whose friendly and efficient service immediately became the face of the brand. The airline's first advertisement featured one of the hostesses,

accompanied with the tagline "This girl's in love with you." The image of the Singapore Girl was refined further in 1974 with the introduction of the sarong kebaya uniform. It was accompanied by the new advertising tagline "Singapore Girl, you're a great way to fly." The slogan was eventually shortened to "A Great Way to Fly."

The image of the Singapore Girl and the slogan remained consistent over the years. Even when SIA was promoting new destinations, aircraft, or services, the Singapore Girl remained a key element in all advertising. Male flight attendants, so-called Singapore Guys, were also hired, but they were rarely seen. On flights, they worked in the background to support the Singapore Girls, who interacted with customers.

SIA expanded its brand to new markets as the airline gained airport access. In 1977 SIA began service to Guam, Honolulu, and San Francisco. Flights to Los Angeles by way of Tokyo were launched in 1980. By 1987 SIA flew to 54 cities in 37 countries. Expansion continued in the following decade. In 1994 SIA's network grew to 68 cities in 40 countries. In 2004 SIA began offering nonstop service to Los Angeles and New York, which attracted considerable press attention that reinforced SIA's reputation for innovation.

SIA also promoted its reputation as a trendsetter by introducing a variety of passenger amenities over the years. During the 1970s it became the first airline to provide a choice of meals and free drinks to economy-class passengers. In the 1990s SIA convened an "International Culinary Panel" to develop a new slate of in-flight meals. SIA was the first to offer satellite telephone service in 1991, and was also a pioneer in audio and video-on-demand services. In addition, SIA became the first airline to fly the new Airbus A380, allowing it to offer the largest first-class cabins in the commercial airline industry.

In time, SIA faced increasing criticism for its reliance on the Singapore Girls. In 2004 SIA launched a brand awareness campaign in the United Kingdom that for the first time did not use the image of a Singapore Girl. In fact, much of the focus of the airline's marketing during this period centered on the A380, along with business-class beds and gourmet foods. As other airlines began adopting the A380, SIA lost that competitive edge. In 2011 SIA returned the Singapore Girls to the focal point of its advertising. Instead of just print and television advertising, SIA now made use of social media and other online tools. For example, the airline released videos on YouTube that documented the making of the new Singapore Girl television commercials, which were filmed in San Francisco, Paris, India, and China. Also unchanged was the slogan "A Great Way to Fly" and the promise of high standards of customer care and service.

BRAND EQUITY

- Strong brand equity allows Singapore Airlines to command a premium fare.
- In 2012 Brand Finance estimated Singapore Airlines' brand value as US$3.2 billion.
- In 2012 Brand Finance listed Singapore Airlines number 351 on its list of the world's 500 most valuable brands.
- Singapore Airlines was Singapore's top brand in 2012 for the fifth consecutive year.
- Singapore Airlines was the second-most valuable airline brand in 2011.

For much of its history, SIA was able to avoid discounting its fares and remain fiscally healthy. It was able to attract passengers who were willing to pay a premium price because of the superior experience it offered, including the sense of safety provided by newer aircraft, the excellent cuisine, entertainment choices, and the attentive service of the air hostesses. Taken altogether, these attributes created brand equity for SIA, allowing the airline to charge a higher fare than most of its competition.

In 2012 Brand Finance estimated a brand value of US$3.2 billion for Singapore Airlines. As a result, the company was ranked 351st on Brand Finance's list of the 500 most valuable global brands. That same year it was awarded the number-1 position on the list of Singapore's top-100 brands. It was the fifth consecutive year SIA achieved that honor. In terms of the top airline brands, Singapore Airlines ranked second in 2011, trailing only Lufthansa.

BRAND AWARENESS

- The popularity of the Singapore Girl has been a key to the brand awareness of Singapore Airlines.
- The Singapore Girl became so iconic that it earned a place in Madame Tussauds museum in London.
- Singapore Airlines is highly regarded for quality, value, image, and customer understanding.

Singapore Airlines enjoys strong brand awareness, due in no small measure to the Singapore Girl. The company's long-time symbol is so well known that a wax figure of a Singapore Girl is on display at Madame Tussauds museum in London. In Asia, becoming a Singapore Girl is the dream of many young women. Even though the perceived glamour of the Singapore Girl is the attraction for this group, Singapore Airlines benefits from improved brand awareness.

Indicative of its recognition and strong reputation, SIA was the second-ranked airline brand in 2011. The airline is also well known for its superior service. In the United Kingdom, for example, a *Reader's Digest* survey on the most trusted brands in the early 2000s revealed that consumers ranked SIA the top airline in terms of quality, value, image, and customer understanding—beating out British Airways, the country's leading airline. SIA also won awards for its service, including being the "World's Best Cabin Crew Service" for 17 straight years in the Business Traveler Asia-Pacific Awards. It was that kind of perception that not only increased brand awareness but also created customer loyalty.

BRAND OUTLOOK

- After other carriers began flying the A380, Singapore Airlines' marketing returned to a focus on the Singapore Girls.
- Criticisms of Singapore Airlines' service increased during the early 2000s.
- To attract cost-conscious travelers, Singapore Airlines developed the Scoot budget brand in 2012.

Singapore Airlines' marketing strategy has remained consistent throughout its history. When the airline took delivery of the superjumbo A380 jet in 2007, it emphasized the aircraft in its marketing. After other carriers began flying the A380, SIA returned its focus to its Singapore Girls, but a lot had changed since the airline's first "This girl's in love with you" ad campaign. To many, the charm of the Singapore Girl had waned. The Singapore Girls themselves were unionized and objected to being forced to retire at such a young age. As the age of the "girls" increased to the late 30s and early 40s, the union bargained for greater job security, seeking a minimum flying career of 20 years. As a result, the youthful image of the Singapore Girl was beginning to fade.

Even though the refocus on the Singapore Girl was meant to play up Singapore Airlines' renown cabin service, the airline's reputation for unmatched service was also coming under question. According to Karamjit Kaur, writing in the *Strait Times* in June 2012, criticism of the carrier's service was growing: "Whether it is the food or website, service on the ground or in the air, SIA is not what it used to be, say a growing number of disgruntled customers. The consensus seems to be that while SIA is still a good airline, others are just as good, if not better—and often cheaper too."

Boding well for SIA was a global travel and tourism industry that was expected to grow despite poor economic conditions. However, much of that growth was likely to come from more cost-conscious travelers. To capture them without diluting the Singapore Airlines brand, SIA launched two new services in 2012: Scoot, a long-haul budget brand, and SilkAir, a regional carrier. Singapore Airlines was likely to retain its status as a premium carrier and continue to attract its share of affluent passengers, but its future was not lacking in challenges.

FURTHER READING

Arnold, Wayne. "For the Singapore Girl, It's Her Time to Shine." *New York Times*, December 31, 1999.

Brand Finance. "Global 500 2012." *Brandirectory.* Accessed January 25, 2013. http://brandirectory.com/league_tables/table/global-500-2012.

Doran, Bernadette. "The Clothes Make the Brand." *Brandweek*, August 23, 1999.

Kaur, Karamjit. "Singapore Girl No Longer Rules Alone." *Strait Times*, June 17, 2012.

Shenon, Philip. "The Last Stewardess." *New York Times*, October 25, 1992.

"Singapore Airlines Limited." *International Director of Company Histories.* Ed. Jay P. Pederson. Vol. 83. Detroit, MI: St. James Press. 2007.

"'Singapore Girl' Makes Comeback as Airline Banks on Superior Service." *Sydney Morning Herald*, August 1, 2011.

SINOPEC

—■—

AT A GLANCE

—■—

Brand Synopsis: The largest producer of refined oil and petrochemical products in China, Sinopec espouses values of innovation, efficiency, and patriotic optimism.

Parent Company: China Petrochemical Corporation (aka Sinopec Group)

22 Chaoyangmen North Street

Chaoyang District

Beijing

China

http://english.sinopec.com

Sector: Energy

Industry Group: Energy

Performance: *Sales*—US$391.5 billion (2011).

Principal Competitors: CNOOC Ltd.; Exxon Mobil Corp.; PetroChina Co. Ltd.

BRAND ORIGINS

- Sinopec was created in 1983 when the Chinese government established the China Petrochemical Corporation to manage China's production and refinement of crude oil.
- In February 2000 China Petrochemical incorporated Sinopec as a subsidiary to compete on the global oil market.

- Sinopec was taken public in October 2000 with listings on the New York, London, and Hong Kong stock exchanges.
- In November 2006 Sinopec purchased a 51 percent share of the Yadavaran oil fields in Iran for a combined deal worth US$128 billion.
- In 2009–10 Sinopec invested US$11.9 billion in Canadian oil companies.

Sinopec was created in 1983 when the Chinese government established the China Petrochemical Corporation (also known as Sinopec Group) to manage China's production and refinement of crude oil. At the time the country was producing more than 600 million barrels of crude oil each year and needed a specialized organization that could manage those resources more effectively and perhaps even expand production. Within a decade of its founding, CPC's production facilities were processing more than 2 million barrels of crude oil per day, and its refineries were producing an additional million barrels of processed oil products each day. As both production and processing improved, CPC began looking at the possibilities of expanding its business into the global market. On February 28, 2000, CPC incorporated the China Petroleum and Chemical Corporation (CPCC), also known as Sinopec Corporation. This new subsidiary would take over full control of all oil production and refinement processes from its parent company. On October 18, 2000, Sinopec Corp. was taken public, simultaneously listing on the New York, Hong Kong, and London stock exchanges with a total issuance of 16.8 billion H shares. On that first day of trading, US$1.9 billion in shares were purchased

974

by three of the largest oil companies in the world—BP Amoco, Exxon Mobil, and Royal Dutch Shell of the Netherlands. By August 8, 2001, Sinopec was also listed on the Shanghai Stock Exchange, issuing an additional 2.8 billion shares.

With plenty of cash reserves now available, Sinopec set out aggressively to increase its territory and resources. On August 24, 2001, it made its first acquisition, the New Star Petroleum Company from its parent CPC. Before Sinopec could proceed with its acquisition strategy, China joined the World Trade Organization (WTO) in December 2001, which opened new options and opportunities for Sinopec in the foreign markets. However, it also meant that foreign companies could now compete in the domestic Chinese market. With the overall picture becoming more competitive on all fronts, Sinopec calculated that the only way to realistically be competitive with the global oil giants was to increase productivity. In order to make this work, the company eliminated unnecessary expenditures and shifted the saved funds into upgrades and purchases of new equipment and research and exploration for new, untapped oil reserves. By the end of 2001 the company had laid off almost 70,000 employees. In 2003 Sinopec spent US$2.4 billion on exploration, with the goal of increasing oil reserves by 25 percent. That same year the company spent another US$1 billion to increase refining capacity. In 2004 and 2005 the three major oil companies that owned stock in Sinopec sold off their shares, making huge profits in the process. Shell and BP nearly doubled their investments, and Exxon earned more than US$6.1 billion in profits alone from the sale.

In 2006 Sinopec picked up its expansion strategy once again and began looking for new opportunities in the foreign markets. In August 2006 the company received a contract worth US$2.8 billion from Iran to upgrade and expand several refineries located in that country. This opened the door to a truly massive acquisition for Sinopec. In November 2006 Sinopec purchased a 51 percent share in the Yadavaran oil fields for US$70 billion. In addition the company agreed to purchase 250 million tons of liquefied natural gas from Iran over the next 25 years. The total value of the deal was about US$128 billion. The Yadavaran field is estimated to hold up to 17 billion barrels of oil. In April 2007 a Sinopec drilling site in Ethiopia was attacked by a Somali rebel group that killed 74 workers, including 9 Chinese employees, and kidnapped 7 others. The attackers later released the 7 hostages but warned against any further trespassing by foreign companies into the region. Sinopec, however, was not deterred from continuing operations at the facility.

In the fall of 2008 a global recession occurred, and no company was spared from its effects. Sinopec suffered a serious downturn in sales, but by 2009 the company had recovered almost fully, once again earning record profits and continuing on its mission of global expansion. In August 2009 Sinopec purchased the Canadian company Addax Petroleum for US$7.2 billion. In April 2010 the company acquired from Conoco Phillips its 9 percent ownership of the Canadian oil sands company Syncrude for US$4.7 billion. In October 2012 Sinopec purchased 20 oil wells in southern Nigeria from Total E&P for US$2.5 billion. In addition, the company paid US$1.5 billion for 49 percent ownership of Talisman Energy Inc. for oil field production in the North Sea.

BRAND ELEMENTS

- The name Sinopec can be broken down into two parts: *Sino* is the Latin prefix for Chinese and *pec* stands for *pe*troleum *c*ompany.
- Sinopec identifies each letter of its name with a particular meaning: Sustainable, International, National, Oil, People, Environment, Cooperation.
- Sinopec refers to its company logo as the "Rising Sun."

The name Sinopec can be broken down into *Sino*, which is a prefix referring to China or anything Chinese, and *pec*, which stands for *pe*troleum *c*orporation. Sino has its roots in the Latin word *sinae* and, further back, from the Greek *sinai*, which is probably of Indo-Aryan origin. On its website Sinopec identifies each letter of its name with its own meaning: Sustainable, International, National, Oil, People, Environment, Cooperation.

The Sinopec logo, internally referred to by the company as the "Rising Sun," contains the outline of a red sun with the name of the company in black western-style lettering in front of it, while inside the "Rising Sun" the name is in black Chinese characters. The Sinopec name at the base of the logo has also been designed into meaningful shapes:

The *S* is in the shape of a fuel pump.

The *I* and *N* are in the elongated shape of an oil derrick.

The *O* represents a container tank.

The *P* represents an oil pipeline.

The *E* represents informatization.

The *C* represents a chemical symbol, which in turn represents petrochemical products.

BRAND IDENTITY

- Sinopec prides itself on being one of the most productive energy companies in the world and one that is innovative and environmentally friendly.
- In 2011 Sinopec was named the "best managed company" in Asia.
- Sinopec advertising uses a combination of patriotic messages and statistics to emphasize its accomplishments.

Sinopec brands itself as more than simply a gigantic, unfeeling corporation. To the contrary, Sinopec takes pride in not only being one of the most productive energy companies in the world, but one that is inventive, resourceful, and environmentally friendly. Sinopec promotes its success as a technological innovator and a leader in production efficiency. The company has applied for 23,031 patents and received 11,939. It has earned 46 national technology invention awards, as well as the 2011 *FinanceAsia* award for Asia's best managed company. In terms of environmental issues, it increased refinery throughput by 108 percent while at the same time reducing the energy consumption of those same refineries by 24 percent. Sinopec also notes that in five years the company reduced its carbon dioxide emissions by 34.7 million metric tons, equivalent to taking 10 million cars off the road for one year.

In its advertising and press releases, Sinopec uses a combination of patriotic messages and statistics to emphasize its accomplishments. For example, in a Sinopec television commercial, the message "In a fast changing world Sinopec safeguards China's energy security" is followed by the company's rankings in refined oil products in China, global oil refining, and global ethylene production. Typical Sinopec advertising promotes a bright future. In one print ad, a little girl in a white dress is holding a potted flower and framed with the words "Making a better future." Another tagline touts the brand as "Dedicated to creating a better tomorrow for our society."

BRAND STRATEGY

- Sinopec's overall growth strategy includes expanding resources, exploring new markets, and increasing competitiveness.
- Sinopec seeks to expand by adding reserves to its current volumes, acquiring companies and resources in foreign markets, and increasing capacity at current refineries.
- Sinopec continually adjusts processes and delivery systems to improve overall production and reduce costs.

In pursuit of creating a world-class integrated energy and chemical company, Sinopec maintains an overall strategy of aggressively expanding resources, exploring new markets, and increasing competitiveness. Sinopec's expansion efforts include both locating new, untapped reserves to add to its current volumes and acquiring companies and resources in foreign markets, notably Canada, South America, and the United Kingdom. Sinopec has also expanded through increasing capacity at its current locations by optimizing the processing of crude oil and gas at each refinery to deliver more end products. In chemical production the focus is on improving the volume and quality generated by the company's chemical facilities.

Finally, Sinopec's overall strategy depends on strengthening current global sales networks and creating new channels when and where possible.

BRAND EQUITY

- Sinopec is the largest producer and supplier of refined oil and petrochemical products in China.
- Sinopec has crude oil reserves of 2.9 billion barrels and 6.7 trillion cubic feet of natural gas as of December 2011.
- On the *Forbes* list of "Global 2000 Leading Companies," Sinopec is number 4 in sales, number 31 in profits, and number 50 in market value.
- Sinopec operates in 38 countries around the world with 377,000 full-time employees.

Sinopec is China's largest producer and supplier of refined oil and petrochemical products. It is also the second largest producer of crude oil behind Petro-China, which in March 2012 surpassed ExxonMobil as the world's largest oil producer. Sinopec has crude oil reserves of 2.9 billion barrels and 6.7 trillion cubic feet of natural gas as of December 2011. The company had US$391.5 billion in sales in 2011 with pre-tax profits of US$11.6 billion.

Sinopec operates 16 oil and gas production fields and 34 refineries in China, and as of the end of 2011 had 522 petroleum engineering and technical services contracts in 38 countries, with a total contract value of US$11.9 billion. Sinopec owns 92 production licenses for operating on an aggregate total of 20,356 square kilometers (7,860 square miles) in China, with an additional 297 exploration licenses covering 966,800 square kilometers (373,280 square miles) in China. Sinopec also owns over 30,000 gas stations and employs more than 377,000 full-time workers. On the *Forbes* list of "Global 2000 Leading Companies," Sinopec is number 4 in sales, number 31 in profits, and number 50 in market value. As of January 20, 2013, Sinopec Corporation had a market capitalization valued at US$105.5 billion.

BRAND AWARENESS

- The Sinopec brand is well known within China, where it owns the largest chain of service stations with over 30,000 locations.
- Although Sinopec is highly regarded among international business and financial analysts, it will likely not make a name for itself with general consumers outside of China.
- Sinopec was one of the first Chinese companies to rank in the top 10 on the *Forbes* list of "Global 2000 Leading Companies."

Sinopec has not generally been a brand name much recognized outside the borders of China, but within China it is very well known. Sinopec is China's largest producer and supplier of gasoline and diesel fuels, as well as other petrochemical products, and it operates the largest service station chain in the country, with more than 30,000 gas stations. It is also the second largest producer of crude oil in China, behind PetroChina, which in 2013 was the largest crude oil producer in the world. Although the company is a titan among global corporations and is highly regarded among business and financial analysts outside of China, Sinopec will likely not make a name for itself with general consumers internationally. It did, however, gain greater brand awareness outside China when it became one of the first Chinese companies to rank in the top 10 on the *Forbes* list of "Global 2000 Leading Companies."

BRAND OUTLOOK

- Sinopec has aggressively been acquiring oil companies in foreign markets, expanding its global reach and has extensive operations in Africa, the Middle East, and Canada.
- In 2013 Sinopec assumes the international oil and gas assets from its parent company, making it among the largest energy companies in the world.
- Sinopec will continue its global expansion in the coming years, both to meet domestic demands in China and to increase its own overall production capabilities and value.

Sinopec has aggressively been acquiring oil companies in foreign markets, expanding its global reach and has extensive operations in Africa, the Middle East, and Canada. On January 10, 2013, Sinopec announced that it was taking over the international gas and oil assets from its parent company China Petrochemical Corp. CPC has invested more than US$34 billion over three years on the acquisition or part ownership of companies in Argentina, Brazil, Canada, the United Kingdom, and the United States. Once the CPC transaction is completed in 2013, Sinopec

will rise to the same level as petroleum giants such as ExxonMobil, Royal Dutch Shell, Chevron, and BP.

China is the second largest economy in the world and consequently has huge and continually growing energy needs. Sinopec will continue its global expansion in the coming years, both to meet domestic demands in China and to increase its own overall production capabilities and value. Sinopec is furthering expansion outside of China to decrease the negative effects on its bottom line of the Chinese government's control of fuel prices within the country. The company is focused on acquiring assets in Colombia, Kazakhstan, and Russia. It has been fairly successful expanding into the UK market, particularly in the North Sea oil fields, where Sinopec owns a 49 percent share of Talisman Energy Inc.

FURTHER READING

Brand Finance. "Sinopec Profile 2012." *Brandirectory.com*, 2013. Accessed January 24, 2013. http://brandirectory.com/profile/sinopec.

"China Petroleum & Chemical Corporation (Sinopec Corp)." *International Directory of Company Histories*. Ed. Derek Jacques and Paula Kepos. Vol. 109. Detroit, MI: St. James Press, 2010.

"Global 2000 Leading Companies—Sinopec Corporation." *Forbes*, April 18, 2012. Accessed January 24, 2013. http://www.forbes.com/search/?q=sinopec.

Nickel, Rod. "Canada Clears Sinopec to Buy Syncrude Stake." Reuters, June 25, 2010.

Quan, Rose. "Sinopec." *Encyclopedia of Business in Today's World*. Ed. Charles Wankel. Vol. 3. Thousand Oaks, CA: Sage Publications, 2009.

"Sinopec to Acquire Parent Assets." *Yahoo! Finance*, January 10, 2013. Accessed January 24, 2013. http://finance.yahoo.com/news/sinopec-acquire-parent-assets-191722099.html.

"Talisman Energy Closes $1.5 Bln North Sea Transaction with Sinopec." RTTNews.com, December 17, 2012. Accessed January 24, 2013. http://www.rttnews.com/2024862/talisman-energy-closes-1-5-bln-north-sea-transaction-with-sinopec-quick-facts.aspx?type=cn.

ŠKODA

─────────■─────────

BRAND ORIGINS

- Like many other European car manufacturers, Škoda began as a bicycle manufacturer.
- Following World War II, Škoda acquired the monopoly of passenger car production in Czechoslovakia.

- In 1987, Škoda introduced the Favorit, its first vehicle to incorporate any hint of modern automotive technology.
- In 1991 Škoda became the fourth brand of the Volkswagen Group alongside Volkswagen, Audi, and Seat, with Škoda occupying the position of entry brand.
- By 2005, Škoda was producing nearly half a million cars annually, and in 2011 it sold a record 875,000 cars.

Like many other European car manufacturers, Škoda originally built two-wheeled, rather than four-wheeled, vehicles. In December 1895, Czechoslovakian bicycle enthusiasts Václav Laurin, a mechanic, and Václav Klement, a bookseller, started manufacturing bikes of their own design, patriotically named Slavia. In 1899, under the name Laurin & Klement, the company began producing motorcycles that were soon successful on the racing circuits that were rapidly growing in popularity. Production of motorcycles, however, was gradually replaced by automobile manufacturing, beginning as early as 1905.

The first Laurin & Klement automobile, the Voiturette, was a success, later becoming the archetype of the Czechoslovakian automobile. The success of its first car helped the company expand into the developing international automobile market. Vehicle production increased rapidly and soon exceeded the potential of a private enterprise, and in 1907 the founders initiated conversion to a joint-stock company.

Due to the country's economic development, a joint venture with a strong industrial partner became essential in the 1920s in order to strengthen and modernize the brand, which by that time was producing numerous types of passenger cars, trucks, buses, airplane engines, and agricultural machinery. In 1925 fusion with the Pilsen Škoda Company was accomplished, marking the end of the Laurin & Klement trademark.

The German occupation of Czechoslovakia during World War II caused a considerable disruption in the history of the company, which was integrated into the industrial structure of the German empire. The civilian production program was immediately limited as production was geared toward military needs. During the course of a large-scale nationalization that began immediately after the war, the company became a national enterprise in 1946. Škoda acquired the monopoly of passenger car production, which it held for much of the next four decades. The vehicles it produced remained largely unchanged during that time, despite the advancements in engineering and manufacturing occurring around the globe. Not until 1987 did Škoda introduce a vehicle, the Favorit, which incorporated some modern automotive technology.

Political changes in the late 1980s resulted in new market conditions, and the government of the new Czech Republic and the management of Škoda began to search for a strong foreign partner whose experience and investments would be capable of securing the long-range international competitiveness of the company. In December 1990 the government chose the Germany-based Volkswagen Group. The Škoda-Volkswagen joint venture began to operate in 1991 under the name Škoda. Škoda became the fourth brand of the Volkswagen Group alongside Volkswagen, Audi, and Seat, with Škoda initially positioned as the entry brand for the Volkswagen Group.

The Volkswagen Group steadily increased its ownership interest in Škoda, raising its equity share to 70 percent by 1995 and making the brand a wholly owned subsidiary in 2000. Backed by expertise and investment from the Volkswagen Group, the design and manufacture of Škoda vehicles improved significantly, and most models today are based on the designs for popular Volkswagen vehicles. With Volkswagen guiding Škoda's development, the brand's image has changed from a dated laughingstock to a hip, small European brand. By 2005, Škoda was producing nearly half a million cars annually, and in 2011 Škoda sold 875,000 cars, a record number for the brand. Škoda's strategic plan includes an aim to double sales by 2018 as part of the Volkswagen Group's plan to become the largest carmaker in the world.

BRAND ELEMENTS

- Škoda has made several significant changes to its logo during its history.

- Early logos featured the names of the company's founders, Václav Laurin and Václav Klement, and showed the influence of the Art Nouveau style.
- Since 1926, the Škoda logo has featured an image of a winged arrow.

Unlike many other auto manufacturers, Škoda made significant changes to its logo, particularly in the company's early years. The first logo, representative of the company's initial focus on the manufacture of bicycles and motorcycles and in use from 1895 to 1905, was based on the images of a wheel and lime leaves. The names of the company's founders, Laurin and Klement, were added and later became the main motif for the new logo introduced in 1905. The design of the logo was influenced by Art Nouveau, a prominent artistic style at the beginning of the 20th century. The initials of the company's two founders were surrounded by a laurel wreath.

When Laurin & Klement became Škoda in 1926, the company's new logo included an oval shape, with the brand name "Škoda" as the dominant central element, surrounded by laurels. Another logo traced to 1926 is the predecessor closest to the current logo: Škoda's famous "winged arrow" shows a right-moving winged arrow with a stylized pinion, in blue on a white background. A black-and-green version was introduced in 1994, with black symbolizing the company's one-hundred-year-old tradition and green representing environmentally sound production.

The current logo, redesigned in 2011, dropped the word "auto" that had been added when the logo went from its blue-and-white to its black-and-green color scheme, and the colors and lines of the winged arrow were sharpened.

BRAND IDENTITY

- Throughout much of the 20th century, the Škoda brand was associated with very mediocre cars.
- Since the Volkswagen Group took over Škoda in 2000, the brand has become known for innovation, customer satisfaction, and style.
- Škoda is an affordable brand of practical, fuel-efficient, low-emission, eco-friendly compact cars that offer an appealing, modern design.
- In the first decade of the 21st century, Škoda's sales have risen dramatically, with particular success in emerging markets like China.

Known for nearly a century as the monopolistic Czech-based brand selling cars that were decades out of date to consumers with practically no other choice for auto transportation, Škoda has been transformed into a hip, "new" European brand. No longer stuck in the manufacturing rut that led to mediocre products, Škoda has become a brand known for customer satisfaction, innovation, and style.

Škoda is positioned as an affordable brand of fuel-efficient, low-emission, eco-friendly compact cars that offer an appealing, modern design inside and out. In general these are basic practical family cars, although some models have a more sporty flair. According to a member of the brand's sales and marketing team, "Clever, good cars at an attractive price is what we make."

The brand includes a range of models, and more are soon to be launched as part of an extensive rebranding effort. One of the models, the Octavia, promises to provide "middle-segment quality at a compact-car price." The Octavia is Škoda's best-selling brand in China, a market that accounts for 25 percent of Škoda's sales worldwide.

BRAND STRATEGY

- When the Volkswagen Group began its takeover of Škoda in the 1990s, it decided to address the brand's image problems head-on.
- Early advertising campaigns after the Volkswagen Group's takeover of Škoda used ironic humor to highlight improvements in Škoda cars.
- Škoda began producing cars in China in 2006, and by 2010 China was Škoda's largest market.
- Škoda plans to introduce a new car every six months through 2015, with new models incorporating a range of innovative designs and technologies.

For decades, Škoda was a byword for poor workmanship and a lack of style. When the Volkswagen Group started its takeover in the 1990s, the brand's leadership decided to tackle the reputation issues head-on by admitting that the Škoda brand had problems. The first wave of television commercials in the United Kingdom—aimed at the more than 60 percent of consumers there who said that they would never buy a Škoda—showed buyers changing their minds at the last minute, even though the facts about Škoda's quality and reliability had been laid out for them. The direct approach worked, with Škoda's sales in the United Kingdom increasing as much as 30 percent annually.

A major turnabout was achieved with the ironic "It is a Škoda, honest" campaign, which was initiated around the turn of the century. In a 2003 advertisement on British television, a new employee on the production line is seen fitting Škoda badges on the car's hoods. When some attractive looking cars come along he stands back and does not fit the badge because the cars look too good to be Škodas.

Škoda's success in the United Kingdom quickly led to its reemergence in other markets around the world. Volkswagen Group Australia reintroduced Škoda to the Australian car market in 2007 after nearly a quarter-century absence. Škoda also started production in China in 2006, and by 2009 the brand was selling close to 125,000 vehicles annually, making China Škoda's largest market by 2010.

Škoda's redesigned Octavia model was set to launch in 2013 and was at the center of the carmaker's strategy to boost annual sales to more than 1.5 million, part of a product onslaught that had Škoda launching a new car every six months through 2015. Future models in the Octavia line were reported to include an estate car, followed by an all-wheel drive Scout, a model powered by compressed natural gas, and a high-performance model that would be the quickest production Škoda to date.

BRAND EQUITY

- Škoda and the other brands that make up the Volkswagen Group claimed a 24 percent share of the European auto market in 2012.
- In 2012, Brand Finance ranked Škoda 302nd among the top 500 global brands with an estimated brand value of US$3.58 billion.
- Škoda has received high marks in recent studies assessing the brand's market strength, environmental performance, and customer satisfaction.

As part of the Volkswagen Group, Škoda has become a brand to be reckoned with in markets around the world. In Europe, for example, the Volkswagen Group and its brands—Volkswagen, Audi, Seat, and Škoda—commanded a market share of 24 percent in 2012, up from about 19 percent in 2004, according to BrandChannel.com. Meanwhile, PSA/Peugeot-Citroen, Europe's second-biggest automaker, saw its market share decline to 12 percent.

In 2012, Škoda made its first showing on Brand Finance's ranking of the world's top 500 brands, placing at number 302 with a brand value of US$3.58 billion. Škoda also broke into the Brand Finance list of the top 30 German brands in 2012 at number 22.

Perhaps the most telling indicator of Škoda's emerging presence was its top 10 ranking in the AutoMarxX brand study. The study, conducted by the brand research house German ADAC, uses such criteria as brand image, market strength, customer satisfaction, product strength, environmental performance, and safety. Of the 33 auto brands studied, Škoda ranked in either sixth or seventh position from 2010 to 2012.

The recent success of Škoda as a brand may also be attributed to its consistently high rankings among consumers. Owner satisfaction studies in Germany, France, and the United Kingdom routinely place Škoda in the top 10 of 22 car brands studied.

BRAND AWARENESS

- Škoda has a longstanding association with motorsports, and in 2010 it won seven events in the International Rally Challenge.
- Škoda's involvement in motorsports has led to increased brand awareness among car researchers and consumers.
- Škoda has long supported the Czech Olympic team, and it plans to emphasize the presence of its brand at the 2014 Winter Olympic Games.
- Škoda sponsors a number of important international cycling events, including the Tour de France, Giro d'Italia, and Vuelta España.

Škoda, like many other car brands, has a strong association with motorsports. Following a long history of class victories in lower levels of motorsport, Škoda became a participant in the World Rally Championships in 1999 and the Intercontinental Rally Challenge (IRC) in 2009. In 2010, Škoda won seven IRC events, taking the manufacturer and driver championships. Škoda has also been involved in auto touring events, and in 2011 the brand announced that it would renew its participation in the British Touring Car Championship.

The brand's expanded involvement in motorsports has led to increased consumer awareness. The growth of Škoda and its expanded line of vehicles has been recognized by car researchers and publications. In 2009, for example, the British television program *Top Gear* named the Škoda Superb its luxury car of the year and the Škoda Yeti its family car of the year.

No longer satisfied with a presence in auto racing, Škoda has sought to engage customers through its association with other popular sports. Škoda has supported the Czech Olympic team for decades, and it plans to emphasize its brand presence at the 2014 Winter Olympic Games in Sochi, Russia. Škoda Auto Russia has been a staunch supporter of the ice hockey world championship tournament and professional cycling. Škoda sponsors several important cycling events, including the Tour de France, Giro d'Italia, Vuelta España, and the UCI Road World Championship.

BRAND OUTLOOK

- Since becoming part of the Volkswagen Group, Škoda has transformed from a local brand to an emerging global brand.
- Despite widespread economic recession, global demand for cars continues to increase in certain markets.
- Škoda's opportunities look most promising in emerging markets such as China, India, and Russia.

Having been a highly localized brand for much of the 20th century, Škoda began the 21st century as one of the emerging brands on the global car market because of the investment in the brand by its parent company, the Volkswagen Group. Since the Volkswagen Group's takeover of the brand in 2000, Škoda has added several new car models and doubled its production while expanding into markets around the world. No longer considered Volkswagen's entry brand, Škoda stands to continue adding to its reputation and market presence as a uniquely European, yet globally appealing, car brand.

Despite a continuing global economic crisis that began in Europe in 2008, worldwide sales of passenger cars increased by 4.8 percent in 2011. Demand for new cars was highest in the United States, China, Russia, and South America. (However, U.S. consumers purchased mostly automobiles manufactured in North America.) Sales in Western Europe continued to lag, although the market had begun to improve in Germany and in Central and Eastern Europe. In Asia and the Pacific region, natural disasters caused a slump in the economy.

Nevertheless, this region is expected to present an enormous opportunity for Škoda and other automakers, because the world's developing countries are becoming home to a growing middle class of people who will want to purchase cars. In 2011 Škoda's largest market was China, where sales increased by 21.9 percent. Škoda's sales increased by 62.5 percent in Russia and 49.9 percent in India. The brand continues to expand its presence in all these markets.

FURTHER READING

Brand Finance. "Škoda." *Brandirectory,* 2012. Accessed December 19, 2012. http://brandirectory.com/profile/Škoda.

Buss, Dale. "European Automaker Rivals Now Mainly Are Eating Volkswagen's Dust." *BrandChannel,* August 22, 2012. Accessed December 21, 2012. http://www.brandchannel.com/home/post/2012/08/22/European-Automaker-Rivals-Now-Mainly-Are-Eating-Volkswagens-Dust.aspx.

Chartered Institute of Marketing. "Škoda: A Joke No Longer." *Brand Strategy,* 2003. Accessed December 21, 2012. http://web.archive.org/web/20081029202605/http://www.cim.co.uk/mediastore/Brand_eGuides/eGuide4.pdf.

Chauhan, Chanchal Pal. "Škoda Cuts All Discounts on Fabia While Reducing Discounts on Rapid, Laura, Superb and Yeti." *Economic Times* [India], October 30, 2012. Accessed December 21, 2012. http://articles.economictimes.indiatimes.com/2012-10-30/news/34817165_1_Škoda-cuts-czech-carmaker-Škoda-fabia.

"China Becomes Škoda's Largest Market." *China AutoWeb,* October 11, 2010. Accessed December 22, 2012. http://china autoweb.com/2010/10/china-became-Škodas-largest-market/.

Davis, Brett. "Škoda VisionD Design Study Reveals New Logo, Design Language." *Car Advice,* March 1, 2011. Accessed December 22, 2012. http://www.caradvice.com.au/107226/Škoda-visiond-design-study-reveals-new-logo-design-language/.

Gardner, Stephen. "Has Your Brand Become Generic?" *Brand-Channel,* February 25, 2002. Accessed December 21, 2012. http://www.brandchannel.com/features_effect.asp?pf_id=81.

"Octavia Set to Boost Škoda Sales." *Just-Auto,* December 18, 2012. Accessed December 22, 2012. http://www.just-auto.com/news/octavia-set-to-boost-Škoda-sales_id129972.aspx.

Škoda Auto Australia. Accessed December 26, 2012. http://www.Škoda.com.au/about/world-history.aspx.

"Škoda Logo—Design and History." *Dinesh.com.* Accessed December 27, 2012. http://www.dinesh.com/history_of_logos/car_logos_-_design_and_history/Škoda_logo_-_design_and_history.html.

"Škoda Supports 2014 Winter Olympics to be Held in Sochi, Russia." *Rush Lane,* September 3, 2012. Accessed December 20, 2012. http://www.rushlane.com/Škoda-supports-2014-winter-olympics-to-be-held-in-sochi-russia-1244184.html.

SyncForce. "Škoda." *RankingtheBrands.com,* 2012. Accessed December 30, 2012. http://www.rankingthebrands.com/Brand-detail.aspx?brandID=1704.

SK TELECOM

AT A GLANCE

Brand Synopsis: At SK Telecom, their vision is to create value that raises the quality of life for all.

Parent Company: SK Holdings Company Ltd.
11, Euljiro 2-Ga
Jung-gu
Seoul
South Korea
http://www.sktelecom.com

Sector: Telecommunications Services

Industry Group: Telecommunications Services

Performance: *Market share*—50.4 percent in South Korea (2011). *Sales*—US$13.88 billion (2011).

Principal Competitors: KT Corp.; LG Corp.; NTT Docomo, Inc.

BRAND ORIGINS

- SK Telecom was established on March 29, 1984, under the name Korea Mobile Telecommunications Services Co. (KMT).
- In March 1997 KMT changed its name to SK Telecom, partly in recognition of its largest shareholder, Sunkyong.
- In January 2005 SK Telecom broke into the U.S. mobile-communications market when it signed a US$440 million contract with Earthlink, a U.S. wireless carrier.

- As of 2012 SK Telecom offered 19 different smart-phone models, 2 tablet PCs, and 2 USB modems, all under its own brand name.

SK Telecom was established on March 29, 1984, under the name Korea Mobile Telecommunications Services Co. It began as a subsidiary of Korea Telecom, the state-owned telephone monopoly of South Korea. By May of that year the new business began selling car-phone services, signing up a total of 2,658 users by the end of its first year. In May 1988 the company's name was changed to Korea Mobile Telecommunications Corp. (KMT). In 1990 KMT initiated its first significant expansion by paying AT&T US$29 million to supply cellular transmission equipment which would expand services throughout South Korea. This upgrade added an additional 60,000 lines to the original 30,000-line mobile network which AT&T had installed the year before.

Beginning in 1987 the South Korean government started efforts to privatize the phone industry. In 1992 it decided to create a second mobile-phone-service carrier and accepted bids from companies who wished to invest in and grow such a business. Sunkyong, a manufacturing conglomerate, initially won the license that year but later lost it due to political controversy. In 1994 Pohang Iron and Steel Co. was awarded the contract to establish South Korea's first private telecom business. In the meantime, Sunkyong acquired a 23 percent stake in KMT, becoming the company's single-largest shareholder. In January 1995 KMT reached its initial goal of 1 million subscribers and in June 1996 became only the third Korean company to be listed on the New York Stock Exchange. During the first five years of the 1990s KMT had experienced incredible growth, both in sales and profits. In each of those years, sales increased an average of 73 percent, while profits jumped 44 percent annually.

In January 1996 KMT became the first telecom in the world to offer its customers the new 2G wireless format called CDMA. By the end of 1996 KMT sales had more than doubled, for total revenues of US$3.17 billion, with approximately 4 million subscribers. In March 1997 KMT changed its name to SK Telecom, partly in recognition of Sunkyong, its largest shareholder. By June 1999 SK Telecom had 7.27 million subscribers, and by August it had upgraded its infrastructure to offer the world's fastest cellular services on its 2G network.

The year 2000 began in a big way for SK Telecom, as it signed a US$200 million, two-year contract with Samsung to collaborate on the development of a superfast, new 3G (third generation) network. The new system would increase overall speed by 30 percent and more than double the traffic capacity. The new system was to be launched by March 2002. Meanwhile SK Telecom was expanding business beyond its country's borders. In September 2001 SK Telecom, in cooperation with SPT (Saigon Postel), cofounded S-Telecom, a Business Cooperation Contract in Vietnam providing mobile telephony and other communications services, using CDMA technology. In April 2002 the company signed a contract with Israeli telecom Pelephone to provide wireless Internet. SK Telecom also was hard at work on collaborations with the Chinese government. One wireless Internet joint venture would involve having China's Unicom set up services using SK Telecom's technology in 2002, and another joint venture with China United Telecommunications would provide additional wireless Internet by early 2003.

In November 2002 SK Telecom launched a new subsidiary company called MONETA, which would provide mobile payment services. By August 2003 SK Telecom became the world's first 3G service to sign one million subscribers. A year later it launched its first DMB (digital multimedia broadcast) satellite in collaboration with Japan's Mobile Broadcasting Corporation. In November 2004 it closed out the year with another new startup, MELON, which was a music portal service. In January 2005 SK Telecom broke into the U.S. mobile-communications market when it signed a US$440 million contract with Earthlink, a U.S. wireless carrier. The new service was initially named SK-Earthlink but was later changed to HELIO. The new venture did poorly and was eventually sold in 2008 to Virgin Mobile for a mere US$39 million, after SK Telecom had already sunk over US$500 million into the investment.

In 2007 SK Telecom continued its penetration into the Chinese market by obtaining an agreement with the Chinese National Development and Reform Commission to develop China's 3G mobile-telecom technology standard, TD-SCDMA (time division synchronous code division multiple access). On March 6, 2008, SK Telecom unveiled a new joint venture with Citibank, called Mobile Money Ventures. The new company was designed to provide mobile financial services and solutions all over the world. It was upwardly scalable to support not only existing mobile banking services but new, up-and-coming services such as P2P (person-to-person) payments. In 2009 SK Telecom celebrated its 25th anniversary. In South Korea 95 percent of the country was using mobile phones and SK Telecom had more than a 50 percent share of that huge market.

In April 2011 the company launched its new 4G LTE (long term evolution) network, which offered ultra-high-speed data service and the ability to handle three times as much data than existing 3G networks. The LTE network was first rolled out in Seoul, with full national coverage projected by 2013. There were two other major developments for the company in 2011. First, it made Apple iPhones and iPads available for purchase by SK Telecom customers, and in September the company showcased its first brand-name LTE smartphone, with a promise of additional products by year's end. As of 2012 SK Telecom was offering 19 different smartphone models, 2 tablet PCs, and 2 USB modems.

BRAND ELEMENTS

- The name SK Telecom was developed in part to acknowledge the company's connection with its major shareholder, Sunkyong, one of the country's largest conglomerates.
- The T-Brand series of SK Telecom subsidiaries offers separate companies and services for individuals aged 10 to 12, 13 to 18, and 19 to 24 years old.
- SK Broadband is the largest of the SK Telecom affiliates and has a 50.6 percent market share in South Korea.

SK Telecom was established in 1984 as Korea Mobile Telecommunications Services Co. Over the next few years the company made dramatic leaps in both technological innovations and total service coverage beyond the borders of South Korea. In 1997 management decided the company needed a new name, not only to better represent this expansion but to also acknowledge the company's connection with its major shareholder Sunkyong, one of the country's largest conglomerates. SK Telecom has cycled through numerous slogans over the years, including "Hug the planet," "Create with You," "Beyond Telecom," and "Beyond Reality," though none have seemed to have any significant longevity.

Over the years as SK Telecom has expanded, it has added dozens of subsidiaries and affiliates, each with its own brand and specialization. Some of the larger brand-name subsidiaries include NATE, which handles both wired and wireless Internet portals; 11th Street, an online marketplace; Leaders Club, which specializes in services for working professionals; and the T-Brand series of wireless-communications subsidiaries, which focus on specific age groups. Under the T-Brand, TTL offers services for 19 to 24 year olds, T-ing has services for 13 to 18 year olds, and T-ing Junior is for 10 to 12 year olds.

In South Korea SK Telecom is so dominant that specific services are divided among a group of major affiliates, each with their own brand and offerings. SK Broadband is the largest of the affiliates and has a 50.6 percent market share in South Korea. Loen Entertainment covers music broadcasts and downloads and has a 63.5 percent market share. Paxnet is a financial online service with a 59.7 percent market share. PS&Marketing specializes in mobile-handset distribution and has a full 100 percent of the South Korean market. MONETA, TU Media Corp., Cyworld, NateON, and many other affiliates serve specific functions in the international telecommunications conglomerate that is SK Telecom.

BRAND IDENTITY

- In May 2001SK Telecom offered the world's first commercial wireless streaming video service.
- SK Telecom has been voted number one in the National Customer Satisfaction Index for 12 consecutive years.
- In April 2007 SK Telecom was selected as one of the "Best Employers in Asia" by the *Wall Street Journal Asia* and Hewitt Associates.

Over the years, SK Telecom has earned a reputation as one of the most innovative technology companies in the telecommunications industry. It has been "first in the world" on several occasions, bringing new technologies and services to market long before any other companies. In January 1996 it became the first telecom in the world to offer its customers the new 2G wireless format called CDMA. In May 2001 SK Telecom offered the world's first commercial, wireless streaming-video service. By August 2003 SK Telecom became the world's first 3G service to sign one million subscribers. In May 2004 it launched a satellite for the world's first digital-media broadcasting service, and the list goes on. SK Telecom continues to invest in advancing wireless technology, bringing its customers products and services which are ever-more-diverse, multifunctional, and entertaining. The ultimate goal is to make everyone's life better, more productive, and happier through the technologies the company develops.

SK Telecom is now following the "Maximizing Happiness" philosophy. This takes the goal of making people's lives better a step further. Rather than achieving that goal through state-of-the-art technology alone, SK Telecom has developed a new Community Involvement program in six specific areas: Social Welfare, Mobile/IT, Education/Scholarship, Volunteer Services, Global Social Contribution, and Environment/Culture/Arts. SK Telecom has won numerous awards in recognition of its commitment to its customers. It has been voted number one in the Mobile Communications Service category of the National Customer Satisfaction Index for 12 consecutive years. In April 2007 it was selected as one of the "Best Employers in Asia" by the *Wall Street Journal Asia* and Hewitt Associates. In September 2008 it was recognized for excellence in global sustainability as a member of the 2008 Dow Jones Sustainability Index, a first among Korean telecommunications companies.

BRAND STRATEGY

- SK Telecom seeks to satisfy four areas of consumer needs and demands: online shopping and banking, wireless Internet, new growth markets, and futuristic technologies.
- In 2010 SK Telecom was involved in a joint venture with China to roll out smartphone-based services across that nation, opening up further opportunities for the brand.
- SK Telecom is currently developing new "Convergence" technologies involving innovative user interfaces, speech recognition, and even artificial intelligence.

SK Telecom's current levels of success are based on satisfying four areas of consumer needs and demands in the wireless telecommunications market. The first area involves online shopping and banking. In September 2009 the company launched T-Store, an online app marketplace with 29,000 items available for download. It ended up delivering 1.5 million downloads to 340,000 customers in its first four months. In 2011 SK Telecom launched its 11th Street online marketplace. After only one year it become a major Korean e-commerce player, generating over US$1.4 billion in sales and more than 10.3 million registered customers.

The second area addressed by SK Telecom is wireless Internet. With the ever-changing trends in wireless technology, specifically smartphones, the company is constantly evolving and expanding the products and services available to its customers, who continue to come up with new uses and adaptations to their equipment and applications. The third area of focus is in expanding SK Telecom's reach through the constant search for new growth markets around the world. In 2010 SK Telecom was involved in a joint venture with China to roll out a smartphone-based group of services across that nation. This will only further open up opportunities in China and globally as well.

Finally, SK Telecom is shaping the technology of "Convergence," in which a number of high-tech fields work together to offer new, even futuristic, services. Some of the technologies currently being researched are innovative user interfaces, e-paper, speech recognition, and artificial intelligence.

BRAND EQUITY

- As of December 31, 2011, SK Telecom's total revenues were US$13.88 billion, with net profits of US$1.38 billion.
- SK Telecom has a domestic market share of 50.4 percent and a total of 4,951 employees.
- SK Telecom is ranked number 538 on the Forbes Global 2000 List of the world's largest companies.

As of December 31, 2011, SK Telecom's total revenues were US$13.88 billion, with net profits of US$1.38 billion. The company has a domestic market share of 50.4 percent and a total of 4,951 employees. It has expanded services to six nations besides its home country of South Korea, including China, Vietnam, Japan, Indonesia, the United States, and the United Kingdom. SK Telecom's market capitalization is valued at US$11.31 billion. On the Forbes Global 2000 List, SK Telecom ranks number 621 in sales, number 431 in profits, number 931 in assets, number 937 in market value, and number 538 overall. On the list of "Top 500 Telecom Brands" for 2012, SK Telecom ranked 51st, while among the Top 50 companies in South Korea, it was ranked 8th.

BRAND AWARENESS

- SK Telecom's products and services are used by more than 50 percent of South Korea's 49.8 million people.
- SK Telecom receives much name recognition through its social and humanitarian ventures, such as the "Maximizing Happiness" series of projects.
- In April 2012 SK Telecom won the "National Customer Satisfaction Index" award for the 12th consecutive year.

SK Telecom has become a ubiquitous name among Pacific Rim nations, which has contributed significantly to its brand awareness. In its home nation of South Korea, SK Telecom's products and services are used by more than 50 percent of the nation's 49.8 million people. The company has also had a series of successful joint ventures developing a wireless and wired infrastructure across the Chinese mainland. In June 2006 SK Telecom purchased US$1 billion worth of convertible bonds of China Unicom, a Chinese, state-owned telecommunications company. SK Telecom also has dozens of subsidiaries and affiliates which fulfill specific services. The company also achieves much name recognition through social and humanitarian

projects, the most recent example being the "Maximizing Happiness" community-involvement series of projects. SK Telecom has also received a great deal of recognition from industry and from international organizations, including an award for being among the "World's Most Innovative Companies," with a ranking of 91st, as listed in *Business Week* magazine (April 2005). Other awards included a "Best Employers in Asia" award by Hewitt Associates and the *Wall Street Journal Asia* in April 2007 and, for the 12th consecutive year, the "National Customer Satisfaction Index" award, in April 2012.

BRAND OUTLOOK

- SK Telecom will be spending US$890 million over the next three years to further develop its new smartphone products and mobile-software business around the globe.
- SK Telecom began building up its products and services to eventually compete with tech giants such as Apple, Facebook, and Google.
- SK Telecom planned to offer 4G LTE mobile services in Brazil by 2013.

In the 2010s, SK Telecom set its sights on handset sales, high-speed Wi-Fi, and expanded 4G network services. In May 2011 the company announced that it would commit approximately US$890 million over the next three years to further develop its new smartphone products and mobile-software business. These ventures would be in direct competition with tech giants such as Apple, Facebook, and Google. SK Telecom is currently looking to open app stores in China and Japan, as well as offering 4G LTE mobile services by 2013 in Brazil, where it would be that country's sixth mobile services provider.

For the global communications industry as a whole, according to a recent report by Global Industry Analysts, Inc., the global telecom services industry is expected to continue its aggressive growth from a current level of US$1.3 trillion to over US$1.8 trillion by 2015. Growth should be particularly significant among the portable devices, such as smart phones, tablet computers, and netbooks/ultrabooks, which are driving the largest portion of the almost exponential growth of mobile broadband subscriptions and data services. SK Telecom is in a particularly good position for solid growth, primarily due to its dominance within the domestic market of South Korea and its significant presence in the Chinese and Brazilian markets.

FURTHER READING

Bills, Steve. "Citi: Mobile Venture Will Go Well beyond Basics." AmericanBanker.com, March 7, 2008. Accessed February 9, 2013. http://www.americanbanker.com/issues/173_46/-347230-1.html.

Block, Ryan. "Helio's Flame Going Out: Stores to Shutter, Customers Heading to Virgin?" Engadget.com, June 20, 2008. Accessed February 9, 2013. http://www.engadget.com/topics/mobile/2008/06/20/helios-flame-going-out-stores-to-shutter-customers-heading-to/.

"Forbes Global 2000 List—SK Telecom." *Forbes*. Accessed February 9, 2013. http://www.forbes.com/companies/sk-telecom/.

Ja-yoong, Yoon. "SK Telecom Sees Falling Market Share." *Korea Times* (Seoul, South Korea), April 4, 2012.

SK Telecom. *2009 Annual Report*. Accessed February 9, 2013. http://www.sktelecom.com.

———. *2010 Sustainability Report*. Accessed February 9, 2013. http://www.sktelecom.com.

"SK Telecom." Yahoo.com. Accessed February 9, 2013. http://finance.yahoo.com/q/is?s=SKM+Income+Statement&annual.

"SK Telecom at 25." Total Telecom Online, March 27, 2009. Accessed February 9, 2013. http://www.totaltele.com/view.aspx?ID=444388.

"SK Telecom Co., Ltd." *International Directory of Company Histories*. Ed. Karen Hill. Vol. 128. Detroit, MI: St. James Press, 2012.

SKY

——— ▪ ———

BRAND ORIGINS

- Satellite Television/Superstation Europe (or Super Station Europe) was the original name of Sky Channel, which later became Sky.
- In 1989, Sky began broadcasting from Luxembourg's Astra satellites.

- British Satellite Television (BSB) merged with Sky to form British Sky Broadcasting (BskyB) in 1990.
- Having switched from analog to digital broadcasting by 2001, Sky began offering high-definition (HD) programming in 2006.
- Other Sky offerings include the recording system Sky+ (also known as Sky Plus) and Sky Broadband, which features services for television, Internet, and phones.

Operating in the early 1980s, Satellite Television/Superstation Europe (or Super Station Europe) was the first satellite television cable channel in Europe. Rupert Murdoch's News Corporation bought this channel and by 1984, it had a new name: Sky Channel. Murdoch hoped that cable and satellite broadcasting would provide British television viewers with alternatives to the limited options available at the time. British law allowed just four broadcast channels to operate: BBC, BBC2, ITV, and Channel 4.

Murdoch, whose media empire would eventually encompass newspapers, television channels, and movie studios in the United Kingdom, the United States, and Australia, was ineligible to receive the satellite broadcasting license because he was not a native Briton. British Satellite Television (BSB) received the license instead and planned to build and launch its own satellites. Without a British license but still eager to enter the British satellite market, Murdoch rented space on Luxembourg's Astra broadcasting satellites.

Sky began broadcasting from these satellites in 1989. Its four initial channels were Sky One (later Sky 1), a version of the original Sky Channel; Sky News; Sky Movies;

and Eurosport. Versions of these channels exist today, along with other Sky channels offering diverse content. Sky also offers other channels from around the world, including the Biography Channel, Comedy Central, Discovery Channel, Disney Channel, FX, History Channel, MTV, National Geographic Channel, and VH1. Sky subscribers with Sky hardware and broadband routers can watch Sky content and other channels, and they can view the previous weeks' programming and access other content by subscribing to Sky's on-demand video option. Sky reaches viewers in the United Kingdom, Ireland, Germany, Austria, Switzerland, Italy, and beyond.

By the early 1990s, Sky was thriving while the official British licensee, British Satellite Television (BSB), still struggled with its new satellites. Sky had practically a monopoly on the British satellite television market, reaching 3.5 million homes in 1994. Since then, competitors have accused Sky of monopolistic practices due to the company's wide reach. Despite its success, Sky was losing money, much like its competitor British Satellite Television (BSB). These financial troubles prompted the two corporations to merge in 1990. The new company took the name British Sky Broadcasting (BskyB). Changes to British laws finally enabled Sky to acquire a broadcasting license.

After the merger, Sky began to add channels and subscribers. It also turned to new technologies, like digital television. It launched the first British digital television service, Sky Digital, in 1998. This service offered more than 140 channels. Other Sky digital services with interactive features included Sky Sports Extra, the shopping channel Open, and Sky News. Sky offered free satellite dishes and hardware boxes to new subscribers, and its digital services proved to be very successful. Sky was the world's first digital-only service provider, dropping its analog television service by 2001. In that year, Sky launched Sky+ (also known as Sky Plus), a system that allows viewers to record, pause, and rewind Sky programming.

A few years later, in 2006, Sky incorporated another technological advancement when it began offering high-definition (HD) television programming. In the same year, it started Sky Broadband, services for television, Internet, and phones. Sky customers can receive discounts if they bundle these services, which means buying them together as a package. These products demonstrate Sky's interest in providing a diverse range of content and technologies to its customers.

BRAND ELEMENTS

- The Sky logo is the word "sky" in lowercase letters, which usually appear in various shades of blue.
- Logos for Sky channels often use a lowercase version of the word "sky," along with the name of the channel in capital letters.

- International Sky channels Sky Italia and Sky Deutschland also feature lowercase versions of the word "sky."
- Sky's channel logos are distinctive but also similar to each other, reinforcing their relationships to each other and to the Sky corporate brand.
- The slogan "Believe in Better" is used in connection with Sky's products, customer service, and corporate giving and outreach.

The Sky logo consists of the word "sky" in lowercase letters in various shades of blue. The company occasionally changes the logo, sometimes using the red, white, and blue Union Jack design of the British flag, for example.

For their own logos, different Sky channels use differently colored versions of the "sky" logo alongside the name of the channel in capital letters, followed by the letters HD (for high definition). These logos appear in badge-like rectangular boxes. Slight variations to these logos include the Sky 1 logo, which uses a lowercase version of the word "sky," the numeral 1, and the letters HD; and the Sky 3-D logo, which uses another lowercase version of the word "sky" followed by "3-D." Sky Italia, Sky's Italian channel, uses a similar logo: sky.it. Meanwhile, Sky Deutschland, which serves Germany, Austria, and Switzerland, uses only the word "sky" as its logo.

The Sky channel logos thus have distinct identities but are also similar to each other, reinforcing their relationships to each other and to the Sky corporate brand. The logos for these channels appear multiple times on their websites, often superimposed over still photographs from the programs these channels offer. These photographs advertise both the channels and their programming. The logos also appear on website photographs representing other Sky offerings. Website photographs of electronic devices feature network logos on the screens of these devices, another instance of Sky advertising its channels and its offerings. The websites also use Sky's corporate blue logo, emphasizing the channels' and products' ties to the parent company and advertising the parent company itself.

Another brand element for Sky is the slogan "Believe in Better," which is sometimes stated as "We believe in better." This slogan appears on Sky advertising and on various webpages in connection with Sky's products, customer service, and corporate giving and outreach.

BRAND IDENTITY

- Sky recognizes that customers have a choice among television providers, so it focuses on making its products affordable, providing exceptional customer service, and finding ways to improve.

- Sky attempts to see the bigger picture by making positive contributions to life in the UK and looking for sustainability solution.
- Sky focuses its corporate responsibility activities on climate change, sport, the arts, and raising young people's aspirations.

The slogan "We believe in better" is an integral component of the way Sky sees itself. Recognizing that customers have a choice among television providers, Sky seeks to "entertain, excite and inspire customers with a great choice of high-quality television in high definition," as stated on the "Our mission" page of the corporate website. To do this, Sky focuses on making its products affordable, providing exceptional customer service, and finding ways to improve.

Sky also defines itself as "seeing the bigger picture." That umbrella covers Sky's efforts to make a positive contribution to life in the UK and to find solutions that improve sustainability. Sky focuses its corporate responsibility activities in four areas: addressing climate change, improving lives through sport, opening up the arts to more people, and raising the aspirations of young people.

For example, Sky has committed money to the creation and production of British programming. In 2012 the Believe in Better campaign focused on the Sky Arts channels. The channels' budgets were enlarged and a number of Sky Arts Ignition art initiatives were launched throughout the United Kingdom. These efforts have promoted both the arts and the Sky brand. In the area of sports, Sky is involved in athletics in several ways. For example, it is the founder and sponsor of Team Sky, a British professional cycling team.

BRAND STRATEGY

- Sky continues to grow through acquisition such as the deal to gain basic pay TV channels from Virgin Media.
- Another Sky strategy is to keep offering its customers the latest in technological advances.
- Other Sky strategies include fostering the development of original British programming, funding arts organizations, and sponsorship of sports.

Sky takes a multi-pronged approach in developing its strategy. It is continuing to grow through the traditional method of acquisitions. For example, in 2010 Sky agreed to acquire several TV channels from rival Virgin Media. This expanded Sky's portfolio of basic pay TV channels.

Another Sky strategy is to keep offering its customers the latest in technological advances. For example, in July 2011, Sky launched a service called Sky Go, which allows Sky TV customers to watch live TV on a wide range of devices such as laptops, smartphones, and tablets. Earlier that year, Sky launched the app (application) Sky News

for iPad, which allows users to control their own news service. In January 2012, Sky entered into partnership with the social networking site zeebox, a "second-screen" service that provides content, interactive features, and social networking features for electronic device users. In 2013, Sky began to launch AdSmart, a service that streams targeted television ads to households based on information the customers themselves provided.

A third Sky strategy is to foster the creation of content. In June 2011, Sky announced that it would increase its investment in the development of original British programming. This effort is related to Sky's fourth strategy—its corporate-responsibility programs, such as its efforts to fund arts organizations and its sponsorship of sports such as cycling events and cycling teams. Sky believes firmly that by giving back to the community, it builds trust and creates more loyal customers. In addition, by sponsoring highly visible activities, Sky promotes its brand by keeping its name in the public eye.

BRAND EQUITY

- In 2008, Sky served more than nine million (about one-third) of the homes in United Kingdom and Ireland.
- By 2010, Sky was providing programming to 10 million (about 36 percent) of homes in the United Kingdom and Ireland.
- In 2012 Brand Finance named Sky the 22nd-best global telecommunications brand and the 149th-best global brand overall.

By 2008, Sky was providing television programming to about nine million homes in the United Kingdom and Ireland, or about one-third of the homes there. Two years later, the number of Sky subscribers reached 10 million, or 36 percent of the homes in the United Kingdom and Ireland. This household presence has translated into significant market share figures. In 2010 the company captured around 80 percent of Britain's pay television market.

The company's channels are also accessible overseas. A Sky News website claimed that the channel reaches more people every day than British broadsheet newspapers.

Its market performance has made Sky a strong global brand. In 2012, Brand Finance named Sky the 22nd-best global telecommunications brand, with a brand value of US$6.4 billion, up from its 2011 value of US$5.8 billion. Sky also placed 149th on Brand Finance's list of the 500 best global brands in all industries.

BRAND AWARENESS

- A 2010 poll found that 19.9 percent of European businesspeople and affluent consumers were aware of the Sky News channel.

- In 2009 the Canaccord Adams Media Magnate Awards named Sky the British media company of the year.
- The United Kingdom's Royal Television Society has designated Sky News as the news channel of the year multiple times.

Sky enjoys strong international brand awareness. A 2010 poll of European businesspeople and affluent consumers found that 19.9 percent of the respondents were aware of the Sky News channel. Other channels in the same poll included the BBC World News, which had a 19.5 percent awareness rate, and the Cable News Network (CNN), which had an awareness rating of 22.4 percent.

In addition to strong market performance, brand assessments, and brand awareness, Sky and its channels have won other recognition. Rewarding excellence in the media industry, the Canaccord Adams Media Magnate Awards named Sky the British media company of the year in 2009. British business periodical *Management Today* also praised Sky in 2009, calling it Britain's most admired company. Sky is the youngest company ever to win this designation.

Sky's individual channels have also won awards. The United Kingdom's Royal Television Society has designated Sky News as its news channel of the year multiple times. In 2012, the United Kingdom's Broadcast Awards named Sky 1 the channel of the year.

BRAND OUTLOOK

- In the 2000s, phone and e-mail hacking scandals involving Rupert Murdoch's media companies affected Sky News, which is partially owned by Murdoch's News Corporation.
- Sky subscribers can watch Sky content on the Internet or via the Sky Go app (application) for smartphones and other electronic devices.
- In 2012, Sky partnered with zeebox to provide content, interactive features, and social networking features for electronic device users.

In less positive news for Sky, Rupert Murdoch's News International newspaper *News of the World* (a British newspaper originally founded in 1843) closed in 2011 after reports surfaced that its journalists allegedly hacked into the voicemail messages of private cellular phone subscribers. A year later, British regulators investigated Sky News, a company partly owned by Murdoch's News Corporation. This investigation followed up claims that a journalist for the channel allegedly hacked into the e-mail messages of criminal suspects. Sky News claimed that it accessed these e-mail messages in the public interest.

In the wake of these scandals, British regulators allowed Sky to keep its broadcast license, although investigations into the News Corporation continued. The ongoing controversy damaged News International's and News Corporation's reputations and prompted BskyB CEO and chairperson James Murdoch (Rupert's son) to resign. Although James Murdoch took a position as BskyB's nonexecutive director later in 2012, a BskyB shareholder questioned whether his reappointment would hurt Sky's reputation among investors.

Despite the scandals, Sky has continued to change and expand. Many recent changes have been technological such as the the Sky Go app and the partnership with zeebox. These developments once again illustrate Sky's commitment to offering diverse content and features to customers. Between Sky's efforts to plan for the long term and the growing consumer demand for digital streaming and video-on-demand, the brand's future looks bright.

FURTHER READING

Brand Finance. "Global 500 2012." *Brandirectory.* Accessed November 13, 2012. http://brandirectory.com/league_tables/table/global-500-2012.

Brand Finance. "Top 500 Telecom Brands 2012." *Brandirectory.* Accessed November 13, 2012. http://brandirectory.com/league_tables/table/top-500-telecom-brands-2012.

BskyB. "About Sky News." 2012. Accessed November 14, 2012. http://skynews.skypressoffice.co.uk/about.

BSkyB. "Timeline." 2012. Accessed November 13, 2012. http://corporate.sky.com/about_sky/timeline.

Clover, Julian. "EMS Shows Brand Awareness Equals Audiences." *Broadband TV News,* September 28, 2010. Accessed November 14, 2012. http://www.broadbandtvnews.com/2010/09/28/ems-shows-brand-awareness-equals-audiences/.

Cohen, M. L., and Christina M. Stansell. "British Sky Broadcasting Group plc." *International Directory of Company Histories.* Ed. Tina Grant and Miranda H. Ferrara. Vol. 60. Detroit: St. James Press, 2004. *Gale Virtual Reference Library.* Accessed November 13, 2012. http://go.galegroup.com/ps/i.do?id=GALE%7CCCX3428700028&v=2.1&u=itsbtrial&it=r&p=GVRL&sw=w.

Prodhan, Georgina. "Murdoch Hacking Scandal Spreads to Sky News." *Live Mint & The Wall Street Journal,* April 5, 2012. Accessed November 13, 2012. http://www.livemint.com/Politics/19WCPVkVMr4Z5roDCsL1PP/Murdoch-hacking-scandal-spreads-to-Sky-News.html.

Sabbagh, Dan. "Sky's Dominance of the UK Television Market." *Beehive City,* September 12, 2010. http://www.beehivecity.com/television/skys-dominance-of-the-uk-television-market123456/.

Spanier, Gideon. "Shareholders' Backing at Sky Boosts James Murdoch." *Independent* [London], November 2, 2012. Accessed November 15, 2012. http://www.independent.co.uk/news/business/news/shareholders-backing-at-sky-boosts-james-murdoch-8274661.html.

SMIRNOFF

BRAND ORIGINS

- Smirnoff vodka had its origins in Russia in 1864.
- The brand was essentially shut down in 1917 because of the Russian Revolution.
- Renamed, Smirnoff vodka was reborn in the United States in the 1930s.
- Smirnoff is the best-selling vodka in the United States and worldwide.

In Moscow in 1864, Pyotr Arsenievich Smirnov opened a vodka distillery under the brand name PA Smirnov. From the first he focused on making and selling a quality product. Between 1877 and 1886, Smirnov's vodka won three double eagles, the highest industrial award Russia offered for the best product in its field. After winning its third double eagle, Smirnov became the purveyor of vodka to the Imperial Court of Tsar Alexander II. He was then given the right to use the Russian State Coat of Arms on his vodka bottles. By the time of his death in 1898, Smirnov was producing and selling millions of bottles annually.

Changes in the political situation in Russia led to catastrophic problems for Pyotr Petrovich Smirnov, who took over the family business. After the Russian Revolution of 1917, the Bolsheviks nationalized the company, essentially ending it. Vladimir Smirnov, Pyotr Arsenievich Smirnov's third son, emigrated to France, registered the (slightly altered) name of Smirnoff vodka in the 1920s, and tried to re-create the secret distilling process.

In 1933 Rudolph Kunett, whose father had worked with the Smirnovs in Russia, convinced Vladimir Smirnov to sell him the American rights for US$2500, just in time for the repeal of Prohibition. A year later, Kunett established Ste. Pierre Smirnoff Fls in Connecticut, the first vodka distillery in the United States. This began the modern production of Smirnoff vodka.

Five years later Kunett's company was only selling 6,000 cases per year. In 1938 Kunett sold out to G.F. Heublein and Brothers, Inc. Sales remained low for the next several years, increasing only to 10,000 cases per year. One reason for slow sales was the false impression Americans had that drinking vodka could result in death, or at least leave a bad hangover, and that it was made from moldy potatoes. No vodka was produced for four years during World War II because of the rationing of grain.

When production resumed, Heublein started marketing vodka as a spirit for mixed drinks. He developed the "Moscow Mule" drink (Smirnoff vodka and ginger beer served in a copper mug) and convinced bartenders to make and sell it. The drink became a fad, and Heublein devised and promoted more vodka drinks, including a revival of the Bloody Mary (first invented in 1921) and the Screwdriver. Such drinks were featured in the first advertising campaigns for Smirnoff in the 1950s, which used the slogan, "It leaves you breathless." The Smirnoff mixed-drink ads continued through the 1950s and 1960s, and featured celebrities like Groucho Marx and Johnny Carson.

As a result of this consumer-oriented advertising campaign, vodka sales increased greatly. By the mid-1950s Smirnoff was selling one million cases per year and sales revenues reached US$250 million. As vodka became more popular in the United States, primarily because of Smirnoff, new vodkas came on the market to compete with it. However, because of its exotic ties with the Russian Tsars and extensive advertising, and with its head start as the first vodka consumed by Americans, Smirnoff remained the number-one vodka in the United States for decades.

The brand was successful not just in the United States. Heublein licensed Smirnoff in other countries, expanding overseas in the early 1950s to England, France, Canada, and Mexico. By 1968 Smirnoff licensees were found in 35 countries. It eventually became the number-one vodka brand in the world as well.

Vodka remained popular in the United States in the 1970s and 1980s, outselling all other spirits. Smirnoff, however, suffered a setback in 1980s when vodkas that presented themselves as prestigious, such as Absolut, came on the market and cut into Smirnoff's sales. While Smirnoff sold 7.45 million cases in 1980, by 1990 that was down to 6.55 million cases. International expansion continued through the early 1990s. Smirnoff was relaunched in the Russian market in the 1980s, for the first time since the predecessor Smirnov's was closed down in 1917. By 1992 Smirnoff was being sold in 117 countries, and in 1994 it entered the Indian market.

Though Smirnoff was dominant in the vodka market, the brand moved into new territory at the end of the 1990s with the launch of a ready-to-drink line in 1999, led by Smirnoff Ice, a malt beverage that was essentially flavored beer. While vodka became increasingly popular during the first decade of the 21st century and Smirnoff remained the world leader in the premium vodka category, the brand achieved dominance in the malt beverage market too. It expanded its vodka offerings to include flavors as varied as blueberry, watermelon, apple, and even whipped cream. And it continued to introduce new products, such as premade

cocktails. With products appealing to every age group and continued expansion in both established and emerging markets, Smirnoff was named the most powerful brand in the wine and spirits industry for several years, through 2012.

BRAND ELEMENTS

- The Smirnoff label features the Regal Eagle, a symbol related to awards won by Pyotr Smirnov for his vodka in the late 19th century.
- The Smirnoff name in all capitals is often featured on a red banner on its label.
- Smirnoff vodka is identified as a quality product.

Though Smirnoff vodka only became popular globally after being revived in the United States beginning in the 1930s, the brand is deeply linked to its Russian roots. The legacy of Pyotr Smirnov can be found on every bottle. Smirnov's vodka won three double eagles, the highest industrial award in Russia in the tsarist period. The label on each bottle of Smirnoff vodka features a version of this double eagle, known as the Regal Eagle. Though the appearance of the double eagle has changed over time, it still symbolizes the brand and provides a visible tie to its origins. Nearly every product produced by the brand, including its ready-to-drink products, features the Regal Eagle.

Other aspects of the label are also closely identified with Smirnoff. On most of the brand's products, the Smirnoff name is written in a distinctive font in all capitals, often on a red, ribbon-like banner. The color scheme, however, varies by product. With the more-than-20 types of flavored vodka, for example, the Smirnoff font and the position of the banner do not change, but the color used reflects the flavor inside.

Quality is also a key element of the Smirnoff brand. Pyotr Smirnov emphasized the importance of pure and superior ingredients in making his vodka. Only the best grains are used to make the alcohol, and its water is of high quality. Smirnov was the first to use charcoal filtration to ensure better taste and a better product. The system remained in use into the 2010s. Smirnoff's modern production process, in which the vodka is distilled three times and filtered through ten stages of charcoal, is designed to maintain high quality.

BRAND IDENTITY

- Smirnoff emphasizes its history and mixability in ads.
- Smirnoff is often identified with music and nightlife, and it sponsors numerous related events.
- The vodka brand has had a long relationship with James Bond.

Smirnoff consistently emphasizes the brand's heritage as the vodka of Russian royalty, allowing those who imbibe to identify with prestige and eliteness. Many advertising campaigns have underscored this effect, most notably the 2007 global campaign, "Signature," which related the history of Smirnoff vodka in various media ads, a redesigned website, and other digital platforms.

Weight is also placed on the vodka's ability to be mixed to create new drinks. Beginning with the "It leaves you breathless" campaign in the United States in the 1950s and to present day, many aspects of brand building have involved promoting Smirnoff's mixability. This includes every launch of a new flavor of Smirnoff vodka.

Smirnoff is also closely identified with music and nightlife. Since 1990 Smirnoff has done a number of promotions related to music. In 2008 the Smirnoff Mix Series linked the production of some of the best-known hip hop songs by well-known producers with a representation of a mixed drink made with Smirnoff's. This particular campaign targeted urban markets and was linked to a key Smirnoff Signature Mix event. The event came about in 2012, when Smirnoff partnered with David LaChappelle to create the Smirnoff Midnight Circus, which went around the globe to celebrate the best nightlife experiences. The Smirnoff website also has featured a section devoted to nightlife, listing the best bars, clubs, and eateries in many cities.

In addition, Smirnoff has long been associated with the prestige and sophistication of the character James Bond. The vodka has been featured in at least 21 Bond films as part of his drink of choice. The relationship began in 1962 with *Dr. No*, and Smirnoff's was mentioned by name in 2006's *Casino Royale*.

BRAND STRATEGY

- Smirnoff created excitement by regularly introducing new vodka flavors.
- Smirnoff's entry into the ready-to-drink market was highly successful.
- The biggest markets for Smirnoff were the United States and the United Kingdom.

While Smirnoff often emphasizes its regal roots and appeals to a wide age-range of drinkers, the brand is built on vibrancy, celebration, entertainment, and youthful qualities. The brand's first two products were Smirnoff Red Label, also known as Smirnoff No. 21 and regularly used as a cocktail base, and Smirnoff Blue Label, which has a slightly higher alcohol content and is sold as an ultra-premium brand. To attract and retain youthful drinkers and to create excitement about the brand, Smirnoff introduced new flavors and variants, including blueberry, coconut, vanilla, whipped cream, "kissed" caramel, and iced cake. In 2010 the brand added the first extensions under Blue Label: Spiced Root Beer and Dark Roasted Espresso.

In 1999 Smirnoff focused on a new market: the young drinker. That year saw the introduction of Smirnoff Red Ice, a flavored malt beverage that did not contain any vodka. With the success of Red Ice, Smirnoff went on to debut Black Ice, and then it added more variants to these basic products, such as cherry lime, green apple, grape, and tropical fruit. These beverages broadened the brand's appeal and brought its name to new, younger markets. Over the years, Smirnoff added branded frozen drinks in a pouch and the single-serving, bottled Smirnoff Premium Malt Mixed Drinks and Smirnoff Cocktails Collection.

Smirnoff's range of products and its successful promotions appealed to wide audiences in many markets around the world, especially where there was an emphasis on nightlife. The biggest markets for Smirnoff were the United States and the United Kingdom. Other significant markets were South Africa, Canada, Brazil, and Australia. Some vodka flavors and other variants were developed for specific international markets, as were many marketing and ad campaigns. Some of Smirnoff's branded products were unique to certain countries. In 2010, for example, Smirnoff Vodka & Cola debuted in the UK.

BRAND EQUITY

- Smirnoff is the best-selling vodka in the world and in many markets such as the United States.
- Millward Brown listed Smirnoff as the top-ranked spirit in 2010, ahead of other popular spirits, such as Johnnie Walker, Bacardi, and Hennessey.
- Intangible Business has ranked Smirnoff atop its best spirit and wine business rankings, though with declining brand value in recent years.

For decades Smirnoff has been the best-selling vodka in the United States and the world. It is also the top vodka in numerous markets, including the United Kingdom and Canada, and it continues to make inroads into emerging markets like Brazil. In 2005 Smirnoff was named the number-one spirits brand based on sales volume and value, at a time when vodka consumption was on the increase.

Smirnoff is highly ranked annually for its brand value. In the 2010 issue of Millward Brown's "BrandZ Top 100 Most Valuable Global Brands," Smirnoff was ranked number 10 among UK brands (its parent company, Diageo, is British-based), with a brand value of US$4.886 billion. That same year it was also the top-ranked spirit, ahead of Bacardi, Johnnie Walker, Jose Cuervo, and Absolut. In 2012 Brand Finance ranked Smirnoff number four in its "Top 50 Drinks Directory," after Johnnie Walker, Bacardi, and Hennessey. It had been ranked number three the previous year. Its brand value was US$1.718 billion in 2012, a slight improvement over 2011 at US$1.704 billion, though Smirnoff's value was US$2.664 billion in 2010 and US$2.827 billion in 2009.

In 2011 Intangible Business ranked Smirnoff the top spirit and wine in the world on its *2011 Power 100*, the brand posting an overall score of 88.9 percent. The Power 100 ranks the brands of spirits and wine which create the most value for their owners. In 2012 Smirnoff retained the number-one position, though with a lower score of 85.2 percent. According to the survey, Smirnoff has been negatively impacted by promotional pricing in the United States, and its brand score was slipping year to year in the face of increased competition.

BRAND AWARENESS

- Smirnoff is sold in 130 countries in both established and emerging markets.
- Smirnoff has high brand awareness in the spirits and wines sector.
- In 2011 it ranked number 45 in the Top 50 Brands in Social Media by Yomego.

Because Smirnoff is the best-selling spirit in the world, and has been the best-selling vodka for some time, it has high brand awareness, including top-of-mind awareness in both established and emerging markets. High consumer awareness was a component of its ranking as the most powerful spirits brand in the world by Intangible Business several times, beginning in 2006 and including 2012. In 2011 it ranked number 45 in the Top 50 Brands in Social Media by Yomego. Being constantly mentioned on social media creates and reflects high brand awareness. In 2009 the Dutch Top 100 Best Brand Awareness survey ranked Smirnoff number 62. This survey, conducted by Je Zuster, looks at the strength of brand awareness among the Dutch.

Though associated with Russia because of its name and Russian roots, Smirnoff is recognized in many countries in the world as the best-known brand of vodka. It is sold in some 130 countries, in both established markets like the United States and emerging markets in Latin America, Asia, and Africa, with both global and local advertising campaigns. In emerging countries, Smirnoff is a brand associated with Western wealth and style, allowing premium pricing.

BRAND OUTLOOK

- Smirnoff's brand value has been on the decline, and sales have struggled since a peak in 2008.
- Smirnoff sold 25.8 million cases in fiscal 2012.
- Smirnoff saw double digit growth in Africa and Latin America, where more growth was expected in the future.

Despite Smirnoff's position as the best-selling vodka and spirit, it has faced numerous challenges in the first years of the 21st century that could impact its long-term positioning. While the brand reached a peak in value in 2009 and is still widely considered the top spirit in the world in terms of brand value, it has been on a decline since then as drinkers have shown an increased interest in other vodkas and other spirits, such as whisky. Smirnoff has also been negatively impacted in 2012 by promotional pricing in the United States; promotional pricing was put in place to address pricing pressure on vodka in that market.

While sales totaled 25.8 million cases in fiscal 2012, this was below the record high of 26.2 million in 2008. Smirnoff had been the industry leader for years in ready-to-drink products, primarily its Smirnoff Ice line, but those sales went into decline as well. Despite these issues, Smirnoff still showed at least 1 percent growth annually into the 2010s. And its wide range of flavored vodkas gave more breadth to and created more interest in the brand.

In contrast to the slow growth in its established markets, Smirnoff saw double-digit growth in markets in Africa and Latin America in fiscal 2012. Because of this success, parent company Diageo considered Smirnoff one of its best products and authorized spending 10 percent more on marketing. Brand experts were not impressed with Diageo's proposed brand strategy, however, and it remained to be seen what contribution it would make to Smirnoff's long-term success.

FURTHER READING

"Best Global Brands 2012." Interbrand. Accessed December 23, 2012. http://www.interbrand.com/en/best-global-brands/2012/Smirnoff.

Brady, Rose. "Smirnoff: The Amazing History of a Brand." *Business Week*, May 20, 2009.

Brand Finance. "Smirnoff." *Brandirectory*. Accessed December 23, 2012. http://brandirectory.com/profile/smirnoff.

"BrandZ Top 100 Most Valuable Global Brands 2010." Millward Brown. Accessed December 23, 2012. http://www.millwardbrown.com/libraries/optimor_brandz_files/2010_brandz_top100_report.sflb.ashx.

Brown, Susan Windisch. "Smirnoff." *Encyclopedia of Global Brands, Volume 1: Consumable Products.* Ed. Janice Jorgensen. Detroit, MI: St. James Press, 1994.

Himselstein, Linda. *The King of Vodka: The Story of Pyotr Smirnov and the Upheaval of an Empire.* New York: HarperCollins, 2009.

Intangible Business. *The Power 100: The World's Most Powerful Spirits & Wine Brands, 2012.* Accessed December 23, 2012. http://www.drinkspowerbrands.com/top-10.html.

Ramshaw, Andre. "Satan's Blood." *National Post's Financial Post & FP Investing*, January 9, 2010.

"Smirnoff." Superbrands East Africa. Accessed December 23, 2012. http://www.superbrandseastafrica.com/wp-content/uploads/file/Vol-1-Pdfs/142-smirnoff.pdf.

Waddell, Ray. "Being There, Doing That." *Billboard*, January 9, 2010.

SODEXO

—■—

AT A GLANCE

—■—

Brand Synopsis: Sodexo is a leading name in foodservice and facilities management services, associated with Quality of Daily Life solutions and "making every day a better day."

Parent Company: Sodexo
255, Quai de la Bataille de Stalingrad
92866 Issy-Les-Moulineaux Cedex 9
France
http://www.sodexo.com

Sector: Consumer Discretionary

Industry Group: Consumer Services

Performance: *Sales*—US$22 billion.

Principal Competitors: ARAMARK Corporation; Compass Group PLC; Elior

BRAND ORIGINS

- Sodexo was founded in France in 1966 as Société d'Exploitation Hotelière.
- The company expanded beyond France in the 1970s.
- U.S. operations are joined under the Sodexho USA subsidiary, creating a company acronym and brand name.
- Sodexho became a well respected business-to-business brand but was little known to general consumers.
- The Sodexo brand was unveiled in 2008.

The Sodexo brand grew out of a company called Société d'Exploitation Hotelière, a food services business in Marseilles, France, established in 1966 by Pierre Bellon. Bellon's family had been involved in serving the cruise ship and luxury liner sectors since the early 1900s. His new venture provided food services to companies, hospitals, and schools. Bellon expanded beyond France in 1971 when he won a contract to supply hospitals in neighboring Belgium. Mid-decade, Bellon began serving offshore drilling platforms and construction sites in Africa and the Middle East. In 1978 he launched a service voucher program to provide meals, gasoline, and medical prescriptions on a prepaid basis. This popular service would eventually make use of smart cards.

Bellon set up subsidiaries in North and South America in 1980. To finance further global ambitions, Bellon took the company public on the Paris Stock Exchange, although he retained majority control. With the funds raised through the stock offer, Bellon engineered several acquisitions of U.S. companies that supplied vending machine vendors, restaurants, and river and harbor cruise shops. These acquisitions led to the formation of Sodexho USA, which made use of an acronym created from the French parent company's name; this name, Sodexho, would become the corporate brand as well.

After negotiating the challenging economic climate of the late 1980s and early 1990s, Sodexho resumed expansion in 1995. The company doubled in size by acquiring Gardner Merchant, a U.K. restaurant and food services operation. The deal was quickly followed in 1996 by the purchase of a Brazil-based service voucher provider, the third largest in the world. In that same year,

Gardner Merchant's U.S. operations were acquired to make Sodexho USA the fourth largest food service company in the United States.

The parent company adopted a new name in 1997, becoming Sodexho Alliance S.A. In 2002 shares of Sodexho Alliance gained a coveted listing on the New York Stock Exchange, adding further luster to the Sodexho brand. The company continued to expand in the new century. With operations in about 80 countries, it became the world's second largest contract foodservice provider. Moreover, it moved beyond foodservice, now considering itself a general services company. Despite the size of the company, Sodexho was a business-to-business brand, little known to general consumers. To rectify that shortcoming and to leverage inherent brand equity, Sodexho launched a major branding program. It culminated in early 2008 with the introduction of a new corporate name and brand, Sodexo, as well as a single global brand strategy.

BRAND ELEMENTS

- The new Sodexo name eliminated the letter "h" as it was unnecessary and culturally difficult to pronounce.
- The "x" in the new logo was depicted as a smile.
- The five stars of the previous logo became a single, larger star in the new logo.
- The tagline "Making every day a better day" is often used as part of the logo.

One of the most important brand elements of Sodexo, the name, was the result of a 2008 global branding effort. The company that had been known as Société d'Exploitation Hotelière until the acronym Sodexho was created eventually became Sodexo. Dropping the letter "h" created a more easily pronounced word in the global market and also shed the idea that the company was strictly a supplier to hotels, the word from which the "h" had derived.

Until 2008 the company's logo was comprised of the name Sodexho rendered in blue upper- and lower-case letters, with the "ex" joined together as a ligature. The name was underlined in red, and in some cases included "alliance." Emanating from the upward sweeping "x" was a group of five expanding stars bending back towards the "o."

In the new Sodexo logo, the entire name was presented in lower-case italicized letters. The "e" and "x" were separated. The red underline was eliminated, and a red stroke was incorporated as one of the slashes in the "x," its upward tilt intentionally evoking a smile. Above it was a single, blue seven-point star, larger than any of the five stars in the previous logo.

In most instances, the Sodexo logo is accompanied by the tagline "Making every day a better day" in blue letters below the Sodexo name and in a smaller type size.

In some instances, a black monochrome version of the logo and tagline are used. On dark backgrounds, a white monochrome of the name by itself is also used.

BRAND IDENTITY

- Sodexo seeks to portray itself as a "quality of daily life" solutions provider.
- The single star of the revised logo symbolizes the company's focusing on its core mission.
- The "Making every day a better day" slogan suggests a daily commitment to Sodexo's mission.
- Philanthropic endeavors reinforce Sodexo's identity.
- Presenting a positive identity to employees is also important to the growth of the company.

Through its branding efforts, Sodexo seeks to portray itself as a "quality of daily life" solutions provider that truly cares about helping to improve the lives of everyday people as well as its clients, shareholders, and employees. The updated Sodexo logo was designed to reflect this personality. The single star that replaced the five stars of the old logo was meant to symbolize the company focusing its energy on its core mission. With seven points, the Sodexo star was uncommon, intended to convey that Sodexo stood out from the competition. The red, upward sweep of one arm of the "x" was reminiscent of a smile, reflecting the brand's friendly and optimistic spirit.

Sodexo's identity is reinforced further by the slogan, "Making every day a better day." As a tagline, the phrase is joined to the logo in all print ads. The stated message is that the company is committed to improving people's daily quality of life. Furthermore, it is a daily commitment, an ongoing commitment.

In keeping with its identity, Sodexo is involved in a number of high-profile philanthropic endeavors. Given the company's lengthy ties to the foodservice industry, Sodexo is especially committed to the problem of world hunger. Activities in this area are coordinated by the STOP Hunger Program, with STOP standing for Sodexo Teams Our People. Not only does the company make food donations, it coordinates the activities of students and its own employees to fight hunger in local communities around the world. In addition, Sodexo reinforces its brand identity through its "Better Tomorrow Plan," which focuses on three areas: reducing the carbon footprint of itself and clients as a way to combat global warming; reducing the use of water by the company and its clients; and promoting health and wellness solutions for customers, clients, and employees.

In addition to communicating to clients and customers, the brand takes pains to present a consistent positive image to employees and potential employees. Influencing the former was important because they are the human face of the brand. To attract the kind of new employees who could be an appropriate face of the brand, Sodexo portrays itself as a responsible, caring employer. Success in this regard is reflected by Sodexo being named "Best Company for Hourly Workers" and "Best Company for Multicultural Women" by *Working Mother Magazine;* being listed by *Fortune* as one of "The World's Most Admired Companies"; attaining the No. 1 rank on DiversityInc.'s on "Top 50 Companies for Diversity Inclusion"; and being named one of the "World's Most Ethical Companies."

BRAND STRATEGY

- The creation of Sodexho USA in 1991 was an effort to raise general brand awareness.
- The company's 1966 logo was not updated until 1995.
- A single brand strategy was introduced in 2008.
- Sodexo manager evaluations are tied to building brand equity.
- Branding is also important to Sodexo's hiring and retention efforts.

Over the course of its corporate history, Sodexo has experienced an evolution in its brand strategy as it has transformed itself from a foodservices company to a service company. Initially, Sodexho was a business-to-business brand, primarily concerned with gaining awareness with collective organizations—the companies, hospitals, and school that might contract for its foodservice services. Over the years, Sodexho extended its business-to-business brand to other parts of the world and into new business sectors. After a major growth spurt in the 1980s, the company established a mission of becoming the world's largest contract feeder. In an effort to meet that goal, the company began taking steps in the early 1990s to improve its image in the marketplace. In the key market of the United States, three recently acquired companies—The Seiler Corporation, Food Dimensions Inc., and Spirit Cruises—were combined in 1991 to create Sodexho USA. Also that year, Sodexho sponsored the World Corporate Games in Lille, France, a prelude to the company's marketing tied to the 1992 Olympics in Spain. It wasn't until 1995 that the company updated the logo that had been in use since 1966. With its red and blue coloring and five stars, the new logo was more colorful and visually interesting than its predecessor.

The corporate brand, however, remained little known with general consumers, a situation that prevailed as the new millennium unfolded. Rather than promote its corporate brand to consumers, Sodexho touted a stable of brands maintained by its Retail Brand Group for its corporate dining, education, and healthcare accounts, with the hope of expanding these dining concepts to shopping malls, airports, and other locations. Sodexho began the consumer branding effort with a pilot program for a

coffeehouse concept, Jazzman's Café, which could operate as a full-service café, kiosk, or cart. Building on Jazzman's success, other branded concepts were introduced. They included Pandini's, an Italian bistro; Sub Connection, a sandwich shop; Sky Ranch Grill, a burger concept; Mein Bowl, offering Asian cuisine; Salsa Rico, offering Mexican food; Pete's Arena, a pizza concept; and Strutters, offering chicken sandwiches and tenders. Sodexho also extended the consumer branding approach to its hospital business, introducing "Total Patient Experience," essentially a patient room service option.

In January 2008, the company unveiled a new single global brand strategy, the result of a year-long process that involved work between the different business groups and geographic regions, as well as branding experts. More than just raising the profile of the company, the new branding program centered on the shortened Sodexo name and was designed to help grow the facilities management business. It was also intended to position the company to become the premier global outsourcing expert so-called Quality of Life services. It was a broad mandate, covering six individual industry sectors, and involved an equally ambitious branding strategy. The new brand was now seen as a valuable asset, one that the company hoped the world could come to know better, love, and with which clients and customers ultimately choose to do business.

The growth of Sodexo's brand equity became a new measuring stick in the evaluation of managers. Hiring and retaining talented employees was also important, and the new brand strategy supported this goal as well. To help build an authentic employment brand, Sodexo created an integrated online presence. It included a full Careers site, discipline-specific microsites, and social media activities. To establish brand awareness with possible future employees, Sodexo began partnering with organizations that worked directly with high school students, such as the Multicultural Food & Hospitality Alliance.

BRAND EQUITY

- Sodexo provides brand value by creating a competitive advantage and by protecting margins.
- Brand Finance estimated Sodexo's brand value at US$2.777 billion.
- Sodexo was listed No. 415 on Brand Finance's 2012 Global 500.
- Sodexo's brand value in 2010 was US$2.078 billion, a performance that received the No. 457 ranking on the 2010 Global 500.

While measuring brand equity is in many ways a subjective exercise, the value of an effective brand is undeniable. In his January 2012 letter to shareholders, Pierre Bellon clearly stated his belief in the importance of the Sodexo brand. He wrote that the brand "must be a source of preference. It is this preference that will give us a competitive advantage and protect our margins."

Several commercial brand consultants have developed ways to quantify the monetary value of brands. One of the leading branding agencies, Brand Finance Plc, assigned a brand value of US$2.777 billion to the Sodexo brand for its 2011 performance. As a result, Sodexo ranked No. 415 on Brand Finance's 2012 Global 500 list of the world's most valuable brands. Sodexo performance was also showing steady improvement. The brand had ranked No. 457 on the 2010 Global 500 with a brand value of US$2.078 billion.

BRAND AWARENESS

- During most of its history, Sodexho Alliance experienced limited brand awareness.
- The awareness of Sodexho Alliance grew as the company entered new industry sectors.
- Brand awareness began to improve following the 2008 launch of a single global brand approach.
- Sodexo's brand awareness is supported by more than 400,000 employees in about 80 countries.

For most of its history, Sodexho Alliance enjoyed scant brand awareness. The company expanded its operations around the world and entered several new industry sectors, yet remained a business-to-business brand. Despite touching the lives of many individual consumers each day, the Sodexho name was little known to the general public. It wasn't until early 2008 that company adopted a global single brand approach to rectify these shortcomings and position itself as leader in facilities management as well as food service.

The spelling of the brand was altered, but the change caused little confusion because Sodexho Alliance was relatively unknown to most people. Essentially, Sodexo was introduced to the marketplace as a new brand. It achieved excellent brand recognition in the industry sectors the parent company served, primarily because of the company's large size. Sodexo maintained operations in 80 countries and employed more than 400,000 employees, making it the 22nd largest employer in the world. It was these legions of employees who would grow Sodexo's brand awareness as they come into contact with the general public in the years ahead.

BRAND OUTLOOK

Given that Sodexo only launched a global branding effort in 2008, the company has only scratched the surfac of the brand's potential. Amplifying that promise is the reach of the company, with involvement in several sectors and doing business in about 80 countries in all corners of the world. There are an abundance of potential contact points between Sodexo employees and consumers. Each day, the company served 50 million consumers. As a result, brand awareness was likely to escalate significantly, as will the equity of the brand.

Sodexo expects much out of its global brand strategy. By making Sodexo a well known and beloved brand that customers and consumers choose, that company has very tangible goals. It seeks to sustain an annual revenue growth rate of 7 percent and a return on capital employed of more than 15 percent. The company estimates in its growth potential to be 50 times its current annual revenues of US$22.85 billion. It would be a heavy lift for any brand and only time would tell if the company's strategy will prove successful.

- The Sodexo brand is young and possesses a great deal of potential.
- The breadth of Sodexo's business bodes well for the growth of the brand.
- Sodexo hopes for a 50-fold revenue increase in the years ahead.

FURTHER READING

Brand Finance. "Global 500 2012." *Brandirectory.* Accessed January 2, 2013. http://brandirectory.com/league_tables/table/global-500-2012.

Herskovits, Beth. "Corporate Case Study: Sodexho Jazzes Up Profile with Consumer Outreach." *PR Week (US).* May 23, 2005.

"Sodexho Alliance SA." *International Directory of Company Histories.* Detroit, MI: St. James Press. Vol. 29. 1999.

"Sodexho Unveils New Brand Strategy." *FoodService Director.* February 15, 2008.

"Sodexho to Change Name, Jump Into '92 Olympics." *Nation's Restaurant News.* June 24, 1991.

"Takin' it to the Streets: Sodexho Pursues Brand Placement in Commercial Settings." FoodService Director. March 15, 2005.

SONY

AT A GLANCE

Brand Synopsis: The Sony brand is associated with innovative electronic products that enhance modern lifestyles.

Parent Company: Sony Corporation
1-7-1 Konan Minato-Ku
Tokyo 108-0075
Japan
http://www.sony.net

Sector: Consumer Discretionary

Industry Group: Consumer Durables and Apparel

Performance: *Market share*—10.9 percent of the global consumer electronics market (2011). *Sales*—US$81 billion (2011–12).

Principal Competitors: Samsung; Panasonic; Universal Music Group; Apple; Microsoft; Canon; LG

BRAND ORIGINS

- Sony began by manufacturing small electric products in the 1940s.
- A strategy of diversification into entertainment was begun in 1968.
- Sony became a major film and record producer in the 1980s.
- The company's strategy for the 21st century encompassed computers and smart phones.

Tokyo Telecommunications Engineering Corporation was founded by Masaru Ibuka and Akio Morita in the wreckage of post–World War II Japan. The company began by repairing radios and then started making simple electric devices such as rice cookers. In the late 1940s Ibuka and Morita designed a reel-to-reel magnetic tape recorder. The trade name of the tape was SONI-TAPE. After visiting the United States, Ibuka and Morita purchased Western Electric transistor patents and developed a line of small transistor radios. The TR-63 model (1956) was extremely small and marketed as a "pocketable" radio. Looking to penetrate the American market for radios and tape recorders, Ibuka and Morita knew that their Totsuko trade name was inappropriate, and in 1958 the company assumed the name of one of its brands, Sony. The founders of the company were both audiophiles and wanted the name to have some association with the world of sound. "Sony" has no meaning in Japanese. That it could be pronounced and understood by English speakers illustrates company's focus on sales outside of Japan.

Having started with tape recorders and radios, Sony then moved into making televisions. The company had found an unexpectedly large market for scaled-down versions of appliances that most families already owned, and it developed a small transistorized television that was highly successful. The introduction of the Trinitron color television in 1968 established the brand as the industry leader in both technology and design. In 1979 Sony introduced its Soundabout audiocassette player. Sony's engineers then reduced its size and cost and called it the Walkman. With the Walkman, Sony established the idea of mobile personal entertainment.

Sony recognized the value of research and development, and the company put a premium on developing new technology that would lead to completely new products. Sony became a leader in the development of videotape recording and in the digital recording of sound and images. The development of the compact disc and DVD formats owed a great deal to Sony's scientific research and enhanced its reputation as a leader in innovation.

In the mid-1960s Sony's leadership sought to establish the company as a major worldwide manufacturer of electronic hardware and software and provider of the music and images that are the focus of consumer electronics. In 1968 they formed a joint venture with CBS Records, a major American record company. They also created a joint venture with Epic Records and set up a music publishing group. In 1983 the newly renamed CBS/Sony Group played a major role in the success of Sony's compact disc, which quickly replaced the vinyl disc as the principal medium for recorded music.

In 1988 the company acquired CBS Records outright and then purchased Columbia Pictures Entertainment, one of the world's major motion picture producers. Columbia Pictures cost Sony US$3.4 billion, which was the largest purchase ever made by a Japanese company, but the acquisition established Sony as a major provider of music and films. The two companies were later renamed Sony Music Entertainment and Sony Pictures Entertainment. In 2004 Sony formed a joint venture with the Bertelsmann Music Group, a move that made Sony BMG Music Entertainment one of the largest record companies and music publishers in the world. Sony took complete control of this company in 2008.

Sony continued to diversify in the 1990s, establishing Sony Computer Entertainment to develop video game consoles and games. The prototype PlayStation was introduced in 1994 in Japan, and its release in the United States in 1995 marked Sony's triumphant entry into the video game market. In 1996 Sony introduced a line of home computers under the VAIO (Video Audio Integrated Operation) brand that extended the company's reputation for top-quality audiovisual technology. The first Cybershot digital camera was also introduced in 1996. Other products, including the CD-ROM and Video CD, also strengthened the brand's multimedia applications.

In 2001 Sony moved into the mobile phone business when it joined with the Swedish telecommunications company Ericsson to form Sony Ericsson. Building on its strong audiovisual expertise, Sony developed multimedia-capable mobile phones, which included innovative features such as cameras.

BRAND ELEMENTS
- Simplicity and modernity are the main elements in Sony's brand identifiers.

- Sony considers the design of its products as an element of its brand.
- Sony has remained faithful to the design of its 1971 logo.

The first Sony logo featured the company's name in a stylized, elongated script that emphasized the "S" and the tail of the "y," making them much longer letters than the "O" and the "N." Enclosed in a rectangle, the logo was registered as a trademark in 1955. Defining the logo was part of the creation of a new brand image and corporate identity that was expressed in the marketing phrase: "Sony—a worldwide brand born in Japan." The company was using large neon signs in many cities, and this led them to make the logo simpler and more compact and discernible from great distances. In the 1957 version of the logo, "Sony" was spelled out in upper case letters in a plain typeface. In 1961 Sony designer Yasuo Kuroki produced another version in which the letters appeared darker and taller. Subsequent revisions of the logo in 1962, 1969, and 1971 introduced only slight changes. When the company reached its 35th anniversary in 1981, it considered a new logo, but management decided to keep the 1971 logo and has used it ever since.

The first major Japanese company to realize the importance of its brand, Sony brought together its research, design, and marketing teams to articulate a consistent brand identity. The company emphasized original materials and designs for its products and was a pioneer in moving away from wooden cabinets and dark colors in the design of its televisions, establishing metallic elements and light-colored plastic cases as the norm.

BRAND IDENTITY
- The Sony brand is based on innovation, originality, and simplicity of design.
- Sony's record of developing new products has enhanced the brand.
- Sony's expansion into film and music production has not helped maintain brand consistency.

As early as 1959, Sony was emphasizing its research and development capabilities with the slogan, "Research Makes the Difference." Since then, it has used such revolutionary products as the Walkman and the compact disc to prove that Sony is at the leading edge of new technology. Being identified with pioneering products like the Walkman has given Sony great prestige among consumers, many of whom used the term "Walkman" for all portable tape players on the market, regardless of manufacturer.

Design and marketing have also been influenced by this emphasis on innovation and originality. Simplicity is highly valued in the company's designs as well as its brand identifiers. Thus, it advertised a new line of televisions with the tag line "The latest Trinitron. So simple, it's naked."

Sony has always been a leader in reducing the size of electronic consumer goods, and this has become an important part of the brand's identity. Terms like "Pocketable" and "Passport-size" have been applied to its products, and thus Sony has been able to add "World's Smallest" to "World's First" in the claims it makes for its products.

The Sony reputation for high-quality products was established in the 1960s with its outstanding television and audio lines. Sony did more than any other Japanese company to dispel the image of the country as a producer of cheap, inferior copies of American or European products that was widespread in the decades after World War II. Companies like Nikon and Toyota followed in Sony's wake and established a new image of Japanese products based on their excellent engineering, pioneering design and technology, and reliability.

For most of the 20th century Sony was able to charge a premium for its products. "It's a Sony!" was a constant refrain in its print and television advertising, emphasizing that the customer was getting high quality and uniqueness in buying Sony products. Sony's marketing strategy is to use one or two catchy words to introduce a new product, which reinforces the brand's association with simplicity and originality of design.

Sony has been far less successful in establishing its brand identity in its music, motion picture, and computer game divisions. Buying Columbia Pictures and CBS Records brought it an enviable library of programming, including the work of famous figures like Michael Jackson, but consumers do not associate such artists with Sony. The global publicity surrounding Sony's acquisitions has given it the appearance of an owner of valuable artistic products rather than a producer of great music or films.

BRAND STRATEGY

- Sony's brand identity is based on its outstanding record of innovation.
- Some of Sony's product names have entered everyday language.
- Product designs and names have been made part of the brand's identity.

Sony's advertising staff has traditionally been involved in product planning. Thus, product names, marketing slogans, and advertising strategies are created in tandem with the products themselves. A prime example of the success of this approach is the name "Walkman." Another example is "Passport-size," which was used to promote the tiny camcorder introduced in 1989. Since the establishment of the Sony brand name, the company has tried to make its product names and catchphrases (such as Walkman and Handycam) part of consumers' everyday language.

Sony's unprecedented record of innovation has often enabled the company to classify and market its products as the "World's First" or "World's Best" products. The burden of being a pioneer in new technology has been a heavy one, however, and there have been several well-documented failures in bringing new inventions to market, such as the Beta format for videotape recorders and the MiniDisc, a digital replacement for the audiocassette tape, both of which failed to catch on and were discontinued.

For decades, Sony's pride in its name and its brand identity was evident in its strategy of turning joint ventures into Sony companies. The CBS and Ericsson names were dropped from the masthead of those companies when Sony acquired them. The company's loyalty to the brand name and logo lessened with the introduction of new product lines in the 1990s and growing competition in the consumer electronics market. PlayStation and VAIO started life with the Sony prefix, but now they stand alone and have different logos. Sony has even dispensed with including the company name in the logo of some of its music products.

BRAND EQUITY

- Sony's brand value declined in 2011 and 2012.
- Sony's market share in consumer electronics fell in 2011.
- Sony Music Group was the world's leading recording company in 2011.

Sony was ranked 61st in the *Brandirectory*'s Global 500 in 2011 but slipped to 69th in 2012 with a brand valuation of US$13 billion. Interbrand ranked Sony 35th among top global brands in 2011. With the exception of its music and digital camera groups, all of Sony's divisions were losing market share during this period. In 2011 Sony claimed only 9 percent of television sales and about 3 percent of mobile phones, and its games market share dropped from 9 percent to 6 percent. Sony Pictures achieved a 12 percent share and was ranked third in film production. Only Sony Music Group led its market, with a 32 percent share.

BRAND AWARENESS

- In the early 21st century Sony's reputation for innovation has suffered.
- Diversification has diluted Sony's brand.
- Sony's competitors are now more focused and agile and have displaced Sony at the forefront of the consumer electronics industry.

As the preeminent global consumer electronics brand, Sony has enjoyed unparalleled brand loyalty. In a 1990 Landor Associates survey of Japanese, American, and European brands, Sony ranked first in terms of esteem and fourth in name recognition to win an overall ranking of second place. The drop in the brand's standing in the early 21st century, however, has provided a case study of how an iconic brand like Sony can go into decline quickly. Sony has failed to keep pace with Samsung and other competitors and can no longer determine the pricing for many of its key products, including televisions.

In recent years, Sony has failed to maintain a balance between the need for brand consistency and the need for constant innovation and growth in the rapidly changing environment of consumer electronics. Sony's diversification into the entertainment business has seriously diluted the brand, while its competitors have strengthened. Some, like Samsung, have focused their efforts in a few dominant businesses, while others, like LG, have been more agile in anticipating market developments. Meanwhile, Apple has taken Sony's mantle as the great innovator in consumer electronics. Although Sony Music Group is the dominant player in the global recording business, it has not produced a star like Michael Jackson or Bruce Springsteen in the 21st century. Compared with its competitors, the Sony brand is now looking distinctly old fashioned.

BRAND OUTLOOK

* Sony endured its worst year in 2012, with an estimated annual loss of US$5.7 billion.
* In 2012 Sony restructured its management and cut its workforce as part of a revitalization effort.
* In the coming years, Sony will have to grapple with the challenges of increased global competition and declining sales.

Sony was immensely profitable throughout the 1990s and early 2000s, in part because of the success of its PlayStation line of video-game consoles. The global financial crisis that began in 2008, the Japanese earthquake in 2011, and an almost a 10 percent drop in sales in 2012 hit the company hard. Sony estimated an annual loss of US$5.7 billion in 2012, the worst result in the history of the company, which also followed four consecutive years of losses. In response, Sony restructured its management in 2012 and planned to lay off 6 percent of its workforce. Given the increased competition in all of its lines of business, however, Sony's revitalization efforts may not prevent further heavy losses.

FURTHER READING

Asakura, Reiji. *Revolutionaries at Sony: The Making of Sony PlayStation*. New York: McGraw Hill, 2000.

"Best Global Brands, 2011." Interbrand. Accessed September 18, 2012. http://www.interbrand.com/en/best-global-brands/best-global-brands-2008/best-global-brands-2011.aspx.

Brand Finance. "Global 500, 2012." *Brandirectory*, 2012. Accessed September 18, 2012. http://brandirectory.com/league_tables/table/global-500-2012.

Chang, Se-jin. *Sony vs. Samsung: The Inside Story of the Electronics Giants' Battle for Global Superiority*. New York: Wiley, 2008.

Mahr, Jackson, and Lesley Keene. "Sony—played." *Brand Channel*, May 9, 2005. Accessed September 20, 2012. http://www.brandchannel.com/features_profile.asp?pr_id=231.

Nathan, John. *Sony: A Private Life*. New York: Houghton Mifflin, 1999.

Roll, Martin. "Brand Rejuvenation: A Case Study of Sony." *Venture Republic*, 2012. Accessed September 25, 2012. http://www.venturerepublic.com/resources/Brand_Rejuvenation_SONY_brand_brand_leadership.asp.

Sony Corporation. "Establishing the Sony Brand." Accessed September 20, 2012. http://www.sony.net/SonyInfo/CorporateInfo/History/SonyHistory/2-23.html.

SPRITE

—■—

BRAND ORIGINS

- Dr. John Styth Pemberton invented Coke, but The Coca-Cola Company owes its early success, both globally and domestically, to Asa G. Candler.
- As The Coca-Cola Company continued to diversify its product line, Sprite was introduced in 1961 in order to compete with 7UP.

- Sprite, both as a product and as a brand, attracts young people from across the globe, making it one of Coca-Cola's top sellers and marketing success stories.

In 1886, in Atlanta, Georgia, Dr. John Styth Pemberton invented Coca-Cola. While Dr. Pemberton did not live to witness the success of his product, The Coca-Cola Company, incorporated in 1891, grew rapidly. Under the ownership of Asa G. Candler, the company expanded its plants, improved the quality of its product, and launched the largest advertising campaign for a single product in history. By 1895 the company had sold the Coca-Cola syrup in every state in America and by 1916 it was being sold in nine countries worldwide.

During the next 50 years The Coca-Cola Company continued to grow despite two world wars and the Great Depression. In fact, it was World War II that catapulted Cola onto the world stage. Bottling plants were set up near fighting fronts in North Africa and throughout Europe to boost troop morale. This effort brought Coca-Cola to new global markets at an unexpected time.

After the war, Coca-Cola expanded its European markets and began to diversify by buying Minute Maid, Duncan Foods Corporation, Belmont Springs Water Company, and several other companies. Additionally, the company began to expand its product line. During the 1960s Fanta, which was invented and sold during World War II in Germany, was brought to the United States. In 1961 Sprite was introduced, followed by Tab in 1963 and Fresca in 1965. New products, particularly Sprite, were introduced to compete with 7UP.

While this competition was fierce at the time Sprite was introduced, it has decreased significantly as Sprite has become the world's number-one seller in the lemon-lime category.

While the brand was initially marketed as a mixer for alcoholic beverages, today Sprite is advertised as a refreshment for the body and the soul. Marketed mostly to the world's youth, specifically the urban teenager, Sprite has used a number of marketing strategies to reach its demographic: Sprite.com, a website designed to encourage young adults to participate in film, music, and sports; an association with the National Basketball Association and professional basketball players; and televised advertising.

BRAND ELEMENTS

- Sprite's clean, crisp, lemon-lime taste was and continues to be at the heart of its brand, marketing, and logo.
- The Sprite brand has consistently aimed to connect with the urban teenager through a series of marketing campaigns and interactive resources.
- Marketing campaigns such as "Obey your thirst" and "Sprite: The spark" have helped boost Sprite's market share and brand equity.

Since its introduction in 1961, Sprite has been identified by its clean, crisp lemon-lime taste, and its short, snappy trademark. Its logo design—traditionally silver, blue, and green—also reflects the product's refreshing quality. The design of the logo has changed over time. In each major marketing campaign, the message is reflected in an updated logo. According to the *Atlanta Journal Constitution*, Sprite's initial advertising goal was to market the product's clean taste as a mixer for alcoholic beverages. This simple message was embodied in the can used in 1966, with its neutral green background and fizzy bubbles. As the brand took on an edgier, urban feel, so did the cans containing the beverage. In the 2006 "SubLYMONal" campaign, for example, the message focused both on Lymon, Sprite's proprietary lemon-lime flavor formula, and on using embedded marketing codes from recorded television commercials to convey exclusive information to consumers. Brand Packaging reported that while the SubLYMONal design retained the familiar silver, blue, and green colors, it added an "S" brand icon embedded into two interlocking yellow and green circular elements. The "S" icon focused on the lemon-lime image in an edgier manner, one that would attract the younger demographic targeted by the brand.

The Sprite brand has continued to represent a product whose thirst-quenching qualities refresh the body and the spirit. From "I like the Sprite in you," a tagline from the 1980s, to its most recent campaign, "Uncontainable,"

Sprite has encouraged its followers to embrace their individuality and connect with the world around them. Within each campaign, Sprite has striven to attract the younger generation, with sometimes spectacular results. As Chris Roush reported in *Knight Ridder/Tribune Business News*, the "Obey your thirst" campaign helped Sprite command 40 percent of Coca-Cola's total U.S. growth in 1996. "Obey your thirst" and its popular connection to the National Basketball Association also helped Sprite beat out competitors Mountain Dew and 7UP during this time.

While sales were strong through 1999, Sprite became less effective as a brand as Coca-Cola spent less and less on its marketing. According to Natalie Zmuda of *Advertising Age*, Coca-Cola slashed measured media spending for Sprite by about 80 percent between 2005 and 2009. In 2010 the company once again ramped up its investment in Sprite's marketing and launched a new campaign, "Sprite: the Spark," that once again targeted the urban teen. This time, however, as noted by Jeremiah McWilliams in the *Atlanta Journal-Constitution*, Sprite made its first major global marketing effort, releasing media to Africa, Asia, North America, and Europe. With major commercial spots, an interactive music and film site, and another relaunch of the logo, the effort paid off, and in 2011 Sprite was included in Interbrand's *Top 100 Global Brands*, its brand value estimated at US$5.6 billion.

BRAND IDENTITY

- While Sprite began as simply a refreshing beverage, it has come to be promoted as a brand that refreshes the soul.
- Historically, Sprite's advertising campaigns have successfully promoted the brand's straightforward yet edgy image with taglines like "Obey your thirst."
- Sprite.com is a way for Coca-Cola to promote Sprite's brand and to connect young adults from all over the world.

In 1961, when Sprite was introduced, it was advertised as a crisp, clean, tart drink that would quench thirst. Since the early 1960s, however, Sprite has become associated with individuality and honesty. Writing for *AdWeek*, Jennifer Comiteau reported in 1995 that Sprite's marketers wanted a straightforward and honest campaign; however, ad executives were worried the strategy might fall flat. The "Obey your thirst" campaign was born. Witty commercials featured such stunts as a basketball player missing his shot—even after drinking a Sprite. The voice-over read, "If you want to make it to the National Basketball Association, practice. If you want a refreshing drink, obey your thirst. Sprite." Variations of this campaign carried the brand successfully for almost 10 years, when Sprite's sales were at their highest. According to Roush, in 1996,

Sprite's market share grew from 5.1 percent to 5.8 percent, and its volume grew 17.6 percent.

Since that time, Sprite has continued to promote itself as a brand for individuals. Sprite.com, Sprite's online interactive site, promotes this same individuality but with an added edge. By providing youth from around the world with an outlet for creativity, a place where they can refresh their passion, Sprite connects to urban teenagers the world over in the only way they can—in cyberspace. Here, teens can mix music, upload original film, upload video for slam-dunk competitions, and connect with other teenagers.

BRAND STRATEGY

- Continuing to invest in award-winning global advertising remains at the heart of Sprite's brand strategy.
- Sprite has paid particular attention to the health-conscious consumer by releasing Sprite Zero and testing such mid-calorie products as Sprite Select.
- Sprite markets specific brand derivatives, such as Sprite Remix, in specialized global markets.

Sprite's main brand strategy has always been effective marketing. Its marketing goals in recent decades have been to connect with its fans, mainly young teens, and to promote its products globally. One example of this dates back to 1999, near the end of the "Obey your thirst" campaign. According to a 1999 report in *Advertising Age International*, the Coca-Cola Company backed up the claim by its Sprite brand that "image is nothing" by placing the labels upside down on the beverage's packaging in Brazil. Commercials soon followed in which teens appeared to climb up to a ceiling to "obey their thirst" and drink Sprite upside down. Inventive advertising pushed the brand into new markets and promoted brand awareness. This type of awareness is particularly necessary for a brand like Sprite in preparation for line extensions.

Line extensions have been an effective way for Sprite to remain competitive in an ever-changing market. Early in its history, Sprite introduced Sugar Free Sprite to appeal to health-conscious consumers. While the concept still exists, the drink has become known as Sprite Zero, Diet Sprite, or Diet Sprite Zero, depending on the country in which it is sold. In 2012 Sprite continued to reach out to consumers seeking a healthier alternative to the original beverage by testing out mid-calorie options like Sprite Select, which has fewer calories and alternate sweeteners like Truvia, according to *Food Manufacturing*. Furthermore, Sprite has released many different flavors that fit regional cultures. Some examples include Aruba Jam Sprite Remix in the Caribbean, Sprite Lemon Finger in China, and Sprite Ice in Australia and India. Sprite 3G was unveiled in 1996 to compete with Red Bull, the world's best-selling energy drink.

BRAND EQUITY

- Sprite's performance in China and India has helped maintained Coca-Cola's number-one spot in the global market.
- In 2011 Sprite's brand was valued at US$5.6 billion, in 63rd place among the top-100 global brands.
- Sprite's brand value beats out its competitors Mountain Dew and 7UP.

While Sprite has never been a top competitor in the total beverage industry, it has always been a consistent seller and a leader in the lemon-lime category. Sprite's popularity contributes in part to Coca-Cola's number one spot in the global market. According to a 2012 ranking by *24/7 Wall St.*, Sprite is the number-one soft drink in China, with a 26.9 percent market share, and, as reported in the Coca-Cola Company's 2011 annual report, Sprite boosted Coca-Cola's 6 percent increase in unit case volume in Eurasia and Africa due to the brand's 17 percent increase in India.

With increasing global sales, consistent domestic sales, and strong marketing, Sprite's brand value remains strong as well. Interbrand's *Best Global Brands 2011* assessed Sprite's value at US$5.6 billion and ranked the brand 63rd among the top-100 global brands. Additionally, *Brandirectory*'s "Global 500" list for 2012 reported Sprite's brand value at almost US$3.9 billion and ranked Sprite fourth in the beverage sector behind Coke (US$31 billion), Pepsi (US$17 billion), and Budweiser (US$5.6 billion). Sprite's ranking of 272 beat out competitor Mountain Dew, which, with a brand value of US$3.5 billion, fell from 269th in 2011 to 311th in 2012.

BRAND AWARENESS

- Coca-Cola's logo is recognized by about 94 percent of people around the world.
- Coca-Cola's other brands, including Sprite, are sold in more than 200 countries because consumers are willing to try almost any Coca-Cola product.
- Brand awareness is a major contributor to Coca-Cola's number-one ranking on the *Top 100 Global Brands* list and to Sprite's ranking of 63.

Although Sprite is just over 50 years old, parent company Coca-Cola celebrated its 125th anniversary in 2011. While Sprite's logo and brand are certainly recognizable throughout the world, its affiliation with its parent company is an extremely valuable asset. According to a July 2012 article in the *Street*, Coca-Cola's unique selling point is its brand recognition. Because the Coca-Cola logo is identifiable by an estimated 94 percent of the world's population, even in places where it has little presence, consumers are more willing to try new products introduced by Coca-Cola. Accordingly, Coca-Cola had plans to make major investments globally in 2012 in Africa, India, Brazil, and China. The awareness of The Coca-Cola Company's brands translates into steep competition for all others and explains in large part why Coca-Cola has been the number one brand on Interbrand's *Top 100 Global Brands* for twelve consecutive years, with a value of US$71.9 billion.

BRAND OUTLOOK

- Coca-Cola continues to pursue its 2020 goals through better advertising and sales.
- Coca-Cola sees and meets the demand for more health-conscious products by testing new sweeteners and mid-calorie drinks under the Sprite and Fanta brands.
- Using its new "PlantBottle" technology, Coca-Cola has collaborated with other companies in effort to go green.

As 2011 came to a close, CEO Muhtar Kent reviewed Coca-Cola's 2020 goals, known as the six Ps, in the *Coca-Cola Annual Review*. Profit, People, Portfolio, Partners, Planet, and Productivity are the six areas that the company will try to pinpoint in the coming decade. According to the report, Coca-Cola has met the first part of its profit goal of striving to double its business over the course of the next decade by earning US$46.5 billion in 2011. Most importantly for the Sprite brand, the company has sought out new ways to enhance fans' affection for its billion-dollar brands through new marketing, effective merchandising, and enhancement of the consumer experience.

While Sprite and Coke remain staples in the Coca-Cola line-up—Kent even calls Coke the "oxygen" of the company—the company has seen the need to invest in new derivatives of these brands and in noncarbonated drinks as more health-conscious consumers enter the market. Additionally, Coca-Cola's use of the no-calorie, all-natural sweetener, Stevia, in Sprite and its return to testing mid-calorie versions of Sprite and Fanta in June of 2012 demonstrate its willingness to respond to the changing market.

Furthermore, Coca-Cola continues to partner with other companies to try out new packaging and products in an effort to remain relevant in a more environmentally conscious world. A good example of both the Partners and Planet aspects of the company's 2020 goals is its collaboration with Heinz to package ketchup using Coca-Cola's "PlantBottle" technology, which utilizes plant-based materials.

FURTHER READING

Acevedo, Jennifer. "Sprite Restage Makes a 'SubLYMONal' Play: Packaging Graphics Redesigned for the First Time in a Decade Are an Integral Part of Sprite's New Marketing Campaign." *Brand Packaging*, May–June 2006.

Brand Finance. "Global 500 2012." *Brandirectory*, 2012. Accessed September 7, 2012. http://brandirectory.com/league_tables/table/global-500-2012.

"Coca-Cola Co." *Advertising Age International*, December 1999.

The Coca-Cola Company. *2011 Annual Report*. Accessed September 9, 2012. http://www.thecoca-colacompany.com/ourcompany/ar/downloads.html.

———. *2011 Annual Review*. Accessed September 9, 2012. http://www.thecoca-colacompany.com/ourcompany/ar/downloads.html.

"The Coca-Cola Company." *International Directory of Company Histories*. Ed. Jay P. Pederson. Vol. 32. Detroit, MI: St. James Press, 2000. *Gale Virtual Reference Library*. Accessed September 8, 2012. http://go.galegroup.com/ps/i.do?id=GALE%7CCX2843600034&v=2.1&u=itsbtrial&it=r&p=GVRL&sw=w.

"Coke, AG Barr Launch Drives to Compete with Red Bull." *Marketing Week*, March 2, 2006.

"Coke Investing Millions in Plant-Based Plastics." *Waste & Recycling News*, September 3, 2012.

Comiteau, Jennifer. "Anti-image Image." *ADWEEK Eastern Edition*, August 21, 1995.

"Five Regions Critical to Coca-Cola's Success." *Street*, July 16, 2012.

Gabert, Krystal. "The Rise of the Mid-calorie Soft Drink." *Food Manufacturing*, June 2012.

McWilliams, Jeremiah. "Coke to Try to Pump up Sprite: Global Ad Campaign to Include Interactive Music, Movie Tools." *Atlanta Journal-Constitution*, February 12, 2010, A17.

"The Most Popular American Companies in China." *24/7 Wall St*, January 3, 2012. Accessed September 10, 2012. http://www.foxbusiness.com/industries/2012/01/03/most-popular-american-companies-in-china/#ixzz25tCwcBhr.

Roush, Chris. "Sprite Moves up in Beverage Rankings." *Knight Ridder/Tribune Business News*, February 5, 1997.

Sicher, John, ed. "U.S. Beverage Results for 2011." *Beverage Digest*, March 20, 2012. Accessed September 7, 2012. http://www.beverage-digest.com/pdf/top-10_2012.pdf.

"2011 Ranking of the Top 100 Brands." Interbrand. Accessed September 7, 2012. http://www.interbrand.com/en/best-global-brands/best-global-brands-2008/best-global-brands-2011.aspx.

Zmuda, Natalie. "Lemon-Lime Gets Boost after Years of Neglect." *Advertising Age*, September 6, 2010.

STARBUCKS

—■—

AT A GLANCE

■

Brand Synopsis: Starbucks offers a full "coffeehouse experience" that includes gourmet beverages, an inviting ambiance, and a reputation for caring about the community and the environment.

Parent Company: Starbucks Corporation
2401 Utah Avenue South
Seattle, Washington 98134-1436
United States
http://www.starbucks.com

Sector: Consumer Discretionary

Industry Group: Hotels, Restaurants & Leisure

Performance: *Market share*—30.9 percent of the whole-bean coffee and 9.5 percent of the ground coffee sold at U.S. food stores, drug stores, and mass merchandisers (excluding Wal-Mart) (2011). *Sales*—US$13.3 billion (2012).

Principal Competitors: Coffee Bean and Tea Leaf; Caribou Coffee Company, Inc.; Costa Coffee; Eight O'Clock Coffee Co.; Peet's Coffee & Tea, Inc.; Tim Hortons; Coffee Beanery; Tully's Coffee Corporation; Folger's; Maxwell House; Dunkin' Donuts; McDonald's; Subway

BRAND ORIGINS

- Starbucks was founded in 1971 by three friends who wanted to provide top-quality gourmet coffee to consumers in the Seattle area.

- Italian coffee bars inspired the owners of Starbucks to reconfigure their company into a chain of full-service coffeehouses.
- The original six Starbucks outlets were sold in 1987 for US$4 million.
- The first Starbucks store outside North America opened in Japan in 1996 and was followed by extraordinary expansion worldwide.
- The company recovered from a slump by relaunching the brand in 2011, a move that increased sales dramatically.

Starbucks was founded in Seattle, Washington, in 1971 by three partners: magazine writer Gordon Bowker, English teacher Jerry Baldwin, and history teacher Zev Siegl. Seattle had long been a haven for coffee aficionados, but by the late 1960s the quality of its coffee had declined. The three friends bought high-grade arabica beans from the famous Peet's Coffee company in Berkeley, California, and began selling coffee, tea, and spices from a store at the Seattle farmer's market. By 1972 the founders had opened a second store and were roasting their own coffee beans. By 1982 the operation had expanded to five stores and was selling coffee to fine restaurants and espresso bars.

In 1983 Howard Schultz, the firm's manager of retail sales and marketing, made a buying trip to Italy and became inspired by the culture and romance of Italian coffee bars. This was a turning point for the Starbucks brand, prompting the company to experiment with the coffeehouse concept in downtown Seattle. Schultz left in 1985 to found Il Giornale, a chain of coffee bars that began serving the Starbucks brand of coffee in Chicago and in Vancouver, Canada. In 1987 Schultz acquired

Starbucks for US$4 million, changed the name of the combined ventures to Starbucks Corporation, and began an aggressive expansion.

The firm went public in 1992 and was operating 165 outlets in North America by the end of that year, 275 in 1993, and 425 in 1994. It moved to its first overseas market, Japan, in 1996. Soon afterward, Starbucks stores opened in Singapore and the Philippines, followed by various other Pacific Rim countries, Kuwait, and Lebanon. In 1998 Starbucks acquired Seattle Coffee Company, an industry leader in the United Kingdom, and began rebranding those locations under the Starbucks name as the company's first step into the European market. By 2005 the corporation was operating 3,000 international outlets.

Meanwhile, in the United States, Starbucks was experimenting with new product lines and wider distribution via retailers such as warehouse clubs, and it also tried operating full-service restaurants and sandwich shops. The company even made an unsuccessful attempt to become an online mega-cybermerchant. Revenues continued to skyrocket for a time as operations expanded at dizzying speed, but by 2007 sales were faltering. It seemed that the company had lost some of its focus on the core brand that had started it all.

In 2008 Starbucks closed 600 underperforming stores and executed a massive relaunch of the brand, returning to some of the basic principles that had proved so effective in the past. The new strategy was remarkably successful. By 2012 Starbucks was the largest coffeehouse chain in the world and the third-most profitable quick-service restaurant chain in the United States.

BRAND ELEMENTS

- A beguiling mermaid logo has helped make Starbucks recognizable and well-liked around the world.
- A satisfying cup of dark, rich, gourmet coffee is the core of the Starbucks brand.
- The enticing aroma of fine coffee is part of a specific ambiance that differentiates Starbucks from its competitors.

When the three partners opened their first store on the waterfront in Seattle's Pike Place Market—renowned for its selection of farm produce, crafts, and fish—they chose the name Starbucks in reference to the coffee-loving first mate in *Moby Dick*. Continuing the nautical theme, the original black-and-white Starbucks logo was based on a 16th-century Norse illustration of a two-tailed mermaid, unclothed and seductive, encircled by the words, "Starbucks Coffee, Tea, Spices." The image was meant to imply that fine coffee was as enticing as a siren. By the 1980s "the Siren" was rendered in a less risqué manner, with her long hair pulled forward to cover most of her body, and the brand name was shortened to "Starbucks Coffee." By

the 1990s the logo had been redesigned again to emphasize the Siren's smiling face and starry crown while almost eliminating the mermaid tails.

The newer logo incorporated the brand's color scheme—green, white, and black—and was used in Starbucks stores worldwide. (In Saudi Arabia, however, the country's Islamic religious leaders objected to the Siren, and for two years a logo consisting of only her crown was used there. Ultimately, the restriction was rescinded.) The logo was printed on the sides of coffee mugs, bags of coffee, and the aprons of employees. It was displayed in the middle of the store's front window, and it often hung as a sign above the sidewalk outside the storefront. This helped create a specific ambiance that was part of the Starbucks brand. Inside a typical Starbucks outlet, a certain type of music would be playing: selections from the company's own line of compilation CDs, which could be purchased in stores. The aroma of coffee would permeate the air, a reminder that the core product of the Starbucks brand was roasted gourmet coffee with a specific kind of taste: dark and rich, with no additional flavors.

BRAND IDENTITY

- Starbucks sells other products to provide customers with a full "coffeehouse experience."
- Starbucks uses advertising slogans that express a resolve to be more than a business that sells coffee for profit.
- Many customers identify with Starbucks because the company emphasizes the need to be socially responsible.
- In 2009 Starbucks was the most popular brand on the social networking site Facebook, surpassing Coca-Cola.

Although coffee remains the centerpiece of every Starbucks establishment, customer engagement and comfort are also an integral part of the brand. The company wants customers to think of Starbucks as "the third place" where they routinely spend time with friendly people when not at home or at work. Instead of the standard seating arrangements found in most cafés, Starbucks promotes social interaction with an assortment of sofas, upholstered chairs, bar stools, and straight-backed chairs around tables. To encourage people to linger, many of the stores provide free reading materials and games, along with free electricity for laptop computers and free Wi-Fi access.

In keeping with the green in its logo and its emphasis on customer engagement, Starbucks has made a point of promoting social responsibility. When the brand was refocused and relaunched in 2011, this idea was reflected in its slogans: "Think beyond coffee" and "You & Starbucks. It's bigger than coffee." The company refers to the sum of all these brand elements as "the Starbucks Experience."

The firm emphasizes that it offers customers "a full and rewarding coffeehouse experience" that includes excellent service by happy employees who enjoy unusually generous benefits and own shares in the company. Starbucks has built a reputation as a responsible, socially conscious corporation that is not entirely focused on profits. The company's stated mission is "to inspire and nurture the human spirit—one person, one cup, and one neighborhood at a time." The company cultivates a friendly, trendy image by promoting its brand via digital and social media such as Facebook and Twitter instead of traditional advertising on television.

BRAND STRATEGY

- Starbucks Corporation markets various brands but carefully differentiates them from each other.
- Less expensive line extensions were detrimental to the Starbucks brand in its early years.
- The brand later benefited from the addition of related products.
- Line extensions have helped Starbucks penetrate the local market in some countries.

Although the Starbucks company also sold tea and spices from the beginning, the brand soon became synonymous with expensive roasted, dark coffee. Later, the offerings expanded to include other types of coffee and beverages, related accessories, pastries and other food, music, books, and gifts. These various product lines are clearly differentiated from the company's core brand, however. For example, the tea has always been called Tazo, not Starbucks. The corporation's portfolio of brands includes Starbucks Coffee, Seattle's Best Coffee, Tazo Tea, Evolution Fresh, La Boulange, and Torrefazione Italia Coffee.

Starbucks Coffee includes line extensions that are carefully tailored to the specific parameters of the brand. In its first years, the company tried selling a less expensive line extension through supermarkets and similar outlets, but it was not particularly successful, and the brand became defined instead as a premium gourmet coffee. The wholesale division of the company was renamed Caravali to avoid sullying the Starbucks name through a connection with coffee that might not be absolutely fresh. During the 1990s, Starbucks teamed with Pepsi-Cola to develop and market new product lines, including a frozen coffee drink called Frappuccino, which resulted in a sales bonanza.

After a sales slump and a subsequent rebranding in 2011, Starbucks introduced new menu items to complement its beverages: breakfast sandwiches, oatmeal, and other healthy foods aimed for the most part at young customers who were willing to pay for premium coffee and food to accompany it. This led to greatly increased sales.

In some instances, Starbucks has introduced a line extension in celebration of a specific country. For example, El Salvador Pacamara, made from rare coffee beans imported from El Salvador, was originally marketed in 2004. When the first Starbucks store opened in El Salvador in 2010, the product was re-released in select stores in the United States, Canada, Japan, and the United Kingdom, along with the El Salvador outlet. To enter the El Salvador market, Starbucks collaborated with a business located in that country, Corporación de Franquicias Americanas, a strategy that Starbucks has often employed in its global expansion.

BRAND EQUITY

- Starbucks owns nearly 18,000 retail stores in 60 countries.
- The company had net sales of US$11.7 billion and gross profit of US$3.1 billion in 2011.
- The company's market value in March 2012 was estimated at US$42 billion.

Starbucks has nearly 18,000 stores in 60 countries, including more than 10,000 stores in the United States. *Fortune* magazine reports that the company ranked 227th among the 500 largest U.S. corporations in 2011, with revenues up 9.3 percent from 2010. For the 39 weeks ending July 1, 2012, revenues increased 15 percent. *Fortune* lists the market value of Starbucks at about US$42 billion as of March 29, 2012. The company's annual income statement for the period ending October 2, 2011, reports net sales of US$11.7 billion (up from US$9.8 billion in 2009); retail sales of US$10.6 billion; net income of US$1.2 billion; and gross profit of US$3.1 billion (up from US$2 billion in 2009).

BRAND AWARENESS

- Starbucks is one of the most recognized brands in the world.
- Operating such a large number of stores has increased the brand's awareness globally.
- The company uses social networking websites to communicate frequently with consumers, which gives the brand constant exposure.
- *Fortune* magazine included Starbucks in its list of "Most Admired Companies in America" annually from 2003 to 2012.
- *Zagat's Survey of National Chain Restaurants* rated Starbucks "No. 1 Most Popular Quick Refreshment Chain" from 2009 to 2011.

Starbucks continues to rank among the top businesses in the world, with recognition and awards including: best coffee, most popular quick refreshment chain, one of the 100 best companies to work for, one of the most admired companies in America, one of the world's 50 most innovative companies, and one of the world's most ethical companies. It is the only coffee brand on the list of 100 most-recognized brands in the world, due in part to the sheer number of its stores. As of September 2012, about 32 million people had visited the Starbucks page on the Facebook social networking site and indicated that they "liked" it. Nearly 3 million people were "following" Starbucks on Twitter.

BRAND OUTLOOK

- The company's long-term goal is to operate 30,000 stores around the world.
- China is expected to become the largest international market for Starbucks.
- Starbucks hopes to contribute one million volunteer hours annually to community service by the year 2015.
- The corporation says it will endeavor to conserve energy and water, recycle, and engage in "green" construction.

Starbucks continues to grow, with new stores opening every year and revenues increasing steadily. The corporation's ultimate goal is 30,000 stores worldwide. CEO Howard Schultz has said he believes that eventually China will be the company's largest market outside the United States. He plans to be operating more than 1,500 stores on the Chinese mainland by 2015. Starbucks entered the Chinese market in 1999, and by 2010 it had a 70 percent market share of coffee-shop sales there.

The company is also planning to expand operations in countries with developing economies, such as India and Brazil. To enter the market in India, Starbucks formed a strategic alliance in 2011 with Tata Coffee, the largest coffee plantation company in Asia. Although Starbucks may need to adjust its prices to compete in India, the new venture is expected to flourish. The company estimates that India could absorb an estimated 4,000 additional coffeehouses.

In addition, Starbucks has announced that by 2015 it hopes to have contributed one million volunteer hours each year to communities where Starbucks is located. The company has a goal of making all of its cups reusable or recyclable and plans to reduce its environmental footprint by conserving energy and water, recycling, and engaging in "green" construction. Starbucks continues its endeavor to use only coffee beans grown according to the highest standards of quality, using ethical sourcing practices. To improve working conditions and provide a superior product, the company plans to collaborate on social projects with farmers and businesses in countries where coffee is grown.

FURTHER READING

Brand Finance. "Global 500 2012." *Brandirectory*. Accessed September 3, 2012. http://brandirectory.com/league_tables/table/global-500-2012.

———. "Profile: Starbucks." *Brandirectory*. Accessed September 3, 2012. http://brandirectory.com/profile/starbucks.

"Brewing up a Storm." *Marketing*, April 15, 2009.

Larkin, Stephanie. "What Makes the Starbucks Coffee Experience Special?" FoodEditorials.com. Accessed September 3, 2012. http://www.streetdirectory.com/food_editorials/beverages/coffee/what_makes_the_starbucks_coffee_experience_special.html.

Morrison, Maureen. "Bang for Its Starbucks: Hits No. 3 Despite Limited Spend." *Advertising Age*, May 2, 2011.

———. "Special Report: Marketer A-List; Starbucks Forges 'Moments of Connection' by Offering Experience." *Advertising Age*, November 7, 2011.

Starbucks Corporation. "Starbucks Celebrates First Store Opening in El Salvador." Accessed September 3, 2012. http://news.starbucks.com/news/starbucks+celebrates+first+store+opening+in+el+salvador.htm.

"Starbucks Corporation." *International Directory of Company Histories*. Ed. Jay P. Pederson. Vol. 77. Detroit, MI: St. James Press, 2006.

"Starbucks Rates Number 1 in Study of Most Socially Engaged Companies by Research Firm PhaseOne." *News Bites US*, March 29, 2012.

Wong, Elaine. "Starbucks' Social Outreach Stirs the Pot." *Adweek*, August 12, 2009.

York, Emily Bryson. "CMOs Discuss Their Brands, Challenges and Agencies." *Advertising Age*, June 14, 2010.

SUBARU

AT A GLANCE

Brand Synopsis: Subaru has staked out an identity that appeals to outdoor-oriented, rugged individualists.

Parent Company: Fuji Heavy Industries Ltd.
Subaru Building
Tokyo
Japan
http://www.fhi.co.jp

Sector: Consumer Discretionary

Industry Group: Automobiles & Components

Performance: *Sales*—US$18.4 billion (2012).

Principal Competitors: Mazda Motor of America, Inc.; Nissan North America, Inc.; Toyota Motor North America, Inc.

BRAND ORIGINS

- Parent company, Fuji Heavy Industries Ltd., was created in Japan in 1953.
- Fuji CEO Kenji Kata chose Subaru, the Japanese name for the Pleiades constellation, to serve as the brand name for a new car.
- Subaru of America was established in 1968.
- Subaru introduced a four-wheel drive station wagon in 1975 that became the official car of the US Ski Team.
- Actor Paul Hogan put a face to the Subaru brand.

Subaru is a brand established by Japan's Fuji Heavy Industries Ltd., which was created in 1953 from five divisions of the Aircraft Research Laboratory, the primary manufacturer of aircraft for Japan during World War II. Following the war, one of these divisions manufactured the Rabbit motor scooter using spare aircraft parts, leading to the development of an automobile. Fuji's chief executive officer, Kenji Kata, provided a brand name, Subaru, the Japanese name for Pleiades, a constellation also known as the Seven Sisters. The first car to bear the Subaru name was the Subaru 1500.

Malcolm Bricklin, a distributor of the Rabbit, struck a deal in 1965 with Fuji to introduce Subaru-branded cars in the United States through the sale of Subaru franchises. In 1968 he and a partner formed Subaru of America in Philadelphia, Pennsylvania. It was in the United States that the Subaru brand developed its unique personality. Initially the company depended on clever advertising and did little to distinguish Subaru from the competition. In 1968 Subaru cars were sold with the tagline "Cheap and ugly does it." Two years later the company adopted another tagline that achieved little or no brand building: "The Subaru is *not* a Japanese Beetle."

In 1975 Subaru employed the tagline, "Inexpensive and built to stay that way." More importantly, the company unveiled a four-wheel drive station wagon and signed an agreement to make the Subaru wagon the official car of the US Ski Team. Although 20 years would pass before they were fully exploited, two key elements of the Subaru brand were established: four-wheel drive and an association with outdoor activities. The brand was also introduced in Canada in 1976 following the successful connection to the US Ski Team.

It wasn't until 1995 that the Subaru brand came into true focus. In that year actor Paul Hogan became the Subaru spokesman. Known for portraying Crocodile Dundee, the main character in a movie of the same name about Australia's outback, Hogan promoted the new Subaru Outback vehicle line. Hogan put a face to the Subaru brand and provided it with a spirit that had been lacking for three decades. Hogan served as spokesman until the new century. A number of other celebrities promoted Subaru in the years that followed, but by now the Subaru brand was well established in the marketplace.

BRAND ELEMENTS

- The Subaru logo depicts six stars against a blue background.
- The largest star in the Subaru logo represents the parent company, Fuji Heavy Industries.
- All-wheel drive is a standard feature on Subaru vehicles and an important brand element.
- Paul Hogan played a key role in building the Subaru brand during his time as spokesperson.
- Tagline "Confidence in Motion" replaced "The Beauty of All-Wheel-Drive."

In markets outside of Japan, any associations attributed to the Subaru name, the Japanese word for the Pleiades constellation, are not recognized. The brand logo, however, is more explicit. It depicts a large star flanked by five smaller stars, set against a blue background within an oval frame. The color evokes the same hot blue emitted by the stars of the Pleiades. Not only does the logo's design represent the star formation, it depicts the corporate structure of Subaru's parent company. In this interpretation, the large star represents Fuji Heavy Industries, and the five smaller stars are the five companies that were brought together to create Fuji. Although the Subaru logo carries a specific meaning from a corporate point of view, it also works in terms of the Subaru brand. Subaru is associated with rugged, outdoor activities. The logo embodying the night sky is an apt symbol for such an identity.

Also in keeping with Subaru's outdoor appeal is another key element of the Subaru brand: all-wheel drive, a standard feature for Subaru cars. For consumers who engage in outdoor activities, all-wheel drive offers a tangible benefit. The Subaru brand also appeals to consumers who identify with the outdoor lifestyle. Moreover, Subaru's all-wheel drive is perceived as a safety feature. As a result the brand receives high scores for safety in consumer surveys.

Subaru vehicles support the brand's identity in other ways. A "4WD" symbol is prominently displayed, touting the brand's all-wheel drive feature. Many of the vehicle model names also reinforce Subaru's rugged, outdoor image. They include Forester and Baja. The most effective model was the Subaru Outback. Australia's vast and remote hinterland, the outback, epitomizes much of Subaru's brand message. To promote the new model, Subaru hired Australian actor Paul Hogan, who played the outback character Crocodile Dundee in a comedic film that was an international hit. Hogan's personality became a key element of the Subaru, as happened with other celebrity spokespeople to follow, albeit with less impact. Another notable brand element is the taglines Subaru has employed over the years, although in many cases the slogan did little in the way of brand building. It wasn't until 1995, when Hogan became the spokesperson, that Subaru unveiled a tagline that served to craft a brand rather than just sell a product: "The Beauty of All-Wheel-Drive." A later tagline, "Confidence in Motion," was a more poetic distillation of Subaru's brand promise.

BRAND IDENTITY

- Early Subaru marketing focused on utility and price.
- The foundation of the Subaru brand was laid in the mid-1970s with the introduction of all-wheel drive transmissions and sponsorship of the US Ski Team.
- Paul Hogan, who starred as Crocodile Dundee, fleshed out the Subaru brand in the mid-1990s.
- Like Crocodile Dundee, Subaru was considered "rugged, adventurous, and outdoorsy."

Subaru's brand identity has evolved over time. For much of its history the company paid little attention to building a consistent image. Early on, Subaru's marketing was merely clever, promoting Subaru cars as ugly but cheap and playfully declaring they were not to be confused with a Japanese Beetle. Then Subaru introduced an all-wheel drive transmission in the mid-1970s and became the official car of the US Ski Team. The development of a strong association with outdoor activities created the conditions for the full flowering of the Subaru brand 20 years later with the Outback campaign, anchored by actor Paul Hogan.

In many respects Hogan came to embody Subaru's brand identity, which would change little after Subaru turned to other celebrity spokespeople and fresh marketing approaches. According to Sal Randazzo, writing in the *Journal of Advertising Research*, Hogan's Crocodile Dundee and the Outback name "gave Subaru a compelling story and its own unique brand identity and personality, which made sense for the brand and connected emotionally with the American consumer."

Crocodile Dundee had been released a decade before Hogan signed with Subaru. It was the most commercially successful Australian film ever produced, and its primary character was still fondly remembered by audiences around the world. It went beyond "Hogan's virtuous charm and humor," Randazzo argues. He adds that Crocodile Dundee "cuts across time and disparate cultures. Women love him. Men want to be like him. He is a uniquely Australian character, and yet he is somehow familiar to us all." It was through the marketing campaign featuring Hogan that Subaru finally created an emotional connection between consumers and its brand. According to Randazzo, Subaru's brand became identified with key attributes of Dundee and the Outback: the brand began to feel "rugged, adventurous, and outdoorsy."

Following the Hogan association, Subaru broadened its appeal to consumers who shared similar traits with outdoor activity enthusiasts but who were often better educated and more affluent. This group also tended to be environmentally aware and socially involved, and Subaru sponsored events and organizations that they supported. Thus Subaru's identity added such traits as social responsibility and environmental friendliness.

BRAND STRATEGY

- Expensive 1993 Super Bowl ad led Subaru to reexamine its marketing approach.
- Subaru differentiated itself from the competition by making all-wheel drive a standard feature.
- Because of enhanced traction, Subaru cars became associated with outdoor activities as well as with safety.
- Subaru sponsored outdoor sports associations to better align the brand with its customers.
- Subaru adjusted marketing to appeal to customers who shared similar traits to outdoor enthusiasts.

Before the early 1990s, Subaru did little in the way of brand building. Rather than building a brand, the company sold automobiles that carried the Subaru brand name. Taglines and marketing campaign strategies changed over time but with little regard to creating a consistent image of Subaru in the mind of consumers. This advertising-centric approach crested in 1993 when Subaru spent about US$2.3 million for 90 seconds of advertising time during the Super Bowl telecast. The company decided that its marketing dollars would be better spent on building the Subaru brand.

The first key strategic decision to be made in the effort to construct a compelling brand was to focus on Subaru's all-wheel drive transmission. By making it standard in all vehicles, Subaru differentiated itself from rival carmakers. The decision also influenced the way the company honed

its image and marketed its products, leading to the pursuit of a benefits-driven strategy. The company introduced the Outback model, which not only brought in Paul Hogan as the Subaru spokesperson to flesh out the brand, but also took Subaru off-road and opened up the growing market of utility vehicles while lending a spirit of fun and adventure to the brand. With improved performance features, the Outback was transformed into a rally racing car that promoted the Subaru brand to racing enthusiasts. In addition, all-wheel drive provided greater traction and control for everyday driving, creating an opening for the brand to associate itself with the concept of safety.

Because of the all-wheel drive focus of Subaru cars and also Hogan's involvement, it became easier to identify the personality of Subaru customers. In an effort to align itself with activities important to those buyers, Subaru pursued a sponsorship strategy. Outdoor-activity associations sponsored by Subaru included the American Canoe Association, the American Association of Snowboard Instructors, and the International Mountain Bicycling Association. In this way Subaru created a sense of good will with a large number of people who were in the market for an all-wheel drive vehicle in pursuit of their hobbies.

After the Hogan relationship ran its course at the turn of the new century, Subaru associated its brand with sports figures. In 2000 Subaru signed tennis star Martina Navratilova. Ensuing celebrity endorsers would be participants in more rugged, outdoor endeavors than tennis, however. They included Olympic skier Diann Roffe-Steinrotter, biker Tara Llanes, and snowboarder Victoria Jealouse.

In the early 2000s Subaru tweaked its brand image to broaden the appeal of Subaru vehicles to people who shared similar traits to outdoor activity enthusiasts. The switch in focus was reflected in the new advertising tagline "Think. Feel. Drive." In 2009 *Advertising Age* reported that Subaru had "linked the brand's core values to those of their active, pet-owning, environmentally aware, socially-involved customers." Just as Subaru supported outdoor sports associations, it also aligned the brand to causes supported by this broader group of customers. For example, Subaru became a sponsor of antianimal cruelty festivals hosted by the ASPCA. The typical Subaru customer was also better educated and enjoyed a higher income, allowing Subaru to be positioned as a more upscale brand. To help appeal to urban customers who were not involved in outdoor activities, Subaru introduced the Tribeca model, a midsize crossover sports utility vehicle, thus aligning itself to the trendy New York City neighborhood. The Tribeca was introduced in the United States in 2005, followed by Australasia a year later, and Europe in 2007.

Subaru was not without missteps in the pursuit of its brand strategy. In the 1990s it made an ill-advised decision to introduce a sports car, a category that was not in keeping with the Subaru image. That was not an isolated error. After winning a Motor Trend Car of the Year award, Subaru ran full-page advertisements touting the honor, but this had little impact on sales. Industry recognition was simply not part of Subaru's brand identity. Its customers were indifferent to what the automobile industry thought about Subaru cars. Even the Tribeca model did not prove as successful as Subaru had wished. It was a perfectly fine car, but the urban appeal of the Tribeca clashed with Subaru's core brand identity.

BRAND EQUITY

- Subaru receives one of the highest repurchase-loyalty ratings in the United States.
- Brand Finance Plc assigned Subaru a brand value of US$2.57 billion in 2012.
- Subaru was listed No. 462 on the Brand Finance Global 500 in 2012.
- Subaru ranked No. 29 on Interbrand's list of the most valuable brands in Japan in 2012.

Although Subaru is not considered a luxury brand, it appeals to a slice of the automobile-buying public that is more affluent than the typical customer. Subaru's brand equity is demonstrated in the higher prices Subaru cars can command. Subaru also enjoys one of the highest repurchase-loyalty ratings in the United States, another reflection of Subaru's high brand equity. Moreover, when the economic crisis of 2008 and 2009 struck and major US automakers were on the verge of going out of business, Subaru enjoyed strong sales despite difficult economic conditions.

According to Brand Finance Plc, a brand evaluation consultancy, the value of the Subaru brand was US$2.57 billion in 2012. As a result, Subaru ranked No. 462 on the Brand Finance Global 500 list of the world's most valuable brands. Using its own methodology, Interbrand, one of the world's leading brand consultancies, assigned a much lower brand value of US$552 million in 2012. According to Interbrand, Subaru was also Japan's 29th most valuable brand, one slot behind another Japanese carmaker, Mazda, but still worth only a fraction of other Japanese car brands. In contrast, Japan's No. 1 brand overall, Toyota, enjoyed a brand value of US$27.8 billion.

BRAND AWARENESS

- General brand awareness of Subaru is limited.
- Subaru builds awareness through ties to associations and events that cater to core customers.
- According to *Consumer Reports*, Subaru's reputation for safe cars is well known.

Subaru does not enjoy especially high brand awareness with the general public, as reflected by Subaru's ranking on the Brand Finance Global 500. On Interbrand's list of Japan's most valuable brands, Subaru trails Mazda, Mitsubishi, Lexus, Nissan, Honda, and Toyota. Subaru fares better with the customers it actively courts, however. The brand aligns itself with a variety of organizations to heighten awareness with potential customers. In addition to the American Association of Snowboard Instructors, the American Canoe Association, and ASPCA, sponsorships include such groups as the Geological Society of America, GRAND-AM Road Racing, International Mountain Bicycling Association, Leave No Trace Center for Outdoor Ethics, Mt. Washington Observatory, and the National Ski Patrol. Subaru is also the official car and sponsor of other outdoor events and venues.

In addition to its association with outdoor activities, Subaru is a well-known automobile brand in terms of safety. In 2008 *Consumer Reports* conducted a survey of brand perception that categorized the order of importance to new-car buyers. Those categories included safety, quality, value, environmentally friendly/green, design/style, and technology/innovation. Subaru ranked third in terms of safety, trailing only Volvo and Toyota, and ahead of Ford and Honda.

BRAND OUTLOOK

- Architect of Outback campaign returned as chief marketing officer in the new century.
- In the early 2000s Subaru placed increasing focus on emotional attachments to the brand.
- New global strategy unveiled in 2010 included new tagline: "Confidence in Motion."
- Future Subaru cars to incorporate more green technology.

Since the mid-1990s Subaru enjoyed success with a brand that identified itself with rugged, independent, outdoor enthusiasts as well as with individuals who identify with such values. It has not been an approach that has allowed Subaru to ascend to a new level. Annual sales of Subaru of North America, for example, increased from US$1.7 billion in 1990 to more than US$4 billion by the early 2000s. Sales flattened around this level as the decade unfolded, however. The chief marketing officer, Tim Mahoney, who had established Subaru's brand image in the mid-1990s and then left the company in 1997, returned in 2006. Under his leadership, Subaru has placed less emphasis on the all-wheel drive message and safety technology, opting instead to focus on the emotional attachment owners have developed with Subaru cars. Reflecting this shift in approach was a new tagline: "Love. It's what makes a Subaru a Subaru."

Subaru's brand messaging shifted again in 2010 with the introduction of the new Subaru Impreza concept car and a fresh tagline, "Confidence in Motion." The concept car's aerodynamic lines and its flair would influence future Subaru models. The company was also looking to incorporate green-car technology, but it was playing catch-up with other car makers in the development of a hybrid car. Subaru had crafted a well-defined image in the 1990s, but in later years the company dropped its reliance on celebrity pitchmen in favor of touting the safety record and resale value of Subaru cars. It was clearly a brand that was in a state of transition, a brand that since the beginning had been on a journey to define itself.

FURTHER READING

Brand Finance. "Global 500 2012." *Brandirectory*. Accessed July 3, 2012. http://brandirectory.com/league_tables/table/global-500-2012.

Cato, Jeremy. "Subaru: It's Time to Go Green." *Globe and Mail*, February 17, 2010.

Gelsi, Steve. "Revving up Brand Appeal." *Brandweek*, January 13, 1997.

Halliday, Jean. "Subaru of America." *Advertising Age*, November 16, 2009.

Kiley, David. "The Love Guru: How Tom Mahoney Got Subaru Back on Track." *Brandweek*, September 13, 2010.

McManus, John. "Driving Home: Subaru Was the Prodigal Car Brand." *Brandweek*, January 5, 1998.

Randazzo, Sal. "Subaru: The Emotional Myths behind the Brand's Growth." *Journal of Advertising Research*, March 2006.

Tellem, Tom. "Subaru Impreza Concept: A New Strategy." *New York Times*, November 18, 2010.

SUBWAY

AT A GLANCE

Brand Synopsis: With thousands of locations in the United States and abroad, Subway has established itself among U.S. consumers as a healthier and "fresher" alternative to other fast-food chains.

Parent Company: Doctor's Associates, Inc.
325 Bic Dr.
Milford, Connecticut 06460
United States
http://www.subway.com

Sector: Consumer Staples

Industry Group: Food, Beverage & Tobacco

Performance: Market share—Largest fast-food restaurant chain in the United States (2012).

Principal Competitors: McDonald's Corporation; Blimpie (subsidiary of Kahala Corp.); Schlotzsky's Franchise, LLC (subsidiary of FOCUS Brands Inc.); Quiznos Corporation (subsidiary of QIP Holder, LLC)

BRAND ORIGINS

- Pete's Super Submarines, Subway's predecessor, opened in Bridgeport, Connecticut, in 1965.
- Pete's Super Submarines became Subway in 1968.
- The first Subway franchise opened in 1974.
- Doctor's Associates, Inc. owns Subway, which is not a public company.

In 1965 Fred DeLuca and Peter Buck opened Pete's Super Submarines in Bridgeport, Connecticut. DeLuca started the restaurant to raise money for college, while Buck, a nuclear physicist and family friend of DeLuca's, provided the startup money. The restaurant offered made-to-order submarine sandwiches with different topping and condiment choices.

DeLuca and Buck went on to open more locations and changed the restaurant's name to Subway in 1968. Wanting to open even more locations, DeLuca convinced a friend to open a Subway franchise in 1974. Franchising would prove to be an important factor driving Subway's growth in the United States and abroad. Worldwide, there were 200 Subways in 1981, 11,000 in 1995, 20,000 in 2003, and 35,000 in 2011. Despite its large number of franchises, Subway is a privately held company owned by Doctor's Associates, Inc., a name chosen not because of the restaurant's reputation as a healthy dining option but because Buck held a doctorate in physics.

BRAND ELEMENTS

- The Subway logo features the company name in all-capital yellow and green letters, with the first and last letters forming arrows. Subway uses this logo frequently.
- The Subway logo and its yellow and green color scheme are repeated in Subway restaurants, in advertisements, on the company website, and on items like cups and bags.
- Subway restaurants feature a central counter for food ordering, preparation, and payment.

- The process of making the food to the customer's specifications in front of the customer is a defining element of the Subway brand.

Subway's logo consists of the word "SUBWAY" in capital letters, with arrows coming from the "S" and the "Y." The first three letters of the word are white and the last three are yellow, while all of the letters have a dark-green outline. Subway uses this logo in its advertisements, on signs located inside and outside its stores, on its corporate website, and on restaurant items like napkins, cups, and take-out bags.

The yellow and green colors of Subway's logo have also been used as the color scheme for its restaurants, advertisements, and website. Another design element of Subway restaurants is wallpaper that features old-fashioned images of subway maps, echoing the Subway name.

The central counter is a primary element at all Subway restaurants. Subway workers stand behind this counter, where they take and fill customer orders and accept payment for these orders. The counter is set up like a cafeteria line, with Subway employees proceeding down the line and asking customers what they would like to eat and how they would like it prepared. The central counter is conveniently located near other important parts of the restaurant, such as its work counters, racks of bread, microwaves, drink dispensers, and displays of accompanying food like cookies and salty snacks. In some smaller Subway restaurants, like those located in food courts in malls and colleges, the counter makes up nearly the entire restaurant.

The process of making the food to the customer's specifications and in full sight of the customer is also a defining element of the Subway brand. Food options at Subway restaurants include a wide variety of meats and seafood, vegetables, cheeses, low-calorie dressings, fresh breads, and other items. Customers at Subway restaurants can order submarine sandwiches on bread, on flatbread, on wrap bread, or without any bread.

BRAND IDENTITY

- Subway's longtime slogan is "Eat Fresh." The chain offers fresh food, such as vegetables, and freshly made food, such as bread baked onsite.
- Subway has offered low-fat menu items on its "7 under 6" menu. Those menu items later became known as "Fresh Fit Choices."
- In 2000 Jared Fogle became a Subway spokesperson after claiming that eating Subway sandwiches helped him lose 245 pounds.

"Eat fresh" has been a longtime advertising slogan for Subway. Its restaurants feature fresh food, such as vegetables and bread that employees bake onsite. This practice

of making food onsite, rather than using premade items (as other fast-food restaurants often do), is another reason why Subway's food is perceived as fresh.

This emphasis on freshness goes along with the brand's emphasis on nutrition. Subway offers a number of menu items for health-conscious consumers. These options include its "7 under 6" menu, which features seven sandwiches with six grams of fat or fewer. These items later became known as "Fresh Fit Choices," a name relating to the "Eat Fresh" slogan and Subway's emphasis on fitness and nutrition.

For most U.S. consumers, no discussion of Subway's focus on nutrition and fitness would be complete without mentioning Jared Fogle. Fogle was a student at Indiana University who claimed that eating Subway's low-calorie sandwiches and exercising helped him lose 245 pounds. Subway hired Fogle as a spokesperson in 2000, and he has been a face of the brand ever since, appearing in Subway advertisements and making personal appearances that promote healthy lifestyles. In 2004 Fogle founded the Jared Foundation, an organization committed to ending childhood obesity. The foundation's board of trustees includes several people affiliated with Subway, including Michael Strahan, a well-known media personality who also once served as a Subway spokesperson. Thus, the Jared Foundation is another way that Subway has associated the brand with health-conscious goals.

BRAND STRATEGY

- US and international athletes have appeared in Subway promotional campaigns, reflecting the brand's emphasis on health and fitness.
- The US$5 footlong sandwich promotion and combination deals target Subway customers looking for a bargain.
- Like its fast-food competitors, Subway offers fast service and meals for children.
- Different Subway menus reflect the religious and dietary practices of Subway's multicultural customers around the world.
- Eager to attract more franchise locations, Subway provides help with financing and training to franchise owners in the United States and abroad.

Other spokespeople have joined Jared Fogle to tout the health-related benefits of eating at Subway. A number of these spokespeople have been athletes, including former National Football League player Michael Strahan. The brand has recruited athletes to become part of what it calls "Subway Famous Fans," including speed skater Apolo Anton Ohno, gymnast Nastia Liukin, swimmer Michael Phelps, and basketball player Blake Griffin. Because many of its "Subway Famous Fans" are Olympic athletes, Subway featured these athletes in commercials and other promotions prior to and during the 2012 Summer Olympics.

Subway has made connections with international athletes as well. Its Australian advertising and company website have featured Australian Olympic athletes, such as swimmer James Magnussen, field hockey player Casey Eastham, and snowboarder Torah Bright. Because Subway markets itself as a brand committed to physical fitness and healthy choices, using athletes as spokespeople is a key element of its brand strategy.

Other Subway promotions have focused on people watching their budgets as well as their waistlines. Customers who visit Subway can purchase combination meals (a meal that typically consists of a sandwich, chips, and a drink, priced lower than the price of purchasing those items individually). In addition to that pricing strategy, in 2008 Subway began selling specific "footlong" sandwiches (its trademark sandwiches that are 12 inches long) for US$5. Each month it rotates one additional sandwich onto its US$5 footlong menu for the duration of the month, and during some months Subway sells an even larger variety of footlong sandwiches. These promotions, and other facets of Subway restaurants, appear in the company's advertising, which has taken the form of commercials, print advertisements, and other promotions.

Although Subway touts a uniquely "fresh" approach to fast food, the restaurant shares some similarities with its fast-food competitors, such as fast service and the offering of combination meals. Subway's meals for children, which it calls "Fresh Fit for Kids," are another similarity. These meals have smaller portion sizes and include apple slices or yogurt, a drink, and often a toy. Subway also created a website specifically for children, which features children's activities and information about Subway products.

Just as McDonald's offers meatless restaurants in India for its vegetarian customers and lamb burgers in Australia, Subway has made concessions to help its restaurants compete in the multicultural global market. For example, Subway restaurants in the United Kingdom serve the "Sag Paneer" sandwich, featuring a patty made of spinach, potatoes, cheese, and other ingredients. Sag paneer (also spelled "saag paneer") is a common dish in India, and the United Kingdom is home to many Indian immigrants. Some Subway restaurants in the Middle East, Africa, and the United Kingdom offer halal menu items that conform to Islamic dietary requirements. Subway also operates kosher Subway restaurants to conform to Jewish dietary standards.

Like its fast-food competitors, Subway has embraced franchising. Subway's franchising has spread the brand name to thousands of locations in the United States and abroad. Subway addresses potential franchise buyers at trade shows, seminars, and online. If a person decides to buy a franchise, Subway offers help with financing, guidelines for the franchise process, and training. Subway trains franchise owners at a collection of centers that is sometimes referred to as "Subway University." There are 12 such training centers around the world, offering instruction in a number of languages and reflecting the restaurant's international reach.

BRAND EQUITY

- Some U.S. military bases in other countries feature Subway restaurants.
- Catering services and nontraditional locations for Subway restaurants, such as grocery stores and hospitals, have broadened the restaurant's reach.
- Subway has more locations than McDonald's does, but McDonald's generates more revenue.
- Subway ranks among the 500 largest global brands.
- Subway and McDonald's are market share leaders in U.S. fast-food breakfast sales and the Australian takeaway food market.

Subway's embrace of franchising has made the restaurant almost a ubiquitous presence in the United States. The restaurant tries to reach Americans far from home by opening locations at military bases around the world.

Subway is the largest fast-food chain in the United States, with more total units than its closest competitor, McDonald's. As of September 2012, Subway had more than 25,000 restaurants in the United States and Canada and 37,581 restaurants worldwide. It operates a large number of restaurants in nontraditional sites, including grocery and convenience stores, truck stops, schools, hospitals, amusement parks, zoos, casinos, riverboats, automobile dealers, construction sites, and even churches. Subway also circulates its products outside its restaurants by offering catering services.

This large presence has led to Subway's emergence as a dominant brand. Brand Finance's Global 500 2012, a ranking of the largest international brands, listed Subway as the 193rd largest brand, with a brand value of around US$5.1 billion. On the same list McDonald's was ranked the 18th biggest brand, with a brand value of around US$22.2 billion. McDonald's has fewer units than Subway does but generates more revenue. McDonald's also dominates sales in other countries where both fast-food chains operate. In 2010 McDonald's held a 19.5 percent share of the takeaway food market in Australia, while Subway captured 2 percent of the same market.

Subway is one of the top-five leaders in U.S. fast-food chains that offer breakfast. In 2010 Subway placed fourth in US market share for fast-food breakfasts, with McDonald's coming in first, Starbucks second, and Dunkin' Donuts third.

BRAND AWARENESS

- Subway's promotional efforts include selling merchandise online, sponsoring NASCAR vehicles and races, and creating floats for parades.
- By sponsoring heart health and childhood obesity initiatives, Subway reinforces its commitment to healthy living.
- Subway created a mutually beneficial relationship with the television show *Chuck* and eventually helped prevent the show's cancellation.
- Surveys have shown that Americans have positive connotations with Subway.

Studies have shown that U.S. consumers have positive connotations with the Subway brand. Results from YouGov's BrandIndex, which studies how people view brands by asking them what they've recently heard about those brands, showed that Subway generated more buzz than any other U.S. brand in 2010, 2011, and 2012. Subway also performed well in the 2012 Harris Poll EquiTrend survey, a poll that measures "brand health," including public familiarity with a brand, positive connotations with a brand, and willingness to do business with or donate to a brand. In this poll, Americans rated Subway the "quick service restaurant brand of the year."

Subway's visibility extends to appearances in a number of movies and television programs. Product placement helped create a mutually beneficial relationship with the U.S. television series *Chuck*. When the show was close to cancellation in 2009, a *Chuck* fan created a campaign called "Finale & Footlong," which urged other *Chuck* fans to buy footlong sandwiches at Subway to demonstrate the fans' economic power and their awareness that the brand sponsored the program. This campaign garnered publicity for the show and for Subway, and *Chuck* was renewed until 2012 and continued to feature Subway product placements and advertisements.

BRAND OUTLOOK

- Subway has begun promoting its environmental efforts, including its recycling initiatives, its use of local distributors, and the establishment of its environmentally efficient Subway ECO-Restaurants.
- The "Eat Fresh. Live Green" slogan of Subway's environmental efforts echoes its "Eat Fresh" slogan.
- International Subway restaurants may outnumber U.S. locations by 2020.
- With its huge population, China is one of the global markets that Subway hopes to capture.

By continuing to embrace health and wellness, Subway is poised to continue its success. In addition to continuing to promote its original concept of fresh fast food, the company is promoting environmental awareness. The brand has operated a number of environmental efforts under the banner "Eat Fresh. Live Green," a slogan that echoes the brand's longtime slogan of "Eat Fresh." In 2007 Subway began establishing "ECO-Restaurants," which include existing Subway restaurants that make more efficient use of energy and water and take measures to reduce waste, and new and remodeled Subway restaurants that feature more environmentally friendly lighting, faucets, and building materials. Subway also uses recycled packaging and makes use of local distribution centers and other local facilities.

While continuing to address health and environmental issues, the brand remains committed to expansion. Although Subway restaurants are common in the United States, the company wants to open even more restaurants in other countries. One Subway executive expects there to be more international Subway locations than U.S. locations by 2020. Like many brands, Subway wants to capture the huge Chinese market, hoping to open 500 stores in China by 2015. These plans reflect Subway's interest in global growth. As Subway's website explains, "Our goal is to be ranked the number one Quick Service Restaurant (QSR) worldwide while maintaining the great-tasting freshness of our products that is our trademark."

FURTHER READING

"Army & Air Force Exchange Service Opens First Subway Shop in Iraq." *Dallas Business Journal*, September 15, 2004.

Brand Finance. "Global 500 2012." *Brandirectory*. Accessed September 14, 2012. http://brandirectory.com/league_tables/table/global-500-2012.

Buss, Dale. "Subway Holds Top Spot in YouGov US Buzz Rankings as Olive Garden Joins Party." Brandchannel.com, July 13, 2012. Accessed September 13, 2012. http://www.brandchannel.com/home/post/2012/07/13/YouGov-QSR-Rankings-Subway-071312.aspx.

"Doctor's Associates." *International Directory of Company Histories*. Ed. Jay P. Pederson and Miranda H. Ferrara. Vol. 67. Detroit, MI: St. James Press, 2005.

Fienberg, Daniel. "NBC Renews 'Chuck,' Embraces Subway Money." HitFix, May 19, 2009. Accessed September 14, 2012. http://www.hitfix.com/articles/nbc-renews-chuck-embraces-subway-money.

Fishkoff, Sue. "Eat Fresh, Eat Kosher: Subway the Largest U.S. Kosher Restaurant Chain." *JTA*, August 5, 2009. Accessed September 14, 2012. http://www.jta.org/news/article/2009/08/05/1007057/the-largest-us-kosher-restaurant-chain-is-subway.

Jargon, Julie. "Subway Runs Past McDonald's Chain." *Wall Street Journal*, March 8, 2011.

Jessop, Alicia. "Subway's Partnership with Michael Phelps Brings the Brand Large-Scale Exposure." *Forbes*, July 17, 2012.

Jimenez, Katherine. "Subway Rolls the Rest to Triumph in Fast-Food Store Wars." *Australian*, March 9, 2011.

Lefton, Terry. "Ohno, Liukin, Griffin Will Carry Torch for Subway Campaign." *SportsBusiness Daily*, July 23, 2012.

Accessed September 13, 2012. http://www.sportsbusiness-daily.com/SB-Blogs/Olympics/London-Olympics/2012/07/LeftonSubway.aspx.

Morrison, Maureen. "Subway, BK Battle It out for Breakfast." *Advertising Age*, February 10, 2011.

"Subway Chain Leads the Pack among Restaurant Chains." Subway. Accessed September 13, 2012. http://www.subway.com/subwayroot/about_us/pressreleases.aspx

"Subway Timeline." Subway. Accessed September 13, 2012. http://www.subway.com/subwayroot/about_us/TimeLine.aspx.

"2012—Top US Buzz Rankings." YouGov's BrandIndex. Accessed September 14, 2012. http://www.brandindex.com/ranking/us/2012-mid/top-buzz-rankings.

"What America Loves to Eat: Subway Continues to Eat Competitors' Lunch in 2012 Harris Poll EquiTrend Study." Harris Interactive. May 10, 2012. Accessed September 14, 2012. http://www.harrisinteractive.com/NewsRoom/PressReleases/tabid/446/mid/1506/articleId/1020/ctl/ReadCustom%20Default/Default.aspx.

York, Emily Bryson. "Subway Caught up in Fan Effort to Save NBC Series 'Chuck.'" *Advertising Age*, April 27, 2009.

SUMITOMO CORPORATION

———————— ■ ————————

BRAND ORIGINS

- The Sumitomo Corporation originated in a small shop in Kyoto started by Masatomo Sumitomo in 1630.
- Thanks to the hard work and initiative of Tomomochi Sumitomo, by the early 18th century the family business grew to produce 20 percent of all the copper mined in Japan.
- After the Japanese surrender at the end of World War II, the Sumitomo company was broken up into smaller independent companies due to American antimonopoly laws.

- The Sumitomo company logo is the ancient symbol for a well frame, called an *igeta*, and has been the company logo since 1590.
- The Sumitomo Corporation has offices in 43 Japanese cities and 93 more cities worldwide.

Born in 1585, Masatomo Sumitomo was the founder and spiritual pillar of a small shop which would, over a period of four centuries, develop into the global conglomerate known as the Sumitomo Corporation. At age 45 Masatomo opened a small shop in Kyoto, Japan, where he sold books and medicines. He named the shop Fujiya. Toward the later years of his life, Masatomo wrote the *Monjuin Shiigaki* ("Aphorisms of Monjuin"). This was a set of instructions to his family and followers on how to honorably conduct business and how to live a good life. These instructions are in the form of five articles, and after nearly four hundred years they are still the bases of the Sumitomo Corporate Charter.

Riemon Soga was a brother-in-law to Masatomo Sumitomo. As a young man, Riemon worked as an apprentice at a copper refinery. In 1590, at the age of 18, he opened his own coppersmithing business, also in Kyoto, not far from Masatomo's shop. Riemon named his new business Izumiya, the "fountainhead shop." For his shop logo he decided to use the *igeta*, which is an ancient character for "well frame." At that time, the symbol was used to represent fresh, sparkling water coming from a spring. Like Masatomo's articles, this symbol would endure to modern times as the logo for the Sumitomo global empire.

In those days, although Japanese refineries processed many tons of copper, they did not have the technology to remove tiny bits of gold and silver which were naturally found in the copper. Foreign traders would purchase great amounts of this copper, take them back to their home cities and separate out the precious metals at a tremendous profit. Riemon eventually learned the secrets to the extraction process called *Nanban-buki* ("Western Refining"). This knowledge made Riemon a very wealthy man. His eldest son Tomomochi Sumitomo became a family member of the House of Sumitomo by marrying one of Masatomo's daughters. When Riemon Soga died in 1636, Tomomochi expanded his father's business to Osaka, where he revealed the Nanban-buki technology to other coppersmiths in the area. Because of this unselfish act, the Sumitomo/Izumiya business became the "head family of Nanban-buki" and Osaka became the leader in copper refining in all of Japan. Tomomochi became a man of great wealth and power. He invested well and diversified in a variety of businesses, including thread, textiles, sugar, and medicines. He also got involved in the copper mining business, opening mines in Ohu, Bicchu Yoshioka, and Besshi in 1691. By the early 18th century the Besshi mines were producing 20 percent of all copper mined in Japan. The Besshi mines were enormously productive, continuing to operate for 283 years.

Over the next 250 years the Sumitomo family would get into and out of a variety of businesses, but the one anchor around which all else revolved was copper production. In 1867 the family business was renamed Sumitomo Honten and was the central headquarters for all other Sumitomo subsidiaries. Finally, in the middle of the 20th century came the Second World War. The Sumitomo refineries, like all other large factories in Japan, became frequent targets for American bombing. By the time Japan surrendered in mid-1945, the country's industrial capabilities had been almost completely wiped out. Japan was placed under the authority of the Allied forces and was subject to a large number of new commercial laws, including one dissolving any form of monopoly. The new law directly affected Sumitomo Honten, which was fragmented into seven fully independent, smaller companies. None of these companies was permitted to use the igeta logo.

In the decade following the end of World War II, the restrictive American laws were gradually relaxed and the fragmented Sumitomo companies began to develop affiliations through limited stock swaps. By June 1, 1952, those affiliates had once again come together as Sumitomo Shoji Kaisha Ltd., the Sumitomo Commercial Affairs Company. Sumitomo Shoji became the trading house for its affiliates at a time when Japan was experiencing incredible economic growth. Shoji quickly expanded and diversified the company's holdings, which would include iron, steel, and other metals, chemicals, textiles, electrical and industrial equipment, agricultural products, petroleum products, and real estate. In 1955 the company saw revenues of US$254 million. Only 10 years later

the revenues had skyrocketed to US$2.3 billion, then to US$26 billion by 1975, and US$74 billion by 1985. In April 2001 there was a major reorganization, separating the main headquarters into 6 corporate groups, 9 business units, and 28 business divisions. Two months later the head office was moved to Chuo-ku, Tokyo, its present location. Today Sumitomo has offices in 43 Japanese cities and 93 more cities worldwide.

BRAND ELEMENTS

- The founder of the Sumitomo Corporation was Masatomo Sumitomo, born in 1585 near Kyoto, Japan.
- The Sumitomo logo, first used by the family in 1590, is called the "igeta" and is based on an ancient Japanese character for a well frame.
- The Sumitomo business goes back to 1590 when Masatomo Sumitomo's brother-in-law, Riemon Soga, opened his first business.

The Sumitomo company name originates with its founder Masatomo Sumitomo, who was born near Kyoto, Japan in 1585. He opened his first business at the age of 45, calling it Fujiya. Though the company name is credited to Masatomo, the 400-year life span of the family business is due to the efforts of Masatomo's brother-in-law, Riemon Soga, who opened a copper refinery and copper works shop in 1590, and Riemon's eldest son Tomomochi Sumitomo, who would expand the modest coppersmithing shop into a national industry.

The Sumitomo logo has an even longer history than the company name. When Riemon Soga opened his copper works in 1590 at the age of 18, he decided to name his business Izumiya, which translates to "fountainhead shop." He wanted an appropriate symbol to go along with the name and so he chose the *igeta*. This is an ancient Japanese symbol for a well frame. The well frame symbolizes fresh, clear water rushing from a fountainhead and then becoming a great river that in turn flows out into the vast ocean. The igeta would become the perfect metaphor for Sumitomo's tiny business, which would grow and flourish over the next four centuries.

BRAND IDENTITY

- When Masatomo Sumitomo, the founder of the Sumitomo Corporation, retired, he moved into a hermitage and lived the life of a Buddhist monk.
- The Sumitomo Corporation bases its operational principles on a small collection of writings by its founder, Masatomo Sumitomo, titled *Monjuin Shiigaki*.
- In 1891 the Sumitomo Corporation selected two articles written by its founder, Masatomo Sumitomo, to represent the foundation of the corporation's operational principles.

The brand identity of the Sumitomo Corporation is based on the writings of its founder, Masatomo Sumitomo. When Masamoto retired from his business, he moved into a hermitage and lived the life of a Buddhist monk. Based on his reflections over a period of several years, he wrote a series of articles that he gathered under the title *Monjuin Shiigaki*, which translates as "Aphorisms of Monjuin." These articles were a set of guidelines written for his family and followers on how to conduct business and how to live a good life. This collection of articles was handed down from generation to generation in the Sumitomo family. Finally, in 1891 two of the articles were officially selected to represent the foundation of the corporation's operational principles. These two principles were stated as follows: "Sumitomo shall achieve strength and prosperity by placing prime importance on integrity and sound management in the conduct of its business; Sumitomo shall manage its activities with foresight and flexibility in order to cope effectively with the changing times. Under no circumstances, however, shall it pursue easy gains or act imprudently."

BRAND STRATEGY

- Since first opening in 1691, the Besshi Copper Mines have been the foundation business for the Sumitomo company for nearly 300 years.
- During its early years, the Sumitomo Corporation believed that business planning should be done for the long term, meaning that results might take several years to appear.
- In the 21st century the Sumitomo Corporation utilizes a wide variety of brand strategies to promote its products and services, including online advertising, seminars, interviews, and multimedia.

Since they first became part of the Sumitomo family business in 1691, the Besshi Copper Mining operations have been the backbone of the company for almost 300 years. During those years Sumitomo developed the belief that all business planning should be done on a long-term basis. The metaphor that was used to visualize this concept was the planting of a seed. If the seed does not bear fruit during the first generation, wait and see what happens in the second and even the third generation.

Today, things have changed considerably. Sumitomo is involved in dozens of categories of business and hundreds, if not thousands, of projects. Global commerce does not have time to wait for two or three generations to see results. Productivity is measured down to the second. In adapting to this fast and ever-changing business environment, Sumitomo has developed aggressive branding strategies to attract attention to new products and services or reposition them from specialty niches to mainstream solutions.

These strategies take the form of multiple operations working reciprocally to get a clear and detailed message across to the potential end-user. These strategies include one or more of the following: an aggressive public relations campaign, an interactive multimedia presentation, print and online advertising, regional seminars and trade shows, and product demonstrations. By applying these strategies to a product known as Air-Blown Fiber Optic Cabling, the results included a dozen feature articles in targeted trade magazines, numerous press release publications, and published interviews about the product.

BRAND EQUITY

- At the end of 2011, Sumitomo had total revenues of US$37.4 billion, with US$2.4 billion in profits.
- Sumitomo Corporation has 18 core companies with 800 subsidiaries and affiliates and over 77,000 employees.
- As of January 2013 Sumitomo Corporation had a market capitalization of US$51.83 billion.

According to its 2012 Annual Report, the Sumitomo Corporation, as of December 31, 2011, generated revenues of US$37.4 billion with US$2.4 billion in profits. The Sumitomo Group is comprised of 18 core companies in industries including finance, electronics and electrical products, construction, chemicals, metals, warehousing, transportation, lumber, and housing. These 18 core companies can be further subdivided into more than 800 subsidiaries and affiliates, with a total of approximately 77,000 employees. The market capitalization for the end of 2011 was estimated at US$15.58 billion, but the company has shown strong positive metrics in the past year. The most recent calculations, as of January 13, 2013, estimate a market cap of US$51.83 billion, according to Bloomberg.com. According to the Forbes Global 2000 rankings, Sumitomo Corporation is listed at number 199 overall among the world's largest companies. It ranks 240th in sales, 253rd in profits, and 273rd in total assets.

BRAND AWARENESS

- Sumitomo tires, first marketed in 1985, are among the few Sumitomo products that carry the brand name of the parent company.
- Sumitomo Rubber Industries, Ltd., is one of the largest tire manufacturers in the world.
- When Sumitomo Rubber Industries purchased TBC Corporation in 2005 and Midas in 2012, they established 2,700 retail stores to market their Sumitomo tires to American consumers.

Despite being a company with a 400-year history and having achieved the status of one of the world's largest companies, Sumitomo Corporation is virtually unknown to the general public outside of Japan. This is because Sumitomo, as a business entity, does not deal directly in any consumer products or services. Sumitomo is specifically known as a "general trading company." This is a form of business unique to Japan in which the purpose of the company is to trade a wide variety of products and commodities. General trading companies also often take on the role of investment banks and private equity firms.

In recent years though, Sumitomo has been revealing their brand name to the consuming public in various ways. Sumitomo tires are a product of Sumitomo Rubber Industries, Ltd., one of the largest tire manufacturers in the world. Though these tires are sold and recognized for their quality and durability in 20 countries around the world, they are not a well-known brand in the United States. In 2005 Sumitomo Rubber Industries purchased TBC Corporation, the largest independent retail-tire chain in the United States. TBC operates 1,200 retail shops in the United States and offers an important branding opportunity for the Sumitomo tires. In April 2012 Sumitomo Rubber Industries went one step further and purchased Midas, the largest and most recognized auto repair service-provider in the entire United States. The Midas brand, with its slogan, "Trust the Midas touch," has a consumer recognition rate of over 90 percent. Midas owns 1,500 stores across the United States, bringing the total, with TBC, to 2,700 retail stores. By capitalizing on TBC's expertise in tires with Midas's general repair and maintenance services, the combination should generate a great deal of revenue for their parent company and significant exposure for the Sumitomo tire brand.

BRAND OUTLOOK

- In the next few years Sumitomo hopes to expand its production of oil drilling pipes and equipment in the North American market, where it currently holds a 20 percent share.
- Sumitomo Financial Services has supplied capital for building power plants that supply 13 percent of the energy to the Java-Bali power grid in Indonesia.
- Sumitomo Corporation is looking to expand its operations in the Japanese consumer market, particularly in retail operations.

In later years, Sumitomo Corporation has made a variety of plans to drive earnings expansion in the global market. This will be done through investing in current and future projects, promoting business model innovation, and deepening partnership strategies. Specific examples include investment in what Sumitomo calls the "Tubular Product Value Chain." It is important because shale gas and oil extraction has expanded dramatically in North America. To meet the rising demands for extended length and horizontal drilling, Sumitomo Corporation, along with recently acquired subsidiary Vallourec S.A., a major French pipe producer, will start operations to produce 350,000 tons of pipes for 2013. Sumitomo currently holds a 20 percent market share in North American oil pipe manufacturing and looks to expand that in the near future.

Sumitomo has also been involved in the expansion of coal-fired thermal power plants in Indonesia. Their financial services division has financed the construction of power plants which now account for 13 percent of the energy supplied to the Java-Bali power grid in Indonesia. Finally, Sumitomo is looking into expanding a variety of retail businesses in the Japanese consumer market. This would include retail operations in electronics stores, supermarkets, drug stores, luxury brands, and the cable TV market. The goal is to expand and strengthen the company's retail businesses in the Japanese markets, while at the same time expanding into new overseas markets with proven business models.

FURTHER READING

Gaens, Bart. "Family, Enterprise, and Corporation: The Organization of Izumiya-Sumitomo in the Tokugawa Period." *Japan Review*, no. 12 (2000).

"Global 2000 Leading Companies – Sumitomo Corporation." *Forbes*. Accessed January 22, 2013. http://www.forbes.com/companies/sumitomo-corp/

"Sumitomo." *History of World Trade since 1450*. Ed. John J. McCusker. Vol. 2. Detroit, MI: Macmillan, 2006.

Sumitomo Corporation. "History of Sumitomo Corp." Accessed January 22, 2013. http://www.sumitomocorp.co.jp/english/company/history/sc_history.html

———. *2012 Annual Report*. Accessed January 22, 2013. http://www.sumitomocorp.co.jp/ir/doc/2012f/ar2012.pdf

"Sumitomo Corporation." *International Directory of Company Histories*. Ed. Tina Grant. Vol. 102. Detroit, MI: St. James Press, 2009.

SUNING

—■—

AT A GLANCE

Brand Synopsis: Heavily identified with electronics and appliance retailing, China's Suning brand is also establishing a presence in online retailing and other fields.

Parent Company: Suning Group
68 Huaihai Road
Nanjing, 210005
China
http://www.suning.com/

Sector: Consumer Discretionary

Industry Group: Consumer Durables & Apparel

Performance: *Net profit*—CNY4.82 billion (US$766 million) (2011).

Principal Competitors: Bailian Group; China 3C Group; Dashang Group Co., Ltd.; Gome Electrical Appliances Holding Ltd.; Shenzhen Sed Electronics Corp.; Telling Telecom Holding Company Ltd.

BRAND ORIGINS

- Beginning in 1990 brothers Zhang Jindong and Zhang Guiping sold air conditioners at their Suning Electrical Appliance store in Nanjing, China.
- Suning has opened discount stores and luxury stores and sells goods online, also operating logistics facilities and undertaking strategic partnerships with other companies like Chinese appliance manufacturer Haier.

- In 2009 Suning bought Citicall Retail Management Ltd., a large chain of electronic stores in Hong Kong. It acquired Japan's Laox chain of stores in 2011 and bought the online retail site Redbaby in 2012.
- Some Chinese Suning branches began operating trial versions of Pizza Hut and KFC restaurants within their stores in 2012.

The early success of giant home appliance and electronics retailer Suning can largely be traced to one of its early products, air conditioners. Beginning in 1990 brothers Zhang Jindong and Zhang Guiping sold air conditioners at their Suning Electrical Appliance store in Nanjing, China. Their timing was auspicious, as the Chinese economy was in transition. State-owned enterprises, businesses owned and operated by the Chinese government, were on the decline, and private businesses like Suning Electrical Appliance were on the rise. Meanwhile, the Chinese middle class and its spending power were growing. By 1999 the Zhang brothers sold a full line of appliances in addition to air conditioners and began opening other stores.

Other retail changes for the company have included the opening of discount stores and luxury stores and Suning's very successful foray into online commerce. It also opened modern logistics facilities to manage its operations more efficiently. Other conditions also helped the company. Suning undertook strategic partnerships with other companies, including major Chinese appliance manufacturer Haier, and took advantage of more favorable trading conditions in China. These efforts helped make Suning a leading retailer, despite increasing competition among other Chinese retailers. In fact, competition was so fierce that

Suning, Hong Kong–based appliance retailer Gome, and Chinese online retailer Jingdong Mall engaged in a price war in 2012, with each trying to best the other's prices.

Suning has expanded in the early 2000s. In late 2009 Suning bought Citicall Retail Management Ltd., one of the largest chains of electronic stores in Hong Kong. It became "China's largest consumer electronics retailer," according to Li Woke in a 2012 piece for *China Daily* in 2012. It acquired more retailers in other regions when it bought Japan's Laox chain of stores in 2011. It also bought the online retail site Redbaby in 2012, which sells items for babies and mothers. These acquisitions have helped Suning diversify its product lines.

Other company developments include new affiliations in its stores. In 2012 some Chinese Suning branches began operating trial versions of Pizza Hut and KFC restaurants within their stores. Pizza Hut and KFC's owner, American company Yum! Brands, announced its plans to open more Yum! restaurants in other Suning stores.

These developments join other Suning businesses. Although retail is a large part of Suning's business, it is not Suning's only business. It owns a chain of luxury hotels and is involved in retail estate and financial operations.

BRAND ELEMENTS

- Suning uses the word Suning in blue letters to identify itself visually, often accompanied by the colors orange or yellow.
- The bright colors of Suning store signs and the Suning.com logo relate to the bright colors of Suning stores, web pages, and advertising, portraying a company that is young, fresh, hip, and happy.
- The company consistently uses bright colors to identify itself visually.

Suning uses the word Suning in blue letters to identify itself visually. Often, the colors orange or yellow accompany these blue letters: Suning storefronts use Suning in blue letters on an orange or yellow background, while Suning.com features Suning in blue and .com in orange (the dot on the Suning i is also in orange).

The bright colors of Suning store signs and the Suning.com logo relate to the bright colors of Suning stores, web pages, and advertising. This brightness, along with the web page's prominent photographs and drawings of children and young people, portrays a company that is young, fresh, hip, and happy.

Continuing this theme, the company employs young women dressed in blue as the Suning girls. They appear at company events. Even the Suning headquarters building in Nanjing sports a Suning sign in large blue letters. Blue and yellow flags reading Suning can be found outside of this headquarters building as well. The company consistently uses bright colors to identify itself visually.

BRAND IDENTITY

- Store and website displays define the Suning brand's interest in retail and reasonable prices.
- The Suning Elite brand and its stores portray themselves as elite and separate from others.
- Suning Elite stores still use the Suning name and blue logo, indicating Suning's recognition of its brand value and position as a brand that offers choice.

Suning's traditional physical and online stores illustrate the brand's interest in retail and low prices. Long lines of products appear in Suning stores and long lines of product photographs appear on its websites. Large colorful price signs appear inside and outside of Suning stores, while Suning websites feature drawings of colorful price tags next to the products being sold. These visual cues inform people what Suning is and what it does, that Suning is a brand in the retail field. Furthermore, Suning's price signs and price tags also inform people of Suning's ability to offer low prices.

Suning Elite, the brand's luxury retailer, communicates different things. Instead of using the bright yellow and other bright colors of traditional Suning stores and websites, Suning Elite stores use a mostly neutral décor and the blue Suning logo accompanied by a script white "elite." The Suning Elite logo is visually related to other Suning retailers, but separated. The stores also feature small room-like areas to demonstrate electronic devices. This segregation physically and psychologically sets people apart. It defines them as elite and separate from other consumers, much like how Suning Elite has separated itself from the traditional Suning retailers. Suning Elite, therefore, uses color and physical space to portray itself as a more elite brand and its customers as more elite customers.

It is significant that it continues to use the Suning name and a blue Suning logo in the Suning Elite stores. In creating these elite stores, Suning could have stopped using the Suning name entirely. Instead, Suning's continued use of its name for these more luxurious stores indicates that the brand knows its own value. With its traditional stores and its Suning Elite ventures, Suning recognizes the power of its name to keep established customers and attract new ones. By offering different stores, Suning portrays itself as a brand that gives customers choices.

BRAND STRATEGY

- Product images, bright colors, and images of young people appear on Suning web pages and on commercials for Hong Kong's Suning Citicall, implying that Suning Citicall is a cool store for young people and for people of all ages who want to live fun lifestyles.
- Suning Citicall commercials have been in Cantonese and English, reflecting the multiculturalism of

Suning Citicall's Hong Kong home and Suning's operations in that area, mainland China, and Japan.

- Suning has converted some of its stores into Suning Expo Super Stores, stores which offer everyday items and expand Suning's product base beyond its usual home appliance and electronics offerings.

The company's use of multiple product images, bright colors, and images of young people is not limited to its web pages. Its commercials have featured these elements. A 2011 brightly colored television commercial for Hong Kong's Suning Citicall stores featured several young people using Suning Citicall products in various settings, such as an amusement park. This advertisement implied that Suning Citicall is a cool store for young people and for people of all ages who want to live fun lifestyles.

This 2011 Suning Citicall commercial was in Cantonese and English, like other Suning Citicall advertisements. The bilingualism reflected the multiculturalism of Hong Kong, Suning Citicall's home. It also reflected Suning's multinational operations that include Suning Citicall stores in Hong Kong, Suning stores in China, and Laox stores in Japan, among other businesses in the region. Suning also offers Green Channel, which provides guides to help expatriates shop at its stores and bilingual signage and advertisements.

In addition to these geographic and cultural concerns, the company has added new types of products and business models. It opened the first of its Suning Expo Super Stores in 2012. The company renovated existing Suning stores to create these stores, which sell Suning's usual assortment of electronics and home appliances but also more general, everyday items. The stores help Suning diversify its product base.

BRAND EQUITY

- A 2012 article by *China Daily* said "Suning ranked [as] China's top retailer in sales in 2011" and stated that Suning's online site, Suning.com, accounted for 3.7 percent of online retail transactions in China.
- In 2012 Suning placed sixth on Interbrand's list of the top retail brands in the Asia Pacific region, prompting Interbrand to call Suning "the leading household appliance retail chain in China."
- In 2012 Suning appeared on Brand Finance's "Global 500," an annual list of the top 500 brands in the world. Suning also appeared on another Brand Finance list, the "China 100," a list of the top 100 brands in China, in 2010 and 2011.

The store occupies a prominent place in Chinese retail. "Suning ranked [as] China's top retailer in sales in 2011," noted a 2012 article by *China Daily*, which called Suning and its retail competitor Gome "home appliance retailing giants." The article also observed that Suning's online site, Suning.com, accounted for 3.7 percent of online retail transactions in China.

This strong brand awareness has made Suning a competitive retail brand. Every year, Interbrand lists the world's top retail brands in various markets. In 2012 Suning placed sixth on Interbrand's list of the top retail brands in the Asia Pacific region, prompting Interbrand to call Suning "the leading household appliance retail chain in China."

Suning is not only a powerful retail brand, but a powerful brand across all industries, both internationally and in its home country. Brand Finance's annual list of the top 500 brands in the world is the "Global 500." In 2012 Suning appeared on this list and ranked 264th out of 500. It also ranked highly on another Brand Finance list, the "China 100," ranking the top 100 brands in China. Suning ranked 21st on this list in 2010 and 30th in 2011.

BRAND AWARENESS

- Respondents to a 2010 Holaba online poll named Suning their favorite IT/appliance retailer.
- Suning customers gave Suning 87.4 points in total service satisfaction and reported 80 percent satisfaction with its after sales services in 2010.
- A 2012 poll found that Suning's stores and online site were popular with Chinese consumers.
- A 2012 *Jiefang Daily* article praised Suning's efficiency in its retail and online operations.

Consumers have also recognized Suning. The online site Holaba asks Internet users about brands by asking them the question, "How likely are you to recommend this Product/Brand to a colleague or friend?" In 2010 it polled about 6,000 respondents, who named Suning their favorite IT/appliance retailer. These respondents also named Suning the company "most likely to increase its market share."

In the *China Home Appliances Chain Industry Service Blue Book for 2010*, Suning noted similar results. This document reported that customers gave Suning 87.4 points in total service satisfaction, while the industry as a whole averaged 76 points. The document also stated that 80 percent of Suning customers reported satisfaction with the brand's after sales services.

Suning has firmly established itself as both a traditional retailer with numerous physical stores and a busy online retailer. According to a *Jiefang Daily* article, a 2012 consumer survey about the Chinese electronics industry addressed Suning's presence in both fields. The poll, which asked Chinese consumers about traditional electronics retailers, online electronics retailers (also known as B2C, or business to consumer websites), and electronic brands, reported that "Suning is the only company that was awarded among the most popular retailers and B2C websites," according to the article, which concluded that "Suning positions its online business in parallel with their physical shops which results in greater efficiency as both channels are fully employed."

BRAND OUTLOOK

- In 2012 Suning opened Laox stores in China to expand its business in shopping malls and use Laox's expertise in various areas and varied product lines to expand its business.
- Suning opened a home appliance training center in China in 2011 to teach Suning employees how to provide installation and maintenance services.
- In a 2013 letter to Suning employees, Suning chairperson Zhang Jindong addressed the company's parent company as the Suning Group, not its previous name of Suning Appliance Group, representing the company's intention to diversify its interests.

Already a major retailer in China, Suning grew even more in 2012. It opened a number of Laox stores in China that year to expand its business in shopping malls. This Chinese business is in addition to Laox's business in Japan at its Japanese stores. This move also expanded Suning Appliance Group/Suning's product line, as Laox stores are department stores that sell items like goods for the home, Japanese animation products, toys, and jewelry; Laox also sells musical instruments at its Musicvox stores. With this move, Suning also hoped to incorporate Laox's experience with design, manufacturing, management, and customer service elements.

Suning has taken other steps to improve its customer service. It opened a Nanjing, China, training center for its employees in 2011. This school provides training for after sales services, the services Suning provides after customers buy the store's products. The first home appliance training center in China, this center teaches Suning employees how to provide installation and maintenance services and represents the company's goal to improve after sales services.

The company hopes to develop its nonretail interests as well. In a 2013 letter to Suning employees, Suning chairperson and cofounder Zhang Jindong addressed the company's parent company as the Suning Group, not its previous name of Suning Appliance Group. The Suning Group name represents the company's intention to diversify its interests in commercial real estate, hotels, and apartments and broaden its financial interests.

FURTHER READING

"Best Retail Brands 2012." Interbrand. Accessed January 6, 2013. http://www.interbrand.com/en/BestRetailBrands/2012-Best-Retail-Brands.aspx#page-wrap.

Brand Finance. "Global 500 2012." *Brandirectory*. Accessed January 1, 2013. http://brandirectory.com/league_tables/table/global-500-2012.

"China Consumer Electronics Suppliers Longing for Brand Strategy." *Jiefang Daily*, June 30, 2012.

"China's Suning Publishes Services Blue Book." *China Retail News*, March 17, 2010.

"IT/Appliance Retailer Brands in China." Holaba, October 2010. Accessed February 20, 2013. http://business.holaba.com.cn/en/uploads/holaba-cms-homepage/pdf/101008Holaba%20IT%20Retailer%20BW%20Overview.pdf.

Poleg, Dror. "Turning Japanese: Suning's Laox Gamble." Buy Buy China, July 6, 2012. Accessed January 6, 2013. http://www.buybuychina.com/turning-japanese-sunings-laox-gamble/.

"Shares of Gome, Suning Slump over Price War." *China Daily*, August 15, 2012.

"Suning Appliance Chain Store Company Ltd." *International Directory of Company Histories*. Ed. Tina Grant. Vol. 120. Detroit, MI: St. James Press, 2011.

"Suning Focuses on Better Retail Training for Its Staff in China." *China Retail News*, August 1, 2011.

"Suning Foraying into Real Estate, Financial Industry." *Want China Daily*, January 3, 2013.

"Suning's Online Business Revenue Surges 130%." ChinaTech-News.com, August 6, 2012. Accessed January 7, 2013. http://www.chinatechnews.com/2012/08/06/16535-sunings-online-business-revenue-surges-130.

Woke, Li. "Suning to Open New Laox Stores." *China Daily*, July 20, 2012.

SUZUKI

—■—

AT A GLANCE

—■—

Brand Synopsis: The fourth-largest automobile manufacturer in Japan and the ninth-largest in the world, Suzuki offers a diverse product line that includes cars, trucks, motorcycles, and all-terrain vehicles.

Parent Company: Suzuki Motor Corporation
300 Takatsuka-cho
Minami-ku, Hamamatsu City
Japan
http://www.globalsuzuki.com

Sector: Consumer Discretionary

Industry Group: Automobiles & Components

Performance: *Market share*—6.20% of the worldwide motorcycle market (2008); 10% of the worldwide ATV market (2008). *Revenues*—US$31.58 billion (2012).

Principal Competitors: Honda Motor Co., Ltd.; Toyota Motor Corporation; Nissan Motor Co., Ltd.; Yamaha Motor Co., Ltd.; Kawasaki Motors Corp.

BRAND ORIGINS

- Suzuki Motor Corporation was founded by Michio Suzuki in 1909 as Suzuki Loom Works, a manufacturer of weaving machines.
- Suzuki entered the motor-vehicle market in 1952 with the release of its first motorized bicycle, debuting its first motorcycle and first passenger sedan in 1955.

- Suzuki entered the U.S. auto market in the 1980s, years behind its competitors, and struggled to establish a strong presence.
- As Suzuki approached the 21st century, it remained primarily a niche manufacturer.
- In 2012, Suzuki's U.S. subsidiary filed for bankruptcy protection and announced that it would discontinue building cars for the U.S. market.

Suzuki Motor Corporation was founded as Suzuki Loom Works, a manufacturer of weaving machines, in 1909. Textile manufacturing was one of Japan's biggest industries in the early 20th century, and Suzuki supplied weaving equipment to hundreds of small fabrics manufacturers. Founder Michio Suzuki took the company public in 1920 and renamed it Suzuki Loom Manufacturing Company.

By 1937, Suzuki had begun producing a variety of war-related materials in addition to its weaving machines. Although the Suzuki factory escaped the bombing campaigns of World War II and was thus able to resume production of textile manufacturing equipment soon after the war, Japan was by then so impoverished that there was little demand for new woven products. In 1947, relying on the manufacturing experience it had gained during the war, Suzuki began working on designs for motorized vehicles. The prospects were favorable, for Japan was a nation of nearly 100 million people, a vast majority of whom lacked access to basic transportation.

In 1952, Suzuki entered the motor-vehicle market with the launch of the Power Free, its first motorized bicycle. A more powerful model, called the Diamond

Free, was released the following year. In 1954 the company changed its name to Suzuki Motor Co., Ltd., and in 1955, Suzuki debuted both its first motorcycle, the Colleda, and its first lightweight passenger sedan, called the Suzulight. In 1961 the company's loom division was officially separated from its motor works. Having gained an important foothold in the Japanese vehicle market, Suzuki continued to expand, developing its first light truck, the Suzulight Carry, in 1961.

While Suzuki had significant early success in establishing itself in the motorcycle market, the prosperity of its chief competitors in the car market, including Honda, Toyota, and Nissan, made it difficult for the company to expand its automotive product line. In its search for growth, Suzuki turned domestically to the expansion of its line of small engines, notably small marine engines, and globally to export markets that were in poor economic condition and in need of vehicles, such as Thailand, Indonesia, and the Philippines.

The oil crisis of the 1970s took a huge toll on Suzuki's car and truck production, with sales in that sector dropping more than 65 percent in Japan during the decade. As a result, Suzuki turned its attention to expanding motorcycle production and entering other markets, including the U.S. auto market. Suzuki, however, was years behind its competitors in introducing its automobiles to American car buyers and struggled to establish a strong foothold for its brand. Suzuki experienced some success in the United States with the introduction of the Samurai, a compact sport utility vehicle (SUV) that sold more than 80,000 units by 1987 and helped to establish the American Suzuki Motor Corporation, the company's subsidiary in the United States. In 1988, however, the company's U.S. sales were thrown into a tailspin when a *Consumer Reports* study declared that the Samurai was unsafe and prone to rollovers. Suzuki's entire U.S. executive team then resigned, a gesture of atonement that was misinterpreted as an abandonment of the company's commitment to the product and to the U.S. market in general.

Suzuki spent much of the 1980s expanding in other countries around the world, leading the company to change its name to Suzuki Motor Corporation in 1990. Suzuki's losses in the automotive sector were partially offset by continuing increases in motorcycle sales and ongoing partnerships with brands such as General Motors Company (GM), but overall company growth stagnated. Nevertheless, Suzuki continued to focus on its presence in the U.S. car market, reinventing its vehicles and increasing its network of dealerships in the United States throughout the 1990s.

As Suzuki approached the 21st century, it remained primarily a niche manufacturer. By the late 1990s, it was deriving about 70 percent of its income from sales of automobiles and selling roughly two million cars a year

worldwide. Suzuki had also become Japan's leading minicar manufacturer, and its motorcycles, which ranged from 50cc scooters to 1100cc touring bikes, were accounting for approximately 15 percent of its business.

Suzuki and the other "Big Four" Japanese motorcycle makers (Honda, Yamaha, and Kawasaki) had for years faced increasing competition from European and U.S. manufacturers, as well as from Chinese companies making pirated copies of their machines. Responding to these threats, Suzuki and Kawasaki announced in 2001 that they had entered into an agreement whereby they would jointly develop new motorcycle models and unify their parts procurement and production operations to cut costs.

As for its line of cars and trucks, Suzuki continued to expand significantly around the globe and lean on its partnership with GM to introduce new models into the U.S. market in hopes of competing with established Japanese brands like Honda and Toyota. Suzuki's U.S. sales peaked in 2007, and GM completed its divestment in the company in 2008. In 2010, Volkswagen AG bought a nearly 20 percent share of Suzuki, making it the company's largest shareholder.

Despite Suzuki's success in numerous automotive markets around the world, sales continued to fall off dramatically in the United States. In 2012 the American Suzuki Motor Corporation filed for Chapter 11 bankruptcy protection, announcing its plans to discontinue building cars for the U.S. market and focus instead on motorcycles, all-terrain vehicles (ATVs), and marine equipment.

BRAND ELEMENTS

- Suzuki's most distinctive brand element is its three-stripe "S" logo.
- The simple and commanding design of Suzuki's logo is meant to symbolize the company's strength.
- The Suzuki "S" logo has undergone some minor revisions but has remained largely unchanged since its introduction in the 1950s.

Suzuki is known by its three-stripe "S" logo, a hallmark element of the Suzuki brand that began appearing on its motorcycles and other vehicles in the 1950s. The strong, simple, and visually appealing red "S" logo is intended to symbolize the company's strength. Over the decades, the lines of the "S" have been slightly sharpened and the logo has been colored in blue and silver on occasion, but the logo has remained largely unchanged during the past half century.

BRAND IDENTITY

- Suzuki is a well-established brand that offers affordability, comfort, quality, reliability, style, and performance.

- Suzuki constantly modernizes its products to meet changing lifestyles and to appeal to customers worldwide.
- The brand's "Way of Life!" slogan implies that every Suzuki will be a pleasure to drive, use, and own.
- The Suzuki brand is meant to be "people-friendly" and fun.

As a well-established global brand with a good reputation, Suzuki offers quality, reliability, and originality, but it also emphasizes the need to modernize products constantly to meet changing lifestyles and to appeal to customers in various cultures around the world.

The Suzuki brand promises to deliver "value-packed products" that meet the needs of consumers while improving their living conditions. The company says its world strategy includes the belief that "people should be able to enjoy economical, eco-friendly motoring without sacrificing style, comfort, practicality, or performance." This is accomplished by applying creativity, enthusiasm, and advanced technologies.

Some Suzukis are designed for customers who live in cities and want small cars that are stylish, enjoyable, and easy on the environment. Others are more elegant and roomy, with an emphasis on comfort. Suzuki motorcycles and ATVs are promoted as sleek, fashionable, high-performance machines that come in many varieties for a wide range of uses. The brand's "Way of Life!" slogan is meant to convey the idea that every Suzuki will be a pleasure to drive, use, and own. In short, the Suzuki brand is meant to be "people-friendly" and fun.

BRAND STRATEGY

- Suzuki's strategy in the United States focused on creating vehicles that combined economy and utility.
- Reflecting its continued attempts to capture the attention of American car buyers, Suzuki ran television commercials during the 2011 and 2012 Super Bowls.
- Increasing competition from Japanese, U.S., and European automakers left Suzuki ultimately unable to effectively compete in the U.S. auto market.

Until Suzuki announced in 2012 its intention to pull out of the U.S. auto market once its remaining vehicles in dealership inventories were sold, the brand's strategy in the United States was focused on continually improving its reputation for combining economy and utility. For example, in 2011, Suzuki entered the most expensive advertising venue on television, the Super Bowl. In a commercial titled "Wicked Weather," a driver in the brand's all-wheel-drive Kizashi compact sport sedan is shown outmaneuvering a pack of snowmen in snowy, off-road conditions. In its 2012 Super Bowl commercial, called

"Sled," Suzuki again highlighted the Kizashi, this time to the soundtrack of a song by rapper 50 Cent.

These advertising campaigns highlighted Suzuki's continued attempts to make strides in the U.S. market against dominant Japanese automakers Honda and Toyota. However, increased competition from other Asian automakers, such as Hyundai and Kia, as well as from U.S. and European makers of compact cars and SUVs, made such an approach untenable.

BRAND EQUITY

- In 2012, Suzuki had a U.S. market share of 0.2 percent, compared to a 14.4 percent market share for fellow Japanese automaker Toyota.
- Suzuki's decision to pull out of the U.S. auto market came on the heels of dismal sales figures and low consumer ratings.
- Suzuki has experienced reputation issues in countries besides the United States, including Japan and France.
- Despite its struggles, Suzuki's brand value has climbed in recent years, with Brand Finance assigning the brand a value of US$4.4 billion in 2012.

Suzuki's 2012 announcement that it would withdraw from the car market in the United States came on the heels of dismal U.S. sales figures for the Japanese manufacturer. In 2012, Suzuki had the smallest U.S. market share among Asian automakers. Suzuki's car sales in the United States during the first 10 months of 2012 fell 4.7 percent, giving it a market share of just 0.2 percent, according to Autodata Corporation. By comparison, Toyota's market share at the time of Autodata's study was 14.4 percent.

Despite some high points during Suzuki's run as an automaker for the U.S. market, it appears American consumers never took to Suzuki as an auto brand. This was reflected in recent findings of the J. D. Power and Associates U.S. Customer Service Index (CSI), which ranks vehicle owners' overall satisfaction with dealer service. In 2012, Suzuki ranked 20th out of 21 auto brands, behind only Dodge, while in 2011 Suzuki was ranked in last place.

Suzuki has struggled with reputation issues in countries besides the United States, including its home country of Japan. In 2012, Suzuki ranked 14th on Interbrand's list of Japan's top global brands, coming in behind automakers Toyota, Honda, Nissan, and Lexus. In 2012, German brand research company ADAC ranked Suzuki 27th out of 33 global auto brands on its AutoMarxX brand study, which includes criteria like brand image, market strength, customer satisfaction, product strength, environmental performance, and safety. Similar results have been posted in studies in countries around the world. In the

J.D. Power and Associates 2011 France Vehicle Ownership Satisfaction Study, for example, French consumers ranked the Suzuki brand 22nd out of the 24 auto brands polled.

Suzuki's struggles in the United States and other countries do not appear to have adversely affected its brand value. Brand Finance gave the company a brand value of US$4.4 billion in 2012, a slight increase over its US$4.3 billion brand value in 2011 and more than double its 2009 brand value of US$2.1 billion. Similarly, while in 2009, Brand Finance ranked Suzuki 331st on its Global 500 list, the company's ranking in 2012 jumped almost 100 spots, to the 232nd position. *Fortune* magazine ranked Suzuki slightly lower on its Global 500 list for 2011, placing the brand in the 316th position. In another promising result for Suzuki's brand reputation, the company was ranked in the 88th spot on the 2012 Global RepTrak 100, a survey of consumers' perception of companies and its effects on purchasing behavior.

BRAND AWARENESS

- Suzuki has struggled to be recognized as a top automaker, but the brand is well-known internationally for its role in motorcycle production and racing.
- A 1988 *Consumer Reports* study faulting the safety of the Samurai SUV dealt a serious blow to Suzuki's reputation in the United States.
- Although Suzuki announced in 2012 that it would discontinue its U.S. car operations, the company plans to continue selling motorcycles and ATVs in the country.

Around the globe, Suzuki has struggled to establish and strengthen its reputation as a car maker. The brand is best known internationally for its role in motorcycle production and racing. Suzuki's motorcycles have been competitive in international racing events since the 1950s, and the company has sponsored numerous motorcycle racing events around the world. The brand also supports several smaller winter sports, such as luge racing and cross-country skiing, as well as soccer events, such as the ASEAN Football Championship.

Suzuki suffered a blow to its reputation among American consumers in 1988, when a *Consumer Reports* study declared that the Suzuki Samurai, the brand's popular compact SUV, was unsafe. The magazine reported that the Samurai's high center of gravity could cause it to flip over while negotiating turns, even at low speeds. Suzuki launched its own investigation and took remedial measures, but the damage had already been done, with sales plunging 31 percent the year the report was published. The *Consumer Reports* study's impact was still evident in the 1990s. In 1995, for example, a U.S. court awarded US$90 million to a woman who was paralyzed

as the result of a Samurai rollover accident, a verdict that was overturned in 2002. Despite Suzuki's decision to stop selling its automobiles in the United States, the company plans to continue promoting its line of motorcycles, ATVs, and marine products to American consumers.

BRAND OUTLOOK

- In 2012, after its car sales declined precipitously, Suzuki announced it would file for bankruptcy and halt car production for the U.S. market.
- Suzuki plans to continue marketing and selling motorcycles, ATVs, and outboard engines in the United States.
- Suzuki's withdrawal from the U.S. auto market will allow it to focus on competing more effectively in markets where it is better established.
- Some analysts predict that Suzuki's pullout from the U.S. auto market will help the brand strengthen its international presence.

American Suzuki Motor Corporation announced in 2012 that it would file for bankruptcy protection and halt car production for the U.S. auto market. According to court documents, American Suzuki claimed US$346 million in debt at the time of its filing. The announcement came on the heels of dismal U.S. sales figures for the Japanese manufacturer. According to *Reuters,* Suzuki sold only 21,188 cars in the United States in the first 10 months of 2012. Those figures were in stark contrast to sales numbers from 2007, when Suzuki sold more than 100,000 vehicles in the country. As to future plans, Suzuki said it would focus on its U.S. motorcycle, ATV, and outboard engine operations and shift its auto business to servicing Suzuki vehicles already on the road.

Suzuki's exit from the U.S. auto market will allow it to focus on emerging markets and innovative products, such as *kei* cars, compact and lightweight automobiles whose owners enjoy tax advantages in Japan and some other countries. Suzuki plans to allocate resources from the United States to areas of the world where its more significant market share is facing increased competition. Part of this defensive focus will be on shoring up the company's lead in India, where it is facing growing competition from Hyundai. In an article from *Reuters* reprinted in the *Chicago Tribune,* Satoshi Yuzaki of Tokyo-based Takagi Securities Co. commented, "Suzuki is no longer among the carmakers like Toyota or Honda to have an advantageous position in the U.S., so why not focus on what it is good at?" Indeed, while it is too early to predict what the future holds for Suzuki, it is possible that its withdrawal from the U.S. market will help the brand strengthen its reputation and sales around the world.

FURTHER READING

Beeler, Jensen. "American Suzuki Expects 9.8% Sales Decrease for Fiscal Year." *Asphalt & Rubber,* February 7, 2012. Accessed December 15, 2012. http://www.asphaltandrubber.com/news/american-suzuki-sales-2011.

Brand Finance. "Suzuki." *Brandirectory.* Accessed December 15, 2012. http://brandirectory.com/profile/suzuki.

Buss, Dale. "Suzuki Joins Joe Isuzu on One-Way Flight Back to Japan." *BrandChannel.com,* November 7, 2012. Accessed December 15, 2012. http://www.brandchannel.com/home/post/2012/11/07/Suzuki-US-Auto-Exit-110712.aspx.

"Fortune Global 500 2011." *CNN Money,* July 25, 2011. Accessed January 6, 2013. http://money.cnn.com/magazines/fortune/global500/2011/snapshots/6749.html.

Riley, Charles. "Suzuki to Stop U.S. Auto Sales, Exit Market." *CNN Money,* November 5, 2012. Accessed December 20, 2012. http://money.cnn.com/2012/11/05/autos/american-suzuki-bankruptcy/index.html.

Simley, John, Susan Windisch Brown, and David E. Salamie. "Suzuki Motor Corporation." *International Directory of Company Histories.* Ed. Jay P. Pederson and Miranda H. Ferrara. Vol. 59. Detroit: St. James Press, 2004. *Gale Virtual Reference Library.* Accessed December 19, 2012.

"Suzuki to End Car Sales in U.S., Focus on Motorcycles." *Chicago Tribune,* November 6, 2012. Accessed December 18, 2012. http://articles.chicagotribune.com/2012-11-06/news/chi-suzuki-to-end-car-sales-in-us-11062012_1_suzuki-shares-suzuki-motor-corp-cami-automotive.

"UPDATE 2-Suzuki to End Car Sales in U.S., Focus on Motorcycles." *Reuters,* November 5, 2012. Accessed January 24, 2012. http://www.reuters.com/article/2012/11/06/americansuzukimotor-chapter-idUSL3E8M58MP20121106.

Woodyard, Chris, and Kelsey Mays. "Suzuki Sees Sales Surge Despite Plans to Leave U.S." *USA Today,* December 23, 2012. Accessed December 26, 2012. http://www.usatoday.com/story/driveon/2012/12/22/suzuki-kazashi-discounts-sale/1786319.

T

BRAND ORIGINS

- Deutsche Telekom AG was formed in 1989 in a reorganization of the government-owned Deutsche Bundespost.
- The company was privatized in 1996 and raised more than US$13 billion in Europe's largest IPO.
- The company's leading unit provides wireless services, landline, and broadband services.
- Germany remains its largest single market.

Deutsche Telekom AG is a German telecommunications company headquartered in Bonn, Germany. The company was formed in 1989 when West Germany's telecommunications services separated from the country's postal system, Deutsche Post. During the early years of telecommunications services in Europe, many countries integrated the postal and telecom operations into government-owned units. This began to change in Germany as early as the 1960s as privatization became a political issue when many complained about the government monopoly's costs and inefficiencies.

Germany's financial, postal, and telecommunications conglomerate, Deutsche Bundespost, was split into three entities on July 1, 1989 as part of a post office reform effort. Those entities became Deutsche Bundespost Telekom, Deutsche Post, and Deutsche Postbank.

Deutsche Bundespost Telekom became Deutsche Telekom AG on January 1, 1995, and the company was privatized in 1996. In the same year, backed by Goldman Sachs, the company raised more than US$13 billion in Europe's largest IPO to date. Its operations as of 2013 include Telekom Deutschland GmbH, which is the division marketing to private customers, providing landline telephone, broadband Internet, mobile telephone, and IPTV services; and T-Systems International, a business division focused on providing services to the public sector and business customers.

The T brand is led by its wireless unit, which served more than 40 percent of the German population as of 2011. This group also offers low-cost mobile, broadband, and VoIP phone service through the subsidiary Congstar. The T brand had been the German monopoly provider of Internet services until its privatization, and thereafter remained the dominant ISP under the unit name T-Online. In its fixed-line business, the brand holds approximately 25 million phone customers and 14 million broadband users in Germany.

Outside Germany and Eastern Europe, the brand's key international wireless subsidiaries are T-Mobile USA and T-Bile (UK). The company attempted to sell T-Mobile USA in 2011, but United States regulator concerns called this sale off. In October of 2012 Deutsche Telekom and MetroPCS agreed to merge their operations in the United States.

Germany remained Deutsche Telekom's largest single market as of 2011, accounting for 45 percent of its sales. The company offers goods and services through subsidiaries in 15 European countries. Additionally the subsidiary T-Systems International has operations in more than 20 countries, although it accounts for less than 15 percent of Deutsche Telekom's overall revenues.

Deutsche Telekom is a large global employer, with approximately 236,000 employees as of 2011.

BRAND ELEMENTS

- The T logo is comprised of a capital letter "T" within a line of pink, square boxes.
- The brand's official colors are magenta and gray.
- The brand's proprietary typefaces are TeleAntiqua and TeleGrotesk, which are based on ITC Century and Neue Helvetica, respectively.

The T brand is exemplified visually by its capital letter "T" placed within a line of pink, square boxes. The line of boxes frequently runs across the top of a webpage or banner, no matter the size of the page. There does not appear to be a design rule as to where the T is placed within this line, as long as both elements are in some way combined. In subsidiaries such as T-Mobile, the "Mobile" will appear after the letter T and several of the boxes. According to the company's website, the simple letter T in the brand's logo represents, "innovation, competence, and simplicity," which are the brand's primary promises to its customers.

The corporate identity agency Zintzmeyer & Lux designed the brand's logo in 1990. The brand's official colors are magenta and gray, and the proprietary typefaces used are TeleAntiqua and TeleGrotesk, which are based on ITC Century and Neue Helvetica, respectively.

BRAND IDENTITY

- Deutsche Telekom's slogan is "Life is for sharing."
- Its objective is to be the first choice for a connected personal and work life.
- The brand's promise is that its state-of-the-art network infrastructure will allow customers to instantly share their major and minor personal events.

"Life is for sharing" is the brand's slogan. Hans-Christian Schwingen, Head of Brand Strategy and Marketing Communications at Deutsche Telekom, explains on the company's website that the slogan "… lies at the very heart of what we do, and serves as the guiding light and constant benchmark for the entire company." The company's objective is to be its customers' first choice for staying connected, both personally and professionally, by sharing major and minor life events with each other through T devices and services.

T's brand mission promises to provide its customers with three things: innovation, competence, and simplicity. These three tenets encompass the company's stated dedication to everything from innovative new technologies and services to excellent customer service to reasonable pricing. Additionally Deutsche Telekom's principles include "customer delight," "respect and integrity," "team together—team apart," "best place to perform and grow," and "I am T—Count on me."

BRAND STRATEGY

- Deutsche Telekom's brand strategy is to be the best-connected telecommunications company, with seamless access technologies available to consumers, businesses, and government.
- It offers seamless access technologies in order to keep its customers connected.
- Telekom is working with both Boku and MasterCard in the mobile payments arena.

Deutsche Telekom's brand strategy is to be the best-connected telecommunications company, with seamless access technologies available to consumers, businesses, and government. The company complements its own innovation with working through partners to provide attractive devices and product portfolios. Partnerships in 2012 included Boku, Inc. and MasterCard, with the former providing a direct billing agreement with Deutsche Telekom offering all Telekom's customers access to Boku's portfolio of merchant partners in order to purchase a variety of digital goods and services, including virtual goods in online games and Facebook credits, and the latter allowing for Telekom's customers to use their mobile phones to pay for goods and services. Additionally as of July 2012 Deutsche Telekom committed to offering Mozilla's Firefox OS-powered devices to their customer base.

In the area of innovation, Deutsche Telekom also committed to offering venture capital and incubator space to start-ups and joint ventures. For businesses of all types, Telekom is working towards enhancing cloud and dynamic computing technologies. It also offers cloud services to consumers and is looking towards providing a consistent user experience across all screens used by delivering modular and flexible bundles of products and services.

BRAND EQUITY

- Business Rankings Annual ranked Deutsche Telekom first among the largest telecommunications company in Europe in 2010.
- The company was listed as the second-most valuable telecommunications company in 2011.
- Deutsche Telekom had 5.6 percent share among wireless telecommunications carriers worldwide in 2011, according to Market Share Reporter.
- BrandZ reported a brand value of US$26.8 billion for Deutsche Telekom in 2012.

Business Rankings Annual ranked Deutsche Telekom first among the largest telecommunications companies in Europe in 2010; second in Europe's most valuable telecommunications companies in 2011; and eighth among the world's most admired telecommunications companies in 2012. Market Share Reporter lists Deutsche Telekom with 3.9 percent market share in fixed line telecom firms worldwide in 2011 as well as having 5.6 percent share among wireless telecommunications carriers worldwide the same year. The top providers in each category are NTT Group with 14.5 percent and China Mobile Ltd. with 6.9 percent respectively.

The BrandZ Top 100 Most Valuable Global Brands 2012 lists Deutsche Telekom with a brand value of US$26.8 billion. It also shows a brand contribution of three on a scale of one to five (with five as the highest ranking) and brand momentum of 2 on a scale of one to 10. The contribution measure is based on the role the brand plays in driving earnings, while the brand momentum describes the prospects for future earnings.

BRAND AWARENESS

- Deutsche Telekom holds an 81 percent market share in its home country of Germany in landline services, furnishing the company with automatic brand recognition and awareness.
- Awareness in its commercial markets is also high and increasing with the introduction of the T M2M Marketplace.
- T-Mobile, the company's wireless brand outside Germany, enjoys the United States as its largest market, where it ranks fourth behind Verizon, AT&T, and Sprint.
- Its acquisition of MetroPCS, the fifth-largest carrier in the United States, will also likely boost the company's brand awareness and recognition.

Deutsche Telekom holds approximately 81 percent of the landline market share in Germany, and the company enjoys high brand recognition among German citizens. Since it is also a leading provider of mobile telecom services, T enjoys large levels of brand awareness and recognition in that arena as well.

Awareness is also strong in the commercial markets with brand awareness likely increasing further due to such innovations and launches such as the company's M2M Marketplace, first launched in spring of 2012. M2M stands for machine to machine, and can include both wired and wireless devices that can communicate together. The M2M Marketplace is a platform for manufacturers and dealers around the world to offer their hardware, software, apps, and full-package solutions relating to M2M communications. Deutsche Telekom plans to also offer SIM cards and SIM chips through this marketplace, likely serving to increase awareness of the T brand in both the business and consumer markets.

T-Mobile is Deutsche Telekom's brand outside Germany, and is located in 11 countries (the largest market being the United States). While T-Mobile is only the fourth-largest carrier in the United States market, behind Verizon, AT&T, and Sprint, its name recognition is quite high. The company also announced the acquisition of MetroPCS, the fifth-largest telecommunications company in the United States, in 2012.

BRAND OUTLOOK

- Deutsche Telekom's T brand has strong geographic diversification, giving the brand strength in the global marketplace.
- The brand enjoys a large customer base, particularly in its home country of Germany.
- While the telecommunications market continues to grow, competitive pressures do as well, from both traditional telecom companies as well as new-style start-ups.
- BrandZ reported a very low brand momentum for Deutsche Telekom, which could point to lower earnings in the coming years.

The T brand possesses many strengths that stem from a company that has strong geographical diversification and successful mobile voice and data services. The T brand also enjoys a large customer base in its home country of Germany as well as in many countries around the world, including the United States. As the global telecommunications market is expected to continue to grow, the demand for the newer technologies in mobile communications, particularly Long Term Evolution (LTE) technology that T-Mobile has plans to launch in 2013, will grow as well.

However telecommunications exhibits a very high industry rivalry since widespread deregulation and privatization occurred in the 1980s through the early 2000s. This has led to price erosion in all markets, but especially in the landline business. Deutsche Telekom also faces additional competition from start-up companies offering digital home network services. Companies such as HomeChoice in London sell a telephone connection, broadband, and on-demand television package, edging in on Deutsche Telekom's traditional markets.

Deutsche Telekom also still faces the challenge of the global economic slowdown that began in 2008. While most markets were growing once again by the end of the first decade of the 21st century, growth has been slow at best, and Europe still faced economic uncertainty in many markets as of 2012. Deutsche Telekom announced a new round of layoffs in 2013 in its home market of Germany. It announced that it would cut 1,200 jobs that are considered overhead, mainly in areas such as marketing, management, and other areas of administration. This layoff followed the elimination of 5,000 jobs in 2012.

In global rankings, Deutsche Telekom dropped from 20th in 2011 to 38th in 2012 in the top-100 companies based on net income. In addition, the BrandZ Top 100 Most Valuable listing shows T with a 10 percent drop in brand value and low brand momentum of two on a scale of one to ten. While the acquisition of MetroPCS in the United States may prove a boon for brand positioning, the fight for both brand recognition and market share remains crucial as Deutsche Telekom enters into the second decade of the 21st century.

FURTHER READING

"Boku Forms Payments Parntership with Deutsche Telekom," *Entertainment Close-up*, May 8, 2012.

"BrandZ Top 100 Most Valuable Global Brands 2012." Millward Brown. Accessed January 26, 2013. http://www.millward-brown.com/brandz/Top_100_Global_Brands.aspx

"Deutsche Telekom Launches M2M Marketplace." *Total Telecom Magazine*, May 30, 2012.

"Global 100." *Total Telecom*, November 2012. Accessed January 28, 2013. http://www.totaltele.com/.

Henning, Dietmar. "Germany: Deutsche Telekom Cuts a Further 1,200 Jobs." *World Socialist Web Site*, January 26, 2103. Accessed January 28, 2013. https://www.wsws.org/en/articles/2013/01/26/tele-j26.html.

"Hip Ma Bells? As Content Becomes Ever More Important, Even Phone Companies Are Starting to Distribute Music, Games, and Movies." *Newsweek International*, September 26, 2005.

TACO BELL

—■—

AT A GLANCE

Brand Synopsis: The largest Mexican-style fast-food brand in the United States, Taco Bell is related to qualities such as youth appeal, inexpensive cost, and regular menu evolution.

Parent Company: Yum! Brands RSC
1900 Colonel Sanders Lane
Louisville, Kentucky 40213
United States
http://www.yum.com/

Sector: Consumer Discretionary

Industry Group: Consumer Services

Performance: *Market share*—58 percent (2011). *Sales*—US$1.8 billion (2011).

Principal Competitors: Burger King Worldwide, Inc.; Chick-Fil-A, Inc.; Chipotle Mexican Grill, Inc.; Del Taco LLC; McDonald's; Qdoba Restaurant Corporation; Subway; Wendy's International, Inc.

BRAND ORIGINS

- Taco Bell was founded by Glenn Bell in 1962.
- PepsiCo acquired the growing regional chain in 1978.
- Taco Bell regularly introduces new menu items and innovative, effective marketing campaigns that have helped position it as the number-one Mexican-style fast-food chain in the United States.

Taco Bell was founded in 1962 by Glen Bell. Bell had begun working in fast food during the early 1950s. A fan of tacos and noting the success of what would become the megachain McDonald's, he was a partner in two small taco chains before establishing his own, Taco Bell. His first restaurant was in Downey, California. Bell introduced franchises in 1964, and the company went public in 1966. By 1967 there were 12 company-owned Taco Bells and 325 franchisees. In 1978 Bell sold his fast-food chain to PepsiCo, Inc., for US$125 million in stock. By that time there were 868 Taco Bells.

PepsiCo believed that it could move Taco Bell from a regional ethnic success into a national fast food chain, so it repositioned Taco Bell to challenge fast-food giants such as McDonald's. By the 1980s Taco Bell dominated the Mexican-style fast-food market in the United States and continued to grow quickly. In 1980 Taco Bell had 1,333 outlets, and in 1983 it had 1,600 outlets and annual sales of US$918 million. By 1986 Taco Bell had 2,400 outlets and over US$1.4 billion in sales; the first international location was opened in London that year. Between 1982 and 1989 Taco Ball saw an annual increase of 25 percent in sales.

Constant menu innovation and effective ad campaigns helped build Taco Bell's audience. In 1984 the brand introduced the Taco Salad and the Taco Bell-Grande. The following year the brand's advertising campaign had the tagline "Just Made for You," which emphasized that most Taco Bell items were custom-made when ordered. In 1986 the brand reminded consumers that Taco Bell was "the cure for the common meal." Two years later, in 1988, Taco Bell started the popular "Run for the Border" campaign.

Taco Bell was not afraid to make radical changes as well. In 1988, amid an economic recession in the United States, the chain lowered prices on many menu items, forcing hamburger chains to follow suit. Despite intense competition, Taco Bell continued to grow by introducing new menu items such as steak burritos and a three-tiered value menu in 1991. Sales increased 60 percent between 1989 and 1991. During the early 1990s Taco Bell pursued several unconventional approaches to expand opportunities for sales in the United States. These included the introduction of Taco Bell Express, which were small outlets with a limited menu and little or no seating in airports, business cafeterias, and sports stadiums.

Because of PepsiCo's desire to focus on other businesses, it combined all its restaurant businesses, including Taco Bell, into one division, then spun it off as TriCon Global Restaurants, Inc., in 1997. (In 2002 TriCon changed its name to Yum! Brands RSC.) In 1997 Taco Bell was the sixth-largest fast-food chain in the United States with 6,500 units in the United States and no national competitors among Mexican fast food.

Taco Bell faced short-term declines between 1999 and 2000, but it remained the number-one Mexican-style fast-food chain with two-thirds of the American market in 1999. It had about 7,000 locations in the United States and 170 abroad. In response, the brand increased the quality of menu items, and in 2001 it launched the US$200 million "Think Outside the Bun" campaign to promote the freshness of Taco Bell's food. More upscale menu items were added, including steak tacos. Beginning in 2001 the brand experienced sustained growth, and it continued to do well over the next few years, despite a worldwide economic downturn that began in 2007.

Even though increased competition in the cutthroat fast-food/quick service industry impacted Taco Bell during this period, it was also affected by the growth of higher quality Mexican restaurants, including Chipotle Mexican Grill. Taco Bell responded in 2012 by placing more emphasis on food as experience instead of food as fuel and introducing several new menu items, including a "First Meal" breakfast menu; a higher quality, chef-created Cantina Bell menu; and the extremely popular Doritos Loco Taco. By 2011 there were 5,670 Taco Bell restaurants in the United States that served 35 million customers every week.

BRAND ELEMENTS

- The original Taco Bell logo was a Hispanic man sleeping under a big sombrero.
- In 1969 Taco Bell began using a mission-style bell as the main piece of its logo.

- In 1997 Dinky the Chihuahua and the tagline "Yo Quiero Taco Bell" were launched, becoming one of the most popular ad campaigns of all time.

By the time Glenn Bell franchised his restaurants in the mid-1960s, the brand's logo was a Hispanic man dozing under a giant sombrero. The logo attracted controversy because the image was considered to be a negative stereotype. In 1969 it was changed to a mission-style bell with the Taco Bell name surrounding it. Originally, the logo featured a yellow bell with green inside on a red yoke, with two orange stripes across the yoke. The Taco Bell name was in brown, and restaurants featured accents in a rainbow of these colors. In 1995 the colors of the brand's logo changed to the current pink and purple with a yellow clapper. The bell was also positioned at an angle and was more active than the previous, upright logo. The change in the logo reflects the brand's continuous growth as both a nationwide and global fast-food brand.

The Taco Bell logo was a part of numerous, memorable advertising campaigns for the brand over the years. One in particular became one of the most popular advertising campaigns of all time and led to an icon associated with the Taco Bell brand. In 1997 Taco Bell launched "Yo Quiero Taco Bell" ("I want Taco Bell") featuring Dinky the talking Chihuahua. He was originally part of another campaign called "Want Some?" which had several television ads set inside a pink room representing a hungry person's stomach. The last ad in the campaign, "Chihuahua," featured Dinky walking down a street looking for a female Chihuahua before approaching a human and saying the memorable line, "Yo Quiero Taco Bell." The popularity of this commercial led to a series of ads with Dinky as well as to Dinky t-shirts and several other products that transcended the Taco Bell brand.

BRAND IDENTITY

- Through its national, and later international, growth, Taco Bell became the definitive Mexican fast food, introducing many people to the concept.
- Campaigns such as "Yo Quiero Taco Bell" ("I want Taco Bell") in 1997 broadened the brand's identity to being both edgy and culturally relevant and widened its appeal.
- By the early 2000s Taco Bell particularly focused on a core audience that consisted mainly of teenagers and young men between the ages of 18 and 34 years.

As a fast-food brand, Taco Bell has long been associated with inexpensive but tasty Mexican food. When Taco Bell was founded during the early 1960s, the concept of fast food in the United States was still a relatively new idea, and the national market was dominated by hamburger chains such as McDonald's. Taco Bell helped expand Mexican food from a regional phenomenon into a food that was consumed across the United States and in certain international markets.

For many who had never had Mexican food before, Taco Bell became the definitive Mexican food experience. Taglines such as "The Cure for the Common Meal" in 1986, "Run for the Border" in 1988, and "Think outside the Bun" in 2001 emphasized that Taco Bell was different from other fast-food brands. Taco Bell was, and still is, an exciting, flavorful alternative to every-day burgers and fries.

By the 1980s Taco Bell was especially favored by college students, even though the brand had a somewhat broad age appeal. Campaigns such as "Yo Quiero Taco Bell" ("I want Taco Bell") in 1997 that featured Dinky the talking Chihuahua garnered the interest of many consumers because of the appeal of the dog and his confident attitude. With this campaign, Taco Bell and its food became an edgy, cultural, popular phenomenon—an identity that the brand fully embraced.

By the early 2000s Taco Bell particularly focused on a core audience that consisted mainly of teenagers and young men between the ages of 18 and 34 years. The "Think outside the Bun" campaign especially targeted these young males. To reach this audience, Taco Bell linked its brand with video games, through an Xbox promotion that was tied into the "Think Outside the Bun" campaign, and with sports, by promoting the X Games on ESPN in 1995 and the National Basketball Association's Skills Challenge in 2012.

With changes such as the introduction of the chef-created Cantina Bell menu in 2012, Taco Bell sought to become a more quality food brand and broaden its audience to include older consumers with more expendable incomes and higher expectations. To further embrace this identity growth, Taco Bell introduced its "Live Más" ("Live Better") campaign in 2013. This campaign included one commercial that featured daring senior citizens living a wild nightlife and an another with an attitude-laden, baby-carrying father walking down a city street gaining the attention of many women. This campaign epitomized Taco Bell's still edgy, but growing appeal, underscored by airing a "Live Más" ad during Super Bowl XLVII.

BRAND STRATEGY
- Taco Bell regularly adds new menu items, such as the Crunchwrap Supreme in 2005.
- To appeal to health-conscious consumers, Taco Bell launched the Fresco menu in 2002.
- The First Meal breakfast line debuted in 2012.

When Taco Bell was launched during the early 1960s, the brand's menu included tacos and burritos. Over the years Taco Bell added several new menu items, including nachos, taco salads, Mexican pizza, border bowls, and wraps, to maintain and build consumer interest. Two of its most successful new products were the Crunchwrap Supreme, which debuted in 2005, and the Doritos Locos Taco, in 2012. The latter was the biggest and most successful product launch for Taco Bell. It was a taco with a shell made of Nacho Cheese Doritos. Taco Bell sold 100 million Doritos Locos Tacos in the first 10 weeks that the product was available on the market.

Even though Taco Bell specialized in fast food, it recognized that there was consumer demand for healthier choices, especially in the early 21st century. In 2002 it launched the Fresco menu, which had less fat and fewer calories. In early 2012 Taco Bell introduced the Cantina Bell menu, which was created in a partnership with the chef Lorena Garcia to compete with higher quality quick-service restaurants such as Chipotle. The menu featured new, fresher ingredients in its gourmet bowls and burritos, each for less than US\$5.

Taco Bell also expanded its menu into breakfast offerings in 2012 with its First Meal menu. The menu's breakfast items included breakfast burritos and wraps, hash browns, and an A.M. Crunchwrap. Some of its breakfast items were cobranded with Cinnabon, Tropicana, and Seattle's Best Coffee. First Meal was to be available nationwide by 2014.

Beginning in 1986 Taco Bell moved into international markets, though it expanded slowly because its menu did not always translate well. In 1992 there were only 11 international locations, and in 1997 there were about 200 outlets outside of the United States. By 2000 Yum! Brands RSC focused on developing Taco Bell as its third international brand after Pizza Hut and KFC. New markets were added in 2009 (Spain and Cyprus) and 2010 (India). International locations sometimes meant that the Taco Bell menu had to be adjusted. In India, for example, there were both vegetarian and non-vegetarian items. Burritos came stuffed with potato and paneer, while there was also a line of spicy items labeled "volcano." By 2011 there were 275 Taco Bell locations outside of the United States in countries such as Canada, Chile, Costa Rica, and Guam.

BRAND EQUITY
- Taco Bell was the top Mexican-style fast-food restaurant in the United States for years.
- In 2012 Taco Bell was ranked number 20 in *Entrepreneur*'s "Franchise 500" rankings for brand performance.

- Among fast-food chains in 2012, Taco Bell was number seven in "BrandZ Top 100 Most Valuable Global Brands."

Even though Taco Bell sometimes suffered through periods of slow sales, the brand was the top Mexican-style fast-food restaurant in the United States for decades, controlling a vast majority of the market. In 2012 Taco Bell was ranked number 20 in *Entrepreneur's* "Franchise 500" rankings for brand performance, after not being ranked the previous year. In 2010 it was ranked number 45 and in 2009 it was ranked number 20.

Taco Bell also has a high brand value globally. According to Brand Finance, Taco Bell had a brand value of US$2.4 billion in 2012, a brand rating of A, and was ranked at number 359 on the "Global 500." In 2008 it had an enterprise value of US$21.7 billion. According to "BrandZ Top 100 Most Valuable Global Brands" in 2012, Taco Bell was number seven with a brand value of US$2 billion, which was an increase of 9 percent over 2011. It was behind McDonald's, Starbucks, Subway, KFC, Pizza Hut, and Tim Hortons.

BRAND AWARENESS

- Taco Bell has had high brand awareness for decades.
- Taco Bell capitalized on this awareness to introduce a line of products in supermarkets in the United States.
- As a brand, Taco Bell has high awareness among both children and adults.

As the leading Mexican-style fast-food restaurant in the United States, Taco Bell has had high brand awareness for decades. The company capitalized on this fact by moving into new types of branded products during the early 1990s. After reviewing several marketing studies indicating that Taco Bell had a higher brand awareness among shoppers than other food companies, the company decided to go into the supermarket retail business.

In 1993 Taco Bell introduced 18 new items in 3,000 stores throughout Georgia, Illinois, Indiana, Michigan, and Ohio. These locations were chosen for diversity in consumer demographics, taste preferences, and Taco Bell brand-name awareness. With virtually no advertising, the new products became successful almost immediately and soon Taco Bell became the number-one or number-two ethnic food brand in supermarket Mexican food sections. By 1994 Taco Bell had expanded into over 10,000 supermarkets nationwide. More supermarket items were added in 1996, including Taco Bell home meal kits manufactured by Kraft, which were available through the early 21st century.

Taco Bell has high brand awareness among both kids and adults. In 2011 Taco Bell was ranked number 86 on Smarty Pants' list of "Kids' Top 100 Most Loved Brands" and number 90 on Smarty Pants' list of "Moms' Top 100 Most Loved Brands." These lists rank the brand's popularity and brand awareness in the United States. Also in 2011 Taco Bell was number 32 on Markenlexikon's list of "Top 50 Facebook Global Brands." Despite Taco Bell's limited international presence, this ranking demonstrates that the brand was strong and universally known.

BRAND OUTLOOK

- Taco Bell has a history of responding well to changes in the fast-food industry.
- In 2011 Taco Bell had US$1.8 billion in sales in the United States alone, with 55 million consumers each week.
- In 2012 Taco Bell opened new concept stores ahead of potential plans to upscale its future restaurants with a more contemporary, sleeker design.

Even though the fast-food industry is highly competitive and impacted by obesity and health concerns, Taco Bell has been able to rise to challenges over the years and retain its position as the number-one Mexican-style fast-food chain in the United States, if not the world. In 2011 Taco Bell had US$1.8 billion in sales in the United States alone, with 55 million consumers each week. Like many fast-food brands, Taco Bell has to spend millions on advertising and marketing to address the competition and constantly creates new menu items to appease sometimes fickle consumers. It has responded well to changes in the industry, including increased competition from chains such as Qdoba Mexican Grill and Chipotle Mexican Grill, by introducing items that are high-quality and/or healthy alternatives. Taco Bell is also becoming more successful internationally and as a result is expanding into more foreign markets. In 2012 Taco Bell opened new concept stores ahead of potential plans to upscale its future restaurants with a more contemporary, sleeker design.

FURTHER READING

Baily, Rayna, and Mariko Fujinaka. "Taco Bell Corp." *Encyclopedia of Major Marketing Campaigns.* Ed. Thomas Riggs. Vol. 2. Detroit, MI: Gale, 2007.

Brand Finance. "Taco Bell." *Brandirectory.* Accessed January 30, 2013. http://brandirectory.com/search/?brand=taco+bell.

"BrandZ Top 100 Most Valuable Global Brands 2012." Millward Brown. Accessed January 29, 2013. http://www.millward brown.com/brandz/2012/Documents/2012_BrandZ_Top100_Report.pdf.

Horovitz, Bruce. "Taco Bell + Doritos = Success? Introducing the Doritos Locos Taco, with a Shell Made from Doritos." *USA Today,* February 20, 2012.

Luna, Nancy. "Doritos Taco Launch Is Taco Bell's No. 1." *Orange County Register* (Santa Ana, CA), June 5, 2012.

Mossman, John. "Prototype Taco Bell Shines Light on Chain's Future." *Denver Post*, October 6, 2012.

"Taco Bell." *Fast Food and Junk Food: An Encyclopedia of What We Love to Eat*. Ed. Andrew F. Smith. Vol. 2. Santa Barbara, CA: Greenwood, 2012.

"Taco Bell." RankingTheBrands.com. Accessed January 30, 2013. http://www.rankingthebrands.com/Brand-detail. aspx?brandID=580.

"Taco Bell Corp." *Company Profiles for Students*. Ed. Donna Craft and Amanda Quick. Vol. 2 Detroit, MI: Gale, 1999.

Vlessing, Etan. "Taco Bell Corporation." *International Directory of Company Histories*. Tina Grant. Vol. 74. Detroit, MI: St. James Press, 2006.

TARGET

■

BRAND ORIGINS

- Target's parent company began as a Minneapolis dry goods store that later became the department store Dayton's.
- Target's parent company acquired other department stores and launched Target as a lower-cost retail alternative in 1962.

- As a result of expansion in the 1970s, 1980s, and 1990s, Target became the focus of its parent company, which sold its department stores and changed its corporate name to the Target Corporation.

Despite Target's emphasis on the latest styles, the company's history reaches back over a century. Target's story began in the American Midwest before becoming a national phenomenon. In Minneapolis, just after the turn of the 20th century, George Draper Dayton bought a dry goods store. This store was known as Goodfellow Dry Goods Company in 1902, the Dayton Dry Goods Company in 1903, and, later, just Dayton's, which would become part of the Dayton Company and the Dayton Corporation.

The company's names reflect its expansion and changes through the years. Having bought and created a number of stores, the company underwent a major expansion in 1969, when the Dayton Corporation merged with the J. L. Hudson Company (Hudson's), a chain of upscale department stores in the Detroit area. This move created the Dayton Hudson Corporation, the fourteenth largest retailer in the United States. In the 1990s, the Dayton Hudson Corporation joined forces with another prominent chain of Midwestern department stores, buying Chicago's famed Marshall Field & Company (Marshall Field's).

While Dayton's, Hudson's, and Marshall Field's all offered upscale goods, the Dayton Hudson Corporation also offered customers more inexpensive options. In 1978 the corporation merged with Mervyn's, a line of department stores featuring more moderately priced items. This merger made the Dayton Hudson Corporation the seventh largest general merchandise retailer in the United States. By the 1970s Target, another Dayton Hudson store offering affordable goods, became the most profitable part of the Dayton Hudson retail empire.

Target represented the Dayton Company's first foray into discount retail stores. The first Target store opened in 1962 in Roseville, Minnesota, near Minneapolis and St. Paul. Other stores in Minnesota followed, and the first Target store outside of Minnesota opened in the Denver, Colorado, metropolitan area in 1966. Target's expansion to other areas in the United States followed, helping Dayton Hudson earn US$1 billion in annual sales by the 1970s and US$10 billion by the 1980s. This expansion accelerated at a dizzying pace in the 1990s, as Target opened eleven stores in the Chicago area on a single day in 1993. The stores themselves expanded during the decade, as Target introduced larger Greatland stores and SuperTargets (stores with grocery sections). In 1995 the retailer introduced the Target Guest Card (later known as the REDcard), the first store credit card for a discount retailer. Target began selling its goods online in 1999.

By the end of the 1990s Target was earning more than three-quarters of the Dayton Hudson Corporation's revenues. The parent company increasingly focused on Target in its changing business plans, and in 2000 the Dayton Hudson Corporation became the Target Corporation. In 2001 the corporation changed the names of its Dayton's and Hudson's department stores to Marshall Field's; later in the decade, the Target Corporation sold all of its Marshall Field's and Mervyn's stores.

BRAND ELEMENTS
- Target has used various bull's-eye designs as its brand logo since the first store opened in 1962.
- Since 1994, Target has also used variations of the slogan "Expect More. Pay Less."
- Target considers the phrase "Expect More. Pay Less." to be a brand promise that represents the corporation's values, as well as an advertising slogan.

Since its first store opened in 1962, Target has used different tools to identify itself in a memorable way. From early on, the company's use of striking visual imagery was evident. Its logo was a bull's-eye of alternating red and white bands, with the word Target superimposed over the bull's-eye. The appearance of the logo has varied throughout Target's history. Since 1999 a painted red bull's-eye has appeared on Bullseye, a dog used in the company's advertisements.

The bull's-eye appears on stores' exterior and interior signs, shopping carts, REDcards, the Target webpage, and in broadcast and print advertisements. Given its prominent use of the bull's-eye, it is not surprising that Target Brands, Inc., has registered the design in addition

to the Target name, thus officially linking the store and its symbol.

Target has also used another registered trademark, "Expect More. Pay Less.," since 1994. Target calls this slogan a brand promise and says that the phrase captures the desire to provide quality, affordability, and charitable involvement. Target has used variations of this slogan, such as the phrase "Eat Well. Pay Less." to promote its SuperTarget stores. Target's repeated use of symbols and phrases has helped create an identity for the brand.

BRAND IDENTITY
- The "Expect More. Pay Less." brand promise extends to Target's stores and merchandise.
- Target stores offer a wide range of store and national brands.
- Target's ties to designers have been financially profitable but have sometimes generated mixed public reviews.
- Both Target and its parent company have given millions to local charities and have sponsored local initiatives across the United States.

With its brand promise of "Expect More. Pay Less." Target strives to offer a superior shopping experience while delivering the low prices of a discount merchandiser—without the negative connotations that are sometimes associated with discount retail. These goals have prompted some consumers to pronounce the company's name as "Tar-*zhay*," as though the store were an exclusive, upscale French boutique and not an American discount retailer with thousands of stores.

A superior shopping experience is considered to start with the stores themselves: the Target Corporation has touted the cleanliness and organization of its stores and has experimented with the format of its stores to enhance shoppers' experience.

Target's merchandise—and the promotion of this merchandise—has been a major factor in the company's "Expect More" promise. The corporation is known for its offerings of trendy merchandise and its collaborations with noted designers. The latter include a line of housewares designed by architect Michael Graves and clothing by Isaac Mizrahi and the Italian fashion house Missoni. The 2011 Missoni offering generated mixed results for the company. Heavy promotion heightened anticipation of the Missoni products, but in some cases, this eagerness led to long lines and aggressive behavior among vying customers. Several customers quickly bought up the merchandise, which made the products unavailable to others and caused the Target website to crash; a number of these buyers then resold their Missoni goods on the Internet at a significant markup. While the Missoni launch was a financial success for the Target brand, the surrounding controversy created a public relations problem for a company accustomed to positive feedback.

In 2012 Target continued to establish ties with other businesses by launching The Shops at Target, an offering of products from boutiques across the United States. In addition to boutique and well-known national brands, Target also offers a number of store brands, which include the Merona and Cherokee clothing lines, Market Pantry and Archer Farms foods, and Up & Up, a brand representing a wide range of personal and household products.

Besides its retailing, Target has made commitments to charities and local endeavors. The Daytons and their companies have donated millions to charities through the years. The Target Corporation has continued this trend, giving more than US$3 million weekly to local charities and sponsoring local initiatives across the United States.

BRAND STRATEGY

- Store renovations are an important part of Target's brand strategy. Target has renovated stores in response to its competitors' strategies and the economic recession that began in 2008.
- A loyalty program for its credit card holders and new promotional efforts helped Target overcome the economic problems of 2008 and 2009.
- Target has experimented with different retail concepts, including a dollar section known as "See. Spot. Save."
- Target has used traditional advertising outlets—commercial, print, and the Internet—and nontraditional promotions, such as sponsorship of an Indy car team and a scientific expedition, to advance its brand.
- Charitable involvement in local communities is an important means of maintaining the Target brand's profile.

The ongoing renovation of its stores reflects the Target Corporation's commitment to design, including store design, as well as its desire to remain fresh, new, and trendy. Renovation has also been a way for the brand to differentiate itself from competitors. In 2004, for example, the corporation renovated stores to focus on women's fashion, a move that paralleled the renewed emphasis on fashion among competitors like Walmart.

Also in 2004 Target rolled out its dollar section, an area of the store initially called the "1 Spot" that eventually became known as "See. Spot. Save." This section, where all prices are under US$5, is reminiscent of dollar stores in offering a wide range of inexpensive products.

Economic necessity has also prompted the company to renovate. In 2008 and 2009 a global recession caused Target's profits to decline, drove shoppers to competitors like Walmart, and prevented Target from opening large numbers of new stores. Instead, the company renovated

a number of stores, redesigning certain departments and focusing on offering a greater variety of food items. Sales rose in 2010, prompted in part by the introduction of Target's loyalty program, which offered REDcard customers a cash return worth 5 percent of the value of their purchases. New advertising efforts promoting Target's low prices also helped to increase the brand's profitability.

Target reaches consumers through television, print, and online advertisements. Some of the company's more unusual promotions have included sponsoring an Indy car team for Chip Ganassi Racing and a 1989 expedition in Antarctica. The corporation's charitable and community efforts have also kept its name before the public, particularly as a result of its contributions to schools and other local entities.

BRAND EQUITY

- Target is the second-largest discount retailer and the second-largest general merchandiser in the United States.
- Target's major competitor in discount and general retailing is Walmart. Among the 500 most valuable brands, Brand Finance ranked Wal-Mart Stores, Inc., as the fifth most valuable brand in 2012 and Target as the 51st.
- Target placed 159th in *Forbes* magazine's list of the 2,000 biggest public companies in the world.
- Target became an international retailer in 2013, when it opened its first stores in Canada.

In 2011 Target ranked as the second-largest discount retailer in the United States after Wal-Mart Stores, Inc. The Target Corporation ranked 38th in the 2012 *Fortune 500* list of largest corporations, in which the company was described as the second-largest general merchandiser, ranking just behind Wal-Mart Stores, Inc., and ahead of Sears Holdings, the parent company of Sears stores and Kmart stores. *Brand Finance's* "Global 500 2012" ranked Target 51st among the top 500 global brands, with a brand value of about US$15.3 billion, down from its brand value in 2001 of about US$16 billion. Major competitor Walmart (of Wal-Mart, Stores, Inc.) ranked fifth on *Brand Finance's* list with a brand value of around US$38.3 billion in 2012. Another competitor, Sears, placed 331st on the same list, with a 2012 brand value of around US$3.3 billion. In another ranking, Target placed 159th on the "Forbes 2000," *Forbes* magazine's list of the 2,000 largest public companies in the world. Wal-Mart Stores, Inc., was 16th on this list and Sears, 823rd.

Target's expansion into Canada in 2013 gave the corporation its first international locations, establishing its presence in a country where Sears stores have been operating since the early 1950s and Walmart stores, since the mid-1990s. Interestingly, Target Australia operates a chain of stores featuring a red bull's-eye logo, a wide range of merchandise, and connections to designers, but it is a separate company.

BRAND AWARENESS

- Target's continuous use of its bull's-eye logo has made it a widely recognized symbol of the brand.
- Target enjoys a better reputation among consumers than many of its rivals, including Walmart and Sears.
- Several business publications have ranked Target among the top retail brands and top discount retailers, citing its more affordable prices and its relationships with designers.
- Target's familiarity has made it a pop culture staple; its stores have provided settings for movies and television programs.

Since the first Target store opened in 1962, the company's trademarked logo has changed very little. Writing in *Strictly Business* magazine, Anne M. Obarski noted that the Target Corporation's consistent use of the bull's-eye has made the symbol synonymous with the company, so recognizable that even a three-year-old "would know exactly what [it] meant."

The Target brand enjoys wide recognition and an excellent reputation among consumers, despite incidents like the Missoni launch in 2011. Target placed 22nd in "America's Most Reputable Companies," a 2012 ranking of large American corporations based on consumer appraisals. Sears ranked 83rd and Walmart ranked 103rd on the list, which was compiled by *Forbes* magazine and the Reputation Institute.

Target ranked second (after Walmart) on *Interbrand's* 2012 list of top retail brands. According to *Interbrand*, this ranking reflected Target's status "as the preferred discount mass merchant of a loyal, satisfied base of affluent shoppers under age 45, while fine-tuning its owned brands and partnering with high fashion designers." As this assessment suggests, Target has successfully maintained its association in consumers' minds with both discount pricing and designer goods.

The popular company has also become a part of popular culture. Much of the 1991 movie *Career Opportunities* is set inside a Target store, while actress Kristen Wiig played the character of the Target Lady on the television series *Saturday Night Live*.

BRAND OUTLOOK

- In 2012 Target began to open more stores, including CityTargets, smaller Targets with merchandise selected for urban shoppers.

- Target's international and multicultural expansion includes the opening of Canadian Target stores, hiring of Indian workers, and creation of advertisements in Spanish.
- The Here for Good plan provides detailed information about Target's corporate responsibility goals; these aims include a drive to raise US$1 billion for education by 2015.

As the economy slowly began to recover from the 2000s recession, Target continued to renovate stores and committed to opening more new stores. In 2012 company began opening stores called CityTargets in urban areas across the United States. As Target has used its renovations to focus on particular aspects of the shopping experience, the company intends to focus on urban life in CityTarget stores, which will be smaller and feature merchandise specially selected for city shoppers.

Target has also expanded internationally. In the year prior to the opening of its Canadian stores in 2013, Target opened a temporary pop-up store in Toronto, offering refreshments and activities as part of its Bull's-eye Beach promotion at various beaches across Canada. The company has also expanded its global reach by hiring employees in India to provide support for its retail stores. In addition, the Target Corporation has made efforts to reach new markets, creating television commercials aimed specifically at Spanish speakers. It also communicates with customers using electronic media, including the social networks Facebook and Twitter, as well as mobile applications.

The Target Corporation also continues to pursue its corporate responsibility goals. Its *2011 Annual Report* discusses Here for Good, a plan aimed at boosting the company's charitable contributions, volunteerism, safety commitments, and environmental efforts. One goal is to raise US$1 billion for education by 2015.

FURTHER READING

"Best Retail Brands 2012." Interbrand. Accessed September 3, 2012. http://www.interbrand.com/en/BestRetailBrands/2012-Best-Retail-Brands.aspx.

Bickers, James. "Missoni for Target Line Sells out, Raises Questions." RetailCustomerExperience.com, September 15, 2011. Accessed September 1, 2012. http://www.retailcustomerexperience.com/article/184615/Missoni-for-Target-line-sells-out-raises-questions.

Bowers, Katherine. "Target's Latest Look: New Lifestyle Focus Boosts Women's Wear." *WWD*, March 31, 2004. Accessed August 31, 2012. http://www.wwd.com/fashion-news/fashion-features/target-8217-s-latest-look-new-lifestyle-focus-boosts-women-8217-s-wear-600437.

Brand Finance. "Global 500 2012." *Brandirectory*. Accessed September 3, 2012. http://brandirectory.com/league_tables/table/global-500-2012.

DeCarlo, Scott, ed. "The World's Biggest Public Companies." *Forbes*, April 18, 2012. Accessed September 3, 2012. http://www.forbes.com/global2000.

Hamstra, Mark. "Target Food Performing Well in Remodeled Stores." *Supermarket News*, May 23, 2011.

Laird, Kristin. "Target Teases Toronto with Pop-up Store." *Marketing*, February 23, 2012. Accessed September 1, 2012. http://www.marketingmag.ca/news/marketer-news/target-teases-toronto-with-pop-up-store-47005.

Obarski, Anne M. "Martha, Target and You—How to Build Brand Recognition." *Strictly Business*. Accessed September 3, 2012. http://www.sbmag.org/AnnMarthaTargetAndYou.html.

Smith, Jacquelyn. "America's Most Reputable Companies." *Forbes*, April 4, 2012.

"Target Celebrates the End of Summer with 'Target Bullseye Beaches' across Canada." Canada Newswire, August 25, 2012.

"Target Corporation." *International Directory of Company Histories*. Ed. Thomas Derdak. Vol. 122. New York: St. James, 2011.

Target Corporation. "Here for Good." Accessed September 4, 2012. http://hereforgood.target.com/?ref=sr_shorturl_hereforgood.

———. "Our History." Accessed August 31, 2012. http://sites.target.com/site/en/company/page.jsp?contentId=WCMP04-031697.

———. "2011 Annual Report." Accessed September 3, 2012. http://sites.target.com/site/en/company/page.jsp?contentId=WCMP04-061641.

Toth, Wendy. "Target Breaks from Dollar Concept." *Supermarket News*, August 14, 2006.

Zmuda, Natalie. "Why the Bad Economy Has Been Good for Target." *Advertising Age*, October 4, 2010.

TATA

AT A GLANCE

Brand Synopsis: The Tata corporate brand supports the wide-ranging business interests of the Tata Group of Companies, India's largest conglomerate and an enterprise known for its competence and ethical conduct.

Parent Company: Tata Group of Companies
Bombay House
Mumbai
India
http://www.tata.com

Sector: Industrials

Industry Group: Capital Goods

Performance: *Revenues*—US$100 billion (2011).

Principal Competitors: Wipro Limited; RPG Enterprises, Inc.; Essar Group

BRAND ORIGINS

- The Tata Group of Companies is India's largest conglomerate.
- Tata Group was founded in 1868 by Jamsetji Nusserwanji Tata.
- A reorganization of the company in 1998 allowed for the creation of a Tata corporate brand.

Tata is the corporate brand of the Tata Group of Companies. India's largest industrial conglomerate, Tata includes more than 100 operating companies in seven business groups: communications and information technology, engineering, materials, services, energy, consumer products, and chemicals. Some of the more significant individual companies are Tata Chemicals, Tata Communications, Tata Global Beverages, Tata Motors, Tata Power, and Indian Hotels.

The man who provided the company with its name was founder Jamsetji Nusserwanji Tata. He was the son of a successful merchant in Bombay (now Mumbai) and worked for his father until the age of 29, when in 1868 he struck out on his own and started a trading company, Tata and Sons. Soon he opened a cotton mill, laying the foundation for Central India Spinning, Weaving and Manufacturing Company, and later built a luxury hotel, the Taj Mahal Hotel in Bombay. Tata harbored greater aspirations, however, and they were realized by members of the Tata family that followed him after his death in 1904. Tata Steel was founded in 1907 and Tata Power in 1910. Jamsetji Tata also wished to open a major science and engineering research institute in India. This dream was realized in 1911 when the Indian Institute of Science in Bangalore first opened its doors to students.

While the dreams of the founder may have been fulfilled, the ambitions of the Tata family were not sated. It became involved in consumer goods in 1917 and aviation and chemicals during the 1930s. Following World War II, the Tata Group expanded into technology, cosmetics, marketing, engineering, and manufacturing. During the 1960s the group became involved in tea production, software services, and publishing. Tata Economic Consultancy Services was established in 1970. A joint venture, Titan Industries, began manufacturing watches in 1984.

In 1991 Ratan Tata, the 54-year-old adoptive great-grandson of Jamsetji Tata, was named chairman of the Tata Group after 10 years at the helm of Tata Industries. He took charge of a balkanized company. In many cases, managers ran individual subsidiaries as personal fiefdoms. There was no centralized control, nor was there any consistent use of the Tata name. Branding was left to the individual companies. For Ratan Tata, who trained as an architect in the United States and graduated from Harvard Business School, this was an unacceptable arrangement. After several years of power struggles, he established a new ownership structure in 1998 that allowed for the creation of a Tata corporate brand.

BRAND ELEMENTS

- More consistent use of the Tata family name has made it an important brand element.
- The stylized *T* of the Tata logo creates an umbrella shape that reflects its status as a holding company.
- The Tata tagline "Leadership with trust" is sometimes combined with the logo.
- Philanthropic programs are a key brand element of Tata.
- The sponsorship of sporting events and music concerts help to create a dynamic and youthful image for the Tata brand.

Unlike many brands, Tata is not a name crafted to convey any particular meaning. It is the family name of the company founder, yet it remains an important brand element because it has developed an esteemed reputation over the past century, especially in India. Moreover, the breadth of Tata's product and service offerings increases the general awareness of the name. Since Tata Group adopted a corporate branding strategy, the Tata name has been used more consistently, adding to its significance.

The Tata name is also an important component of the brand's logo. The uppercase rendering of *TATA* eliminates the crossbars in the letter *A*s. Above the brand name is a stylized white *T* divided into two parts and placed within a blue oval. The same shade is used to render the brand name. Because of the way the *T* is split within the oval, a picture of an umbrella is created. Given that this is a logo for a holding company, a so-called umbrella company, the image is particularly apt.

In some cases the Tata logo is combined with a tagline: "Leadership with trust." It is an important element because it reflects the core of the brand's identity. A previous tagline, "Improving the quality of life," served a similar purpose. Since the founding of Tata and Sons in the mid-19th century, philanthropy has been an important element of the Tata brand. Well before the group's corporate branding approach, the Tata family had developed a reputation for good works. Thus, the associations that the group keeps are a significant key element. Community development efforts include health, education, and art programs. To project an image of currency with the brand, the group also sponsors sporting events and music concerts.

BRAND IDENTITY

- Tata portrays itself as a trustworthy and competent company that places ethics above profit.
- A reputation for ethics preceded Tata's corporate branding efforts.
- Chairman Ratan Tata in many ways served as the embodiment of Tata's brand identity.

Because the Tata corporate brand is applied to companies involved in a wide variety of industries doing business in many countries, its identity may vary depending on the context. Nevertheless, there is a core Tata identity the company seeks to present to the world. In essence, Tata portrays itself as a trustworthy and candid yet highly effective and technically proficient company that places ethics above profit.

Much of Tata's brand identity is personality driven, reflective of both the founder, Jamsetji Tata, and his great-grandson, Ratan Tata. The elder Tata espoused, in his own words, "a patchwork philanthropy which clothes the ragged, feeds the poor, and heals the sick." Among his endeavors, he began JN Tata Endowment Scheme for higher education in 1892 to fund the schooling of impoverished but talented students. It was this spirit that was embraced by the generations of the Tata family to follow as well as the companies the family owned and operated.

When the Tata Group pursued a corporate branding strategy at the behest of Ratan Tata, the brand's identity very much mirrored the group's chairman who carried on the spirit of his great-grandfather. Both privately and publicly, he opposed corruption in India. According to *The Economist* in a 2012 profile, Ratan Tata kept a "polite distance" from India's political class: "He has long attacked what he calls 'vested interests'—code for crony capitalism, in which firms make profits by buying favours from officials and politicians." Ratan Tata was also ahead of his time in advocating for globalization, laying the groundwork for the emergence of the Indian economy in the new millennium. A vast enterprise, Tata Group has not been immune from controversy, but the personal rectitude of Ratan Tata, the public face of the group, and the actions he has taken in running the group have played an important role in grounding Tata's brand identity.

The good works supported by the Tata Group and its generosity toward its employees further reflect the brand. The importance of advertising should not be overlooked. Two primary taglines—"Improving the quality of life" and "Leadership with trust"—state and support the core of Tata's brand identity.

BRAND STRATEGY

- Tata's corporate brand was introduced in 1999.
- Tata's global branding approach was accompanied by a series of international acquisitions.
- Tata umbrella companies include "Tata" in their names, whereas acquisitions with strong name recognition include the corporate tagline "A Tata Enterprise."

Before the 1990s the Tata Group had few interests outside of India, and the brand identity of Tata was very much tied to Indian culture and history. Chairman Ratan Tata was eager to expand the group internationally and believed that growth could accelerate if there was more central control over the individual companies and a corporate brand identity that was more global in approach. After several years of modifying the ownership structure to give him greater authority, Ratan Tata was able in 1998 to begin the development of a corporate brand with consistent rules on its use.

One of the first steps taken in creating a global Tata brand was the design of a unified mark. The Tata "T" logo was designed by Wolf Ollins, an international brand consultancy. AC Nielsen was also hired to survey the perception of the Tata brand before it was rolled out in 1999. In 2000 an advertising campaign was launched to promote the brand making use of the logo's graphic design. Advertising featured the "T" embedded in various images, such as a chandelier at the Taj Hotel, a tea garden, a car wheel, a twin waterfall. Each of the backgrounds also represented one of Tata's businesses. The tagline "Improving the quality of life" helped to establish a core principle of the brand. Next, Tata began sponsoring sporting events and musical concerts, and it worked with the India Today Conclave to organize "knowledge events." These associations helped to portray the Tata brand as energetic, youthful, and involved.

Tata Group fleshed out its brand identity with another advertising campaign in 2002. It featured examples of how Tata companies used information and technology to improve the lives of ordinary people. A 2004 campaign promoted Tata's deep roots (and by implication its trustworthiness) by commemorating the 100th anniversary of the death of Jamsetji Tata. The following year, an advertising campaign focused on the work Tata companies do in support of the communities in which they work, emphasizing its commitment to ethics over profits.

While Tata's global brand was being nurtured, the group was expanding internationally through a series of acquisitions and joint ventures. The first major addition took place in 2000 with the acquisition of London-based Tetley Tea in 2000. The following year, Tata Group established Tata-AIG in a partnership with American International Group. South Korea's Daewoo Motors was acquired in 2004. The steelmaker Corus followed in 2007, Jaguar Land Rover was acquired in 2008, and a number of small acquisitions also took place in Europe and North America.

As practiced, Tata Group's brand strategy allows for some flexibility. There are essentially two ways that the corporate brand is applied. In many cases it serves as an umbrella brand, directly connected to a group company. Examples include Tata Chemicals, Tata Steel, and Tata Motors. A half-umbrella approach is taken with the remaining companies, which do not include "Tata" in the company name but employ a tagline for the corporate brand: "A Tata Enterprise." Two types of companies fall into the half-umbrella category: those with strong brands, such as Indian Hotels, that could lose value through a name change, and younger companies or riskier ventures, the uncertain performance of which might have an adverse impact on the corporate brand. For acquisitions, the company only rebrands if the change will clearly add value. There is also a great deal of latitude given to the branding of individual products and services. In this way for example, Tata Tea, Tetley Tea, and Good Earth Tea coexisted and prospered within the Tata Global Beverages subsidiary.

BRAND EQUITY

- The importance of Tata's brand varies between industries and countries.
- Tata is the most valuable Indian brand according to independent brand consultancies.
- According to Brand Finance, Tata's brand value at the end of 2011 was US$16.3 billion.
- Tata was number 45 on the Brand Finance "Global 500" list of the world's most valuable brands in 2012.
- In 2012 Tata became the first Indian brand to rank in the top 50 in Brand Finance's "Global 500."

The importance of the Tata brand is very much dependent on the industry as well as the country in which the product or service is sold. Because of its long tradition in India and the scope of its operations in that country, the Tata brand carries far greater weight in its home country than in the United States. Particular group companies like Tata Steel or consumer products like Tetley Tea, however, carry considerable brand equity in the United States. The same could be said for Tata's brand equity around the world.

The attention paid to the development of a corporate brand, nevertheless, paid dividends for Tata. While it is hard to determine a brand's true equity (generally defined as the difference in price between a branded product and a generic equivalent) some brand consultancies and business publications have developed methodologies to assign a monetary value to a brand that help to gauge the importance of a brand to its parent company. The Tata corporate brand has steadily risen in value since the start of the millennium. According to Brand Finance, the value of the Tata brand was US$7.4 billion at the end of 2007. As a result, Tata was ranked number 51 on the Brand Finance "Global 500" list of the world's most valuable brands in 2008. Tata's brand value increased to US$16.3 billion at the close of 2011, a performance that warranted a number 45 listing on the 2012 "Global 500." It was the first time that an Indian brand had ranked in the top 50 of the "Global 500." The European Brand Institute also ranked Tata as the 45th most valuable brand in its 2012 "Top 100 Brand Corporations Worldwide" list.

BRAND AWARENESS

- Tata enjoys high brand awareness in India.
- Operations in more than 80 countries across six continents create general awareness of the Tata corporate brand.
- Tata's brand awareness is dependent on industry and location.

Awareness of the Tata brand is not as great as the scope and longevity of the Tata Group might warrant. Tata as a corporate global brand is extremely young. As a result, brand awareness is spotty. In India the brand enjoys high awareness because so many products and services offered by Tata Group companies have a daily impact on people's lives. In addition, the Tata family has been well known in the country for many years. In some respects the Tata family is the Tata brand, and individual family members, in particular the founder and Ratan Tata, are held in high esteem.

The Tata brand enjoys some level of brand awareness internationally because of the Tata Group's many holdings. The group maintains operations in more than 80 countries on six continents, encompassing seven business sectors. About 30 of those companies are publicly traded. By sheer scale alone, Tata makes its name known around the world. How well it is known is again a matter of industry and location. As an example, the Tata Sky direct-to-home satellite television service in India enjoyed 38 percent top-of-mind brand awareness in a study conducted in 2011. The market leader, Dish TV, which had 14 million subscribers to Tata Sky's 10 million subscribers, had a brand awareness of 24 percent. It was a significant difference between the two services, attributed in large part to the recognition of the Tata name among Indian consumers. In its home market, at least, the Tata corporate brand is well known and influential.

BRAND OUTLOOK

- As a young corporate brand, Tata should have room for future growth.
- Individual business sectors and countries offer opportunities for targeted growth of the Tata brand.
- The retirement of Chairman Ratan Tata in December 2012 brings a degree of uncertainty to the future of the Tata corporate brand.

The Tata corporate brand has enjoyed steady growth since a shift in strategy at the turn of the millennium, as demonstrated by the increasing valuation of the brand by independent entities that now rank it among the world's 50 most valuable brands. There is reason to believe that considerable room remains to grow the brand further. The group is involved in seven different business sectors, each one offering opportunities to expand the Tata brand. Further, opportunities exist to expand the brand in major markets such as the United States, where there is little awareness of the Tata brand among general consumers.

The future of the Tata brand is not without challenge, however. As 2012 came to an end, Ratan Tata stepped down as the chairman of Tata Group. He had become the face of the brand, and his departure might have an adverse impact on the Tata Group and the Tata corporate brand. In his more than 20 years at the helm, he created an executive team that shared his values, which in turn informed the Tata brand. There was every reason to believe that the corporate culture he left behind would be strong enough to carry on the Tata brand identity that he took pains to nurture. Whether Ratan Tata's successors would live up to the brand he left them was a question yet to be answered.

FURTHER READING

Babu, Santhosh. "Understanding Brand Ratan Tata." Exchange4media.com, December 29, 2012. Accessed February 27, 2013. http://www.exchange4media.com/49248_understanding-brand-ratan-tata.html.

Brand Finance. "Global 500 2012." *Brandirectory*. Accessed February 15, 2013. http://brandirectory.com/league_tables/table/global-500-2012.

"Dish TV, Tata Sky Show Brand Power." *Hindustan Times*, November 4, 2012.

"Ratan Tata's Legacy; Capitalism in India." *Economist*, December 2012.

Sharma, Sukalp. "Worth Its Salt: Tata among Top 50 Global Brands." *Financial Express*, March 22, 2011.

"Tata Steel Ltd." *International Directory of Company Histories*. Ed. Derek Jacques and Paula Kepos. Vol. 109. Detroit, MI: St. James Press, 2010.

Vijayraghavan, Kala. "How Tatas Plan to Build Consumer Trust Abroad." *Economic Times*, October 28, 2010.

Witzel, Morgen. "Case Study: Tata." *Financial Times*, December 29, 2010.

TESCO

—◾—

AT A GLANCE

◆

Brand Synopsis: The self-effacing slogan "Every little helps" belies the fact that the Tesco brand represents the United Kingdom' largest supermarket chain.

Parent Company: Tesco PLC
New Tesco House, Delamare Road
Cheshunt, Hertfordshire EN8 9SL
United Kingdom
http://www.tesco.co.uk

Sector: Food & Staples

Industry Group: Food & Staples Retailing

Performance: *Sales*—£47.4 billion (US$61.2 billion) in the United Kingdom; £11.4 billion (US$14.7 billion) in Europe; £638 million (US$823.9 million) in the United States (2011).

Principal Competitors: Asda Stores Ltd; Sainsbury's Supermarket's Ltd; Waitrose; Marks and Spencer PLC

BRAND ORIGINS

- John Edwards Cohen founded Tesco Stores Limited in 1932.
- The first Tesco self-service store opened its doors in 1947.
- Ian McLaurin began a modernization project in 1977 by upgrading existing stores, opening more superstore formats, and entering the chain market.

- In the 1990s Tesco began expanding outside Great Britain by buying supermarket chains in France, Hungary, Poland, and Scotland.
- In 1997 Tesco gained leading market share positions in both the Republic of Ireland and Northern Ireland.

In 1919 John Edwards Cohen, a previous owner of a small grocery stall, began a career as a market trader. After experiencing success outside of London's East End, he branched into wholesaling. In 1932 Cohen founded Tesco Stores Limited. The name originated from the initials of the tea merchant T.E. Stockwell and the first letters of Cohen's surname. In 1935 Cohen was invited by several American suppliers to learn the system of the American self-service supermarket, and Cohen brought this system back to the United Kingdom after World War II.

The company grew over the next decade, and the first Tesco self-service store opened its doors in 1947. Tesco stores continued to spread across the United Kingdom throughout the 1950s, eventually carrying fresh goods as well as dry in its supermarket in Maldon, Essex, in 1956.

In 1960 Tesco established a department in its larger stores called Home'n'Wear, carrying high margin nonfood items including household appliances and clothing. During this decade Tesco also opened its first 40,000 square foot superstore in Crawley, Sussex, which carried a wide selection of food and nonfood items. By 1976 Tesco owned nearly 900 supermarkets and superstores in the United Kingdom. Unfortunately, the company also had slim margins due to the changing market, which now valued merchandise over quantity.

The job of bringing Tesco up to speed with demand fell to Ian McLaurin in 1973. In 1977 Tesco cut prices in an attempt to increase sales, which incited a price war with J. Sainsbury PLC, Tesco's major rival. Tesco's modernization strategy also involved upgrading existing stores, opening more superstore formats, and entering the chain market. To support the new stores and its new high-quality image, Tesco introduced private-label product lines, computerized its distribution system, and opened its own centralized inventory warehouses. In 1981 food sales were settling into a slump, prompting Tesco's Checkout '82, which cut prices on 1,500 food items, once again setting off a price battle with J. Sainsbury.

In 1983 the company name was changed to Tesco PLC, and a year later it joined forces with Marks & Spencer to develop shopping centers in the United Kingdom, which included a 65,000 square foot Tesco superstore at Brookfield Center, Cheshunt. In 1985 Tesco launched a massive capital spending program for store and warehouse expansion. The investment in a sophisticated distribution system allowed Tesco to incorporate its acquisition of the 40 store Hillards PLC chain, giving the brand visibility in Yorkshire. In the late 1980s the company also improved service to its stores by instituting a six-warehouse distribution system.

In the 1990s Tesco began its expansion outside Great Britain by paying £175 million (US$226 million) to purchase Catteau S.A., a grocery chain in northern France. Catteau struggled against other large chains and was eventually sold back to Promodes, but other expansion moves, such as the Scottish chain William Low in 1994, the Hungarian chain Global in the same year, and the Polish chain Savia in 1995, were more successful. In 1996 the brand bought 17 Kmart stores in the Czech Republic and Slovakia, which it converted to the Tesco name. The following year Tesco acquired Irish food retailing businesses of Associated British Food PLC, gaining leading market share positions in both the Republic of Ireland and Northern Ireland.

BRAND ELEMENTS

- Tesco's characteristic brand slogan is "Every Little Helps."
- The Tesco logo text was modernized and introduced in 1996.
- In 2011 Tesco introduced the "Just Discovered" brand logo.

Tesco's tagline "Every little helps" originated in a series of ads in the 1980s, which boosted Tesco's brand awareness to 89 percent. The Tesco logo text in its current form (a red font with reflections underneath) was introduced in 1996, after years of featuring a typewriter text that had been in use since the 1970s, a decision which was part of the brand's desire to bring its image out of the past. The

brand has consistently used a red and blue color scheme for its branding images, suggesting the basic colors of the British flag (red connotes prosperity and happiness, while blue represents excellence and trustworthiness).

In 2011 Tesco introduced the "Just Discovered" brand logo, which was designed to be placed on new Tesco products and product lines. The Tesco's Finest and Everyday Value brands are the two largest food brands in the U.K., with more than £1 billion (US$1.3 billion) in sales per year.

BRAND IDENTITY

- Tesco aims to be the most highly valued brand in the United Kingdom.
- The Tesco brand wishes to be seen as innovative and adaptable.
- Tesco's increased focus is on customer loyalty.

Tesco is the United Kingdom's leading supermarket group, controlling about 30 percent of all supermarket sales and two-thirds of its revenue generated inside the country, which accounts for 70 percent of the brand's trading profit. However, a lack of innovation in Tesco's home market has, in recent years, given its competitors the chance to match its sales. To address the slipping sales, owners of the brand began investing in the refurbishment of Tesco's core stores, a move which was not seen as moving upmarket but rather providing the brand's already existent customer base with effective solutions to customer needs and expectations.

Tesco aims to be the most highly valued brand in the United Kingdom, not only by focusing on growth, both in the U.K. and internationally, but also by cultivating loyalty among customers. Tesco planned to accomplish its goals by adding new stores, revamping existing stores, and offering Tesco-branded products. With its stores and products widely available, it hoped to maintain top-of-mind awareness.

BRAND STRATEGY

- Tesco's growth strategy involves focus on the growth of efficient retail services in stores and online.
- Tesco aims to capitalize on the online shopping market through programs like the Click & Collect loyalty/online buying platform.
- The Tesco Direct website, which is configured for mobile devices, offers shoppers access to Tesco's food products and Tesco's other websites.

To address the losses of the U.K. operations, Tesco has formulated a specific plan for its home businesses: (1) improvement of service and staff, including investment in recruitment, training, and new equipment, (2) improvement of Tesco stores and store development, (3) prioritizing price, value and brand marketing, (4) offering a wide range of Tesco brand products, and making these products store and format specific, and (5) promoting online services such as Click & Collect.

In 1995 a new series of advertisements featuring British actress Prunella Scales called the "Dotty" campaign allowed Tesco to promote their brand values and Clubcard. The Tesco Clubcard was part of the first such loyalty program in British retail. In 1997 Tesco introduced the first of its financial services, including the Tesco Visa Card, Tesco savings accounts, Tesco Travel Money and Insurance, and Clubcard Plus (a combination loyalty car and savings account).

In 1992 the brand introduced the Tesco Metro stores, a smaller shopping outlet designed specifically for urban areas, to compete with Marks and Spencer. Other formats, including Extra, Superstore, Express, One Stop, Tesco Homeplus, and Dobbies, were likewise introduced in years to come, differentiating between outlet size and the range of products carried. In 1994 the brand diversified into the fuel market, and the first Tesco Express gasoline stations, combination filling and convenience stores, were opened in London.

Tesco's controlled brand products account for a large part of Tesco's markets. In 2012 Tesco expanded their product offering, introducing Venture Brands in the U.K. and Europe (including Chokablok chocolate and Carousel children's toys). Tesco store formats include Extra, Superstore, Metro, and Express, but in 2012 Tesco put particular energy into improving the larger format stores and introducing online shopping services, which the brand owners recognized as a necessary component in pleasing customers. The Click & Collect program (the option of ordering a product online and picking it up in-store) was a convenient way for customers to shop and collect loyalty points. Configured for cellular devices, the Tesco Direct website offers shoppers access to Tesco's food products and, soon, Tesco's other U.K. Clothing and Entertainment websites. In 2011 Tesco acquired BzzAgent, a business that combines word-of-mouth-marketing with commercial application of social media to promote customer advocacy. Tesco staff also use Yammer (a social network for businesses) to discuss business practices and successes.

BRAND EQUITY

- In 2012 Tesco was named top U.K. brand by Interbrand.
- In 2012 Tesco reported group sales of £72 billion (US$93 billion) and final dividends of 10.13 percent per share.
- Tesco's international businesses recorded sales in Europe growing by 8 percent, in Asia by over 10 percent, and in the United States by 27 percent.

In 2011 Tesco's brand rating according to YouGov's Brand Index (which includes measures such as reputation, recommendation, value, quality, and satisfaction) had fallen 12 points over the course of the year; nevertheless, by 2012 Tesco was named Interbrand's top U.K. brand ahead of Marks & Spencer, Boots, and Asda.

In 2012 Tesco reported group sales of £72 billion (US$93 billion) and a group trading increase of 1.3 percent from the previous year. Group capital expenditure was £3.8 billion (US$4.9 billion) and group return of 13.3 percent. The brand's final dividends were 10.13 percent per share, an increase of 2.1 percent on the previous year. Tesco's trading profit in the United Kingdom was down overall in 2012 by 1 percent. Tesco's international businesses performed favorably, with sales in Europe growing by 8 percent, in Asia by over 10 percent, and in the United States by 27 percent.

BRAND AWARENESS

- In 1979 Terry Leahy assumed the position of CEO of Tesco, beginning Tesco's rise to prominence in the U.K. food market.
- Tesco's market research tracks consumer buying habits and resulted in services such as the Tesco loyalty card.
- In 2007 Tesco opened its first supermarket chain in the United States, called Fresh'n'Easy, which boasted healthy food products at affordable prices.

In 1979 Terry Leahy assumed the position of CEO of Tesco, and it was his involvement in the brand that aided in Tesco's rise to prominence in the U.K. food market. Leahy's strategic vision led the supermarket chain to other allied markets such as consumer financial services. This willingness to innovate succeeded in earning Tesco sales in nonfood items of £10.4 billion (US$13.4 billion) in 2011, which was nearly a quarter of the parent brand's revenue. (Tesco's nonfood products and services are currently growing at roughly twice the rate of its food products.) Tesco has additionally expanded into housing with the Tesco Property Market, lauded as "A one-stop online property shop."

One of Tesco's most effective methods of brand promotion is acting on in-depth customer research, which they perform more than any of their competitors in the sector. Tesco's market research tracks consumer buying habits and resulted in services such as the Tesco loyalty card, which in 2011 was the largest loyalty scheme in the United Kingdom with an estimated 13 million members. These cards communicate still more information to the brand owners about logistics and products lines. Tesco also places considerable importance on brand positioning, expanding its customer base by increased efforts to reach a range of income brackets. To this end, they released a luxury food product line called "Tesco Finest" and a budget version titled "Tesco Value."

The growth of the brand's awareness in the United States proved to be more of a struggle than in the United Kingdom. In 2007 Tesco opened its first supermarket chain in the United States, called Fresh'n'Easy, which boasted healthy food products at affordable prices (suggested by the chain's green color scheme and leaf-themed logo). The initial stores were located along the West Coast where the healthy products line was expected to garner more business, however, the Fresh'n'Easy enfranchisement only expects to break even by 2013.

Perhaps the biggest threat to Tesco's favorable brand recognition was a documentary produced by the BBC called "Whistleblower," which took cameras behind Tesco counters and revealed serious breaches of hygiene and food safety. The documentary was viewed by 4.5 million people, but Tesco's swift damage control resulted in minimal damage. The Tesco trading director at the time immediately set up a video link and fielded concerns within 48 hours of the documentary's broadcast, resulting in a strengthened connection with its customer base. Internal investigations were also launched, employees were retrained, and the overall effect on Tesco's reputation was contained.

BRAND OUTLOOK

- In 2011 Tesco's sales in the United Kingdom consisted of £47.4 billion (US$61.2 billion), trading profit of £2.5 billion (US$3.2 billion), and 14.8 percent dividends per market share.
- In 2012 Tesco made a £1 billion (US$1.3 billion) commitment to improving in-store customer experience.

Tesco is the United Kingdom's leading retailer. In 2011 the brand's sales in the United Kingdom consisted of £47.4

billion (US$61.2 billion), trading profit of £2.5 billion (US$3.2 billion), and 14.8 percent dividends per market share. With a core focus on food products and strengthening its core group of supermarkets, in 2012 Tesco made a £1 billion (US$1.3 billion) commitment to improving in-store customer experience in categories including service, range, quality, price, availability, and effective store format.

Part of Tesco's strategy for future growth involves entering the markets of China, growing online shopping services, continued use of social media outlets like BzzAgent, and buying on large scale to achieve better cost prices.

FURTHER READING

Askey, Katy. "Tesco's New Customer Focus Will Put Squeeze on Rivals." *just-food*, March 6, 2012. Accessed October 3, 2012. http://www.just-food.com/comment/tescos-new-customer-focus-will-put-squeeze-on-rivals_id118508.aspx.

Baker, Rosie. "Tesco Introduces 'Just Discovered' Brand." *MarketingWeek*, August 15, 2011.

Church, Chris. "How Tesco Took the Low Road to Scotland." *Grocer*, September 30, 1995.

Corina, Maurice. *Pile It High, Sell It Cheap: The Authorized Biography of Sir John Cohen.* London: Weidenfeld & Nicolson, 1971.

Jacobsen, Ken. "What Tesco Can Teach Us." Growthbusiness. co.uk, September 13, 2007. Accessed October 2, 2012. http://www.growthbusiness.co.uk/growing-a-business/business-planning-and-expansion/259636/what-tesco-can-teach-us.thtml.

"Tesco—How 'Every Little Helps' Was a Big Help to Tesco." *thinkbox*. Accessed October 2, 2012. http://www.thinkbox.tv/server/show/ConCaseStudy.1642.

"Tesco PLC." *International Directory of Company Histories*. Ed. Jay P. Pederson. Vol. 24. Detroit, MI: St. James Press, 1999.

Woof, India. "How Important Is Brand Awareness?" University of Sheffield. Accessed October 2, 2012. http://enterprise.shef.ac.uk/2011/06/important-brand-awareness.

THOMSON REUTERS

———————◆———————

AT A GLANCE

Brand Synopsis: Combining a wide range of information-related products and services, Thomson Reuters offers businesses and professionals a combination of industry expertise and innovative technology.

Parent Company: Thomson Reuters Corporation
Three Times Square
New York, New York 10036
United States
http://thomsonreuters.com/

Sector: Industrials

Industry Group: Commercial & Professional Services

Performance: *Revenues*—US$13.3 billion (2012).

Principal Competitors: Bloomberg; Reed Elsevier; Wolters Kluwer

BRAND ORIGINS

- Reuters pioneered news delivery for the financial industry as well as for the mainstream media.
- Thomson established a strong position in publishing and educational information services.
- Both companies moved consistently to incorporate technology and focus on digital information.
- Merger of the two companies in 2008 produced a good business fit but created a branding challenge.

The Thomson Reuters brand can be traced all the way back to 1851, when Paul Julius Reuter established the first news service to use telegraphy. Reuters initially served commercial news directly to banks and other businesses, but soon began providing information to newspapers. The company acquired an excellent reputation for the speed and reliability of its news coverage, and in 1923 it began transmitting news by radio. Reuters became, and remains, a major news agency, supplying newspapers, and later other media outlets, with text and images from around the world.

In the meantime, Roy Thomson, a Canadian businessperson, bought his first newspaper in 1934, expanded his Canadian publishing interests, and, in 1953, bought the first of several newspapers in the United Kingdom. In the 1960s Thomson branched out into book and periodical publication, while Reuters began using computers to transmit market data. During the following decade, Reuters intensified its information focus, but Thomson diversified its interests to include the travel and petroleum industries.

Both companies continued to grow by acquiring businesses and products. In 1978 Thomson entered the specialized information field by purchasing Wadsworth Publishing and, over the course of the next two decades, gradually shifted toward a focus on digital information delivery, selling off most of its print holdings. Reuters purchased Instinet, one of the first computer-based trading systems, in 1987, and in 1999 Reuters entered an agreement with Dow Jones to combine their interactive services for the corporate and professional markets.

By the early 2000s, Thomson and Reuters were on a course toward convergence, but the two companies did not enter formal discussions until 2007. At that time Thomson sold off its educational assets to focus on business and financial information, and a merger with Reuters was announced in 2008. Both Thomson and Reuters were well established in electronic information-delivery, but in terms of brand image, Thomson was still widely perceived as a publishing company and Reuters as a news service. Therefore the branding challenge for the newly created Thomson Reuters was not only to develop a unified brand identity but also to clarify its business focus.

Both companies also had diversified product lines, making it difficult to establish an effective business structure. Initially there were two large divisions, but in 2011 Thomson Reuters organized its product lines into four main business units: Financial and Risk; Legal; Tax and Accounting; and Intellectual Property and Science. The Reuters news service and other media holdings are grouped separately, and a new unit was created for Global Growth and Operations.

BRAND ELEMENTS

- In 2008 a new brandmark and tagline provide a unified brand identity after Thomson and Reuters merge.
- In 2010 a rebranding campaign focuses attention on synergy effects created by a range of Thomson Reuters products.
- Taglines "Intelligent Information" and "Knowledge Effect" are used together in Thomson Reuters messaging.
- Thomson Reuters blog and other marketing communications leverage business storytelling.

Thomson and Reuters had to combine two different brands, as well as two corporate cultures, when the companies merged in 2008. In order to create a new, unified brand-identity, Thomson Reuters adopted a new brandmark. The mark has two components: the "Kinesis," a complex circular symbol based on the Fibonacci sequence (a mathematical progression found in many naturally occurring patterns), and the Thomson Reuters wordmark. The customized wordmark utilizes a distinctive typeface with rounded corners that create a softer, more approachable feel, and a heavy line weight that suggests strength and solidity. The wordmark is capitalized to communicate the company's stature. This new look, which was also used in redesigning the company's website, included nature images that convey a message of organic integration.

Initially the combined company used the tagline "Intelligent Information" across all its entities, in order to establish a common theme. This approach was successful in terms of linking various products to the new brand identity. In 2010 the company evolved this tagline into a campaign organized around the "Knowledge Effect." That approach emphasized the value of synergistic connections

that can be derived from the broad range of Thomson Reuters products. This identity campaign includes the Knowledge Effect blog, which offers business stories highlighting the benefits of using Thomson Reuters information products. The campaign also offers a bold visual presentation that capitalizes on the Reuters reputation for award-winning photojournalism.

In the process of acquiring businesses and products over several decades, both Thomson and Reuters added a long list of technology patents to their assets, along with copyrights and trademarks. The combined entity has continued to focus on obtaining competitive advantages by developing or purchasing advanced technologies for information-processing and delivery.

BRAND IDENTITY

- Brand identity is built around the value of "intelligent information," as well as the name recognition and good will previously accrued by both companies.
- The brand image is still vague, due to the diversity of products and services, many of which are not clearly connected to the parent brand.
- Thomson Reuters has intensified its focus on closing the gap between brand identity and brand image.

Thomson Reuters bases its brand image on the ability to deliver "intelligent information," which is sometimes described by the company as "information that thinks for itself." Marketing communications emphasize that the company can provide enhanced, "smarter" information to customers, giving them the "freedom to achieve." This messaging has been driven at the corporate level across a wide range of platforms, including traditional media, advertising, digital delivery, marketing materials, and investor communications. Thomson Reuters has worked to develop a reputation for industry leadership in its market sectors and to connect its various markets through a consistent top-level message. Furthermore, Thomson Reuters promotes its identity as a global enterprise, with customers in dozens of countries and employees located around the world.

The challenge that confronts Thomson Reuters is the wide variety of its products and services, which address a diverse assortment of business customers and end users. Because many Thomson Reuters products have independent histories and brand images, often users do not identify the products they are using with the Thomson Reuters brand. Additionally, users in a specific vertical market may be aware that they are using one or several Thomson Reuters products, but they may not be aware of related Thomson Reuters products. Thus the company's flagship brands, well-positioned in various market sectors, may not be identified with the parent brand. Beginning in 2012, changes in the management team and the business structure were specifically targeted to develop a more coherent brand identity.

BRAND STRATEGY

- Strategic priorities include targeting opportunities more effectively, building products across business units, and increasing the role of news and insight.
- Strategic improvements will address customer satisfaction and sales enrichment for Eikon and other Financial and Risk products.
- A new Global Growth unit will focus on identifying and exploiting international opportunities.

The 2011 Knowledge Effect campaign was heavily digital and included the launch of a microsite, as well as use of traditional media, digital display advertising, mobile marketing, an iPad app, and social media. This brand update, which focused heavily on business storytelling, helped Thomson Reuters move up from 39th to 37th in Interbrand's survey of the 100 Best Global Brands for 2011. Interbrand noted in its 2011 assessment that "consistent and compelling branding for such a global and complex company can be difficult," but concluded that the Knowledge Effect campaign had enabled Thomson Reuters to improve its brand definition and product alignment. Also part of the company's strategic plan for 2011 was the launch of Eikon, a financial intelligence platform intended to consolidate Thomson Reuters's advantage over Bloomberg, its leading competitor. Despite an expensive launch, however, Eikon performed less well than expected, leading to substantial changes in company leadership.

Addressing stockholder and analyst concerns in the 2011 Annual Report, Thomson Reuters announced four key priorities for 2012. The first priority was to foster growth in the Financial and Risk business unit, which accounts for the major share of company revenue. Specific steps to implement priority included improvements in the customer experience and enrichment of the product pipeline. The second priority was to invest in higher-growing segments, with a strategic goal to refine the company's focus on where to compete, targeting opportunities at the intersection of regulation and finance. The third priority was to exploit franchise strengths, primarily by building products that cross business units and by increasing the role of news and insight across all flagship products. The fourth priority was to accelerate fast-growing geographies. To support this priority, Thomson Reuters launched a new Global Growth and Operations unit and directed two-thirds of its 2011 acquisition dollars outside North America.

BRAND EQUITY

- Thomson Reuters lost market share to major competitor Bloomberg in 2011, but still leads in the information delivery market.

- Disappointing performance of Eikon, a new financial data flagship product, influenced industry assessment of Thomson Reuters.
- In 2012 Thomson Reuters dropped from 37th to 44th on Interbrand's list of 100 Best Global Brands and moved down on Brandirectory's Global 500 league table.
- The Financial and Risk business unit has been unsettled, but other units, notably Legal, as well as Tax and Accounting, have maintained their brand equity.

Since its Financial and Risk unit provides more than half of Thomson Reuters's total revenue, this segment of the company represents a substantial portion of its brand equity. In 2010 Thomson Reuters controlled more than 33 percent of the financial-data market, well ahead of its nearest competitor, Bloomberg, and its market share was growing. However, the disappointing performance in 2011 of its financial intelligence platform, Eikon, raised questions concerning Thomson Reuters's branding and business development strategies. Despite efforts to reverse the damage, Thomson Reuters slipped from 37th to 44th in Interbrand's 2012 survey of the 100 Best Global Brands. Interbrand acknowledged that a new management team had "already refocused the company on its core competencies," but noted that "the brand's lack of communication to the market regarding these changes (and in response to negative press) has influenced customer confidence." At the same time, however, other Thomson Reuters business units, including Legal, which provides about a quarter of the company's revenue, have retained or improved their brand equity. Although not a major revenue contributor, the Reuters news service retains a high level of name recognition and consumer confidence, which enhances the Thomson Reuters brand. Thomson Reuters ranked 163rd in the Brandirectory Global 500 league table for 2012, sharply down from its number 122 ranking in 2010.

BRAND AWARENESS

- Brand awareness is fragmented, with some products well known in their own vertical markets but not associated with the Thomson Reuters brand.
- Legacy products and acquisitions may have a weak or nonexistent identification with Thomson Reuters.
- Although Thomson Reuters outperforms Bloomberg in the financial data market, Bloomberg has a stronger brand identity and a higher level of brand awareness.

Many products within the Thomson Reuters portfolio have a high level of brand awareness within their market segments, but may not be generally identified with the parent brand. Both Thomson and Reuters took on a variety of products through acquisition before their merger, and while some of these products (particularly in Finance and Risk) have been clearly rebranded as part of Thomson Reuters, other products and services (especially smaller entities within the company, such as Westlaw and Tradeweb) have little or no obvious association with the parent brand. Some products, such as Thomson ONE and Thomson Innovation, still retain their earlier brand names, although they now display the Thomson Reuters logo. Similarly, Reuters news service uses Thomson Reuters brand elements only minimally. The news service is now a very small part of the Thomson Reuters portfolio, but it is much better-known to the general public than any other component of the company, due to its longevity and media associations. Additionally, competitor Bloomberg is better known, both to the public and within the financial industry, than Thomson Reuters, even though Thomson Reuters still has the larger market share. Due to industry news surrounding the competition between Thomson Reuters and Bloomberg, as well as the problems with Eikon, the Thomson Reuters parent brand may, ironically, be best known in connection with its most problematic business unit.

BRAND OUTLOOK

- The outlook for Thomson Reuters depends on the success of its recent restructuring and newly defined strategic priorities.
- Thomson Reuters continues to acquire new products and expand globally, reflecting its targeted growth strategy.
- Volatility in the international economy may continue to affect Thomson Reuters's performance.

In its 2012 analysis, Interbrand noted that despite the loss of market share in 2011, "Thomson Reuters continues to successfully align its brand and business strategies." Looking ahead, Interbrand projected that "Thomson Reuters has an opportunity to assert influence and leadership through its ongoing commitment to corporate citizenship and its 'customer first' initiative—both within its Financial and Risk business and across the organization." In 2011 Thomson Reuters issued its first Corporate Responsibility report, communicating company-wide performance and progress in a single, all-inclusive presentation. This move serves to highlight Thomson Reuters's growing emphasis on sustainability and its inclusion for the fourth consecutive year on Ethisphere's list of the World's Most Ethical Companies. Strengthening its overall image and name recognition should support the priorities announced in the Thomson Reuters 2011 Annual Report, especially as these relate to exploiting franchise strengths and focusing on the customer experience.

Thomson Reuters management projected growth in the low single digits for 2012 and reaffirmed that estimate as of the second quarter. However, the company's primary revenue stream comes from a volatile market sector, marked by unpredictable performance and strong competition. Thomson Reuters's Eikon has yet to gain traction, but management expects it to grow. The company continues to grow its global position, and it has focused in particular on developing its Legal unit and Tax and Accounting unit in Latin America. Through strategic acquisitions, Thomson Reuters has grown its Latin American revenues from less than US$35 million in 2009 to a projected US$200 million in 2012. Acquisitions in other business areas have also continued, exemplified by the addition of MarkMonitor, a leading provider of brand protection technology, to the Intellectual Property portfolio.

From a brand perspective, the outlook for Thomson Reuters depends partly on whether its new business structure can drive sales and marketing more effectively, and partly on whether new products and services, whether developed or acquired, can be successfully integrated into a unified brand. Analyst consensus suggests continuing growth in the low single-digits in 2013, based on the company's 2012 performance, and a higher rate of growth over the next five years. However, Thomson Reuters has indicated that unsettled economic conditions in Europe impacted a key market for its Financial and Risk products in 2012, and the effect is likely to continue or worsen, depending on future financial and political events.

FURTHER READING

Brand Finance. "Thomson Reuters Profile." *Brandirectory.* Accessed October 29, 2012. http://brandirectory.com/profile/thomson-reuters.

Goldenberg, Susan. *The Thomson Empire.* New York: Beaufort Books, 1984.

Massaro, Kerry. "Thomson Reuters Eikon: What Went Wrong?" *Wall Street & Technology.* Accessed October 28, 2012. http://www.wallstreetandtech.com/trading-technology/thomson-reuters-eikon-what-went-wrong/232301134.

Pachner, Joanna. "Thomson Reuters' Eikon Fails to Unseat Bloomberg." *Canadian Business,* February 14, 2012.

Read, Donald. *The Power of News: The History of Reuters, 1849–1989.* Oxford: Oxford University Press, 1992.

Thomson Reuters. *2011 Annual Report.* Accessed October 28, 2012. http://ar.thomsonreuters.com/home.html.

"Thomson Reuters." *Rebrand.* Accessed October 30 2012. http://www.rebrand.com/2010-merit-thomson-reuters.

"Thomson Reuters Harnesses Storytelling in Knowledge Effect Corporate Branding Campaign." BrandChannel, January 24, 2011. Accessed October 29, 2012. http://www.brandchannel.com/home/post/2011/01/24/Thomson-Reuters-Harnesses-Storytelling-in-Knowledge-Effect-Corporate-Branding-Campaign.aspx.

"2012 Ranking of the Top 100 Brands." Interbrand. Accessed October 30, 2012. http://www.interbrand.com/en/best-global-brands/2012/ThomsonReuters.

Wong, Elaine. "Thomson Reuters Touts 'Knowledge Effect' in New Corporate Branding Campaign." *Forbes,* January 24, 2011.

3M

AT A GLANCE

Brand Synopsis: The maker of Post-It, Scotch tape, and more than 55,000 other products around the world, 3M is a widely admired brand known for innovation.

Parent Company: 3M Company
3M Center
St. Paul, Minnesota 55144-1000
United States
http://www.3m.com

Sector: Industrials

Industry Group: Capital Goods

Performance: *Market share*—70.2 percent of adhesive tape market (2011). *Sales*—US$29.6 billion (2011).

Principal Competitors: Avery Dennison Corporation; E. I. du Pont de Nemours and Company; Henkel AG & Co. KGaA; Johnson & Johnson; S. C. Johnson & Son, Inc.

BRAND ORIGINS

- 3M began in 1902 as the Minnesota Mining and Manufacturing Company, a mining venture that soon began manufacturing sandpaper.
- 3M's most recognizable consumer brands include Scotch, Post-it, Scotchgard, Nexcare, Thinsulate, and Command.
- Business-to-business sales are an integral part of 3M's business in U.S. and international markets. 3M creates manufacturing and high-tech materials, as well as business processes and systems.
- In 1976 3M became one of the 30 companies whose stock prices are used to calculate the Dow Jones Industrial Average.
- In 1992 3M's international sales surpassed its domestic sales. By 2011 around two-thirds of its sales came from its overseas business.

Originally known as the Minnesota Mining and Manufacturing Company, 3M began in 1902 as a mining venture and became a sandpaper manufacturer shortly afterward. 3M is now a multinational corporation that produces thousands of products. 3M's commitments to invention and expansion have created a corporation with an influence that extends far beyond its Minnesota headquarters.

3M's approach to invention and expansion can be seen in the way it conducts sales. Rather than dispatching salespeople to meet with purchasing agents, 3M instructs its sales teams to address the people who actually use its products. In this way, the salespeople are able to ascertain customer needs and help 3M develop ways to meet those needs. 3M sales representatives now span the globe, selling products and helping the company develop new products.

Although 3M's products still include abrasive products like sandpaper, the company now manufactures more than 55,000 different items. Consumers are probably most familiar with 3M's consumer products, which include the Scotch brand of tape, the Post-it brand of adhesive notes, the Scotchgard line of cleaning supplies,

Nexcare health care products, Thinsulate insulation products, and Command adhesive items.

As popular and profitable as these products are, they make up just a fraction of 3M's portfolio. In fact, the company's core business is selling to other businesses in the United States and worldwide. For example, business-to-business sales account for around 85 percent of 3M India's sales. 3M's business products include manufacturing materials, such as abrasives, adhesives, resins, and tubing. They also include high-tech products, such as touch-screen, lighting, optical, computer, and software systems, as well as graphics solutions. In addition, 3M develops business processes, including delivery systems for businesses in a wide range of fields.

3M's size and productivity are indicators of its success in the United States and abroad. In 1976 3M became one of the 30 companies in the Dow Jones Industrial Average, an index of prominent companies whose stock prices are used to determine the health of the stock market and the U.S. economy as a whole. The company's success is also reflected in its international revenue. In 1992 3M made more money through international sales than through domestic sales. By 2011 international sales accounted for around two-thirds of the company's total sales, reflecting 3M's position as a global corporation.

BRAND ELEMENTS

- Since 1906, the company has used "3M" as part of its logo, even though it did not officially adopt the name until 2002.
- The current logo for 3M is the numeral 3 and a capital M, both in red.
- 3M provides specific instructions regarding the use of its logo and considers the logo to be a "company asset" and part of its "brand identity."
- Individual 3M brands share distinctive brand looks, like the tartan designs used for Scotch and Scotchgard products.

Although it is a huge, complex company with thousands of products, 3M has a simple logo: the numeral 3 and the letter M, both in red. 3M's website includes specific instructions for the correct use of this logo, advising users about the proper shade of red, the proportions of the logo and its font size, and the number of times the logo may be used per project. 3M is careful to control use of its logo because, as the 3M website explains, the company considers the logo to be "a key element of our brand identity. It is one of our most valuable company assets." The company has used the numeral 3 and the letter M as part of its logo in different ways since 1906, even though the company did not officially change its name to 3M until 2002.

Some of 3M's best-known individual brands also have distinctive looks and trademark names. Packaging for Scotch office supply products features a green, black, and yellow pattern that looks like a Scottish tartan plaid. The Scotchgard line of cleaning products also features packaging with Scottish tartan designs, this time in shades of red. Packaging for another 3M office supply line, the Post-it brand, includes in its logo the word "Post-it" over a drawing of notes in various shades of yellow. Some of 3M's other brands, such as the Nexcare line of health care products, are packaged using less distinctive logos or designs but still include the red 3M logo.

BRAND IDENTITY

- Innovation is a key concept for 3M and a key word in its promotions.
- 3M's emphasis on innovation translates into a research and development budget of more than US$1 billion annually.
- 3M is a multinational brand, with impressive sales figures, a significant number of products, thousands of employees, and operations in more than 60 countries.
- 3M's large size has necessitated the company's division into smaller parts; as of 2012, the company included six separate business segments.

3M prides itself on its history of innovation and actively promotes future innovation. The word "innovation" appears prominently and frequently throughout 3M's website and literature. The company defines itself as "a global innovation company that never stops inventing," uses the phrase "Innovation Lighting the Way" in a discussion of some of its products, and has posted an online pamphlet titled "Culture of Innovation."

This focus on invention is a large part of 3M's corporate culture. For 2011, 3M reported a research and development (R & D) budget of around US$1.6 billion. In the five-year span ending in 2011, the company spent around US$7.1 billion on R & D. This spending is consistent with the company's history of focusing heavily on new products. For example, the company's divisions have set goals in which they strive to make 25 percent to 30 percent of their earnings from sales of new products.

Size is another characteristic of 3M. It is the largest public company and the largest manufacturing company in the state of Minnesota. 3M's large size is evidenced by the number of products it manufactures, its US$29.6 billion in net sales (in 2011), its more than 80,000 employees, the 60-plus countries in which it operates, and the almost 200 countries in which 3M products are sold.

3M's large size has required that the corporation organize into smaller divisions. 3M has been divided in various ways throughout its history, but as of 2012, it was divided into six business segments: Consumer and Office; Display and Graphics; Electro and Communications; Health Care; Industrial and Transportation; and Safety, Security, and Protection Services.

BRAND STRATEGY

- 3M has created "fighter brands," less expensive versions of its existing brands, to protect the value and market share of its brands.
- 3M established the 3M Innovative Properties Company to protect its patents, trademarks, and other intellectual properties.
- 3M has attempted to protect its brands by engaging in court battles with competitors.
- By sponsoring brand awareness seminars and international awards presentations, 3M seeks to expand awareness of its brand internationally.

Given 3M's focus on innovation and creating new products, it is not surprising that the company has protected its brand identity by creating "fighter brands." A fighter brand is a less expensive version of an existing product offered by the same company. If successful with consumers, a fighter brand can minimize the success of, or eliminate altogether, other companies' competing brands, allowing the fighter brand's manufacturer to maintain its share of the market without having to alter the premium brand. 3M adopted this strategy, creating products like its popular Highland adhesive notes, a more basic and less expensive version of its Post-it notes. Thus, 3M has protected its premium brands and its market share by creating even more products.

3M has taken other steps to protect its brands, including engaging in court battles with competitors. In one litigation, 3M and Avery Dennison Corporation both argued for the right to sell their versions of retroreflective sheeting, a material used for traffic signs. Pending further judgment, both companies as of 2012 have been permitted to sell the sheeting. Because 3M produces a number of inventions and processes every year, its fundamental business model drives its interest in legal matters. The 3M Innovative Properties Company employs intellectual property attorneys who work to protect 3M's patents, trademarks, and other assets against illegal copying and other illegal tactics.

The company has taken various measures to increase its international brand awareness. In 2010 3M hosted a seminar in the United Arab Emirates about brand awareness. 3M also sponsored the 2012 BioProcess International Awards, where it highlighted its involvement in the life sciences industry. These actions were designed to showcase the fact that the 3M brand conducts much of its business on an international level and that this global business shows no signs of slowing.

BRAND EQUITY

- 3M creates new types of products and, as a result, new markets. The company dominates these new markets and has a strong presence in others.
- In 1994 3M introduced the Nexcare bandage line. By 1998 it had a 13.8 percent market share.
- In 2012 3M ranked 102nd on the Fortune 500, and Brand Finance listed 3M among the 500 largest companies in the world.
- Interbrand ranked 3M among the most valuable international brands in 2011.

Because 3M produces so many different types of products, it operates in a number of markets in the United States and abroad. The company's emphasis on innovation has even created new markets. As an innovator, 3M dominates certain types of markets, but it also competes in areas in which the company would not be considered a pioneer. For example, 3M created a retroreflective sheeting used for traffic signs, and its 2010 estimated market share for this product was almost 100 percent, while it held at least a 70 percent market share for other types of sheeting. In contrast, 3M's Nexcare bandages held a 13.8 percent market share in the bandage market as early as 1998, compared to industry giant Johnson & Johnson's 55 percent share with its well-known Band-Aid line. 3M's market share in this area was noteworthy, however, because Nexcare bandages were not sold before 1994.

Its competitive success has vaulted 3M to the tops of many lists of prominent U.S. corporations. In *Fortune* magazine's Fortune 500, 3M ranked 97th in 2011 and 102nd in 2012. In comparison, 3M's competitor Avery Dennison Corporation finished 356th in 2011 and 367th in 2012. In 2012 3M dropped a proposed plan to purchase Avery Dennison Corporation. This plan would have helped 3M capture even greater portions of some markets.

3M ranked 79th on Brand Finance's Global 500 2012, a list of the world's 500 largest companies, with a brand value of US$10.7 billion. In brand consultancy Interbrand's 2011 ranking of the top 100 global brands, 3M ranked 85th, with an estimated brand value of US$3.9 billion.

BRAND AWARENESS

- 3M brands such as Post-it and Scotch have top-of-mind awareness among consumers.
- *Fortune* magazine named 3M the 15th most admired company in the world in 2011. 3M placed 18th on the same list in 2012.
- The Reputation Institute's Global RepTrak 100 poll determined that 3M had a favorable reputation in 2011 and 2012.
- Interbrand ranked 3M second best on its Best Global Green Brand list in 2011 and as the 12th best in 2012.

The strength of 3M's brand value can be traced partly to the popularity of its products. Some 3M products are so popular that they have top-of-mind awareness among consumers. This means that consumers cite these products or brands when they are asked to name products in a particular category. A disposable adhesive note is commonly known as a Post-it, the name of a 3M brand. Clear cellophane tape is known commonly as Scotch tape, the name of another 3M brand.

Besides a high level of consumer awareness, 3M enjoys a favorable reputation. *Fortune* magazine included 3M in its list of the world's most admired companies, ranking it 15th in 2011 and 18th in 2012. The Reputation Institute's Global RepTrak 100, a poll that studies how people feel about international businesses and determines those brands' reputations, ranked 3M 24th in 2011 and 30th in 2012.

3M has also received acclaim for its environmental record. In 2011 Interbrand ranked 3M second in its Best Global Green Brand list, with Toyota in the top spot. 3M placed 12th on the same list in 2012. Similarly, *Newsweek* praised 3M for its environmental responsibility in the magazine's 2010 and 2011 Green Rankings, which assess the environmental records and reputations of the largest companies in the United States.

BRAND OUTLOOK

- It is unclear how an environmental lawsuit filed in 2010 against 3M by the state of Minnesota will affect the brand.
- 3M continues to introduce new products, including Post-it PopNotes, an "app" that allows users to create digital Post-it notes on electronic devices.
- 3M offers websites for different countries in several languages.
- Emerging markets, including Brazil, China, and India, accounted for around one-third of 3M's profits in 2011.
- Large affiliates like 3M India signify the size and global presence of 3M.

In a blow to 3M's reputation as an environmentally friendly company, in 2010 the state of Minnesota sued the company for what the state claimed was the improper disposal of perfluorochemicals (PFCs), chemicals frequently used in manufacturing. The following year, the Twin Cities Metropolitan Council joined Minnesota in the lawsuit against 3M. The lawsuit claimed that 3M's improper disposal of PFCs had harmed Minnesota's waterways and groundwater. 3M countered that it was cleaning up the disposal sites and taking measures to prevent future spills, adding that the impact of PFCs on the environment was not as great as Minnesota claimed. Brand Finance has questioned whether this environmental lawsuit will affect the brand.

Regardless of developments surrounding the company's image, 3M continues to launch new products,

some of which are digital. In 2011 it launched Post-it PopNotes, an "app" (application software) that allows users to write or draw on digital Post-it notes pictured on the screens of electronic devices. 3M features new products like Post-it PopNotes on its corporate websites. The company offers corporate websites in more than 25 languages for a number of countries. These sites reflect 3M's global presence and the fact that international sales make up a large percentage of its business.

International business will continue to be a focus for 3M. In 2011 the company estimated that approximately one-third of its profits came from such emerging markets as India, China, and Brazil. A variety of 3M's branded and unbranded products have helped it capture certain consumer markets in India. Its affiliate there, 3M India, is a large company in its own right, with a corporate office, innovation laboratories, and multiple manufacturing facilities and branch offices. 3M India has filed for patents and introduced a number of innovations. In 2010 a 3M India executive expressed hope that 3M India would earn US$1 billion by 2015.

FURTHER READING

Bhandari, Bhupesh. "Q&A: Ajay Nanavati, MD, 3M India." *Business Standard*, August 2, 2010. Accessed September 27, 2012. http://www.business-standard.com/india/news/qa-ajay-nanavati-md-3m-india/403170/.

Brand Finance. "Global 500 2012." *Brandirectory*. Accessed September 20, 2012. http://brandirectory.com/league_tables/table/global-500-2012.

"Fortune 500." *CNN Money*, May 23, 2011. Accessed September 24, 2012. http://money.cnn.com/magazines/fortune/fortune500/2011/full_list/301_400.html.

Interbrand. "2011 Ranking of the Top 100 Brands." Accessed September 24, 2012. http://www.interbrand.com/en/best-global-brands/best-global-brands-2008/best-global-brands-2011.aspx.

Ritson, Mark. "Fighter Brand Strategy Considerations." *Branding Strategy Insider*, October 7, 2009. Accessed September 21, 2012. http://www.brandingstrategyinsider.com/2009/10/fighter-brand-strategy-considerations.html.

SyncForce. "2012 Rankings per Brand." Accessed September 24, 2012. http://www.rankingthebrands.com/Brand-detail.aspx?brandID=1418.

3M Company. "3M Performance." Accessed September 20, 2012. http://solutions.3m.com/wps/portal/3M/en_US/3M-Company/Information/Profile/Performance/.

3M Company. "Fundamentals—Snapshot." Accessed September 20, 2012. http://phx.corporate-ir.net/phoenix.zhtml?c=80574&p=irol-fundsnapshot.

"3M Company." *International Directory of Company Histories*. Ed. Jay P. Pederson. Vol. 122. Detroit, MI: St. James Press, 2011.

Vomhof, John, Jr. "3M, Best Buy Tops in Overseas Sales." *Minneapolis St. Paul Business Journal*, June 29, 2012. Accessed October 18, 2012. http://www.bizjournals.com/twincities/print-edition/2012/06/29/intl-markets-boon-for-minnesota-biz.html.

TIFFANY & CO.

AT A GLANCE

Brand Synopsis: Considered an affordable luxury store chain, Tiffany prides itself on its unique, artful design of exquisite jewelry, always delivered in a signature blue box.

Parent Company: Tiffany & Co.
Fifth Avenue and 57th Street
New York, New York 10022
United States
http://www.tiffany.com

Sector: Consumer Discretionary

Industry Group: Retailing

Performance: *Market share*—5 percent of the jewelry market (2011). *Sales*—US$3.6 billion (2011).

Principal Competitors: Signet Group; Blue Nile; Zale

BRAND ORIGINS

- The company name was shortened to Tiffany & Co. in 1853, 16 years after the first store opened.
- The iconic flagship store opened in its current location in Manhattan in 1940.
- In 1978 Tiffany & Co. was sold to Avon Products Inc., resulting in a decline in quality of services and products.
- In 1987 Tiffany & Co. became a public corporation.

Initially operating primarily as a stationery and fancy goods emporium in Lower Manhattan, Tiffany & Co. was founded in 1837 by Charles Lewis Tiffany. The store originally bore the name Tiffany & Young, and, after the addition of a third partner, it was changed to Tiffany, Young & Ellis. In 1853, when Tiffany took control of the company, he shortened the name to Tiffany & Co. Also at this time the company's focus shifted to fine jewelry sales and design.

From the beginning, Tiffany set his store apart from others at the time by clearly marking items with a set price and only accepting cash payments. Both practices were considered unusual in the 1800s. In 1845 Tiffany published the first ever mail-order catalogue, which still comes out every fall. Tiffany also made a name for his company in 1878 when he purchased one of the world's largest yellow diamonds and named it the Tiffany Diamond. It remains on display at the flagship store today. Tiffany further established the store's luxury by purchasing the French crown jewels, a step that earned him the title "The King of Diamonds." In 1878 Tiffany & Co. won the highest honors for its Japanesque silver at the Paris World Exposition, which brought the company worldwide recognition for its jewelry design.

In a further attempt to establish its identity as a luxury jewelry brand, Tiffany introduced its solitaire diamond engagement ring in 1886, simultaneously creating a style and niche for the engagement ring industry. The simple design is recognized throughout the world. The Tiffany Setting diamond ring is still made and sold today and is the most popular engagement ring that Tiffany sells.

In the latter part of the 1800s Tiffany's gemologist, George Kunz, traveled the world in search of unique gemstones. He returned with a pink stone, known as Kunzite, and thereby initiated the Tiffany tradition of designing with rare and unusual gemstones. In the early 1900s Charles Lewis Tiffany's son, Louis Comfort Tiffany, became Tiffany's design director and was a prominent figure in the Art Nouveau movement because of his jewelry designs, as well as his stained-glass designs for lamps and windows.

In the early 1940s Tiffany built its flagship store in Manhattan, known today for its extravagant and theatrical window displays. The flagship store has served as a backdrop in several movies and television shows, such as *Breakfast at Tiffany's*, "Ugly Betty," and "Sweet Home Alabama." Tiffany & Co. is also mentioned in such popular songs as "Diamonds Are a Girl's Best Friend" and "Santa Baby."

In November 1978 Tiffany was sold to Avon Products, Inc. In 1984 the company was sold to an investment group led by William R. Cheney. The company went public in 1987. After being sold to Avon Products, Inc., the quality of products and services at Tiffany declined, and it had begun to resemble a department store. Since going public, the company has regained its reputation for luxury and fine jewelry.

The Tiffany brand has also established links with U.S. history. In the 1880s Tiffany redesigned the seal of the United States of America, and the redesign still appears on the back of the one-dollar bill. From 1917 to 1942 Tiffany made the Congressional Medal of Honor, known as the Tiffany Cross. Since 1967 Tiffany has designed and created the Vince Lombardi trophy, awarded each year to the winner of the National Football League's Super Bowl Championship. In 1968 First Lady Lady Bird Johnson commissioned Tiffany to create the presidential china.

In 2012 Tiffany & Co. was a publicly owned company with more than 250 store locations worldwide.

BRAND ELEMENTS

- The Tiffany Blue Box is a well-recognized wrapping and, when presented as a gift package, is commonly assumed to contain an engagement ring.
- Louis Comfort Tiffany's glasswork is still part of Tiffany & Co.'s brand image.
- Tiffany & Co. began using dramatic window displays in 1955 to attract customers.

In 1845 Tiffany, Young & Ellis, as the company was called at the time, began producing an annual mail-order catalogue, known as the "Blue Book" for "Useful and Fancy Articles." This was the first catalogue of its kind, and it originally marketed a wide array of products, from horse whips to French sugarplums. The catalogue still comes out every fall; however, it now offers fine and luxury jewelry.

In 1878, while at the Paris World Exposition, Charles Lewis Tiffany purchased some of the crown jewels

of France as well as a large yellow diamond that is still on display at the Tiffany & Co. flagship store in Manhattan, New York. As a result, Tiffany became known as "The King of Diamonds." He followed up the title by designing and creating the Tiffany Setting diamond engagement ring, a solitaire diamond on a gold band that is still the best-selling ring at Tiffany & Co. All Tiffany & Co. jewelry has been packaged since the founding of the company in the distinctive Tiffany Blue Box wrapped with a white ribbon tied in a bow.

After the death of his father, Louis Comfort Tiffany became the first design director of Tiffany & Co. Prior to working with his father's company, Tiffany had made a name for himself as an artist working in stained glass. His artworks contained primarily used glass, which contained impurities that, according to Tiffany, resulted in an original look and made the glass more desirable. In joining Tiffany & Co., Louis Comfort Tiffany brought with him his designs and experience, thus helping launch Tiffany & Co. in the Art Nouveau movement. Tiffany's stained glass work also influenced the designs of the company.

In 1955 Tiffany & Co. hired window dresser Gene Moore to decorate their store windows in the flagship store in Manhattan. As a result, Tiffany & Co. became well known for their theatrical and extravagant window displays, which often contained contemporary art that incorporated the actual jewelry. The windows also commonly display jewelry in unusual scenes. Because of this, Tiffany & Co.'s windows attract tourists and shoppers alike.

BRAND IDENTITY

- Tiffany has used the Tiffany Blue Box as packaging since the first store opened in 1837.
- In 1845 Tiffany started using a mail-order catalogue for marketing.
- Since going public in 1987, Tiffany has reaffirmed its reputation for luxury and fine jewelry.
- In 2012 Tiffany & Co. launched its Rubedo line in honor of its 175th anniversary.

Tiffany & Co. has been considered the premier jeweler in the United States since the 1800s and is the world's second-largest jewelry retailer, behind British-based Signet Jewelers Limited. Setting itself apart from competitors such as Kay Jewelers and Blue Nile, Tiffany & Co. works to ensure that consumers feel special about the jewelry they are buying or receiving, right down to the exclusive Tiffany Blue Box. Tiffany defined its uniqueness as a retailer from the beginning, by only accepting cash payments as well as by designing and making jewelry in-house, as opposed to importing it. The original Tiffany Setting diamond engagement ring, designed in the 1880s, is still portrayed in advertising as the quintessential diamond engagement ring. The Tiffany mail-order catalogue, first distributed in

1845, is still used by Tiffany & Co. to market its products and has also become a signature of the brand.

After Tiffany & Co. was purchased by Avon Products in 1978, both the quality of and rarity of Tiffany products were reported to have declined, and Tiffany locations were compared to the department store Macy's. This brand discrepancy was resolved when Tiffany & Co. became a public company in 1987. Although only 60 percent of Tiffany products are produced by Tiffany & Co. today, the brand's reputation for original designs still stands. Tiffany is also still known for its discovery and creation of unique gems and alloys. In 2012 Tiffany introduced the distinctive Rubedo pink alloy for use in jewelry designed in honor of the brand's 175th anniversary.

BRAND STRATEGY

- Tiffany & Co. established itself as a global competitor in the mid-19th century.
- After Charles Lewis Tiffany took control of the company, he established Tiffany & Co. as a high-end jeweler.
- Tiffany has created products besides jewelry, such as the "Tiffany" fragrance, that have also been highly successful.
- Tiffany & Co. has been worn by many celebrities and well-known families, which has furthered its reputation as a high-end jeweler.

According to Tiffany & Co.'s *2011 Annual Report*, the brand Tiffany is the single most important asset of the company. The brand is intended to be associated with high-end gemstones (specifically diamonds), romance, and sophistication. Every customer expects excellence in service, product, and packaging, specifically with regard to the Tiffany Blue Box that accompanies each purchase.

Tiffany & Co.'s global presence has always been a part of their marketing strategy. Having opened its first international location in the mid-19th century in Paris, Tiffany has been established as an international luxury brand almost from the beginning. The first London location opened in 1868, further expanding the brand's international presence. In 1972 Mitsukoshi Ltd., a high-end department store chain in Asia, began selling Tiffany products and quickly became successful. Because of the Tiffany engagement ring, engagement rings became popular in Asia, where they had not been a tradition before.

Since the beginning of Tiffany & Co., the brand has undergone few identity changes. When Charles Lewis Tiffany took control of the company in 1853, he shifted the focus from varied fine goods and costume jewelry to hone in on the fine jewelry market. The focus on jewelry helped establish the identity that Tiffany's still has today as a supplier of luxury. The only spinoff company that Tiffany & Co. has attempted in its history was a short-lived jeweler

called Iridesse, which dealt solely in pearl jewelry. The model was abandoned within five years, and the company cited the poor economy as the cause.

In 1902 Louis Comfort Tiffany, son of Charles Lewis Tiffany, was placed in charge of design at Tiffany & Co. Prior to joining his father's company, Tiffany's stained glass artwork had been featured in various high-end locations, from the Mark Twain House to the White House. Tiffany brought the Art Nouveau style to bear on Tiffany's jewelry design.

In 1987 Tiffany ventured into the fragrance market for the first time, introducing "Tiffany," a perfume for women. This venture proved very successful: in addition to Tiffany & Co. stores, the fragrance is also sold in various department stores. The masculine counterpart to "Tiffany," "Tiffany for Men," was launched in 1989 and also continues to be successful for Tiffany & Co. In 2012 "Tiffany" remained a consistent seller, with an average cost of US$220 per ounce.

In the 20th century, Tiffany & Co. incorporated celebrities, artists, and well-known designers as part of their branding. Their flagship window on Fifth Avenue in New York has featured many celebrated artists, from Andy Warhol to Jasper Johns. Additionally, Tiffany has been worn by many famous American families, such as the Astors, Huttons, and Vanderbilts, which has furthered the brand's reputation for luxury. In 2012 Tiffany continued to feature collections by famous designers, such as Paloma Picasso and Elsa Peretti.

BRAND EQUITY

- In recent years, Tiffany's sales have continued to improve, rising from US$3.1 billion in 2010 to US$3.6 billion in 2011.
- In 2011 Tiffany & Co. was ranked the 73rd most successful global brand, with Cartier in 70th place. Competitor Signet Jewelers was not ranked.
- In 2012 Tiffany & Co.'s brand value was estimated at US$2.95 to US$4.4 billion.

Tiffany & Co. is considered the second-most successful jewelry retailer in the world, after Signet Jewelers Limited. According to RetailSails, diamond engagement rings account for more than 23 percent of all of Tiffany's sales, reinforcing Tiffany's association with romance and luxury.

According to Interbrand's *2011 Ranking of the Top 100 Brands*, Tiffany & Co. ranked 73rd with a brand value of US$4.4 billion, whereas France's Cartier ranked 70th, with a brand value of US$4.7 billion. Tiffany ranked fifth in the luxury sector, according to the same poll, coming in well ahead of Giorgio Armani in 93rd place and Burberry in 95th. Brand Finance's "Global 500 2012" ranked Tiffany & Co. 384th overall and estimates its brand value at US$2.95 billion. Cartier was ranked 357th on the same list.

BRAND AWARENESS

- Tiffany's has been associated with the color Tiffany Blue, and the Tiffany Blue Box, since the company was founded.
- In 2011 Tiffany & Co. estimated that diamond engagement rings made up more than 23 percent of its total sales.
- Tiffany & Co. is oftentimes associated with Truman Capote's novella "Breakfast at Tiffany's," as well as by the 1961 film adaptation starring Audrey Hepburn.

The Tiffany brand has been around since 1837 and has changed relatively little. The best-known symbol of the brand is the distinctive packaging, known as the Tiffany Blue Box, which is provided with each purchase. The color Tiffany Blue has also been used in all marketing since the founding of the company. Tiffany & Co. is also commonly associated with the novella "Breakfast at Tiffany's," by Truman Capote, which prominently features the Manhattan flagship store. The popularity of the story and the 1961 film adaptation starring Audrey Hepburn has engrained the store in the memory of consumers beyond the luxury target-market of Tiffany & Co.

The Tiffany Setting diamond engagement ring has proven successful in international markets, including Asia, where there was no previously existing engagement ring tradition. According to Tiffany's *2011 Annual Report*, diamond engagement rings made up more than 23 percent of its sales and provided a strong measure of consumers' awareness of the brand.

BRAND OUTLOOK

- According to Tiffany & Co.'s *2011 Annual Report*, Tiffany will continue to focus on maintaining its identity as a high-end jeweler.
- As a discretionary retailer, Tiffany is directly affected by the economy.
- In 2012 Tiffany & Co. maintained a commitment to its policy of using only conflict-free diamonds and responsibly mined gold.

As explained in Tiffany & Co.'s *2011 Annual Report*, the company will continue to focus on maintaining its brand identity. In order to do this, Tiffany has outlined a strategy containing such points as keeping stores "well-staffed with knowledgeable professionals," maintaining brand packaging, making use of in-store displays, and keeping stores in the best "high street" locations to reinforce the brand's high-end aspirations. The company has had steady growth; sales increased from US$3.1 billion in 2010 to US$3.6 in 2011. Historically, the worst downslide Tiffany has experienced was during the Great Depression, when sales dropped more than 40 percent.

Tiffany & Co. faces its strongest competition in the market for diamond engagement rings. Rather than engage in price wars with competitors, however, Tiffany continues to emphasize the quality of its product as opposed to the price associated with it. According to its *2011 Annual Report*, Tiffany will continue to follow that already successful model. Because Tiffany & Co.'s products are considered discretionary, their sales are directly affected by the health of the economy. As faith in the economy wanes, fewer consumers are willing to spend money on luxurious products. Additionally, more than one-third of Tiffany's annual sales occur during the fourth quarter, and a weak economy during that season could dramatically affect Tiffany's sales for the year.

Tiffany has reinforced its image as a responsible business by adopting "a zero tolerance policy" toward both "conflict diamonds" and "dirty gold." It has joined with other jewelers from around the world to develop processes to ensure that its gems and metals are mined in a humane and environmentally responsible manner.

FURTHER READING

Besler, Carol. "Holiday Shoppers Love Luxury." *World One.* Accessed September 6, 2012. http://www.worldone-journal.com/cgi-bin/adframe/watches/article.html?ADFRAME_MCMS_ID=195&id=13453241766624972161232 60.

Brand Finance. "Global 500 2012." *Brandirectory.* Accessed September 3, 2012. http://brandirectory.com/league_tables/table/global-500-2012.

———. "Global 500 2012, The Annual Report." *Brandirectory.* Accessed September 6, 2012. http://brandfinance.com/images/upload/bf_g500_2012_web_dp.pdf.

Gassman, Ken. "Jewelry Sales Hit $68.3B." *National Jeweler,* February 2, 2012. Accessed September 4, 2012. http://www.nationaljeweler.com/nj/independents/a/~27759-IDEX-Online-Research-Jewelry-sales.

———. "The Complete 2011 U.S. Jewelry Sales Roundup & 2012 Outlook." *IDEX Online News,* February 27, 2012. Accessed September 4, 2012. http://www.idexonline.com/portal_FullNews.asp?id=36477.

Rosen, John. "Tiffany's Losing Luster in Luxury Slowdown." *Bloomberg News,* January 9, 2012.

Tiffany & Co. *2011 Annual Report.* Accessed September 5, 2012. http://viewer.zmags.com/publication/a0b9bb3c#/a0b9bb3c/1.

———. *The World of Tiffany.* Accessed September 2, 2012. http://www.tiffany.com/About/Default.aspx?isMenu=1.

Tiffany & Co. Profile. RetailSails. Accessed September 5, 2012. http://retailsails.com/monthly-sales-summary/tif/.

"2011 Ranking of the Top 100 Brands." Interbrand. Accessed July 3, 2012. http://www.interbrand.com/en/best-global-brands/best-global-brands-2008/best-global-brands-2011.aspx.

TIME WARNER CABLE

———————————•———————————

AT A GLANCE

Brand Synopsis: Time Warner Cable, one of the top providers of cable, broadband Internet, and digital voice services in the United States, draws upon its rich history to connect people and businesses with the information and entertainment they seek.

Parent Company: Time Warner Cable, Inc.
60 Columbus Circle
New York, New York 10023
United States
http://www.timewarnercable.com

Sector: Consumer Discretionary

Industry Group: Media

Performance: *Market share*—14% of U.S. cable television market (2011). *Sales*—US$19.7 billion (2011).

Principal Competitors: Comcast Corporation; DIREC-TV; DISH Network Corporation; Cox Communications, Inc. (subsidiary of Cox Enterprises); Verizon Communications Inc.; AT&T Inc.

BRAND ORIGINS

- Time Warner Cable originated in the 1989 merger between the cable divisions of Time, Inc., and Warner Communications, which created former parent company Time Warner.

- In the mid-1990s, Time Warner Cable launched Road Runner, the first cable-based high-speed Internet service.
- In 2009, Time Warner Cable spun off from parent corporation Time Warner and now operates as an entirely independent company.
- By 2011, Time Warner Cable was operating in 28 states and serving more than 14.5 million subscribers.

Time Warner Cable, Inc., is the offspring of a 1989 merger between the cable divisions of media titans Time, Inc., and Warner Communications. The initial merger brought together 6.1 million cable subscribers under one organizational umbrella, which was named Time Warner.

Just two weeks after the merger was announced, Paramount Communications attempted a hostile takeover of Time. The takeover attempt was unsuccessful, but Time was forced to raise its bid for Warner to US$14.9 billion in cash and stocks. Although Paramount filed a lawsuit to block the merger, the courts ruled in favor of Time, and the deal for the merger officially closed in 1990. In 1992 the two businesses were formally combined into a single entity, and the Time Warner Cable subsidiary was created to house the corporation's cable television, video programming, and high-speed data services.

In 1994, Time Warner Cable launched the Full Service Network (FSN), which combined traditional cable, interactive television, telephone, and high-speed Internet services into one package. Touted as the most high-tech development of its day, the FSN was the precursor to set-top boxes offering interactive services, which would gain

1069

popularity in the following years. In 1995 the company introduced its Line Runner high-speed Internet service in the test market of Elmira, New York. Following its successful test, the service was made available nationally in 1996 as Road Runner, the first cable-based high-speed Internet service. In 1996, Time Warner acquired Turner Broadcasting System, effectively reentering the basic cable television market and regaining the rights to thousands of pre-1950 films, which previously had been purchased by Turner Broadcasting. In 1998, Time Warner Cable introduced Road Runner Business Class, offering video and high-speed data services to the small business community.

In 2000, Time Warner merged with AOL in a massive, US$183 billion deal, and the new corporation became known as AOL Time Warner, Inc. The deal was seen as a major win for both companies, as AOL would gain 13 million new cable subscribers, while Time Warner would gain access to huge domestic and international markets in the digital realm. However, the 2000-01 collapse of the dot-com bubble resulted in a major downturn in advertising revenues and new subscribers. This effect was further compounded by the terrorist attacks of September 11, 2001, and the subsequent economic recession. Just a year after the merger, the company's value had plunged significantly, and in 2002, AOL Time Warner reported a loss of US$99 billion, one of the largest in corporate history. The company's value had fallen to US$66 billion by 2008, by which time the late-2000s global recession had begun. Time Warner would eventually spin off AOL as a separate, independent company, with the official change occurring in 2009.

Despite the turbulence affecting its parent company, Time Warner Cable continued to move forward during the first decade of the 21st century. In 2006, Time Warner Cable and Comcast combined resources to purchase Adelphia Communications Corp. for US$17 billion. Through the purchase, Time Warner Cable gained more than 3.3 million cable subscribers, while Comcast gained 1.7 million cable subscribers. To maximize the impact of the gains, the two companies traded some subscribers in order to consolidate important regions. For example, all Houston-area subscribers went to Comcast, while Dallas-area subscribers went to Time Warner Cable. Bolstered by the liquidation of a large competitor and a significant gain in subscribers, Time Warner Cable went public and began trading on the New York Stock Exchange in 2007.

In 2009, as part of a larger restructuring, Time Warner Cable spun off from parent company Time Warner, Inc. Time Warner Cable continues to use the Time Warner and Road Runner brands under license from its former parent company, but the cable provider now operates as an entirely independent entity. In 2011, Time Warner Cable purchased NaviSite for US$230 million, adding cloud and hosting options to its menu of services.

This was followed by the purchase of Insight Communications for US$3 billion that same year, through which the company acquired 760,000 new subscribers. By 2011, Time Warner Cable was serving more than 14.5 million subscribers in 28 states.

BRAND ELEMENTS

- Following its split from parent company Time Warner in 2009, Time Warner Cable retained its name, logo, and other brand elements through licensing.
- The Time Warner Cable logo, updated in 2010, features the company name alongside a graphic representing a hybrid of the human eye and ear.
- The slogan "Enjoy better," launched in 2012, was meant to tie the Time Warner Cable brand to the products and services that customers love.

After separating from its parent company in 2009, Time Warner Cable retained its name through brand licensing. At that time Time Warner was, and continues to be, one of the world's largest media and entertainment conglomerates, and so the cable provider kept the "Time Warner" in its name to continue enjoying the benefits of that brand recognition.

The Time Warner Cable logo, meant to symbolize the visual and audio services the company offers, features a simple graphic that represents a hybrid of the human eye and ear, with the company name appearing alongside. This logo was introduced in 2010, as the cable provider felt it needed an updated logo that represented its focus on cable services following the split from Time Warner. The new design included a more prominent eye and ear graphic, proportional in size to the company name, and the words "Time Warner" and "Cable" appeared in a heavier sans serif font. While the previous logo had rendered the word "Cable" in a smaller font so it would stand out, all words in the new version were equally sized. Additionally, the color of the logo was altered from a stark navy blue to a softer, more vibrant baby blue.

The original slogan for Time Warner Cable was "Now anything's possible." This was changed to "The Power of You" in 2005 as part of a minor adjustment to the company's logo. In 2012, Time Warner Cable launched a new slogan during the Super Bowl that encouraged customers to "Enjoy better." The advertising campaign accompanying the slogan focused heavily on the Time Warner Cable brand in addition to its services. Jeffrey A. Hirsch, the company's chief marketing officer, said the new slogan was meant "to tie the things that consumers love to do and get through us, to us."

BRAND IDENTITY

- The long history of Time Warner Cable and its antecedents is an important aspect of its brand identity.

- Strategic acquisitions and partnerships in 2011 allowed Time Warner Cable to add Internet hosting and new wireless options to its services.
- Recent blemishes on Time Warner Cable's brand image include lawsuits alleging poor customer service and public relations blunders.

Time Warner Cable has been recognized as a major brand for more than 20 years, while the histories of the parents of the 1989 Time Warner merger, Warner Communications and Time, Inc., extend back much further into the 20th century. History is arguably the single most influential factor in Time Warner Cable's brand identity, and the company has made sure to capitalize on that history. In 2010, for example, it launched the tagline "Moving technology forward to bring you back," which tied the brand to its successful past while emphasizing its use of modern technology.

Time Warner Cable has also sought to demonstrate a commitment to giving customers more control, more options, and a better experience overall. The company has delivered on these goals with a variety of innovations and developments, including the 2011 release of the Time Warner Cable mobile application (app) for iPad. The first of its kind among cable media companies, the app gave customers the ability to watch live programming on their tablets. Around the same time, Time Warner Cable upgraded and expanded its broadband capability; acquired NaviSite and began offering Internet cloud services; and added several new wireless options through joint ventures with Verizon Wireless, Comcast, and Bright House Networks.

Despite strides forward, the Time Warner Cable brand has experienced its share of public relations blunders. In 2008 the Los Angeles city attorney's office filed a lawsuit claiming Time Warner Cable had failed to live up to parts of its franchise cable agreement, alleging that excessive repair delays and long waits for service calls had caused "major havoc and distress" when the company became the top pay-TV provider in the area. In 2010, Time Warner Cable was forced to issue an apology when adult programming from the Playboy Channel was mistakenly aired on two of its children's channels in the company's North Carolina markets. In 2011, *Business Insider* magazine cited these incidents, among others, when it listed Time Warner Cable in the third spot on a list called "The 19 Most Hated Companies in America." Top competitor Comcast appeared in the fourth spot on the same list.

BRAND STRATEGY

- Time Warner Cable's goal is to enrich the experiences of viewers without making them conscious of the technology involved.

- In 2012, Time Warner Cable unveiled the new slogan "Enjoy better," which was a variation of a slogan used by chemical company BASF.
- Time Warner Cable has a history of striving to provide its customers with the latest technology and services through innovations and acquisitions.

Time Warner Cable has been on a steady and focused path to becoming one of the largest and best providers of high-speed data, voice, and video in the United States. The goal and the challenge have been to provide products and services that significantly enrich the consumer's experience while leaving the user unaware of the technology involved in the process. Jeffrey A. Hirsch, Time Warner Cable's chief marketing officer, compared the brand's strategy to the slogan used by chemical company BASF that reads, "We don't make a lot of the products you buy. We make a lot of the products you buy better." In 2012, with the guidance of public relations agency Ogilvy, Time Warner Cable came up with its own variation of the BASF concept with a new slogan, "Enjoy better."

Throughout Time Warner Cable's evolution there have been examples of technological innovations, business transactions, and joint ventures designed to offer subscribers a better, richer, and yet simpler experience. An excellent example of this was the 1994 launch of the Full Service Network (FSN), the first attempt by a cable provider to integrate interactive television, telephone, and high-speed Internet services through the same cable network. In 1996, Time Warner Cable introduced Road Runner, the first cable-based high-speed Internet service, and in 2011 the company became the first cable provider to release an iPad application (app). That same year, the purchase of NaviSite allowed Time Warner to add cloud and web hosting options to its ever-increasing menu of products and services, demonstrating the brand's willingness to use acquisitions and partnerships to provide its customers with the latest technology and services.

BRAND EQUITY

- In 2011, Time Warner Cable was the second largest cable provider in the United States in terms of the number of subscribers.
- In 2012, Brand Finance ranked Time Warner Cable 95th on the Global 500 list, with a brand value of US$9.1 billion.
- Time Warner Cable was listed as the 142nd largest U.S. corporation on the 2012 Fortune 500 list.
- Although its top competitor, Comcast, operates in all 50 states, Time Warner Cable's coverage extends to only 28 states.

In 2011, Time Warner Cable was the second largest cable provider in the United States in terms of number of subscribers, behind only Comcast. In 2011 the company's revenues were US$19.7 billion, a 4.3 percent increase over 2010, while the number of its video, high-speed data, and voice subscribers grew to approximately 14.5 million. More than 60 percent of those customers subscribed to a bundle of at least two services.

In 2012, Brand Finance estimated Time Warner Cable's brand value at US$9.1 billion, placing it in the 95th spot on the Global 500 list for that year. This was a significant jump from the brand's 107th spot on the same list in 2011, but still a long way from its highest ranking of 41st in 2008. The 2012 Fortune 500, *Fortune* magazine's annual ranking of the largest U.S. corporations, placed Time Warner Cable in the 142nd spot, down slightly from its ranking of 137th the previous year.

Although top U.S. cable provider Comcast has consistently demonstrated higher brand rankings and subscriber numbers than Time Warner Cable, those numbers are somewhat misleading, for Comcast operates in all 50 states, while Time Warner Cable operates in only 28.

BRAND AWARENESS

- Time Warner Cable is a highly recognized brand, thanks primarily to its role as the second largest U.S. cable provider and its familiar name.
- In 2012, Time Warner Cable sought to increase its brand recognition by emphasizing high-profile content partners, celebrity spokespeople, and the slogan "Enjoy better."
- Time Warner Cable holds naming rights to two sports arenas, one in North Carolina and one in Wisconsin.
- Time Warner Cable's signature philanthropic initiative, Connect a Million Minds, aims to increase proficiency in science, technology, engineering, and math among young Americans.

As the second largest cable provider in the United States, with approximately 14.5 million customers subscribing to one or more of its three primary services in 2011, Time Warner Cable is a highly recognized brand. This recognition is helped by the company's continued use of the Time Warner name despite severing ties with its parent corporation in 2009.

Unlike top competitor Comcast, Time Warner Cable does not operate in all 50 states. Rather, the company provides services in 28 states located in five geographic areas. In 2012, Time Warner Cable launched a US$80 million advertising campaign in its local markets featuring the new slogan "Enjoy better." Names of content partners like Facebook, ESPN, and Netflix were displayed between the words "Enjoy" and "better" (for example, "Enjoy Netflix better"), an attempt to communicate to customers that Time Warner Cable provides a superior way of accessing their favorite content

providers. The company also hired popular celebrities like Ricky Gervais and Mary-Louise Parker to star in the campaign's commercials.

To boost its brand awareness, Time Warner Cable also holds naming rights to two sports arenas. The Time Warner Cable Arena in Charlotte, North Carolina, is home to the Charlotte Bobcats National Basketball Association (NBA) team and also acts as an entertainment and sports venue for the city. Located in Wisconsin, the Time Warner Cable Field at Fox Cities Stadium is the home field of the Wisconsin Timber Rattlers minor league baseball team and has also hosted the NCAA Division III College World Series. Time Warner Cable has also sought to boost its brand recognition through its signature philanthropic initiative, Connect a Million Minds, the goal of which is to support proficiency in science, technology, engineering, and math among young Americans.

BRAND OUTLOOK

- In 2011, Time Warner Cable added more than two dozen new products and features and saw its total annual revenues rise 4.3 percent.
- In 2011, Time Warner Cable was ranked among the most successful companies in the United States by *Institutional Investor* magazine.
- In 2012, Time Warner Cable purchased Insight Communications for US$3 billion and acquired 760,000 new subscribers in three states.
- Future goals for Time Warner Cable include expanding business services offerings and Wi-Fi capabilities and using targeted marketing and sales to expand residential services.

In 2011, Time Warner Cable saw several positive developments. The cable provider added more than two dozen new products and features, including the cloud-based services gained through the acquisition of NaviSite. The company also strengthened its financial position in 2011, with an increase in total revenues of 4.3 percent from 2010. Business services revenues rose an impressive 32.7 percent, and operating income rose 10.3 percent. Thanks to numbers like these, in 2011 *Institutional Investor* magazine ranked Time Warner Cable among the most successful companies in the United States.

In 2012, Time Warner Cable completed a US$3 billion purchase of Insight Communications, acquiring 760,000 subscribers in Indiana, Kentucky, and Ohio. According to the company's 2011 annual report, it planned on instituting numerous company-wide initiatives over the following years, including expanding business services offerings, growing its sales force, expanding residential services through targeted marketing and sales, expanding Wi-Fi capabilities, and enhancing its line of advanced home-security systems.

FURTHER READING

Cohen, M. L., et al. "Time Warner Inc." *International Directory of Company Histories.* Ed. Derek Jacques and Paula Kepos. Vol. 109. Detroit: St. James Press, 2010. *Gale Virtual Reference Library.* Accessed November 5, 2012. http://go.galegroup. com/ps/i.do?id=GALE%7CCX1302700100&v=2.1&u=itsbtr ial&it=r&p=GVRL&sw=w.

Dan, Avi. "Turning Time Warner Cable from a 'Dumb Pipe' to a Powerful Brand." *Forbes,* August 9, 2012. Accessed November 5, 2012. http://www.forbes.com/sites/avidan/2012/08/09/ turning-time-warner-cable-from-a-dumb-pipe-to-a-powerful-brand.

Dudley, Alex. "Time Warner Cable Launches 'Enjoy Better' Brand Platform during Super Bowl Sunday." *Enhanced Online News,* February 1, 2012. Accessed November 5, 2012. http:// eon.businesswire.com/news/eon/20120201006574/en.

Elliot, Stuart. "Time Warner Cable Campaign Focuses on Brand More than Services." *New York Times,* January 31, 2012. Accessed November 5, 2012. http://mediadecoder.blogs.nytimes.com/2012/01/31/ time-warner-cable-campaign-focuses-on-brand-more-than-services.

Hampp, Andrew. "Why Time Warner Cable Stuck With Its Name." *Ad Age,* October 4, 2010. Accessed November 5, 2012. http://adage.com/article/media/ marketing-time-warner-cable-stuck/146251.

Johnson, Tom. "That's AOL folks …" *CNN Money,* January 10, 2000. Accessed November 5, 2012. http://money.cnn. com/2000/01/10/deals/aol_warner.

Time Warner Cable, Inc. "Time Warner Cable 2011 Annual Report." Accessed November 5, 2012. http:// www.pdfdownload.org/pdf2html/view_online.php? url=http%3A%2F%2Fir.timewarnercable.com% 2Ffiles%2Fdoc_financials%2FAnnual%2520Reports% 2FTWC_2011_Annual_Report.pdf.

———. "Time Warner Cable History." Accessed November 5, 2012. http://history.timewarnercable.com.

Vit, Armin. "Brand New: Eye Hear You." *Under Consideration,* October 25, 2010. Accessed November 5, 2012. http://www. underconsideration.com/brandnew/archives/eye_hear_you.php.

T-MOBILE

BRAND ORIGINS

- World War II destroyed most of the telephone infrastructure in Germany.
- For many years, telephone service in Germany was under the control of the Deutsche Bundespost, or German postal system.
- Deutsche Telekom, owned by the German government, is the parent company of T-Mobile, its global cellular telephone brand.

The optical telegraph (a communications system using visual signals) was first introduced in the German state of Prussia in 1833. Thirteen years later, the first telegraph line connected the two largest cities of the state, Berlin and Potsdam. However, another 31 years passed before the human voice was first successfully transmitted over a wire in Germany. In 1877 the first postmaster of Germany's united postal system, Deutsche Bundespost, approved an experiment with two telephones built by U.S. inventor Alexander Graham Bell. For the first time in Germany, voices were transmitted over a distance of more than two kilometers. The postmaster realized the potential of the new medium and put telephone services under the control of the Deutsche Bundespost.

By 1880, 16,000 German households subscribed to telephone services. In the following decades, the telephone won wider acceptance in Germany, and the technology was greatly improved. Automated systems started replacing operator-based telephone systems in the early 1900s. The 1920s brought self-dialing, long-distance, and mobile phone service to Germany. In 1926, for the first time, train passengers traveling between Berlin and Hamburg could call anywhere in the world. In 1933 public telex service was introduced between the two cities.

After Adolf Hitler came to power in January 1933, the Deutsche Bundespost became an instrument of the Nazi regime. Letters and telephone calls were routinely intercepted and used to identify Jews and dissidents. During World War II telephone services of the Bundespost continued to function right up until the Allied occupation of Germany. However, the service was in chaos by the time of Germany's surrender on May 7, 1945. Of the

3,420 buildings the Bundespost had owned before the war, 1,483 had been completely destroyed or damaged by bombing between 1940 and 1945, as well as during the fighting within Germany before its surrender. Many of the Bundespost's former personnel were dead or missing, and many telephone lines were cut.

As U.S., British, and Soviet forces assumed control of Germany's government, they also took over postal and telephone services. Postal services in the eastern part of Germany were turned over to the new East German state established by the Soviets in 1949. The Deutsche Bundespost, reborn as a state body under the control of a cabinet ministry, became responsible for the postal service, telephones, and telegraphs in the new Federal Republic of Germany, or West Germany.

The issue of freeing the Bundespost, including its telephone service, from political control came to the forefront when West Germany experienced an unprecedented economic boom after World War II and many business and consumer groups began criticizing the post office monopoly for inefficiency. In 1989, Germany's parliament, the Bundestag, passed a law dividing Deutsche Bundespost into three separate companies: Deutsche Bundespost Postdienst (postal services), Deutsche Bundespost Postbank (bank services), and Deutsche Bundespost Telekom (telecommunications). Each company had its own board of management, but the government's Ministry of Posts and Communication still had ultimate supervisory and regulatory authority.

The collapse of East Germany's government in 1989, and Germany's subsequent reunification in 1990, brought with it the integration of East Germany's own telecommunications monopoly, Deutsche Post, with the Bundespost. To make telephone connections available quickly, Telekom made it a priority to establish a mobile telecommunications infrastructure in eastern Germany. Following completion of an ambitious construction schedule, by 1997 the former East Germany had the most modern and efficient telecommunications infrastructure in the world.

The enormous costs of updating the former East German telephone system caused many politicians to drop their objections to privatizing Deutsche Bundespost. On January 1, 1995, Deutsche Bundespost Telekom was transformed into a public stock company and renamed Deutsche Telekom AG. In 2001, Deutsche Telekom once again restructured its business organization. Corresponding with the company's new strategy, all activities were organized in four divisions: T-Mobile, T-Online, T-Systems, and T-Com.

Deutsche Telekom finalized its takeover of U.S. mobile phone service providers VoiceStream and Powertel in 2001 and rebranded the service T-Mobile USA. By the end of the decade, Deutsche Telekom had expanded its T-Mobile European network to include operations in Germany, the United Kingdom, the Netherlands, Austria, the Czech Republic, Croatia, Hungary, Poland, and Slovakia, as well as stakes in operators in Montenegro and elsewhere.

BRAND ELEMENTS

- T-Mobile's television and Internet ads feature a distinctive five-note ringtone that serves as an audio logo.
- The magenta color used in T-Mobile advertising has been trademarked in Germany by T-Mobile and Deutsche Telekom.
- New T-Mobile ads in the United States are meant to show T-Mobile as a challenger to the current brand leaders in cell phone plans.

In 1996, Deutsche Telekom launched a vast image campaign to attract private investors, including a new "T" logo for Telekom. Within two years of its introduction, nine out of ten Germans recognized the pink "T" as Telekom's logo. The current T-Mobile logo includes the same pink capital letter "T" next to "Mobile" in plain black lettering. The magenta color is so closely identified with the brand that Deutsche Telekom and T-Mobile own a German trademark on its use in relation to their branding. Television ads also feature a distinctive ringtone that has become an audio logo for the brand.

T-Mobile has relied on celebrities featured in their advertising to bring appeal and prestige to the brand. Well-known actresses Jamie Lee Curtis and Catherine Zeta Jones have both been featured in television and print ads for T-Mobile USA. T-Mobile has also used the flash mob concept for advertising videos that have been huge hits on the Internet, including flash mobs in a suburban Chicago mall and in London's Liverpool Street Station, Heathrow Airport, and Trafalgar Square. T-Mobile had the second-most watched video ad on YouTube in 2011. The ad depicted a high-spirited version of the wedding of Prince William and Kate Middleton. A song used in T-Mobile ads for British television became a hit single in the United Kingdom.

Ads featuring Canadian actress Carly Foulkes began running in 2010. They showed the actress in a striking magenta summer dress that became a recognizable symbol of T-Mobile. In 2012, T-Mobile re-launched the brand with a series of commercials featuring an edgier, leather-clad Carly on a motorcycle, a metaphor meant to invoke T-Mobile as a brand challenging the status quo, with the motorcycle representing the speeds achieved by the T-Mobile network.

BRAND IDENTITY

- T-Mobile brand identity has been disjointed as the carrier has worked to define itself in the competitive telecommunications industry.

- T-Mobile has endeavored to find its niche by targeting consumers looking to avoid long and costly cell phone contracts.
- T-Mobile placed first in 11 of 16 surveys asking wireless customers to rate their satisfaction with their wireless carriers.

Since its inception, T-Mobile has struggled to find its identity in the highly competitive telecommunications industry. Viewed primarily as a discount cellular telephone carrier, the company worked to change its brand image and began realigning itself to become known as the telecommunications brand that provided more features of greater value to customers.

Without the popular Apple iPhone in its product offerings, consumers were shunning the brand in favor of companies who could provide the phone. T-Mobile continued to wrestle with its identity as customers with lucrative contract deals chose other providers. The company shifted its focus back again to consumers searching for a bargain who didn't want to get locked into a costly contract. T-Mobile aggressively sought out these customers by offering no-contract, cheap, prepaid phones.

T-Mobile had placed first 11 of 16 times in the annual J. D. Power Wireless Customer Care report, a survey of wireless customers' satisfaction with their carriers. Even with its stellar customer service and cheaper rates, consumers continued leaving T-Mobile because of issues with coverage. Dropped calls and slow data-transfer speeds have plagued the network, leaving subscribers frustrated and T-Mobile with the continued image of a beleaguered company endeavoring to find its place.

BRAND STRATEGY

- T-Mobile has a presence in ten European countries primarily through mergers and acquisitions involving its parent company, Deutsche Telekom.
- A T-Mobile joint venture in the United Kingdom with France Telecom's Orange telecommunications brand has produced a new company called Everything Everywhere (EE).
- T-Mobile uses sponsorship of various sports teams and tournaments to promote its brand to a wider audience.

T-Mobile has continued to grow internationally primarily through mergers and acquisitions. In 2011, T-Mobile re-branded one of the most popular Polish telecommunications brands, Era, which Deutsche Telekom acquired from Era's parent company, PTC. In 2010, France Telecom's Orange and Deutsche Telekom announced plans to merge Orange and T-Mobile in the United Kingdom. The new company was named "Everything Everywhere" (commonly known as "EE"); both Orange and T-Mobile continued operating as brands alongside that of the new company. EE is the United Kingdom's largest cellular phone operator.

To aid in global expansion, T-Mobile has also used a number of promotions to help boost its brand. The brand has been a sponsor of various professional sports teams, with the T-Mobile logo prominently displayed on everything from banners to clothing and buses. In Germany, T-Mobile has a lucrative deal as the jersey sponsor for the immensely popular German Bundesliga (association football) club FC Bayern Munich. T-Mobile also sponsors the Austrian Football Bundesliga, the highest-ranking national league club competition in Austrian football. T-Mobile previously sponsored several English football clubs and Scottish Premier League football clubs. T-Mobile was the official global mobile phone carrier for the 2006 FIFA World Cup football tournament in Germany. In the United States, T-Mobile has a multi-year contract as the official wireless services partner for the NBA and the WNBA. T-Mobile also sponsors numerous youth sports tournaments.

BRAND EQUITY

- In 2011, T-Mobile was ranked 70th in Brand Finance's Global 500, with a brand value of US$12 billion.
- T-Mobile had a brand value of US$13 billion, according to the *Financial Times'* 2010 Most Valuable Continental European Brands.
- T-Mobile's parent company, Deutsche Telekom, had an estimated brand value of US$29.8 billion in 2011.

In Brand Finance's Global 500 in 2011, T-Mobile was ranked 70th, with a brand value of US$12 billion, and it placed first among Germany's most valuable telecommunications brands, also with a brand value of US$12 billion. The *Financial Times* ranked T-Mobile sixth, with a brand value of US$13 billion, in its 2010 World's Most Valuable Mobile Operators Brands and tenth, with a brand value of US$13 billion, in its Most Valuable Continental European Brands in 2010. The *Financial Times* also ranked T-Mobile's parent company, Deutsche Telekom, fifth in its World's Most Valuable Telecommunication Provider Brands in 2011, with a brand value of US$29.8 billion.

BRAND AWARENESS

- With 265.9 million subscribers in 2009, T-Mobile enjoys a strong market presence throughout Europe and the United States.
- T-Mobile had a 2.7 percent market share globally in 2010.
- T-Mobile USA is the fourth-largest cellular provider in the United States, behind AT&T, Verizon Wireless, and Sprint.

As a reflection of its brand awareness, T-Mobile had a 2.7 percent market share worldwide in 2010. This included a 40 percent market share in the Czech Republic, a 46 percent market share in Hungary, a 21.5 percent market share in the United Kingdom, a 45.4 percent market share in Croatia, and a 35.6 percent market share in Germany. In 2009, *Brandweek* placed T-Mobile fourth among the top telecommunications brands, with 265.9 million subscribers globally.

According to *Advertising Age,* T-Mobile USA was the fourth-largest wireless provider in the United States, with a 12.2 percent market share in 2010, up from an 11.9 percent market share in 2009. T-Mobile USA had 33.7 million subscribers in 2009.

BRAND OUTLOOK

- A proposed deal announced by Deutsche Telekom would merge MetroPCS with T-Mobile, with both continuing to operate under the T-Mobile brand.
- T-Mobile has seen the defection of scores of subscribers because of slow data speeds and spotty coverage within its network.
- The only major carrier in the United States to not sell Apple's iPhone, T-Mobile instead offers cheaper plans to consumers with older, unlocked iPhones.

In 2011, AT&T offered Deutsche Telekom US$39 billion for the T-Mobile USA brand. Federal regulators filed an antitrust lawsuit to block the sale. AT&T gave up on the proposition late in the year, and the failed sale negatively affected investors' interest in T-Mobile. Hoping to bounce back, in October 2012, Deutsche Telekom announced a plan to buy the regional prepaid carrier MetroPCS and merge it with the T-Mobile brand. The planned merger is expected to close in 2013 and to help T-Mobile overtake rival Sprint, which would make T-Mobile the third-largest cellular provider in the United States.

As part of its re-branding efforts in 2012, T-Mobile has been upgrading its infrastructure to the faster speeds of 4G. Subscribers have also been disappointed with T-Mobile's throttling of data speeds once a preset limit of data has been reached. In response, T-Mobile has announced plans to offer subscriptions with full-speed service regardless of the amount of data transferred.

T-Mobile is the only major carrier in the United States to not have a deal with Apple to sell its iPhone. T-Mobile has been targeting customers with older, unlocked iPhones (phones that are no longer under contract with other carriers), enticing them to join the T-Mobile network with substantially lower monthly rates. Even though joining T-Mobile means switching to slower data speeds, T-Mobile has more than 1 million iPhones running on its network.

A completely integrated 4G network would allow iPhones on the T-Mobile network to run at full speeds.

FURTHER READING

Delo, Cotton. "Another T-Mobile Flash Mob Video Strikes Viral Gold: Cellphone Carrier's Latest Spot Features 'Home for the Holidays' Sung in a Mall." *Ad Age Digital,* December 22, 2011. Accessed October 20, 2012. http://adage.com/article/the-viral-video-chart/t-mobile-flash-mob-video-strikes-viral-gold/231720.

Fried, Ina. "T-Mobile Looks to Put the 'Unlimited' Back in Its Unlimited Data Plan." *All Things D,* August 21, 2012. Accessed October 20, 2012. http://allthingsd.com/20120821/t-mobile-looks-to-put-the-unlimited-back-in-its-unlimited-data-plan.

Masnick, Mike. "Engadget Mobile Threatened for Using T-Mobile's Trademarked Magenta." *techdirt,* March 31, 2008. Accessed October 20, 2012. http://www.techdirt.com/articles/20080331/134624706.shtml.

Reardon, Marguerite. "What T-Mobile's merger with MetroPCS means to you (FAQ)." *CNET,* October 4, 2012. Accessed October 20, 2012. http://news.cnet.com/8301-1035_3-57526200-94/what-t-mobiles-merger-with-metropcs-means-to-you-faq.

Siewert, Clark, Evelyn Hauser, and M. L. Cohen. "Deutsche Telekom AG." *International Directory of Company Histories.* Ed. Jay P. Pederson. Vol. 108. Detroit: St. James Press, 2010, 205-13. *Gale Virtual Reference Library.* Accessed October 20, 2012. http://go.galegroup.com/ps/i.do?id=GALE%7CCX1302600045&v=2.1&u=itsbtrial&it=r&p=GVRL&sw=w.

"Top Telecommunication Brands, 2009." *Business Rankings Annual.* Ed. Deborah J. Draper. Detroit: Gale, 2012. *Business Insights: Global.* Accessed October 20, 2012. http://bi.galegroup.com/global/article/GALE%7CI2501277530/8095f16db1a2be07953cef9d13c8e560?u=itsbtrial.

"Top Wireless Service Firms, 2011." *Market Share Reporter.* Ed. Robert S. Lazich and Virgil L. Burton III. Detroit: Gale, 2012. *Business Insights: Global.* Accessed October 20, 2012. http://bi.galegroup.com/global/article/GALE%7CI2502039967/62a4ca1f3a0171ed83c5f642c55382ac?u=itsbtrial.

"Top Wireless Subscribers, 2010." *Market Share Reporter.* Ed. Robert S. Lazich and Virgil L. Burton III. Detroit: Gale, 2012. *Business Insights: Global.* Accessed October 20, 2012. http://bi.galegroup.com/global/article/GALE%7CI2502038132/54000a0773e0fff94dc7461ba6098387?u=itsbtrial.

"US- T-Mobile USA looks to overtake Sprint in US mobile market." *America's Intelligence Wire,* October 18, 2012. *Business Insights: Global.* Accessed October 20, 2012. http://bi.galegroup.com/global/article/GALE%7CA305834021/407265f1981985d8a7db84364d2fbd7c?u=itsbtrial.

Wingfield, Nick. "T-Mobile USA Says Bring Us Your iPhones." *New York Times,* September 11, 2012. Accessed October 20, 2012. http://bits.blogs.nytimes.com/2012/09/11/t-mobile-usa-says-bring-us-your-iphones.

TOSHIBA

AT A GLANCE

Brand Synopsis: Toshiba, a Japanese company known worldwide for its innovative electronic technologies as well as for a diverse line of consumer products, enjoys a loyal following based on its reputation for quality and reliability.

Parent Company: Toshiba Corporation
1-1, Shibaura 1-chome, Minato-ku
Tokyo 105-8001
Japan
http://www.toshiba.co.jp/

Sector: Consumer Discretionary; Information Technology

Industry Group: Consumer Durables and Apparel; Technology Hardware and Equipment

Performance: Market share—5.50% of computers, worldwide (2010). Sales—US$77.26 billion (2012).

Principal Competitors: Hitachi, Ltd.; Fujitsu Limited; NEC Corporation; Mitsubishi Electric Corporation; Samsung Electronics Co., Ltd.; Hewlett-Packard Company; Sony Corporation

BRAND ORIGINS

- Toshiba was created in 1939 through the merger of two established electronics firms.
- The company adopted its Toshiba nickname as its official corporate name in 1984.

- Toshiba began expanding through the export of its consumer products in the late 1950s.
- Toshiba brought the first laptop computers to market in 1985.

Toshiba is a Japanese-based company that originated in the combination of two enterprises that created and manufactured telegraphic and electrical equipment. Tanaka Engineering Works and Tokyo Electric Co. were already well established, thriving Japanese companies when the firms merged in 1939. Both had been founded in the 1870s. The new concern became known as Tokyo Shibaura Electric Co., Ltd. The company ultimately became popularly known as Toshiba, and it adopted the name officially in 1984. Its goal was to become an internationally renowned electrical equipment manufacturer. With the advent of World War II, the company focused on providing the nation with products such as generators, radios, and military supplies. During the postwar reconstruction period, the company's primary focus was on manufacturing heavy electrical machinery.

The company achieved numerous technological firsts in Japan throughout its history, including developing the first radar, first fluorescent lights, and the first electric rice cooker, which remains a key domestic product for Toshiba. The company started experimenting with using electricity to cook rice in the 1920s and offered its first electrical rice cooker in 1955. Within the first year, Toshiba was producing 200,000 rice cookers a month. By 1960 automatic rice cookers could be found in half of all Japanese households. It was, however, soon eclipsed by other appliances available in postwar Japan that became known as the "three sacred treasures" of modern living: the television, washing machine, and refrigerator. Still, in 1970, Toshiba was selling 12.35 million rice cookers annually. The company has stated that it remains a modern, relevant appliance "as it is the product that boils the staple food for the Japanese people."

In the late 1950s Toshiba began producing goods for export, initiating a period of expansion. The company opened new manufacturing facilities and sales offices in overseas markets to support its international growth. However, Toshiba is noted for being a traditional, conservative business, according to Tetsuo Abo, writing in the *Encyclopedia of Japanese Business and Management:* "Historically its domestic market, relying on its traditional brand name and based on a reputation of innovative products, [was] more profitable than its overseas markets. …[T]he company has preferred to implement the main part of its strategic R&D and manufacturing activities at its home facilities and to export its products to foreign markets."

Because the traditional Japanese management style was ill-suited to diverse cultural backgrounds, Toshiba adopted a merger and acquisition strategy to launch its foreign operations. It also sought joint ventures and alliances with such companies as IBM, Motorola, and Siemens.

Toshiba has manufactured a wide-ranging product line, including medical imaging equipment, computer peripheral devices, high definition DVD players and recorders, LCD TVs, semiconductors, and home appliances. Among consumers, particularly outside Japan, the Toshiba brand became closely associated with laptop computers because the company brought the first laptop to market in 1985.

With economic conditions stagnating in Japan in the 1990s, Toshiba realigned its business through a massive restructuring plan that sought to focus its efforts on the semiconductor and personal computer markets. At the end of the decade, Toshiba established eight different in-house companies to promote faster decision-making. In 2007 it decided to leave the music and recording business after 50 years.

Continually challenged by economic conditions worldwide, Toshiba frequently refines and realigns its business structure to remain a vital enterprise worldwide. Toshiba now consists of more than 550 consolidated companies worldwide with 202,000 employees and net annual sales of ¥6.1 trillion (US$6.6 billion).

BRAND ELEMENTS
- The company used its name as its brand symbol until 2006.
- In 2006, Toshiba adopted a logo featuring the company name in bold red capitals and the tagline

"Leading Innovation," followed by three right-pointing chevrons.
- Toshiba's logo and tagline are used in advertising and catalogs, and on business cards and websites.

Until the 21st century, Toshiba's name essentially functioned as its brand. This is known as "the branded house," a branding strategy in which the company is the brand. Other corporations using this strategy include GE and Virgin. The silver, all capital letters are emblazoned on Toshiba products, which range from rice cookers to personal computers.

In 2006, the logo was revised. It now features the name "Toshiba" in red, all-capital letters in a contemporary, bold, sans-serif font. Below the name is the tagline "Leading Innovation" in black letters, with only the first letters capitalized. Following the tagline is a graphic of three right-pointing chevrons. The left chevron is gray, the middle chevron is darker, and the right chevron is black. The graphic conveys the idea of motion or progress. Toshiba uses its logo and tagline in corporate and product advertising, in catalogs, on business cards, and on the company website.

BRAND IDENTITY
- Toshiba has long enjoyed a reputation for excellence.
- The company began focusing on managing its global brand in 2001.
- In 2006, Toshiba introduced a new logo and tagline, and it issued a new brand statement that emphasized innovation.

As a corporation with a long, rich history, Toshiba is deeply rooted in Japanese culture. The company, like many multinational Japanese firms, has enjoyed a reputation for excellent products since its founding in the late 1930s.

Although the name on Toshiba's wide range of consumer products is the same, Jean-Noël Kapferer, writing in *The New Strategic Brand Management: Creating and Sustaining Brand Equity Long Term,* notes that the products do not have the same brand image. Toshiba computers, for example, have a different brand image from its television sets. It was not until 2001 that the corporation sought to manage its global brand. "The Toshiba Corporation up until now never thought of itself as a brand that needed to be managed globally as such," observes Kapferer. "It is only recently that a VP was named with that objective, with worldwide responsibilities and authority."

Under the leadership of Atsutoshi Nishida, president and chief executive officer from 2005 to 2009, Toshiba management was radically restructured to create "a lively more clearly defined Toshiba Group that channels ceaseless innovation into achieving sustained growth with profit across Toshiba business." In 2006 the "TOSHIBA Leading Innovation" branding was adopted.

In addition, the theme of corporate social responsibility became infused across the business under Nishida's principle, "Be truthful in thought, word, and deed." The company, using this principle as a guide, says it is resolved to be responsible to its stakeholders by establishing guidelines that addressed such issues as bribery prevention and anti-trust compliance.

In 2006, at the same time Toshiba launched its new logo and tagline, it issued a new brand statement. That statement read, "Toshiba delivers technology and products remarkable for their innovation and artistry—contributing to a safer, more comfortable, more productive life. We bring together the spirit of innovation with our passion and conviction to shape the future and help protect the global environment—our shared heritage. We foster close relationships, rooted in trust and respect, with all our customers, business partners and communities around the world."

BRAND STRATEGY

- Since the early 2000s, Toshiba has made a concerted effort to establish innovation at the center of its brand image.
- Two examples of campaigns that stressed innovation were the "light, lighter" television ads of 2007 and the TabletMan character introduced in 2012.
- Toshiba also seeks to reinforce its image as a sustainable brand by promoting initiatives such as the National No-Print Day.

Since the early 2000s, Toshiba has made a concerted effort to place innovation at the center of its brand image. In an advertising campaign launched at the end of 2007 in the United Kingdom, for example, the images in the commercial, which featured pictures of Toshiba's product development technology, were accompanied by a narrator saying, "We make light, lighter; fast, faster; bright, brighter; small, smaller." In a more recent example, in 2012 the company introduced its TabletMan global communication character at a Singapore technology conference, with plans to launch a global brand awareness campaign based on the character. TabletMan was a person wearing a black rubber body suit enlivened by electro-luminescent lights and 11 Toshiba tablets, on which passersby were encouraged to record their wishes for the future. These messages were then played on Toshiba's YouTube site and Facebook page. The goal of the campaign was to promote Toshiba's tablet computer products worldwide as well as to capture attention for Toshiba as an edgy, innovative brand.

To reinforce its image as a sustainable brand, in 2012 Toshiba announced the National No-Print Day campaign to encourage individuals and companies to commit to not using a printer for one day. Bill Melo of Toshiba America Business Solutions, the spokesperson for the initiative, pointed out that "approximately 336,000,000 sheets of paper are wasted daily—that's more than 40,000 trees."

BRAND EQUITY

- As of 2011, Toshiba was the most valuable international electronics brand.
- Toshiba's brand value increased from US$11.14 billion in 2011 to US$14.19 billion in 2012.
- Toshiba's ranking in Brand Finance's Global 500 rose from 74 in 2011 to 58 in 2012.
- Toshiba plans to sustain its high brand equity by moving into new international markets such as Africa and the Middle East.

According to Brand Finance, Toshiba was the leading brand in the 2012 ranking of world's most valuable electronics brands, with a brand value of US$14.19 billion, up from a value of US$11.14 billion in 2011. In both years the brand rating was AA-. Toshiba's rank in Brand Finance's Global 500 was 58 in 2012. This was a significant improvement over its 2011 rank of 74.

Toshiba plans to sustain its high brand equity by moving into new international markets. For example, according to the website ChannelEMEA, the brand equity of Toshiba notebooks in the Gulf region is the highest worldwide, and in the first half of 2012, the company experienced 50 percent year-on-year sales growth. Toshiba wants to extend its brand equity and reputation for value throughout the Middle East and Africa. The company's goal is a minimum 20 percent target share in East Africa.

BRAND AWARENESS

- As a manufacturer of products for both the industrial and consumer sectors, Toshiba faces a challenge in its attempts to unify its brand.
- Toshiba consumers are loyal to the brand.
- Toshiba is known worldwide as a reputable company.

Toshiba has functioned more as a corporate name than as a familiar brand with a global reputation for excellence. However, it produces not only consumer electronics and appliances but equipment that can be found in industrial settings such as power-generation plants and building infrastructures. Although the name inscribed on its range of products may be the same, consumer perception of the brand is not consistent. Consumers view Toshiba computers, for example, in a very different light than they view its television sets. The company established an executive position to oversee corporate branding in 2001 and has undertaken a variety of campaigns aimed at unifying the brand. Most recently, Toshiba launched its TabletMan campaign to promote both its global brand and its tablet computer products.

Among consumers, "[p]eople who are aware of Toshiba know and love it; they are good brand advocates and they are loyal," stated Matt McDowell, Toshiba's United Kingdom marketing director, in a 2008 interview. "But the problem is, it's not enough and we have to look to engage new audiences." On the positive side, Toshiba is known internationally as a trustworthy company. According to *Forbes,* in 2009 the Reputation Institute ranked Toshiba as the 190th-most reputable company in the world.

BRAND OUTLOOK

- In the near future, Toshiba intends to focus on expanding into emerging markets.
- Toshiba has a leading market position in sales of various industrial and consumer products.
- Executives plan to restructure Toshiba to enable it to respond nimbly to changes in the global economy.

In its 2012 Annual Report Toshiba stated that its primary goal is "to be an even stronger global contender." To realize this ambition, it intends to allocate its resources to strategic growth areas.

The company has indicated it will focus on emerging markets in 2013, as these are the only regions appearing to show growth potential. The emerging economies are expected to post double-digit growth through at least the 2014 fiscal year, according to the company's 2012 annual report. It is expecting overseas sales to grow from 55 percent of total sales in fiscal year 2011 to 65 percent by fiscal year 2014. Toshiba is, for example, continuing to expand its operations in the Middle East and Africa into East and South Africa. Sales in East and South Africa are expected to boost revenues by 30 percent in the 2012–13 fiscal year, according to sales executives. Toshiba is also opening a washing machine production facility in Indonesia, the largest market in Southeast Asia, to meet growing demand.

In many of the markets for which it produces goods, Toshiba has a leading market share. It leads, for example, the world market in nuclear power generation with a 28 percent global market share and has a 25 percent share of the geothermal power generation market. Toshiba is the number-two producer of NAND flash memory worldwide.

Looking forward, Toshiba executives plan to transform the company's business structure, restructure its businesses to withstand both global economic and market changes, and continue its focus on sustainability and corporate social responsibility. "[W]e will work to enhance our brand recognition and to clarify our brand positioning through CDI (corporate design identity)," stated Norio Sasaki, Toshiba's president and chief executive officer, "and we will strive to become a dominant player in the emerging economies."

FURTHER READING

Bird, Allan, ed. *The Encyclopedia of Japanese Business and Management.* New York: Routledge, 2002.

"BRAND LOVE: Do you really love me?" *Brand Strategy,* December 10, 2008, 27.

Deakin, Simon, and D. Hugh Whittaker, eds. *Corporate Governance and Managerial Reform in Japan.* New York: Oxford University Press, 2010.

Francks, Penelope, and Janet Hunter, eds. *The Historical Consumer: Consumption and Everyday Life in Japan, 1850–2000.* New York: Palgrave Macmillan, 2012.

Gasbarre, April Dougal, and David E. Salamie. *International Directory of Company Histories.* Ed. Jay P. Pederson. Vol. 99. Detroit: St. James Press, 2009.

"Japan's Most Valuable Brands, 2011." *Business Rankings Annual.* Ed. Deborah J. Draper. Detroit: Gale, 2013. http://bi.galegroup.com/global/article/GALE%7CI2501281239/ebbbd2b843a0e0afb6760c0d6e9bebd1?u=itsbtrial.

Kapferer, Jean-Noël. *The New Strategic Brand Management: Creating and Sustaining Brand Equity Long Term.* Philadelphia: Kogan Page Publishers, 2008.

"OPINION: Make yourself crystal clear." *Brand Strategy,* February 23, 2009, 13.

"World's Most Valuable Electronics Brands, 2011." *Business Rankings Annual.* Ed. Deborah J. Draper. Detroit: Gale, 2013. http://bi.galegroup.com/global/article/GALE%7CI2501283084/983f6bcbd37a279aca026c173d3aa7a4?u=itsbtrial.

TOTAL

BRAND ORIGINS

- The Compagnie française des pétroles, the forerunner of the French oil and gas company Total, began in 1924.
- After World War II, the Compagnie française des pétroles explored for oil and gas in Canada and Africa.

- Total works in oil and gas exploration, production, refining, transporting, trading, marketing, and energy operations, and it produces chemicals.
- Varied names for Total's companies through the years have included the Compagnie française des pétroles, Total-Compagnie Française des Pétroles, Total Fina, Total Fina Elf, and Total S.A.

Total has been a multinational company from the very beginning. The Compagnie française des pétroles (CFP) began on March 28, 1924. This French company controlled France's oil rights in Mesopotamia, a region that encompasses the modern countries of Iraq, Turkey, and Syria. The company also worked to develop oil production in France's colonies and other countries with French affiliations.

After World War II, CFP embarked on these international ventures. It explored for oil in Canada and the territories of French Equatorial Africa, four territories that are now independent countries: the Central African Republic, Chad, Gabon, and the Republic of the Congo. CFP was particularly successful in Algeria, finding productive and lucrative oil and gas fields in that country.

The company then worked with other companies and Algeria's French territorial government to work in all aspects of the oil and gas industries. This diversified work continues, as the company, now known as Total, works in oil and gas exploration, production, refining, transporting, trading, marketing, and energy operations. It operates service stations (gas stations), produces chemicals, and sells oil products to consumers. It also works on developing environmentally conscious products and technologies. It conducts this varied work in more than 130 countries.

In addition to its varied operations, the company has also used a number of names through the years. It began using the Total name in 1954 and changed its name to Total-Compagnie Française des Pétroles in 1985 and Total S.A. in 1991. Company expansions brought about further name changes. Total's 1999 acquisition of Belgian petroleum company Petrofina created the new company name Total Fina. The next year, Total Fina merged with French oil company Elf Aquitaine and became Total Fina Elf. Finally, in 2003, the company reverted back to the Total S.A. name. These changes reflect the company's growth, widespread geographic affiliations, and heavy involvement in the oil and gas industries.

BRAND ELEMENTS

- Total has used red letters to depict the company name since 2003 and has used red logo letters throughout its history.
- Since the 1980s, Total has used red, orange, blue, and white, as brand colors.
- Red, orange, and blue ribbons form a spherical shape that Total uses as a logo.
- Red, orange, and blue ribbons also represent Foundation Total, Total's organization that sponsors health, community, scientific, and cultural efforts.

Since 2003 Total has used the word "Total" in red letters. This red name logo symbolizes the company and its history, as it has intermittently used a red Total logo since 1954. This red logo was symbolic in another way, since it appeared on a blue and white background on the 1954 logo. The company chose the colors red, white, and blue to echo the colors of France's flag and remind people of Total's home country.

The company has used red, orange, blue, and white as brand colors since the 1980s. According to the company, the use of the color red symbolizes strength. Total uses the color it calls warm orange to convey friendliness. Beginning in 2003, Total has used bold red, orange, and blue ribbons of color to form a ball- or sphere-shaped logo. The shape also resembles a globe and helps to convey Total's international presence.

The red, orange, and blue ribbons that create Total's spherical logo also appear on the Facebook page for Foundation Total, an organization that sponsors health, community, scientific, and cultural efforts. In addition, the colors red, orange, and blue adorn posters and other promotional materials for Oil Cup Total, a soccer tournament sponsored by Total.

BRAND IDENTITY

- Oil storage tanks and oil trucks, gas stations, and motor oil cans all use Total's red, orange, and blue sphere logo.
- Total's tricolor sphere adorns Total fuel cards and the Club Cards issued by Total Parco Pakistan Limited.
- Other Total S.A. brands include Elf, Elan, and AS 24.

Total's red, orange, and blue sphere logo appears in various places, illustrating its participation in various operations. The Total tricolored sphere appears on oil storage tanks and tanker trucks, on signs at its gas stations, and on containers of motor oil.

The Total name and sphere also appear on Total fuel cards for fuel and travel expenses, demonstrating Total's ties to the financial side of the energy industry. Other cards affiliated with Total include the Club Cards issued by Total Parco Pakistan Limited, a partnership between Total and Pakistan's Pak Arab Refinery Limited, or Parco. These cards help show Total's range of activities and its geographic span.

Parent company Total S.A. has a number of different brands. In addition to Total, other company brands include Elf, Elan, and AS 24. Some of these companies use symbolic logos and colors. While Total company Elf uses a plain text logo with a horizontal band for its corporate logo, its brand symbol uses the lowercase word "elf" accompanied by a stylized drawing of a drill bit in blue and red. This is yet another example of a Total company using visual images to identify itself and its industries.

BRAND STRATEGY

- Recognizing Qatar's interests in horses and racing, Total E&P Qatar has sponsored The Emir's Sword Race, a horse race in Doha, Qatar.
- Total E&P Italia is heavily involved in Italian soccer, sponsoring the Oil Cup Total soccer tournament there.
- In India, Total company Totalgaz sponsored the Total Quartz Safety Run in several Indian cities in 2012.
- Foundation Total has helped create Département des Arts de l'Islam, an Islamic art section in the Louvre museum in Paris, France, that opened in 2012.

A number of Total companies have ties to various sports. Total E&P Qatar has been a longtime title sponsor of The Emir's Sword Race, a horse race held at the Qatar Racing and Equestrian Club in Doha, Qatar. This sponsorship promoted Total in Qatar and represented the company's intention "to support Qatar through investments in the community," in the words of Total Managing Director Stephane Michel. According to Michel, this involvement represented the company's commitment to Qatar and its recognition of the country's culture, as Total E&P Qatar intended "to encourage events of cultural and traditional significance such as horse racing, through our sustained sponsorship."

Total E&P Italia is heavily involved in Italian soccer. In addition to its sponsorship of the Oil Cup Total soccer tournament, it has sponsored a soccer team and exhibitions highlighting soccer uniforms. Totalgaz, a Total company in India, sponsored the Total Quartz Safety Run as part of its Total Quartz Safety Month in 2012. Staged in 21 cities in India, this three-kilometer run promoted road safety.

Other Total activities support other efforts. Foundation Total has helped create Département des Arts de l'Islam, an Islamic art section in the Louvre museum in Paris, France. This wing of the museum opened in September 2012. This involvement joined other Foundation Total initiatives, which include environmental and biodiversity efforts, community support efforts, and other activities related to culture and heritage.

BRAND EQUITY

- Operating service stations/gas stations in several countries under the Total, Elf, Elan, and AS24 brands, Total has captured a portion of this market.
- Total ranked 18th on *Forbes* magazine's list of the largest companies in the world, the "Forbes Global 2000."
- In 2012 a Seeking Alpha website called Total "the largest energy company in France" as well as "one of the six 'supermajor' oil companies which places it as one of the largest energy companies on the planet."

The company competes in a number of markets in a number of geographic areas. It has several service stations/gas stations under the Total, Elf, and Elan names in France alone. Its subsidiary, AS24, operates unmanned gas stations throughout Europe that serve people who drive for a living. In Africa, Total has thousands of gas stations in more than 40 countries. As a result, Total held 11 percent of the African market in 2008.

Given this market share, it is not surprising that Total is one of the largest public companies in the world. In 2012 it placed 18th on the "Forbes Global 2000," *Forbes* magazine's list of the largest companies in the world. Compared to other companies on this list, Total ranked as the largest French company and one of the ten largest oil and gas companies in the world.

Other commentators have discussed Total's prominence in France and within its industry. In 2012 a contributor to the Seeking Alpha website called Total "the largest energy company in France" as well as "one of the six 'supermajor' oil companies which places it as one of the largest energy companies on the planet."

BRAND AWARENESS

- In 2012 Total encountered gas leaks in the North Sea near Scotland and in Nigeria's Niger Delta.
- Total has been heavily involved in the liquid natural gas industry in different countries, including Algeria, Qatar, Yemen, Indonesia, Australia, and Russia.
- Its shareholder services have garnered 2010 and 2011 Boursoscan prizes for Total for excellence in investor relations.
- Nobel Peace Prize winner and Myanmar (Burma) parliament member Aung San Suu Kyi said in 2012 that "Total is a responsible investor in Burma."

Two unfortunate incidents in 2012 brought unwanted attention to Total. The company experienced two gas leaks that year, one in the North Sea near Scotland, the other in Nigeria's Niger Delta. A *New York Times* article reported that the North Sea leak cost the company millions of dollars and speculated on whether this would affect Total's reputation, although the company did stop the leaks in May 2012.

The incidents in Nigeria and near Scotland, Total's sporting involvements in Italy and Qatar, and its cultural affiliations in France all demonstrate the corporation's global reach. It also has a long affiliation with the LNG (liquid natural gas or liquefied natural gas) industry in several regions, beginning in the 1960s in Algeria. Total has since conducted LNG operations in Indonesia, Australia, Russia, and a number of Middle Eastern countries, including Qatar and Yemen. Total's heavy involvement in LNG in so many regions has made the company "an integral proponent of LNG's remarkable growth story," wrote Daniel Canty in a 2012 article on the ArabianOilandGas.com website about the oil and gas industry. Canty added that "the company is well-positioned to lead LNG expansion in the years ahead."

Total's varied business interests have brought it recognition. Its services to shareholders have garnered various honors, such 2010 and 2011 Boursoscan prizes for excellence in investor relations. Prominent people have also discussed Total. In 2012 Aung San Suu Kyi, a Nobel Peace Prize winner and a member of the parliament in Myanmar (Burma), called the company "a responsible investor in Burma." She acknowledged that although there were once questions about Total's support of Myanmar's past military regime, she stated that Total now "is sensitive to the issue of human rights."

BRAND OUTLOOK

- Total's Eco 10 program is intended to limit fuel use.
- Since the early 1980s, Total has worked to research, develop, and promote photovoltaic solar energy systems that capture sunlight and convert it into electricity.

- In 2010 Total began a partnership with renewable-product company Amyris to develop renewable fuels made from plant sugars and develop ways to produce these fuels for mass markets.

The company has also intensified its environmental efforts. Total claims that consumers can use its Eco 10 program to limit fuel use. The program encourages the use of Total fuel and oil and encourages vehicle owners to maintain their vehicles and keep the vehicles' tires properly inflated. This program simultaneously aims to limit the consumption of fuel while promoting the specific, judicious use of Total products.

Total's other environmental interests include its affiliations with alternative energy. It has been interested in photovoltaic solar energy since the early 1980s. Photovoltaic solar energy systems capture sunlight and convert it into electricity. Total has put resources into research and development to study and develop these systems. It has created and provided materials promoting solar energy at a number of its gas stations.

In other environmental developments for the company, Total has worked to develop renewable fuels, or fuels from renewable sources, as opposed to nonrenewable fossil fuels like oil. In 2010 it began a partnership with Amyris, a company specializing in renewable products. Total and Amyris have worked to convert plant sugars into a type of renewable diesel fuel and produce this fuel for mass markets. This project is another instance of Total applying its oil and gas interests to environmental issues.

FURTHER READING

Canty, Daniel. "Golden Age of Gas: Total's LNG Chief." ArabianOilandGas.com, September 12, 2012. Accessed January 28, 2013. http://www.arabianoilandgas.com/article-10602-golden-age-of-gas-totals-lng-chief/.

DeCarlo, Scott. "Forbes Global 2000." *Forbes*, April 18, 2012.

"Total Qatar Extends Partnership with QREC up to 2018." *Qatar Tribune*, September 20, 2012.

Total S.A. "Aung San Suu Kyi Calls Total a 'Responsible Investor in Burma.'" June 15, 2012. Accessed January 28, 2013. http://www.total.com/en/about-total/news/news-940500.html&idActu=2818.

———. "Group Presentation." Accessed January 18, 2013. http://www.total.com/en/about-total/group-presentation/group-history/total-group-history-922650.html.

———. "Total and Amyris Partner to Produce Renewable Fuels." November 30, 2011. Accessed January 28, 2013. http://www.total.com/en/about-total/news/news-940500.html&idActu=2690. USE?

———. "Total Marketing in the U.A.E." Accessed January 20, 2013. http://www.totalmarketingmiddleeast.com/Lub/LubUAE.nsf/VS_OPM/30254C155691FA90C12572790035 4AF0?OpenDocument.

"Total S.A." *International Directory of Company Histories*. Ed. Jay P. Pederson. Vol. 118. Detroit, MI: St. James Press, 2011.

"2 High-Yielding European Oil and Gas Majors with Strong Reserves." SeekingAlpha.com, February 28, 2012. Accessed January 21, 2013. http://seekingalpha.com/article/396641-2-high-yielding-european-oil-and-gas-majors-with-strong-reserves.

Werdigier, Julia. "Oil Company Says Gas Leak Costs $2.5 Million a Day." *New York Times*, April 2, 2012.

TOYOTA

—■—

AT A GLANCE

Brand Synopsis: Toyota's three-oval logo has come to stand for some of the most popular automobile models in the world, as well as for the company's pioneering work in environmentally friendly hybrid vehicles.

Parent Company: Toyota Motor Corporation
1, Toyota-Cho
Toyota-Shi Ach 471-8571
Japan
http://www.toyota-global.com/

Sector: Consumer Discretionary

Industry Group: Automobiles and Components

Performance: *Market share*—15.2 percent worldwide (2010); 27.6 percent in Japan and 12.6 percent in the United States (2011). *Sales*—US$3.5 billion worldwide (2012).

Principal Competitors: Chrysler Group LLC; Ford Motor Company; General Motors Company; Honda Motor Company, Ltd.

BRAND ORIGINS

- Toyota began as the automobile division of Toyoda Automatic Loom Works in the 1930s.
- Among popular Toyota series introduced in the 1950s and 1960s were the Land Cruiser, Crown, Corona, and Corolla.

- Toyota entered the U.S. market in 1957 and by 1975 had surpassed Volkswagen as the leading supplier of imported vehicles to the United States.
- In the late 1980s Toyota established Lexus as a luxury division, and in the late 1990s it introduced the gas- and electric-powered hybrid Prius.
- During the early 21st century Toyota weathered the global financial crisis, worldwide recalls, and a massive earthquake and tsunami in Japan.

After a visit to several U.S. automobile manufacturing plants in 1933, Kiichiro Toyoda established the auto division of his father's company, Toyoda Automatic Loom Works. The division produced its first prototype vehicle in 1936 and, with a new spelling, became Toyota Motor Company in 1937. After focusing on war production in the 1940s, Toyota in the 1950s introduced a number of enduring series, including the four-wheel-drive Land Cruiser (1951), the full-size Crown (1955), and the mid-size Corona (1957). Another popular model, the Corolla compact, followed in 1966.

Toyota entered the U.S. market in 1957, and by 1975 it had surpassed Volkswagen Group as the leading supplier of imported vehicles to the United States. By 1980 it ranked second only to General Motors Company (GM) in total car production worldwide. In 1982, the year it debuted the Camry, Toyota Motor Company merged with Toyota Motor Sales to form the Toyota Motor Corporation. It began producing cars in the United States, first through a 1984 joint venture with GM, and after 1986, through Toyota Motor Manufacturing, USA, Inc.

Expanding its product line, Toyota in 1989 established Lexus as a luxury division and in 1993 entered the U.S. full-size pickup truck market with the T100. Several sport-utility vehicle lines followed, along with the gas- and electric-powered hybrid Prius in 1997 and the sporty Scion in 2003. During the early 21st century Toyota weathered a number of challenges, including the global financial crisis, worldwide recalls of some 8 million vehicles in 2009 and 2010, and a massive earthquake and tsunami in Japan in March 2011.

BRAND ELEMENTS

- Founder Kiichiro Toyoda's sister-in-law suggested a company name change to "Toyota" in 1936.
- Among the reasons for the name change was the fact that "Toyoda" means "fertile rice paddies," which hardly seemed fitting for a car manufacturer.
- The Toyota logo used outside of Japan features three ovals in red against a white backdrop.
- Two of the ovals in the Toyota logo form a "T," while the larger oval surrounding them symbolizes the global reach and technological potential of the brand.
- Well-known advertising slogans used by Toyota in North America and elsewhere include "You asked for it! You got it! Toyota" and "Oh, what a feeling!"

In 1936, during a public contest for a new logo, Toyota founder Kiichiro Toyoda's sister-in-law, Rizaburo, suggested a company name change on aesthetic grounds. Not only did "Toyota" sound better when spoken, Rizaburo maintained, but it also looked better when written in Japanese, and the fact that it required eight brush strokes seemed auspicious in a culture that regarded eight as a lucky number. Perhaps most important was the fact that the word "Toyoda" means "fertile rice paddies," an image that hardly seemed fitting for a forward-looking industrial firm.

The 1936 logo, which renders the company name in stylized Japanese characters within a red circle, remains in use in Japan. Throughout the rest of the world, however, Toyota uses a logo composed of three ovals in red against a white backdrop. The largest of these ovals, which symbolizes the global reach and technological potential of the Toyota brand, surrounds the smaller two, which form a capital "T." Besides representing the brand name, the overlapping ovals of the "T" illustrate a relationship of mutual trust and benefit between customer and company.

Well-known advertising slogans used by Toyota in North America and elsewhere include "You asked for it! You got it! Toyota" (1975–79), "Oh, what a feeling!" (1979–85), "Who could ask for anything more?" (1985–89), and "I love what you do for me, Toyota!" (1989–97).

BRAND IDENTITY

- Toyota changed its brand name from "Toyopet" to "Toyota" in the face of a negative response from U.S. buyers in the 1950s.
- The company adopted its logo in 1989 to present a consistent image worldwide.
- Marketing slogans in the late 20th century emphasized a positive customer experience, while those in the early 21st century have depicted Toyota as the wave of the future.
- Besides its logo and marketing campaigns, Toyota's brand image is characterized by a set of principles known as "the Toyota Way."

Just as it changed its name from "Toyoda" to "Toyota" for reasons relating to its Japanese base, Toyota has made a number of brand-identity adjustments with an eye toward global marketing. During the decade prior to entering the U.S. market in 1957, the company used the brand name "Toyopet," but U.S. buyers did not respond well to this name, with its suggestion of playthings. Thus, the company began selling its cars in the United States (and, after the mid-1960s, globally) under the Toyota brand name.

Similarly, the adoption of the three-oval logo in 1989 was a response to the needs of the international marketplace. Though ostensibly the company made the change to commemorate a half century in business, it also did so in order to establish a consistent identity in overseas markets and to differentiate Toyota from the newly created Lexus line.

Toyota advertising slogans of the late 20th century (e.g., "Oh, what a feeling!") emphasized the positive experience of owning a Toyota. In the 21st century, taglines such as "Moving Forward" and "Today Tomorrow Toyota," used respectively in North America and Europe, depicted the company and its brand as the wave of the future.

Besides its logo and marketing campaigns, Toyota's brand image is characterized by a set of principles known as "the Toyota Way." These became formalized as "Toyota Way 2001," which outlines five principles: Challenge, *Kaizen* ("improvement"), *Genchi Genbutsu* ("go and see"), Respect, and Teamwork. Together, these principles reflect the stated company values of "Respect for People" and "Continuous Improvement."

BRAND STRATEGY

- Like its original 1936 Model AA, most of the 70-plus models Toyota offered in the early 21st century were passenger sedans.
- The names of the Corolla and Camry are variations (in Latin and Japanese, respectively) of the word "crown."
- Toyota's various model names vary greatly by region. For example, the same vehicle is marketed as the

"ist" in Japan, the Scion xD in North America, and the Urban Cruiser in Europe.

- Toyota's most popular hybrid is called the Prius, a name taken from the Latin term for "before" to signify the company's early interest in environmental issues.
- Nearly half of Toyota's worldwide sales come from its native Japan, while the North American market accounts for a fifth of total sales.

Like its original 1936 Model AA, most of the 70-plus models Toyota offered in the early 21st century were passenger sedans. These included subcompacts known as the Yaris, Vios, and Echo, depending on the region in which they were marketed, as well as the compact Corolla (Latin for "crown"), the midsize Camry (a name based on the Japanese word for "crown," *kanmuri*), and the full-size luxury Crown.

Toyota vans include the Verso, a compact multipurpose vehicle (MPV) sold in Europe; the Alphard, an Asian luxury hybrid; the Tarago, an MPV for the Australian market; and the Sienna, made for the US market. Toyota also offers a subcompact MPV known in Japan as the "ist" (from the English suffix "–ist"), the Scion xD in North America, and the Urban Cruiser in Europe.

Toyota's sport-utility vehicles include the RAV4, a crossover that offers the fuel efficiency of a smaller car; the midsize 4Runner; the Land Cruiser, Toyota's oldest series; and the FJ Cruiser, which has a design that recalls that of early Land Cruisers. Besides its highly popular pickup trucks, including the Tacoma in North America and the Hilux in other parts of the world, Toyota markets commercial trucks under the Dyna name. It also sells a minibus, the Coaster.

In the 21st century Toyota has focused particularly on hybrids, vehicles that supplement gasoline power by using electricity. Most notable among its hybrid offerings was the midsize hatchback Prius, a name that comes from a Latin term meaning "before," signifying the fact that Toyota designers conceived it before environmental concerns became a prominent feature of everyday life.

As of 2012, Toyota had more than 500 consolidated subsidiaries and more than 200 affiliated companies selling to approximately 170 countries. Nearly half of Toyota's sales came from its native Japan, with Asian sales overall accounting for about 60 percent of the total. North America constituted another 20 percent of its global business.

BRAND EQUITY

- Toyota ranked 11th on Interbrand's 2011 list of the top-100 global brands, making Toyota the most valuable of the 12 automotive brands on the list.
- Interbrand estimated Toyota's brand value at nearly US$28 billion for 2011, a 6 percent increase over 2010.

- Among the many high rankings Toyota earned in 2010 and 2011 was a first-place position on *Consumer Reports*' "Car Brand Perception Survey."
- In 2011 the Toyota Camry was the third best-selling automobile worldwide and the best-selling midsize automobile worldwide.
- Toyota's Corolla/Matrix sold more than 240,000 units in 2011, making it the world's best-selling compact car for that year.

Toyota ranked 11th on leading brand consultancy Interbrand's "Best Global Brands" list in 2011. With a brand value of US$27.8 billion, a 6 percent increase over the previous year, Toyota was the most valuable of the 12 automotive brands on the 2011 list. *Brandirectory*, which ranked Toyota 15th for 2012, valued the brand at US$24.5 billion. Toyota also placed high on other lists between 2010 and 2012. Among these were the ADAC-AutomarxX Brand Ranking (eighth place for 2010 and 2011), the Harris Poll EquiTrend study (fourth place in the 2012 "Full Line Automotive" category), Interbrand's "Best Global Green Brands" and "Japan's Best Global Brands" (first place in 2010 and 2011), and the *Consumer Reports* "Car Brand Perception Survey" (first place in 2010 and 2011).

In 2011 *Business Rankings Annual*, published by Gale, ranked Toyota as the world's most valuable automobile and parts company and also the world's most valuable Japanese company. Toyota's estimated worth of more than US$139 billion made it nearly twice as valuable as second-place Daimler AG and far ahead of fifth-place Ford Motor Company (Ford) at US$56.4 billion and seventh-place General Motors Company (GM) at US$48.4 billion. Toyota came in second only to GM in global unit sales for 2009, with US$1.8 million in units sold worldwide as compared to GM's US$2.1 million and Ford's US$1.7 million. According to *Market Share Reporter*, also published by Gale, Toyota was the top automaker in Japan for 2011, with more than twice as many units produced as second-place Nissan Motor Company Ltd (Nissan). Toyota ranked third, after GM and Ford, among top automakers worldwide for 2010.

In 2011, with nearly 309,000 units sold worldwide, the Toyota Camry was the third best-selling automobile worldwide (after the Ford F-Series and the Chevrolet Silverado) and the best-selling midsize automobile worldwide. The Toyota Corolla/Matrix, with more than 240,000 units sold worldwide, ranked first among compact models for that year.

BRAND AWARENESS

- In 2009 Toyota spent US$2.3 billion on advertising worldwide, placing it seventh among all companies.

- With high consumer awareness of the brand, Toyota has often focused on building a favorable image, particularly among U.S. buyers.
- Toyota scored third place in a 2012 car brand awareness survey by *Consumer Reports*.

Toyota ranks high among advertisers in all industries, not just the automobile trade. In 2009 it spent more than US$2.3 billion on advertising worldwide, placing it seventh among all companies. In comparison, fourth-ranked General Motors Company (GM) spent nearly US$3.3 billion, while the world's number-one advertiser, the Procter and Gamble Company, spent almost US$8.7 billion. Toyota held a ninth-place position among television advertisers in 2011, with more than US$767 million spent, compared to US$1.1 billion for third-ranked GM, US$890 million for fifth-ranked Chrysler Group LLC, and US$781 million for eighth-ranked Ford Motor Company (Ford). The Procter and Gamble Company also led the TV advertising list in 2011, spending more than US$1.7 billion.

Toyota's marketing efforts have tended to be directed not so much toward making consumers aware of the brand as toward shaping that awareness in ways favorable to the Japanese carmaker. In the United States, for instance, Toyota has sought to remind buyers of the fact that its U.S. manufacturing plants provide jobs to Americans and contribute economically to their communities.

A 2012 car brand awareness survey by *Consumer Reports* found Toyota in third place for the second year in a row. When asked to name an automotive brand, consumers mentioned Toyota 70 percent of the time, up from 68 percent in 2011. In first place was Ford with 87 percent, second was Chevrolet with 76 percent, and fourth was Honda with 57 percent. Most other brands had less than 40 percent. After the results were scored for overall brand perception across seven categories (safety, quality, value, performance, environmentally friendly/green, design/style, and technology/innovation) Toyota had the lead with a total of 131 points. Ford was second with 121, and Honda was third with 94. Although Toyota's score had slipped from 147 in 2011, the brand received the highest marks for quality and environmental friendliness.

BRAND OUTLOOK

- Despite the 2009 and 2010 recalls and a devastating 2011 earthquake and tsunami in Japan, Toyota was able to bounce back to its pre-2010 market share within just two years.
- Toyota has aggressively sought (and, in large part, achieved) a leading position in the growing market for hybrid cars.

- As of August 2009, Toyota had sold more than 2 million hybrids, three-quarters of them under the Prius name.
- *Market Share Reporter* predicted that by 2015, Toyota would hold a 39 percent share of the electric vehicle market, more than Ford, Nissan, and GM combined.

In the midst of Toyota's recall troubles, Derrick Daye and Brad VanAuken of *Branding Strategy Insider* expressed concerns regarding the company's brand architecture. Like other Japanese firms, Toyota had largely used a single brand, unlike General Motors Company (GM), which as of 2009 had 11 distinct brands. "Focusing on a sub-brand approach," the authors wrote, "in which most of its cars are linked to a single corporate brand, means that a problem with any vehicle at Toyota will not only affect sales of the model in question, but also spread across the whole range."

Despite the recalls and other challenges, including an earthquake and tsunami that struck Japan (and Toyota's profits) in March 2011, the brand has shown great resiliency. Brand consultant Lisa Merriam, recalling a colleague's prediction that it would take Toyota a decade or two to recover from the recalls and the tsunami, wrote in March 2012 that, after just two years, "The Toyota brand is definitely back." Along the way, she maintained, Toyota had "become a textbook example of how a brand can bounce back." She attributed its success in part to effective communication with the public but went on to note that "by far the most credit for Toyota's recovery is due to decades of delivering on its brand promise of durable, affordable high quality cars."

In line with its corporate principle of "Continuous Improvement," Toyota has aggressively sought (and, in large part, achieved) a leading position in the growing market for hybrid cars. In addition to the Prius, the best-selling hybrid in the United States, Toyota has marketed hybrid versions of the Camry and Auris sedans, as well as the Highlander sport-utility vehicle. As of August 2009, Toyota had sold more than 2 million hybrids (three-quarters of them under the Prius name) to buyers in more than 50 countries. *Market Share Reporter* predicted that by 2015, Toyota would hold a 39 percent share of the electric vehicle market, more than Ford Motor Company (Ford), Nissan Motor Company Ltd (Nissan), and General Motors Company (GM) combined.

FURTHER READING

Bartlett, Jeff. "2012 Car Brand Perception Survey: Ford Leads All in Brand Awareness." *Consumer Reports*, January 26, 2012. Accessed February 13, 2013. http://news.consumerreports. org/cars/2012/01/2012-car-brand-perception-survey-ford-leads-all-brands-in-awareness.html.

Daye, Derrick, and Brad VanAuken. "Toyota's Brand Problems Begin at Its Core." *Branding Strategy Insider*, March 22, 2010. Accessed September 27, 2012. http://www.brandingstrategy-insider.com/2010/03/toyotas-brand-problems-begin-at-its-core.html.

Halliday, Jean. "VW and Toyota Want Owners to Tout Their Brands." *Forbes*, September 17, 2012.

Kelly, Anne Marie. "Has Toyota's Image Recovered from the Brand's Recall Crisis?" *Forbes*, March 5, 2012. Accessed September 27, 2012. http://www.forbes.com/sites/annemariekelly/2012/03/05/has-toyotas-image-recovered-from-the-brands-recall-crisis/print/.

Lassa, Todd. "US Market Share for the Top Five Automakers: Closing in on Western Europe's 18-18-18 Model?" *Motor Trend*, February 2012. Accessed September 27, 2012. http://www.motortrend.com/features/auto_news/2011/1202_u_s_markets_share_for_the_top_five_automakers/?ti=v2&rec=1.

Merriam, Lisa. "The Toyota Brand Bounces Back." Merriam Associates, March 6, 2012. Accessed September 27, 2012. http://merriamassociates.com/2012/03/the-toyota-brand-bounces-back/.

"Toyota." RankingTheBrands.com. Accessed September 27, 2012. http://www.rankingthebrands.com/Brand-detail.aspx?brandID=13.

Toyota Motor Corporation. "Annual Report 2011." Accessed September 27, 2012. http://www.toyota-global.com/investors/ir_library/annual/pdf/2011/ar11_e.pdf.

"Toyota Motor Corporation." *International Directory of Company Histories*. Ed. Tina Grant. Vol. 100. Detroit, MI: St. James Press, 2009.

"2011 Ranking of the Top 100 Brands." Interbrand. Accessed September 27, 2012. http://www.interbrand.com/en/best-global-brands/best-global-brands-2008/best-global-brands-2011.aspx.

TWITTER

———■———

AT A GLANCE

———■———

Brand Synopsis: As one of the most popular social media websites in the world, Twitter emphasizes its commitment to the free and open exchange of information.

Parent Company: Twitter, Inc.
1355 Market Street, Suite 900
San Francisco, California 94103
United States
http://www.twitter.com

Sector: Telecommunication Services

Industry Group: Telecommunication Services

Performance: *Market share*—2% among social networking websites (August 2012). *Sales*—US$45 million (2010).

Principal Competitors: AOL, Inc.; Facebook, Inc.; Google Inc.; Pinterest; Myspace

BRAND ORIGINS

- Internet entrepreneurs Jack Dorsey, Evan Williams, and Biz Stone launched Twitter in 2006.
- Twitter is often referred to as a microblogging service, as messages shared on Twitter are limited to 140 characters.
- Initially, Twitter relied heavily on investors and venture capital for financing, but in 2010 the company began generating revenue through paid advertising.

The birth of the concept underpinning Twitter can be traced to founder Jack Dorsey, who began his software development career as a teenager. At the age of 14, Dorsey started writing programming code for a dispatch company in his hometown of St. Louis, Missouri, developing open source software that enabled taxi drivers, limousine drivers, and couriers to communicate. Dorsey's interest in dispatch software continued as he progressed through his teenage and college years.

Dorsey was a 10-year veteran of writing dispatch programs by the time he launched his career as an entrepreneur at the age of 24. In 2000 he started a company in Oakland, California, that dispatched couriers, taxis, and emergency services via the Internet. Around the same time, Dorsey began exploring the idea of instant status communication, prompting him to tinker with fusing together dispatch software, instant messaging, and text messaging. His work in this area continued for several years, reaching fruition when he joined forces with the two other architects of Twitter's formation, Evan Williams and Christopher Isaac "Biz" Stone.

Intent on entering the technology sector, Evan Williams left the University of Nebraska midway through his sophomore year. He worked for several start-up firms in Texas and Florida before moving to California. In 1999, at the age of 27, Williams started his entrepreneurial career. He cofounded Pyra Labs, a start-up firm whose first product was a web application functioning as a project manager, contact manager, and to-do list. Williams then developed an offshoot of the product, a web application that created and managed web logs. Williams named the application "Blogger," giving the technology sector one of its most frequently used words of the early 21st century.

Google acquired Pyra Labs in early 2003, and Williams went with the company, serving as a Google employee until 2004, when he left to cofound a podcasting company called Odeo. Joining him in launching Odeo was Biz Stone, who had also helped Williams create Blogger. In 2006, Dorsey met Williams and Stone at Odeo's headquarters in San Francisco, a meeting that would ultimately lead to the creation of Twitter.

Dorsey and Stone collaborated on the first Twitter prototype at Odeo's offices. The pair spent two weeks creating a program that would enable short messages to be shared among mobile devices. They launched a limited version of the service in early 2006 for Odeo employees, who used the program to communicate with one another. In July 2006 a full-scale version of Twitter was released to the public. Referred to as a "microblog," Twitter limited its messages (called "tweets") to 140 characters, giving the public a new way to communicate that ignited frenzied use in staccato fragments.

Twitter experienced rapid growth in its first few years. In 2007 there were approximately 400,000 tweets posted per quarter, but by 2010 that number had grown to 65 million tweets posted each day. In March 2012, Twitter celebrated its sixth birthday by announcing it had reached 140 million active users, an increase of 40 percent from September 2011. By 2012, Twitter had become one of the top three social networking websites based on market share of visits, its top competitors being Facebook and YouTube.

Despite the rapid growth in the number of Twitter users, concerns have been raised about the company's financial viability. During its first years in business, Twitter relied mostly on venture capital and investors to stay afloat. In 2010, however, the company began generating revenue through a paid advertising program, which was extended to mobile devices in 2012. Although Twitter remained a privately held company in 2012, some analysts have predicted it may begin its transformation into a public company as early as 2013.

BRAND ELEMENTS

- In 2012 the Twitter name was removed from the company's logo, which now features only the image of a small, blue bird.
- The company's name was chosen because the definition of "twitter" ("short bursts of inconsequential information") was deemed to fit the product.
- The widespread use of Twitter has introduced new terms like "tweet," "hashtag," and "trending" into everyday conversation.

Twitter's original logo featured the company name in lowercase, rounded, light-blue lettering. A redesign in 2010 retained the font style of the company name but changed the coloring from blue to black. A small, blue bird was also added to the right of the company name. At that time the Twitter brand was also symbolized by a blue, lowercase "t," which was outlined in white and placed within a blue square.

In mid-2012 the Twitter logo underwent another redesign. The company name was dropped, and the logo's only element became the light-blue bird that had been added in 2010, although the design of the bird was streamlined slightly. In explanation of the new logo, Twitter said it felt that "a bird in flight is the ultimate representation of freedom, hope, and limitless possibility."

When Jack Dorsey was developing Twitter, he used the project code name "twttr," immortalized by Dorsey's first message on the service, which read, "just setting up my twttr." In a 2009 interview with the *Los Angeles Times,* Dorsey explained the reasoning behind the company name, saying, "We came across the word 'twitter,' and it was just perfect. The definition was 'a short burst of inconsequential information,' and 'chirps from birds.' And that's exactly what the product was."

The popularity of Twitter has introduced new terms into informal, everyday vernacular. Posted messages on Twitter are known as "tweets." Registered users can subscribe to other users' tweets by "following" those users. "Hashtags," or words or phrases preceded by the "#"symbol, are used to group together multiple posts about the same topic. When a user is replying to or mentioning another person on Twitter, that person's username is placed after the "@" symbol. This combination of the "@" symbol followed by a username is referred to as a "handle." The most popular words or phrases being used in tweets at any given time are referred to as "trending topics."

BRAND IDENTITY

- By giving users the ability to share information instantaneously with a large number of people, Twitter has in many ways transformed the way the world communicates.
- Twitter is the "fastest, simplest way to stay close to everything you care about."
- Although much "inconsequential information" is shared on Twitter, the service also facilitates communication about significant world events and natural disasters.

Twitter's brand identity has evolved throughout the company's history. Viewed initially as a unique way to keep tabs on busy friends, Twitter has in many ways changed the way the world communicates. The defining characteristic of Twitter is the open exchange of information, and the company is proud of its status as a real-time information network that encourages both public and private interactions, whether they be one-to-one or one-to-a-crowd.

According to the "About Twitter" section on the Twitter website, Twitter is the "fastest, simplest way to stay close to everything you care about." Keeping things simple is at the core of the Twitter brand identity. Twitter conveys this straightforward and simple identity by focusing on Twitter content and emphasizing that Twitter is an information network. Twitter's image is not weighed down by extraneous details. The Twitter website itself is very clean and simple, and the company information section provides few details about the company's location, its staff, or its corporate values.

Twitter has become a conversation hub where users have the freedom to express thoughts and opinions at any time. Millions of people use Twitter as an instantaneous way to share and find information after hurricanes, floods, and other natural disasters. Tweets have helped spark revolts and revolutions in countries like Egypt, Iran, and Tunisia, causing some governments to attempt to block the service.

BRAND STRATEGY

- Twitter's application programming code is available to the public, which has enabled third-party software developers to create thousands of applications for the service.
- In 2010, Twitter began offering advertising opportunities with Promoted Tweets, Promoted Accounts, and Promoted Trends, which account for much of the company's revenue.
- Twitter also offers self-serve advertising, a more affordable option for smaller businesses.

Twitter makes its application programming code available to the public, enabling third-party software developers to create applications for the service. This strategy is a win–win situation. Twitter increases its consumer appeal without the cost of additional programming and third-party programmers make revenues from their applications. Thousands of applications have been created, such as TweetDeck, which lets users segment and rearrange tweets on a computer screen. The application Twitpic enables users to share photos in their tweets, while Twitterfeed gives users the ability to post messages to Twitter and to several other microblogging platforms at the same time. Other popular Twitter applications include Twhirl, which enables users to post and view tweets on their computer desktop without logging on to the Twitter website, and HootSuite, which allows users to manage multiple social networking profiles through one dashboard.

In 2010 Twitter debuted Promoted Tweets, its first advertising platform, featuring ads that appear at the top of a Twitter user search. Users can "re-tweet" (or share) the ad to pass it on to other users. Although Promoted Tweets initially appeared only on the Twitter website, the company distributed them to mobile devices in 2012. As a companion to the Promoted Tweets program, Twitter launched Promoted Accounts as a way for advertisers to grow a loyal follower base. Through the Promoted Account program, Twitter studies current Twitter users to look for people who might be interested in the advertiser. When it finds a match, Twitter places the advertiser in that user's "Who to Follow" section. Similarly, Twitter's Promoted Trends program matches advertisers with trending topics. When a business advertises using Promoted Trends, its ad tweets are automatically placed at the top of a trending conversation.

By 2012, Promoted Tweets, Promoted Accounts, and Promoted Trends had become major sources of revenue for Twitter. In 2011, buying a Promoted Trend on Twitter cost approximately US$120,000 per day, and large corporations proved quite willing to pay such premium rates to advertise their products and services to Twitter's huge number of users. For smaller businesses, Twitter launched self-serve advertising, which is similar to Promoted Tweets and Promoted Accounts but charges the advertiser only when its account is followed or when a user engages with the advertiser's promoted tweet.

BRAND EQUITY

- Brand ranking agency BV4 assigned Twitter a brand value of US$13.3 billion in 2012 and ranked it the third most valuable social media brand.
- Twitter's 2011 earnings were estimated to have been between US$100 million and US$110 million.
- Twitter could see advertising revenues rise to US$1 billion by 2014, according to *Bloomberg*.

In 2012 the brand ranking agency BV4 assigned Twitter a brand value of US$13.3 billion and ranked it the third most valuable social media brand, behind only Facebook and YouTube. The 2012 Siegel+Gale Global Brand Simplicity Index, a ranking of brands with a simplicity value that inspires brand loyalty, ranked Twitter at number 70, with brands like Google, McDonald's, and Apple appearing at the top of the list.

As a privately held company, Twitter declines to release revenue data. However, in 2011 the *Wall Street Journal* reported that Twitter generated 2010 revenues of approximately US$45 million and estimated its 2011 revenues at between US$100 million and US$110 million. Meanwhile, Internet market research company eMarketer estimated that Twitter would earn US$288 million in 2012 advertising revenues, while *Bloomberg* reported that Twitter could see advertising revenues rise to US$1 billion by 2014.

Twitter has also been commended for its creative and cutting-edge corporate image and culture. In 2012, *Fast Company* ranked Twitter sixth on its Most Innovative Companies list, a ranking of businesses that provide creativity in the global marketplace. In 2010, Allegro234 ranked Twitter 16th on its global Coolest Brands list, while in 2012 the Centre for Brand Analysis ranked Twitter fourth on a list called the Top 20 Cool Brands.

BRAND AWARENESS

- According to a 2010 report by Experian, the average American user spent 2 hours and 12 minutes on Twitter every month.
- Although originally released in English, Twitter was available in 33 languages by 2012.
- The number of tweets posted on Twitter spikes during significant events around the globe.

In 2010, 79 of the top 100 companies on *Fortune* magazine's Global 500 list had active Twitter accounts. In 2010 global information services group Experian reported that the total amount of time the average American user spent on Twitter every month was 2 hours and 12 minutes. Approximately 39 percent of those users were between the ages of 18 and 24. These numbers suggest that Twitter has an extremely high brand awareness.

In 2012, Twitter was estimated to hold a 2 percent market share among social networking websites, with Facebook and YouTube serving as its closest competitors. In 2012, Twitter announced it was handling 340 million tweets per day and had 140 million active users. In 2012, Twitter was available in 33 languages, including Japanese, Ukrainian, Farsi, and Hebrew.

Twitter is one of the 10 most visited websites on the Internet. The number of tweets posted on the site spikes during significant global events, such as political elections and rallies, major sporting events, and natural disasters. In late 2012 the Twitter users with the most followers were primarily celebrities, although U.S. president Barack Obama was the fifth most-followed user on the site.

BRAND OUTLOOK

- Twitter is evolving from a young start-up company with a casual attitude into a media entity with more rules and restrictions.
- Critics charge that Twitter has become more concerned with generating advertising revenue than with serving the users who helped build its popularity.
- Some analysts expect Twitter to launch an initial public offering as early as 2013, though the company must consider the risk of a disappointing IPO.

In 2012, Twitter was in the process of evolving from an open platform to one that was more private and controlled. Third-party developers have begun to find more restrictions placed on applications designed to run on Twitter. The company has also started to buy third-party software to create official Twitter applications for various platforms, blocking popular applications that it feels may be in direct competition with its own interests.

Some former fans of Twitter have become critics, charging that the company that once embraced a free-wheeling environment is now more concerned with advertisers and revenue than with its users. Critics have also asserted that Twitter wants to control more of its users' content so that it can place a value on its growing audience via advertising. As Twitter transforms from a young start-up into a media entity, users will need to decide if they want to remain loyal despite the company's new ambitions and the controls, restrictions, and advertising messages that come with them.

Although Twitter has expressed hopes of remaining an independent company, some expect it to launch an initial public offering as early as 2013. Such a move would have Twitter following in the uncertain footsteps of its top competitor, Facebook, whose initial public offering in 2012 generated a great deal of hype but was ultimately disappointing. Now operating in a culture wary of such letdowns, Twitter is facing increasing pressure to justify the valuation of its brand.

FURTHER READING

Ante, Spencer E., Amir Efrati, and Anupreeta Das. "Twitter as Tech Bubble Barometer." *Wall Street Journal,* February 10, 2011. Accessed December 15, 2012. http://online.wsj.com/article/SB10001424052748703716904576134543029279426.html?KEYWORDS=twitter#.

Arrington, Michael. "Odeo Releases Twttr." *TechCrunch,* July 15, 2006. Accessed December 7, 2012. http://techcrunch.com/2006/07/15/is-twttr-interesting.

Clay, Kelly. "Twitter Possibly Worth More Than $10 Billion." *Forbes,* July 27, 2012. Accessed December 7, 2012. http://www.forbes.com/sites/kellyclay/2012/07/27/twitter-possibly-worth-more-than-10-billion.

Covell, Jeffrey L. "Twitter, Inc." *International Directory of Company Histories.* Ed. Jay P. Pederson. Vol. 118. Detroit: St. James Press, 2011. *Gale Virtual Reference Library.* Accessed December 7, 2012. http://go.galegroup.com/ps/i.do?id=GALE%7CCX1722000098&v=2.1&u=itsbtrial&it=r&p=GVRL&sw=w.

Griggs, Brandon. "Twitter's bird logo gets a makeover." *CNN,* June 7, 2012. Accessed December 7, 2012. http://edition.cnn.com/2012/06/06/tech/social-media/twitter-bird-logo.

"Leaders in Online Advertising Revenues, 2011." *Market Share Reporter.* Detroit: Gale, 2012. *Business Insights: Global.* Accessed December 7, 2012. http://bi.galegroup.com/global/

article/GALE%7CI2502040125/e47af76df32b70795243dc846e564bc3?u=itsbtrial.

Miller, Claire Cain. "Twitter Unveils Plans to Draw Money From Ads." *New York Times,* April 12, 2012. Accessed December 7, 2012. http://www.nytimes.com/2010/04/13/technology/internet/13twitter.html?_r=0.

Taylor, Chris. "Twitter Has 100 Million Active Users." *Mashable,* September 8, 2011. Accessed December 7, 2012. http://mashable.com/2011/09/08/twitter-has-100-million-active-users.

Terdiman, Daniel. "It was six years ago today that twttr began to play." *CNET,* March 21, 2012. Accessed December 7, 2012. http://news.cnet.com/8301-13772_3-57401830-52/it-was-six-years-ago-today-that-twttr-began-to-play.

"Who Uses Twitter, 2009-2010." *Market Share Reporter.* Ed. Robert S. Lazich and Virgil L. Burton III. Detroit: Gale, 2012. *Business Insights: Global.* Accessed November 7, 2012. http://bi.galegroup.com/global/article/GALE%7CI2502038137/343d12b5e1182e3ceccb6c88b11b96a1?u=itsbtrial.

UBS

―――――― ∎ ――――――

AT A GLANCE

――――― ∎ ―――――

Brand Synopsis: Despite a series of scandals, UBS portrays itself as a knowledgeable and trustworthy advisor, dedicated to serving the needs of high net-worth individuals, companies, and institutional investors.

Parent Company: UBS AG

Bahnhofstrasse 45

Zurich

Switzerland

http://www.ubs.com

Sector: Financials

Industry Group: Banks

Performance: *Revenues*— CHF25.4 billion (US$26.9 billion) (2011).

Principal Competitors: Credit Suisse Group AG; HSBC Holdings plc; Citigroup Inc.

BRAND ORIGINS

- The Swiss Bank Corporation was established in 1854.
- Union Bank of Switzerland was created in 1912.
- The 1998 merger of Swiss Bank Corporation and Union Bank of Switzerland created UBS AG.
- A global branding effort in 2000 created the UBS units.
- UBS adopted a "one firm" brand strategy in 2003.

A variety of banks and financial services companies were brought together to create the UBS global brand. The oldest entity was Swiss Bank Corporation, established in 1854 when six private Basel, Switzerland-based banks formed a consortium. The English name, Swiss Bank Corporation (SBC), was adopted in 1917. The other major component was Union Bank of Switzerland (UBS). It was created in 1912 through the merger of two banks with roots dating back to the 1860s. UBS began to expand internationally following World War II, opening a representative office in New York, but primarily the bank focused on its domestic market. By the early 1960s, UBS had become Switzerland's largest bank with 81 branch offices.

Switzerland offered limited growth opportunities for UBS. In the 1980s and 1990s, UBS expanded internationally and became involved in the life insurance market, while continuing to acquire smaller Swiss banks. Despite these steps, UBS in the mid-1990s became the target of dissident shareholders, critical of the bank's conservative management. UBS managed to fend off a takeover attempt, but faced challenges on other fronts as well. In addition to the adverse impact of a Swiss recession, the bank had to contend with the public relations fallout from published reports about its dealings with Nazi Germany and the efforts of Jewish groups demanding reclamation of money that victims of the Holocaust had placed into Swiss bank accounts in anticipation of World War II.

It was against this backdrop that SBC approached UBS about a merger. Although the transaction was characterized as a merger of equals, it became apparent that SBC, despite bringing fewer assets to the marriage, was the dominant partner: about 80 percent of the top posts went to SBC executives. SBC and UBS had planned to call the combined entity United Bank of Switzerland, but because there was already a United Bank Switzerland, they elected to use UBS AG as the bank's new name to avoid any confusion.

In 2000 UBS consolidated its business brands into a UBS global brand to emphasize that UBS was an integrated investment services firm. The result was three sub-brands: UBS Switzerland for domestic retail and private banking; USB Warburg for international private banking as well as investment banking; and USB Asset Management, responsible for institutional asset management and mutual funds. Later in 2000 UBS acquired Paine Webber Group Inc., the United States' fourth largest brokerage firm, which now became known as UBS Paine Webber. In 2003 UBS went one step further and brought its four groups under a single overarching UBS brand, adopting a "one firm" strategy.

BRAND ELEMENTS

- The relative youth of the UBS brand prevents the brand elements from being well established.
- The three keys in the UBS logo are meant to symbolize confidence, security, and discretion.
- The "You & Us" theme was used as a tagline in the formative years of the brand.

The elements that comprise the UBS brand are neither plentiful nor striking. The UBS name is hardly evocative, chosen merely to avoid confusion with another Swiss financial services firm. The initials have some resonance in the Swiss market, where one of UBS's successor companies, Union Bank of Switzerland, was highly recognizable. Outside of Switzerland, however, UBS was little known. UBS's "one firm" global branding strategy is also relatively new, allowing the bank little time to establish positive connections with the name in the minds of consumers. Moreover, the early years of the brand coincided with financial collapse and corruption in the banking sector. All too often, UBS was linked to these matters, casting a negative light on the brand name.

The primary image of the UBS logo, three overlapping keys, was essentially inherited from the other major component of the 1998 merger: Swiss Bank Corporation. The keys are meant to symbolize confidence, security, and discretion. At the very least, any kind of key represents security. The UBS keys are traditional mortice keys, the old-fashioned look reinforcing an image of confidence and discretion. In the UBS logo, the keys are generally rendered in black while the brand name is red. These colors are not especially important in distinguishing the UBS brand from its competition. The logo as used in signage at UBS buildings and branches, however, helps to build brand awareness.

UBS has no slogan that is closely associated with its brand. Rather, the brand relies on whatever tagline or theme is employed in its latest advertising campaign. Much use was made of "You & Us" in the formative years of the brand. Later, after the bank and its brand were tarnished by scandal, a new theme emerged: "We will not rest."

BRAND IDENTITY

- UBS presents itself as a trusted adviser.
- UBS appeals to high net-worth individuals who do not think of themselves as wealthy.
- The "You & Us" theme in UBS advertising supported the idea of a bank-client partnership.
- The "We will not rest" theme carried an implied apology for improprieties.

UBS attempts to portray itself as a trusted adviser, a valuable partner with the expertise, heft, and, most importantly, the concern necessary to help customers reach their financial goals. While UBS seeks to build its corporate and institutional businesses, the bulk of its branding efforts target individual investors. In particular, UBS appeals to high net-worth individuals who do not think of themselves as wealthy. For the most part, these people have earned their wealth, rather than inherited it, and are more focused on their businesses or careers than they are on their investments. They are the type of people who want to delegate much of their investment responsibilities to someone knowledgeable and trustworthy, and are therefore receptive to the promise of the USB brand.

All aspects of the USB brand reinforce the trusted adviser image. The keys used in the USB logo connote security. Longevity and solidity of the brand are suggested by the traditional style of the keys. The long-used "You & Us" theme in UBS's advertising made claims that supported the brand identity. The ads offered the expressed promise that UBS was concerned about a customer's individual needs and would take the time necessary to understand those needs and goals, and that together they would form a "two-person organization" to achieve a common end.

In the wake of adverse publicity, the UBS tagline was revamped as part of a new brand campaign in 2010. The "We will not rest" theme reaffirmed the bank's commitment to its clients and the value of partnership. The campaign's advertisements featured clients who, with the support of USB, achieved success. The earlier recipe remained essentially unchanged, albeit seasoned with an implied apology and promise to try harder to deserve the trust of clients.

BRAND STRATEGY

- A "one firm, one brand" strategy was adopted in 2003.
- Branding campaigns support the overarching UBS brand as well as UBS divisions.

- The "You & Us" tagline was a major element in the early years of UBS's "one firm, one brand" strategy.
- Subprime mortgage investment losses and the need for a government bailout undercut UBS's brand message.
- The "We will not rest" theme was adopted as part of an effort to repair brand damage.

Since late 2003 UBS has pursued a "one firm, one brand" strategy. After UBS AG was formed through the 1998 merger of Swiss Bank Corporation and Union Bank Corporation, an attempt was made to use UBS as a corporate brand prefix, dividing the business among three sub-brands: UBS Switzerland, UBS Warburg, and USB Asset Management. A short time later, Paine Webber Group Inc. was acquired, creating a fourth sub-brand, UBS Paine Webber. USB also began development on a long-term brand strategy that would provide clarity on USB's identity not only to customers but to employees as well. The commitment of employees was deemed essential because if the brand was to be more than just sloganeering, the people on the front lines had to embody it. Because the linchpin of the new strategy was the portrayal of the brand as a knowledgeable and trustworthy advisor, USB's actual advisors had to believe in the brand and make the brand promise a personal commitment.

The new branding strategy was announced in late 2003, and in February 2004 UBS launched its "You & Us" global branding campaign. Executions focused on the overarching brand and also on UBS Wealth Management and UBS Investment Bank. The campaign proved so successful that in just one year USB was recognized by *Business Week* as one of only five financial service firms on its list of the top 100 global brands.

The "You & Us" campaign was refined in 2006. The UBS logo and tagline were given more prominence, and the photographs were crafted to better emphasize relationship and empathy. Because of the financial crisis that enveloped the world in 2008 and tarnished the reputation of banks and many other financial services companies, UBS became more defensive in its messaging. Despite the difficulties, UBS pledged that relationships developed with clients were unchanged. In further support of this commitment, the bank issued a "manifesto" in 2009, explicitly stating that UBS was financially secure. Given that UBS had written down more than US$50 billion in bad subprime mortgage investments and had only been kept afloat by a Swiss government bailout of nearly US$60 billion, reassurance was clearly in order. The manifesto also renewed a commitment to clients, claiming "We're redoubling our efforts to listen, to understand, and to do the fundamentals better than ever."

In 2010 UBS retired the "You & Us" tagline. The firm replaced it with "We will not rest." Advertising now claimed that UBS would work even harder and refuse to be satisfied until a client's goals were met. The underlying strategy remained unaltered, however. The bank relied on a corporate brand that promised to be a trustworthy partner. The fact that some of the bank's actions in the fact-based world, and those of the entire financial services industry, contradicted this image lent a hint of desperation to the "We will not rest" declaration. A rogue trader scandal that followed in 2011 and the Libor manipulation scandal the year after only served to compromise the brand further.

BRAND EQUITY

- Intense competition in the financial services industry makes brand equity critically important.
- UBS was ranked by Brand Finance as the 6th most valuable banking brand in 2007 and number 36 on the Global 250.
- At the end of 2012, UBS's brand value was estimated to be US$7.29 billion by Brand Finance.
- UBS was ranked number 160 on Brand Finance's 2012 Global 500 list of the world's most valuable brands.
- UBS was ranked number 30 on Brand Finance's Banking 500 list of the world's most valuable bank brands.

Brand equity is especially important to a financial services brand because intense competition in the industry renders differences in price or product features negligible. Customers give less rational consideration to the choice of a financial services company and instead depend on emotional, subjective reasons. Thus, a strong brand is of utmost importance to a firm like UBS. In the simplest measure, the equity of the brand is how many more customers it attracts than the competition.

According to brand consultancy Brand Finance plc, which employs a methodology to assign a monetary value to brands, the UBS brand was worth US$7.29 billion at the end of 2012. As a result, UBS was ranked number 30 on the Brand Finance Banking 500 list of the world's most valuable bank brands in 2013. It was a significant improvement over the performance of UBS in 2011, when at year's end its brand value was US$5.944 billion. For much of the decade, UBS's brand valuation fluctuated greatly in response to downturns and scandal. Before the turmoil caused by the subprime mortgage disaster, UBS was ranked as the 6th most valuable banking brand in 2007 and number 36 on the Global 250 list of the world's most valuable brands.

BRAND AWARENESS

- A strong retail banking network provides strong brand awareness in Switzerland.
- The "one firm, one brand" strategy increased international brand awareness when launched in 2004.
- Scandal has brought unwanted brand awareness since 2007.

Relatively high awareness of the UBS brand has been both a blessing and a curse. In Switzerland, the UBS brand is well known due to the extensive, long-standing retail branch operations of Union Bank of Switzerland. While the use of three keys in the UBS logo was contributed by Swiss Bank Corporation, the UBS initials were well familiar in Switzerland where they were displayed by dozens of Union Bank branches.

The UBS initials were barely known internationally, providing more of a blank slate for UBS AG when it was formed through merger in 1998. The "one firm, one brand" strategy that was launched in 2004 enjoyed solid success in building awareness of UBS and developing positive associations to the brand. After a year of the strategy, UBS reported significant increases in brand awareness in many markets. This claim was supported by UBS stock, which outperformed the Swiss Market Index and average bank share prices. UBS was also recognized as the 45th most valuable brand on the *Business Week* Global 100 list.

BRAND OUTLOOK

- A series of scandals may have a lasting impact on the UBS brand.
- Widespread problems in the financial services industry may diminish UBS's individual culpability.
- Despite damage, the UBS brand remains valuable.
- Emerging markets hold promise for UBS.

The future of the UBS brand is far from certain. A single scandal can have an enduring negative impact on a brand, but UBS suffered a series of scandals in a five-year window. The firm's Wall Street unit was the first New York firm in early 2007 to announce it was taking heavy losses in the subprime mortgage sector, and a few months later UBS's internal hedge fund, Dillon Read Capital Management, folded. Matters grew worse in 2008 when the global financial crisis struck. UBS suffered the worst single-year loss of any Swiss company in history, and if not for a Swiss government bailout would have faced complete collapse. In addition, UBS became the subject of a United States government inquiry that would lead to USB paying a US$780 million settlement in 2009 for helping wealthy Americans to evade taxes.

UBS attempted to repair the damage done to its brand, but the company continued to be tarnished by its conduct. In the fall of 2011, it came to light that the activities of a rogue UBS trader, 31-year-old Kweku Adoboli, that had begun in 2008 had cost UBS US$2.3 billion. A more systemic problem for UBS (and for other banks but not to same level of culpability) was the manipulation of Libor and other interest rate benchmarks. In December 2012 UBS agreed to a US$1.5 billion settlement with regulators in the United States, United Kingdom, and Switzerland. It was one of the largest fines ever imposed on a bank. Separately, a Japanese subsidiary pleaded guilty in U.S. criminal court to a count of fraud related to benchmark manipulation. Two UBS traders were also charged with fraud and antitrust violations, ensuring that the damage to the reputation of UBS and its brand would continue.

The reputation of the entire financial services sector was tarnished during this period, creating a sense of distrust associated with all financial services brands. For UBS, which made trustworthiness an essential part of its identity, the damage may be substantial and long lasting. Despite its blemishes and a loss in equity, UBS remains a very valuable brand. Because the financial services sector has experienced so many widespread scandals in so short a period of time, the entire industry has been held collectively guilty. Thus, UBS has been provided with some measure of cover. Even if they adopt an attitude of "a pox on all of their houses," people and institutions will still needed to do business with banks. It is very likely that UBS will not be singled out for punishment. Whether UBS would ever truly embody its brand and be seen as a trustworthy advisor and committed partner to its clients is a question only time could answer.

FURTHER READING

Bart, Katharina, Tom Miles, and Aruna Viswanatha. "USB Traders Charged, Bank Fined $1.5 Billion in Libor Scandal." Reuters, December 19, 2012.

Brand Finance. "Global 500 2012." *Brandirectory*. Accessed February 12, 2013. http://brandirectory.com/league_tables/table/global-500-2012.

Elliott, Stuart. "Great Recession Takes Great Toll on Value of Brand Names." *New York Times*, September 18, 2009.

Ferrell, O. C., John Fraedrich, and Lind Ferrell. "Banking Industry Meltdown." *Business Ethics: Ethical Decision Making and Cases*. Boston, MA: Houghton Mifflin College Division 2009.

Loch, Oliver, and Patricia Kidd. "Building the Corporate Brand." ESOMAR Conference on Financial Services, February 2005. http://www.harrisinteractive.com/vault/ESOMAR_Research_Paper_Corp_Brand.pdf. Accessed February 12, 2013.

Shoffman, Marc. "UBS Faces Action by UK and Swiss Regulators." *Financial Times*, February 9, 2012.

Slater, Steve, and Katharina Bart. "USB Faces $1 Billion Day of Reckoning over Interest Rate Rigging." Reuters, December 16, 2012.

"Swiss Bank to Open Secret Files." *Information Management Journal*, May–June 2009.

"UBS AG." *International Directory of Company Histories*. Ed. Tina Grant. Vol. 134. Detroit, MI: St. James Press, 2012.

"UBS Centralizes Global Identity to Raise Awareness." *Marketing*, February 10, 2000.

UNITEDHEALTHCARE

■

BRAND ORIGINS

- UnitedHealthcare's founding dates to 1973.
- UnitedHealthcare acquired Humana, Inc., to create UnitedHealthcare Group.
- UnitedHealthcare's first major national branding campaign was launched in 2000.
- A 2003 branding campaign relied on the "UnitedHealthcare: It just makes sense" tagline.

The visionary behind the founding of UnitedHealth Group Inc. was Dr. Paul Ellwood, who is considered the father of the managed health care (HMO) model. In 1970 he founded Interstudy, a Minnesota-based think tank that developed the HMO concept. A year later, he hired Richard Burke make the HMO a reality. In 1974 Burke launched Charter Med Inc., a for-profit company that managed Physicians Health Plan of Minnesota, an HMO that by law had to operate as a nonprofit company. UnitedHealthcare Corporation was created in 1977 to acquire Charter Med and serve as an acquisition vehicle.

UnitedHealthcare was operating 11 HMOs in ten states in 1984 when it was taken public and began a national expansion program. By the end of the decade, UnitedHealthcare was one of the country's largest publicly traded HMOs, operating in 15 states and serving about one million people. Along the way, the company learned the painful lesson that there were no significant efficiencies to be gained by becoming national in scope. In fact, health care needed to operate on a regional basis in order to more effectively control medical costs and operating costs. To this end, UnitedHealthcare began acquiring specialty companies that focused on specific aspects of health care, including prescription drugs, organ transplants, and mental health.

One of UnitedHealthcare's specialty companies operated under the Optum name. A mental health provider, it offered employee assistance services, such as the Optum Care 24 telephone hotline service that did not limit itself to dealing with mental health and medical problems. Counselors also helped employees with financial problems and domestic violence situations.

UnitedHealthcare continued to acquire smaller HMOs. In 1998 it reached an agreement to acquire Humana Inc. in a deal that promised to create the largest

HMO company in the United States. Even before a corporate restructuring was completed in 2000, the company began calling itself UnitedHealth Group. UnitedHealthcare became the flagship brand.

In the new century, UnitedHealthcare became a major health care brand as the company maintained a strong pattern of growth under Chief Executive Officer Dr. William McGuire. In 2000 UnitedHealth launched a national branding effort, the first time that it presented a consistent look and message to all of the markets in which it operated. The company then began to fashion a brand identity based on the doctor-patient relationship. UnitedHealth's branding approach grew more sophisticated in 2003. A series of humorous commercials depicted situations in which access to an HMO might be helpful. In one, for example a bride throws a bouquet to bridesmaids who in their eagerness jump off a nearby cliff. The voiceover states "People don't always use common sense," and concludes with the tagline "UnitedHealthcare: It just makes sense."

In 2007 UnitedHealth was reorganized into four units: Health Care Services, which included United-Healthcare and three other health delivery operations; Ingenix; Prescription Solutions; and OptumHealth. UnitedHealthcare and OptumHealth were clearly the parent company's most valuable brands, both enjoying high valuations by independent branding agencies.

BRAND ELEMENTS

- The UnitedHealthcare logo relies on blue and orange.
- The UnitedHealthcare logo is often combined with the slogan "Healing Health care. Together."
- The Optum logo colors are orange, black, and shades of gray.
- The Optum slogan is "Good for the system."

The UnitedHealthcare and Optum brands have their own unique brand elements. The UnitedHealthcare logo relies on blue and gold coloring, although it is sometimes rendered in black and white. A stylized "u" accompanies the UnitedHealthcare name. In the full-color version, the left arm of the "u" is colored blue, while the right arm is broken into three strands that transition from blue to gold. The symbol is either positioned directly above or to the left of "UnitedHealthcare" or "UnitedHealth Group." The logo is sometimes combined with the name of a UnitedHealth Group division, such as Community Plan or Medicare Solutions. In other versions, the corporate slogan is positioned below the symbol and name in smaller type. Also used as an advertising tagline, the slogan is "Healing Health care. Together."

The Optum logo makes use of orange, black, and shades of gray. The Optum name is presented in capital block letters. To the left is an orange and gray diamond,

textured and slightly twisted to give a three-dimensional appearance. This primary logo is also combined with the names of individual Optum businesses, including OptumHealth, OptimumRX, and OptumInsight. Depending on the usage, the logo may also be rendered in black and grays. The logo is also used with the Optum slogan "Good for the system" and business-specific slogans, such as "Optimizing Health and Well-Being" or "Behavioral Solutions" with OptimumHealth.

BRAND IDENTITY

- The brand identities of UnitedHealthcare and Optum overlap.
- At the heart of UnitedHealthcare's identity is a commitment to serve as a collaborator between doctors, patients, and the insurer.
- Optum's brand identity is primarily patient-focused.
- Both UnitedHealthcare and Optum make improving the health care system part of their brand identities.

UnitedHealthcare and Optum enjoy similar yet slightly different brand identities because much of UnitedHealthcare's image lays the groundwork for Optum. The parent company views its mission as helping people to live healthier lives by working to improve the health care system, expanding access to quality health care, and providing patients and their doctors with the information and necessary tools they need to manifest healthy lives. In order to achieve these goals, UnitedHealthcare fosters an image that espouses integrity and compassion on the one hand while demonstrating a commitment to innovation and excellent performance on the other.

UnitedHealthcare's identity is embodied in its slogan: "Healing Health care. Together." The use of the word "together" sends the message that the brand supports the idea of collaboration between doctors, patients, and the insurer. The opening phrase is more subtle in its meaning, however. In one reading, "healing" is used as an adjective, so that UnitedHealth is portrayed as providing high-quality "healing" health care. In another interpretation, "healing" is used as a verb. UnitedHealthcare, thus, presents itself as a catalyst for improving the health care system.

Optum also makes the promise of helping to improve the health care system. The brand places greater emphasis, however, on helping people to stay healthy. Specifically, this goal is achieved by helping people to understand their benefits and how to navigate the health care system to attain those benefits. As is the case with UnitedHealthcare, Optum's identity is reflected in a slogan with multiple meanings: "Good for the system." In one sense, the word "system" is synonymous with "body," suggesting that the brand offers good health. On another level, "system" refers to the health care system, implying that Optum makes valuable contributions to the improvement of the health care system. Inherent in either interpretation is the underlying assumption that Optum is caring and trustworthy, other core elements of the brand's identity.

BRAND STRATEGY

- UnitedHealth Group's branding strategy evolved over time.
- By the early 2000s UnitedHealth housed six brands between two primary business units.
- In 2011 UnitedHealth divided its business between two master brands.
- Health benefits businesses operated under United-Healthcare brand following the 2011 master branding initiative.
- Operating under the Optum brand are Optum-Health, OptumInsight, and OptumRx.

UnitedHealth Group's brand strategy has evolved over the years. Initially, the parent company was simply an HMO doing business in Minnesota and made little effort at brand building. As other local HMOs were acquired under the UnitedHealthcare banner and the company began establishing a national footprint, a brand began to take shape, but there was little effort to create a consistent look or message. With the acquisition of specialty companies in the early 1990s, several other brands were added, including United Resource Networks, Diversified Pharmaceutical Services, Healthmarc, and Optum.

Following the merger with Humana that created UnitedHealth Group, an effort was finally made to fashion a true brand out of UnitedHealthcare. The company continued to maintain a number of business units within the health care service segment that used their own brands, including Ovations, a unit that delivered health care to people over 50 years old, and AmeriChoice, which focused on Medicaid. On the specialty business side of UnitedHealth Group, there were three additional companies, each maintaining a unique brand. There was Uniprise, a provider of health and well-being services, business-to-business transaction processing services, consumer connectivity, and technology support services. Another brand was Ingenix, which focused on health care data collection, analysis, and application. Finally, there was OptumHealth, the best known of the three specialty subsidiaries. It had grown out of the Optum employee assistance services business of the early 1990s that now offered personalized management solutions, specialized benefits, and health financial services.

In 2011 UnitedHealth Group decided the time had come to refine its approach to branding. The health benefits businesses were now aligned under the UnitedHealthcare master brand, and the health services businesses were organized under the Optum brand. While OptumHealth retained its name, Ingenix became

OptumInsight, and Prescriptions Solutions became known as OptumRx. As a result, UnitedHealth Group now relied on two master brands: UnitedHealthcare for the health benefits businesses and Optum for the individual health services businesses.

To support its new branding approach, UnitedHealth Group launched an image and reputation campaign. Based on the "Health in Numbers" tagline and theme, the campaign commercials provided specific examples of how UnitedHealth units made positive contributions to the health of everyday people. Because it was operating in a mature market, the United States, UnitedHealth now looked to international markets as a way to expand its brands. In 2011 Optum developed a joint venture to open up the fast growing health IT services market in the Middle East. A year later UnitedHealth reached an agreement to acquire Brazil's largest health care company, opening the door for future growth in Latin America.

BRAND EQUITY

- According to Brand Finance, UnitedHealthcare had a brand value of US$9.92 billion at the end of 2011.
- UnitedHealthcare was ranked No. 85 on Brand Finance's 2012 Global 500.
- Before the switch to a master branding strategy, OptumHealth had a brand value of US$3,483 billion at the end of 2009.
- OptumHealth was listed No. 243 on Interbrand's 2010 Global 500.

Both of UnitedHealth Group's master brands enjoy strong brand equity. According to Brand Finance plc, a leading brand consultancy that employs a proprietary brand evaluation model, UnitedHealthcare possessed a brand value of US$9.92 billion at the end of 2011. As a result, UnitedHealthcare was ranked No. 85 on Brand Finance's Global 500 list of the world's most valuable brands.

Optum also enjoyed strong brand value. Combining to generate US$25 billion in annual sales, the subsidiaries operating under the Optum banner were large enough collectively to qualify for Fortune 500 status. While Brand Finance did not provide a brand value for Optum, a sense of its worth can be surmised by an earlier estimation of the OptumHealth brand. At the end of 2009, the agency assigned a brand value of US$3.483 billion, a performance good enough to place OptumHealth No. 243 on the 2010 Global 500.

BRAND AWARENESS

- Because of the size of UnitedHealth Group, the UnitedHealthcare and Optum brands enjoy strong brand awareness in the United States and certain parts of the world.

- UnitedHealth Group companies serve about 75 million people around the world.
- Diverse operations create strong brand awareness for UnitedHealthcare and Optum with employers, healthcare providers, and other potential clients.

The sheer scale of UnitedHealth Group ensures strong awareness of the company's UnitedHealthcare and Optum brands. It is just one of 22 publicly trade companies to produce more than US$100 billion in annual revenues. In addition to operations throughout the United States, UnitedHealth has a growing international presence. The company is involved in Canada and Brazil, as well as countries in Europe, the Middle East, and the Asia Pacific region. About 70 million people in the United States are served by UnitedHealth Group, and about 5 million in international markets, providing ample opportunity for the UnitedHealthcare and Optum brands to grow awareness in the general population.

Helping to increase recognition of the brands is the diversification of UnitedHealth Group's business. Both the UnitedHealthcare and Optum brands serve employers, a wide range of healthcare service providers, and insurers. As a result, the brands are well familiar to key decision makers, an important factor in the success of UnitedHealth Group.

BRAND OUTLOOK

- UnitedHealth Group's dual branding approach is just beginning to realize its potential.
- Growing levels of health care spending in the United States is expected to benefit both the UnitedHealthcare and Optum brands.
- UnitedHealthcare and Optum are looking to international markets for future growth.

UnitedHealth Group's dual master brand strategy is relatively young, offering ample room for growth in brand equity for both UnitedHealthcare and Optum. Although the United States is a mature market for insurance, they are also well positioned to enjoy growth in the years ahead. Healthcare spending is projected to increase steadily, due in large measure to the aging Baby Boom generation. By 2020 the share of health care spending is expected to exceed 20 percent of the United States' gross national product.

In addition to projected domestic growth, the UnitedHealth Group brands are likely to expand outside of the country. The large and rapidly growing country of Brazil appears especially promising. In 2012 United-Health Group reached an agreement to acquire 90 percent of Amil Participacoes, Brazil's leading insurer and hospital operator. With that foundation, UnitedHealthcare might very well become a dominant brand in all of Latin America in the years ahead. The Optum brand holds similar potential. In the Middle East, for example, the Optum division in 2011 forged a joint venture with the Abu Dhabi health system Lifeline Hospital Group to introduce its health IT services to this potentially lucrative market. The initial focus was on the six Arab states that comprise the Gulf Cooperation Council: Bahrain, Kuwait, Oman, Qatar, Saudi Arabia, and United Arab Emirates.

FURTHER READING

Brand Finance. "Global 500 2012." *http://brandirectory.com*. Accessed January 4, 2013.

Crosby, Jackie. "UnitedHealth Reaches $100 Billion Milestone." *Star Tribune* (Minneapolis, MN), May 6, 2012.

———. "UnitedHealth Sees New Market in Middle East." *Star Tribune* (Minneapolis, MN), November 6, 2011.

Crosby, Jackie, and Jennifer Bjorhus. "United Makes $4.9B Move into Brazilian Health Care." *Star Tribune* (Minneapolis, MN), October 9, 2012.

Haugh, Richard. "Building a National Image." *H&HN Hospitals & Health Networks*, September 2000.

Howatt, Glenn. "United HealthCare Resuscitates Itself." *Star Tribune* (Minneapolis, MN), February 28, 1994.

Neurath, Peter. "First Local Step for National Giant United HealthCare." *Puget Sound Business Journal*, March 29, 1996.

"UnitedHealth Group Inc." *International Directory of Company Histories*. Ed. Jay P. Pederson. Vol. 103. Detroit, MI: St. James Press, 2009.

Wasserman, Todd. "UHC Looks on Light Side of Pain, Injuries." *Brandweek*, July 14, 2003.

UPS

BRAND ORIGINS

- The company that would become UPS was established in 1907 by Seattle messenger James E. Casey, who espoused the brand's values of "Best Service and Lowest Rates."
- Casey's company underwent its first expansion in 1919 in Oakland, California. In 1922 service began in Los Angeles, where the company offered common-carrier.
- Continued growth brought the company into opposition with the Interstate Commerce Commission, which prevented further expansion until World War II.
- In 1975 the ICC granted UPS the authority to connect its existing operations in various states and expand them across the country. With the connections provided by this "Golden Link," UPS became the first company of its kind to offer delivery to any address throughout the contiguous United States.

In 1907, 19-year-old James E. Casey established the American Messenger Company in Seattle, Washington, to meet the growing demand for private messenger and delivery services. To compete with numerous other messenger companies, Casey introduced strict policies of round-the-clock service, low rates, and exemplary customer care. These principles were summed up in Casey's slogan, "Best Service and Lowest Rates."

The company came to rely on deliveries on behalf of retail stores as an increase in the use of automobiles caused a downturn in the messenger business. During this time, the company's most reliable client was the U.S. Post Office, for whom Casey's messengers delivered all special mail entering Seattle. American Messenger Company also began using the method of consolidated delivery, by which one vehicle delivered all packages addressed to homes or businesses in the same neighborhood. The company's first vehicle, a Model T Ford, was one of several significant improvements made to the company in 1913. The company also took a new name, Merchant's Parcel Delivery, after it merged with a rival company run by Evert McCabe. In 1916 a third partner, Charlie Soderstrom, joined the company, contributing automobiles and prompting the business to once again change its name to Merchants Parcel Delivery.

The company made its first expansion, from Seattle to Oakland, California, in 1919, and adopted the name United Parcel Service in the same year. In 1922 UPS acquired a Los Angeles common-carrier company. Among its many modern features, the common-carrier service provided daily pickup calls, immediate return of undeliverable items, and an updated documentation system with weekly billing, all of which allowed UPS to continue to compete with other courier services and the standard parcel post at low rates. In 1924 the technological implement that would change the future for UPS—the conveyor belt—made its debut, resulting in a faster, more efficient system for handing packages. Simultaneously, the company expanded its service to include all major cities on the U.S. Pacific Coast.

Despite fuel shortages during World War II, UPS continued its expansion by negotiating rights to deliver packages between both private and commercial customers. This development brought UPS into direct competition with the U.S. Postal Service, as well as opposition with the regulations of the Interstate Commerce Commission (ICC). To escape the authority of the ICC, UPS began common-carrier operations in cities such as Chicago and sought an extension of its operating platform in California. The latter move prompted a succession of legal battles and applications for greater operating rights.

Following World War II UPS was able to offer delivery services by air. This service, called UPS Blue Label Air, was available in every U.S. state by 1978, despite the fact that the company was still fighting federal authorities for the right to operate across the country. UPS provided customers in Europe, Asia, Latin America, and the Caribbean region with postal and shipping services following the establishment of air hubs in Miami; Cologne, Germany; and Hong Kong, Shanghai, and Shenzhen in China.

BRAND ELEMENTS
- UPS mounted its first major television campaign in 1988, with the slogan "We run the tightest ship in the shipping business."
- Known in the industry as "Big Brown," UPS adopted the familiar brown color of its vehicles and the well-known acronym as its official brand mark in 2003.
- In 2009 UPS unveiled an updated version of its logo, which showcases both the brand's traditional values and its modern adaptability.

In 1988, after incorporating consistently up-to-date technology in its shipping practices, UPS introduced its first major television campaign, featuring the slogan "We run the tightest ship in the shipping business." UPS's sponsorship of the 1996 Olympics was a bid to make the signature

brown trucks better known outside the United States. The introduction of Worldwide Logistics meant that UPS offered more than simple package deliveries. Early in the 21st century, the brand also became a resource providing inventory management and financial and mail services to business customers. UPS is known as "Big Brown" in the shipping industry because of the recognizable brown logo featuring the trademarked acronym that was adopted as the company's official brand name in 2003. UPS has become increasingly known over the years for its leadership in the transportation of goods and the superior management of finances and information related to the movement of goods.

The brand strategist FutureBrand was instrumental in updating the UPS brand mark in 2009. The three-dimensional brand mark represents consistent progress and an understanding of modern sensibilities and technologies while retaining the brand's traditional brown shield, the shape of which suggests the stability and reliability of UPS's service. This brand mark appears on all UPS' visible accoutrements, including vehicles and packaging.

BRAND IDENTITY
- In 1989 Kent C. Nelson assumed leadership of UPS and began a transformation that affected all aspects of its operations, from its internal systems to its public image.
- Challenged primarily by Federal Express, UPS introduced new technology to improve its services in the 1990s.
- UPS moved its headquarters to Atlanta, Georgia, in 1991, hoping through the publicity generated by its sponsorship of the Centennial Olympics in 1996.
- UPS launched a global expansion effort to establish itself as an international brand.
- In recent years, UPS has attempted to improve its public image for social responsibility by promoting greener business solutions, negotiating with the Teamsters, and contributing to international relief efforts.

Beginning in the 1990s, under the leadership of chairman and CEO Kent C. Nelson, UPS embarked on a transformation extending from the inner workings of the corporation to the brand's public image. The aim was to give UPS a much-needed boost in its competition with Federal Express. UPS promoted and launched a series of new services and technologies, including the DIAD (delivery information acquisition device), which combined a barcode scanner, technology for capturing customer signatures electronically, and a cellular tracking network in a single, handheld tool. These changes to the details of the company's system were implemented to reflect the brand's continuing dedication to its traditional values of efficiency and superior customer satisfaction.

In keeping with its desire to be identified as a global rival to Federal Express, UPS embarked on a period of expansion during the 1990s. The first step was to move the UPS headquarters to Atlanta, Georgia, in 1991, a few years prior to the Centennial Olympic Games, which were held there in 1996. This bold move was intended to bring publicity to the company. Over the following years, UPS's international network eventually extended to 200 countries worldwide.

UPS also wants to be perceived as a socially responsible brand. One aspect of this goal is to be viewed as a worldwide leader in promoting greener business solutions. To that end, UPS publishes an annual sustainability report that outlines the goals, accomplishments, and challenges of its efforts to balance its business and environmental concerns. UPS also wants its public image to be one of dealing fairly with employees. In recent years UPS has been compelled to negotiate with Teamsters American chapters in order to ensure the continued success of that aspect of the brand's mission. UPS continued its focus on social responsibility in 2009 by committing to a multimillion dollar initiative to improve the capabilities of relief organizations that respond to global emergencies, such as the American Red Cross, UNICEF, the World Food Program, CARE, and the Aidmatrix Foundation. UPS forged connections with these organizations through its delivery of aid and logistics expertise following earthquakes in American Samoa in 2009 and Haiti in 2010.

BRAND STRATEGY

- UPS began its global expansion in 1975 by establishing a franchise in Toronto, Ontario, and opening air hubs in Louisville, Kentucky, and Cologne, Germany.
- UPS acquired Mail Boxes Etc. in 2001 and rebranded the franchise The UPS Store.
- In 2002 UPS launched its "What can brown do for you?" campaign to promote its wide array of shipping and logistical services.
- UPS sponsors large complex athletic events to highlight its capabilities in transport and logistics.

Efforts to make the UPS brand known worldwide began in 1975 in Toronto, Ontario, where the first air hub outside the United States was established. By the 1980s, competition with Federal Express forced UPS to expand its air services, and the brand opened air hubs in Louisville, Kentucky, and Cologne, Germany. With the brand under the control of Kent C. Nelson during the 1990s, UPS began a renewed campaign to move into global prominence. The effort included the promotion of numerous new services, such as timed and same-day deliveries, two- and three-day delivery services, and a Worldwide Logistics subsidiary, which offered clients inventory management and

warehousing services. In 2001 UPS acquired Mail Boxes Etc., a retail chain offering shipping and other services, and renamed it The UPS Store. The acquisition enabled UPS to offer even lower shipping rates. In 2002 UPS launched the campaign most representative of its brand's aim to extend its services beyond shipping. The campaign, which carried the tagline "What can brown do for you?" was intended to promote UPS's lesser-known services and further the brand's global recognition, an aim that has consistently been at the forefront of the brand's strategy.

The brand's competitive strengths lie primarily in its capacity to maintain global reach and scale through an integrated ground and air network, up-to-date technology, a wide portfolio of services, and long-term customer relationships. In the future, U.S. and international economies will become more interconnected due to the increase in free trade agreements, and UPS is in an excellent position to take advantage of such growth. By building on the brand's leadership in its U.S. branches, continuing to provide supply-chain solutions, and advocating for the expansion of free trade, UPS can ensure it takes a leading role in emerging markets.

UPS also uses corporate sponsorships to promote its identity as a worldwide leader in delivery, transportation, and logistics. To that end, in 2011 it launched a partnership with Live Nation Entertainment to try to make the touring industry a greener business. UPS also sponsors a range of athletic events, such as NASCAR, the Olympics, the NCAA, and the European Golf Tour, thereby promoting its ability to deliver huge amounts of equipment and to assist with setting up complex events and streamlining supply chains.

BRAND EQUITY

- The brand's losses throughout the 1990s, brought on by consistent efforts to push into European markets, reached nearly US$1 billion.
- According to its 2011 annual report, UPS had a balance of cash and marketable securities worth approximately US$4.275 billion and shareholders' equity of US$7.108 billion.
- According to BrandZ's 2011 survey, UPS was ranked among the top three most valuable brands in the world.
- Despite market volatility in 2011, UPS experienced generally favorable revenue growth, with a slowdown toward the end of the year.

Despite the renewed effort to make the brand known internationally, UPS lost money throughout the 1990s. Backed by patient shareholders, however, UPS managed to survive its intensified competition with Federal Express and expanded its international network to include 200 countries. It also announced plans to invest more than US$1 billion in the expansion of its European operations and US$130 million in its Asian operations. According to its 2011 annual report, as of December 31, 2011, UPS had a balance of cash and marketable securities worth approximately US$4.275 billion and shareholders' equity of US$7.108 billion. The brand's service portfolio and investments have been rewarded with some of the highest returns on invested capital. According to a study by BrandZ's Millward Brown, UPS is among the top three most valuable brands in the world. In 2012 its brand value of US$37.1 billion was ranked 16th in the world, up one spot from 2011.

The continued slow economic recovery in the United States in 2011 put extra pressure on volume and revenue growth in UPS's domestic package segment. Despite ongoing volatility in world markets, UPS experienced favorable revenue growth for most of 2011, though this slowed toward the end of the year.

BRAND AWARENESS

- *American City Business Journals* cited UPS as one of the most recognizable brands in America.
- UPS was ranked in the top 25 brands in 2010 and 2011.
- UPS ranked tenth in the 2012 Harris Interactive's Reputation Quotient Survey.

UPS consistently ranks high in brand awareness. In 2011 UPS was cited as one of the top three most recognizable brands in the United States in a survey by *American City Business Journals*. The survey noted UPS's "strong commitment to sustainability, further brandishing its image." In 2010 and 2009, UPS held third place in the same survey.

UPS is not only highly recognizable with its signature brown trucks and shield logo, it also has an enviable reputation. In the 2012 Harris Interactive's Reputation Quotient Survey, UPS ranked tenth. (It rose from thirteenth the year before.) Harris Interactive also found that UPS ranked third in the subcategory of emotional appeal. In 2011, UPS earned the ranking of America's sixth most reputable company in a survey conducted by the Reputation Institute.

BRAND OUTLOOK

- UPS sets long-term goals of increasing earnings-per-share to 15 percent from 10, return on invested capital in excess of 25 percent, and free cash flow conversion greater than 100 percent of net income.
- In October 2011, UPS launched UPS My Choice, a service which allows receivers of UPS shipments to control aspects of their delivery.
- UPS achieved an A+ rating for transparency in 2012 and received one of the top scores worldwide in the Carbon Disclosure Project, which aims to measure and manage carbon emissions.

UPS has set long term goals for increasing earnings-per-share 10 percent to 15 percent, return on invested

capital more than 25 percent, and free cash flow conversion greater than 100 percent of net income. In order to upgrade the shipping solutions promoted as part of the brand's expansion plan, UPS launched UPS My Choice in the United States, which allows the receivers of UPS shipments to control aspects of the delivery. The service was unveiled in October 2011, and by the end of the year, the number of subscribers had reached nearly 750,000.

In 2005 UPS partnered with TNT Express, an international courier service, to provide humanitarian logistics expertise to the World Food Program and continued to work with the WFP in Haiti, Nigeria, and Turkey. UPS has also worked to develop environmentally conscious business practices, issuing its first Corporate Sustainability report in 2003, which highlighted the importance of balancing economic, social, and environmental objectives. The 2012 sustainability report announced that the brand had achieved A+ status for superior transparency and earned the highest Carbon Disclosure Project score among all U.S. companies while tying with three others for the top score in the world.

Since 1903 UPS has consistently updated its business model, progressing from a small-scale messenger service to a dominant global provider of air, ocean, ground, and electronic transportation services.

FURTHER READING

Berman, Jeff. "UPS, FedEx Receive Limited Domestic Delivery Licenses in China." *Logistics Management.* Accessed September 27, 2012. http://www.logisticsmgmt.com/article/ups_fedex_receive_limited_domestic_delivery_licenses_in_china/.

Bonney, Joseph. "UPS Bets a Billion." *American Shipper*, January 1993.

Burnson, Patrick. "UPS Calls for Federal Fiscal Leadership." *Logistics Management.* Accessed September 27 2012. http://www.logisticsmgmt.com/article/ups_asks_for_fiscal_leadership/.

Greenwald, John. "Hauling UPS' Freight." *Time*, January 29, 1996.

Madden, Stephen J. "Big Changes at Big Brown." *Fortune*, January 18, 1988.

Steiner, D. M. "Parcel Post Demand Is Elastic." *Transportation Journal*, Summer 1964.

United Parcel Service. *2011 Annual Report.* Accessed September 7, 2012. http://thomson.mobular.net/thomson/7/3275/4584/.

"United Parcel Service of America, Inc." *International Directory of Company Histories.* Ed. Tina Grant. Vol. 17. Detroit, MI: St. James Press, 1997.

Woodward, Kevin. "UPS's Domestic Volume Was Flat in 2011." *Internet Retailer.* Accessed September 27, 2012. http://www.internetretailer.com/2012/01/31/ups-domestic-volume-was-flat-2011.

VAUXHALL

—■—

BRAND ORIGINS

- The first Vauxhall car was built in 1903.
- In its first decade, the company focused on the construction of vehicles that blended elegance with touring and sporting elements.
- In 1925, General Motors purchased Vauxhall for US$2.5 million.
- During World War II, Vauxhall focused its wartime production on one tank—the Churchill, whose armor could withstand the German Tiger tank's weaponry.

- Vauxhall focused attention in the early part of the 21st century on making its vehicles greener, safer, and more efficient performers.
- Vauxhall manufactures 17 models of cars and vans in the United Kingdom, and the brand has a significant presence throughout Europe.

The first Vauxhall car was built in 1903. In its first decade, the company focused on the construction of vehicles that blended elegance with touring and sporting elements for a distinguished, affluent customer base. By the early 1920s, Vauxhall was regularly engaged in motoring events, and the company increased its production of sport cars and racing vehicles. The Vauxhall E-type, for example, became the fastest catalogued car in Britain by 1923.

In 1925, General Motors (GM) purchased Vauxhall for US$2.5 million. GM immediately increased Vauxhall production, and sales throughout the United Kingdom soared during the 1930s.

During World War II, Vauxhall focused its wartime production on one tank—the Churchill, which became known as the only British tank whose armor could withstand the German Tiger tank's weaponry. Following the war, Vauxhall returned to manufacturing cars, though British consumers faced a waiting list of a year or more as the manufacturer exported half its production to keep up with demand for vehicles throughout war-torn Europe.

American influences marked the Vauxhall during the 1950s, and the 1960s brought Vauxhall into the economy car market for the first time with the introduction of its Viva model. When its production run ended in 1979, Vauxhall had sold more than 600,000 Vivas.

The 1970s and 1980s were a period of innovation for Vauxhall. From the introduction of fiberglass body components and its first five-speed transmission to its first four-wheel drivetrain and V-6 engine, Vauxhall produced some of its most successful cars during this time, including the Cavalier, which remained in production for 20 years; the Nova, which sold more than a half million units over its decade-long run; and the Astra, a vehicle still in production today.

As it moved into the 1990s, Vauxhall returned to its roots, renewing its attention to developing sporty yet elegant vehicles for upper-class consumers. The 1989 Carton not only cost £48,000 (about US$59,000) but came with a suspension developed by Lotus, a high-end sports car manufacturer, and a 377-horsepower twin-turbo engine that could reach speeds in excess of 170 miles per hour. The development of luxury and sports cars added breadth to Vauxhall's vehicle lineup and depth to its reputation as an auto manufacturer.

While Vauxhall was expanding its brand in the 1990s, it was also strengthening many of its foundations, including its commitment to small-car production and environmental protection. The 1993 Corsa, a small-car model, had available features such as power steering, anti-lock brakes, and a car alarm. It was painted with water-based paints, used CFC-free air conditioning, and was constructed to be 90 percent recyclable.

With awards such as Engine of the Year (for the 2005 Vauxhall VXR) and Car of the Year (for the 2009 Insignia), Vauxhall's brand value gained strength in the first decades of the 21st century. Like most other auto manufacturers, Vauxhall focused much of its attention in the early part of the century on making its vehicles greener, safer, and more efficient performers. Three of its innovations included adaptive forward lighting, the FlexRide adaptive stability system, and Voltec extended-range electric vehicle technology, also called E-REV. Adaptive forward lighting, for example, enhances the effectiveness of headlights while negotiating curves, as movable elements in the headlights automatically adjust themselves to different conditions, improving road illumination up to 90 percent.

As of 2012, Vauxhall manufactured 17 models of cars and vans in the United Kingdom, and the brand had a significant presence throughout Europe, where the Ampera beat out three dozen competitors to win the 2012 European Car of the Year award at the historic Geneva Motor Show.

BRAND ELEMENTS

- Since the early 1970s, Vauxhall cars have essentially been rebadged Opels.
- Critics have often suggested that parent company General Motors abandon the Vauxhall name in favor of the better-known Opel brand.

- Both Vauxhall's name and its emblem are linked to the historical figure Falkes de Bréauté, a thirteenth-century soldier in the service of King John.

Since the early 1970s, Vauxhalls have in essence been rebadged Opels. In its UK marketing campaigns since 2005, for example, Vauxhall has used Opel advertising and simply tagged its logo into the end frame. According to the BBC, critics of Vauxhall have suggested for years that its parent company, General Motors (GM), drop the Vauxhall name and market all Vauxhall vehicles under the more recognized name of Opel, another GM subsidiary.

The Vauxhall badge, or emblem, is based on the mythical griffin, which has the body of a lion and the head, and often the wings, of an eagle. Thought to be an especially powerful and majestic creature, the griffin is known for guarding treasure. The Vauxhall griffin emblem is derived from the coat of arms of Falkes de Bréauté, a mercenary soldier who was granted the manor of Luton for services to King John in the thirteenth century. The house he built, Falkes Hall, became known in time as Vauxhall. Vauxhall Iron Works, the original name of the company that became Vauxhall Motors, adopted this emblem from the coat of arms to emphasize its links to the area. Since its introduction in 1903, the Vauxhall emblem has been redesigned several times, though it has always kept the griffin as its core symbol.

BRAND IDENTITY

- The Vauxhall brand is generally considered to have a weak identity.
- Vauxhalls are thought to be better-than-average cars, though not distinctive.
- Many people associate the Vauxhall brand with functionality rather artistry.

Vauxhall's brand identity is based in large part on its design philosophy: "sculptural artistry meets manufacturing precision." While this philosophy is reflected to some degree in Vauxhall's current and future vehicles, its brand identity is weak, according to critics. "When you think Vauxhall, you probably don't think of cool. Or hip. Or flash. Or snazzy. Or any of those other diaphanous terms that marketing men trade in," observed the BBC's Finlo Rohrer. "If you think anything of Vauxhalls, you think of economy and functionality—cars for families and fleets." While at one time, the brand may have represented luxury, and while the brand may claim to celebrate artistry and precision, the brand has become more synonymous with cars that people learn to drive in rather than cars they desire to purchase. A Vauxhall is considered a better-than-average car, but not much more. "It has a Cinderella-type stigma to it," commented Fred Dukes, membership secretary of the Vauxhall Owners Club. "It's difficult to describe what a classic is. It isn't in the same vein as the Mini or the MGB or the Morris Minor. It hasn't taken that mass interest, but in its own right it isn't a badly designed car." Unlike the identity established by other UK automakers, the identity of Vauxhall appears to be one of functionality rather than artistry.

BRAND STRATEGY

- One strategy of Vauxhall is the development, production, and marketing of alternative fuel-cell vehicles.
- Vauxhall's HydroGen4 car—its fourth-generation fuel-cell vehicle—is the result of more than 10 years of research into fuel cells and hydrogen.
- Vauxhall's RAD e is the first e-bike concept to be designed around automotive manufacturing mass-production methods.

One strategy Vauxhall has undertaken to bolster its brand is the development, production, and marketing of alternative fuel-cell vehicles. The selling point of the Ampera, for example, is that when its battery runs out after 50 miles of electric power, a gasoline engine provides backup power for another 300 miles or more. Because the fuel still drives the electric motor, however, the company says the vehicle should be considered a "range extender" rather than a hybrid car, like the popular Toyota Prius.

In addition to offering the electric Ampera and the forthcoming Flextreme model, Vauxhall has developed the HydroGen4 car, its fourth-generation fuel-cell vehicle that is the result of more than 10 years of research into fuel cells and hydrogen. Instead of combustion, the Gen4 uses an electro-chemical reaction to power the electric drive, therefore producing no harmful emissions, according to the manufacturer. Further, the overall efficiency is about twice that of a car propelled by an internal combustion engine, essentially halving energy consumption.

Vauxhall has extended its commitment to alternative transportation beyond that of many, if not all, of its competitors. Its electric bicycle (or e-bike), the RAD e, is a concept vehicle for getting around when car use is restricted or not possible, as is often the case in many areas of its primary market in Europe. Marketed primarily to urban travelers and developed at a time when e-bikes are predicted to play an increasing role in integrated urban transport, the RAD e incorporates the boomerang design cues that also appear in the Ampera, according to the manufacturer.

The RAD e is the first e-bike concept to be designed around automotive manufacturing mass-production methods, from its pressed-steel frame—which is also lightweight, strong, flexible, and easy to make—to its "pedelec" propulsion system, which is based on a 250-watt electric motor that is charged as the bike's operator pedals.

Overall, Vauxhall's strategy appears focused on the future of transportation: small cars, innovative and alternative fuel sources combined with progressive designs, and alternative forms of transportation.

BRAND EQUITY

- The value of the Vauxhall brand declined drastically during the global economic recession.
- Vauxhall is the second-largest automaker in the United Kingdom, but consumers have recently given the brand a poor rating.
- MPP Consulting ranked Vauxhall 88th among the most valuable British brands.

Vauxhall's brand performance suffered a giant fall in the first decade of the 21st century because of significant drops in sales during the worldwide recession. The decline led to calls for an end to the brand, despite its more than 100 years of production history. Vauxhall is the second-largest auto manufacturer in the United Kingdom, but owners in its home country are not satisfied, ranking the brand 26th among auto manufacturers. Vauxhall continues to spend significant dollars on advertising, including social media outlets such as Twitter. Brand researcher MPP Consulting, however, ranks the auto manufacturer 88th among the most valuable British brands. Recent sales figures suggest that Vauxhall's brand value may be on the rise, but studies of consumer satisfaction and brand equity continue to indicate that the manufacturer has plenty of room for improvement.

BRAND AWARENESS

- Despite its recent difficulties, the Vauxhall brand enjoys strong brand awareness among consumers.
- Unlike many other automakers, Vauxhall is not a prominent supporter of motor sports.
- Vauxhall sponsors a large number of soccer and rugby teams in the United Kingdom.
- Vauxhall also provides significant support for events in the arts and entertainment.

Despite challenges facing the Vauxhall brand, consumers have a strong affiliation with and awareness of it. This may be due to the brand's unique approach to community involvement and sponsorship. For example, the brand is not nearly as involved in motoring events as many other car manufacturers. Instead, the brand supports other types of sporting events and, more significantly, the arts.

Vauxhall is a prominent supporter of two of the most popular sports in the United Kingdom, soccer and rugby. It sponsors more than 30 different age-level groups for the national soccer teams of all four countries in the United Kingdom: England, Ireland, Scotland, and Wales.

Vauxhall's commitment to soccer is surpassed only by its support for the arts. From art to fashion design and from popular music to the performing arts, Vauxhall sponsors numerous well-known events in the United Kingdom, including the UK Beatbox Championships, the Ampera Theatre, the Art Car Boot Fair, and the Fashion Scout. These efforts increase its already high European brand awareness.

BRAND OUTLOOK

- The outlook for Vauxhall is clearly tied to the future of its parent company, U.S. auto-manufacturing giant General Motors.
- Vauxhall is part of major losses for GM's European division, which registered shortfalls of more than $1 billion between 2011 and the first quarter of 2012.
- In 2012, Vauxhall had one of the strongest product portfolios that British consumers had seen in decades, and its sales were improving.
- Although both GM and Vauxhall have struggled recently, the Vauxhall brand maintained its place in the European auto market.
- In May 2012, sales of the Vauxhall Corsa topped the British charts for new cars, the first time sales of the Corsa outpaced those of the Ford Fiesta.

Despite positive growth in Vauxhall's 2012 sales figures, the outlook for the brand is clearly tied to the future of its parent company, U.S. auto-manufacturing giant General Motors (GM). Some indicators suggest that GM is on the way back from the government bailout it received in 2009, particularly with its growth in emerging markets such as China and India. Others suggest that GM's future in the United Kingdom and Europe, Vauxhall's primary markets, is not a bright one.

According to British auto blogger Tom Gibbs, GM's shares neared a 52-week price low of US$19 per share in July 2012, and Karl-Friedrich Stracke, who took over GM's European division from the retiring Nick Reilly just six months earlier, stepped down from the leadership position to take on "special assignments." The news came just two weeks after GM presented a new plan to rebuild the Vauxhall brand, leaving investors increasingly uncomfortable regarding its future outlook.

Gibbs wrote that "there is no doubt that it is crunch time for General Motors." Less than two years after GM's relaunch into the market following its bailout, Vauxhall had one of the strongest product portfolios that consumers had seen in decades, and its sales were improving. However, Vauxhall continued to be part of major losses for GM's European division, which

registered shortfalls of more than US$1 billion between 2011 and the first quarter of 2012, bringing the cumulative division loss to more than US$16 billion between 1999 and 2012.

GM's overall struggles in Europe led the manufacturer to consider other tactics, including adding even more models (as it appeared to be doing in the planned introduction of the Flextreme electric vehicle) to the Vauxhall lineup, attempting to market the brand in some emerging markets, and relocating production of some of the brand's lineup.

Despite the impact of GM's challenges and questionable future on Vauxhall, the brand still has a significant consumer following in the United Kingdom. The Vauxhall brand has also maintained its place in the European auto market.

Vauxhall's strengthening performance was supported by new-car sales figures, which rose at their fastest rate in more than two years in 2012 and landed the Vauxhall Corsa ahead of the Ford Fiesta at the top of the UK best-seller charts for the first time. In fact, Vauxhall placed three models on the list of the top 10 best-selling new cars for May 2012 in the UK, its best performance in quite some time.

FURTHER READING

Brand Finance. "Vauxhall." *Brandirectory.com*. Accessed November 26, 2012. http://brandirectory.com/profile/vauxhall.

Gibbs, Tom. "GM Surprises Market—Not in a Good Way." *Motley Fool* (UK), July 7, 2012. Accessed November 22, 2012. http://beta.fool.com/gibbstom13/2012/07/12/gms-announcement-surprises-market-shares-approach-/7082/.

Rohrer, Finlo. "A Car You Learned to Drive In." *BBC News Magazine*. June 2, 2009. Accessed November 21, 2012. http://news.bbc.co.uk/2/hi/uk_news/magazine/8078754.stm.

SyncForce. "Vauxhall." *RankingtheBrands.com*. Accessed November 12, 2012. http://www.rankingthebrands.com/Brand-detail.aspx?brandID=217.

Vaughan, Adam. "Vauxhall Predicts Ampera Will Boost Electric Car Sales." *Guardian* (London), May 1, 2012. Accessed November 24, 2012. http://www.guardian.co.uk/environment/2012/may/01/vauxhall-ampera-electric-cars.

Vauxhall Motors. "Future Models and Concepts." Accessed November 24, 2012. http://www.vauxhall.co.uk/vehicles/future-models-and-concepts/range/index.html.

Vauxhall Motors. "History and Heritage." Accessed November 15, 2012. http://www.vauxhall.co.uk/about-vauxhall/about-us/history.html.

"Vauxhall Topples Ford as New Car Sales Rise." *MSN.com* (UK), June 13, 2012. Accessed November 19, 2012. http://cars.uk.msn.com/news/vauxhall-topples-ford-as-new-car-sales-rise.

VEOLIA

■

BRAND ORIGINS

- The water division of Veolia originated in 1853, when Napoleon III called for a company to distribute water in France.

- In 1905, CGE research demonstrated the benefits of using ozone to filter and sterilize water.
- Veolia has expanded to include four divisions: water, environmental services, energy, and transportation.
- The company changed its name to Vivendi in 1998 and was listed on the Paris and New York stock exchanges in 2000 and 2001, respectively.
- In 2003, Vivendi became Veolia Environnement, and the name was further simplified, becoming Veolia, in 2005.

Veolia is a global brand based in France. Its divisions of water, environmental services, energy, and transportation fulfill the needs of global cities and municipalities.

Veolia began developing its business in water services in the mid-1850s. In 1853, Napoleon III decreed that a company should be formed to provide water and irrigation to the cities and countryside of France. Compagnie Générale des Eaux (CGE) began by providing services to Lyon. Seven years later, the company secured a 50-year contract to serve Paris.

CGE began to expand its water services outside of France in 1880, when it received water production and distribution rights in Venice and elsewhere in Italy. Expansion continued in 1882 with the establishment of services in Constantinople (Istanbul). By 1884, the company was also serving the cities of Porto, Portugal, and Reims, France.

In 1905, CGE discovered that ozone could be used to filter and sterilize water, which helped replace the use of chloride. The company was able to implement this technology in 1909. By the company's 100th anniversary in 1953, it was supplying water to eight million people in France.

CGE's environmental services division was organized when the municipality of Nantes, France, contracted with François Grandjouan to, "clear the streets of sewage and waste and convert the latter into manure." In 1870, another company that would become part of CGE, Soulier Brothers, was established. The company recycled old rags and paper.

The transportation division of CGE began as Compagnie Générale Française de Tramways (CGFT). French civic planner Baron Haussmann founded the business in 1875. His creation of the horse-drawn tram led to the first light rail service in Le Havre, Nancy, and Marseille. The transportation division of CGE evolved further in 1912, when Charles Blum used Georges Latil's "front-end" design to create a fleet of industrial vehicles. The new subsidiary's name was Compagnie Générale d'Entreprises Automobiles (CGEA).

The transportation and environmental service divisions of the CGE brand worked together in 1919, when CGEA operated as a household waste collection business in Paris. By its 100th anniversary, CGE was collecting waste for multiple municipalities. In 1967, the company began operating its first waste incinerators. In 1975, CGE created SARP Industries, which recycled hazardous waste, and it became the first European center for the treatment of liquid toxic waste. The first waste drop-off centers opened in 1986.

In 1935, Léon Dewailly started a business that built heating and air-conditioning systems named Chauffage Service. Established in 1944, Compagnie Générale de Chauffe (CGC), also a heating and cooling company, went on to maintain NATO bases in France in 1958. The two businesses merged in 1960, and in 1967 they joined CGE. In 1973, CGC responded to the oil crisis with research in geothermal energy and the recovery of wasted energy. CGE's Energy Services division was created in 1995 by merging CGC and a company called Groupe Montenay.

CGE opened a training center in 1994. The Institut de l'Environnement Urbain (IEU) in Jouy-le-Moutier helped demonstrate CGE's leadership role in the environmental services industry. The center provides vocational education and apprenticeships in environmental services.

In 1998, the name of the CGE Group (with the exception of the water division) was changed to Vivendi. Vivendi Environnement was listed on the Paris Stock Exchange in 2000. A year later, the company was listed on the New York Stock Exchange. The company changed its name to Veolia Environnement in 2003. In 2005, to further streamline the company, Veolia Environnement placed the water division under its name, which it changed to Veolia, and designed a unified company logo.

BRAND ELEMENTS

- Veolia's mission is "Creative solutions for our environment."
- During the brand's 150-year existence, its name and services have evolved into one cohesive brand under the name Veolia.
- The company's name appears in a customized font in the company logo, which features a graphic of a person embracing the world.
- The red-on-white design of Veolia's logo is clean and fresh, representing the brand's endeavors to improve the environment.

The Veolia mission is "Creative solutions for our environment." Veolia's original name, Compagnie Générale des Eaux (CGE), represented a company that managed the distribution of water. During the brand's 150 years, its operations have expanded to include waste management, transportation, and energy services.

The Veolia brand has been reinvented numerous times as a result of consolidations and new names. The simplified name of Veolia was adopted in 2005, along with a sleek, red logo, which represents a person embracing the world. The person's head is represented by an upside-down drop of water. The red-on-white design is clean and fresh, suggestive of the brand's endeavors to improve the environment. The company's name appears in a customized modern font, which is also used by all of its subsidiaries.

BRAND IDENTITY

- Veolia is "Dedicated to Protecting People and Improving the Environment" with its management of water, environmental waste, energy, and transportation services.
- Veolia leads the environmental services industry with high safety ratings and strong compliance records.
- The Veolia brand is known for its innovations and research into ways to reduce the environmental footprints of communities and businesses.

According to the company's website, Veolia's ambition is "to provide comprehensive, high-value-added solutions that balance growth and environmental protection." Research and innovation have helped the brand to create ways of making the environment around cities and municipalities more livable. Veolia's website also declares in a slogan that the company is "Dedicated to Protecting People and Improving the Environment."

Veolia's Transdev brand in the United States is dedicated to customer satisfaction and sustainable practices. Its motto is "Mobility inspired by you," and its goal is to provide reliable transportation with "quality service [and] economic performance … while ensuring the preservation of our planet."

Veolia prides itself on leading the industry with high safety ratings and strong compliance records. The brand presents itself to cities and municipalities as one that provides environmental, utility, and transportation services that cater to new global regulations and help reduce environmental footprints. That company also states that its "commitment to providing first-class service as your partner of choice across our full set of capabilities has never been stronger."

BRAND STRATEGY

- In the late 20th century, mergers among Veolia's subsidiaries led to the formation of four divisions: Omnium de Traitement et de Valorisation (OTV), Connex, Onyx, and Dalkia.
- Veolia has experienced financial troubles in the early 21st century due to the global economic downturn and overzealous expansion.
- In 2012, Veolia restructured in order to reduce debt and costs.

In the 1980s and 1990s, a set of mergers among the company's subsidiaries occurred and made CGE a more cohesive entity. Four businesses were brought together: Omnium de Traitement et de Valorisation (OTV), which "specialized in the design, engineering and manufacture of water and wastewater treatment equipment"; Connex, derived from CGEA; Onyx, which provided hazardous waste services; and Dalkia, which became the Energy Services division in 1998 after CGE acquired a controlling interest in the company. Onyx included one of Europe's biggest paper and plastic recyclers in its portfolio when it acquired Groupe Soulier in 1990. In 1996, the Onyx cleaning division was established through the merger of USP (rail stations and trains), Comatec (urban transportation), and Rénosol. Each division was supported by investments to create the Water Research Center; the Energy and Waste Management Research Center; and the Transportation Research Center. In 1999, Vivendi Environnement was created to consolidate all of these environmental service activities.

Economic problems, combined with the overzealous expansion of the brand into 250 different types of business, led to declines in profitability as Veolia entered the 21st century. In 2012, the company reorganized, focusing on a strategy aimed at reducing debt through divestment, streamlining the company's portfolio of services through convergence, and cutting expenditures.

BRAND EQUITY

- *Brandirectory* ranked Veolia 254th among the top 500 global brands in 2012.
- The Global Fortune 500 ranked Veolia 175th in 2011.

- In 2012, ADS Waste Holdings acquired Veolia's U.S. solid waste business for approximately US$2 billion.

Brandirectory ranked Veolia 254th top 500 global brands in 2012, down from 241st in 2011. The brand's value was estimated to be US$4.08 billion. The Global Fortune 500 ranked the brand 175th in 2011, and, according to *Engineering News-Record,* Veolia was third among the top 200 Environmental Firms in both 2011 and 2012. In the most significant change for the company since consolidation and rebranding under the Veolia name in 2005, ADS Waste Holdings (a subsidiary of Highstar Capital) acquired Veolia's solid waste business in the United States in 2012. In a *Waste & Recycling News* article, the acquisition price of approximately US$2 billion was described as "8.3 times the company's [2011] earnings before interest, taxes, depreciation and amortization."

BRAND AWARENESS

- Veolia is a global leader in a wide range of environmental services, and it is a European leader in energy and transportation services.
- Veolia is the leading private operator of public transportation services in Europe, and it is one of France's largest private-sector employers.
- Veolia is the 33rd-largest corporate employer worldwide, and it was portrayed positively on the television show *Undercover Boss* in Australia.

Veolia claims that it is "the only global operator to provide a complete range of waste management solutions." It is a European leader in energy services, and it is the leading private operator of public transportation systems in Europe. According to the *Economist* magazine, Veolia is one of France's largest private-sector employers, and according to the company itself, it is the 33rd-largest corporate employer worldwide.

An episode of the television program *Undercover Boss* in Australia presented a positive view of the company from the perspective of its employees and did much to boost brand awareness. Employees interviewed on the show generally expressed pride in their work for the company. One employee had been working for Veolia 35 years and expressed the desire to continue working part-time after retirement. The willingness of the director to visit with employees and implement their input was demonstrated to a large audience by the television program.

BRAND OUTLOOK

- CEO Antoine Frérot's strategy to reduce Veolia's debt stirred controversy among members of the company's board of directors.

- In 2012, Veolia Transdev was in the process of being transferred to state-owned Caisse des Depots et Consignations (CDC).
- Veolia's goal in the second decade of the 21st century was continued growth in hazardous waste and industrial services in North America and Europe.

Historically, Veolia has been a successful global brand, but it has struggled recently as a result of the worldwide economic downturn. As reported in the *Economist,* there was controversy regarding Veolia's leadership in 2011. Chief Executive Henri Proglio appointed Antoine Frérot as his successor in 2009. Frérot's strategy for bringing the brand back to its previous level in the market was to remove extraneous branches acquired by Proglio. Proglio had expanded Veolia to 77 countries and 250 varieties of business. The expansion left the brand with extensive debt and a loss of 60 percent in share value from 2011 to 2012. Frérot's plan was to bring focus to the brand and make it more modern. Frérot announced a sale of assets worth EUR 5 billion (US$6.6 billion) and a retreat to 40 markets, as well as an overhaul of the company's culture. His reorganization and divestments were intended to remove the brand's heavy debt in Europe and North America. These changes were not universally accepted within the company, however. Per Lekander, an analyst with the Parisian investment bank UBS, commented, "It was entirely clear that something radical needed to be done to focus the business. But Frérot's rebellion has infuriated Proglio, who has reportedly been briefing fellow board members of Veolia that they need to replace him."

On November 21, 2012, Veolia Environnement announced the completion of its sale of its solid waste business in the United States to ADS Waste Holdings. The total transaction value was approximately US$2 billion (around EUR 1.5 billion). According to the *Wall Street Journal,* the sale will help the company in its goal to divest EUR 5 billion (US$6.6 billion) in assets by the end of 2013.

A *Reuters* article of October 23, 2012, discussed the future of Veolia Transdev, noting that the subsidiary brand of Veolia was slated to come under the control of state-owned Caisse des Depots et Consignations (CDC). According to the report, "Veolia put its 50 percent stake in Veolia Transdev up for sale in December [2011] as part of a plan to shed 5 billion euros in assets and cut its borrowing to below 12 billion euros from 14.7 billion euros last year."

In November 2012, Veolia Environnement also offered a cash tender for "dollar-denominated notes due 2018." In order to reduce debt, the company offered to pay up to US$200 million for notes that would mature at a 6-percent interest rate to US$700 million in 2018.

A new CEO, Jeff Adix, was appointed for Veolia Environmental Services North America (VESNA) in 2012. Adix remarked that what worked in the past may not work at this time in history, and he stated that he looks forward to the challenge of helping the United States branch of the brand return to its previous level of operation. Adix declared, "Industrial cleaning, maintenance and hazardous waste management capabilities in North America are core to Veolia's strategy and backed by the expertise and resources of our global business."

As the Veolia brand entered the second decade of the 21st century, the company's leadership planned to continue pursuing growth in hazardous waste and the industrial services businesses in North America, as well as other regions, including France, Central Europe, Germany, and Australia. The company is also "[p]reparing for unrestricted competition in the European passenger transportation market."

FURTHER READING

Bender, Ruth. "Veolia Environment Completes Sale of US Solid Waste Business." *Wall Street Journal,* November 21, 2012. Accessed December 13, 2012. http://online.wsj.com/article/BT-CO-20121121-701094.html.

Berton, Elena. "Update 2—Veolia to Cut Transport JV Stake to Reduce Debt." *Reuters,* October 23, 2012. Accessed December 14, 2012. http://www.reuters.com/article/2012/10/23/veolia-cdc-transdev-idUSL5E8LN25M20121023.

Brand Finance. "Veolia." *Brandirectory.* Accessed December 19, 2012. http://brandirectory.com/search/?brand=veolia.

"Jean-Marc Janaillac Appointed Chairman and Chief Executive Officer of Veolia Transdev." *Bloomberg,* December 3, 2012. Accessed December 13, 2012. http://www.bloomberg.com/article/2012-12-03/apccZ.fwlytho.html.

Johnson, Jim. "Veolia ES Solid Waste Price May Scare Others, Analysts Say." *Waste & Recycling News,* July 30, 2012. Accessed January 8, 2013. http://www.wasterecyclingnews.com/article/20120730/NEWS01/120739998/veolia-es-solid-waste-price-may-scare-others-analysts-say.

"Plumbing the Depths." *Economist,* February 25, 2012. Accessed December 10, 2012. http://www.economist.com/node/21548256.

"The Top 200 Environmental Firms: 2012." *Engineering News-Record.* Accessed December 12, 2012. http://enr.construction.com/toplists/Top-Environmental-Firms/001-100.asp.

"Undercover Boss—Veolia." *YouTube,* December 30, 2010. Accessed December 19, 2012. http://www.youtube.com/watch?v=ezlmRTAvUmc&feature=endscreen.

Veolia. Accessed December 10, 2012. http://www.veolia.com.

"Veolia Environnement Launches Cash Tender Offer to Purchase Certain of its Dollar-Denominated Notes Due 2018." *Bloomberg,* November 28, 2012. Accessed December 14, 2012. http://www.bloomberg.com/article/2012-11-29/acFD7e9xdSn0.html.

VERIZON

BRAND ORIGINS

- Verizon was established in 2000 through a series of mergers and acquisitions that united the Bell Atlantic Corporation with GTE, AirTouch, NYNEX, and Vodafone.

- Verizon was a leading wireless brand from the first, a position enhanced with its "Can You Hear Me Now?" campaign in 2002.
- In 2012 Verizon had more than 100 million subscribers, and revenues reached US$115.8 billion.
- Verizon Wireless was the number-two wireless firm in the world after China Mobile.

Verizon was established in 2000 through a series of mergers and acquisitions that united the Bell Atlantic Corporation with GTE, AirTouch, NYNEX, and Vodafone. The new organization, Verizon Communications, Inc., began with 28 million customers, 63 million phone lines, and coverage in 67 of the biggest cities in the United States.

Bringing together the extensive Bell Atlantic and GTE telecommunications networks was a daunting task as each had previously operated in separate markets and offered distinct products. Verizon began by focusing on its consumer and business services and invested in its wireless enterprise, Verizon Wireless, which started out with 32 million subscribers, the combined number from Bell Atlantic and Vodafone. Although at its inception Verizon Wireless became an industry leader by size, it had little name recognition in the marketplace and soon undertook one of the largest renaming campaigns in history. Print ads featuring Verizon employees promised customers that they would receive the same dependable and reliable service they had experienced with Bell Atlantic and Vodafone. By 2001 Verizon also offered wired long-distance telephone service in certain states and high-speed Internet access nationwide. After only one year, Verizon Communications was operating in 40 countries, had 27.5 million customers, and US$65 billion in revenues.

From its earliest days, Verizon was not only concerned with expanding its markets, products, and services, but also with investing in technology and voice capacity to improve its network. By 2002 Verizon Wireless was the largest cellular telephone service provider in the United States and had high customer satisfaction. Verizon was spending an estimated US$1 billion every 90 days to improve service quality and expand its coverage footprint. Verizon was considered the most reliable wireless provider in the United States.

Competitors such as Sprint and Cingular soon initiated a price war by offering low-priced calling plans, but their coverage, service, and sustained-call rates could not match Verizon's. Verizon avoided the price war and rebranded itself as a premium service provider. It launched the "Can You Hear Me Now?" campaign in January 2002. Featuring television commercials and print ads, the campaign helped position Verizon as superior to its competitors and became a pop culture phenomenon in the process. "Can You Hear Me Now?" contributed to Verizon gaining five million subscribers between 2002 and 2003 and reducing customer turnover from 2.5 percent to 1.8 percent annually by 2004.

By 2003 Verizon had become one of the largest telecommunications brands in the United States and in some markets globally. However, it faced new competition from cable companies that were expanding into voice services. To stay competitive, Verizon teamed up with Direct TV to offer customers digital broadcast satellite services along with voice and Internet services.

By the start of 2004 Verizon had 43.8 million subscribers. Verizon remained the number-one wireless company in the United States until AT&T Wireless merged with Cingular in 2005. That year Verizon sales reached US$75.1 billion, and it was second largest wireless provider, connecting 1.5 billion telephone calls per day. Verizon had 51 million customers in the United States. By this time, Verizon divided its business into Verizon Wireless, domestic telecom (wireline and telecommunications services including broadband), information services (directory publishing and electronic commerce service), and international (wireline and wireless operations in the Americas and Europe). Verizon's advertising for its wireless services began asking "Are You In?" beginning in 2005, which sought to brand the benefit of using Verizon and its mobile-to-mobile offerings.

To further expand it products and services, Verizon acquired rival MCI, Inc., a global communications provider, in 2005. With the deal, Verizon added advanced communications and information technology solutions, primarily for large business and government customers. Also in 2005, Verizon separately launched its FiOS, a fiber-optic-based video service, first in Texas, and then in other markets over the next few years. FiOS had 4.7

million customers by the end of 2012. In 2007 Verizon Wireless introduced the first truly live mobile television service with eight channels of live TV.

By 2008 Verizon Communications was the second largest telecommunications company in the United States, and Verizon Wireless was the second largest mobile carrier in the United States. The following year Verizon Wireless sales alone reached US$43.9 billion. In 2010 the Verizon Wireless income and customer base expanded when it began selling the iPhone, a device that had previously only been available from AT&T. By 2010 Verizon Wireless had 31.3 percent of the market in the United States and was the leading wireless provider. In 2011 Verizon acquired Terremark Worldwide Inc. and CloudSwitch; the latter acquisition enhanced Verizon's ability to offer cloud services. Sales for Verizon Communications reached US$110.9 billion, with Verizon Wireless reaching US$70.2 billion. In addition to retaining the number-one position among cellular telephone companies in the United States, Verizon also was the number-four U.S. broadband firm and number-two U.S. wired telecommunications firm.

Although Verizon had been competing with Time Warner Cable in various areas such as broadband and voice, the two companies started a joint venture in 2012 to cross-sell products. Verizon continued improvements to its technology infrastructure, investing US$66 billion to maintain, upgrade, and expand it between 2009 and 2012 alone. Verizon also enhanced its content offerings and delivery options through a joint venture with Redbox to allow streaming movies. By 2012 Verizon had more than 100 million subscribers, and revenues reached US$115.8 billion. Verizon Wireless was the number-two wireless firm in the world after China Mobile. As a brand, Verizon had adopted the tagline "What Do We Want to Build Next?" emphasizing its belief that technology could offer a wide range of solutions for consumers, businesses, and governments.

BRAND ELEMENTS

- The Verizon name was created by combining the words "veritas" and "horizon."
- "Can You Hear Me Now?" is the definitive advertising campaign for Verizon.
- Verizon's "Can You Hear Me Now?" transcended the brand to become a pop culture phenomenon.

When Bell Atlantic merged with GTE Corporation and combined operations with NYNEX, Vodafone, and AirTouch, the resulting telecommunications conglomerate took on a new name and logo. The brand name "Verizon" was selected as a combination of the Latin word "veritas," which means truth, and the word "horizon." From the first, then, Verizon emphasized its place as a leading, quality telecommunications brand with a broad, forward-thinking perspective. These ideas are reflected in the Verizon logo. The logo is focused on the Verizon name primarily in black with two elements in red, an echo of the *V* moving upward out to infinity and the *z* with its bottom stroke stretching forward underneath the *on*. The logo suggests speed, another key aspect of Verizon as a telecommunications company.

Two years after Verizon became a brand, it introduced a brand-defining campaign and tagline. "Can You Hear Me Now?" debuted in 2002 as part of Verizon's attempt to stay above the price war started by Sprint and Cingular, two of its major competitors at the time. Verizon wanted to avoid taking part in the war and lowering the prices of its calling plans. Instead, Verizon responded by positioning itself as a premium brand with a superior network and better reliability; the ad campaign emphasized the ability to place calls anytime and anywhere for its target audience of 25 to 54 year olds.

Although it had some print ads, "Can You Hear Me Now?" was primarily focused on television commercials featuring a bespectacled actor depicting a Verizon field tester. Known as Testman, the character dropped in on locations ranging from the mundane to the outlandish, including wheat fields, snowy mountains, and the set of *Jeopardy*, asking "Can You Hear Me Now?" into a Verizon cell phone. Presumably hearing an affirmative on the other end, Testman responded "Good!" Later spots, after 2004, still used the tagline and featured Testman but in different situations. "Can You Hear Me Now?" became an iconic advertising slogan and campaign.

BRAND IDENTITY

- Verizon has positioned itself as a superior brand with an outstanding wireless network.
- Taglines and campaigns including "Can You Hear Me Now?" and "Rule the Air" underscored Verizon's identity as a quality wireless brand.
- Verizon emphasized the power of its technology to be a significant part of the search for innovative solutions to the biggest challenges in the world.

Two years after the Verizon brand was created, it began identifying itself as a premium wireless brand in the United States with its "Can You Hear Me Now?" tagline and campaign. Over the course of more than 100 commercials, Verizon emphasized that it was the most dependable U.S. national wireless provider, with high quality service because its superior network was always being validated. Verizon did not position itself as low-cost nor did it emphasize promotional deals or phone giveaways as was common among its competitors. Instead, Verizon operated on high ground, reminding consumers it had spent

millions expanding and improving its wireless network and network coverage.

Verizon would not lower subscriber fees, yet it had the least number of customer complaints in the industry and a low customer turnover rate because consumers bought into its strong identity as a superior brand with an outstanding network. Although "Can You Hear Me Now?" had essentially run its course by 2009, Verizon's advertising continued to focus on its better network coverage, favorably comparing its wide 3G coverage in the United States to that of such competitors as AT&T. In 2010 Verizon promised consumers they could "Rule the Air" and be empowered ahead of its introduction of its 4G LTE network. By 2012 Verizon was reminding consumers that it still had "the nation's most reliable wireless network."

Other Verizon branded services also emphasized their superiority. To promote its broadband in 2006, for example, Verizon introduced Verizon the Beatbox Mixer, targeting web users, music lovers, and people considering broadband purchase. The Beatbox Mixer was an online interactive sampler that allowed users to create their own mixes. This campaign also included a tagline, "Richer Deeper Broader." Through such ad campaigns, Verizon intended to show its broadband was more powerful than other broadband services and linked Verizon to hipness as well. By 2012 Verizon was emphasizing the power of its technology to be a significant part of the search for innovative solutions to the biggest challenges in the world. With such taglines as "What Do We Want to Build Next?" and "Powerful Answers," Verizon underscored its position as a top-quality telecommunications brand through services like wireless networking, fiber optics, and cloud computing.

BRAND STRATEGY

- Verizon originally divided its business between domestic wireless and wireline.
- Verizon lived up to its identity as a high quality, reliable telecommunications brand by constantly expanding and improving its network and related technology.
- In 2011 Verizon began offering cloud services after acquiring Terremark Worldwide, Inc.

When Verizon was formed in 2000, its business was divided into two major segments. Domestic wireless focused on products and services in the United States, including wireless voice and data services and the sale of equipment. Wireline focused on voice, Internet services, broadband video and data, Internet protocol network services, network access, and long distance. Wireline's customers included consumers, carriers, businesses, and government agencies in the United States and international markets.

Over the years Verizon emphasized improving its wireless network and its available technology, living up to its identity as the high quality, superior telecommunications brand. After building its 3G network for wireless, Verizon created the first wireless consumer 3G multimedia service. In December 2010 it launched what became the largest, fastest, and most advanced 4G LTE network in the United States, adding new markets throughout 2011 so that its coverage area was available to more then 273 million people in 476 markets by the end of that year.

Verizon also regularly added new products and services in line with the way telecommunications brands generally expanded their offerings. In 2005, for example, Verizon launched FiOS, a next generation broadband service. FiOS was an advanced fiber-optics-based service that included Internet, phone, and television offerings and reached more than 17 million homes in the United States by 2012. In 2011 Verizon acquired Terremark Worldwide, Inc., a recognized cloud leader, allowing the brand to enter the cloud computing market with a global network of data centers and other IT products. Verizon had a presence in 200 locations in 140 countries, primarily in its data products and services like the cloud.

BRAND EQUITY

- Verizon was the number-two telecommunications services company and the largest wireless company in the United States in 2011.
- Verizon Communications sales reached US$115.8 billion in 2012.
- Verizon was ranked number 12 on Brand Finance's "Global 500" in 2012.

Since its formation, Verizon has been a leading telecommunications brand, and it achieved revenues of US$115.8 billion in 2012. In 2011 it was the number-two telecommunications services company in the United States, based on size, after AT&T. Verizon also was the largest U.S. wireless company with 107.8 million total connections, including 92.2 million retail customers. In addition, Verizon was the number-four U.S. broadband firm, with 10.2 percent market share. It had high customer loyalty based on a turnover rate of 1.26 percent as of 2011.

Verizon has maintained a high brand value for the whole of its existence. It was ranked number 12 on Brand Finance's "Global 500" and number three in its "Top 500 Telecom Brands" in 2012. Brand Finance estimated that Verizon had a brand value of US$27.6 billion and an enterprise value of US$203.3 billion. In the "BrandZ Top 100 Brand Ranking" in 2012, Verizon Communications ranked number nine with a brand value of US$49.2 billion. The same report also placed Verizon at number nine on its list of "Top 10 North America" and number two on the report's list of "Telecom Provider's Movers

and Shakers." The *Forbes* list of the "World's Most Powerful Brands" for 2012 placed Verizon Communications at number 55 with a brand value of US$19.4 billion.

BRAND AWARENESS

- Verizon focused on building awareness of its brand name since it was formed in 2000.
- The popularity of the "Can You Hear Me Now?" campaign brought Verizon years of strategic awareness.
- Verizon was number 40 on Harris Interactive's ranking of the "Reputations of the Most Visible Companies" in 2012.

Because Verizon was created out of a series of mergers, acquisitions, and partnerships between GTE, Bell Atlantic, and other leading telecommunications companies, the new conglomerate launched a massive campaign in 2000 to introduce its brand name; this effort successfully raised brand awareness in key markets such as the United States. Two years later, the wireless division of Verizon Communications developed an extremely effective marketing campaign that not only defined the brand's high quality and reliability, but also became a pop culture phenomenon. The popular campaign "Can You Hear Me Now?" brought Verizon years of strategic awareness, primarily in the United States, although the brand had a presence in 140 countries. Verizon's subsequent campaigns did not have the same impact as "Can You Hear Me Now?," yet Verizon Communications maintained its position in the marketplace and placed at number 40 on Harris Interactive's ranking of the "Reputations of the Most Visible Companies" in 2012. This survey of the American general public offered a ranking of brand popularity. Verizon Wireless also placed high on Brand Keys' "Customer Loyalty Leaders," a ranking of customer satisfaction. It was number 88 in 2012, number 93 in 2011, and number 79 in 2010.

BRAND OUTLOOK

- Verizon had to continually improve its offerings and technologies to retain its customers in the second decade of the 21st century.
- Verizon was expected to thrive because of its long-term investments in network development and its successful marketing strategies.
- To ensure its growth, Verizon sought strategic uses for its technology in such rising areas as health care and education.

Because some major markets had achieved 100 percent penetration for wireless services, telecommunication companies attempted to increase customer loyalty and lure new customers by continually updating offerings and adding capacity. Verizon and its competitors added new business segments such as storage, improved broadband, and cloud computing, and offered bundled services for phone, cable, and Internet access. Because Verizon was financially stable, had years of positive growth despite the economic recession, and had invested heavily in developing its network and technologies, it was expected to continue thrive in the second decade of the 21st century.

To ensure its growth, Verizon sought strategic uses for its technology in such rising areas as health care and education. As it looked to the future, Verizon emphasized its commitment to finding innovative solutions to global challenges and its belief that technology could solve problems. Verizon not only sponsored the Powerful Answer Awards in 2013, which celebrated solutions for health, education, and sustainability, but also made effective use of a related online community it created, Thinkfinity, which focused on corporate social responsibility efforts in education.

FURTHER READING

Brand Finance. "Verizon." *Brandirectory*. Brand Finance. Accessed February 10, 2013. http://brandirectory.com/profile/verizon.

"BrandZ Top 100 Most Valuable Global Brands 2012." Millward Brown. Accessed February 11, 2013. http://www.millwardbrown.com/brandz/2012/Documents/2012_BrandZ_Top100_Report.pdf.

"Cellco Partnership." *Encyclopedia of Major Marketing Campaigns*. Ed. Thomas Riggs. Vol. 2. Detroit, MI: Gale, 2007.

Springer, Paul. "Verizon the Beatbox Mixer." *Ads to Icons: How Advertising Succeeds in a Multimedia Age*. London: Kogan Page, 2007.

"Verizon Communications." *Forbes*. Accessed February 10, 2013. http://www.forbes.com/companies/verizon-communications/.

"Verizon Communications." RankingTheBrands.com. Accessed February 10, 2013. http://www.rankingthebrands.com/Brand-detail.aspx?brandID=525.

"Verizon Communications, Inc." *International Directory of Company Histories*. Ed. Tina Grant. Vol. 78. Detroit, MI: St. James Press, 2006.

"Verizon Wireless." RankingTheBrands.com. Accessed February 10, 2013. http://www.rankingthebrands.com/Brand-detail.aspx?brandID=80.

VISA

BRAND ORIGINS

- Dee Ward Hock was the driving force behind Visa's explosive growth.
- National BankAmericard Inc. (NBI), a consortium of banks that issued the BankAmericard, was established in 1970.
- In 1974 all foreign credit card operations held by Bank of America were sold to IBANCO, of which the domestic BankAmericard system became a subsidiary.
- In 1976 BankAmericard was rebranded as the Visa card, NBI rebranded as Visa U.S.A., and IBANCO became Visa International.
- By 1992 Visa's Gold Card had become the most widely used and best recognized credit card in the world.

The driving force behind Visa's explosive growth was Dee Ward Hock. Born in 1930, Hock was raised in North Ogden, Utah. He attended a local junior college, married his childhood sweetheart soon after school, and worked in a slaughterhouse and for a brick mason. In the early 1950s Hock joined the consumer finance department of Pacific Finance Company and soon became a local branch manager.

In 1965 Hock began working for National Bank of Commerce in Seattle, eventually becoming assistant vice-president. At the same time, Bank of America was in the process of licensing BankAmericard, its credit card operation, to other banks. National Bank became one of BankAmericard's first licensees, and Hock was promoted to manager of the bank's credit card program. However, many of the new licensee banks complained of delayed payment transfers and lack of adequate measures to prevent user fraud. At a meeting of over 100 bank licensees in 1968, Hock prodded the members to restructure the entire credit card operation. Hock was elected head of the committee to resolve recurring problems.

The success of Bank of America's credit card operation was accompanied by problems, which Hock, in his capacity as head of the banks' committee, was responsible for solving. He urged the member banks to take control of the BankAmericard program, and in 1970 they created National BankAmericard Inc. (NBI), a consortium of banks that issued the BankAmericard. This independent, non-stock membership corporation purchased the entire bank card operation from Bank of America over the next few years and then began to administer and develop the BankAmericard system. Hock was chosen to lead the new organization.

Hock headed an entirely domestic bank card system. Outside the United States, BankAmericard was issued by Bank of America's licensee banks in over 15 countries. In 1974 Hock negotiated the sale of all foreign credit card operations held by Bank of America to IBANCO, a group of bank licensees that formed a multinational, non-stock corporation to administer and develop the international operations of the BankAmericard program. He then made the entire domestic BankAmericard system a subsidiary of IBANCO, and served as this group's chief executive officer.

When it came to Hock's attention that in many foreign countries there was resistance to issuing a card associated with Bank of America, despite the fact that the association was nominal only, he decided to rebrand both the card and the company. In 1976 BankAmericard was renamed the Visa card. Hock chose the name "Visa" because it implied no national identification, it was relatively easy to pronounce in any language, and it made no reference to a bank, which Hock thought might limit how customers perceived they could use the card. Concurrently, NBI was renamed Visa U.S.A., and IBANCO became Visa International.

Under Hock's leadership, customer billings for the Visa card rose dramatically, and worldwide brand recognition grew at an astronomical rate. The first Visa Classic card was issued in 1977, and in 1979 Visa Travelers Cheques were introduced. In 1983 Hock implemented one of the most important and far-reaching services known in the credit card industry: a global network of automated teller machines (ATMs) that allowed Visa cardholders to obtain cash at locations far away from the banks or credit unions that originally issued them the card. In January 1987 Visa won a contract to operate Interlink, the largest retailer, or point-of-sale (POS), network that accepted debit cards in restaurants and stores in the United States.

By 1992 Visa's Gold Card, previously the Premiere Card, had become the most widely used and best-recognized credit card in the world. That year, total worldwide billings under the Visa name exceeded US$500 billion; more than 300 million cards were issued to customers around the world, more than six billion card and check transactions were made, and Visa operated more than 160,000 ATMs in 60 nations. As of 2012 Visa

was the most widely recognized financial services brand in the world according to the company's website.

BRAND ELEMENTS
- In 2013 Visa communicated the essence of its brand through the catchphrase, "Better Money for Better Living."
- The Visa brand has been represented by the phrase, "More People Go with Visa," which resulted from the brand's first global advertising campaign in 2009.
- The main Visa brand is represented by a logo displaying the brand name in blue capital letters. The letter "V" includes a golden-colored winged element on the left side.
- There are a number of different variations of the main logo, in which it is combined with other words, sub-brands, or global brands.

Over the years, a number of taglines have been used to promote Visa. The slogan, "Better Money for Better Living" was introduced in 2013. The catchphrase, "More People Go with Visa," resulted from the brand's first global advertising campaign in 2009.

The main Visa brand is represented by a logo displaying the brand name in blue capital letters. The letter "V" includes a golden-colored winged element on the left side. There are a number of different variations of the main logo, in which it is combined with other words, sub-brands, or global brands. For example, dedicated versions of the logo are used for "Visa Commercial," "Visa Processing Services," and "Verified by Visa." The letter "V" from the main brand logo, depicting the golden-colored winged element, has been used on its own to promote Visa's "V.me" digital wallet technology. One example of the Visa logo used in conjunction with another global brand is a dedicated Disney Visa logo, which includes the word "Disney" in stylized type next to the Visa name. Both brands appear above a subhead that reads: "wishes. dreams. magic."

BRAND IDENTITY
- In 2013 Visa communicated the essence of its brand identity through the catchphrase, "Better Money for Better Living."
- Because a strong association exists between the brand and credit cards, consumers often perceive Visa to be a credit card company, when in fact it is a global payments technology business.
- The Visa name is meant to convey payment acceptance and security, but the company does not directly issue credit cards or make loans.

In 2013 Visa communicated the essence of its brand identity through the catchphrase, "Better Money for Better

Living." This conveyed key attributes, such as convenience, trust, acceptance, reliability, and security. Additionally, according to Visa, the statement also communicated a number of "emotional truths." These included "the empowerment of choice, the richness of meaningful experience and the pervasive peace of mind that your Visa card is accepted and secure, wherever you go." Visa's brand identity also has been represented by the phrase, "More People Go with Visa," which stemmed from the brand's first global advertising campaign in 2009.

A strong association exists between the Visa brand and credit cards. For this reason, consumers often perceive Visa to be a credit card company, when in fact it is a global payments technology business. The company's positioning emphasizes its broader role in developing a wide range of payment products, including cash-access programs, debit cards, and prepaid cards. Visa also has developed real-time technologies that utilize email and text messages to notify account holders about potentially fraudulent activity, or if certain account-related criteria are met.

While the Visa logo is widely recognized and appears on numerous payment products, consumers sometimes mistakenly associate the brand with card issuing. Although the Visa name is meant to convey payment acceptance and security, the company does not directly issue credit cards or make loans. Because one of its primary roles is transaction processing, the company typically interacts with financial institutions, and not directly with merchants or consumers.

BRAND STRATEGY

- In 2012 Visa's strategy was defined by three overarching themes: advancing international growth, developing new payment technologies, and delivering shared value.
- By 2015 Visa's objective is to generate better than 50 percent of its revenues from international markets.
- Visa has partnered with world governments to introduce electronic payment technologies that expand the brand's global footprint while advancing economic development in emerging markets.
- Sponsorships with the U.S. National Football League, Olympic Games, and FIFA are key elements of Visa's global brand strategy.
- Visa has tailored its brand strategy to reach specific markets across the globe.

As Chairman Joseph W. Saunders explained in the company's 2012 annual report, Visa is guided by a vision to be "the Best Way to Pay and Be Paid." That year, the company's strategy was defined by three overarching themes. These included advancing international growth, developing new payment technologies, and delivering shared value.

By 2015 Visa's objective is to generate better than 50 percent of its revenues from international markets. The company has identified significant opportunities in global markets where the majority of transactions are made with cash. One example is Russia, where cash accounts for about 80 percent of consumer transactions. In 2012 Visa bolstered its position in Russia when its payment products became accepted at the country's largest grocery store chain. In addition to Russia, other markets with significant opportunity included Mexico, sub-Saharan Africa, Brazil, the Gulf Cooperation Council, and Japan. Visa's strategy appeared to be working, as international revenues increased 16 percent during its 2012 fiscal year.

Growing international revenues also goes hand-in-hand with Visa's focus on new payment technologies. For example, the company has developed a virtual prepaid product that enables consumers in developing markets like Uganda and Nigeria to pay bills and make purchases using their mobile phones, without the need for physical debit or credit cards. In 2012 Visa introduced V.me, a digital wallet option that positioned the company for additional growth within the e-commerce market.

Visa's goal of delivering shared value has involved partnerships with world governments and other entities. These have focused on the advantages and benefits associated with electronic payments. According to Visa, in 2012 basic financial services were out of reach for approximately 2.5 billion people. The introduction of electronic payment technologies had the dual benefit of expanding Visa's global footprint and advancing economic development.

Sponsorships also are a core element of Visa's global brand strategy. In the sponsorship arena, Visa has benefited from an association with the U.S. National Football League since 1995, providing strong exposure during high-profile events such as the Super Bowl. The brand also has benefited from its status as an Olympic partner since 1986, and has agreed to be the Olympic Games' official payment service through 2020. Finally, Visa reaches soccer fans through its connection with FIFA.

Visa also has tailored its brand strategy to reach specific racial and ethnic markets. For example, in 2011 the company sponsored the Essence Music Festival in New Orleans. This enabled Visa to promote its prepaid card products to the African-American market. Related promotions involved television, outdoor, radio, and online advertising. In 2011 Visa also employed a targeted approach to market its prepaid products to the Hispanic market. Although the company utilized social media, it had not yet embraced a Spanish-language advertising campaign, which surprised some analysts.

BRAND EQUITY

- With roots dating back to the credit card industry's formative days, Visa has amassed tremendous equity over more than 50 years of operation.
- In 2013 Visa claimed to be the most recognized financial services brand in the world.
- More than 80 billion transactions occurred with Visa's payment products in 2012, worth US$6.3 trillion, and approximately 2 billion Visa cards were in circulation.
- Visa ranked 74th on Interbrand's listing of the Best 100 Global Brands in 2012.
- According to the *The Nilson Report*, in 2011 Visa had a commanding 56.7 percent share of the US$3.6 trillion in purchases that were made with general-purpose credit and debit cards in the United States.

With roots dating back to the credit card industry's formative days, Visa has amassed tremendous equity over more than 50 years of operation. In 2013 Visa claimed to be the most recognized financial services brand in the world. At that time it was in the enviable position of operating the largest global retail electronic payments network.

In 2012 more than 80 billion transactions occurred with Visa's payment products, worth US$6.3 trillion. Worldwide, approximately 2 billion Visa cards were in circulation. In 2012 Visa ranked 74th on Interbrand's listing of the Best 100 Global Brands. Interbrand estimated the brand's value at US$4.9 billion, a 10 percent increase from the previous year.

According to the *The Nilson Report*, in 2011 Visa had a commanding 56.7 percent share of the US$3.6 trillion in purchases that were made with general purpose credit and debit cards in the United States. This compared to MasterCard (25.1 percent), American Express (15 percent), and Discover (3.2 percent). Visa's share of the US$2.1 trillion in United States credit card purchases made during 2011 totaled 43.3 percent. Second-place American Express accounted for 26.3 percent, followed by MasterCard (24.8 percent) and Discover (5.6 percent).

BRAND AWARENESS

- In 2013 Visa claimed to be the most recognized financial services brand in the world, representing the largest global retail electronic payments network.
- Worldwide, approximately 2 billion Visa cards were in circulation during 2012.
- The Visa brand benefits from billions of impressions received through its branded payment products.
- Visa unveiled its very first global advertising campaign in 2009, which featured the tagline, "More People Go with Visa."
- In the sponsorship arena, Visa benefits from an association with the U.S. National Football League, Olympic Games, and FIFA.

In 2013 Visa claimed to be the most recognized financial services brand in the world, representing the largest global retail electronic payments network. Worldwide, approximately 2 billion Visa cards were in circulation during 2012. As the company explains, its brand "transcends language, cultures and geography under a common payment mark that we believe symbolizes convenience, flexibility and security to hundreds of millions of consumers across the world."

Beyond the billions of impressions received through its branded payment products, Visa has built and maintained top-of-mind awareness in other ways. These include both traditional advertising and sponsorships that provide the brand with international exposure. Visa unveiled its very first global advertising campaign in 2009, which featured the tagline, "More People Go with Visa."

In the sponsorship arena, the Visa brand has benefited from an association with the U.S. National Football League since 1995, providing strong exposure during high-profile event such as the Super Bowl. The brand also has benefited from its status as an Olympic partner since 1986, and has agreed to be the Olympic Games' official payment service through 2020. Finally, Visa reaches soccer fans through its connection with FIFA.

BRAND OUTLOOK

- The continued development of digital and mobile payment technologies, as well as emerging economies, represents the future of the Visa brand.
- In 2012 Visa introduced a digital wallet option named V.me, which positioned the company for additional growth within the e-commerce market.
- Visa has invested in Square, a payment processing start-up company that allows merchants to accept credit card payments without traditional equipment.
- In November of 2012 Visa named Charles W. Scharf as its new CEO.

The continued development of digital and mobile payment technologies, as well as emerging economies, represents the future of the Visa brand. By 2013, tremendous opportunity existed in economies that were still maturing, resulting in a growing number of middle-class citizens. In turn, markets such as these would see a rise in electronic payment volume, especially with debit cards.

According to a report from Capgemini, in 2011 there were approximately 28.3 billion electronic and mobile payment transactions worldwide. Mobile payments were a particularly promising market. Capgemini's report indicated that only 2 percent of mobile users made mobile payments. However, volumes were projected to reach 17 billion in 2013. In general, exponential growth was anticipated for cash alternatives.

One example of an innovative new payment technology developed by Visa is a digital wallet option named V.me, which was introduced in 2012. This positioned the company for additional growth within the e-commerce market. In addition, the company also has invested in Square, a payment processing start-up company established by Jack Dorsey, the founder of Twitter. The developer of mobile point-of-sale technology allows merchants to accept credit card payments without traditional equipment and infrastructure.

In 2012 Visa generated record net operating revenues of US$10.4 billion, an increase of 13 percent over the previous year. In November of that year the company named Charles W. Scharf as its new CEO, following an extensive succession plan executed by Visa's board of directors. As the company headed into 2013, Visa appeared to be positioned for continued success.

FURTHER READING

"Debit Cards Continue to Win Market Share from Credit Cards." *Yahoo! Finance*, October 9, 2012. Accessed January 3, 2013. http://finance.yahoo.com/news/debit-cards-continue-win-market-063000767.html#.

"General Purpose Cards—U.S. 2011." *Nilson Report*, February 2012. Accessed January 1, 2013. http://www.nilsonreport.com/pdf/news/aemc.pdf

Swartz, Jon. "Visa CEO Talks Consumer Tech, Future of Mobile Payments." *USA Today*, September 21, 2012.

Visa Inc. "Brand and Sponsorships." Accessed January 1, 2013. http://corporate.visa.com.

———. "2012 Annual Report." Accessed January 1, 2013. http://investor.visa.com.

"Visa Inc." *International Directory of Company Histories*. Ed. Jay P. Pederson and Tina Grant. Vol. 104. Farmington Hills, MI: St. James Press, 2009.

Worthham, Jenna. "Visa to Offer Mobile Payments in Developing Nations." *New York Times*, November 16, 2011.

VODAFONE

—■—

AT A GLANCE

■

Brand Synopsis: The second-largest mobile phone company, Vodafone has made itself a recognized brand by being "customer-obsessed."

Parent Company: Vodafone Group, Plc.
Vodafone House, The Connection
Newbury, Berkshire RG14 2FN
United Kingdom
http://www.vodafone.com

Sector: Telecommunication Services

Industry Group: Telecommunications

Performance: *Market share*—11 percent in UK market (2011). *Sales*—US$74.83 billion (2011).

Principal Competitors: Deutsche Telecom; Orange; Telefónica Europe

BRAND ORIGINS

- Vodafone was created as a mobile telecommunications division of British-based Racal Electronics, with the name combining the concept of voice and data.
- The company left Racal and became independent in 1991.
- Vodafone adopted the concept of Partner Networks in 2001, allowing the company to provide its services in cooperation with existing local providers.

Racal Electronics Group, a British electronics firm, won the bidding for one of two private sector cellular licenses in the United Kingdom in 1982 and set up a telecommunications division. The other bid went to British Telecom, a UK-based multinational telecommunications company. The Racal division was named "Vodafone," combining the concept of voice and data services over mobile phones. By 1985 the Vodafone network became the first cellular network launched in the United Kingdom. Vodafone continued to grow, creating the Vodafone Recall, a voicemail as well as paging service. Vodafone had become the world's largest mobile network by 1987, providing a paging network that covered 80 percent of the British population. Vodafone's parent company, Racal Telecomms, appeared on the London and New York stock exchange in 1988.

The Vodafone division of Racal left its parent company in 1991, and Vodafone appeared on the London and New York stock exchanges as an independent company. Also in 1991, Vodafone introduced digital mobile phone service, further expanding the availability of its services. During the same year, Vodafone successfully made the world's first roaming call, working with Telecom Finland. Instead of being able to use their phones only when within range of a Vodafone cellular tower, users were able to access cell towers from other networks to continue using their mobile devices. After the success with roaming, Vodafone signed an international roaming agreement with Telecom Finland in 1992. As the market began to become multinational, Vodafone created a division called Vodafone Group International to help with the acquisition of licenses and overseas interests.

In 1994 Vodafone continued advancing, becoming the first network operator in the United Kingdom to release data, fax, and text messaging services within its digital network. Also in 1994 Vodafone joined Globalstar consortium to help develop and launch a Low Earth Orbiting Satellite for mobile phone service. As the capabilities of the company changed, the offers to consumers also began to change. Vodafone altered its billing system to include time used down to the second, allow consumers to purchase bundled minutes, and permit off-peak local calls to landlines. The billing changes were the first in the revolution of charging per minute and per text message and allotting the usage of data.

The company ventured many changes at the turn of the 21st century. In 2000 Vodafone and Microsoft went into a joint venture, allowing Microsoft Outlook, the company's email software, to operate on Vodafone devices. The same year, the company acquired Mannesmann AG, a Germany-based company that operated Germany's cellular network carrier D2 Mannesmann. The acquisition made Vodafone the largest mobile telecommunications company in the world at the time, only later to be surpassed by China Mobile.

A major shift for the company came in 2001, when Vodafone introduced the concept of Partner Networks in a deal with Denmark's TDC Mobil. The purpose was to allow the Vodafone brand and services into international local markets without Vodafone having to make an investment in local operating companies there. It could instead market its services under a dual brand, such as TDC Mobil-Vodafone.

Vodafone was able to enter the U.S. mobile market in 1999 through a joint venture with Bell Atlantic Corp., an American telecommunications company. The business was called Verizon Wireless. Verizon Communications, the company created out of a merger between Bell Atlantic and GTE 2000, owned the majority of Verizon Wireless, and the brand Vodafone was not used. As of 2013 Vodafone still owned 45 percent of Verizon Wireless and was in a standoff with Verizon, each company seeking to purchase the other's remaining share.

BRAND ELEMENTS

- The name "Vodafone" is a combination of the words "voice," "data," and "fone" (for phone), as pertaining to mobile devices.
- Vodafone's logo is a simple, red, single-quotation mark that replaced the brand name in 1997.
- The latest slogan for the company is "Power to you," encouraging consumers to make their own decisions about switching from feature phones to smartphones.

The Vodafone brand was started by the Racal Electronics Company in 1982, after the company acquired a license to become a UK-based cellular company. The name was a combination of the words "voice," "data," and "fone" (for phone). The brand became independent of Racal in 1991 and served as the company's name. As of 2013 the company still utilized "Vodafone" as its brand name. In partnerships and other joint ventures, the brand name is often combined with the partner company. For example, when Vodafone signed a Partner Network agreement with Denmark's TDC Mobil, the brand in Denmark became TDC Mobil-Vodafone.

Since the company has been in existence it has only used two logos. The original logo, the word "Vodafone" in black capital letters with a white line running through, was utilized until 1997. That year the company began using a smaller, more subtle logo: a single-quotation mark in red. As opposed to stating explicitly which company the logo represented, Vodafone cleverly forced consumers to infer the brand from the bare symbol alone. As the company was already very well-known in the United Kingdom and Europe, the new, sleeker logo and the branding ploy probably enhanced brand recognition and interest.

Vodafone has gone through several slogan changes. The most-used global slogan for the brand was "How are you?" which was used from 2003 to 2006 in Britain. This catchy and short slogan was changed in 2008 to "Make the most of NOW," encouraging consumers to live in the moment. However, in many countries "How are you?" stayed in use. The official slogan was changed again in 2012 to "Power to you." The company stated that the change was to empower the customer to make his or her own decision to switch from feature phones to smartphones.

BRAND IDENTITY

- Vodafone has successfully expanded its international brand through Partnership Networks.
- The company has striven to stay on the forefront of technology ever since it provided the first cellular phone call in 1985.
- Through supporting charities, Vodafone maintains a society-driven corporate brand image.

Vodafone defines its brand in two ways: as a world competitor in mobile telecommunications and as a customer-based company. The brand became recognized worldwide as Vodafone developed the concept of Partnership Networks with local telecom providers to further both sales and the brand itself. A Partnership Network is created when Vodafone signs an agreement with a local telecommunications company to help them with mobile availability, in return for which the Vodafone brand is added to the local company's name. For example, when Vodafone formed a partnership with Denmark's TDC Mobil, the brand became TDC Mobil-Vodafone. By using the international networks, Vodafone was able to further the exposure of its brand, making it one of the most recognizable mobile networks in the world.

The company also markets itself as being customer-oriented, or "customer-obsessed" as it proclaims on its website. Essential to Vodafone's customer-friendliness is always to release the best available technology to its customers. Vodafone has been cutting-edge right from its founding; it made the first-ever cellular phone call in 1985. With this history, Vodafone has been able to present the brand as one that offers the best information and expertise available. Additionally, part of the company's mission statement is to bring far-flung families together through Vodafone's advanced technology.

Vodafone also strives to contribute to society through supporting local charities as part of its World of Difference program. Under it, the company supports employment of individuals to work for a participating charity, providing salary and expenses. Vodafone also started a charity in 2012 called JustTextGiving, through which charities of all sizes can raise money via text messages, at no cost to the charity. Because the brand gives back to the communities that utilize its services, it portrays itself, not as revenue-driven, but as "society-driven."

BRAND STRATEGY

- The Vodafone brand was created after Racal Electronics won a cellular network bid from the UK in 1982.
- Vodafone became an independent company in 1991.
- Vodafone created and revolutionized the concept of roaming, allowing consumers to use their mobile devices when out of range of a Vodafone network.
- The company has expanded internationally by forming partnerships with local networks.

The brand name Vodafone was created by Racal Electronics after winning a UK cellular network license in 1982. Racal held control of the brand until the division became a separate company in 1991. Since then Vodafone has maintained its name intact, without introducing any brand extensions. The word "Vodafone" comes from a combination of "voice," "data" and "fone" (for phone). In the United Kingdom, all Vodafone products have been released under the Vodafone brand.

The company established international relationships with other network providers through two primary means. The first was to seek agreements to limit roaming charges for Vodafone subscribers using other networks. Roaming occurs when a subscriber is out of range of a cell tower for his or her network and has to use another network, which ultimately would result in a high usage bill. The first roaming agreement that Vodafone signed was with Telecom Finland in 1992. As the market began to expand to include multinational capabilities, Vodafone created a division called Vodafone Group International to help with the acquisition of licenses and overseas interests.

The second tool that the company has used in international relationships is to establish Partner Networks. Through these arrangements, Vodafone makes its products available to smaller networks, and in return the networks take on the Vodafone brand. When Vodafone signed a partnership with Denmark's TDC Mobil, the company became known as TDC Mobil-Vodafone. This concept has usually been successful with the company, with a few exceptions. When Vodafone attempted to penetrate the market in the United States, which was behind Europe in mobile communication, Vodafone joined with Bell Atlantic Corp., an American telecommunications company, to form Verizon Wireless. In this deal, however, Verizon Communications, the company created out of a merger between Bell Atlantic and GTE 2000, owned the majority of Verizon Wireless. Vodafone held 45 percent of Verizon Wireless's shares, but the brand Vodafone was not allowed to be used.

BRAND EQUITY

- Vodafone built brand equity by breaking into emerging markets, successfully buying out smaller networks before other mobile networks expanded.
- As the market changes for Vodafone, the company responds by adapting and creating new mobile technology.
- Brand Finance ranked Vodafone as the ninth-most-valuable global brand, with a value of US$30.04 billion, making it the most valuable telecommunications brand in the world.

Vodafone has significantly enhanced its brand value since 2002 by expanding actively into developing economies, taking control of international mobile markets in the early stages. The company bought out partner network Essar, an Indian operating network, in 2011. As the market has changed for Vodafone, the company has been able to adapt and create new mobile technology.

Brand Finance's "Global 500 2012" listed Vodafone as ninth in the Top 20 Most Valuable Brands, with a brand value of US$30.04 billion, down from the previous year's ranking of fifth. Competitor Deutsche Telekom was ranked 161st, with a brand value of US$5.867 billion, and France's Orange telecommunications network was ranked 31st, down from 29th, with a brand value of US$18.557 billion.

BRAND AWARENESS

- With the company's expansion into emerging markets, Vodafone continues to enjoy high levels of brand awareness.

- When Vodafone establishes agreements with partner networks, the Vodafone name is attached to the local network's name, furthering the brand exposure.
- Vodafone has greatly encouraged and invested in charities, starting JustTextGiving in 2012.

Despite a drop in its brand value in 2012, Vodafone continued to be the most successful telecom brand on Brand Finance's "Global 500 2012" ranking. The company enjoyed high levels of brand awareness with both developed and emerging markets. Since the company performed the first cellular phone call in 1985, Vodafone has been a staple among the mobile brands. The brand was originally part of Racal Electronics but became independent of its parent company in 1991. Additionally, through agreements with partner networks the Vodafone name has expanded into emerging markets. With partner networks, the Vodafone name is attached to the local network's name, furthering the brand exposure.

The company has also generated brand awareness by supporting charities. Vodafone expanded its ongoing efforts in this area in 2012 with its new charity sponsorship JustTextGiving, a method through which charities of all sizes can raise money via text messages at no cost. As the brand is able to give back to the communities that utilize its services, the brand can be presented, not as revenue-driven, but as society-driven, thereby further enhancing positive awareness.

BRAND OUTLOOK

- Vodafone saw a slump in share prices, attributable mainly to corporate underinvestment.
- Vodafone reported that its revenues increased 8.4 percent between 2010 and 2011.
- Vodafone has been growing as a company due expansion into emerging markets.

Despite the company's growth in emerging markets across the globe, Vodafone did see a slump in share price in 2012. Part of the slump was attributed to inadequate capital investment. Also putting downward pressure on shares was Vodafone's attempt to purchase the remaining shares beyond its 45 percent stake in U.S.-based Verizon Wireless, which has simultaneously attempted to buy out Vodafone's shares. The possibility of losing Verizon's shares caused Vodafone's share price to fall. However, by the end of 2012 share prices had stabilized.

Vodafone has reported increased revenues from targeted growth markets. The company has also reported that 33 percent of its revenue is generated from products as opposed to service plans. The company's growth has slowed during the global economy's recovery from the 2008 recession. Although consumer contracts did not fall during the height of the recession, the company suffered lower income from roaming fees because fewer subscribers were traveling. Nevertheless, group revenues for the company increased 8.4 percent between 2010 and 2011, providing a positive sign for the company's and the brand's fortunes. This, combined with Vodafone's solid global base of over 340 million subscribers, provides a basis for optimism about the future.

FURTHER READING

Brand Finance. "Global 500 2012." *Brandirectory*. Accessed December 12, 2012. http://brandfinance.com/images/upload/bf_g500_2012_web_dp.pdf.

Carew, Sinead. "Verizon Says No Verizon Wireless Buyout Talks with Vodafone." *Telecom Engine*, January 11, 2013. Accessed January 13, 2013. http://www.telecomengine.com/article/verizon-says-no-verizon-wireless-buyout-talks-vodafone.

Colao, Vittorio. "Chief Executive's Review." Vodafone Group, Plc. Accessed January 13, 2013. http://www.vodafone.com/content/annualreport/annual_report10/exec_summary/chief_executives_review.html.

Jones, Dan. "How Secure Is Vodafone's Dividend Outlook?" *InvestmentWeek*, October 1, 2012.

O'Sullivan, Cian. "Power to Who? Vodafone Rebrand Aimed at Pulling App Buyers to Operators." *GoMo News*, September 21, 2012.

Quinn, James. "Vodafone: A Difficult Call to Make." *Telegraph* (London), November 11, 2012.

Vodafone Group, Plc. "About Us." Accessed January 9, 2013. http://www.vodafone.com/content/index/about.html.

———. "Annual Report 2011." Accessed January 10, 2013. http://www.vodafone.com/content/annualreport/annual_report11/business-review/key-market-review.html.

———. "Vodafone Group Plc Factsheet." Accessed January 11, 2013. http://www.vodafone.com/content/dam/vodafone/investors/factsheet/group_factsheet.pdf.

VOLKSWAGEN

AT A GLANCE

Brand Synopsis: The most successful multibrand group in the automotive industry, the Volkswagen brand has evolved from the German auto manufacturer best known for the inexpensive "love bug" to a global brand characterized by innovative designs and quality engineering.

Parent Company: Volkswagen Aktiengesellschaft
VHH 11th Floor
P.O. Box 1849
D-38436 Wolfsburg
Germany
http://www.vw.com/

Sector: Consumer Discretionary

Industry Group: Automobiles & Components

Performance: *Market share*—7.30 percent of the global market in cars and light-duty vehicles (2011). *Sales*—US$196.57 billion (2011).

Principal Competitors: Ford; General Motors; Toyota; Honda

BRAND ORIGINS

- In 1933 Adolf Hitler met with Daimler-Benz's former chief designer Ferdinand Porsche to discuss Hitler's idea of a "people's car."
- Volkswagen was founded in 1937 as a direct response to the luxury car at the center of the early German auto industry.

- Besides the Beetle (launched in 1946), two other Volkswagen models, the Golf and the Passat, have enjoyed tremendous production success.
- Marketing primarily to younger consumers, Volkswagen print ads of the 1960s and 1970s became tremendously popular.
- Volkswagen is part of the Volkswagen Group, which includes the car brands Audi, Skoda, Seat, Man, Bentley, Scania, Lamborghini, Bugatti, and Porsche.

Volkswagen was founded in 1937 as a direct response to the popularity of the luxury car at the center of the early German auto industry. Almost all cars before 1930 cost more than a year's wages, even if they were designed for the average German worker. The average German citizen of the 1930s could not afford a car, particularly a luxury car such as a Mercedes-Benz, and Volkswagen (which translates to "people's car") was developed to meet the demand for a cheaper automobile.

In 1933 Adolf Hitler met with Daimler-Benz's former chief designer, Ferdinand Porsche, to discuss Hitler's idea of a "Volkswagen," or a people's car for all German citizens. Hitler proposed a car that could carry at least four people, cruise at speeds of 60 miles per hour, average 30 to 40 miles per gallon, and cost no more than 1,000 marks.

Porsche viewed this as an opportunity to push his own idea of a small car forward, and he completed his first designs by 1935. Porsche went on to build a total of 50 Volkswagen prototypes between 1935 and 1937. In 1938, to celebrate the production of the "people's car," construction began on the Wolfsburg factory, which remains one of the largest manufacturing facilities in the world. By the late 1930s, the Volkswagen had incorporated front-hinged doors, a rear split window, and an oversized hood, establishing a look that would characterize the highest-volume car produced in the history of the automobile. Built on a cheap and reliable flat, four-cylinder, rear-mounted, air-cooled engine, this early edition of the car was the basis of the later VW Beetle, which appeared after World War II.

In 1946 the Wolfsburg plant, located in the British zone of occupied postwar Germany, was placed under the responsibility of Major Ivan Hirst. Using blueprints discovered in the factory, Hirst put the original Volkswagen Beetle (referred to by the manufacturer as "Type 1" or "T1") into full production by 1949, producing one million cars by 1955. The car would be produced in Germany until 1980 and then in Mexico until 2003.

The original Beetle remained in production until 2003. The "new" version was produced from 1997 through 2010, and the redesigned version launched in 2011. Two other VW models, the Golf and the Passat, have enjoyed tremendous production success, thus strengthening the brand's legacy. These three cars, all currently in production, are recognized as three of the ten best-selling cars worldwide of all time.

Although only two Beetles sold in the United States in 1949, U.S. consumer interest in the T1 and T2 grew during the next two decades and beyond, in large part due to creative advertisements. Targeting younger consumers, the Volkswagen print ads of the 1960s and 1970s became incredibly popular, solidifying the brand's identity within an entire generation of American consumers. Due to its success, Volkswagen introduced several new models during this time, including the Karmann Ghia and the Golf.

After a period of decline in the 1980s largely due to increased competition in the small car market from automakers in the United States and Japan, Volkswagen reignited its brand in the 1990s with the introduction of new models designed for a more sophisticated car buyer and the reintroduction of creative, catchy advertising. With its popular Golf and Beetle redesigned for a new generation of car buyers with more upscale tastes, Volkswagen's sales increased dramatically, leading the brand to acquire several other smaller European brands and to extend its reach across the full range of car buyers.

This decline-rebound scenario was enacted again in the early 2000s, with the first half of the decade witnessing scandals and significant sales declines. New models were not well received by consumers, and by 2005 nearly all Volkswagen models sat near the bottom of reliability and quality ratings. However, in 2007, under the leadership of CEO Martin Winterkorn, Volkswagen significantly strengthened its position both on a national and international level by focusing on diesel engine design, its history in making cars for the common people, the brand's creative work in advertising, and the introduction of flex-fuel vehicles, hybrids, electric cars, and mini vehicles.

Today, Volkswagen is part of the Volkswagen Group, which includes the car brands Audi, Skoda, Seat, Man, Bentley, Scania, Lamborghini, Bugatti, and Porsche, along with Volkswagen Financial Services.

BRAND ELEMENTS

- Besides its famous name and its timeless designs like the "bug" and the "bus," Volkswagen is known worldwide for its VW logo.
- Volkswagen's unique approach to nomenclature has involved both the manufacturer and the consumer in the process of naming vehicle models.
- The Volkswagen brand is recognized for its catchy, enduring slogans and taglines.
- Other than perhaps BMW, the VW brand is the most recognized brand in the auto industry.

In addition to its famous name and such timeless designs as the "bug" and the "bus," Volkswagen is known worldwide for its VW logo. The initial logo, designed in 1939 by a Porsche employee named Franz Xavier Reimspiess as part of a design competition, was heavily influenced by designs associated with Hitler's Third Reich and the German Nazi party. The original black-and-white logo encircled the bold letters "V" and "W" in what looked like a ship's wheel with four fans around it, similar in some respects to the swastika. The postwar version removed the fans but retained the "VW" inside a wheel-like circle. Later changes included removing the wheel elements from the circle and adding a now widely recognized blue coloring.

The Volkswagen brand has also relied on a unique approach to nomenclature. For much of the brand's existence, Volkswagen representatives and purists preferred the manufacturing model names (Type 1, Type 2, and so on). It was not until 1968 that the name "Beetle" appeared in advertisements, though millions had been built by that time. In this way, the Volkswagen to some extent encouraged owners to invent their own names for its vehicles. From the "hippie bus" (Type 2) to the "slug bug" (Type 1), the lack of traditional nomenclature allowed VW owners to create their own associations with the brand. In the 21st century, Volkswagen uses model names similar to those of its competitors, but its early approach to nomenclature was unique in the auto industry.

The Volkswagen brand is also recognized for its catchy, enduring slogans and taglines. From earlier taglines such as "it makes you look bigger" and "every new one comes slightly used" to more recent slogans like "Fahrvergnügen" ("driving enjoyment"), "for the love of the car," and "drivers wanted," Volkswagen is rivaled only by BMW in the auto manufacturing sector with regard to consumer recognition of brand elements.

Volkswagen's newest advertisements have adopted the simple tagline "Das Auto," German for "the car." Volkswagen wants people to think of Volkswagen when they think of cars, in the same way that people think of McDonald's when they think of hamburgers and Coca Cola when they think of soft drinks.

BRAND IDENTITY

- The Volkswagen brand is enduring, with a strong brand image and brand personality.
- Despite its young-at-heart, adventurous identity, the brand has been repositioning itself since the 1990s to expand its market presence.
- Despite its reputation for spotty quality and the poor customer satisfaction, Volkswagen's overall identity seems sufficiently robust to overcome these negative aspects.

Whenever a consumer hears of Volkswagen, he or she is likely to instantly connect the brand with target audiences of all kinds: car enthusiasts, young drivers, and even recovered hippies. The brand is iconic in terms of its enduring brand image and personality.

Despite its young-at-heart, adventurous identity, the brand has been repositioning itself since the 1990s in order to expand its market presence. For nearly three-quarters of a century, Volkswagen held on to its humble "for the people" origins even as the brand moved into the luxury, sport utility, and sports car markets. While some critics suggested that any significant overhaul of its identity was likely to be unsuccessful, Volkswagen's approach to connecting its "for the people" identity of the past with its "for the planet" identity of the future seems poised for success. "Social responsibility makes good sense [for VW]," notes a writer for Brand Talk, "in the same way that it made sense for Dove to redefine beauty and give women more self-confidence."

Despite its reputation for spotty quality and poor customer satisfaction, VW's overall brand identity remains sturdy. For example, the revitalized Beetle, designed to help reestablish Volkswagen's brand identity with mainstream consumers, helps to perpetuate an identity with a storied history.

BRAND STRATEGY

- The first component of Volkswagen's threefold brand strategy is a return to its roots as a maker of cars for the people.
- Second, Volkswagen wants to be a car for all kinds of people.
- Third, Volkswagen's brand strategy emphasizes partnerships and ventures in new markets.

Besides rebranding itself as the auto brand with an environmental conscience, Volkswagen's current brand strategy is threefold. First, Volkswagen is returning to its roots as a maker of cars for the people. It has abandoned a decades-long practice of "trying to convince Americans to buy cars engineered and priced for European tastes," writes Mark Phelan, an auto columnist for the *Detroit Free Press*. For example, Volkswagen has reduced prices on its Jetta model to compete with the likes of the Honda Civic, and its new Passat model is competing with the Ford Fusion and Toyota Camry. In doing so, Volkswagen is no longer competing so much with fellow European brands but with heavyweight car makers such as Ford, Honda, and Toyota.

Second, Volkswagen wants to be a car for all kinds of people. On one hand, Volkswagen is in the process of building an electric car for cost-conscious consumers. On the other, Volkswagen, through its Audi brand, has purchased Ducati, a maker of upscale motorcycles, and has been rumored to be once again exploring the purchase of Alfa Romeo, a premium-car brand from Italy. Alfa Romeo would add to Volkswagen's recent acquisition of the premium sports car brand Porsche and earlier acquisitions of such super luxury brands as Bentley, Lamborghini, and Bugatti.

Third, Volkswagen's strategy emphasizes partnerships and ventures in new markets. According to the *Economist* in 2012, Volkswagen "bet on China nearly 30 years ago. Now it is the world's biggest car market and VW has 18 percent of it, through two joint ventures. They sell 2 [million] vehicles a year and plan to double this by 2018." Similar ventures have reaped success in countries from Brazil to Russia.

BRAND EQUITY

- The Volkswagen Group's profits more than doubled to a record US$23.8 billion in 2012.
- Volkswagen is ranked behind only Toyota, Johnson & Johnson, and Honda among Interbrand's "Best Global Green Brands for 2012."
- Volkswagen is currently ranked ahead of brands like BMW and Mercedes-Benz as the "Best Business Brand in Germany."

With Volkswagen ranked behind only Toyota, Johnson & Johnson, and Honda at number four in its "Best Global Green Brands for 2012," Interbrand calls the German automaker "of the world's most innovative and sustainable car manufacturers." Through major investments, including the more than US$700 million it committed to the development of renewable energy plants and such creative concepts as its new "e-scooter," Volkswagen, more than any other manufacturer in any industry, has tied its brand to the environment, and Interbrand believes this approach has had a significant positive impact on the Volkswagen's brand equity.

This impact can be seen in Volkswagen's being ranked ahead of brands like BMW and Mercedes-Benz as the "Best Business Brand in Germany" by Das Deutsche Markenranking in 2011, as well as in other brand rankings. Volkswagen jumped eleven spots in overall brand performance from number 22 to number 11 on Sync-Force's "Ranking the Brands Top 100" for 2012. This gives Volkswagen its highest-ever ranking and places it fourth among automakers and ahead of such heavyweight brands as Sony, Microsoft, and even McDonald's.

Recent performance has dramatically affected Volkswagen's brand equity. According to the *Economist*, the Volkswagen Group's profits more than doubled to a record US$23.8 billion in 2012. As most European carmakers were closing factories and cutting jobs, VW was "seizing market share in Europe, booming in China and staging a comeback in America." Setting its sights on top-ranked Toyota, Volkswagen and its brand equity are on the rise.

BRAND AWARENESS

- Volkswagen has maintained a significant presence in motorsports since the early 1960s.
- Besides its presence in competitive motoring, the Volkswagen brand has appeared in numerous movies, including as Disney's "Herbie" in *The Love Bug* series.
- A 2012 *Consumer Reports* survey of car buyers ranked Volkswagen twentieth in "Best Car Brand Perception."

Volkswagen has maintained a significant presence in motorsports since the early 1960s. It first marked its presence in the sport with "Formula Vee" and "Super Formula Vee" racing, in which the racecars were constructed of used Beetle parts. Formula Vee became perhaps the first popular, low-cost form of formula auto racing, and Volkswagen acknowledged it by introducing the *Formula Vee* edition of the Beetle in the early 1970s and making a name for itself in formula racing in events across the United States, Europe, China, and South Africa in the first decades of the 21st century.

Besides its presence in competitive motoring, the Volkswagen brand has appeared in numerous movies, including as Disney's "Herbie" in *The Love Bug* series from 1968 to 2005, in the animated *Transformers* series in the 1980s, and in Disney's *Cars* of 2006. Not necessarily by design, the Volkswagen brand's unique marketing efforts for its vehicles also helped to bring about a new approach to advertising in general, as companies across the United States and around the world used the Beetle, Bus, and other models to promote their own products. Through a unique and distinctive design that has endeared it to target audiences around the world, the brand image of Volkswagen has achieved cult status among consumers.

While Volkswagen's brand image and equity have strengthened globally in the early years of the 21st century, it must be noted that its brand awareness has still suffered to some extent in the United States during the same period. For example, a 2012 *Consumer Reports* survey of car buyers ranked Volkswagen twentieth in "Best Car Brand Perception," and it had been ranked as low as 35th of 37 automakers in the past.

BRAND OUTLOOK

- Despite a host of ups and downs over the past few decades, the outlook for the Volkswagen brand in 2012 was solid.
- The Volkswagen brand was poised to succeed as the "world's most profitable, fascinating and sustainable automobile company by 2018."
- Integrating innovations in fuel-efficient, low-emission mobility solutions, Volkswagen intends to launch the first "e-vehicle" for everyone, the Up "blue-e-motion."

By incorporating sustainability throughout its product line, increasing fuel efficiency and fuel options for its vehicles, pushing the envelope with its design of hybrid and electric vehicles, and committing to developing "green" production facilities, Volkswagen's "Think Blue" model of the 2000s has the brand poised for success in the 21st century. By adopting the popular "Think Green" phrase and adding Volkswagen's classic blue logo, Volkswagen has creatively made the global push for environmental sustainability its own.

Long gone are the brand associations of the "hippie bus" and "slug bug" that led to its own kind of "Beetle-mania" in the 1960s. In 2012 the Volkswagen brand was poised to compete with other auto manufacturers in an effort to become the "world's most profitable, fascinating and sustainable automobile company by 2018." Volkswagen CEO Martin Winterkorn has gone on record to say his aim is to pass Toyota as the world's largest automaker by 2018. To do so, Volkswagen set four goals as part of its "Group Strategy 2018" plan. These four goals included deploying intelligent innovations and technologies to become a world leader in customer satisfaction and quality, increasing unit sales by focusing on above-average share of the development of the major growth markets, increasing the return on sales to ensure that the group's solid financial position and ability to act are guaranteed even in difficult market periods, and aiming to become the top employer across all brands, companies, and regions.

Integrating a wide range of innovations into fuel-efficient, low-emission mobility solutions, Volkswagen is on its way to launching the first "e-vehicle" for everyone, the Up "blue-e-motion." With the intention of reminding consumers that it is the auto manufacturer for the people, Volkswagen strives to be the best brand for the environment and for the consumer. With such an approach, the Volkswagen brand strategy seems well timed and well positioned for success.

FURTHER READING

"Best Global Green Brands 2012: Top 50 Brands." Interbrand. Accessed September 15, 2012. http://www.interbrand.com/en/best-global-brands/Best-Global-Green-Brands/2012-Report/BestGlobalGreenBrandsTable-2012.aspx.

Brand Finance. "Volkswagen." *Brandirectory*. Accessed September 18, 2012. http://brandirectory.com/profile/volkswagen.

Dougherty, Tom. "The Volkswagen Brand Feels Right—And Its Sales Do Too." StealingShare.com, June 4, 2012. Accessed September 15, 2012. http://www.stealingshare.com/blog/?p=3680.

Forbes, Thom. "VW's U.S. Sales Zoom." *Marketing Daily*, June 4, 2012. Accessed September 16, 2012. http://www.mediapost.com/publications/article/176036/vws-us-sales-zoom-shifts-gears-globally.html?edition=47533.

Hamer, Tony, and Michele Hamer. "History of the Volkswagen." About.com, 2012. Accessed September 19, 2012. http://classiccars.about.com/od/classiccarsaz/a/volkswagen.htm.

Johnson, Ben. "Case Study of Volkswagen Logo: From 1939 to Present Day." LogoInn.net, September 5, 2009. Accessed 20 September, 2012. http://www.logoinn.net/case-study-of-volkswagen-logo-from-1939-to-present-day/.

"The People's Branded and Wanted Icon." *BrandTalk*, October 2011. Accessed September 18, 2012. http://www.peopalove.com/brandtalk/2011/oct/wanted.html.

Phelan, Mark. "VW Elbows Way into Mainstream Market." *Detroit Free Press*, June 3, 2012.

Volkswagen Group. "Annual Report 2011." Accessed September 14, 2012. http://annualreport2011.volkswagenag.com/servicepages/filelibrary/files/collection.php.

———. "Sustainability and Responsibility." Accessed September 20, 2012. http://www.volkswagenag.com/content/vwcorp/content/en/sustainability_and_responsibility.html.

"VW (Volkswagen)." RankingtheBrands.com, 2012. Accessed September 17, 2012. http://www.rankingthebrands.com/Brand-detail.aspx?brandID=189.

"VW Conquers the World: Germany's Biggest Carmaker Is Leaving Rivals in the Dust." *Economist*, July 7, 2012.

WALGREENS

AT A GLANCE

Brand Synopsis: Walgreens aims to embody the "Well Experience" for retail consumers and institutional clients.

Parent Company: Walgreen Co.
200 Wilmot Road
Deerfield, Illinois 60015
United States
http://www.walgreens.com

Sector: Consumer Staples; Health Care

Industry Group: Food, Beverage & Tobacco; Health Care Equipment & Services

Performance: *Market share*—20 percent of pharmacy prescriptions in the United States (2011). *Sales*—US$72.2 billion (2011).

Principal Competitors: CVS Caremark Corporation; Rite Aid Corporation; Wal-Mart Stores, Inc.

BRAND ORIGINS

- Charles R. Walgreen opened his first pharmacy in 1901.
- Walgreens introduced the self-service format in 1952.
- Starting in the 1980s, the number of Walgreens drugstores rapidly expanded.
- New management adjusted Walgreens' course starting in 2008.

In 1901 Charles R. Walgreen bought the drugstore on the south side of Chicago at which he had been working as a pharmacist. By 1915 there were five Walgreen drugstores. He added soda fountains that featured luncheon service. He also began to make his own line of drug products and offer them at lower prices than competitors. The Walgreens chain expanded across neighboring Midwestern states and opened its first outlet in New York City in 1927. In 1946 Walgreen Co. purchased a minority share of Mexican retailer Sanborns, which it maintained until the 1980s. In 1960 Walgreens entered Puerto Rico.

In the 1960s and 1970s the Walgreen Co. operated several chains of department stores and restaurants, which the company sold by the late 1980s to concentrate on its drugstore business. Walgreens expanded rapidly nationwide, reaching nearly 1,500 units in 1990, as it banked on increased demand from the rising population of older persons. The company preferred to build new, freestanding stores with a consistent appearance and format and located on prominent street corners.

In 2007 the Walgreens chain opened its 6,000th store. However, economic shocks prompted an adjustment in approach in 2008. A new management team cut back Walgreens' retail expansion plans and launched programs such as the Take Care in-store health clinics and the Complete Care and Well-Being initiative providing cost-effective health and wellness solutions for employers. In 2010 Walgreen Co. acquired the Duane Reade chain of 258 drugstores, followed by drugstore.com in 2011 with a customer base of 3 million and access to numerous online vendors. As of August 31, 2012, Walgreens counted 7,929 drugstores in every U.S. state and Puerto Rico and recorded 6.1 million customers served each day.

BRAND ELEMENTS

- The Walgreens logo has remained almost unchanged since 1951.
- "My Walgreens" is Walgreens' current marketing tagline.
- Walgreens slogans reinforce the brand's association with health and wellness.

Walgreens drugstores have used the same basic logo since 1951—in cursive script with a prominent W—while many competitors have updated their logos to make them more contemporary. This old-style logo subtly underlines Walgreens' heritage and tradition. The "W" itself also serves as a brand identifier. In 2010 Walgreen Co. sued U.S. supermarket chain Wegmans, asserting that the Wegmans logo, which also featured a prominent initial W, infringed on the Walgreens logo. In April 2011, Wegmans announced it had settled with Walgreens and agreed to stop using the "W" separately in promotions while it retained the right to use its full logo.

Walgreens has been known for catchy taglines since founder Charles R. Walgreen introduced "Drugs with a Reputation." For several years after 2000, Walgreens used the slogan "The Pharmacy America Trusts," coupled with the tagline "Our Focus Is Pharmacy. Our Focus Is You." As Stephen Winzenburg put it, writing in *Advertising Age* in January 2008, "'The pharmacy America trusts' clearly states that Walgreens deals in prescription drugs, is available across the country and is a secure place to go when sick." "My Walgreens" is the overarching tagline for the company in 2012, which positions Walgreens as consumers' preferred source for all health and wellness-related products and services under the "Well Experience" theme.

BRAND IDENTITY

- Walgreens competes across the United States with CVS and Rite Aid.
- Walgreens faces competition not only from drugstores but also from convenience stores, mass merchandisers, and supermarkets.
- Walgreens sought to strengthen its brand identity with the "There's a Way" campaign.

For much of its history, Walgreens rested on its image of quality service and competed mainly with independent pharmacists and regional chains. In the late 20th century, Walgreens became associated with competitors also aggressively spreading nationwide, chiefly CVS and Rite Aid. Together these brands came to define the contemporary drugstore in many U.S. consumers' minds as many independent pharmacists went out of business. After spreading across the continental United States, Walgreens and CVS headed to Hawaii; after Walgreens entered the market in late 2007, CVS purchased chief local competitor Longs Drug Store the

following year. Meanwhile, in Puerto Rico Walgreens competed strongly with domestic retailer Farmacias El Amal until it shut down in February 2011, leaving Walgreens the clear leader.

Walgreens found itself competing against not only chained drugstores but also convenience stores, mass merchandisers, and even supermarkets. As Walgreens stocked more food products and general merchandise, other retail formats were introducing in-store pharmacies. The concept of Walgreens is to provide a variety of convenient products that consumers can find within minutes, perhaps while they are also picking up prescriptions or OTC medicines. Store positioning on corners with easy vehicle access and drive-through windows fosters speed and convenience. Speaking to *Retail Management* in December 2000, marketing expert David Rogers stated, "They [Walgreens] are the female convenience store now." He went on to note that it appeals to women with its extensive assortments of beauty products, greeting cards, and home care items, which contrasts with the male-centered focus of conventional convenience stores on tobacco and alcohol. Walgreens has also, in an increasingly diverse nation, taken the lead among drugstores in stocking health and beauty products aimed at African Americans and Latinos.

According to chief marketing officer Kim Feil in an interview with *Brandweek* published in December 2008, despite its success, Walgreens had failed to develop a distinctive brand identity, other than being professional and convenient, and was even regarded by some consumers as old-fashioned. To rectify this, the "There's a Way" campaign in 2009 promoted Walgreens as the first-stop provider of resources for staying "well." In 2011 Walgreens took more steps to differentiate itself from CVS. First, it sold its pharmacy management benefit unit, Walgreens Health Initiatives Inc., which had competed directly with CVS's Caremark unit. Then Walgreens acquired drugstore.com, which had over 3 million customers, strengthening its online retailing position.

BRAND STRATEGY

- Most stores operate under the Walgreens name, while some stores operate under their previous brand identity.
- Walgreens stores feature a wide array of both private label and branded products.
- Walgreens began its first national promotional campaign for private label products in 2011.
- Walgreens was one of the first drugstore retailers to develop an Internet presence.

The Walgreen Co. operates nearly all of its own established drugstores under the Walgreens brand. When the company purchases drugstore chains, it selectively rebrands stores based on location and competition. For example, when Walgreen Co. purchased the regional drugstore chain Happy Harry's in 2006, it converted the outlets in Pennsylvania to Walgreens right away in places where the brand was already prominent. Meanwhile, in Happy Harry's core market of Delaware, the logo changed to "Happy Harry's, a Walgreens Pharmacy," but in 2011 some outlets began adopting the Walgreens banner. When Walgreen Co. purchased 258 Duane Reade drugstores in 2010, it converted most of the outlets to the Walgreens name while keeping the Duane Reade name on several Manhattan stores, to take advantage of its local name recognition. In fact Duane Reade and Walgreens outlets are located almost side-by-side in some high-traffic locations, such as Times Square in Manhattan, where the Walgreens store sports a 17-story-high digital billboard that provides splendid advertising opportunities for Walgreens and favored suppliers.

Walgreens drugstores offer private label products in many retail categories, as well as a wide selection of popular brand-name items. By 2002 Walgreens' private label products accounted for 13 percent of the brand's front-end sales and a 29 percent share of all drugstore private label sales. At the time, many of Walgreens' private labels echoed names of popular-branded competitors: for example, its decongestant was named Wal-phed, after Sudafed; likewise, its Wal-tussin cough medicine referred to Robitussin. The Walgreens Apothecary line introduced in 2007 evokes the company's heritage with old-style labeling and is positioned as a premium private label at prices that are below those of branded leaders. Although Walgreens' private labels often are shelved beside branded competitors at lower prices, branded manufacturers are eager to have their products stocked in Walgreens stores because the chain's customer traffic drives sales.

In 2008 Walgreens began revamping its private label strategy as recession-stressed consumers flocked to private label products at the expense of brand names. In February 2011 Walgreens launched its first nationwide promotional campaign for the Walgreens line of private label health and wellness products on network television and websites. That October the chain introduced Nice! as a unifying label for common grocery and household items. Walgreens kept and expanded several of its other private labels, including Good & Delish for premium snacks and beverages, Petshoppe for pet products, Studio 35 for beauty products, and Café W for chilled prepared foods.

Walgreens' Internet branding began with the introduction of the Walgreens.com website in 1996. By 1999 the site offered online pharmacy purchases as well as extensive health information cobranded by the prestigious Mayo Clinic. In 2003 Walgreens was the first major drugstore chain to create a dedicated Spanish-language website. Facebook provided another web-based platform for Walgreens to promote its brand and interact with customers. There were more than 800,000 Facebook fans by March 2011. The newly acquired drugstore.com provided Walgreens with a large new customer base and fostered more effective e-commerce programs.

BRAND EQUITY

- In 2012 Walgreens was ranked as the number two drugstore retailer in the U.S. behind CVS, according to Interbrand.
- Walgreens was ranked as the ninth leading retailer worldwide in 2010, according to *Stores*.
- In fiscal year 2011 Walgreens dispensed around 20 percent of all prescriptions in the US.

According to Interbrand's *Best Retail Brands Report 2012*, Walgreens ranked sixth with a brand value of US$15.0 billion, up 4 percent from the previous year. Walgreens ranked far behind industry leader Walmart, with a brand value of US$139.2 billion, but more closely behind its chief drugstore competitor CVS, with a US$17.3 billion value. Walgreen Co. was ranked by the *Financial Times* as the second most valuable food and drug retailer behind CVS Caremark and was assigned a market value of US$37.0 billion as of March 2011. *Stores* ranked the company as the ninth leading retailer worldwide in 2010, with revenues of US$67.4 billion. Walgreens reported filling 819 million prescriptions in fiscal year 2011, accounting for approximately 20 percent of all prescriptions filled in the the U.S. pharmacy market. Industry analyst Adam J. Fein estimated Walgreens' total prescription revenues at US$45.1 billion in 2011, giving it a 16.5 percent value share.

BRAND AWARENESS

- According to *Prevention*, Walgreens is one of the brands most frequently mentioned by middle-aged women consumers.
- In 2012 the Harris Poll ranked Walgreens as the leading drugstore brand in the United States.
- International brand awareness might increase with the Walgreens-Boots partnership.

Walgreens brand awareness spread gradually across the United States in the late 20th century with the chain's expansion. Walgreens needs to drive particularly strong brand awareness among women, who made up an estimated 75 percent of its customer base in 2007. Its success at this can be judged from a 2008 study conducted for *Prevention* magazine that revealed that Walgreens was the fourth most often mentioned brand among boomer women (aged 43 to 62), the most influential group in word-of-mouth communication about brands.

According to a May 2008 Zandl Group survey, 61 percent of young consumers were becoming more frugal and Walgreens was one of the retailers that remained in favor with the thrifty crowd. The 2012 Harris Poll Equi-Trend study conducted in February 2012 ranked Walgreens as Drugstore Brand of the Year and found further that U.S. consumers still preferred drugstores over value retailers (e.g., Walmart and Target) for pharmacy purchases. Walgreens ranked number one under the rubrics of Familiarity and Purchase Consideration.

International brand awareness of Walgreens has been minimal so far. The partnership and planned merger of Walgreen Co. with Alliance Boots announced in 2012 will provide access for Walgreens-branded products in several European markets. However, unless Walgreens stores open abroad under this merger, brand exposure will remain limited.

BRAND OUTLOOK

- Many Walgreens stores have adopted the Consumer Centric Initiative format.
- Walgreens' Balance Rewards loyalty program was introduced in September 2012.
- Walgreens outlets are increasingly providing medical services.
- Walgreen Co. is planning a merger with UK-based drugstore retailer Alliance Boots.

By 2012 the majority of Walgreens stores followed the Customer Centric Initiative format, which involves destocking slow-moving items, reconfiguring private label ranges, and opening up sight lines on the store floor. Walgreens is introducing expanded selections of prepared foods in many outlets. It has pledged to set up 1,000 "food oasis" stores providing fresh and healthy foods in underserved areas. Meanwhile more upscale outlets are presenting indulgent offerings, such as sushi and frozen yogurt. Walgreens introduced its first branded loyalty program, Balance Rewards, in September 2012, long after many retail competitors had done so.

The continued aging of the population and the increasing centrality of healthcare in the U.S. economy augur further growth opportunity. Walgreens seeks to foster market-driven healthcare reform, combining its assets in drugstore retailing, store-based and employer health clinics, and specialized pharmacy and medical equipment to drive down prices and improve health outcomes for organizations and individual consumers. Walgreens stores are increasingly offering medical services, such as vaccinations, routine checkups, and disease screenings. Walgreens is aligning its brand with campaigns promoting public health, such as Walk with Walgreens and the Walgreens "Way to Well" Fund, which receives one cent for each purchase of a Walgreens-branded product.

In June 2012 Walgreen Co. announced it would purchase a 45 percent stake in UK-based Alliance Boots, the leading chained pharmacy operator in Europe. A complete merger is planned by 2015, which will create a company with some 11,000 outlets in 12 countries. Walgreens stores will be able to stock Boots labels already present in some of its stateside rivals, while Boots stores could carry Walgreens and Duane Reade private labels.

FURTHER READING

Alexander, James. "Deal to Buy Happy Harry's Vaults Walgreens into Delaware." *Drug Store News*, June 26, 2006.

Buss, Dale. "Walgreens and Boots Join Brands to Create Global Pharmacy Giant." *Brandchannel*, June 19, 2012. Accessed October 9, 2012. http://www.brandchannel.com/home/post/2012/06/19/Walgreens-Boots-Deal-061912.aspx

"The Economy Is Impacting Gen X/Y's Brand Choices." *Brandweek*, June 23, 2008.

Eder, Rob. "Tailoring the Mix to Make Mi Walgreens Su Walgreens." *Drug Store News*, March 22, 2004.

———. "Walgreens: Destination Self-Care." *Drug Store News*, October 16, 2000.

Fein, Adam J. "2011 Market Share of Top Pharmacies." *Drug Channels*, January 4, 2012.

Frederick, James. "Walgreens the Best of the Century." *Drug Store News*, April 10, 2000.

"It's a Walgreens, Farmacias El Amal Market in Pharmacy." *MMR*, June 18, 2007.

Johnsen, Michael. "Walgreens: Wired for Well." *Drug Store News*, February 27, 2012.

Kruger, Renée Marisa, and Jay L. Johnson. "Walgreens: America's Corner Drugstore." *Retail Merchandiser*, December 2000.

"Marketing Touts Single Identity." *Chain Drug Review*, December 6, 2010.

Monks, Richard. "Walgreens Lights up New York." *Chain Drug Review*, November 24, 2008.

"Most Valuable US Food and Drug Retailers, 2011." *Financial Times*, June 24, 2011.

Prior, Molly. "Tailored Mix Complements Aggressive Expansion." *Drug Store News*, March 23, 2003.

"Report: Listen to Lady Boomers." *Brandweek*, November 17, 2008.

"Top Global Retailers by Revenue." *Stores*, January 2012.

"Top Retailers in 2012 Harris Poll EquiTrend Study: Walgreens Is Drug Store Brand of the Year; Target Stores Is Top-Ranked for Second Straight Year." *PR Newswire*, May 14, 2012.

Vega, Tenziga. "Walgreens Starts Campaign to Push Store-Brand Products." *New York Times*, February 11, 2011.

"Walgreen Co." *International Directory of Company Histories*. Ed. Jay P. Pederson. Vol. 133. Detroit, MI: St. James Press, 2012.

Watson, Stephen T. "Wegmans to Drop Script 'W' Logo." *Buffalo News*, April 24, 2011.

Woldt, Jeffrey. "Walgreens Ups the Ante with Loyalty Program." *MMR*, September 17, 2012.

Wong, Elaine. "Feil Reveals Resolution for the New Walgreens." *Brandweek*, December 1, 2008.

WALMART

—■—

BRAND ORIGINS

- Wal-Mart Stores, Inc., was founded in 1962 in Arkansas by two brothers who owned a chain of Ben Franklin variety stores.
- The innovative concept of prices so low that customers would drive some distance to shop there differentiated Walmart stores from competitors.

- By 1990 Wal-Mart Stores, Inc., was the largest retailer in the United States.
- Mexico has more Walmart stores than any other country except the United States.

Wal-Mart Stores, Inc., was founded in Rogers, Arkansas, in 1962 by two brothers named Sam Walton and J. L. (Bud) Walton, who had been operating a small chain of Ben Franklin variety stores since the 1950s. After studying mass-merchandising techniques, Sam Walton decided that a department-size store could make a profit in a town of about 5,000 to 25,000 people if its prices were low enough to attract customers from the surrounding areas. The new venture, named Wal-Mart Discount City, was so successful that within five years the enterprise had grown into a chain of 24 stores with revenues of US$12.7 million. In 1969 the company was combined with the family's Ben Franklin chain to form Wal-Mart Stores, Inc.

During the 1970s the business went national and became a publicly traded company, and the home office was moved to Bentonville, Arkansas. By 1976 the Waltons had phased out their Ben Franklin stores so they could focus on Walmart stores, which were expanded to include pharmacy, auto service, jewelry, and shoe divisions. By 1980 the corporation had 276 outlets and sales of US$1 billion. A subsidiary chain of wholesale stores called Sam's Club opened in 1983, followed in 1988 by the introduction of huge Walmart "supercenters" that offered a broad inventory of general merchandise and a complete supermarket under one roof. By the end of the decade, Wal-Mart Stores, Inc., had become the largest retailer in the United States.

The corporation's first international outlet was a Sam's Club initially known as Club Aurrera, which opened in Mexico City in 1991 as a joint venture with a firm named Cifra. By the year 2000 Cifra had become Walmart de México, and in 2009 it acquired Walmart Centroamérica. Since 2007 Walmart de México has also operated a bank called Banco Wal-Mart, serving Mexico and several Central American nations.

In 1994 Wal-Mart Stores, Inc., acquired a chain of 122 retail stores called Woolco Canada and rebranded the chain as Walmart Canada, followed by expansion into China in 1996, Germany and South Korea in 1998, and the United Kingdom in 1999. During the next decade, Wal-Mart Stores, Inc., experienced rapid growth globally, including development in Africa and India. As of 2012 the corporation was operating about 2,000 stores in Mexico, 1,000 in Central and South America, 300 in Canada, 500 in the United Kingdom, 300 in China, and 400 in Japan.

BRAND ELEMENTS

- Wal-Mart Stores, Inc., is the corporation that owns the Walmart brand.
- The size and characteristic design of Walmart stores contribute to the brand's unique identity.
- The Walmart stores logo has always featured the brand name with slight variations in font, color, and small graphic elements.

The company's first logo, known as the "Frontier Font Logo," was simply the word "Wal-Mart" written in all-capital black letters in a western-style font. In 1981 the color of the letters was changed to brown and the "frontier" font was replaced with a more modern one. In 1992 the hyphen between "Wal" and "Mart" was replaced with a star, and the lettering became blue. In 2008 the color of the lettering was changed to a lighter blue and only the "W" was upper case, while the brand name became one word ("Walmart") and a gold-colored "spark" resembling a sunburst was added after the name.

The brand is named after its founders, the Walton brothers. The corporation's name includes a hyphen, while the brand name does not. Wal-Mart Stores, Inc., operates three business segments: Walmart U.S., Walmart International, and Sam's Club.

One of the most recognizable characteristics of the Walmart brand is the design of the stores themselves. In the United States most are "supercenters," enormous buildings full of merchandise arranged in open, brightly lit departments not separated by walls. The inclusion of a supermarket in each supercenter helps differentiate Walmart from competitors that offer only merchandise. The sheer size of these stores (182,000 square feet of floor space) contributes to the brand's distinctive personality. The company also operates smaller discount stores (106,000 square feet) that look like supercenters but have no supermarket. Even smaller and yet displaying the same branded appearance are Walmart Neighborhood Markets (38,000 square feet), Walmart Express stores (15,000 square feet), and very small Walmart on Campus outlets. In countries outside the United States, a store bearing the Walmart brand name is usually a supercenter or a standard discount store.

BRAND IDENTITY

- "Everyday low prices" is the core promise of the Walmart stores brand.
- The official company purpose of Wal-Mart Stores, Inc., is to work together to lower the cost of living and improve people's lives.
- Wal-Mart Stores, Inc., wants people to associate its brand with social responsibility and integrity.

The Walmart stores brand is built on a commitment to providing a wide assortment of merchandise at affordable prices to help customers improve their lives. The fundamental brand promise was initially stated in the tagline "The lowest prices anytime, anywhere," which evolved into the enduring catchphrase "Everyday low prices."

Company founder Sam Walton said, "If we work together, we'll lower the cost of living for everyone.... We'll give the world an opportunity to see what it's like to save and have a better life." This is the official company purpose of Wal-Mart Stores, Inc.

In addition, the company promotes a perception of Wal-Mart Stores, Inc., as a socially responsible organization that strives to improve communities where its Walmart stores are located. Sam Walton said, "Each Walmart store should reflect the values of its customers and support the vision they hold for their community," adding that the company's fundamental values of "personal and moral integrity" should start with its personnel. In the Wal-Mart Stores, Inc., 2011 Annual Report, the company expressed a resolve to improve operations by reducing waste, buying locally grown produce, making healthy food more affordable, donating to charities and disaster victims, helping small farmers worldwide to earn higher profits, and fostering the careers of women and minorities.

BRAND STRATEGY

- Wal-Mart Stores, Inc., operates several types of stores under the Walmart brand name, most of them offering similar merchandise.
- Affiliates without the Walmart brand name are common in foreign nations.

- "Powered by Walmart" refers to the company's ability to leverage global buying power and expertise to keep its prices low.

The Walmart stores brand name appears on stores of various sizes in the United States and abroad, most of them selling the same general types of products, although the format and merchandise assortment of each store may be modified somewhat to fit the store's specific location. Wal-Mart Stores, Inc., also owns Sam's Club, a subsidiary that functions as its own business segment separate from Walmart U.S., which operates all Walmart stores in the United States and Puerto Rico, as well as the company's online retail operations. Outside the United States, the Walmart brand name is sometimes attached to businesses such as banks, pharmacies, and restaurants. Wal-Mart Stores, Inc., also operates numerous foreign enterprises without the Walmart name, such as a chain of discount stores called Bodega Aurrera and a department store chain called Suburbia, both located in Mexico.

Globally, the company uses its enormous buying power and expertise to keep its myriad of stores operating efficiently and to sell merchandise at low prices, a strategy summarized in the slogan "Powered by Walmart." Despite its low prices, the company makes a profit through sales volume.

BRAND EQUITY

- Based on revenues, Wal-Mart Stores, Inc., was the second-largest corporation in the United States in 2011.
- The estimated market value of Wal-Mart Stores, Inc., in March 2012 was US$207 billion, according to *Fortune* magazine. Interbrand valued the corporation at US$139 billion in 2012.
- As of 2012 there were 3,925 Walmart stores in the United States and 5,850 in 26 other countries.
- More than one-third of the foreign operations of Wal-Mart Stores, Inc., are in Mexico, including a bank that also serves Central America.
- Each new Walmart supercenter creates about 300 jobs with benefits.

As of 2012 Wal-Mart Stores, Inc., was operating more than 10,000 retail outlets worldwide, including 3,925 Walmart stores in the United States (up from 3,595 in 2008) and 5,850 in 26 other countries (up from 3,093 in 2008). More than one-third of these retail outlets are in Mexico, including 216 Walmart supercenters. The company also operates a bank in Mexico, called Banco Wal-Mart, which serves five Central American nations as well. Wal-Mart Stores, Inc., serves more than 200 million customers each week. It employs 2.2 million people worldwide, including 1.4 million in the United States. Each new opening of a Walmart supercenter creates about 300 jobs with benefits.

According to *Fortune* magazine, Wal-Mart Stores, Inc., was the second-largest U.S. corporation in 2011,

with revenues of US$447 billion, up 6 percent from 2010. The company had been in first place for the previous two years but was forced to slash prices in response to declining sales during a nationwide economic downturn. The price cuts increased sales but decreased profits by 4.6 percent. Meanwhile, international sales reached US$35.5 billion in 2011, an increase of 13.1 percent. *Fortune* magazine listed the market value of Wal-Mart Stores, Inc., at US$207 billion as of March 2012.

Interbrand, a branding consultancy firm, calculated the value of the Wal-Mart Stores, Inc., brand at US$139 billion in 2012, in first place among U.S. retail brands but down 2 percent from its value the previous year. Target Corporation (Target) placed second at US$23 billion, followed by Home Depot, Inc. (Home Depot), CVS Caremark Corporation (CVS), and Best Buy Co., Inc. (Best Buy). Interbrand reported that Wal-Mart Stores, Inc., was earning US$260 billion in domestic sales in 2012, which amounted to "a legitimate claim" of 1.7 percent of the gross domestic product (GDP) in the United States. Interbrand also noted that Wal-Mart Stores, Inc., continues to hold the top spot on the firm's list of the most valuable U.S. retail brands "by a huge margin."

Another brand valuation consultancy, Brand Finance, calculated the value of the Wal-Mart Stores, Inc., brand at US$38.3 billion in 2012, up from US$36.2 billion in 2011. Brand Finance ranked the company as the fifth top brand worldwide in 2012, down from third in 2011. It ranked Wal-Mart Stores, Inc., as the top retail brand for both 2011 and 2012. Wal-Mart Stores, Inc., retained its AA brand rating despite fluctuating brand value because, thanks largely to its low prices and customer loyalty, the company continued to dominate the retail market during a time of economic uncertainty.

BRAND AWARENESS

- The Walmart brand is so well-known that "Walmarting" has become a verb with both positive and negative connotations.
- Some U.S. customers feel such a strong connection with Walmart stores that they camp overnight in store parking lots.
- As one of the world's most admired companies, Wal-Mart Stores, Inc., receives numerous awards each year.

The Walmart brand is so widely recognized that the name is sometimes used as a verb. "Walmarting" can refer to the negative effect that such a large enterprise can have on society. For example, introducing many thousands of almost identical stores in communities nationwide tends to reduce the distinctive character of those individual towns. Conversely, "Walmarting" can also refer to the most admirable qualities of U.S. business practices, holding up this successful corporation and brand as an example of how an enterprise can excel.

Customers feel such an attachment to Walmart stores that tens of thousands of them regularly camp overnight in the stores' parking lots. While planning a vacation, many Americans traveling in recreational vehicles (RVs) will consult a "Walmart Atlas" to locate stores in towns along the way, where they will buy groceries and other items and then, rather than locating a campground, sleep in their RVs in the Walmart store parking lot.

Each year Wal-Mart Stores, Inc., receives awards for its business practices, social involvement, and environmental responsibility. In 2011 Central American business magazine *Estrategia & Negocios* called Walmart Central America the most admired multinational company in Central America for the third consecutive year. Canadian newspaper the *National Post* included Wal-Mart Stores, Inc., on its list of the 10 companies with the most admired corporate cultures. For its Green Rankings Global List, *Newsweek* magazine ranked Wal-Mart Stores, Inc., the number-one retailer globally, first in all sectors in Mexico, and second in all sectors in Latin America.

BRAND OUTLOOK

- U.S. sales for Wal-Mart Stores, Inc., continue to increase, but the company expects to grow most rapidly in other countries.
- To keep prices low, the company will strive to reduce expenses and improve productivity.
- The company is pursuing ways to expand its online retailing business to reach customers in emerging e-commerce markets.

Wal-Mart Stores, Inc., continues to experience steady domestic growth and rapid expansion outside the United States. In 2011 sales increased 1.5 percent for its U.S. stores. To provide the comprehensive inventory that customers want, the company added back more than 10,000 products and launched a two-year investment of US$2 billion to reduce expenses and increase productivity, which is expected to enable a further lowering of prices. The company is also investing in its online store, along with supercenters and smaller enterprises, to offer customers a variety of shopping options.

Internationally, Wal-Mart Stores, Inc., sales increased 15.2 percent in 2011. The company has announced its intent to be the low-cost leader in every market where it operates. In January 2012 the company announced it had added 1,094 new stores and acquisitions (or 42.2 million square feet of retail space) in foreign countries in just 12 months. The company expects to have added another 30 to 33 million square feet of retail space by January 2013.

Wal-Mart Stores, Inc., plans to expand its online retailing operations to take advantage of a trend toward enormous e-commerce growth in countries such as the United Kingdom, Canada, Brazil, Japan, and China. As of 2012 the company was pursuing a majority share in Yihaodian, one of China's largest online retailers, to make the Walmart brand more widely available in that country. The corporation has also established a digital technology division called @WalmartLabs to strengthen its online presence and has purchased certain Internet businesses that will provide useful new talent.

FURTHER READING

Askew, Katy. "Talking Shop: Is Wal-Mart's EDLP Focus Enough to Drive Sustained Growth?" *just-food*, August 16, 2012. Accessed September 12, 2012. http://www.just-food.com/analysis/is-wal-marts-edlp-focus-enough-to-drive-sustained-growth_id120198.aspx.

Bartlett, Jeff. "2012 Car Brand Perception Survey: Ford Leads All Brands in Awareness." *Consumer Reports*, January 26, 2012. Accessed February 13, 2013. http://news.consumerreports.org/cars/2012/01/2012-car-brand-perception-survey-ford-leads-all-brands-in-awareness.html.

Berg, Natalie. "Walmart Must Box Clever in the Internet Age." *Grocer*, March 31, 2012.

"Best Retail Brands 2012." Interbrand. Accessed September 10, 2012. http://www.interbrand.com/en/BestRetailBrands/2012-Best-Retail-Brands.aspx.

Brand Finance. "Global 500 2012." *Brandirectory*. Accessed September 9, 2012. http://brandirectory.com/league_tables/table/global-500-2012.

———. "Walmart." *Brandirectory*. Accessed September 9, 2012. http://brandirectory.com/profile/walmart.

Clifford, Stephanie. "Big Retailers Fill More Aisles with Groceries." *New York Times*, January 16, 2011.

Edelson, Sharon. "Firms Battle Dangers of Overseas Markets." *Women's Wear Daily*, June 13, 2012.

"Global 500 2012." *CNN Money*. Accessed September 9, 2012. http://money.cnn.com/magazines/fortune/global500/2012/performers/companies/biggest/.

Hall, Ron. "Wal-Mart vs. Target, Costco: Best Discount Store Stock." Seeking Alpha, April 26, 2012. Accessed September 14, 2012. http://seekingalpha.com/article/532521-wal-mart-vs-target-costco-best-discount-store-stock.

Pogoda, Dianne M. "Timeline: Wal-Mart at 50." *Women's Wear Daily*, March 28, 2012.

Troy, Mike. "Familiar Strategy Yields Familiar Results." *Drug Store News*, April 23, 2012.

"Wal-Mart Stores, Inc." *International Directory of Company Histories*. Ed. Adele Hast. Vol. 5. Chicago, IL: St. James Press, 1992.

Walton, Sam, and John Huey. *Sam Walton, Made in America: My Story*. New York: Random House, 1993.

Wilson, Marianne. "Sizing up Brand Value." *Chain Store Age*, February 22, 2012. Accessed September 10, 2012. http://www.chainstoreage.com/article/sizing-brand-value.

WHOLE FOODS

———— ◆ ————

BRAND ORIGINS

- Since 1980, Whole Foods Market has grown to a chain of more than 300 stores in multiple countries, with more than 60,000 workers.
- John Mackey, Renee Lawson Hardy, Mark Skiles, and Craig Weller combined their retail operations to open the first Whole Foods Market.

- The first international Whole Foods Market opened in Canada in 2001.
- Quality Assurance International named Whole Foods Market the first national certified organic grocer in the United States.

Whole Foods Market is the biggest company, and biggest name, in natural and organic foods in the United States. Its first store opened in Austin, Texas, in 1980, and the company has grown to become a chain of more than 300 stores in multiple countries, with more than 60,000 employees worldwide.

Since the company's founding, consolidation has often fueled the growth of Whole Foods. John Mackey and Renee Lawson Hardy owned the Austin health food store Safer Way Foods, and Mark Skiles and Craig Weller owned the Clarksville Natural Grocery. They decided to combine their businesses in order to open a supermarket, Whole Foods Market. Throughout the 1980s, the group opened additional Whole Foods Markets in Texas and other areas, and they also started acquiring other stores at that time. These acquisitions included natural foods stores or store chains, such as the Wellspring supermarkets of North Carolina, the Bread & Circus food and toy stores of Massachusetts and Rhode Island, the Los Angeles-based chain Mrs. Gooch's Natural Food Markets, the 22 Fresh Field stores in various states, the Merchant of Vino stores of metropolitan Detroit, California's Natural Abilities stores, and other stores throughout the United States. The company's largest acquisition came in 2007 with the purchase of Wild Oats, a large chain of stores operating in the United States and Canada.

1143

The name of each newly-acquired store is usually changed to Whole Foods Market. Exceptions to this procedure are the Harry's Farmers Markets of Georgia. Although Whole Foods Market owns a number of these stores, they are often known by the Harry's name and their location, such as Alpharetta Harry's or Harry's Farmers Market Marietta. By acquiring these stores and opening new stores, Whole Foods Market has expanded the number of its stores and its geographic reach.

In addition to stores, Whole Foods Market has also bought companies that helped it stock its shelves. It bought a majority interest in Sourdough: A European Bakery in 1993. Long a supplier of baked goods for Whole Foods Markets in Texas and Louisiana, this bakery helped the company open more bakery facilities in stores in different regions and trained apprentice bakers. Whole Foods Market bought another supplier, Allegro Coffee, and also acquired Amiron, Inc., a company that makes and markets health supplements and vitamins. Amiron has provided products for Whole Foods Market and has lent the stores its experience in catalog and Internet sales.

Already a major retailer in the United States, Whole Foods Market became an international company when it opened a store in Toronto, Ontario, Canada, in 2001, which was soon followed by other openings in Canada. The company entered the United Kingdom by purchasing the British Fresh & Wild chain of organic stores in 2004. It has continued to use the Fresh & Wild name, and it opened its first British Whole Foods Market in London in 2007.

Throughout all of this growth, Whole Foods Market has retained its emphasis on natural, organic food and its promotion of healthful lifestyle practices. Quality Assurance International named Whole Foods Market as the first national certified organic grocer in the United States, and a number of Whole Foods Market products have received national organic certification.

BRAND ELEMENTS
- The Whole Foods Market logo features the color green as well as leaf-like shapes springing from the O in the word Whole.
- Drawings and photographs of vegetables and fruit appear on the Whole Foods Market website.
- Whole Foods Market refers to healthful food and the environment by using the registered slogan "America's Healthiest Grocery Store."

Not surprisingly, the Whole Foods Market logo incorporates natural elements and refers to its healthful products. Leaf-like shapes project from the O in the word Whole. This logo often appears in green or on a green background, the color green echoing the color of fresh vegetables and

other plants. Sometimes the company abbreviates this leafy logo and just uses the term Whole Foods.

Photographs and drawings of vegetables and fruits and other foods also appear on Whole Foods Market websites. These websites incorporate other natural items, using images of such natural materials as wood and stone as background.

The company refers to healthful foods with its registered slogan, "America's Healthiest Grocery Store." It has also used the pro-health and pro-environment motto "Whole Foods, Whole People, Whole Planet," a motto that often accompanies a drawing of a farmer. This drawing and phrase again link the company to fresh, healthful food acquired from natural sources.

BRAND IDENTITY
- Whole Foods trademarked the phrase "America's Healthiest Grocery Store."
- Whole Foods works hard to promote an image of high quality and excellent service.
- Whole Foods launched a campaign in 2008 to emphasize value.

Whole Foods wishes to be known as "America's Healthiest Grocery Store" so much that it has trademarked that phrase. The company works hard to promote an image of high quality and excellent service, both in partnering with other companies and serving customers. Whole Foods also emphasizes the importance of its "team members."

The company's emphasis on quality and natural and organic foods has upon occasion hurt its brand identity. Many jokingly refer to Whole Foods as "Whole Paycheck" because of its premium products and high prices. The downturn in the U.S. economy in the early 21st century also impacted Whole Foods as customers turned to lower-priced alternatives. To combat the perception that Whole Foods is not affordable to the masses, in 2008 the company began stressing value. Some store locations provided employee-led tours that focused on budget, and the company added store brands with lower price points.

BRAND STRATEGY
- The 365 Everyday Value store brand introduces Whole Foods products and stores to people who might find other Whole Foods brands to be too expensive.
- Whole Foods Market has launched a pilot program of wellness clubs at select locations.
- In 2011 Whole Foods Markets opened smaller stores in smaller cities to serve younger people who grew up with the brand.
- Whole Foods Market has launched a pilot program of wellness clubs at select locations.

The Whole Foods Market logo with the leafy O appears on the packaging of foods sold under the Whole Foods Market brand, a private store brand that features organic and natural products. Other Whole Foods Market private brands include Whole Foods Market Exclusive, which includes products unique to the chain; the budget-friendly 365 Everyday Value brand; and the Whole Foods Market Premium Body Care line of personal products. All of these products are meant to capture the brand's identity—a commitment to natural, fresh foods that help people maintain a healthy lifestyle.

To further serve its customers and extend its brand name, Whole Foods started its Whole Foods Market Wellness Clubs. It launched these clubs at selected locations as a pilot program in 2011. Members of these doctor-affiliated clubs can receive health information, participate in classes and demonstrations, receive discounts on health products at Whole Foods Market, buy premade meals from the stores' supper clubs, and receive other membership benefits. These clubs are yet another way Whole Foods Market offers health-related information and products to consumers.

In addition to its store brands and wellness club program, Whole Foods Market has used new stores to advance its name. In 2011 it opened a number of smaller stores in smaller cities, including a number of university towns. Analysts said that this strategy would help capture younger consumers who were raised with the brand, not to mention consumers that could have potentially high earnings in their futures and a potentially long retail relationship with the Whole Foods brand.

BRAND EQUITY

- Whole Foods Market is the largest retailer of natural and organic foods in the United States.
- In 2012, Whole Foods Market captured 26 percent of the natural and organic foods market.
- While Whole Foods Market does not have a large share in the overall food retailing market, it has a good "mind share" among consumers.
- *Fortune* magazine named Whole Foods Market the eighth-largest food and drug store corporation in the United States in 2012.

As a decades-old chain of stores across the United States, Canada, and the United Kingdom, Whole Foods Market is, not surprisingly, a prominent retailer. It is the largest retailer of natural and organic foods in the United States. In fact, Whole Foods Market captured 26 percent of this market, according to one business writer in 2012.

The company does not have a significant market share in the larger food retailing market, but analysts have argued that it has other strengths. Marketing consultant John Moore has said that, while its competitors have a greater share of the overall food retailing market, Whole Foods Market has a large "mind share." Mind share represents consumers' awareness of a brand. Moore explained that Whole Foods Market was a "strong brand" and that "people talk about the brand … a lot."

In addition to its brand strength, the company enjoys size and recognition. It is a Fortune 500 company, one of the largest 500 corporations in the United States, as determined by *Fortune* magazine. In 2012 the magazine also named Whole Foods Market the eighth-largest food and drug store corporation in the United States.

BRAND AWARENESS

- Phrases like "Selling the Highest Quality Natural and Organic Products Available" have helped build brand awareness for Whole Foods.
- A brand analyst has found that social media users rate Whole Foods Market positively and use phrases like "Love it" when discussing the brand.
- Whole Foods Market has appeared in *Fortune* magazine's "100 Best Companies to Work for in America" poll every year since 1998.

Whole Foods Market's success and consistent interests have helped build awareness for its brand. Marketing consultant John Moore has said that, while its competitors have a greater share of the overall food retailing market, Whole Foods Market has a large "mind share." Mind share represents consumers' awareness of a brand. To achieve this awareness, Whole Foods has repeatedly manifested its interest in natural and organic foods through the use of images and language. "Selling the Highest Quality Natural and Organic Products Available" is a slogan that appears on its website. The phrase also appears in its "on hold" messages, the messages people hear while waiting on the telephone to speak with a Whole Foods representative.

The company has built brand awareness and a positive reputation by satisfying customers. Brand analyst Daniel Baur has studied Whole Foods Market's social media profile. Baur observed that Facebook users have used phrases like "Love it" when discussing the company. He noted that in a sampling of social media users, 48 percent had positive impressions of the brand, 5 percent had negative impressions, while 47 percent had no impression at all.

Employees of Whole Foods Market also hold positive opinions about the company. Every year since 1998, *Fortune* magazine has published the "100 Best Companies to Work for in America" poll. Whole Foods has performed well in this poll, making this list every year since 1998. Employee surveys and other questions determine these rankings, which make clear that Whole Foods employee respondents think highly of their employer.

BRAND OUTLOOK

- Internet publication *Store Brand Decisions* named Whole Foods Market its retailer innovator of the year in 2012.
- Unlike other retailers, Whole Foods Market does not have established procedures for building and opening new stores.
- A 2012 article stated that the organic foods and drink market could reach US$78 billion by 2015, which could benefit Whole Foods.

As Whole Foods Market has continued to develop products for its private store brands, it has received awards for these brands. In 2012, *Store Brand Decisions,* an Internet publication that analyzes private store brands, awarded four of its Retailer Innovation Awards to Whole Foods Market's 365 Everyday Value brand, including three awards for product development and one for packaging. *Store Brand Decisions* also named Whole Foods Market its retailer innovator of the year.

Whole Foods Market's approach to new stores is also noteworthy. It does not have an established procedure to building and opening new stores, like other retail chains. Marketing consultant and former Whole Foods employee John Moore noted that this flexibility allows the company to make refinements and improvements with each new store, but also means that it takes Whole Foods longer to open each new store. He wondered if the process will help strengthen the brand or hurt it, as the lengthier building process prohibits Whole Foods from building as many stores as its competitors.

Other analysts have studied Whole Foods Market and its competitors. In a 2012 article posted on the Seeking Alpha website, business analyst Garrett Dallas cited estimates from research firm Packaged Facts that stated that sales of organic foods and beverages could top US$78 billion by 2015. Dallas admitted that Whole Foods could lose ground in this market, as competitors like Walmart have increased their own sales of organic foods since 2006. Dallas also noted that Whole Foods Market's retail share could increase, as the organic foods market could grow more than expected, especially as people become more conscious of their health and their food. He also noted that the brand might see market increases due to its opening of smaller stores in smaller markets. Despite this

uncertainty, Dallas observed that "Whole Foods is a juggernaut in the natural and organic foods space."

FURTHER READING

Andrejczak, Matt. "Whole Foods: Smaller Is More Profitable." *Wall Street Journal,* February 9, 2012. Accessed February 25, 2013. http://blogs.marketwatch.com/thetell/2012/02/09/whole-foods-smaller-is-more-profitable/.

Baur, Daniel. "Brand Image—Whole Foods Market: 'Love, Love, Love.'" *Social Brand Value,* July 12, 2010. Accessed November 16, 2012. http://social-brand-value.com/2010/07/12/brand-image-whole-foods-market-love-love-love/.

Dallas, Garrett. "The Road to 1,000 Stores for Whole Foods Market." *Seeking Alpha,* November 7, 2012. Accessed November 17, 2012. http://seekingalpha.com/article/986091-the-road-to-1-000-stores-for-whole-foods-market.

Martin, Andrew. "Whole Foods Looks for a Fresh Image in Lean Times." *New York Times,* August 2, 2008. Accessed March 1, 2013. http://www.nytimes.com/2008/08/02/business/02food.html?pagewanted=all&_r=0.

Moore, John. "The Biggest Challenge Facing Whole Foods Market." *Brand Autopsy,* December 4, 2006. Accessed November 17, 2012. http://www.brandautopsy.com/2006/12/the_biggest_cha.html.

Vosburgh, Robert. "SN Whole Health: Natural Food Chains Are on the Move." *Supermarket News,* February 27, 2012. Accessed December 17, 2012. http://supermarketnews.com/natural-food-stores/sn-whole-health-natural-food-chains-are-move.

"Whole Foods Builds Brand Awareness in 30 Seconds Using On Hold Advertising." *The Original On Hold,* February 16, 2011. Accessed November 16, 2012. http://www.onholdinc.com/blog/post/Whole-Foods-Builds-Brand-Awareness-in-30-Seconds-using-on-hold-advertising.aspx.

Whole Foods Market. "2011 Annual Report." Accessed November 15, 2012. http://www.wholefoodsmarket.com/sites/default/files/media/Global/Company%20Info/PDFs/ar11.pdf.

"Whole Foods Market, Inc." *International Directory of Company Histories.* Ed. Tina Grant. Vol. 110. Detroit: St. James Press, 2010. *Gale Virtual Reference Library.* Accessed November 15, 2012. http://go.galegroup.com/ps/i.do?id=GALE%7CCCX1302800104&v=2.1&u=itsbtrial&it=r&p=GVRL&sw=w.

"Whole Foods Named Retail Innovator of the Year, 17 Retailers Win Category Awards." *Store Brand Decisions,* November 14, 2012. Accessed November 17, 2012. http://www.storebrandsdecisions.com/news/2012/11/14/whole-foods-named-retail-innovator-of-the-year-17-retailers-win-category-awards.

WOOLWORTHS

AT A GLANCE

Brand Synopsis: Woolworths, a popular supermarket chain committed to freshness, is one of the most powerful brands in Australia and New Zealand.

Parent Company: Woolworths Limited
1 Woolworths Way
Bella Vista, New South Wales 2153
Australia
http://www.woolworthslimited.com.au

Sector: Consumer Staples

Industry Group: Food & Staples Retailing

Performance: *Market share*—28% of Australia's fresh food market (2011). *Sales*—AUD54.1 billion (US$59.99 billion) (2011).

Principal Competitors: Coles Supermarkets (owned by Wesfarmers Limited); Metcash Limited; IGA (Independent Grocers of Australia; owned by Metcash Limited); ALDI Group

BRAND ORIGINS

- The first Woolworths variety store opened in 1924 in Sydney, Australia.
- By 1930 more Woolworths variety stores had opened throughout New South Wales, Queensland, Western Australia, and New Zealand.
- Woolworths Limited opened its first supermarket in 1960.
- Woolworths Limited has no connection to the popular chain of discount stores once operated by F. W. Woolworth Company.
- Other Woolworths Limited stores include Big W, Dick Smith Electronics, Dan Murphy's, Masters Home Improvement, and various online retailers.

Woolworths Limited started in 1924 as Woolworths Stupendous Bargain Basement in Sydney, New South Wales, Australia. The company founders chose the store name to borrow on the success of the Woolworth discount store chain operated by F. W. Woolworth Company (now Foot Locker, Inc.) in the United States and United Kingdom. The two companies are not related. Woolworths Limited has become a retailing giant in Australia and New Zealand, with more than 100 stores in a variety of formats, including the Woolworths supermarket chain, referred to colloquially as "Woolies."

More stores opened following the launch of the first Woolworths variety store in Sydney, and by 1930 the company had 16 stores across New South Wales, Queensland, Western Australia, and New Zealand. Woolworths opened its first "food" store, which offered a limited selection of fresh vegetables and delicatessen items, in Sydney in 1957, while the first Woolworths supermarket opened in 1960 in Warrawong, New South Wales. Supermarkets would soon become a major part of the company's business.

In addition to supermarkets, Woolworths Limited owns Big W, a chain of discount department stores resembling Walmart stores. Other stores owned by Woolworths Limited include consumer electronics retailer Dick Smith Electronics, liquor retailer Dan Murphy's, and a chain of home improvement stores called Masters Home Improvement. Among Woolworths Limited's additional holdings are a number of gas (petrol) stations, several liquor stores and an online wine auction house, other online retailing sites, and the hotel group Australian Leisure and Hospitality Limited. Because of its many retail holdings, Woolworths Limited is a major retail force in Australia and New Zealand.

BRAND ELEMENTS

- In 2012, Woolworths supermarket changed its slogan from "The Fresh Food People" to "Australia's Fresh Food People."
- The Woolworths supermarket logo features a fruit-like shape in a fresh green color, which echoes the chain's freshness slogan.
- The color green features prominently in the Woolworths supermarket logo, its stores, its website, and its catalogs.
- Apple Inc. has contested Woolworths' use of a fruit in its logo, but the grocery store chain continues to use it.

Since the 1980s, Woolworths supermarket has used the slogan "The Fresh Food People." In 2012 the company modified this slogan slightly, changing it to "Australia's Fresh Food People." This modified slogan and the Woolworths name appear as part of the logo for its chain of supermarkets.

The Woolworths supermarket logo features the word "Woolworths," with "Australia's fresh food people" written underneath. Above "Woolworths" is a swirly shape that resembles a piece of fruit, like an apple or a pumpkin, rendered in a fresh green color. All three elements of the logo (the fruitlike shape, the Woolworths name, and its fresh food slogan) are often displayed in shades of green. The use of the color green reinforces the idea of freshness and represents the produce customers can find at Woolworths supermarket stores.

The website for Woolworths supermarket reinforces the brand's connection to freshness. The website uses the Woolworths supermarket logo and incorporates different shades of green for different parts of the site. In addition to using the stylized fruit of the logo, the site has featured photographs of actual fruit, like watermelons and bananas, as background decoration. Photographs of fruit, vegetables, and other goods have also appeared in online catalogs linked with the website, which were also designed using the Woolworths supermarket logo and various shades of green.

The Woolworths supermarket logo made news in 2009, when U.S.-based Apple Inc. claimed that the logo's fruitlike shape too closely resembled the apple in its own famous logo. Woolworths supermarket, however, has continued to use the logo, even on Woolworths applications (apps) that customers can buy at Apple's iTunes store.

BRAND IDENTITY

- The Woolworths supermarket website frequently mentions the freshness of its products.
- A key element of Woolworths' brand identity is "consistent quality fresh food."
- The 2012 rebranding campaign for Woolworths supermarket aimed to prove to customers that the stores' items are fresh and created onsite.

Woolworths supermarkets promote the company's commitment to freshness. The stores use the Woolworths supermarket logo with its fruitlike shape, along with various shades of green, including green signage decorated with pictures of plantlike material. The Woolworths supermarket website also touts freshness, with sections called "Your Guide to Fresh Food," "Buying Fresh Food," and "Fresh Market Update Videos." Another section of the website discusses what Woolworths supermarket calls its "consistent quality fresh food." The website also contains information about and photographs of some of the people who grow food for Woolworths supermarket, and it claims that 96 percent of the fresh fruit and vegetables and 100 percent of the fresh meat sold in its stores are from Australia.

This promotion of freshness intensified when Woolworths Limited launched a rebranding campaign for Woolworths supermarket in 2012. With the relaunch, remodeled Woolworths supermarket stores allowed customers to see "behind the scenes," where they could watch butchers carving meats and bakers making bread and other baked goods. Woolworths supermarket displayed these employees creating and preparing food onsite to refute customer complaints that most of the stores' goods were imported from elsewhere. Indeed, Woolworths supermarket so identifies itself with freshness that it named its charity drive to raise money for children's hospitals "Fresh Food Kids Hospital Appeal."

BRAND STRATEGY

- Store brands at Woolworths supermarket include Macro Wholefoods Market, Woolworths Homebrand, Woolworths Select, Fresh, Woolworths Naytura, and Woolworths Free From.
- Some companies have accused Woolworths supermarket of copying the packaging of brand-name products for its store brands and then selling the latter for less.

- Woolworths Limited's Countdown supermarkets in New Zealand feature the Australian Woolworths supermarket store brands, as well as their own store brand, Signature Range.
- Woolworths Limited's Big W stores carry store brands offering a wide range of items.

Woolworths supermarket sells a number of store brands, many of which reinforce the Woolworths name. Its Macro Wholefoods Market products are a line of foods aimed at health-conscious consumers. In the logo for this line, the "O" in Macro is shaped like an apple or other piece of fruit, implying that the foods in the line are natural. The apple-shaped "O" also echoes the fruitlike shape in the Woolworths supermarket logo and provides a subtle reminder of the brand's promise of freshness.

Another store brand, Woolworths Homebrand, features a wide range of products that include food, cleaning supplies, and baby care items. These items, targeted to the budget shopper, feature a red-colored logo. Woolworths supermarket promotes the more expensive Woolworths Select food products, which feature the stylized fruitlike shape from the store's logo, to customers who would ordinarily buy brand-name products. The companies behind these brand names have complained about this strategy, claiming that Woolworths Select products mimic the packaging of brand-name products but cost less. Another Woolworths supermarket store brand, called Fresh, features prepared meals and soups, along with prepared vegetables that can be used as meal elements.

Other Woolworths supermarket store brands include Woolworths Naytura, a line of natural foods, and Woolworths Free From, food items that are "free from" certain ingredients. A number of these store brands can also be found in New Zealand's Countdown supermarkets, which are owned by Woolworths Limited and feature their own store brand, called Signature Range.

Store brands are not limited to Woolworths supermarket. Woolworths Limited's Big W stores feature the Smart Value brand, a diverse line of goods that includes quilts, eating utensils, and buckets. Big W sells electronics through its AWA brand, baby items through its Dymples brand, and apparel through its Emerson brand. The diversity of Big W's store brands reflects the wide range of items that Big W stores sell.

BRAND EQUITY

- A 2011 study found that Woolworths Limited and competitor Coles Supermarkets accounted for about 40 percent of consumer spending in Australia.
- Other studies have estimated that Woolworths supermarket and Coles Supermarkets together control 75 to 80 percent of the Australian food retail market.

- Because of their domination of Australian food retail, Woolworths and Coles Supermarkets are considered a duopoly by some consumers.
- In 2012, Brand Finance named Woolworths Limited the 16th most valuable international retail brand and the 130th largest global brand.
- Brand Finance named Woolworths Limited the most valuable brand in Australia from 2009 to 2012.

A study published in 2011 found that Woolworths Limited and its closest competitor, Coles Supermarkets, accounted for nearly 40 percent of Australian retail spending, or almost 40 cents for every dollar Australians spent. Other estimates have stated that Woolworths supermarket and Coles Supermarkets dominate 75 to 80 percent of the food retailing market in Australia. This dominance has led to charges that the two corporations constitute a duopoly, prompting some customers to boycott the chains.

Given its dominance, Woolworths Limited is a prominent international brand. In Brand Finance's "Global 500 2012," a ranking of the largest global brands, Woolworths Limited ranked 130th, with a brand value of around US$7.3 billion. Brand Finance named Woolworths Limited the world's 16th most valuable retail brand in 2012.

Woolworths Limited is also a powerful brand in its home country. Brand Finance named it Australia's most valuable brand every year between 2009 and 2012, with Coles Supermarket coming in third.

BRAND AWARENESS

- Woolworths supermarket and competitor Coles Supermarkets engaged in price wars for milk and fresh produce in 2011 and 2012.
- In 2012, Coles Supermarkets adopted the slogan "There's no freshness like Coles freshness," challenging Woolworths supermarkets "fresh food" pledge.
- Commercials shot in New York City in 2010 introduced Woolworths supermarket to New Yorkers and the brand's reputation for fresh, high-quality meat.

Woolworths supermarket and Coles Supermarkets are the two largest supermarket chains in Australia. Their visibility increased after the two companies battled each other over prices in 2011 and 2012. In 2011 the two corporations waged what the media called "milk wars," with each brand seeking to provide the lowest prices on staples like milk, bread, and laundry detergent. In 2012 the two companies engaged in another price battle, this time cutting prices on fresh vegetables and fruit. The Woolworths supermarket slogan, "Australia's Fresh Food People," is well known to Australians, and in 2012 Coles supermarket adopted the new advertising slogan "There's no freshness like Coles freshness."

Although Woolworths Limited is a dominant brand in Australia and New Zealand, it is not as well known in other countries. In 2010, Woolworths supermarket launched an advertising campaign in the United States to help bring awareness to the brand name. Television commercials filmed on the streets of New York City featured an Australian actor posing as a Woolworths supermarket butcher. This "butcher" gave free Woolworths supermarket meat samples to New Yorkers. Over a shot of beef cooking on a barbecue, a tagline at the end of the commercial read, "The world loves Australian beef. Australians love Woolworths beef." This commercial reinforced the position of Woolworths supermarket as a leading Australian food retailer and helped introduce the brand to a new market (New Yorkers). Woolworths Limited has also made Americans aware of its brand by partnering with U.S. home improvement retailer Lowe's Companies to form the Australia-based chain of home improvement stores Masters Home Improvement.

BRAND OUTLOOK

- Woolworths Limited wants to increase its Australian fresh food market share from 28 percent to 36 percent.
- In 2012, Woolworths Limited introduced "virtual supermarkets" at Australian train stations, which allowed customers to shop using their smartphones.
- Woolworths Limited's brand may become better known in India, where the company provides supplies, training, and other assistance for the Indian chain Croma.

Already a dominant presence in Australian retail, Woolworths Limited hopes to increase its market share of Australia's fresh food market from the 28 percent share it held in 2011 to 36 percent. The brand plans to do this partly by renovating existing supermarkets and adding new supermarket locations.

Woolworths Limited is also trying new retailing models. In 2012 the company opened "virtual supermarkets" in Australian train stations. With this system, a customer can download an app onto his or her digital device (such as a smartphone), browse displays of Woolworths products in the train station, and then scan the product codes with the digital device to place an order online. A local Woolworths supermarket nearby then fills the order and, for a fee, delivers it to the customer's home. A customer can also order items with his or her smartphone or computer without using such displays.

Woolworths Limited is also expanding geographically. The company provides supplies, training, and other assistance to Croma, a chain of stores in India that sells electronics and durable goods, such as appliances and phones. This alliance spreads awareness of Woolworths

Limited's brand name and products to the huge Indian market. It is possible that this expansion into international markets may someday help Woolworths Limited become a prominent and recognizable brand overseas as well as in its home country of Australia.

FURTHER READING

Addington, Tim. "Big W." *B&T*, November 2, 2007. Accessed September 19, 2012. http://www.bandt.com.au/news/archive/big-w.

Aldridge, Mark M. "National Boycott of Coles & Woolworths July 2012." *GoPetition*, July 19, 2012. Accessed September 19, 2012. http://www.gopetition.com/petitions/national-boycott-of-coles-woolworths-july-2012.html.

Brand Finance. "Global 500 2012." *Brandirectory*. Accessed September 17, 2012. http://brandirectory.com/league_tables/table/global-500-2012.

"Corbett, Roger 1942-." *International Directory of Business Biographies*. Ed. Neil Schlager. Vol. 1. Detroit: St. James Press, 2005. *Gale Virtual Reference Library*. Accessed September 18, 2012.

Griffith, Chris. "Woolworths Unveils Virtual Supermarket in Sydney." *The Australian*, February 20, 2012. Accessed September 19, 2002. http://www.theaustralian.com.au/australian-it/exec-tech/woolworths-unveils-virtual-supermarket-in-sydney/story-e6frgazf-1226275454280.

Hernandez, Vittorio. "Woolworths to Renovate 170 Stores in 2013 to Boost Share of Fresh Food Market to 36%." *International Business Times*, June 18, 2012. Accessed September 19, 2002. http://au.ibtimes.com/articles/353167/20120618/woolworths-renovate-170-stores-2013-boost-share.htm.

Lambert, Elisabeth. "Woolworths Launches First Virtual Australian Supermarket." *Power Retail*, February 20, 2012. Accessed September 17, 2012. http://www.powerretail.com.au/news/woolworths-launches-first-virtual-australian-supermarket/.

Lee, Julian. "Apple Bites over Woolworths Logo." *The Age*, October 5, 2009. Accessed September 19, 2012. http://www.theage.com.au/business/apple-bites-over-woolworths-logo-20091005-ghzr.html.

Marian, Petah. "Woolworths Full-Year Sales Grow." *just-food*, July 20, 2011. Accessed September 18, 2012. http://www.just-food.com/news/woolworths-full-year-sales-grow_id116002.aspx.

Marshall, Andrew. "Woolies Boom Meat Week." *Stock & Land*, September 16, 2010. Accessed September 19, 2012. http://sl.farmonline.com.au/news/state/livestock/news/woolies-boom-meat-week/1943573.aspx.

Maxwell, Miranda. "UPDATE 1-Australia's Woolworths Faces More Sluggish Trade after H1 Edges Up." *Reuters*, February 29, 2012. Accessed September 19, 2012. http://www.reuters.com/article/2012/02/29/woolworths-idUSL4E8DT82V20120229.

Myatt, Glenn, "Why Coles Is 'Better' Than Woolworths." *Brand Truth*, June 23, 2012. Accessed September 19, 2012. http://brandtruth.com.au/2012/06/23/why-coles-is-better-than-woolworths/.

"The New Lowes/Masters Stores in Australia, via Easy Home Renovating." *Easy Home Renovating*, July 31, 2010. Accessed

September 19, 2012. http://easyhomerenovating.com/2581/thw-new-lowes-masters-stores-in-australia/.

Silmalis, Linda. "Woolworths Now Made in Australia." *Sunday Mail*, June 17, 2012. Accessed September 18, 2012. http://www.news.com.au/business/woolworths-now-made-in-australia/story-e6frfm1i-1226397873047.

———. "A Home-Brand War for Woolworths as Supermarket Launches New Advertising Blitz." *Sunday Telegraph*, April 8, 2012. Accessed September 18, 2012. http://www.dailytelegraph.com.au/news/a-home-brand-war-for-woolworths/story-e6freuy9-1226321058714.

Swiss-Australian Chamber of Commerce and Industry. "Importance of the Major Australian Retailers." Accessed September 18, 2002. http://www.sacci.com.au/index.php?option=com_content&view=article&id=251:importance-of-the-major-australian-retailers&catid=53:importfromaexporttoaustralia&Itemid=93.

University of New South Wales. "Milking the Market: What's Behind the Coles-Woolworths Price War?" *Knowledge@Australian School of Business*, April 11, 2011. Accessed September 19, 2012. http://knowledge.asb.unsw.edu.au/article.cfm?articleid=1373.

Viellaris, Renee, and Nick Gardner. "Coles and Woolworths Receive Almost 40 Per Cent of Australian Retail Spending." *Sunday Mail*, April 24, 2011. Accessed September 18, 2012. http://www.news.com.au/money/money-matters/coles-and-woolworths-receive-almost-40-per-cent-of-australian-retail-spending/story-e6frfmd9-1226043866311.

Withers, Stephen. "Review: Woolworths App." *iTWire*, February 17, 2012. Accessed September 18, 2012. http://www.itwire.com/reviews/software/52850-review-woolworths-app/52850-review-woolworths-app?start=2.

Woolworths Limited. *2011 Annual Report*. Bella Vista, NSW, Australia: Woolworths Limited. Accessed September 17, 2012. http://www.woolworthslimited.com.au/page/Invest_In_Us/Reports_Results_and_Presentations/.

"Woolworths' Profits Up 5.1%" *RetailBiz*, August 29, 2011. Accessed September 18, 2012. http://www.retailbiz.com.au/2011/08/29/article/Woolworths-profits-up-5-1/EQEYDAQFYI.

"Woolworths Relaunches Brand with New Droga5 Work but Retains Emphasis on Fresh Food People." *mUmBRELLA*, June 17, 2012. Accessed September 17, 2012. http://mumbrella.com.au/woolworths-relaunches-brand-with-new-droga5-work-but-retains-emphasis-on-fresh-food-people-97277.

"Woolworths Sales Up 4.7%." *Macro Business*, July 20, 2011. Accessed September 18, 2012. http://www.macrobusiness.com.au/2011/07/woolworths-sales-up-4-7/.

Woolworths.com. Accessed September 18, 2012. http://www.woolworths.com.au.

XEROX

—————— ■ ——————

AT A GLANCE

■

Brand Synopsis: A leading business process and document management company, Xerox is "ready for real business."

Parent Company: Xerox Corporation
45 Glover Avenue
Norwalk, Connecticut 06850
United States
http://www.xerox.com

Sector: Information Technology

Industry Group: Technology Hardware & Equipment; Software & Services

Performance: *Market share*—15.4 percent of color laser printers (2010); 4.7 percent of mono laser printers (2010). *Sales*—US$22.4 billion (2012).

Principal Competitors: Accenture plc; Canon Inc.; Hewlett-Packard Company; Pitney Bowes Inc.; Ricoh Company, Ltd.; Seiko Epson Corporation

BRAND ORIGINS

- Xerox can trace its roots to 1906, when the Haloid Company, a photography-paper business, was established in Rochester, New York.
- In 1947 Haloid entered into an agreement with Battelle Memorial Institute, a nonprofit research organization in Columbus, Ohio, to produce a machine based on a new process called xerography.
- In 1958 Haloid changed its name to Haloid Xerox Inc., reflecting its belief that the company's future lay with xerography.
- Introduced in 1960, the Xerox 914 copier was the first automatic Xerox copier and the first marketable plain-paper copier.
- In 1961 Haloid Xerox Inc. changed its name to Xerox Corporation and was listed on the New York Stock Exchange.

Xerox traces its roots to 1906, when the Haloid Company, a photography-paper business, was established in Rochester, New York. Its neighbor, Eastman Kodak Company, ignored the company, so Haloid was able to build a business on the fringe of the photography market. In 1912 control of the company was sold for US$50,000 to the Rochester businessman Gilbert E. Mosher, who became president but left responsibility for daily operations to its founders.

Mosher kept Haloid profitable and opened sales offices in Chicago, Boston, and New York City. To broaden the company's market share, Haloid's board decided to develop a better paper. It took several years, but when Haloid Record finally came out in 1933, it was so successful that it saved the company from the worst of the Great Depression. By 1934 Haloid's sales were approaching US$1 million. In 1935 Joseph R. Wilson, the son of one of the founders, decided that Haloid should buy the Rectigraph Company, a photocopying machine manufacturer that used Haloid's paper. To help pay for the acquisition, Haloid went public in 1936, and selling Rectigraphs became an important part of Haloid's business.

In 1947 Haloid entered into an agreement with the Battelle Memorial Institute, a nonprofit research organization in Columbus, Ohio, to produce a machine based on a new process called xerography. Xerography, a word derived from the Greek words for "dry" and "writing," was invented by Chester Carlson. Carlson was a patent lawyer and worked for a New York electronics firm. Frustrated by the difficulty and expense of copying documents, Carlson invented in 1938 a method of transferring images from one piece of paper to another using static electricity. In 1947 Battelle signed a royalty sharing agreement with Carlson and began developing commercial applications for xerography.

Two years later Haloid introduced the XeroX Copier, which was initially spelled with a capital *X* at the end. Requiring much of the processing to be done manually, the machine proved to be difficult and messy to use and made errors frequently. Many in the financial community thought that Haloid's large investment in xerography was a big mistake. However, Battelle engineers discovered that the XeroX made excellent masters for offset printing, which was an unforeseen quality that sold many machines. Haloid invested earnings from these sales into research on a second-generation xerographic copier.

In 1950 Haloid sold its first commercial contract for a xerographic copier to the state of Michigan. Meanwhile, Haloid's other products were again highly profitable, with paper sales increasing and several successful new office photocopying machines selling well. In 1955 Haloid revamped its 18 regional offices into showrooms for its new generation of Xerox machines, hired 200 sales and service people, began building the first Xerox factory in Webster, New York, and introduced three new types of photography paper. Haloid also introduced the Copyflo, Haloid's semiautomatic copying machine.

In 1958 Haloid changed its name to Haloid Xerox Inc., reflecting its belief that the company's future lay with xerography, even though photography products were still more profitable. That balance quickly changed with the success of the Xerox 914 copier. Introduced in 1960, it was the first automatic Xerox copier and the first marketable plain-paper copier. The company could not afford a blanket advertising campaign, so it placed ads in magazines and on television programs where it hoped business owners would see them. The company also offered the machines for monthly lease to make xerography affordable for smaller businesses.

Demand for the 650-pound 914 model exceeded Haloid Xerox's most optimistic projections. Sales and rental of xerographic products doubled in 1961 and kept growing. In 1961 the company was listed on the New York Stock Exchange, changed its name to Xerox

Corporation, and photography operations were placed under the newly created Haloid photo division.

BRAND ELEMENTS

- In 1961 Xerox's visual trademark was established, with the brand name appearing in black capital letters in a stylized font.
- During the mid-1990s a red version of Xerox logo was introduced, consisting of a large *X*, the upper right arm of which was pixelated to convey digital capabilities.
- Xerox introduced "The Document Company" tagline during the mid-1990s, but stopped using it in 2004.
- During the latter half of the first decade of the 21st century the Xerox brand was refreshed, and a red spherical graphic, overlaid with a white X-like element, was added to the right of the brand name.

From the late 1940s through the late 1950s the Xerox brand was intertwined with that of Haloid. Beginning in 1961 a new visual trademark was established for the Xerox Corporation. The brand name appeared in black capital letters in a stylized font that included extenders on the lower portions of the letters *X* and *R*. During the mid-1990s a red version of the brand's visual trademark was introduced. This consisted of a large *X*, the upper right arm of which was pixelated to convey the company's digital capabilities. In addition, the supporting tagline "The Document Company" was introduced.

A simpler, more contemporary typeface was instituted in 2004. The Xerox name appeared in its entirety, with the letters remaining in red. Also, the tagline "The Document Company" was replaced with "Technology/Document Management/Consulting Services."

Toward the end of the decade Xerox's brand identity was refreshed once again. Red, lowercased characters were used, and a red spherical graphic that was overlaid with a white X-like element was added to the right of the brand name. In 2011 the cover of Xerox's annual report read: "You'll find us everywhere business gets done." This phrase signified the brand's transformation from a document focus to one that encompassed a broad range of business services, which it communicated through the tagline "Ready for Real Business."

BRAND IDENTITY

- Because of its pioneering role and early market dominance, Xerox's brand name was long synonymous with making copies.
- By 2012 the tagline "Ready for Real Business" signified Xerox's transformation from a document focus to one that encompassed a broad range of business services.

- Xerox's US$6.4 billion acquisition of Affiliated Computer Services in 2009 marked the company's foray into the categories of outsourcing and business process management.

Because of its pioneering role and early market dominance, Xerox's brand name was long synonymous with making copies. Office workers frequently used the term *xeroxing* instead of *photocopying*. Although this initially was advantageous for Xerox, it presented challenges as digital technology grew in prominence. This prompted the company to brand itself as "The Document Company" during the mid-1990s.

By 2012 the evolution of the Xerox brand continued. The tagline "Ready for Real Business" signified its transformation from a document focus to one that encompassed a broad range of business services. This was made possible by the US$6.4 billion acquisition of Affiliated Computer Services in 2009, which marked the company's foray into the categories of outsourcing and business process management.

In Xerox's 2011 annual report, CEO Ursula Burns captured the essence of the company's brand identity, explaining: "We're the new Xerox. We don't make the hottest new gadget on store shelves or run a hospital that saves lives or get you to work on time or manufacture the safest aircraft on the planet. But we do something every bit as important. We're behind the scenes, managing the 'must do work' that enables every one of those things to happen. It's a noble mission. To take some very complex business processes and make them appear simple to those who need them."

BRAND STRATEGY

- The US$6.4 billion acquisition of Affiliated Computer Services in 2009 was a key evolutionary milestone for the Xerox brand, as its scope was broadened to include business services.
- In 2011 Xerox generated 48 percent of its revenues from business services.
- The global growth of Xerox's information technology outsourcing and business process services was a key aspect of its strategy in 2012, especially in emerging markets.

Xerox's brand strategy is focused on the company's capabilities in the area of business services. Although its long association with plain paper copying was beneficial for many decades, it also presented challenges as the Xerox brand attempted to evolve. One key evolutionary milestone took place during the 1990s, when Xerox rebranded itself as "The Document Company," positioning itself for a future that was focused more on digital technology.

The US$6.4 billion acquisition of Affiliated Computer Services in 2009 was another key evolutionary milestone for the Xerox brand, as its scope was broadened to include business services such as outsourcing and business process management. In September 2010 Xerox launched an advertising campaign that featured how the company was helping high-profile customers such as Marriott International Inc. and Target Corporation on the business services front.

By 2012 Xerox's strategy, which was promoted by the tagline "Ready for Real Business," had expanded beyond traditional advertising to include an online presence at Realbusiness.com. The site promoted Xerox's capabilities in categories such as customer care, human resources, document management, finance and accounting, and information technology outsourcing. As with advertising, Realbusiness.com showcased how Xerox was helping well-known companies such as Michelin with "back-end processes."

The success of Xerox's brand strategy was clear by 2011, when the company generated 48 percent of its revenues from business services. Moving forward, the company was focused on growing its information technology outsourcing and business process services globally. This especially was the case in emerging markets. By 2012 Xerox was concentrating on markets such as Brazil, Chile, Colombia, India, Mexico, Peru, Poland, Russia, and Turkey. Strong opportunities existed where public-sector expansion was taking place.

BRAND EQUITY

- According to Interbrand, the Xerox brand was valued at US$6.7 billion in 2012, an increase of 5 percent from the previous year.
- In 2012 Xerox ranked 59th on Interbrand's listing of the "100 Best Global Brands."
- By the end of 2011 Xerox's design and utility patents exceeded 10,500, and the company held approximately 550 U.S. trademarks.

In Xerox's 2011 annual report, CEO Ursula Burns commented: "Our brand is known and respected around the world. Its multi-billion-dollar value is the sum total of millions upon millions of decisions made, actions taken and values lived by our people for several decades."

According to Interbrand, the Xerox brand was valued at US$6.7 billion in 2012, an increase of 5 percent from the previous year. Xerox ranked 59th on Interbrand's listing of the "100 Best Global Brands." Citing figures from NPD Group Inc., *CRN* reported in March 2011 that Xerox was the second-leading manufacturer of color laser printers in 2010, with a market share of 15.4 percent. The company trailed Hewlett-Packard

(58.5 percent), but led Lexmark (13.1 percent). Similarly, the publication indicated that Xerox ranked third in market share for mono laser printers (4.7 percent), behind Hewlett-Packard (65.4 percent) and Lexmark (19.6 percent).

As Burns commented, Xerox's brand equity is rooted in many decades' worth of work. Collectively, the efforts of the company's employees have produced a tremendous body of intellectual property. In 2011 alone Xerox was awarded 1,030 patents in the United States, ranking 19th. By the end of that year the company's design and utility patents exceeded 10,500. In addition, it held approximately 550 U.S. trademarks. In 2012 Xerox continued its research and development activities at five global research centers.

BRAND AWARENESS

- The term *xeroxing* is often used instead of *photocopying*, and *xerox* appears in many dictionaries as a verb.
- The strong association between the Xerox brand and the act of making copies did not naturally extend to the brand's connection with business services, prompting the need for significant advertising.
- By 2012 the Xerox brand was widely recognized throughout the world. From small businesses to large organizations, Xerox served a wide range of customers in more than 160 countries.

The Xerox brand name has long been associated with plain paper copying, beginning with its pioneering role in the commercialization of xerographic technology. This association was so strong that the term *xeroxing* was commonly used instead of *photocopying*. In addition, *xerox* eventually appeared in many dictionaries as a verb.

For many decades, this strong top-of-mind awareness ensured that the Xerox brand was a part of the business community's collective psyche. However, trademark concerns during the 1970s prompted Xerox to discourage the use of its brand name as a verb. According to the June 10, 2011, issue of the London *Independent*, one advertisement stated: "You cannot xerox a document, but you can copy it on a Xerox brand copying machine."

The association between the Xerox trademark and the act of plain paper copying has always been strong. However, this same top-of-mind awareness has not naturally extended to the brand's connection with business services. Since the 2009 acquisition of Affiliated Computer Services, Xerox has devoted significant resources to promote its capabilities in areas such as outsourcing and business process management. By 2012 the Xerox brand was widely recognized throughout the world.

From small businesses to large organizations, Xerox served a wide range of customers in more than 160 countries.

BRAND OUTLOOK

- In 2011 Xerox attributed 48 percent (US$10.8 billion) of its revenues to business services, compared with 23 percent (US$3.5 billion) in 2009.
- In 2011 Xerox competed in a market that was valued at US$600 billion.
- By 2012 Xerox was looking to emerging markets for continued growth. These were accompanied by varying degrees of opportunity and risk.

Despite challenging economic times, Xerox was in a strong position in 2012. The company's revenues increased from US$15.2 billion in 2009, to US$21.6 billion in 2010, and to US$22.6 billion in 2011. The brand's expansion to encompass business services had much to do with Xerox's growth. In 2009 Xerox attributed 23 percent (US$3.5 billion) of its revenues to business services. This percentage nearly doubled to 45 percent (US$9.6 billion) in 2009 and to 48 percent (US$10.8 billion) in 2011.

Xerox competed in a market that was valued at US$600 billion in 2011. To capitalize on this, Xerox was focused on several key areas. These included a commitment to the continued global expansion of the company's business services offerings. Additionally, Xerox remained focused on maintaining its technology leadership position, especially with advancements in color copying technology and offerings for smaller and medium-sized businesses. While pursuing these areas, Xerox was equally conscious about maximizing its quality performance and efficiency on the operational side.

Innovation is critical for the continued evolution of organizations and their brands, and Xerox is no exception. In this regard, the company carried out important research and development activities at five global research centers. In 2011 alone Xerox was awarded 1,030 patents in the United States, ranking 19th. By the end of that year the company's design and utility patents exceeded 10,500. In addition, it held approximately 550 U.S. trademarks.

By 2012 Xerox was looking to emerging markets for additional growth. Examples included Brazil, Chile, Colombia, India, Mexico, Peru, Poland, Russia, and Turkey. Strong opportunities existed where public-sector expansion was taking place. Even though emerging markets presented opportunities, they were also accompanied by their own challenges. These included complicated labor laws, complex tax codes, and political instability.

FURTHER READING

"Corporate Strategy: Company Profile—Can Xerox Duplicate Its Paper Success?" *Foreign Direct Investment*, April 1, 2012.

Deutsch, Claudia. "New Logo and Tagline for Xerox." *New York Times*, September 13, 2004.

Dignan, Larry. "Xerox Buys ECS for $6.4 Billion." *CNET News*, September 28, 2009.

Marsden, Rhodri. "'Genericide': When Brands Get Too Big." *Independent* (London), June 10, 2011.

Schultz, E. J. "When Other Marketers Are the Ad's 'Talent.'" *Advertising Age*, October 3, 2011.

Spector, Nicole. "The Reimaging of Xerox's Brand." *DM News*, August 2012.

Xerox Corporation. "2011 Annual Report." Accessed December 5, 2012. http://www.xerox.com/assets/pdf/2011_Annual_Report.pdf.

"Xerox Corporation." *International Directory of Company Histories*. Ed. Jay P. Pederson. Vol. 69. Farmington Hills, MI: St. James Press, 2005.

YAHOO!

AT A GLANCE

Brand Synopsis: With a loud yodel and an ostentatious exclamation point, Yahoo! strives to make its homepage the destination for millions of Internet users worldwide.

Parent Company: Yahoo! Inc.
701 First Avenue
Sunnyvale, California 94089
United States
http://www.yahoo.com

Sector: Information Technology

Industry Group: Internet Services

Performance: *Market share*—17 percent of online display advertising worldwide (2010); 7 percent of search engines worldwide (2012). *Sales*—US$5 billion (2011).

Principal Competitors: America Online, Inc.; About Inc.; Google Inc.; Microsoft Corporation

BRAND ORIGINS

- Stanford University students Jerry Yang and David Filo founded Yahoo! in the 1990s under the name Jerry's Guide to the World Wide Web.
- The name Yahoo! comes from the term Yet Another Hierarchical Officious Oracle, the definition of a "Yahoo" as a rude person, and "Yahoo!" as an exclamation of excitement.
- In addition to Yahoo! Internet searches, Yahoo! offers a variety of communication, content, and commerce services.

- Partnerships with SBC Communications and Nextel Communications and the acquisition of the photo-sharing site Flickr have helped Yahoo! expand its services beyond computers.

In the early 1990s, Stanford University graduate students Jerry Yang and David Filo created their own website, Jerry's Guide to the World Wide Web. This website included links to Yang and Filo's favorite web pages and was a precursor to the Yahoo! homepage Internet users are familiar with today.

As Jerry's Guide to the World Wide Web grew in popularity, Yang and Filo customized the site into an online space where visitors could search for and locate other websites. Looking to rebrand, the two founders took the name of the Unix computer program Yet Another Compiler Compiler (YACC) as a cue, coming up with Yet Another Hierarchical Officious Oracle, or YAHOO. Yang and Filo liked the fact that the term "Yahoo" could mean a rude or uncouth person, and that "Yahoo!" is also an expression of excitement, infusing the brand with a sense of fun and irreverence.

Yahoo saw significant growth in 1995 as Yang and Filo moved Yahoo! from the Stanford University servers to servers at Netscape Communications. Also in 1995 another Stanford engineer, Tim Koogle, joined the company as chairperson and chief executive, and Jeff Mallett joined as its chief operating officer. Another Stanford graduate, Karen Edwards, joined the company the following year as its brand marketer.

Yahoo! continued to grow, earning revenues by selling banner advertisements on its web page. Internet users could click on advertisements to get instant access to the advertisers' websites and products. On occasion Yahoo! entered into distribution agreements with companies wishing to advertise on Yahoo!, receiving a percentage of the profits the companies received when customers purchased products through Yahoo!-linked advertisements.

As Yahoo! usership expanded, so did Yahoo! services. In addition to search engine services, Yahoo! integrated communication-based services such as Yahoo! Mail and Yahoo! Messenger, commerce-based services such as Yahoo! Small Business, Yahoo! Shopping, and Yahoo!-hosted domains, and content-based services such as shopping, news, movies, music, and games into its business model.

Yahoo! acquired thirteen Internet companies from 2000 to 2004, and continues to partner with companies across varying markets and platforms in order to expand market share and provide relevant services to Internet users around the globe. These partnerships have included alliances with SBC Communications and Nextel Communications, which brought Yahoo! services to portable electronic devices. Yahoo! also acquired the photo-sharing website Flickr in 2005, further expanding the company's reach beyond personal computers.

BRAND ELEMENTS

- A 1995 Yahoo! logo featured yellow and red letters, movement marks, and misaligned letters, which created a vibrant visual brand representation for the young, growing company.
- A 1997 Yahoo! logo featured more movement: a drawing of a jumping y-shaped person, called the "jumping Y guy."
- Later Yahoo! logos featured the word "Yahoo!" in purple capital letters as well as an encircled capital *Y* next to an exclamation point. The second logo is called the "Y! Bang" since typesetters call exclamation marks "bangs."
- Another Yahoo! brand identifier is the Yahoo! yodel, a yodeled version of the word "Yahoo!"

As Yahoo! evolved, so did the company's logo. When the company was officially incorporated in 1995, its logo was comprised of red letters outlined in an orange-yellow color alongside a black exclamation mark, which was outlined in the same orange-yellow color. The logo featured marks near the *Y* and first *o* of "Yahoo," a spiral in red and orange-yellow representing the last *o*. In addition, the letters were not aligned but staggered, giving the appearance of moving type. These touches animated the word, an appropriate touch for a young and growing company.

In 1997 the logo for Yahoo! changed to incorporate slightly staggered capital letters followed by an exclamation point. This version of the company logo has had both purple and red iterations. Yahoo! has also made use of a drawing of a jumping y-shaped person, called the "jumping Y guy." The company has also used a capital *Y* in a circle next to an exclamation mark. This logo is known as the "Y! Bang" because typesetters refer to an exclamation mark as a "bang."

The Yahoo! brand is also identified by the Yahoo! yodel, used in television commercials and other forms of multimedia advertising. The yodel sounds as if someone is singing the word "yahoo," with the second part of the word drawn out in multiple syllables. The Yahoo! yodel relates to the expression "Yahoo!" as an exclamation of excitement.

BRAND IDENTITY

- Yahoo! wishes to be viewed as a trustworthy and helpful brand.
- Yahoo! has had several missteps in its attempts to overhaul its brand identity.
- The 2009 "It's Y!ou" global campaign failed to meet its goals.

As Yahoo! entered the 21st century, it was unclear what its brand identity truly was. According to Yahoo!'s website, the company wished to be viewed as a brand that is trustworthy and helpful and asserted that "Yahoo! stands out as one of the most visited and trusted Internet destinations because we uniquely pair innovative technology with a human touch to personalize the digital world." In the statement Yahoo! largely dwelled on its long-standing reputation, however, and offered little information on its unique technological advancements or innovations.

Yahoo! has attempted to revitalize its brand on a number of occasions. In 2009, for instance, the company announced a major brand overhaul with its US$100 million "It's Y!ou" marketing campaign. The campaign, Yahoo!'s first global effort, launched in the fall of 2009 with a flurry of advertisements, including online and outdoor ads, and guerrilla marketing. The campaign's goal was not only to increase brand awareness but also to further engage Yahoo! users and promote Yahoo! as a relevant brand.

By the following spring, however, the "It's Y!ou" campaign had been declared a failure because it had not clarified the identity of the Yahoo! brand. As reporter Kara Swisher wrote on the AllThingsD website, "Yahoo never really answered what exactly 'you' was, which is why CEO Carol Bartz finally admitted to a group of reporters in March that the effort 'didn't have a really good call to action.'"

BRAND STRATEGY

- The Yahoo! logo and Y! Bang logo appear on various Yahoo! websites.
- Yahoo! promotional campaigns have included the 1990s campaign "Do you Yahoo!?" and the 2000s campaign "It's Y!ou."

- Yahoo! offers original programming on its Y! Screen pages. These pages also promote Yahoo!, as they feature Yahoo! logos and link to other Yahoo! pages.

In addition to serving as an Internet search engine, Yahoo! makes a variety of other content and services available to the global Internet-browsing public. Its homepage features news and links to other Yahoo! pages such as weather, sports, travel, My Yahoo!, music, and movies. Each of these individual Yahoo! pages features the Yahoo! logo or the Y! Bang logo, reinforcing the brand with every click.

Yahoo! has deployed several catchphrases and slogans throughout the years as a part of the company's brand strategy. In 2009 Yahoo! featured the tagline "It's Y!ou" in a promotional campaign, emphasizing the personal, customizable nature of Yahoo! features and services. An earlier campaign from the 1990s featured the slogan "Do you Yahoo!?" alongside various other recognizable brand features such as the Yahoo! yodel and the Y! Bang logo. The slogan "Do you Yahoo!?" also reinforced the company's emphasis on Yahoo! as a brand that catered to individuals and their diverse online needs.

Yahoo! also promotes and reinforces its brand through its original programming features. Visitors to the service Y! Screen can watch comedy, advice, and interview series on the web. Yahoo! created these programs as visible products that could entertain and help consumers. While it can be hard to describe what Yahoo! does, these programs represent a more tangible product of the Yahoo! brand. These programs appear on Y! Screen pages featuring links to other Yahoo! sites as well as the omnipresent Yahoo! and Y! Bang logos. Yahoo! thus provides its users a wide range of content while simultaneously promoting itself.

BRAND EQUITY

- In 2012 digital analyst comScore found that Yahoo! held a 13 percent market share for American Internet searches.
- A 2012 study by Net Applications and Net Market Share determined that Yahoo! possessed a 7 percent market share for global Internet searches. A 2012 study by communications firm Karma Snack determined that Yahoo's global market share for Internet usage was 2.4 percent.
- Interbrand's Global 500 list included Yahoo! as the 97th largest company in the world in 2012.
- Also in 2012 Byte Level Research listed Yahoo! among its top 25 websites for international users.

In a June 2012 study on Internet searches in the United States, digital business analyst comScore found that North American users accessing Internet sites used Yahoo! search engines 13 percent of the time, with Google at 66.8 percent and Microsoft at 15.6 percent. A similar comScore survey found that, during October 2011, North American Internet users accessed Yahoo! sites 15.2 percent of the time, Google sites 65.6 percent of the time, and Microsoft sites 14.8 percent of the time.

A 2012 market share study by Net Applications and Net Market Share determined that Yahoo! held a 7 percent market share for global Internet searches, Google, an 86 percent share, Bing, a 4 percent share, the Chinese company Baidu, a 2 percent share, and Ask.com, a 1 percent share. In 2012 the American Internet communications firm Karma Snack found that global Internet users chose Yahoo! search engines for 2.4 percent of their searches, Google search engines for 88.8 percent of their searches, Bing for 4.2 percent, Baidu for 3.5 percent, Ask.com for 0.6 percent, and other sites for 0.5 percent.

Despite fierce global competition and modest market shares, Yahoo! remains a prominent global brand. Yahoo! placed 97th on Interbrand's Global 500 list in 2012, with a brand value of US$3.9 billion. In 2012 Byte Level Research, an American firm interested in global Internet usage, listed Yahoo! among its 25 best websites. The study noted that Yahoo! was adept at incorporating other languages and country information into its web page designs, such as the Yahoo! en Español feature, which allows users to see Yahoo! homepage information in Spanish at the click of a button. Yahoo! users can also access Yahoo! sites in languages other than Spanish and English.

BRAND AWARENESS

- Times Square, New York City, San Francisco, California, and North Sydney, Australia are all places that have had prominent Yahoo! physical advertising campaigns.
- In 2012 the Nielsen Company determined that Yahoo! had the third-most visitors of any online video site and ranked it the fourth-best web parent company in the world and in the United States.
- In the 2012 Reputation Institute's Global RepTrak 100, more than 40,000 international customers determined that Yahoo! had the 75th best company reputation in the world.

Yahoo! not only promotes its brand in the virtual world, but in the physical world as well. Yahoo! has made use of prominent signs and billboards in bustling hubs like New York City's Times Square and metropolises such as San Francisco, California and Sydney, Australia. Many of the company's signs and billboards featured changing, electronic content advertising Yahoo! products and services, displayed seasonal messages, and once even featured a marriage proposal. The Yahoo! logo also appears on the company's offices throughout the world, such as the large yellow neon letters that grace the company's office in North Sydney, Australia. By featuring brand logos on both physical and cyber promotional materials, Yahoo!

has consistently made a conscious effort to promote its name and logos both in the physical world and the virtual world of the World Wide Web.

In an August 2012 study, The Nielsen Company ranked Yahoo! as the fourth-best global web parent company as well as the fourth-best U.S. web parent company. Also in 2012 Nielsen determined that Yahoo! had the third-most visitors of any online video site, with more than 42 million unique viewers.

Yahoo! users have been shown to rate the company's services highly. More than 40,000 consumers in 15 countries determined that Yahoo! had the 75th best company reputation in the world, according to the Reputation Institute's 2012 Global RepTrak 100 survey.

BRAND OUTLOOK

- Nokia and Yahoo! have partnered to provide content for computer and personal electronic device applications.
- Microsoft search engine Bing partnered with Yahoo! in 2012 to help advertisers target search engine users.
- Yahoo! and Chinese Internet company Alibaba Group Holding Ltd. were involved in the buying and selling of company stock in 2012. The resulting alliance has been profitable for Yahoo! as it involves Yahoo! gaining access to the world's largest Internet market, China.

Yahoo! continues to expand and diversify its offerings, which includes the pursuit of more original programming. Yahoo! laid plans to begin airing the web series *Suit Up* in 2013. The producers of *Suit Up*, which depicts a college athletic department, believed that Yahoo! would be a good fit for the program because Yahoo! already features sports news as a part of its content delivery.

Users can enjoy Yahoo! content through several different channels, since Yahoo! content is accessible on more than just personal computers. Users can access Yahoo! content and services on their tablets or Yahoo! Mobile on their phones. In 2010 Yahoo! partnered with the technology company Nokia. In this partnership, Yahoo! provided e-mail and search services for Nokia products and Nokia provided content for the popular Yahoo! Maps and navigation services. Additionally, Yahoo! partnered with Microsoft's search engine Bing in 2012 to form the Yahoo! Bing Network, a site enabling companies to target their advertisements to reach specific group Internet searchers.

Ties to other companies have been profitable for Yahoo! The company has welcomed and pursued these partnerships as Google and other companies continue to expand their market share. In 2012 the Chinese Internet company Alibaba Group Holding Ltd. repurchased some of the shares of its company that Yahoo! had bought in 2005. Yahoo! made approximately US$4.3 billion on the deal and retained stock in Alibaba. Business analysts have given positive ratings to the Yahoo! and Alibaba alliance due to the booming market of the Chinese Internet-using public.

FURTHER READING

"Best Global Brands 2012." Interbrand. Accessed October 7, 2012. http://www.interbrand.com/en/best-global-brands/2012/Best-Global-Brands-2012.aspx.

Byte Level Research. "The Web Globalization Report Card 2012." Accessed October 7, 2012. http://www.bytelevel.com/reportcard2012/.

"comScore Releases June 2012 U.S. Search Engine Rankings." comScore.com, July 11, 2012. Accessed October 7, 2012. http://www.comscore.com/Press_Events/Press_Releases/2012/6/comScore_Releases_June_2012_U.S._Search_Engine_Rankings.

Eaton, Kit. "The 5 Things Yahoo's New CEO Scott Thompson Should Do Right Away." *Fast Company*, January 4, 2012. Accessed February 22, 2013. http://www.fastcompany.com/1805464/5-things-yahoos-new-ceo-scott-thompson-should-do-right-away.

Karma Snack. "Oct 2012—Updated // Search Engine Market Share." KarmaSnack.com, October, 2012. Accessed October 7, 2012. http://www.karmasnack.com/about/search-engine-market-share/.

Net Applications and Net Market Share. "Search Engine Market Share." NetApplications.com, 2012. Accessed October 7, 2012. http://www.netmarketshare.com/search-engine-market-share.aspx?qprid=4.

Nielsen. "Internet." Accessed October 9, 2012. http://www.nielsen.com/us/en/insights/top10s/internet.html.

O'Malley, Gavin. "Yahoo, DirecTV 'Suit Up' for Cross-Platform Entertainment." *MediaPost*, August 29, 2012. Accessed October 8, 2012. http://www.mediapost.com/publications/article/181830/yahoo-directv-suit-up-for-cross-platform-entert.html.

"Rankings per Brand." SyncForce, 2012. RankingTheBrands.com. Accessed October 7, 2012. http://www.rankingthebrands.com/Brand-detail.aspx?brandID=100.

Swisher, Kara. "Yahoo Sticks with 'It's Y!ou,' Expanding Pricey Ad Campaign by Pushing 'Hero Products' and Relevance." AllThingsD, December 15, 2009. Accessed February 22, 2013. http://allthingsd.com/20091215/yahoo-sticks-with-the-its-you-expanding-pricey-ad-campaign-and-pushing-hero-products/.

"Yahoo! Inc." *International Directory of Company Histories*. Ed. Tina Grant. Vol. 70. Detroit, MI: St. James Press, 2005.

Yahoo Investor Relations. "Yahoo Reports Fourth Quarter and Full Year 2011 Results." Yahoo.com, January 24, 2012. Accessed October 7, 2012. http://investor.yahoo.net/releases.cfm?Year=&ReleasesType=&PageNum=3.

YAMADA DENKI

BRAND ORIGINS

- Norboru Yamada launched a Matsushita electronics store in 1973, which developed into a chain that would bear his name.
- Yamada Denki became an independent company in 1983.
- The Yamada Denki brand expanded beyond the northern region of Japan in 1992.
- National expansion was accelerated in the late 1990s.
- The Yamada Denki brand was introduced in China in 2010.

Yamada Denki Co., Ltd., is a Japanese holding company for several subsidiaries and brands, the most important of which is Yamada Denki, Japan's largest chain of consumer electronics retail stores. The Yamada Denki brand can trace its origins to the 1973 founding of the Matsushita retail store chain for home electronics. Matsushita enlisted the help of retail veteran Norboru Yamada to start its retail operations. Under Yamada, a single store was opened in Maebashi, the capital city of the Gunma prefecture in the northern Kanto region of Japan. Over the course of the next decade, Yamada not only opened other outlets in the region, he forged distribution agreements with additional manufacturers. In 1983, Yamada Denki was incorporated as an independent company. Literally translated, "denki" means electricity, so that in effect Yamada Denki is Yamada Electronics.

Still a regional player, Yamada Denki relied more on high levels of service than price in order to compete. The company was also quick to embrace the large-scale store format, opening its first large store in 1987 under the Tecc Land banner. To support further growth, Yamada Denki made an initial public offering of stock in 1989 and secured a listing on the Tokyo Stock Exchange.

It wasn't until 1992 that Yamada Denki opened its first store outside of the northern Kanto region. It was also during this period that the retail chain made a greater commitment to larger format stores, closing many of the smaller outlets. This fundamental change allowed Yamada Denki to increase its product range and gain a volume purchasing advantage that allowed it to now compete on price.

In the late 1990s, Yamada Denki launched an expansion program, opening large stores in high-traffic locations as part of a push to become a national brand. By the start of the new century, the chain boasted 120 stores and sales of more than Y750 billion, making it Japan's third largest specialty electronics retailer. Into the early 2000s, Yamada Denki continued its aggressive growth strategy, primarily through the acquisition of smaller, weaker electronics retail chains. It also acquired the Daikuma discount chain to add a second retail format. Also during this period, the Yamada Denki chain took a major step in improving its competitive position. It opened a new experimental retail format under the Digital 21 brand rather than Tecc Land. The store was used to test a points-based customer loyalty program that offered discounts as large as 15 percent and proved highly popular with customers.

Yamada Denki had mostly engineered its growth by focusing on smaller cities and suburban areas. The first urban store opened in Hiroshima in 2004. Moreover, this store laid the groundwork for the new "Labi" superstore format, which at 20,000 square meters in size was suited for urban markets. The chain continued, however, to operate and open smaller stores in rural markets. In 2005, Yamada Denki became the first specialty electronics retailer to reach Y1 trillion in annual sales. The new chain looked to expand its brand beyond Japan, meeting this goal in 2010 by opening a Yamada Denki store in China.

BRAND ELEMENTS
- Blue and orange are the primary colors of the Yamada Denki logo.
- "For Your Just" serves as the Yamada Denki slogan.
- A Yamada Denki theme song is played on commercials and in stores.

The outward representation of the Yamada Denki brand is comprised of several elements. The Yamada name is prominently displayed on store signage, rendered in blue, with part of the letter "y" forming an orange triangle. In some signage, the blue and orange colors are reversed. The word is often accompanied by a logo in which a white "y" trisects an orange pentagon. This house-like shape is then enclosed in a blue line that forms a square perimeter. This symbol is also linked to the name "Labi," the brand logo of Yamada Denki superstores.

Another important element of the Yamada Denki brand is the English-sounding slogan "For Your Just." To native speakers of English, it is a curious phrase, but it emerged in a culture in which English words and phrases sometimes gain acceptance because they are easy to say or simply sound interesting. The slogan is meant to convey the idea that Yamada is dedicated to satisfying the customer and has an extensive inventory to supply everything a customer might

desire. The slogan is often found on signage and used in communications.

Another unique brand element is the Yamada Denki song. The pop-sounding jingle includes the lyrics, "Yamada Denki and its jolly friends." The song is featured in Yamada Denki commercials. The ending, in which a female singer shouts "Yamada Denki," is also played in the retail stores. This randomly interrupts the background music, often startling customers unfamiliar with the practice.

BRAND IDENTITY
- Yamada Denki is a brand that seeks to show that it cares about its customers.
- Trustworthiness is a key part of Yamada Denki's brand identity.
- Philanthropic endeavors help to support the brand's identity.
- Good environmental stewardship is a key aspect of the Yamada Denki's brand identity.
- Yamada Denki espouses the belief that customer satisfaction is linked to employee satisfaction.

At its core, Yamada Denki portrays itself as a brand that cares about its customers, mostly by offering a wide variety of merchandise at low prices. This approach is embodied in the "For Your Just" slogan and reflected by the upbeat tone of its well known jingle. The logo is bright and optimistic. The graphic that uses a "y" to divide a figure shaped like a house, evokes a connection between the brand and the customer's family. The message of low prices is also supported by the retailer's customer loyalty card.

To further support an identity as a caring brand, Yamada Denki pursues programs that benefit the communities in which it does business. The stores house charity boxes for the collection of donations, and also host local events. Yamada Denki stores are involved in education and general cultural events, and donate and raise funds for local charitable causes. In addition, Yamada Denki extends its image as a good corporate citizen by supporting efforts to reduce harmful impacts on the environment, including the reduction of carbon emissions. At the consumer level, this means store associates provide information on the energy-saving qualities of individual electric appliances. The chain also offers "Smart House" solutions to help customers reduce their energy usage. To play its part, Yamada Denki follows an "Eco-Store" program to reduce the chain's carbon footprint. In addition, Yamada Denki stores maintain an electric appliance reuse system and accept used ink cartridges for proper recycling.

Much of the operating philosophy of Yamada Denki, and a reflection of its brand identity, is distilled in the management slogan "Appreciation and Trust." Not only does Yamada Denki seek to present itself as a brand that is grateful for the business of its customers and worthy of their trust, the message extends to employees. Customer satisfaction and employee satisfaction are seen as inextricably linked. To reflect that belief, the company instituted an "Everybody's Improvement Proposal Program" to allow all levels of the workforce to make management proposals. Yamada Denki also promotes a "work-life balance" for all of its employees, and for female employees a program was crafted to support career development and to elevate more women to management ranks.

BRAND STRATEGY

- Yamada Denki Co. employs a multifaceted brand strategy.
- In addition to organic growth and acquisitions, the Yamada Denki brand has grown through franchising.
- The Tecc Land and Labi brands have been used for large-format Yamada Denki stores.
- Frontier brand was created for personal computers and other in-house products.
- Yamada Denki Co. controls other brands through subsidiary companies.

Yamada Denki Co. pursues a multifaceted brand strategy. At the core is the Yamada Denki retail store brand that the company has nurtured since 1973. Steadily, the brand was expanded to all regions of Japan and migrated from smaller communities to the country's urban areas. The chain began opening larger format stores under the Tecc Land name in the late 1980s. When restrictions on even larger format stores were lifted in the early 2000s, the company entered this sector as well, creating another standalone brand known as Labi. To maintain a connection to the flagship Yamada Denki brand, the Labi logo made use of the orange house symbol in the Yamada Denki's logo. Yamada Denki grew organically or through acquisitions until 2005, when it launched a franchising system to accelerate the growth of the brand.

In 2010 Yamada Denki introduced its brand in China, marking the first time the company ventured beyond Japan's borders. Because there was already entrenched competition in the market, the chain moved cautiously, avoiding major cities such as Beijing and Shanghai. Instead, it chose Shenyang City in the northeastern Liaoning Province. The chain also adopted a more decentralized approach in China, allowing local store managers greater pricing authority.

Yamada Denki solidified its hold on the Japanese electronics market by acquiring majority control of a smaller rival, publicly traded Best Denki Co., in a deal completed in December 2012. Best Denki would retain its listing, and its 500 stores would continue to operate under its own brand. Not only did Yamada Denki expand its footprint to include new markets in Japan through Best Denki, it gained operations in Singapore, Malaysia, Taiwan, Indonesia, and Vietnam.

In addition to store formats, Yamada Denki developed an in-house product brand, Frontier, initially used for personal computers. In 2005 the company became the first Japanese retailer to offer digital electronics under a house brand, again making use of the Frontier label. Yamada Denki also extended its brand beyond retailing through joint ventures. Working with a system developer, the company in 2002 began selling computer systems to restaurants to help manage customer orders. In another joint venture in 2007 Yamada Denki subsidiary Kouziro Co., a computer manufacturer, became involved in the production of electronic medical chart systems. In 2009 Yamada Denki teamed up with a home builder to sell solar power generation systems. Two years later, Yamada Denki acquired another homebuilder, SxL. Corp., to offer housing bundled with solar power systems, energy-efficient home appliances, and electric vehicles.

Yamada Denki Co. owns several other businesses that offer their own brands. The Daikuma discount store chain was acquired in 2002. Later, the Tecc Land stores were folded into this subsidiary. Another company in the group, Project White Co., Ltd., develops and markets PCs and Peripherals. Kimuraya Select Co., Ltd., operates five variety stores located in front of Greater Tokyo train stations. Another unit, CIC Co., Ltd., operates the Sairaku Replus business that repairs appliances and refurbishes appliance for resale. The Yamada Eco Solutions Co., Ltd., subsidiary promotes solar generation systems providing employee training for the Yamada Denki Group. Inversenet Co., Ltd., recycles personal computers and manufactures communication and electronic devices for Yamada Denki. Yamada Broadband C., Ltd., markets broadband products and services at many Yamada Denki stores. Yamada Financial Co., Ltd., is responsible for Yamada LABI cards and affiliated credit cards.

BRAND EQUITY

- Brand Finance estimated Yamada Denki's brand value at US$2.647 billion in 2012.
- Yamada Denki was ranked No. 441 on the Brand Finance Global 500 list of the world's most valuable brands in 2012.
- Interbrand listed Yamada Denki is the 10th most valuable retail brand in the Asia Pacific region in 2012.

As Japan's largest consumer electronics retail chain, Yamada Denki commands considerable brand equity in its domestic market, enough to make it one of the world's most valuable brands. According to brand consultancy Brand Finance plc, Yamada Denki possessed a brand value of US$2.647 billion, good enough in 2012 for the No. 441 ranking on the Brand Finance Global 500 list of the world's most valuable brands. Two years earlier, the value of the brand was estimated at US$1.909 billion. Yamada Denki was placed at No. 492 on the 2010 Global 500.

Using it own methodology, major branding agency Interbrand assigned Yamada Denki a brand value of US$265 million. As a result, Interbrand listed Yamada Denki as the 10th most valuable retail brand in the Asia Pacific market. The agency also recognized a growth in value for the brand, which was worth US$240 million in 2011. On the other hand, Yamada Denki enjoyed a higher ranking among Asia-Pacific retail brands, listed at No. 8 in 2011. With more than 500 stores in six countries, Best Denki also possessed some level of brand equity, but not enough to make the lists of any of the major branding agencies.

BRAND AWARENESS

- Yamada Denki enjoys its strongest brand awareness in the northern Kyushu and southern Kyushu areas of Japan.
- A diverse portfolio of products and services helps to elevate awareness of the Yamada Denki brand.
- Subsidiary Best Denki enjoys greater brand recognition than does Yamada Denki outside of Japan.

Yamada Denki enjoys strong brand awareness in Japan. It is the largest consumer electronics retailer in the country with about 600 company-owned outlets in 47 prefectures, helping to raise the profile of the brand with Japanese consumers. The brand is especially well known in the northern Kyushu and southern Kyushu areas. In addition, franchise operations elevate brand awareness. Also serving to promote the Yamada Denki brand is the company's diverse product and service portfolio. Although best known as a purveyor of electronics, Yamada Denki also sells washing machines, refrigerators, air conditioners, stoves, and other major home appliances. Through subsidiaries bearing the Yamada name, the brand is also involved in broadband products, environment-related services, and "smart house" construction.

Yamada Denki is little known outside of Japan. By the end of 2012 the chain only operated three retail stores outside of the country, all located in smaller markets in China. The company-controlled Best Denki brand is smaller but possesses higher brand awareness outside of Japan, operating 60 outlets in five Asian countries. With nearly 500 stores in Japan, Best Denki is also a well-known brand to Japanese consumers.

BRAND OUTLOOK

- Despite its diverse product range, Yamada Denki remains very much dependent on a single segment, consumer electronics.
- Future brand growth will most likely come outside of Japan.
- Both the Yamada Denki and Best Denki brands possess international potential.

Although Yamada Denki boasts a diverse product portfolio, it remains very much dependent on a single segment, consumer electronics, in a highly saturated market. To gain an edge over Japanese rivals, the chain decided in recent years to increase the sale of products from foreign manufacturers, such as LG, Samsung, and Haier. The addition of Best Denki also added to the scale of Yamada Denki Co., creating an improved competitive position that redounded to the benefit of both brands.

Yamada Denki will most likely need to look overseas for future brand growth. China no longer appears to be as promising a market as it once had, and many Japanese companies are beginning to reduce their exposure to the market, despite its vast size. The foothold of Best Denki in other Asian markets provides Yamada Denki Co. with a platform on which to build. Whether it chooses to use the platform to grow the Best Denki brand or the Yamada Denki brand, or both, remains to be seen. Another strong possibility is that Yamada Denki Co. will enter another large, tempting market: India.

FURTHER READING

"Best Retail Brands 2012." Interbrand. Accessed February 15, 2013. http://www.interbrand.com/en/BestRetailBrands/2012-Best-Retail-Brands.aspx

"Japan's Yamada Denki to Double Stores to More than 500." *AsiaPulse News*, February 14, 2005.

"Japan's Yamada Denki to Launch House-Brand Digital Electronics." *AsiaPulse News*, December 6, 2004.

"Shopaholics and Shopaphobes; Retailing in Japan." *Economist*, September 11, 2010.

"With Norms Eased, Japan Retailers Too Eyeing India." *Financial Express*, October 1, 2012.

"Yamada Denki Becomes 1st Specialty Retailers with 1 Tril. Yen Sales." *Japan Consumer Electronics Scan*, February 28, 2005.

"Yamada Denki to Buy Best Electronics." *SinoCast Daily Energy Beat*, July 13, 2012.

"Yamada Denki Co., Ltd." *International Directory of Company Histories*. Ed. Tina Grant. Vol. 86. Detroit, MI: St. James Press, 2007.

"Yamada Denki Needs New Business Model If It Hopes to Compete in China—Analyst." *China Business News*, May 13, 2008.

ZARA

AT A GLANCE

Brand Synopsis: Eschewing traditional marketing, Zara is known for its beautiful retail locations and ever-changing inventory of economical fashions.

Parent Company: Inditex Group, S.A. (Industria de Diseño Textil)
Edificio Inditex
Avenida de la Diputacion
15142 Arteixo, A Coruña
Spain
http://www.zara.com

Sector: Consumer Discretionary

Industry Group: Consumer Durables and Apparel

Performance: *Market share*—65 percent of all sales for Inditex (2011). *Sales*—EUR11.4 billion (US$14.8 billion) (2011).

Principal Competitors: Gap, Inc.; H&M Hennes and Mauritz AB; Arcadia Group Ltd.; Esprit International; Benetton Group S.p.A.

BRAND ORIGINS

- Zara, founded in Spain in 1975 by Amancio Ortega Gaona, initially catered to an influx of women entering the workforce.
- Zara began its global expansion by opening a store in Portugal in 1988, followed by stores in New York and Paris in 1989.

- One facet of Zara's success is the control maintained over all aspects of its production processes.

Zara International, Inc., one of the world's fastest-growing leaders of the "fast fashion" retail movement, was founded by reclusive Spanish clothier Amancio Ortega Gaona, said to be one of the world's richest men. Born in 1936, Gaona began his career in the clothing industry at the age of 14 as an errand boy for a local A Coruña-based shirtmaker. There, Ortega recognized the difficulties and high expense of depending on third-party suppliers for fabrics, materials, and other goods required for manufacturing clothing. By the early 1960s Ortega had taken a position as a clerk at an A Coruña clothing retailer. Ortega's experience there played an important role in the development of his career. In 1963 Ortega decided to launch his own clothing manufacturing company. With just 5,000 pesetas (equivalent to approximately US$25 in the 2000s), Ortega set up a small workshop in his home in Arteixo, where he began producing bathrobes, nightgowns, pajamas, and lingerie. Ortega named his company Confecciones Goa, reversing the initials of his name, and began his manufacturing career producing clothing for other brands.

Ortega also began laying plans to open his own retail operation. The Spanish clothing market of the 1960s and 1970s, which remained under tight dress-code regulations enforced by the Franco dictatorship, was not yet ripe for Ortega's ideas. At the same time, the relatively low numbers of women in the workplace left this important consumer base with little discretionary income.

Ortega recognized that the death of Franco in 1975 offered new opportunities for the retail market, and he opened his first retail store in A Coruña. Called Zara, the

1165

store featured inexpensive yet fashionable clothing and proved an immediate hit among the new generation of young Spanish women then entering the workplace by the thousands. An important feature of the Zara clothing line, and one of the keys to the retail chain's later success, was its ability not merely to anticipate its customers' fashion desires but to react quickly to changing trends. While most other clothing retailers remained limited to a seasonal model, changing their collections only twice per year, Ortega's company instituted a policy of constantly turning over its collection.

This nonseasonal production model, which was based on small and limited production runs, presented a number of important advantages. For one, Zara customers soon learned to make purchases quickly because a particular design was not likely to remain in the store for long and most likely would not be available again. In this way, Zara customers could be reassured that not everyone would be wearing the same clothing. At the same time, the system encouraged Zara customers to return frequently to the store, in order to discover the latest designs.

The small production runs also helped the company avoid costly design mistakes; when a particular design failed to sell, the company's financial exposure remained limited, and the design could be quickly replaced. The company was also able to sound out its customers for their own design interests, and Zara store managers and employees soon became an informal but important part of the company's design team. By responding quickly to customer feedback, as well as reacting to prevailing fashion industry trends, Zara was able to anticipate customer demand. This helped boost the success rate of the company's designs, and a large percentage of Zara's designs sold out quickly.

Another important factor in Zara's success was the decision to maintain tight control over its production processes by developing a degree of vertical integration unparalleled throughout most of the retail world. The company developed a network of some 14 factories, as well as a contracted network of some 400 local garment cooperatives in the A Coruña region. In this way, the company controlled every stage of a clothing design's development, from the initial design idea to its twice-weekly distribution to the company's stores. By controlling its processes, Zara was able to produce a new clothing design and place it on store shelves in as little as two weeks, compared to many months for most of its competitors.

Based on the success of the first store, Ortega soon laid plans to open new Zara stores elsewhere in Spain. By the mid-1980s Zara had risen to the top of the national clothing retail market, placing stores in all of the country's major cities. At the end of the decade, Zara

already operated more than 85 stores in Spain. By then, Ortega had begun to lay the foundations for the company's future expansion, both internationally and into new retail formats. As part of that effort, Ortega's retail and production operations were reorganized under a new holding company, Industria de Diseno Textil, S.A., or Inditex.

The Zara chain, which had grown steadily yet quietly through the 1980s, made its first modest entry into the international market in 1988, with the opening of a store in Oporto, Portugal. The experience convinced the company of the exportability of its fashion and retail model, and in 1989 the company made headlines, opening a store in New York that boasted some 10,000 square feet of selling space. That store was soon followed by a store in Paris.

Zara maintained strong growth through the 1990s. In 1994 the company operated 165 stores, 47 of which were outside of Spain. By the end of 1997 there were 550 Zara stores in operation, including 250 franchised stores. By the early 2000s Zara had become something of a fashion steamroller with nearly 950 stores in 64 countries. As it laid plans for its future growth, the Zara brand had become recognized as an important role model not only for clothing retailers but for the global retail industry itself.

BRAND ELEMENTS

- Founder Amancio Ortega Gaona's first choice for his new brand name was Zorba, but the name was already in use by a local proprietor.
- The Zara logo is suggestive of high-end retailer Prada's logo, with an elegant black wordmark.
- There has been criticism that the Zara logo is too generic and simplistic.

According to the company, the name Zara was not the founder's first choice for the brand. Amancio Ortega Gaona wanted to name his stores Zorba after the name of the lead character in a popular novel and movie, but there was already a bar named Zorba located near the new clothing shop, and the bar owner did not want to cause confusion among his patrons. Since the letters for the sign had already been made into a mold, they were simply rearranged, and the Zara brand was formed.

Updated in 2010, the Zara logo is reminiscent of luxury retailer Prada's logo. The wordmark is presented in all black capital letters, with significant spacing between the letters. It is a clean and straightforward logo with the black coloring signifying style and elegance. As Zara does not advertise, the logo is part of the distinctive visual identity of the brand. Some critics have charged that the logo is too simplistic and common.

BRAND IDENTITY

- Zara's retail spaces evoke the look and feel of high-end fashion boutiques, reinforcing the brand's image.
- Zara does not spend money on advertising, relying instead on its store windows to be all the advertising it needs.
- Zara stores feature fast turnover of clothing which encourages repeat shopping and creates excitement within the brand.

Zara is unique in the global retail market in that it does not spend money on advertising to promote its brand, investing money instead in new store openings. Unlike its closest competitors, Zara shuns splashy ad campaigns and celebrity collaborations, relying on stores strategically built in heavily trafficked and high-end retail areas to be its only advertising. The Zara store format, standardized throughout the chain, features sparse interiors reminiscent of luxury retailers. The design of Zara stores is also an integral part of its brand image. Zara stores are built to appear light and airy, to give a shopper the illusion of being in a much higher-end, exclusive boutique. Floor layouts and displays are patterned after those of luxury brands found throughout Europe.

The allure of the Zara brand lies in the ability of consumers to walk into any Zara store and find a well-made item that appeals to their own sense of fashion. Zara clothes promote the image of quality and sophistication, emphasizing design, quality of fabrics, and tailoring more than many other retailers at the same price point, which provides shoppers high-fashion looks at affordable prices.

Zara works to promote its brand as cutting-edge and desirable, and its designers have developed a reputation for being able to anticipate clothing trends and quickly translating those trends into wearable clothes that have mass appeal. Zara devotees are not worried that everyone else will be wearing the same dress; Zara spreads the supply of its clothing thinly among its stores. Once an item is gone from shelves—often within days—it may never reappear. New clothing products are introduced on a near-daily basis, breaking the traditional seasonal stock rotation found in the retail clothing industry.

BRAND STRATEGY

- Zara's strong brand image has been helped by the launch of other Inditex brands.
- An unparalleled vertical integration in its operations allows Zara to introduce roughly 10,000 new items a year into its stores, with turnover in as little as two weeks.
- Keeping the majority of its production in Spain has allowed Zara to avoid many of the problems associated with poor working conditions in Asian factories.

In contrast to most of its rivals, Zara has resisted outsourcing to countries in the developing world, maintaining as much as 60 percent of its production, and especially its fashion-forward production, near its headquarters in Arteixo, in the A Coruña province of northwestern Spain. Vertical integration, with operations including design, textile manufacturing, and dying, permits the company to respond extremely quickly to market conditions and fashion trends. With a staff of 200 designers, the company is able to bring a garment from initial design to the selling floor in as little as two weeks.

Inditex has been largely dependent for its revenues on Europe, which accounted for 70 percent of 2011 sales. Continuing its push into new markets, Inditex opened 179 new stores in Asia in 2011, with 156 of them in China. While Zara remains Inditex's global phenomenon, the Zara brand is helped by the expansion of other Inditex brands, including the 2003 launch of Zara Home, which features home furnishings and textiles. Inditex itself went public in 2001 and continued to expand its range of store brands, a process begun in the early 1990s with the creation of the Pull & Bear retail chain and continuing with the retail brands Bershka, Massimo Dutti, Oysho, Stradivarius, Tempe, Uterque, and Lefties. In 2009 the diversity of its brands helped give Inditex a 1.7 percent market share of the global retail clothing and footwear market.

BRAND EQUITY

- Zara's brand value placement among global luxury brands is a reflection of its strong brand image.
- Zara's brisk expansion rate is reflected in their ranking as the third fastest-growing brand in the world in 2008–09.
- In 2011 Zara ranked 44th among the top-100 global brands.
- Zara's strong brand image is reflected in its 24th-place ranking among the best retail brands.

Brand Finance's *Top 500 Most Valuable Global Brands 2012* ranked Zara at number 215, with a brand value of US$4.7 billion, which positioned Zara in the elite company of luxury brands such as Louis Vuitton, which was ranked at number 202 with a brand value of US$5 billion. Zara was also ahead of luxury retailer Prada, ranked at number 329 with a brand value of US$3.3 billion, and Ralph Lauren, at number 325 with a brand value of US$3.4 billion.

According to Interbrand's *2011 Ranking of the Top 100 Brands*, Zara ranked 44th with a brand value of US$8 billion, the second highest ranking for an apparel company. *Business Week* ranked Zara third with a 14 percent annual growth in brand value in their *World's Fastest-Growing Brands 2008–09*. Zara ranked 66th with a brand value of US$12.6 billion in BrandZ's *Top 100 Brand Ranking of the World's Most Trusted Brands* and 24th with a brand value of US$4.7 billion in Brand Finance's *Best Retail Brands*.

BRAND AWARENESS

- The Zara brand enjoys free publicity when their clothes are photographed being worn by celebrities.
- Zara has built a loyal brand following by incorporating consumers' ideas into their design strategies.
- Inditex and Zara have pushed into global markets and built a strong brand following throughout the world.

Kate Middleton, duchess of Cambridge, made headlines when she appeared the morning after her 2011 wedding to Prince William wearing a blue Zara dress. The dress sold out instantly and reinforced the image of Zara as a maker of high-fashion yet wearable clothing.

Since Amancio Gaona founded Zara in Spain in 1975 with an emphasis on trendy clothing styled after high-fashion concepts and coupled with moderate pricing, the essence of Zara has changed very little. Zara has built a strong brand image by putting the consumer at the core of their business. Zara actively seeks out consumer comments and translates those ideas into the designs that appear on store shelves. Not only anticipating trends but also incorporating those trends into clothing that works for everyday shoppers have helped Zara to build a loyal brand following.

Steady expansion into world markets has helped broaden the brand awareness. With Zara at its forefront, Inditex has become a global force. In 2009 Inditex was ranked ninth by *Business Week* in their listing of the top 40 of *The World's Best Companies*, the only apparel company on the list. Inditex also ranks 94th in the European Brand Institute's *Top 100 Brand Corporations Worldwide*, with a brand value of US$9.8 billion, and it placed 41st among the *Top 50 Europe's Brand Corporations*, a listing of Europe's most valuable brand corporations.

BRAND OUTLOOK

- Zara's vertical integration means that it is dependent only on itself for all aspects of its production process.
- China and the United States offer Zara enormous expansion opportunities.
- Zara began offering online shopping in limited European countries in 2010 and in the United States in 2011.

Zara's vertical integration is central to their success. With control over every facet of the production process, from design to manufacturing to the shop floor, Zara is able to react quickly to the changing marketplace and stay in front of the competition. There are lingering concerns, however, that the company's insistence on keeping production in Spain could harm further global expansion, given rising transportation costs.

With Spain in the midst of an economic recession and consumers pulling back on spending, Zara is not opening new stores in its homeland. The company is instead concentrating on plans for China and the United States. While both countries offer enormous expansion opportunities, Zara has announced intentions to open 400 stores in China with only a limited number to be open in the United States, with customer demand given as the reason for the disparity.

Both Zara and rival clothier H&M were slow in reacting to online commerce, with the Zara brand stating that the reluctance came from its desire to have direct contact with its customers. Zara began its e-commerce trade in 2010 in six European countries, while slowly integrating more countries throughout 2011. The company has stated that it will continue enabling online shopping until it is fully realized in all operating markets.

FURTHER READING

Brand Finance. "Top 500 Most Valuable Global Brands 2012." Accessed September 5, 2012. http://www.brandfinance.com/images/upload/bf_g500_2012_web_dp.pdf.

Chu, Jeff. "Cheap, Chic and Made for All: How Uniqlo Plans Take over of Casual Fashion." *Fast Company*, June 18, 2012. Accessed September 17, 2012. http://www.fastcompany.com/1839302/cheap-chic-and-made-all-how-uniqlo-plans-take-over-casual-fashion.

Dishman, Lydia. "The Strategic Retail Genius behind Zara." *Forbes*, March 23, 2012.

"Fashion Forward: Zara, Spain's Most Successful Brand, Is Trying to Go Global." *Economist*, March 24, 2012.

"Rankings Per Brand." RankingTheBrands.com. Accessed September 17, 2012. http://www.rankingthebrands.com/Brand-detail.aspx?brandID=56.

"Top Clothing and Footwear Specialist Retailers Worldwide, 2009." *Market Share Reporter*. Ed. Robert S. Lazich and Virgil L. Burton III. Detroit, MI: Gale, 2012.

"2011 Ranking of the Top 100 Brands." Interbrand. Accessed September 17, 2012. http://www.interbrand.com/en/best-global-brands/best-global-brands-2008/best-global-brands-2011.aspx.

"World's Fastest-Growing Brands, 2008–2009." *Business Rankings Annual*. Deborah J. Draper. Detroit, MI: Gale, 2011.

ZURICH

———◼———

AT A GLANCE

Brand Synopsis: Since its founding, Zurich, the largest insurer in Switzerland, has worked to see that its clients receive uncomplicated claim payouts for its accident, general, Farmers, and Global Life insurance.

Parent Company: Zurich Insurance Group Limited
Mythenquai 2, Zurich, 8022
Switzerland
http://www.zurich.com

Sector: Financials

Industry Group: Insurance

Performance: *Market share*—7.7 percent (2010). *Sales*—US$34.57 billion (2011).

Principal Competitors: AXA; Allianz; Aviva; Assicurazioni Generali

BRAND ORIGINS

- The company started in transport and marine reinsurance in 1872.
- In 1875 Zurich began dealing in accident insurance and quickly made that the primary focus of its business.
- Because Switzerland was neutral during World War I, Zurich was strong enough to profit from the postwar bankruptcies of other European insurance firms.
- In 2005 Zurich launched its "Zurich. Because Change Happenz" campaign.

Zurich Insurance Group was founded in Zurich under the name Versicherungs-Verein, or "Insurance Association," in 1872 as a subsidiary of Schweiz Marine Co. In the beginning its primary purpose was to write marine reinsurance for its parent company. From the start, the company had global clients as far away as New York. In 1875 the company expanded its insurance policies and began to offer accident insurance, changing its name to Zurich Transport and Accident Insurance Limited. Within just one year, Zurich opened new offices in Germany, Austria, Sweden, Norway, and Denmark.

The company continued its policy expansion and began to target a previously untapped market: the middle and lower classes. In 1878 Zurich began offering "micro-insurance," individual accident policies for workers, at a price that was affordable. That same year, it opened offices in France and the Netherlands. In its annual report the following year, the company debated the practice of microinsurance, citing concerns that offering insurance at a low rate could result in more claims and payouts that did not meet expectations, thus tarnishing the company's reputation. Zurich addressed this in 1923 by writing into its mission "no business without a sufficient premium but, on the other hand, far reaching goodwill in claims regulation." Paying customers, no matter how much they paid, were to be valued and provided with the best service possible.

In 1879 Zurich rented an office at the Zurich Stock Exchange to effectively market to visitors and introduce the concept of insurance. After a large loss that had to be covered by capital reserves, Zurich dropped marine insurance from its offerings, and this led to a turnaround for the business. Headed by Heinrich Müller, Zurich began focusing on casualty insurance. It was at this time that gross premium income reached CHF1 million. In the 1880s Zurich's largest market was Germany, where it provided 53 percent of policies, followed by France (21 percent) and Switzerland (19 percent). In 1881 Zurich began marketing accident insurance to factory owners as a way for them to reduce loss due to accidents, which had become more of a problem as industrialization spread across Europe. When an accident at a large textile factory in France killed 11 people and injured 18 others, Zurich established itself as a "no fuss" brand by paying the resulting claims without delay.

The company faced another financial blow in 1886, when Germany nationalized worker's compensation, making accident insurance redundant. It was the first time that Zurich's premium income fell. The hardship was offset the following year, however, when Zurich entered into an agreement with the Swiss government to insure soldiers during training. That success was brief; the government created its own version of accident insurance for the military in 1893.

In 1894 Zurich changed its name to Zurich General and Accident Liability Insurance Limited. In 1898 the company had a large profit because of a new law in France that required companies to carry workman's compensation insurance for employees. Zurich quickly became France's largest insurer. Belgium and Italy adopted similar laws in 1905. By 1913 Zurich had obtained the necessary license to offer accident insurance in the United States, and by the end of the year, business in the United States accounted for 9 percent of Zurich's premium income. Zurich purchased the struggling Spanish insurance company Hispania Compania General de Seguros in 1915, adopting the strategy of making profits through corporate takeovers.

In the 1920s insurers in other countries focused on domestic growth and postwar recovery, but Switzerland had not participated in World War I, leaving Zurich in a position to continue to expand internationally. It absorbed many of the German insurance companies that were bankrupted by hyperinflation following the war, creating a new company called VITA in the process. In 1926 Zurich introduced the "Ford Scheme," which was the first car insurance offered to new Ford automobile owners. That same year, VITA began offering free physicals to its life insurance customers and followed up by offering customers a health care advisor and guidance for healthy lifestyles.

For the next 60 years Zurich continued its expansion, opening branches in South America, Asia, and Northern Africa. In the 1970s Zurich also began offering umbrella plans that included multiple policies. In 2005 the company launched a rebranding under the slogan "Zurich. Because Change Happenz."

BRAND ELEMENTS

- Although the company's name has changed several times, "Zurich" has always remained part of the name.
- In identifying the city where the company was founded and is still based, the name Zurich emphasizes the brand's history and consistency.
- The slogan "Zurich. Because Change Happenz" was introduced in 2005.

The company name is Zurich's best-known brand element. The original name, Versicherungs-Verein, was changed after the company became successful enough to separate from its parent in 1875, and the name was changed to Zurich Transport and Accident Insurance Limited. Although the name has changed several times since the company was founded, the element "Zurich" has remained constant. Zurich represents the city where the company was founded and where it continues to have its headquarters.

Zurich's marketing successes began in its early days, when it targeted Zurich Stock Exchange workers, and continued into the 21st century, when in 2005 it introduced the "Zurich. Because Change Happenz" slogan as a catchy way of advertising insurance as a preparation for the unexpected. In the same year, two hurricanes, Katrina and Wilma, and extensive flooding in Europe gave emphasis to the slogan's point.

BRAND IDENTITY

- Since its creation, Zurich has projected the image of being a fair insurer.
- Zurich's commitment to fairness in claims processing is written into the company's mission.
- Zurich innovated by providing annual physicals and health advice to life insurance clients.

From the beginning, the image that Zurich has projected is that of a fair and trustworthy insurer. Part of that concept was written into the company's mission in 1923: "No business without a sufficient premium but, on the other hand, far reaching goodwill in claims regulation." No matter what premium a client paid, every claim filed would be processed quickly and with a fair payout. Although Zurich is a Swiss brand and global in scope, it still works with and helps the individual. In the 1920s and 1930s, for example, it began offering physicals to life insurance policy holders and providing advisors to help clients maintain a healthy lifestyle. The strategy works for both parties involved in a life insurance claim: a healthy client is less of a risk, and the client may benefit from a longer and more enjoyable life.

BRAND STRATEGY

- Zurich has worked to be a global brand since the company was founded in 1872.
- Zurich has acquired many companies since World War I.
- Zurich has three primary sub-brands: Zurich General, Global Life, and Farmers Insurance.

From its inception, Zurich aimed to be an international organization. It contracted with its first documented international client, based in New York, not long after the company was founded. Global expansion has been a key to success: claims resulting from a natural disaster in one part of the world are offset by premiums paid by customers in other regions, lessening the impact of any one disaster. Despite the number of claims filed after Hurricane Katrina in 2005, the company did not suffer a loss in revenue that year. In 2011, however, the company suffered financially because of the tsunami in Japan and an earthquake in New Zealand. The occurrence of two disasters of such magnitude within a short time frame is uncommon, but it is a potential drawback for a global insurance company.

Another part of Zurich's strategy has been the acquisition of failing insurance companies. The origin of this strategy dates back to the end of World War I, when Zurich was able to purchase German insurers bankrupted by inflation following the war. This approach has continued to the present day. In 2000, for example, Zurich acquired American-owned Farmers Insurance Group, the third-largest U.S. provider of home, auto, and commercial insurance.

The Zurich brand represents three primary groups. The primary subsidiary is Zurich General Insurance, which is based on the original model of the company. Additionally, Zurich offers plans under the subsidiary Global Life, which offers pensions, life insurance, savings, and investments. The final group is Farmers, which is well-known in the United States.

BRAND EQUITY

- Zurich suffered a 12 percent operating loss in 2011 due to natural disasters in Japan and New Zealand.
- In 2011 Zurich was ranked 94th among the top-100 brands, but it did not make the list in 2012.
- According to Brand Finance, Zurich's brand value was about US$5.38 billion in 2012.

Zurich Insurance Group is the largest insurer in Switzerland and the sixth-largest insurance company globally in terms of revenue. The company suffered a large loss in 2011 due to claim payouts after the tsunami in Japan and earthquake in New Zealand, reporting a 12 percent loss for 2011. In the first half of 2012, however, Zurich

reported an increase in operating profit of 17 percent over the same period during the previous year.

According to Interbrand's "2011 Ranking of the Top 100 Brands," Zurich ranked 94th with a brand value of US$3.79 billion. However, Zurich did not make the list in 2012. Competitor Allianz was ranked at 67th in the 2011 Interbrand ranking and moved up to 62nd in 2012, with a brand value of US$6.18 billion. Brand Finance's "Global 500 2012" ranked Zurich 176th overall, with an estimated brand value of US$5.38 billion. In 2011 Brand Finance ranked Zurich 123rd. Competitor Allianz was ranked 77th on the 2012 list, with a brand value of US$10.95 billion, up from 78th in 2011.

BRAND AWARENESS

- Farmers Insurance Group, a Zurich subsidiary, is well known in the United States and has several consistent marketing strategies, including sports sponsorships.
- Zurich Insurance Group is best known in Europe due to its long history there.
- In the slogan "Because change happenz," the "z" in "happenz" was intended to remind consumers that the slogan belongs to Zurich.

In the United States, Zurich's most successful subsidiary is Farmers Insurance Group. After acquiring Farmers in 2000, Zurich was able to use the company's history and level of recognition in the United States as an advantage. In 2012 the best-known slogan for Farmers was the simple "We are Farmers" jingle that ran on radio and television. The previous slogan was "Farmers. Gets you back where you belong." Farmers also used sports sponsorships to advertise the brand. In February 2011 Farmers announced that it was sponsoring a football stadium in Los Angeles, to be named Farmers Field. Farmers also became the lead sponsor for the San Diego Open golf tournament, subsequently renamed the Farmers Insurance Open, in 2010. Since 1926 Farmers has also sponsored a Los Angeles tennis tournament, the Farmers Classic, the longest-running sports event in the city.

Zurich General Insurance began using the slogan "Zurich. Because Change Happenz" in 2005. The misspelling of the word "happens," with the "s" replaced by a "z," was intended to help the consumer recall that the slogan belongs to Zurich. Although Zurich has had a global presence since shortly after its founding, the company is better known in Europe than it is elsewhere in the world. With the push for nationalized insurance in European countries, Zurich has focused on accident insurance.

In 2012 Zurich had a presence in more than 170 countries.

BRAND OUTLOOK

- Zurich suffered a 12 percent loss in 2011 due to natural disasters in Japan and New Zealand.
- Zurich reported higher profits for the first half of 2012, reassuring its shareholders.
- In 2012 Zurich signed an alliance with Banco Santander with the aim of gaining entry to the Latin American market.

The worst loss that Zurich has reported was in 2011, after two devastating events: a tsunami in Japan and an earthquake in New Zealand. The only other time in the company's history when capital was affected was not long after the company was created, when it suffered a loss due to a significant marine accident. After the accident, Zurich stopped dealing in transport insurance. After the disasters of 2011, however, Zurich reported higher profits in the first half of 2012 than for the same period the previous year, and this contributed to the company's positive outlook. To assure concerned shareholders after the dramatic loss of 2011, Zurich launched a marketing campaign with the tagline "Tomorrow is insured" representing the company's endurance despite the loss. In 2012 Zurich signed an alliance with Spain-based Banco Santander, one of the largest banks in the world, with the aim of reaching the previously untouched Latin American market and its 36 million potential customers.

FURTHER READING

Bandel, Carolyn. "Zurich Insurance Profit Drops after Year-Earlier Asset Sale." *Bloomberg*, August 16, 2012.

———. "Zurich Insurance May Say Net Fell after Year Earlier Asset Sale." *Bloomberg Businessweek*, August 10, 2012.

Brand Finance. "Global 500 2012." *Brandirectory*. Accessed October 17, 2012. http://brandfinance.com/images/upload/bf_g500_2012_web_dp.pdf.

"Industry News." *Vanilla Life*, 2011. Accessed October 18, 2012. http://www.vanilla-life.co.uk/articles/zurich_grows_market_share.php.

"Leading Global Insurance Companies." *Statista*, 2012. Accessed October 11, 2012. http://www.statista.com/statistics/185746/revenue-of-the-leading-global-insruance-companies/.

"2011 Ranking of the Top 100 Brands." Interbrand. Accessed October 15, 2012. http://www.interbrand.com/en/best-global-brands/previous-years/best-global-brands-2011.aspx

"2012 Ranking of the Top 100 Brands." Interbrand. Accessed October 10, 2012. http://www.interbrand.com/en/best-global-brands/2012/Best-Global-Brands-2012.aspx.

Zurich Insurance Group. "Annual Report." Accessed October 18, 2012. http://www.bloomberg.com/news/2012-08-16/zurich-insurance-profit-drops-after-year-earlier-asset-sale-1-.html.

———. "Heritage." Accessed October 14, 2012. http://www.zurich.com/aboutus/heritage/.

"Zurich Insurance Profit Drops after Year-Earlier Asset Sale." *Bloomberg*, August 16, 2012.

Brand Sector Index

Person/Company Index

Geographic Index